IMMIGRATION OPTIONS FOR INVESTORS AND ENTREPRENEURS
SECOND EDITION

AILA TITLES OF INTEREST

AILA'S OCCUPATIONAL GUIDEBOOKS

Immigration Options for Artists and Entertainers

Immigration Options for Essential Workers

Immigration Options for Physicians

Immigration Options for Nurses & Allied Health Care Professionals

Immigration Options for Religious Workers

Immigration Options for Academics and Researchers

Immigration Options for Investors and Entrepreneurs

STATUTES, REGULATIONS, AGENCY MATERIALS & CASE LAW

Immigration & Nationality Act (INA)

Immigration Regulations (CFR)

Agency Interpretations of Immigration Policy (Cables, Memos, and Liaison Minutes)

CORE CURRICULUM

Navigating the Fundamentals of Immigration Law

Immigration Law for Paralegals*

AILA's Guide to Technology and Legal Research for the Immigration Lawyer

TOOLBOX SERIES

AILA's Immigration Practice Toolbox

AILA's Litigation Toolbox

FOR YOUR CLIENTS

Client Brochures (10 Titles)

U.S. Tax Guides for Foreign Persons and Those Who Pay Them, 4 volumes— (H-1Bs, L-1s, J-1s, B-1s)*

AILA'S FOCUS SERIES

EB-2 & EB-3 Degree Equivalency
by Ronald Wada

Waivers Under the INA
by Julie Ferguson

Private Bills & Pardons in Immigration
by Anna Gallagher

The Child Status Protection Act
by Charles Wheeler

Immigration Practice Under AC21
by A. James Vazquez-Azpiri & Eleanor Pelta

TREATISES & PRIMERS

Kurzban's Immigration Law Sourcebook
by Ira J. Kurzban

Professionals: A Matter of Degree
by Martin J. Lawler

AILA's Asylum Primer
by Regina Germain

Immigration Consequences of Criminal Activity
by Mary E. Kramer

Representing Clients in Immigration Court
by CLINIC

Essentials of Immigration Law
by Richard A. Boswell

Litigating Immigration Cases in Federal Court
by Robert Pauw

Immigration Law & the Family
edited and written by Charles Wheeler

Immigration Law & the Transgender Client
by Transgender Law Center & Immigration Equality

OTHER TITLES

Immigration Practice Pointers

AILA's Guide to Worksite Enforcement and Corporate Compliance

David Stanton Manual on Labor Certification

Going Global: Trends in Outbound Immigration

AILA's Global Immigration Guide: A Country-by-Country Survey

Immigration & Nationality Law Handbook

The Consular Practice Handbook

Immigration Practice Under NAFTA and Other Free Trade Agreements

The International Adoption Sourcebook

GOVERNMENT REPRINTS

BIA Practice Manual

Immigration Judge Benchbook

Citizenship Laws of the World

CBP Inspector's Field Manual

EOIR Immigration Court Practice Manual

Affirmative Asylum Procedures Manual

ONLINE RESEARCH TOOLS

AILALink Online

Tables of Contents and other information about these publications can be found at *www.ailapubs.org*. Orders may be placed at that site or by calling 1-800-982-2839.

*An AILA-distributed title

AN **A**ILA
OCCUPATIONAL
GUIDEBOOK

Immigration Options for
INVESTORS &
ENTREPRENEURS
Second Edition

Editor-In-Chief: Lincoln Stone

Associate Editors:

Edward J. Carroll

Amy R. Novick

Susan L. Pilcher

Cletus M. Weber

Managing Editor: Danielle Polen

Website for Corrections and Updates

Corrections and other updates to AILA publications can be found online at: *www.aila.org/BookUpdates*.

If you have any corrections or updates to the information in this book, please let us know by sending a note to the address below, or e-mail us at *books@aila.org*.

This publication is designed to provide accurate and authoritative information in regard to the subject matter covered. It is distributed with the understanding that the publisher is not engaged in rendering legal, accounting, or other professional service. If legal advice or other expert assistance is required, the services of a competent professional should be sought.

—from a Declaration of Principles jointly adopted by a committee of the American Bar Association and a committee of publishers

Proceeds from the sales of AILA publications are reinvested in the association to help support member programs and services in the areas of federal and state advocacy, government liaison, practice assistance, ethics education, media outreach, and timely dissemination of members-only information via InfoNet. In addition, contributions are made to the American Immigration Council (formerly known as American Immigration Law Foundation (AILF)).

Copyright © 2006, 2010 by the American Immigration Lawyers Association

All rights reserved. No part of this publication may be reproduced or transmitted in any form or by any means, electronic or mechanical, including photocopy, recording, or any information storage retrieval system, without written permission from the publisher. No copyright claimed on U.S. government material.

Requests for permission to make electronic or print copies of any part of this work should be mailed to Director of Publications, American Immigration Lawyers Association, 1331 G Street NW, Washington, D.C. 20005, or e-mailed to *books@aila.org*.

Printed in the United States of America

ISBN 978-1-57370-304-8
Stock No. 53-04

TABLE OF CONTENTS

Preface xi
About the Editors xiii
Table of Appendices 435
Index 661

IMMIGRATION OPTIONS FOR ENTREPRENEURS IN STARTUPS AND SMALL BUSINESS

Immigrant Entrepreneurs and the American Dream
    by Stuart Anderson 3

Special Issues in Using Nonimmigrant Classifications Other Than
E-2 for Investors and Entrepreneurs
    by William L. Coffman 5

E-2 Visas for Investors in Smaller Businesses
    by Henry J. Chang 13

Permanent Residence Without Labor Certification—Using the EB-1 and EB-2
Classifications for Small Businesses and Entrepreneurs
    by Susan L. Pilcher 31

Alien Influence and Control Over the Job Opportunity
    by Allen E. Kaye 45

PERMANENT RESIDENCE FOR EMPLOYMENT-CREATING INVESTMENT

EB-5 Immigrant Investors
    by Stephen Yale-Loehr, Carolyn S. Lee, & Nicolai Hinrichsen 61

EB-5 Immigrant Investor Program—A Changing Landscape
    by Bernard P. Wolfsdorf, Naveen R. Bhora, & Tien-Li Loke Walsh 79

Practical Guidance in Preparing I-526 and I-829 Petitions
    by Elsie Hui Arias and Susan L. Pilcher 91

Reading the TEA Leaves: Exploring the "Targeted Employment Area"
Rules of the EB-5 Investor Visa Program
    by David M. Morris 105

The Meaning of "At Risk" in EB-5 Investment
    by Carolyn S. Lee 113

Navigating the Lawful Source Requirement for EB-5 Immigration
 by Elsie Hui Arias and Lincoln Stone.. 119

Country-Specific Issues and Challenges in Representing EB-5 Petitioners
from the People's Republic of China
 by Robert P. Gaffney 131

Russian EB-5 Investors—"Unwrapping" the Mystery
 by Kenneth White.. 139

Selected Issues in EB-5 Cases: Job Creation, Two-Year Periods,
and Indirect Employment
 by Edward J. Carroll.. 145

EB-5 Job Creation—What to Do When Plans Change
 by H. Ronald Klasko... 153

Conditional Permanent Residence and Immigration Risk for Investors
 by Lincoln Stone 165

Strategies for Overcoming Denials of I-829 Petitions to Remove Conditions
from Permanent Residence
 by Martin J. Lawler and Estelle Mckee 193

Litigating the Immigrant Investor's Case
 by Ira J. Kurzban... 217

HISTORICAL ROOTS OF INVESTOR IMMIGRATION

The Evolution of Legal Precedent in Treaty Investor Visa Cases
 by H. Richard Sindelar III and Stephen K. Fischel 229

A Synopsis of the Former Nonpreference Investor Category
 by Lincoln Stone 245

Legislative History of the EB-5 Category for Immigrant Investors
 by Cristina Perez Gonzalez, Humberto R. Gray, & Lincoln Stone 257

CRITICAL INTERDISCIPLINARY CONSIDERATION FOR
IMMIGRATION COUNSEL IN REPRESENTING INVESTORS

A Roundtable on Ethical Considerations and Professional
Risks in Investment Immigration
 by Robert E. Juceam, Denyse Sabagh, & Roxana C. Bacon 265

Federal Laws and Regulations Affecting the Foreign Investor
in the United States
 Updated by Doreen Edelman 279

Table of Contents

Business Considerations for Investors
    by Mark H. Scribner 293

The Legal and Non-Legal Professionals Behind a Viable EB-5 Regional Center
    by Linda Lau and Tina Lee 297

Marketing and Promoting EB-5 Investments: Securities Issues for
Regional Centers and Immigration Lawyers to Consider
    by Jennifer Mercier Moseley 303

Anti-Money Laundering and OFAC Sanctions Concerns for
Immigration Practitioners Assisting Foreign Investors
    by Edward J. Krauland and Jack Hayes 309

An Overview of Business Entities
    by Paul Applebaum 331

Accounting for Investor-Based Immigration: More to It
Than Just Federal Tax Returns
    by Christopher K. Zilafro 339

Tax Implications of and Planning for Immigrant and Nonimmigrant Visas
    by Albert S. Golbert and Miriam J. Golbert 359

COMPARATIVE INVESTMENT IMMIGRATION

Entrepreneurs and Investors—Australia
    by Robert J. Walsh 397

Canadian Immigration for International Investors and Entrepreneurs
in the Current Global Economy
    by David L.P. Garson and Lainie M. Appleby 407

Hong Kong Resident Visas for Entrepreneurs and Investors
    by Eugene Chow 415

New Zealand Residency for Investors
    by Eugene Chow 421

Understanding Investment-Based Immigration to the United Kingdom
    by Linda Lau 429

APPENDICES

A. AAO Precedents

1. *Matter of Soffici*, 22 I&N Dec. 158 (Assoc. Comm'r, Examinations 1998), AILA InfoNet Doc. No. 98070290 437

2. *Matter of Izummi*, 22 I&N Dec. 169 (Assoc. Comm'r, Examinations 1998), AILA InfoNet Doc. No. 98082091 449

3. *Matter of Ho*, 22 I&N Dec. 201 (Assoc. Comm'r, Examinations 1998), AILA InfoNet Doc. No. 98081291 481

4. *Matter of Hsiung*, 22 I&N Dec. 206 (Assoc. Comm'r, Examinations 1998) AILA InfoNet Doc. No. 98081290 491

B. Federal Court Decisions:

- *Chang v. United States*, 327 F.3d 911 (9th Cir. 2003), AILA InfoNet Doc. No. 03043045 497

C. USCIS/INS Memos:

1. USCIS Memorandum, W. Yates, "Establishment of an Investor and Regional Center Unit" (Jan. 19, 2005), AILA InfoNet Doc. No. 05012663 529

2. Legacy INS Memorandum, M. Pearson, "EB-5 Field Memorandum No. 9: Form I-829 Processing" (Mar. 3, 2000), AILA InfoNet Doc. No. 00060702 533

3. USCIS Memorandum, W. Yates, "Amendments Affecting Adjudication of Petitions for Alien Entrepreneur" (June 10, 2003), AILA InfoNet Doc. No. 03061744 555

4. USCIS Memorandum, D. Neufeld, "EB-5 Entrepreneurs—Job Creation and Full-Time Positions (AFM Update AD 09-04)" (June 17, 2009), AILA InfoNet Doc. No. 09061964 559

5. USCIS Memorandum, D. Neufeld, "Adjudication of EB-5 Regional Center Proposals and Affiliated Form I-526 and Form I-829 Petitions; Adjudicator's Field Manual (AFM) Update to Chapters 22.4 and 25.2 (AD09-38)" (Dec. 11, 2009), AILA InfoNet Doc. No. 09121561 567

D. USCIS Adjudicator's Field Manual

1. Chapter 22, Section 22.4: Employment Creation Entrepreneur Cases 591

2. Chapter 25, Section 25.2: Entrepreneurs 605

E. Highlights, GAO Report on Immigrant Investors

- U.S. Government Accountability Office (GAO) Report to Congressional Committees, "Immigrant Investors: Small Number of Participants Attributed to Pending Regulations and Other Factors," No. GAO-05-256 (Apr. 2005), AILA InfoNet Doc. No. 05040475 619

F. CIS Ombudsman Report

- Office of the CIS Ombudsman, "Employment Creation Immigrant Visa (EB-5) Program Recommendations" (Mar. 18, 2009), AILA InfoNet Doc. No. 09031868 621

G. USCIS Response to Ombudsman Report

- USCIS Memorandum, M. Aytes, "Response to Recommendation 40, Employment Creation Immigrant Visa (EB-5) Program Recommendations" (June 12, 2009), AILA InfoNet Doc. No. 09061770 639

H. USCIS Q&A from Stakeholder Session

- USCIS Q&A from Stakeholder Session with AILA EB-5 Committee and Invest in the USA" (Dec. 14, 2009), AILA InfoNet Doc. No. 10010462 643

I. Index of Online Resources, *compiled by* Susan Pilcher 659

PREFACE

The first edition of AILA's *Immigration Options for Investors and Entrepreneurs* was a singular piece, helping to establish investor immigration as a subspecialty practice area and thereby filling the void in the immigration law publishing field where no book previously had covered exclusively the subject of investor immigration. That first edition covered the historical roots of investor immigration, the EB-5 category of immigration practice, alternatives to EB-5 practice, interdisciplinary subjects, as well as a comparative survey of investor immigration laws in other countries.

When I signed off on the first edition four years ago, I could faintly see on the distant horizon a second edition that would benefit tangibly from the cumulative practice experience of more AILA attorneys. This second edition has fulfilled my expectation.

The historical material on investor immigration has been reproduced here in the second edition. Other materials have been carefully shuffled and edited with the aim of delivering significant improvements in the offering of articles across the spectrum of subjects that make up the field of investor immigration.

Where this second edition is vastly changed from the first edition is in the section on EB-5 practice. And this should be no surprise, as EB-5 practice has shed its former pariah status, or so it seems. Over the past four years, U.S. Citizenship and Immigration Services (USCIS) and other agencies have dedicated significant resources to the management of the EB-5 immigrant investor program, and ever-increasing numbers of AILA lawyers have made EB-5 practice a specialty area within their law firms. Naturally, then, there are new voices to be heard and featured in this second edition on *Immigration Practice for Investors and Entrepreneurs*. In October 2009, AILA sponsored its first ever continuing legal education conference on the EB-5 investor visa. A second such conference is scheduled for August 2010. These guidebooks and conferences signal more than merely an uptick in the prospects of those professionally invested in the EB-5 program, but more importantly, they represent a widespread commitment to the success of a practice area. A consequence is that more creativity, ideas, context, and experience are present when critical work must be done, whether that is in legal scholarship, liaison, advocacy, or client representation.

This second edition is graced by the exceptional legal skills and editorial talents of Cletus Weber, Susan Pilcher, Ed Carroll, and Amy Novick. They contributed hundreds of hours to working with individual authors to improve articles within a tight timeframe. We certainly could not have produced a book without their stalwart efforts.

Danielle Polen and the entire staff at AILA Publications ably managed this project, and we in the immigration bar thank Danielle, Tatia L. Gordon-Troy, and their team at AILA Publications for their dedication in completing this second edition.

In closing, some of the works are informational—a digest of history and current practice. Other works, especially in the EB-5 practice area, are more inclined to challenge the ever-evolving standards revealed by USCIS. It is not a stretch to call these latter works empowering, serving to convert disappointment, frustration, and even anger into something useful and durable. I have little doubt that the readers of this second edition will find much within the pages that follow to inspire, guide, and enrich the practice of representing investors and entrepreneurs.

Lincoln Stone
August 2010

ABOUT AILA

The American Immigration Lawyers Association (AILA) is a national bar association of more than 11,000 attorneys who practice immigration law and/or work as teaching professionals. AILA member attorneys represent tens of thousands of U.S. families who have applied for permanent residence for their spouses, children, and other close relatives for lawful entry and residence in the United States. AILA members also represent thousands of U.S. businesses and industries who sponsor highly skilled foreign workers seeking to enter the United States on a temporary or permanent basis. In addition, AILA members represent foreign students, entertainers, athletes, and asylum-seekers, often on a pro bono basis. Founded in 1946, AILA is a nonpartisan, not-for-profit organization that provides its members with continuing legal education, publications, information, professional services, and expertise through its 36 chapters and over 50 national committees. AILA is an affiliated organization of the American Bar Association and is represented in the ABA House of Delegates.

American Immigration Lawyers Association
1331 G Street, NW
Washington, D.C. 20005
Tel: (202) 507-7600
Fax: (202) 783-7853
www.aila.org

ABOUT THE EDITORS

Lincoln Stone (Editor-in-Chief) practices immigration law at Stone & Grzegorek LLP in Los Angeles. His legal training includes the University of Notre Dame Law School, a federal court clerkship with the Honorable Robert A. Grant, trial attorney experience with the legacy Immigration and Naturalization Service, and private practice experience in business transactions and litigation. Mr. Stone's writing in the immigrant investor field includes such works as "Immigrant Investment in Local Clusters," "Policy Considerations in the Immigrant Investor Pilot Program," and "Conditional Permanent Residence and Immigration Risk for Investors." He served for five years as chair of the American Immigration Lawyers Association's (AILA) Investor Visa Committee, chair of AILA's National Pro Bono Committee, and chair of the State Bar of California Board of Legal Specialization's Immigration and Nationality Law Advisory Commission. He is the conference program chair for AILA's EB-5 Investor Visa Conference, and editor-in-chief of the first and second editions of AILA's *Immigration Options for Investors and Entrepreneurs*. Mr. Stone holds the degrees of Juris Doctor, Master of Arts in Humanities, and Bachelor of Science in Business Administration.

Edward Carroll (Associate Editor) was an advisor to the state of Vermont on its initial EB-5 Regional Center application during the state's regional center recertification process, and he continues to counsel on regional center amendments and operational issues. He is the advisor to many U.S. enterprises regarding EB-5 issues. Mr. Carroll practices immigration law at the firm of Carroll & Scribner, P.C., in Burlington, VT. Articles authored by Mr. Carroll have appeared in AILA publications, publications for the American Bar Association (ABA) and the Vermont Bar Association, and in Canadian publications. Mr. Carroll has served as a member of AILA's Investor (EB-5) Committee and several other substantive law committees and as co-chair of the Vermont Service Center Liaison Committee. He has been liaison to U.S. Citizenship and Immigration Services (USCIS), U.S. Customs and Border Protection (CBP) in Vermont, and liaison to Vermont's Congressional Delegation for AILA's New England Chapter. He also has served as vice-chair of the ABA Immigration Law Committee, General Practice Section. Mr. Carroll is a frequent presenter on U.S. immigration law to legal and business groups in the United States, Canada, and Asia. He has taught immigration law to adjudicators at the Vermont Service Center and has been a commentator for radio and television in the United States and Canada on U.S. immigration issues. Mr. Carroll is a graduate of Harpur College/SUNY–Binghamton (B.A. 1966) and Brooklyn Law School (J.D. 1969). He is listed in *Best Lawyers in America*.

Amy Novick (Associate Editor) is of counsel with The Haynes Immigration Law Firm in Washington, D.C., where she focuses her practice on obtaining visas for highly skilled professionals, waivers of the two-year home residency requirement for exchange visitors, and issues of concern to diplomats and international workers, investors, naturalization and citizenship, foreign adoptions, and family-based immigration matters. Ms. Novick also serves as executive director of Immigrants' List, the leading bipartisan, pro-immigration political action committee supporting pro-immigration candidates for Congress. Ms. Novick is a member of the Board of Trustees of the American Immigration Council and is listed in the 2010 edition of *The International Who's Who of Business Lawyers*. A frequent speaker on employment-based immigration and immigration policy, Ms. Novick has extensive publication editing experience, having served as deputy director of AILA, managing editor of the *Immigration & Nationality Law Handbook*, and other AILA titles, including *The Visa Processing Guide, Selected Fundamentals of Immigration Law and Practice*, AILA's

Family Immigration Law Handbook, *Immigration Options for Academics and Researchers*, and *Immigration Options for Investors and Entrepreneurs*.

Susan L. Pilcher (Associate Editor) is of counsel to the firm of Carroll & Scribner, P.C., in Burlington, VT, where her general immigration practice includes a substantial focus on EB-5 and investment-related matters. Ms. Pilcher's professional background includes nearly a decade of full-time law teaching, including general and specialized immigration law courses, at the University of Arkansas School of Law (Fayetteville); a federal court clerkship in San Diego; commercial law practice; and many years of diverse and rewarding experience representing clients in virtually all types of immigration-related matters. She obtained her J.D. with distinction from Stanford Law School, where she served as managing editor of the *Stanford Law Review*. Ms. Pilcher has published and lectured extensively on immigration law topics, and she is active in agency liaison functions for AILA.

Cletus Weber (Associate Editor) is a co-founder and managing member of Peng & Weber, PLLC, a Mercer Island, WA (suburban Seattle) immigration law firm focusing on assisting investors, entrepreneurs, and highly talented persons. In addition to serving as associate editor of AILA's *Immigration Options for Investors and Entrepreneurs*, 2nd edition, and associate editor of AILA's 2010–11 *Immigration Practice Pointers*, Mr. Weber is vice chair of AILA's Board of Publications and a member of AILA's 2010–11 Topics Conference Committee (EB-5 Investors). He chaired AILA's Washington State Chapter in 2005–06. With a strong interest in categories that reflect his clients' excellence, major contributions, or substantial investment in job creation and the overall betterment of the United States, his practice focuses on national interest waivers, aliens of extraordinary ability, outstanding professors or researchers, J-1 waivers, and E-1/E-2 and EB-5 investors, as well as PERM labor certification and other employment-based immigrant and nonimmigrant visas. Mr. Weber achieved Beta Gamma Sigma honors while earning his undergraduate business degree at the College of William and Mary in Williamsburg, VA, in 1986, and earned his law degree from George Washington University in Washington, D.C., in 1989. He served as managing editor of the *George Washington Law Review*, 1988–89. Mr. Weber has written and spoken nationally on immigration law and practice and has been quoted in *HR Magazine*, *Seattle Times*, *Daily Telegraph* (UK), *Workforce Management*, and other major media.

AILA
OCCUPATIONAL
GUIDEBOOK

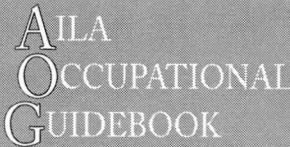

IMMIGRATION OPTIONS FOR ENTREPRENEURS IN STARTUPS AND SMALL BUSINESSES

IMMIGRANT ENTREPRENEURS AND THE AMERICAN DREAM

by Stuart Anderson[*]

Immigrant entrepreneurs capture the imagination and provide economic benefits to the United States. Nothing more symbolizes the American Dream than the "rags to riches" stories of immigrants who came to this country with little more than the clothes on their backs and started a successful business. Immigrants like Ovidiu Colea.

As a young man in Romania, Ovidiu Colea was arrested and sent to a prison camp. "What was my crime? I wanted liberty, I wanted freedom. I wanted to reach America. I endured five years of starvation, torture, beatings, long hours of labor in boiling hot and cold, freezing weather, sleeping on a dirty floor, long hours of physical labor, eating plant roots ... I was not allowed to communicate with my family," said Ovidiu.

The thawing of the cold war allowed him to receive a visa to the United States. "It was the best day of my life. When I came to America I was penniless but this country gave me great hope and opportunity."

Ovidiu worked three jobs, saved his money and within four years, in 1982, he started his own business, which produced small replicas. By 1985, his company had landed a contract to make replicas, ironically enough, of the Statue of Liberty. Today, Ovidiu's company Colbar Art employs 20 people in Queens, New York and stands as a symbol of the possibilities that America offers.

There are at least three types of immigrant entrepreneurs. First, is the refugee or family-sponsored immigrant who starts a business and sometimes gets by in the early stages with help from relatives working as employees. Taiwanese-born John Tu, president and CEO of Kingston Technology, must be one of America's most successful family-sponsored immigrants. He sold his company for $1 billion and distributed a large portion of the sale to employees, some receiving $100,000 to $300,000 each. He later bought back the company, which employs about 4,000 people. Sergey Brin, the enormously successful co-founder of Google, came to America as a child through the refugee program.

A second type of immigrant entrepreneur is the international student turned H-1B professional/green card holder. A National Venture Capital Association study, which I co-authored with Michaela Platzer, found that 25 percent of the venture-backed companies that became publicly traded since 1990 had at least one immigrant founder. Many of these companies were started by skilled, foreign-born professionals who started on temporary work visas, such as an H-1B.

A third way immigrant entrepreneurs make their mark on America is through the immigrant investor visa program. While underutilized in the past, renewed interest exists in the financial community and among lawmakers in the possibilities this visa category offers to create more jobs and companies in the United States.

Starting a successful business is difficult. Achieving that success in a land you were not born in is even more challenging. The ability of many immigrants to overcome these challenges and achieve success as an entrepreneur remains an important part of the American Dream.

---

[*] **Stuart Anderson**, former staff director of the Senate Immigration Subcommittee, is executive director of the National Foundation for American Policy, a nonpartisan research group in Arlington, VA.

SPECIAL ISSUES IN USING NONIMMIGRANT CLASSIFICATIONS OTHER THAN E-2 FOR INVESTORS AND ENTREPRENEURS

by Bill Coffman[*]

In addition to the traditional nonimmigrant investor vehicle of the E-2 visa, it is also possible for foreign investors to qualify for work status in the United States through other nonimmigrant categories. Recently, U.S. Citizenship and Immigration Services (USCIS), through apparent changes in adjudication standards at the Administrative Appeals Office (AAO) and by agency memo (referred to in this article as the "Neufeld Memo"),[1] have made this procedure more difficult and maybe even impossible for a sole owner/investor who is also the beneficiary of the petition. Please note that the Neufeld Memo is highly controversial and may be withdrawn or modified by USCIS, or may be rendered moot by subsequent congressional or regulatory action or by federal court action. Until that happens, practitioners representing investors and entrepreneurs in the non–E-2 nonimmigrant classifications will need to deal with the Neufeld Memo and heed its guidance. This article will address the special challenges that investors and entrepreneurs face in qualifying for such classifications as H-1B, L-1, or O-1 in light of these changes. The article also will provide some suggested strategies for dealing with these issues in the investor/owner context.

RECENT USCIS ADJUDICATION STANDARDS AND THE NEUFELD MEMO

Over the past year, practitioners undoubtedly have noticed an increase in Requests for Evidence (RFE) and even denials for H-1B and L-1 petitions where the petitioning company is small and the sole owner is also the beneficiary of the petition. These adjudicatory changes are rooted, in part, in the USCIS regulation defining "United States employer" in the H-1B context. USCIS regulations define a U.S. employer, for H-1B purposes, as a "person, firm, corporation, contractor, or other association, or organization in the United States which (1) [e]ngages [another] person to work within the United States; (2) [h]as an employer-employee relationship with respect to employees under this part ...."[2] This provision clearly contemplates that it is impossible for an individual to self-petition for H-1B status. However, a separately chartered entity, legally separate from the H-1B employee, could petition for that employee even if all the shares of the entity are owned by the H-1B employee.[3] For example, in certain circumstances, a corporation could file an H-1B visa for the employee/owner.[4] However, the concept has now found its way into adjudications of other nonimmigrant work visa petitions and even the I-140 multinational petition.

Traditionally, this concept simply meant the employer and beneficiary could not be the same person. In the investor context, it was quite possible for a prospective investor to form a separate legal entity and have that separate legal entity serve as the petitioner.

---

[*] **Bill Coffman** practices immigration law at the Boston office of Mintz, Levin, Cohn, Ferris, Glovsky, and Popeo, P.C. His legal work focuses on U.S. immigration and nationality law, as well as outbound emigration and related international law. Bill regularly speaks at local and national American Immigration Lawyers Association (AILA) conferences and has written immigration related articles for AILA publications and Massachusetts Continuing Legal Education courses and manuals. He authored "Organization Membership and Political Opinion as Grounds for Refugee Status" for the 1996 Winter issue of the *Houston Journal of International Law* and he co-authored "The Changing Face of Equal Protection: Gender Bias In U.S. Citizenship Law," for the March 1995 issue of *Immigration Briefings*. He received his J.D., cum laude, from the University of Houston Law Center (1996), where he served on the editorial board of the *Houston Journal of International Law*.

[1] U.S. Citizenship and Immigration Services (USCIS) Memorandum, D. Neufeld, "Determining Employer-Employee Relationship for Adjudication of H-1B Petitions, Including Third-Party Site Placements. Additions to Officer's Field Manual (AFM) Chapter 31.3(g)(15) (AFM Update AD 10-24)" (Jan. 8, 2010), *published on* AILA InfoNet at Doc. No. 10011363 (*posted* Jan. 13, 2010) (Neufeld Memo). For AILA's legal analysis of recent Administrative Appeals Office (AAO) opinions and the Neufeld Memo, see the January 26, 2010, letter from AILA-USCIS HQ Liaison Committee to Roxanna Bacon, USCIS Chief Counsel, *published on* AILA InfoNet at Doc. No. 10012760 (*posted* Jan. 27, 2010).

[2] 8 CFR §214.2(h)(4)(ii).

[3] *Matter of [name not provided]*, SRC 98 101 50785 (AAO Aug. 1999); *see also Matter of [name not provided]*, LIN 99 100 52016 (AAO Sept. 19, 2000).

[4] 8 CFR §214.2(h)(4)(ii).

Until recently, practitioners could rely on a long line of appeals unit cases that dealt with this requirement and concluded that a separate legal entity can serve as the petitioner in this context as long as it is truly a separate entity.[5] These cases even concluded that this separate entity can serve as the petitioner/employer even when the beneficiary/employee is the 100 percent owner of the petitioning entity.

The Neufeld Memo

The Neufeld Memo primarily deals with the requirement of an employer-employee relationship in the consulting services sector, where H-1B employees often are placed at third-party sites to provide consulting services on behalf of the H-1B petitioner. USCIS is concerned that the petitioner/employer has the right to control and direct the employee as understood by common-law agency principles. The memo gives a number of examples where a valid employer-employee relationship is present, and some where there is not a valid employer-employee relationship. The primary concern in the investor context is the example that self-employed beneficiaries do not present a valid employer-employee relationship for H-1B purposes. The example given in the memo is as follows:

> The petitioner is a fashion merchandising company that is owned by the beneficiary. The beneficiary is a fashion analyst. The beneficiary is the sole operator, manager, and employee of the petitioning company. The beneficiary cannot be fired by the petitioning company. There is no outside entity which can exercise control over the beneficiary. The petitioner has not provided evidence that the corporation, and not the beneficiary herself, will be controlling her work. **[No Separation between Individual and Employing Entity; No Independent Control Exercised and No Right to Control Exists]**

The memo includes two lengthy footnotes in this example. The first footnote acknowledges prior case law recognizing that a sole shareholder of a corporation can be employed by that corporation because the corporation is a separate legal entity from the owners even if there is only one owner. The footnote then distinguishes this for the H-1B context based on the control issue. The footnote states that "an H-1B beneficiary/employee who owns a majority of the sponsoring entity and who reports to no one but himself or herself may not be able to establish that a valid employment relationship exists in that the beneficiary, who is also the petitioner, cannot establish the requisite 'control.'"

The second footnote acknowledges prior AAO unpublished decisions that confirm a beneficiary may be employed by the petitioner even though the beneficiary is a sole owner and operator of the petitioner. The AAO analysis in these decisions followed the same analysis that corporations (and presumably other separately formed business entities) are separate and distinct from their owners and that as a separate legal entity, the corporation may petition for, and hire, their principal stockholders as H-1B employees. Here, the footnote, citing *Matter of Allan Gee, Inc.*,[6] strains to make a distinction in the analysis between who or what can be an "employer" and who can be an "employee" for H-1B purposes. The footnote goes on to say that "the AAO did not reach the question of how, or whether, petitioners must establish that beneficiaries are bona fide 'employees' of 'United States employers' having an 'employer-employee' relationship." The footnote then concludes that prior case law is correct in saying that a petitioner may employ an H-1B who also happens to have a significant ownership interest in the petitioner, but that this does not automatically mean that the beneficiary is a bona fide employee.

This article will not engage in a criticism of this newfound distinction in analysis between "employer" and "employee" for nonimmigrant visa petition purposes. The best arguments against this analysis have been presented by a January 26, 2010, letter from the American Immigration Lawyers Association (AILA)-USCIS HQ Liaison Committee to Roxanna Bacon, Chief Counsel, USCIS.[7]

The author received an RFE from the Vermont Service Center for a pending H-1B in August of 2009—four months before the Neufeld Memo—that clearly shows USCIS was heading in this direction. The RFE states as follows:

> It is not presently evident that an employer-employee relationship exists between the petitioner and the beneficiary because it appears the beneficiary may be an owner/partner of the petitioning company. A public search of the Secre-

---

[5] *Matter of X*, File No. EAC *[number not provided]*, (AAO Feb. 23, 2006); *Matter of [name not provided]*, SRC 98 101 50785, 21 *Immigr. Rptr.* B2-6 (AAU Aug. 9, 1999).

[6] 17 I&N Dec. 296 (Acting Reg. Comm'r 1979).

[7] *See* letter to Roxanna Bacon, *supra* note 1.

tary of State's Office indicates that the petitioner has no managers and that the beneficiary is the only person listed on the Certificate of Organization authorized to "execute, acknowledge, deliver and record any recordable instrument on behalf of the LLC purporting to affect an interest in real property ...."

To establish that an employer-employee relationship exists between the petitioner and the beneficiary, submit evidence which clearly establishes who supervises and assigns work to the beneficiary, who has the authority to hire, fire, pay, and change the beneficiary's job duties, or otherwise control his or her work. Such documentation may include, but is not limited to, an organizational chart, employment contract, or any other document describing the beneficiary's claimed employment relationship with the petitioner. Include a statement concerning:

- the beneficiary's influence on the petitioning business if he or she reports to a higher authority,
- whether it is intended that the beneficiary be an employee, and
- whether the beneficiary shares in profits, losses, and liabilities of the business.

In addition, submit evidence which will establish the ownership and control of the petitioning company. The evidence to submit may include, but is not limited to, copies of stock ledgers, stock certificates, articles of incorporation, joint-venture agreements, etc., which delineate the ownership and control of the U.S. petitioner.

This RFE also clearly shows USCIS's willingness to research online corporate records of secretaries of state to find out the level of involvement with the initial incorporation process.

STRATEGIES FOR DEALING WITH THE NEUFELD MEMO FOR OWNERS/INVESTORS

In its letter to USCIS's Chief Counsel, AILA has requested complete retraction of the Neufeld Memo as a violation of the Administrative Procedures Act.[8] It remains to be seen whether USCIS will stand by this memo, retract it, or possibly publish an amended memo. As indicated above, even before the memo, USCIS service centers were sending RFEs and denials related to the issue of owner/beneficiaries. So, for the foreseeable future, it appears all practitioners will have to deal with the Neufeld Memo as it stands now. Practitioners should be prepared to warn clients and, if necessary, advise on restructuring corporate ownership to comply with the guidance in the memo. Fortunately, the memo provides some suggestions for evidence to help establish the employer-employee relationship, and establish that the beneficiary also qualifies as a bona fide "employee." The memo lists a number of suggestions for evidence. Listed below are the suggestions from the memo that apply to the owner/beneficiary situation, along with a discussion of how each may be implemented in the owner/beneficiary context.

- *Copy of signed Employment Agreement between the petitioner and beneficiary detailing the terms and conditions of employment.*

A signed employment agreement is quite possible with the beneficiary signing for himself or herself as the prospective employee, and an officer or director of the legal entity signing on behalf of the separate petitioner/entity. The sole owner of a corporation can appoint someone to serve as an officer or director for the purposes of providing independent counsel and advice to the corporation and its owner(s), and that individual can sign the employment agreement on behalf of the corporation. It is probably in the best interests of both parties to have the terms of employment committed to a written document anyway.

- *Copy of employment offer letter that clearly describes the nature of the employer-employee relationship and the services to be performed by the beneficiary.*

As with the written agreement above, a less formal offer letter could outline sufficient terms of the relationship and be put on the petitioner's letterhead and signed by an officer or director who is not the owner/beneficiary.

- *Copy of position description or any other documentation that describes the skills required to perform the job offered, the source of the instrumentalities and tools needed to perform the job, the product to be developed or the service to be provided, the location where the beneficiary will perform the duties, the duration of the relationship between the petitioner and beneficiary, whether the petitioner has the right to assign ad-*

---

[8] Administrative Procedure Act (APA), Pub. L. 79-404, 60 Stat. 237, 238; (codified at 5 USC §§551–59, 701–06, 1305, 3105, 3344, 5372, 7521).

ditional duties, the extent of petitioner's discretion over when and how long the beneficiary will work, the method of payment, the petitioner's role in paying and hiring assistants to be utilized by the beneficiary, whether the work to be performed is part of the regular business of the petitioner, the provision of employee benefits, and the tax treatment of the beneficiary in relation to the petitioner.

The way the job description is presented as part of the petitioner support letter can focus attention not only on specific duties, but also on the direction and control of the owner/beneficiary by other officers, a board, or even other owners if the owner/beneficiary is not the sole owner. The job description can clarify which duties require consultation or direction from these other corporate bodies. Furthermore, companies whose product or service is highly technical often enlist services of outside experts by appointing an independent advisory board to provide collective guidance to the company and owner(s) and review decisions before they are implemented. For example, biotechnology companies often have a scientific advisory board. These board members do not take the place of a corporate board of directors, but instead, provide sector-specific advice and consultation to the company to ensure actions taken are in line with the overall goals of the company. This could be part of a larger company business plan or independent document appointing the advisory board and should be documented appropriately in the petition filing.

- *A description of the performance review process.*

Here again, performance review could be vested by the owner(s) with another officer of the company or an independent board of directors or advisory board. This can be outlined as part of the corporate governance documents or in a business plan for the company.

- *Copy of petitioner's organizational chart, demonstrating beneficiary's supervisory chain.*

Inclusion of this type of chart provides a visual aid to show clearly the owner/beneficiary's place within the company with respect to other officers, the board of directors, or a separate advisory board.

The Neufeld Memo also outlines evidence that can be included with the petition extension. This includes documentation that typically would not be available at the time of an initial petition filing such as pay records (to clearly show payment from the separate corporation), work product created during the previous nonimmigrant validity period, dated performance reviews, and employment history records showing changes in pay, promotions, etc.

Finally, it is worth noting that the Neufeld Memo has made specific changes to the USCIS *Adjudicator's Field Manual* (AFM). The AFM is the day-to-day guidebook used by service center officers during the adjudication process. A quick review of the AFM shows that much of its language finds its way into RFEs and Notices of Intent to Deny sent by the service centers so it is likely we will see even more of these in the sole owner/investor context for H-1B and other non-E work visa petitions. Information gleaned from USCIS at the February 18, 2010, public stakeholders meeting specifically to discuss the Neufeld Memo indicates that the memo's analysis would not be extended to L-1A petitions even though practitioners have reported the receipt of numerous RFEs, both before and after the memo, with requests to demonstrate clearly employer-employee relationships.

OTHER SPECIAL ISSUES IN THE H-1B CONTEXT

Ability to Pay

In recent years, a common RFE from the service centers for small H-1B companies requests additional evidence to demonstrate that the prospective employer has the ability to pay the offered wage if the H-1B petition is approved. USCIS appears to be borrowing this from its I-140 regulations and attempting to apply it in the H-1B context. However, in 2000, a pair of AAO decisions clarified that since all H-1B petitioners must prepare and file a labor condition application with the U.S. Department of Labor (DOL), jurisdiction for ability to pay issues is the sole responsibility of the DOL.[9] Today, ability to pay is not an issue directly raised. It is couched in questions of the company's viability.

USCIS regulations require that H-1B classification be accorded a foreign national who *will* perform services in a specialty occupation.[10] This highlights the policy that USCIS will not approve an H-1B petition for "speculative employment." So, to avoid RFEs on these issues for the new and smaller company typically formed by a sole investor, practitioners should prepare H-1Bs with sufficient financial and other in-

---

[9] *Matter of [name not provided]*, LIN 99 243 50365 (AAU May 23, 2000), *published on* AILA InfoNet at Doc. No. 00061301 (*posted* June 13, 2000).

[10] 8 CFR §214.2(h)(4)(i).

formation to show the legitimacy of the company and the need for the H-1B worker. As in the new office L context discussed above, petitioners should include a copy of the office bank accounts, wire transfers of money deposited in corporate bank accounts, business plans, contracts with U.S. clients, etc.

H-1Bs for Owners/Managers

In most cases, for an owner/beneficiary, the beneficiary will be filling a managerial position for the company. In this situation, it must be proven that the managerial position is a "specialty occupation" requiring the attainment of at least a bachelor's degree.

In previous generations, there was an established business tradition of promoting employees from within companies to higher level managerial positions once the employee had sufficient experience. While this is no longer the business model today, service center examiners still may be under the impression that managerial positions do not normally require attainment of a degree. Additionally, general manager positions that could be performed by anyone with managerial experience have been found not to be "professional" because they do not require a specific bachelor's degree. It is therefore critical to the company to describe the duties of the manager in detail to prove the complexity of the duties and/or knowledge required in a specific field to perform the duties. The H-1B is best utilized where the manager has education and experience in either a specific business area such as financial analysis, accounting, etc. or in the subject matter of the product or service provided by the business.

It is also common to find managers who have not completed at least a bachelor's degree. In these situations, it will be necessary to qualify the manager based on a degree equivalency using any higher education the manager does have, in addition to work experience.[11]

Size of the Business

While current cases say company size does not matter for the H-1B visa,[12] in practice, often it does. As with the L-1 manager for a small company, USCIS examiners may question whether the company is large enough and has enough complex activity to support the need for an H-1B worker. A small business with few employees all engaged in work that clearly would not meet the definition of "specialty occupation" may lead a USCIS examiner to conclude that the offered H-1B position is, similarly, not a "specialty occupation," or that the beneficiary will perform some specialty occupation duties in combination with other non-specialty occupation duties. Therefore, it is necessary for small businesses to submit substantial evidence about the nature of the business as well as the need for the position, and that it will be filled by a degreed person.

For the investor/entrepreneur of a smaller business, the H-1B petition must be supported by a detailed letter explaining the complexity of the position. This job description should not be generic. For example, the need for the position and the duties must be detailed, and explain why the job requires a degree. Perhaps the company has recently grown as a result of additional investment, or is now under contract to provide services to a larger company and requires significant project management experience. The complexity of the job duties is one basis for specialist classification, and a specific and detailed lengthy letter is the way to prove this criteria.

SPECIAL ISSUES IN THE L-1 INTRACOMPANY TRANSFER CONTEXT

As indicated previously, the Neufeld Memo and many of the AAO opinions dealt with the employer/employee relationship in the H-1B context. However, there are increasing signs that USCIS may be applying these same criteria to other classifications including the L-1 intracompany transfer even though there is no similar definition of "U.S. employer" in the L-1 regulations. Because the L-1 is based on an intracompany transfer—*i.e.*, the transferee has been employed by a related company outside the United States for at least one year—the employer/employee relationship issue should be easier to prove. Furthermore, USCIS regulations contemplate that an L-1 beneficiary may be an owner or major stockholder. The purpose of the regulation is to require the petitioner to provide additional evidence that "the beneficiary's services are to be used for a temporary period and evidence that the beneficiary will be transferred

---

[11] USCIS regulations allow three years of work experience to equal one year of college or an educational equivalency opinion to be rendered by a college or university official who has authority to grant academic credits for prior work experience. See 8 CFR §214.2(h)(4)(iii)(D)(1).

[12] *Young China Daily v. Chappell,* 742 F. Supp. 552 (N.D. Cal. 1989).

to an assignment abroad upon the completion of the temporary services in the United States."[13]

Even in the case of a sole owner of the foreign company or sole owner of both the foreign and U.S. companies, it is much more likely that the owner has an established business abroad with an established board of directors or other officers who can continue to serve in similar capacities for the U.S. company. If possible, the U.S. company should be set up as a subsidiary of the foreign company so that ownership need only be traced to the foreign parent to show the qualifying relationship. It is always possible USCIS will ask for evidence of ownership of the foreign company. Even if the L-1 beneficiary is the sole owner of the foreign company, evidence of control through the foreign parent's board of directors or specialty advisory board, as indicated above, can be included to demonstrate the employer-employee relationship.

Specific Requirements for the "New Office" L-1

As with the traditional E-2 investment vehicle, the L-1 regulations specifically recognize the need for a foreign company to establish a new office in the United States, and have regulations to address that. A new investor or entrepreneur may use the "new office" provisions of the L-1 regulations to start up a new enterprise as long as it meets the standard L-1 requirements. The regulations require detailed documentation to establish the legitimacy of the L-1 employer in the United States.

- *Sufficient Physical Premises*

This requires, at a minimum, a lease for office space sufficient to house the new business.[14] While a "home office" situation rarely will be sufficient, a lease for relatively small preliminary office space is usually acceptable. A commercial lease is better than a lease in an administrative office suite that shares reception and secretarial duties, but the latter also usually is accepted. Photographs of the interior and exterior of the physical premises are helpful evidence to satisfy this requirement, and often are requested by USCIS if not provided with the initial filing.

- *U.S. Operation will support executive/manager within one year*

A new office L-1 petition can be approved only for a maximum of one year.[15] At the conclusion of that one-year period, the petitioning business will need to show that the company is of a sufficient size that it will need the services of an executive or manager, or that it is engaged in business that continues to need a specialized-knowledge employee.[16] A staff of employees to be supervised or a significantly budgeted department within the company will be necessary to convince USCIS that a manager is needed. Furthermore, if the L-1A employee is a functional manager, the extension after the first year must provide evidence that there are sufficient other employees to relieve the L-1A of non-managerial duties so that he or she can perform predominantly managerial responsibilities.

At the initial new office L-1 filing, a detailed business plan may be helpful to demonstrate the company will be successful. While not mentioned by name, the concept of a business plan is suggested by the regulations.[17] Additional supporting documentation may include evidence of sufficient investment in the U.S. company and/or financial ability of the foreign company to pay the L-1 employee's salary and to commence business operations in the United States.[18] Typically, evidence of a U.S. corporate bank account with initial capital on deposit, is used to satisfy this requirement. USCIS regulations further indicate that showing the organizational structure of the foreign company also is needed to satisfy this requirement.[19] Any additional documentation that helps establish that the new U.S. office is ready to conduct actual business operations is also helpful. Such documentation might include contracts with U.S. clients, invoices from vendors, bank statements showing deposit and check writing activity, payroll records, a business license, tax filings, brochures, and so forth.

A strategic alternative to qualifying the new office L-1 as an L-1A manager or executive is to utilize the L-1B specialized knowledge provision. The regulations allow for a new-office L transfer under either option.[20] It may be easier to show that the beneficiary/investor has specialized knowledge of the company's products or services to meet the L-1B

---

[13] 8 CFR §214.2(*l*)(3)(vii).
[14] 8 CFR §214.2(*l*)(3)(v)(A).
[15] 8 CFR §214.2(*l*)(7)(i)(A)(*3*).
[16] 8 CFR §214.2(*l*)(3)(v).
[17] 8 CFR §§214.2(*l*)(3)(v) & (6).
[18] 8 CFR §214.2(*l*)(3)(v)(C)(2).
[19] 8 CFR §214.2(*l*)(3)(v)(C)(3).
[20] 8 CFR §§214.2(*l*)(3)(v) & (6).

criteria. Since the L-1B does not require an additional showing of the ongoing need for a manager at the conclusion of the first year of operation, the L-1B extension may be an easier case to prove. Once the business has grown enough to support a manager, the L-1B investor can be bumped up to L-1A. However, practitioners should be warned that L-1B petitions are under additional government scrutiny after the legacy Immigration and Naturalization Service (INS)-issued memoranda of March 9, 1994,[21] and December 20, 2002.[22] While ostensibly written to ease adjudication standards of L-1B petitions, these memos have given examiners new language to use in L-1B RFEs, and made the process of securing L-1B approval more difficult.

- *Post-Approval Considerations*

After visa approval, it is advisable to explain the difficulties that may be encountered in a year, when the new-office L expires and significant documentation will be needed to support the extension application. Regular meetings and document review during the year also may be useful for the client.

SPECIAL ISSUES IN THE O-1 EXTRAORDINARY ABILITY CONTEXT

The O-1 visa is for a person of extraordinary ability. As with the H-1B, the O-1 requires a petition be filed by a legal entity distinct from the beneficiary.[23] Note that there is no self-petitioning allowed with the O-1 visa as there is with the first preference employment-based immigrant visa category for individuals with extraordinary ability. Also, the O-1 category specifically encompasses individuals who have extraordinary ability in a variety of fields, including science, arts, education, business, or athletics, or who "have . . . a demonstrated record of extraordinary achievement in the motion picture or television industry."[24] An entrepreneur/businessman with documented success abroad or in the United States may qualify as an O-1 with substantial documentation.

CONCLUSION

Nonimmigrant work visa categories outside the E context traditionally have been useful when foreign nationals do not qualify for the E visa because they are not citizens of a treaty country. USCIS policy is certainly evolving with respect to dealing with these categories where the owner is also the beneficiary. Hopefully, all is not lost with recent AAO decisions and the Neufeld Memo so that careful advocacy in the right cases still will allow investors to take advantage of these visa classifications.

---

[21] Legacy Immigration and Naturalization Service (INS) Memorandum, J. Puleo, "Interpretation of Specialized Knowledge" (Mar. 9, 1994), *published on* AILA InfoNet at Doc. No. 01052171 (*posted on* May 21, 2001).

[22] Legacy INS Memorandum, F. Ohata, "Interpretation of Specialized Knowledge" (Dec. 20, 2002), *published on* AILA InfoNet at Doc. No. 03020548 (*posted* Feb. 5, 2003).

[23] 8 CFR §214.2(o)(2)(i).

[24] 8 CFR §214.2(o)(1)(i).

E-2 VISAS FOR INVESTORS IN SMALLER BUSINESSES

*by Henry J. Chang**

INTRODUCTION

The E-2 nonimmigrant category is a useful but sometimes overlooked alternative to the EB-5 immigrant investor category. In many ways, the E-2 classification resembles lawful permanent residence (LPR) status. For example, E-2 nonimmigrants may engage in self-employment (in furtherance of the qualifying investment), may remain in the United States for an indefinite period, and are not required to maintain ties to their home country. In light of these facts, the E-2 classification may be a realistic alternative to the EB-5 category.

The requirements for E-2 eligibility are discussed in greater detail below.

RELEVANT AUTHORITIES

The statutory authority for the E-2 category appears at §101(a)(15)(E)(ii) of the Immigration and Nationality Act (INA).[1] According to INA §101(a)(15)(E)(ii), an E-2 nonimmigrant is defined as follows:

[A]n alien entitled to enter the United States under and in pursuance of the provisions of a treaty of commerce and navigation between the United States and the foreign state of which he is a national, and the spouse and children of any such alien if accompanying or following to join him:

(ii) Solely to develop and direct the operations of an enterprise in which he has invested, or of an enterprise in which he is actively in the process of investing, a substantial amount of capital.

In addition to the statutory definition above, practitioners should refer to Department of State (DOS) regulations on the E-2 classification, which appear at 22 CFR §41.51, and the regulations of U.S. Citizenship and Immigration Services[2] (USCIS), which appear at 8 CFR §214.2(e). The DOS and USCIS rules are similar, but not identical to each other.

The DOS and USCIS regulations pertaining to the E-2 classification were initially published in the *Federal Register* on September 12, 1997.[3] The DOS regulations were subsequently amended again in 2005 but these amendments did not result in any substantive changes to the E-2 classification.[4]

Although the proposed USCIS regulations had differed from the DOS regulations, legacy INS subsequently altered them so that the final regulations would more closely track the DOS regulations, which were also published on the same date. Legacy INS's willingness to alter its own regulations to conform to DOS regulations reflected the general consensus that primary jurisdiction over the adjudication of E nonimmigrant cases rests with DOS. Although practitioners should always refer first to the USCIS regulations in cases involving a change of status or extension of stay, DOS guidance should also carry significant weight at the USCIS Service Centers in the absence of specific USCIS guidance.

Another extremely useful authority is §41.51 to Title 9 of the *Foreign Affairs Manual* (FAM), which is used by consular posts. Although the guidance contained in the FAM is not binding on consular officers, it can be a valuable source of guidance for practitioners. Where relevant, the FAM should be cited in visa cases filed with consular posts abroad

---

* **Henry J. Chang** is a partner with the firm of Chang & Boos in its Toronto office. He has practiced exclusively in the field of United States immigration law for more than 18 years. Mr. Chang is a member of the State Bar of California, the Law Society of Upper Canada, and currently holds the position of Immediate Past Chair for the Canadian Chapter of the American Immigration Lawyers Association (AILA).

[1] Immigration and Nationality Act of 1952, Pub. L. No. 82-414, 66 Stat. 163 (*codified as amended at* 8 USC §§1101–1524) (INA).

[2] USCIS was formerly known as the Bureau of Citizenship and Immigration Services (BCIS) and also as the Immigration and Naturalization Service (legacy INS).

[3] Department of State (DOS) regulations appeared at 62 Fed. Reg. 48149 (Sept. 12, 1997) and became effective on November 12, 1997. The USCIS regulations appeared at 62 Fed. Reg. 48138 (Sept. 12, 1997) and became effective on November 12, 1997.

[4] 70 Fed. Reg. 52292 (Sept. 2, 2005). The amendments resulted from the insertion of regulations relating to the E-3 classification for Australian nationals. Relevant section numbers relating to the E-2 classification were modified but the substantive requirements for E-2 eligibility remain the same as in the 1997 regulation.

and even in change of status or extension of stay cases filed with USCIS.

ELIGIBILITY REQUIREMENTS

Existence of Treaty

The basis of the E-2 classification lies in treaties that were intended to enhance and facilitate economic and commercial interaction between the United States and the treaty country. Therefore, a treaty of Freedom, Commerce, and Navigation (FCN) must exist between the United States and the country of the applicant's nationality.[5] Bilateral investment treaties (BITs) also have been held to be equivalent to an FCN treaty.[6] A treaty country also includes a foreign state that is accorded treaty visa privileges by specific legislation,[7] such as the North American Free Trade Agreement Implementation Act.[8]

A list of treaties or the equivalent in effect between the United States and other countries, which give rise to E classification eligibility, appear in the FAM.[9] This list is also reproduced at the end of this article as Exhibit A. The most recent additions to the list of eligible countries are Chile[10] and Singapore.[11]

Some treaties allow a national of that treaty country to seek either E-1 treaty trader status or E-2 treaty investor status, but not both.[12] In addition, some treaties may contain specific restrictions on E visa eligibility.[13] In order to determine whether a particular foreign national will be eligible for E-2 status, practitioners should refer to the list contained in the FAM and, if necessary, the text of the treaty itself.

Nationality

In order to qualify for E-2 investor status, the applicant must possess the nationality of a treaty country.[14] In most cases, determining nationality is simple. However, establishing the requisite nationality can be difficult in certain situations.

According to DOS regulations, the authorities of the foreign state of which the alien is a national determine the nationality of an individual treaty trader or treaty investor.[15] In unclear cases, practitioners should examine the nationality laws of the treaty country and the language of the relevant treaty in order to determine whether the individual qualifies for E-2 status. For example, in treaty countries where the doctrine of *jus sanguinis* exclusively applies, an individual born within the country's jurisdiction may not be a national of that country.

The nationality of a business is determined by the nationality of the individual owners of that business.[16] The country of incorporation is irrelevant to the nationality requirement for E-2 purposes.[17] A business that is at least 50 percent owned by nationals of the relevant treaty country will be eligible for E status.[18] Where two aliens equally own a company, both of which possess different nationality, the company will possess both nationalities.[19]

Applicants who hold dual nationality (other than U.S. citizenship) may qualify for E status but they must hold themselves out as nationals of the treaty country in question.[20] Such applicants must be documented and be admitted into the United States as nationals of the treaty country from which the treaty benefits accrue. However, nationals of a treaty country who also hold U.S. citizenship[21] or U.S. LPR

---

[5] INA §101(a)(15)(E); 22 CFR §41.51(b)(5); 9 *Foreign Affairs Manual* (FAM) 41.51 N3.

[6] 9 FAM 41.51 N3.

[7] 22 CFR §41.51(b)(5).

[8] Pub. L. No. 103-182, 107 Stat. 2057 (Dec. 8, 1993).

[9] 9 FAM 41.51, Exhibit I. The list of treaty countries currently appears online at: http://travel.state.gov/visa/frvi/reciprocity/reciprocity_3726.html.

[10] U.S.-Chile Free Trade Agreement Implementation Act, Pub. L. 108-77 (effective Jan. 1, 2004).

[11] U.S.-Singapore Free Trade Agreement Implementation Act, Pub. L. 108-78 (effective Jan. 1, 2004).

[12] For example, nationals of Brunei, Denmark, Greece and Israel may seek E-1 status but not E-2.

[13] For example, "A Convention to Regulate Commerce Between the Territories of the United States and of His Britannick Majesty," July 3, 1815, *entered into force* July 3, 1815, 8 Stat. 228; TS 110; 12 Bevans 49, permits nationals of the United Kingdom to seek E-1 and E-2 status but applies only to British territory in Europe (the British Isles (except the Republic of Ireland), the Channel Islands and Gibraltar) and to "inhabitants" of such territory. This term, as used in the Convention, means "one who resides actually and permanently in a given place, and has his domicile there."

continued

---

tion, means "one who resides actually and permanently in a given place, and has his domicile there."

[14] 22 CFR §41.51(b)(6); 9 FAM 41.51 N2.

[15] *Id.*

[16] *Id.*

[17] 9 FAM 41.51 N3.2.

[18] 9 FAM 41.51 N3.1.

[19] 9 FAM 41.51 N3.3.

[20] *Id.*

[21] Verbally confirmed by Jeff Gorsky, of the DOS Visa Office, at the 2002 AILA Annual Conference.

status[22] are not considered nationals of the treaty country for the purposes of E-2 eligibility.

The source of investment capital is clearly not relevant to the issue of nationality. For example, a corporation that is 50 percent owned by a treaty national will have the nationality of the treaty country, even if 100 percent of the investment capital comes from non-treaty investors. Although this scenario might create other eligibility problems, such as the treaty investor's inability to satisfy the substantial investment requirement (unless the corporation acted as the treaty investor), the nationality requirement would clearly be satisfied.

The nationality requirement is easy to satisfy when the treaty business is at least fifty percent owned by treaty nationals. However, nationality problems will arise when the treaty business is less than fifty percent owned by treaty nationals. In such cases, the attorney may need to restructure the treaty business in order to satisfy the nationality requirement.

One possible solution is to sell an appropriate amount of shares from the non-treaty national to the treaty national. As payment for the shares, the treaty national could then execute a loan agreement with an option for the non-treaty national to later repurchase the shares at the original price. This option could be exercisable only after the expiration date of the treaty national's visa or upon certain earlier events such as the treaty national's departure from the business or her insolvency. This strategy should satisfy the nationality requirement while also protecting the interests of the non-treaty national.

Under common law, a trust is not a separate legal entity from the trustee; the trustee is the legal owner of trust assets. If this principle were applied, a non-treaty national beneficiary could become eligible for E-2 status simply by placing the investment funds into a trust and hiring a treaty national trustee to administer it. However, DOS has confirmed that it will look to the beneficiaries, rather than to the trustee, when determining the nationality of the treaty business.[23]

Meaning of "Investment"

The term "investment" means the treaty investor's placing of capital, including funds and other assets, at risk in the commercial sense with the objective of generating a profit.[24] These requirements are discussed in greater detail below.

Investor Must Have Possession and Control of the Funds Invested

The treaty investor must be in possession of and have control over the capital invested or being invested.[25] If the investor has received funds by legitimate means (*i.e.,* savings, gift, inheritance, contest, etc.), and has control and possession over the funds, the proper employment of the funds may constitute a proper investment.[26] The source of the funds need not be outside the United States.[27] However, inheriting the treaty business itself will not constitute an investment.[28]

As funds either gifted or loaned (without security being placed on the business assets) can be attributed to the recipient for E-2 purposes, it may be possible to make another individual the principal investor where the original owner of the funds is not eligible for E-2 status. For example, a U.S. permanent resident who is ineligible for E-2 status may not bring in an E-2 employee. However, by gifting or lending the funds to an alien holding treaty nationality, that alien can qualify for E-2 status as the principal investor. Similarly, where two investors seek E-2 status for the same business, but neither individually is investing sufficient funds to meet the proportionality or substantiality requirements, one investor can gift or loan his or her funds to the other and then seek status as an E-2 employee.

It is also be possible to pool investment capital through the use of a holding corporation. Where there are several investors, none of whom is investing sufficient funds to qualify as the principal investor, it still may be possible to establish a holding corporation that will qualify. If this holding corporation possesses treaty nationality, it could act as the principal investor for the purposes of E-2 eligibility. The holding corporation could invest in the treaty enterprise, establishing 100-percent proportionality of its investment and its ability to develop and direct the treaty enterprise. Some or all of the shareholders

---

[22] 9 FAM 41.51 N14.1.

[23] Verbally confirmed by the late Stephen Fischel, former Director of Legislation, Regulations and Advisory Assistance for the DOS Visa Office, during the 1999 AILA Annual Conference.

[24] 22 CFR 41.51(b)(7).

[25] *Id.*

[26] 9 FAM 41.51 N8.1-1

[27] *Id.*

[28] *Id.*

of the holding corporation can then seek E-2 status as employees thereof.

The Investment Must Be at Risk

The investment capital must be subject to partial or total loss if investment fortunes reverse.[29] Such investment capital must be the investor's unsecured personal business capital or capital secured by personal assets.[30]

Indebtedness secured by the assets of the treaty business is not considered a qualifying investment.[31] This is true even where personal assets in addition to the assets of the business secure the indebtedness.[32] However, unsecured loans or loans secured solely by the alien's own personal assets are considered qualifying investments.[33]

In other words, a small investor could obtain the investment capital from personal sources (*i.e.,* savings, proceeds from the sale of personal property, gifts from friends and relatives), from a mortgage securing his or her personal residence, or from an unsecured personal loan (*i.e.,* a personal line of credit or a credit card). The only investment capital that may not be counted is a loan secured on the assets of the business (*i.e.,* capital obtained from a mortgage securing a commercial building that will be used in the treaty business).

The Investment Must Be Irrevocably Committed

Capital that is "in the process of being invested" must be irrevocably committed to the enterprise.[34] However, it is possible to use various legal mechanisms, such as holding funds in escrow, to establish the necessary commitment of funds.[35]

For the alien to be "in the process of investing", the alien must be close to the start of actual business operations, not simply in the stage of signing contracts (which may be broken) or scouting for suitable locations and property.[36] Mere intent to invest, or possession of uncommitted funds in a bank account, or even prospective investment arrangements entailing no present commitment, will not suffice.[37] However, a reasonable amount of cash, held in a business bank account or similar fund to be used for routine business operations, may be counted as investment funds.[38]

Where the applicant is purchasing an established business, it is easy to show that the entire qualifying investment has been irrevocably committed, even where the purchase has not been completed. A binding agreement of purchase and sale coupled with the use of an escrow agreement (which mandates the payment of the investment funds to the vendor upon issuance of the visa) will satisfy the requirement. Similarly, an irrevocable direction by the applicant to his or her own lawyer, directing the lawyer to apply the funds to the purchase of the business (subject to visa issuance) may also provide the necessary irrevocable commitment.

Where the applicant is starting a new business, it is much more difficult to show an irrevocable commitment of the entire qualifying investment. In such cases, the applicant will be expected to spend a sufficient percentage of the investment capital before irrevocability will be established. However, the applicant is not required to spend the entire qualifying investment before a visa will be issued.

As stated above, the FAM specifically states that a reasonable amount of cash, held in a business bank account or similar fund, to be used for routine business operations, may be counted as irrevocably committed investment funds.[39] The amount of capital actually committed must only be enough to demonstrate that the applicant intends to follow through with the entire investment once the visa is approved.[40]

Other Financial Transactions as Investments

Payments in the form of leases or rents for property or equipment may be calculated toward the investment in an amount limited to the funds devoted to that item in any one month, since the remaining payments presumably will be paid out of earnings

---

[29] 22 CFR §41.51(b)(7).

[30] *Id.*

[31] 9 FAM 41.51 N8.1-2.

[32] *Id.* However, it may still be possible to argue that the portion of the loan that exceeds the value of the secured business assets can be counted as an investment, since it will not be secured by the assets of the business.

[33] *Id.*

[34] 22 CFR §41.51(b)(7).

[35] *Id.*

[36] 9 FAM 41.51 N8.1-3.

[37] *Id.*

[38] 9 FAM 41.51 N8.1-2.

[39] *Id.*

[40] Verbally confirmed by the late Stephen Fischel, former Director of Legislation, Regulations and Advisory Assistance for the DOS Visa Office, during the 2000 AILA Annual Conference.

from the treaty business.[41] However, more than one month of payments may be counted if they are made in advance.[42] For example, if the treaty investor prepays her equipment lease for one year, the entire year's worth of payments may be counted as part of the qualifying investment.

The amount spent for the purchase of equipment and for inventory already in the possession of the treaty investor may be counted as part of the qualifying investment.[43] The value of goods or equipment transferred to the United States may be considered part of the qualifying investment if it can be demonstrated that the goods or machinery will be put to use in an ongoing commercial enterprise.[44] The treaty investor must establish that the purchased goods or equipment are for business, not personal purposes.[45] While a company car might not meet this burden if it will also be used for personal purposes, inventory or industrial equipment clearly will.

The issue of book value versus market value of transferred assets should also be considered. Either the historical cost (*i.e.*, original purchase price, less depreciation) or market value of an existing asset would appear to be acceptable for the purposes of calculating the qualifying investment. The FAM makes reference to both the "amount spent" and the "value of goods or equipment."[46] From the practitioner's perspective, it usually makes sense to use the higher of the two figures.

Rights to intangible or intellectual property may also be considered capital assets to the extent to which their value can reasonably be determined.[47] Where no market value is available for a copyright or patent, the value of current publishing or manufacturing contracts generated by the asset may be used.[48] If none exist, the opinions of experts in the particular field in question may be submitted for consideration and acceptance.[49]

Where the applicant is seeking E-2 status based on an established business that he or she has operated for an extended period of time (perhaps under a different nonimmigrant status), it is sometimes difficult to document the investment. However, in the author's opinion, it is not enough to simply show the current market value of the business as evidence that an investment has been made. Practitioners should first document the initial capital contribution made to the treaty business and then document that the proportionality of the investment is still sufficient at the time of the application.

Where the applicant began with a small initial investment but has operated an established business for a period of time, much of the investment may now be in the form of retained earnings. In such cases, the current investment may be considered too small to be substantial unless these retained earnings are also counted.

Retained earnings represent previously earned income that has been retained in the treaty enterprise instead of being paid out to the shareholders. Although in the EB-5 context, it is often stated that retained earnings do not qualify because they are not sufficiently personal to the investor, even where the corporation is wholly owned and controlled by that investor, this appears to be less of a problem in the E-2 context.

The author's own experiences confirm that retained earnings will usually be considered part of the qualifying E-2 investment. This is especially true in the context of E-2 renewals, where the investor has operated the treaty business for several years and its asset value has now increased by means of retained earnings.

In the EB-5 immigrant investor context, USCIS often takes the position that retained earnings are not part of the investment because the capital is not personal to the investor (even if the corporate entity is 100 percent owned and controlled by the investor). It instead requires that investor to personally receive the retained earnings (*i.e.*, as a dividend), pay income tax on the income, and then reinvest the funds into the corporation. However, the negative tax implications often make this very undesirable. Fortunately, DOS appears to take a more relaxed position in the E-2 context.

Retained earnings would appear to comply with the concept of "investment," as that term is defined in the DOS regulations and in the FAM.[50] The FAM clearly states that the INA does not require the source of the funds to be from outside the United

---

[41] 9 FAM 41.51 N8.2-1.
[42] *Id.*
[43] 9 FAM 41.51 N8.2-2.
[44] *Id.*
[45] *Id.*
[46] *Id.*
[47] 9 FAM 41.51 N8.2-3.
[48] *Id.*
[49] *Id.*

---

[50] 22 CFR §41.51(b)(7); 9 FAM 41.51 N8.

States.[51] Further, if the treaty business is wholly owned or controlled by the investor, he or she should be able to demonstrate possession and control of the funds invested, as required by the FAM.[52]

However, some consular officers may still allege that retained earnings held by a corporation are not personal to a shareholder until paid out as dividends. If this occurs, the attorney should consider characterizing the corporation that operates the treaty business as the treaty investor. In that situation, the retained earnings of the corporation would clearly be personal to the corporation. The corporation's shareholders could then seek status as E-2 managerial or supervisory employees.

The Enterprise Must Be a Bona Fide Commercial or Entrepreneurial Undertaking

The enterprise must be a real and active commercial or entrepreneurial undertaking, producing some service or commodity for profit and must meet applicable legal requirements for doing business in the particular jurisdiction in the United States.[53] It cannot be a paper organization or an idle speculative investment held for potential appreciation in value, such as underdeveloped land or stocks held by an investor without the intent to direct the enterprise.[54] As the investment must be a commercial enterprise, E-2 status is not available to nonprofit organizations.[55]

Investing in a residential property in Scottsdale, Arizona, clearly would not qualify since it would be considered a passive investment, even if some limited management activities are required to rent the property to a tenant. Investing in more than one investment property would not change the passive nature of the investment, unless the investment portfolio was so large that it required the establishment of an active property management business to administer it. In such cases, the property management business might qualify as a treaty enterprise.

The Investment Must Be Substantial

One of the most common reasons for investors in small businesses being denied E-2 visas is that their investment is not considered substantial. For this reason, practitioners acting on behalf of such investors should carefully address this issue.

According to INA §101(a)(45), the term "substantial" means "such an amount of trade or capital as is established by the Secretary of State, after consultation with appropriate agencies of Government." DOS's position continues to be that there is no set minimum dollar amount that will be considered "substantial" for purposes of E-2 eligibility. The FAM states that, as long as all the other requirements for E-2 status are met, the cost of the business per se is not independently relevant or determinative of qualification for E-2 status.[56] While a manufacturing business might easily cost millions of dollars, the cost of purchasing or establishing a consulting firm may be relatively low.[57]

In practice, some consular posts still apply an informal minimum investment threshold in addition to the proportionality test, although there appears to be no legal basis for such a position. In the past, many consulates would accept investments approaching $50,000, since the FAM made specific reference to an investment of $50,000.[58] However, it no longer contains specific examples of substantial investments. They were apparently deleted because too many consular officers were using them as brightline tests instead of considering substantiality on a case-by-case basis.[59]

According to the current FAM, the purpose of the substantiality requirement is to ensure to a reason-

---

[51] 9 FAM §41.51 N8.1-1.

[52] Id. If the investor did not own the entire E business, retained earnings would likely have to be prorated according to the investor's actual ownership interest.

[53] 22 CFR §41.51(b)(8).

[54] 9 FAM 41.51 N9.

[55] Id.

[56] 9 FAM 41.51 N10.3.

[57] Id.

[58] The former 9 FAM 41.51 N.9.3 (TL:Visa-78; 5-7-93) included the following specific examples: (a) in the case of a $50,000 investment, an investment approaching 90–100 percent would easily meet the test; (b) a business costing $100,000 might require an investment of 75–100 percent to meet the test; (c) a business costing $500,000 would demand generally upwards of a 60 percent investment, with a $375,000 investment clearly meeting the test; (d) in the case of a million dollar business, a lesser percentage might be needed, but 50–60 percent investment would qualify; (e) a business requiring $10 million to purchase or establish would require a much lower percentage—a $3 million investment might suffice in view of the sheer magnitude of the dollar amount invested; and (f) an investment of $10 million in a $100 million business would qualify based on the sheer magnitude of the investment itself.

[59] The current 9 FAM 41.51 N10.4 simply states that investments of 100 percent or a higher percentage would normally automatically qualify for a small business of $100,000 or less.

able extent that the business invested in is not speculative, but is, or soon will be a successful enterprise as the result of the exercise of sound business and financial judgment.[60] It further states that the rules regarding the amount of funds committed to the commercial enterprise and the character of the funds, primarily personal or loans based on personal collateral, are intended to weed out risky undertakings and to ensure that the investor is unquestionably committed to the success of the business.[61]

The FAM still states that the requirement of substantiality is met by satisfying the "proportionality test." It defines the proportionality test as a comparison between two figures:

(i) The amount of qualifying funds invested; and

(ii) The cost of an established business or, if a newly created business, the cost of establishing such a business.[62]

The cost of an established business is, generally, its purchase price, which is normally considered to be the fair market value.[63] The cost of a newly created business is the actual cost needed to establish such a business to the point of being operational.[64] In addition, an element of judgment to be factored into the requirement of substantial investment concerns an assessment of the extent of the investor's commitment to the successful operation of the project in view of the amount invested.[65]

Although some consular posts may still be willing to approve an E-2 based on an investment of $50,000, the elimination of the specific examples contained in the FAM has made it more difficult to qualify based on investments at this level. Given the current environment, a more realistic minimum investment is probably $100,000 or more. Of course, it is still theoretically possible for investments of less than $100,000 to qualify in appropriate cases.

Investment Must Not Be Marginal

The marginality of a business is also one of the most common reasons why investors in smaller businesses are denied E-2 visas. For this reason, practitioners acting on behalf of such investors should address this issue carefully as well.

In order to qualify for E-2 status, the applicant must not have invested in a marginal enterprise solely for the purpose of earning a living for him– or herself and his or her family.[66] A marginal business is an enterprise that does not have a present or future capacity to generate more than enough income to provide a minimal living for the treaty investor and his or her family.[67] However, an enterprise that does not have the capacity to generate such income but does have a present or future capacity to make a significant economic contribution is not considered a marginal enterprise.[68]

In other words, if the investment will indirectly expand job opportunities locally or otherwise have a positive significant impact on the local economy, the applicant may still qualify even though the income from the business may only be enough to sustain the investor and his or her family.[69] For example, an investment that *indirectly* creates jobs in the local area (in the same manner as an EB-5 regional center investment) should be able to establish that it is not a marginal business.

The projected future capacity (either to generate more than marginal income or to make a significant contribution) should generally be realizable within five years from the date the alien commences normal business activity of the enterprise.[70] Therefore, a treaty enterprise does not necessarily have to realize this projected future capacity within the first year. Of course, the sooner it occurs, the stronger the case will be.

It was previously possible to establish that the treaty enterprise was not a marginal enterprise by showing independent sources of income to support the applicant and her dependents. If the applicant possessed other sources of income for support, the treaty enterprise would not exist solely to earn a living for the applicant and his or her family; it therefore could not be a marginal business.[71] However, this is no longer possible. The applicant must now

---

[60] 9 FAM 41.51 N10.1.

[61] *Id.*

[62] 9 FAM 41.51 N10.2. *See also* 22 CFR §41.51(b)(9)(ii).

[63] 9 FAM 41.51 N10.2.

[64] *Id.*

[65] 9 FAM 41.51 N10.5.

[66] 22 CFR §41.51(b)(1)(i); 9 FAM 41.51 N11.

[67] 22 CFR §41.51(b)(10).

[68] *Id.*

[69] The expansion of job opportunities was accepted in *Matter of Walsh and Pollard*, 20 I&N Dec. 60, 68 (BIA 1988).

[70] 22 CFR §41.51(b)(10); 9 FAM 41.51 N11.

[71] *Matter of Kung*, 17 I&N Dec. 260 (Comm'r 1978).

establish that the income from the treaty business alone is sufficient.[72]

Practitioners should provide as much evidence as they can to address the question of marginality. It is recommended that the applicant submit a reliable business plan to verify the capacity to realize a sufficient profit within a maximum of five years.[73] It also may be a good idea to obtain one or more expert opinions from business consultants or other experts who are familiar with the type of business in the area where the treaty enterprise will commence business activity. An opinion letter should describe the expert's background and then confirm that the expert: (a) has reviewed the business plan (including the projected financial statements contained therein); and (b) has concluded that the business plan is realistic. In addition, if the applicant is purchasing an existing business, he or she should consider submitting financial statements and tax returns for previous years, if they establish that the treaty enterprise will generate sufficient profit.

Ability to Develop and Direct the Business

A treaty investor (but not E-2 employees) must be seeking entry solely to develop and direct the treaty business.[74] The ability to develop and direct can be established by owning at least 50 percent of the treaty business (if the owner retains full rights of control over that portion of the business and has not assigned them to another), by possessing operational control through a managerial position or other corporate device, or by other means.[75]

In instances in which a sole proprietor or an individual who is a majority owner wishes to enter the United States as an "investor," or to send an employee to the United States as his or her personal employee, or as an employee of the U.S. enterprise, the owner must demonstrate that he or she personally develops and directs the enterprise.[76] Likewise, if a foreign corporation owns at least 50 percent of a U.S. enterprise and wishes its employee to enter the U.S. as an employee of the parent corporation, or as an employee of the U.S. business, the foreign corporation must demonstrate that it develops and directs the U.S. enterprise.[77]

Factors considered include ownership, control of stock by proxy, management position and authority, etc.[78] Where the treaty investor does not own at least 50 percent of the treaty business, the attorney may wish to consider the use of proxy agreements and/or management agreements to evidence his or her ability to develop and direct the business.

An equal share of the investment in a joint venture or an equal partnership of two parties generally does give controlling interest, if the joint venture and partner each retain full management rights and responsibilities.[79] However, an equal partnership with more than two partners would not give any of the parties control based on ownership, as the element of control would be too remote.[80]

In instances in which treaty country ownership may be too diffuse to permit one individual or company to demonstrate the ability to direct and develop the U.S. enterprise, the owners having treaty country nationality must:

- Show that together they own 50 percent of the U.S. enterprise; and
- Demonstrate that, at least collectively, they have the ability to develop and direct the U.S. enterprise.[81]

In these cases, an individual owner will not be eligible to receive an E-2 visa as the "investor," nor

---

[72] 22 CFR §41.51(b)(10); 9 FAM 41.51 N11.

[73] 9 FAM 41.51 N11.

[74] 22 CFR §41.51(b)(1)(ii); confirmation that this requirement does not apply to E-2 employees (and presumably E-1 employees as well) appears in *Matter of Walsh and Pollard*, 20 I&N Dec. 60 (BIA 1988), Visa Office Response to Interrogatory 17, digested at 66 *Interpreter Releases* 369 (Apr. 3, 1989).

[75] 22 CFR §41.51(b)(11).

[76] 9 FAM 41.51 N12.2.

[77] *Id.*

[78] *Matter of Walsh and Pollard,* Visa Office Response to Interrogatory 17, *supra* note 74.

[79] 9 FAM 41.51 N12. This note actually incorrectly defines the concept of "negative control." It states that "[w]ith each of the two parties possessing equal responsibilities, they each have the capacity of making decisions that are binding on the other party." This instead describes the nature of a partnership, where both parties have equal ownership and control over the entire partnership. Negative control actually contemplates each party having a veto power over decision making, as in the case of a joint venture where two shareholders both own 50 percent of the voting shares of the corporation. Neither may make a decision without the consent of the other, which results in negative control. However, this error does not affect DOS's position that both equal partnerships and joint ventures involving two parties is sufficient to give each party the ability to develop and direct the enterprise.

[80] *Id.*

[81] 9 FAM 41.51 N12.3.

may an employee be considered to be an employee of an owner for E-2 purposes.[82] However, an owner and any other employee may still qualify for E-2 status as an employee of the U.S. enterprise, which will be the treaty investor.[83]

In the case of franchised businesses, many franchise agreements contain restrictions on how the franchisee can operate the business. If the restrictions are too onerous, a consular officer may conclude that the franchisee has assigned its operational control to the franchiser by contract. However, a franchise business may still qualify for E-2 status if the franchisee retains sufficient control over the management of the business, including the ability: (i) to hire and fire employees; (ii) to set wage scales; and (iii) to set the hours of business.[84] In most cases, the ability to develop and direct the treaty enterprise will not become an issue as a result of the franchise agreement. However, if it does, practitioners should be prepared to explain how the franchisee continues to retain operational control.

Employees of E-1 and E-2 Principal Aliens

In most small businesses, an owner will seek E-2 status based on his or her investment in the treaty enterprise. However, there are circumstances where the investor will be required to seek E-2 status as an employee of his or her own company. For example, where the capital attributed to a particular owner is too small to qualify as an investor, he or she will have to file the application on behalf of the corporate entity as the treaty investor and then seek E-2 status as an employee thereof. In addition, the investor may wish to seek E-2 status on behalf of friends or relatives who intend to join in the treaty business. Such aliens will need to establish their eligibility as executives, supervisory employees, or essential skills workers.

General Requirements for Employees

As mentioned above, an alien employee of a treaty investor may be classified E-2 if the employee is in or is coming to the United States to engage in duties of an executive or supervisory character or, if employed in a lesser capacity, the employee has special qualifications that make the services to be rendered essential to the efficient operation of the enterprise.[85] Employees of treaty investors seeking E status must also have the same nationality as their employer.[86]

In order to support an E-2 application filed on behalf of an alien employee of a treaty trader or treaty investor, the employer must be:

- A person having the nationality of the treaty country, who is maintaining the status of treaty trader or treaty investor if in the United States or if not in the United States would be classifiable as a treaty trader or treaty investor; or

- An organization at least 50 percent owned by persons having the nationality of the treaty country who are maintaining nonimmigrant treaty trader or treaty investor status if residing in the United States or, if not residing in the United States, who would be classifiable as treaty traders or treaty investors.[87]

In other words, where the employer is residing in the United States in some capacity other than E-2, it is not possible to seek treaty investor status on behalf of employees. The same applies in the case of a corporate employer, where more than 50 percent of the individuals who own the employer are residing in the United States in some capacity other than E-2.

Executive or Supervisory Character

Executive or supervisory duties grant the employee ultimate control and responsibility for the enterprise's overall operation or a major component thereof.[88] An executive position provides the employee great authority to determine policy of and direction for the enterprise.[89] A supervisory position grants the employee supervisory responsibility for a significant proportion of an enterprise's operations and does not generally involve the direct supervision of low-level employees.[90]

In order to qualify as an executive or supervisory employee, the executive or supervisory element of the employee's position must be a principal and pri-

---

[82] *Id.*

[83] *Id.*

[84] *Matter of Kung*, 17 I&N Dec. 260 (Comm'r 1978). The franchise agreement in this case was fairly restrictive and yet the franchisee was still found to have sufficient control over the treaty enterprise. This suggests that the franchisor would require an extremely high level of control over the franchisee before the latter became ineligible for E-2 status.

[85] 22 CFR §41.51(b)(2).

[86] 9 FAM 41.51 N14.1.

[87] 22 CFR §41.51(b)(2).

[88] 22 CFR §41.51(b)(12).

[89] *Id.*

[90] *Id.*

mary function of the position and not an incidental or collateral function.[91] For example, if the position principally requires management skills or entails key supervisory responsibility for a large portion of a firm's operations and only incidentally involves routine substantive staff work, an E classification would generally be appropriate.[92] Conversely, if the position chiefly involves routine work and secondarily entails supervision of low-level employees, the position could not be termed executive or supervisory.[93]

In determining whether the proposed position is executive or supervisory, consular officers will consider the title of the position, its place in the company's organizational structure, the duties of the position, the degree to which the applicant will have ultimate control and responsibility for the company's overall operations or a major component thereof, the number and skill levels of the employees the applicant will supervise, the level of pay, and whether the applicant possesses qualifying executive or supervisory experience.[94]

The weight given to a particular factor will vary from case to case.[95] For example, the position title of "vice president" or "manager" might be of use in assessing the supervisory nature of a position if the applicant were coming to a major operation having numerous employees.[96] However, if the applicant were coming to a small, two-person office, such a title in and of itself would be of little significance.[97]

In the case of a small business, the company may only have a few employees and the manager may be required to perform some routine staff work in addition to traditional managerial duties. Unfortunately, the concept of a "functional manager," which is recognized in USCIS regulations for L-1A multinational managers,[98] is not expressly recognized for the E classification. However, there is also no specific requirement that an E-2 supervisory employee manage any subordinate workers. The definition of "supervisory character" states only that it does not involve the direct supervision of low-level employees.[99] A similar limitation applies to L-1A multinational managers as well.[100] Therefore, a functional manager might be considered a supervisory employee within the E-2 context, even though he or she does not directly manage any subordinate employees.

Essential Skills
General

Given the ongoing need to show that such an employee's special qualifications are essential to the treaty enterprise, it is normally not appropriate for investors to seek E-2 status in this capacity. However, it can still be used to bring other foreign nationals into the United States as employees of the treaty enterprise.

The applicant bears the burden of establishing at the time of application not only the need for the special qualifications that he or she offers but also the length of time that such skills will be needed.[101] In general, the E classification is intended for specialists and not for ordinary skilled workers.[102]

Special qualifications are those skills and/or aptitudes that an employee in a lesser capacity brings to a position or role that are essential to the successful or efficient operation of the enterprise.[103] The essential nature of the alien's skills to the employing firm is determined by assessing the degree of proven expertise of the alien in the area of operations involved, the uniqueness of the specific skill or aptitude, the length of experience and/or training with the firm, the period of training or other experience necessary to perform effectively the projected duties, and the salary that the special qualifications can command.[104]

Whether the special qualifications are essential will be assessed in light of all circumstances at the time of each visa application, on a case-by-case basis.[105] In assessing the specialized skills and their essentiality, the consular officer should consider such factors as:

- The degree of proven expertise of the alien in the area of specialization;

---

[91] Id.
[92] 9 FAM 41.51 N14.2
[93] Id.
[94] Id.
[95] Id.
[96] Id.
[97] Id.
[98] 8 CFR §214.2(l)(1)(ii)(B). Functional managers are not required to directly supervise any employees.
[99] 22 CFR §41.51(b)(12)(ii).
[100] 8 CFR §214.2(l)(1)(ii)(B).
[101] 9 FAM 41.51 N14.3-1.
[102] Id.
[103] 22 CFR §41.51(b)(13).
[104] Id.
[105] Id.

- The uniqueness of the specific skills;
- The function of the job to which the alien is destined; and
- The salary such special expertise can command.[106]

The availability of U.S. workers provides another factor in assessing the degree of specialization the applicant possesses and the essentiality of this skilled worker to the successful operation of the business.[107] This consideration is not a labor certification test, but a measure of the degree of specialization of the skills in question and the need for such skills.[108] For example, a TV technician coming to train U.S. workers in new TV technology not generally available in the U.S. market probably would qualify for a visa.[109] If the essential skills question cannot be resolved on the basis of initial documentation, the consular officer might ask the firm to provide statements from such sources as chambers of commerce, labor organizations, industry trade sources, or state employment services as to the unavailability of U.S. workers in the skill areas concerned.[110]

There is no requirement that an "essential" employee have any previous employment with the treaty enterprise.[111] The only time that such previous employment is a factor is when the needed skills can only be obtained by that employment.[112] The above criteria are similar, but not identical, to those applied in the context of L-1B specialized knowledge worker cases.

In the L-1B context, "specialized knowledge" means special knowledge possessed by an individual of the petitioning organization's product, service, research, equipment, techniques, management, or other interests and its application in international markets, or an advanced level of knowledge or expertise in the organization's processes and procedures.[113] This "specialized knowledge" definition clearly emphasizes knowledge of the petitioning organization that is gained while working with that organization abroad. In contrast, the definition of "essential skills" makes clear that an employee can be essential without having previously worked for the treaty enterprise.

There are two distinct types of essential skills workers: (a) short-term essential skills workers; and (b) long-term essential skills workers. Each type is briefly discussed below.

Short-Term Need

In the case of short-term essential workers, the employer may need the skills for only a relatively short period of time when the purpose of the employee's admission relates to start-up operations (of either the business or a new activity by the business), or to the training and supervision of technicians employed in manufacturing, maintenance, and repair functions.[114] Ordinarily skilled workers can qualify as essential employees but this almost always involves workers needed for start-up or training purposes.[115]

A new business or an established business expanding into a new field in the United States might need employees who are ordinarily skilled workers for a short period of time.[116] Such employees derive their essentiality from their familiarity with the overseas operations rather than the nature of their skills.[117]

Employers in such cases are expected to train U.S. workers to replace these employees, usually within one or two years.[118] Short-term essential skills workers are therefore in a less desirable position than L-1B specialized knowledge workers, who are not required to demonstrate that U.S. workers will be trained to replace them.[119]

To illustrate the above, it may be useful to consider *In Re: X*.[120] In that case, the treaty investor employee sought an extension of stay for its E-2 employee as a "tatami service specialist" in a Japanese restaurant. The employer described her position as follows:

---

[106] 9 FAM 41.51 N14.3-2.
[107] *Id.*
[108] *Id.*
[109] *Id.*
[110] *Id.*
[111] 9 FAM 41.51 N14.3-4.
[112] *Id.*
[113] 8 CFR §214.2(*l*)(1)(ii)(D).

[114] 9 FAM 41.51 N14.3-1.
[115] 9 FAM 41.51 N14.3-3.
[116] *Id.*
[117] *Id.*
[118] 9 FAM 41.51 N14.3-1, N14.3-3. *See also* 8 CFR §214.2(e)(18)(ii).
[119] L-1B specialized knowledge workers rarely have difficulty extending their status up to the five-year maximum described in INA §214(c)(2)(D).
[120] 11 *Immig. Rptr.* B2-79 (AAU 1993).

The gourmet cuisine and service in a "Tatami" room is the most highly specialized, intricate and important in Japanese gastronomy, and requires intimate familiarity with the Japanese arts of the tea ceremony and flower arrangement. Because of her four years of experience, and her high level of linguistic proficiency, acquired at the Tokyo Foreign Language School, [the E-2 employee] is uniquely qualified for her position.

One year of training was required for the applicant to learn how to perform the duties of her position, and she earned $29,705 a year for her services.

Relying upon the guidance contained in the FAM, the Administrative Appeals Unit (AAU) stated that applicant had to demonstrate that she was either a highly trained and specially qualified technician, or a start-up employee of a new enterprise whose essentially was based on her familiarity with the overseas operations of the employer rather than on the nature of her skills. It concluded that the applicant was not a technician or a highly trained employee. She had not been shown to have any familiarity with an overseas operation of her employer in the United States and the employer's business operation was not a new enterprise. The absence of a training program intended to replace the alien with a U.S. worker was also considered a negative factor. The AAU concluded that she was an ordinary skilled worker and denied her extension of stay.

The situation may have been different if the employee (although an ordinary skills worker) had previously worked for the employer's foreign operation, the U.S. operation was still considered a new enterprise, and/or the employer had a training program in place designed to eventually replace the employee.

Long-Term Need

Long-term essentiality may be established in connection with continuous activities in such areas as product improvement, quality control, or the provision of a service not generally available in the United States.[121] If an applicant establishes that he or she has special qualifications and, on a long-term basis, these qualifications are essential for the efficient operation of the treaty enterprise, the training of United States workers as replacement workers is not required.[122] It should therefore be possible for such an employee to remain in the United States in E-2 status for an indefinite period of time.

The precedent decision relating to long-term essential skills workers is *Matter of Walsh and Pollard*.[123] The employees in that case were automotive design engineers from Britain who were coming to the United States (pursuant to a contract between the treaty investor and General Motors) for the purpose of redesigning General Motors's line of cars in a smaller, more European fashion. It was established that a worker with an engineering degree would still require approximately 10 years of training to become an automotive design engineer and that there were not sufficient numbers of U.S. automotive design engineers to fill the present needs of the automotive industry. The Board of Immigration Appeals (BIA) concluded that the employees were long-term essential skills workers and the treaty investor was not expected to replace the employees with U.S. workers in the future.

Intention to Depart from the United States

In order to qualify for E-2 classification, the alien must intend to depart from the United States upon the termination of his or her status.[124] However, an applicant does not have to establish an intention to remain in the United States for a specific temporary period of time or the existence of a residence in a foreign country that the applicant does not intend to abandon.[125] The applicant's expression of an unequivocal intent to return when the E-2 status ends is normally sufficient, in the absence of specific evidence to the contrary.[126] This intent normally can be expressed by way of a written statement submitted with the E-2 visa application.

A limited form of dual intent is recognized for E-2 nonimmigrants. DOS's position is that an applicant who is the beneficiary of an immigrant petition may still be eligible for E-2 status by showing that he or she will not remain in the United States to adjust status to lawful permanent resident or otherwise remain in the United States regardless of the legality of his or her status.[127] USCIS's position is that an application for initial admission, change of status, or

---

[121] 22 CFR §41.51(b)(13)(ii).
[122] 9 FAM 41.51 N14.3-3.
[123] *Matter of Walsh and Pollard*, 20 I&N Dec. 60 (BIA 1988).
[124] 22 CFR §41.51(b)(1)(iii).
[125] 9 FAM 41.51 N15.
[126] *Id.*
[127] *Id.*

extension of stay in E-2 classification may not be denied solely on the basis of an approved request for permanent labor certification or a filed or approved immigrant visa preference petition.[128] In addition, an applicant who has already filed an application for adjustment of status may still file for an extension of E-2 status after that date.[129] This clearly shows that an E-2 nonimmigrant may be the beneficiary of a labor certification, immigrant petition, or have an adjustment of status application pending, and still remain eligible for E status.

Notwithstanding the above, INA §214(b) still applies to E-2 nonimmigrants. A prior overstay or violation of status while in the United States will often strongly infer that the applicant does not intend to depart from the United States upon termination of his or her status and it will be very difficult to overcome such an inference. The only way to overcome the presumption of immigrant intent in such situations is to establish (if possible) that the violation or overstay was brief and inadvertent.

Labor Disputes (Citizens of Canada, Mexico, Chile, and Singapore Only)

Citizens of Canada and Mexico are not entitled to E-2 classification if there is a strike or lockout in progress in the course of a labor dispute in the occupational classification at the place or intended place of employment, unless such alien establishes, pursuant to the regulations, that the alien's entry will not affect adversely the settlement of the strike or lockout or the employment of any person who is involved in the strike or lockout.[130] A similar restriction also applies to citizens of Chile and Singapore.[131]

INCIDENTAL ACTIVITIES WHILE IN E-2 STATUS

Treaty investors are entitled to engage in incidental activities as long as their primary purpose for coming to the United States is to develop and direct the treaty enterprise.[132] However, these incidental activities are limited to those activities in which a visitor could engage. In addition, as dependents of treaty traders and investors are permitted to attend school,[133] it is probable that the treaty trader or investor will also be permitted to do so.

However, a treaty investor or treaty employee may only engage in employment that is consistent with the terms and conditions of his or her status and the activity forming the basis for the E-2 treaty status.[134] For example, in *Matter of Laigo*,[135] the BIA found that a self-employed treaty investor (who controlled companies that were engaged in the development of a Philippine Cultural and Trade Center) violated her status when she began selling cemetery plots on behalf of an unrelated third party company, in return for commissions.

The one exception is employment with a subsidiary of the treaty enterprise. Performing work for subsidiaries of a common parent enterprise or organization will not be deemed to constitute a substantive change in the terms and conditions of the underlying E treaty employment if, at the time the E-2 treaty status was determined, the applicant presented evidence establishing:

- The enterprise or organization, and any subsidiaries thereof, where the work will be performed; the requisite parent-subsidiary relationship; and that the subsidiary independently qualifies as a treaty organization or enterprise;

- In the case of an employee of a treaty trader or treaty investor, the work to be performed requires executive, supervisory, or essential skills; and

- The work is consistent with the terms and conditions of the activity forming the basis of the classification.[136]

DEPENDENTS OF E-2 NONIMMIGRANTS

The spouse and dependent children (unmarried and under age 21) of an E-2 nonimmigrant are entitled to the same classification as the principal alien.[137] The nationality of a spouse and child is not material to their eligibility.[138]

Such treaty dependents are permitted to engage in incidental activities, such as engaging in tour-

---

[128] 8 CFR §214.2(e)(5).

[129] Legacy INS Memorandum, P. Virtue, Acting Executive Commissioner, HQ 70/6.2.5, 70/6.2.9 (Aug. 5, 1997), reprinted in 74 Interpreter Releases 1226–29 (Aug. 11, 1997).

[130] INA §214(j)(1); see also 22 CFR §41.51(b)(14).

[131] INA §214(j)(2).

[132] 9 FAM 41.11 N3.1.

[133] 8 CFR §248.3(e)(2); 9 FAM 41.11 N5.2.

[134] 8 CFR §214.2(e)(8)(i).

[135] *Matter of Laigo*, 15 I&N Dec. 65 (BIA 1974).

[136] 8 CFR §214.2(e)(8)(ii).

[137] 22 CFR §41.51(b)(3).

[138] *Id.*

ism[139] or attending school.[140] However, this does not mean that treaty dependents are entitled to engage in employment without authorization. According to 8 CFR §214.1(e), a nonimmigrant may not engage in any employment unless she has been accorded a nonimmigrant classification, which authorizes employment, or she has been granted permission to engage in employment. Any unauthorized employment by a nonimmigrant constitutes a failure to maintain status, which may give rise to removal proceedings.

Fortunately, as a result of legislation enacted in 2002, dependent spouses of E-2 nonimmigrants who have been admitted in E-2 status may now apply for an open-market employment authorization (EAD).[141] This employment authorization permits dependent spouses holding E-2 status to work for any employer, once they have received an employment authorization document. However, the legislation does not extend employment eligibility to dependent children of the principal alien.

Although the INA now permits the issuance of an EAD to dependent spouses of E-2 nonimmigrants, USCIS's regulations have not been amended to reflect this fact. The instructions to Form I-765 state that dependent spouses of E-2 nonimmigrants should make reference to 8 CFR §274a.12(a)(17); however, this subsection does not yet exist. Nevertheless, USCIS has been issuing EADs to dependent spouses of E-2 nonimmigrants in the absence of these implementing regulations.

PERIOD OF VISA VALIDITY AND PERIOD OF ADMISSION

The maximum validity period for an E visa will depend upon reciprocity with the country of the alien's nationality. The maximum visa validity period for each country is shown in the reciprocity schedules that appear in the FAM, but in many cases, will be five years.[142]

The period of validity of a nonimmigrant visa is the period during which the alien may use it in making an application for admission.[143] This has no relationship to the period of time the immigration authorities at a port of entry may authorize the alien to remain in the United States.[144]

To determine the maximum period of admission to the United States, one must refer to USCIS regulations. According to these regulations, an E-2 nonimmigrant (including dependents) may be admitted for an initial period of not more than two years at a time.[145] This is the period that will be shown on the alien's Form I-94. However, as long as the alien continues to hold a valid E-2 visa, he or she may depart from the United States before the expiration of this two-year period and then reenter the United States using the visa. At the time of admission, the alien may request a new Form I-94 from the port of entry for an additional two years.

As the validity period of the visa has no relationship to the period of admission, the alien may seek a two-year period of admission even if the visa is due to expire within a shorter period of time. Even if the alien enters the United States one day before the visa is due to expire, the immigration officer at the port of entry should issue a Form I-94 for a period of two years. However, if the alien subsequently leaves the United States prior to the expiration of his or her Form I-94, he or she will not be readmitted for the remainder of his or her status without a valid visa (since a visa is required for admission to the United States).

This can still be useful in light of the long delays in adjudicating E visa applications at consulates abroad. An alien whose visa is about to expire may depart from the United States and then reenter (using the still valid visa), obtain a new Form I-94 for a period of two years, and then continue working in the United States while his or her visa application is pending abroad.

WHERE TO APPLY

Aliens who are currently in the United States under some other status may seek E-2 status from USCIS by applying for a change of status through the California Service Center. However, in most cases it is preferable for the alien to apply for an E visa through a consulate abroad.

In contrast to most other nonimmigrant employment classifications, U.S. consulates issue E-2 visas

---

[139] 9 FAM 41.11 N3.1.

[140] 8 CFR §248.3(e)(2); 9 FAM 41.11 N5.2.

[141] Pub. Law. 107-124 (Jan. 16, 2002).

[142] 9 FAM Appendix C. The reciprocity tables currently appear online at: http://travel.state.gov/visa/frvi/reciprocity/reciprocity_3272.html.

[143] 22 CFR §41.112(a).

[144] Id.

[145] 8 CFR §214.2(e)(19).

abroad without prior petition approval from USCIS. Also, because E-2 visa eligibility is derived from treaties negotiated by the United States, the general consensus is that DOS has primary jurisdiction over E-2 adjudications.

Visa applicants who previously acquired E-2 status through a change of status in the United States will find that many consular posts do not simply issue E-2 visas based on a prior USCIS adjudication. Instead, they will require the alien to submit a new application to the consular post along with completed forms, fees, and supporting documentation. For this reason, it is usually more efficient to simply apply through a consular post.

Of course, there are exceptions to the general rule. Where the consular post having jurisdiction over the applicant's country of citizenship or residence is particularly tough, it may be preferable to apply initially through the California Service Center and apply for a visa abroad after the treaty business has established a track record of success and the applicant's investment therein has grown. In addition, where the applicant must immediately begin his or her management of the treaty business, it may be quicker to seek a change of status (using premium processing) and apply for the E-2 visa later.

Aliens who acquire E-2 status by means of a change of status will be unable to travel abroad until they have obtained an E-2 visa at a consular post abroad. However, they should be permitted to travel to a contiguous territory and then reenter the United States, despite the fact that they do not possess a valid E-2 visa, pursuant to 22 CFR §41.112(d).

Unfortunately, Canadian citizens who change status to E-2 will be unable to take advantage of 22 CFR §41.112(d). This is because Canadians are visa exempt under most nonimmigrant categories. As they will not have initially entered the United States using a visa, there will be no visa to revalidate under 22 CFR §41.112(d).

Until recently, aliens who were already in E-2 status in the United States could also choose to revalidate their visas through the DOS Visa Office in St. Louis, Missouri, instead of applying at a consulate abroad. However, DOS announced that visa revalidation would no longer be available for E-2 nonimmigrants as of July 16, 2004.[146]

E-2 VISA RENEWALS

Practitioners should remember to treat E-2 visa renewals and extensions of stay with the same care as initial E-2 applications. Several years will have elapsed since the initial visa application or change of status was adjudicated. During this time, any number of events may have occurred, which will affect the nonimmigrant's E-2 eligibility.

For example, a subsequent change of ownership may have altered the nationality of the treaty business. In addition, the economic downturn may have reduced the net income of the business to the point where it is considered a marginal enterprise. The treaty business also may have acquired real property that is subject to a mortgage, which would alter the proportionality of the investment.

An E-2 nonimmigrant seeking a visa renewal or extension of stay will be expected to establish his or her eligibility for E-2 status *ab initio*. All E-2 eligibility requirements should therefore be re-assessed based on the alien's current fact situation.

CONCLUSION

The E-2 category allows aliens who may be unwilling or unable to meet the more stringent requirements of the EB-5 immigrant investor category to nonetheless pursue entrepreneurial activities in the United States. In addition, aliens who wish to avoid tax obligations imposed on lawful permanent residents may prefer the E-2 over the EB-5. As a result, practitioners should always consider the E-2 category when representing prospective entrepreneurs and investors.

---

[146] "AILA Practice Advisory—Additional Information on Termination of Visa Revalidations," *published on* AILA InfoNet at Doc. No. 04062363 (*posted* June 23, 2004).

EXHIBIT A—LIST OF TREATY COUNTRIES

Country	Visa	Date
Albania	E-2	January 04, 1998
Argentina	E-1	December 20, 1854
Argentina	E-2	December 20, 1854
Armenia	E-2	March 29, 1996
Australia	E-1	December 16, 1991
Australia	E-2	December 27, 1991
Austria	E-1	May 27, 1931
Austria	E-2	May 27, 1931
Azerbaijan	E-2	August 02, 2001
Bahrain	E-2	May 31, 2001
Bangladesh	E-2	July 25, 1989
Belgium	E-1	October 03, 1963
Belgium	E-2	October 03, 1963
Bolivia	E-1	November 09, 1862
Bolivia	E-2	June 06, 2001
Bosnia and Herzegovina[11]	E-1	November 15, 1882
Bosnia and Herzegovina[11]	E-2	November 15, 1882
Brunei	E-1	July 11, 1853
Bulgaria	E-2	June 02, 1994
Cameroon	E-2	April 06, 1989
Canada	E-1	January 01, 1993
Canada	E-2	January 01, 1993
Chile	E-1	January 01, 2004
Chile	E-2	January 01, 2004
China (Taiwan)[1]	E-1	November 30, 1948
China (Taiwan)[1]	E-2	November 30, 1948
Colombia	E-1	June 10, 1848
Colombia	E-2	June 10, 1848
Congo (Brazzaville)	E-2	August 13, 1994
Congo (Kinshasa)	E-2	July 28, 1989
Costa Rica	E-1	May 26, 1852
Costa Rica	E-2	May 26, 1852
Croatia[11]	E-1	November 15, 1882
Croatia[11]	E-2	November 15, 1882
Czech Republic[2]	E-2	January 01, 1993
Denmark[3]	E-1	July 30, 1961
Ecuador	E-2	May 11, 1997
Egypt	E-2	June 27, 1992
Estonia	E-1	May 22, 1926
Estonia	E-2	February 16, 1997
Ethiopia	E-1	October 08, 1953
Ethiopia	E-2	October 08, 1953
Finland	E-1	August 10, 1934
Finland	E-2	December 01, 1992
France[4]	E-1	December 21, 1960
France[4]	E-2	December 21, 1960
Georgia	E-2	August 17, 1997
Germany	E-1	July 14, 1956
Germany	E-2	July 14, 1956
Greece	E-1	October 13, 1954
Grenada	E-2	March 03, 1989
Honduras	E-1	July 19, 1928
Honduras	E-2	July 19, 1928
Iran	E-1	June 16, 1957
Iran	E-2	June 16, 1957
Ireland	E-1	September 14, 1950
Ireland	E-2	November 18, 1992
Israel	E-1	April 03, 1954
Italy	E-1	July 26, 1949
Italy	E-2	July 26, 1949
Jamaica	E-2	March 07, 1997
Japan[5]	E-1	October 30, 1953
Japan[5]	E-2	October 30, 1953
Jordan	E-1	December 17, 2001
Jordan	E-2	December 17, 2001
Kazakhstan	E-2	January 12, 1994
Korea (South)	E-1	November 07, 1957
Korea (South)	E-2	November 07, 1957
Kyrgyzstan	E-2	January 12, 1994
Latvia	E-1	July 25, 1928
Latvia	E-2	December 26, 1996
Liberia	E-1	November 21, 1939
Liberia	E-2	November 21, 1939
Lithuania	E-2	November 22, 2001
Luxembourg	E-1	March 28, 1963
Luxembourg	E-2	March 28, 1963
Macedonia, the Former Yugoslav Republic of (FRY)	E-1	November 15, 1882

Macedonia, the Former Yugoslav Republic of (FRY)	E-2	November 15, 1882
Mexico	E-1	January 01, 1994
Mexico	E-2	January 01, 1994
Moldova	E-2	November 25, 1994
Mongolia	E-2	January 01, 1997
Morocco	E-2	May 29, 1991
Netherlands[6]	E-1	December 05, 1957
Netherlands[6]	E-2	December 05, 1957
Norway[7]	E-1	January 18, 1928
Norway[7]	E-2	January 18, 1928
Oman	E-1	June 11, 1960
Oman	E-2	June 11, 1960
Pakistan	E-1	February 12, 1961
Pakistan	E-2	February 12, 1961
Panama	E-2	May 30, 1991
Paraguay	E-1	March 07, 1860
Paraguay	E-2	March 07, 1860
Philippines	E-1	September 06, 1955
Philippines	E-2	September 06, 1955
Poland	E-1	August 06, 1994
Poland	E-2	August 06, 1994
Romania	E-2	January 15, 1994
Senegal	E-2	October 25, 1990
Singapore	E-1	January 01, 2004
Singapore	E-2	January 01, 2004
Slovak Republic[2]	E-2	January 01, 1993
Slovenia[11]	E-1	November 15, 1882
Slovenia[11]	E-2	November 15, 1882
Spain[8]	E-1	April 14, 1903
Spain[8]	E-2	April 14, 1903
Sri Lanka	E-2	May 01, 1993
Suriname[9]	E-1	February 10, 1963
Suriname[9]	E-2	February 10, 1963
Sweden	E-1	February 20, 1992
Sweden	E-2	February 20, 1992
Switzerland	E-1	November 08, 1855
Switzerland	E-2	November 08, 1855
Thailand	E-1	June 08, 1968
Thailand	E-2	June 08, 1968
Togo	E-1	February 05, 1967
Togo	E-2	February 05, 1967
Trinidad & Tobago	E-2	December 26, 1996
Tunisia	E-2	February 07, 1993
Turkey	E-1	February 15, 1933
Turkey	E-2	May 18, 1990
Ukraine	E-2	November 16, 1996
United Kingdom[10]	E-1	July 03, 1815
United Kingdom[10]	E-2	July 03, 1815
Yugoslavia[11]	E-1	November 15, 1882
Yugoslavia[11]	E-2	November 15, 1882

[1] **China (Taiwan)**—Pursuant to Section 6 of the TRA and Executive Order 12143, 44 Fed. Reg. 37191, this agreement which was concluded with the Taiwan authorities prior to January 1, 1979, is administered on a nongovernmental basis by the American Institute in Taiwan, a nonprofit District of Columbia corporation, and constitutes neither recognition of the Taiwan authorities nor the continuation of any official relationship with Taiwan.

[2] **Czech Republic and Slovak Republic**—The Treaty with the Czech and Slovak Federal Republic entered into force on December 19, 1992; entered into force for the Czech Republic and Slovak Republic as separate states on January 1, 1993.

[3] **Denmark**—The Convention of 1826 does not apply to the Faroe Islands of Greenland. The Treaty, which entered into force on July 30, 1961, does not apply to Greenland.

[4] **France**—The Treaty, which entered into force on December 21, 1960, applies to the departments of Martinique, Guadeloupe, French Guiana, and Reunion.

[5] **Japan**—The Treaty, which entered into force on October 30, 1953, was made applicable to the Bonin Islands on June 26, 1968, and to the Ryukyu Islands on May 15, 1972.

[6] **Netherlands**—The Treaty, which entered into force on December 5, 1957, is applicable to Aruba and Netherlands Antilles.

[7] **Norway**—The Treaty, which entered into force on September 13, 1932, does not apply to Svalbard (Spitzbergen and certain lesser islands).

[8] **Spain**—The Treaty, which entered into force on April 14, 1903, is applicable to all territories.

[9] **Suriname**—The Treaty with the Netherlands, which entered into force December 5, 1957, was made applicable to Suriname on February 10, 1963.

[10] **United Kingdom**—The Convention which entered into force on July 3, 1815, applies only to British territory in Europe (the British Isles (except the Republic of Ireland), the Channel Islands, and Gibraltar) and to "inhabitants" of such territory. This term, as used in the Convention, means "one who resides actually and permanently in a given place, and has his domicile there." Also, in order to qualify for treaty trader or treaty investor status under this treaty, the alien must be a national of the United Kingdom. Individuals having the nationality of members of the Commonwealth other

than the United Kingdom do not qualify for treaty trader or treaty investor status under this treaty.

[11] **Yugoslavia**—The U.S. view is that the Socialist Federal Republic of Yugoslavia (SFRY) has dissolved and that the successors that formerly made up the SFRY—Bosnia and Herzegovina, Croatia, the Former Yugoslav Republic of Macedonia, Slovenia, and the Federal Republic of Yugoslavia continue to be bound by the treaty in force with the SFRY and the time of dissolution.

Permanent Residence Without Labor Certification—Using the EB-1 and EB-2 Classifications for Small Businesses and Entrepreneurs

by Susan L. Pilcher[*]

Small business owners and investors, self-employed individuals, and entrepreneurs face a number of unique challenges in establishing eligibility for permanent residence in the United States. Obstacles inherent in the labor certification process mean that foreign nationals in these circumstances may need to explore the first and second employment-based preference classifications for additional options statutorily exempt from the labor certification requirement. Where viable, these options further present tremendous advantages in terms of visa availability and processing time. Understanding the primary hurdles facing self-petitioners, business owners, or small businesses within each of these narrow frameworks is key to developing an effective and successful strategy.

Accordingly, this article reviews the fundamentals of petitions in the five employment-based classifications known as: (a) Aliens with Extraordinary Ability; (b) Multinational Managers and Executives; (c) Outstanding Professors or Researchers; (d) Exceptional Ability (Schedule A, Group II); and (e) National Interest Waivers.[1] It also highlights some of the issues, obstacles, and opportunities that may be encountered by small business owners, investors, and entrepreneurs who pursue one of these paths to permanent residence.

With the exception of the Multinational Managers and Executives classification, these petitions are based on records of accomplishment and relative merit. While the regulations may appear rigorously objective on their face, their application tends to be more a matter of drawing subjective impressions. Consequently, successful petitions are primarily the result of skillful advocacy, with the supporting documentation painting persuasive portraits of relative merit. Readers should understand at the outset that this article's intended audience of "self-petitioners, business owners, and entrepreneurs" encompasses individuals with wildly diverse profiles. As among these applicants, experienced practitioners will agree that those individuals with clearly articulable individual accomplishments and solid or impressive financials will find U.S. Citizenship and Immigration Services (USCIS) a more welcoming audience, notwithstanding theoretical hurdles that could be raised by a skeptical adjudicator. For those with modest resources and a less well developed record of commercial, professional, or academic successes, a more conservative approach may be warranted. Thus, this article aims both to articulate technical legal risks, for the particular benefit of those whose efforts may prove marginal, as well as

---

[*] **Susan L. Pilcher**, *spilcher@cslaw.us*, is Of Counsel to the firm of Carroll & Scribner, P.C. in Burlington, Vermont, where her general immigration practice includes a substantial focus on EB-5 and investment-related matters. Ms. Pilcher's professional background includes nearly a decade of full-time law teaching, including general and specialized immigration law courses, at the University of Arkansas School of Law (Fayetteville), a federal court clerkship in San Diego, California, commercial law practice, and many years of diverse and rewarding experience representing clients in virtually all types of immigration-related matters. She obtained her J.D. with distinction from Stanford Law School, where she served as Managing Editor of the Stanford Law Review. Ms. Pilcher has published and lectured extensively on immigration law topics, and she is active in agency liaison functions for the American Immigration Lawyers Association (AILA).

[1] Due to the breadth of its subject matter, this article is intended only to provide an overview of possible petition types and issues that will be of common concern to many readers of this book. While covering the essential contours of the statute and regulations, it should be understood that in-depth treatment is beyond the article's scope. Where appropriate, *continued*

the notes will direct readers to particularly useful articles and other resources that explore each of the covered topics in more detail. As a general matter, the author acknowledges three previously published works surveying the same subject matter: J. Quill, "Employment-Based Sponsorship Exempt from Labor Certification—Issues for Small Businesses and Entrepreneurs," *Immigration Options for Investors and Entrepreneurs* 29 (AILA 2006); and A. Chehrazi et al., "Employment-Based Petitions Exempt from Labor Certification," *Immigration & Nationality Law Handbook* 291 (AILA 2005–06 Ed.); C. Weber, "Immigration Without Labor Certification: When and Why to File an EB-1 or NIW Petition," 9 *Bender's Immigr. Bull.* 571 (May 1, 2004).

to explore the practical opportunities for those whose achievements may open doors.

EB-1(A) EXTRAORDINARY ABILITY: THE CREAM OF THE CROP

First-preference immigrant classification as a "priority worker" is available to a select few foreign nationals who have extraordinary ability in the sciences, arts, education, business, or athletics. The statute specifies that the prospective immigrant's extraordinary ability must have been demonstrated by sustained national or international acclaim and his achievements recognized in the field through extensive documentation. Finally, the beneficiary must establish intent to enter the United States to continue work in the area of extraordinary ability, and that his or her entry will substantially benefit prospectively the United States.[2] The regulations define "extraordinary ability" as a level of expertise indicating that the individual is one of that small percentage who have risen to the very top the field of endeavor.[3]

The statute's reference to "extensive documentation" is taken a step further by the regulations, which require that the beneficiary's sustained acclaim and recognition within his or her field of expertise be persuasively documented with evidence of one major, internationally recognized award (such as a Nobel prize or an Olympic medal), or alternatively, with evidence that satisfies at least three of ten substantive criteria, as follows:

(i) Documentation of the alien's receipt of lesser nationally or internationally recognized prizes or awards for excellence in the field of endeavor;

(ii) Documentation of the alien's membership in associations in the field for which classification is sought, which require outstanding achievements of their members, as judged by recognized national or international experts in their disciplines or fields;

(iii) Published material about the alien in professional or major trade publications or other major media, relating to the alien's work in the field for which classification is sought. Such evidence shall include the title, date, and author of the material, and any necessary translation;

(iv) Evidence of the alien's participation, either individually or on a panel, as a judge of the work of others in the same or an allied field of specification for which classification is sought;

(v) Evidence of the alien's original scientific, scholarly, artistic, athletic, or business-related contributions of major significance in the field;

(vi) Evidence of the alien's authorship of scholarly articles in the field, in professional or major trade publications or other major media;

(vii) Evidence of the display of the alien's work in the field at artistic exhibitions or showcases;

(viii) Evidence that the alien has performed in a leading or critical role for organizations or establishments that have a distinguished reputation;

(ix) Evidence that the alien has commanded a high salary or other significantly high remuneration for services, in relation to others in the field; or

(x) Evidence of commercial successes in the performing arts, as shown by box office receipts or record, cassette, compact disk, or video sales.[4]

USCIS takes the position that not every beneficiary who meets at least three of the ten criteria will qualify as an alien with extraordinary ability. In keeping with its interpretation that extraordinary ability can describe only a "small percentage who have risen to the very top," USCIS adjudications reportedly involve skeptical qualitative review of the evidence submitted in support of each of the qualifying criteria, to determine the extent to which the petitioner's showing demonstrates that the beneficiary is genuinely among the elite in his or her field. Art-

---

[2] Immigration and Nationality Act (INA) §203(b)(1)(A). The regulations do not prescribe evidence required to establish prospective benefit to the United States, as in most cases the evidence that a foreign national with extraordinary ability will continue to work in his field of expertise is, itself, indicative of substantial prospective benefit. U.S. Citizenship and Immigration Services (USCIS) (legacy Immigration and Naturalization Service (INS)) has acknowledged that in the vast majority of cases, the evidence of the beneficiary's extraordinary ability itself, without more, will satisfy this requirement. *See* Letter, Skerrett, Chief, Immig. Branch, Adjudications, HQ 204.24-C (Aug. 10, 1995), *reprinted in* 72 *Interpreter Releases* 1281–82 (Sept. 18, 1995) (Skerrett Letter). However, as it is an essential statutory element of eligibility, petitioners should ensure that the matter of prospective benefit is not overlooked, particularly where there may be questions of marginality or controversial features to the beneficiary's work.

[3] 8 CFR §204.5(h)(2).

[4] 8 CFR §204.5(h)(3).

fully defining the beneficiary's field of expertise in a way that highlights the beneficiary's relative merit can be the determinative feature of a well-crafted and approvable extraordinary ability petition.[5]

Notably, the regulation invites the submission of "comparable evidence" (without defining what that might be) wholly in lieu of the ten specified criteria where the criteria "do not readily apply to the beneficiary's occupation."[6] Precedent suggests that the agency reads this regulation narrowly, accepting and considering "comparable evidence" in the absence of probative documentation relating to three of the criteria only where it is persuaded that the specified criteria cannot be used to assess the beneficiary's relative stature among others in the field.[7] In practice, however, whether one frames the case using the specified criteria or the "comparable evidence" catch-all, it is important to document the beneficiary's accomplishments using both direct evidence (*i.e.*, award, publication, membership certificate, etc.) and indirect evidence (*i.e.*, expert opinion letters, documents evidencing third-party recognition, etc.). The indirect, qualitative evidence generally serves as the quintessential evidence of sustained acclaim and recognition within the field. The required showing ultimately is one of sustained national or international recognition for achievement. If a well crafted presentation can demonstrate this degree of relative merit as compared to others in the field, there is considerable opportunity for favorable adjudication.

Importantly, the regulation explicitly provides that an offer of employment is not required.[8] The beneficiary, or any person on behalf of the beneficiary, may serve as the petitioner.[9] However, the regulations suggest the petition must include "clear evidence" that the alien will continue working in the area of expertise, which evidence may include, among other things, prearranged contracts or job offer(s).[10]

Because self-petitioning is expressly permitted and job offers are unnecessary, the extraordinary ability classification is a particularly appealing classification for the independent investor or entrepreneur. If the prospective immigrant may be able to satisfy the qualitative criteria relating to sustained national or international acclaim and recognition in the field, counsel should carefully consider the following potential obstacles:

Where there is no employer, USCIS may be more rigorous in terms of proof that the alien will continue work in the area of expertise. The regulation states that "a statement from the beneficiary detailing plans on how he or she intends to continue his or her work in the United States" could satisfy the "clear evidence" requirement. In many cases, the necessary inferences may be drawn from the nature of the beneficiary's work and stated agenda alone. The self-petitioner who is more risk averse will want to document not only the specifics of a plan, but also provide objective indicia of an ability to implement it with a likelihood of success. Such indicia could include, for example, business dealings falling technically short of contracts and job offers, such as a strong past history of contract work for U.S. employers, specific inquiries and expressions of interest from such employers (or ongoing negotiations with the same), a history of commanding and receiving a high level of remuneration as compared to others in the field, and a history of affiliation with renowned or prestigious organizations.[11] Beneficiaries nearing retirement age or whose achievements are not of recent vintage, in particular, would do well to address this criterion adequately in the initial petition.

---

[5] For excellent recent discussion of the art of field delineation in the context of USCIS adjudications, see N. Waxman, "What a Difference a Field Makes: Field Delineation in the EB-1 and EB-2 Classifications," *Immigration & Nationality Law Handbook* 129 (AILA 2008–09 Ed.); R. Sostrin *et al.*, "Responding to Difficult RFEs: The Secret" to Winning EB-1-1, EB-1-2, and NIW Cases," *Immigration & Nationality Law Handbook* 335 (2009–10 Ed.) (also including detailed discussion of common Request for Evidence (RFE) issues, evidentiary standards, and practical tips for preparing successful petitions).

[6] 8 CFR §204.5(h)(4).

[7] *See, e.g., Matter of [name not provided]*, EAC 04 033 50279 (AAO May 2, 2007) (corporate banker may not rely on "comparable evidence"), *published on* AILA InfoNet at Doc. No. 08051464 (*posted* May 14, 2008); *Matter of [name not provided]*, LIN 96 203 50280 (AAO Apr. 27, 1998), 19 Immgr. Rptr. B2-9 (10 specified criteria inapplicable to showman and driver of Clydesdale draft horses; petition approved on "comparable evidence").

[8] 8 CFR §204.5(h)(5).

[9] 8 CFR §204.5(h)(1). As used in this section, "person" is used in its legal sense, which includes both individuals and legal entities. *See Matter of M–*, 8 I&N Dec. 24 (BIA 1958, AG 1958) (corporation may petition for owner in extraordinary ability classification).

[10] 8 CFR §204.5(h)(5).

[11] The author is indebted to an article by John Quill, *supra* note 1, for several of these examples.

Entrepreneurs and investors intending to embark on a new venture, start a new company, or take their talents in a new direction, may face additional hurdles. USCIS could question whether the beneficiary will be working "in the area of expertise" if oversight of a new venture will involve taking on administrative or financial responsibilities, or managing subordinates, in addition to working at his or her craft.[12] Although rarely raised in the context of clearly qualifying petitions, a skeptical adjudicator could also question whether an entrepreneur with a new, untested venture can persuasively establish the required prospective substantial benefit to the United States.[13] Thus, in cases involving new ventures, a carefully crafted petition could benefit from including ample evidence relating to the business plan and objective indicia that it can likely be successfully implemented. As a final observation, although "ability to pay" is not a required element of proof *per se*, evidence that the new venture will be viable, sustainable, and likely to succeed can add substantial credibility to the beneficiary's assertions regarding his or her future work in the field.

EB-1-2 OUTSTANDING PROFESSORS OR RESEARCHERS

Prospective immigrants with an internationally known record of accomplishment as a professor or researcher may find even more useful the first-preference Outstanding Professors or Researchers classification. The Immigration and Nationality Act (INA) designates as priority workers those who are recognized internationally as outstanding in a specific academic area, have at least three years of experience in teaching or research in that area, and are either taking up a tenured or tenure-track teaching or research position at a college or university, or will be employed in a "comparable" full-time research position for a qualifying private employer.[14] To qualify, private employers must employ at least three full-time researchers and have achieved documented accomplishments in an academic field.[15] Petitions may be filed only by a prospective "United States employer."[16]

The beneficiary's eligibility must document that he or she has at least three years of experience in teaching and/or research in the academic field,[17] and is internationally recognized as outstanding in his or her academic field. In contrast to the extraordinary ability classification, which is limited to "the sciences, arts, education, business or athletics," this classification is available across the full spectrum of *academic* fields, defined as "a body of specialized knowledge offered for study at an accredited United States university or institution of higher education."[18] The applicable regulations provide that initial evidence must meet at least two of six specified criteria, as follows:

1. Documentation of the alien's receipt of major prizes or awards for outstanding achievement in the academic field;
2. Documentation of the alien's membership in associations in the academic field which require outstanding achievement of their members;
3. Published material in professional publications written by others about the alien's work in the academic field;
4. Evidence of the alien's participation, individually or on a panel, as a judge of the work of others in the same or an allied field;
5. Evidence of the alien's original scientific or scholarly research contributions to the academic field; or
6. Evidence of the alien's authorship of scholarly books or articles (in scholarly journals with international circulation) in the academic field.[19]

Unlike the extraordinary ability criteria, these six criteria comprise a finite, closed set of alternatives ("comparable evidence" cannot provide the sole basis for approval). Much like the extraordinary ability

---

[12] This issue typically arises where a beneficiary is seeking to close one chapter of a career and begin another, such as when a competitive athlete is ceasing a heralded career as a competitor and seeks to undertake coaching positions in the United States.

[13] While prospective substantial benefit is an element of a prima facie case for an alien of extraordinary ability, it is an issue that rarely receives independent attention in practice. *See supra* note 2 (discussing the Skerrett Letter).

[14] INA §203(b)(1)(B).

[15] INA §203(b)(1)(B)(iii).

[16] 8 CFR §§204.5(i)(1), 204.5(i)(3)(iii).

[17] 8 CFR §204.5(i)(3)(ii). The regulation further specifies the form of the beneficiary's evidence of experience, and it prescribes conditions under which research or teaching while in a graduate degree program may be accepted toward the experience requirement.

[18] 8 CFR §204.5(i)(2).

[19] 8 CFR §204.5(i)(3)(i).

criteria, however, the outstanding professor or researcher criteria invite qualitative assessments of relative merit as compared to the field as a whole, involving adjudication of whether prizes are sufficiently "major" or for achievements that are sufficiently "outstanding," whether contributions are sufficiently "original," whether publications are sufficiently "scholarly," and so on. Importantly, although only one of the criteria so specifies, the evidence as a whole must establish that recognition of the beneficiary's work is international in scope.[20]

Of particular interest to investors and entrepreneurs is the extent to which private employers may qualify to petition on behalf of outstanding researchers. Evidentiary requirements for non-university petitioners are significant and can present hurdles to some prospective employers in the private sector, particularly if they have a small business model in mind. Other investors and entrepreneurs, whose ventures or prospective employers may be larger or more well financed, may find the substantive requirements readily addressed, inviting substantial flexibility in this type of a case. The regulations require that a "department, division or institute" of a petitioning private employer establish:

1. That it employs at least three persons full-time in research positions;
2. That it has achieved documented accomplishments in an academic field; and
3. That it has extended to the beneficiary an offer of employment in a "permanent research position" in the beneficiary's academic field.[21]

Additionally, as with any employment-based petition that requires a job offer, the petitioning employer must affirmatively establish that it has the ability to pay the beneficiary the proffered wage as of the priority date of the petition.[22]

Documented accomplishments in an academic field may be demonstrated by any relevant evidence. Notably, in contrast to other provisions, this part of the regulation does not specify that the employer's accomplishments must have been in *the beneficiary's* academic field, suggesting there need not be a precise fit between the employer's past accomplishments and its research agenda for the beneficiary. Nevertheless, the petitioner's record of accomplishments must relate to an "academic" field. Practitioners suggest this requirement is designed to reflect a "level of research commitment that would merit the services of an academic researcher" and report that USCIS adjudicators examine whether the petitioner has a sufficiently strong record of research pursuits to be credibly offering indefinite employment to a high-caliber academic researcher, or whether the offered position is credibly characterized as "research"-related.[23]

The same issues regarding the credibility of the petitioner's institutional commitment to research activities are similarly likely to inform USCIS review of the positions of the required three full-time researchers. The term "research" is not defined in the statute or the governing regulations relating specifically to the outstanding researcher classification, but it is clear that USCIS will examine the nature of these employees' work to determine whether their positions are primarily research-driven. The Administrative Appeals Office (AAO) has held that engineering and product design are not fundamentally research activities, because they involve "the technological application of existing research."[24] However, one author notes that the H-1B regulations relating to "nonprofit research organizations" helpfully define research as including a broad range of inquiry, specifically including "applied research" that may have a fundamentally commercial objective. In practice, one should be careful to articulate and emphasize the research orientation of any relevant activities undertaken in the private sector.

---

[20] Excellent discussion of the criteria for evaluating the beneficiary's qualifications as "outstanding" can be found in R. Sostrin *et al.*, *supra* note 5; D. Berger *et al.*, "EB-1-2 Outstanding Researcher Cases: Issues and Trends," *Immigration & Nationality Law Handbook* 321 (2009–10 Ed.); and E. Farrell *et al.*, *Immigration Options for Academics & Researchers* 149 (AILA 2005).

[21] 8 CFR §204.5(i)(3)(iii).

[22] 8 CFR §204.5(g)(2).

[23] *See* R. Sostrin *et al.*, *supra* note 5, at 346–49 (suggesting a record of research commitment may be demonstrated with such evidence as an ongoing R&D budget, a history of patent applications, publications and presentations by research staff, and documentation that the company publicly emphasizes its research achievements); *see also* C. Weber, *supra* note 1, at 573 (also noting that for start-up companies the reputation and accomplishments of the company's other researchers, as opposed to those of the company itself, could prove useful).

[24] *Matter of [name not provided]*, WAC 99 016 52605 (AAO Feb. 6, 2001), *reported in* 7 Bender's Immigr. Bull. 1095–1104 (Sept. 15, 2002).

The petitioning employer's mere statement of its intention to employ the beneficiary will not meet the "permanent job offer" requirement of the outstanding researcher regulations. Instead, a copy of the employer's actual job offer to the beneficiary, outlining the nature, terms and conditions of the proposed employment is specified as required initial evidence in support of the petition. The regulations provide that offered research positions must be "permanent," defined as "for a term of indefinite or unlimited duration, and in which the employee will ordinarily have an expectation of continued employment unless there is good cause for termination."[25] In the private sector, of course, companies rarely do or can undertake contractual commitments for permanent employment absent a showing of good cause, and in the arena of grant-funded research particularly, this requirement appears onerous. Following a history of denials on this ground,[26] however, USCIS has acknowledged the realities of modern business practices and clarified in a recent guidance memorandum that the "permanence" of the offer will not turn strictly on the presence or absence of a contractual requirement of good cause for termination. Instead, the specifics of the job offer and the business context of the petitioner's employment arrangements will be reviewed for evidence of intent to continue employing the beneficiary indefinitely, in combination with an objectively reasonable expectation that it will be able to do so.[27] The memorandum suggested, by way of example, that where an employer's one-year employment contracts were demonstrably a function of its receipt of annual grants, a documented history of grant renewals and evidence of the employer's intention to continue seeking the funding would sufficiently demonstrate a reasonable expectation of continued employment indefinitely.[28]

Particularly in cases where the beneficiary has a minimally sufficient record of achievement, or where they are thinly capitalized, start-up companies and new ventures could have substantial difficulty petitioning in the Outstanding Researchers classification, for many of the reasons outlined above. Without a solid history of ongoing business operations and research successes over time, it could be more difficult to make a persuasive showing as to the petitioner's documented research achievements, employment of three full-time researchers, or reasonable expectation of sustaining long-term (permanent) employment of a world-class academic researcher. Without a history of investments, project records, and work product, documentation of the nature of the work as full-time "research" could similarly prove elusive. And, as with any new venture, it will of course be challenging to establish to USCIS standards the petitioner's ability to pay the beneficiary's wage.[29]

In a potentially problematic turn of events, investors and entrepreneurs with an ownership stake in the petitioning entity could face challenge from USCIS as to whether the petitioner and beneficiary have a bona fide "employer-employee" relationship. Historically, due to restrictive and detailed U.S. Department of Labor regulations, owner-beneficiaries have encountered substantial difficulty petitioning through their own entities in classifications requiring labor certification, but they have found a more favorable landscape in labor certification-exempt contexts such as EB-1 and EB-2. The INA and USCIS regulations are in general conspicuously silent with respect to definitions of the terms "employer" or "employee."[30] More usefully, three longstanding precedent decisions have held squarely that a corporation could legitimately serve as a petitioner in an employment-based petition on behalf of its owner, reasoning that a corporation and its owner are separate legal persons.[31] However, troubling recent adju-

---

[25] 8 CFR §204.5(i)(2).

[26] For a review of Administrative Appeals Office (AAO) decisions prior to 2006 which uniformly denied Outstanding Professor and Researcher petitions where "good cause for termination" language was absent from the employment arrangement, see D. Berger *et al.*, *supra* note 20, at 321, 323 & nn.6–10.

[27] USCIS Memorandum, M. Aytes, "Guidance on the Requirement of a 'Permanent Offer of Employment' for Outstanding Professors and Researchers" (June 6, 2006), *published on* AILA InfoNet at Doc. No. 06060860 (*posted* June 8, 2006) (amending the USCIS *Adjudicator's Field Manual* (AFM) accordingly).

[28] *Id.* For additional practice pointers on this issue and others, see generally D. Berger *et al.*, *supra* note 20; *see also* R. Sostrin *et al.*, *supra* note 5, at 348.

[29] For current USCIS criteria regarding "ability to pay," see USCIS Memorandum, M. Aytes, "Determinations of Ability to Pay Under 8 CFR §204.5(g)(2)" (May 4, 2004), *published on* AILA InfoNet at Doc. No. 04051262 (*posted* May 12, 2004).

[30] Limited exceptions include 8 CFR §274A (relating to the Immigration Reform and Control Act of 1986 (IRCA)), and 8 CFR §214.2(h)(4)(ii) (relating to H-1B employment).

[31] *Matter of M–*, 8 I&N Dec. 24 (BIA 1958, AG 1958); *Matter of Aphrodite Investments Ltd.*, 17 I&N Dec. 530 (Comm.'r 1980); *Matter of Allan Gee, Inc.*, 17 I&N Dec. 296 (Acting Reg. Comm'r 1979).

dication trends suggest that owner/beneficiaries may need to be prepared to marshall additional legal arguments in categories where the petitioner must be an "employer."

In January 2010, USCIS issued guidance to its adjudicators regarding the evaluation of employer-employee relationships in connection with H-1B petitions (the Neufeld Memo).[32] Drawing on the common law of agency and seeking to distinguish agency precedent, the Neufeld Memo concluded (among other things) that because a beneficiary/owner cannot be "controlled by" the petitioning entity if he owns it, such an individual could not legitimately be an "employee" within the meaning of the INA. Although restricted on its face to H-1B nonimmigrant petitions, the analysis in the Neufeld Memo is much broader and distinguishes away all of the contrary precedent, such that it would be equally applicable in the context of nearly all other employment-based immigrant and nonimmigrant petitions. Indeed, practitioners report having seen the identical legal analysis in AAO and USCIS decisions in the EB-1-3 and L-1A classifications, as well as with H-1B.[33] The analysis and conclusions of the Neufeld Memo are sharply criticized in a January 26, 2010, letter to USCIS Chief Counsel Roxana Bacon from the American Immigration Lawyers Association (AILA)-USCIS HQ Liaison Committee.[34] AILA's January 26, 2010, letter offers a detailed challenge to the legal reasoning in the Neufeld Memo, and it expresses deep concern that the effect of this agency action may be to narrow all immigrant and nonimmigrant classifications to exclude beneficiary/owners. To date, USCIS has offered no formal public response.[35]

Despite the potentially far-reaching applications of this new interpretation, there is to date no reason to believe that USCIS adjudications in EB-1 and EB-2 classifications are or will be routinely incorporating this inquiry into their decision-making process. To the extent there have been denials on this ground, they continue to appear to be the exception, rather than the rule. Therefore, owner/beneficiaries with otherwise solid cases for EB-1 or EB-2 eligibility, while cognizant of the risk, should not hesitate to proceed as usual, provided they understand they may need to be prepared to advocate vigorously on this issue should it be challenged in an Request for Evidence (RFE).

EB-1-3 CERTAIN MULTINATIONAL MANAGERS AND EXECUTIVES

Permanent residence may be available in the first-preference Priority Worker category to those multinational managers and executives who have been employed outside the United States for at least one of the most recent three years, in a capacity that is "managerial or executive," by the petitioning employer or its subsidiary or affiliate.[36] For those who are familiar with the closely related L-1A nonimmigrant classification for multinational managers and executives,[37] there are four distinct differences which make the EB-1-3 option more limited:

1. The prospective U.S. employer must have been regularly, systematically, and continuously doing business in the United States for at least one year,[38] effectively eliminating the option for start-up U.S. enterprises;

2. Petitions may only be filed by a U.S. employer, and the petitioner must supply a job offer indicating the beneficiary's managerial or executive role in the United States and clearly describing the job duties of the position;[39]

3. The beneficiary's qualifying employment abroad must have been in a managerial or executive capacity and not merely in a capacity

---

[32] USCIS Memorandum, D. Neufeld, "Determining Employer-Employee Relationship for Adjudication of H-1B Petitions, Including Third-Party Site Placements" (Jan. 8, 2010) (Neufeld Memo), *published on* AILA InfoNet at Doc. No. 10011363 (*posted* Jan. 13, 2010).

[33] Examples of numerous such decisions are catalogued in an appendix to a letter dated January 26, 2010, from AILA-USCIS HQ Liaison Committee to USCIS Chief Counsel Roxana Bacon, *published on* AILA InfoNet at Doc. No. 10012760 (*posted* Jan. 27, 2010) (urging recission of the Neufeld Memo).

[34] *Id.*

[35] Notably, during a February 18, 2010, public stakeholders meeting, a caller specifically asked USCIS whether the Neufeld Memo would be extended to L-1A petitions, and the response was "No." If there is consensus on this issue within

continued

the agency (which is not at all clear), guidance on the same has not yet made its way to adjudicating officers.

[36] INA §203(b)(1)(C).

[37] *See, e.g.,* INA §101(a)(15)(L); 8 CFR §214.2(l).

[38] 8 CFR §204.5(j)(2) (defining "doing business"); 8 CFR §204.5(j)(3)(D).

[39] 8 CFR §§204.5(j)(1), (j)(5).

involving the application of specialized knowledge (meaning that managers or executives who have been promoted to managerial/executive positions subsequent to their transfer to the U.S. will not qualify); and

4. As with all employment-based petitions requiring a job offer, the petition must establish the petitioner's "ability to pay" the beneficiary's wage.[40]

In one respect, the EB-1-3 classification is more forgiving: Both the EB-1-3 and L-1A categories permit the one year of qualifying employment abroad to have occurred within one of the three years prior to admission to the United States (as opposed to strictly within one of the most recent three calendar years);[41] however, the immigrant petition regulations do not include the requirement that the qualifying employment have been "continuous."[42]

In other respects, the EB-1-3 classification closely parallels its nonimmigrant partner: Although qualifying relationships between the U.S. and foreign employers in the EB-1-3 context do not include "branch" relationships, but are instead limited to the same employer or its subsidiary[43] or affiliate;[44] the definition of "branch" in the L-1A regulations[45] will coincide with the EB-1-3 "same employer" alternative, provided the overseas office is a branch of the U.S. entity (but not vice versa). The regulations defining "managerial" and "executive" capacity are identical in the immigrant and nonimmigrant contexts,[46] both requiring that qualifying positions involve spending the majority of one's time on the exercise of upper-level operational or policy management responsibilities, as opposed to administrative tasks, supervision, or productive work providing the company's products or services.[47]

Some investors and entrepreneurs, particularly those with startups and smaller or less-well-financed operations, may find the EB-1-3 classification inhospitable. As noted above, the petitioning U.S. employer must have had an ongoing, viable, and productive business operation in the United States for at least one year prior to filing the petition.[48] Fledgling operations, even with a year of business behind them, frequently require their managerial and executive personnel to perform a variety of duties out of necessity—including administrative tasks, customer relations, direct supervision, and the like—until the organization matures. Because USCIS generally takes the position that primarily managerial and executive positions are not realistically necessary or sustainable (read: credible) in new and smaller businesses, such petitions must generally provide more extensive documentation regarding the nature of the business and the day-to-day responsibilities of the beneficiary.[49] Because of the one-year-of-systematic-operations requirement, even larger organizations, such as large-scale multinational employers establishing an initial U.S. presence, cannot immediately utilize the EB-1-3 category until their U.S. operations have successfully launched and become sustain-

---

[40] 8 CFR §204.5(g)(2); *see also* note 29 *supra*.

[41] 8 CFR §§204.5(j)(3)(B), 214.2(*l*)(1)(ii)(A).

[42] "Continuous" employment abroad for purposes of L-1 eligibility may still be established provided that periods interruptive of such status were spent in the United States in lawful status for an employer with a qualifying relationship, or in the United States on brief trips for business or pleasure; however, each such trip may not be "counted" toward the required one year of continuous employment. 8 CFR §214.2(*l*)(1)(ii)(A). In contrast, qualifying employment abroad for EB-1-3 purposes need only be "for at least one year." 8 CFR §204.5(j)(3)(B). The USCIS *Adjudicator's Field Manual* acknowledges that cumulative periods of interrupted employment abroad may be combined to establish a total of one year. AFM ch. 22.2(i)(3).

[43] "Subsidiary" is a legal entity of which the parent entity owns at least 50 percent and maintains no less than 50 percent control, or a legal entity of which the parent owns less than 50 percent but maintains de facto control. 8 CFR §204.5(j)(2); *see also Matter of Arctic Storm, Inc.*, A73 426 962 (AAU Nov. 29, 1999) (de facto control in case of joint venture may include negative [veto] control).

[44] "Affiliate" is one of two "subsidiaries," *see id.*, both of which are owned and controlled by the same parent or individual; one of two legal entities owned and controlled by the same individuals in approximately the same proportions; or qualifies for unique treatment as one of certain international accounting firms that market their services under an internationally recognized name. *Id.*

[45] 8 CFR §214.2(*l*)(1)(ii)(J) ("an operating division or office of the same organization housed in a different location").

[46] *See* 8 CFR §§204.5(j)(2), 214.2(*l*)(1)(ii).

[47] For an excellent review of key issues and common pitfalls in seeking to establish "managerial" or "executive" capacity, see D. Butte *et al.*, "L-1A Visas—A Quick Way to Work, Fraught With Traps for the Unwary," *Immigration & Nationality Law Handbook* 126 (AILA 2007–08 Ed.). *See also* the review of nonimmigrant options elsewhere in this volume.

[48] *See supra* note 38.

[49] *See* D. Butte *et al.*, *supra* note 47; *see also* the outstanding practical guidance provided in D. Butte, "Representing Small Companies—The Devil is . . . Everywhere," *Immigration & Nationality Law Handbook* 187 (AILA 2009–10 Ed.).

able. Petitioners whose business plans may benefit from the EB-1-3 classification in the longer term may elect to transition into permanent residence with an L-1A nonimmigrant status for the purpose of establishing a new office (limited by statute to one year), thereafter renewing the L-1A upon a showing of ongoing, sustainable and mature business operations, and finally petitioning for permanent residence based upon a solid record of U.S. business activity.

"Ability to pay" is a notoriously problematic requirement for new or smaller organizations, even those that have a solid record of viability after the first year of operations. Because of the substantial risk of denial without RFE on this issue, particular care must be taken in these cases to establishing the ability to pay using, where possible, documentation deemed acceptable in USCIS guidance.[50]

Owner/beneficiaries may likewise encounter hurdles. Although years of agency decisions have permitted U.S. companies to petition on behalf of executive officers who were also their shareholders or sole owners, recent developments in USCIS policy and adjudications[51] have raised concerns about the long-term viability of this strategy. As is explained in more detail above,[52] USCIS's newly published guidance suggests that U.S. companies petitioning on behalf of their owners may be challenged by the agency to establish that they are "employers" within the meaning of the INA, suggesting that may not be possible where the owners themselves control the fact and conditions of their own employment.[53] The new guidance contradicts several precedent decisions holding that corporations may legitimately petition on behalf of their shareholders.[54] At this time, it is far from clear that this interpretation, which was drafted specifically for application in H-1B adjudications, will be routinely extended into the context of EB-1 immigrant petitions. Practitioners have expressed concern that a number of EB-1-3 denials and AAO decisions raising this issue may evidence a trend in adjudications. In a positive sign, USCIS has informally signaled that it does not presently intend to inject the issue systematically into L-1A decision-making.[55] Prudence dictates that counsel prepare for vigorous advocacy in cases where the prospective employer is owned, wholly or partially, by the beneficiary.

EB-2 EXCEPTIONAL ABILITY: SCHEDULE A, GROUP II

Foreign nationals with "exceptional ability" by U.S. Department of Labor (DOL) standards may avoid the permanent labor certification process associated with second-preference employment-based petitions through its Schedule A, Group II "precertification" procedures.[56] The INA provides that second-preference classification may be accorded to qualified immigrants who, because of their exceptional ability in the sciences, arts, or business, will substantially benefit prospectively the national economy, cultural or educational interests, or welfare of the United States, and whose services in the sciences, arts, professions, or business are sought by an employer in the United States.[57]

USCIS regulations defining "exceptional ability" for the EB-2 category itself (as opposed to the DOL regulatory definition of "exceptional ability") present a substantially lower eligibility threshold than exists for either of the first two EB-1 (extraordinary ability or outstanding researcher) classifications.[58] In general, however, foreign nationals with exceptional ability remain subject to the labor certification requirement. To avail themselves of the exemption from formal labor certification, eligible persons of EB-2 exceptional ability (those with exceptional ability in the sciences or the arts[59]) must document that they can satisfy even higher standards prescribed by the DOL. The DOL standards, which in

---

[50] *See supra* note 29. In particular, it may be prudent to determine whether expending funds on an audit to bolster the credibility of the petitioner's financials could significantly affect an adjudicator's initial assessment of the case.

[51] *See* Neufeld Memo, *supra* note 32.

[52] *See supra* notes 32–35 and accompanying text.

[53] *See* Neufeld Memo, *supra* note 32.

[54] *See, e.g.,* cases cited in note 31 *supra*.

[55] *See* note 35 *supra*.

[56] Because the classification is infrequently used, guidance in this area is scarce. Useful discussions of the topic may be found in A. Chehrazi et al., *supra* note 1; N. Waxman, *supra* note 5, at 135; F. Retman, "Schedule A, Group II: A Reason to Exist, *Immigration Options for Academics & Researchers* 185 (AILA 2005).

[57] INA §203(b)(2).

[58] 8 CFR §§204.5(k)(1), (3)(ii). In essence, the USCIS standards focus on whether the alien's expertise is "significantly above that ordinarily encountered," and is supported by documentation demonstrating "recognition for achievements and significant contributions to the industry or field."

[59] 20 CFR §656.15(d)(1). Foreign nationals with exceptional ability in the performing arts are also eligible but must satisfy different regulatory criteria. *See* 20 CFR §656.15(d)(2).

many respects mirror the criteria for establishing EB-1 eligibility under the extraordinary ability or outstanding researcher classifications, require that the alien document:

1. Widespread acclaim and international recognition accorded the alien by recognized experts in his or her field;
2. That his or her work in that field during the past year required exceptional ability;
3. That his or her intended work in the United States will require exceptional ability; and
4. That documentation be presented meeting at least two of seven specified criteria, in summary as follows:
   a. Receipt of internationally recognized prizes or awards for excellence in the field of intended employment;
   b. Membership in international associations, in the field of intended employment, which require outstanding achievement of their members, as judged by recognized international experts in their disciplines or fields;
   c. Published material in professional publications about the alien and his or her work in the field of intended employment;
   d. Participation on a panel, or individually, as a judge of the work of others in the same or in an allied field of specialization to the field of intended employment;
   e. Original scientific or scholarly research contributions of major significance in the field for which certification is sought;
   f. Authorship of published scientific or scholarly articles in the field of intended employment, in international professional journals with an international circulation;
   g. Display of his or her work, in the field of intended employment, at artistic exhibitions in more than one country.

Bypassing DOL altogether, employers seeking Schedule A, Group II certification file their DOL labor certification applications directly with USCIS along with the EB-2 immigrant petition and documentation supporting eligibility for precertification. USCIS has jurisdiction to determine whether the documentation satisfies DOL regulatory standards.[60] Although adjudicated by USCIS, these Schedule A, Group II labor certification applications must also be supported by a satisfactory Notice of Filing and prevailing wage determination in compliance with DOL rules.[61]

In practice, the Schedule A Group II procedures are infrequently used, primarily because many beneficiaries who would be eligible for precertification would also qualify in one of the EB-1 classifications, but undoubtedly also because the discrete roles and substantial mismatch of USCIS and DOL standards for "exceptional ability" create confusion and because guidance in the area is scarce. The utility of the procedure should not be overlooked, however, particularly for those individuals whose EB-1 eligibility is somewhat uncertain or has perhaps been subjected to an excessively rigorous EB-1 adjudication. For example, Schedule A, Group II could be ideal for those individuals whose achievements are indeed "extraordinary" but whose acclaim cannot yet establish that it has been "sustained." As for those who are recognized as "outstanding," the procedure may prove particularly useful to those who:

1. May not be readily classified as "researchers";
2. Have less than three years of experience;
3. Will work for an employer with fewer than three full-time researchers;
4. Work in an area of expertise not readily recognized as "academic"; or
5. Have a job offer that might not meet the EB-1-2 requirements for "permanent" employment.

Schedule A, Group II labor certification applications, and their accompanying immigrant petitions, may only be filed by a "United States employer."[62] Furthermore, the INA requires that they must be accompanied by evidence of a job offer,[63] which in turn subjects the petitioner to the requirement that it also document its "ability to pay."[64] These requirements may well prove burdensome to certain investors and entrepreneurs. As previously discussed, new and/or small business employers, in particular, may find it more challenging to establish the ability to pay to the

---

[60] 20 CFR §656.15(e).

[61] 20 CFR §656.15(b).

[62] 20 CFR §656.15(a); 8 CFR §204.5(k)(1).

[63] INA §203(b)(2); *see also* 8 CFR §§204.5(k)(1), (4)(i). Unlike the distinctly substantive "job offer" requirements of the EB-1-2 classification, this requirement may be satisfied merely by the employer's representations in the labor certification application and supporting documentation.

[64] *See* §204.5(g); *see also supra* note 29.

satisfaction of USCIS.[65] Additionally here, as in the EB-1 context, the requirement of a petitioning "employer" carries with it a risk that USCIS may dispute the eligibility of an entity owned by the beneficiary to qualify as an "employer," on the ground that companies cannot legitimately claim a bona fide "employer-employee" relationship with their (working) owners.[66]

Despite the fact that the DOL criteria require a record of only one year of work (the most recent) evidencing exceptional ability, petitioners should not presume that start-ups, fledgling U.S. enterprises, and beneficiaries with more limited records of experience will find the Schedule A, Group II adjudication fully hospitable and without risk relating to these features. The DOL criteria clearly mandate that the position in which the beneficiary has worked for one year, and the position in which the beneficiary will work in the United States, *require(d)* exceptional ability. Agency decisions relating to EB-1 and various nonimmigrant classifications (such as H-1B and L-1A) could well portend heightened scrutiny on these issues for small or new businesses, or for individuals newly embarked on their field of expertise.[67] In essence, these are credibility issues, and they warrant carefully crafted support in the first instance. And as with all credibility issues, they are more likely to take a back seat, or not arise at all, where the petition makes a persuasive showing on the fundamentally determinative issue of the beneficiary's relative merit.

Two further technical requirements warrant mention. First, although the showing in an Exceptional Ability case may not be as demanding as that required in the context of a National Interest Waiver case,[68] all EB-2 petitions must establish that the beneficiary's proposed work will "substantially benefit prospectively the national economy, cultural or educational interests, or welfare of the United States."[69] Exceptional ability petitions should articulate the substantial benefit, which will most likely be premised on the fact that an individual of exceptional ability will be utilizing his or her exceptional talents in the service of a U.S. employer. Just as in the EB-1 extraordinary ability context, however, it is most likely that the supporting evidence of exceptional ability will itself, without more, suffice to establish substantial prospective benefit.[70]

Second, petitioners in these cases must not overlook the necessity of establishing the beneficiary's exceptional ability pursuant to the separate USCIS criteria (unless the beneficiary has a master's degree or equivalent education and experience).[71] Although as previously noted these criteria establish a substantially lower threshold than do the DOL criteria and may for all practical purposes be a formality once the DOL criteria are met, the USCIS criteria define eligibility for EB-2 classification. The USCIS standards require documentation relating to three criteria, as opposed to only two in the DOL arena.

EB-2 NATIONAL INTEREST WAIVER

In contrast to the EB-2 Exceptional Ability classification, which is subject to the dual requirements of labor certification and job offer (but is deemed "precertified"), the EB-2 National Interest Waiver (NIW) classification is genuinely exempt from both. Notably, as a result, NIW EB-2 cases may be self-petitioned and need not rely on an arrangement for full-time work for a single U.S. employer.

National interest waiver beneficiaries must qualify initially for statutory EB-2 classification as professionals with advanced degrees or individuals with exceptional ability, as defined by USCIS regulations.[72] Additionally, to establish eligibility for a waiver of both the job offer and the related labor certification, a prospective NIW immigrant must show that his or her U.S. employment will be in the "national interest." USCIS guidance dictates that the "national interest" standard requires a showing of "significantly more than [the] 'prospective national

---

[65] *See* discussion at *supra* note 29 and accompanying text.

[66] *See* discussion at *supra* notes 32–35 and accompanying text. As the reported developments in this area are still evolving, applicable sections of the AFM note only that self-petitioning is precluded, and the new guidance applies on its face only to H-1B petitions, practitioners should be prepared for inquiry and advocacy on this issue but need not at this time conclude such a petition is not viable.

[67] RFEs questioning why and how a small employer can sustain or justify the need for qualifying executive/managerial personnel or employees in specialty occupations are common in the H-1B, L-1A and EB-1-3 contexts, so small business petitioners documenting how exceptional ability was/will be "required" should freely draw guidance from the practice literature in those areas.

[68] *See generally* notes 72–79 *infra* and accompanying text.

[69] INA §203(b)(2).

[70] *See* discussion at note 2 *supra*.

[71] 8 CFR §204.5(k)(3)(ii).

[72] 8 CFR §§204.5(k)(1), (3).

benefit' required of all aliens seeking to qualify as having exceptional ability."[73]

The seminal AAO precedent decision governing current adjudication of NIW cases is *Matter of New York State Department of Transportation (NYSDOT)*.[74] In *NYSDOT*, the AAO determined that for one's work to be in the "national interest" within the meaning of the statutory EB-2 classification, it would have to satisfy three criteria:

1. The beneficiary must be seeking employment in an area of "substantial intrinsic merit;"[75]
2. The benefit to be provided will be "national in scope";[76] and
3. The "national interest would be adversely affected if a labor certification were required," in the sense that the beneficiary would benefit the United States to a "substantially greater degree" than minimally qualified U.S. workers who might compete with the beneficiary in the job market.[77]

The available literature and guidance regarding agency application of each of the *NYSDOT* criteria is extensive and growing,[78] and because none of these criteria draws a bright line, each of them invites artful advocacy in connection with each petition's unique facts. Successful NIW cases generally benefit from carefully crafted expert opinion letters attesting to the national significance and impact of the beneficiary's work.[79]

The NIW route to permanent residence is significantly more flexible than the EB-1 or Schedule A, Group II options, in that it is not constrained to particular fields of endeavor or types of expertise. The doors are wide open to any beneficiary who can articulate a credible case. Because an NIW approval waives the requirement of a job offer, beneficiaries may self-petition and need not demonstrate the ability to pay.[80] For all of these reasons, it provides a highly attractive option for investors and entrepreneurs involved in solo, smaller, or start-up pursuits, or those whose financing might not bear rigorous scrutiny if analyzed for "ability to pay." As an added bonus, the option of self-petitioning eliminates the uncertainties faced specifically by owner/beneficiaries in many of the other EB-1 and EB-2 classifications.

Given the ad hoc nature of adjudications, an NIW case can be challenging under the best of circumstances, and requests for evidence are routine. Self-petitioners with smaller and start-up businesses should anticipate that issues will be raised on several fronts. New ventures without a substantial track record may be challenged to demonstrate how the work will have an objectively measurable impact on the field. Those with smaller businesses, solo pursuits, or with local clientele, in particular, may encounter resistance pertaining to whether their work is national in scope and of broader, national significance. The extent to which these hurdles can be overcome turns

---

[73] USCIS *Adjudicator's Field Manual* ch. 22.2(j).

[74] 22 I&N. Dec. 215 (Acting Assoc. Comm'r 1998).

[75] "Substantial intrinsic merit" appears to be standard exploring the overall societal importance of the beneficiary's type of work. In *NYSDOT*, the AAO found that work on highway bridges as a structural engineer had substantial intrinsic merit. *Id*. By way of contrast, the AFM suggests that the work of a juggler who proposes to perform at children's birthday parties, while not deleterious, would not be of *substantial* intrinsic merit. AFM ch. 22.2(j)(4).

[76] The concern that the work be "national in scope" constrains petitions for occupations which cannot credibly demonstrate how the beneficiary's work may have an impact reaching beyond his or her local or regional community. *NYSDOT's* engineer satisfied this standard because his work involved making improvements to the national transportation infrastructure. Examples of successful showings abound in the National Interest Waiver (NIW) literature, *see, e.g.*, note 78 *infra*, and surveying the cases can be most instructive. The AFM suggests that the *primary purpose* of the beneficiary's work must be advancing a national interest. *See* AFM ch. 22.2(j)(4).

[77] Substantially greater national benefit generally requires a demonstration that the beneficiary's work has a measurable impact on the field of endeavor at large. *See* S. Koehler *et al.*, "National Interest Waiver Petitions for Researchers: Demonstrating a Measurable Impact on a Larger Field," *Immigration Options for Academics & Researchers* 171 (AILA 2005); N. Waxman, *supra* note 5, at 133–35.

[78] *See, e.g.*, S. Koehler *et al.*, *supra* note 77; N. Waxman, *supra* note 5, at 132–35; R. Sostrin *et al.*, *supra* note 5; M. Lawler, *Professionals: A Matter of Degree* 30–34 (AILA 2003); J. Quill, *supra* note 1, at 33–37; I. Kurzban, *Immigration Law Sourcebook* ch. 7, §III(F) (cataloguing cases); AFM ch. 22.2(j)(4).

[79] For helpful guidance on the effective use of experts in the NIW context, see particularly R. Sostrin *et al.*, *supra* note 5, at 349–52; N. Waxman, "National Interest Waiver: Case Study," *Immigration & Nationality Law Handbook* 454 (AILA 2006–07 Ed.).

[80] Again, however, while the rule regarding "ability to pay," 8 CFR §204.5(g), may strictly speaking be inapplicable in NIW cases, the objective viability of the planned enterprise may well affect the determination of its "substantial prospective benefit."

largely on the nature of the beneficiary's proposed activity. Even more so, it turns on counsel's skill in shaping the case and effectively harnessing and presenting the available supporting documentation. Investors and entrepreneurs would do well to explore whether this more flexible classification may indeed provide a viable option where other, more straightforward routes may be foreclosed.

CONCLUSION

Investors and entrepreneurs seeking permanent residence may well qualify in the first and second employment-based preference classifications, particularly where they can demonstrate that their level of expertise or achievement is noteworthy. When a client appears to have a personal history that includes extraordinary, outstanding, exceptional, or downright important accomplishments, any of the merit-based immigration options may well prove fruitful. The key in each of these cases is to persuade a USCIS adjudicator that, with due homage to U.S. Supreme Court Justice Potter Stewart, "you know it when you see it." Although discrete features of the legal landscape in the EB-1 and EB-2 arenas can be inhospitable to self-petitioners, small businesses, or start-up ventures, in many circumstances the challenges presented may be readily anticipated and, with creative lawyering and solid documentation, successfully addressed.

ALIEN INFLUENCE AND CONTROL OVER THE JOB OPPORTUNITY

by Allen E. Kaye[*]

When an alien invests in, or otherwise owns or controls, a company or is related to those who own or control a company that will file an application under the Program Electronic Review Management (PERM) System for the alien, practitioners face what could be a very delicate situation that requires a good deal of planning and preparation. The following article will explain why this is so and will help in the preparation of the application.

The PERM regulation, when proposed by the U.S. Department of Labor (DOL),[1] discussed the topic of "Alien Influence and Control Over Job Opportunity." The supplementary information preceding the proposed PERM regulation stated that:

> [w]hen an employer seeks a labor certification for an alien who is in a position to unduly influence hiring decisions or who has such a dominant role in, or close personal relationship with the employer and/or employer's business that it is unlikely that the employer would replace the alien with a qualified U.S. applicant, [Board of Alien Labor Certification Appeals] BALCA decisions allow the Certifying Officer to determine that the job opportunity has not been clearly open to any qualified U.S. worker.

---

[*] Updated from an article first published in 3rd edition of *The David Stanton Manual on Labor Certification* (AILA 2005).

Allen Kaye is an attorney residing in New York City, who has practiced U.S. immigration, naturalization, visa, and consular law for over 35 years. Mr. Kaye is a graduate (Phi Beta Kappa and *cum laude*) of Queens College of the City University of New York (B.A.), Columbia University Law School (J.D.), and New York University Law School (LL.M.). He is a past national president of the American Immigration Lawyers Association (AILA). Mr. Kaye is a regular columnist on U.S. immigration and naturalization law for the newspaper *India Abroad* and many other newspapers across the United States. Mr. Kaye is listed in Martindale-Hubbell's *Bar Register of Preeminent Lawyers* and in *The Best Lawyers in America for Immigration and Naturalization Law*. He is a founding member of IMMLAW, the national consortium of immigration law firms.

[1] U.S. Dep't of Labor (DOL), Employment and Training Administration (ETA), "Labor Certification for the Permanent Employment of Aliens in the United States; Implementation of New System" (Proposed PERM Rule), 67 Fed. Reg. 30466, 30466–521 (May 6, 2002), *published* on AILA InfoNet at Doc. No. 02050740 (*posted* May 7, 2002).

DOL then cited "the leading BALCA decision," *Modular Container Systems, Inc.*,[2] as articulating several factors that should be considered by certifying officers (COs) "to determine whether or not the job opportunity is bona fide or clearly open to any qualified U.S. worker."[3] The CO should consider whether the employer had complied with former 20 CFR §§656.20(c)(8) and 656.21(b)(6). Former §656.20(c)(8), now codified at 20 CFR §656.10(c)(8), requires the employer to show that a bona fide job opportunity exists. Former §656.21(b)(6), now codified at 20 CFR §656.10(c)(9), requires the employer to show that U.S. workers were rejected solely for lawful, job-related reasons. In making such determination, the CO should consider whether the alien's investment in the employer's business was so great that employment of the alien was tantamount to self-employment in violation of 20 CFR §656.3, which defines employment as (permanent full-time) work by an employee for an employer other than oneself.

Interestingly, §656.3 also states that, for purposes of the definition of employment, "an investor is not an employee." One would think that would preclude labor certification for an investor. Yet, even before PERM, some alien investors were considered employees and, as such, obtained labor certification. The fact that an alien was an investor, or had some other special relationship with the employer, did not establish *per se* the absence of a bona fide job opportunity. Ultimately, the question of whether a *bona fide* job opportunity existed turned on "whether a genuine determination of need for alien labor can be made by the employer corporation and whether a genuine opportunity exists for American workers to compete for the opening."[4]

Today's PERM regulation at 20 CFR §656.17(*l*) essentially and significantly codifies BALCA's seminal decision in *Modular Container Systems, Inc.* This article discusses BALCA's test for a bona fide job opportunity as articulated in *Modular Container*;

---

[2] *Matter of Modular Container Systems, Inc.*, 89 INA 228 (BALCA July 16, 1991) (*en banc*).

[3] Proposed PERM Rule, *supra* note 1, at 30474.

[4] *Matter of Modular Container Systems, Inc.*, *supra* note 2, citing *Hall v. McLaughlin*, 864 F.2d 868 (D.C. Cir. 1989).

discusses other BALCA decisions including pre-*Modular Container* cases and post-*Modular Container* cases including a case filed pre-PERM but decided post-PERM; discusses PERM provisions specifically relating to "alien influence and control over the job opportunity," and Items on ETA Form 9089 that might trigger an audit; and, finally, discusses the evidence that the employer is required to present as well as additional evidence that the employer may want to gather in anticipation of an audit, where an application relates to investors or other employees with close relationships to the employer.

BALCA's Test for a Bona Fide Job Opportunity—Also Called the *Modular Container* Test

In *Modular Container Systems, Inc.*, BALCA clarified the test for the existence of a bona fide job opportunity where the alien is an investor or has some other special relationship with the employer. Before *Modular Container*, BALCA had applied a variety of tests to determine whether a bona fide job opportunity existed. In one line of cases, BALCA applied a two-part test: (1) whether the employment was only a scheme for obtaining the alien's labor certification and, therefore, a sham; and (2) whether the employer was inseparable from the beneficiary.[5] Other BALCA decisions determined whether the alien had such significant ownership and control that a bona fide job opportunity did not exist.[6] Some cases, such as *B.F. Hope Construction, Inc.*,[7] applied both tests. *Modular Container* sets a totality of the circumstances test that embraces the elements of the older tests and provides flexibility for the Board to consider other relevant factors.

Under *Modular Container*, the factors to be examined may include, but are not limited to, whether the alien:

- is in the position to control or influence hiring decisions regarding the job for which labor certification is sought;
- is related to the corporate directors, officers, or employees;
- was an incorporator or founder of the company;
- has an ownership interest in the company;
- is involved in the management of the company;
- is one of a small number of employees;
- has qualifications for the job that are identical to specialized or unusual job duties and requirements stated in the application; and
- is so inseparable from the sponsoring employer because of his or her pervasive presence and personal attributes that the employer would be unlikely to continue in operation without the alien.

The totality of the circumstances standard also includes a consideration of the employer's level of compliance and good faith in the processing of the case. Moreover, the business cannot have been established for the sole purpose of obtaining certification for the alien.

Other BALCA Decisions: Historical Perspective

Pre-*Modular Container* BALCA Cases

Listed below is a sampling of BALCA cases decided **before** the July 1991 decision in *Modular Container*, which indicate the reasoning and factors that comprise the "totality of circumstances" test:

- *Matter of Kafko Partnership*, 89 INA 297 (BALCA May 14, 1991). There is no bona fide job opportunity where the alien and his brother were partners, the alien exercised complete control, the alien was closely involved in creation and development of the enterprise, and the partnership relied on the alien's knowledge, experience, and participation. Labor Certification denied.

- *Matter of Japanese Motor International, Inc.*, 89 INA 246 (BALCA Jan. 30, 1991). Position: Import Manager. Alien is son of President, who owns 60 percent of Employer. Citing *Paris Bakery*, the denial based per se upon familial relationship was not warranted. Labor Certification granted.

- *Matter of Rimaco, Inc.*, 89 INA 362 (BALCA Nov. 16, 1990). There is no genuine test of labor market where the alien and one partner were incorporators, owners, directors, and officers; the alien was the only employee in United States; and business would cease without the alien. Labor Certification denied.

- *Matter of GHR Atlanta Realty, Inc.*, 89 INA 123 (BALCA Mar. 26, 1990). Alien was the sole employee, one of two directors, and was transferred to the United States to establish presence for

---

[5] *See, e.g., Matter of Lignomat, USA, Ltd.*, 88 INA 276 (BALCA Oct. 24, 1989) (*en banc*) (sham and inseparability).

[6] *See, e.g., Matter of Keyjoy Trading Co.*, 87 INA 592 (BALCA Dec. 15, 1987) (*en banc*) (significant ownership and control); *Matter of Ocean Paradise of Hawaii*, 89 INA 188 (BALCA Nov. 21, 1989) (significant ownership and control).

[7] *Matter of B.F. Hope Construction, Inc.*, 89 INA 162 (BALCA Feb. 27, 1990).

South African parent company. Labor Certification denied.

- *Matter of B.F. Hope Construction, Inc.*, 89 INA 162 (BALCA Feb. 27, 1990). There is no bona fide job opportunity where the alien was one of two employees, had previously served as vice president and as one of two directors, had been 50 percent owner and may have retained financial interest in employer. Labor Certification denied.
- *Matter of Paris Bakery*, 88 INA 337 (BALCA Jan. 4, 1990) (en banc). Alien, with four years of qualifying experience, sought position of French Baker. Alien is owner's brother. Where Employer proves "genuine need for an employee with the alien's qualification, the job has not been specifically tailored .... Employer has undertaken recruitment ... and same has not produced applicants who are qualified, the relationship ... does not require denial of certification." Where there were no U.S. applicants with required experience, fraternal relationship does not require denial. Labor Certification granted.
- *Matter of Bulk Farms, Inc.*, 89 INA 51 (BALCA Jan. 3, 1990). Alien was president and sole stockholder, was involved in marketing business, and employer's brochure contained personal message from the alien and his wife to prospective customers. Labor Certification denied.
- *Matter of Lignomat, USA, Ltd.*, 88 INA 276 (BALCA Oct. 24, 1989) (en banc). A genuine test of labor market was unlikely where the alien and his wife were 49 percent shareholders, were two of three directors, comprised the officers of the corporation, and the alien was one of five employees and had developed the employer's product. Labor Certification denied.
- *Young Seal of America*, 88 INA 121 (BALCA May 17, 1989) (en banc). No bona fide job opportunity was deemed to exist where, inter alia, the alien's wife was director, chief financial officer, corporate secretary of the employer corporation, signed all correspondence concerning the application and was the contact person. Alien arrived at time of incorporation. Position does not reflect a legitimate job opportunity. Labor Certification denied.
- *Matter of Medical Equipment Designs, Inc.*, 87 INA 673 (BALCA May 6, 1988). Alien was intimate with foreign inventors of product, active in product development, owned royalty rights to product, was deemed essential by employer to manufacturing and marketing product in United States and to position offered, was sales director and had primary duty to direct marketing. Labor Certification denied.
- *Matter of Keyjoy Trading Co.*, 87 INA 592 (BALCA Dec. 15, 1987) (en banc). There is no genuine test of labor market where the alien owned 10 percent of corporation and occupied several high-ranking positions. Labor Certification denied.
- *Matter of Amger Corp.*, 87 INA 545 (BALCA Oct. 15, 1987). There is no bona fide job opportunity where the alien was 100 percent shareholder, director, president, and founder of employer; and the single qualified U.S. applicant was hired for another position.[8] Labor Certification denied.

Post-Modular Container BALCA Cases

Modular Container has been directly cited by BALCA over 125 times since being issued in July 1991. Listed below is a sampling of BALCA cases decided since July 1991, revealing that *Modular Container* is still the standard and suggesting, as we move further along in the PERM era, that practitioners should expect the "totality of circumstances" test to be applied, first, by DOL in its audits, and then by BALCA in its adjudication of inevitable appeals. The following list of cases is an illustrative rather than exhaustive review of BALCA decisions since *Modular Container* that dealt with the issue of "alien control"—most resulting in denial but some resulting in certification.

Alien's Investment, Managerial Involvement, or Familial Relationship Precluding Labor Certification

Labor certification has been frequently denied to aliens who were also investors, officers, directors or relatives of the sponsoring employer. The following cases—although not all decided under the totality of the circumstances test—illustrate instances in which the alien's familial relationship, level of investment, or managerial involvement prevented a finding of a bona fide job opportunity:

---

[8] To the same effect, see *Matter of Young Seal of America, Inc.*, 88 INA 121 (BALCA May 17, 1988) (en banc); *Matter of Pan Ocean Aquarium, Inc.*, 87 INA 691 (BALCA Feb. 17, 1988); *Matter of Friendly Starts, Inc.*, 87 INA 517 (BALCA Jan. 29, 1988). See also A. Kaye and E. Litwin, "The Issue of Alien Ownership of the Employer—A Review of BALCA Decisions," 2 *Immigration & Nationality Law Handbook* 338–42 (AILA 1990–91 Ed.).

- *Matter of Umrani Aquatic Limited,* 06 INA 51 (BALCA Apr. 24, 2007). This case commenced pre-PERM. The President and Secretary of the employer were the alien's parents. Labor certification was denied because the employer had failed to sufficiently respond to the CO's request to document that the company is sufficiently independent of the alien to create a bona fide opportunity which is open to any qualified U.S. worker. Although this case was filed in 2001 before PERM was enacted, BALCA made its decision in 2007. This case, therefore, is significant because it is the first case decided post-PERM and underscores the importance of using documentation to rebut issues of concern.
- *Matter of JIL Industries, Ltd,* 00 INA 63 (BALCA Aug. 22, 2000). Although the alien only holds 11.4 percent of the shares of the employer's business, the alien is one of only two limited partners. Bare assertions without supporting reasoning or evidence are insufficient to establish a bona fide job opportunity. Labor certification denied.
- *Matter of Cleanex House Cleaning Service, Inc.,* 03 INA 208 (BALCA Sept. 7, 2004). Alien's brother is President, Treasurer, Clerk, sole Director and contact person of employer. Labor Certification denied.
- *Matter of Star Custom Industries, Inc.,* 98 INA 286 (BALCA June 18, 1999). Alien does not appear to have equity interest but his brother is owner, sole director, and chief executive officer. Labor Certification denied.
- *Matter of Nakano Warehouse & Transportation Corp.,* 92 INA 337 (BALCA Nov. 23, 1993). Alien, who held E-2 visa and sought certification as Chief Executive Officer, held the most senior position in the United States, senior to person signing the application, and, although he had no ownership interest, did exercise control or influence over the recruitment process. Labor Certification denied.
- *Matter of Topco USA, Inc.,* 93 INA 516 (BALCA Feb. 23, 1996). Alien is the brother-in-law of the sole shareholder's wife (and wife is Vice-President and Secretary to the corporation and member of the Board of Directors). Evidence submitted did not establish that a bona fide position exists. Applying "strict scrutiny," Labor Certification denied.
- *Matter of Ridhi Gems,* 93 INA 312 (BALCA Oct. 25, 1994). Alien is brother of proprietor and owner of employer and, thus "in the position to control or influence hiring decisions ...." Labor Certification denied.
- *Matter of Morex, Inc.,* 91 INA 206 (BALCA, Oct. 27, 1992). Alien holds 25 percent of the shares of employer, a closely held corporation, and alien's three brothers (one of whom is the employer's president) hold the remaining 75 percent. Based on a totality of circumstances test and especially, the investment and family relationships between the alien and the employer, there is not a bona fide job opportunity. Labor Certification denied.
- *Matter of Asseman (Sky) Travel Agency,* 90 INA 496 (BALCA May 26, 1992). Alien has considerable influence over employer, since he is the brother of employer's single other officer and related to other shareholders. Labor Certification denied.
- *Matter of Malone & Associates,* 90 INA 360 (BALCA July 16, 1991) (en banc). This case was decided the same day as *Modular Container*. BALCA determined that there is no bona fide job opportunity where the employer was a law firm, founded and wholly owned by the alien, bearing the alien's name, until recently located in the alien's home, and applications were reviewed by a permanent employee of the alien/employer. Labor Certification denied.

Investment or Involvement Does Not Preclude Labor Certification

Where, considering the totality of the circumstances, it appears that an employer is offering a genuine job opportunity, certification may properly be granted despite the alien's investment or management involvement in the employer. Accordingly, in the case of *Human Performance Measurement, Inc.*, 89 INA 269 (Oct. 25, 1991) (en banc), BALCA held that even though the alien had "a collegial and professional relationship with the sponsoring employer" and was a stockholder, member of the board of directors, treasurer, and vice president for finance and marketing, labor certification should be granted where it appeared that a genuine job opportunity existed. Circumstances found persuasive by the Board included:

- the alien's ownership of just four percent of the employer's stock along with 30 other shareholders made it unlikely that the alien had a controlling say regarding the hiring of employees (However, four Board members did not join in this finding, noting the record did not establish that four percent was an insignificant level of stock ownership);

- the alien had no family relationship with key company personnel;
- the employer's history indicated that other persons were the prime movers in corporate affairs;
- although the job requirements matched the alien's qualifications, the job was unique because it involved a new theory and new technology derived from original research, with which the alien was familiar because of his graduate studies;
- the alien's work experience for the job was gained through an employer, which, although engaged in joint research with the sponsoring employer, appeared to be independent; and
- the employer would have accepted U.S. applicants with experience in a related field, but none applied.

Interestingly, *Human Performance* has only been cited in BALCA decisions seven times since its publication and has not been specifically referenced this decade. However, as it has not been directly overruled, it remains the benchmark reference point for successful PERM applications involving alien ownership and control.[9]

Alien's Familial Relationship to the Employer Does Not Preclude Certification

One of the factors considered under *Modular Container's* totality of the circumstances test is whether the alien for whom certification is sought is related to the employer's directors, officers, or employees. Prior to *Modular Container*, the family relationship between the alien and employer was the focus of only a few decisions.

As noted above, in the pre-*Modular Container* case of *Young Seal of America*,[10] BALCA held that no bona fide job opportunity existed where, inter alia, the alien's wife was director, chief financial officer, and corporate secretary of the employer corporation. However, in the ensuing pre-*Modular Container* case of *Paris Bakery*,[11] BALCA stated that a close family relationship between the person having the authority to hire and the alien (brother of the owner) does not, standing alone, establish that the job is not bona fide or available to U.S. workers. BALCA stated in *Paris Bakery* that while a family relationship increases the level of scrutiny to be paid to the application, it is only one factor to be considered. If the employer genuinely needs an employee with the alien's qualifications, the job has not been tailored to the alien, and good faith recruitment has not produced qualified applicants, a family relationship does not *per se* require denial of certification.[12]

In the post-*Modular Container* case of *Altobeli's Fine Italian Cuisine*,[13] the panel noted that *Paris Bakery* invites a higher level of scrutiny where there is a family relationship. Nevertheless, applying the *Modular Container* totality of the circumstances test, the panel found that the employer had demonstrated it was genuinely independent from the alien, despite the alien's family relationship to two of the employer's board members and shareholders. Specifically, the panel noted that the alien had no ownership interest, was not an incorporator or founder, was not on the board of directors, and was not currently an employee. In addition, the panel noted that the job duties did not appear to be tailored to the alien's qualifications, the business had been operating without the alien, and there was no reason to think it would not continue to do so without him, and the CO did not challenge the propriety of the recruitment.

Similarly, in *H&R Auto Paint & Body Repair*,[14] the panel granted certification, noting that despite the familial relationship (alien is brother of sole proprietor), the evidence produced established that the business had been operating for over seven years without the alien, that the alien had 13 years of qualifying experience as an Automobile Body Repairer, and employer's recruitment had not produced any qualified applicants.

---

[9] *E.g., Matter of Tridus International, Inc.*, 98 INA 287 (BALCA Mar. 1, 1999).

[10] *Matter of Young Seal of America*, 88 INA 121 (BALCA May 17, 1989) (en banc).

[11] *Matter of Paris Bakery*, 88 INA 337 (BALCA Jan. 4, 1990) (en banc).

[12] *See also Matter of Japanese Motors International, Inc.*, 89 INA 246 (BALCA Jan. 30, 1991) (reversing denial based only on the alien's close family relationship to the employer's president).

[13] *Matter of Altobeli's Fine Italian Cuisine*, 90 INA 130 (BALCA Oct. 16, 1991).

[14] *Matter of H & R Auto Repair*, 02 INA 169 (BALCA Aug. 5, 2003).

PERM Provisions Establishing Alien Influence and Control, and Items on Form ETA-9089 That Might Possibly Trigger an Audit

As mentioned above, when the PERM regulation was implemented on March 28, 2005, and codified at 20 CFR §656.17(*l*),[15] it suggested what constitutes "alien influence and control over [the] job opportunity." In so doing, the regulation reveals when an audit is likely to ensue. Section 656.17(*l*) provides:

> ***Alien influence and control over job opportunity.*** If the employer is a closely held corporation or partnership in which the alien has an ownership interest, or if there is a familial relationship between the stockholders, corporate officers, incorporators, or partners and the alien, or if the alien is one of a small number of employees, the employer, in the event of an audit, must be able to demonstrate the existence of a bona fide job opportunity, *i.e.*, the job is available to all U.S. workers, and must provide to the Certifying Officer, [enumerated] following supporting documentation:

Based on a clear reading of §656.17(*l*), an audit is likely to result when any of the following exists: (1) the alien has an ownership interest in a closely held corporation, partnership or sole proprietorship or a position that carries control over the business's operations; (2) the alien has a familial relationship with the owners, stockholders or officers; or (3) the employer only has a few employees. Thus, and as discussed below, the practitioner should expect an audit when its answers on ETA Form 9089 suggest any of the above issues exist.

Alien Has Ownership Interest in Employer

The PERM regulation suggests that an audit is likely to arise if the answer is "yes" to the following question: "Is the employer a closely held corporation, partnership, or sole proprietorship **in which the foreign worker has an ownership interest?**" (emphasis supplied). Indeed, Section C, Item 16 on ETA Form 9089 asks this very question.

"Closely held corporation" is defined in 20 CFR §656.3 as "a corporation that typically has relatively few shareholders and whose shares are not generally traded in the securities market."[16] It is expected that a "yes" answer to Section C, Item 16 would trigger an audit. Despite numerous BALCA decisions discussing alien ownership and percentages of shares held, it is not clear what amount of "ownership interest" would result in a denial of certification on the basis of undue alien influence or control, establishing the lack of a bona fide job opportunity.

The PERM regulation does not define what constitutes "significant" ownership in order to establish what an alien's undue influence over the employer would entail. However, and in the Form I-864, Affidavit of Support context, U.S. Citizenship and Immigration Services (USCIS) regulations define "significant ownership interest" as meaning "an ownership interest of 5 percent or more."[17]

Alien Has Familial Relationship with Employer's Owners, Stockholders or Officer

The PERM regulation also suggests that an audit is likely to arise if the answer is "yes" to the question: "Is there a familial relationship between the foreign worker and the owners, stockholders, partners, corporate officers, and/or incorporators?" Not surprisingly, Section C, Item 17 on ETA Form 9089 asks this very question. This item is ambiguous in two ways.

One, PERM does not clarify whether a familial relationship to "owners or stockholders" of a public company requires answering Item 17 with a "yes." One would think not, but it is not clear.

Two, PERM does not define what is meant by "familial relationship." Guidance, however, can once again be found in the USCIS regulation regarding Form I-864, Affidavit of Support. 8 CFR §213a.1 defines the term "relative" to mean, "a husband, wife, father, mother, child, adult son, adult daughter, brother, or sister." Relatives, including but not limited to in-laws, step-parents, aunts, uncles, nieces and nephews, are omitted, leaving the practitioner and employer to wonder if a relationship which the alien considers to be familial should be disclosed.[18] This author takes a conservative ap-

---

[15] DOL, ETA, "Labor Certification for the Permanent Employment of Aliens in the United States; Implementation of New System" (Final PERM Rule), 69 Fed. Reg. 77325, 77395 (Dec. 27, 2004) (*codified at* 20 CFR §656.17(*l*)), *published on* AILA InfoNet at Doc. No. 04122312 (*posted* Dec. 27, 2004).

[16] *Id.*

[17] 8 CFR §213a.1.

[18] *See generally* R. Kapoor *et al.*, "A Magical Mystery Tour: Selected PERM Issues," *Immigration & Nationality Law Handbook* 180 (AILA 2007–08 Ed.) (referencing *Matter of Young Seal of America*, 88 INA 121 (BALCA May 17, 1989) (en banc); *Matter of Paris Bakery*, 88 INA 337 (BALCA Jan. 4, 1990) (en banc); *Matter of Altobeli's Fine*

continued

proach and often errs on the side of disclosure when confronted with issues of extended family member sponsorship in the PERM context.

Employer Only Has a Few Employees

The PERM regulation also suggests that an audit is likely to ensue where the employer has few employees. ETA Form 9089 asks at Section C, Item 12: "Number of employees currently on the employer's payroll in the area of intended employment."

Interestingly, during the comment period that preceded the Final PERM rule, two commentators recommended that the employer be required to specify its number of employees, noting that "if the alien is one of a few employees, the job may not be open to U.S. workers."[19] The DOL obviously agreed. Significantly, the PERM regulation provides: If the alien is one of 10 or fewer employees, the employer must document any family relationship between the employees and the alien. This suggests that an audit might not occur if the employer (only) has 10 employees but the alien has no familial relationship, per Section C, Item 17 of ETA Form 9089, with the "owners, stockholders, partners, corporate officers, and/or stockholders."

Other Items That Might Trigger an Audit

An answer to an additional item, alone or in combination with the answer to another item on ETA Form 9089, also might trigger an audit. Section C, Item 13 which asks "year commenced business" also may trigger an audit depending on the alien's work history, delineated in Section J, Item e. For example, the answer to Item 13 (evidencing that the employer was recently established) and the answer to Section J, item e (evidencing the alien's past employment overseas with an affiliate of the U.S. employer) might cause the adjudicator to suspect alien control. In such instance, an audit might result.

The answer to section J, Item 16 ("class of admission") also may trigger an audit for an alien on an E-1 or E-2 visa if the answers to Section C, Items 12 and 13 ("number of employees and year commenced business") indicate that the newly established employer has few employees and/or the answer to Section J, item e ("alien's employment history") indicate that the alien has considerable authority. In *Driessen*

Aircraft Interior Systems,[20] BALCA held that an E-2 visa holder, who is not an investor but is highly trained and holds considerable authority, would not permit his replacement by any qualified U.S. worker, in the absence of evidence to the contrary. BALCA found that the CO had reasonably questioned whether a bona fide job opening existed in view of the alien's E-2 visa status. In this case, BALCA determined that the employer had not submitted relevant and reasonably obtainable documentation requested by the CO to prove that a bona fide opportunity existed.[21] As a result, the denial of labor certification was upheld. However, there are numerous examples of BALCA decisions that permit an E visa holder to obtain labor certification when present in the United States in either a supervisory or essential skills position for larger corporate entities.[22]

In addition, other respected practitioners report receiving labor certification on behalf of an alien in E-2 status without an audit. In the event of an audit, practitioners should be prepared to submit relevant and reasonably obtainable documentation to prove the absence of "control" and the existence of a bona fide job opportunity.

Surviving the Audit

Importantly, before the PERM regulation was implemented, the American Immigration Lawyers Association (AILA) offered its comment that the regulations should allow the employer, when audited, to provide evidence on the issue of undue influence and bona fide job opportunity. DOL agreed and stated in the Supplementary Information that "in determining whether the job is subject to the alien's influence and control, we will evaluate the totality of the circumstances, using the *Modular Container Systems* crite-

---

Italian Cuisine, 90 INA 130 (BALCA Oct. 16, 1991); *Matter of Ibes, Inc.* 89 INA 187 (BALCA July 23, 1990)).

[19] Final PERM Rule, *supra* note 15, at 77356.

[20] *Matter of Driessen Aircraft Interior Systems*, 93 INA 82 (BALCA Jan. 11, 1995).

[21] *Matter of Gencorp*, 87 INA 659 (BALCA Jan. 13, 1988) (Region V). This important case stands for the proposition that once the certifying officer (CO) asks for documentation evidencing "no alien control" and the existence of a bona fide job opportunity, the employer should not submit self-serving assertions, but has the burden to submit documentation that evidences and establishes that a bona fide job opportunity exists.

[22] *E.g., Matter of D Koby Enterprises, Inc.*, 06 INA 53 (BALCA Apr. 24, 2007). In this case the CO assumed incorrectly that the alien had an ownership interest. BALCA certified the case because the employer was able to provide the requested documentation evidencing otherwise, in line with the *Gencorp* guidance.

ria...." and that "no single factor, such as a familial relationship between the alien and the employer, or the size of the employer, shall be controlling."[23]

The PERM regulation sets forth at 20 CFR §656.17(*l*) the documentation required in the event of an audit. Such documentation includes:

(1) A copy of the articles of incorporation, partnership agreement, business license or similar documents that establish the business entity;

(2) A list of all corporate/company officers and shareholders/partners of the corporation/firm/business/their titles and positions in the business's structures, and a description of the relationships to each other and to the alien beneficiary;

(3) The financial history of the corporation/company/partnership, including the total investment in the business entity and the amount of investment of each officer/incorporator/partner and the alien beneficiary;

(4) The name of the business's official with primary responsibility for interviewing and hiring applicants for positions within the organization and the name(s) of the business's official(s) having control or influence over hiring decisions involving the position for which labor certification is sought;

(5) If the alien is one of 10 or fewer employees, the employer must document any family relationship between the employees and the alien.

The above list, in whole or in part, comprises most audit requests. The prudent practitioner will anticipate an audit and will have such documentation compiled before the PERM application has been filed. The practitioner additionally and importantly should compile and be ready to submit, in the event of an audit, additional documents that demonstrate that, despite the identified adverse factors (such as familial relationship), a real and bona fide business opportunity existed and exists. Such documentation may include copies of advertisements before the PERM process was contemplated and pursued, evidencing that the employer was trying (unsuccessfully and continuously) to fill the position before employing the alien to assume same.

Such documentation also may include copies of advertisements placed by similar or competing employers, evidencing that this position is a "shortage" position and known to be difficult to fill. Such documentation could include copies of correspondence and work product from the alien, showing that he has no authority relating to the hiring function. Indeed, there is considerable opportunity for creative lawyering. Opinions of outside experts in corporate law also might be solicited and included to develop facts and an explanation showing that despite some indicia of ownership, family relationship, and/or control, the employer is truly offering a bona fide job opportunity to qualified U.S. workers.

LOOKING AT AN ACTUAL AUDIT UNDER PERM

On December 20, 2005, this author's office filed a PERM application, disclosing at Section C, Item 16 that the employer is a closely held corporation, partnership, or sole proprietorship and a familial relationship existed between the alien and an officer. On April 24, 2006, the case was selected for audit. The alien was a Senior Quality Surveyor. He was also the brother of the Secretary/Treasurer of the company.

A special attachment in the audit notice stated as follows: "The application shows that the employer is a closely held corporation, partnership, or sole proprietorship. Per §656.17(*1*), please submit the following documentation:

- A copy of the articles of incorporation, partnership agreement, business license, or similar documents that establish the business entity;

- A list of all corporate/company officers and shareholders/partners of the corporation/firm/business, their titles and positions in the business' structure, and a description of the relationships to each other and to the alien beneficiary;

- The financial history of the corporation/company/partnership, including the total investment in the business entity and the amount of investment of each officer, incorporator/partner and the alien beneficiary; and

- The name of the business's official with primary responsibility for interviewing and hiring applicants for positions within the organization and the name(s) of the business's official(s) having control of influence over hiring decisions involving the position for which labor certification is sought.

On or about May 24, 2006, the author's office submitted a response to the audit notice, together with a Memorandum of Law. The response to the audit notification furnished the complete recruitment documentation. It established that this was a bona fide

---

[23] *Id.*

position supported by a bona fide recruitment effort, that the requisites for the position were standard and basic to the industry in question, and that there were no qualified U.S. workers located for the position.

- **List of all company officers and shareholders/partners of the corporation/firm/business, their titles and positions in the business's structure, and a description of the relationships to each other and to the alien beneficiary.**

The response to the special attachment explained that the company was owned in its entirety by its sole shareholder, its CEO and President Mr. R.T.P. All other corporate officers were non-owner employees of the company. The alien (Mr. B.W.) was not an officer of the company, nor did he have an ownership interest in it.

The position of Senior Quality Surveyor reports directly to the Vice President. As such, we asserted, there was no "alien influence or control over the job opportunity." This "is a bona fide opportunity which requires significant industry-related experience to serve as a company team member contributing a full range of specialized experience to normal, industry business operations." Hence, we said, the PERM application met the standard of a bona fide job opportunity.

- **The name of the business's official with primary responsibility for interviewing and hiring applicants for positions within the organization and the name(s) of the business's official(s) having control or influence over hiring decisions involving the position for which labor certification is sought.**

The employer's Human Resources Director, Mr. J.W.W., has primary responsibility for interviewing and hiring applicants for company positions. However, the President and CEO of the company has ultimate control over hiring for all positions.

The Memorandum of Law

The Memorandum of Law gave information about the company, including its sole shareholder, the Board of Directors, and its officers.

The total number of employees for the company was 188 and adding employees of the affiliate companies, the total was 457.

It discussed the financial investment—all by Mr. R.T.B., the business officers responsible for interviewing and hiring applicants—Mr. J.W.W., and the business officers with control over hiring decisions involving the position of Senior Quality Surveyor—the owner, Mr. R.T.B.

A discussion of the law followed.

Question Presented

The issue presented and discussed in the Memorandum of Law was "is the job offered by RTB associates, Inc. (the employer) for Mr. B.W. (the alien) a bona fide job offer under §656.21(c)(8)?"

Excerpts from the Memorandum of Law follow.

Discussion

BALCA's Test for Bona Fide Job Opportunity

In *Modular Container Systems, Inc.*, BALCA clarified the test for the existence of a bona fide job opportunity where the alien is an investor or has some other special relationship with the employer. *Modular Container* sets a totality of circumstances test that embraces the elements of older tests and provides flexibility for looking at other relevant factors.

Under *Modular Container*, the factors to be examined include, but are not limited to, whether the alien:

- is in the position to control or influence hiring decisions regarding the job for which the labor certification is sought; **This is not the case concerning this application.**

- is related to the corporate directors, officers or employees;

- was an incorporator or founder of the company; **Not the case here.**

- has an ownership interest in the company; **Not the case here.**

- is involved in the management of the company; **Not the case here.**

- is one of a small number of employees; **Not the case here.**

- has qualifications for the job that are identical to specialized or unusual job duties and requirements stated in the application; and **same with most labor certification applications.**

- is so inseparable from the sponsoring employer because of his or her pervasive presence and personal attributes that the employer would be unlikely to continue in operation without the alien. **Not the case here.**

The totality of circumstances standard also includes a consideration of the employer's level of compliance and good faith in the processing of the claim.

Application of BALCA Tests of Bona Fide Job Opportunity

1. <u>Significant investment of managerial involvement.</u> Labor certification was frequently denied to aliens who were also investors, officers, or directors of the sponsoring employer.

2. <u>Investment or involvement not significant enough to find lack of bona fide job opportunity.</u> Where, considering the totality of circumstances, it appears that an employer is offering a genuine job opportunity, certification may properly be granted despite the alien's investment or management involvement by Mr. B.W., the alien.

3. <u>Alien's family relationship to the employer.</u> One of the factors considered under *Modular Container's* totality of circumstances test is whether the alien for whom certification is sought is related to the employer's directors, officers, or employees. Prior to *Modular Container*, the family relationship between the alien and the employer was the focus of only a few decisions.

   In *Young Seal of America* (88 INA 121 (BALCA May 17, 1989) (en banc)), BALCA held that no bona fide job opportunity existed where, inter alia, the alien's wife was director, chief financial officer, and corporate secretary of the employer corporation. However, in *Paris Bakery*, BALCA stated that a close family relationship between the person having the authority to hire and the alien (brother of the owner) does not, standing alone, establish that the job is not bona fide or available to the U.S. workers. BALCA stated in *Paris Bakery* that, while a family relationship increased the level of scrutiny to be paid to the application, it is only one factor to be considered. If the employer genuinely needs an employee with the alien's qualifications, the job has not been tailored to the alien, and good faith requirement has not produced qualified applicants, a family relationship does not per se require denial of certification.

   In *Altobeli's Fine Italian Cuisine* (90 INA 120 (BALCA Oct. 16, 2004)), the panel noted that *Paris Bakery* invites a higher level of scrutiny where there is a family relationship. Nevertheless, applying the *Modular Container* totality of circumstances test, the panel found that the employer had demonstrated it was genuinely independent from the alien despite the alien's family relationship to two of the employer's board members and shareholders. Specifically, the panel noted that the alien has no ownership interest, was not an incorporator or founder, was not on the board of directors, and was not currently an employee. In addition, the panel noted that the job duties did not appear to be tailored to the alien's qualifications, the business had been operating without the alien, and there was no reason to think it would not continue to do so without him, and the CO did not challenge the propriety of the recruitment.

From the Proposed to the Final PERM Rule

The Supplementary Information to the final PERM rule discussed how DOL modified the regulation in the area of alien influence and control.

<u>Familial Relationship Between Alien and Employer.</u> DOL stated that "in determining whether the job is subject to the alien's influence and control, we will evaluate the totality of circumstances, using the *Modular Container Systems* criteria listed in the preamble to the NPRM" and that "no single factor, such as familial relationship between the alien and the employer, or the size of the employer, shall be controlling."

The regulations define closely held corporations and discuss corporations where the alien is "related" to any shareholders. We have no definition of what is meant by "related." Are in-laws treated as related? Nor do we have a definition of "familial relationship." The final rule reads as follows:

"Alien influence and control over job opportunity. If the employer is a closely held corporation or partnership in which the alien has an ownership interest, or if there is a familial relationship between the stockholders, corporate officers, incorporators, or partners, and the alien, or if the alien is one of a small number of employees, the employer in the event of an audit must be able to demonstrate the existence of a bona fide opportunity, *i.e.*, the job is available to all U.S. workers, and must provide to the Certifying Officer, the following supporting documentation."

Conclusion (of Memorandum of Law)

- The job offered by R.T.B. Associates, Inc. to Mr. B.W. was and is a bona fide job offer under §656.21(c)(8).

- The employer completed an extensive recruitment effort for the position of Senior Quality Surveyor. However, there was absolutely no response whatsoever to any of its efforts.
- Mr. B.W. operates under the supervision of the Vice President of Operations, Mr. K.L. While Mr. B.W. is the brother of the Secretary/Treasurer, Ms. E.A.B., he is not in a position to control or influence hiring decisions regarding the job for which the labor certification is sought. He operates strictly in the job/work area described in the PERM application. He has no ownership interest of any sort in any of the companies described above. He makes no managerial decisions outside the areas of his assigned work.
- While Mr. B.W. contributes his time and talents, they are only as regular employee in his assigned areas of business.
- The company clearly could exist without the alien employee, Mr. B.W., and he is not so intensively involved in the company that he is not likely to be replaced.
- DOL stated in the preamble that in determining whether the job is subject to the alien's influence and control, it would evaluate the totality of circumstances, using the *Modular Systems* criteria. DOL stated that "no single factor, such as a familial relationship between the alien and the employer or the size of the employer, shall be controlling." Under the "totality of the circumstances" in this case, this application should be approved.

[The PERM application was approved.]

CONCLUSION

Labor certification denials can be appealed to BALCA and eventually BALCA will issue decisions in these PERM cases. BALCA will either approve or deny, as it can no longer remand cases back to the CO.

In the preamble to the final PERM regulations, DOL stated that AILA had noted a familial relationship alone should not invalidate the job opportunity and suggested that the regulations allow the employer to provide evidence on the issue of bona fide opportunity beyond the items listed in the regulation. This was not done. However, and as suggested in this article, nothing stops the attorney from submitting additional evidence (including work product, copies of correspondence and a history of real-world ads) to substantiate, when applicable, the existence of a bona fide job opportunity and/or the absence of alien control.

DOL stated in the preamble that, in determining whether the job is subject to the alien's influence and control, it would evaluate the totality of the employer's circumstances, using the *Modular Systems* criteria. DOL stated that "no single factor, such as a familial relationship between the alien and the employer or the size of the employer, shall be controlling."

Where the employer maintains that a real job opportunity exists and it would not be able to recruit and hire a qualified U.S. worker for the job opportunity, the practitioner should take the guidance provided by BALCA decisions and, hopefully, this article, to compile, before the PERM application is submitted, the documentation that will convincingly show that, despite the alien's familial relationship and/or the alien's investment in the company, a real and bona fide job opportunity exists.

POSTSCRIPT: POST–PERM LABOR CERTIFICATION APPROVAL ISSUES

Once the PERM labor certification application is approved, we are usually past the time of ownership and control. The next step is to file the Form I-140, Immigrant Visa Petition, with or without the I-485 application for Adjustment of Status.

However, recent developments may indicate continued problems with USCIS in cases where individuals have controlling or substantial interests in a petitioning U.S. company.

USCIS Memo on Determining Employer-Employee Relationship for Adjudication of H-1B Petitions, Including Third-Party Site Placements

A January 8, 2010, memorandum from Donald Neufeld (Neufeld Memo), Assistant Director of Service Center Operations, provided guidance, in the context of H-1B petitions, on the requirement that a petitioner establish that an employer-employee relationship exists and will continue to exist with the beneficiary through the duration of the H-1B validity period.[24]

In a March 19, 2010, letter to Alejandro Mayorkas, Director of USCIS, and Roxana Bacon, Chief Counsel, the author discusses the impact of policies

---

[24] U.S. Citizenship and Immigration Services (USCIS) Memorandum, D. Neufeld, "Determining Employer-Employee Relationship for Adjudication of H-1B Petitions, Including Third-Party Site Placements" (Jan. 10, 2010), *published on* AILA InfoNet at Doc. No. 10011363 (*posted* Jan. 13, 2010).

adopted by the Neufeld Memo on adjudication outside the H-1B context as follows:

> The factors defining the employer-employee relationship adopted by the Neufeld Memo, particularly relating to beneficiaries who have ownership interests in the petitioning firms, have found their way in adjudications outside the H-1B context for some time, specifically, in the L context and in the I-140 context. The Darden-Clackamas doctrine has been relied on by the AAO to deny an executive-manager I-140 petition to senior corporate executive or manager beneficiaries who are sole owners or significant shareholders of the petitioning corporations. (*In re [name not provided]*, SRC 07 800 23180 (AAO Sept. 23, 2009 [www.uscis.gov/err/B4%20-%20Multinational%20Managers%20and%20Executives/Decisions_Issued_in_2009/Sep232009_01B4203.pdf.]). More recently, an AILA member has reported receiving a denial of an EB-1-3 I-140 petition for a CEO and President of a multinational corporation on the grounds that the beneficiary owned a majority of the shares of the company and that no one supervised the beneficiary's work. (*In re [name redacted]*, SRC 09 157 52345 (NSC Feb. 3, 2010)). Clearly, this is not a basis for denial of a multinational manager/executive petition. Indeed, the fact that no one supervised the President and CEO of the company would seem to constitute evidence that the beneficiary qualified for the classification of multinational manager or executive. Similarly, several AILA members have reported denials based on the employer-beneficiary language found in the Neufeld Memo in L-1A and O-1 visa contexts. The doctrines underlying the Neufeld Memo are infecting adjudication of other categories of temporary worker petitions.

AILA submitted a memorandum[25] on January 26, 2010, to Roxana Bacon, Chief Counsel of USCIS, concerning the recent USCIS application of *Nationwide Mutual Insurance Company v. Darden*[26] and *Clackamas Gastroenterology Associates, P.C. v. Wells*[27] to nonimmigrant and immigrant visa petitions.

The memorandum reads as follows:

Dear Ms. Bacon:

AILA is deeply concerned about a line of recent USCIS Administrative Appeals Office decisions, subsequent USCIS Service Center adjudications, and the January 8, 2010, Memorandum and Additions to the Officer's Field Manual. These actions constitute a clear and significant shift from prior policy and practice without the notice and comment afforded by a proper regulatory process. In the required rulemaking process, USCIS would have learned that it has erroneously concluded that an individual who has a controlling or substantial interest in a petitioning U.S. company or that company's foreign parent company (hereinafter a "working-owner") cannot—in most cases—be a beneficiary of a nonimmigrant (*e.g.*, L-1, H-1, and O-1) or immigrant employment-based petition.

Although the Neufeld Memorandum purports to address only H-1B petitions and related third-party worksite placements, AILA believes the effect could be much broader because the reasoning underlying the guidance potentially reaches into all areas of employment-based immigration and already has been getting so used of late. As such, it may have the effect of frustrating clear congressional intent to attract foreign talent and investment and to liberalize our procedures for doing so. AILA and its members will address its additional, specific concerns with the Neufeld Memorandum in subsequent correspondence to USCIS.

AILA considers the issuance of the Neufeld Memorandum to be in violation of the Administrative Procedure Act (APA), because the Memorandum is a substantive rule even though its "guidance" to Service Center Directors as to petition adjudications is characterized as interpretative. We note with interest the comments of the U.S. Court of Appeals for the District of Columbia Circuit in *Appalachian Power Company, et al. v. Environmental Protection Agency*:[28]

---

[25] Memorandum from AILA's USCIS Liaison Committee to USCIS's Chief Counsel presenting legal arguments on eligibility for nonimmigrant status of owners of substantial interests in the petitioning company (Jan. 26, 2010), *published on* AILA InfoNet at Doc. No. 10012760 (*posted* Jan. 27, 2010).

[26] *Nationwide Mutual Insurance Company v. Darden*, 503 U.S. 318 (1996).

[27] *Clackamas Gastroenterology Associates, P.C. v. Wells*, 538 U.S. 440 (2003).

[28] *Appalachian Power Company, et al. v. Environmental Protection Agency*, 208 F.3d 1015, 1024 (D.C. Cir. 2000).

It is well-established that an agency may not escape the notice and comment requirements (here, of 42 USC §7607(d)) by labeling a major substantive legal addition to a rule a mere interpretation. See *Paralyzed Veterans v. D.C. Arena L.P.*, 117 F.3d 579, 588 (D.C. Cir. 1997); *American Mining Congress v. MSHA*, 995 F.2d 1106, 1109–10 (D.C. Cir. 1993) "We must still look to whether the interpretation itself carries the force and effect of law, ... or rather whether it spells out a duty fairly encompassed within the regulation that the interpretation purports to construe." (citations and internal quotations omitted). See *Paralyzed Veterans*, 117 F.3d at 588.

In addition, we note the court's comments that an agency's guidance can have a binding effect for APA purposes regardless of language to the contrary:

> But we have also recognized that an agency's other pronouncements can, as a practical matter, have a binding effect. See, e.g., *McLouth Steel Prods. Corp. v. Thomas*, 838 F.2d 1317, 1321 (D.C. Cir. 1988). If an agency acts as if a document issued at headquarters is controlling in the field, if it treats the document in the same manner as it treats a legislative rule, if it bases enforcement actions on the policies or interpretations formulated in the document, if it leads private parties or State permitting authorities to believe that it will declare permits invalid unless they comply with the terms of the document, then the agency's document is for all practical purposes 'binding.' See Robert A. Anthony, *Interpretative Rules, Policy Statements, Guidances, Manuals, and the Like—Should Federal Agencies Use Them to Bind the Public?*, 41 Duke L.J. 1311, 1328–29 (1992), and cases there cited.[29]

208 F.3d at 1021.

The Neufeld Memorandum revises the Adjudicator's Field Manual, which is binding on adjudicators pursuant to AFM Section 3.4.

Again, AILA will provide detailed comments on the specifics of the Neufeld Memorandum separately; we believe that the Neufeld Memorandum should be set aside in its entirety and that appropriate notice and comment be provided to the public as required by §553 of the APA. The agency cannot change longstanding interpretation or established practice by ukase. The APA and related federal court decisions require agencies to seeking to alter longstanding interpretations or established practices to engage in notice and comment rulemaking.

The instant correspondence relates to recent USCIS Administrative Appeals Office decisions and USCIS Service Center adjudications, as well as the Neufeld Memorandum, that misapply the reasoning of Supreme Court cases *Nationwide Mutual Insurance Company v. Darden*[30] (hereinafter "Darden") and *Clackamas Gastroenterology Associates, P.C. v. Wells*[31] (hereinafter "Clackamas") to reach the conclusion that individuals with controlling or substantial interests in a petitioning U.S. company or its foreign parent company cannot—in most cases—be a beneficiary of a nonimmigrant (*e.g.*, L-1, H-1B and O-1) or immigrant employment-based petition. We strongly believe that this USCIS position departs from longstanding binding precedent, ignores the plain language of the Immigration and Nationality Act (INA) and its implementing regulations, thwarts Congressional intent respecting the purpose of the INA, and leads to absurd results.

Copies of examples of AAO decisions and Service Center adjudications are attached to this memorandum and summarized in Exhibit A.

The AAO's analysis contained in non-precedent decisions but cited repeatedly by adjudicators to justify RFEs, NOIDs and Denials—and now expressed in the AFM revisions regarding H-1B petitions—begins with the proposition that the beneficiary in any employment-based nonimmigrant or immigrant petition must be an "employee" of the petitioning employer. The AAO then notes that the term "employee" is not clearly defined anywhere in the INA and concludes that absent such a definition, under *Darden* and *Clackamas,* it must look to the common law definition of employee to determine who is and is not eligible for employment-based benefits under the INA.2 While the common law definition employs a multi-factor test, the AAO and subse-

---

[29] 208 F.3d at 1021.

[30] *Nationwide Mutual Insurance Company v. Darden*, 503 U.S. 318 (1992).

[31] *Clackamas Gastroenterology Associates, P.C. v. Wells*, 538 U.S. 440 (2003).

quent adjudications, and the Neufeld Memorandum, have focused almost exclusively on one element: control. They have concluded that anyone with a significant ownership interest in the petitioning employer cannot be an "employee" for purposes of eligibility for employer-sponsored nonimmigrant visa status or employment-based immigrant preference classification because the individual is not "controlled" by the employer. AILA believes that this sweeping conclusion is inconsistent with the statutory language, thwarts the purpose and intent of the statute and ignores decades of precedent decisions.[32]

We await a final resolution of these new USCIS policies which, unless modified or changed, will obviously impact investors and entrepreneurs who obtain PERM labor certification when they file I-140 petitions.

---

[32] See Memorandum from AILA's USCIS Liaison Committee to USCIS's Chief Counsel, *supra* note 25, for the rest of this extensive memorandum.

AILA
OCCUPATIONAL
GUIDEBOOK

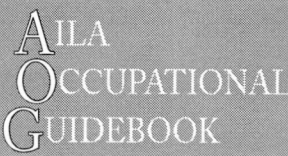

PERMANENT RESIDENCE FOR EMPLOYMENT-CREATING INVESTMENT

EB-5 IMMIGRANT INVESTORS

by Stephen Yale-Loehr, Carolyn S. Lee, & Nicolai Hinrichsen[*]

OVERVIEW

Congress created the fifth employment-based preference (EB-5) immigrant visa category in 1990 for immigrants seeking to enter to engage in a commercial enterprise that will benefit the U.S. economy and create at least 10 full-time jobs.[1] The basic amount required to invest is $1 million, although that amount may be $500,000 if the investment is made in a "targeted employment area."[2] Of the approximately 10,000 numbers available for this preference each year, 3,000 are reserved for entrepreneurs who invest in targeted employment areas.[3] A separate allocation of 3,000 visas is set aside for entrepreneurs who immigrate through a regional center pilot program discussed below.

The statutory requirements of the EB-5 visa category are onerous. At most, fewer than 1,500 people a year have immigrated in this category, just over one-tenth of the visas available.[4] In FY 2005, only 346 people, including derivatives, immigrated in this category.[5] In FY 2006 the number increased to 749,; in FY 2007 it increased to 806; and in FY 2008 it increased to 1,306.[6]

Legacy Immigration and Naturalization Service (INS) (now U.S. Citizenship and Immigration Services (USCIS)) made it even harder to qualify in this category by issuing four precedent decisions in 1998 that significantly restricted eligibility for EB-5 status.[7] Since then, the Administrative Appeals Office (AAO) has issued numerous nonprecedent decisions.[8]

---

[*] Updated from an article published at *Immigration & Nationality Law Handbook* 63 (AILA 2008–09 Ed.). Copyright © 2009 Stephen Yale-Loehr. All rights reserved.

Stephen Yale-Loehr (*syl@millermayer.com*) is co-author of *Immigration Law and Procedure*, the leading immigration law treatise, published by LexisNexis/Matthew Bender. He also teaches immigration law and asylum law at Cornell Law School, and is of counsel at Miller Mayer LLP (*www.millermayer.com*) in Ithaca, NY. Mr. Yale-Loehr is a member of the American Immigration Lawyers Association's (AILA) Business Immigration Committee. He graduated from Cornell Law School in 1981 cum laude, where he was editor-in-chief of the *Cornell International Law Journal*.

Carolyn S. Lee (*csl@millermayer.com*) is a partner at Miller Mayer LLP. She graduated cum laude from Williams College in 1993 and received her J.D. from Cornell Law School in 1999, where she graduated with a specialization in International Legal Affairs.

Nicolai Hinrichsen (*nh@millermayer.com*) is an associate attorney at Miller Mayer LLP. He received his J.D. from Boston University School of Law in 1998. Before joining Miller Mayer he practiced international corporate law in Paris for a U.S. Fortune 500 company and then corporate and securities law in San Francisco for a large U.S.-based law firm.

[1] Immigration and Nationality Act of 1952 (INA), §203(b)(5), 8 U.S. Code (USC) §1153(b)(5), Pub. L. No. 82-414, 66 Stat. 163, (codified as amended at 8 USC §§1101 *et seq*.), For a detailed treatment of the EB-5 immigrant investor category, see C. Gordon, S. Mailman, & S. Yale-Loehr, *Immigration Law and Procedure* §39.07 (rev. ed. 2009).

[2] INA §203(b)(5)(C)(ii), 8 USC §1153(b)(5)(C)(ii).

[3] INA §203(b)(5)(B)(i), 8 USC §1153(b)(5)(B)(i).

[4] Office of Immigration Statistics, U.S. Department of Homeland Security, *2008 Yearbook of Immigration Statistics* 18 (2008) (Table 6), available at www.dhs.gov/xlibrary/assets/statistics/yearbook/2008/ois_yb_2008.pdf (last visited Feb. 9, 2010) [hereinafter 2008 Yearbook of Immigration Statistics].

[5] *Id.*

[6] *Id.*

[7] *Matter of Soffici*, 22 I&N Dec. 158, 19 *Immigr. Rep.* B2-25 (Assoc. Comm'r, Examinations 1998); *Matter of Izummi*, 22 I&N Dec. 169, 19 *Immigr. Rep.* B2-32 (Assoc. Comm'r, Examinations 1998); *Matter of Hsiung*, 22 I&N Dec. 201, 19 *Immigr. Rep.* B2-106 (Assoc. Comm'r, Examinations 1998); *Matter of Ho*, 22 I&N Dec. 206, 19 *Immigr. Rep.* B2-99 (Assoc. Comm'r, Examinations 1998). *Soffici, Izummi, Hsiung,* & *Ho* are all reproduced in Appendix A.

[8] *See generally* H. Joe, R. Oh, S. Smalley, & S. Yale-Loehr, "More AAO EB-5 Decisions," 7 *Bender's Immigr. Bull.* 251 (Mar. 1, 2002); 6 *Bender's Immigr. Bull.* 945 (Sept. 15, 2001) (summaries of four AAO EB-5 decisions); L. Stone, W. Mason, B. Stern Wasser, & S. Yale-Loehr, "Immigrant Investors Strike Out Again at AAO," 6 *Bender's Immigr. Bull.* 709 (July 15, 2001); S. Park & S. Yale-Loehr, "More Bad News from the AAO for Immigrant Investors," 6 *Bender's Immigr. Bull.* 309 (Mar. 15, 2001); L. Stone, R. Oh, & S. Yale-Loehr, "Recent AAO Decisions Continue Trend of Limiting Immigrant Investor Visas," 5 *Bender's Immigr. Bull.* 1031 (Dec. 15, 2000); B. Palmer, "Recent EB-5 Denials," 4 *Bender's Immigr. Bull.* 1139 (Dec. 1, 1999); 4 *Bender's Immigr. Bull.* 810 (Aug. 15, 1999) (summaries of four AAO EB-5 denials). Some AAO EB-5 decisions are available at *www.uscis.gov/uscis-ext-templating/uscis/jspoverride/errFrameset.jsp* (last visited Feb. 25, 2009) (category B7).

In 2002, Congress enacted the 21st Century Department of Justice Appropriations Act (2002 law) a law designed to help certain stranded immigrant investors hurt by the 1998 decisions.[9] Those provisions are discussed in detail below. As of February 2010, regulations to implement the 2002 law had not been published.[10]

In 2003, Congress asked the U.S. Government Accountability Office (GAO) to study the EB-5 program.[11] The GAO report concluded that the program has been under-used for a variety of reasons, including the rigorous application process and the failure to issue regulations implementing the 2002 law.[12] The report found that even though few people have used the EB-5 category, EB-5 participants have invested an estimated $1 billion in a variety of U.S. businesses.[13]

STATUTORY REQUIREMENTS

The Regular Program

Immigration and Nationality Act (INA) §203(b)(5)[14] provides a yearly maximum of approximately 10,000 visas for applicants to invest in a new commercial enterprise employing at least 10 full-time U.S. workers. To qualify under the EB-5 category, the new enterprise must: (1) be one in which the person has invested (or is in the process of investing) at least $1 million (or at least $500,000 if investing in a "targeted employment area," discussed below) after November 29, 1990; (2) benefit the U.S. economy; and (3) create full-time employment for at least 10 U.S. workers. Moreover, the investor must have at least a policy-making role in the enterprise.

The Pilot Program

To encourage immigration through the EB-5 category, Congress created a temporary pilot program in 1993.[15] The Immigrant Investor Pilot Program (pilot program) directs the attorney general and secretary of state to set aside 3,000 visas each year for people who invest in "designated regional centers." The pilot program has been renewed several times, and is currently due to expire September 30, 2012.[16] Efforts are underway in Congress to extend the pilot program beyond this date. At the time of the last sunset, USCIS issued instructions on what would happen with pending cases if Congress failed to renew the pilot program.[17]

The pilot program does not require that the immigrant investor's enterprise itself employ 10 U.S. workers. Instead, it is enough if 10 or more jobs will be created directly or indirectly as a result of the investment.[18] This program also differs from the regular EB-5 provisions in that it permits private and governmental agencies to be certified as regional centers if they meet certain criteria.[19]

[See further discussion of the pilot program in "Regional Centers," *infra*.]

Qualified Immigrants

Outside of the investment and employment requisites, the statute does not specifically address who may be a qualified applicant. USCIS appears to preclude corporate or other nonindividual investors from this category. However, two or more individuals may join to make an EB-5 investment. A single new commercial enterprise may be used for inves-

---

[9] 21st Century Department of Justice Appropriations Authorization Act, Pub. L. No. 107-273, 116 Stat. 1758 (2002). The immigrant investor provisions are in §§11031–37. The conference committee report is H.R. Conf. Rep. No. 107-685 (2002).

[10] U.S. Citizenship and Immigration Services (USCIS) has published interim field guidance pending publication of the regulations. USCIS Memorandum, W. Yates, "Amendments Affecting Adjudication of Petitions for Alien Entrepreneur (EB-5)," (June 10, 2003), *published on* AILA InfoNet at Doc. No. 03061744 (*posted* June 17, 2003); *reprinted in* 8 *Bender's Immigr. Bull.* 1179 (July 1, 2003) [hereinafter Yates Memo]. The Yates Memo is reproduced in Appendix C of this volume.

[11] Basic Pilot Program Extension and Expansion Act of 2003, Pub. L. No. 108-156, §5, 117 Stat. 1944.

[12] U.S. Government Accountability Office (GAO), No. GAO-05-256, "Immigrant Investors: Small Number of Participants Attributed to Pending Regulations and Other Factors" (Apr. 2005), *available at* www.gao.gov/new.items/d05256.pdf (last visited Feb. 25, 2009). Highlights of the GAO Report are reproduced in Appendix E.

[13] *Id.* at 1.

[14] INA §203(b)(5), 8 USC §1153(b)(5).

[15] Departments of Commerce, Justice, and State, the Judiciary, and Related Agencies Appropriations Act of 1993, Pub. L. No. 102-395, §610, 106 Stat. 1828; S. Rep. No. 102-918 (1992).

[16] Department of Homeland Security Appropriations Act, 2010, Pub. L. No. 111-83, § 548, 123 Stat. 2142.

[17] USCIS Update, *Sunset Date to Affect Regional Center Proposals Under the Immigrant Investor Program* (Feb. 19, 2009), *published on* AILA InfoNet at Doc. No. 09022072 (*posted* Feb. 20, 2009).

[18] 21st Century Department of Justice Appropriations Authorization Act, *supra* note 9, §11037(a)(3).

[19] 8 CFR §204.6(m)(3). *See* www.millermayer.com/LinkClick.aspx?fileticket=JYnsmgwj6hM%3d&tabid=126&mid=863 for a list of approved EB-5 regional centers.

tor/employment-creation classification by more than one investor, provided that: (1) each petitioning investor has invested (or is actively in the process of investing) the required amount; and (2) the creation of at least 10 qualifying full-time jobs may be attributable to each investor.[20] In fact, a new commercial enterprise may be used for investor/employment-creation classification even though there are several owners of the enterprise, including persons not seeking classification, if: (1) the source(s) of all capital invested is (are) identified; and (2) all invested capital has been derived by lawful means.[21] The lawful source of funds issue is discussed in more detail in "Legal Acquisition of Capital," *infra*.

The New Commercial Enterprise

There are two basic requirements for showing a new commercial enterprise. First, the enterprise must be "new"—*i.e.*, formed after November 29, 1990.[22] However, an enterprise formed before this date may qualify if an investor "restructures"[23] or "expands"[24] an existing business. Second, it must be a "commercial" enterprise. Any for-profit entity formed for the ongoing conduct of lawful business may serve as a commercial enterprise. This includes sole proprietorships, partnerships (whether limited or general),[25] holding companies, joint ventures, corporations, business trusts, or other entities publicly or privately owned.[26] This definition would even include a holding company and its wholly owned subsidiaries, if each such subsidiary is engaged in a for-profit activity formed for the ongoing conduct of a lawful business. However, the term "new commercial enterprise" does not include noncommercial activity, such as owning and operating a personal residence or nonprofit enterprise.[27]

Creating an Original Business—According to a 1998 precedent decision, an EB-5 petitioner had to have a hand in the creation of the enterprise and must be present at the enterprise's inception.[28] This posed particular problems for people investing in partnerships. The partnership usually will be created first, and then the general partner will seek individuals to invest as limited partners. Under legacy INS's interpretation, such investors could not qualify for EB-5 classification because they were not partners at the establishment of the original partnership. In 2002, Congress eliminated the "establishment" requirement for EB-5 investors.[29] Instead of proving that they have "established" a commercial enterprise themselves, investors now need only show that they have "invested" in a commercial enterprise.

Restructuring an Existing Business—By reorganizing or restructuring an existing business, an investor may create a "new commercial enterprise" and therefore qualify for a visa. The statute and regulations provide little insight into what degree of restructuring or reorganization must be done to establish a new enterprise. The AAO has held that simply changing the legal form of the enterprise does not satisfy this requirement.[30] There is only one known case where the AAO agreed the business was sufficiently restructured or reorganized.[31]

Regardless of the forms used to create a new enterprise, the focus of the law is on the creation of at least 10 new employment opportunities. Investments creating a new enterprise but failing to create 10 new jobs also will fail to qualify for EB-5 classification.

Expanding an Existing Business—An investor also can create a new enterprise by expanding an existing business. Only an expansion resulting in an increase of at least 40 percent in the net worth of the business or in the number of employees of the business will satisfy the visa requirements.[32] This could require

---

[20] 8 CFR §204.6(g)(1).

[21] *Id.*

[22] *See, e.g., Matter of [name not provided]*, EAC 91 184 50136, 12 *Immigr. Rep.* B2-51 (AAU Aug. 12, 1993) (denying petition as investment made before Nov. 29, 1990; investor's documentation of "expanded business" deemed insufficient). *See also* Yates Memo, *supra* note 10, at ¶2.

[23] 8 CFR §204.6(h)(2).

[24] 8 CFR §204.6(h)(3).

[25] The 21st Century Department of Justice Appropriations Authorization Act, *supra* note 9, clarifies that a "commercial enterprise" may include a limited partnership. *Id.* §11036(b)(3).

[26] 8 CFR §204.6(e) (definition of commercial enterprise).

[27] *Id.*

[28] *Matter of Izummi*, 22 I&N Dec. 169, 198, 19 *Immigr. Rep.* B2-32 (Assoc. Comm'r, Examinations 1998).

[29] 21st Century Department of Justice Appropriations Authorization Act, *supra* note 9, §11036(a)(2). *See also* Yates Memo, *supra* note 10, at ¶1.

[30] *Matter of Soffici*, 22 I&N Dec. 158, 166, 19 Immigr. Rep. B2-25 (Assoc. Comm'r, Examinations 1998) ("A few cosmetic changes to the decor and a new marketing strategy for success do not constitute the kind of restructuring contemplated by the regulations, nor does a simple change in ownership.").

[31] *Matter of [name redacted]* (AAO July 11, 2001) (approved case involved the "restructuring" of a horse breeding business into a new business for horse breeding and training).

[32] 8 CFR §204.6(h)(3). *See also* Yates Memo, *supra* note 10, at ¶2.

the investor to create more than 10 new jobs to qualify for a visa if the pre-expansion number of employees was more than 25. The larger the business that the investor expands, the more onerous his or her burden to qualify for a visa under this standard. However, an investor need not show that his or her investment alone caused the 40 percent increase.[33] The AAO has insisted that proof of expansion of the company requires audited financial statements concerning the company's former net worth at the time of investment.[34]

Pooling Arrangements—The regulations specifically allow immigrant investors to pool their investments with others seeking EB-5 status.[35] Each investor must invest the applicable statutory amount. All of the new jobs created by the new commercial enterprise will be allocated among those within the pool seeking permanent investor visas.[36]

The AAO has injected a restriction on pooling investments by requiring the petitioner to show that *every* investor in the partnership identify the source of their funds and prove that they were derived by lawful means.[37]

"Engaging" in a New Commercial Enterprise

The statute requires an EB-5 applicant to enter the United States to engage in a new commercial enterprise.[38] To qualify, an investor must maintain more than a purely passive role in the new enterprise upon which the petition is based. The regulations require an EB-5 immigrant to be involved in the management of the new commercial enterprise.[39] The petitioner either must be involved in the day-to-day managerial control of the commercial enterprise or manage it through policy formulation. The regulations state that if the EB-5 petitioner is a corporate officer or board member, or, in the case of a limited partnership, is a limited partner under the provisions of the Uniform Limited Partnership Act (ULPA), he or she satisfies the requirement of engaging in the management of the new commercial enterprise.[40] The AAO, however, has found that merely calling the investor a limited partner pursuant to the ULPA in a partnership agreement does not automatically mean that the person is involved in the management of the new commercial enterprise.[41]

"Investing" or "Actively in the Process of Investing" "Capital"

The statute requires an EB-5 petitioner to have invested or be in the process of investing. Although the statute explicitly states that an EB-5 petitioner may be "in the process" of investing the required capital,[42] USCIS effectively requires the entire capital amount to be already invested and at risk in the commercial enterprise at the time the I-526 petition is filed. This interpretation appears to contravene the statute, but shows USCIS's desire to have the full amount committed and immediately available for use in job-creation.

The term "invest" means to contribute capital. A contribution of capital in exchange for a note, bond, convertible debt, obligation, or any other debt arrangement between the entrepreneur and the new

---

[33] Legacy Immigration and Naturalization Service (INS) Memorandum, T. Alexander Aleinikoff, INS General Counsel, to Louis D. Crochetti, Jr., Acting Assoc. Comm'r for Examinations, "Whether a Pool of Alien Immigrant Investors Can Create a New Commercial Enterprise by Expanding an Existing Business by at Least 40%," HQ 204.27-C (Jan. 31, 1995), *reprinted in* 73 Interpreter Releases 1625 (Nov. 18, 1996).

[34] *Matter of [name not provided]*, WAC 99 010 50117 (AAO Dec. 15, 2000).

[35] 8 CFR §204.6(g).

[36] *See generally* 8 CFR §204.6(g); H.R. Klasko, "Pooled Investment Arrangements: Unraveling the Controversy," 2 *Immigration & Nationality Law Handbook* 107 (AILA 1998–99 Ed.) [hereinafter Klasko]; A.J. Vasquez-Aspiri, "The Role of Commercial Organizations in the EB-5 Employment Process," 2 *Bender's Immigr. Bull.* 813 (Oct. 15, 1997).

[37] *See, e.g., Matter of [name not provided]*, WAC 98 106 51072, slip op. at 20 (AAO July 6, 2000); *Matter of [name not provided]*, WAC 98 106 51583, slip. op. at 22 (AAO Sept. 11, 2000). This requirement is discussed further *infra*.

[38] INA §203(b)(5)(A), 8 USC §1153(b)(5)(A).

[39] 8 CFR §204.6(j)(5).

[40] *Id. See also* 73 *Interpreter Releases* 48, 55 (Jan. 10, 1996).

[41] *See, e.g., Matter of [name not provided]*, WAC 98 111 53508, slip op. at 23 (AAO Mar. 20, 2000) ("Despite the superficial language in the limited partnership agreement referring to the ULPA and to 8 CFR §204.6(j)(5)(iii), it is clear that the petitioner here does not in fact have the rights normally granted to limited partners under the ULPA").

[42] INA §203(b)(5)(A)(i), 8 USC §1153(b)(5)(A)(i). *See also* 8 CFR §204.6(j)(2) (allowing an investor to be "actively in the process of investing the required amount of capital"). Indeed, even the regulations governing removal of an EB-5 investor's conditional resident status two years later acknowledge that an investor may not have invested all of his or her money by then. The regulations simply require an investor to provide evidence that the alien "invested or was actively in the process of investing the requisite capital." 8 CFR §216.6(a)(4)(ii).

commercial enterprise does not constitute a contribution of capital and will not constitute an investment.[43]

The regulations define "capital" as cash and cash equivalents, equipment, inventory, and other tangible property.[44] According to USCIS, retained earnings cannot count as "capital."[45]

Capital does not include loans by the petitioner or other parties.[46] Indebtedness secured by assets owned by the entrepreneur may be considered capital, provided the investor is personally and primarily liable for the debts and the assets of the enterprise upon which the petition is based are not used to secure any of the indebtedness.[47]

Indebtedness typically consists of a promissory note signed by the petitioner that specifies a payment schedule to the new commercial enterprise. Absent fraud, a signed promissory note that is secured by the petitioner's personal assets constitutes a contribution of capital by the petitioner.[48] The issuer of the promissory note—*i.e.*, the investor—is considered to be "at risk" if the petitioner is clearly obligated to make all the required payments on the note and there are no "escape" clauses. The investor cannot receive any bond, note, or other debt arrangement from the enterprise for the capital contributed to it. This includes any stock redeemable at the holder's request, a form of a put option. All capital is valued at fair market value in U.S. dollars at the time it is given.[49]

Debt arrangements are extremely complicated. A prudent practitioner must do careful research and analysis to determine current USCIS positions and policies on this issue.[50]

Benefiting the U.S. Economy

The statute requires that investments "benefit the U.S. economy" to qualify the investor for an EB-5 visa or status.[51] The statute provides no guidance on which investments benefit the economy. This silence means USCIS adjudicators are left to their subjective interpretations of the investment and its relative benefits when reviewing the petition. Arguably, the petitioner has benefited the economy merely by meeting the employment and investment requirements of the visa classification. However, because the statute specifically identifies the "benefit" element as distinct from other components of the visa, it appears that the applicant must show independently that the enterprise, in the conduct of its business, will benefit the U.S. economy. Therefore, a consulting firm exclusively serving customers abroad with no return benefit to the U.S. economy (other than employing the requisite number of workers) might not support an EB-5 petition. In contrast, showing that the new enterprise provides goods or services to U.S. markets should satisfy this requirement.

Federal regulation of foreign investments is extensive. Some regulations restrict foreign investments in aviation, banking, shipping, communications, land use, energy resources, and government contracting. Additionally, Congress has imposed several disclosure and data requirements on foreign investments.[52] An investment may not be deemed beneficial to the U.S. economy if it runs afoul of any statutory limitation on foreign investment.

Creating or Saving Jobs

To qualify for EB-5 status, an investment normally must create full-time employment for at least 10 U.S. citizens, lawful permanent residents, or oth-

---

[43] *See* 8 CFR §204.6(e) (definition of "invest").

[44] *Id.* (definition of "capital").

[45] Letter from E. Hernandez, Chief, USCIS Business and Trade Branch, to S. Yale-Loehr, File No. HOOPRD 70/6.2.8 (June 4, 2004), *available at* www.usa-immigration.com/litigation.htm (last visited Feb. 25, 2009). *See also Kenkhuis v. INS*, No. 3:01-CV-2224-N, 2003 U.S. Dist. LEXIS 3334, at *6 (N.D. Tex. Mar. 6, 2003) ("[t]he definition of 'invest' . . . requires an infusion of new capital, not merely a retention of profits of the enterprise"); *De Jong v. INS*, No. 6:94 CV 850 (E.D. Tex. Jan. 17, 1997).

[46] *Matter of Soffici*, 22 I&N Dec. 158, 19 *Immigr. Rep.* B2-25 (Assoc. Comm'r, Examinations 1998).

[47] 8 CFR §204.6(e) (definition of "capital").

[48] *Matter of Hsiung*, 22 I&N Dec. 201, 19 *Immigr. Rep.* B2-106 (Assoc. Comm'r, Examinations 1998).

[49] *Matter of Izummi*, 22 I&N Dec. 169, 192–93, 19 Immigr. Rep. B2-32 (Assoc. Comm'r, Examinations 1998) (finding that investor failed to show how bank accounts in Japan were in trust or otherwise secured the note, as required by 8 CFR §204.6(e), and that the note was not readily enforceable and
continued

was in any event not now worth its face value payable over six years).

[50] *See generally* W. Cook, "Somewhere, Over the Rainbow . . . Lies the EB-5 Pot of Gold," 3 *Bender's Immigr. Bull.* 1205 (Dec. 1, 1998); Klasko, *supra* note 36.

[51] INA §203(b)(5)(A)(ii), 8 USC §1153(b)(5)(A)(ii).

[52] For a comprehensive summary of the regulations, see Marans, Williams, Griffin, & Pattison, *Manual of Foreign Investment in the United States* (3d ed. 2004); *United States Law of Trade and Investment* (B. Kozolchyk & J. Molloy eds., 2000).

er immigrants lawfully authorized to be employed in the United States.[53] Neither the investor nor the investor's spouse and children count toward the 10-employee minimum.[54] Nonimmigrants also are excluded from the count. The "other immigrants" provision means that conditional residents, temporary residents, asylees, refugees, and recipients of suspension of deportation or cancellation of removal may all be considered employees for EB-5 purposes.

The regulations define an "employee" for EB-5 purposes as an individual who (1) provides services or labor for the new commercial enterprise and (2) receives wages or other remuneration directly from the new commercial enterprise.[55] This definition excludes independent contractors.[56]

The EB-5 pilot program does not require the investment to directly create 10 U.S. jobs. Instead, pilot program investments only require an indirect creation of jobs.[57]

The Types of Jobs—The jobs created must be full-time. This means employment of a qualified employee in a position that requires a minimum of 35 working hours per week, regardless of who fills the position.[58] Job-sharing arrangements, where two or more qualifying employees share a full-time position, also will serve as full-time employment if the hourly requirement per week is met.[59] Job-sharing does not include combinations of part-time positions even if, when combined, such positions meet the hourly requirement per week.[60]

When the Jobs Must Exist—The law is unclear about when new jobs must exist. The statutory language is prospective and therefore does not require jobs to exist at the time of initial investment or before the I-526 petition is filed. USCIS does not require retention of employees until a reasonable time after conditional visa issuance. In fact, a petitioner may support a petition with a comprehensive business plan demonstrating a need for at least 10 employees within the next two years. The business plan need only indicate the approximate dates during the following two years when the employees will be hired.[61] The temporary vacancy of a position during the two-year conditional period does not disqualify an investor, as long as good-faith attempts to re-staff the position are made.

Note that arguably different standards apply in the pilot program context. There, the regulations do not appear to call for any specific time period, but rather require "reasonable methodologies" to show that not fewer than 10 full-time jobs will be created either directly or indirectly.[62]

Where the Jobs Must be Located—When enacting the EB-5 program, Congress took an affirmative step toward creating jobs in the geographic areas that need them most. The statute sets aside 3,000 of the approximately 10,000 EB-5 visas available annually for foreign citizens who invest in "targeted employment areas."[63] The statute defines a "targeted employment area" as a rural area or an area that has experienced high unemployment of at least 150 percent of the national average.[64] An area not within a metropolitan statistical area (as designated by the Office of Management and Budget) or the outer boundary of any city or town having a population of 20,000 or more is considered a rural area.[65] Each state notifies USCIS which state agency will apply these guidelines, and determines targeted employment areas for that state.[66]

Troubled Businesses—Special rules govern investments in "troubled" businesses. A troubled business is one that has been in existence for at least two years, has incurred a net loss for accounting purposes during the 12- or 24-month period before the petition was filed, and the loss for such period is at least equal to 20 percent of the business's net worth before the loss.[67] To establish an investment in a

---

[53] INA §203(b)(5)(A)(ii), 8 USC §1153(b)(5)(A)(ii).

[54] *Id.*

[55] 8 CFR §204.6(e) (definition of "qualifying employee").

[56] *Id.*

[57] See 8 CFR §204.6(m)(7)(ii).

[58] 21st Century Department of Justice Appropriations Authorization Act, *supra* note 9, §11031(f). *See also* Yates Memo, *supra* note 10, at ¶4.

[59] 8 CFR §204.6(e) (definition of "full-time employment").

[60] *Id.*

[61] *Matter of Ho*, 22 I&N Dec. 206, 19 *Immigr. Rep.* B2-99 (Assoc. Comm'r, Examinations 1998).

[62] See 8 CFR §204.6(j)(4)(iii).

[63] INA §203(b)(5)(B), 8 USC §1153(b)(5)(B).

[64] INA §203(b)(5)(B)(ii), 8 USC §1153(b)(5)(B)(ii).

[65] INA §203(b)(5)(B)(iii), 8 USC §1153(b)(5)(B)(iii).

[66] Several states have websites that can help determine whether a particular area in the state qualifies as a "targeted employment area" for EB-5 purposes. *See, e.g., www.labor.ca.gov/calBIS/cbfederalvisaprog.pdf* (last updated May 2008) (last visited Feb. 25, 2009).

[67] 8 CFR §204.6(e) (definition of "troubled business").

troubled business, the petitioner must show that the number of existing employees will be maintained at no less than the pre-investment level for at least two years. Thus, this provision includes a significant incentive, in that it does not require the creation of 10 new jobs. Instead, it requires only that the business maintain the number of existing employees during the conditional status period.[68] However, 10 jobs must be saved for every EB-5 investor.[69] As a caveat, if the troubled business does not remain afloat for at least two years after the investment, the investor might lose his or her conditional residency status.

EB-5 PROCEDURES: INITIAL EVIDENCE

The regular EB-5 program and the pilot program have similar requirements to begin the process. The distinction between the two processes is that the former requires the petitioner to submit all of the described evidence; the latter requires the designated regional center to certify that the investor has met its criteria.

In either case, the investor files for EB-5 classification using Form I-526. The petition must be signed by the investor, not someone acting on his or her behalf. All EB-5 related petitions are filed with the California Service Center.[70]

Initial Evidence for the Regular EB-5 Program

The following paragraphs detail the evidence that should be submitted with an I-526 petition for EB-5 classification under the regular program.

The New Commercial Enterprise—To qualify for EB-5 classification, an investor must show that an investment has been made in a qualified commercial enterprise. The applicant should include:

- An organizational document for the new enterprise, including articles of incorporation, certificates of merger and consolidation, or partnership agreements;
- A business license or authorization to transact business in a state or city, if applicable; and
- For investments in an existing business, proof that the required amount of capital was transferred to the business after November 29, 1990, and that the investment has increased the net worth or number of employees by 40 percent or more.[71]

Capitalization—To show that the petitioner has invested (or is actively in the process of investing) the required amount of capital, the petition must be accompanied by evidence that the petitioner has placed the required amount of capital "at risk." A mere intention to invest will not demonstrate that the petitioner is actively in the process of investing. The investor must show actual commitment of the required amount of capital. Such evidence may include:

- Bank statements showing deposits in the U.S. account of the enterprise;
- Evidence of assets purchased for use in the enterprise;
- Evidence of property transferred from abroad;
- Evidence of funds invested in the enterprise in exchange for stock, except for stock redeemable at the holder's request; or
- Evidence of debts secured by the investor's assets and for which the investor is personally and primarily liable.[72]

The AAO has held that merely putting cash into the corporate account of a business does not show that the capital is "at risk" for the purpose of generating a return.[73] The AAO also has held that the full amount of the required capital must be expended by the enterprise directly toward job creation; otherwise that capital is not at risk of loss.[74] Based on these statements, it is difficult to know what a petitioner must do to show that the money is truly at risk.

Legal Acquisition of Capital[75]—The regulations require filing the following types of documentation

---

[68] 8 CFR §§204.6(h)(3), 204.6(j)(4)(ii).

[69] Summary of December 4, 2008, USCIS Stakeholders Conference with Invest in the USA and American Immigration Lawyers Association (Dec. 12, 2008), *published on* AILA InfoNet at Doc. No. 08121567 (*posted* Dec. 15, 2008) (Q&A No. 9).

[70] *See* 74 Fed. Reg. 912 (Jan. 9, 2009).

[71] 8 CFR §204.6(j)(1).

[72] 8 CFR §204.6(j)(2).

[73] *See Matter of [name not provided]*, file no. redacted (AAO July 7, 2000).

[74] *See, e.g., Matter of [name redacted]*, WAC 98 194 50913 (AAO Aug. 16, 2002). For a good discussion of the immigration agency's overly restrictive interpretation of the "at risk" requirement, see L. Stone, "Immigrant Investment in Local Clusters: Part II," 80 *Interpreter Releases* 937, 941–45 (July 14, 2003) [hereinafter Stone].

[75] For an in-depth discussion of the requirement that an investor's capital be from a lawful source, see Stone, *supra* note 74, at 946–50; S. Yale-Loehr & Christopher Repole, "Show Me the Money: Proving Lawful Source of Funds for EB-5 Immigrant Investors," available at *www.millermayer.com/Immigration/EB5Investors/SourceofFunds/tabid/159/Default.aspx* (last visited Feb. 25, 2009); L. Stone & S. Yale-Loehr, "Evi-
continued

to establish that capital used in the new enterprise was acquired by legitimate means:

- Foreign business registration records;
- Personal and business tax returns, or other tax returns of any kind filed anywhere in the world within the previous five years;
- Documents identifying any other source of money; or
- Certified copies of all pending governmental civil or criminal actions and proceedings, or any private civil actions involving money judgments against the investor within the past 15 years.[76]

Although the regulations list these requirements in the disjunctive, meaning that submission of any one type of document should suffice, the AAO requires investors to submit tax returns for the previous five years.[77] This interpretation makes it harder for investors to qualify for EB-5 status, and appears to violate the regulations.

The regulations further define "capital" as only those assets acquired through lawful means.[78] The AAO has held that money earned or assets acquired while in the United States in an unlawful status are not considered lawful means to acquire capital.[79] This interpretation goes far beyond Congress' original concern to prevent drug smugglers or other criminals to use their ill-gotten gains to be able to obtain permanent residents status in the United States through the EB-5 category.

Earned income is generally the most straightforward source of funds, but it is necessary to document exactly how the money was earned and to provide tax returns documenting that all due taxes were paid in full. As an example, the authors' office handled a successful EB-5 case for a French academic with 20 years of tax-exempt public sector service. To prove his lengthy and complicated income stream, the client provided tax returns, an accountant's letter explaining the tax-exempt income, and income receipts accounting for five years of earned income.

Gift money usually requires more complex documentation of source of funds, as the donor must document lawful obtainment of funds, as well as provide tax returns. Additionally, the donor and/or investor must pay any gift taxes due from the transaction.

"Old money" also presents challenges in documenting how funds obtained by inheritance were obtained lawfully.[80]

The importance of tracing funds is present in all of the above scenarios. The sticky issues involving gifting, disposition of a trust, inheritance, and other complex fact patterns must be accompanied by full documentation of the history of the funds and objective confirmation that all taxes have been paid on the acquisition and disposition of the funds.

Creating Employment—To show that a new commercial enterprise will create at least 10 full-time positions for qualified employees, the petition must be accompanied by:

- Photocopies of relevant tax records, Forms I-9, or similar documents for 10 qualifying employees; or
- A comprehensive business plan showing the need for at least 10 qualifying employees, and when the employees will be hired.[81] The plan should include a description of the business; the business' objectives; a market analysis including names of competing businesses and their relative strengths and weaknesses; a comparison of the competition's products and pricing structures; a description of the target market and prospective customers; a description of any manufacturing or production processes, materials required and supply sources; details of any contracts executed; marketing strategy including pricing, advertising, and servicing; organizational structure; and sales, cost and income projections and details of the bases therefore. In addition, specifically with respect to employment, the business plan must set

---

dence of Source of Capital in Immigrant Investor Cases," 6 *Bender's Immigr. Bull.* 972 (Oct. 1, 2001).

[76] 8 CFR §204.6(j)(3).

[77] *See, e.g.*, *Matter of [name not provided]*, file no. redacted, slip op. at 12 (AAO July 7, 2000) ("In addition, the petitioner has not submitted his corporate and personal tax records for at least the five years preceding filing the petition as required by 8 CFR §204.6(j)(3).").

[78] *See* 8 CFR §204.6(e) (definition of "capital).

[79] *See, e.g.*, *Matter of [name not provided]*, file no. redacted, slip op. at 12 (AAO July 7, 2000); *Matter of [name not provided]*, file no. redacted, slip op. at 12 (AAO July 11, 2000); *Matter of [name not provided]*, WAC 98 106 51583, slip. op. at 22 (AAO Sept. 11, 2000).

---

[80] *See, e.g.*, *Matter of [name not provided]*, file no. WAC 00 070 52366, slip. op. at 3–6 (AAO Apr. 21, 2005) (petitioner failed to adequately document transfer of money from family trust to her).

[81] 8 CFR §204.6(j)(4)(i).

forth the company's personnel experience, staffing requirements, job descriptions for all positions, and a timetable for hiring.[82]

Troubled Business—To show that a new enterprise, established through capital investment in a troubled business, meets the statutory requirement, the petition must show that the number of existing employees will be maintained at no less than the pre-investment level for a period of at least two years. The applicant should include photocopies of the I-9 forms, tax records or payroll documents, and a comprehensive business plan.[83]

Managerial Capacity of the Investor—An EB-5 immigrant must be involved in the management of a new commercial enterprise to qualify for a visa. The petitioner either must be involved in the day-to-day managerial control of the enterprise, or manage it through policy formulation. These requirements may be evidenced by:

- A comprehensive job description for the position occupied by the investor. The petitioner's title should also be indicated;
- Evidence that the petitioner is a corporate officer or on the board of directors; or
- Evidence that the petitioner is involved in direct management activities or policymaking activities of a general or limited partnership. A limited partner also must show that he has rights, powers and duties commensurate with those normally granted under the ULPA.[84] The AAO, however, has found that merely calling the investor a limited partner pursuant to the ULPA in a partnership agreement does not automatically mean that the person is involved in the management of the new commercial enterprise.[85]

Designation of a High Unemployment Area—The state government may designate a particular geographic or political subdivision as an area of high unemployment (at least 150 percent of the national average rate). Evidence of such designation may be provided with Form I-526. Such evidence should include:

- Boundaries of the subdivision;
- The date of the designation; and
- The methods by which the statistics were gathered.[86]

Creation of Employment in a Targeted Employment Area—To show that the new commercial enterprise has created, or will create, employment in a targeted employment area, the petition must be accompanied by:

- For a rural area, evidence that the new commercial enterprise is not located within any standard metropolitan statistical area, or within any city or town having a population of 20,000 or more; or
- For a high unemployment area, evidence that the metropolitan statistical area, or the county in which a city or town with a population of 20,000 or more is located, in which the new commercial enterprise is principally doing business has experienced an average unemployment rate of 150 percent of the national average rate; or a letter from the state in which the new commercial enterprise is located that certifies that the area has been designated as a high unemployment area.[87]

Regional Centers

An investment under the EB-5 pilot program must be made in a commercial enterprise located within a "regional center," which is defined as "any economic unit, public or private, which is involved with the promotion of economic growth, including increased export sales, improved regional productivity, job creation, or increased domestic capital investment."[88]

A center seeking USCIS approval must submit a proposal showing how it plans to focus on a geographical region within the United States and achieve the required growth by the means specified.[89] The proposal is filed with the California Service Center.[90]

---

[82] *Matter of Ho*, 22 I&N Dec. 206, 19 Immigr. Rep. B2-99 (Assoc. Comm'r, Examinations 1998).

[83] 8 CFR §204.6(j)(4)(ii).

[84] 8 CFR §204.6(j)(5).

[85] *See* 8 CFR §204.6(j)(5); *Matter of [name not provided]*, WAC 98 111 53508, slip op. at 23 (AAO Mar. 20, 2000) ("Despite the superficial language in the limited partnership agreement referring to the ULPA and to 8 CFR §204.6(j)(5)(iii), it is clear that the petitioner here does not in fact have the rights normally granted to limited partners under the ULPA.").

[86] 8 CFR §204.6(i).

[87] 8 CFR §204.6(j)(6).

[88] 21st Century Department of Justice Appropriations Authorization Act, *supra* note 9, §11037(a)(2); 8 CFR §204.6(e) (definition of "regional center").

[89] 8 CFR §204.6(m)(3).

[90] 74 Fed. Reg. 912 (Jan. 9, 2009).

The proposal must show "in verifiable detail how jobs will be created indirectly through increased exports," as well as the amount and source of capital committed and the promotional efforts made and planned.[91]

The USCIS is backlogged in reviewing applications for regional center designation under the pilot program. In 2000, legacy INS issued five decisions on regional center applications, denying or remanding all of them.[92] The decisions set forth restrictive new requirements to qualify as a regional center.[93]

To counteract this trend, in 2002, Congress amended the EB-5 regional center designation provisions.[94] Under the 2002 law, USCIS should approve applications for EB-5 regional center status as long as the applications are based on a general prediction concerning: (1) the kinds of commercial enterprises that will receive capital from investor; (2) the jobs that will be created directly or indirectly as a result of the investment of capital; and (3) the other positive economic impacts that will result from the investment of capital.[95]

USCIS is currently stepping up its review of new regional center applications and increasing oversight of existing regional centers to ensure that the EB-5 program grows in a responsible way.[96] For example, in June 2007, Maurice Berez, then-Program Manager for the USCIS Foreign Trader, Investor & Regional Center Program, sent an advisory letter to the Metropolitan Milwaukee Association of Commerce (MMAC), a regional center in Wisconsin.[97] The letter outlines 17 types of information that approved regional centers must track to keep their regional center designation.

The reporting requirements set forth in the MMAC letter mirror recent regional center decisions, which are growing ever longer and more detailed. In essence, USCIS is exercising greater oversight of regional centers in all aspects of the EB-5 process, including: (1) granting or denying regional center status; (2) maintaining regional center status; and (3) monitoring compliance through immigrant investors' I-526 and I-829 petitions filed through regional centers.

Assuming a regional center application has been approved, an applicant seeking EB-5 status under the pilot program must make the qualifying investment (*i.e.*, the amount required under the regular program) within an approved regional center. However, the requirement of creating at least 10 new jobs is met by a showing that as a result of the new enterprise, such jobs will be created directly or indirectly.[98] USCIS will only count construction jobs as direct jobs if they are expected to last at least two years.[99]

To file an I-526 form under the pilot program, attach a copy of legacy INS or USCIS letter designating the regional center. The petitioner's new commercial enterprise must be within the area specified in that letter. If the commercial enterprise is involved directly or indirectly in lending money to job-creating businesses, it may only lend money to businesses located within targeted employment areas to take advantage of the lesser capital requirement ($500,000).[100] The businesses receiving the loans must be within the geographic limits of the regional center if the enterprise is to qualify under the pilot

---

[91] *Id.* A list of designated regional centers can be found at http://www.millermayer.com/LinkClick.aspx?fileticket =mldVsHggmUY%3d&tabid=126&mid=863. Another two dozen or more applications for regional center designation are pending.

[92] *See generally* L. Stone, "INS Decisions Cloud Future of Investor Pilot Program," 6 *Bender's Immigr. Bull.* 233 (Mar. 1, 2001).

[93] *Id.*

[94] 21st Century Department of Justice Appropriations Authorization Act, *supra* note 9, §11037.

[95] *Id.* §11037(a)(3). For a good analysis of the kinds of economic benefits EB-5 regional centers could potentially create, see L. Stone, "Immigrant Investment in Local Clusters: Part I," 80 *Interpreter Releases* 837 (June 16, 2003).

[96] *See* Stephen Yale-Loehr & Lindsay Schoonmaker, "USCIS Increases Oversight of EB-5 Regional Centers," 12 *Bender's Immigr. Bull.* 1713 (Dec. 1, 2007), *reprinted at* www.millermayer.com/Immigration/EB5Investors/USCIS IncreasesOversightoEB5RegionalCenters/tabid/157/ Default.aspx (last visited Feb. 25, 2009).

[97] *See* letter from M. Berez, Program Manager, USCIS Foreign Trader, Investor & Regional Center Program, to Metropolitan Milwaukee Association of Commerce (June 12, 2007), *published on* AILA InfoNet at Doc. No. 07061360) (*posted* June 13, 2007).

[98] 8 CFR §§204.6(j)(4)(iii), 204.6(m)(7).

[99] "Summary of December 4, 2008, USCIS Stakeholders Conference with Invest in the USA and American Immigration Lawyers Association" (Dec. 12, 2008), *published on* AILA InfoNet at Doc. No. 08121567) (*posted* Dec. 15, 2008) (Q&A No. 3); USCIS Memorandum, D. Neufeld, "EB-5 Alien Entrepreneurs—Job Creation and Full-Time Positions (June 17, 2009), *published on* AILA InfoNet at Doc. No. 09061964 (*posted* June 19, 2009). The Neufeld Memo is reproduced in Appendix C of this volume.

[100] *Matter of Izummi*, 22 I&N Dec. 169, 19 *Immigr. Rep.* B2-32 (Assoc. Comm'r, Examinations 1998).

program. Otherwise the enterprise is not promoting economic growth through "improved regional activity" as required by the regulations.[101]

In 2003 Congress gave USCIS discretion to "give priority" to EB-5 petitions filed through a regional center.[102] USCIS exercises this authority judiciously, and specific criteria must be met before USCIS will expedite an I-526 petition filed through a regional center.

EB-5 PROCEDURES: REMOVING THE CONDITIONS

Assuming USCIS approves an investor's I-526 petition under either the regular or pilot program, he or she becomes a conditional resident for two years following the approval of an adjustment application or admission under an immigrant visa.[103] The procedure to remove the conditions is analogous to that followed by people who obtain conditional residence through marriage to a U.S. citizen or lawful permanent resident.[104] An immigrant investor's petition to remove the conditions should be filed on Form I-829 with the California Service Center.[105] It must be accompanied by evidence that the individual invested, or was in the process of investing, the required capital, and that the investment created or will create 10 full-time jobs. These jobs may be filled by eligible U.S. workers with payroll records, relevant tax documentation, and Forms I-9.[106] The individual also must show that he or she "sustained the actions" required for removal of conditions during the person's residence in the United States. An entrepreneur will have met this requirement if he or she has "substantially met" the capital investment requirement and has continuously maintained this investment during the conditional period.[107]

Failure to File Form I-829

An immigrant investor in conditional resident status must submit Form I-829 to the appropriate service center within the 90-day period immediately preceding the second anniversary of his or her admission to the United States as a conditional permanent resident.[108] Failure to do so will result in automatic termination of the conditional resident's status and initiation of removal proceedings.[109]

Working with a Regional Center to Prepare Form I-829

If an immigrant investor has an approved I-526 petition by investing in a regional center, it is important to work with the regional center well in advance to prepare the I-829 documentation. The regional center should provide each immigrant investor with verification of employment for the employees hired because of the immigrant investor's investment, as well as documentary proof of the immigrant investor's complete deposit of funds.

Adjudication of Form I-829 by a Service Center

Initial Review of Form I-829—An immigration service center may (1) approve an I-829 petition without review, (2) issue a request for further evidence, or (3) refer it for adjudication (with or without the interview) by a district office.[110]

Approval of Form I-829 by the USCIS Service Center—A service center may approve an I-829 petition if the petition establishes the requirements for removing the conditions outlined above. If approved, the service center director will remove the conditions on the conditional resident's status as of the second anniversary of his or her admission as a conditional resident.[111] The service center will then mail the new permanent residence card directly to the applicant.

Request for Further Evidence—A service center also may issue a request for further evidence (RFE). An RFE must be based on a determination by the service center director that the conditional resident must provide further documentation or answer certain questions in writing.[112] If the questions cannot be answered in writing, the petition must be referred

---

[101] *Id.*

[102] Basic Pilot Program Extension and Expansion Act of 2003, *supra* note 11, §4(a)(2).

[103] *See* INA §216A, 8 USC §1186b; 8 CFR §216.6.

[104] *See* INA §216, 8 USC §1186a.

[105] 8 CFR §§216.6, 1216.6; *See also* 74 Fed. Reg. 912 (Jan. 9, 2009).

[106] *See* 8 CFR §216.6(a)(4)(iv).

[107] 8 CFR §§216.6(a)(4), 1216.6(a)(4).

[108] 8 CFR §§216.6(a)(1), 1216.6(a)(1).

[109] 8 CFR §§216.6(a)(5), 1216.6(a)(5); legacy INS Memorandum, M. Pearson, "EB-5 Field Memorandum No. 9: Form I-829 Processing" (Mar. 3, 2000), *published on* AILA InfoNet at Doc. No. 00060702 (*posted* June 7, 2000), and reproduced in Appendix C of this volume (amending legacy INS's *Adjudicator's Field Manual* ch. 25.2) [hereinafter I-829 Memo]. *See also* L. Stone, "Removal of the Conditions on Permanent Residence for Immigrant Investors," *Immigration & Nationality Law Handbook* 329 (AILA 2005–06 Ed.).

[110] *Id.*

[111] 8 CFR §§216.6(d)(1), 1216.6(d)(1).

[112] *Id.*

for an interview. An RFE will not be issued if the petition is clearly deniable on grounds other than those for which the RFE might be issued. The RFE will specify the deadline for responding.[113] Upon receipt of the RFE, the service center director must either approve or refer the Form I-829 petition to the district office.[114]

An RFE may be issued for many reasons. One issue that sometimes arises in I-829 adjudications is whether the proper number of jobs has been created. The regulations state that an investor must submit evidence that he or she created or can be expected to create 10 jobs "within a reasonable time."[115] Asked to define that phrase, USCIS responded:

> "USCIS cannot articulate a bright line rule to define what constitutes a "reasonable period of time" as such period will depend on the factors of each individual case. USCIS will consider all appropriate evidence that would (a) clearly justify not having completed the job creation by the end of the two years of conditional residence (*e.g.*, the nature of the investment, the industry involved, etc.) and (b) show that the full number of requisite new jobs will be created within a clear, defined and credible period of time."[116]

Determination that Referral to District Office is Appropriate—A service center will refer the petition to a district director if the initial review of the petition or the response to a request for additional evidence reveals that (1) the requirements for removal of conditions have not been met and the case should be denied without an interview, or (2) an interview is necessary to approve or deny the petition.[117]

Adjudication of Form I-829 by the District Office

Approval of Form I-829 by the District Director—A district office may approve an I-829 petition if it is satisfied that the petition satisfies the requirements for removing the condition outlined above.[118]

Denial of Form I-829 by the District Director—A district director must deny an I-829 petition if the petition does not establish the requirements for removing the condition. There is no appeal from this decision. The conditional resident may seek review of the district director's decision in removal proceedings.[119]

Status of Conditional Residents While I-829 is Pending

Immigrant investors remain in valid status while their I-829 petition is pending. Their status is supposed to be extended automatically in one-year increments until USCIS acts on the petition. During that time they are authorized to travel.[120] Practitioners have complained, however, that many offices are unaware of this procedure. Extending conditional resident status, obtaining re-entry permits, and proving authorization to travel can be particularly difficult for spouses and children of EB-5 investors.

USCIS issued a memorandum in January 2005, intended to help conditional residents with pending or denied I-829 petitions that might benefit from the 2002 law discussed below.[121] The memo instructs USCIS adjudicators to extend conditional resident status for affected EB-5 petitioners. The memo also instructs agency officials to assist pending I-829 petitioners with travel and parole requests.[122]

Conditional permanent residents with pending I-829 petitions should travel with an attorney "pocket letter" describing their status with a copy of the January 2005 memorandum validating their claims.

TERMINATION OF EB-5 STATUS

The statute provides three separate grounds for terminating an EB-5 investor's status during the two-year conditional period.[123] Immigrant status will be terminated if USCIS determines that:

- The investment in the new commercial enterprise was to evade the immigration laws of the United States.[124] This provision requires termination on-

---

[113] 8 CFR §103.2(b)(8).

[114] I-829 Memo, *supra* note 109.

[115] 8 CFR §216.6(a)(4)(iv).

[116] "USCIS-AILA Liaison Committee Agenda" (Apr. 2, 2008), at 10, *published on* AILA InfoNet at Doc. No. 08040235 (*posted* Apr. 2, 2008).

[117] I-829 Memo, *supra* note 109.

[118] *Id.*

[119] 8 CFR §§216.6(d)(2), 1216.6(d)(2); I-829 Memo, *supra* note 109.

[120] I-829 Memo, *supra* note 109.

[121] USCIS Memorandum, W. Yates, "Extension of Status for Conditional Residents with Pending or Denied Form I-829 Petitions Subject to Public Law 107-273 (Jan. 18, 2005), *published on* AILA InfoNet at Doc. No. 05012167 (*posted* Jan. 21, 2005), *reprinted in* 10 *Bender's Immigr. Bull.* 236 (Feb. 15, 2005).

[122] *Id.*

[123] INA §216A(b), 8 USC §1186b(b).

[124] INA §216A(b)(1)(A), 8 USC §1186b(b)(1)(A).

ly if the investment of the enterprise was "solely" to evade immigration laws. This suggests that if the investment was made with legitimate intentions, in addition to an intention to fraudulently procure permanent resident status, termination would not be proper under this ground;

- The investor failed to invest (or was not in the process of investing) the requisite capital, or failed to sustain the investments during the two-year conditional period;[125] or

- The individual was otherwise not conforming to the requirements of the employment-creation status provisions of INA §203(b)(5).[126] This catch-all provision is dangerous because it does not define the conduct giving rise to termination of status. USCIS potentially could apply this provision broadly to terminate the investor status of an applicant for any infraction of the section. Fortunately, however, it does not appear that USCIS has ever invoked this provision to terminate the status of an immigrant investor.

An EB-5 investor admitted under the pilot program is also subject to the same conditions and restrictions.

DETERRING FRAUDULENT INVESTMENTS

In enacting the EB-5 program, Congress expressed concern about the possibility of fraudulent investments. To deter such fraud, establishing a commercial enterprise for the purpose of "evading any provision of the immigration laws" is a felony punishable by up to five years imprisonment.[127] One reason Congress provided for two-year conditional permanent residency status for EB-5 investors is to aid in this deterrence. This two-year continuum for business activity and investment requires a significant investment and is a strong deterrent to fraud. Nonetheless, should USCIS discover fraud before the two-year conditional period ends, it will terminate the investor's status.[128] So far it appears that USCIS has not prosecuted any EB-5 investors for fraud.[129]

---

[125] INA §216A(b)(1)(B), 8 USC §1186b(b)(1)(B).

[126] INA §216A(b)(1)(C), 8 USC §1186b(b)(1)(C).

[127] INA §275(d), 8 USC §1325(d).

[128] INA §216A(b)(1), 8 USC §1186b(b)(1).

[129] For an interesting case, rife with intrigue, fraud, and shady dealings surrounding two EB-5 promoters, see *United States v. O'Connor*, 158 F. Supp. 2d 697 (E.D. Va. 2001).

continued

EB-5 PETITIONS: THEORY vs. REALITY

The statutory and regulatory provisions discussed above are onerous.[130] For this reason, immigration through the EB-5 category has never approached the maximum of about 10,000 a year. Yet the legacy INS radically restricted the EB-5 program even further in 1998 by issuing four precedent AAO decisions that made it even harder to obtain EB-5 status.[131]

A complete discussion of the four precedent decisions is beyond the scope of this article. Below is a summary of the changes created by the four decisions.[132] The post-1998 requirements are listed first; prior law or policy is listed in italics.[133]

Post-1998: Promissory note valued at fair market value.

Pre-1998: Promissory note valued at face value.

Post-1998: Promissory note generally must be paid after two years.

Pre-1998: No limit on term of promissory note.

Individual EB-5 investors appear to have been victims, not perpetrators, of the fraud. *See also Serova v. Teplen*, No. 05 CIV.6748 (HB), 2006 U.S. Dist. LEXIS 5781 (S.D.N.Y. Feb. 16, 2006) (EB-5 investor claims her attorney failed to represent her adequately, in part by failing to disclose that he also represented the company in which she invested).

[130] For information on litigation and other developments surrounding EB-5 provisions, see the EB-5 Litigation Document Web page at *www.usa-immigration.com/litigation.htm* (last visited Feb. 25, 2010).

[131] *Matter of Soffici*, 22 I&N Dec. 158, 19 *Immigr. Rep.* B2-25 (Assoc. Comm'r, Examinations 1998); *Matter of Izummi*, 22 I&N Dec. 169, 19 *Immigr. Rep.* B2-32 (Assoc. Comm'r, Examinations 1998); *Matter of Hsiung*, 22 I&N Dec. 201, 19 *Immigr. Rep.* B2-106 (Assoc. Comm'r, Examinations 1998); *Matter of Ho*, 22 I&N Dec. 206, 19 *Immigr. Rep.* B2-99 (Assoc. Comm'r, Examinations 1998). *See generally* W. Cook, "Somewhere, Over the Rainbow … Lies the EB-5 Pot of Gold," 3 *Bender's Immigr. Bull.* 1205 (Dec. 1, 1998).

[132] Note that the requirements established by these cases may be applied retroactively, even if they contravene practices established by earlier unpublished decisions or other guidance. *See Golden Rainbow Freedom Fund v. Ashcroft*, 24 Fed. Appx. 698, 2001 U.S. App. LEXIS 25482 (9th Cir. Nov. 26, 2001). *See also R.L. Inv. Ltd. Partners v. INS*, 86 F. Supp. 2d 1014 (D. Haw. 2000), *aff'd*, 273 F.3d 874 (9th Cir. 2001). *But see Chang v. United States*, 327 F.3d 911 (9th Cir. 2003) (ruling that retroactive application of the newly established requirements is impermissible if the applicant was granted conditional residency before the new requirements came into effect); *Sang Geun An v. United States*, No. C03-3184P (W.D. Wash. Feb. 16, 2005) (following *Chang*).

[133] Thanks to H. Ronald Klasko, who drafted the original version of this list and allowed it to be reprinted here.

Post-1998: Security for promissory note needs to be perfected under the UCC.

Pre-1998: *Security does not need to meet UCC perfected security interest requirements.*

Post-1998: Bank accounts cannot be used as security.

Pre-1998: *Bank accounts can be used as security.*

Post-1998: Reduce the fair market value of promissory note by "considerable expense and effort" to execute on foreign assets.

Pre-1998: *Promissory note valued at face value.*

Post-1998: No redemption provisions can be agreed to before end of conditional residence and before conclusion of payments on promissory note.

Pre-1998: *Redemption provisions can be agreed to so long as redemption does not occur until after promissory note has been paid in full.*

Post-1998: Amounts attributable to expenses to start new commercial enterprise must be deducted from capital contribution.

Pre-1998: *Start-up costs and expenses included in amount of capital contribution.*

Post-1998: New ownership and new corporation are not sufficient to establish new commercial enterprise.

Pre-1998: *Restructuring or reorganization sufficient to establish new commercial enterprise.*

Post-1998: All of the activities must benefit the targeted geographical area to count indirect employment.

Pre-1998: *The qualifying investment must be within the approved regional center; there is no separate requirement to prove benefit solely to the regional center.*

Below is a summary of additional restrictive interpretations created by the AAO in nonprecedent decisions:

Post-1998: Money earned or assets acquired while in the United States in an unlawful status are not considered lawful means to acquire capital.

Pre-1998: *Drug smugglers or other criminals cannot use their ill-gotten gains to obtain permanent resident status in the United States through the EB-5 category; nothing specified about others illegally in the United States.*

Post-1998: All investors in the partnership must identify the source of their funds to prove that they were derived by lawful means.

Pre-1998: *Only the petitioning investor must identify the source of his or her funds in the partnership to prove that they were derived by lawful means.*

Post-1998: Merely injecting cash into the corporate account of a business does not show that the capital is "at risk" for the purpose of generating a return.

Pre-1998: *Injecting cash into a corporate account could show that the capital is "at risk" for the purpose of generating a return.*

2002 AMENDMENTS

Investors who were hurt by changes the immigration agency made in 1998 lobbied Congress for relief. Eventually, in 2002, Congress enacted changes to the EB-5 program as part of a U.S. Department of Justice authorization bill.[134] To qualify under the new law, an investor must have filed a petition for EB-5 classification (Form I-526) and had it approved between January 1, 1995 and August 31, 1998.[135] The law took effect November 2, 2002.

Section 11031(c) of the 2002 law sets forth procedures to determine whether investors can have their conditions removed. The government must decide three things: whether (1) the I-829 petition contains any material misrepresentations; (2) the investment created or saved 10 jobs; and (3) the investor has complied substantially with the investment requirement ($1 million or $500,000).[136] Investments in regional centers or in troubled businesses count.[137] The law gives investors a choice of three dates by which to measure their compliance: (1) the date the I-829 petition was filed; (2) six months after the I-829 peti-

---

[134] 21st Century Department of Justice Appropriations Authorization Act, *supra* note 9, §§11031–37. *See generally* S. Yale-Loehr, "Congress Helps Stranded Immigrant Investors," 7 *Bender's Immigr. Bull.* 1306 (Nov. 1, 2002), and at www.millermayer.com/Immigration/EB5Investors/Congress HelpsStrandedImmigrantInvestors/tabid/162/Default.aspx (last visited Feb. 25, 2009).

[135] 21st Century Department of Justice Appropriations Authorization Act, *supra* note 9, §§11031(b)(1), 11032(b).

[136] *Id.* §11031(c)(1)(A).

[137] *Id.* §11031(c)(1)(B), (C).

tion was filed; or (3) the date the government makes its determination under the new law.[138]

If the investor meets the jobs and investment requirements and has not made a material misrepresentation, the government will remove the conditional resident status and the investor and family members will become permanent residents as of the second anniversary of the date they became conditional residents.[139] If the government finds against an investor on any of the three grounds, the government must notify the investor, and provide the investor with an opportunity to submit evidence to rebut the adverse determination.[140] If the investor loses on the jobs or investment requirement, the government will continue the investor's conditional resident status for an additional two years.[141] During that time the investor can try to meet those requirements.

If the government finds that the investor made a material misrepresentation, the government will terminate the investor's conditional resident status.[142] The investor can appeal to the Board of Immigration Appeals and then seek judicial review.[143] During administrative or judicial review proceedings, the investor and his or her family members remain in conditional resident status.[144]

Most investors are unlikely to persuade the government that they fully met the capital investment and jobs creation requirement. The new law gives them an additional two years to make another investment. During that time they can combine investments made earlier with new investments to show that altogether they invested the total amount required.[145] This includes investments in limited partnerships.[146]

An investor must file another I-829 during the 90 days preceding the new two-year anniversary.[147] Failure to file normally will terminate a conditional resident's status.[148] There is a good cause exception.[149]

Assuming an investor files another I-829 petition, the government has 90 days to decide three things: whether (1) the I-829 petition has any material misrepresentations; (2) the investment created or saved 10 jobs; and (3) the investor has substantially complied with the investment requirement ($1 million or $500,000).[150] The investor can aggregate money invested before and jobs created or saved from the initial investment.[151] Investments in regional centers or in troubled businesses count.[152]

If the investor meets the job creation and investment requirements and has not made a material misrepresentation, the government will remove the conditional resident status of the investor and family members. They will become permanent residents as of the second anniversary of the date their conditional resident status was continued.[153] If the government finds against an investor on any of the three grounds, the government must notify the investor, who may attempt to rebut the adverse facts.[154] If the investor loses, the government will terminate the investor's conditional resident status.[155]

Section 11032 of the 2002 law provides similar procedures for EB-5 investors whose I-526 petitions were approved, but who never became conditional residents because legacy INS never acted on their adjustment of status applications or because they remained overseas. This section defines an eligible individual as an investor who filed an I-526 petition that was approved between January 1, 1995, and August 31, 1998, and who then timely filed an adjustment of status application or applied for an immigrant visa overseas. Investors are not eligible if they are inadmissible or deportable on any ground.[156]

If legacy INS revoked the I-526 petition on the ground that the investor failed to meet the capital investment requirement, that revocation is to be disregarded.[157] If the adjustment of status application or immigrant visa application overseas was not pending on November 2, 2002, the date of enactment, it is to

---

[138] *Id.* §11031(c)(1)(D).
[139] *Id.* §11031(c)(1)(E).
[140] *Id.* §11031(c)(1)(F)(i).
[141] *Id.* §11031(c)(1)(F)(ii).
[142] *Id.* §11031(c)(1)(F)(iii).
[143] *Id.* §11031(c)(1)(F)(iv).
[144] *Id.*
[145] *Id.* §11031(c)(2)(A).
[146] *Id.*
[147] *Id.* §11031(c)(2)(C)(i).
[148] *Id.* §11031(c)(2)(D).
[149] *Id.* §11031(c)(2)(C)(ii).
[150] *Id.* §11031(c)(2)(E).
[151] *Id.*
[152] *Id.*
[153] *Id.* §11031(c)(2)(F).
[154] *Id.* §11031(c)(2)(G)(i).
[155] *Id.* §11031(c)(2)(G)(ii).
[156] *Id.* §11032(b).
[157] *Id.* §11032(c)(1).

be treated as reopened if: (i) it is not pending because the government claims the investor never complied with the capital investment requirement; or (ii) the investor left the United States without advance parole.[158] If an investor applied for adjustment of status in the United States but is now overseas, the government will establish a process to let them return to the United States if necessary to obtain adjustment.[159]

The government was supposed to approve adjustment of status applications for eligible investors by May 1, 2003, 180 days after enactment.[160] However, that has not happened yet, because USCIS has not yet published regulations to implement the 2002 law. The investors eventually will be in conditional resident status. Such investors must file an I-829 petition within two years of becoming a conditional resident.[161] The determinations and process are similar for both §11031 and §11032 investors. For example, the government must credit the investor with funds invested and jobs created or saved both before and after November 2, 2002, the date of enactment.[162] This section gives investors a choice of two dates by which to measure their compliance: (1) the date they filed their adjustment of status application; or (2) the date the government decides the I-829 petition.[163]

Finally, the new law states that a noncitizen who was admitted on a conditional basis by virtue of being the child of an EB-5 investor still shall be considered a child for purposes of the new law, even if they turn 21 or marry.[164]

ETHICAL CONSIDERATIONS[165]

It is important for an attorney to consider the ethical considerations before beginning to represent a client in the complex EB-5 category. The American Bar Association's (ABA's) Model Rules of Professional Conduct's first rule states: "A lawyer shall provide competent representation to a client. Competent representation requires the legal knowledge, skill, thoroughness and preparation reasonably necessary for the representation."[166] Therefore, representing an immigrant investor client without a good base of EB-5 knowledge could be considered a breach of ethical rules.

If an attorney feels inadequate to represent a client in an EB-5 matter, he or she may comply with competence rules either by consulting with an EB-5 expert or by bifurcating representation between EB-5 and non-EB-5 related counsel, such as an attorney handling adjustment of status. In a joint counsel scenario, most jurisdictions require that the client be made aware of any joint representation, and that the fees be split to reflect the proportional amount of work that each law firm is providing.

Finally, there is an ethical consideration concerning the referral fees that many regional centers offer to someone who recommends an investor to the regional center. Accepting such fees may involve a conflict of interest, since an attorney's representation of a client may be materially impaired by the prospect of a pecuniary gain from a regional center. An attorney has a duty of undivided loyalty to a client, and would be best advised to consult the relevant state's ethics rules before both accepting referral fees from a third party and representing the client in his or her EB-5 petition filing. Referral fees also may trigger U.S. securities laws regulating broker/dealers. Both regional centers offering referral fees and attorneys seeking to accept them should seek securities counsel to ensure no contravention of securities laws.[167]

CONCLUSION

Qualifying a person for EB-5 status is one of the most complicated subspecialties in immigration law. A sophisticated knowledge of corporate, tax, investment, securities, and immigration law are all required. Moreover, the four 1998 precedent AAO decisions and subsequent nonprecedent decisions have made it even harder to obtain approvals of EB-

---

[158] *Id.* §11032(c)(2)(A).

[159] *Id.* §11032(c)(2)(B).

[160] *Id.* §11032(a).

[161] *Id.* §11032(e).

[162] *Id.* §11032(e)(2).

[163] *Id.* §11032(e)(3).

[164] *Id.* §§11031(e), 11032(f).

[165] *See* C. Lee, "Ethical and Practical Considerations in EB-5 Representation," at www.ilw.com/articles/2007,1120-lee.shtm, and at www.millermayer.com/Immigration/EB5Investors/EthicalAndPractical/tabid/158/Default.aspx, reprinted in 13 *Bender's Immigr. Bull.* 332 (Mar. 15, 2008).

[166] *See generally* Model Rules of Professional Conduct R. 1.1. The New York Disciplinary Rules of the Code of Professional Responsibility, the California Rules of Professional Conduct, and the Maine Code of Professional Responsibility are not based on the ABA Model Rules of Professional Conduct.

[167] *See* J. Moseley, A. Paparelli, C. Lee, & M. Ladd, "The Relevance of U.S. Securities Laws to Immigrant Investors, EB-5 Regional Centers, and their Advisors," in 14 *Bender's Immigr. Bull.* 938 (Aug. 1, 2009).

5 petitions. Investors must discard normal investment opportunities in favor of investments structured to meet the unrealistic requirements of the precedent decisions. Attorneys, in turn, must proceed at their peril in advising clients. In many cases it may be more practicable for investors to come to the United States through other visa categories such as the E-2 investor, L-1 intracompany transferee, or EB-1-3 multinational executive or manager routes.

Nevertheless, the EB-5 category has engendered rising interest, both within the immigration bar and USCIS. In January 2005, USCIS established a new Investor and Regional Center Unit (IRCU) at USCIS headquarters. IRCU, since renamed the Foreign Trader, Investor and Regional Center Program, provides oversight for EB-5 policy and regulatory development, field guidance, and training. According to USCIS, establishing IRCU will "strengthen and protect the integrity of the [EB-5] program while promoting the intent of Congress to encourage investment and increase employment within the United States."[168] Indeed, while only 129 individuals were admitted as EB-5 conditional residents in FY 2004, 1,360 individuals obtained conditional resident status in FY 2008.[169]

These changes mark a major leap forward in the usage of the EB-5 visa category. Recent policy memoranda issuing from USCIS show that the agency is struggling to manage the novel and complex issues that this category raises within the relatively spare statutory and regulatory framework. These memoranda raise as many issues as they purport to resolve. Moreover, the sunset of the pilot program is approaching. Hopefully, it will be renewed, perhaps permanently. Time will tell whether the EB-5 program continues growing.

---

[168] USCIS Memorandum, W. Yates, "Establishment of an Investor and Regional Center Unit," (Jan. 19, 2005), *published on* AILA InfoNet at Doc. No. 05012663 (*posted* Jan. 26, 2005), *reprinted in* 10 *Bender's Immigr. Bull.* 195 (Feb. 15, 2005), and reproduced in Appendix C of this volume.

[169] *See* 2008 Yearbook of Immigration Statistics, *supra* note 4, at 18 (Table 6).

EB-5 IMMIGRANT INVESTOR PROGRAM—A CHANGING LANDSCAPE

by Bernard P. Wolfsdorf, Naveen R. Bhora, Tien-Li Loke Walsh[*]

The employment-based fifth preference (EB-5) Immigrant Investor Program is one of the most controversial and challenging provisions in the Immigration Act of 1990 (IMMACT90).[1] The program's instability, the changing economic environment, and friendlier immigrant investor programs offered by other nations have all led to its underutilization. Of the 130,000 visas allocated between 1992 and 2004, only 6,024 visas were issued to immigrant investors and their dependent family members. Of this group, only 643 investors were successful in removing the conditional requirement and receiving full permanent resident status.[2] However, due to some positive developments in recent years, we now have seen a surge in EB-5 investor petitions and U.S. Citizenship and Immigration Services (USCIS) approval rates. This article aims to review the program's history and recent developments, and show that the program now provides an excellent path to permanent residence for foreign investors and entrepreneurs, and is sure to boost the economy.

THE STATUTORY FRAMEWORK

IMMACT90 was enacted during a different era—one that reflected a relatively prosperous, pro-immigrant period in U.S. immigration history. Congress recognized that "it is unlikely that enough U.S. workers will be trained quickly enough to meet legitimate employment needs, and . . . immigration can and should be incorporated into an overall strategy that promotes the creation of the type of workforce needed in an increasingly global economy."[3]

IMMACT90 allocated 140,000 visas annually to employment-based immigrants, almost tripling the number allocated in prior years.[4] The EB-5 program,

---

[*] © Copyright © 2010 Bernard P. Wolfsdorf, A Professional Law Corporation/Wolfsdorf Immigration Law Group (all rights reserved).

Bernard P. Wolfsdorf is the national president of the American Immigration Lawyers Association (AILA). He is a California State Bar-Certified Specialist in Immigration and Nationality Law and has been managing partner of Wolfsdorf Immigration Law Group since 1986. *Chambers USA 2009* lists Mr. Wolfsdorf as the highest ranked immigration lawyer in Southern California, with "star" designation. He was recently named one of the "Top 10 Immigration Attorneys in the U.S." by the *Human Resource Executive* magazine. He is also listed in the *Best Lawyers in America 2010*, Martindale Hubbell's *Pre-eminent Specialist Directory*, *Southern California Super Lawyers 2010*, *Chambers USA 2010*, and the *Chambers Global World's Leading Lawyers for Business 2010*. Mr. Wolfsdorf can be reached at *bernard@wolfsdorf.com*.

Naveen R. Bhora is a senior attorney in the firm's New York Office. She represents a wide range of clients in U.S. immigration matters, from individuals and small and emerging businesses to major hospitals and universities. Ms. Bhora has developed a particular expertise in extraordinary/exceptional ability and outstanding researcher/professor matters, and represents physicians, registered nurses and allied health care workers, among others. She is the former treasurer of the AILA Southern California Chapter and is currently serving her second term on AILA's Vermont Service Center (VSC) Liaison Committee. Ms. Bhora has written extensively on various advanced immigration law topics and continues to present to local and national audiences. Ms. Bhora can be contacted at *nbhora@wolfsdorf.com*.

Tien-Li Loke Walsh practices exclusively in the area of immigration and nationality law with the firm. She previously served as vice-chair of AILA's Department of State (DOS) Liaison Committee, as well as the AILA/California Service Center (CSC) Liaison Committee. Ms. Loke Walsh is listed in the current edition of *Best Lawyers in America*, International and California editions of *Who's Who of Corporate Immigration Lawyers*, and the *Southern California Super Lawyers*, Rising Stars edition. She can be contacted at *tloke@wolfsdorf.com*.

The authors wish to graciously acknowledge attorney Lincoln Stone for his excellent article from the previous edition of this book, which is incorporated extensively herein. *See* L. Stone, "A Comparison of the EB-5 Category with Alternative Immigration Strategies," *Immigration Options for Investors and Entrepreneurs* (AILA 2006).

[1] Immigration Act of 1990 (IMMACT90), Pub. L. No. 101-649, 104 Stat. 4978. INA §203(b)(5).

[2] U.S. Government Accountability Office (GAO) Report to Congressional Committees, "Immigrant Investors: Small Number of Participants Attributed to Pending Regulations and Other Factors," GAO-05-256 (Apr. 2005), *published on* AILA InfoNet at Doc. No. 05040475 (*posted* Apr. 4, 2005) (GAO Report). Highlights of the GAO Report are reproduced in Appendix E.

[3] H.R. Rep. No. 723, 101st Cong., 2d Sess., pt. 1, at 41 (1990).

[4] L.C. Lee, "The 'Immigrant Entrepreneur' Provision of the Immigration Act of 1990: Is a Single Entrepreneur Category Sufficient?," 12 *J.L. & Com.* 147, 149 (1992).

created for immigrant investors, is the category for the new Employment Creation Pilot Program, aimed at "creat[ing] new employment for U.S. workers and to infuse new capital into the country."[5] To achieve this, Congress allocated approximately 10,000 visas each year for immigrant investors who invest at least $1 million in a business and generate a minimum of 10 new jobs for U.S. workers.[6]

Of the 10,000 visas available annually for immigrant investors, 3,000 visas are reserved for investment in targeted employment areas. Another 3,000 are set aside for investment through the Regional Center Pilot Program.[7] The Pilot Program allows investors to meet the criteria of the 10-minimum job creation by allowing for indirect employment by individuals who invest their capital in a "designated" regional center that promotes economic growth or creates jobs. A regional center is "any economic unit, public or private, which is involved with the promotion of economic growth, including increased export sales, improved regional productivity, job creation, and increased domestic capital investment."[8]

Furthermore, if the regional center or individual commercial enterprise is in a targeted employment area, the capital investment is reduced to $500,000.[9] A targeted employment area is an area that, at the time of the investment, is a rural area or an area that has experienced unemployment of at least 150 percent of the national average.[10]

The Regional Center Pilot Program was initially set to expire in 2000, but the Visa Waiver Permanent Program Act of 2000,[11] extended the Pilot Program for three years until September 30, 2003. On the eve of its expiration, Senator Chuck Grassley (R-IA) introduced the Basic Pilot Program Extension and Expansion Act of 2003 to extend the Pilot Program for another five years until September 30, 2008.[12] Thereafter, Senator Patrick Leahy (D-VT) had tried to push for another five-year extension of the Pilot Program and even introduced legislation to make the program permanent; however, on September 30, 2008, just in time to avoid a gap, the Regional Center Pilot Program was extended until March 6, 2009,[13] and then extended again until September 30, 2009.[14] On October 1, 2009, President Obama signed a stopgap bill to extend the program until October 31, 2009. Thereafter, on October 28, 2009, he signed into law the fiscal year (FY) 2010 Department of Homeland Security Appropriations bill, which extended the EB-5 Program through September 30, 2012.[15]

The extensions of the Pilot Program are an important sign of strong bipartisan support and congressional commitment to the Immigrant Investor Program. However, unless Congress makes the Regional Center Pilot Program permanent, the program will continue to be marred with uncertainty and deter potential investors.

REQUIREMENTS AND RESTRICTIONS

Immigrant investor eligibility requires proof that: (1) petitioner has invested or is actively in the process of investing the required amount of capital in a new commercial enterprise; (2) the investment is at risk; and (3) petitioner is or will be engaged in the management of the new commercial enterprise, either through day-to-day managerial control or policy formulation.16 An investor qualifies by initially filing Form I-526, Immigrant Petition by Alien Entrepreneur.[17] After the petition is approved, the investor must apply for adjustment of status in the United

---

[5] *See* S. Rep. No. 55 (1989).

[6] The proposed S. 1348 Senate immigration bill would cut overall EB-5 immigrant investor numbers from 10,000 to just 2,800 a year, and EB-5 regional center green card numbers from the current 3,000 to just 1,500 a year. INA §203(b)(5)(A); 8 CFR §204.6.

[7] 8 CFR §204.6(j)(4)(iii).

[8] 8 CFR §204.6(e).

[9] 8 CFR §204.6(f)(2).

[10] INA §203(b)(5)(B); 8 CFR §204.6(e).

[11] Visa Waiver Permanent Program Act of 2000, Pub. L. No. 106-396, 114 Stat. 1631, §402(a).

[12] President George W. Bush extended the Pilot Program until September 30, 2008, when he signed Senate bill 1685 into law on December 3, 2003.

[13] Consolidated Security, Disaster Assistance, and Continuing Appropriations Act, 2009, Pub. L. No. 110-329, 122 Stat. 3574.

[14] Omnibus Appropriations Act, 2009, Pub. L. No. 111-8, 123 Stat. 524.

[15] Department of Homeland Security Appropriations Act, 2010, Pub. L. No. P.L.111-83, 123 Stat. 2142.

[16] 8 CFR §204.6. However, the establishment requirement was later eliminated by the 21st Century Department of Justice Appropriations Authorization Act (DOJ Amendments), Pub. L. No. 107-273, 116 Stat. 1758, signed into law on November 2, 2002.

[17] 8 CFR §204.6(a).

States or at a U.S. consulate/embassy overseas.[18] Upon approval, the investor is granted a two-year conditional green card.

During the 90-day period prior to expiration of the conditional period, Form I-829, Petition by Entrepreneur to Remove Conditions, must be filed.[19] In this petition, the investor must demonstrate the stated investment was made or still sustained over the two-year conditional period, and the requisite full-time jobs were created or will be created within a reasonable period of time. Only upon approval of the I-829 petition is the conditional nature of the green card lifted and full permanent residence granted.

Restrictive Interpretation of Regulatory Goals

During the first 15 years, the restrictive interpretation of the regulations drastically limited the types of investment permitted under the program. For example, a purely passive investment of more than $1 million that created at least 10 jobs would be denied for failure to meet the managerial requirement.[20] Likewise, if an investor sought to expand an already existing business that did not result in a substantial change, *i.e.*, an increase of at least 40 percent in either the net worth or number of employees, the petition would be denied for failure to meet the establishment requirement.[21] A strict reading of the regulation would mean that if an investor wished to risk $1 million in an existing enterprise that already has 100 employees, he or she had to create at least 40 new jobs with his or her investment, despite the statutory requirement of creating only 10 new jobs, as clearly designated by Congress. These restrictions enormously altered the statutory goals of the EB-5 program and made investment in existing businesses difficult. While a passive investment or an expansion of a business may have met the goals of employment creation and infusion of capital, it would not meet the government's restrictive interpretations and would thereby lose its eligibility under the EB-5 regulations.

Restrictive Standard of Adjudication

Not only did the regulations alter the statutory goals, but the legacy Immigration and Naturalization Service's (INS) restrictive standards of adjudication further stifled the EB-5 program. In 1997, the Office of General Counsel issued an opinion that drastically altered the existing regulations and devastated an already faltering program.[22] The General Counsel's legal opinion prohibited certain types of business arrangements, such as: (1) the use of a down payment of cash with the remainder of the alien's contribution in the form of a promissory note; (2) a multi-year installment plan on a promissory note with a substantial "balloon" payment after the removal of the conditional status of the alien's permanent residence; (3) an option given to the alien to sell his or her investment for a fixed price that may be less than, equal to, or greater than the alien's cash contribution; (4) an option given to the enterprise or limited partnership to buy the investment at a fixed price; (5) a provision that allows or requires the commercial enterprise to place sufficient cash into a bank account to guarantee that funds will be available to repay the alien if the alien exercises an option to sell; (6) the withholding of a portion of the alien's capital contribution for attorneys' and finders' fees and other costs; and (7) a guaranteed return on the cash portion of the alien's investment.[23]

Many of the initial EB-5 applications involved business plans where the creation of a limited partnership was used to pool multiple investors' money to invest in either a new or a troubled business in the United States. Unfortunately, some of these limited partnership agreements were designed to reduce the investor's risk, so that only a small amount of the investment capital actually reached the business enterprise, and much of the investment included promissory notes of collateral where it was clear the actual, designated cash amount was not at risk.[24] Furthermore, the General Counsel's legal opinion also directed legacy INS to use not only these new standards going forward, but to retroactively apply these new standards to previously approved EB-5 petitions at the I-829 stage.

In 1998, the Administrative Appeals Office (AAO) issued a series of opinions (*Matter of Soffici, Matter of Izumii, Matter of Hsiung,* and *Matter of Ho*), collectively known as the "1998 precedent decisions," that not only echoed the 1997 legacy INS

---

[18] As of the date of this article, U.S. Citizenship and Immigration Services (USCIS) does not permit concurrent filing of the application to adjust status with the I-526 petition.

[19] 8 CFR §216.6.

[20] 8 CFR §204.6(j)(5).

[21] 8 CFR §204.6(h)(3).

[22] D. Hirson and C.I. Mayou, "The Sinking of the Titanic, or the Rising of the Phoenix? An Update on Immigrant Investor Visas," 98-09 *Immigration Briefings* (Sept. 1998).

[23] 75 *Interpreter Releases* 332 (Mar. 9, 1998).

[24] 8 CFR §204.6(j)(2).

mandate, but that effectively signaled the end of the road for the EB-5 program.[25]

For example, under the initial regulation, a promissory note could be valued at face value, but under the new standard, the promissory note had to be valued at fair market value. Under the old standard, the term of the promissory note was limitless, but under the new standard, the note had to be paid after two years. Furthermore, bank accounts could no longer be used as security.[26]

These decisions applied a restrictive approach and, even worse, retroactively applied the 1998 interpretations to investors who already had received I-526 approvals but were still subject to the two-year conditional residency requirement. As a result, hundreds of I-829 petitions filed by immigrant investors were denied based on the retroactive criteria. Most of the I-526 investor petitions filed after 1998 never had a chance, as investors relied on plausible interpretations of published regulations and invested in what appeared to be lawful investment plans, but ultimately became entangled in the government's restrictive interpretation of the law.

Restrictive Evidentiary Requirements

Consistent with the restrictive standards of adjudication and ever wary of fraud, USCIS requests extensive documentation. To cite a few examples, both I-526 and I-829 petitions require extensive proof that an investment has been made or is in the process of being made and must include evidence that the petitioner's personal capital was placed at risk.[27] USCIS will not recognize investments made directly through a petitioner's incorporated or limited liability business because the corporate assets are not considered the petitioner's personal assets.[28] Furthermore, the investment arrangement cannot be structured to shift the financial risk from the investor to the commercial enterprise.

USCIS also has been particularly concerned about whether the capital used for the investment was obtained through lawful means. The regulations instruct the petitioner to document the source of funds by providing foreign business registration, five years of tax return filings (within and outside the United States), and evidence identifying any other source of capital (*e.g.*, inheritance).[29]

In practice, the petitioner may have to trace the lawful source of funds back by several decades to the origin—which can be a daunting, if not impossible, task. Business in many countries is conducted on a trust basis and parties may agree to a contract with a handshake. This is a common problem with emerging economies that do not have the sophisticated documentary paper trails which U.S. businesses are generally required to possess. Thus, investors from certain countries often do not have credible records of income tax documents. Moreover, even where the investment can be traced to an original source, USCIS continues to use every technical basis to deny cases, leaving some potential investors discouraged from pursuing the EB-5 category because of the rigorous evidentiary requirements for the initial I-526 and the subsequent I-829 petitions.

Another example of unduly strict interpretation affects investors who transfer exactly $500,000 or $1 million, as required, but neglect to calculate the cost of the nominal bank wire transfer fee. USCIS will routinely reject these investors based on such minor technical grounds.

THE LANDSCAPE CHANGES

Several positive developments in the last few years indicate the landscape may be changing, as USCIS begins to approve EB-5 applications. Investors applying through the Employment Creation Pilot Program's regional centers appear to have met with considerably more success recently. This may be due to a perceived preference in adjudication on the part of USCIS, which seems to be approving EB-5 Pilot Program petitions at a substantially higher rate than in prior years. Unfortunately, most of the previously designated regional centers are now defunct, and investors are encouraged to under-

---

[25] *Matter of Soffici*, 22 I&N Dec. 158, 19 *Immigr. Rep.* B2-25 (AAO June 25, 1998); *Matter of Izumii*, 22 I&N Dec. 169, 19 *Immigr. Rep.* B2-32 (AAO June 13, 1998); *Matter of Hsiung*, 22 I&N Dec. 201, 19 *Immigr. Rep.* B2-106 (AAO July 31, 1998); and *Matter of Ho*, 22 I&N Dec. 206, 19 *Immigr. Rep.* B2-99 (AAO July 31, 1998). All four of these precedent decisions are reproduced in the Appendix materials to this volume.

[26] S. Yale-Loehr, "EB-5 Immigrant Investors: An Overview," *Immigration Options for Investors* 51, 62 (AILA 2006).

[27] 8 CFR §204.6(j)(2); 8 CFR §§216.6(a)(4)(ii), 1216.6(a)(4)(ii). For more on this topic, see C. Lee, "The Meaning of 'At Risk' in EB-5 Investment," elsewhere in this volume.

[28] *See Matter of M–*, I&N Dec. 24, 50 (BIA 1958, AG 1958).

[29] 8 CFR §204.6(j)(3). For more on this topic, see E. Arias & L. Stone, "Navigating the Lawful Source Requirement for EB-5 Immigration," elsewhere in this volume.

take extensive due diligence analysis before applying for EB-5 status.

Judicial Involvement

In May 2001, a California federal district court in *Chang v. United States* chastised the government and ruled that INS could not apply the new standards of adjudication retroactively in connection with approved I-526 petitions.[30] The court held that:

> INS could not "change the rules of the game" by automatically applying its new more restrictive interpretations retroactively to investors who had already received conditional green cards and who are now trying to have those conditions removed. Instead, the agency must allow some investors an opportunity to show how such a retroactive application would hurt them.

Despite this apparent victory for immigrant investors, this decision actually had the effect of curtailing the program. The court ordered that the merits of the retroactivity claim be remanded to the administrative courts for review. Unfortunately, INS refused to hear the retroactivity claims. Even though the parties argued the issue of retroactivity before the district court, the subject was left unresolved.

Two years later, on April 29, 2003, the Ninth Circuit Court of Appeals issued its review of *Chang v. United States*.[31] The court held that no further exhaustion of the administrative process was necessary and that it had jurisdiction to review the claims. More significantly, the court performed the retroactivity analysis, noting that the district court's actions were irrational because it "wasted judicial resources by remanding to the INS for it to do what it firmly states it may not and will not do . . . The district court was itself fully capable of doing what it asked the INS to do against its will. The remand was thus an abuse of discretion."[32] The Ninth Circuit determined that retroactive application of the 1998 AAO precedent decisions was impermissible. It further chastised the government, stating:

> INS's approving and receiving the benefits of [immigrant] investments, only to renege on the promise of LPR status once those benefits were garnered, must seem very unfair. It is hard to imagine how the INS has a compelling statutory interest in such an outcome. Congress has not repealed the EB-5 program; it still intends for it to continue. The reputation and integrity of the EB-5 program is ill-served by the proposition that INS approval of an I-526 petition as satisfying EB-5's requirements cannot be relied upon.[33]

Consequently, for those investors caught in the midst of the rule changes, this landmark decision provided the first indication that the 10-year pattern of negative, restrictive adjudication might be drawing to a close based on the appellate court's conclusion that retroactive application of the 1998 precedent decisions was impermissible.

Congressional Involvement

While the federal courts breathed new life into an otherwise moribund program, Congress also tried to revive the program with the 21st Century Department of Justice Appropriations Authorization Act (DOJ Amendments), signed into law on November 2, 2002.[34] This law was specifically designed to reform the program and provide some regulatory guidance. The DOJ Amendments considerably eased the regulations by providing relief to investors left in limbo by the restrictive 1998 precedent decisions, outlining special procedures for investors with I-526 petition approvals between January 1, 1995, and August 31, 1998, and who had filed an adjustment of status application or had applied for an immigrant visa overseas.[35]

Some investor applicants with denied I-829 petitions were given an opportunity to file a motion to reopen, and others with approved I-526 petitions awaiting removal of conditional resident status in the United States were given a second chance at compliance.[36] Even investor applicants outside of the United States with approved I-526 petitions were given an opportunity to return to the United States, if necessary, to obtain adjustment.[37]

The DOJ Amendments eliminated the "establishment" requirement—that EB-5 investors have "established" a commercial enterprise.[38] Instead, investors

---

[30] *Chang v. United States*, No. CV-99-10518-GHK (AJWx) (C.D. Cal. May 3, 2001).

[31] *Chang v. United States*, 327 F.3d 911 (9th Cir. 2003). The *Chang* decision is reproduced at Appendix B.

[32] *Id.* at 925.

[33] *Id.* at 929.

[34] 21st Century Department of Justice Appropriations Authorization Act, *supra* note 16.

[35] *Id.* at §§11031–32.

[36] *Id.* at §11031(b).

[37] *Id.* at §11032(c)(2)(B).

[38] *Supra* note 12, at 53.

only needed to show they have "invested" in a commercial enterprise. Thus, immigrant investors who invest in an existing enterprise no longer had to prove they expanded the net worth or the number of employees by 40 percent.[39] This significantly altered the original regulations and eliminated one of the biggest obstacles created by the 1998 precedent decisions. For instance, in *Matter of Izumii*, the AAO determined that the limited partners who had joined the general partnership over varying periods had used these "pooling agreements" to circumvent the establishment of a new business enterprise requirement. Because the DOJ Amendments eliminated the "establishment" requirement, the finding stated in *Matter of Izumii* is no longer applicable.

For advocates of the investor visa program, Congress's decision to eliminate the establishment requirement was seen as a significant positive development. However, soon after those judicial and statutory victories were celebrated, USCIS once again dealt the program another setback. On June 10, 2003, USCIS issued an interim guidance memo confirming that although an "alien entrepreneur is no longer required to establish a commercial enterprise,"[40] the new law does not remove the requirement that the enterprise be "new," as defined in 8 CFR §204.6(e). From this restrictive interpretation, it appeared that the "establishment of a new commercial enterprise" requirement still pertained to those enterprises established prior to November 29, 1990.

Most disturbing, however, is that USCIS has yet to issue conforming regulations to implement the DOJ amendments. Investors remain stuck in the quagmire from the prior confusion and guessing as to how they can extract themselves from the regulatory and adjudicatory mess.

Investors should continue to exercise caution in applying for immigrant investor visas as restrictive adjudications continue. For this reason, most EB-5 investors choose to participate in recently approved Pilot Program-designated regional centers, as they allow for creation of indirect employment, and the alien investor is not required to engage in the day-to-day management of the new commercial enterprise.[41] Also, USCIS appears to be approving Pilot Program cases for designated regional centers at a higher rate than traditional cases. However, the investor is cautioned that the strict reading of the source of the funds issue continues to be rigorously enforced for all cases. Also, with so many new regional centers being established, there are now concerns as to whether some will be economically viable, and if they will be able to meet the requirements to remove the conditional nature of the residency that is granted for an initial two-year period.

THE EFFECTIVENESS OF THE PROGRAM

The Basic Pilot Program Extension and Expansion Act of 2003 mandated that the Government Accountability Office (GAO) study the efficacy of the EB-5 program.[42] The GAO found that despite its turbulent history and negative perception by the government and potential investors, the program has been beneficial to the economy.[43] The 653 immigrant investors who have managed to attain permanent residency have collectively invested approximately $1 billion. This is a small estimate of the total investment in the U.S. economy because it only accounts for just over 10 percent of all EB-5 participants who have invested over a 13-year period. The GAO found that investments were made in various industries, including real estate, hotels/motels, manufacturing, import/export, agriculture, and technology, and across 17 states. However, California was the primary recipient, having drawn 41 percent of the investors.

The GAO concluded that the EB-5 program has a worthy mandate that can be beneficial to the U.S. economy and recommended that DHS issue the long-awaited regulations, thereby providing relief to the hundreds of investors whose status and cases have been in limbo for years. Furthermore, the GAO determined that the regulations will help provide guidance for adjudicators and potential investors.

ON THE BRIGHT SIDE

As mentioned above, participation in the EB-5 program through the Pilot Program appears to be the

---

[39] 8 CFR §204.6(h)(3).

[40] USCIS Memorandum, W. Yates, "Amendments Affecting Adjudication of Petitions for Alien Entrepreneur" (June 10, 2003), 8 *Bender's Immigr. Bull.* 1306 (Aug. 1, 2003), *published* on AILA InfoNet at Doc. No. 03061744 (*posted* June 17, 2003).

[41] Citizenship and Immigration Services Ombudsman "Annual Report 2009" (June 30, 2009), *published* on AILA InfoNet at Doc. No. 09063065 (*posted* June 30, 2009).

[42] The Basic Pilot Program Extension and Expansion Act of 2003, Pub. L. No. 108-156, 117 Stat. 1944, §5.

[43] GAO Report, *supra* note 2.

best option for prospective investors. By investing in commercial enterprises located within a designated regional center and targeted employment area, the investment amount is reduced to $500,000, and the petitioner does not have to directly prove job creation. USCIS appears to show preference for these types of cases, and there have been several reports confirming the higher rate of approval for investments made under the Pilot Program. This positive development provides greater certainty that both the I-526 and I-829 petitions will be approved, and the investor will eventually succeed in obtaining permanent residence status.

Another positive development occurred in January 2005, when USCIS established within the agency the Investor and Regional Center Unit (IRCU) to provide oversight for policy and regulatory development, field design, case auditing, and training on regional center adjudication. USCIS believes that this will encourage foreign investment and job creation without damaging the integrity of the EB-5 program.[44] IRCU is now known as the USCIS Foreign Trader, Investor and Regional Center Program (FTIRCP) and also oversees the E treaty traders and investors visa programs.

Currently, prospective investors may choose from 49 approved regional centers operating in 21 states.[45] USCIS maintains a public list of all approved regional centers[46] and recently confirmed that another 41 regional center applications are pending at the California Service Center.[47]

JOB CREATION METHODOLOGY

In a further sign that that the government is warming up to the EB-5 investor program, USCIS recently issued two important memoranda clarifying key program questions and stakeholder concerns. Michael Aytes, Acting Deputy Director of USCIS issued the first memo, titled "Response to Recommendation 40, Employment Creation Immigrant Visa (EB-5) Program Recommendations," on June 12, 2009.[48] The memo provides responses to eight issues highlighted by Acting USCIS Ombudsman Richard Flowers concerning the improvements to the immigrant investor program. Among other recommendations, Mr. Flowers had urged USCIS to issue procedures "specifically direct[ing] EB-5 adjudicators to not reconsider or re-adjudicate the indirect job creation methodology in Regional Center cases, absent clear error or evidence of fraud."[49] In response, the Aytes Memo states:[50]

> USCIS concurs with the intent of this recommendation to the extent that EB-5 adjudicators should not re-adjudicate the indirect job creation methodology for Regional Center cases absent clear error or evidence of fraud. USCIS will, however, continue to review the I-829 petitions to ensure that all measurable variables and assumptions that underlie the indirect job creation methodology have, in fact, been met. For example, an investor may make a proposal to create a shopping center that would be leased to various businesses. At the I-526 stage, the investor may claim that this proposal would result in the hiring of a certain number of employees by the tenant businesses and that a certain number of indirect jobs would be created as well. USCIS must ensure that the tenant jobs have substantially been filled to support the indirect job count. This is not re-adjudicating the job creation methodology, merely verification of an assertion previously made during the I-526 stage. In the alternative, if the job creation was based on total expenditure of capital to create the shopping center, USCIS must make sure the full amount has, in fact, been invested in the job creating enterprise to support the job count.

---

[44] USCIS Memorandum, W. Yates, "Establishment of an Investor and Regional Center Unit" (Jan. 19, 2005), *published on* AILA InfoNet at Doc. No. 05012663 (*posted* Jan. 26, 2005). The Yates Memo is reproduced at Appendix C.

[45] *See* "Q&As from EB-5 Stakeholders Meeting Hosted by Invest in the USA (IIUSA) and the American Immigration Lawyers Association (AILA)" (June 24, 2009), *published on* AILA InfoNet at Doc. No. 09071362 (*posted* July 13, 2009), at Q&A No. 4.

[46] The list is posted at: www.uscis.gov/portal/site/uscis/menuitem.5af9bb95919f35e66f614176543f6d1a/?vgnextoid=3df2b199cb011210VgnVCM1000004718190aRCRD&vgnextchannel=4f719c7755cb9010VgnVCM10000045f3d6a1RCRD.

[47] *See* "Q&As from EB-5 Stakeholders Meeting Hosted by IIUSA and AILA," *supra* note 45, at Q&A No. 5.

[48] *See* USCIS Memorandum, M. Aytes, Acting Deputy Director, USCIS, to Richard Flowers, Acting Ombudsman, USCIS, "Response to Recommendation 40, Employment Creation Immigrant Visa (EB-5) Program Recommendations" (June 12, 2009), *published on* AILA InfoNet at Doc 09061770 (*posted* June 17, 2009), and reproduced at Appendix G (Aytes Memo).

[49] *Id.* at 2.

[50] *Id.*

As is apparent, USCIS conceded that the job creation methodology "is an issue"[51] and should not be re-adjudicated in Regional Center EB-5 cases. USCIS also stated that the government's goal is not to re-adjudicate issues "previously decided in instances where circumstances remain unchanged."[52] USCIS further stated that it was in the process of drafting a guidance memo that would clarify which issues should be decided at each stage of the process.[53]

On the other hand, the agency appears to retain the right to review this same methodology at the stage of the I-829 petition to remove conditions. Presently, California Service Center (CSC) adjudicators continue to demand proof of indirect job creation and issue challenges regarding previously cleared methodologies to both I-526 and I-829 petitioners. Furthermore, CSC continues to question the factors and models that formed the basis for gaining approval of Regional Centers every step of the process. Thus, it remains to be seen what impact such half-hearted concessions will have on future EB-5 cases and petition approval rates.

Timing of Job Creation

On June 17, 2009, USCIS published a memorandum from Donald Neufeld, Acting Associate Director, USCIS Domestics Operations, titled "EB-5 Entrepreneurs—Job Creation and Full-Time Positions."[54] Under USCIS regulations, I-526 petitions must be accompanied by "a comprehensive business plan showing that, due to the nature and projected size of the new commercial enterprise, the need for not fewer than ten (10) qualifying employees will result, including approximate dates, within the next two years, and when such employees will be hired."[55] The Neufeld Memo updates the *Adjudicators Field Manual* (AFM), clarifying that "each petitioner must submit a business plan"[56] and that the requirement that the requisite jobs will be created in two years "applies to all Form I-526 petitions, including those filed under the Regional Center Program, [which] rely on indirect job creation to satisfy the statutory employment creation requirement."[57]

The memo acknowledges that USCIS regulations do not specify *when* the two-year period begins for purposes of adjudicating I-526 petitions and that the phrase "next two years" referenced in 8 CFR §204.6(j)(4)(i)(B) "relates to the two-year period of conditional residence."[58] In other words, at the end of the two-year period of conditional residence, the alien investor must demonstrate with his or her I-829 petition that he or she has either "created or can be expected to create within a reasonable period of time" the necessary jobs, in order to have the conditions removed and full residence granted.[59] Thus, USCIS decided to fix the start of the two-year period with respect to the petitioner's job creation obligation since "the officer adjudicating Form I-526 cannot be certain when the period of conditional residence will in fact commence,"[60] among others. In particular,

> USCIS has determined that the average processing times for EB-5 petitioners filing for immigrant visas via consular processing and EB-5 petitioners filing for adjustment of status [to obtain conditional resident status] is approximately six months. Accordingly, in order to best approximate the two-year period of conditional residence the two-year period described in 8 CFR §204.6(j)(4)(i)(B) will be deemed to commence six months after the adjudication of Form I-526. USCIS officers should ensure that the business plan filed along with Form I-526 reasonably demonstrates that *the requisite number of jobs will be created by the alien's investment by the end of the two-year period that commences six months after the adjudication of the petition.*[61] [Emphasis added.]

In essence, USCIS has extended the timing of job creation from two years to two years and six months, which, in turn, means that an I-526 petitioner must produce a business plan detailing how and when the required number of qualifying (full-time[62]) jobs will

---

[51] *See* "Q&As from EB-5 Stakeholders Meeting Hosted by IIUSA and AILA," *supra* note 45, at Q&A No. 12.

[52] *Id.*

[53] *Id.*

[54] USCIS Memorandum, D. Neufeld, "EB-5 Entrepreneurs—Job Creation and Full-Time Positions (AFM Update AD 09-04)" (June 17, 2009), *published on* AILA InfoNet at Doc. No. 09061964 (*posted* June 19, 2009) (Neufeld Memo). The memo is reproduced at Appenidx C.

[55] 8 CFR §204.6(j)(4)(i)(B).

[56] Neufeld Memo, *supra* note 54, at 1.

[57] *Id.* at 3.

[58] *Id.*

[59] 8 CFR §216.6(c)(1)(iv).

[60] Neufeld Memo, *supra* note 54, at 3.

[61] *Id.* at 3–4.

[62] The Neufeld Memo clarified that "direct and indirect construction jobs that are created by the petitioner's investment and that are expected to last at least 2 years, inclusive of

continued

be created within two and a half years of I-526 approval. USCIS assumes, however, that an investor will require, "on average," six months to receive conditional permanent residence either via consular processing or adjustment of status. If either one of these processes takes more than six months (which is not unusual), will the alien still have to meet the job creation requirement "by the end of the two-year period that commences six months after the adjudication of the petition"? Thus, fixing the start of the job creation period, while adding some certainty to USCIS adjudications, may end up creating more uncertainty for EB-5 petitioners. It might additionally have the effect of ruling out EB-5 projects that take longer than two and a half years to create the requisite jobs.[63] Although USCIS has the discretion to approve major projects that are delayed because of circumstances beyond the applicant's control, such as delays in issuing building permits, or where there are less than 10 jobs because an employer unknowingly hires an undocumented worker, but regrettably, we have not seen much favorable exercise of discretion for substantial good faith compliance.

Initial Review of Form I-829 Petitions Where Jobs Have Not Been Created

The Neufeld Memo states that I-829 petitions are "intended to examine whether the alien entrepreneur has satisfied the conditions of his or her admission to the United States."[64] USCIS must determine "whether the alien has invested the requisite capital and created the requisite jobs through that investment."[65] Because USCIS regulations provide that I-829 petitions must be accompanied by evidence that "the alien created or can be expected to create within a reasonable time ten full-time jobs for qualifying employees,"[66] the memo advises that:

> In making the "reasonable time" determination, officers should consider the evidence submitted along with the petition that demonstrates when the jobs are expected to be created, the reasons that the jobs were not created as predicted in Form I-526, the nature of the industry or industries in which the jobs are to be created, and any other evidence submitted by the petitioner. If, after considering the evidence, the officer determines that the jobs are more likely to be created within a reasonable time, Form I-829 should be approved consistent with 8 CFR §2166(d)(1) if the petitioner is otherwise eligible to have his or her conditions removed. If, however, the officer determines that the jobs will not be created within a reasonable period of time, Form I-829 should be denied consistent with 8 CFR §216.6(d)(2).[67]

This portion of the Neufeld memo provides needed flexibility in I-829 adjudications for investments where jobs have not yet been created and directs adjudicating officers to consider various factors in determining whether the required job creation may be shown "within a reasonable period of time."

TEA DESIGNATIONS

Another area of concern is that USCIS continues its position of requiring different investment levels ($500,000 versus $1,000,000) in multi-year projects located within designated "targeted employment areas" (TEAs) where the area's TEA designation is withdrawn but the project is ongoing and requires further investments. USCIS's position is that once the TEA designation is lost, the amount of investment in this same project is $1,000,000. This issue was captured in the June 24, 2009, EB-5 stakeholders meeting:[68]

> Most states update census tracts and counties/cities once a year. Assume that a regional center starts a project in a census tract that is a TEA for the current period but may not be a TEA for the following year. If funding is not completed until the second year, when the tract may no longer qualify as a TEA, can EB-5 investors who come into the project the second year nevertheless invest $500,000 rather than $1 million? It makes little sense to require investors invested in a project at different amounts, based on the sole fortuity of when a state updates its TEA list.
>
> *USCIS Answer:* The project location has to qualify as a TEA at the time of filing the I-526, so if

---

when the petitioner's I-829 is filed, may now count" as "full-time" jobs. *Id.* at 5.

[63] *See* S. Yale-Loehr, "USCIS Clarifies Key Aspects of EB-5 Program" *available at www.abil.com/articles/USCIS%20 Clarifies%20Key%20Aspects%20of%20EB-5%20Program %20(Yale-Loehr).pdf* (last accessed Sept. 11, 2009).

[64] Neufeld Memo, *supra* note 54, at 6.

[65] *Id.*

[66] See 8 CFR §§ 216.6(4)(iv) and 216.6(c)(1)(iv).

[67] Neufeld Memo, *supra* note 54, at 6, 7.

[68] *See* "Q&As from EB-5 Stakeholders Meeting Hosted by IIUSA and AILA," *supra* note 45, at Q&A No. 15.

the area does not qualify then the minimum investment is one million dollars.

Although extremely unfair to EB-5 investors who come to the project perhaps a year later from their predecessors, the above answer implies USCIS's respect for TEA designations by state governments. In fact, adjudicators often question such designations, creating more uncertainty for the program and inconsistency in both regional center and individual petition adjudications. USCIS has finally recognized this concern and appears willing to issue a memo "instructing adjudicators not to question TEA designations."[69] The agency stated that it was not "in the business of questioning the governors or the state designation in this regard."[70]

A larger issue underlying TEA designations is that robust regional center investments and the resulting job growth in a targeted employment may lead to the loss of the area's TEA designation.[71] Basically, the commercial success of a regional center may be fatal to its very existence if the area in which it is located has seen improved economic activity and significant reduction in unemployment rates thanks to EB-5 investments.

EB-5 PROGRAM – STILL THE BEST CHOICE FOR INVESTORS AND ENTREPRENEURS?

Despite the EB-5 Program's turbulent history, it has many advantages over other employment-based immigrant visa classifications. First, it does not require an offer of employment and approved labor certification application. Second, as a historically underutilized program, prospective investors will have immigrant visas immediately available to them and need not wait years for a visa number.[72]

Since the EB-5 Program most closely parallels the EB-1C classification for multinational executives and managers, it is worthwhile to compare the attributes and nuances of the two visa categories. Practitioners should consider the EB-1C classification first, as it does not require a two-year conditional residence period. If the investor is qualified and if the investment can be structured to meet the requirements for EB-1C classification, then the practitioner should prepare and file the Form I-140 petition based on the EB-1C classification and avoid conditional residency.[73] If EB-1C classification is not available, then consider the EB-5 classification.[74]

Characteristics of Investor and Control of the Enterprise

The investor applying for permanent residence based on the EB-5 classification need not have a particular background or any experience at all. Regulations for the EB-5 classification are silent on characteristics of the investor. Successful petitioners have included students, relatively young adults, retirees, petitioners with limited English language ability and no prior investment, managerial, or entrepreneurial skills or experience, and investors with no management experience or entrepreneurial skills.[75]

Not only is the EB-5 petitioner excused from presenting evidence of past experience, but the EB-5 classification, in essence, minimizes the significance of what the investor actually will do in the U.S. enterprise. The EB-5 classification mandates only that the investor will be "engaged" in the enterprise, which can be as minimal as having a role in policy formulation.[76] The investor does not have to be a manager, executive, or even an employee in the business, and does not have to direct and control the business. The EB-5 regulation requires some participation in the management of the enterprise, either day-to-day managerial control or a role in policy formulation.[77] Presumably, an officer or director position would satisfy the requirement to be engaged in the enterprise.

---

[69] *Id.*, at follow-up Q&A.

[70] *Id.*

[71] 8 CFR §204.6(m)(6).

[72] Visa retrogression is of particular concern for Indian and Chinese-born nationals who are currently subject to five- and nine-year waits in the EB-2 and EB-3 categories, respectively. *See Visa Bulletin* (Mar. 2010).

[73] An added benefit is that the I-140 petition, unlike the I-526 petition, can be concurrently processed with an I-485 application for adjustment of status. Interim Rule, 67 Fed. Reg. 49561 (July 31, 2002), *published on* AILA InfoNet at Doc. No. 02073171 (*posted* July 31, 2002).

[74] For an in-depth analysis of the EB-5 classification as it compares to other visa classifications, *see* L. Stone, "A Comparison of the EB-5 Category with Alternative Immigration Strategies" *Immigration Options for Investors and Entrepreneurs* (AILA 2006). *See also* Exhibit I to this article—a checklist to help determine if an investment would qualify for EB-5 classification.

[75] Holders of the EB-1C classification, on the other hand, must have worked as an executive, manager, or specialized knowledge employee for an affiliated business.

[76] INA §203(b)(5)(A); 8 CFR §204.6(j)(5).

[77] 8 CFR §204.6(j)(5).

EMPLOYMENT IMPACTS

The EB-5 Program stresses the employment consequences of the investment and, thus, is named the "employment creation" visa category. As noted above, the investment must lead to the creation of at least 10 jobs.[78] The jobs filled by the investor or the investor's immediate family do not count toward meeting the requirement.[79] The jobs must be full-time (*i.e.*, at least 35 hours weekly), although part-time positions can be combined in cases of job sharing.[80] The I-526 petition must demonstrate either that at the time of filing the petition the investment already has created the requisite 10 full-time jobs, or the petition may include evidence of a comprehensive business plan that provides details on how the jobs will be created during the investor's conditional residence period.[81] In contrast, the EB-1C regulations, for instance, do not prescribe the number of employees an enterprise must have to qualify an applicant as "manager," but experienced practitioners know well that USCIS examiners look for depth in company organization charts and are more favorable towards businesses that employ numerous U.S. workers.

For those clients who have sufficient funds to invest, but who do not maintain a multinational business with offices abroad and in the United States, the EB-5 permanent residence classification can be an attractive vehicle to achieve U.S. permanent residence.

BE ENCOURAGED BUT PROCEED WITH CAUTION

Following a decade of turbulence, there have been positive developments for investors who are able to demonstrate the lawful source of funds used for investment in designated regional centers under the Pilot Program. Moreover, Congress has historically expressed support for the EB-5 program. Whenever legacy INS interpreted the regulations restrictively, Congress took action and passed new laws, attempting to soften the blow on immigrant investors. Congress's continuous extension of the Pilot Program reiterates the government's commitment to the EB-5 program. Regrettably, USCIS continues to delay the issuance of final enabling regulations that may help those lost in the labyrinth of restrictive adjudication, leaving previous investors without clear directions as to how to emerge from the quagmire. Hopefully, USCIS will recognize the clear congressional intent and draft regulations that will stabilize and energize a program that has the potential to reduce unemployment and revive the economy.

The Regional Center Pilot Program appears to be the best option for many prospective investors. It now appears that approximately 90 percent of all EB-5 petitions are filed through the Regional Centers.[82] By investing in commercial enterprises located within a designated regional center located in a targeted employment area, the investment amount is reduced to $500,000 and the investor does not have to directly prove job creation but can do so through a combination of direct and indirect jobs. USCIS therefore appears to continue to show preference for these types of cases. There have also been several reports of expeditious approvals, and a higher rate of approval for investments made under the Regional Center Pilot Program. This positive development provides greater certainty for some investors seeking to obtain permanent residence status.

---

[78] 8 CFR §204.6(j)(4)(i).
[79] 8 CFR §204.6(e), defining "Qualifying employee."
[80] 8 CFR §204.6(e), defining "Full-time employment."
[81] 8 CFR §204.6(j)(4).

[82] "USCIS Q&A from Stakeholder Session with AILA EB-5 Committee and Invest in the USA" (Dec. 14, 2009), *published on* AILA InfoNet at Doc. No. 10010462 (*posted* Jan. 4, 2010), and reproduced at Appendix H.

EXHIBIT I

The following checklist may be handy in determining whether an investment will qualify for the EB-5 classification:

- The investment must be made after November 29, 1990, the effective date of the enabling legislation.
- Only an individual can make the investment. Allowing for the possible exception where the petitioner owns 100 percent of the investing entity, in most instances, if an entity makes the investment, the immigration benefits will be limited to the L-1 and E-2 visa categories and the EB-1C immigrant classification.
- The investment must be for a for-profit commercial enterprise formed for the ongoing conduct of lawful business.
- Location of the investment is pivotal for the requisite amount of capital and if the investment is in a Regional Center, the task of proving job creation is simplified. In contrast, investment location is irrelevant for seeking EB-1C classification.
- The EB-5 classification stipulates a minimum capital investment of $1 million. As indicated above, if the investment is in a "targeted employment area," the minimum capital that must be invested is reduced to $500,000. Capital that is not cash, such as equipment or inventory, is credited in the amount of its fair market value. Regulations for the EB-5 permanent residence classification do not require considerations of substantiality, proportionality, or marginality, as in E-2 visa practice.
- The petitioner must demonstrate that the invested capital was "obtained through lawful means."[83]
- The investment capital must be at risk. The invested funds may be escrowed pending the approvals of the I-526 petition and immigrant visa, as in E-2 visa practice, to protect the investor. But adjudicators are likely to require firm and detailed evidence of how the escrowed funds will be expended by the enterprise immediately after approval of the I-526 petition and visa issuance.[84]

---

[83] 8 CFR §204.6(j)(3).

[84] Legacy Immigration and Naturalization Service (INS) Memorandum, R. Bach, "Immigrant Investor Petitions—Placement of Invested Funds in Escrow and Extension of Time to Withdraw a Held Petition and File a New Petition in its Place" (Aug. 28, 1998), *published on* AILA InfoNet at Doc. No. 98083198 (*posted* Aug. 31, 1998); *see also* 22 CFR §41.51(b)(7); 8 CFR §214.2(e)(12).

PRACTICAL GUIDANCE IN PREPARING I-526 AND I-829 PETITIONS

by Elsie Hui Arias and Susan L. Pilcher[*]

INITIAL CASE ASSESSMENT FOR I-526 IMMIGRANT PETITION FOR ALIEN ENTREPRENEUR

- Conduct due diligence—consider issues of inadmissibility grounds, age-out of dependents, source and tracing documentation, etc.

- Examine key legal issues—New or pre-existing business, amount of capital required, job creation, lawful source of funds, etc.

- Review legal requirements—INA §203(b)(5) and 8 CFR §204.6, recent U.S. Citizenship and Immigration Services (USCIS) memoranda, and precedent decisions of the Administrative Appeals Office (AAO).

- Analyze Form I-526—Prepare detailed memorandum and organize supporting documents. File with USCIS, California Service Center, with $1,435 filing fee. See Appendix A for guidance in drafting Form I-526, Immigrant Petition by Alien Entrepreneur.

---

[*] **Elsie Hui Arias** (*elsie@lskglaw.com*) is an associate attorney with Stone & Grzegorek LLP, an immigration law firm in Los Angeles. Certified as a specialist in Immigration and Nationality Law by the California State Bar, Ms. Arias practices in all areas of immigration law and has served as a conference speaker on various immigration topics. She is a graduate of the University of California at Berkeley and the University of California at Davis School of Law.

Susan L. Pilcher (*spilcher@cslaw.us*) is Of Counsel to the firm of Carroll & Scribner, P.C. in Burlington, Vermont, where her general immigration practice includes a substantial focus on EB-5 and investment-related matters. Ms. Pilcher's professional background includes nearly a decade of full-time law teaching, including general and specialized immigration law courses, at the University of Arkansas School of Law (Fayetteville), a federal court clerkship in San Diego, California, commercial law practice, and many years of diverse and rewarding experience representing clients in virtually all types of immigration-related matters. She obtained her J.D. with distinction from Stanford Law School, where she served as Managing Editor of the Stanford Law Review. Ms. Pilcher has published and lectured extensively on immigration law topics, and she is active in agency liaison functions for the American Immigration Lawyers Association.

WHAT CONSTITUTES INVESTMENT OF CAPITAL?

Law requires an investor to have invested or be in the process of investing the required capital.

- Evidence of investment—*e.g.*, wire transfer of cash funds to EB-5 business, or transfer of inventory or equipment to EB-5 business.

Amount of Capital

Required capital is $1 million—provide evidence of investment amount in petition.

Required capital is reduced to $500,000 if investment is located in a "Targeted Employment Area" (TEA), which is an area of high unemployment (at least 150 percent of national average rate) or can be characterized as rural (enterprise is located in a city or town outside a metropolitan statistical area (MSA) and has a population of no more than 20,000).

- State designation of TEA area describing the basis for its designation, *e.g.*, letter from State of Washington—Employment Security Department; *or*

- Statistical evidence of TEA qualification, *e.g.*, for high unemployment area, compare national average unemployment rate through U.S. Department of Labor (*www.dol.gov*) and local area in which enterprise is located, *e.g.*, research statistics published by state workforce agency; *or*

- Population data, county identification, and information on MSA affiliation (from U.S. Census Bureau) to establish "rural" area.

Equity Capital/Type of Capital

Investment = contribution of equity capital. Loans of capital to enterprise do not count. Investor cannot receive any bond, note, or other debt arrangement from enterprise in exchange for contribution of capital. Also, investor's personal guarantee of a loan that is primary obligation of enterprise does not constitute equity investment capital.

Capital can include cash and cash equivalents, equipment, inventory, other tangible property, and debts. All capital shall be valued at fair market value at time of investment.

Escrow can be used, but escrow agreement should reflect that sole condition for release of funds is approval of I-526 petition or conditional resident status. Escrow must release funds directly into commercial enterprise's account for "job-creation purposes."

Investment Capital Must Be "At Risk"

Simply transferring funds into account of enterprise does not meet "at risk" requirement. USCIS focuses on actual and intended uses of capital to confirm that it will be used for job creation and profit-generating activity (for example, capital used for partnership expenses and reserve accounts does not count for EB-5 purposes). Evidence that investment capital is at risk may include:

- Details of how capital has been or will be utilized, *e.g.*, purchase agreements, receipts, invoices, bank statements reflecting withdrawals of funds, etc.
- Comprehensive business plan: description of business, products, and services; marketing analysis, including review of competition; marketing strategy; organizational chart, hiring plan/timeline for employees; and five-year pro forma.
- Financial documents, *e.g.*, income tax returns, financial statements, federal and state quarterly income tax filings.
- Business operation documents, *e.g.*, business license.
- Sample business transaction details, *e.g.*, customer invoices, office improvements, utility bills, lease agreement, recent bank statements, marketing materials, website.

INVESTMENT MUST BE MADE IN A "NEW" COMMERCIAL ENTERPRISE

Enterprise is *"new"* if formed after November 29, 1990 (Immigration Act of 1990's (IMMACT90) date of passage).

- Evidence that enterprise was formed *after* November 29, 1990, such as articles of incorporation

If investor contributes capital to an *"existing"* business, *i.e.*, formed prior to November 29, 1990, investment may count for EB-5 purposes in two separate situations:

1. Investor substantially reorganizes or restructures existing business.

    - Evidence that enterprise was formed *before* November 29, 1990, such as articles of incorporation.
    - Evidence that required capital was invested into business *after* November 29, 1990.
    - Evidence of substantial reorganization or restructuring. Mere change of ownership or form of entity (*e.g.*, corporation, LLC, limited partnership), cosmetic changes to business site, and implementation of new marketing strategy are insufficient alone to constitute reorganization into a "new" commercial enterprise.

    Or

2. Investor expands existing business, resulting in either: (a) increase of at least 40 percent in net worth of business *or* (b) increase of at least 40 percent in number of employees.

    - Evidence that enterprise was formed *before* November 29, 1990, such as articles of incorporation.
    - Evidence that required capital was invested into business *after* November 29, 1990.
    - Evidence that subsequent to investment, existing business has increased its net worth or number of employees by 40 percent, such as income tax returns, audited financial statements, and employment tax filings.

Commercial Enterprise

For-profit enterprise can be structured as sole proprietorship, partnership (limited or general), holding company (including its wholly owned subsidiaries), joint venture, corporation, or other entities privately and/or publicly owned. Documents required depend on structure, for example:

- Corporation—articles of incorporation, bylaws, shareholder list, stock certificate.
- Limited partnership—partnership agreement, list of limited partners.
- Limited liability company—articles of organization, operating agreement, member schedule.

Practice tip: In forming or investing in a commercial enterprise, EB-5 client should be advised to consult with a business attorney regarding appropriate business structure for enterprise. Issues that the EB-5 investor should be aware of include liability, taxation, complexity of creation and termination, and management capability and control.

DOCUMENTING SOURCE AND TRACING OF INVESTMENT FUNDS

EB-5 law requires that source of investment capital is lawful, and that capital originated from investor's personal funds.

- Background of investor: last five years of income tax returns (personal and business); curriculum vitae; if applicable, certified copies of judgments or evidence of pending civil or criminal actions involving monetary judgments against petitioner.

- Detailed explanation and documentation regarding actual source of investment capital, *e.g.*, employment earnings, stock sale, gift, loan proceeds, sale of real property or business, inheritance.
  - Where funds originated from a gift or a loan, provide background documentation of donor or lender to verify lawfulness of source of funds, *e.g.*, income tax returns (if source not evident from returns alone, may need additional tracing of donor's or lender's source).
  - Evidence reflecting path of investment funds from source to investor, *e.g.*, investor's bank statement reflecting deposit of real estate sale proceeds, is sometimes required.

- Detailed documentation tracing investment capital from investor to EB-5 commercial enterprise, *e.g.*, bank statements reflecting outgoing transfers and corresponding deposits of investment funds.

EMPLOYMENT CREATION: CREATING (OR SAVING) JOBS

Jobs must be created for at least 10 employees (not independent contractors), on a full-time basis (minimum 35 hours per week). Neither the investor nor his or her spouse or children count toward the 10-employee minimum. U.S. workers include U.S. citizens, lawful and conditional permanent residents, asylees, and refugees. Job-sharing arrangements of full-time positions are permissible, but combinations of part-time positions do not count. Commercial enterprises affiliated with an EB-5 Pilot Program (regional center) may rely on indirect employment creation.

- If EB-5 investment has created jobs for 10 full-time U.S. workers at time of I-526 filing: payroll records, W-2 forms, I-9 forms, organizational chart, detailed list of employees/job descriptions, etc.

- If requisite employees not hired at time of I-526 filing: comprehensive business plan reflecting hiring plan/timeline for employees within two years, proposed organizational chart, detailed list of employees/job descriptions.

- If "troubled business": Provide evidence that number of existing employees will be maintained at no less than pre-investment level for a period of at least two years, *e.g.*, payroll records, W-2 forms, I-9 forms of employees, business plan, etc. Evidence of "troubled business" will require credible financial statement and tax returns.

- If regional center: Business plan and economist report discussing creation of employment—directly and/or indirectly—resulting from investment.

Practice tip: If investment funds are pooled together with other EB-5 investors, employment creation must be sufficient to support all EB-5 investors cumulatively (*e.g.*, creation of 20 jobs could support petitions filed by two EB-5 investors).

MANAGEMENT RESPONSIBILITIES OF EB-5 INVESTOR

Law requires investor to "engage" in management of enterprise. Role in enterprise must be *active, not passive*—can consist of day-to-day management *or* policy formulation. Evidence may include:

- Formal agreement, *e.g.*, limited partnership agreement, shareholder agreement, operating agreement, corporate resolution.

- Declaration (if sole proprietor).

ADDITIONAL REQUIREMENTS: WHERE I-526 PETITION IS BASED ON INVESTMENT IN EB-5 PILOT PROGRAM (REGIONAL CENTER)

Above legal and regulatory requirements must be met. Must also include:

- Legacy Immigration and Naturalization Service (INS) or USCIS letter designating regional center.

- Documentation to establish that new commercial enterprise is located geographically within boundaries of designated regional center territory as defined in designation letter.

- Documentation to show that new commercial enterprise is within scope of target industries or activities approved by USCIS in regional center designation (*i.e.*, consistent with the regional center's business plan).

- If applicable, economist report detailing proof of indirect job creation based on reasonable methodologies (*i.e.*, report that discusses accepted statistical or economic models, how new commercial enterprise will create direct and/or indirect employment within a particular period of time).

REMOVING CONDITIONS FROM EB-5 INVESTOR'S RESIDENT STATUS: PREPARATION AND ANALYSIS OF I-829 PETITION

Regulations require filing within the 90-day period immediately prior to expiration of two-year conditional residence period. Failure to file timely will result in automatic termination of conditional resident status and possible initiation of removal proceedings. See Appendix B for guidance in drafting Form I-829. Requirements include:

- Form I-829 is filed with California Service Center. Filing fee is presently $2,850, plus $80 biometrics fee for investor and each dependent seeking removal of conditions. Dependents with conditional residence period different from the principal may require separate I-829 petitions and filing fees.

- Evidence that investment of requisite capital has been completed, *e.g.,* bank statements reflecting transfer of investment funds from investor to EB-5 commercial enterprise, confirmation of release of funds where escrow used.

- Evidence that investment has been sustained throughout two-year conditional residence period and utilized for job creation purposes, *e.g.,* investment capital has not been returned to investor, ongoing business operations. Evidence may include: business invoices/receipts, bank statements, contracts, business licenses, audited or reviewed financial statements, federal or state income tax returns and quarterly tax statements, etc.

- Evidence that new commercial enterprise as described in I-526 business plan has been created and its business plan objectives have been met, *e.g.,* business plan, organizational documents, evidence of project status, federal tax returns, etc.

    Practice tip: If the business plan and/or capital investment project has changed since approval of the I-526 petition, analyze whether change is "material" and requires an amendment to business plan and filing of new I-526 petition.

- Evidence that investment resulted in creation of 10 full-time jobs within conditional residence period (or will create jobs within reasonable period of time).

    – If I-526 petition based on non-regional center enterprise, submit evidence of direct job creation:
        - Number of full-time employees at time of investment and at time of I-829 filing, *e.g.,* business payroll records, relevant tax documents, and employee W-2 and I-9 forms.
        - Jobs created were for "qualifying employees," *i.e.,* U.S. citizens, lawful permanent residents, or other work-authorized immigrants, excluding investor and immediate family.
        - Jobs created are full-time, *i.e.,* at least 35 hours per week.
    – If I-526 petition based on "troubled business," submit evidence that minimum 10 jobs were "saved" (and created, if necessary for 10-job requirement) during two-year conditional residence period.
    – If I-526 petition based on investment in a regional center affiliated entity, submit economic analysis regarding employment creation in support of "indirect" job numbers, and provide evidence that investment was made in accordance with regional center's business plan to receive credit for job creation.

- If applicable, documentation relating to arrests, charges, and convictions during conditional residence period of investor or immediate family, as requested on Form I-829.

ANALYZING AND DRAFTING FORM I-526, IMMIGRANT PETITION BY ALIEN ENTREPRENEUR

The following is practical guidance to completing Form I-526, Immigrant Petition by Alien Entrepreneur, which is required of EB-5 petitioners. The reproduced exemplar of Form I-526 (rev. 01/06/10), found at the end of this article, is annotated by letters (A-Z), which are cross-referenced to comments in the accompanying text below. The comments are designed to alert the practitioner to legal issues implicated by each of the fields and/or sections on the USCIS form, excepting those that are self-explanatory.

Part 1. Information About You

A - *Petitioner's current status and entry information*: Being out of status does not preclude I-526 approval or subsequent lawful admission if otherwise eligible. The timing of investment and I-526 filing relative to date and class of admission may implicate issues of immigrant or preconceived intent.

Part 2. Application Type

B - *Box "a"* should be checked if the petitioner's investment qualifies for a minimum $500,000 investment because the enterprise is located in a TEA, *i.e.*, a rural area or designated area of high unemployment. The petition must be supported by evidence that the qualifying TEA or rural area satisfies the criteria in 8 CFR §204.6(i) and recent USCIS guidance.

C - *Box "b"* should not, at present, be checked for any petition. Under INA §203(b)(5)(C)(iii), USCIS has the authority to require up to three times the standard amount of required capital for certain MSAs with low unemployment rates. However, to date, USCIS has not adjusted the required capital investment upward in any geographic area.

D - *Box "c"* should be checked if the petitioner's investment is not within an area of high unemployment or a rural area meeting TEA requirements, and is thus subject to the minimum investment amount of $1 million.

Part 3. Information About Your Investment

E - *Street Address*: Where eligibility for reduced capital investment depends on the location of the enterprise in an area meeting TEA requirements, USCIS will request evidence that the enterprise is geographically located within the qualifying area. Any discrepancy between this address and the qualifying area as described in the petition should be fully documented and explained in the support letter.

F - *Date established*: This date is relevant to whether the enterprise is "new," *i.e.*, created after November 29, 1990, or if special requirements regarding "existing business" should apply (*i.e.*, substantially restructuring or reorganization, or 40 percent expansion in net worth or employees).

G - *IRS Tax #:* This field refers to the IRS-issued Federal Employer Identification Number (FEIN) applicable to the enterprise. The FEIN may be used to identify the employer for purposes of evaluating the creation of "direct" jobs resulting from the petitioner's capital investment.

H - *Total capital investment to date*. This amount should in most cases meet or exceed the required minimum capital investment amount of $500,000 or $1 million, as applicable.

I - *Names and immigration plans of other investors*. This information is not specifically required under the law or regulation but may relate to sharing credit for employment creation. To the extent it is known or readily available, it should be provided with Form I-526.

J - *County and State*. Complete if you checked Box "a" or Box "b" in Part 2. The data in these fields must be consistent with the basis for the reduced or increased amount of the required capital investment.

Part 4. Information About Your Investment

K - *"Creation of a new business"* box should be checked if the investor created the enterprise after November 29, 1990 (*i.e.*, eligibility rests on 8 CFR §204.6(h)(1)).

L - *"Purchase of an existing business"* box should be checked where eligibility rests on 8 CFR §204.6(h)(2). Checking this box will require supporting documentation of simultaneous or subsequent restructuring or reorganization of the enterprise.

M - *"Capital investment in an existing business"* box should be checked where eligibility rests on 8 CFR §204.6(h)(3). Checking this box will require supporting documentation of expansion of the net worth or number of employees by at least 40 percent as a result of the contribution of capital.

N - *Composition of the Petitioner's Investment*. Figures in these fields relate only to the makeup of the investor's contributed capital as of the time of filing the I-526 petition; for each type of capital contributed, the regulations prescribe required supporting evidence (8 CFR §204.6(j)). These entries also define the nature of the capital investment for purposes of showing at the removal of conditions stage that the investment has been sustained.

O - *Income*. This question relates to the income of the enterprise, not of the investor.

P - *Net worth*. These are the fields in which to assert a 40 percent expansion in the net worth of the business, if applicable, to show a qualifying "capital investment in an existing business" (see field "M" above). May enter "N/A" in other circumstances.

Part 5. Employment Creation Information

Q - *Difference in Number of Employees*. This field, resulting from comparison of data in the preceding two fields, is used to assert expansion of the number of employees by 40 percent, if applicable, to show a qualifying "capital investment in an existing business" (see field "M" above). Alternatively, this field is used to establish a baseline for assessing the required creation of 10 jobs per qualifying investment. If the enterprise qualifies as a "troubled business," this will be the baseline for determining whether existing direct jobs are maintained throughout the conditional residence period.

R - *Number of new jobs created by your investment.* This field is for designating how many of the jobs in the "difference" field above are attributable to the particular investment outlined in this petition. Where there are multiple investors in an enterprise, this is where specific job numbers could be assigned to each investor.

S - *Additional new jobs to be created by additional investment.* Although this field implies it should be used only when the investor's capital contribution has not yet been completed, this field may be used to project additional direct—and if applicable, indirect job creation—that will be attributable to the investor's capital contribution. Ensure the total of this field and the previous field totals at least the minimum required for approval (in some cases, such as with troubled businesses, an annotation is advised—"saving jobs").

T - *Position, office, or title.* Although the investor need not be an employee of the enterprise, entries in this field should reflect that the investor is engaged in the management of the business, either as an employee, officer, director, or partner.

U - *Duties, activities, responsibilities.* Entries in this field must reflect an "active" role in the management of the enterprise, via day-to-day control or policy formulation. Limited partners should include evidence of the right to participate in policymaking and certain key decision-making to the extent normally permitted by the Uniform Limited Partnership Act.

V - *Salary and benefits.* The regulations do not require that the investor be salaried, but data in these fields should be consistent with entries in the previous two fields.

Part 6. Processing Information

W - *Applicant intending to adjust status.* Concurrent filing of the I-485 application is not presently permitted. If this box is checked, USCIS will retain the petition instead of forwarding it to the National Visa Center.

Practice tip: Checking this box is not recommended unless the investor is certain that he or she will utilize the adjustment of status process, as changing procedures after approval of the I-526 petition may require a Form I-824 (Application for Action on an Approved Application or Petition), resulting in significant delay.

X - *Applicant intending to consular process.* Checking this box will result in USCIS forwarding the approved petition to the National Visa Center for consular processing of the immigrant visas. Entries in the fields will be used by the National Visa Center to make an initial determination of consular jurisdiction.

Practice tip: Although there is no place on the I-526 form to name derivative beneficiaries of the petition, in practice if you identify them and document their identities and relationships to the petitioner (*i.e.*, name, birthdate, passport identification, and birth and/or marriage certificate), the National Visa Center will open visa cases for all family members upon receipt of the petition from USCIS. Also, unlike with the preceding field, a subsequent change from consular processing to adjustment of status should not entail a delay, as USCIS will simply recall the petition from the National Visa Center upon receipt of a Form I-485 adjustment application.

Y - *Deportation or removal proceedings.* Being in removal proceedings should not disqualify an investor from I-526 approval. It is possible for an I-526 investor—if otherwise eligible—to adjust status in immigration court.

Z - *Work in the United States without permission.* Having worked in the United States without permission does not disqualify an investor from I-526 approval. However, it may be considered in reviewing the lawfulness of the investor's source of funds, and it may affect the investor's eligibility for adjustment of status and/or admissibility.

ANALYZING AND DRAFTING FORM I-829, PETITION BY ENTREPRENEUR TO REMOVE CONDITIONS

The following is practical guidance to completing Form I-829, Petition by Entrepreneur to Remove Conditions, which is required of EB-5 conditional residents. The reproduced exemplar of Form I-829 (rev. 04/27/09), found at the end of this article, is annotated by letters (A-O), which are cross-referenced to comments in the accompanying text below. The comments are designed to alert the practitioner to legal issues implicated by each of the fields and/or sections on the form, excepting those that are self-explanatory.

Part 1. Information About You

A - *Criminal/arrest record.* This question relates to incidents occurring since the date of admission to permanent residence, and asks only about such incidents involving the person named in Part 1. Although not required by the regulation, the I-829 Form Instructions (Rev. 4/27/09) specify that supporting documentation should be submitted in relation to any such incident. Note that the petitioner and all dependents included on the I-829 petition who are over age 14 will also be fingerprinted in connection with a biometrics appointment, and criminal record checks are a standard part of I-829 petition processing. These issues may lead to reexamination of the lawfulness of the investor's source of capital, per 8 CFR §216.6(c)(2), in addition to removability.

Part 2. Basis for Petition

B - *Box "a"* should be checked where the investor is filing the I-829 petition on behalf of himself and any eligible dependents.

C - *Box "d"* should be checked in the case of a "stand-alone" I-829 for a derivative family member whose removal of conditions could not be processed in connection with the investor's I-829, *e.g.*, his or her conditional residence period differs from the principal's conditional resident period.

D - *Box "e"* should be checked where the investor is deceased, but the investment was sustained and resulted in the requisite job creation for removal of conditions purposes—eligibility per 8 CFR §216.6(a)(6).

Part 3. Information About Your Husband or Wife

E - Complete this section for the spouse of the person named in Part 1, even if the spouse will require a separate I-829 petition or if the person named in Part 1 is not the alien entrepreneur.

Part 4. Information About Your Children

F - Include all children of the person named in Part 1, regardless of whether they are over 21, married, or not yet eligible for removal of conditions.

G - *Living with you*. The response to this question does not affect eligibility for removal of conditions.

Part 5. Information About Your Commercial Enterprise

H - *"Creation of a new business."* This box should be checked if the basis for eligibility in the underlying I-526 was premised on 8 CFR §204.6(h)(1) (creation of enterprise after November 29, 1990).

I - *"Reorganization of an existing business."* This box should be checked if the basis for eligibility in the underlying I-526 petition was premised on 8 CFR §204.6(h)(2), and the I-526 petition included evidence of substantial reorganization or restructuring.

J - *"Capital investment in an existing business."* This box should be checked if the basis for eligibility in the underlying I-526 was premised on 8 CFR §204.6(h)(3), and the I-526 included evidence of 40 percent increase in net worth or number of employees.

K - *Kind of business*. This should be consistent with the parallel entry on the underlying I-526. See recent USCIS guidance if the business plan or investment structure have materially changed.

L - *Number of full-time employees in the enterprise*. While this question asks about number of employees in the enterprise, presumably this query is intended to confirm total number of employment positions created as a result of the investment. Therefore, the third field of this question should generally state a sufficient number, *e.g.*, "10+." Note that Form I-829 does not include a field for number of indirect jobs created, which relates to petitions based on an investment in a regional center-affiliated business. In this event, the number of direct and/or indirect jobs created should be indicated on the form, with a notation to refer to the economist report or similar supporting documentation.

M - *Subsequent investment in the enterprise*. This should include all of the I-526 petitioner's capital investment that post-dates the signing of the I-526 petition. "Type of investment" should specify the nature of the capital, consistent with the definition of "capital" in 8 CFR §204.6(e).

N - *Business changes*. Failure to "sustain" the investment and fulfill the objectives of the business plan underlying the I-526 can lead to denial of the I-829 petition. If changes to the business have materially altered the objectives of the business plan, see recent USCIS guidance regarding whether an amendment and a new I-526 petition may be required.

O - *Disposition of capital*. These questions are relevant to whether the petitioner has "sustained" the capital investment throughout the conditional residence period.

FORM I-526, IMMIGRANT PETITION BY ALIEN ENTREPRENEUR (ANNOTATED)

Department of Homeland Security
U.S. Citizenship and Immigration Services

OMB No. 1615-0026; Exp. 01/31/2012

I-526, Immigrant Petition by Alien Entrepreneur

Do Not Write in This Block - For USCIS Use Only (Except G-28 Block Below)

Classification

Action Block

Fee Receipt

Priority Date

To be completed by Attorney or Representative, if any
☐ G-28 is attached
Attorney's State License No. _____

Remarks:

START HERE - Type or print in black ink.

Part 1. Information About You

Family Name | Given Name | Middle Name

Address:
In care of
Number and Street | Apt. #
City | State or Province | Country | Zip/Postal Code
Date of Birth (mm/dd/yyyy) | Country of Birth | Social Security # (if any) | A # (if any)

If you are in the United States, provide the following information: Ⓐ
Date of Arrival (mm/dd/yyyy) | I-94 #
Current Nonimmigrant Status | Date Current Status Expires (mm/dd/yyyy) | Daytime Phone # with Area Code

Part 2. Application Type (Check one)

a. Ⓑ This petition is based on an investment in a commercial enterprise in a targeted employment area for which the required amount of capital invested has been adjusted downward.

b. Ⓒ This petition is based on an investment in a commercial enterprise in an area for which the required amount of capital invested has been adjusted upward.

c. Ⓓ This petition is based on an investment in a commercial enterprise that is not in either a targeted area or in an upward adjustment area.

Part 3. Information About Your Investment

Name of commercial enterprise in which funds are invested

Street Address Ⓔ

Phone # with Area Code | Business organized as (corporation, partnership, etc.)

Kind of business (e.g. furniture manufacturer) | Date established (mm/dd/yyyy) Ⓕ | IRS Tax # Ⓖ

RECEIVED: _____ RESUBMITTED: _____ RELOCATED: SENT _____ REC'D _____

Form I-526 (Rev. 01/06/10)Y

PRACTICAL GUIDANCE IN PREPARING I-526 AND I-829 PETITIONS

Part 3. Information About Your Investment *(Continued)*

Date of your initial investment (mm/dd/yyyy): [   ]

Amount of your initial investment $ [   ]

Your total capital investment in the enterprise to date $ [(H)   ]

Percentage of the enterprise you own [   ]

If you are not the sole investor in the new commercial enterprise, list on separate paper the names of all other parties (natural and non-natural) who hold a percentage share of ownership of the new enterprise and indicate whether any of these parties is seeking classification as an alien entrepreneur. Include the name, percentage of ownership, and whether or not the person is seeking classification under section 203(b)(5). **NOTE:** A "natural" party would be an individual person and a "non-natural" party would be an entity such as a corporation, consortium, investment group, partnership, etc. **(I)**

If you indicated in **Part 2** that the enterprise is in a targeted employment area or in an upward adjustment area, name the county and State: County [(J)] State [   ]

Part 4. Additional Information About the Enterprise

Type of Enterprise (check one):

(K) New commercial enterprise resulting from the creation of a new business.

(L) New commercial enterprise resulting from the purchase of an existing business.

(M) New commercial enterprise resulting from a capital investment in an existing business.

Composition of the Petitioner's Investment: (N)

Total amount in U.S. bank account .... $ [   ]

Total value of all assets purchased for use in the enterprise........................... $ [   ]

Total value of all property transferred from abroad to the new enterprise......... $ [   ]

Total of all debt financing... $ [   ]

Total stock purchases... $ [   ]

Other (explain on separate paper)... $ [   ]

Total $ [   ]

Income: (O)

When you made the investment.......... Gross $ [   ]   Net $ [   ]

Now.. Gross $ [   ]   Net $ [   ]

Net worth: (P)

When you made investment............... Gross $ [   ]   Now $ [   ]

Form I-526 (Rev. 01/06/10)Y Page 2

Part 5. Employment Creation Information

Number of full-time employees in the enterprise in U.S. (excluding you, your spouse, sons, and daughters)

When you made your initial investment? [ ] Now [ ] Difference [**Q**]

How many of these new jobs were created by your investment? [**R**] How many additional new jobs will be created by your additional investment? [**S**]

What is your position, office, or title with the new commercial enterprise?
[**T**]

Briefly describe your duties, activities, and responsibilities.
[**U**]

What is your salary? $ [**V**] What is the cost of your benefits? $ [ ]

Part 6. Processing Information

Check One:

[**W**] The person named in **Part 1** is now in the United States, and an application to adjust status to permanent resident will be filed if this petition is approved.

[**X**] If the petition is approved and the person named in **Part 1** wishes to apply for an immigrant visa abroad, complete the following for that person:

Country of nationality: [ ]

Country of current residence or, if now in the United States, last permanent residence abroad: [ ]

If you provided a United States address in **Part 1**, print the person's foreign address:
[ ]

If the person's native alphabet is other than Roman letters, write the foreign address in the native alphabet:
[ ]

Are you in deportation or removal proceedings? [**Y**] ☐ Yes (Explain on separate paper) ☐ No
Have you ever worked in the United States without permission? [**Z**] ☐ Yes (Explain on separate paper) ☐ No

Part 7. Signature *Read the information on penalties in the instructions before completing this section.*

I certify, under penalty of perjury under the laws of the United States of America, that this petition and the evidence submitted with it is all true and correct. I authorize the release of any information from my records that the U.S. Citizenship and Immigration Services needs to determine eligibility for the benefit I am seeking.

Signature [ ] Date [ ]

NOTE: *If you do not completely fill out this form or fail to the submit the required documents listed in the instructions, you may not be found eligible for the immigration benefit you are seeking and this petition may be denied.*

Part 8. Signature of Person Preparing Form, If Other Than Above (Sign below)

I declare that I prepared this application at the request of the above person, and it is based on all information of which I have knowledge.

Signature [ ] Print Your Name [ ] Date [ ]

Firm Name [ ] Daytime phone # with area code [ ]

Address [ ]

Form I-526 (Rev. 01/06/10)Y Page 3

FORM I-829, PETITION BY ENTREPRENEUR TO REMOVE CONDITIONS (ANNOTATED)

Department of Homeland Security
U.S. Citizenship and Immigration Services

OMB No. 1615-0045; Expires 04/30/2011
I-829, Petition by Entrepreneur to Remove Conditions

Do not write in this block - For USCIS use only (Except G-28 Block Below)		
☐ Applicant Interviewed	Action Block	Fee Receipt
		To be completed by Attorney or Representative, if any ☐ G-28 is attached Attorney's State License No. _____

Remarks:

START HERE - Type or print in black ink.

Part 1. Information About You

A # (if any) [   ]   Form I-526 Receipt Number [   ]

Family Name [   ]   Given Name [   ]   Middle Name [   ]

Address:
In care of [   ]
Number and Street [   ] Apt. # [   ]
City [   ]   State or Province [   ]
Country [   ]   Zip/Postal Code [   ]   Daytime Phone # [   ]
Date of Birth (mm/dd/yyyy) [   ]   Country of Birth [   ]   U.S. Social Security # (if any) [   ]

Since becoming a conditional permanent resident, have you ever been arrested, cited, charged, indicted, convicted, fined, or imprisoned for breaking or violating any law or ordinance (excluding traffic regulations), or committed any crime for which you were not arrested?
☐ Yes   ☐ No   (If yes, explain on separate sheet(s) of paper, including disposition, if any.) **(A)**

Part 2. Basis for Petition *(Check one)*

(B) a. ☐ My conditional permanent residence is based on an investment in a commercial enterprise.
b. ☐ Reserved.
c. ☐ Reserved.
(C) d. ☐ I am a conditional permanent resident spouse or child of an entrepreneur, and I am unable to be included in a Petition by Entrepreneur to Remove Conditions (Form I-829) filed by my conditional resident spouse or parent.
(D) e. ☐ I am a conditional permanent resident spouse or child of an entrepreneur who is deceased.

Part 3. Information About Your Husband or Wife **(E)**

Family Name [   ]   Given Name [   ]   Middle Name [   ]

Gender ☐ Male ☐ Female   Date of Birth (mm/dd/yyyy) [   ]   Date of Marriage (mm/dd/yyyy) [   ]

Other names used (including maiden name or aliases) [   ]

A# (If any) [   ]   Current Immigration Status [   ]   Is your current immigration status based on the petitioner's current status? ☐ Yes ☐ No

RECEIVED: _____   RESUBMITTED: _____   RELOCATED: SENT _____   REC'D _____

Form I-829 (Rev. 04/27/09)Y

Part 4. Children *(List all your children. Attach another sheet(s) of paper, if necessary.)* **(F)**

Family Name		Given Name		Middle Name	
A# (if any)		Current Immigration Status		Date of Birth (mm/dd/yyyy)	Living with you? ☐ Yes ☐ No **(G)**

Family Name		Given Name		Middle Name	
A# (if any)		Current Immigration Status		Date of Birth (mm/dd/yyyy)	Living with you? ☐ Yes ☐ No

Family Name		Given Name		Middle Name	
A# (if any)		Current Immigration Status		Date of Birth (mm/dd/yyyy)	Living with you? ☐ Yes ☐ No

Family Name		Given Name		Middle Name	
A# (if any)		Current Immigration Status		Date of Birth (mm/dd/yyyy)	Living with you? ☐ Yes ☐ No

Family Name		Given Name		Middle Name	
A# (if any)		Current Immigration Status		Date of Birth (mm/dd/yyyy)	Living with you? ☐ Yes ☐ No

Family Name		Given Name		Middle Name	
A# (if any)		Current Immigration Status		Date of Birth (mm/dd/yyyy)	Living with you? ☐ Yes ☐ No

Part 5. Information About Your Commercial Enterprise

Type of Enterprise *(Check one)*:

(H) ☐ New commercial enterprise resulting from the creation of a new business.

(I) ☐ New commercial enterprise resulting from the reorganization of an existing business.

(J) ☐ New commercial enterprise resulting from a capital investment in an existing business.

Kind of Business *(Be as specific as possible)*: **(K)**

Date Business Established *(mm/dd/yyyy)*

Amount of Initial Investment

Date of Initial Investment *(mm/dd/yyyy)*

% of Enterprise You Own

Number of full-time employees in enterprise in United States (excluding you, your spouse, sons, and daughters):

(L) At the time of your initial investment: ____ Presently: ____ Difference: ____

How many of these new jobs were created by your investment?

Form I-829 (Rev. 04/27/09)Y Page 2

Part 5. Information About Your Commercial Enterprise (continued)

Subsequent Investment in the Enterprise:

Date of Investment	Amount of Investment	Type of Investment

Provide the gross and net incomes generated annually by the commercial enterprise since your initial investment. Include all income generated up to date during the present year.

Year	Gross Income	Net Income

Has your commercial enterprise filed for bankruptcy, ceased business operations, or have any changes in its business organization or ownership occurred since the date of your initial investment? ☐ Yes (Explain on separate sheet) ☐ No

Has your commercial enterprise sold any corporate assets, shares, property, or had any capital withdrawn since the date of your initial investment? ☐ Yes (Explain on separate sheet) ☐ No

Part 6. Signature (Read the information on penalties in the instructions before completing this section.)

I certify, under penalty of perjury under the laws of the United States of America, that this petition and the evidence submitted with it is all true and correct. I further certify that the investment was made in accordance with the laws of the United States and was not for the purpose of evading United States immigration laws. I also authorize the release of any information from my records that the U.S. Citizenship and Immigration Services needs to determine eligibility for the benefit being sought.

Signature of Applicant	Print Name	Date

NOTE: If you do not completely fill out this form or fail to submit any required documents listed in the instructions, you may not be found eligible for the requested benefit and this petition may be denied.

Part 7. Signature of Person Preparing Form, If Other Than Above

I declare that I prepared this petition at the request of the above person and it is based on all information of which I have knowledge.

Signature	Print Name	Date

Firm Name and Address (Include Telephone Number with Area Code and E-Mail Address.)

READING THE TEA LEAVES: EXPLORING THE "TARGETED EMPLOYMENT AREA" RULES OF THE EB-5 INVESTOR VISA PROGRAM

by David M. Morris, Esq.[*]

Under the EB-5 Immigrant Investor Visa program regulations, a foreign entrepreneur who invests a minimum of $1 million into a new commercial enterprise has no geographical restrictions on the location of the investment. In other words, that entrepreneur could seek immigrant visa classification for an investment located in America's richest neighborhoods such as Beverly Hills, West Palm Beach, or Old Greenwich.

But if the foreign entrepreneur is prepared to invest only $500,000 of capital, the new commercial enterprise must be located within a specially defined geographical area—called a "Targeted Employment Area" (TEA).[1] The same rule applies to EB-5 Regional Center programs. An entrepreneur may claim the $500,000 reduced investment threshold if the Regional Center activities benefit companies operating principally within a TEA.[2]

U.S. Citizenship and Immigration Services (USCIS) reported recently that approximately 90 percent of all EB-5 Immigrant Investor Visa petitions filed in FY2009 involved entrepreneurs participating in Regional Center programs.[3] In the absence of official statistics, an informal survey reveals most all Regional Centers claim they operate within TEAs and claim eligibility for the $500,000 reduced investment threshold.

Despite its prominent role in the expanding EB-5 program, the TEA provision is criticized as being unduly restrictive, confusing, and unreliable. This article examines the current rules defining the TEA provision and several emerging issues that may impact future USCIS policy.

BACKGROUND ON THE EB-5

Congress established the fifth employment-based (EB-5) preference category in 1990 for immigrants seeking to enter the United States to invest in a new commercial enterprise that will benefit the U.S. economy and directly create at least 10 full-time jobs for U.S. workers.[4]

The minimum amount of capital an entrepreneur is required to invest is $1 million.[5] That investment threshold is reduced to $500,000 if the new commercial enterprise is located in a "targeted employment area."[6] When an entrepreneur's investment is coordinated through a regional center, the new commercial enterprise must "benefit companies located in targeted employment areas" to claim the reduced $500,000 investment amount.[7]

For EB-5 program purposes, a "targeted employment area" is either a "rural area" or a "high unemployment area."[8] Over the years, the Service has issued a number of policy guidelines interpreting these two TEA options. Understanding and applying these rules are critical to petition success.

OPTION #1—MEETING THE "RURAL AREA" TEA TEST

The regulations allow for a reduced investment of $500,000 if the new commercial enterprise has

---

[*] **David M. Morris** is an American Immigration Lawyers Association (AILA) member practicing business-based immigration law for 18 years, and currently the Managing Member at Visa Law Group PLLC, a boutique immigration law firm in Washington, D.C. He founded and co-manages the EB-5 Sugarbush project in the State of Vermont Regional Center and he established the EB-5 America—Washington, D.C. Regional Center. He has been a regularly invited speaker on EB-5 investor visa law topics, including national conferences sponsored by AILA and Immigration Law Weekly (ILW). His recent article on proposed legislative improvements to the current Targeted Employment Area (TEA) provisions of the EB-5 program appeared in 14 *Bender's Immigr. Bull.* 1290 (Oct. 15, 2009). Morris@VisaLawGroup.com.

[1] INA §203(b)(5)(B), 8 USC §1153(b)(5)(B).

[2] *Matter of Izummi*, 22 I&N Dec. 169, 19 *Immigr. Rep.* B2-32 (Assoc. Comm'r, Examinations 1998).

[3] Statement of Alexandra Haskell, U.S. Citizenship and Immigration Services (USCIS) Senior Adjudications Officer, USCIS EB-5 Program Stakeholders Meeting at the USCIS California Service Center (Mar. 16, 2010).

[4] INA §203(b)(5), 8 USC §1153(b)(5).

[5] INA §203(b)(5)(C)(ii), 8 USC §1153(b)(5)(C)(ii).

[6] *Id.* See also 8 CFR §204.6(f).

[7] *Matter of Izummi*, 22 I&N Dec. 169, 172–73.

[8] INA §203(b)(5)(B)(ii), 8 USC §1153(b)(5)(B)(ii).

created or will create employment in a qualified "rural area." In general, this is the easier TEA option to understand and document—as compared to the "high unemployment area" alternative.

Webster's Dictionary defines a "rural area" as "of or relating to the country, country people or life, or agriculture."[9] However, USCIS takes a much more restrictive and empirical view with respect to the EB-5 program. To show a targeted employment area in a "rural area" for EB-5 program purposes, the regulations provide that the petition must be accompanied by:

> evidence that the new commercial enterprise is principally doing business within a civil jurisdiction not located within any standard metropolitan statistical area as designated by the Office of Management and Budget, or within any city or town having a population of 20,000 or more as based on the most recent decennial census of the United States;[10]

At first blush, the plain language of the regulation appears to provide two alternatives to meeting the definition of "rural area." However, USCIS has correctly interpreted the provision to require that the entrepreneur prove the investment target is:

(1) Not located within any standard metropolitan statistical area, *AND ALSO*

(2) Not located within any city or town having a population of 20,000 or more as based on the most recent decennial census of the United States.

Failing to provide evidence satisfying both of these tests precludes "rural area" TEA designation and thereby requires a minimum $1 million investment by the entrepreneur. These two prongs are further analyzed below.

Located Within a Metropolitan Statistical Area (MSA)?

Metropolitan statistical areas (MSAs) are geographic entities defined by the U.S. Office of Management and Budget (OMB) for use by Federal agencies in collecting, tabulating, and publishing federal statistics.[11]

An MSA contains a core urban area of 50,000 or more population, and consists of one or more counties and includes the counties containing the core urban area, as well as any adjacent counties that have a high degree of social and economic integration (as measured by commuting to work) with the urban core.

These MSAs are seemingly omnipresent. According to a U.S. General Accountability Office (GAO) report issued in 2004, approximately 83 percent of the American population lives within metropolitan statistical areas.[12] There are currently 1,090 counties in the United States that fall within existing MSAs.[13] And many states are entirely consumed by MSAs.[14]

For example, the entire state of Maryland falls within the Washington-Baltimore-Virginia MSA, except for five remote counties. The entire state of Massachusetts, but for the Island of Nantucket, is covered by the Boston-Worcester-Manchester MSA. The geographies of Rhode Island and New Jersey are covered by their respective MSAs. In California, the entire state is covered by several MSAs, but for 20 remote counties.[15]

For EB-5 program purposes, the simplest way for an entrepreneur to determine if a new commercial enterprise is located within an MSA is to search the U.S. Census Bureau's website.[16] Several online research tools are available. For example, the agency provides "static" page-size state maps depicting state and county boundaries as well as any MSA zones defined by the OMB. Maps are provided for each of the 50 states, the District of Columbia, and Puerto Rico. Additionally, the agency provides "dynamic" mapping such as the Tiger Map Service.[17] This free service allows users to input an address to generate a customized map containing geographic entities including MSA lines.

---

[9] www.merriam-webster.com/dictionary/rural.

[10] 8 CFR §204.6(j)(6)(i).

[11] www.census.gov/population/www/metroareas/metrodef.html.

[12] Government Accountability Office (GAO) Report to Congressional Committees, "Immigrant Investors: Small Number of Participants Attributed to Pending Regulations and Other Factors," GAO-05-256 (Apr. 2005), *published on* AILA InfoNet at Doc. No. 05040475 (*posted* Apr. 4, 2005) (GAO Report), at 3. Highlights of the GAO Report are reproduced in Appendix E.

[13] *Id.*

[14] www.census.gov/geo/www/maps/stcbsa_pg/stBased_2004 11_nov.htm.

[15] http://ftp2.census.gov/geo/maps/metroarea/stcbsa_pg/Nov 2004/cbsa2004_CA.pdf.

[16] www.census.gov/geo/www/maps/stcbsa_pg/stBased_2004 11_nov.htm.

[17] http://tiger.census.gov.

It is important to recognize that, according to USCIS, "8 CFR 204.6(i) does not provide states with the authority to make TEA designations regarding whether a certain area qualifies as rural."[18] The authority to designate a TEA under this regulation is limited to determinations of high unemployment.

So step one of the "rural area" test requires the entrepreneur to determine if the new commercial enterprise is located within an MSA. If the answer is yes, the project fails the "rural" component of the test. If the project is located outside any MSA, then the entrepreneur must proceed to the "population" prong of the test.

Located Within a City or Town with a Population Exceeding 20,000?

If a new commercial enterprise is not located within an MSA, the entrepreneur should demonstrate that the job-creating entity is not located within any city or town having a population of 20,000 or more, based on the most recent decennial census of the United States.

For this test, USCIS expects evidence from the U.S. Census Bureau. Perhaps the best resource to determine a city or town population is the American Fact Finder section of the Census Bureau's website. This interactive application supports the Economic Census, the American Community Survey, the 1990 Census, Census 2000, and the latest Population Estimates.

In particular, the "Population Finder"[19] search engine permits the entrepreneur to input a specific street address and then receive a detailed population report based upon the Census 2000 data. That report may be submitted as part of the Form I-526 petition to demonstrate that a new commercial enterprise is not "located within any city or town having a population of 20,000 or more as based on the most recent decennial census of the United States."[20]

Thus, to satisfy the "rural area" TEA definition, USCIS must receive two sets of records: (1) evidence that the project is not located within any MSA; and (2) evidence that the project is not within any city or town having a population of 20,000 or more as based on the most recent decennial census of the United States. It is strongly recommended that all evidence come from the OMB and the Census Bureau; records from state and local governments may not be accepted by USCIS, given the availability of federal statistics. Only if both prongs of the test are satisfied may the entrepreneur claim the reduced investment threshold of $500,000. Failing to prove both of the prongs, an entrepreneur must invest a minimum of $1 million.

Emerging Issues for the "Rural Area" TEA Option

While providing greater stability and predictability then the dynamic "high unemployment area" option, the "rural area" definition is no panacea; it has many shortcomings and is the subject of significant criticism. Two examples include:

- **Changes to MSA Boundaries Because of the 2010 Census.** Shifting populations occurring in states, counties, and cities over the past 10 years will be quantified by the 2010 Census, resulting in redrawn MSA boundaries. These forthcoming changes may disqualify some EB-5 projects currently meeting the "rural area" classification because they will be reclassified inside newly defined MSAs. This is especially important because on December 11, 2009, USCIS updated the *Adjudicators Field Manual* (AFM) to require the petitioner to prove that the new commercial enterprise is located in a TEA as of the date he files his Form I-526 petition or when the investment was made. As USCIS notes, "the fact that a business may be located in an area that was once rural, for example, does not mean that the area is still rural."[21] The OMB defines metropolitan statistical areas according to published standards that are applied to Census Bureau data. Since the 1950 census, changes in the definitions of MSAs have consisted chiefly of:

---

[18] "USCIS Q&A from Stakeholder Session with AILA EB-5 Committee and Invest in the USA" (Dec. 14, 2009), *published on* AILA InfoNet at Doc. No. 10010462 (*posted* Jan. 4, 2010), and reproduced at Appendix H.

[19] http://factfinder.census.gov/servlet/SAFFPopulation?_submenuId=population_0&_sse=on.

[20] *See supra* note 10.

[21] USCIS Memorandum, D. Neufeld, "Adjudication of EB-5 Regional Center Proposals and Affiliated Form I-526 and Form I-829 Petitions; *Adjudicators Field Manual* (AFM) update to chapters 22.4 and 25.2 (AD09-38)" (Dec. 11, 2009), *published on* AILA InfoNet at Doc. No. 09121561 (*posted* Dec. 15, 2009). *See also Matter of Soffici*, 22 I&N Dec. 158, 159 (Assoc. Comm'r, Examinations 1998). Both the Neufeld Memo and *Soffici* are reproduced in the Appendix materials to this volume.

- The recognition of new areas as they reached the minimum required city or urbanized area population; and
- The addition of counties to existing areas as new decennial census data showed them to qualify.

In some instances, formerly separate areas have been merged, components of an area have been transferred from one area to another, or components have been dropped from an area. The large majority of changes have taken place on the basis of decennial census data.

In 2004, the GAO conducted a study of the OMB changes to the MSA standards that occurred for the 2000 Census. The GAO reported that the number of counties within MSAs increased by 243 to 1,090.[22] In other words, the United States experienced a change of nearly 20 percent in the number of counties that were added to MSAs after the last decennial census.

For EB-5 program purposes, entrepreneurs must consider the possible impact of redrawn MSAs resulting from the 2010 Census. The issue, perhaps more for Regional Center programs seeking to enroll investors in projects that span months or years, is whether their new commercial enterprise will move into or out of a redrawn MSA? This seems almost certain to occur in some measure and may impact entrepreneurs seeking "rural area" designation in those areas.

According to USCIS, "each alien must establish that his or her capital investment qualifies for the reduced investment threshold, and cannot reply on previous TEA determinations made based upon facts that have subsequently changed."[23] Changes to MSA boundaries may result in some investment project losing "rural" status requiring entrepreneurs document an investment of the full $1 million.

- **MSAs Cover Approximately 83 Percent of the U.S. Population**

The omnipresence of MSAs has frustrated many an entrepreneur and Regional Center operator who fail the "rural area" TEA test despite a sincere belief that their new commercial enterprise is located in a traditionally recognized rural area. For example, at least one ski resort in Vermont falls within the Burlington MSA, yet the resort is located in a region most would reasonably agree is very rural. Similarly, many West Virginians are surprised to learn that despite a minimum two-hour commute to Washington D.C., parts of the "Wild and Wonderful" state fall within the D.C. MSA.

Legislators are responding to this criticism by introducing bills that would eliminate MSA testing from the "rural area" definition. In particular, Congressman Jared Polis (D-CO) announced in December 2009 his initiative, H.R. 4259[24] (the Employment Benefit Act of 2009), to expand the TEA provision in several ways—including the elimination of any MSA testing from to the "rural area" definition.

OPTION #2—MEETING THE "HIGH UNEMPLOYMENT" TEA TEST

As an alternative to the "rural area" option, the TEA definition also allows an entrepreneur to qualify for the reduced $500,000 investment if the new commercial enterprise is located within a "high unemployment area." To qualify, the regulations provide that the petition must be accompanied by:

(A) Evidence that the metropolitan statistical area, the specific county within a metropolitan statistical area, or the county in which a city or town with a population of 20,000 or more is located, in which the new commercial enterprise is principally doing business has experienced an average unemployment rate of 150 percent of the national average rate;[25] or

(B) A letter from an authorized body of the government of the state in which the new commercial enterprise is located which certifies that the geographic or political subdivision of the metropolitan statistical area or of the city or town with a population of 20,000 or more in which the enterprise is principally doing business has been designated a high unemployment area. The letter must meet the requirements of 8 CFR §204.6(i).[26]

Unlike the rigid "rural area" option, the "high unemployment area" definition affords an entrepre-

---

[22] GAO Report, *supra* note 12, at 3.

[23] Neufeld Memo, *supra* note 21, at 17.

[24] http://thomas.loc.gov/cgi-bin/query/z?c111:H.R.4259.

[25] 8 CFR §204.6(j)(6)(ii)(A).

[26] 8 CFR §204.6(j)(6)(ii)(B).

neur some evidentiary flexibility in meeting the requirements. Not surprisingly, conflict has resulted between entrepreneurs seeking to "exploit" the flexibility and USCIS seeking to "uphold congressional intent."[27]

Federal Government Evidence of "High Unemployment Areas"

The first opportunity to demonstrate a "high unemployment area" relies upon evidence gathered from the federal government—more specifically the Bureau of Labor Statistics (BLS).

A unit of the U.S. Department of Labor, the BLS is the principal fact-finding agency for the U.S. government in the broad field of labor economics and statistics. The BLS is an agency that collects, processes, analyzes, and disseminates essential statistical data to the American public, the U.S. Congress, other federal agencies, state and local governments, business, and labor representatives.[28]

A number of BLS programs provide information about joblessness, two of which are directly related to collecting and calculating "high unemployment area" data for the EB-5 program. This process can be broken into two steps.

Step 1. Establish the 150-Percent Rate

The BLS publishes the National Unemployment Rate Report[29] as part of the Current Population Survey. Available on the agency's website, this monthly report provides comprehensive information on the employment and unemployment of the American population. For EB-5 program purposes, this report establishes the "national average" unemployment rate as defined in 8 CFR §204.6(j)(6)(ii)(A).

According to this regulation, an entrepreneur is required to take 150 percent of the national average rate (presumably reported by BLS[30]) to yield the "high unemployment area" rate defined by the TEA rules[31]. For example, BLS currently reports an average national unemployment rate of 5.8 percent for 2008. Taking 150 percent of that figure yields a TEA rate of 8.7 percent. That means an entrepreneur's new commercial enterprise must be located within a defined geographical area with an unemployment rate of at least 8.7 percent to meet the "high unemployment area" TEA test.

Step 2. Establish Local Rate from LAUS Reports

Having used the BLS national average data to determine the 150-percent rate, the entrepreneur should next look to a separate BLS report to obtain "local" unemployment statistics for the area specifically covering the new commercial enterprise. This BLS report, generated by the agency's Local Area Unemployment Statistics (LAUS) program,[32] is a federal-state cooperative effort in which monthly estimates of total employment and unemployment are prepared for approximately 7,300 areas, including:

- State Metropolitan Statistical Areas
- Small Labor Market Areas
- Counties and county equivalents
- Cities of 25,000 population or more

The LAUS estimates are key indicators of local economic conditions. The BLS is responsible for the concepts, definitions, technical procedures, validation, and publication of the estimates that State employment security agencies prepare under agreement with BLS.[33]

For EB-5 purposes, an entrepreneur should access the LAUS program and select the map or table that provides unemployment statistics for the geographic location of the new commercial enterprise. For example, if the target investment will be located in downtown Washington, D.C., the LAUS 2008 report reveals the city had a Labor Force of 334,143 and Employed of 312,155, yielding a reported Unemployment Rate of 6.6 percent.

Since the national average unemployment rate report by BLS for 2008 is 5.8 percent, the 150-percent rate calculation yields a benchmark rate of 8.7 percent. Because the LAUS program reports a local unemployment rate of only 6.6 percent, the entrepreneur cannot claim that the entire geography of Washington, D.C. meets the "high unemployment area" definition. Accordingly, an entrepreneur would be required to make a minimum investment of $1 million.

Because publicly available LAUS reports cover only very large geographical areas (states, counties, MSAs, and large cities) the aggregate unemploy-

---

[27] USCIS Q&A from Stakeholder Session, *supra* note 18, at 7.

[28] www.bls.gov/bls/blsmissn.htm; see generally: www.bls.gov.

[29] www.bls.gov/cps/.

[30] USCIS specifically cites to this Bureau of Labor Statistics (BLS) report but does not state it is the exclusive authority. *See,* Neufeld Memo, *supra* note 21, at 18.

[31] 8 CFR §204.6(j)(6)(ii)(A).

[32] www.bls.gov/lau/lauov.htm.

[33] *Id.*

ment data for the region mutes the high unemployment rates of small neighborhoods. Thus, these generalized LAUS reports published by BLS tend to be less helpful to entrepreneurs seeking to satisfy the "high unemployment area" definition.

But even if the publicly available LAUS reports fail to satisfy the "high unemployment" definition, the entrepreneur may still qualify under the "State Designation" test.

State Designation of "High Unemployment Area"

As an alternative to the public LAUS unemployment reports, which cover very large geographies, the EB-5 regulations allow an entrepreneur the flexibility to narrow the reporting to smaller geographical areas or political subdivisions encompassing the new commercial enterprise. For example, an entrepreneur could elect to shrink the unemployment survey down to the geography of a single town, neighborhood, or census tract.[34]

But because distinct unemployment data is not readily available to the general public from the BLS for these smaller geographies, an entrepreneur must obtain a special "high unemployment" certification letter from a qualified state government agency.[35] The regulation defines the procedures a state government must follow to issue a qualified designation letter, as follows:

> *State designation of a high unemployment area.* The state government of any state of the United States may designate a particular geographic or political subdivision located within a metropolitan statistical area or within a city or town having a population of 20,000 or more within such state as an area of high unemployment (at least 150 percent of the national average rate). Evidence of such designation, including a description of the boundaries of the geographic or political subdivision and the method or methods by which the unemployment statistics were obtained, may be provided to a prospective alien entrepreneur for submission with Form 1-526.

Before any such designation is made, an official of the state must notify the Associate Commissioner for Examinations of the agency, board, or other appropriate governmental body of the state which shall be delegated the authority to certify that the geographic or political subdivision is a high unemployment area.[36]

A USCIS memorandum updating the AFM further interprets the procedures established in 8 CFR §204.6(j).[37] At first blush, this memo appears to cede "high unemployment area" designation authority to each state government, thereby creating a "safe harbor" for an entrepreneur who receives a state certification letter. Specifically, the memorandum provides:

> The designation of high unemployment areas are within the purview of each U.S. state governor, or if applicable, his or her designee. *USCIS personnel have no substantive authority to question or challenge such high unemployment designations*, and therefore must rely on the high unemployment designations that conform to the requirements outlined above that are made by a U.S. state governor or his or her designee. (Emphasis added)[38]

But in the same paragraph, the agency affirms its retained authority to reject a state's bona fide certification letter. For example, USCIS can deny a state's designation if the letter "utilizes statistics that do not reflect the national and local unemployment rates at the time of the alien investor's capital investment."[39] Likewise, USCIS can reject a state's designation as failing to identify the "methods by which the unemployment statistics were obtained."[40]

USCIS also says it can reject the state's prerogative to identify and assemble selected political subdivisions or census tracts establishing a contiguous geographical area when it believes "gerrymandering" has occurred. In particular, USCIS writes:

> While state governments clearly have the authority to make TEA designations, state governments do not have the authority to designate areas as high unemployment that do not in reality qualify as a targeted area under INA §203(b)(5)(B).

---

[34] 8 CFR §204.6(i). (USCIS has accepted a census tract as meeting "a particular geographic or political subdivision" as defined in the regulation).

[35] Several states have websites that can help determine whether a particular area in the state qualifies as a "targeted employment area" for EB-5 purposes. *See, e.g.*, website for State of California—Business, Transportation, and Housing Agency which contains their "Qualifying High Unemployment Census Tracts" Report (2008) (last visited Apr. 7, 2010).

[36] 8 CFR §204.6(i).

[37] *See*, Neufeld Memo, *supra* note 21, at 16–19.

[38] *Id.* at 19.

[39] *Id.*

[40] *Id.*

It appears that this question solicits confirmation from USCIS that state-sanctioned attempts to "gerrymander" a finding of high unemployment that is not in accordance with the statutory requirement, through cobbling together various portions of political subdivisions so that an investment in a commercial enterprise in a location that is not a high unemployment area would ultimately qualify as one, is an acceptable business practice for EB-5 purposes. On its face, this supposition blatantly frustrates the congressional intent behind INA §203(b)(5)(B). As such, USCIS cannot confirm that this is an acceptable business practice for states to use in making TEA designations.[41]

USCIS's claim to hold veto authority over bona fide state-issued designation letters is unsupported by the regulations. Moreover, rejecting a designation letter sends an unmistakably clear message to the state that its work is untrustworthy and its methods unreliable. And here is the ironic part. While reserving the right to second guess and reject a state's reported unemployment data and methodologies, USCIS has never provided the states with any rules identifying acceptable standards. As a result, states and entrepreneurs are left to speculate on the agency's adjudication standards—which assumes they exist.

In many ways, this dilemma is very familiar to the EB-5 program. For many years, the Service failed to provide entrepreneurs with acceptable methodologies and standards for claiming indirect job creation. Only by de facto adjudications, rather than published policy, have entrepreneurs been assured that the Service will accept REDYN, RIMS II or IMPLAN economic models.

At a minimum, USCIS should immediately issue guidance that approves any state designation letter that utilizes certain BLS-established unemployment reporting methodologies. For example, the BLS has long relied upon both the "Population Claims Method" and the "Census Share Method" to determine unemployment statistics for small geographical areas not part of the published LAUS reports. With procedures on both already defined in the "BLS Handbook of Methods,"[42] many state and local governments already rely on these programs to disseminate unemployment data. The Service should always accept a state designation letter that relies upon these proven methods and should publish this policy to eliminate confusion.

Emerging Issues for the "High Unemployment Areas"

While providing greater evidentiary flexibility then the static "rural area" option, the "high unemployment area" definition is burdened with unresolved adjudication issues that create inherent unreliability for entrepreneurs. Some emerging issues include the following:

- USCIS has declined to establish a formal policy that recognizes a state designation letter as automatically valid for a certain, period—for example, 12 months. The best immigration analogy would be the Department of Labor recognizing the validity period of state-issued prevailing wage determinations for a period of 12 months in the context of the H-1B visa and PERM programs. By USCIS failing to recognize a predetermined validity period for state designation letters, entrepreneurs are unable to determine if a state letter meets the "most recently available public data" standard.

- Under what circumstances will USCIS refuse to accept the state's prerogative to identify and assemble selected political subdivisions or census tracts establishing a contiguous geographical area?

- State, county, and local government agencies share overlapping management responsibilities on issues of unemployment and population. So, which agencies have USCIS authority to issue TEA certification letters? May more than one agency be designated by a governor to issue designation letters?

- USCIS has declined to establish a formal policy that "grandfathers" a regional center project as located within a TEA for the duration of the project. Rather, USCIS policy places the burden on the entrepreneur filing the I-526 petition to prove that the new commercial enterprise is located within a TEA *at the time the petition is filed*. For an ongoing project operating within the regional center context, that had qualified as a TEA and enrolled $500,000 investors, it is not difficult to imagine a change in the MSA boundaries, an increase in the population over 20,000, or an improvement in the local unemployment rate below 150 percent of the national average rate for the area covering the new commercial enterprise. Under current USCIS policy, all subsequent en-

---

[41] USCIS Q&A from Stakeholder Session, *supra* note 18, at 7.

[42] *www.bls.gov/opub/hom/*.

trepreneurs would be required to invest a full $1 million.

CONCLUSION

For many foreign entrepreneurs, the EB-5 program provides a viable path to permanent residence but only as long as the minimum investment threshold is $500,000. The key to qualifying for that reduced investment amount is the viability and reliability of the "targeted employment area" provision of the law. And to be sure, the "rural area" and "high unemployment area" alternatives have been relied upon by many entrepreneurs and regional center operators over the past several years. However, current adjudication policies for both options are inadequate or ill conceived to meet the stakeholder's reasonable demands for reliability and clarity.

THE MEANING OF "AT RISK" IN EB-5 INVESTMENT

by Carolyn S. Lee[*]

As recent U.S. Citizenship and Immigration Services (USCIS) requests for evidence and surveyed Administrative Appeals Office (AAO) decisions show, there is confusion both within USCIS and the immigration bar concerning the meaning of the "at risk" requirement in the employment-based fifth preference visa (EB-5) context. This article seeks to provide clarifying guidance on the proper construction of this evidentiary requirement.

"AT RISK" ELEMENT: SOURCES AND MEANING.

The requirement that an EB-5 investor's capital be "at risk" is found in the EB-5 regulations' description of evidence required to prove "investment." These regulations state:

> To show that the petitioner has invested or is actively in the process of investing the required amount of capital, the petition must be accompanied by evidence that the petition has placed the required amount of capital at risk for purposes of generating a return on the capital placed at risk. Evidence of mere intent to invest or of prospective investment arrangements entailing no present commitment will not suffice to show that the petitioner is actively in the process of investing. The alien must show actual commitment of the required amount of capital.[1]

The first sentence of the above regulations relates directly to the "at risk" element. The second and third sentences relate to the "actual commitment" of the funds—an issue that arises most often in situations where the investor has yet to fully invest the required amount of capital at the time of filing the petition.

There is no independent statutory reference to capital being placed "at risk." The regulations themselves derive from the statutory requirement that the alien investor have "invested . . . or [be] actively in the process of investing, capital in the amount not less than the amount specified."[2]

When Congress created the EB-5 immigrant category in 1990, it intended that the investor have a personal stake in the success of the enterprise receiving the EB-5 capital.[3] Congress specifically required investors to commit equity rather than debt into the new commercial enterprise, but did not limit the form of investment in any other way.

The preamble to the final EB-5 regulations[4] points to the Department of State requirements for E-2 nonimmigrant treaty investors as the model for the "at risk" evidentiary requirement.[5] The preamble states: "As with that program, the concept of investment here connotes the placing of funds or other capital assets at risk for the purpose of generating a return on the funds placed at risk." Accordingly, the EB-5 regulations mirror the E-2 regulations' investment requirement, which state:

> An alien is classifiable as a nonimmigrant treaty investor (E-2) if the consular officer is satisfied that the alien qualifies under the provisions of INA 101(a)(15)(E)(ii) and that the alien:
>
> (1) Has invested or is actively in the process of investing a substantial amount of capital in bona fide enterprise in the United States . . . .[6]

The E-2 regulations lucidly explain the meaning of "investment" in the E-2 context:

> Investment means the treaty investor's placing of capital, including funds and other assets, *at risk in the commercial sense* with the objective of generating a profit. The treaty investor must be in pos-

---

[*] **Carolyn S. Lee** is a partner at Miller Mayer LLP in Ithaca, NY. Her email is csl@millermayer.com.

[1] 8 CFR §204.6(j)(2).

[2] INA §203(b)(5)(A)(ii), 8 USC §1153(b)(5)(A)(ii).

[3] Letter from U.S. Senate, Committee on the Judiciary, Subcommittee on Immigration and Refugee Affairs, to Gene McNary, Comm'r, legacy Immigration and Naturalization Service (INS) (Aug. 2, 1991), commenting on the proposed EB-5 regulations ("We agree with the thrust of the proposed regulations that the alien must have a personal stake in the long range success of the enterprise and be willing to suffer a loss if the business fails. We do not believe that the investor should qualify merely by loaning money to the new enterprise, nor do we believe that the investment should be raised by securing a loan against the assets of the U.S. company. In short, we expect the investor to put his money at risk.").

[4] 56 Fed. Reg. 60897 (Nov. 29, 1991).

[5] *Id.* at 60905.

[6] 22 CFR §41.51(b)(1).

session of and have control over the capital invested or being invested. The capital must be subject to partial or total loss if investment fortunes reverse. Such investment capital must be the investor's unsecured personal business capital or capital secured by personal assets. Capital in the process of being invested or that has been invested must be irrevocably committed to the enterprise. The alien has the burden of establishing such irrevocable commitment given to the particular circumstances of each case. The alien may use any legal mechanism available, such as by placing invested funds in escrow pending visa issuance, that would not only irrevocably commit funds to the enterprise but that might also extend some personal liability protection to the treaty investor.[7]

This E-2 regulation is essential in understanding the proper meaning of the "at risk" element in the EB-5 regulation, notwithstanding the interpretations of the Service Centers and the AAO:

- *First*, for the capital invested to be "at risk," the objective must be to generate profit. Not-for-profit enterprises do not qualify for E-2 purposes.[8] Nor do they qualify for EB-5 purposes.

- *Second*, the capital must belong to the investor. The investor must have possession and control of the invested funds, even if derived from third-party sources such as by gift or inheritance.[9] This requirement ties the investment directly to the beneficiary of the immigration benefit. The qualifying capital must be that of the investor in order for the investor to derive the immigration benefit.

- *Third*, the money must be subject to both gain and loss.[10] This concept comports most closely with the common definition of "investment," which involves using money with the hope and expectation of gain.[11]

- *Fourth*, as further assurance that the investor personally bears the full risk of loss where the capital comes from indebtedness, the security must be the investor's personal assets if the capital is provided from a secured loan.[12]

- *Fifth*, the capital must be irrevocably committed to the enterprise in which the capital is invested. This is the E-2 analogue to the "actual commitment" component in the EB-5 regulations. Accordingly, this fifth element is not strictly germane to the "at risk" analysis, but rather is a part of understanding the larger "investment" requirement. The E-2 regulations are open as to the method of showing irrevocable commitment. The investor may use "any legal mechanism available," as long as the consular officer can determine that the funds are irrevocably committed.[13]

Four of these five components of the E-2 definition thus relate to whether capital is "at risk," and they may be distilled into three core principles. The first principle is that the objective of the investment must be to use the money to create profit, and the target of the funds must be a for-profit entity. The second principle is that the money must be the investor's and no one else's. This principle is straightforward. The third principle is that the money must be subject to gain and loss.

Below we will see how USCIS has confused these principles and elements in its EB-5 adjudication. The purpose of this analysis is to guide USCIS back to a proper understanding of the "at risk" evidentiary requirement in the EB-5 context.

MATTER OF IZUMMI

Four precedent AAO decisions,[14] in particular, *Matter of Izummi* and *Matter of Ho*, elaborate on the "at risk" element. However, they misconstrue

---

[7] 22 CFR §41.51(b)(7) (emphasis added).

[8] *See* 9 *Foreign Affairs Manual* (FAM) 41.51 N8.1-2(a).

[9] *See* 9 FAM 41.51 N8.1-1, N8.1-2(b).

[10] *See* 9 FAM 41.51 N8.1-2.

[11] An accessible definition of "to invest" is the following: "To put (money) to use, by purchase or expenditure, in something offering potential profitable returns, as interest, income, or appreciation in value." http://dictionary.reference.com/browse/invest

[12] *See* 9 FAM 41.51 N8.1-2.

[13] Because both the EB-5 and E-2 provisions in the Immigration and Nationality Act (INA) permit the investor to be "in the process" of investing as opposed to having already invested, the "irrevocable commitment" requirement assures the adjudicator that the required capital has parted from the investor and is poised to be united with the enterprise subject to some "personal liability" protection.

[14] *Matter of Soffici*, 22 I&N Dec. 158, 19 Immigr. Rep. B2-25 (Assoc. Comm'r, Examinations 1998); *Matter of Izummi*, 22 I&N Dec. 169, 19 Immigr. Rep. B2-32 (Assoc. Comm'r, Examinations 1998); *Matter of Hsiung*, 22 I&N Dec. 201, 19 Immigr. Rep. B2-106 (Assoc. Comm'r, Examinations 1998); *Matter of Ho*, 22 I&N Dec. 206, 19 Immigr. Rep. B2-99 (Assoc. Comm'r, Examinations 1998). All four of these cases are reproduced in the Appendix materials to this volume.

the meaning of "at risk" and impose burdens without foundation in either the regulations or their original intent.

Matter of Izummi involved a regional center-based petition in which the new commercial enterprise, AELP, invested in its affiliate, American Commercial and Export Credit Company, which then made loans to various other target companies. The EB-5 investors contributed their capital to AELP, which then deducted various partnership expenses with the remainder of the investors' capital remaining in escrow until approval of the visa application. The AAO ruled, "As the payment of initial partnership expenses and costs was not the type of profit-generating activity contemplated by the regulations, no more than [the amount remaining in escrow] could be considered to have been 'invested.'"[15] The AAO distinguished deduction for partnership expenses at the AELP level in this instance from partnership expenses such as initial salaries where "the employment-creating entity is spending the money."[16] The AAO ruled, "The full amount of money must be made available to the business(es) most closely responsible for creating the employment upon which the petition is based."[17]

First, this interpretation confuses the investment requirement—of which the "at risk" element is an evidentiary component—with the job creation requirement. Recall the three-fold purpose of the "at risk" evidentiary test: to ensure that the investor's intent is to generate a profit, to ensure that the capital invested belongs to the investor, and to ensure that the investment is subject to personal gain or loss. **The "at risk" requirement does not prescribe *the manner of capital's use*.** Indeed, Congress specifically avoided constraining the business activities benefiting from EB-5 capital.[18] As long as the EB-5 petitioner satisfies the evidentiary requirements for placing the required capital at risk, it is improper for the Service to examine how the capital is used.

---

[15] *Matter of Izummi, supra* note 14, at 178.

[16] *Id.* at 179.

[17] *Id.*

[18] *See* 136 Cong. Rec. S17112 (daily ed. Oct. 26, 1990) (Immigration Act of 1990 Conference Report) (Senator Simon stated, "[a]s long as the employment goal is met, it is unnecessary to needlessly regulate the type of business—manufacturing service, retail or the like—nor the character of the investment, corporations, partnerships, proprietors—all legal types of business—are appropriate.").

Izummi's rule expresses concern over the possible dissociation of the investment from job creation. However, job creation is a separate requirement with its own schema of evidentiary requirements, both at the I-526 phase and at the I-829 phase. One can easily contemplate, and certainly skilled entrepreneurs and professional managers may create, an investment structure that is highly efficient in creating jobs with only a small amount of capital, without any impairment of the investment requirement. Where the deployment of the investment capital appears not sufficiently related to job creation, the adjudicator should review the business plan to assess whether there are adequate projections for required job creation. Indeed, where the I-526 is based on 10 jobs already created, there is no analysis of the investment's use; rather, the focus is on whether the required investment was made. Thus, not only does *Izummi*'s rule violate the language and spirit of the regulations, it makes little commercial sense and is inconsistent with the regulations themselves.

Second, this holding has a capricious impact on large-scale transactions where the ultimate deployment of capital rests on fulfillment of certain conditions precedent. By requiring that the full amount of required capital be "made available" to the job-creating entity in the regional center context, *Izummi* raises the question of what suffices as a factual matter to make the capital "available." For example, placing investment capital in escrow pending the approval of the I-526 appears acceptable globally as satisfying the "at risk" evidentiary requirement. However, placing investment capital in escrow pending the fulfillment of certain commercially accepted conditions precedent, such as securing a construction loan, appears problematic.[19] It is hard to discern the principle behind the distinction.

Similarly, *Izummi* has created confusion regarding the use of cash reserves, particularly in the regional center context. In *Izummi,* the partnership agreement permitted the creation of a reserve account for the purpose of satisfying partnership obligations, including its obligation to buy back the partnership interest from an investor.[20] The AAO found this a violation of the "at risk" provision because "these reserve funds are, by agreement, not available for purposes of job creation and therefore

---

[19] Administrative Appeals Office (AAO) decision, on file with author.

[20] *Matter of Izummi, supra* note 14, at 189.

cannot be considered capital placed at risk for the purpose of generating a return on the capital placed at risk."[21] Again, the AAO conflates the job creation mission of EB-5 investments with the independent investment requirement. The problem in *Izummi* was not the mere existence of cash reserves. Rather, the problem was narrower: **the cash reserves here were created for the purpose of buying back partnership interests** rather than being deployed (or in the process of being deployed) for generating profit, which the AAO found impermissible. This is consistent with the purpose of the "at risk" evidentiary requirement as discussed in the above section. However, the AAO makes an analytical error in linking the "at risk" element expressly with job creation.

Izummi also produced a narrow rule regarding so-called guaranteed payments that has created more confusion than warranted among USCIS and the bar. The petitioner in *Izummi* had a right to receive a 12 percent annual return on his capital contribution under an investment agreement between the petitioner and the partnership.[22] While stating that it did not reach the issue of whether distribution of profits is permissible to a petitioner who still owes investment capital, the AAO stated that the "problem addressed here is that the annual returns are **guaranteed**."[23] The AAO found it problematic that "the Partnership receives no infusion of new funds from the petitioner,"[24] because the petitioner may receive the obligated returns from the Partnership and use them to satisfy his investment. There is an obvious problem here, but it is not a violation of the "at risk" element. Rather, the problem as described by *Izummi* is a violation of the statutory **amount of capital** requirement. The Immigration and Nationality Act (INA) at §203(b)(5)(A)(ii) requires an investment of an amount set forth in subparagraph (C), which in general requires $1 million, unless downward adjusted in the case of investment made in a targeted employment area.[25] Where the enterprise is required by contract to reimburse set amounts to the investor before the investor has completed the required EB-5 investment, the investment fails to meet the capital amount required by statute. The *Izummi* rule, therefore, prohibits contractual returns for preset amounts that would in essence vitiate the requirement that the investor place an infusion of new funds in the required amount.

Some circles have misinterpreted this rule as prohibiting legal guarantees, a specific form of contract. Guarantees are agreements entered into by third parties to assure performance of obligations by an obligor under a separate contract.[26] As an example, a borrower X agrees to pay lender Y $500,000 under a note. The borrower's guarantor Z guarantees payment of $500,000 to Y if the X defaults under the note. These arrangements are **not** prohibited by *Izummi* or elsewhere in EB-5 law and regulations. However, in the EB-5 context, such guarantees do not relieve the petitioner of her investment requirement.[27] The petitioner herself must make the full capital contribution of $1 million, or $500,000 if the investment is in a targeted employment area.

Suppose in a regional center context that it is the business of the new commercial enterprise, a partnership, to make loans as was the case in *Izummi*. Also suppose that a borrower, the target company responsible for job creation, provides a guarantee for its debt obligation to the partnership. Again, this arrangement does not violate *Izummi*. *Izummi* merely prohibits the enterprise from providing the investor with the contractual right to receive a preset return on capital.

Finally, *Izummi* found that the redemption agreement at play in that case to violate the "at risk" requirement. While the holding is sensible under *Izummi*'s particular facts, USCIS has construed the holding as a broader adjudicative principle. In *Izummi*, the investment agreement vested an unconditional right in the petitioner to sell his partnership interest back to the partnership after six years.[28] The AAO reasoned that the petitioner's investment is not at risk because "it is guaranteed to be returned, regardless of the success or failure of the business."[29]

---

[21] *Id.*

[22] The investment agreement provided: "I shall receive a return on the cash I have contributed to the Partnership in the amount of 12% per annum, payable annually, commencing one year from the date I am admitted to the Partnership as a Limited Partner and ending five years thereafter." *Id.* at 180.

[23] *Id.* at 181 (emphasis in original).

[24] *Id.*

[25] INA §203(b)(5)(A)(ii), (C); 8 USC §1153(b)(5)(A)(ii), (C).

[26] Black's Law Dictionary (6th ed. 1990).

[27] In *Matter of Soffici,* the petitioner was the guarantor on the enterprise's debt. The AAO held that the petitioner's guarantee does not transform the enterprise's debt into the petitioner's debt so as to satisfy the petitioner's investment requirement. See *Matter of Soffici, supra* note 14.

[28] *Matter of Izummi, supra* note 14, at 183.

[29] *Id.* at 184.

It found that the arrangement is "in essence, a debt arrangement, in which [the investor] provides funds in exchange for an unconditional, contractual promise that it will be repaid later at a fixed maturity date[.]"[30] The AAO provided two rulings in this respect. Making clear that the investor may at some point sell back his partnership interest, the AAO first ruleds that the partnership may not grant a right to sell back the interest before the investor completes his payments under a note.[31] Second, the AAO ruled that no such agreements may be entered into before the end of the conditional residency period.[32] The reasoning is critical. The AAO stated:

> The alien must go into the investment not knowing for sure if he will be able to sell his interest at all after he obtains his unconditional permanent resident status; and if he is successful in selling his interest, the sale price may be disappointingly low (or surprisingly high and more than what he paid). This way, the alien risks both gain and loss. To allow otherwise transforms the arrangement into a loan.[33]

USCIS recently prohibited agreements by certain regional centers to return the investment capital if the I-829 is denied. USCIS reasoned that such agreements were impermissible redemption agreements. Looking at the precise facts and holdings of *Izummi*, it is clear that this interpretation misapplies *Izummi*. The AAO's concern in *Izummi* was the guaranteed right to sell for a fixed price after obtaining unconditional permanent residency, regardless of how the business fared. The AAO contemplated a fact pattern where the alien investor anticipates what he would do after USCIS lifts the conditions. The lifting of conditions was assumed. In contrast, an agreement to return the investment if the conditions are not lifted is not an attempt to hedge a risk against business loss as *Izumii* contemplates. As long as there is no other provision allowing the return of capital for a fixed price at a fixed date, there is no *Izumii* violation.

Note that the E-2 regulations specifically permit the capital to be placed in escrow pending visa issuance. Interim escrows in the E-2 context, therefore, do not violate the "irrevocable commitment" requirement. This is further evidence that contractual arrangements in the EB-5 context allowing for return of capital in the event of I-829 denial do not and should not be found to violate the investment requirement.[34]

MATTER OF HO

Matter of Ho[35] most notably elaborates the standard for business plan content. However, it is also notable for confusing the "at risk" standard with the separate "actual commitment" standard. Both are evidentiary elements of the investment requirement as set forth in the regulations, but each is analytically distinct.

In *Matter of Ho*, the petitioner was the sole owner of the enterprise, King's Wheel, whose putative business was importing steel and aluminum automobile wheels from Taiwan. The AAO found that the petitioner failed to make an at risk investment because the petitioner had merely placed the capital into a corporate bank account over which the petitioner exercised sole control. "Simply formulating an idea for future business activity," the AAO held, "without taking meaningful concrete action, is similarly insufficient for a petitioner to meet the at-risk requirement." The AAO ruled:

> Before it can be said that capital made available to a commercial enterprise has been placed at risk, a petitioner must present some evidence of the actual undertaking of business activity; otherwise, no assurance exists that the funds will in fact be used to carry out the business of the commercial enterprise.[36]

Recall that the EB-5 regulations treat "at risk" and "actual commitment" together as components of the required evidence of "investment." The portion of the regulations relating to "actual commitment" states: "Evidence of mere intent to invest, or of prospective investment arrangements entailing no present commitment will not suffice to show that the petitioner is actively in the process of investing. The alien must show actual commitment of the required amount of capital."[37] Recall also that the E-2 regulations separately call for "irrevocable commitment" to satisfy the investment requirement (the fifth element of the E-2 definition of investment discussed

---

[30] *Id.*
[31] *Id.* at 186.
[32] *Id.*
[33] *Id.* at 187.

[34] 22 CFR §41.51(l).
[35] *Matter of Ho, supra* note 14.
[36] *Id.* at 210.
[37] 8 CFR §204.6(j)(2).

above). Concomitantly, the "at risk" element and the "actual commitment" element have different evidentiary standards and purposes that *Ho* confuses. As long as the petitioner invests his capital for profit, subject to both loss and gain, the "at risk" requirement is satisfied.

The "actual commitment" requirement's purpose is to allow the adjudicator to determine whether there is sufficient union between the capital and the enterprise to find satisfaction of the investment requirement. Because the EB-5 statute permits the petitioner to qualify even if she is merely "in the process" of investing as opposed to having invested already at the time of the EB-5 petition, the "actual commitment" requirement makes sense. This is made clear in the E-2 regulations and the FAM portions governing "irrevocable commitment." The FAM states: "To be 'in the process of investing' for E-2 purposes, the funds or assets to be invested must be committed to the investment and the commitment must be real and irrevocable."[38] The FAM then elaborates on the standard that *Matter of Ho* erroneously enunciates as an "at risk" rule:

> Moreover, for the alien to be "in the process of investing," the alien must be close to the start of actual business operations, not simply in the stage of signing contracts (which may be broken) or scouting for suitable locations and property. Mere intent to invest, or possession of uncommitted funds in a bank account, or even prospective investment arrangements entailing no present commitment, will not suffice.[39]

As to what specific facts show sufficient "irrevocable commitment," the E-2 regulations remain sensibly agnostic. The E-2 regulations acknowledge that diverse business arrangements may be fashioned using "any legal mechanism," including those to protect the investor from personal liability.[40] The adjudicators are responsible, then, for analyzing the particular facts to determine whether there is sufficient commitment of capital to the enterprise.

So when an EB-5 adjudicator raises concern about capital in reserve or sub-escrow accounts, for example, she is mistaken in invoking the "at risk" standard. Rather, the concern she expresses is whether the funds are "actually committed" to the enterprise. Correctly identifying the issue will help the adjudicator apply the correct standard and invoke the proper rationale underlying the standard.

Applying the correct standard to the example of reserve or interim accounts, the adjudicative questions should be: Has the investor actually invested—meaning parted with the money such that it is no longer his or under his control? What business activity has been undertaken? The facts at hand should be measured against the problematic facts in *Matter of Ho*, where the petitioner had sole control of the funds, merely sitting in a corporate account, with no other evidence of preparation or operational business activity.

CONCLUSION

It is clear that recent USCIS adjudication has departed from the actual meaning of the "at risk" evidentiary component of the EB-5 "investment" requirement. This is due in part to overreaching rules in precedent decisions, themselves misconstruing the meaning and source of the "at risk" concept. USCIS corrupts the proper standard further by misapplying the regulations and the precedent decisions' limited rules. USCIS must return to the source of the "at risk" standard to properly adjudicate EB-5 cases.

---

[38] 9 FAM 41.51 N8.1-3(a).
[39] 9 FAM 41.51 N8.1-3(b).
[40] 22 CFR §41.51(l).

NAVIGATING THE LAWFUL SOURCE REQUIREMENT FOR EB-5 IMMIGRATION

by Elsie Hui Arias and Lincoln Stone[*]

For foreign nationals with the means to invest a substantial amount of capital into a U.S. commercial enterprise, and who do not qualify for or wish to endure the extensive backlog of certain family– or employment-based categories, EB-5 immigration may be an attractive and increasingly popular option. However, prospective EB-5 petitioners should be advised of the complex requirements concomitant with this immigrant visa category, including the need to identify and document thoroughly the origin of their investment funds.

As reflected in the regulations concerning EB-5 petitions, the investor is required to show that he or she "has invested, or is actively in the process of investing, capital obtained through *lawful means*"[1] (emphasis added). Since 1998, the Administrative Appeals Office (AAO) has demonstrated a clear pattern of adhering to a stringent standard for documentation of lawful source of funds.

This article discusses how—based on the authors' experience—diverse types of sources of capital can be addressed in immigrant investor petitions. It is important to note that in documenting this requirement, practitioners should be flexible—an approach for one client may be different from that suited to another client, depending on the client's background and what documentation the client can produce.

Also, due diligence is critical in this practice area of immigration law. Conduct a background check on your client using public sources—such as online research—as U.S. Citizenship and Immigration Services (USCIS) will conduct similar background investigation of the petitioner.[2]

REGULATORY REQUIREMENTS FOR DOCUMENTATION

The regulation concerning the contents of an immigrant investor petition includes a distinct provision addressing what the petitioner must present as evidence "[t]o show that the petitioner has invested, or is actively in the process of investing, capital obtained through lawful means."[3] The structure of the regulation is stated in the alternative: The petitioner may present evidence of business records, tax returns, *or* any other evidence of lawful source of funds. In practice, however, we respond to the regulation by instructing our clients to produce evidence of tax returns and business records as a minimum, and then extracting from our clients adequate information to articulate the actual source of funds.

Also, where applicable, the petitioner should present evidence of any pending civil, criminal, or administrative actions, or proceedings, and of any monetary judgments against the petitioner within the past 15 years.[4] USCIS conducts background investigations of EB-5 petitioners and their dependents in regard to this latter requirement. In one particular case, USCIS issued a request for evidence regarding a charge of embezzlement pending against the petitioner's spouse in his home country, raising the question of whether the investment funds were derived from improper conduct.

In preparing the client's documents, the practitioner should keep in mind another important regulation which applies to all immigration-related applications and petitions—8 CFR §103.2(b)(3). Foreign documents must be supported by a certified English translation—otherwise, USCIS will not consider the document as evidence. While this would appear to be an obvious requirement, a surprising number of

---

[*] **Elsie Hui Arias** is an associate attorney at Stone & Grzegorek LLP, an immigration law firm in Los Angeles. Certified as a specialist in Immigration and Nationality Law by the California State Bar, Ms. Arias practices all areas of immigration law and has served as a conference speaker on various immigration topics. She is a graduate of the University of California at Berkeley and the University of California at Davis School of Law.

Lincoln Stone practices immigration law in Los Angeles with Stone & Grzegorek LLP, *www.lskglaw.com*.

[1] 8 CFR §204.6(j)(3).

[2] *See, e.g., www.bis.doc.gov/complianceandenforcement/liststocheck.htm*.

[3] *Id.*

[4] 8 CFR §204.6(j)(3)(iv).

the AAO's nonprecedent decisions concerning immigrant investor petitions reflected the AAO's consternation over the presentation of foreign documents without English translations. Consequently, these documents were not included as part of the AAO record. Even financial documents such as bank statements and tax returns, in which the key data appears in numerical form, must be translated so terms such as "account number," "debit/credit," and "balance" will be accurately understood.

Income Tax Returns

USCIS expects the petitioner to submit five years of income tax returns, both for the individual petitioner and businesses owned, in any jurisdiction where tax returns have been filed.[5] In practice, we require all clients to present evidence of five years of income tax returns or offer an explanation as to why a petitioner has not filed. Information reflected in the tax returns, such as reported proceeds from employment or a specific financial transaction, can serve as further evidence of the lawful source of funds. The evidence of income tax returns is not intended to prove that the petitioner has paid taxes in the home country or in the United States, if applicable. Whether the petitioner has paid or failed to pay income taxes should not serve a basis for approval or denial of an investor petition.

Reasons as to why income tax returns have not been filed may include: income tax returns have not been prepared and filed yet; the petitioner was not obligated to file income tax returns for the period of time in question; or the foreign country in which the petitioner resides does not have income tax return requirements.[6] These reasons should be supported by the petitioner's declaration and, where possible, a letter from an accountant or tax attorney familiar with taxation requirements in the petitioner's country of residence.

Business Records

The regulation also requires that the petitioner submit "foreign business registration records,"[7] which we interpret to mean documentation concerning any businesses the petitioner owns. Thus, the petitioner should submit copies of registration certificates, articles of incorporation, share certificates, and other like documentation concerning the business.

ACTUAL SOURCE OF FUNDS

Beyond providing income tax returns (and business records, if applicable), the petitioner must provide an explanation and supporting evidence of the actual source of the investment capital—whether it is employment or business earnings, loan or gift from a relative or friend, proceeds from a specific transaction, or a combination of these sources.

As the AAO has admonished throughout its nonprecedent decisions in the last 12 years, a petitioner's failure to explain the source of the investment capital and present sufficient supporting evidence may result in a determination that the petitioner did not demonstrate that the investment capital was obtained through lawful means.[8] The AAO has held that merely submitting bank letters or statements documenting the deposit of funds may not establish the lawful source of investment capital.[9]

It is important to remind practitioners that—in presenting evidence of the investor's source of funds (as well as other requirements of EB-5 immigration not addressed in this article)—unsupported assertions of counsel are not considered evidence by USCIS. Facts presented in the petition must be supported by documentary evidence. Facts that cannot be supported by documents can be presented by declaration of the investor and/or any other relevant party. Where primary evidence is not available, the petitioner must document this fact.[10]

In our experience, declarations by the petitioner—and by parties with personal knowledge about the source or tracing of the investment capital—have been invaluable in summarizing succinctly the transactions that may have occurred in accumulating or transferring the investment funds, or generally filling in evidentiary holes where documents may not be available. Successful petitions that relied in part on declarations are weaved throughout our discussion below.

---

[5] 8 CFR §204.6(j)(3)(ii).

[6] See, e.g., www.deloitte.com/view/en_GX/global/services/tax/international-tax/international-tax-and-business-guides/index.htm for information on tax reporting requirements worldwide.

[7] 8 CFR §204.6(j)(3)(i).

[8] See, e.g., Matter of [name redacted] (AAO Apr. 20, 2009).

[9] Matter of Izumii, 22 I&N Dec. 169, 195, 19 Immig. Rptr. B2-32 (AAO July 13, 1998); Matter of Ho, 22 I&N Dec. 206, 210–11, 19 Immigr. Rptr. B2-99 (AAO July 31, 1998). Both Izumii and Ho are reproduced in the Appendix materials to this volume.

[10] 8 CFR §103.2(b)(2)(i).

We now address the types of documentation and challenges that may emerge with specific sources of investment capital.

Earnings from Business Owned by Petitioner

Where the investor derives the source of the investment funds from earnings of a business he or she owns (as opposed to earnings from employment), documentation about the earnings and business should be submitted with the petition. First, the petitioner should establish the lawful nature of the business. As described earlier in this article, the regulations indicate that documentation of a business owned by the petitioner should include income tax returns, registration certificates, business license, articles of incorporation, stock holdings list (reflecting equity percentage), and other similar documentation. Where available, we also include further details about the business, such as website printouts, marketing materials, and evidence of products or services offered by the business.

Second, the petitioner should characterize the nature of any earnings received from the company, whether the earnings are salary, profit distributions, and/or bonuses. Evidence of earnings received by the petitioner also should be included, such as tax records. If tax records are not available, evidence of these earnings may include bank statements reflecting deposits into the petitioner's individual bank account, distributions of earnings reflected in the business income tax returns or financial statements, and/or corporate minutes or resolutions.

For example, a cardiac surgeon that we successfully represented derived his investment capital from dividend payments he received from a company that he jointly established to develop and manufacture medical devices in Brazil. Documentation submitted in support of the petition included: his individual and company bank statements confirming the payment and receipt of the dividend payments; business registration and license of the company; income tax returns filed by the company; and background information about the petitioner, such as his medical degree and license.

Difficulties will likely arise where the petitioner transfers investment capital directly from the account of his business to the account of the EB-5 commercial enterprise. Some investors consider this route possibly to avoid taxation or to expedite the transfer of the investment funds.

USCIS personnel have stated informally that the agency has denied I-526 petitions where the investment funds were sent directly to the EB-5 commercial enterprise from the bank account of the petitioner's business. The denials were made on the basis that the investment appeared to be made by the business, not by the individual. USCIS has cited several administrative decisions in support of its view that a corporation is a separate and distinct legal entity from its owners or shareholders,[11] and therefore, the funds transferred directly from the petitioner's business should not be credited to the petitioner. However, USCIS personnel also indicated that if the petitioner provides evidence that the wired funds reflected the petitioner's personal funds—such as confirmation from the company's other shareholders—USCIS may credit the investment capital to the petitioner.[12]

Loan

In the case where the petitioner is deriving his or her investment capital from the proceeds of a loan, there are several issues to consider. Principally, the law is clear that if the petitioner uses the proceeds of a loan to invest in the commercial enterprise, repayment of the loan cannot be secured by the assets of the enterprise—otherwise, USCIS will not count the investment of the loan proceeds as capital for EB-5 purposes.[13]

If repayment of the loan, on the other hand, is secured by other assets of the petitioner, the loan proceeds that are invested as capital in the commercial enterprise can be counted toward the minimum capital requirement. We have also represented successfully EB-5 petitioners who invested the proceeds of unsecured loans into U.S. commercial enterprises.

---

[11] *See, e.g., Matter of M*, 8 I&N Dec. 24 (BIA 1958), and *Matter of Aphrodite Investments, Ltd.*, 17 I&N Dec. 530 (Comm'r 1980).

[12] It should be noted that in unpublished nonprecedent decisions, the Administrative Appeals Office (AAO) has indicated that it does not view the contribution of retained earnings as an investment of "capital" for EB-5 purposes. "Retained earnings" refers to a company's net earnings that are not paid out as dividends to shareholders but are retained by the company for other purposes, such as reinvestment in its core business or to pay off debt obligations.

[13] 8 CFR §204.6(j)(2)(v); *see Matter of Soffici*, 22 I&N Dec. 158, 19 *Immig. Rptr.* B2–25 (AAO June 25, 1998) (*Soffici* is reproduced in the Appendix materials to this volume). The same rule applies in E-2 visa adjudications. *See* 9 *Foreign Affairs Manual* (FAM) 41.51 N8.1-2.

Petitioners without apparent financial means to repay a sizeable loan may receive additional scrutiny.[14]

In regard to the supporting documents for the I-526 petition: The petition should include documentation reflecting the terms of the loan arrangement, such as the written agreement and promissory note. If the loan arrangement was made verbally or a formal written agreement was not drafted, then declarations from both the lender and petitioner addressing the loan terms should be submitted. Similarly, if the loan is unsecured and the loan documentation is silent with respect to security, this issue should be clarified with declarations.

Another critical requirement in documenting this form of investment source is to provide evidence about the lender where the lender is an individual (as opposed to a bank or lending institution). We usually submit documentation about the individual lender's background, including relationship to the petitioner, and provide detail regarding how the lender obtained the capital that they loan to the EB-5 petitioner.

How far back does the petitioner have to reach to document the lawfulness of the lender's funds? In a nonprecedent case in which the source of investment funds was a gift (although the same guidance would logically apply to a loan), the AAO stated that "[if] the original source is a gift, the petitioner must establish that the individual gifting the funds obtained those funds through lawful income."[15] Fortunately, the AAO also indicated that "the petitioner need not trace back the specific funds transferred by the [donor] to their previous source," but that "the petitioner must provide at least basic evidence that [the donor] has lawful income or a legitimate business or investment interest that could account for the lawful accumulation of significant cash."[16]

In light of this guidance, such documentation should include income tax returns (and business income tax returns, if applicable), evidence tracing the funds from the lender to the petitioner/borrower, and an explanation (perhaps by declaration) regarding the circumstances of the loan, for example, the lender and petitioner are family members. Sufficient documentation regarding the lender will help alleviate concern that unlawful funds originating from the petitioner were funneled through the lender, and then returned to the petitioner under the auspices of a "loan."

Specific case examples shed light on what has constituted sufficient evidence for USCIS approval. In one particular case, a petitioner invested the proceeds of an unsecured loan from her uncle, the president of a manufacturing facility in Japan. The uncle indicated that the loan was derived from accumulated employment earnings. The initial petition included proof of the familial relationship, loan agreement, bank statements reflecting the transfer of the loan proceeds from the uncle to the petitioner, and evidence of the uncle's background, including individual and business income tax returns.

Observing that the uncle's bank statement reflected a small balance of funds over a period of several years, but revealed a single large deposit of funds approximately one month before the loan proceeds were transferred to the petitioner, USCIS requested additional evidence regarding the uncle's source of income. In response, the petitioner submitted her uncle's income certificates and record of tax withholdings from his employment earnings. She also submitted a declaration from the uncle explaining that he held his earnings in several bank accounts, and that he consolidated some savings in a single transaction through the bank account from which he ultimately wired the proceeds to the petitioner. Based on this additional evidence, USCIS approved the I-526 petition.

Gift

If the actual source of the petitioner's investment funds is the proceeds of a gift, the petitioner should submit documentation similar to those required where the source of the EB-5 investment capital is a personal loan. Appropriate documents should include: background information regarding the donor; income tax returns; details of how the donor accumulated sufficient assets; evidence of the path of funds from the donor to the petitioner; and a summary of why the gift was made (again, a declaration should be sufficient).

Our experience with this type of transaction has indicated that the I-526 petition may be approved even though the petition is not supported with evidence that the donor has paid a gift tax that may or may not be due under the laws of a certain jurisdiction. Of course, if a gift tax has been paid, evidence of the payment should be included in the petition.

In one particular case that was approved by USCIS, a client aggregated her employment earn-

---

[14] *See, e.g., Matter of [name redacted]* (AAO Apr. 16, 2009).

[15] *Matter of [name redacted]* (AAO Apr. 20, 2009).

[16] *Id.*

ings with substantial gifts she received from her parents. Substantial background documentation from the parents included income tax returns and lease agreements of properties they owned and from which they derived significant rental income. Due to the banking regulations in India at that time, individuals could not transfer annually more than $200,000 overseas. As the EB-5 investment amount exceeded the regulatory limit, the petitioner's parents sent individual wires directly to the U.S. commercial enterprise with a notation that the transfers were solely for the credit of the petitioner. As further support of these transfers, the petitioner included regulations from the Reserve Bank of India that referred to the currency transfer restrictions.

Inheritance

A successful petition also may be based on investment of funds that were received by inheritance. The petition should be supported with evidence concerning the relationship between the petitioner and the decedent, probate court documents, bank statement reflecting deposit of proceeds, and death certificate of the decedent. Additionally, background information regarding how the decedent accumulated the estate assets should be included.

It is not uncommon where the inheritance was received many years prior and documentation such as probate court documents or financial information of the decedent are not readily available. Also, the events may be so remote that the petitioner lacks documentation that would trace funds from the decedent's estate to the petitioner. In these circumstances, the petition should be supported with declarations of the petitioner and other parties with personal knowledge of the decedent, estate assets, and/or inheritance transfer, such as a statement from the probate attorney. These statements should explain thoroughly the assets inherited by the petitioner (and value of the assets, if possible), background information of the decedent, and other relevant facts concerning the inheritance.

In one illustrative case, the petitioner received an inheritance upon the death of his father, but documentation of the will was not available. The documentation filed in support of the petition included the death certificate, evidence of the investor's receipt of the inherited funds, certification of payment of inheritance tax, receipts for payment of inheritance tax, and a declaration from the attorney-executor listing the beneficiaries and describing the contents of the estate.

Transaction

The actual source of funds may be based on the proceeds of a certain transaction—such as a sale or a loan—involving real property, stocks, or a business.

When the actual source of funds can be isolated to a specific transaction, most petitioners can pull together documentation concerning the surrounding circumstances, including deeds, closing statements, account statements, and like documentation. The petitioner also should address how and when they acquired or purchased the subject asset of the transaction, *e.g.*, residence, business, stocks, or retirement account.

Real Estate

In a transaction involving real estate, it is common for the petitioner to have purchased the home with employment earnings and bank financing many years ago. Often following substantial appreciation of the property's value, the petitioner obtains a significant line of credit or realizes substantial capital gains following the sale of the home.

Where the petitioner sold a residence or obtained a home-equity loan and has used the proceeds of the transaction to invest, the petitioner should produce documentation such as the purchase or loan agreement, final settlement statement, and verification that the proceeds were received in the petitioner's individual bank account.

Documentation of the sale of property may vary between countries. For example, in the United Kingdom, investors often are able to provide a solicitor's statement confirming completion of the sale and amount of the net proceeds. This documentation can be supplemented with the investor's bank statement showing the deposit of the proceeds.

For other countries, documentation of the sale of real estate may be more difficult to obtain. For example, an investor using proceeds from the sale of real estate in Iran may only have the real estate sales contract as evidence of the completed transaction. In this case, the petition should be supported by an explanation as to how the funds were transferred, and documentation as to the petitioner's general sources of income. To complicate the matter, in Iran, the payment of property transfer taxes is sometimes made before the recording of the property transfer. In this event, it would be helpful to include documentation regarding Iranian tax obligations in the form of a declaration from a professional with expertise in the area.

As an alternative to selling their home, a petitioner may obtain a bank loan secured by their residential or commercial real estate, and use the proceeds for investment purposes. As indicated earlier, many petitioners have benefited from the significant appreciation in real estate markets worldwide, and are able to obtain a loan or line of credit against the equity in their real property. In such cases, the EB-5 petitioner should provide documentation supporting this transaction, such as the loan or line-of-credit agreement, settlement statement, and personal bank statement (and related bank documents) confirming receipt of funds from the lending institution. An appraisal of the property should be submitted as well, if available.

Stocks

A substantial stock portfolio is also often the actual source of the investment capital. Petitioners may opt to sell their securities—which may have increased in value over a lengthy period of time—or obtain institutional loans that are secured by assets contained in their securities portfolio.

In one particular case, a retired investment banker from the United Kingdom regularly invested his employment earnings in an equities account held at a major brokerage firm. To enable his wife to invest in a commercial enterprise, he obtained a loan of $530,000 from the brokerage firm, for which his securities portfolio of approximately $5 million served as collateral. The petition included the loan agreement between the spouse and the brokerage firm, the spouse's brokerage statement reflecting a balance of $5 million, the petitioner's account statement reflecting deposit of the loan proceeds, and a declaration from the petitioner detailing the circumstances in which she obtained the proceeds. The petitioner also included evidence of her husband's prior earnings, including income tax returns.

In another case that was also approved by USCIS, the petitioner sold stocks held in different companies in the United States and Korea. To document the proceeds she received from both stock sales, she submitted her passbook which reflected the deposits, stock purchase and sale agreement, stock ledger, and a detailed declaration confirming how she acquired the stocks.

Sale of Business Assets

Where the petitioner obtained proceeds from the sale of his or her business assets, supporting documents should include copies of the purchase agreement, bank statement reflecting the receipt of sale proceeds, evidence that the petitioner owned the business (such as corporate registration and business license), and evidence of the business' value, such as financial statements and tax records.

If the sale occurred many years ago and such documents are not readily available, the practitioner will need to work with the petitioner in identifying other types of reliable documentation that can evidence the sales transaction and receipt of proceeds.

In an illustrative case, to document the sale of assets in a Nigerian company in which he held 10 percent interest, a client provided substantial evidence, including: the asset purchase agreement, wire instructions directing the deposits of the proceeds, bank statement reflecting a credit from the sale, and various corporate documents (registration, memorandum and articles of association). As the client's father established the company and held a majority interest, background information of the father was also included, such as news articles discussing his accomplishments and business interests, as well as a detailed declaration.

Retirement Funds

Successful EB-5 petitioners have also derived their investment capital from accumulated funds in their retirement accounts. In these cases, the petitioner should present evidence of their employment, periodic contributions to their retirement account, application or written request to withdraw the funds, and their individual bank statement reflecting the deposit of the proceeds.

In cases we have prepared that have utilized this form of investment capital, the proceeds often were not credited into the petitioner's bank account but directly transferred to the commercial enterprise by the pension management company on the petitioner's behalf. To avoid the appearance that the company is the investor, it is imperative to submit evidence that the transfer reflected personal funds owned by the petitioner, and that the transfer was conducted for the benefit of the petitioner. Evidence may include the petitioner's account statement and wire instructions directing the transfer of the retirement funds to the enterprise on behalf of the petitioner.

General Wealth Accumulation

For some investors, the income reported on their income tax returns in the last five years may demonstrate that they earned sufficient income to invest in the commercial enterprise. Alternatively, as described earlier, the petitioner may be able to isolate a specific event or transaction that demonstrates the receipt of sufficient funds for the EB-5 investment.

For other investors, the income reported on the last five years of tax returns may not obviously reflect a "level of income" that would allow investment of the capital amount they invested into the commercial enterprise. These individuals may have accumulated their wealth from more modest employment, business, and/or investment earnings over a period of many years.

In these cases, the investor will need to be able to provide other forms of reliable evidence that demonstrate how the capital was accumulated over time from lawful sources. Based on our experience, USCIS has been reasonable in considering a petitioner's overall financial background without imposing an onerous demand for a detailed analysis of historical earnings over a particular period of time.

Two AAO precedent decisions—*Matter of Izumii*[17] and *Matter of Ho*[18]—addressed the issue of "level of income." The petitioner in *Izumii* claimed he earned sufficient income in a jeans-trading business, but he presented only two years of income tax returns and scant further evidence, leading the AAO to reason that he lacked sufficient evidence of having discretionary funds that could be used for investment. The petitioner in *Ho* claimed he earned income as a medical doctor. However, the AAO noted that he presented no evidence supporting this assertion, and thus, it determined that the record did not contain evidence of his income.

With respect to the requirement that the investment capital originated from a lawful source, these AAO precedent decisions are significant for illustrating that a petitioner cannot succeed by presenting little or no evidence of financial background. In noting the paucity of evidence in these cases, the AAO did not establish a rule requiring petitioners to prove—by way of evidence of earnings as well as evidence of the cost of living—that the level of income only in recent years is sufficient for the EB-5 investment.

Rather, the AAO has indicated that USCIS examiners can consider evidence of lifetime earnings, if such evidence is probative of general wealth accumulation. In a telling nonprecedent EB-5 case, the AAO approved the petition, remarking: "While the petitioner has not demonstrated an unusually large income, she has demonstrated a pattern of steady income and 26 years of professional employment that is not inconsistent with the accumulation of $500,000 at the time of retirement."[19]

One particularly challenging case we prepared involved a French citizen who invested in small residential properties in France, and parlayed the capital gains into other real estate and stock investments. The client produced a list of the properties that he could recall purchasing and selling over the last 20 years in France. Because he conducted numerous transactions over the years, he determined it would be nearly impossible to produce evidence of all proceeds that he received. However, he was able to retrieve a representative sampling of real estate transactions. Coupled with a detailed declaration, a letter from an accountant examining his tax records, and letters from his real estate attorneys in France, the petition was ultimately approved by USCIS following the response to a request for additional evidence.

In preparing the source documentation for these petitions, the practitioner should take note that the burden on the petitioner in visa petition proceedings is usually that of a preponderance of the evidence,[20] and that "preponderance of the evidence" means "more likely than not."[21] Where a petitioner presents credible evidence in support of proving a particular fact and no contradicting evidence is available, USCIS should conclude that the petitioner has satisfied his or her burden of proving that fact.[22]

TRACING

In addition to providing evidence of the lawful source of the investment capital, the petitioner must document carefully the path of funds from the petitioner to the EB-5 enterprise. The AAO has held that

---

[17] *Supra* note 9.

[18] *Id.*

[19] *Matter of [name redacted]* (AAO Dec. 30, 2004).

[20] *Matter of Soo Hoo*, 11 I&N Dec. 151 (BIA 1965); *Matter of Patel*, 19 I&N Dec. 774 (BIA 1988); *Matter of Martinez*, 21 I&N Dec. 1035 (BIA 1997).

[21] *Matter of J–E–*, 23 I&N Dec. 291 (BIA 2002).

[22] *See, e.g., Young China Daily v. Chappell*, 724 F. Supp. 552 (N.D. Cal. 1989); *Augat, Inc. v. Tabor*, 719 F. Supp. 1158 (D. Mass. 1989); *Globenet, Inc. v. Att'y Gen.*, Civil Action No. 88-1261 (HHG), 1989 U.S. Dist. LEXIS 7154 (D.D.C. Jan. 10, 1989); *Hong Kong T.V. Video Program, Inc. v. Ilchert*, 685 F. Supp. 712 (N.D. Cal. 1988) (petitioner's proof was sufficient to establish eligibility for H-1B classification).

without documentation of the path of funds, the petitioner cannot meet his burden of establishing that the funds are his own funds.[23] The AAO also has stressed that if the U.S. enterprise receives invested funds from an account that is not clearly identified as the account of the petitioner, the petitioner will be requested to provide further evidence.

To trace the funds to the petitioner, documentation should reflect that the petitioner transferred personal funds to the commercial enterprise. Such evidence would typically include the bank statement of the enterprise confirming receipt of the petitioner's investment funds, and the petitioner's bank statement reflecting a corresponding transfer or withdrawal of funds to the enterprise. Where applicable, other related bank documentation, such as cancelled checks or wire receipts and instructions should also be submitted.

Currency Transfer Laws

Tracing the investment funds from the enterprise to the petitioner will be more difficult to document in some cases due to various factors, such as the currency transfer laws of the petitioner's home country.

Certain countries have laws that restrict the transfer of funds out of the country. This has the effect of encumbering the investor's ability to freely transfer funds held in a personal bank account to a U.S. commercial enterprise. It is not advisable to counsel the investor to transfer the funds in a particular manner to the U.S. commercial enterprise, or to be directly involved in the transfer of funds, such as accepting the transferred funds into the attorney's account. Engaging in any of these practices may result in a money-laundering charge against the attorney and/or the client, and/or civil or criminal penalties for the client in his or her home country. Clients seeking assistance with transferring funds overseas should be advised to consult local counsel on this matter.

In our experience, petitioners often transfer their investment capital to the United States by employing the assistance of third-party intermediaries. USCIS has not withheld approval of I-526 petitions in which the petitioner has used this practice but did not submit documentation reflecting compliance with currency transfer laws. We have stressed in earlier publications that it would be *ultra vires* action to require such proof.[24] USCIS personnel have informally expressed that examiners will not insist on compliance with such foreign laws, which is on a par with E-2 visa adjudication in regards to this particular consideration.[25]

Copies of bank statements, wire receipts and instructions, and cancelled checks should be included to demonstrate the path of funds. Where some documents may not be available, declarations have been invaluable in detailing how and why the funds were transferred in a particular manner. Declarations are also helpful in confirming that the third parties involved in coursing the funds to the United States are not equity investors in the U.S. commercial enterprise. We counsel clients that transparency is paramount to show that the funds originated from the petitioner, and remained within the petitioner's control and direction at all times.

With Iranian investors, for example, it is a common practice for funds to be transferred to intermediaries who in turn will transfer funds to the United States for the credit of the particular Iranian national. The petition should be supported with ample documentation concerning the transfers to and from the intermediary entities, as well as an explanation as to this common practice of transferring funds out of Iran.

The People's Republic of China (PRC) also has laws restricting the transfer of currency overseas. Currently, the PRC limits the annual overseas remittance per individual to $50,000.[26] To transfer investment capital of $500,000 to the United States, some of our Chinese clients have enlisted the assistance of 10 individuals to facilitate the transfer of funds.

In one illustrative case, a Chinese national asked 10 friends and family members to each transfer $50,000 to his son (the petitioner), an F-1 student in

---

[23] *Supra* note 7.

[24] *See* L. Stone & S. Yale-Loehr, "Evidence of Source of Capital in Immigrant Investor Cases," 6 *Bender's Immigr. Bull.* 972 (Oct. 1, 2001).

[25] *See, e.g.*, INA §101(a)(15)(E)(ii), and 9 FAM 41.51 N.8.1-1, which lack any mention of compliance with laws of the foreign country as a requirement for E-2 visa issuance.

[26] *See* Circular of the State Administration of Foreign Exchange on Printing and Distributing the Detailed Rules on the Implementation of the Measures for the Administration of Individual Foreign Exchange (July 13, 2009), published in English on the website of the State Administration of Foreign Exchange (SAFE), at *www.safe.gov.cn/model_safe_en/* (last visited Mar. 31, 2010).

the United States who wished to obtain conditional resident status through an EB-5 investment. Evidence submitted in support of this petition included: the father's bank book reflecting 10 withdrawals of $50,000 each; the bank books and outgoing wire remittance receipts of the 10 individuals, confirming receipt of the funds from the father and outgoing transfer to the petitioner; and the petitioner's U.S. bank statement, reflecting 10 deposits totaling $500,000. The father also provided a declaration confirming that the funds represented a gift, and detailing how and why the gift funds were transferred to his son through third parties.[27]

Another country with restrictive transfer laws is India.[28] In one particularly challenging case, an Indian national sold his company for approximately $29 million, which was deposited into an account shared with his wife, the petitioner. To transfer investment funds to the U.S. commercial enterprise, she consulted tax professionals in India about Indian laws that regulate overseas transfers of personal funds. They advised her to course the investment funds held in her joint account through an Indian company's "second level investment," *e.g.*, wholly-owned subsidiary.

Following this advice, she transferred the funds through another Indian company she fully owned and controlled, and set up a U.S. subsidiary of this Indian company. She subsequently transferred her personal investment funds through the account of the Indian company, and then onto the account of the U.S. subsidiary, from which she eventually wired the investment funds to the EB-5 enterprise. USCIS issued a request for evidence that the funds reflected the petitioner's *personal* funds—not the funds of the business. After submitting a detailed letter from her tax advisor, excerpts of the relevant currency transfer laws in India, and a declaration from the petitioner in response to the request for evidence, USCIS approved the petition.

CHALLENGES SPECIFIC TO CERTAIN COUNTRIES

In addition to country-related tracing issues, sources of investment capital originating from certain countries—such as China and Iran—may invite closer scrutiny by USCIS examiners, presumably due to national security and documentation challenges.

Petitioners from these countries may lack evidence of income tax filings, which are often viewed as reliable documentation concerning individual wealth accumulation. Due to currency transfer laws as discussed above, transfers of funds to the United States are not typically straightforward. There may also be cultural attitudes towards the government, such as a desire to keep financial information confidential. Although USCIS has been approving meritorious cases on behalf of petitioners from these countries, practitioners should be advised that all of these factors in the aggregate can present formidable challenges in documenting evidence of the lawful source of investment capital.[29]

For example, documentation of the transfer of funds and business transactions in Iran is often sparse. In one particular case, the petitioner received a gift from his father, who derived the capital from the sale of commercial property in Iran. The father could only produce a "transaction letter," which provided details of property sale, and a document entitled "Property Deliver Minute," confirming transfer of the assets and receipt of the sale proceeds. The documents tracing the gift funds directly to the father were also intermittent. To address the evidentiary holes in the petition, the petitioner provided a detailed declaration that served as a narrative of the events that transpired, including the source of the gift funds.

Clients from Iran also should be counseled to consult an attorney knowledgeable about the Iranian Transaction Regulations and Related Executive Orders—enforced by the U.S. Department of Treasury's Office of Foreign Assets Control (OFAC)—which prohibit the receipt of funds that pass through certain banks in Iran.[30] Petitions on behalf of Iranian

---

[27] The ability to transfer the funds through third parties may now be more difficult, in light of a recent directive issued by the People's Republic of China (PRC) government. *See* Circular of the State Administration of Foreign Exchange Settlement and Sale Business for Individuals (Dec. 23, 2009), published in English on the website of SAFE, at *www.safe.gov.cn/model_safe_en/* (last visited Mar. 31, 2010).

[28] *See www.rbi.org.in.*

---

[29] *See, e.g.,* K. White, "Russian EB-5 Investors—'Unwrapping the Mystery,'" elsewhere in this volume, for a detailed discussion of Russian nationals and EB-5 immigration.

[30] *See www.treas.gov/offices/enforcement/ofac/programs/iran/iran.pdf.* For a detailed discussion of these regulations and executive orders, see E. Krauland and J. Hayes, "Anti-
continued

investors that include an approval letter from OFAC have been approved by USCIS.

For EB-5 petitions involving Chinese nationals, practitioners will discover that tax filing requirements will differ, depending on when and how the income was earned.[31] Chinese clients may be able to provide tax payment receipts as evidence that they earned income that was taxable by the Chinese government. In other situations, employers may have paid income taxes on behalf of the Chinese employee. In these instances, we request a letter from the employer attesting to the wages earned by the petitioner and taxes paid on behalf of the petitioner, as well as evidence of the tax payments.

UNLAWFUL STATUS—OBSTACLE TO EB-5 IMMIGRATION?

Certain nonprecedent AAO decisions have raised the question of whether a petitioner who has resided unlawfully in the United States may be able to qualify for the EB-5 category.[32] Such cases suggest that a petitioner in unlawful status must prove that the invested funds were not earned as the result of unauthorized stay or unauthorized employment in the United States. Note that this is merely a question of lawful status, not a question of whether the invested funds must come from abroad; legacy Immigration and Naturalization Service has stated clearly that invested funds need not originate from abroad.[33]

In adjudicating EB-5 petitions, USCIS will note whether the petitioner is in lawful status in the United States. This information is elicited on Form I-526, specifically: the status the petitioner currently holds in the United States; when the status will expire; and whether the petitioner has ever worked without authorization in the United States. Where the petitioner claims that the investment funds were derived from employment earnings, USCIS may question whether the investment funds were earned without authorization. If so, USCIS may characterize such funds as not lawfully obtained.

In this situation, it would be advisable to explore with the petitioner whether he has alternative sources of investment capital other than employment income that may have been earned without proper authorization from USCIS. Bearing this issue in mind, we have successfully represented clients who were in the United States unlawfully, but had the means to invest in a commercial enterprise and were otherwise eligible to adjust their status to conditional resident under INA §245(i).[34]

In one such case, the petitioner had overstayed the period authorized to him as a tourist. While in the United States, he was severely injured in an automobile accident and received a settlement of several million dollars, from which he derived his investment funds. Documentation of the lawfully-obtained funds included copies of the settlement checks, account statement from the court acting as trustee of the settlement funds, and court order confirming settlement of the lawsuit.

In another case, the petitioner obtained his investment capital from the sale of real estate that he had inherited from his lawful permanent resident mother, and a personal loan from his U.S citizen domestic partner. Supporting documents included evidence tracing the funds from the real estate sale and loan transaction to the petitioner's bank account, real estate sale agreement, promissory note issued by the domestic partner, and evidence of the domestic partner's U.S. citizenship.

RAMIFICATIONS FOR I-829 PETITION

Towards the end of the two-year conditional resident period, the EB-5 petitioner will be required to file Form I-829 to remove the conditions from his or her resident status. It is important to note that the law governing the adjudication of I-829 petitions

---

Money Laundering and OFAC Sanctions Concerns for Immigration Practitioners Assisting Foreign Investors," elsewhere in this volume.

[31] See R. Gaffney, "Country-Specific Issues and Challenges in Representing EB-5 Petitioners from the People's Republic of China," elsewhere in this volume, for a detailed discussion about Chinese taxation laws and complications for Chinese EB-5 investor cases.

[32] See Matter of [name redacted] (AAO Apr. 7, 2009); see also cases reviewed in L. Stone, "Immigrant Investment in Local Clusters: Part II," 80 Interpreter Releases 946, 948 (July 14, 2003).

[33] 56 Fed Reg. 60897, 60902 (Nov. 29, 1991); see also Department of State E-2 visa guidance at 9 FAM 41.51 N8.1-1.

[34] Notwithstanding failure to maintain lawful status or engagement in unauthorized employment, some petitioners may be eligible to adjust status to conditional or permanent resident status under INA §245(i). Practitioners should note that INA §245(k)—which authorizes adjustment of status for certain employment-based immigrants who failed to maintain lawful status for less than 180 days—does not include EB-5 petitioners.

does not require submission of evidence that the source of the investment capital was lawful.[35]

If USCIS questions the source of funds during the adjudication of the I-829 petition, it must detail with particularity why this evidence is being requested. Specifically, the regulations state that if "it becomes known to the government that the entrepreneur obtained his or her investment funds through other than legal means (such as through the sale of illegal drugs)," USCIS "shall offer the alien entrepreneur the opportunity to rebut such information."[36] If the petitioner "fails to overcome such derogatory information or evidence" that the source of funds was unlawful, USCIS may deny the I-829 petition, terminate resident status, and issue a notice to appear in removal proceedings.[37]

CONCLUSION

Successfully representing the EB-5 petitioner requires careful review of the legal and regulatory requirements, as well as close collaboration with the petitioner in identifying and documenting thoroughly the source and tracing of his or her investment capital. Addressing this requirement early in the planning stages will help guide client expectations and address clearly one of the more thorny requirements of EB-5 immigration.

---

[35] For a detailed discussion of the requirements for removal of conditions of EB-5 investors, *see* L. Stone, "Conditional Permanent Residence and Immigration Risk for Investors," elsewhere in this volume.

[36] 8 CFR §216.6(c)(2).

[37] *Id.*

COUNTRY-SPECIFIC ISSUES AND CHALLENGES IN REPRESENTING EB-5 PETITIONERS FROM THE PEOPLE'S REPUBLIC OF CHINA

*by Robert P. Gaffney**

The People's Republic of China (PRC) is the country of origin of a significant percentage of persons immigrating under the EB-5 provisions. Due to a rapidly changing economic, social, political, and legal environment and the persistence of substantial regional variations in business and financial reporting practices within China, representing PRC persons seeking immigrant investor status presents special challenges to EB-5 practitioners. This article highlights a number of issues that commonly arise in this context and offers practice pointers that may be of assistance to practitioners, including an overview of common PRC commercial practices, tips on proving lawful source of funds, and a brief discussion of the challenges PRC investors face in transferring investment funds to the United States in light of currency-export limitations.[1]

---

* **Robert P. Gaffney**, a California State Bar Certified Specialist in immigration and nationality law, has over 25 years of experience counseling a wide range of corporate and individual clients in areas of employment-related, investment, and family-based visa and immigration matters. Through his law firm in San Francisco he has a strong practice focus on representing individual investors in obtaining permanent residence, and counseling U.S. businesses in the development of investment opportunities designed to qualify foreign direct investors for immigrant status under the EB5 provisions. Mr. Gaffney, who is fluent in Mandarin Chinese, received his B.A. degree in Chinese Studies, summa cum laude, from U.C. San Diego (1973), completed graduate studies at the University of Michigan, Center for Chinese Studies (1973–76), and received his J.D. degree from U.C. Hastings College of the Law (1980).

[1] Our discussion is limited to issues pertaining to residents of those areas of China under the direct control of the Central People's Government and does not include a consideration of issues arising under the laws of the Hong Kong or Macao Special Administrative Regions, which, under the principle of "one country, two systems" now in place, maintain distinct legal and economic systems reflecting their divergent colonial heritage. Nor do we address issues pertaining to the representation of EB-5 petitioners from Taiwan, which while considered a part of China by governments on both sides of the Formosa Straits, effectively continues to maintain governmental, legal, and economic independence from the PRC.

PROOF OF LAWFUL SOURCE OF FUNDS FOR PRC NATIONALS

The regulations provide that to show that a petitioner has invested, or is actively in the process of investing, capital obtained through lawful means, the I-526 petition must be accompanied, as applicable, by foreign business registration records,[2] and personal tax records and tax returns of any kind filed by a corporation, partnership, or any other entity with any taxing jurisdiction in or outside the United States by or on behalf of the petitioner within the prior five years.[3] The regulations further provide that a petitioner may submit evidence identifying any other sources of capital.[4] When the source of capital to be invested derives by way of gift, inheritance or loan from a third party, counsel must be prepared to fully document the lawful manner in which the funds were accumulated by the benefactor or creditor.

In advising a prospective EB-5 petitioner from the PRC, counsel should cast a wide net at the outset of the case-preparation stage, gathering as much evidence as possible about the client's income-producing activities and investments, tax filings and valuable assets. As most prospective EB-5 investors from China will be aware of the lawful source documentation requirement and will have given the matter considerable thought, counsel should actively encourage the client's input and suggestions as to how best to address this issue.

In planning and preparing to file an I-526 petition, counsel will typically consider several approaches to establishing the lawful source of the funds to be invested in the U.S. enterprise. An EB-5 practitioner may look initially to evidence of the client's earned income, which, when available, is generally the most obvious and easily demonstrated source of invested funds. A review of tax returns filed by the petitioner and any profitable enterprises

---

[2] 8 CFR §204.6(j)(3)(i).
[3] 8 CFR §204.6(j)(3)(ii).
[4] 8 CFR §204.6(j)(3)(iii).

owned by the petitioner is the standard starting point of this inquiry.

UNDERSTANDING CHINA'S GENERAL TAXATION SYSTEMS

As with the United States, China has several layers of taxation systems, which can vary from jurisdiction to jurisdiction. Understanding the basics of these systems can help the EB-5 practitioner with planning and presenting evidence to prove the lawful source of funds and to comply with the EB-5 regulations' requirement regarding investor tax returns. The subsections below provide a general overview of the most common taxation systems in China.

Individual Income Taxation

Pre-2006: Employers withheld and reported employees' income tax.

Before 2006, Chinese citizens were not required to file individual income tax returns. Rather, in accord with the Chinese Personal Income Tax Law, employing business entities withheld the income tax owed by an employee on earnings, paid the taxes to the government on the employee's behalf, and filed the required tax returns with the tax-collecting authority on a monthly basis.[5] Copies of the monthly tax-payment reports filed by the employer and tax-payment receipts issued by the local tax-collection agency are typically available.

2006-Present: Individuals must self-report/pay income tax.

Changes in the Chinese taxation law implemented in 2006 now require the self-reporting of income by individuals earning over RMB120,000, or approximately US$17,500 at current exchange rates.[6] Under the Self-Declaration Rules Concerning Individual Income Tax, any taxpayer with annual income above the threshold reporting amount is required to declare all items of annual income within three months after the end of a tax year. Income to be declared includes salary and wages, income from the production and operation of individually owned businesses, income from contract operations, compensation for labor services, author's remuneration, royalties, interest, dividend and bonus income, income from the lease of property, income from the transfer of property, incidental income, and other types of taxable income.[7]

Sole proprietors: Dual-tax obligation abolished in 2006.

Previously, sole proprietors (as opposed to employees) faced dual taxation, but the rule has since been abolished. Specifically, until 2000, sole proprietors in the PRC were subject to a dual tax, paying a 20-percent personal income tax out of the profits of an enterprise, net of a 33-percent enterprise income tax. The dual tax was the subject of considerable debate during the drafting of the Sole Proprietorship Enterprise Law, which took effect in January 2000. In September 2006, in response to the concerns of sole proprietors, the State Council, the Ministry of Finance, and the State Tax Bureau released the "Regulation Concerning the Personal Income Tax of the Investor in Sole Proprietorship Enterprises and Partnership Enterprises," which, under Article 2, abolished the dual-tax system, requiring sole proprietors to pay only personal income tax.[8]

Under-reporting of earnings is common.

It is a relatively common practice for entrepreneurs in the PRC to report only a relatively modest monthly wage to the tax authorities, and to rely upon substantial "off-book" expense allowances to meet all personal expenses in excess of the reported wage amount. Due to this practice and the significant under-reporting of individual income, documentation of the reporting and payment of taxes on individual income provided by Chinese clients will frequently fail to show a stream of income sufficient to sustain a viable I-526 petition, requiring counsel to look to other forms of lawful source documentation, which may require the leveraging of aged assets, personal or company loans, the receipt of one-time dividends from profitable enterprises, inter-generational gifts, and other creative solutions.

---

[5] Article 8 of the Personal Income Tax Law of the People's Republic of China, enacted Sept. 10, 1989, provides, "For the purpose of personal income tax, the income earner is the taxpayer, and the unit or individual paying such income is the withholding agent."

[6] *See* Publicity Material for Self-Declaration Rules Concerning Individual Income Tax, available online at the English language website of the PRC National Administration of Taxation at *www.chinatax.gov.cn/n6669073/n6888589/6889238.html* (last visited Feb. 1, 2010).

[7] *Id.*

[8] Available on the English language website of the Chinese State Administration of Taxation at *http://202.108.90.130/ n6669073/n6669088/8965437.html*. *See also* Jian Fu, "Private Enterprises and the Law," *China's Third Economic Transformation: The Rise of the Private Economy* (Ross Garnaut and Ligang Song eds., Routledge 2004).

Corporate Income Tax

To establish the lawful source of a client's invested capital and comply with the regulations calling for the submission of a wide range of corporate and other tax records, counsel should review financial statements and tax filings submitted by profitable enterprises owned in whole or in part by the petitioner. In this context, a basic knowledge of the statutory framework for the organization and management of the most commonly seen PRC business entities is helpful.

Common PRC commercial entities.

In addition to the sole proprietorship enterprise, the most common forms of Chinese commercial entities likely to be encountered by EB-5 practitioners are the limited liability company (LLC) *(youxian zeren gongsi)* and "company limited by shares" *(gufen youxian zeren gongsi)*. Under the Company Law of the People's Republic of China, both limited liability companies and companies limited by shares will typically have a board of directors with chief executive authority vested in a general manager who is responsible to the board of directors. In lieu of a board of directors, a Chinese LLC with a relatively small number of shareholders may have an executive director who may also serve as the company's general manager. A Chinese company limited by shares will have a chairperson who is the legal representative of the company, and may have one or two vice-chairpersons. Both the LLC and company limited by shares are required, at the end of each fiscal year, to prepare a financial statement that should include a balance sheet, profit and loss statement, statement of financial changes, explanation of financial condition, and profit-distribution statement.[9]

Corporate income tax requirements.

PRC companies, whether an LLC or a company limited by shares, are required to pay corporate income tax.[10] Under the new Corporate Income Tax Law of the People's Republic of China and Implementation Regulations that came into effect on January 1, 2008, the corporate income tax rate has been unified to 25 percent of taxable income. Lower tax rates apply to enterprises defined as "Advanced and New Technology Enterprises."[11]

Tax incentives, exemptions, holidays, and reductions are extended under laws and regulations applicable to enterprises engaged in certain types of state-encouraged activities, or located in "ethnic autonomous regions" or a variety national, provincial or municipal-level Economic and Technological Development Zones.[12] A PRC entrepreneur may establish a company to engage in a tax-favored activity, or operate in a development zone for the duration of a period of tax exemption and/or reduction, and then shut down that company and reopen a new company in the same line of business in the same enterprise zone, thereby effectively extending a limited tax holiday into one of indefinite duration.

Corporate tax reporting.

Although reporting practices vary considerably by region, a Chinese company will typically submit quarterly financial reports and pay taxes on quarterly revenues to local tax-collecting agencies. At the end of the tax year, the company will submit an annual tax report for review and possible auditing and adjustment by the tax authorities. Following review of the annual tax report, the local tax agency will provide the company with a copy of the report bearing the seal of the agency confirming approval. Copies of quarterly and annual tax reports filed by companies, and certification of payment of corporate income taxes issued by the tax collection agency, are generally available. Banks processing tax payments on behalf of the tax agency will also routinely provide tax payment receipts.

Other Tax Obligations of PRC Business and Individuals

Knowledge of the wide range of tax obligations imposed on EB-5 petitioners from the PRC will assist counsel in producing the requisite five years of tax records called for in the EB-5 regulations. Below are some of the common ones.

VAT.

Since 1984, Chinese individuals and enterprises engaged in non-service or production-related activities, such as trading or manufacturing, are subject to

---

[9] *See* Chinese Company Law, adopted at the Fifth Session of the Standing Committee of the 8th National People's Congress on Dec. 29, 1993, with amendments as of Dec. 25, 1999.

[10] *See* Corporate Income Tax Law of the People's Republic of China, adopted by 10th National People's Congress of the PRC on Mar. 16, 2007, and effective Jan. 1, 2008.

[11] *Id.* at Article 28.

[12] *See* complete list of National Economic and Technological Zones on the website of the Chinese Ministry of Commerce at *www.mofcom.gov.cn/xglj/kaifaqu.shtml* (last visited Feb. 15, 2010).

Value-Added Tax (VAT). VAT, which is one of the single largest sources of revenue to the Chinese government, applies in the sale of taxable goods, excluding intangible assets and real estate, the provision of taxable labor services (*i.e.*, processing and repairing services), and the import of taxable goods into China.[13]

Business tax.

Business tax is payable by all business entities that provide taxable services (*e.g.*, transportation, construction, finance and insurance, entertainment, and professional services), or transfer possession of immovable properties, such as real estate and intangible assets. Business tax is levied on the gross income from services and non-production activities regardless of whether a foreign entity has a permanent establishment in China or not. Business tax rates vary in accordance with different industries and jurisdictions.[14]

Consumption tax.

All enterprises and individuals engaged in production or importation of taxable consumer goods, such as cosmetics, motor vehicles, jewelry, and alcoholic beverages are required to report and pay a Consumption Tax.[15]

Other common tax obligations.

In addition to VAT, business tax, and consumption tax, Chinese individuals and enterprises typically will also be able to provide documentation of the payment of myriad other national, provincial and local taxes, including, inter alia, real estate transfer tax, urban land-use tax, farmland occupation tax, and education tax.[16]

---

[13] *See* Provisional Regulations on Value Added Tax of the People's Republic of China, Promulgated on the Order of the State Council [1993] No.134, Dec. 13,1993.

[14] *See* Provisional Regulations on Business Tax of the People's Republic of China, promulgated on Order [1993] No. 136 of the State Council on Dec. 12, 1993, available in Chinese and English at the website of the State Administration of Tax at *http://202.108.90.130/n6669073/n6669088/index.html*. (last visited Jan. 30, 2010).

[15] *See* Provisional Regulations of the People's Republic of China on Consumption Tax, promulgated on Order [1993] No. 135 of the State Council on Dec. 13, 1993.

[16] *See* the text of numerous tax laws in force at the English website of the PRC State Administration of Tax, at *http://202.108.90.130/n6669073/index.html* (last visited Feb. 1, 2010).

USE OF THIRD-PARTY ACCOUNTING PRESENTATIONS TO PROVE LAWFUL SOURCE OF FUNDS

To address the daunting challenge of sifting through a large volume of Chinese-language tax returns, bank records, and other business and financial documents of varying degrees of relevance and utility, practitioners may wish to outsource a portion of this work to a third-party accountancy firm with a presence in China willing and able to prepare a detailed compilation of documentation evidencing a client's historical income, ownership of valuable assets, and net worth.

While this may provide a practical solution to some of the linguistic and cultural barriers confronted by counsel, expense may be a consideration, as reputable international accounting firms understandably charge substantial fees for this service. Of equal importance, however, is the fact that EB-5 investors from the PRC are often pleased to learn that participation in the U.S. immigrant investor program does not require a complete disclosure of assets. The "net worth" approach typically employed in third-party presentations prepared in this context is often not well-suited to PRC petitioners who may be reticent to make the types of disclosures required for a meaningful "net worth" presentation. Counsel should discuss the trade-offs of using such third-party accountants to prepare presentations on lawful source of funds.

CREATIVE APPROACHES AND CAVEATS TO SELECTING THE ASSET(S) TO SERVE AS THE LAWFUL SOURCE OF FUNDS

Faced with the frequent inability of PRC clients to produce tax returns and financial documents evidencing a stream of income sufficient to allow for the accumulation of the capital required for a qualifying EB-5 investment, counsel must be prepared to discuss the "lawful source" issue with a prospective client at the outset of the case-planning process.

It is of critical importance in PRC EB-5 cases that counsel clearly communicates with the client to explain the documentary requirements of the EB-5 regulations and to collaboratively develop solutions to evidentiary challenges before the client's remittance of the investment capital to the United States. Inadequate communication and poor case planning can result in the inbound remittance of capital of uncertain origin, setting the stage for petition denial.

Counsel may wish to propose that a PRC client identify one or more "aged assets," which can be liquidated, or used as collateral for a loan. If the client is a major investor in a closely held company that has substantial liquid assets, the client may be able to obtain formal shareholder and board approval of a substantial one-time dividend distribution, or a loan of some portion or even all of the funds required for the client's investment in the EB-5 enterprise. If a loan is extended to the petitioner by a creditor that is not a bank or licensed lending institution, counsel must be prepared to adequately document the financial ability of the creditor to extend the loan. In addressing a private loan arrangement, counsel should also document the manner in which the petitioner intends to repay the loan.

A reading of the language of INA §203(b)(5) gives no indication that Congress intended to impose upon an investor-petitioner the burden of proving that the source of the invested funds derived from lawful means. Nevertheless, the regulations at 8 CFR §204.6(j)(3) require a petitioner to show that he or she "has invested, or is actively in the process of investing, capital obtained through lawful means." Strictly enforced, this rule would function to create a presumption of "unlawful source," which all EB-5 petitioners would be required to overcome in the same manner that applicants for various nonimmigrant visas must overcome the presumption of immigrant intent under INA §214(b).[17]

Setting aside valid concerns regarding the *ultra vires* nature of this requirement, in the exercise of due diligence on behalf of an EB-5 petitioner, counsel must be cognizant of the relative prevalence in China's modernizing economy of a variety of business practices which, at best, may be described as legally questionable. Of obvious concern is the receipt of a "kickback" in the form of a commercial bribe paid by a seller to a purchasing agent acting on behalf of a government entity in order to induce the agent to enter into the transaction. The payment and receipt of kickbacks or other types of compensation not disclosed to both parties to a transaction is expressly prohibited by Article 8 of the Anti-Unfair Competition Law of the People's Republic of China.[18]

CURRENCY RESTRICTIONS AND CHALLENGES IN TRACING THE PATH OF FUNDS

In the globalized economy and business environment of today, immigration practitioners active in the EB-5 field are regularly called upon to provide counsel with regard to transactions that cross national borders, requiring familiarity with foreign law. The PRC restricts the exchange of Chinese currency *(renminbi)* and generally limits the remittance of foreign currency to $50,000 per year per individual.[19] A "work around" frequently seen in the EB-5 context involves the cooperation of family, friends, and acquaintances willing to serve as "accommodation remitters" to collectively accomplish the remittance.[20] Various informal private currency exchange and/or remittance arrangements involving friends or business associates outside of China are also common and have been found acceptable by U.S. Citizenship and Immigration Services (USCIS) when thoroughly documented.

In recent years, USCIS adjudicators have not imposed an obligation on I-526 petitioners to establish the lawfulness of remittances under foreign law, and have readily approved otherwise approvable I-526

---

[17] The actual purpose of the agency in imposing the "unlawful source" standard is unclear, as the existing statutory bars to admission authorize U.S. Citizenship and Immigration Services (USCIS) and consular officers to deny U.S. immigration benefits to any alien who would attempt to use the proceeds of criminal activity to invest in and immigrate to the United States. (*See* 9 *Foreign Affairs Manual* (FAM) 40.28.)

[18] Adopted by the Third Session of the Standing Committee of the Eighth National People's Congress on Sept. 2, 1993. Text available on the English language public website of the Supreme People's Court of the People's Republic of China, at *http://en.chinacourt.org/public/* (Last visited Sept. 4, 2009).

[19] *See* Circular of the State Administration of Foreign Exchange on Printing and Distributing the Detailed Rules on the Implementation of the Measures for the Administration of Individual Foreign Exchange (July 13, 2009), published in English on the website of the State Administration of Foreign Exchange, at *www.safe.gov.cn/model_safe_en/* (last visited Feb. 1, 2010).

[20] The continued viability of these types of arrangements is very much in doubt in light of a recent directive issued by the State Administration of Foreign Exchange which expressly prohibits the use of multiple parties to accomplish serial remittances in excess of the permissible annual limitation. *See* "Circular of the SAFE Concerning Further Improving Administration of Foreign Exchange Settlement and Sale Business", published Nov. 15, 2009 on the Chinese language website of the State Administration of Foreign Exchange, available online in Chinese and English at *www.safe.gov.cn/model_safe/index.html* (last visited Feb. 1, 2010).

petitions accompanied by probative evidence clearly tracing the invested funds from the PRC investor to the EB-5 enterprise. Ideally, counsel will discuss issues related to documenting the path of investor capital with a prospective investor prior to the actual remittance of funds to the United States. In this manner, issues arising from remittances lacking adequate tracing documentation may hopefully be avoided.[21]

Counsel will often be asked by a prospective PRC investor to propose methods to avoid or circumvent Chinese currency remittance restrictions. Such inquiries raise issues as to the ethical obligation of counsel when a client proposes to take an action that may violate some rule of foreign law, and whether the U.S. practitioner has an ethical obligation to offer advice or refrain from offering advice concerning such a course of action.

The ABA Model Rules of Professional Conduct (2003), at Rule 1.2 (d), provide: "A lawyer shall not counsel a client to engage, or assist a client, in conduct that the lawyer knows is criminal or fraudulent, but a lawyer may discuss the legal consequences of any proposed course of conduct with a client and may counsel or assist a client to make a good faith effort to determine the validity, scope, meaning or application of the law." While Rule 1.2 is not restricted by political or geographic boundaries, it is by no means settled law that there are ethical requirements placed upon an attorney licensed to practice in the United States by the mere fact of a foreign law mandate.[22] This question is particularly nuanced where, as in the case of foreign exchange violations, the conduct in question does not violate U.S. laws.

Obviously, counsel must exercise extreme caution in advising a client on issues involving possible violations of foreign law, which advice, if relied upon, may expose the client to civil administrative penalties or criminal liability in his or her home country. In light of these considerations, the most prudent path for the attorney confronted with such issues may be to direct the client to local counsel who can interpret the foreign-law requirement, what it means in practice, and its realistic contours.

CONSULAR PROCESSING IN CHINA

The U.S. Consulate General in Guangzhou, which issues more immigrant visas annually than all consular posts worldwide with the exception of Ciudad Juarez and Manila, is responsible for processing all immigrant visa applications in China.[23] The National Visa Center (NVC) will send a letter to counsel when a case is transferred electronically to Guangzhou. The interview cannot take place, however, until the physical file arrives at post. Due to delays in getting files through Chinese customs, it typically takes about three months for a file to arrive at the consulate after being shipped by the NVC. Once the consulate receives the physical file, and all security checks have been completed, the consulate will schedule the interview and notify the applicant. Interviews are typically scheduled three to six weeks in advance.

The EB-5 visa process is a high-stakes endeavor, typically involving substantial legal fees and financial risk on the part of the visa applicant. It is therefore essential that every prospective EB-5 case begin with a thorough review of all possible grounds of inadmissibility. Of particular importance in the case of EB-5 visa candidates from the PRC is the need to rule out inadmissibility under INA §212(a)(3)(D) which, with specific statutory exceptions, and subject to a discretionary waiver for qualified applicants, excludes any "immigrant who is or has been a member of or affiliated with the Communist or any other totalitarian party (or subdivision or affiliate thereof), domestic or foreign." Under the exception for past membership, an immigrant applying for a visa from a country such as China, which is under the control of a totalitarian party, who has terminated membership in or affiliation with the party for at least five years at the time of applying for a visa or admission to the United States is not inadmissible if he or she is not determined to be a threat to the security of the United States. INA §212(a)(3)(D)(iii).[24]

---

[21] Confronted with a remittance lacking the necessary documentation, the best option may be for counsel to advise a "re-do" of the remittance in a fully documented manner.

[22] These comments are, of course, restricted to the ethical sanctions that may be imposed by a lawyer's jurisdiction of admission as a result of actions violating foreign laws. Unquestionably, certain U.S. laws such as the Foreign Corrupt Practices Act of 1977 (15 USC §§78dd-1, *et seq*), attach criminal liability to acts which will frequently also violate foreign laws.

---

[23] *See* Summary of Visas Issued by Issuing Office, Fiscal 2008, available at www.travel.state.gov/visa/frvi/statistics/statistics_4391.html. (Last visited Sept. 4, 2009).

[24] Other exceptions extend to party membership or affiliation that is found to be: (1) involuntary; (2) solely when under 16 years of age; (3) by operation of law; or (4) to obtain employment, funds, or other essentials of living. INA §212(a)(3)(D)(iv). INA §212(a)(3) also authorizes a discre-
continued

Successful applicants seeking visas through investment in designated regional centers report that the consular officers in Guangzhou are not requiring an in-depth knowledge of the details of the regional center's business plan on the part of the investor. Applicants may expect to be asked to identify the project in which they have invested, the amount of their investment, and the manner in which their funds were remitted to the United States. EB-5 visa seekers who are applying outside of the regional center program, and who may be required to take a more "hands on" management role in the U.S. enterprise than that granted to most regional center investors, may be required to have a more thorough knowledge of the business of the enterprise. Consular officers in Guangzhou often request the submission of family photographs to verify the parentage of accompanying minor dependents.

Reports have been received that over-zealous agents in China acting on behalf of some regional centers have on occasion made representations to investors with regard to an early return of the investor's capital following I-829 approval. Counsel should actively educate visa applicants that USCIS deems any redemption agreement made prior to I-829 approval impermissible and that information substantiating such representations may result in the return of an approved I-526 to USCIS for possible revocation.

CONCLUSION

The representation of PRC citizens seeking to immigrate under the alien entrepreneur provisions presents a number of daunting challenges to the EB-5 practitioner. These challenges, which are aggravated by the lack of national uniformity in financial and tax reporting practices, include the absence of financial records demonstrating a source of income adequate to generate the necessary capital to be invested in the target enterprise in the United States and difficulties tracing remitted capital to the U.S. enterprise due to the Chinese government's prohibition on the conversion and outbound remittance of substantial sums. In light of these factors, success in representing EB-5 candidates from the People's Republic of China must be built upon clear and effective communication of evidentiary requirements by the attorney to the client and the active engagement of the client in the process beginning at the case-planning stage and continuing through to case completion.

---

tionary waiver of this ground of inadmissibility for an immigrant who is the parent, spouse, son, daughter, brother, or sister of a U.S. citizen or a spouse, son, or daughter of a permanent resident. This waiver may be based upon humanitarian purposes, to ensure family unity, or when it is otherwise in the public interest, if the noncitizen is not a threat to U.S. security.

RUSSIAN EB-5 INVESTORS—"UNWRAPPING" THE MYSTERY

*by Kenneth White**

Winston Churchill's words still ring true today, that Russia can indeed be a "riddle, wrapped in a mystery, inside an enigma." This mystique is compounded by the dual legacies of its Soviet past and the "Wild West" atmosphere of the 1990s. Nevertheless, Russia has made substantial strides in transforming itself into a modern, open economy. This transformation is marked by integration into the global economy; until recently, booming consumer, real estate and financial markets; better corporate governance; greater tax compliance; and improved transparency.

For EB-5 practitioners, this means that legitimate Russian[1] investors are usually able to evidence the source of their funds without significant complications. Russians are less inclined to evade taxes because its tax rates are among the lowest in the world: a flat 13 percent tax on income;[2] 9 percent on dividends;[3] 6 percent on certain types of entrepreneurial activity;[4] and no taxation on gifts between close relatives[5] or on profits from real estate transactions if the property has been held for at least three years.[6] This tax framework has had the effect of bringing Russian capital out of the shadows. For EB-5 lawyers, it has eased the burden of documenting client cases.

BACKGROUND

Compared to emigration from China, India, and Korea, Russian immigration to the United States is negligible. This is also reflected in the EB-5 program. For fiscal years (FYs) 2008 and 2009 combined, less than 100 Russians have obtained permanent resident status through EB-5.[7] Besides the greatly improved economic situation in Russia since the early 1990s and the overall political stability, specific reasons cited by potential EB-5 investors for a reluctance to participate include: (1) U.S. worldwide taxation on permanent residents; (2) the perceived riskiness of EB-5 investments and the two-year conditional status; (3) low return on investments (Russian entrepreneurs are accustomed to 15–30 percent annual return); and (4) an inability to collateralize existing assets to finance an investment due to high Russian interest rates (14–17 percent). Other factors contributing to these spartan EB-5 statistics include a short-term mentality;[8] little EB-5 marketing in Russia; widespread gray and corrupt sources of funds; and the existence of other residency and passport alternatives (*e.g.*, UK, Canada, St. Kitts, and Bulgaria).[9]

For the EB-5 program, this is unfortunate because Russians represent a truly large pool of potential participants. In the 1990s, Russians were able to privatize their apartments for a nominal fee, and employees and management of large factories received free privatization vouchers. Virtually overnight, millions of Russians became owners of apartments—mortgage free—and shareholders in factories. Poor *babushkas* became real-estate rich. During the boom times of the 2000s, real estate

---

* **Kenneth White** is a member of the District of Columbia bar and was a long-time resident of Moscow, Russia. He is the coauthor of the Russian-language books: *U.S. Nonimmigrant Visas*; *Handbook for Immigrants to Canada*; and the soon-to-be-released *Immigration to the United States*. His law firm specializes in consular matters and U.S. immigration issues, including EB-5.

[1] While the term "Russian investor" is used in this article for simplicity purposes, it encompasses individuals of various nationalities from countries and regions throughout the former Soviet Union who are currently resident in Russia.

[2] Article 224(1) of the Russian Tax Code.

[3] Article 224(4) of the Russian Tax Code.

[4] Article 346(20) of the Russian Tax Code.

[5] Article 217(18.1) of the Russian Tax Code.

[6] Article 217(17.1) of the Russian Tax Code.

[7] 2008 and 2009 Reports of the Visa Office, Table V, Part 3.

[8] Typified by the Russian expression: "Until it starts to thunder, a man will not make the sign of the cross."

[9] In contrast to the substantial number of multinational companies based in the UK, Germany, Canada, and other Western countries with operations in the United States, Russian-origin multinationals with offices in the United States are very few. As a result, the number of EB-1 intra-company transferees within Russian multinational companies is small. Russian EB-1 executives have tended to be owner-operators of both the Russian and U.S. entities. With the recent change in U.S. Citizenship and Immigration Services (USCIS) policy regarding owner-operator Ls and EB-1s—potentially foreclosing this immigration option for owner-operators—and the ineligibility of Russians for E visas, this policy change may have the unintended effect of bolstering the number of Russian EB-5 petitions.

prices increased on average 7–8 times, with prices in Moscow rivaling New York and London.[10] In short, the greatest state giveaway in history created a class of asset-rich owners.

PRELIMINARY SCREENING OF INVESTORS BEFORE UNDERTAKING REPRESENTATION

Before undertaking representation of a Russian EB-5 client, EB-5 practitioners should be particularly cognizant of inadmissibility issues. In the 1990s and early 2000s, amidst the Russian mafia frenzy portrayed in the Western press, the Embassy in Moscow was "bar happy": it slapped numerous applicants—legitimate and not so legitimate—with a variety of admissibility bars, including alien smuggling, material misrepresentation, criminal, security, and fraud. Many individuals who had not even applied for a visa were also subject to visa "hits"; some individuals who did apply and were found ineligible for a visa under §214(b) of the Immigration and Nationality Act (INA)[11] were not advised of an admissibility problem.

Section 212(a)(3)(A)(ii) of the INA deserves particular attention. This provision states that a visa applicant is inadmissible if the consular officer has "reasonable ground to believe" that the applicant "seeks to enter the United States to engage solely, principally, or incidentally … in any other unlawful activity." In 1995, this section of the INA became applicable to organized crime groups operating in countries of the former Soviet Union. While the *Foreign Affairs Manual* (FAM) discusses *membership* in an organized crime group as grounds for a finding of inadmissibility,[12] the U.S. Embassy in Moscow has applied §212(a)(3)(A)(ii) far outside this circle: to family members, friends, and even individuals who merely had been seen in public with mafia members.

While the "bar-happy" trend has moderated, §212(a)(3)(A)(ii) continues to be broadly applied to all kinds of unlawful activity. For example, a legitimate Russian businessman who engaged in importing cars from Germany in 2000–03, and has received numerous Shengen and UK visas since, is subject to a §212(a)(3)(A)(ii) bar for suspicion of money laundering relating to the German transactions. "Poison-pen" letters can be deemed sufficient to trigger a finding of inadmissibility under this provision of the INA. Individuals who have made their money in the gas and metal industries seem to be particularly targeted. Someone who visited the United States five years ago may find out that he has been recently "black listed" under this provision of the INA, although he is engaged in the same activity he was five years ago. The author recently encountered a "by-the-way" moment after spending 30 minutes with a potential EB-5 investor: "by the way, I have had a B visa application pending for more than one year at the Embassy in Moscow."

Therefore, besides the general efficacy of having an investor visit potential EB-5 targets before making an investment, if the investor is a businessman and has not received a visa in the past two years, it is advisable to have him make an application for a B visa before making an investment to ensure that there are no admissibility issues.

Once the risk of admissibility problems has been minimized, counsel most likely will spend time with a potential Russian investor dispelling popular myths circulating in Russia about the EB-5 program. For example, the most widely disseminated fiction is how 10 family members—regardless of age and level of relationship—can receive green cards based on an investor's EB-5 participation. Other urban legends include: (1) a Regional Center project does not need to create 10 jobs; (2) guaranteed condition removal; (3) exorbitant returns on investment; and (4) guaranteed buybacks. Thus, it is imperative to ensure that the potential client has a proper understanding of the risks, requirements, and benefits before proceeding with the representation.

TRACKING THE PATH OF FUNDS

Once the representation has been undertaken, the practitioner is likely to encounter a variety of tax, corporate governance, technical, cultural, and logistical issues in documenting the lawful source of the investment funds. For example, Russian law does not require the filing of tax declarations for most indi-

---

[10] "Global Property Guide," Feb. 6, 2009, www.globalpropertyguide.com/press-relations/Most-expensive-real-estate-markets-in-2009#. Notwithstanding the recent collapse of the market, real estate in Moscow and St. Petersburg remains an expensive commodity.

[11] Immigration and Nationality Act of 1952 (INA), Pub. L. No. 82-414, 66 Stat. 163 (codified as amended at 8 USC §§1101 *et seq.*).`

[12] 9 *Foreign Affairs Manual* (FAM) 40.31 N5.3.

viduals.[13] Conflict of interest questions sometimes arise. Resumes and business promotional materials are foreign concepts among many Russian entrepreneurs over the age of 45. Technical and logistical issues that frequently arise relate to the constantly fluctuating exchange rate (33 percent depreciation of the ruble over the past year); bank statements which often do not reflect daily balances or even the names of the owners of the account; delays in transferring of funds to the EB-5 entity or escrow account because some banks have little experience with international transactions or require the translation of all investment-related documentation; and a general lack of automation and public accessibility to personal and corporate records, hindering due diligence efforts.

One issue that counsel does not need to be concerned about relates to currency restrictions. In contrast to the currency restrictions faced by Chinese and Korean EB-5 investors, there are no limitations in Russian law on transferring funds abroad to escrow accounts or EB-5 entities. However, tracking the pre-investment path of funds can be particularly nettlesome in Russia because of the traditional distrust of banks.[14] This distrust is manifested in numerous ways: for example, when a transaction of considerable value is consummated, funds paid to an account at a Russian bank are often transferred abroad or to a Western bank in Russia for safekeeping. Because there are no escrow accounts in Russia and relatively few mortgage transactions, the overwhelming majority of real estate deals are cash transactions, with safe deposit boxes serving as the conduit for the transaction and handwritten receipts utilized.

As noted, Russian tax law is very liberal and has been relatively effective in ensuring greater tax compliance. This is not to say that all Russians diligently pay their taxes. High pension and social fund taxes have the effect of discouraging employers from reporting full salaries or any salaries at all. Offshore companies continue to be commonplace, acting as invoicing mechanisms for business transactions, "piggy banks" for accumulating funds, and investment structures.[15] Real estate held for less than three years is subject to income tax. Transactions which may not pass a "laugh test" in the West—such as a $500,000 apartment being sold on paper for $30,000—are not uncommon.[16] With the corruptibility of tax inspectors, it may be easier and cheaper to pay off a tax official than to pay one's taxes.

Other pertinent Russian law provisions that arise in the EB-5 context include corporate governance laws, which cover certain conflict-of-interest situations.[17] For example, it is not unusual for antiquated Soviet-era factories to have unused premises. An executive for the successor organization may also own an outside company, and acting in the name of the organization, lease out the unused premises to his own company, which in turn subleases the premises to another company. As long as the Board of Directors of the successor organization approves the transaction, it is permissible under Russian law. In contrast, Russian anti-corruption legislation is unequivocal in prohibiting government officials from profiting from their positions.[18] While not having the desired effect of curbing widespread corruption, these provisions, along with U.S. source-of-funds

---

[13] Usually, employers will issue W-2-like forms to employees and shareholders reflecting the payment of salaries and dividends. The employers withhold the relevant taxes and file the necessary reports with the Russian Tax Inspectorate. For those individuals who do file declarations, they must file for the previous calendar year by April 30th and pay the tax owed by July 15th. Articles 227–229 of the Russian Tax Code. In the EB-5 context, this issue may be particularly acute for investors whose source of income for the investment was earned in the most recent tax year, and who have yet to file tax declarations or pay taxes on that income. In such instances, it would be appropriate to point out these tax deadlines to USCIS and have the client provide counsel with copies of the declaration and receipt of tax payment once these obligations have been met.

[14] This distrust proved well-founded when numerous banks went bankrupt in 1998, and hundreds of thousands of Russians lost their life savings.

[15] Companies based in offshore havens such as Cyprus are among the top investors in Russia. *Russia Today*, Aug. 25, 2009, *http://rt.com/Business/2009-08-25/fdi-russia-slide-rebound.html*.

[16] A typical transaction chain would encompass two stages. The first stage would be at the construction phase of a residential building, when a real estate investor will execute an agreement with the developer to purchase an apartment. The agreement will not reflect the actual price—for example, instead of $150,000, a price of $25,000. The second stage takes place after the building has been completed, say, 18 months later, and the real estate investor seeks to sell the apartment. His asking price may be $500,000, with a paper price of $30,000. In this way, the real estate investor will have "economized" on tax payments by more than $50,000.

[17] Articles 81–84 of the Russian "Federal Law on Joint Stock Companies."

[18] *E.g.*, Russian Federal Laws 273, 274, and 280 "On Counteracting Corruption."

requirements, seem to have deterred EB-5 petitions by such individuals.

OTHER ADVICE FOR THE PETITION-PREPARATION STAGE

The practitioner will often deal with other Russia-specific issues in the course of preparing a petition for an investor. For example, one of the legacies of the Soviet era is the Labor Book, the official confirmation of one's work experience. It contains information on an individual's education level; specialization; starting and ending dates for each place of employment; corresponding positions; and internal organization protocol number serving as the basis for the hire or termination. This becomes relevant when the information listed in an individual's resume or employer's salary records diverges from the data specified in the Labor Book. Blank Labor Books are sold in metro stations and kiosks, and because they are subject to manipulation, the U.S. Embassy in Moscow gives little credibility to them. Obviously, the practitioner should be alert to any inconsistencies in work history, particularly if that work experience and salaries earned from that experience form the basis for the investment.

Another Soviet-era legacy is the Russian residential registration system, or *propiska*. The system was put into place to track and control the movements of the population. Today, this comes into play when a client is registered at one address, but actually lives at a different address, which may be in a different city. It is imperative to stress to the client that the actual address, not the registration address, be used in all documentation, including for purposes of obtaining police certificates.

While basic business information is available online, detailed, Internet-accessible business, property, and criminal records are nearly nonexistent in Russia. However, clients are able to obtain a variety of public records reflecting property and corporate ownership, as well as criminal and judicial files. These records can be supplemented by the omnipresent *spravka*, or reference, a staple of Russian bureaucratic life. The *spravka* can be used to confirm any type of official matter: from attendance at a university, to the payment of taxes, to medical conditions, to how many individuals are registered in an apartment.[19]

Finally, because of the various Russian legal issues which crop up during the preparation of the petition, it often makes sense to include a Legal Opinion of a licensed Russian attorney.

SPECIAL CONSIDERATIONS FOR THE IMMIGRANT VISA INTERVIEW IN MOSCOW

There are minimal delays at the National Visa Center (NVC) in processing Russian cases and at the U.S. Embassy in Moscow in interviewing applicants. After payment of the immigrant visa (IV) fees and submission of the supporting documents, NVC schedules the interview.[20] The interview is usually scheduled approximately three to four months after the submission of the documents. On average, the visa is issued within three to five business days after the interview.

The post has been quite helpful in rectifying errors and handling post-interview issues. E-mail inquiries (consulmo@state.gov) are generally answered within one to three business days; after the interview, if additional documents are required, they can be sent to the post by e-mail; courier; or hand-delivered to the embassy's 221(g) drop box at the north gate.

To date, the post has been cooperative in processing EB-5 cases. Interviews have tended to be a relative formality. Questions focus on (1) how the investor earned his capital for the investment; (2) plans for the United States (not related to the investment); (3) past visa issuances and time spent in the United States; and (4) admissibility issues. As a rule, the officer requests confirmation of the transfer of the funds to the U.S. entity or the escrow account; although this documentation was submitted with the I-526 petition, the investor applicant should have a copy with him at the time of the interview.

CONCLUSION

The Russian proclivity to operate in cash and not adhere to the letter of Russian legislation certainly poses challenges to counsel in preparing EB-5 petitions. Nevertheless, the overall trend is towards the gradual "civilizing" of Russian business, including increased transparency and tax compliance. While

---

[19] Again, counsel should be alert to the overall corruption in Russian officialdom, and that such references can be bought and sold with relative ease.

[20] The Embassy previously had an online immigrant visa appointment system. The system allowed for the monitoring of the appointment date based on the USCIS case number. However, that system was discontinued recently.

this positive trend and the underlying wealth of asset-rich Russians would seem to augur well for Russian participation in the EB-5 program, the Russians, true to Winston Churchill's words, have remained an enigma. Now that they are free to emigrate and have the financial ability to do so, they have generally chosen—at least for now—not to pursue immigration opportunities for themselves or their children in the United States.

SELECTED ISSUES IN EB-5 CASES:
JOB CREATION, TWO-YEAR PERIODS, AND INDIRECT EMPLOYMENT

by Edward J. Carroll[*]

Since the inception of the EB-5, Alien Entrepreneur program in 1990, investors, their lawyers, legacy Immigration and Nationality Service (INS), and U.S. Citizenship and Immigration Services (USCIS) have grappled with issues that determine the success of an I-526, Immigrant Petition by Alien Entrepreneurs. The complexities of assembling an approvable I-526 petition became more challenging with the creation of the Regional Center Pilot Program,[1] and the law of I-526 petitions was further modified by four precedent decisions issued by legacy INS in 1998.[2] USCIS also has illustrated its changing interpretations of law and regulations via the issuance of Requests for Evidence (RFE) and denials of petitions.

Practitioners understand that the planning and documentation of an I-526 petition ought to be done with an awareness of what an investor will be expected to demonstrate when the I-829, Petition by Entrepreneur to Remove Conditions, is filed. In particular, projects in the I-526 phase are advised to address the peculiar requirements of timing of job creation and the methodology for demonstrating the establishment of jobs that vary among non-regional center cases, troubled business cases, and regional center filings. During the I-829 process, USCIS will test for compliance with these requirements. Failure to meet these tests during the I-829 process subjects an investor to the risk of removal, so the I-526 case ought to create a framework within which an investor can implement an enterprise and demonstrate compliance with applicable I-829 requirements.

As the process of reviewing I-829 Petitions has evolved, investors now are subjected to retroactive and increasingly detailed scrutiny of their compliance with I-526 petition requirements long ago adjudicated favorably and thought to be resolved. Some investors are experiencing new analysis of the input/output job creation model and the source of funds information provided during the I-526 adjudication. Others are finding that indirect employment created outside the geographical boundaries of a regional center, projected and approved during the I-526 phase, now must be excluded from job creation figures at the I-829 stage. There does not appear to be any limit on USCIS's appetite to revisit the entire I-526 case during an I-829 filing, although the agency has said recently that it does not routinely review I-526 adjudications. These reviews are troubling to investors who have made irrevocable investments, relocated their families to the United States, started businesses, or gained employment and, in every sense, made this country their home. Difficulties for investors whose previously approved I-526 petitions are now in question are often traceable to the effort by USCIS to impose rigid standards that ease the ability of examiners to count jobs and measure time periods without sufficient regard for the vagaries of legitimate, worthwhile business projects that unfold unevenly and are not susceptible to rigid deadlines and scientific-like certainty.

Further to its efforts to create fixed deadlines and identify each newly employed worker attributable to all EB-5 projects during an I-829 adjudication, on June 17, 2009, USCIS released a memorandum entitled *EB-5 Alien Entrepreneurs—Job Creation and Full-Time Positions (AFM Update AD 09-04)*.[3] The

---

[*] **Edward J. Carroll** (*ecarroll@cslaw.us*) practices immigration law in Burlington, VT. with Carroll & Scribner, P.C. All rights reserved.

The author would like to thank Lincoln Stone and Martin Lawler for their cogent writings and helpful discussions on the topics addressed in this article, which he has tried to synthesize accurately. Thank you, also, to Steven Yale-Loehr for guiding so many discussions among stakeholders in the EB-5 community.

[1] Departments of Commerce, Justice, and State, the Judiciary, and Related Agencies Appropriations Act, 1993, §610, Pub. L. 102-395, 106 Stat. 1874, Oct. 6, 1992, as amended.

[2] *Matter of Soffici*, 22 I&N Dec. 158, 19 *Immig. Rptr.* B2-25 (AAO, June 25, 1998); *Matter of Izumii*, 22 I&N Dec. 169, 19 Immig. Rptr. B2-32 (AAO, July 13, 1998); *Matter of Hsiung*, 22 I&N Dec. 201, 19 *Immig. Rptr.* B2-106 (AAO, July 31, 1998); and, *Matter of Ho*, 22 I&N Dec. 206, 19 *Immig. Rptr.* B2-106 (AAO, July 31, 1998). All four of these cases are reproduced in the Appendix materials to this volume.

[3] USCIS Memorandum, D. Neufeld, "EB-5 Alien Entrepreneurs—Job Creation and Full-Time Positions (AFM Update AD 09-04)" (June 17, 2009), *published on* AILA InfoNet at

continued

Memorandum (Memo) updates the *Adjudicator's Field Manual* (AFM) on several significant issues affecting the adjudication of I-526 and I-829 petitions.[4]

The Memo cites Immigration and Nationality Act (INA)[5] §216A(d)(1)(B), which says that an alien investor's petition to remove conditions requires the submission of evidence that the alien "is otherwise conforming to the requirements of Section 203(b)(5)" of the INA,[6] the statute to which I-526 petitions must conform. The Memo's reference to this provision,[7] for inclusion in the AFM, likely means, despite the agency's denials, that examiners will make increasing use of the I-829 process to re-examine an alien investor's compliance with I-526 criteria previously thought to have been adjudicated conclusively. So long as this statutory provision remains on the books, investors and their lawyers can expect USCIS to continue revisiting I-526 compliance during I-829 adjudications.

JOB CREATION REQUIREMENTS

The Memo asserts that petitioners must submit "a comprehensive business plan" to demonstrate that the commercial enterprise requires at least 10 qualifying employees who will be hired *"within the next two years."*[8] It emphasizes that this requirement also applies in I-526 regional center cases "that will rely on indirect job creation to satisfy the statutory employment creation requirement."[9]

To support this position, the Memo cites 8 Code of Federal Regulations (CFR) §204.6(j)(4)(i)(B).[10] However, this regulation does not control the obligations of an investor in a regional center case. A review of the construction of the subsections of this rule, the meaning and logic of the English expression in the subsections, and the legislative history of the subsections, leave no doubt that USCIS is imposing requirements on regional center cases without lawful authority.

8 CFR §204.6(j)(4) describes three distinct EB-5 cases: "(i) *General*" filings, which may be thought of as non-regional center cases, "(ii) *Troubled business*" filings, and "(iii) *Immigrant Investor Pilot Program*" cases. It is no accident that each case type is accorded a separately enumerated paragraph, and that the requirements listed in subsections (i) and (ii) vary from the requirements in subsection (iii).

In subsection (i) *General*, the petitioner is expected to prove that the requisite employment has taken place at the time of filing by providing "(A) tax records, Form I-9 or other similar documents;" or, if the employment is prospective, the investor must rely on "(B) A copy of a comprehensive business plan."[11] In subsection (ii) *Troubled business* filings, the petitioner also must include "tax records, Form I-9 or other relevant documents" as evidence of maintenance of employment at pre-investment levels, "and a comprehensive business plan."[12]

However, in subsection (iii) *Immigrant Investor Pilot Program* cases, there is no mention of employment records or a business plan. Instead, the investor is permitted to establish that the requisite jobs will be created by submitting evidence that relies upon "reasonable methodologies," later defined to mean "valid forecasting tools, including, but not limited to feasibility studies, analyses of foreign and domestic markets . . . and/or multiplier tables."[13]

This distinction, plainly seen, between the requirements in (i) and (ii) as compared to (iii), highlights the erroneous assertion that all I-526 cases must be supported by the submission of a business plan. The Memo also twists the meaning of 8 CFR §204.6(j)(4)(i) by claiming that "USCIS regulations *generally* require evidence to obtain approval of a Form I-526, including a business plan."[14] By misinterpreting the word "General," used in the regulation as a descriptor of one type of case, to mean "generally," as in a universal requirement, the Memo self-servingly restates USCIS's on-going effort to impose the same job creation standards in Pilot Pro-

---

Doc. No. 09061964 (*posted* June 19, 2009) [hereinafter Neufeld Memo]. The Neufeld Memo is reproduced in Appendix C of this volume.

[4] *Id.* at 1.

[5] Immigration and Nationality Act of 1952 (INA), Pub. L. No. 82-414, 66 Stat. 163, (codified as amended at 8 USC §§1101 et seq.).

[6] INA §203(b)(5); 8 USC §1153(b)(5).

[7] Neufeld Memo, *supra* note 3, at 2.

[8] *Id.* at 3.

[9] *Id.*

[10] *Id.*

---

[11] 8 CFR §204.6(j)(4)(i). Emphasis supplied.

[12] 8 CFR §204.6(j)(4)(ii). Emphasis supplied.

[13] 8 CFR §204.6(j)(4)(iii); 8 CFR §204.6(m)(3)(v).

[14] Neufeld Memo, *supra* note 3, at 2. Emphasis supplied.

gram cases as apply only in (i) *General*; and, (ii) *Troubled business* cases.

USCIS interpretation disregards the fact that the original regulation contained only subsections (i) and (ii), both of which refer to a business plan.[15] If, as USCIS contends, subsection (i) is the statement of a general requirement for all I-526 cases, why is the requirement repeated in subsection (ii)? There would be no need for repetition if, as USCIS maintains, business plans are "generally" (meaning universally) required. The repetition makes sense only if the requirements for different case types are read disjunctively.[16] Likewise, because the requirement of a business plan was stated separately in subsections (i) and (ii), but omitted from subsection (iii), the requirement is not applicable to (iii), regional center petitions.

Subsection (iii) *Immigrant Investor Pilot Program* was added after the adoption of the Pilot Program.[17] This subsection does not include any obligation to establish through a comprehensive business plan the "time within the next two years" when 10 qualifying employees will be hired.[18] USCIS's imposition of this requirement on regional center-based petitions is the result of the agency's erroneous interpretation of the regulation, arguably contrary to congressional intent, and this practice undermines the purpose of the Pilot Program.

The Pilot Program was conceived after the initial EB-5 program "in order to increase interest in the existing alien entrepreneur immigrant classification under section 203(b)(5) of the Act."[19] To encourage greater use of the EB-5 program, the Pilot Program "expressly relaxes the job creation requirement"[20] found previously in 8 CFR §204.6 by permitting regional center investors to rely upon reasonable methodologies for determining job creation. This provision, in stark contrast to the mandate to count jobs precisely in subsections (i) and (ii) of the regulation, recognizes that where indirect jobs may be relied upon in regional centers to meet job creation requirements, it is impossible to identify each new position created in the economy or each employee hired on account of an investment. Adherence to the requirement of identifying each new position or each new indirectly employed worker, or mandating that indirect jobs be created within the period of conditional residence, violates the provisions of the regulation and discourages the use of the EB-5 program, thus defeating the reason for creating regional centers.

THE "TWO-YEAR PERIOD"

USCIS has created a new way to count to two. Its new method appears to have been implemented as an extension of the erroneous position by USCIS that jobs in all EB-5 projects, including regional center projects, must be created within a two-year period. But for this intractable, incorrect view, USCIS would not have the need to further complicate I-526 processing by the imposition of a new, extra-legal two-year period, within which prospective employment must be projected to occur.

An alien entrepreneur is admitted to lawful permanent resident status conditionally and must persuade USCIS to remove these conditions or risk removal.[21] The period of conditional lawful permanent resident status (CLPR) begins when the investor first enters the United States in reliance upon an immigrant visa, or is first adjusted to this status. In the even of either, the status is conferred after approval of an I-526 petition. CLPR is initially granted for a period of two years.[22] During the 90-day period before the second anniversary, the alien must file a petition seeking the removal of conditions.[23] These are the only statutory provisions that mark the beginning and the end of the period of CLPR for an alien entrepreneur. There is no statutory authorization for any other two-year period in the EB-5, Alien Entrepreneur program.

This notwithstanding, the Memo has announced a new two-year period, deemed to begin six months after the approval of an I-526 petition and ending two years later. USCIS explains that this period is being manufactured to provide examiners with a uniform method of determining during an I-526 ad-

---

[15] *See* Final Rule, 56 Fed. Reg. 60897 (Nov. 29, 1991).

[16] Lincoln Stone, Esq., was among the first to argue ably that these subsections must be read disjunctively. He noted that the repetition of requirements in subsections (i) and (ii) belies the concept that subsection (i) is a general requirement, meant to apply to all types of I-526 cases.

[17] *See* Final Rule, 59 Fed. Reg. 17920 (Apr. 15, 1994).

[18] Neufeld Memo, *supra* note 3, at 3.

[19] Interim Rule, 58 Fed. Reg. 44606 (Aug. 24, 1993).

[20] *Id.*

[21] INA §§216A(a)(1), (c)(1)(A), (c)(3)(D); 8 USC §§1186b(a)(1), (c)(1)(A), (c)(3)(D).

[22] INA §216A(d)(2); 8 USC §1186b(d)(2).

[23] *Id.*

judication when the CLPR period will begin and end. USCIS contends that without such an arbitrary period, it is unable to know during I-526 adjudications if the requisite job creation will take place within two years.[24]

The Memo says this time period is the two-year period of conditional residence "described in 8 CFR §204.6(j)(4)(i)(B)."[25] This position disregards the meaning of the regulation, which is best understood by giving appropriate deference to the clear meaning of the language, logic, and legislative history of each subsection, all of which is discussed above. To summarize that discussion: there is little basis for USCIS to require a business plan demonstrating job creation within a two-year period. Sub-sections (i)(B) and (ii) of 8 CFR §204.6(j)(4) do contain, however, clear references to some circumstances—in *General* cases and in *Troubled business* cases—where this might be the case. References are not made in subsection (i)(A), where jobs already have been created by the time of the I-526 filing. There is no authorization to impose a two-year job creation requirement in an *Immigrant Investor Pilot Program* case.

The Memo also fails to mention that there is no authorization in INA §203(b)(5) or any other statute to impose any time frame within which jobs must be created in an EB-5 project. The absence of any such authorization belies the right of USCIS to require an alien investor to project or prove job creation *in a two-year period* in any EB-5 case.

For discussion's sake, let us assume that demonstrating requisite job creation in a two-year period is a valid requirement in an I-526 petition for a (i) *General* or (ii) *Troubled business* case. In its effort to alleviate its adjudicatory burden,[26] USCIS has violated the provisions of unambiguous language in INA §216A, declaring that the period of CLPR shall commence six months after approval of the I-526 for the purpose of measuring timely job creation in I-526 petitions. The Memo says six months after an I-526 is approved is the approximate[27] time that investors will require in order to be admitted in CLPR status. This is merely a guess[28] that provides a rationalization to commence counting a new two-year period created by the agency for its own convenience.

The only mention of a two-year period of CLPR in the EB-5 program is found in INA §216A concerning the grant of conditional residence and the removal of those conditions.[29] Since CLPR begins when the alien investor is admitted in this status, it appears that the Memo's new measuring period is without legal foundation, as it is not linked to the actual admission of the investor.

The question that USCIS should be required to address as a result of its new standard in I-526 adjudications is this: On what legal basis may USCIS deny an EB-5 investor the opportunity to file an I-829 petition by denying the investor's I-526 petition for failure to meet *ultra vires* requirements? Doesn't this new, extra-legal standard potentially deprive an alien investor of the right to lawful permanent residence, a benefit of the EB-5 program under the INA? This new I-526 standard joins the growing list of agency actions that deter the use of the EB-5 program.

In regional center-based I-526 cases, USCIS attempts unsuccessfully to reconcile the new standard with the undeniable right of an investor to rely upon "reasonable methodologies" to establish job creation.[30] Try as it may, USCIS cannot extricate itself from its extra-legal approach, because it persists in requiring that regional center cases provide a business plan that "shows jobs will be created in two years."[31] This unsupportable position, discussed earlier, requires an interpretation of 8 CFR §204.6(j)(4)(iii) that cannot be justified by the language and logic of the entire regulation or by the legacy INS discussion of the Interim Rule, which says that the enabling legislation of the Immigrant Investor Pilot Program[32] "ex-

---

[24] Neufeld Memo, *supra* note 3, at 2, 3–4.

[25] *Id.* at 4.

[26] *Id.* at 3 ("The regulations, however, do not clearly state when the two-year period commences for the purpose of adjudicating the Form I-526.").

[27] *Id.* at 4.

[28] *Id.* at 3–4 ("USCIS has determined that the *average* processing times for EB-5 petitioners filing for immigrant visas via consular processing and EB-5 petitioners filing for adjustment of status is *approximately* six months. Accordingly, in order to best *approximate* the two-year period of conditional residence, the two-year period described in 8 CFR §204.6(j)(4)(i)(B) will be deemed to commence six months after the adjudication of Form I-526." (Emphasis supplied)).

[29] INA §216A; 8 USC §1186b.

[30] Neufeld Memo, *supra* note 3, at 3–4.

[31] *Id.* at 3.

[32] 1993 Appropriations Act, supra note 1.

pressly relaxes the job creation requirement currently set forth in 8 CFR 204.6 . . . ."[33]

Each of the circumstances described in the Memo, on the matter of when jobs will be created within a Regional Center, is linked to the requirement that job creation must occur in a two-year period. Examiners are directed to look for indications within the input/output economic model that there will be "compliance with the two-year requirement."[34] Absent such language, examiners are to determine if the "required infusion of capital or the creation of indirect jobs will occur within two years."[35] USCIS is unwilling to abandon insistence on a two-year job creation requirement in I-526 regional center cases.

It is ironic that in a discussion of I-829 standards in the Memo, USCIS advises examiners:

> If after considering the evidence, the office determines that the jobs are more likely than not going to be created within a reasonable time, Form I-829 should be approved ... if the petitioner is otherwise eligible to have ... conditions removed.[36]

How is it that USCIS would approve an I-829 petition to remove conditions that failed to meet the strict requirement of job creation within two-years but deny an I-526 that does not contain a business plan demonstrating such compliance, or in a regional center case, does not contain some other compelling proof that jobs will be created in two years?

In addition to the clear disenfranchisement of the rights accorded to alien investors by the EB-5 statutes and regulations, USCIS's insistence on an extra-legal two-year job creation requirement disregards the effect this requirement will have on large projects with multiple investors in regional centers, where job creation may not be completed in two years. The imposition of this requirement will result in the denial of otherwise approvable I-526 petitions and the coincident loss of new employment and economic stimulus.

CREDITING INDIRECT EMPLOYMENT

USCIS has focused attention recently on indirect job creation in regional center petitions by declaring that it will not count towards requisite job creation any indirect employment generated outside the boundaries of a regional center. Potentially, this is problematic for a small regional center that cannot reasonably be expected to create all employment within its borders, for large projects that by dint of size or complexity spur employment outside of regional center boundaries, or for many projects situated near the boundary of a regional center. USCIS has not said if this newly declared approach will be applied to existing projects that have some subscribed investors but are continuing to seek new subscribers. However, since all EB-5 petitions are adjudicated separately, on facts existing at the time of filing, it seems likely that new investors in an existing project will be judged differently from those whose petitions have been approved prior to the announcement. This announcement also casts doubt on whether the business plan supporting a previously approved I-526 petition will be acceptable when the investor seeks removal of conditions.

In 2002, USCIS added the language below to the AFM:

> **(2) Regional Center Pilot Program.**
>
> Under a Pilot Program . . . visas . . . are set aside for aliens who invest in a "regional center" . . . for the promotion of economic growth, including improved regional productivity, job creation, and increased domestic capital investment . . . . Under the Pilot Program, aliens investing in new commercial enterprises located in regional centers are not required to demonstrate that the new commercial enterprise itself employs ten U.S. workers; a showing of indirect job creation and improved regional productivity will suffice. Implementing regulations for the Pilot Program are found at 8 CFR 204.6(m).[37]

The inclusion of this language in the AFM honored congressional intent to increase regional productivity *and* promote job creation. Notably, however, neither Congress nor the AFM say that all qualified indirect job creation must occur within a regional center. This makes good sense. It is not difficult to con-

---

[33] Interim Rule, 58 Fed. Reg. 44606 (Aug. 24, 1993), *reprinted in* 70 Interpreter Releases 1142 (Aug. 30, 1993).

[34] Neufeld Memo, *supra* note 3, at 4.

[35] *Id.* at 5.

[36] *Id.* at 7.

[37] USCIS Memorandum, M. Aytes, "AFM Update: Chapter 22: Employment-Based Petitions (AD03-01)" (Sept. 12, 2006), *published on* AILA InfoNet at Doc. No. 06101910 (*posted* Oct. 19, 2006) [hereinafter AFM Update].

ceive of an EB-5 project that creates employment outside of a regional center at the same time as it increases productivity within the regional center. These results are not mutually exclusive. In some cases, indirect employment creation outside a regional center may be necessary to the function of the regional center project—*e.g.*, where goods or services provided from outside the region are critical to implementing the project. In this situation, without extra-regional employment creation there would be no increased direct or indirect employment within the regional center. It is also understandable that very small regional centers may not be able to confine all indirect employment within their boundaries, and that projects situated close to the boundaries of a regional center may create employment outside the perimeter of the regional center.

USCIS, having abided these concepts and its own language in the AFM since September 2002, announced in December 2009 that it would no longer permit an investor to count indirect employment created outside the boundaries of the regional center towards requisite job creation. This revelation came during a stakeholder information session hosted by USCIS.[38] This change was visited upon the EB-5 community without warning and without any amendment in the governing statues or regulations, neither of which, as currently written, support this position.

An EB-5 project operating within a regional center must promote economic growth, regional productivity, and increased domestic capital investment.[39] These activities help to assure achievement of the overarching goal of the EB-5 program found in the enabling statute. The seminal EB-5 legislation, codified at INA §203(b)(5)(A)(iii),[40] provides EB-5 classification if the new commercial enterprise *"will benefit the United States economy* and create full-time employment for not fewer than 10" qualified persons. The primary purpose of the EB-5 program is, then, to aid the entire U.S. economy.

The new stance taken by USCIS ignores this core policy—the sole purpose of the EB-5 program—and casts the success of a regional center project (measured by increased employment, albeit sometimes partially outside its borders) as a failure to the extent that the new employment is too far flung. Regional centers, by stimulating economic growth, regional productivity and increased domestic capital investment, are a tool to help benefit the overall economy. Bearing this objective in mind, what rational basis is there to deny investor I-526 petitions that achieve this goal by stimulating new jobs outside the regional center? How has the U.S. economy benefitted overall by the suppression of job-creating enterprises, the result of denying EB-5 projects the ability to count indirect employment they generated outside the regional center? The artificiality of the distinction drawn by USCIS between indirect employment within versus employment outside a regional center is not mandated by statute or regulation, and it very clearly contradicts and defeats the singular purpose of the EB-5 program.

In announcing this new policy, USCIS said during a stakeholder information session[41] that it:

> interprets the statutory and regulatory prescribed focus to mean that the economic analysis methodology used by regional centers should also be focused on job creation within the bounds of the regional center. [See also *Matter of Izumii*.]

USCIS' reliance on *Matter of Izumii*[42] is unpersuasive. *Izumii* did not address the matter of indirect job creation outside a regional center. The *Izumii* decision rested in part on the finding that all activity central to the investors' business plan took place outside regional center boundaries. For this reason, *Izumii* held that all employment must be direct. This is quite distinct from the matter of whether investment and business activities within such boundaries generate indirect employment beyond the boundaries for which investors should be credited. Inasmuch as *Izumii* does not by *dicta* or mandate hold that discounting indirect employment outside the boundaries of a regional center is necessary, USCIS's new policy cannot be justified by reliance upon this decision.[43]

---

[38] "Questions and Answers: American Immigration Lawyers Association EB-5 Committee and Invest in the USA (IIUSA) USCIS" (Dec. 14, 2009), *published on* AILA InfoNet at Doc. No. 10010462 (*posted* Jan. 4, 2010) [hereinafter Stakeholder's Meeting]. The Stakeholder Meeting Q&As are reproduced in Appendix H of this volume.

[39] *Adjudicator's Field Manual* (AFM) Update, *supra* note 37.

[40] INA §203(b)(5)(iii); 8 USC §1153(b)(5)(iii) (emphasis supplied).

---

[41] Stakeholder Meeting Q&As, *supra* note 38.

[42] *Izumii*, *supra* note 2.

[43] Further to its explanation during the Stakeholder's Meeting, *supra* note 38, USCIS discussed the misuse of economic input models when "most of the direct inputs are not locally produced." This discussion is not relevant to the new USCIS policy, because jobs created outside a regional center bound-
continued

Speaking during a seminar on EB-5 issues, a USCIS representative opined that counting only indirect employment inside a regional center was appropriate because "how big or how small an individual seeks to make their regional center is entirely their call."[44] This suggests that were one to have a regional center consisting of all forty-eight contiguous U.S. states, the agency would not object to counting indirect employment generated throughout most of the country. Setting aside issues one might anticipate relating to the formation and operation of this regional center, one must ask how this scenario differs materially from creating the same number of indirect jobs inside almost the entire country but outside the boundaries of a smaller regional center. Inasmuch as equal employment creation and economic stimulation result in either case, what is the rational basis for USCIS to object, especially when doing so contradicts the policy made and the statutory language written while creating the EB-5 program?

It is interesting that during the discussion of this topic in a recent seminar,[45] USCIS suggested to regional center applicants that they consider requesting larger centers so that indirect employment would occur inside center boundaries. This is the clear import of saying that the size of a regional center is "your call."[46] If applicants take this suggestion to seek larger regional centers, will USCIS object, claiming that applicants are gerrymandering borders to overcome the agency's policy of discounting indirect employment created outside regional center borders? This is the same objection that some projects have encountered when defining the boundaries of targeted employment areas, and USCIS concluded that those boundaries were gerrymandered merely to comport with TEA requirements. How will the USCIS reaction differ when regional center applicants follow USCIS advice?

Regional centers are becoming profligate with USCIS's blessing. The agency scrutinizes these regional centers and the many projects within them with a vigilant eye for non-compliance and fraud. The new policy to discount legitimate indirect job creation outside regional center boundaries seems to stem from the perception that some projects or regional centers do not or cannot meet mandated job creation requirements and, consequently, investors should not receive immigration benefits for supporting such projects. How does USCIS expect its concerns for enforcement to be taken seriously if it suggests that the solution for investors is to create larger regional centers? Are investors being encouraged to create *bona fide*, worthwhile projects which legitimately create employment inside and outside a regional center? Or, are they being encouraged to use the artifice or larger boundaries that permit approval of projects which otherwise cannot stimulate focused regional growth?

USCIS intended to inform EB-5 adjudicators, investors and lawyers of its most recent interpretation of job-creation requirements by publishing the Memo, by holding a face-to-face meeting with stakeholders,[47] and by speaking to stakeholders during a telephonic seminar.[48] The efforts made by USCIS to provide guidance to stakeholders are laudable. Unfortunately, in the process, USCIS has memorialized compliance issues in the I-526 process that may be *ultra vires*. Practitioners are advised to plan I-526 presentations that adapt where possible to these requirements until Congress has the good sense to forbid these new approaches. Until then, the true risk to investors in the EB-5 program may come from their treatment by USCIS, not from the prospect of the economic failure of an enterprise.

---

ary could be indirect only if they resulted from investment and economic activity inside the boundaries. USCIS also contends that it is improper to claim jobs inside a regional center's boundaries by relying on data derived outside the regional center. Assuming this to be so, it is unclear how this concern bears any relation to the creation of indirect employment outside the boundaries of a regional center on account of investment and economic activity within the regional center's boundaries.

[44] *Investors for Experts* seminar sponsored by ILW.com (Jan. 21, 2010).

[45] *Id.*

[46] *Id.*

[47] See supra note 38

[48] See supra note 44.

EB-5 JOB CREATION—WHAT TO DO WHEN PLANS CHANGE

*by H. Ronald Klasko**

INTRODUCTION

This article is intended to fill a void in the existing employment-based fifth preference (EB-5) visa literature. There are plenty of articles discussing the requirements of job creation in EB-5 cases.[1] There also are articles challenging, with good reason, the U.S. Citizenship and Immigration Services (USCIS) interpretation of the job creation requirements both at the I-526 EB-5 petition stage and, most significantly, at the I-829 condition removal stage.[2] But little, to date, has been written on the topic of job creation.

The purpose of this article is to deal with the issue of what happens when anticipated job creation doesn't happen, or falls behind schedule, or is revised in some way. Specifically, the article will address the USCIS "material change" standard as it relates specifically to job creation. The article also identifies flaws in the USCIS proposed solution, and proposes a revised procedure for USCIS to consider that would be more consistent with both the law and the policy behind the EB-5 program. Finally, the article evaluates the impact upon the investor and the various options and strategies that might be available to the investor. This will be done in the context of both individual EB-5 petitions and regional center EB-5 petitions.

This article incorporates both the law (*i.e.*, statute, regulations, and precedent decisions) and the lore (*i.e.*, USCIS memoranda, advisory opinions, liaison or stakeholders meetings answers, and the *Adjudicator's Field Manual* (AFM)). Although all elements of the lore are subject to question and challenge in federal court (and the author believes many should be challenged), for purposes of this article, it is assumed that this is all part of the body of "law" with which the investor must cope and comply.

SUMMARY OF LAW ON JOB CREATION

EB-5 Petition Stage

The law on job creation must be analyzed with an understanding of the differences between requirements at the I-526 stage and requirements at the I-829 stage. It also must be analyzed with respect to requirements for individual EB-5 investors vs. requirements for regional center EB-5 investors.

The basic job creation requirement is contained in Immigration and Nationality Act (INA)[3] §203(b)(5)(a)(ii), which requires the investor to "create full-time employment for not fewer than 10 United States citizens or aliens lawfully admitted for permanent residence or other immigrants lawfully authorized to be employed in the United States (other than the immigrant and the immigrant's spouse, sons, or daughters)."

The relevant regulatory section is 8 Code of Federal Regulations (CFR) §204.6. In addition to defining "employee," "full-time employment," and "qualifying employee" in 8 §204.6(e), the regulation focuses on job creation at 8 CFR §204.6(j)(4). It is significant to note that these regulations require that the employment created by the new commercial enterprise be for W-2 "employees." Arguably, under the statutory language, if the new commercial enterprise enters into full-time independent contractor arrangements, "employment" would have been "cre-

---

* H. Ronald Klasko is one of the country's leading lawyers representing investors in EB-5 and treaty investor (E-2) cases. He is the Chair of the American Immigration Lawyers Association's (AILA) EB-5 Committee. Mr. Klasko was the lead attorney on the famous *Walsh and Pollard* case, which established the key precedent for treaty investor visas. Mr. Klasko is the Philadelphia-based Managing Partner of Klasko, Rulon, Stock & Seltzer, LLP, chosen as one of six top tier immigration firms by Chambers Global. He is a former national president and three-term General Counsel of AILA and has been a member of its Board of Governors since 1980. He is one of only three practicing attorneys ever honored with the AILA Founders Award for his contributions to immigration jurisprudence. His website is www.eb5immigration.com.

[1] See, e.g., E. Carroll, "Selected Issues in EB-5 Cases: Job Creation, Two-Year Periods, and Indirect Employment"; B. Wolfsdorf et al., "EB-5 Immigrant Investor Program—A Changing Landscape," both of which are included elsewhere in this volume.

[2] See, e.g., L. Stone, "Conditional Permanent Residence and Immigration Risk for Investors," included elsewhere in this volume.

[3] Immigration and Nationality Act of 1952 (INA), Pub. L. No. 82-414, 66 Stat. 163, (codified as amended at 8 USC §§1101 *et seq.*).

ated" for 10 qualified individuals. However, such employment creation would not qualify under the regulations since the individuals are not "employees."[4]

8 CFR §204.6(j)(4) provides four options for proving employment creation:

- For an individual, non-regional center EB-5 petition, if the 10 qualifying employees have been hired at the time of the filing of the I-526 petition, documentation of the 10 employees should be provided;

- If the 10 employees have not been hired at the time of the I-526 petition, a comprehensive business plan must be provided showing "the need" for at least 10 qualifying employees "will result" within the next two years, including when such employees will be hired;

- In the case of a "troubled business,"[5] the comprehensive business plan must show the number of existing employees is being or will be maintained at no less than the pre-investment level for at least two years; and

- In the case of a regional center investment (for which there is no mention of a business plan), the I-526 must include evidence that the investment will create full-time positions for not fewer than 10 persons either directly or indirectly through "reasonable methodologies."

Significantly, 8 CFR §204.6(j)(4)(i)(B)(iii), relating to regional centers, does not reference a business plan, and references 10 "persons" rather than 10 "qualifying employees." This regulatory section is amplified by 8 CFR §204.6(m)(7)(ii), which references "reasonable methodologies" that may be used to "indicate the likelihood that the business will result in increased employment." It is important to contrast the regulatory requirement at the I-526 stage—*i.e*, that the new commercial enterprise for an individual, non-regional center investment "will create" requisite employment—with the requirement for the regional center investor to show "the likelihood" that the increased employment will result. The latter represents, arguably, a significantly lesser burden of proof.

USCIS added potentially significant gloss to the regulations regarding employment creation in a December 11, 2009, memorandum from Donald Neufeld, Acting Associate Director, Domestic Operations at USCIS (December 2009 Neufeld Memo).[6] The following points are worth noting:

- There is no requirement to show that indirect or induced jobs created through a regional center investment are full-time;

- Direct construction jobs count as "permanent jobs" if they are expected to last at least two years;

- It is the position—and not the employee—that is critical, meaning that the occupants of the position can vary as long as the position remains the same;

- Independent contractor positions can qualify to establish indirect employment for regional center petitions, but not for individual, non-regional center petitions;

- Full-time employment cannot be seasonal—it must be year-round.

Condition Removal Stage

The major area of controversy relating to job creation involves exactly what needs to be proven at the time of filing the I-829 condition removal petition. The statute is completely silent regarding any test of employment creation at the I-829 stage. Rather, in INA §216A(d)(1), in order to remove the conditions on permanent residence status, the investor must demonstrate that he or she: "invested, or is actively in the process of investing," the requisite capital; "sustained" the investment of the requisite capital throughout the period of conditional residence; and "is otherwise conforming to the requirements of section 203(b)(5)."

Although both the legislative history and an earlier legacy Immigration and Naturalization Service

---

[4] 8 Code of Federal Regulations (CFR) §204.6(e).

[5] "Troubled business" is defined as a business that has been in existence for at least two years, has incurred a net loss for accounting purposes during the previous 12– or 24-month period, and the loss for such period is at least equal to 20 percent of the troubled business's net worth prior to the loss. 8 CFR §204.6(e).

[6] U.S. Citizenship and Immigration Services (USCIS) Memorandum, D. Neufeld, "Adjudication of EB-5 Regional Center Proposals and Affiliated Form I-526 and Form I-829 Petitions; *Adjudicator's Field Manual* (AFM) Update to Chapters 22.4 and 25.2 (AD09-38)" (Dec. 11, 2009), *published on* AILA InfoNet at Doc. No. 09121561 (*posted* Dec. 15, 2009). The memo is reproduced at Appendix C.

(INS) memorandum[7] indicate that counting of jobs is not and should not be part of the adjudication of a condition removal petition, USCIS has created that requirement by regulation. Specifically, 8 CFR §216.6(c)(1)(iv) requires proof that the conditional resident investor either created, "or can be expected to create within a reasonable period of time," the requisite number of employees. USCIS takes the position that this is a reasonable interpretation of the statutory requirement regarding the alien "conforming" to the requirements in INA §203(b)(5). Especially in the context of a regional center investment, it is a stretch to argue that Congress felt that an alien was not conforming to the requirements if, for reasons totally beyond his or her control, the regional center failed to create the necessary jobs, causing the investor, who did nothing wrong and relocated with his or her family to the United States, to be removed from the country.

WHEN MUST THE JOBS BE CREATED?

Given the present adjudication standards of USCIS, when must the jobs be created in order to obtain approval of an I-526 petition and an I-829 petition? For the first time, in a memorandum dated June 17, 2009 (June 2009 Neufeld memo),[8] USCIS instituted a requirement applicable to both individual investors and regional center investors, stating that the requisite employment must be created within two years. Since the regulation at 8 CFR §204.6(j)(4)(i)(B) had created the two-year employment creation requirement only for individual EB-5 investors (and not regional center investors), and since there is no two-year employment creation requirement in the statute, this new requirement by memorandum is certainly subject to challenge. Nevertheless, given that this memorandum now has been incorporated into the AFM at ch. 22.4(c)(4)(D)(ii), it is critical to understand USCIS's present requirements.

Assuming for purposes of an individual EB-5 petition, or a regional center EB-5 petition, that a showing must be made of job creation within two years, the next question is: when does the two-year period start? This question is answered for the first time in the June 2009, Neufeld Memo, incorporated in the AFM, as being two and a half years from the approval of the I-526 petition.[9] How did USCIS come up with this date? The reasoning needs some explanation. For the purpose of determining the outcome of an I-829 petition, USCIS believes that the two year conditional residence period dates from the acquisition of conditional residence (following the approval of the I-485 or the consular immigrant visa application). However, for purposes of adjudicating the I-526, the adjudicator does not know when that will occur; USCIS estimates that it will occur within six months. Therefore, in adjudicating the I-526 petition, the adjudicator will require proof that the jobs will be created within two years, plus the estimated six months.

The "Reasonable Time" Standard

Assuming the I-526 petition is approved, what happens if all of the jobs are not created by the time of the filing of the I-829? Even though the investor had the burden of proving that the jobs would be created by the time of filing the I-829, the regulations only require that the jobs "can be expected to [be created] within a reasonable period of time."[10] There is no definition of what constitutes a "reasonable time." The AFM, as amended by the June 2009 Neufeld Memo, states the following at ch. 25.2(e)(4)(D):

> In making the "reasonable time" determination, officers should consider the evidence submitted along with the petition that demonstrates when the jobs are expected to be created, the reasons that the jobs were not created as predicted in form I-526, the nature of the industry or industries in which the jobs are to be created, and any other evidence submitted by the petitioner.

The AFM states that the officer should approve the I-829 if it appears "more likely than not" that the jobs will be created within a reasonable time; otherwise, the officer should deny the I-829.

What evidence should be submitted if all of the jobs have not been created in order to show that it is "more likely than not" that they will be created within a "reasonable time?" There is no guidance on this

---

[7] Legacy Immigration and Naturalization Service (INS) Memorandum, J. Puleo, "Removing Conditional Residence Status for Aliens Admitted as Conditional Resident Investors," No. HQ204.27-P [date unknown].

[8] USCIS Memorandum, D. Neufeld, "EB-5 Alien Entrepreneurs—Job Creation and Full-time Positions (AFM Update AD09-04)" (June 17, 2009), *published on* AILA InfoNet at Doc. No. 09061964 (*posted* June 19, 2009). The memo is reproduced at Appendix C.

[9] *Adjudicator's Field Manual* (AFM) ch. 22.4(c)(4)(D)(ii)(a).
[10] 8 CFR §216.6(c)(1)(iv).

whatsoever. Presumably, the evidence to be submitted will be very case specific. A starting point likely would be a logical explanation, with documentation, of what events specific to the business or external to the business resulted in a delay in job creation compared to what was anticipated at the time of approval of the I-526 petition. In addition to documenting all of the jobs that have already been created, and in addition to providing an anticipated time schedule for the creation of the remaining jobs, documentation might include the following evidence:

- Weather conditions that created delays;
- Acts of god, such as hurricanes, earthquake, fires, etc.;
- Unanticipated economic or industry downturns;
- Recent business activity that leads to an optimistic near term future for the business;
- Recent marketing efforts and results of those marketing efforts;
- Employees having left the business and attempts to replace them;
- Recent contracts or anticipated contracts;
- Additional capital influx;
- Industry or geographic positive predictions for future near term growth;
- A new product line; and
- Anything else that may be persuasive to explain both the delay in job creation and the anticipated increase in job creation in the near future.

How does all of this apply in the case of a regional center where many, most, or sometimes all of the jobs are indirect or induced employment? The December 2009, Neufeld Memo states that the adjudicator should not readjudicate the job creation methodology that resulted in the economic projection of the requisite amount of direct or indirect employment.[11] In responding to a question at an EB-5 stakeholders meeting on June 24, 2009, USCIS stated that the I-829 inquiry in a regional center case is "limited to assessing milestones that were predicted at the I-526 stage of the process." Their answer gives the following example:

> At the I-526 stage the plan was to build a shopping center and lease out the space. At the I-829 stage we would want to know if the space had substantially leased as predicted. In the alternative, if jobs were predicted based on total expenditure, we would want to know if the funds had been spent as planned.[12]

Therefore, documentation should be provided at the I-829 stage to show that the foundational elements of the econometric model, filed with the I-526 petition, have occurred or will occur within a "reasonable time." These foundational elements often include expenditure of capital, creation of direct jobs, construction of the building, leasing of units, net sales revenue and other developments specific to the business model.

Problems with Job Creation

What if most or all of the jobs were only recently created? Although this could create a credibility issue, it does not create a problem under the statute or the regulations. The statute requires that the investment was "sustained" during the period of conditional residence.[13] Likewise, the regulations require that the commercial enterprise and the investment capital must have been "sustained" during the conditional residence period.[14] Neither the statute nor the regulations require that the employment be sustained for any particular period of time. Therefore, fluctuating levels of employment during the two year period, or an increase in employment near the end of the two year period, should not be disqualifying.

What if a Request for Evidence is issued subsequent to the filing of the I-829 and the response indicates that, although the requisite employment was created at the time of filing the I-829, there has been a reduction in employment subsequent to such filing? Since the regulatory language is in the past tense—"the alien created"[15]—there would seem to be no requirement for continuing such employment beyond the statutory two year period. Arguably, any request for evidence relating to activity subsequent to the filing would be ultra vires the statute and regulation. However, it is not at all clear that USCIS would agree with this analysis.

However, if the requisite employment was not created at the time of the filing of the I-829, the is-

---

[11] AFM ch. 22.4(a)(2)(E).

[12] "EB-5 Stakeholders Meeting hosted by Invest in the USA (IIUSA) and AILA" (answer to question 12) (June 24, 2009), *published on* AILA InfoNet at Doc. No. 09071362 (*posted* July 13, 2009).

[13] INA §216A(b)(1)(B)(ii).

[14] 8 CFR §216.6(c)(1)(iii).

[15] 8 CFR §216.6(a)(4)(iv).

sue of post-filing activity is a more complicated one. Presumably, if jobs were actually created subsequent to the filing of the I-829 petition, the investor would be eager to provide such information to the adjudicator to prove that the projection of creation of jobs within a reasonable time actually has occurred. On the other hand, if post-filing activity is less robust, there is a good argument that the "reasonable time" determination must be made based upon facts existent at the time of the filing of the I-829, and that subsequent events are irrelevant. If a denial is based on a determination that the jobs were unlikely to be created within a reasonable time, presumably the fact that the jobs ultimately are created within a reasonable time would be a basis for the filing of a motion to reopen.

Another issue seen in recent adjudications involves the immigration status of the employees. The issue is a difficult one. On one hand, the statute requires the employees to be U.S. citizens, permanent residents, or other immigrants lawfully authorized to be employed in the United States.[16] The regulation also requires the employees to be "qualifying employees."[17] On the other hand, the employing entity is prohibited from inquiring beyond the employee's choice of documents to present in the I-9 process (as long as they reasonably appear to be genuine) upon penalty of a discrimination charge.[18] Although legacy INS previously resolved that balance in favor of the investor,[19] the present USCIS position requires the employer to violate the antidiscrimination provisions in order to ensure compliance with the job creation requirements.[20] Employing entities may wish to enroll in E-Verify in order to know in advance whether the government database reflects the authorized work status of the employees. However, E-Verify will not confirm whether the employees are citizens or residents, as opposed to nonimmigrants with work authorization.

---

[16] INA §203(b)(5)(A)(ii).

[17] 8 CFR §204.6(e).

[18] INA §274B(a)(6).

[19] See INS I-829 Standard Operating Procedure ("The Service Center may not hold the employers to a higher standard of care in determining the employees [sic] authorization to work than the Immigration Reform Act of 1986").

[20] See "USCIS Q&As from Stakeholder Session with AILA EB-5 Committee and Invest in the USA" (answers to questions 15, 16, and 17) (Dec. 14, 2009), *published on* AILA InfoNet at Doc. No. 10010462 (*posted* Jan. 4, 2010). The stakeholder meeting Q&As are reproduced at Appendix H.

NEW PROCEDURE CREATED BY DECEMBER 11, 2009, NEUFELD MEMORANDUM

Until recently, neither the regulations nor the AFM created an option beyond approval or denial of the I-829 petition in the event USCIS was not satisfied that the job creation requirement was met, or likely would be met, within a reasonable time. USCIS takes the position that the I-526 business plan may not be "materially changed" after the petition has been filed, and there is no provision for extending the time period for the filing of the I-829 petition to provide the investor more time to meet requirements. Historically, in the event of a material change, whereby the investor could not demonstrate compliance during the period of conditional residence with the business plan approved in the I-526 case, the I-829 very likely would be denied. However, a third option was introduced by the December 2009 Neufeld Memo.[21] If there is a material change that otherwise would lead to this unwanted result, the investor has the option of filing a new I-526 petition and starting a new conditional residence period. If USCIS is satisfied that the new I-526 can be approved, the investor may file a new application for conditional permanent residence.[22]

This new procedure begs many questions:

- What is a material change necessitating a new I-526?
- Can this procedure be utilized after the denial of the I-829?
- What is the status of the investor while the new I-526 is being adjudicated?
- Is the investor eligible for adjustment of status?
- What about the conditional resident children who have subsequently turned 21?

The following sections attempt to deal with each of these issues.

What is a "Material Change"?

"Material change" is not expressly defined either for EB-5 purposes or, for that matter, with respect to other petitions filed with USCIS. However, we are not drawing on a blank slate. In a memorandum dated August 22, 1996, entitled "Amended H-1B

---

[21] Dec. 11, 2009, Neufeld Memo, *supra* note 6.

[22] AFM ch. 22.4(c)(4)(G).

Petitions,"[23] legacy INS stated that a "material change" exists when a change substantially alters the terms or conditions of an H-1B employee's employment. The AFM provides examples of changes that are not "material":

- Transfer of a beneficiary from one branch of a firm to another branch of the firm;
- Change of petitioner's name; and
- Changes in the ownership structure of the petitioning entity.

Examples of material change in the AFM are rather obvious:

- Transfer of employee from one employer to another employer;
- Change from one specialty occupation to another specialty occupation; and
- Merger that creates a new employing entity.[24]

With respect to L-1 petitions, legacy INS stated that even a change from one managerial position to a completely different managerial position is not a material change. Only if there is a change from a specialized knowledge to a managerial/executive position, or if there is a transfer from one company to another company, is the change material.[25]

Applying these standards in the EB-5 context, the analogy would be that, if there is a completely new entity in which the investment is made, the change is "material." As long as the statutory requirements regarding making the investment and sustaining the investment are met, the only change that is material should be one that results in the investor not creating the requisite jobs within a reasonable time after the filing of the I-829 petition. If there are changes in the business plan, timing of the investment, timing of job creation, nature of the jobs, nature of the business, or other changes that would not result in a denial of the original I-526 petition, the changes should not be considered material.

What if some or all of these changes affect the indirect employment creation calculations in the econometric report using one of the established input/output models? If the changes would result in the requisite indirect employment not being created within a reasonable time using the designated input/output model, the change may well be "material." However, if the model still would result in a conclusion that the requisite indirect employment will be created within a reasonable time, the change arguably should not be considered "material." In that case, perhaps the new econometric report, based on the new and updated facts and circumstances, should be filed with the I-829 condition removal petition.

What is USCIS's position? The agency's position appears to be that any change in the business plan, even if all of the necessary jobs have been created, is a "material change."[26] For example, if the original plan on which the I-526 was approved envisioned the creation of a restaurant with employment being in the form of cooks and waiters, but in the end the company evolved into a catering business with employees being drivers, menu planners, and order takers, even though the investment was sustained and even though the employment was created, the I-829 petition might be denied under this policy. This is subject to challenge, however, since the investor has met all statutory and regulatory requirements, none of which requires that the jobs created be the same jobs as envisioned in the I-526 filing, and since it is inconsistent with USCIS standards for other visa categories.

What if the I-526 business plan envisions a business that will be multi-faceted over time, including creating a restaurant, a catering business, and possibly other businesses? Would the I-829 be approved because there is no material change? USCIS's position is, at best, unclear. If the business plan clearly articulated multiple business opportunities, but if the specific job creation at the I-526 stage was premised upon only the first of the specific businesses, there is some indication, including the above language from the AFM, that USCIS would not approve the I-829 if it did not pre-approve this specific job creation in this specific business at the I-526 stage. If that is, in fact, USCIS's adjudicatory position in a case where the investor sustained the investment and the jobs actually were created, the USCIS position would appear to be especially vulnerable in litigation.

USCIS answers to questions posed by the AILA EB-5 Committee at a December 14, 2009, EB-5

---

[23] INS Memorandum, T. Aleinikoff, "Amended H-1B Petitions" (Aug. 22, 1996).

[24] AFM ch. 31.2(e)

[25] INS Memorandum, J. Hogan, "Guidelines for the Filing of Amended H and L Petitions," (Oct. 22, 1992).

[26] See AFM ch. 22.4(c)(4)(G), as amended by the December 11, 2009, Neufeld Memorandum (the actual project identified in the business plan and approved in the I-526 petition must serve as the basis for determining whether the I-829 petition should be approved; if there is a material change, a new I-526 petition must be filed).

stakeholders meeting[27] are instructive. One particular question read as follows:

> If a business plan provides for investments in multiple job-creating businesses over time, and if the commercial enterprise moves the money from one job-creating business to another consistent with the business plan, does every such movement of funds require an amended I-526?

USCIS's response was that the business plan must provide specifically for investment in multiple job-creating businesses over time in order for USCIS to determine that it is feasible. The business plan also must demonstrate that the requisite jobs will be created through the succession of capital investments through the commercial enterprise. "In such an instance, an amended petition would not be required as long as the capital investment activities … are in keeping with the approved business plan."[28]

New Petition or Amended Petition

In the December 2009, Neufeld Memo, USCIS states that the result of a material change should be the requirement to file a new petition. This is not consistent with the agency's past practice with respect to other types of applications. The AFM states that a material change in the terms and conditions of employment or in the beneficiary's eligibility for the benefit does not require a new petition. Rather, it requires an amended petition.[29]

[For comparison, see also 8 CFR §214.2(h)(11)(i)(A), which requires an amended petition—and not a new petition—when there are changes in the terms and conditions of employment of a beneficiary which may affect eligibility for H-1B status. The procedure for O-1 visa beneficiaries is consistent with the H-1B petition procedures. The AFM requires a new petition if there is a change of petitioning employers. However, if the conditions of employment change, even if the changes are "material changes in the terms and conditions of employment or the beneficiary's eligibility," no new petition is required—only an amended petition.][30]

With respect to immigrant petitions, perhaps the I-140 petition is the most analogous to the I-526 petition. If there is a material change in the job opportunity necessitating a new labor certification application, the labor certification can be submitted in support of the pending I-140 petition without requiring a new I-140 petition.[31] Previous legacy INS memoranda either stated specifically that a "material change in the terms and conditions of employment or the beneficiary's eligibility" requires an amended petition, or refer to new and amended petitions interchangeably.[32]

Therefore, if the change is not material, no additional petition should be required, and USCIS can be advised of the change at the I-829 stage. If there is a material change consistent with USCIS policy as stated above, the remedy should be an amended I-526 petition and not a new I-526 petition.[33]

Ramifications of New I-526 Petition

The distinction between new and amended petitions is critically important. An amended I-526 petition would not affect the timing of the filing of the condition removal petition, and would not require the investor to obtain a new period of conditional residence status. On the other hand, a new petition would create the necessity for a new application for conditional permanent residence and a new two year period. The significance of this cannot be overstated. Not only does filing a new application require additional time and expense for obtaining conditional permanent residence, and not only does it require the investor to delay obtaining full permanent residence for another two years, it also has the following impacts:

- Any children of the investor who obtained conditional permanent status but are now over age 21, or any spouse who has been divorced, would now be ineligible to obtain a new period of conditional residence;
- The investor likely would be ineligible for adjustment of status to conditional permanent residence;

---

[27] See "EB-5 Stakeholders Meeting," *supra* note 12.

[28] *Id.* at question 12. Note USCIS's reference to an "amended petition" rather than a "new petition," which can be highly significant.

[29] AFM ch. 31.2(e).

[30] AFM ch. 33.4(a).

[31] AFM ch. 22.2(E).

[32] *See supra* notes 23 and 25.

[33] One of the precedent decisions, *Matter of Izummi*, 22 I&N Dec. 169 (BIA 1998), is often cited for the proposition that an investor may not make material changes to a petition that has been filed in order to make a deficient petition approvable. However, *Matter of Izummi* arguably has no relevance to an I-526 petition that was approvable when filed and actually approved.

- If the conditional permanent residence application was filed under INA §245(i), eligibility for adjustment of status may be lost because the petition that grandfathered the alien under that section cannot be used a second time for §245(i) grandfathering purposes;[34]
- A new five year period for purposes of naturalization would start from the grant of the new conditional permanent residence status.

These issues will be explored separately.

What happens to the investor's children, who subsequently have become age 21 or older, and the investor's previous spouse, who now has become an ex-spouse? Both the December 2009 Neufeld Memo and the amended AFM[35] state that the adult son and daughter and the ex-spouse, all of whom are now ineligible to be classified as EB-5 dependents at the time of the filing of the new I-485 application, are left without remedy. Presumably, these individuals would be subject to removal. This result would not inure in the event of the filing of an amended petition, since the original grant of conditional permanent residence that protected the dependents would remain in effect and still would be the basis for the pendency of the conditional removal petition.

One of many ways in which the December 2009 Neufeld memo appears to be legally incorrect is its statement that the conditional resident who abandons conditional residence is eligible to adjust status to a new period of conditional residence. A closer analysis fails to reveal a legal basis for this conclusion. The analysis starts with INA §245(f), which prohibits the adjustment of status of an alien lawfully admitted for conditional residence under INA §216A. In *Matter of Stockwell*,[36] the Board of Immigration Appeals (BIA) interpreted the implementing regulations, now contained at 8 CFR §245.1(c)(5), as barring from adjustment only those aliens currently holding conditional permanent resident status, and not those whose conditional status has been terminated. On this basis, USCIS suggests in the AFM that the investor should abandon permanent residence status on Form I-407.[37]

However, once the alien terminates conditional permanent residence status, under what subsection of INA §245 is the alien adjusting? This remains a mystery. The problem is INA §245(c)(7), which prohibits an alien from adjusting status to an immigrant under INA §203(b) (EB-5 is under §203(b)(5)) if the alien is "not in a lawful nonimmigrant status." With abandonment concurrently filed with the adjustment, the alien may be in a lawful immigrant status, but clearly not in a lawful nonimmigrant status. Therefore, the alien who ends his or her conditional permanent residence could apply for adjustment of status to conditional permanent residence upon marriage to a U.S. citizen spouse (under INA §201(b)(2)), or based on any family-sponsored category under §203(a), but not under §203(b), which applies to employment-based immigrants.

Doesn't INA §245(k) save the day, allowing an employment-based immigrant to adjust irrespective of the prohibition in INA §245(c)(7)? Unfortunately, §245(k) only applies to employment-based immigrants under INA §§203(b)(1), (2) and (3) (and sometimes (4)), but does not apply to §203(b)(5) immigrants. It appears to this author that attempting to utilize the procedure suggested by the December 2009, Neufeld Memo is an invitation to a denial of adjustment of status, especially since USCIS states that it is not bound by its own memoranda,[38] and certainly not bound where its memoranda violate statutory language.

Of course, if an alien is grandfathered under INA §245(i), he or she would be eligible to utilize this procedure, right? Not necessarily. Legacy INS took the position that a petition filed before the relevant date (January 14, 1998, or April 30, 2001) can only be used to grandfather an alien for adjustment of status one time.[39] Presumably, the investor used the

---

[34] USCIS Memorandum, W. Yates, "Clarification of Certain Eligibility Requirements Pertaining to an Application to Adjust Status under Section 245(i) of the Immigration and Nationality Act" (Mar. 9, 2005), at 6, *published on* AILA InfoNet at Doc. No. 05031468 (*posted* Mar. 14, 2005).

[35] AFM ch. 22.4(c)(4)(G).

[36] *Matter of Stockwell*, 20 I&N Dec. 309 (BIA 1991).

[37] This leaves open the question whether abandonment is the same as a termination for purposes of the holding in *Stockwell*. Arguably the answer should be in the affirmative. *See also Matter of Mendez*, 20 I&N Dec. 833 (BIA 1994) (withdrawal of support by petitioning spouse to jointly-filed I-751 condition removal petition effectuated a termination of the conditional permanent residence status).

[38] *Matter of Izummi*, 22 I&N Dec.(BIA 1998).

[39] *See* INS Memorandum, R. Bach, "Accepting Applications for Adjustment of Status under Section 245(i) of the Immigration and Nationality Act" (Apr. 14, 1999), at 4. *See also* Yates Memorandum, *supra* note 34, at ¶3(E)(2).

petition to enable adjustment of status under §245(i) for the first filing, which could make it unavailable a second time.

Therefore, the December 2009 Neufeld Memo clearly needs to be revised both as a matter of policy and as a matter of law. In addition to defining material change as indicated above, the revised memorandum should clearly indicate that a material change—assuming it does not involve a different commercial entity—requires an amended petition and not a new petition, and, therefore, does not require abandonment of previous conditional permanent residence status or a new application for conditional permanent residence status. The suggested revision would put I-526 practice in conformity with I-140 practice, which allows for the transfer of a filed adjustment of status application based on an approved I-140 petition to a new approved I-140 petition, without the need to withdraw the adjustment of status application and file a new one, as long as there is no break in the continuity of the adjustment of status application.[40]

Investor's Choice— I-829 or New I-526

At least for now, an investor who has any change whatsoever in the business from the business plan—even if only that the vicissitudes of the business, the economy, acts of nature, etc. resulted in the jobs being created on a slower schedule than anticipated—clearly is faced with a dilemma. Should the investor file the I-829 petition with an explanation of all of the extenuating circumstances that resulted in a delay in job creation, together with documentation establishing the likelihood that the jobs will be created within a reasonable time; or should the investor choose not to take the risk of filing the I-829 petition, and instead file a new I-526 petition with a new business plan taking into account the changed circumstances?

- USCIS provided two examples in a superseded portion of the AFM that may be helpful in gleaning how an I-829 may be treated:
  – A conditional resident has created positions for only seven full-time employees. If the conditional resident states that he intends to create three additional positions at an indefinite time in the future, the I-829 petition should be denied. If the conditional resident provides credible evidence to demonstrate recruitment for the remaining full-time positions, that the positions are in the process of being actively recruited, and that they will clearly be filled, the I-829 petition may be approved.
  – Although a conditional resident claims to have created positions for ten full-time employees, only nine are actually working. If a conditional resident presents evidence that she actively recruited the tenth employee, and the tenth employee is expected to be hired and begin employment, the I-829 petition may be approved.[41]

Examples abound of other scenarios that would create a difficult choice for the investor:

- A construction project is behind schedule. Most jobs have not been created. It is likely to be another year or two until the construction is completed and jobs are created. Is this a material change? Will the jobs be created within a "reasonable time?"

- More than 10 jobs were created, but recent events have resulted in a significant slowdown of business and some of the employees have been laid off. The plan is to rehire when business conditions improve. Is this a "material change? Will business conditions improve within a "reasonable time?"

- The expected start date of the business was delayed. However, since the launch date, everything has gone as originally planned. The plan will now be a three year plan instead of a two year plan. Is this a "material change?" Will the jobs be created within a "reasonable time?"

- The original plan was to hire 10 employees up front. The plan changed, and the employees were not hired until later; but all 10 were hired by the end of the two years. Is this a "material change?"

- All 10 employees were hired during the two years, but the job positions and titles are very different than originally anticipated. Is this a "material change?"

- A regional center's construction project was delayed because of weather conditions, unavailability of capital, economic conditions, etc. As a result, all of the foundational elements of the econometric model have not yet occurred. However, the project is now moving forward. Is this a

---

[40] AFM ch. 23.2(l).

[41] These examples appeared in a superseded version of the AFM at ch. 15.2(h).

"material change?" Will the jobs be created within a "reasonable time?"

The answers to all of these factual scenarios are unclear and ultimately would depend upon the unknown definitions of "material change" and "reasonable time." Although there is a good argument that none of these is a "material change" and that the jobs would be created within a "reasonable time," in all of the scenarios the investor may choose not to take the risk of getting an I-829 denial, and may prefer to file a new I-526 petition.

Procedure for New I-526 Petition

Let's assume the investor chooses the conservative option and files a new I-526 petition. What is the procedure? The AFM, as amended by the December 2009 Neufeld Memo, sets forth the new procedure for filing new I-526 petitions in the event of either a material change that results in an inability to satisfy the I-829 requirements, or in the event of a complete failure of the project and the initiation of a new capital investment project.[42] The revisions to the AFM set forth three scenarios regarding timing, and leave open a fourth.

The first scenario occurs before the alien becomes a conditional permanent resident. In that event, the approval of the new I-526 would be the basis for the approval of the existing application for adjustment of status or immigrant visa.

The second scenario is if the new I-526 petition is filed after the alien becomes a conditional permanent resident, but before the due date of the filing of the I-829 petition. Upon approval of the new I-526, the investor files an abandonment of permanent residence application (Form I-407) with a new I-485 adjustment of status application. The result is that the investor has a new two-year period of conditional residence.

Finally, if the I-829 petition is pending, the investor may request the withdrawal of the I-829 petition upon approval of the new I-526 petition, and then file a new application for adjustment of status.

Many questions remain:

- If the I-829 is already filed, will the adjudication be deferred pending action on the new I-526?
- If the I-829 is filed, there has been a material change but the necessary jobs have been created. Can the new I-526 petition be co-filed with the existing I-829 petition, or must it be accompanied by a new I-829 petition?
- Can the same procedure allowing for adjustment of status be applied in the case of a new I-526 petition filed after an I-829 petition has been denied?

An earlier legacy INS Memorandum, "EB-5 Field Memorandum 9: Form I-829 Processing,"[43] is instructive. That memorandum, and the accompanying amendment to the AFM, stated that, where an I-526 was approved prior to the issuance of the four EB-5 precedent decisions, and the I-829 cannot be approved because of the changes created by those decisions, the investor could file a new I-526 based upon the same business plan with changes to conform to the precedent decisions. Legacy INS would suspend adjudication of the I-829 until the new I-526 petition was adjudicated. Upon approval, the investor would abandon his previous conditional permanent residence status, leave the United States, and obtain a new period of conditional residence status.

Another question involves whether the filing of the new I-526 petition eliminates the need to file an I-829 petition before the end of the original two-year conditional residence period. Nothing in the aforementioned memorandum or the AFM so indicates. Presumably, in order to have conditional permanent residence status continue, the investor would have to timely file the I-829 petition before the expiration of the initial conditional residence, while concurrently pursuing the new I-526 petition. Otherwise, the conditional resident status of the investor likely would be terminated, leaving the investor with no lawful status in the United States.

EFFECT OF I-829 DENIAL

Let's now visit the option of the investor who chooses not to file a new I-526 petition, chooses to proceed with the I-829 petition and attempts to prove that there has been no material change and that the jobs will be created within a reasonable time. If the I-829 application is denied, what are the options?

Although the December 2009 Neufeld Memo does not reference the possibility of a new I-526 petition after the denial of the I-829, it is not expressly precluded. Therefore, this should still be an option.

---

[42] AFM ch. 22.4(c)(4)(G).

[43] INS Memorandum, M. Pearson, Executive Associate Commissioner, Office of Field Operations, (Mar. 3, 2000), adding AFM 25.2(f)(9)(B) (since superseded).

What is the status of the alien and his or her family once the I-829 petition is denied? Although there is some confusing and apparently contradictory language, the end result is somewhat clearer. 8 CFR §216.6(d)(2) states the lawful permanent residence status is terminated as of the date of the I-829 denial, and the investor must surrender his permanent residence card. However, this is inconsistent with *Matter of Lok*,[44] which makes clear that the lawful permanent resident status of an alien is not terminated until the entry of a final administrative order of deportation. USCIS resolves this discrepancy in the AFM.[45] It states that if the I-829 is denied, until a final order of removal is entered, the alien must be issued a temporary extension of his or her conditional resident status. This procedure was recently reaffirmed at a USCIS EB-5 stakeholders meeting ("an alien investor retains conditional residence status and is entitled to proof of that status while he or she obtains review of the USCIS termination in removal proceedings").[46] Presumably, proof of conditional resident status would be issued in the form of a temporary I-551 stamp in the passport.

What if the investor wants to challenge the I-829 denial? First, there is no appeal of an I-829 denial.[47] However, the investor may seek review of the I-829 in removal proceedings. In such event, the burden of proof rests with USCIS to establish by a preponderance of the evidence that the facts and information in the investor's removal petition are not true and that the petition was properly denied.[48] This would leave it to an immigration judge to sort out legal issues, such as whether job counting is a proper basis for an I-829 adjudication; whether there was a material change to the I-526; whether the investor has created the requisite employment; and whether the requisite employment will be created within a reasonable time.

If the investor wants to obtain judicial review of the denial of an I-829 by an immigration judge, as with any other removal proceeding, the investor can appeal to the BIA. During such appeal, the investor continues to be entitled to proof of conditional residence status.[49] Ultimately, if the BIA denies the appeal, judicial review is available in a court of appeals. However, once the order is administratively final, the investor is no longer entitled to proof of conditional residence status.[50] If, despite the investor's efforts, no Notice to Appear is issued (and, therefore the investor is unable to renew his condition removal petition before an immigration judge), it may be possible to go to federal district court.[51]

CONCLUSION

Recent positions taken by USCIS put EB-5 investors in a precarious position when there are any deviations in the planned course of job creation. At least until USCIS revises its current policies, or until there is a successful administrative or judicial challenge, investors have difficult choices to make with very serious ramifications to their ability to remain in the United States with their families, and to become unconditional permanent residents and ultimately naturalized citizens.

---

[44] *Matter of Lok*, 18 I&N Dec.101 (BIA 1981), *aff'd*, 681 F.2d 107 (2d Cir. 1982).

[45] AFM ch. 25.2(k).

[46] *See* "USCIS Q&A" (answer to question 37), *supra* note 20.

[47] 8 CFR §216.6(d)(2).

[48] 8 CFR §216.6(d)(2).

[49] AFM ch. 25.2(k).

[50] *Id.*

[51] *See Iddir v. Immigration and Naturalization Service*, 301 F.3d 492 (7th Cir. 2002); *Chang v. United States*, 327 F.3d 911 (9th Cir. 2003). The *Chang* decision is reproduced at Appendix B.

CONDITIONAL PERMANENT RESIDENCE AND IMMIGRATION RISK FOR INVESTORS

by Lincoln Stone[*]

INTRODUCTION

Interest in the employment-based fifth preference category (EB-5) for immigrant investors has been on the rise. Were visa issuances to reach the annual cap of 10,000 visas, the EB-5 investor visa program administered by U.S. Citizenship and Immigration Services (USCIS) could legitimately lay claim to attracting some $1.5 billion in investment capital and fueling the creation of approximately 30,000 jobs in the U.S. economy *each year*.

Congress indeed intended to set forth a clear path to unconditional permanent residence—one that would entice foreign persons to invest in the U.S. economy. As written by Congress, the EB-5 statutes require the investor to undertake investment (or commercial) risk. When the investor combines that investment risk with a credible plan to create 10 jobs in a U.S. business, the investor is well on the way to satisfying the requirements for a visa in the EB-5 category. Permanent residence in the EB-5 category is conditional, and at the end of a two-year period the investor must file with USCIS a petition for removal of the conditions on permanent residence.[1] Congress intended that the conditions on permanent residence should be removed if the investor has sustained the investment. In devising a statutory scheme that would attract job-creating capital to the United States, Congress imposed no other requirements for achieving unconditional permanent residence. Put your money at risk in the U.S. economy, and sustain the investment—that is the formula prescribed by Congress.

A more sobering reality, however, is that the EB-5 category does not amount to a clear path to unconditional permanent residence. Courtesy of the restrictive standards USCIS has introduced into the EB-5 petition process, numerous pitfalls line the path to unconditional permanent residence. Experience in hundreds of successful cases involving petitions for removal of conditions—usually involving difficult Requests for Evidence (RFEs), and even petition denials in some cases—teaches that USCIS's approval of the petition for removal of conditions is not lightly given. To be sure, by way of two sets of instructions to field offices, USCIS recently memorialized certain rigid adjudication standards that promise to bedevil investors and their counsel seeking removal of conditions.[2] It is perhaps unpopular to say it but, in effect, USCIS has introduced "immigration risk"—*i.e.*, difficult-to-meet or murky adjudication standards that hinder the process of achieving unconditional permanent residence, although the investor has met the legislative standard of sustaining the investment. Experience reveals that immigration risk in the EB-5 petition process is substantial.

This article sets forth the statutory framework for defining the conditions on permanent residence, and then reveals the ways in which the rigid mindset that USCIS imposes on adjudication of EB-5 petitions results in extra-legal transformation of the conditions on permanent residence. Putting aside for the most part the question whether a court would provide relief to an investor aggrieved by extra-legal standards, this transformation of the conditions on permanent residence imposes untenable immigration risk on the EB-5 petition process. The article concludes that significant changes in the adjudication standards are necessary in order to build confidence that the EB-5 laws

---

[*] **Lincoln Stone** practices law in Los Angeles with Stone & Grzegorek LLP, *www.lskglaw.com*, an immigration law firm. Copyright ©2010 Lincoln Stone. All rights reserved.

[1] For a primer on the law and procedure concerning removal of the conditions for EB-5 investors, *see* L. Stone, "Removal of the Conditions on Permanent Residence for Immigrant Investors," *Immigration Options for Investors and Entrepreneurs* (AILA 2006).

[2] U.S. Citizenship and Immigration Services (USCIS) Memorandum, D. Neufeld, Acting Associate Director, Domestic Operations, "EB-5 Alien Entrepreneurs—Job Creation and Full-Time Positions" (AFM Update AD 09-04) (June 17, 2009), *published on* AILA InfoNet at Doc. No. 09061964 (*posted* June 19, 2009) (hereinafter Neufeld I); USCIS Memorandum, D. Neufeld, Acting Associate Director, Domestic Operations, "Adjudication of EB-5 Regional Center Proposals and Affiliated Form I-526 and Form I-829 Petitions" (AFM Update AD 09-38) (Dec. 11, 2009), *published on* AILA InfoNet at Doc. No. 09121561 (*posted* Dec. 15, 2009) (hereinafter Neufeld II). Both of these memoranda are reproduced at Appendix C.

are fair and the promised immigration outcomes are reasonably achievable.

PERMANENT RESIDENCE ON A CONDITIONAL BASIS

Congress articulated in clear and unambiguous language the conditions on the EB-5 investor's permanent residence, and in so doing, Congress clarified that the narrow objective of the conditional period is deterrence of fraud. As will be demonstrated, though, the legislative intent has been subverted over time by agency actions that have transformed the conditions on permanent residence. As a consequence, whether the petition for removal of conditions is approved will depend not so much on compliance with statutory criteria as on compliance with onerous and extra-legal interpretations that legacy Immigration and Naturalization Service (INS) and USCIS have imposed on the adjudication process.

A Statutory Framework Defining the Conditions on Permanent Residence

As conceived by Congress in the Immigration Act of 1990 (IMMACT90), the EB-5 investor obtains lawful permanent residence status on a conditional basis.[3] The conditional concept already existed in law as of 1986, as immigrants via marriage also could be subject to conditions under the provisions of the Immigration Marriage Fraud Amendments of 1986 (IMFA), codified at §216 of the Immigration and Nationality Act of 1952 (INA). Indeed, instead of making EB-5 investors subject to the same conditions set forth in IMFA for married applicants, INA §216A was created specifically for conditional permanent residents in the EB-5 investor category. INA §216A is a relatively lengthy body of law—approximately three times the length of the statute describing the requirements for initial eligibility for the EB-5 category visa—and it articulates precisely what conditions Congress intended for EB-5 investors.

As contemplated in the original regulations first promulgated in 1988 to support IMFA, prior to enactment of the EB-5 investor category, permanent residence on a conditional basis is tantamount to permanent residence in all its attributes, the only exception being the conditional permanent resident is also subject to certain conditions:

A conditional permanent resident is an alien who has been lawfully admitted for permanent residence within the meaning of section 101(a)(20) of the Act, except that a conditional permanent resident is also subject to the conditions and responsibilities set forth in §§216 or 216A of the Act, whichever is applicable, and part 216 of this chapter.[4]

(Note the above reference to §216A of the Act was added in 1994 when legacy INS promulgated regulations for removal of conditions for EB-5 investors.)

The same regulation puts the conditional permanent resident on equal footing with any other permanent resident:

Unless otherwise specified, the rights, privileges, responsibilities and duties which apply to all other lawful permanent residents apply equally to conditional permanent residents, including but not limited to the right to apply for naturalization (if otherwise eligible), the right to file petitions on behalf of qualifying relatives, the privilege of residing permanently in the United States as an immigrant in accordance with the immigration laws, such status not having changed; the duty to register with the Selective Service System, when required; and the responsibility for complying with all laws and regulations of the United States.

Consequently, when in IMMACT90 Congress elected to make EB-5 investors subject to conditions, it did so in the context of an already existing legal framework and firm understanding for what is meant by a conditional permanent resident. Congress apprehended well that the conditional status is a permanent residence status by any other measure, except there would be certain specific conditions to that permanent residence status. For EB-5 investors, those conditions were identified by Congress with the utmost particularity.

As articulated in the statute, when the EB-5 investor obtains lawful permanent residence on a conditional basis, the investor should receive notice of the requirement to file a petition to remove the con-

---

[3] INA §216A(a)(1).

[4] 8 CFR §§216.1, 1216.1. The cited statute, INA §101(a)(20), provides: "The term 'lawfully admitted for permanent residence' means the status of having been lawfully accorded the privilege of residing permanently in the United States as an immigrant in accordance with the immigration laws, such status not having changed."

ditions.[5] The petition to remove the conditions must be filed within the 90-day period before the second anniversary of the investor's admission for permanent residence,[6] and that petition must set forth "the facts and information described in subsection (d)(1)" of INA §216A.[7] It could not be any clearer that Congress intended that the conditions on permanent residence be removed for the EB-5 investor if the investor's petition satisfies the requirements of subsection (d)(1).

Congress also clarified that the government could initiate proceedings to terminate permanent residence on a conditional basis *during* the two-year conditional period if it determined that the investment was a sham or a mere immigration artifice, the investment was not in the process or sustained, or the investor was not otherwise conforming to the requirements of the EB-5 statute.[8]

In sum, the actual conditions Congress imposed on the permanent residence of the EB-5 investor can be grouped in three categories which have a sequential relevance:

(i) *during the two-year conditional period* the status can be terminated if the investment was a sham or a mere immigration artifice, the investment was not in the process or sustained, or the investor was not otherwise conforming to the requirements of the EB-5 statute (the "maintenance of status conditions");

(ii) *during the 90-day window* immediately prior to the two-year anniversary of obtaining permanent resident status, the petition to remove the conditions must be filed (the "petition filing conditions"); and

(iii) *upon filing the petition for removal of conditions* the documentation in support of the petition must set forth "the facts and information described in subsection (d)(1)" of INA §216A (the "petition adjudication conditions").

According to the intent of Congress, no conditions other than the three categories of conditions itemized above can be imposed on the EB-5 investor.

Turning to the question of what the EB-5 investor must do to obtain a favorable USCIS decision removing the conditions on permanent residence, we can quickly dispose of two of the above-described categories of conditions so that we can focus on just the one category of conditions that controls the USCIS adjudication of the petition to remove the conditions. The maintenance of status conditions have little significance in normal practice—because they apply only during the initial two-year period of conditional permanent residence, the government is required to initiate and make a determination that a maintenance of status condition has not been met, and the government bears the burden of proof in any contested proceedings. In nearly two decades of EB-5 practice involving some 1,000 EB-5 cases, I am unaware of any case where the maintenance of status conditions have been questioned.

The petition filing conditions—the filing of a petition to remove the conditions—are satisfied by a timely filing of the petition or even later if there is "good cause and extenuating circumstances" for filing the petition after the statutory deadline.[9] In the vast majority of cases, suffice to say, once the EB-5 investor files the petition to remove the conditions, the investor has cleared the hurdles of the maintenance of status conditions and petition filing conditions.[10]

Therefore, when it comes time to adjudicate the petition for removal of conditions, the lone hurdle remaining for the EB-5 investor to clear is the brief listing of petition adjudication conditions which are the specific requirements enumerated by Congress for removal of conditions.

We know exactly what Congress intended in the way of petition adjudication conditions because Congress pointedly stated that the petition must set forth "the facts and information described in subsection (d)(1)" of INA §216A. That provision of the law, following its amendment in 2002, clearly provides that the petition for removal of conditions:

> shall contain facts and information demonstrating that the alien—
>
> (A)(i) invested, or is actively in the process of investing, the requisite capital; (the "investment requirement") and

---

[5] INA §216A(a)(2).
[6] INA §216A(d)(2)(A).
[7] INA §216A(c)(1)(A).
[8] INA §216A(b)(1), as amended.

[9] INA §216A(d)(2).
[10] USCIS lacks the authority, for instance, to require the investor to prove a maintenance of status condition (such as proving that the investment is not a mere immigration artifice) as if it were one of the petition adjudication conditions.

(ii) sustained the actions described in clause (i) throughout the period of the alien's residence in the United States; (the "sustained requirement") and

(B) is otherwise conforming to the requirements of section 1153(b)(5) of this title. (the "otherwise conforming requirement")[11]

Of utmost importance, the statutory authority for removal of conditions is significantly distinct from the statutory authority for initial eligibility in the EB-5 category.[12] To demonstrate initial EB-5 eligibility the investor must present documents concerning not only investment, but also concerning a "new" business that is a "commercial enterprise," management participation, and past or future job creation. The statutory criteria for removal of conditions are abbreviated, including in specifics only the investment requirement and the sustained requirement.[13]

The statute is by no means silent or ambiguous about what Congress expects an investor to prove for removal of conditions purposes. In instances where Congress has delineated clearly what it requires, the agency "must give effect to the intent of Congress" and not attempt to impose additional requirements not found in the statute.[14] This limitation on agency power is dictated by the maxim of statutory construction *expressio unius est exclusio alterius* ("the explicit mention of one is the exclusion of the other").[15]

Congress authorized USCIS to make a determination as to "whether the facts and information described in subsection (d)(1) of this section and alleged in the petition are true with respect to the qualifying commercial enterprise."[16] If it is true, in other words, that the investor is at least in the process of investing the requisite capital and has sustained the investment, the statute requires USCIS to approve the petition for removal of conditions. The statutory language is a clear indication that Congress intended the two-year conditional residence period and the petition to remove conditions to serve limited purposes.

As is plain from the statutory language, Congress originally intended only that the conditional residence period serve as a mechanism to ensure that the investor has made or is in the process of making a real investment that the investor is sustaining. The limited purpose of the conditional residence period is to deter investor fraud. As it was first introduced, section 204 of the Immigration Act of 1989 was entitled "Deterring Immigration-Related Entrepreneur Fraud,"[17] it required a two-year conditional permanent residence status, and authorized termination of such status on proof that the business was established solely as a means of evading the immigration laws.[18] The provision was adopted later in the EB-5 statutes enacted into law with IMMACT90 and codified at INA §216A. The statutory scheme furthers the goal of fraud deterrence by requiring proof in support of the petition to remove conditions that the investment in the new commercial enterprise is real and has been sustained.[19]

Agency Actions Transforming the Conditions on Permanent Residence

No fair consideration of the EB-5 investor program can be accomplished without acknowledging that USCIS has made significant gains in productivity and transparency. With respect to substantive standards, there should be little doubt that USCIS officials have labored toward getting it right, for all interests concerned. Even so, there exists substantial immigration risk in the EB-5 investor program. And that immigration risk stems from the reality that USCIS does not adjudicate EB-5 investor cases in accord with the petition adjudication conditions. It is not enough in the eyes of USCIS for the investor to

---

[11] INA §216A(d)(1), as amended.

[12] *Compare* INA §216A *with* INA §203(b)(5).

[13] The general, catch-all "otherwise conforming requirement" was added in 2002, Pub. L. No. 107-273, 116 Stat. 1758, Title I, Subtitle B, Ch. 1, §11036(b) (2002), and is addressed later in this article. The 2002 amendments also eliminated from the petition adjudication conditions the requirement that the investor "established" the new commercial enterprise.

[14] *See, e.g., Coronado-Durazo v. INS*, 123 F.3d 1322 (9th Cir. 1997); *Almero v. INS*, 18 F.3d 757, 760 (9th Cir. 1994). Deference to the agency is not warranted if the agency's standards are contrary to statute. *Chevron USA v. Natural Resources Defense Council*, 467 U.S. 837 (1984); *INS v. Aguirre-Aguirre*, 526 U.S. 415 (1999).

[15] *See, e.g., Ardestani v. INS*, 502 U.S. 129, 145-46 (1991); *Carlson v. Reed*, 249 F.3d 876, 882 (9th Cir. 2001); *Gee v. INS*, 875 F. Supp. 666 (N.D. Cal. 1994).

[16] INA §216A(c)(3)(A).

[17] S. 358, 101st Cong. §204 (1989).

[18] S. Rep. No. 101-55, at 22 (1989).

[19] Investors are "admitted as conditional permanent residents as a means to deter immigration-related entrepreneurship fraud." Commentary to Final Rule, 59 Fed. Reg. 26587 (May 23, 1994), *quoting* S. Rep. No. 101-55, at 22 (1989).

satisfy the investment requirement and the sustained requirement.

Of first importance, although evidence of job creation is not one of the statutory petition adjudication conditions, legacy INS nonetheless adopted a regulation imposing the requirement that the petition for removal of conditions include evidence of job creation: "The alien created or can be expected to create within a reasonable period of time ten full-time jobs for qualifying employees."[20] Inasmuch as Congress specifically identified the petition adjudication conditions, it may not be presupposed that it simply lost its collective head and neglected to include job creation as a petition adjudication condition. The longstanding precept of statutory construction—*expressio unius est exclusio alterius* ("the explicit mention of one is the exclusion of the other")—requires the opposite conclusion that Congress intended to omit job creation as a petition adjudication condition. This regulation, therefore, is ultra vires and subject to legal challenge. To mask the ultra vires action in the shape of a regulation does not lend legality to the agency action because an agency cannot promulgate regulations that are beyond its statutory authority.[21]

Job creation, without a doubt, is a goal of the EB-5 investor program. Therefore, this regulation and its application to specific EB-5 investor cases will be scrutinized at length in a later section of this article. It is enough to observe for now that the fact job creation is a goal of the EB-5 investor program does not justify the agency action in transforming the petition adjudication conditions that have been carefully crafted by Congress. To the extent proof of job creation factors into adjudications of petitions for removal of conditions, it is due solely to the ultra vires regulation.

More recently, in June 2009, in a USCIS Memorandum transmitting field instructions to agency officers (Neufeld I), USCIS memorialized its view that not only is job creation one of the petition adjudication conditions, but also that proof of having created jobs is a central purpose of the conditional residence period, meaning all the requisite jobs must be created as of the time the petition for removal of conditions is adjudicated. Neufeld I adds language to the *Adjudicator's Field Manual* (AFM), stating that the primary purpose of the I-829 adjudication is to determine the petitioner "has invested the requisite capital and created the requisite jobs through investment."[22]

Suffice to say, the plain language of the statute does not support this proof-of-jobs declaration by USCIS. When questioned before the Senate Judiciary Committee in July 2009 about the limited fraud-deterrent objectives of the conditional residence period, and how USCIS's self-appointed task of counting jobs at the removal of conditions stage seemed to transform the original intent of the law and unduly burden the process, USCIS countered that it interprets the law in a way that it must demand that all required job creation occur within the two-year conditional period.[23] It is a substantial expansion of agency power, and one subject to challenge, which interprets a statute that purposefully does not mention job creation as a petition adjudication condition such that USCIS requires not only proof of some jobs but proof of 10 jobs as a petition adjudication condition.

In another measure that transforms petition adjudication conditions, a December 2009 USCIS Memorandum transmitting field instructions to agency officers (Neufeld II), USCIS states that EB-5 law requires that adjudication of the petition for removal of conditions must be based on the same capital investment project and business plan (*without material change*) that formed the basis for the approval of the investor's conditional permanent residence. Neufeld II adds a section to the AFM, stating:

> The structure of the EB-5 program is inflexible in that the capital investment project identified in the business plan in the approved Form I-526 petition must serve as the basis for determining at the Form I-829 petition stage whether the requisite capital investment has been sustained throughout the alien's two-year period of conditional resi-

---

[20] Final Rule, 59 Fed. Reg. 26587 (May 23, 1994), *codified at* 8 CFR §216.6(a)(4)(iv).

[21] The legal claim would be advanced under the Administrative Procedures Act (APA), 5 USC §706(2)(C); *United States v. Larianoff*, 431 U.S. 864, 872 (1977). *See also Mart v. Beebe*, No. CIV. 99 1391 JO, 2001 WL 13624 (D. Or. Jan. 5, 2001); *Ali v. Smith*, 39 F. Supp. 2d 1254 (W.D. Wash. 1999); *Tenacre Foundation v. INS*, 892 F. Supp. 289 (D.D.C. 1995).

[22] *Adjudicator's Field Manual* (AFM), ch. 25.2(e)(1), excerpted in Neufeld I, *supra* note 2, at 6. The AFM is available at *www.ailapubs.org/*.

[23] Promoting Job Creation and Foreign Investment in the U.S.: An Assessment of the EB-5 Regional Center Program: Hearing Before the S. Comm. on the Judiciary, 111th Cong. (July 22, 2009).

dency and that at least ten jobs have been or will be created within a reasonable period of time as a result of the alien's capital investment. The business plan in the Form I-526 petition may not be materially changed after the petition has been filed. In addition, USCIS may not act favorably on requests to delay the filing or adjudication of Form I-829 petitions beyond the timeframes outlined in 8 CFR 216.6(a) and (c).[24]

Where there is material change, Neufeld II mandates that the investor must relinquish conditional permanent residence and commence the EB-5 petition process from the start. It is a harsh outcome. Given the difficulty, too, of ascertaining where "material change" exists, large black clouds of uncertainty loom over the entire conditional residence period. It is difficult to square this agency position, grounded in a suggested "inflexible" statutory scheme, with a reasonable reading of the EB-5 statutes which appear to call for flexible interpretation. By imposing the added requirement of no variation from the originally-conceived capital investment project and business plan, Neufeld II further transforms the petition adjudication conditions. Later sections of this article elaborate on how this new standard is without legal basis and is misguided in terms of the overall objectives of the EB-5 investor program.

As USCIS has transformed petition adjudication conditions, it has utilized a transformed conception of conditional residence to reach desired outcomes in other forums. For example, for naturalization purposes, by statutory directive, a conditional permanent resident "shall be considered to have been admitted as an alien lawfully admitted for permanent residence and to be in the United States as an alien lawfully admitted to the United States for permanent residence."[25] USCIS nonetheless routinely challenges the conditional resident's eligibility for naturalization if the petition for removal of conditions has not yet been approved, declaring in direct contradiction of the statute that where the petition for removal of conditions remains pending the investor "has not been lawfully admitted." In one illustrative case USCIS stated:

> Because of the nature of the EB-5 visa, Congress specifically created the two-year conditional resident status as a mechanism to allow USCIS *to ensure that an alien complied with his or her investment plan and did, in fact, create the jobs.* The I-829 petition to remove conditions is a vital and critical component of the overall immigration process for alien entrepreneurs because the I-526 petition, upon which alien entrepreneurs are admitted to the United States, is in essence a promise by the alien to do certain things after admission. Without having successfully completed the process of removing the conditions from the alien entrepreneur's status, the alien entrepreneur has not been lawfully admitted in compliance with all applicable provisions of the INA, as required by section 318 of the INA. (italics added)

In another case involving the application for naturalization filed by a derivative family member, USCIS put it more succinctly and perhaps more confusingly too:

> A review of your file, and that of your father, the principal EB-5 applicant, reveals that he did not make the required investment or *create and maintain at least (10) full-time positions for qualifying employees at the time he was accorded permanent resident status under section 216A of the INA*, and you were accorded such status derivatively. Because your father, the principal, failed to comply with the statutory requirements under section 216A, you did not lawfully obtain your permanent resident status. (italics added)

While the holdings of these cases are limited to the specific realm of naturalization and do not apply directly to the adjudication of EB-5 cases (neither the initial I-526 petition nor the I-829 petition for removal of conditions), the underlying reasoning employed by USCIS in these cases is that the petition adjudication conditions include the requirement to create 10 full-time jobs; the failure to present such proof should mean denial of the I-829 petition for removal of conditions;[26] and, without approval of the I-829 petition, the EB-5 investor cannot be deter-

---

[24] AFM, ch. 22.4(c)(4)(G), excerpted in Neufeld II, *supra* note 2, at 19.

[25] INA §216A(e).

[26] The referenced naturalization cases involve investors and families referred to in USCIS parlance as the "Public Law investors," as they are the subject of a 2002 statute whereby the government is barred from denying their I-829 petitions. Pub. L. No. 107-273, 116 Stat. 1758, Title I, Subtitle B, ch. 1 §11031 et seq. (2002). This statute provides a path for several hundred families to "fix" the deficiencies in their cases; however, that path has been unavailable to them as the agency has not yet issued implementing regulations.

mined to have *ever* lawfully obtained permanent residence status, even though a statutory directive says exactly the opposite, and even though there is no allegation of fraud or misrepresentation.[27] Apart from the fact that the underlying reasoning in these cases stands as an incredible feat of legal analysis (making unmistakable statutory provisions disappear), the central significance is that where the agency is left to create the conditions on permanent residence as it chooses, the outcomes in legal terms are limitless and entirely unpredictable. These legal gymnastics, grounded in the re-conceptualization of the conditions on permanent residence, do not bode well in terms of sizing up the immigration risk faced by EB-5 investors.

It cannot be reasonably contended that Congress established the conditional residence timeframe as a two-year crucible for completing the ramp-up of a new business, operating the business without change from its original business plan, and creating 10 jobs in the U.S. economy. This is clear from the plain language of the EB-5 statutes.

To be sure, a majority of EB-5 investors and their families uproot themselves from homelands during the conditional residence period, and arrive in the United States with every intention of promptly settling in for the long term, establishing a home, enrolling children in schools, and initiating the process of assimilation to U.S. society. These families are relying heavily—indeed, betting the entire future of their families—on the legal foundation of conditional permanent residence, that it is permanent residence without diluted rights, privileges, and value, which will be unconditional permanent residence upon satisfaction of clear and reasonable conditions.

As described above, over time legacy INS and now USCIS have transformed the conditions on permanent residence. By conceptualizing the conditional aspect of permanent residence in a new and onerous manner, USCIS has injected into the removal of conditions process substantial "immigration risk" that well-informed investors are not likely to accept. The recent field instructions confirm that USCIS is depriving the removal of conditions process of any semblance of predictability. Unless there is a radical change in direction, the appeal of the EB-5 visa category to prospective investors likely will be diminished.

THE PETITION TO REMOVE CONDITIONS

The earlier discussion introduced the subject of petition adjudication conditions. The discussion that follows will delve deeper into the substance of those conditions—the investment requirement and the sustained requirement, as well as the "otherwise conforming requirement" as it is related to the agency-imposed job creation requirement. For the sake of completeness, the discussion begins with guidance on procedures concerning petitions for removal of conditions and a few observations concerning the controlling legal sources for removal of conditions.

Procedure

As indicated above, the petition filing conditions require the filing of the I-829 petition for removal of conditions during the 90-day period before the second anniversary of being admitted as a conditional permanent resident.[28] Failure to file the I-829 petition will result in termination of permanent resident status, and possible commencement of removal (deportation) proceedings.[29] A late filing may be considered if for "good cause and extenuating circumstances."[30]

Only the principal investor is required to file the I-829 petition, as the spouse and dependent children are automatically included.[31] Children who have reached the age of 21 or have married during the two-year period of conditional status do not lose the benefits of riding with the principal. Even the former spouse who divorced during the conditional period is protected by the principal's petition or by a separate petition.[32]

Upon the filing of the I-829 petition with USCIS, lawful resident status is automatically extended and will remain valid until such time as the petition is adjudicated.[33] USCIS should issue a receipt notice

---

[27] In a slightly different analysis, one federal district court judge concluded that notwithstanding the statutory authority to apply for naturalization, USCIS may withhold naturalization until the petition for removal of conditions has been approved. *Abghari v. Gonzales*, 596 F. Supp. 2d 1336 (C.D. Cal. 2009).

[28] INA §216A(d)(2)(A); 8 CFR §§216.6(a)(1), 1216.6(a)(1).

[29] INA §216A(c)(2).

[30] INA §216A(d)(2)(B); 8 CFR §§216.6(a)(5), 1216.6(a)(5).

[31] 8 CFR §§216.6(a)(1), 1216.6(a)(1). Note, however, that USCIS has stated informally that a dependent who follows to join the principal investor and commences conditional permanent residence more than 90 days after the principal's commencement of conditional permanent residence must file an independent I-829 petition.

[32] 8 CFR §§216.6(a)(1), 1216.6(a)(1).

[33] *Id.*

that provides documentary proof of a one-year extension of conditional resident status.[34] The receipt notice also serves as a travel document. Separate verification notices for each of the investor's dependents serve the same purpose as the investor's receipt notice.

Service center processing times for I-829 petitions can vary widely, although as of the date of this writing, USCIS is adjudicating petitions for removal of conditions within three to four months of filing. During the time the I-829 petition remains pending, the principal investor and dependent family members are entitled to obtain in their passports I-551 stamps valid for 12 months as evidence of continuing residence status.[35]

If USCIS approves the I-829 petition, it will issue an approval notice and advise the petitioner of the need to visit a local USCIS office for processing of a new resident alien card. If, on the other hand, USCIS denies the I-829 petition, it advises the petitioner that status is terminated and there is no right to appeal. Any doubts about the gravity of the I-829 petition for an investor and dependent family members who may have become rooted in the United States should be resolved by a quick review of a standard I-829 denial notice:

NOTICE OF DECISION

It is ordered that Form I-829, Petition by Entrepreneur to Remove Conditions, seeking removal of his or her conditional permanent residence status, be denied as a matter of law because:

SEE ATTACHMENT

In accordance with the provisions of section 216A(b)(1) of the Act, the conditional resident's status and the statuses of the following dependents are terminated as of the date of this decision …

The conditional residents are hereby directed to immediately surrender their Alien Registration Cards, Form I-551, and any evidence of authorized temporary conditional residence to a local U.S. Citizenship and Immigration office.

This decision leaves you without lawful immigration status and you are therefore present in the United States in violation of the law. You are required to depart the United States. Remaining in the United States without authorization may result in the initiation of removal proceedings against you and may affect your ability to return to the United States in the future.

This decision may not be appealed. However, the petitioner may request a review of this decision before an immigration judge while in proceedings pursuant to 8 CFR 216.6(d)(2).

USCIS should cause issuance of a Notice to Appear representing the commencement of proceedings before an immigration judge to remove (or deport) the investor from the United States.[36] However, there is no guarantee the Notice to Appear will issue. Before the immigration judge, the government bears the burden of proving that the investor is not eligible for removal of conditions.[37] Absent the commencement of proceedings in an immigration court where the investor might plead the merits of the underlying case, the investor may be required to file motions for reconsideration of the USCIS decision to deny the petition for removal of conditions, or possibly to file a lawsuit in federal court in order to obtain prompt, meaningful review.[38]

Legal Authorities

The sources of law concerning the removal of conditions for investors include the statute, regulations, and case law. The statutory authority for removal of the conditions sets forth what the petitioner must prove when submitting the I-829 petition and

---

[34] Legacy Immigration and Naturalization Service (INS) Memorandum, M. Pearson, Exec. Assoc. Comm'r Field Operations, "EB-5 Field Memorandum Number 9: Form I-829 Processing" (Mar. 3, 2000), *published on* AILA InfoNet at Doc. No. 00060702 (*posted* June 7, 2000), at 3. The Pearson Memo is reproduced at Appendix C.

[35] *Id.* at 13 and 15.

[36] 8 CFR §§216.6(d)(2), 1216.6(d)(2).

[37] INA §216A(c)(3)(D). In one case litigated in 2007 before the immigration court in Seattle, the immigration judge concluded that the government failed to sustain its burden of proving that the investor's contribution of inventory to the commercial enterprise was a loan from a third party rather than a capital contribution by the investor.

[38] Possible motion strategies following denial of the petition for removal of conditions are addressed in M. Lawler & E. McKee, "Strategies for Overcoming Denials of I-829 Petitions to Remove Conditions from Permanent Residence," elsewhere in this volume. Federal court jurisdiction of cases involving EB-5 investors is addressed in I. Kurzban, "Litigating the Immigrant Investor's Case," also found elsewhere in this volume.

supporting documents.[39] In 2002, Congress amended the removal of conditions statute significantly by eliminating the requirement that the investor "established" the commercial enterprise.[40] As a consequence, the statute for removal of conditions now requires evidence that: (i) the petitioner has invested or is actively in the process of investing the requisite capital; and (ii) the investment and commercial enterprise have been sustained throughout the period of residence.[41] The regulations add a third substantive item of proof, requiring the I-829 petition to prove: "The alien created or can be expected to create within a reasonable period of time ten full-time jobs for qualifying employees."[42] If the theory of job creation is based on a "troubled business," then the I-829 petition must be supported by evidence that "the alien maintained the number of existing employees at no less than the pre-investment level for the previous two years."[43]

The Administrative Appeals Office (AAO) issued four precedent decisions in 1998 (AAO precedent decisions), which have the binding authority of regulation.[44] Those decisions, however, concerned only I-526 petitions and the separate statutory and regulatory authority for becoming a conditional permanent resident. Consequently, the AAO precedent decisions should not directly apply in the realm of USCIS adjudication of the I-829 petition for removal of conditions.

Further to the statute and regulations for removal of conditions, the only other binding source of law concerning removal of conditions is a Ninth Circuit Court of Appeals decision. In *Chang v. United States*,[45] the court considered the argument that new standards set forth in the AAO precedent decisions could not be imposed retroactively to deny the investor's I-829 petition. The court found that in light of the related but distinct legal schemes for becoming a conditional permanent resident at first and removing the conditions thereafter, the adjudication of the petition for removal of conditions is not an *ab initio* review of the petitioner's eligibility for becoming a conditional permanent resident, but rather is an adjudication based on current facts according to the statute and regulations providing for removal of the conditions. The court held that in adjudicating the I-829 petition, USCIS cannot apply new standards that did not exist when the petitioner became a conditional resident, without first weighing the degree of burden imposed by the retroactive application of the new standards.

USCIS and legacy INS also have issued various interpretive memoranda and instructions to field offices that constitute guidance to USCIS officers. But these memoranda do not carry the weight of binding legal authority and may be modified or withdrawn entirely without prior notice or opportunity for comment.[46]

While it seems clear on the face of the statutes that USCIS should be adjudicating I-829 petitions for removal of conditions based on the limited authority granted to it in INA §216A, one cannot tell that is the case by reading the work product of USCIS. Again and again, in one RFE after another, USCIS cites to the statute and regulations concerning initial EB-5 eligibility as its authority for adjudication of removal of conditions cases:

> "The petitioner's Form I-829 Petition by Entrepreneur to Remove Conditions has been reviewed carefully for eligibility in accordance with Section 203(b)(5) of the Immigration and Nationality Act and Title 8 Code of Federal Regulations Section 204.6 as well as four precedent decisions issued by the Administrative Appeals Office."

In case after case involving adjudication of the I-829 petition, where INA §216A is the paramount authority, USCIS makes not even a mention of the statute. Instead, the investor seeking removal of conditions is issued the closing instruction:

---

[39] INA §216A(d)(1).

[40] Pub. L. No. 107-273, 116 Stat. 1758, Title I, Subtitle B, ch. 1 §11036(b) (2002). USCIS has not yet promulgated regulations to implement the statutory amendments enacted in 2002, although the amendments are effective upon enactment.

[41] The 2002 amendments also added language (*codified at* INA §216A(d)(1)(B)) requiring evidence that petitioner "is otherwise conforming to the requirements of section 203(b)(5)."

[42] 8 CFR §§216.6(c)(1)(iv), 1216.6(c)(1)(iv).

[43] *Id.*

[44] *Matter of Soffici*, 22 I&N Dec. 158, 19 *Immigr. Rptr.* B2–25 (AAO June 25, 1998); *Matter of Izumii*, 22 I&N Dec. 169, 19 *Immigr. Rptr.* B2–32 (AAO July 13, 1998); *Matter of Hsiung*, 22 I&N Dec. 201, 19 *Immigr. Rptr.* B2–106 (AAO July 31, 1998); *Matter of Ho*, 22 I&N Dec. 206, 19 *Immigr. Rptr.* B2–99 (AAO July 31, 1998). All four of these precedent decisions are reproduced in Appendix A.

[45] *Chang v. United States*, 327 F.3d 911 (9th Cir. 2003). The *Chang* decision is reproduced in Appendix B.

[46] *See, e.g.*, "Neufeld I" and "Neufeld II," *supra* note 2.

"In addition to the evidence requested above, submit a letter clearly explaining how the evidence submitted establishes compliance with each requirement of Section 203(b)(5) of the Immigration and Nationality Act enumerated at the beginning."

Some seven years after the decision in *Chang*, it remains unclear whether USCIS genuinely follows the court of appeals directive to refrain from revisiting initial EB-5 eligibility, let alone the very statute, INA §216A, that invests USCIS with the authority to adjudicate a petition for removal of conditions. Inasmuch as Neufeld II was issued by USCIS only a few months ago, as of this writing, it is too early to form conclusions about the intentions of USCIS with respect to certain aspects of its revisions to the AFM. The AFM revisions include a section entitled "I-829 Consideration of Form I-526 EB-5 Eligibility Requirements,"[47] which appears to invite adjudicators of petitions for removal of conditions to re-adjudicate initial EB-5 eligibility quite apart from the petition adjudication conditions already discussed herein. In public but informal comments, USCIS officials have replied to the concern with the statement that the AFM revisions do not condone *ab initio* review of EB-5 eligibility. But if USCIS does in practice use the I-829 petition process as a mechanism to re-adjudicate the investor's eligibility under INA §203(b)(5), then USCIS effectively will have eliminated INA §216A from the statute books.

The Investment Requirement

For the time being, INA §216A remains the law of the land in terms of adjudication of petitions for removal of conditions. As the first of the petition adjudication conditions, the investment requirement demands documentation demonstrating that the petitioner has invested or is actively in the process of investing the requisite capital.[48] Among other things, the following discussion shines a bright light on the difficulties posed by the "in the process of investing" language of the statute. It is not too far a stretch to suggest that legacy INS and now USCIS have eliminated the statutory phrase from its considera-

tion of the petition adjudication conditions. Satisfying the investment requirement may involve several subsidiary investment issues which are discussed below in turn.

Required Amount of Capital Investment

The requisite amount of capital is determined in the adjudication of the initial I-526 petition;[49] that determination should not be revisited in the adjudication of the I-829 petition. As the court stated in *Chang*, in adjudicating the I-829 petition USCIS should not conduct an *ab initio* assessment of the petitioner's eligibility for obtaining conditional permanent residence. The statute and regulations providing for initial EB-5 eligibility stipulate that if the commercial enterprise is located in a targeted employment area (TEA) (because the location is either a rural or high unemployment area), the minimum capital threshold is lowered to $500,000.[50] Whether the commercial enterprise is located in a TEA depends on the rural or high unemployment character of the business location as of the time of investment.[51] Therefore, the fact that population data or unemployment rates may have changed during the two-year conditional period is not material to whether the business continues to be located in a TEA. Neufeld II acknowledges that subsequent data changes of this kind do not alter the earlier TEA determination.

Source of Capital Investment

Just as the TEA determination should not be revisited, so too the petitioner's ("lawful" or "unlawful") source of funds is not a required element of the investor's prima facie case for removal of conditions. To be sure, the investor is required to present evidence of lawful source of funds in support of the I-526 petition to demonstrate initial eligibility in the EB-5 category.[52] And during the two-year condi-

---

[47] Neufeld II, supra note 2, at 21. Recently filed lawsuits in part challenge USCIS denials of I-829 petitions on the theory that USCIS improperly re-adjudicated the earlier-approved I-526 petitions. *Kim v. U.S.*, Case No. 10-CV-2019 DPP (C.D. Cal. 2010); *Song v. U.S.*, Case No. 10-CV-2017-SJQ (C.D. Cal. 2010).

[48] INA §216A(d)(1)(A)(i), as amended.

[49] 8 CFR §204.6(j)(6).

[50] INA §203(b)(5)(C)(ii); 8 CFR 204.6(f)(2).

[51] 8 CFR §204.6(e), "targeted employment area" (TEA) defined. Citing *Matter of Soffici*, supra note 44, Neufeld II provides that the TEA determination may be based on data existing at the time the I-526 petition is filed with USCIS in cases where the investor's capital is deposited in escrow pending the USCIS adjudication.

[52] 8 CFR 204.6(j)(3). For a more detailed treatment of source of funds issues, see Administrative Appeals Office (AAO) cases reviewed and arguments presented in L. Stone, "Immigrant Investment in Local Clusters: Part II," 80 *Interpreter Releases* 937, 946–50 (July 14, 2003); *See also* E. Arias & L. Stone, "Navigating the Lawful Source Requirement for EB-5 Immigration," elsewhere in this volume.

tional period, USCIS can initiate proceedings to terminate a conditional resident's status based on evidence it has of unlawful sources of investment.[53] But neither the statute nor the regulations require the I-829 petitioner to make an affirmative showing of the investor's source of funds. The commentary to the removal of conditions regulations provides that questions of lawful source of funds are more appropriately addressed at the I-526 petition stage.[54]

Nonetheless, an occasional RFE probes the question of lawful source of funds. In one case, where the petitioner's investment capital was earned via trading in the stock market, USCIS queried how it was that petitioner was able to invest in the stock market in the first place:

> The I-526 petition notes that the monies were gained through investments in the stock market, for a gain of $1,803,933, when the petitioner sold his shares in a number of companies. The source of initial funds for investments was, however, not documented and therefore never established.... Like the I-526 petition, the I-829 lacks evidence to establish the source of initial funds for investment and those funds were lawfully acquired. The petitioner is requested to submit this evidence in order to complete the filing of the petition in this category.

It may be advisable in responding to RFEs to provide "more documents and less argument," but in this case, the investor already had provided the relevant documentation, including all income tax filings and earnings schedules, *five years earlier* in the course of the adjudication of the I-526 petition. Legal arguments helped nudge this case to a successful outcome.

Although generally it is true that lawful source of funds should not be a factor in the adjudication of the petition for removal of conditions, the regulations provide that if "it becomes known to the government that the entrepreneur obtained his or her investment funds through other than legal means (such as through the sale of illegal drugs)," then the source of funds becomes germane to adjudication of the I-829 petition.[55] Importantly, USCIS must raise the issue and support the charge with its findings. If USCIS appropriately raises a question about the investor's source of funds, the petitioner must present the appropriate evidence to rebut the charge. In one recent case, the RFE on the I-829 petition demanded a burdensome list of documents concerning the investor's source of funds, but without identifying anything in particular in the case that would warrant the demand. A request for review of the RFE by USCIS management led to withdrawal of the RFE.

A final observation on source of funds relates to investors from Iran. USCIS has issued RFEs to Iranian investors seeking removal of conditions, requesting the investor to present clearance or a license from the U.S. Department of Treasury Office of Foreign Asset Control (OFAC).[56] Upon our presentation of the OFAC license or a letter from OFAC indicating that no license is required, these petitions for removal of conditions have been approved by USCIS.

Shortfall of Capital Investment by the Investor

Especially in these difficult economic times it should not be surprising that clients have not been perfect in following their business plans. In certain cases for removal of conditions, at the time the petition is filed, the investor may not have invested the entire capital amount required by law—for example, the investor has invested $800,000 but not the entire $1 million the law requires. The statute provides that a petitioner for removal of conditions may be "in the process of investing" the required amount of capital, suggesting a safe harbor exists for investors running into difficulties during the conditional residence period. Unfortunately by way of regulation, AAO precedent decisions, and adjudication practices, as described below, legacy INS and USCIS have built more of an inhospitable coral reef rather than a safe harbor for those investors hoping to use the "in the process of investing" prong of the statute.

The regulation describing the documentation needed to satisfy the investment requirement is terse and of little aid, merely stating that documentation of proof of investment "may include, but is not limited to, an audited financial statement or other probative evidence."[57] As if the drafter of regulations

---

[53] 8 CFR §§216.3, 1216.3.

[54] Commentary to Final Rule, *supra* note 19, at 26589.

[55] 8 CFR §§216.6(c)(2), 1216.6(c)(2).

[56] The topic of U.S. Department of Treasury, Office of Foreign Asset Control (OFAC) regulations and their application in EB-5 cases is addressed in E. Krauland & J. Hayes, "Anti-Money Laundering and OFAC Sanctions Concerns for Immigration Practitioners Assisting Foreign Investors," elsewhere in this volume.

[57] 8 CFR §§216.6(a)(4)(ii), 1216.6(a)(4)(ii). USCIS is unlikely to require a petitioner to spend the exorbitant sums attendant to securing an audited financial statement. The
continued

elected to ignore the statute, there is no further explication in this part of the regulation of what "in the process of investing" might mean for purposes of the adjudication of a petition for removal of conditions.

Has the "in the process of investing" prong of the statute simply disappeared from the landscape for purposes of adjudication of petitions for removal of conditions? Not exactly, but in brief, for purposes of the petition for removal of conditions, a line of argument grounded on the "in the process of investing" concept seems to have limited utility. The agency's analysis of legal concepts relevant to this prong of the statute has been woefully confused. The confusion in large part is due to legacy INS mixing the concept of "in the process of investing" with the concept of an "at risk" investment, a confusion that is exacerbated by AAO precedent decisions. This confused analysis occasionally wreaks havoc with I-526 petition and I-829 petition adjudications alike.

In order to fully deconstruct the misguided agency analysis of these concepts, it is helpful to review the roots of the "in the process of investing" prong in the EB-5 statutes. When the investor petitions for initial EB-5 eligibility, the I-526 petition must be supported with evidence that the capital is "at risk."[58] The EB-5 "at risk" requirement is based on the standards used in adjudication of applications for the E–2 treaty investor visa, as noted in its comments to the final regulation.[59] As with the EB-5 immigrant investor status, the E-2 treaty investor visa may be granted on either of two bases: (a) the investor already invested the required capital; or (b) the investor is in the process of investing the required capital. With respect to the first alternative (*i.e.*, "invested"), the source of law for E-2 visas, the *Foreign Affairs Manual* (FAM), emphasizes that whether the investor already made a complying "investment" depends on risk of loss: "If the funds are not subject to partial or total loss if business fortunes reverse, then it is not an 'investment' in the sense intended by INA §101(a)(15)(E)(ii)."[60] Conversely, therefore, if the invested capital is subject to risk of loss, then the investor has made a qualifying investment.

With respect to the latter alternative (*i.e.*, "in the process of investing"), the FAM emphasizes that the funds must be irrevocably committed to the business: "To be 'in the process of investing' for E-2 visa purposes, the funds or assets to be invested must be committed to the investment, and the commitment must be real and irrevocable."[61] In this case, the investor has not yet deposited the capital in the enterprise but is in the process of doing so, and typically the issue arises because the investor maintains control over the funds either in a sole proprietor or close corporation form of business, in a manner that the funds are indistinguishable from the funds for personal use. The FAM elaborates:

> Moreover, for the alien to be "n the process of investing,"the alien must be close to the start of actual business operations, not simply in the stage of signing contracts (which may be broken) or scouting for suitable locations and property. Mere intent to invest, or possession of uncommitted funds in a bank account, or even prospective investment arrangements entailing no present commitment, will not suffice."[62]

Thus, to be "in the process of investing" means that the investor has irrevocably committed the funds to the business, such as in the case of an escrow that releases funds to the business without further action by the investor upon approval of a petition.[63]

---

commentary to the regulations acknowledges that audited statements might be too onerous for petitioners. Commentary to Final Rule, *supra* note 19, at 26588.

[58] 8 CFR §204.6(j)(2).

[59] Final Rule, 56 Fed. Reg. 60897 (Nov. 29, 1991), at 60904: "The evidentiary showing necessary to establish that the petitioner either has invested or is in the process of investing the required amount of capital is modeled after requirements used by the Department of State for nonimmigrant 'treaty investors.' As with that program, the concept of investment here connotes the placing of funds or other capital assets at risk for purpose of generating a return on the funds placed at risk."

[60] 9 *Foreign Affairs Manual* (FAM) 41.51 N8.1-2 (note entitled "Investment Connotes Risk").

[61] 9 FAM 41.51 N8.1-3 (note entitled "Funds Must be Irrevocably Committed").

[62] *Id.*

[63] Or, the investor could satisfy the requirement by use of a promissory note that irrevocably commits funds to the business, so long as the promissory note meets the stringent criteria set forth by the AAO's *Hsiung* decision, *supra* note 44. Although the *Hsiung* case concerned only the adjudication for initial eligibility in the EB-5 category, it is an open question whether its principles would be applied in a case for removal of the conditions. The AAO held that the promissory note must be secured by specifically identified personal assets of the investor, the security interest must be perfected in the jurisdiction where the assets are located and must be amenable to seizure, and the assets must have a fair market value exceeding the face amount of the note.

Another factor for the investor who has not yet invested all the required capital is that regulations for the sustained requirement have significant implications that limit how we view the "in the process of investing" concept. Sustaining the investment is a petition adjudication condition. The regulations for the sustained requirement state that the requirement is deemed satisfied if the petitioner "in good faith, has substantially met the capital investment requirement of the statute and continuously maintained his or her capital investment over the two years of conditional residence."[64] In its comment to the final regulations, legacy INS observed that "[w]hile there is no statutory requirement with respect to when the requisite capital must have been invested during the two-year period," Congress nonetheless "expressed its intent that substantially all of the requisite capital be invested by the alien entrepreneur before the expiration of the conditional resident status."[65] Legacy INS's conclusion rests on the flimsy reasoning that the statutory language "invested" is in the past tense; this incomplete rationale of course ignores the alternative statutory prong with the "in the process of investing" language. One might contend the regulation concerning the term "sustained" entirely negates the statutory language "in the process of investing," which may amount to ultra vires agency action. Until the government is challenged on the regulation, the substantial completion test is likely to be the adjudication standard in individual cases.

The regulatory commentary cautioned that there is no black and white rule that the agency will apply, since the determination of whether an alien entrepreneur had invested a substantial portion of the requisite capital in good faith must be made on a case-by-case basis. However, in posing hypothetical qualifying and disqualifying scenarios, the agency suggested strongly that the determination of whether the petitioner "substantially met" the capital investment requirement depends directly on the petitioner's evidence concerning the ability to complete the investment "within a reasonable time." The regulatory commentary poses the hypothetical where the investor was granted conditional residence based on a business plan that envisioned an investment of $1.2 million, but by the end of the conditional residence period the investor has invested only $800,000 in a non-targeted employment area, because through circumstances beyond the investor's control, construction of a facility took longer than anticipated. The comment concludes:

> The Service may remove the conditions if the entrepreneur can show that he or she can and will invest the additional capital within a reasonable time to complete the investment. On the other hand, if the entrepreneur cannot show that he or she will be able to generate additional capital within a reasonable time, regardless of his or her good-faith efforts, the Service will not remove the conditions.[66]

Legacy INS elaborated to indicate that in determining whether the investor has demonstrated that he or she invested in good faith, it examines the investor's intent based on both objective and subjective standards. Legacy INS used a similar hypothetical to illustrate the appropriate "good faith" analysis. If, at the time the investor obtained conditional residence, the investor had "no realistic prospect of obtaining funds to meet the capital investment requirement and in fact is unable to acquire" the additional funds required to complete the investment, then, under the objective part of the good faith analysis, the investor will be unable to establish that he or she substantially met the capital investment requirement in good faith.[67]

In sum, assuming the regulatory commentary sets forth the relevant litmus test that USCIS examiners will follow, if the petitioner has not yet completed the investment of capital at the time the I-829 petition must be filed, then the supporting evidence should include proof that the investor can promptly complete the investment. The evidence should indicate the specific timing of the additional investment (*i.e.*, link the investment to a specific event), the client's intention to complete the investment (*e.g.*, submit proof of a contractual commitment that must be met), and the client's financial ability to complete the investment (*e.g.*, submit probative financial records). With such evidence, the case is well-supported for demonstrating that the investor is "in the process of investing" and therefore met the capital investment requirement.

---

[64] 8 CFR §§216.6(c)(1)(iii), 1216.6(c)(1)(iii), and 8 CFR 216.6(a)(4)(iii), 1216.6(a)(4)(iii).
[65] Commentary to Final Rule, *supra* note 19, at 26588–89.
[66] Commentary to Proposed Rule, 59 Fed. Reg. 1317 (Jan. 19, 1994).
[67] *Id.*

Use of Capital by the Commercial Enterprise

Another issue raised by USCIS in the context of the investment requirement is the extent of use of EB-5 capital by the commercial enterprise. USCIS has declared the petition for removal of conditions insufficient in cases where the commercial enterprise has not yet expended all EB-5 investor capital toward job-creating uses. The rationale advanced by USCIS is that the capital is not "at risk" if all of it has not yet been expended in job-creating activities. In such cases, USCIS has found that the investor has not met the investment requirement.

In one case that is representative of dozens of RFEs, the agency observed that a company tax return from two years earlier suggested:

> The partnership equity is invested in passive activities, not in job creation. Thus, the record fails to show that the funds have been placed at risk in job-creating activities. Submit evidence that the claimed $500,000 has actually been placed at risk in conducting the business activities of the commercial enterprise. Merely showing that these funds will be available for investment at some point in the future is not sufficient.

In cases involving partners invested in partnerships of numerous investors, USCIS has likened the arrangement to a "blind pool trust" which, in the eyes of USCIS examiners, serves to obfuscate the true factual circumstances and hinder the analysis of whether the petitioner's capital is genuinely at risk:

> Since all of the partnership's funds are held in a pooled trust fund and notwithstanding evidence which indicates the petitioner is not precluded from investing in other capital ventures, for the petitioner to make a qualifying investment, the evidence must establish either that all of the capital contribution held by the partnership has been made available for the purchase and renovation of the building(s) in question, or that all of the petitioner's contribution has been made available for the purchase and renovation of the building(s) in question ... Like a holding company, monies held in a "blind pool trust" must be made fully available to the business(es) most closely responsible for creating the employment upon which the petition is based.

In order to disentangle the analysis that USCIS applies in these cases, begin with the regulations for initial EB-5 eligibility, which state:

> To show that the petitioner has invested or is actively in the process of investing the required amount of capital, the petition must be accompanied by evidence that the petition has placed the required amount of capital at risk for purposes of generating a return on the capital placed at risk. Evidence of mere intent to invest or of prospective investment arrangements entailing no present commitment will not suffice to show that the petitioner is actively in the process of investing. The alien must show actual commitment of the required amount of capital.[68]

It also is helpful to return to the source of the EB-5 standards. As stated above in the brief overview of the standards applicable to E-2 visas, legacy INS acknowledged that the intent of the immigrant investor law is to incorporate legal standards that echo the E-2 visa standards. To ascertain whether the petitioner has "invested" the required capital, focus on whether the capital is at risk of loss. If the investor contends that he or she is "in the process of investing" the required capital, focus on whether there is an irrevocable commitment of the capital to the commercial enterprise. Thus, it is clear that of the three sentences quoted above from the EB-5 regulations, the first sentence relates to the "at risk" requirement but the second and third sentences relate only to the scenario where the investor is claiming to be "in the process of investing" the required capital.

The brief review of the source of law illustrates just how far USCIS has drifted from the moorings of the E-2 visa standards. For one, USCIS has collapsed the two alternatives (the "invested" alternative and the "in the process of investing" alternative) into one very restrictive standard. USCIS has formulated the very restrictive standard by juggling components of the two alternatives. It has eliminated any concept of being "in the process of investing" and determined that a petitioner has not "invested" the required capital unless the deposited capital has been irrevocably committed by the business to certain expenditures. This misguided trend in adjudications is based on incorrect interpretation of regulations and the erroneous and expansive use of dicta found in AAO precedent decisions. In rearranging these standards, USCIS also has modified the consideration of whether the capital is at risk. In effect, USCIS seeks to transform the "at risk" issue into a consideration of how the business would expend its capital, and specifically, whether the capital would

---

[68] 8 CFR §204.6(j)(2).

be expended toward job-creating activities. This new legal standard is not supported by the E-2 visa sources of law, the EB-5 regulations, or the AAO precedent decisions in EB-5 investor cases.[69]

In the *Ho* case,[70] the AAO held that where the petitioner controls the business and its accounts, the mere deposit of the required amount of capital in a bank account and the signing of a lease agreement—without any further indicia of a business—do not place that capital at risk. Rather, according to the AAO, the regulation requires the petitioner to present evidence of "meaningful concrete action" and the "actual undertaking of business activity" in order to provide sufficient assurance that the deposited capital would be used to carry out the business objectives of the commercial enterprise.

The other relevant AAO precedent decision, the *Izumii* case,[71] involved a limited partnership that used capital from its limited partner investors to fund a subsidiary credit company that extended loans to exporter businesses. The limited partner entered into an investment agreement that included a promissory note with a payment schedule that exceeded the two-year conditional period; a provision for the limited partnership to pay guaranteed returns to the investor; a sell option that the investor could exercise to redeem the limited partner ownership interest; and a provision for reserve funds that could be used by the partnership to fund the redemption to the investor. The AAO held that this combination of investment features all but eliminated the risk of loss and, therefore, the capital had not been invested. Also, the AAO held that the portion of capital used to pay the partnership's administrative expenses prior to the partnership's transfer of invested capital to the credit company was not at risk. Because administrative expenses were deducted prior to transfer of that capital to the credit company, the AAO stated:

"The full amount of money must be made available to the business(es) most closely responsible for creating the employment upon which the petition is based."[72] Similarly, with respect to the partnership's maintaining reserve funds that might be used to fund a redemption, the AAO declared that "these reserve funds are, by agreement, not available for purposes of job creation and therefore cannot be considered capital placed at risk for the purpose of generating a return on the capital being placed at risk."[73]

Read in a reasonable light, the latter references in the *Izumii* decision, which refer to a requirement that capital must be made available for job creation, should be interpreted narrowly given the unusual facts of that case. In *Izumii* the capital set aside as reserves and the funds used to pay administrative expenses did not constitute an investment under the law because, according to the AAO, the capital was never exposed to loss in the actual business. In ascertaining which entity in the investment structure (limited partnership, subsidiary credit company, or borrower company) should be the analytical focus in the determination of whether the petitioner actually has invested in the commercial enterprise, the AAO observed that the "job-creating" entity must receive the investor's capital. Insofar as the fund for reserves and the administrative expenses were established within the limited partnership, before the remaining capital was transferred to the credit company that was in the business of extending loans, the AAO decided that the limited partnership was not the job creator.[74] Thus, the investor could not have "invested" the capital set aside to fund reserves and to pay administrative expenses because that capital would never be at risk of loss in the underlying credit company business.

The decisions in *Ho* and *Izumii* would appear to have limited application on the adjudication of a petition for removal of conditions. Both of these cases involve the law on adjudication of I-526 petitions, not the law on adjudication of I-829 petitions. Even so, the facts of these cases would appear to be the kind rarely encountered in the adjudication of a petition for removal of conditions. The core facts of *Ho* concerned the mere deposit of capital in the bank account of a company in the exclusive control of the petitioner, without any other evidence of business

---

[69] For a discussion of how the AAO analysis in nonprecedent cases is not true to the E-2 visa standards, see L. Stone, "Immigrant Investment in Local Clusters: Part II," 80 *Interpreter Releases* 937, 941 (July 14, 2003); *See also* C. Lee, "The Meaning of 'At Risk' Requirement in EB-5 Investment," elsewhere in this volume.

[70] *Matter of Ho, supra* note 44.

[71] *Matter of Izumii, supra* note 44.

[72] *Id.* at 12.

[73] *Id.* at 24.

[74] The AAO also decided that where capital is placed in reserves to fund a redemption (an agreement to refund capital to the investor), it is clear the investor has loaned money to the enterprise in violation of the requirement to invest equity capital.

activity. The principal facts of *Izumii* concerned the diversion of EB-5 capital for administrative expenses prior to the capitalization of the entity that would engage in business.

These precedent decisions, however, in no way stand for the proposition that the petition for removal of conditions should be denied if the fully capitalized commercial enterprise has not yet entirely expended its EB-5 capital. Far from that. Instead, to the extent these case precedents stand for anything relevant to the adjudication of the petition for removal of conditions it is that the investor's capital is at risk when the capital has been exposed to at least partial loss. To meet the requirements imposed by the *Ho* decision, the investor also would present evidence of "meaningful concrete action" and the "actual undertaking of business activity." This should be sufficient since there is no legal authority to require the commercial enterprise to expend all of its EB-5 capital prior to the filing of the petition to remove conditions. The entire purpose of the EB-5 program is to attract capital that is used reasonably in genuine U.S. businesses that stimulate job creation. Congress did not impose timelines on such commercial enterprises for the use of EB-5 capital.

With these legal principles in mind, it is evident that USCIS misapprehends the significance of large "pools" of investor capital that are commonly found in regional center affiliated entities. Instead of a "blind pool trust" there may be a limited partnership that "pools" the capital of dozens of investors into one business; the limited partnership is not "blind" in any sense whatsoever, given that the use of partnership capital is very specifically allocated for investment in a specific business or for the specific use of purchasing, developing, and managing a particular property or asset and nothing else; the investor's capital already is "fully available" to the business most closely responsible for creating employment, the limited partnership; and the limited partnership is actively expending its capital in a customary and commercially reasonable manner in accordance with its business plan to develop the particular property. In the circumstances USCIS should not hesitate to conclude that the petitioner has made an investment that is exposed to commercial risk in the commercial enterprise.

A described herein, the administrative interpretations adopted by legacy INS and USCIS have confused adjudications of petitions for removal of conditions. Of particular significance are the many cases that incorrectly apply dicta from AAO precedent decisions, resulting in the near disappearance of the "in the process of investing" standard as a component of the statutory EB-5 investment requirement that is the foundation of the petition adjudication conditions. Note that this discussion has not addressed the somewhat different subject of what happens when the investment capital was not expended toward the subject business but was instead diverted to different uses.

The Sustained Requirement

The second of the petition adjudication conditions is the requirement that the investor sustained the investment throughout the period of conditional residence.[75] Earlier, in the discussion of an investor who has not yet invested all the required capital, we touched on the regulations for the sustained requirement, which provide that the requirement is deemed satisfied if the petitioner "in good faith, has substantially met the capital investment requirement of the statute and continuously maintained his or her capital investment over the two years of conditional residence."[76]

The sustained concept requires a showing that the petitioner "continuously maintained" the investment.[77] Legacy INS stated that it intended for the "sustained" concept to be *liberally interpreted*. In the comment to the final rule, legacy INS explained:

> This liberal interpretation of the term "sustained" permits the Service maximum flexibility in determining whether the requirements for removal of conditional resident status have been met, as well as following Congress'[s] intent to ensure that "all aliens receiving visas in this section . . ." continue their new commercial enterprises so that the creation of U.S. jobs and the infusion of capital into the U.S. economy is sustained.[78]

Insofar as the regulatory comment suggests that the "sustained" concept should be construed in the context of the desired lasting impacts for the U.S. economy, counsel may emphasize both the present and future positive economic impacts that flow from petitioner's investment. In appropriate cases, other probative evi-

---

[75] INA §216A(d)(1)(A)(ii), as amended.

[76] 8 CFR §§216.6(c)(1)(iii), 1216.6(c)(1)(iii), and 8 CFR §§216.6(a)(4)(iii), 1216.6(a)(4)(iii).

[77] Evidence of sustaining the investment "may include, but is not limited to, bank statements, invoices, receipts, contracts, business licenses, Federal or State income tax returns, and Federal or State quarterly tax statements." 8 CFR §§216.6(a)(4)(iii), 1216.6(a)(4)(iii).

[78] Commentary to Final Rule, *supra* note 19, at 26588.

dence might include marketing brochures, contracts, proposals, business plans, and related documentation concerning future business operations.

Under this topic heading, USCIS has struggled with the complexities of entity income tax returns. For example, where the Schedule K-1 issued to a limited partner indicates a capital account balance lower than the minimum $500,000 threshold for EB-5 investment, USCIS has interpreted the document to mean that the investor has withdrawn capital from the commercial enterprise. The response to the RFE must describe partnership accounting practices, and specifically the fact that depreciation, amortization, and casualty losses are considered losses for tax purposes and therefore reduce a partner's capital account. The reduction to the capital account is not necessarily a withdrawal of capital by the investor.

Given the current recessionary U.S. economy, practitioners also must be prepared to handle the unexpected business downturns experienced by investor clients and the inevitable changes in business plans. It should be little surprise that early-stage business ventures will need to modify their initial startup plans and adjust to commercial realities as they are encountered, particularly in the current credit-starved economy.

This brings us back to Neufeld II and the "material change" discussion. The sustained requirement is a central feature of the adjudication petition conditions. Nothing in the statute, however, would suggest that the sustained requirement should be inflexibly interpreted. Legacy INS viewed the requirement in a flexible manner, and was concerned only with the objective of ensuring that the investment is continuously maintained. Neufeld II nonetheless veers off into a different direction as it pronounces a new "material change" standard for adjudication of EB-5 investor petitions.

The new section of the AFM reads:

(G) Eligibility Requirements for the Review of a Form I-526 Petition that Seeks Consideration of a Business Plan that Differs from the Business Plan in a Previously Approved Form I-526 Petition.

Some EB-5 aliens may encounter difficulties when unforeseen circumstances cause the achievement of the requisite job creation outlined in Form I-526 petition to be cast in doubt. This may occur when the job creation capital investment project or commercial enterprise that was relied upon for the approval of the Form I-526 petition fails or otherwise cannot be completed with the alien's two-year period of conditional residence. The structure of the EB-5 program is inflexible in that the capital investment project identified in the business plan in the approved Form I-526 petition must serve as the basis for determining at the Form I-829 petition stage whether the requisite capital investment has been sustained throughout the alien's two-year period of conditional residency and that at least 10 jobs have been or will be created within a reasonable period of time as a result of the alien's capital investment. The business plan in the Form I-526 petition may not be materially changed after the petition has been filed. In addition, USCIS may not act favorably on requests to delay the filing or adjudication of Form I-829 petitions beyond the timeframes outlined in 8 CFR 216.6(a) and (c).[79]

Since the time of release of Neufeld II, which is neither statute nor regulation, USCIS has explained that it merely intended to extend a remedy in cases where the factual circumstances would not support approval of the I-829 petition. Conditional resident investors welcome that avenue of relief. It is particularly welcome in cases where the underlying commercial enterprise is no longer viable and the investor seeks to start anew with a modified investment plan or an entirely new investment. But the "material change" concept announced in Neufeld II is entirely unwelcome in many other cases where the "change" has been commercially reasonable.

Specifically, Neufeld II purports to transform the petition adjudication conditions. It reaches far beyond requiring that the petitioner's investment in the commercial enterprise have been continuously maintained. It adds the requirement that the "capital investment project" (a new, undefined term) that is identified in the business plan supporting the I-526 petition must continue to be the basis for the adjudication of the I-829 petition.

The first deficiency in this approach to adjudication of the I-829 petition is that the term "capital investment project" is not a term found in the statute or in the regulations. Nor does Neufeld II bother to define it. The statute and regulations use the term "commercial enterprise" but it is obvious that Neufeld II intends the term "capital investment project" differently.

---

[79] AFM, ch. 22.4(c)(4)(G), excerpted in Neufeld II, *supra* note 2, at 19.

A second deficiency in this approach to adjudication is that it is based on an extra-legal premise: It states that:

> the capital investment project identified in the business plan in the approved Form I-526 petition must serve as the basis for determining at the Form I-829 petition stage whether the requisite capital investment has been sustained throughout the alien's two-year period of conditional residency and that at least 10 jobs have been or will be created within a reasonable period of time as a result of the alien's capital investment.

This bald statement concerning the primacy of the original capital investment project for purposes of the petition for removal of conditions is made without legal citation, and that is because there is no legal authority supporting it.

The third deficiency relates to the outcome that Neufeld II requires. If this aspect of Neufeld II is upheld, an investor could prove that he has continuously maintained the investment in the commercial enterprise, but due to some change in the original business plan, the Neufeld II standard would require denial of the petition for removal of conditions. The application of an adjudication standard that is clearly not grounded in statute or regulation, and that has negative adjudication consequences, is subject to legal challenge.

Neufeld II pronounces that in cases of "material change" the investor cannot proceed with the I-829 petition for removal of conditions, but instead must relinquish conditional residence and begin anew with a fresh I-526 petition based on the modified plan and embark on another two-year period of conditional residence.[80] Although an exhaustive analysis of Neufeld II is beyond the scope of this article, it is enough to observe that the "inflexible" structure that Neufeld II finds central to formulating this new policy is directly opposed to the "maximum flexibility" and "liberal interpretation" that legacy INS indicated would be central considerations in determining eligibility for removal of conditions.

In our experience responding to dozens of RFEs in cases for removal of conditions, we have witnessed a multitude of unexpected business developments—substantial delays in build-out of a business, building code changes, water shortages and drought, environmental hazards, structural engineering problems, building permit backlogs, and substantially increased costs due to rising construction costs and design modifications. Is it a "material change" for the project to be delayed one year? Three years? If the costs of the project double, requiring a complete overhaul of the capital investment structure, would that be a "material change"?

Since the time of release of Neufeld II, in public but informal comments USCIS has not been able to offer any particular guidance on what amounts to a material change. USCIS also indicated that no work was underway in terms of formulating further guidance, but hinted at the possibility an AAO decision covering the subject matter might provide guidance.

In June 2010, USCIS released an AAO decision dated April 23, 2010, but pointed out that it is not a published or precedent AAO decision. In that case the I-526 petition had been based on investment in a regional center affiliated entity (a limited partnership) that used the capital provided by five EB-5 investors to make a $2.5 million loan to a home improvement materials supplier. During the two-year conditional residence period the supplier company advised the limited partnership that it would default on its obligations—not entirely a surprise, in a tumbling economy it was losing money and was slashing, not increasing, employment levels. Accordingly, the limited partnership sought to cut its losses by withdrawing its EB-5 investment capital from the supplier company and switching it over to a second company doing business as a restaurant. The investors sought removal of conditions based on the reinvestment of capital with the restaurant business.

In denying the I-829 petition for removal of conditions and a motion to reopen/reconsider the denial of one of the investor cases, the California Service (CSC) declared that:

> [D]uring the entire two years of conditional status the investment funds must be made available to the business engaged in the approved job creating activity which was [the supplier business]. An investment in [the restaurant business] was never presented as an investment project when the I-526 was filed and therefore, should not be considered with the filing of the I-829.

Because the investor did not prove that he "sustained his investment in the job creating enterprise, [the supplier business], for the two-year conditional period as required at section 216A(d)(1) of the INA

---

[80] *But see* H.R. Klasko, "EB-5 Job Creation—What to Do When Plans Change," elsewhere in this volume, arguing that a fairer and legally justifiable result would be an amended petition rather than a new petition.

and 8 CFR 216.6(a)(4)(iii)," the petition for removal of conditions could not be approved.

The AAO adopted this reasoning in upholding the denial of the I-829 petition filed by one of the investors in the group. Citing Neufeld II, the AAO found that the I-829 petition must be based on the same "capital investment project" that was identified in the original business plan as part of the I-526 adjudication. By focusing on the need for continuity of the "capital investment project" from the time of the I-526 filing and throughout the conditional residence period, the AAO stepped around the "material change" concept and was not required to decide what is or is not a material change. In a related finding, the AAO would deny the I-829 petition for the reason that the capital was not expended for business expansion but instead was used to refinance a mortgage and repay a loan, which uses were not identified in the I-526 petition.

In light of the above—where both Neufeld II and the recent CSC and AAO decisions do not permit significant *changes* in the underlying business—it seems that a *business failure* is likely to doom the petition for removal of conditions. No existing source of law is immediately helpful in the circumstances. The petitioner may be able to demonstrate sufficient capital was invested prior to business failure; however, in order to satisfy the requirement to "sustain" the investment, the petitioner also must demonstrate that the investment was "continuously maintained." No matter the equities, then, in favor of the client's case—such as the good faith investment of the required capital, and the hiring of the required number of employees during the conditional period—if the business has failed prior to the filing of the I-829 petition, USCIS is likely to deny the petition. Of course, certain investors may have the resources to start anew with a fresh I-526 petition (and new capital) and follow the readjustment procedures outlined in Neufeld II.

These outcomes demonstrate clearly the relatively unfavorable aspects of the form of conditional residence enjoyed by an investor. Unlike the immigrant who becomes a conditional resident based on a recently contracted marriage, the investor has no statutory or other legal basis for arguing that the conditions should be removed due to the investor's good faith investment or due to the extreme hardship that would result if the conditions are not removed.[81] It is difficult to understand why USCIS is vested with the authority to distinguish between a good faith marriage and a bad faith marriage in one statutory scheme, but is not delegated the authority to distinguish between a good faith investment and a bad faith investment in the other statutory scheme. This failure to provide such discretion to the agency (or the resistance of the agency to concluding that it has such discretion) points to the need for a "good faith" exception that would permit removing conditions for investors in worthy cases. Legislative action by Congress, though, likely would be required before this form of relief is available.

The Agency-Imposed Job Creation Requirement

As already discussed, the statute authorizing removal of conditions does not require the petitioner to present evidence of employment. Even the statute providing for the initial conditional residence status does not require the requisite job creation prior to the end of the conditional residence period; it merely states that the petitioner is required to create ten jobs, without specifying the time frame for such job creation.[82] Consequently, as far as Congress is concerned, job creation is not a petition adjudication condition.

We already featured the regulation promulgated by legacy INS which requires evidence that the petitioner "created or can be expected to create within a reasonable period of time ten full-time jobs for qualifying employees" and indicated that litigation was underway to challenge the ultra vires nature of the regulation.[83]

Still, inasmuch as a main objective of the EB-5 investor program is job creation in the U.S. economy, why object to a regulation that concerns job creation even if it is ultra vires? The short answer is that nobody is objecting to the regulation as written, if it truly is cemented in reasonableness. Objections arise, however, in the unreasonable application of the regulation to individual investor petitions for removal of conditions. In applying the regulation to individual petitions, is there room for examiner dis-

---

[81] Not only are good faith and extreme hardship relevant in the case of the recently married conditional resident, INA §216(c)(4), if the marriage exceeds two years' duration by the time the applicant becomes an immigrant, there is no conditional status at all. INA §216(g).

[82] INA §203(b)(5)(A)(iii).

[83] 8 CFR §§216.6(c)(1)(iv), 1216.6(c)(1)(iv). See cases cited, *supra* note 47.

cretion in adjudicating individual petitions? If so, what are the guidelines for examiner discretion? Is the regulation reasonably applied, considering both the "micro" (individual circumstances with particular commercial enterprises) and the "macro" (general health of the economy and specific industry trends) facts and circumstances? These factors will be considered below throughout the discussion of removal of conditions for standard EB-5 cases (not tied to a regional center) and regional center affiliated EB-5 cases.

Employment Eligibility

One obstacle to removal of conditions for investors is documentation of the employment eligibility of U.S. workers. In a typical EB-5 case, the documentation of job creation may consist of payroll registers and employer tax filings (to demonstrate the number of full-time employment positions) as well as Form I-9 (to demonstrate the employment eligibility of each of the employees). In recent adjudications of petitions for removal of conditions, however, USCIS has demanded documentation of employment authorization that far exceeds the standard requirements imposed on U.S. employers. In brief, USCIS has insisted on proof of the immigration status of the individual employee and has not accepted standard documentation of the employee's eligibility for employment.

The statute for initial EB-5 eligibility provides that the claimed employment creation must be for "United States citizens or aliens lawfully admitted for permanent residence or other immigrants lawfully authorized to be employed in the United States (other than the immigrant and the immigrant's spouse, sons, or daughters)."[84] In turn, the regulation provides that a "qualifying employee" includes several categories of persons who are authorized to work in the United States but it does not include a nonimmigrant.[85] Significantly, there is nothing in the regulation that requires any specific type of evidence beyond "photocopies of relevant tax records, Form I-9, or other similar documents" for proving worker qualification for EB-5 job creation purposes.[86]

Pursuant to federal law,[87] a U.S. employer is obligated to use the Form I-9 to verify the employment authorization of its workforce. An employee, regardless of citizenship or immigration status, must provide for the employer's review a List A document (establishing both identity and employment authorization) such as a U.S. passport, or the combination of a List B document (establishing identity) such as a driver's license with a List C document (establishing employment authorization) such as a Social Security card. An employer is obligated to accept a document that reasonably appears to be genuine on its face. Under federal anti-discrimination laws an employer may be heavily penalized for prescribing which documents an employee must provide in the I-9 process.[88]

Nevertheless, in the adjudication of petitions for removal of conditions, and even though the investor often is not the employer, USCIS has insisted that the investor provide substantial evidence of the immigration status of the employer's workforce. In one RFE, for example, USCIS stated:

> For U.S. citizens such documents would include birth certificates, passports, driver's licenses and social security cards. Driver's licenses and Social Security cards alone do not establish citizenship. Permanent residents must have clear and legible copies of I-551s (Green Cards) that clearly show the A number and they must also have Social Security cards. You must provide copies of their I-551s and Social Security Cards.

In a different case, where USCIS initially denied the petition for removal of conditions due to the investor's failure to provide like documentation, the denial notice explained that USCIS is not requiring the investor to demonstrate that the commercial enterprise has hired work-authorized employees but instead is requiring convincing proof of the immigrant status of the employees:

> "Proof of the immigrant qualifications of the workers hired to fill the employment creation requirements of the regulations is a separate issue from the work eligibility requirements of the Form I-9, Employment Eligibility Verification."

For investors who require specific guidance on how to proceed—between the rock of USCIS which demands specific documentation of immigrant status and the hard place of federal anti-discrimination laws—USCIS offers little. Where the RFE indicated that the I-9 information was compared with the "Service database" and USCIS had determined that

---

[84] INA §203(b)(5)(A)(iii).
[85] 8 CFR §204.6(e).
[86] 8 CFR §204.6(j)(4)(i).
[87] INA §274A(b)(1).

[88] INA §274B(a)(6).

a certain percentage of the employees' information "did not match" and therefore those employees could not be "verified" as qualifying employees, the Service did not specify which of the employees could not be verified. Consequently, the employer was required to treat all employees as unverified. In such cases it may be advisable for clients to obtain the advice and guidance of separate counsel on re-verification of the employment authorization of each member of the workforce.

In yet another case for removal of conditions, USCIS indicated:

> Finally, it is advisable to check green cards and A-numbers with BCIS or E-Verify before providing copies of them in response to this request for evidence. The A numbers on the I-551s will be checked in the Electronic Database and if the names do not match the names of the employees, they will not be counted as Qualified Employees.

The upshot of this trend in adjudications of petitions for removal of conditions is that USCIS is requiring the investor to present documentation concerning the immigration status of each employee. The rigid adjudication position puts the investor in jeopardy of violating federal anti-discrimination law. Insofar as it is a restrictive interpretation that arguably conflicts with a different statute with a clear statutory mandate, it is of dubious merit.[89] The adjudication stance also tends to defeat the overriding purpose of attracting capital via the EB-5 investor program, which seems imprudent given the alternative mechanisms the government has for ensuring an employment-eligible workforce.

Shortage of Jobs

According to regulations, in order to obtain the initial conditional permanent residence *in a standard EB-5 case*, the investor must have demonstrated that at least 10 jobs had been created at the time of filing the I-526 petition, or that at least 10 jobs would be created during the two-year conditional residence period in accordance with a comprehensive business plan.[90] Likewise, the regulation concerning removal of the conditions requires proof of job creation.[91] If there are not at least 10 employment positions at the end of the conditional residence period, the petitioner is in jeopardy of not qualifying for removal of the conditions on residence. If the investor has not met these requirements when the petition for removal of conditions is filed, how should counsel advise the investor?

The phrase "within a reasonable period of time" should be the principal focus for consultations with clients who have not yet created the 10 employment positions. Where the commercial enterprise, for instance, involves a long-term initial build-out—assume a three-year period for construction of a solar energy project requiring hundreds of employees—it may be reasonable in the circumstances to expect that the business will not hire employees until several months after the I-829 petition is filed. Insofar as the regulation contemplates the possibility that the required job creation may not have occurred yet, but *will occur*, the evidence in support of the I-829 petition may include job offer letters, prospective contract engagements, business plans, and other appropriate documentation concerning future business activities.

Notwithstanding that the regulation is ultra vires, it would be better tolerated by investors if USCIS were understanding of commercial realities when determining the acceptable range of a reasonable period of time. In testimony before the Senate Judiciary Committee, USCIS allowed that "unexpected weather" that delayed progress in a project could be the justification for the job creation occurring after the filing of the I-829 petition.[92] No other possibilities were offered. But Neufeld I allowed that a determination of "reasonable period of time" might be shaped by various considerations:

> Officers should consider the evidence submitted along with the petition that demonstrates when the jobs are expected to be created, the reasons that the jobs have not been created as predicted in Form I-526, the nature of the industry or industries in which the jobs are to be created, and any other evidence submitted by the petitioner.[93]

In practice, USCIS routinely issues RFEs in cases for removal of conditions finding deficiencies in evidence of job creation. The following is illustrative of the RFEs in these cases:

---

[89] Well-accepted principles of statutory construction mandate an interpretation of statutory language so as to avoid conflicts with other statutes that have specific aims. *See, e.g.,* Morton v. Mancari, 417 U.S. 535, 550–51 (1974).

[90] 8 CFR §204.6(j)(4)(i). Standards relating to regional center-affiliated petitions are discussed later in the text.

[91] 8 CFR §§216.6(c)(1)(iv), 1216.6(c)(1)(iv).

[92] Senate Hearing, *supra* note 23, response to question 5.

[93] Neufeld I, *supra* note 2, at 6–7.

The copy of the business plan submitted fails to identify sufficient time frames leading to the completion of the project or job creation. Please provide updated information regarding the following: Estimated dates when the projects will be completed; estimated time frame for job creation; estimated time that the investor money will be placed with the job creating entity. Please provide information on any of the projects or portions of the project that have been completed. Please provide an update regarding whether the current state of the economy has had an impact on project projections. Any other relevant milestones with dates leading to the completion of the projects and creation of the jobs.

Reviews of many of our case histories show that a fully documented response that provides current status on a business or project development has been sufficient to garner approval of the petition for removal of conditions. To the extent these favorable outcomes indicate that USCIS examiners do apply the "reasonable period of time" regulation in a reasonable manner, at least most of the time, objections to the ultra vires regulation are likely to be muted. If, on the other hand, USCIS examiners turn to using two years as a rigid timeframe for job creation, expect investors to resort to the courts to protect their rights.

Regional Center-Affiliated Petitions

Separate consideration must be given to petitions for removal of conditions that are based on investments with designated regional centers. Such petitions may be supported by evidence of job creation based on expert economic analysis that does not include actual payroll records and I-9 forms. In short, regional center-affiliated petitions for removal of conditions should not be subject to the same job creation requirements that apply in standard EB-5 cases.

When Congress first introduced the Immigrant Investor Pilot Program in 1992, it intended to catalyze immigrant investment in defined geographic areas, and, thus, it hatched the concept of "regional centers" for EB-5 investment.[94] The Pilot Program is designed to amass and pool capital for targeted investment, *i.e.*, it contemplates "pooling investments in a region of the United States in order to develop interrelated enterprises which would increase the employment base and economic productivity of that region."[95]

A "regional center" may be identified with city or county boundaries, a redevelopment area, an enterprise zone, or any similar geographic area with definite boundaries. A "regional center" is designated by the immigration agency on the basis of a proposal for economic growth in the particular geographic area.[96] The applicant for regional center designation may be a private or public economic development agency, or a for-profit private entity that advances a general plan to use immigrant investor capital to fuel economic growth within the defined geographic area.[97]

Not only does the regional center have a territorial boundary, it also has a conceptual focus. Each regional center is designated by USCIS upon presentation of a general regional center plan. For example, the plan may be to focus investment in certain industry clusters in order to enhance regional economic productivity in consonance with the particular needs and attributes of the region. The general regional center plan also is supported by a job creation methodology intended to measure job impacts that result from investments in the particular regional center area. Based on the territorial focus, the general regional center plan, and the particular job creation methodology, USCIS designates the applicant as a regional center authorized to participate in the Pilot Program and, thereby, sanctions the job creation analysis for investors who base their petitions on investment with the regional center entity.

In the filing of I-526 petitions to obtain conditional permanent residence, regional center investors are not required to rely on proof of direct job creation. Instead, investors may include in their petitions

---

[94] Departments of Commerce, Justice, and State, the Judiciary, and Related Agencies Appropriations Act of 1993 (Appropriations Act), Pub. L. No. 102–395, §610, 106 Stat. 1828; S. Rep. No. 102–918 (1992).

[95] *See* S. Rep. No. 102–331 (1992); Immigrant Investor Pilot Program, Final Rule, 59 Fed. Reg. 17920–21 (Apr. 14, 1994); Pub. L. No. 107-273, 116 Stat. 1758, Title I, Subtit. B. ch. 1 §11037 (2002). For a thorough discussion of the investor pilot program and regional centers, see L. Stone, "Policy Considerations in the Immigrant Investor Pilot Program," *Immigration Options for Investors and Entrepreneurs* (AILA 2006).

[96] See 8 CFR §204.6(m) for the requirements of regional center designation.

[97] According to the regulations, "*[r]egional center* means any economic unit, public or private, which is involved with the promotion of economic growth, including increased export sales, improved regional productivity, job creation, and increased domestic capital investment." 8 CFR §204.6(e).

proof of indirect job creation based on "reasonable methodologies" that, if already approved by the USCIS, are presumed to identify job impacts throughout the economy.[98] A major objective of Congress in enacting the Pilot Program was to "increase interest" in the EB-5 classification, and, thus, USCIS is directed to implement a relaxation of the evidentiary standards for job creation that otherwise govern in the cases of immigrant investor petitions.[99] Consequently, the initial success of the Pilot Program in attracting large concentrations of capital that will fuel higher levels of job creation is entirely dependent upon USCIS permitting investor-petitioners to use reasonable and credible job-estimating tools that are by nature general predictions of future events and estimates of job creation. Adjudication of regional center-affiliated petitions should be in accordance with these clear objectives.

The I-829 petition and earlier I-526 petition are based on a particular employment methodology that has been approved by USCIS when it initially approved the regional center. In passing through to conditional permanent residence, the individual petitioner has relied on "economically or statistically valid forecasting devices which indicate the likelihood that the business will result in increased employment,"[100] and in approving the I-526 petition, USCIS has approved of the application of the employment methodology to the specific investor's case. In many regional center projects, the measurement of job impacts is largely a matter of economic analysis, input-output models, and estimating the likely job impacts throughout the regional economy.

Just as the agency, without statutory authority, has created the requirement of proof of all jobs within two years, it has compounded the error in cases of investors who file regional center-affiliated petitions. By subjecting regional center-affiliated investors to the two-year temporal requirement, USCIS ignores its own regulations.

Neufeld I, which primarily concerns the imposition of a job creation requirement that USCIS examiners can administer as they adjudicate petitions, overlooks the reality that Congress did not identify job creation as a petition adjudication condition.

USCIS uses an incomplete and unbalanced picture of the applicable law to rationalize its ultra vires requirement, including a faulty syllogism consisting of four statements about the relevant law.

First, Neufeld I observes that the statute providing for initial EB-5 eligibility is based in part on future job creation.

Second, with respect to removal of conditions Neufeld I states:

> INA 216A places conditions upon the permanent resident status of aliens admitted in the EB-5 classification that must be removed at the end of a two-year period of conditional residency. In order to have the conditions removed, EB-5 visa holders must file a Form I-829 that demonstrates that the petitioner is, among other requirements, "conforming to the requirements of INA 203(b)(5)." INA 216A(d)(1)(B).

This combination of sentences is baffling, as it turns the requirements for removal of conditions upside down. It emphasizes the general statement concerning requirements of INA §203(b)(5) but entirely buries without mention the specific adjudication requirements that are itemized in INA §216A(d).[101] The otherwise confirming requirement found in the statute for removal of conditions is the very same language found in the maintenance of status conditions. If, during the conditional residence period, an investor is not conducting himself in conformity with the requirements of an EB-5 category investor (*i.e.*, the investor is not at least in the process of investing, is not sustaining the investment, and so on), then USCIS could initiate proceedings to terminate the permanent resident status. However, that statutory provision has no relevance to any requirement of proof of job creation within a two-year timeframe. Perhaps the reference to the otherwise conforming requirement is merely a harbinger of the curveballs to come with statements three and four.

Third, Neufeld I then cites the regulation applicable to standard EB-5 petitions requiring a business plan that estimates job creation within two years:

> Consistent with the two-year period of conditional residency, USCIS regulations generally require

---

[98] *See* the Appropriations Act, *supra* note 94, §610(c), and 8 CFR §§204.6(j)(4)(iii) and (m)(7)(ii).

[99] Immigrant Investor Pilot Program, Commentary to Interim Rule, 58 Fed. Reg. 44606 (Aug. 24, 1993).

[100] 8 CFR §§204.6(m)(7)(ii) and (j)(4)(iii).

[101] Why Neufeld II would conceal the specific statute-based petition adjudication conditions—the investment requirement and the sustained requirement—under the phrase "among other requirements" and instead specifically identify the otherwise conforming requirement as if it is a more significant factor for removal of conditions is a troubling question.

evidence to obtain approval of a Form I-526, including a business plan that demonstrates that jobs will be created within the two-year period of conditional residence. 8 CFR §204.6(j)(4)(i)(B).

This statement is correct, as far as it goes. Significantly, however, it omits to mention that part (iii) of the same regulation, 8 CFR §204.6(j)(4), which specifically relates to petitions filed for regional center-affiliated investors, does not require a business plan providing for job creation within the two-year period. The regulation concerning regional center-affiliated cases has no temporal dimension, yet Neufeld I makes no mention of part (iii) relating to regional center-affiliated petitions.

And *fourth*, Neufeld I cites to the regulation for removal of conditions that is based on job creation within a reasonable period of time:

> USCIS regulations relating to the removal [of] conditions from the lawful permanent resident status of alien entrepreneurs status provide that a petitioner must demonstrate "the alien has created or can be expected to create within a reasonable period of time" the required jobs. 8 CFR §216.6(c)(1)(iv).

This excerpt from Neufeld I, however, does not completely present the text of the cited regulation. The actual language of the agency regulation for removal of conditions does not refer to "the required jobs" as suggested in Neufeld I. Rather, the actual regulation refers to jobs for "qualifying employees," which is the term reserved in the regulatory framework for the workers in a standard EB-5 case, *i.e.*, 8 CFR §204.6(j)(4)(i) or (ii), as distinct from a regional center-affiliated case. The regulation at 8 CFR §204.6(j)(4)(iii) relating to proof of job creation in regional center-affiliated cases provides for proof in the form of "reasonable methodologies" that estimate jobs for 10 "persons," which clearly is not the same as "qualified employees," as that latter term is defined in regulations. The principal statements of Neufeld I seem to skirt these distinctions in definition with the objective of corralling regional center affiliated petitions into a two-year timeframe for job creation with a parallel requirement of presenting documentation for "qualifying employees."

Neufeld I ignores a clear design that is evident in the regulations concerning job creation. The regulation requiring job creation evidence in support of the I-526 petition has three parts—(i) *General*, (ii) *Troubled business*, and (iii) *Immigrant Investor Pilot Program*:

> 8 CFR 204.6(j)(4) Job creation—
>
> (i) *General*. To show that a new commercial enterprise will create not fewer than ten (10) full-time positions for qualifying employees, the petition must be accompanied by:
>
>> (A) Documentation consisting of photocopies of relevant tax records, Form I–9, or other similar documents for ten (10) qualifying employees, if such employees have already been hired following the establishment of the new commercial enterprise; or
>>
>> (B) A copy of a comprehensive business plan showing that, due to the nature and projected size of the new commercial enterprise, the need for not fewer than ten (10) qualifying employees will result, including approximate dates, within the next two years, and when such employees will be hired.
>
> (ii) *Troubled business*. To show that a new commercial enterprise which has been established through a capital investment in a troubled business meets the statutory employment creation requirement, the petition must be accompanied by evidence that the number of existing employees is being or will be maintained at no less than the pre-investment level for a period of at least two years. Photocopies of tax records, Forms I–9, or other relevant documents for the qualifying employees and a comprehensive business plan shall be submitted in support of the petition.
>
> (iii) *Immigrant Investor Pilot Program*. To show that the new commercial enterprise located within a regional center approved for participation in the Immigrant Investor Pilot Program meets the statutory employment creation requirement, the petition must be accompanied by evidence that the investment will create full-time positions for not fewer than 10 persons either directly or indirectly through revenues generated from increased exports resulting from the Pilot Program. Such evidence may be demonstrated by reasonable methodologies including those set forth in paragraph (m)(3) of this section.

It is evident from the obvious framework of 8 §CFR 204.6(j)(4) that each of its parts—(i), (ii), and (iii)—is intended to be read disjunctively. That is, where part (i) is applicable to adjudication of the I-526 petition, parts (ii) and (iii) do not also apply. Conversely, if part (iii) were to govern the adjudication of the I-526 petition, then neither part (i) nor part (ii) would be applicable. This interpretation is manifest from the actual language of the regulation. For example, part (i) *General* requires evidence of tax records and I-9 forms for employees. Part (ii) *Troubled business* also explicitly requires evidence of tax records and I-9 forms for employees. There would be no need for this explicit reference in part (ii) if part (i) were intended to be interpreted as a catch-all set of requirements for all I-526 petitions. The correct reading, rather, is that parts (i), (ii), and (iii) are separate and alternative requirements; the petitioner satisfies the job creation aspect of the regulation by fitting within just one of these alternatives.

That part (iii) of the regulation stands on its own, and is the exclusive standard for Pilot Program-based cases, is clear from the history of regulatory development. When first promulgated, 8 CFR §204.6(j)(4) included only parts (i) and (ii).[102] The Pilot Program was enacted thereafter and legacy INS promulgated the implementing regulations by adding part (iii) to indicate what is required for Pilot Program-based petitions.[103]

It is clear that both parts (i) and (ii) require evidence of tax records and I-9 forms of the "qualifying employees" of the commercial enterprise. Notably, part (iii) relating to Pilot Program-based investor petitions does not require evidence of tax records and I-9 forms for "qualifying employees," but instead refers to reasonable methodologies for creating positions for 10 "persons."

Similarly, part (iii) relating to *Immigrant Investor Pilot Program*-affiliated petitions does not impose a time requirement for job creation. Whereas part (i) relating to *General* petitions clearly states that job creation should occur "within the next two years" and part (ii) relating to *Troubled business* petitions clearly requires maintaining employees "for a period of at least two years," there is no such temporal requirement in part (iii) relating to *Immigrant Investor Pilot Program* petitions.

Notwithstanding the clear architecture of the controlling regulations that have been parsed above, drafted to treat regional center-affiliated petitions differently, USCIS has imposed a near-absolute temporal requirement for creating regional center-affiliated jobs, which cannot be reconciled with the expansive intent of the Pilot Program or with the laws that bind USCIS adjudications.

Legacy INS and Congress understood well that indirect employees in the regional center sense of the term are different from the directly employed workers of a business. In the regulation quoted in full above, which addresses the required evidence of job creation in an EB-5 case, use of the term "qualifying employees" is in the subpart relating to *General*—that is, for a standard EB-5 case that is not regional center affiliated. The petition must demonstrate that the investor "will create not fewer than ten (10) full-time positions for qualifying employees." On the other hand, where the regulation treats the required evidence for *Immigrant Investor Pilot Program*—that is, for a regional center-affiliated EB-5 case—the regulation requires "evidence that the investment will create full-time positions for not fewer than 10 persons."

The two different terms are used because there is a specific purpose in making the distinction. Evidence of jobs in a standard EB-5 case consists of identified "employees" who are working directly for and on the payroll of the new commercial enterprise. Evidence of jobs in a regional center-affiliated EB-5 case, on the other hand, consists of a much broader category of unknown "persons" who may work in jobs throughout the economy, as estimated by reasonable methodologies in the opinion of an expert economist. Consequently, when legacy INS promulgated the regulation concerning removal of conditions—just one month after promulgating regulations for regional center-affiliated cases—and required the I-829 petition to include evidence of "qualifying employees," it clearly intended that requirement to apply only to standard EB-5 petitions not to regional center affiliated EB-5 petitions.

This distinction was sanctioned and reaffirmed by Congress in the removal of conditions legislation enacted in 2002. Well after the 1994 promulgation of the regulation for removal of conditions, in 2002 Congress effectively ingrained the principle that standard EB-5 petitions and regional center-affiliated EB-5 petitions are to be adjudicated based on a different set of evidentiary rules. In the legislation enacted to fashion a remedy for investors marooned by a change in adjudication standards, Congress indicated that in a standard EB-5 case the investor must demonstrate eligibility for removal of conditions by proving job creation, capital investment, and no material misrepresentation.[104] But in

---

[102] Final Rule, 56 Fed. Reg. 60897 (Nov. 29, 1991).
[103] Final Rule, 59 Fed. Reg. 17920 (Apr. 15, 1994).

[104] Pub. L. No. 107-273, 116 Stat. 1758, tit. I, subtit. B, ch 1, §11031(c)(1)(A) (2002).

stark contrast, in a regional center-affiliated case, Congress provided that if the investment is based on one of the acceptable "reasonable methodologies" then it shall be deemed to satisfy the job creation requirements for removal of conditions.[105]

Although the 2002 statutory provision relates only to the "Public Law class" of EB-5 investors, the disparate treatment of investors with standard EB-5 petitions and investors with regional center-affiliated EB-5 petitions is an unmistakable directive by Congress that the removal of conditions for regional center-affiliated EB-5 investors who have placed capital at risk in pursuit of the business plan is not to be burdened by additional evidentiary requirements for proof of jobs. Where there is evidence of a sustained investment, Congress does not intend the removal of conditions for a regional center-affiliated investor to be withheld for want of further proof of job creation beyond the initial job creation methodology. This legislative objective is recognized too in the regulation for removal of conditions, requiring evidence of "qualifying employees" which can be only a reference to standard EB-5 cases, not regional center-affiliated cases.

In view of the objectives of deterring fraud and maximizing capital attraction and job creation, Congress did not intend to hamstring the Pilot Program by imposing onerous requirements for proof of job creation at the time the investor-petitioner files the I-829 petition. The goal of deterring fraud is accomplished by requiring proof of a real investment. In regional center-affiliated cases, the process of I-829 petition adjudication should not be reduced to a counting of the jobs created within two years. Petitioners should be able to rely on the reasonable methodologies for estimating job creation that formed the basis for the I-526 petition approval, coupled with evidence of a real investment. Where USCIS uses the removal of conditions process to re-evaluate the job creation methodology it already approved before, as in the *Song* and *Kim* regional center-affiliated cases cited above,[106] investors are likely to bring their grievances about denials of I-829 petitions before the federal courts.

From a policy perspective which recognizes massive capital attraction and job creation as the paramount objectives of the Immigrant Investor Pilot Program, to hold the view that the law does not authorize USCIS to count jobs in the course of adjudicating the petition for removal of conditions does not make one "anti-jobs" in the least. We can assume there is common ground in wanting to maximize job creation in the U.S. economy. We can respectfully disagree, however, on the means for achieving the goal. Above all else, the clear statutory scheme devised by Congress should not be eliminated in order to make room for an alternative policy scheme advanced by USCIS.

CONCLUSION: TIME FOR A CHANGE

USCIS, for its part, believes it must function as a counter of jobs; it apparently sees no other way to manage the EB-5 investor program, and it therefore interprets the law at every turn in ways that entrust it with the maximum authority for counting jobs and confining the activities of EB-5-funded U.S. businesses throughout the process. There is a different perspective: The law does not entrust USCIS with the authority it has wrested, but instead the law contemplates a forward-looking plan of investment and job creation, and removal of conditions based on good faith investment and actual business activity in pursuit of commercial gain. USCIS need not penalize EB-5 investors for normal and ordinary business events which they cannot possibly control. It is the latter perspective, not the rigid USCIS position, that is more likely to maximize capital attraction and thereby maximize job creation.

The earlier pages of this article featured a form Notice of Decision advising the I-829 petitioner of a USCIS decision to deny the removal of conditions. For the investor and dependent family members, lawful residence status is terminated immediately. The family is ordered to depart the United States. The only hope to remain lawfully in the United States rests with the uncertain path of a court hearing before an immigration judge. This is the outcome for an investor and dependent family members even in cases where the investor has already invested the requisite capital, and the investor has at all times acted in good faith and was not at fault in the failure to remove the conditions. Causes for the denied petition for removal of conditions might range from being unable to prove: that the commercial enterprise has adhered strictly to its original business plan; that the commercial enterprise expended all of the business's capital; that the business has hired enough employees; or that the employees are lawful citizens and immigrants. Each of these reasons for denial is a creation of USCIS field guidance and adjudication; denial for any one of these

---

[105] *Id.*, §11031(c)(1)(B).

[106] *Supra* note 47.

reasons does not appear to be compelled by existing law. In ways that are subject to legal challenge, USCIS has transformed the petition adjudication conditions.

As a policy matter, these unfair outcomes for well-intended EB-5 investors tarnish the U.S. immigrant investor program. As dreams are dashed, through no fault of the investors, the cumulative effect makes the EB-5 investor category decidedly unappealing. Whatever the analytical failings of Neufeld I and Neufeld II, it is unfortunate that USCIS has not recognized that its adjudication stance will do more to harm rather than help its mission to meet the objectives of the EB-5 investor program. Once prospective investors fully grasp the inherent immigration risk attendant to the removal of conditions process as conceived by USCIS, many will forego the EB-5 investor program.

Whether Congress steps in to remedy these incongruous circumstances is anybody's guess. But when it does, Congress should explore the following: clarifying that the sole purpose of the conditional residence period is to deter fraud; emphasizing that the conditional residence period is not to test whether the commercial enterprise fully expended all of its capital and created all 10 jobs; curtailing the USCIS practice that requires investors to prove the immigration status of employees; and adding a good faith waiver provision that will benefit genuine investors who followed the directive of the EB-5 law to undertake commercial risk.

If Congress is stymied in the short term by the political reality that it must package a bill within "comprehensive immigration reform," then USCIS should act in the interim to do what is best for attracting EB-5 capital. The most effective strategy for USCIS would be to eliminate the immigration risk from the petition process by providing clarity and adjudication standards that reflect the broader vision advanced by Congress.[107] Whether by formal regulation or by field instructions and memoranda, USCIS can throw its considerable weight behind an initiative to make the process for removal of conditions more fair, reasonable and consistent with national economic objectives.

---

[107] In a report dated April 2005, upon reviewing the entire history of the immigrant investor program, the U.S. Government Accountability Office (GAO) concluded that one of the principal obstacles to success of the program was the lack of regulations and clear guidance from USCIS. GAO Report to Congressional Committees, "Immigrant Investors: Small Number of Participants Attributed to Pending Regulations and Other Factors," GAO-05-256 (Apr. 2005), *published on* AILA InfoNet at Doc. No. 05040475 (*posted* Apr. 4, 2005). The "Highlights" section of the GAO Report is reproduced in Appendix E. In a March 18, 2009, report by the USCIS Office of the Ombudsman, USCIS was urged to engage in regulation development in order to provide more certainty in the EB-5 process. Office of the CIS Ombudsman, "Employment Creation Immigrant Visa (EB-5) Program Recommendations" (Mar. 18, 2009), *published on* AILA InfoNet at Doc. No. 09031868 (*posted* Mar. 18, 2009), and reproduced in Appendix F.

STRATEGIES FOR OVERCOMING DENIALS OF I-829 PETITIONS TO REMOVE CONDITIONS FROM PERMANENT RESIDENCE

*by Martin J. Lawler and Estelle McKee**

INTRODUCTION

When U.S. Citizenship and Immigration Services (USCIS) denies an immigrant investor's I-829 petition to remove the conditions from his or her permanent residence, there is no procedure for appeal. The application may be renewed before the Immigration Judge in removal proceedings.[1] There are however other strategies available to obtain further administrative review or review in federal court. This article will address these strategies. It will also address some of the reasons USCIS denies I-829 petitions, and arguments counsel may wish to consider when seeking the reversal of an I-829 denial.

---

* **Martin J. Lawler** is a California immigration lawyer with over 30 years of experience. He is the author of *Professionals: A Matter of Degree*, a treatise on business visas and permanent residence. *Professionals*, published by the American Immigration Lawyers Association (AILA), is in its fifth edition. The *Wall Street Journal* published two of Martin's opinion page articles in 2007. Martin was a guest speaker on National Public Radio's Science Friday program about visas for scientists. Martin has spoken at many universities, including Harvard, Stanford, San Jose State, and San Francisco State. He is a regular speaker at AILA conferences, including its EB-5 Investor Visa conference. He has also lectured at the American Law Institute, the San Francisco Bar Association, Innovation Norway, and American Chemical Society, among other venues. He chaired AILA's H-1B visa committee and is a member of AILA's EB-5 Investor Committee 2008–10. Martin is the recipient of the AILA Jack Wasserman Memorial Award for excellence in immigration litigation. He is Martindale-Hubbell A rated and listed in *Best Lawyers in America*, the Bar Register of Preeminent Lawyers, and *San Francisco Magazine*'s Super Lawyers.

Estelle McKee is an Associate Attorney at Lawler & Lawler. She was formerly an Associate Clinical Professor at Cornell Law School. She has published articles in *Bender's Immigration Bulletin*, and has contributed to the book *Professionals: A Matter of Degree*, by Martin J. Lawler and Margaret Stock, and the legal treatise *Immigration Law & Procedure*, by Charles Gordon, Stanley Mailman, and Stephen Yale-Loehr.

Edward Carroll, a foremost expert on EB-5 visas, also contributed to this article.

Hope M. Frye, former AILA President and book author, substantially drafted the *Steenblik v. Chertoff* complaint that follows this chapter.

[1] INA §216A(b)(2), 8 USC §1186b(b)(2).

PROCEDURAL OPTIONS FOR SEEKING REVIEW OF A DENIAL

Immigration Court

Immigration courts have jurisdiction to review denials of I-829 petitions in removal proceedings.[2] It is important to note, in such cases, the government has the burden to establish by a preponderance of evidence at least one of the following:

- the investment in the commercial enterprise was intended solely as a means of evading the immigration laws of the United States;

- the immigrant investor did not invest, or was not actively in the process of investing, the requisite capital, or did not sustain the investment throughout the period of his or her conditional residence; or

- the immigrant investor was otherwise not conforming to the requirements of the statute.[3]

Although the government has the burden in removal proceedings, immigrant investors may not want to wait until they are in removal proceedings before challenging the I-829 denial. While awaiting a removal hearing, an immigrant investor may find it difficult to manage a business without legal status. International travel will not be permitted. Loans may not be renewed and work authorization not permitted, which may affect driver's license validity. Further, the Department of Homeland Security (DHS) must first initiate removal proceedings by issuing a Notice to Appear, but there is no requirement to do so.

Motions to Reopen or Reconsider

The regulations[4] permit petitioners to file motions to reopen or reconsider within 30 days of a denial. Motions to reopen (but not motions to reconsider) that are filed beyond that time may be excused in the adjudicator's discretion where the delay was

---

[2] INA §216A(c)(3)(D), 8 USC §1186b(c)(3)(D).

[3] INA §203(b)(5), 8 USC §1153(b)(5). The requirements for filing a petition for classification as an entrepreneur, INA §216A(c)(3)(D), 8 USC §1186b(c)(3)(D).

[4] 8 CFR §103.5.

reasonable and beyond the petitioner's control.[5] Motions to reopen or reconsider should be submitted on Form I-290B. Specific filing requirements are provided at 8 CFR §103.5(a)(1)(iii). Although not required, counsel should always submit a brief synopsis of the arguments for reversal of the decision.

A motion to reopen seeks to present new facts that would result in the approval of the I-829 petition. The regulations require such a motion to state the new facts that will be provided in the reopened proceeding. The motion must include affidavits or other documentary evidence.[6]

A motion to reconsider is based on developments in the law or other legal reasons for reversal. According to the regulations,[7] it must state the reasons for reconsideration and cite cases, regulations, or other law to demonstrate that the denial was based on an incorrect application of law or USCIS policy. A motion to reconsider a decision must also establish that the decision was incorrect based on the record evidence at the time of the initial decision.

The regulations do not limit the number of motions that an immigrant investor may file. However, each subsequent motion should have a new basis that could not have been raised earlier, such as an argument addressing a new finding or legal conclusion in the adjudicator's decision on the previous motion, or new facts that came to light since the previous motion.

Even if one believes that the adjudicator will deny a motion, practitioners should not disregard this option. Motions can be very useful to narrow issues before filing a complaint in federal court. In *Steenblik v. Chertoff*,[8] three motions to reopen were filed. With each new denial the issues narrowed. USCIS accepted counsel's argument that, although *Steenblik* owned his dairy farm land separately from his farm corporation, the land was intricately intertwined with the farm corporation and it was one EB-5 enterprise (this issue is further discussed later in this article). The motions thus made the case less complex to litigate.

Motions may be accompanied by expert witness testimony about the evidence in the record or to rebut conclusions in the decision. Experts may include accountants to explain amended tax returns or a construction expert may explain delays in the project and how soon it will be completed. A business law and/or financial expert may provide testimony to prove funds are at risk. The investor may also give an affidavit to address issues raised in the denial.

The examiner may be reluctant to accept new evidence with a motion which was previously requested in a Request for Evidence (RFE). RFEs are, however, often vague, confusing, or fail to explain why the evidence previously provided is insufficient. The RFE may have one meaning to the examiner and another to the investor. Since the denial of an I-829 can have dire economic, social, psychological and other consequences to the investor and his or her family, the business, its employees, as well as to the community if the business is abandoned, the USCIS should be encouraged to accept the new evidence even if it was requested by an RFE. The investor's affidavit should explain any confusion or her interpretation of the RFE and explain why certain evidence was not previously provided. Evidence from the community about the economic impact of losing the employer may also be helpful to convince the USCIS to accept new evidence.

Federal Court Action

When administrative remedies fail, an immigrant investor may seek review of a denied I-829 in federal court. There are several grounds on which an investor may seek relief.

The Administrative Procedure Act (APA) provides for review when it is alleged that an agency's actions are arbitrary, capricious, and otherwise violate the law.[9] The APA can provide relief where an agency applies the wrong standard of review, its decision is not supported by substantial evidence, or ignores probative testimony or evidence.[10]

Similarly, federal courts may provide relief when an agency exceeds its statutory authority, thus acting ultra vires of the law. In the I-829 context, an argument can be made that USCIS acts illegally when it readjudicates matters that it already adjudicated when it approved the immigrant investor's I-526 petition, such as by redetermining that the immigrant

---

[5] 8 CFR §103.5(a)(1)(i).

[6] 8 CFR §103.5(a)(2).

[7] 8 CFR §103.5(a)(3).

[8] No. 8:08-cv-01156-AHS-MLG (C.D. Cal. Dec. 5, 2008). A copy of the complaint follows this chapter.

[9] 5 USC §706.

[10] *Hong Kong T.V. Video Program, Inc. v. Ilchert*, 685 F. Supp. 712 (N.D. Cal. 1988).

investor's commercial enterprise is located within a targeted employment area (TEA) or revisiting the source of funds.[11] USCIS's failure to follow the law and its own published rules may also constitute a violation of the immigrant investor's constitutional right to due process.[12]

USCIS may challenge a federal court action on the ground that the immigrant investor has not exhausted his or her administrative remedies by renewing the case in removal proceedings. The immigrant investor's complaint should explain the consequences of further administrative remedies. For example, in *Steenblik v. Chertoff*, the denial deprived Mr. Steenblik due process, which is an issue that an immigration court would not be able to address. There may also be irreparable harm to a business if an investor cannot maintain loans or work authorization in protracted removal proceedings, which would jeopardize the entire enterprise and possibly the investor's life savings. The federal court may be asked to enjoin USCIS from revoking the conditional residence and/or work and travel authorization.

In *Gulen v. Chertoff*,[13] an EB-1 petitioner filed a complaint in federal court while his AAO appeal was pending. The complaint was amended to incorporate the AAO denial. While courts often will dismiss a complaint because administrative remedies have not been exhausted, filing a complaint in court will involve a U.S. Attorney who may view the case more objectively than the agency, opening the way for possible settlement.

CHANG V. INS

In adjudicating an I-829 petition, USCIS, in reliance upon INA §216A(b)(1)(c), frequently readjudicates matters already settled by its approval of the I-526 petition. When USCIS does so, it disregards the only federal court case that has addressed this issue: *Chang v. INS*.[14] In *Chang*, the Ninth Circuit concluded that USCIS may not apply precedent decisions,[15] establishing new investment rules, to deny immigrant investors' I-829 petitions when these investors had followed USCIS's previous investment rules, which governed at the time they submitted their I-526 petitions. In so deciding, the court stated that USCIS must approve the I-829 petition upon finding that the petitioners made no material misrepresentations in the I-526 petition and that they complied with the EB-5 requirements.[16] The decision on the Form I-829 is not meant to be a re-adjudication of the investment plan, source of funds or any other matter covered by the Form I-526 process.[17]

In *Chang*, the government argued that the precedent decisions had no improper retroactive effect on the immigrant investors' approved I-526 petitions because the I-829 required a complete re-adjudication of I-526 petitions. In response, the court stated the following:

[I]f I-526 approval is decoupled from I-829 approval, then petitioners whose I-526 petitions had been approved would have no reasonable reliance that the rules set out in 8 C.F.R. §216.6 would not change in midstream. If, on the other hand, approval of the I-526 petition was *an official provisional approval of the petitioner's plan, contingent on its effectuation*, then a retroactivity analysis is required. (emphasis added.)[18]

The court concluded that the approval of an I-526 petition was a tacit approval of the business plan and, therefore, it conducted a "retroactivity analysis." This analysis resulted in the finding that the three precedent decisions established new investment rules (all of which involved I-526 petitions), had impermissible retroactive effect on the immigrant investors' approved I-526 petitions and, therefore, were impermissibly applied to the adjudication of the petitioner's I-829 filing. The court said:

---

[11] Although INA §216A(d)(1)(B) allows the agency to examine whether the investor is "otherwise conforming to the requirements of section 1153(b)(5) of this title [INA §203(b)(5)]," the Ninth Circuit in *Chang v. INS*, 327 F.3d 911 (9th Cir. 2003), limited the agency's ability to conduct an entirely de novo readjudication of issues it already decided. This case is discussed later in this article.

[12] For a discussion of Administrative Procedure Act (APA) and due process claims, see M. Lawler and M. Stock, *Professionals: A Matter of Degree*, ch. 34, and I. Kurzban, *Kurzban's Immigration Law Sourcebook*, at 1085–88, 1213.

[13] No. 07-2148, 2008 U.S. Dist. LEXIS 54607 (E.D. Pa. July 17, 2008).

[14] 327 F.3d 911 (9th Cir. 2003).

[15] These decisions were *Matter of Izummi*, 22 I&N Dec. 169 (Assoc. Comm'r, Examinations 1998); *Matter of Soffici*, 22 I&N Dec. 158 (Assoc. Comm'r, Examinations 1998); and *Matter of Ho*, 22 I&N Dec. 206 (Assoc. Comm'r, Examinations 1998), all of which are reproduced in Appendix A.

[16] *Chang*, 327 F.3d at 916.

[17] *Id.* at 927; compare 8 CFR §204.6(j) *with* 8 CFR §216.6(a)(4) and (c)(1).

[18] *Chang*, 327 F.3d at 927.

The government argues that I-526 approval neither guarantees nor predicts I-829 approval, but the latter is clearly untrue. I-526 approval does not guarantee I-829 approval—the petitioner might not successfully "sustain the actions . . . throughout the period of . . . residence"—but it certainly predicts it. No one obtains I-829 approval without prior I-526 approval. The government provides no reason to believe that the combination of I-526 approval, successful execution of the approved plan, and absence of material misrepresentation in the I-526 petition—all characteristics that Appellants claim apply to them—was not an excellent predictor of I-829 approval up until the precedent decisions appeared.[19]

To be clear, the *Chang* decision does not preclude the imposition of new standards in I-526 petitions if the standards are announced in advance of the filing of the petitions. The *Chang* court objected, instead, to using the I-829 review as an opportunity to retroactively impose new standards for approval on I-526 cases previously approved. Such action is impermissible because it disregards the I-526 approval as an "...excellent predictor of I-829 approval."

Elsewhere, the court says, "We conclude that Appellants reasonably relied on the application of 8 C.F.R. §216.6 extant when their I-526 petitions were approved. We conclude that the INS's refashioning of 8 C.F.R. §216.6 into an independent *ab initio* assessment of Appellants' satisfaction of the EB-5 program standards raises serious retroactivity concerns."[20]

On December 11, 2009, USCIS issued a new policy memorandum and amended the *Adjudicator's Field Manual* (AFM). The revised language pays lip service to *Chang*'s prohibition against *ab initio* review of I-526 petitions:

> Pursuant to section 216A(c)(3) of the Act, USCIS must determine that the facts and information contained in the petition are true. ISOs [Immigration Service Officers] should generally give deference to the approval of EB-5 eligibility requirements previously made in the alien investor's Form I-526 petition and affiliated regional center designation, as applicable, if the facts presented in the earlier proceedings remain unchanged to include:
>
> – The new commercial enterprise's capital investment structure;
>
> – That the commercial enterprise qualifies as "new" for EB-5 purposes;
>
> – If the commercial enterprise is affiliated with a regional center, the direct and indirect job creation methodology;
>
> – If the Form I-526 petition was approved for reduced capital investment threshold of $500,000, that the new commercial enterprise was located in a TEA at the time of filing of the Form I-526, and;
>
> – That the alien investor's investment capital was lawfully obtained.[21]

This language does not absolutely prohibit adjudicators from revisiting issues decided in the I-526 petition but instead directs ISOs to "generally give deference" to the previous I-526 and regional center approval unless some material change in the facts is determined.

The memorandum also provides that:

> The CSC EB-5 program manager should be notified to determine the appropriate action to take if an ISO discovers during the adjudication of the Form I-829 petition that:
>
> – Documentation relating to the regional center's capital investment structure or job creation methodologies or the eligibility requirements favorably decided-upon in the Form I-526 petition have materially changed post-approval of the regional center designation or Form I-526 petition;
>
> – The record contains evidence of fraud or misrepresentation; or
>
> – The evidence of record indicates that the previously favorable decision to approve the regional center proposal (or amendment) was legally deficient.[22]

These provisions, authorizing a review of issues decided in the I-526 petition, are general and permissive and appear to defeat the concept of deference that ISOs are directed earlier in the memorandum to give to adjudicated I-526 petitions.

---

[19] *Id.*

[20] *Id.*

[21] *Adjudicator's Field Manual* (AFM) ch. 25.2. The AFM is available at *www.ailapubs.org/*.

[22] *Id.*

As noted by Lincoln Stone, one of the foremost experts in this area, the legislative history of the I-829 process demonstrates that its goal was to deter fraud, not readjudicate the I-526 petition:

> Section 204 in the 1989 Bill was entitled "Deterring Immigration-Related Entrepreneur Fraud,"[23] it required a two-year conditional permanent residence status, and authorized termination of such status on proof that the business was established solely as a means of evading the immigration laws.[24] The provision was adopted in the EB-5 statute and codified at INA §216A.[25]

Mr. Stone also observes that:

> Early on, when legacy INS initially promulgated regulations for the EB-5 category, it stated that the two-year conditional residence status exists in the EB-5 category for the primary purpose of ensuring that investors continue their new commercial enterprises so that the creation of U.S. jobs and the infusion of capital into the U.S. economy are sustained.[26] In other words, the agency viewed its fraud deterrent role to be one of confirming that the investment and enterprise would be sustained beyond the completion of the immigration processing. That made considerable sense then as Congress envisioned the EB-5 category as an attractor of foreign capital. It continues to make sense today.[27]

Practitioners are advised to review the *Chang* decision as well as the USCIS December 11, 2009, memorandum, if confronted with an RFE, Notice of Intent to Deny, or a denial of an I-829 petition predicated on a deficient I-526 filing.

STEENBLIK V. CHERTOFF

Steenblik v. Chertoff[28] involved denial of an I-829 for a very successful dairy farm investment. Like many self-investor projects, it started out as an E-2 enterprise. The principal issue was whether USCIS, at the I-829 petition stage, could readjudicate the I-526 in violation of *Chang*. Three motions to reopen/reconsider were granted and a new denial was issued. The motions addressed a number of issues including that Mr. Steenblik's personal ownership of the farmland was part of his dairy farm corporation investment. USCIS's final denial concluded that Mr. Steenblik was ineligible for the original grant of conditional permanent resident status. The denial had three bases:

(a) the alleged failure of Plaintiff to document the source of two cash payments, which he used to purchase farmland, pay for crop expansion, and pay off a chattel mortgage crop loan. Defendants claim that Plaintiff did not submit evidence to show that the funds had originated from him and not from the retained earnings of the farm;

(b) the alleged failure of the record to clearly show whether the payments originated from Plaintiff or from loans made to Plaintiff and secured by the assets of the dairy farm; and

(c) the alleged failure of prior counsel's cover letter and an accountant's reconciliation letter to establish that the claimed investment originated from Plaintiff and not retained earnings from the farm.

In addition to claiming that the plaintiff's I-526 was illegally readjudicated, the complaint claimed: (1) the denial applied an illegal "clear and convincing" standard of proof instead of the "preponderance" standard; (2) the denial illegally revoked the I-526 in violation of USCIS rules; (3) the denial arbitrarily misconstrued and ignored evidence; and (4) Mr. Steenblik executed his business plan submitted with the I-526.

Steenblik v. Chertoff was settled and Plaintiff Steenblik's I-829 was granted.

SELECTED ISSUES FOR I-829 PETITIONS

USCIS regulations governing I-829s provide as follows:

Documentation. The petition for removal of conditions must be accompanied by the following evidence:

(i) Evidence that a commercial enterprise was established by the alien. Such evidence may include, but is not limited to, federal income tax returns;

(ii) Evidence that the alien invested or was actively in the process of investing the requisite capital. Such evidence may include, but

---

[23] Immigration Act of 1989, S. 358, 101st Cong. (1989).
[24] S. Rep. No. 101-55, at 22 (1989).
[25] L. Stone, "Revisiting Removal of the Conditions for Immigrant Investors: Time for a Change," *EB-5 Investors—New Opportunities for Your Clients and Your Practice* (2009 AILA Fall Topics CLE Conference).
[26] Commentary to Final Rule, *supra* note 3, at 26588.
[27] *Id.*
[28] No. 8:08-cv-01156-AHS-MLG (C.D. Cal. Dec. 5, 2008). A copy of the complaint follows this chapter.

is not limited to, an audited financial statement or other probative evidence; and

(iii) Evidence that the alien sustained the actions described in paragraph (a)(4)(i) and (a)(4)(ii) of this section throughout the period of the alien's residence in the United States. The alien will be considered to have sustained the actions required for removal of conditions if he or she has, in good faith, substantially met the capital investment requirement of the statute and continuously maintained his or her capital investment over the two years of conditional residence. Such evidence may include, but is not limited to, bank statements, invoices, receipts, contracts, business licenses, Federal or State income tax returns, and Federal or State quarterly tax statements.

(iv) Evidence that the alien created or can be expected to create within a reasonable time ten full-time jobs for qualifying employees.

In the case of a "troubled business," as defined in 8 CFR §204.6(j)(4)(ii), the alien entrepreneur must submit evidence that the commercial enterprise maintained the number of existing employees at no less than the pre-investment level for the period following his or her admission as a conditional permanent resident. Such evidence may include payroll records, relevant tax documents, and Forms I-9.[29]

Practitioners should advise clients of these requirements as early as possible. The proper preparation of business and tax records from the time the I-526 is filed can determine the success of the I-829 petition.

The Commercial Enterprise

USCIS has objected to the division of a commercial enterprise into two or more legal entities, each owned by the investors. It is common in certain industries, such as farming, for land to be personally owned by the investor while the farming operations taking place on that land are owned by the investor's corporation. Similarly, investors commonly purchase land on which to locate hotels, restaurants, and the like, but choose for accounting or risk-reduction purposes to keep the land under personal ownership and lease it to the business, which is operated in a different entity. This arrangement is rife with problems for the immigrant investor.

In the I-526 context, the AAO has rejected arguments that the corporate-owned business was merely a holding company for a subsidiary real estate business where the investor owned the land on which his corporate-owned farm operated.[30] It is the view of USCIS that if the corporation—the farm, hotel, or restaurant, for example—is the commercial enterprise, then the investor must transfer the land to the corporation so that it has formal title to the land. Otherwise, USCIS may find the investment is not an asset of the enterprise.[31] Likewise, where the investor retains personal ownership of the land, questions may arise as to whether the funds used to purchase the land are truly at risk, given that the investor will still own the land even if the corporation fails.

Finally, the capital must contribute to the employment-generating activities of the enterprise. This was one of the reasons that the AAO affirmed the denial of an I-526 petition filed by an investor who invested in a corporation operating a restaurant and a separate corporation that purchased the land on which the restaurant was located. The AAO refused to consider as invested capital the funds used to purchase the land even though the land may have been very valuable to the restaurant. Aside from other issues, including the petitioner's investment in two separate corporations instead of a single commercial enterprise, the AAO noted that the restaurant's lease payments "are funds that the restaurant would not owe had the petitioner infused the funds for the purchase of this land directly into the corporation operating the restaurant. Thus, we fail to see how the purchase of this land contributes to the employment generating activities of the restaurant." The AAO did not explain how the restaurant could have created more jobs if it did not have to make lease payments.[32]

Practitioners can avoid the above problems by advising investors to purchase land and transfer formal title of the land into the corporation that will

---

[29] 8 CFR §1216.6(a)(4); *see* INA §203(b)(5), 8 USC §1153(b)(5); INA §216A, 8 USC §1186b.

[30] *Cf. Matter of [name not provided]*, WAC 07 004 50015 (AAO Sept. 24, 2008) (affirming denial of I-526 petition where farming corporation and land were separately owned).

[31] *Cf. Matter of [name not provided]*, SRC 07 096 51387 (AAO Jan. 26, 2009) (allowing funds used to purchase land to be counted as invested capital because land was transferred to corporation listed as commercial enterprise).

[32] *Matter of [name not provided]*, WAC 00 070 50236 (AAO Apr. 21, 2005).

be generating employment. When this has not been done, the following arguments may be available.

In certain industries, such as farming, where land is traditionally held separately from the operating entity, practitioners may argue that the law recognizes specific industry traditions in which farming operations are so closely entwined with the land that the separately owned assets are deemed a part of the same enterprise and subject to risk if the operating business fails.[33] In this situation the farmer owns both the land and the operating farm business and bears the risk of failure, regardless of the formal ownership structure.

Federal law has recognized this distinct situation and granted exceptions for farmers where the ownership structure of their business would otherwise prevent them from acquiring the same benefits available only where one business entity was involved. For example, the Tax Code's estate tax provisions provide that family members renting land to their wholly owned farming corporations have one enterprise because in doing so they necessarily retain the risks of farming.[34]

Similarly, under the FLSA, courts have long recognized that wage and hour claims against farming operations cannot turn on the technicalities of corporate organization because separate entities can be "uniquely integrated into [an] overall agricultural enterprise."[35] Likewise, when the same people own a farming corporation and a partnership that leases its land to the corporation, the two entities are a "single agricultural enterprise," allowing the corporation to claim an agricultural exception to overtime wage and hour claims even though employees work on the partnership's land.[36] Such entities are so intertwined and interrelated that courts have concluded they comprise a single agricultural enterprise.[37]

Despite the position of USCIS in the EB-5 context that a corporation is a separate and distinct entity from its owners and may petition for the owners, USCIS has recently taken a different position in the H-1B context. On January 8, 2010, USCIS issued a memo stating that a corporation owned by the foreign national H-1B visa applicant is not distinct from the owner and the owner has no employer-employee relationship with the corporation.[38] If this policy stands, and it is legally questionable at best,[39] one may argue that USCIS has an inconsistent standard by piercing the corporate veil for H-1B sole owners, yet for EB-5 purposes, maintaining that a sole-owner corporation is a separate, distinct entity from its owners. It is irrational for USCIS to maintain two contrary standards toward sole-owner corporations for H-1B and EB-5 purposes. Irrational decisions are arbitrary and capricious and often found by courts to be illegal.[40]

---

[33] *See, e.g.*, K. Esch & P. Spaccarotella, "Limited Liability Companies as an Alternative Choice of Entity for Farming and Ranching Operations in the State of Nebraska," 28 Creighton L. Rev. 19, 31 (1994) (discussing strategies for farmers when incorporating a farm, including retaining ownership of the land and leasing it to the farming corporation that the farmer owns); *see also* Note, "Tax Consequences for Owners of Farmland: Why Land Owners Who Rent Their Land to Farming Employers are Probably Liable for Self-Employment Tax on Rent Received and Why Congress Should Change the Current Policy," 76 N.D. L. Rev. 605, 628 (2000) (advocating change in self-employment tax policy to recognize the distinctive roles of an individual farmer, who may individually own farmland and also hold shares in a farm corporation); Pennsylvania Center for Farm Transitions, Pennsylvania Dep't of Agriculture, Business Structures and Strategies 4, *available at* www.iplantofarm.com/resources.aspx (last visited Feb. 8, 2010) (follow "Business Structures and Strategies" hyperlink) ("Once the decision to incorporate has been made, however, a very important issue that will need addressing will be which property to incorporate. Does one incorporate every asset that the farm owns or should it be split, holding in the operational assets and leaving out the land capital? Including just the operating assets is the most common method.").

[34] *See* Treas. Reg. §20.2032A-3(b)(1); *Minter v. United States*, 19 F.3d 426, 427, 429 (8th Cir. 1994); *see generally* 26 USC §2032A(c)(1)(B).

[35] *Wirtz v. Jackson & Perkins Co.*, 312 F.2d 48, 50 (2d Cir. 1963); *see Ares v. Manuel Diaz Farms, Inc.*, 318 F.3d 1054, 1057–58 (11th Cir. 2003); *De La Cruz v. Gill Corn Farms, Inc.*, 2005 U.S. Dist. LEXIS 44676, at *2, 11–2 (N.D.N.Y. 2005).

[36] *De La Cruz*, 2005 U.S. Dist. LEXIS 44676, at *11–2; *see also see Dofflemyer v. NLRB*, 206 F.2d 813, 814 (9th Cir. 1953) (packing and storage plant owned by partnership comprised of three farmers to handle crops from their separate farms was still part of the separate farming operations).

[37] *See Farmers Reservoir & Irrigation Co. v. McComb*, 337 U.S. 755, 767–8 (1949).

[38] USCIS Memorandum, D. Neufeld, "Determining Empoyer-Employee Relationship for Adjudication of H-1B Petitions, Including Third-Party Site Placements" (Jan. 8, 2010), *published on* AILA InfoNet at Doc. No. 10011363 (*posted* Jan. 13, 2010).

[39] *See* Memorandum from AILA's USCIS Liaison Committee to USCIS's Chief Counsel (Jan. 26, 2010), *published on* AILA InfoNet at Doc. No. 10012760 (*posted* Jan. 27, 2010).

[40] *See* 5 USC §706(2)(A); *INS v. Yueh-Shaio Yang*, 519 U.S. 26, 32 (1996); *Virk v. INS*, 295 F.3d 1055, 1059 (9th Cir. 2002).

Classification of the Capital Investment as a Shareholder Loan

A problem may arise for immigrant investors when accountants, acting according to accounting standards and in an effort to afford clients the maximum flexibility in business operations, characterize equity capital as loans to the enterprise.

Although the regulations allow for many types of evidence to establish an immigrant investor's capital investment, Schedule L of the commercial entity's federal tax returns will weigh heavily in its evaluations. Schedule L is part of the tax returns that corporations and partnerships must file, and is like a balance sheet of the corporation.

For immigrant investors, two of the most important lines in the Schedule L are the lines providing the company's capital stock and additional paid-in capital. USCIS considers these lines as reflecting the immigrant investor's contribution of capital. However, the line for capital stock typically does not reflect the immigrant investor's actual contribution to the company. Instead, it usually only provides the par value of the company's stock, which is the stock's theoretical, minimum value. Because setting par value high limits corporate flexibility in pricing the stock and may increase corporate taxes in certain states, corporations have incentive to set it very low, such as a penny per share or less (and some states do not require any par value at all). If the capital stock amount is merely its par value, an immigrant investor's actual contribution must be noted elsewhere. Accountants may classify it as either additional paid-in capital or a shareholder loan.

A problem arises for immigrant investors when accountants classify their contributions as shareholder loans, because an EB-5 investor must contribute capital to the enterprise—not loan it funds.[41] Even if Schedule L lists the funds as a loan, the funds may not in fact be shareholder loans because the shareholder does not expect repayment or is willing to forego it to maintain the health of the business, a situation that is likely when the shareholder is the primary owner of a small corporation. Nonetheless, this classification is fairly common for tax purposes—to reduce taxes, give the shareholder more flexibility to withdraw the money, or for other reasons.[42] In such cases, the capital contribution may appear in full or in part on the line titled "Loans from Shareholders."

In this situation, an accountant's goal will be at cross-purposes with an immigrant investor's goal of establishing and maintaining a capital contribution. Shareholder loans are not an investment because they are a debt arrangement under 8 CFR §204.6(e). Once an immigrant investor's capital contribution has been classified as a "shareholder loan," USCIS may reject explanations that the funds are actually a capital investment and were simply booked as a loan by mistake or for tax purposes.[43] USCIS may rely on the amount of capital stock and additional paid-in capital as the immigrant investor's capital contribution.

If, however, at the time an I-829 is prepared it appears that the immigrant investor's capital contribution has been misclassified on the Schedule L, then tax law may afford the immigrant investor the opportunity to amend his tax returns within three years.

Counsel may also be able to argue that the immigrant investor's contribution was legally a capital contribution and not a loan, regardless of what is said on the Schedule L. For example, in the Sixth Circuit,[44] an advance from a shareholder to a corporation is a capital contribution, regardless of how it is classified on a tax return, when the objective facts establish that the shareholder did not intend to create

---

[41] *Matter of Soffici*, 22 I&N Dec. 158, 162 (Assoc. Comm'r, Examinations 1998); 8 CFR §204.6(e).

[42] Accounting rules may govern when shareholder contributions can be classified as loans versus capital stock, and accountants themselves may disagree on the benefits and disadvantages of doing so. *See, e.g., www.taxalmanac.org/index.php/Discussion:S_CORP--Loan_from_Shareholder_vs._Capital_Contribution%3F* (last visited Feb. 3, 2010); *http://www.taxalmanac.org/index.php/Discussion:APIC_vs._S/H_Loans_-_Am_I_wrong%3F_(S-Corp)* (last visited Feb. 3, 2010). However, such discussions are beyond the scope of this article.

[43] *See, e.g., Matter of [name not provided]*, WAC 07 229 54388 (AAO Apr. 27, 2009) (rejecting argument that shareholder loan was actually capital); *Matter of [name not provided]*, WAC 00 070 50236 (AAO Apr. 21, 2005) (refusing to count shareholder loan as capital, especially when tax returns show it was repaid).

[44] When determining whether money advanced by a shareholder is a loan or not, the federal circuit law where the case arose governs. *See Matter of K–S–*, 20 I&N Dec. 715, 719–20 (BIA 1996) (listing cases) (noting a federal agency's obligation to follow the law of a circuit court but not a district court); *cf. Jama v. Immigration & Customs Enforcement*, 543 U.S. 335, 351 n.10 (2005) (noting that the BIA follows the law of the circuit where an individual case arises).

an unconditional obligation for the corporation to repay the advances.[45] This determination is based on the following factors: (1) the lack of any loan instruments indicating indebtedness; (2) the lack of a fixed maturity date and repayment schedule; (3) the lack of a fixed rate of interest and interest payments; (4) the lack of any security for the advances; (5) the lack of any sinking fund to provide repayments; (6) the source of repayments; (7) the inadequacy of capitalization; (8) the extent to which the advances were used to acquire capital assets; (9) the inability of the corporation to obtain other financing; (10) the identity of the creditor's and the stockholder's interests; and (11) the extent to which the advances were subordinated to the claims of outside creditors. The less a shareholder's advance resembles an arm's-length transaction, the less likely it is a loan.[46]

These factors worked in favor of the immigrant investor in *Steenblik v. Chertoff*. The dairy farmer's corporate tax return Schedule L showed that his cash advances to his S-corporation were loans that had been paid back, albeit sporadically and in varying amounts. The immigrant investor argued that he never intended to recoup that advance until the farm was sold. He submitted a declaration stating that he had designated it as a "shareholder loan" only upon the advice of his accountants. An expert witness in accounting explained that designating funds as "loans from shareholders" is merely an accounting technique to balance the entry showing an assignment of assets into the corporation. The immigrant investor's cash advance was hardly an arm's length transaction given that the immigrant investor and his wife were the sole owners of the corporation. Further, the varying payments the dairy farm corporation subsequently made to them—which never exceeded retained earnings and profits—had all the characteristics of dividends, and none of loan repayments.

When dealing with accounting issues and other areas requiring technical knowledge, expert witnesses may provide assistance, not only by ensuring that counsel understands the immigrant investor's position, but also by providing evidence and explaining it to USCIS.[47] Similarly, those within the banking industry can often provide simple explanations of terms that may otherwise be easily misconstrued. In one recent case, USCIS misunderstood the term "credit memo" to represent a line of credit. A letter from a banking official involved in the transaction clarified that a "credit memo" is actually an asset owned by a company free of any financial obligation, not a line of credit.[48] Online business dictionaries confirm that a "credit memo" or a "credit note" is a form or letter sent by a seller to a buyer, stating that a certain amount has been credited to the buyer's account, and that it is issued in various situations to correct a mistake, such as when: (1) an invoice amount is overstated; (2) correct discount rate is not applied; (3) goods spoil within guaranty period; or (4) they do not meet the buyer's specifications and are returned.

Employment Creation

An I-829 petition must include evidence establishing that the immigrant investor's capital created 10 full-time jobs for qualifying employees (individuals who are authorized to work). The regulations merely state that such evidence "may" include payroll records, tax documents, and I-9 forms.[49] Nonetheless, as a matter of practice for all I-829 petitions based on direct employment, USCIS requires the state payroll tax returns filed by the commercial enterprise, I-9 forms, and passports, employment authorization cards, lawful permanent resident cards, naturalization certificates or other documentation establishing that the 10 employees are authorized to work. Although a commercial enterprise will probably be able to provide I-9 forms, it may not be able to provide the documentation that the employees are authorized to work. Employers are not required to keep this infor-

---

[45] See *Roth Steel Tube Co. v. Comm'r*, 800 F.2d 625, 630 (6th Cir. 1986).

[46] *Indmar Products*, 444 F.3d at 777. A professor at Eastern Michigan University has written an interesting article addressing the converse problem from an accountant's point of view. This article discusses the law in other circuits as well. See L. Burilovich, "Planning Techniques to Avoid the Reclassification of Shareholder Debt as Equity," *available at* www.thefreelibrary.com/Planning+techniques+to+avoid +the+reclassification+of+shareholder+debt-a0155919006 (last visited Feb. 3, 2010).

---

[47] See generally, *Hong Kong T.V. Video Program, Inc. v. Ilchert*, 685 F. Supp. 712, 717 (N.D. Cal. 1988) (taking expert testimony as true where the government failed to question the expert's qualifications or contradict his testimony).

[48] *Matter of D–L–*, A [numbers withheld], Respondent's Prehearing Statement and Motion for Judgment on the Pleadings (Seattle Immigr. Ct. Sept. 13, 2007), filed by Attorney Robert Gibbs.

[49] 8 CFR §216.6(a)(4)(iv).

mation on file.[50] Moreover, once employees show this documentation to the enterprise so that an I-9 form can be completed, no law requires the employee to provide it again. Arguably, it is a violation of the Immigration Reform and Control Act to require documents not offered by the employee if the offered documents meet I-9 requirements.

Another problem arises if the I-9 forms are not correctly completed. Often these forms contain errors that are easily made when the forms are filled out quickly. Improper documents may be used to establish identity or employment authorization. Submission of incorrect I-9 forms to USCIS all but asks for an I-9 audit by U.S. Immigration and Customs Enforcement (ICE). These audits can result in penalties for the commercial enterprise.

At the I-526 stage, the immigrant investor should be made aware of the importance of maintaining proper I-9 forms and supporting documentation and may wish to enroll in the government's E-Verify program to ensure the enterprise's workers are legal. However, to the extent that an I-829 denial rests on the failure to produce documentation of work authorization or proper I-9 forms, counsel may argue in court that USCIS has no authority to force the immigrant investor to produce documentation that he or she has no legal right to obtain. Regarding I-9 forms, counsel may argue that requiring their production essentially enables the Department of Homeland Security to conduct an I-9 audit without following the requisite procedure, as provided in 8 CFR §274a.9.

Also, it may be wise to advise investors to use the E-Verify system when hiring workers and keep the records for the I-829.

CONCLUSION

Despite the lack of any appeal process, immigrant investors are not without avenues for relief to win reversal of I-829 denials. Strategic use of motion practice and the availability of federal court review can afford immigrant investors redress, and strong arguments remain for overcoming many grounds of I-829 denials.

---

[50] *See* Form I-9 Employment Eligibility Verification instructions at 1.

Martin Lawler, Esq. (CA State Bar No.: 77127)
LAWLER & LAWLER
50 Francisco Street, Suite 118
San Francisco, CA 94133
Tel: (415) 391-2010
Fax: (415) 781-6181
Attorney for Plaintiffs

UNITED STATES DISTRICT COURT FOR THE
CENTRAL DISTRICT OF CALIFORNIA

Herman A. STEENBLIK,
Elsken N. STEENBLIK,
Johanna STEENBLIK,
Derkje STEENBLIK,
Elsken A. STEENBLIK;
    Plaintiffs,
vs.
The United States of America; Michael CHERTOFF, Secretary, U.S. Dept. of Homeland Security; Jonathan SCHARFEN, Acting Director, U.S. Citizenship & Immigration Services; Christina POULOS, Director, U.S. Citizenship & Immigration Service, California Service Center;
    Defendants.
	Case No.:
	COMPLAINT FOR DECLARATORY JUDGMENT[51]

PRELIMINARY STATEMENT

1. This is a civil action brought under 28 U.S.C. §2201(a) (Declaratory Judgment) and 5 U.S.C. §701 *et seq.* (Administrative Procedure Act), which accord this Court jurisdiction over this action. In addition, this Court has jurisdiction under 28 U.S.C. §§1331 and 1346(a)(2) because this action challenges federal administrative agency policies, procedures and legal interpretations as being arbitrary, capricious and *ultra vires* of the law, particularly the Immigration and Nationality Act, related agency regulations, and the due process guarantees of the U.S. Constitution.

---

[51] This Complaint was drafted primarily by Hope M. Frye, Esq.

2. Plaintiff Herman Steenblik is a dairy farmer from the Netherlands. Sixteen years ago he sold his Dutch dairy farm and home and used the proceeds to purchase a half-a-million-dollar dairy farm in Pewamo, Michigan.

3. Plaintiff and his wife structured ownership of their dairy farm in a way common to many family farms – they own the operational assets as sole shareholders of a small corporation and own the farmland and buildings in their own names.

4. Plaintiff obtained a temporary work visa and began expanding his Michigan farm. He then filed an Immigrant Petition by Alien Entrepreneur (Form I-526). The purpose of the Form I-526 is to petition the U.S. Citizenship and Immigration Service (USCIS) for immigrant status as an investor in a commercial enterprise.

5. Through the I-526 petition and its attachments, Plaintiff proved that he had invested more than $500,000 in an enterprise which would benefit the U.S. economy and that the business would create 10 full-time jobs.

6. Defendant granted Plaintiff's Form I-526 on September 20, 2001. Approval of the Form I-526 proves that the investment described in the petition is qualifying under the legislation and regulations and will support a grant of conditional permanent residence (if the individual and his family are otherwise admissible).

7. Based on their I-526 approval, Plaintiff and his family filed applications for Adjustment of Status, Forms I-485, and were granted conditional permanent residence on October 15, 2004.

8. Plaintiff and his wife continued to expand the dairy. Today they own 376 acres and 3,726 cows. They rent 2,489 additional acres to grow feed for the cows. The dairy is valued at over $19 million.

9. On November 22, 2006, Plaintiff filed a Petition by Entrepreneur to Remove the Conditions (Form I-829) seeking removal of the conditional nature of his and his family's immigration status so they could become full permanent residents.

10. This action challenges Defendants' denial of their Form I-829. This denial has resulted in Plaintiffs' complete loss of legal status, loss of the right to remain here to operate their business, and potential inability to maintain the dairy farm while they remain here seeking legal recourse.

11. Plaintiffs seek declaratory judgment relief under 5 U.S.C. §706(2) (Administrative Procedure Act) and 28 U.S.C. §2201 (Declaratory Judgment Act) that as a matter of law they are entitled to approval of the Form I-829 and to full, unconditional permanent residence in the United States as mandated by the Immigration and Nationality Act (INA) of 1990 §§216A(c)(3)(A)–(C) and (d)(1), 8 U.S.C. §§1186b(c)(3)(A)–(C) and (d)(1), and USCIS regulations at 8 C.F.R. §216.6.

JURISDICTION

12. The court has jurisdiction over the subject matter of this action pursuant to 28 U.S.C. §§1331 (federal question jurisdiction) and 1346(a)(2) (Tucker Act: United States as a defendant) under the laws of the United States, particularly the Immigration and Nationality Act and related agency regulations. In addition, this Court has jurisdiction under 28 U.S.C. §2201(a) (Declaratory Judgment Act) and 5 U.S.C. §701 *et seq.* (the Administrative Procedure Act).

13. Plaintiffs have exhausted their administrative remedies. They made multiple motions to re-open and requests for reconsideration (none of which are required), as well as other requests of Defendants to grant their Form I-829. Plaintiffs have no right to any other administrative remedies to redress the grievances described in this Complaint.

14. Although the Form I-829 can be reviewed in removal proceedings (seeking Plaintiffs' deportation) under INA §216A(b)(2), 8 U.S.C. §1186b(b)(2) and 8 C.F.R. §216.6(d)(2), such a remedy is inadequate and not efficacious as the Immigration Court lacks jurisdiction over the basic issue in this case – whether Defendants have the right to re-adjudicate the Form I-526 once approved (absent fraud or misrepresentation).

15. Plaintiffs have no access to removal proceedings. Although the first denial was over a year ago, Defendants have not initiated removal proceedings. It is well settled that the Defendants may or may not begin removal proceedings, as that decision is solely within their discretion.

16. Removal proceedings are not designed to develop an adequate record for judicial review, which includes issues beyond the evidence supporting Plaintiff's Form I-829. These issues include whether Defendants: (a) applied the wrong standard of proof to Plaintiff's I-829; (b) failed to follow Ninth Circuit law; (c) violated Constitutional due process requirements and (d) failed to comply with the APA and Defendants' own regulations.

17. Pursuant to INA §216A(c)(3)(B), 8 U.S.C. §1186b(c)(3)(B), the denial of Plaintiff's Form I-829 for which judicial review is sought is not a discretionary decision. Therefore, jurisdictional limitations under INA §242(a)(2)(b)(ii), 8 U.S.C. §1252(a)(2)(b)(ii), and 5 U.S.C. §701(a) do not apply.

VENUE

18. Venue lies in the Central District of California under 28 U.S.C. §1391(e)(1), as this is an action against officers and employees of the United States acting in their official capacities, brought in the district where one of the Defendants resides. Defendant Poulos performs a significant amount of her official duties and maintains her office in Laguna Niguel, California.

19. Venue also properly lies within the Central District of California pursuant to 28 U.S.C. §1391(e)(2), as the events giving rise to the Plaintiffs' claims occurred in this district, *i.e.*, at Defendant Poulos's office in Laguna Niguel, California, which issued the denial of Plaintiff Steenblik's Form I-829.

THE PARTIES

20. Plaintiffs to this action are Herman A. Steenblik, an individual immigrant investor, his wife, Elsken N. Steenblik, and their children, Johanna, Derkje, and Elsken. Plaintiff's wife and children derive their immigration status from him.

21. Defendant Chertoff is the Secretary of the Department of Homeland Security (DHS), whose office address is DHS, 245 Murray Lane, Building 410, SW, Washington, DC 20528. He is sued in his official capacity.

22. Defendant Scharfen is the Director of USCIS, a subdivision of DHS, whose office address is USCIS, 20 Massachusetts Avenue, NW, Washington, DC 20529. He is sued in his official capacity.

23. Defendant Poulos is the Director of the USCIS California Service Center, whose office address is 24000 Avila Road, Laguna Niguel, CA 92677. She is sued in her official capacity.

STATUTORY AND REGULATORY FRAMEWORK
The Immigrant Investor Law

24. In 1990, Congress enacted the Immigrant Investor Law, INA §203(b)(5), 8 U.S.C. §1153(b)(5), creating a fifth employment-based visa category for foreign nationals who have invested, or are in the process of investing, a designated amount of lawfully obtained capital in commercial enterprises that will benefit the United States economy and create 10 or more jobs. This category is known as "EB-5." Under this law, qualified immigrant investors may obtain permanent residence in the United States for themselves and their dependents.

25. The law is intended to attract foreign capital; encourage economic development, especially in depressed areas; promote job creation or job retention; and generally benefit the United States economy and labor market.

26. The law made 10,000 immigrant visas available for qualified foreign nationals who invest in a "commercial enterprise" and create employment. To qualify, the foreign national must invest or be actively in the process of investing $1 million. When the investment is made in a "targeted employment area" the amount is reduced to $500,000. The foreign national must also demonstrate that the investment creates full-time employment for no fewer than 10 U.S. workers. INA §203(b)(5), 8 U.S.C. §1153(b)(5).

27. Defendant's regulations at 8 C.F.R. §204.6 interpret the law and provide the definitions for deciding a Form I-526.

The Process for Obtaining Permanent Residence

28. The application for an EB-5 immigrant investor visa begins with the filing of a Form I-526 (Immigrant Petition by Alien Entrepreneur) with supporting documentation. The documents must include a detailed overall investment plan and proof that the required amount of capital is at risk in a commercial enterprise for the purpose of generating a return. 8 C.F.R. §204.6(j).

29. Documents establishing that the investor has placed capital at risk include, but are not limited to, bank statements showing amounts deposited by the investor in the enterprise's accounts and/or evidence of

assets which have been purchased for use in the U.S. enterprise (which includes invoices and sales receipts). 8 C.F.R. §204.6(j)(2).

30. Defendant USCIS's Service Center at Laguna Vista, California, adjudicates the Form I-526. If Defendant USCIS determines the immigrant investor has established a qualifying investment (*i.e.*, is entitled to EB-5 status), the Form I-526 is approved and a Notice of Approval generated.

31. Once the Form I-526 is approved, the immigrant investor may obtain "conditional" permanent resident status by filing an Application to Register Permanent Residence or Adjust Status, Form I-485, if residing in the United States, or by applying for an immigrant visa at an American Consulate if residing abroad.

32. Within 90 days of the second anniversary of the grant of conditional residence, the immigrant investor must file a Form I-829 (Petition by Entrepreneur to Remove Conditions) to terminate the conditional nature of the permanent resident status.

33. If the immigrant investor fulfills the investment plan submitted with his previously approved Form I-526, sustains this investment for two years, and creates 10 jobs, Defendants must approve the Form I-829 (absent any fraud or material misrepresentation). *Chang v. INS*, 327 F.3d 911, 927 (9th Cir. 2003); *see* INA §§216A(c)(3)(A)–(B) and (d)(1), 8 U.S.C. §§1186b(c)(3)(A)–(B) and (d)(1); *compare* 8 C.F.R. §204.6(j) *with* 8 C.F.R. §§216.6(a)(4) and (c)(1).

34. The decision on the Form I-829 is *not* a readjudication of whether the investor's investment and creation of a commercial enterprise satisfies EB-5 requirements.

35. The documentary requirements at 8 C.F.R. §216.6(a)(4) for the Form I-829 are minimal because similar but more substantial documentation must be presented at the first stage of the process in connection with the Form I-526.

36. Upon approval of the Form I-829, the investor's conditional status is removed and the investor becomes a full permanent resident of the United States. USCIS shall decide the Form I-829 within the later of 90 days of the date of filing the Form I-829 or within 90 days of an interview, unless the interview is waived. 8 C.F.R. §216.6(c).

STATEMENT OF THE CASE

37. In 1994, after selling his dairy farm and home in the Netherlands, Plaintiff made the first of four wire transfers, depositing $743,847 to his U.S. account. He purchased a dairy farm in Pewamo, Michigan, now called "Steenblik Dairy." Plaintiff and his wife wholly own the dairy farm. The U.S. Consul in Amsterdam issued nonimmigrant visas to the family to allow them to live temporarily in the United States to run their dairy farm.

38. Plaintiff filed Form I-526 based on his investment in the dairy farm. Plaintiff provided an investment plan for his dairy farm and proof that his capital investment in the dairy farm was in excess of $500,000. He submitted real estate closing statements and a money transfer showing a cash contribution of $504,900, which included a cash down payment of $154,900. He also provided checks, and invoices documenting another cash contribution of $74,982.50 for farm equipment, construction, and other farm needs. Wire transfers in 1994 and early 1995 established that these contributions were part of a total of $858,795 that Steenblik brought from the Netherlands after selling his Dutch farm there. All of Steenblik's investment originated in these wire transfers. He had no other capital.

39. Defendants approved the Form I-526 on September 20, 2001. The approval established that the investment is qualifying under the EB-5 legislation and regulations. Plaintiffs then filed their Forms I-485 applications for permanent residence. Based on the approved Form I-526, Defendants granted Plaintiff and his family conditional permanent resident status on October 15, 2004.

40. Plaintiff rapidly expanded his dairy in reliance on: (1) the approval of Form I-526; (2) the grant of conditional permanent resident status; and (3) Defendants' rules, interpretations, and procedures concerning the EB-5 category.

41. On November 22, 2006, Plaintiff filed a Form I-829 to remove the conditions on permanent residence for himself and his family. He attached proof that he still owned and operated the farm, had expanded it and increased the value to over $19 million. He also documented that he created more than 10 jobs.

42. On July 23, 2007, Defendant USCIS denied Plaintiff's Form I-829. The bases for the denial are issues that only involve the original investment. These issues were covered by the approved Form I-526.

43. Plaintiff filed a motion to reopen or reconsider which Defendants denied on December 3, 2007.

44. Plaintiff again moved to reopen or reconsider on December 27, 2007, and submitted additional evidence. This evidence included expert testimony from Geoffrey Kulik, CPA, explaining certain tax and accounting issues and establishing that under normal rules of accounting and usual business practices, and considering Defendant's regulatory definition of "invest," Plaintiff had invested over $858,781 in his dairy farm in 1994 and 1995. This was proved by documents which had been submitted with the Form I-526. Kulik also calculated Plaintiff's total investment as $4.7 million as of 2006, not including debts and retained earnings.

45. Defendants agreed to reopen the case, but then denied the Form I-829 again on February 25, 2008. Plaintiff moved to reopen and reconsider this latest decision on March 26, 2008. Defendants agreed to reconsider the case and ultimately denied the Form I-829 a fourth time on August 11, 2008.

46. Defendants' final denial concluded that Plaintiff was ineligible for the original grant of conditional permanent resident status. The denial has three bases:

(a) the alleged failure of Plaintiff to document the source of the 1994 cash payments of $154,900 and $74,982.50, which he used to purchase farmland, pay for crop expansion, and pay off a chattel mortgage crop loan. Defendants claim that Plaintiff did not submit evidence to show that the funds had originated from him and not from the retained earnings of the farm;

(b) the alleged failure of the record to clearly show whether the $154,900 and $74,982.50 originated from Plaintiff or from loans made to Plaintiff and secured by the assets of the dairy farm; and

(c) the alleged failure of prior counsel's cover letter dated June 8, 2007, and an accountant's reconciliation letter for the tax period of 1994 to 2005 to establish that the claimed investment originated from Plaintiff and not retained earnings from the farm.

47. By relying on the grounds listed above to deny Plaintiff's Form I-829, Defendants revoked the approval of the Form I-526 without going through the mandatory revocation procedures at 8 C.F.R. §103.5(a)(5)(ii).

48. Moreover, Defendants conducted a *de novo* review of the Form I-526 and reached conclusions that conflict with their decision on that petition. Defendants' conclusion that Plaintiff failed to document whether the $154,900 and $74,982.50 originated from him or from loans made to him conflicts with Defendants' approval of the Form I-526. In approving the Form I-526, Defendants implicitly concluded that the capital Plaintiff had already invested in 1994, including the two amounts at issue, was not from a loan made to Plaintiff. In any event, Defendants' conclusion that Plaintiff had "not adequately documented the source of funds" was unlawful because the Defendants may only inquire into an investor's source of funds when adjudicating an I-526 petition and not an I-829 petition to remove conditions. *Compare* 8 C.F.R. §§204.6(j) *and* (j)(3)(iii) (requiring proof of lawful source of funds) *with* 8 C.F.R. §216.6 (containing no requirement that an investor demonstrate the source of funds).

49. Defendants applied an improperly stringent standard of proof by requiring the record to be "clear" as to whether the $154,900 and $74,982.50 originated from Plaintiff or from loans made to him. The proper standard is whether a preponderance of the evidence in the record shows that the claimed investments originated from Plaintiff or from loans made to him.

50. The bank letter dated September 27, 2006, cited in Defendants' final denial of the Form I-829 refers only to bank loans given in 2006, not 12 years earlier, when Plaintiff invested the two amounts of capital at issue.

51. The reconciliation letter that Defendants cite does not address the tax period from 1994 to 2005. It only addresses the tax period from 1997 to 2000, well after Plaintiff invested the amounts of capital at issue. It also does not address retained earnings as alleged by Defendants.

52. Defendants' decision ignores CPA Kulik's expert testimony confirming that Plaintiff sustained his capital investment in his dairy farm from 2004 to 2006, and that the farm's Schedule L tax return could not reflect Plaintiff's entire investment, because some of the farm's assets were not corporate-owned,

but instead were personally owned by the Plaintiffs. The denial also fails to consider other evidence of Plaintiffs' investment in their dairy farm.

53. At the very least, Plaintiff made and sustained a capital investment of more than $500,000 in his dairy farm through his two 1994 capital contributions of $154,900 and $74,982.50 and the capital stock and additional paid-in capital of $271,688.

54. Defendants also failed to consider Plaintiff's additional investment of $61,128 in the form of cash to pay off a crop mortgage in early 1995 and $17,645 in the form of installment payments for farmland pursuant to a land contract. Both of these contributions were made before Steenblik had any retained earnings or secured loans that could have been the source of these contributions.

55. Plaintiff honestly presented all aspects of his case. Defendants have never taken issue with his veracity or the authenticity of the evidence used to support the Form I-526 or Form I-829.

56. Plaintiff successfully executed the plan set out in Form I-526 and Defendants, in their August 11, 2008, decision, did not state otherwise.

57. Due to Defendants denial of Plaintiff's Form I-829, Plaintiff and his family have suffered irreparable loss and extreme emotional distress. Plaintiffs are deeply worried that their banks will not renew the loans needed to run the farm because of their uncertain immigration status. If the banks refuse to issue and reissue farm and crop loans, the farm will collapse.

58. If Plaintiff's Form I-829 denial is left standing, Plaintiff and his family stand to lose the family farm and creditworthiness established through 14 years of hard work. In this difficult economic time, this would amount to an irrational and draconian punishment.

CAUSES OF ACTION

Count I: Arbitrary and Capricious in Violation of the Administration Procedure Act

59. Plaintiffs incorporate paragraphs 1 through 58 as if fully stated in this Count.

60. Defendants' practices, policies, interpretations of law, and conduct violate the Administrative Procedure Act (APA), and should be set aside under 5 U.S.C. §706(2)(A) as arbitrary, capricious and other-

wise not in accordance with law and under 5 U.S.C. §706(2)(D) as without observance of procedure required by law.

61. Defendants' denial of Plaintiff's Form I-829 violates the APA because it readjudicates matters already approved in Defendants' decision on the Form I-526.

62. Defendants' denial of Plaintiff's Form I-829 is arbitrary and capricious in that it is not supported by substantial evidence.

63. Defendants' denial of Plaintiff's Form I-829 improperly applied a "clear and convincing" standard of proof instead of the requisite "preponderance of the evidence" standard.

64. The regulation at 8 C.F.R. §216.6 requires Defendants to conclude that an investor has sustained his capital investment when he has, in good faith, substantially met the investment requirement of the statute and maintained that investment during two years of conditional residence, and created 10 jobs. Defendants do not take issue with this. Rather, they deny the Form I-829 solely because they now decide that Plaintiff's paperwork supporting the Form I-526 was not entirely complete.

65. Through the denial, Defendants revoked the prior approval of the Form I-526 without following their revocation procedures at 8 C.F.R. 103.5(a)(5)(ii).

66. The denial ignores the testimony of Plaintiff's certified public accountant. A decision which ignores probative testimony is arbitrary and capricious.

Count II: Exceeding Statutory Authority

67. Plaintiffs incorporate paragraphs 1 through 58 as if fully stated in this Count.

68. Defendants' review of the Form I-829 is limited by law to whether the investor has executed the investment plan proposed in his approved Form I-526, sustained the required investment in his commercial enterprise for his two years of conditional residence, and created 10 jobs, and whether he made any material misrepresentations that would require revocation of Form I-526 approval through a formal revocation process described at 8 C.F.R. §103.5(a)(5)(ii). The decision on the Form I-829 is not a readjudication of the investment plan, source of funds, or any other matter covered by the Form I-526 process. *Chang v. INS*, 327 F.3d 911, 927 (9th Cir. 2003); *compare* 8 C.F.R. §204.6(j) *with* 8 C.F.R. §§216.6(a)(4) and (c)(1). Therefore

in their denial, Defendants have acted *ultra vires* of the law at INA §§216A(c)(3)(A)–(C) and (d)(1), 8 U.S.C. §§1186b(c)(3)(A)–(C) and (d)(1).

Count III: Violation of Due Process

69. Plaintiffs incorporate paragraphs 1 through 58 as if fully stated in this Count.

70. Defendants' denial of the Form I-829 violates Plaintiffs' constitutional right to due process by their failure to follow the law and their own rules and procedures.

ATTORNEY'S FEES

71. As a result of the Defendants' unlawful actions, Plaintiff was required to hire counsel and pay fees and expenses. Because Defendants were not substantially justified in pursuing this action, Plaintiffs are entitled to recover legal fees and all costs and expenses under the Equal Access to Justice Act, 5 U.S.C. §504 and 28 U.S.C. §2412.

RELIEF REQUESTED

WHEREFORE, Plaintiffs respectfully request this Court enter judgment on their behalf and issue the following:

a. an order declaring that Plaintiff's capital investment in his dairy farm satisfies the requirements of INA §216A, 8 U.S.C. §1186b and the implementing regulations;

b. an order directing Defendants and their agents to promptly approve Plaintiff's Form I-829 to remove conditions from his lawful permanent resident status;

c. an order directing Defendants and their agents to immediately issue all necessary and appropriate documentation to Plaintiff and his family evidencing continuing permanent resident status and right to work in the United States;

d. an order declaring the practices of Defendants and their agents challenged here as violating the Plaintiffs' right to due process under the Constitution of the United States, the Administrative Procedure Act, the INA, and federal regulations;

e. an order directing Defendants and their agents not to consider the Plaintiffs' presence in the United States as unlawful during the period of time between the denial of Form I-829 and the disposition of this litigation;

f. an order awarding Plaintiffs their attorney's fees and costs; and

g. an order granting such other relief as the Court may deem just, equitable, and proper.

Dated: October 14, 2008

Respectfully submitted,

_____

Martin Lawler, Esq. (CA State Bar No.: 77127)
LAWLER & LAWLER
50 Francisco Street, Suite 118
San Francisco, CA 94133
Tel: (415) 391-2010
Fax: (415) 781-6181
ATTORNEY FOR PLAINTIFFS

LITIGATING THE IMMIGRANT INVESTOR'S CASE

by Ira J. Kurzban[*]

Over the past decade, the administration of the employment-based fifth preference (EB-5) immigrant investor program by legacy Immigration and Naturalization Service (INS) and U.S. Citizenship and Immigration Services (USCIS) has resulted in substantial litigation over the failure to comply with the language and spirit of the EB-5 program. The government's decision to apply unpublished rules retroactively to hapless investors caught between initially described criteria and radically altered ones has resulted in continued litigation since the late 1990s. Although the companies litigating those cases did not fare well,[1] individual investors have been quite successful in defeating the government's efforts to change the rules in midstream and deny their applications.[2] In fact, some even have won attorney's fees.[3]

Lawsuits also have been filed to force the government to adjudicate EB-5 cases. These cases have been stalled in the administrative process because USCIS, in the face of new legislation[4] and old litigation, developed administrative paralysis. As a result, individual investors, frustrated by the endless years of waiting for the adjudication of their I-526s or, more likely, their I-829s, brought actions in the form of mandamus in the federal courts. These cases were designed to seek some final resolution of their clients' investor status.[5]

More recently, litigation has challenged USCIS' position that conditional residents under the EB-5 program may not naturalize prior to the approval of their I-829 applications.[6] Other litigation has challenged the substantive criteria that USCIS uses to determine the employer-employee relationship and the methodology for indirect job creation.[7]

As in any litigation, the lawyer and client must formulate a strategy for victory that outlines the:

- Issues at stake;
- Type of litigation that is appropriate for those issues;
- Government's jurisdictional and other defenses to the litigation; and
- Likelihood of success on the merits in the venue chosen.

This article addresses each of these aspects of EB-5 litigation in an effort to encourage lawyers to bring legal action, while highlighting the pitfalls that arise in such litigation.

ISSUES LIKELY TO ARISE IN EB-5 INVESTOR CASES

The investor process is, by its nature, a four-step process. Therefore, issues can arise at each step, including when the applicant submits: (1) the initial I-526 petition to be classified in the EB-5 Green Card category; (2) the application for adjustment of status (I-485) or an immigrant visa (IV) abroad; (3) the

---

[*] **Ira Kurzban** is a partner in the Miami law firm of Kurzban, Kurzban, Weinger, Tetzeli & Pratt. Mr. Kurzban's firm has specialized in litigating immigration cases for over 30 years and he is currently litigating a number of EB-5 cases including *Chang v. U.S.*, 327 F.3d 911 (9th Cir. 2003). An honorary fellow of the University of Pennsylvania Law School, he also teaches immigration and nationality law, serving as adjunct faculty at the University of Miami School of Law and the Shepard Broad Law Center of Nova Southeastern University. He received his J.D. and M.A. from the University of California, Berkeley. Mr. Kurzban is also author of *Kurzban's Immigration Law Sourcebook*.

[1] *Spencer Enterprises Inc v. United States*, 345 F.3d 683, 693 (9th Cir. 2003); *R.L. Investment Limited Partners v. INS*, 86 F. Supp. 2d 1014 (D. Haw. 2000), *aff'd*, 273 F.3d 874 (9th Cir. 2001); *Golden Rainbow Freedom Fund v. Ashcroft*, 2001 U.S. App. LEXIS 25482 (9th Cir. Nov. 26, 2001).

[2] *Chang v. United States*, 327 F.3d 911 (9th Cir. 2003); *Sang Geun An v. United States*, Case No. C03-3184P (W.D. Wash. 2005).

[3] *Sang Geun An v. United States*, Case No. C03-3184P (W.D. Wash. Apr. 20, 2005) (order granting $54,970 in fees and costs to plaintiffs).

[4] 21st Century Department of Justice Appropriations Authorization Act (DOJ Act), Pub. L. No. 107-273, 116 Stat. 1758, Subtitle B, *published on* AILA InfoNet at Doc. No. 02110441 (*posted* Nov. 4, 2002).

[5] *Romiti v. Neufeld*, Case No. 02-CV-1161 (C.D. Cal. Dec. 17, 2002); *Arcis v. INS*, Case No. 02-CV-939 (C.D. Cal. Oct. 9, 2002).

[6] *Abghari v. Gonzales*, 596 F.Supp.2d 1336 (C.D. Cal. 2009); *Buhler v. U.S.*, Case No. CV 99-10518-GHK (C.D. Cal. 2010) (submission of Fourth Amended complaint in *Chang* litigation raising naturalization issue).

[7] *Kim v. U.S.*, Case No. 10-CV-2019 DPP (C.D. Cal. 2010); *Song v. U.S.*, Case No. 10-CV-2017-SJQ (C.D. Cal. 2010).

petition to remove his or her conditional residence (I-829); and (4) the application for naturalization. As we know from the potentially confusing language of the EB-5 statute, the latter two steps do not necessarily occur *in seriatim*. An applicant may apply for naturalization even if his or her I-829 has not been adjudicated,[8] although USCIS claims that it will not actually grant naturalization until it decides the investor's I-829 petition.

Legal actions challenging the denial of an I-526 petition raise issues typically associated with the denial of any petition, but also include some that are unique to EB-5 petitioners. For example, lawsuits have challenged unsuccessfully the application of legacy INS's changes in the regulatory criteria to approve an I-526.[9] In one case, the lower court believed that there was no estoppel bar to deny I-526 petitions when legacy INS changed the criteria for approving the petitions before they were adjudicated.[10] The U.S. Court of Appeals for the Ninth Circuit affirmed this ruling,[11] and in a separate unpublished decision, rejected a retroactivity claim brought by a company sponsoring investors.[12]

Other issues that have arisen include whether: (1) the nature of the investment comports with the EB-5 law; (2) the employees will be permanent employees; (3) the investor actually invested the full amount required under law;[13] (4) the source of the money was lawful; and (5) the business plan was credible.[14] The petitioner often faces a difficult time challenging a decision by USCIS on the merits because of the deference usually accorded the agency, as well as the substantial evidence standard of review under *INS v. Elias-Zacarias*, which requires a court to rule for the agency unless the facts "compel" a different finding.[15]

The submission of an adjustment of status application before USCIS, or an immigrant visa at the consulate abroad, typically generates a different set of issues. In these instances, the adjudicator or the consular officer no longer accepts the approved I-526 (or, for that matter, any approved petition) at face value. The officer is not precluded, in many cases, from re-examining the I-526 if he or she is inclined to do so. The officer may ask USCIS to review and, if appropriate, revoke the approved petition pursuant to Immigration and Nationality Act (INA) §205. Although the U.S. Department of State has sought to restrict consular officers' decisions to return petitions to USCIS,[16] they are not barred from doing so.[17] USCIS officers obviously also have the authority to review the bona fides of an I-526 at an adjustment interview, and to revoke the petition if they suspect wrongdoing or ineligibility.[18] How USCIS frames the revocation, and what reasons are advanced for its decision often will determine the nature of the litigation to be brought.[19]

The adjudication of the I-829 petition will raise a multitude of issues—*e.g.*, the legality of re-adjudicating the facts raised in the I-526 approval; the retroactive application of new standards to the adjudication of the I-829 petition—that were not raised in the review and approval of the I-526 petition. The retroactive application of new standards claim by the government has been flatly rejected by two courts,[20] and the former appears contrary to the regulations[21] and also has been rejected.[22]

---

[8] *See* Immigration and Nationality Act of 1952 (INA), Pub. L. No. 82-414, 66 Stat. 163 (codified as amended at 8 USC §§1101 *et seq.*), §216A(e).

[9] *R.L. Investment Limited Partners v. INS*, 86 F. Supp. 2d 1014 (D. Haw. 2000), *aff'd*, 273 F.3d 874 (9th Cir. 2001).

[10] *R.L. Investment Limited Partners*, 86 F. Supp. 2d at 1026–27.

[11] *R.L. Investment Limited Partners v. INS*, 273 F.3d 874 (9th Cir. 2001). *See also Spencer Enterprises, Inc. v. United States*, 345 F.3d 683, 693 (9th Cir. 2003).

[12] *Golden Rainbow Freedom Fund v. Ashcroft*, 2001 U.S. App. LEXIS 25482 (9th Cir. Nov. 26, 2001).

[13] *Kenkhuis v. INS*, 2003 U.S. Dist. LEXIS 3334, Case No. 3:01-CV-2224-N (N.D. Tex. Mar. 7, 2003).

[14] *See, e.g., Spencer Enterprises*, 345 F.3d at 694.

[15] *INS v. Elias-Zacarias*, 502 U.S. 478, 481 n.1 (1992).

[16] 9 *Foreign Affairs Manual* (FAM) 42.43; Guidance on Petition Revocations, 01-State-121801 (July 13, 2001), *published on* AILA InfoNet at Doc. No. 01071333 (posted July 13, 2001); *Matter of Arias*, 19 I&N Dec. 568 (BIA 1988).

[17] Guidelines and Changes for Returning DHS/BCIS Approved IV and NIV Petitions, 04-State-41682 (Feb. 25, 2004) at ¶¶6–10, *published on* AILA InfoNet at Doc. No. 04030364 (*posted* Mar. 3, 2004).

[18] 8 Code of Federal Regulations (CFR) §205.2.

[19] *Compare Matter of Estime*, 19 I&N Dec. 450 (BIA 1987), *and Matter of Arias*, 19 I&N Dec. 568 (BIA 1988), *with Ghaly v. INS*, 58 F.3d 1425, 1434 (9th Cir. 1995).

[20] *Chang v. United States*, 327 F.3d 911 (9th Cir. 2003); *Sang Geun An v. United States*, Case No. C03-3184P (W.D. Wash. 2005).

[21] 8 CFR §§216.6, 1216.6.

[22] *Chang v. United States*, 327 F.3d at 926–28.

In light of the spate of substantial memos and changes to the *Adjudicator's Field Manual* (AFM) by USCIS,[23] new issues undoubtedly will arise, including:

- What constitutes full-time employment and when do you count that employment;
- The methodology for indirect job creation;
- The employer-employee relationship;
- The nature of "material changes" in an application requiring the filing of an amended or new I-526; and
- When an "erroneously approved" I-526 warrants a denial of an I-829.

At the core of many of these issues will be litigation that determines the role of USCIS in adjudicating the I-829. Will it be a readjudication of the I-526, as USCIS seems want to do, or will it be the limited role that the statute and regulations require?

Even naturalization issues appear to creep into the EB-5 immigrant investor process. First, USCIS, in taking an aggressive posture in naturalization interviews, can review (and in effect readjudicate) any issue concerning applicants' residency, on the theory that they would be ineligible for citizenship if they illegally procured their residency.[24] Illegal procurement claims have led to substantial litigation particularly in the denaturalization of former Nazis.[25] A separate issue arises over the right to obtain citizenship even if USCIS has failed to adjudicate a pending I-829 petition. INA §216A(e) explicitly states that an immigrant investor admitted as an EB-5 conditional resident "shall be considered to have been admitted as an alien lawfully admitted for permanent residence" for naturalization purposes. Thus, a conditional resident should not have to wait years for the I-829 petition to be approved before he or she can become a naturalized U.S. citizen.[26] USCIS sought to lay the issue to rest in its August 4, 2009, memorandum,[27] asserting that an I-829 applicant cannot naturalize until the I-829 application is approved. To date, this position has been sustained in the *Abghari* decision,[28] but major litigation remains in the *Chang* class action lawsuit.[29]

THE FORM OF LITIGATION IN FEDERAL COURT

Litigation of EB-5 issues may arise in several different contexts. First, an unsuccessful applicant challenging USCIS procedures or rules to a given case may file an action in the U.S. District Court under appropriate rules of venue[30] and personal jurisdiction. These actions usually are brought under the Administrative Procedure Act (APA),[31] pursuant to federal question jurisdiction,[32] because the APA is not an independent source of jurisdiction. An APA challenge typically will seek reversal of USCIS's decision because it is "arbitrary, capricious, an abuse of discretion, or otherwise not in accordance with law,"[33] or because it is "in excess of statutory jurisdiction, authority, or limitations."[34] The former challenge will be subject to a substantial evidence standard of review;[35] the latter will be subject to de novo review because whether the agency has acted ultra vires is a question of law, and questions of law are reviewed de novo.[36] The litigation of the government's "arbitrariness" often requires a detailed study of how it has treated other similarly situated cases,[37] whether it departed from

---

[23] *See e.g.*, USCIS Memorandum, D. Neufeld, "EB-5 Alien Entrepreneurs—Job Creation and Full-Time Positions (AFM Update AD 09-04)" (June 17, 2009), *published on* AILA InfoNet at Doc. No. 09061964 (*posted* June 19, 2009); USCIS Memorandum, D. Neufeld *et al.*, "Conditional Permanent Residents and Naturalization under Section 319(b) of the Act; Revision to Adjudicator's Field Manual Chapter 25 (AFM Update AD09-28)" (Aug. 4, 2009), *published on* AILA InfoNet at Doc. No. 09080761 (*posted* Aug. 7, 2009); USCIS Memorandum, D. Neufeld, "Adjudication of EB-5 Regional Center Proposals and Affiliated Form I-526 and Form I-829 Petitions; Adjudicators Field Manual (AFM) Update to Chapters 22.4 and 25.2 (AD09-38)" (Dec. 11, 2009), *published on* AILA InfoNet at Doc. No. 09121561 (*posted* Dec. 15, 2009); AFM ch. 22.4(a)(2),(c)(3), (c)(4).

[24] *Fedorenko v. United States*, 449 U.S. 490 (1981).

[25] *Id.*

[26] *See also* 8 CFR §§216.1, 1216.1.

[27] See Aug. 4, 2009, Neufeld Memo, *supra* at note 23.

[28] *Abghari*, *supra* note 6.

[29] *Id.*

[30] 28 U.S. Code (USC) §1391 *et seq.*

[31] 5 USC §701 *et seq.*

[32] 28 USC §1331.

[33] 5 USC §706(2)(A).

[34] 5 USC §706(2)(C).

[35] *Spencer Enterprises Inc. v. United States*, 345 F.3d 683, 694 (9th Cir. 2003).

[36] *McNary v. Haitian Refugee Center*, 498 U.S. 479, 493 (1991).

[37] *Johnson v. Ashcroft*, 286 F.3d 696 (3d Cir. 2002) (finding that the Board of Immigration Appeals (BIA) inexplicably

continued

previous consistent interpretations of its rules without explanation,[38] or whether it failed to consider all relevant factors in making its determination.[39] A review of this nature also is limited to the administrative record that exists,[40] unless the record is inadequate to permit review.[41]

Litigation to determine whether the government's regulations or procedures are ultra vires, although subject to the court's de novo review, also may be subject to USCIS's deference under *Chevron USA v. Natural Resources Defense Council*.[42] However, *Chevron* deference is not unbounded, and both regulations[43] and procedures[44] may be invalidated if they are contrary to the statute. One area ripe for such litigation is USCIS's insistence on determining sufficient job creation at the I-829 stage, since the statute does not require proof of job creation at that point.[45]

Judicial review also may arise in the context of a mandamus petition to compel USCIS to adjudicate an I-526 or I-829 petition. Mandamus traditionally has been used to force the government to comply with its duty to decide a case that has remained unadjudicated for months or years.[46] To be entitled to mandamus, a party must establish that: (1) a clear and certain claim exists; (2) the duty owed is ministerial and so plainly prescribed as to be free from doubt; and (3) no other adequate remedy is available.[47] The issue in EB-5 immigrant investor cases will be whether the duty to decide a case within a particular time frame is discretionary or a clear and certain claim that is free from any doubt. Some courts have taken the view that mandamus is appropriate where USCIS or legacy INS has failed to adjudicate a petition within a reasonable period of time.[48] Others have determined that because the timing of an interview or decision is discretionary, mandamus is an inappropriate remedy.[49] However, this does not preclude an action under the APA to compel the agency to act "within a reasonable time."[50]

Another vehicle for judicial review of issues arising under the EB-5 program is through the judicial review of a removal hearing. An EB-5 investor is subject to removal if his or her status as a conditional resident investor is terminated, or if he or she is found otherwise ineligible for the removal of conditional status.[51] In the removal hearing, the investor may raise the bona fides of his or her investment, as well as any errors the agency made in terminating conditional resident status or refusing to grant permanent residency. The decision by the immigration judge (IJ), if unfavorable, may be appealed to the Board of Immigration Appeals (BIA). The BIA's decision is subject to appeal to the circuit court of appeals where the removal proceeding arose.[52] Review of the BIA's decision is subject to de novo review for errors of law, and the substantial evidence standard for issues of fact. The substantial evidence standard is established by statute,[53] and "the administrative findings of fact are conclusive unless any

---

had departed from *Matter of Patel* regarding what an immigration judge (IJ) may consider on remand).

[38] *Osei v. INS*, 305 F.3d 1205 (10th Cir. 2002); *Virk v. INS*, 295 F.3d 1055 (9th Cir. 2002).

[39] *Urban v. INS*, 123 F.3d 644 (7th Cir. 1997); *Watkins v. INS*, 63 F.3d 844, 850 (9th Cir. 1995).

[40] *Bolaton, Inc. v. Reno*, 93 F. Supp. 2d 61 (D.D.C. 2000) (claim that Administrative Appeals Unit (AAU) always affirms denials of small company L-1s is not a basis for discovery to supplement administrative record). *See also* INA §242(b)(4)(A).

[41] *See, e.g., Yang v. McElroy*, 277 F.3d 158 (2d Cir. 2002).

[42] *Chevron USA v. Natural Resources Defense Council*, 467 U.S. 837, 843–44 (1984); *INS v. Aguirre-Aguirre*, 526 U.S. 415, 424 (1999).

[43] *INS v. Cardoza-Fonseca*, 480 U.S. 421, 446 n.30 (1987) (regarding asylum interpretation); *Iavorski v. INS*, 232 F.3d 124, 133 (2d Cir. 2000) (challenge to interpretation of 90-day reopening period).

[44] *United States v. Mead Corp.*, 533 U.S. 218, 228–31 (2000) (where rules not promulgated under APA, deference is inapplicable).

[45] INA §216A(d)(1).

[46] *Jefrey v. INS*, 710 F. Supp. 486 (S.D.N.Y. 1989).

[47] *Yu v. Brown*, 36 F. Supp. 2d 922, 933–34 (D.N.M. 1999) (juvenile required to wait over two years for adjudication of special immigrant petition could file mandamus).

[48] *Jefrey v. INS*, 710 F. Supp. 486; *Yu*, 36 F. Supp. 2d 922.

[49] *Saleh v. Ridge*, 347 F. Supp. 2d 508, 511 (S.D.N.Y. 2005) (because adjustment of status is discretionary, mandamus does not lie to compel decision on adjustment application pending for five years, although action may be brought under §1331 pursuant to APA §555); *Zheng v. Reno*, 166 F. Supp. 2d 875 (S.D.N.Y. 2001) (because adjustment is discretionary, mandamus cannot be used to require the scheduling of an interview); *Rahman v. McElroy*, 884 F. Supp. 782, 786–87 (S.D.N.Y. 1995) (no duty to schedule adjustment interview for lottery winner).

[50] *Saleh*, 347 F. Supp. 2d 508.

[51] INA §237(a)(1)(D)(i).

[52] INA §§242(a)(1), (b)(2).

[53] INA §242(a)(4)(B).

reasonable adjudicator would be compelled to conclude to the contrary."[54]

An action also potentially may be brought in an immigrant investor case where USCIS failed to naturalize a conditional resident. This scenario typically arises where USCIS fails to take any action to remove conditional residency, the applicant files an application for citizenship, and the five-year time period has accrued for citizenship. Although the merits of this approach have not been the subject of any judicial scrutiny thus far, an action may be brought against USCIS when it fails to adjudicate a naturalization case within 120 days of a naturalization interview.[55]

THE GOVERNMENT'S DEFENSES TO EB-5 LITIGATION

The major problem confronting any counsel who intends to litigate against the government in an immigrant investor case is the array of jurisdictional and other defenses raised by the government. The government will often raise these defenses either in a motion to dismiss a petitioner's complaint or in a motion for summary judgment. In virtually every case, the court must first wade through numerous jurisdictional arguments before it can address the merits. *Spencer Enterprises, Inc. v. United States*[56] and *Chang v. United States*[57] are two cases in point.

In *Spencer Enterprises*, the government argued, as it has in similar cases,[58] that Congress precluded review of all discretionary decisions of USCIS when it enacted INA §242(a)(2)(B)(ii). This section provides that: "Notwithstanding any other provision of law, no court shall have jurisdiction to review . . . any . . . decision or action of the Attorney General the authority for which is specified under this subchapter to be in the discretion of the Attorney General. . . ."[59] The issue in *Spencer Enterprises* was whether legacy INS had abused its discretion and violated the INA when it denied the investor's I-526 petition. The government argued that the decision to grant or deny an employment-based petition was in the sole discretion of legacy INS and that, because it was a discretionary decision, it was barred from review in the federal courts. The Ninth Circuit disagreed. The court focused on the language in INA §242(a)(2)(B)(ii) precluding judicial review only for an action or decision "the authority for which is specified" under the statute to be in the attorney general's discretion. The court reasoned that Congress typically specified this type of broad discretionary authority in matters related to relief from removal, not as to whether a person qualifies for a particular category of residency. The statute governing the attorney general's decision to grant or deny an I-526 petition therefore was not written to vest sole discretionary authority in the attorney general and could not bar review.[60]

The Ninth Circuit's decision follows sound principles of judicial review. Under our legal system, there is a strong presumption of judicial review.[61]

---

[54] *Id.*

[55] INA §336(b).

[56] 345 F.3d 683 (9th Cir. 2003).

[57] 327 F.3d 911 (9th Cir. 2003).

[58] *Compare El-Khader v. Monica*, 366 F.3d 562, 565–67 (7th Cir. 2004) (finding that the discretionary decision bar under INA §242(a)(2)(B)(ii) is *not* limited solely to matters arising in removal, deportation, or exclusion proceeding, thereby barring judicial review of the revocation of a visa petition); *Systronics Corp. v. INS*, 153 F. Supp. 2d 7 (D.D.C. 2001) (no jurisdiction, but even if there was jurisdiction, the standard of review is highly deferential); *Ana International Inc. v. Way*, 393 F.3d 886, 893–95 (9th Cir. 2005) (following *Spencer Enterprises* and holding that INA §242(a)(2)(B)(ii) does not bar judicial review of an I-140 visa revocation of an EB-1 decision under 8 USC §1155 because the "good and sufficient cause" language of the statute provides a legal standard, as does the "managerial capacity" criteria of EB-1); *Soltane v. U.S. DOJ*, 381 F.3d 143, 146–48 (3d Cir. 2004) (following *Spencer Enterprises* in regard to special immigrant religious worker cases and finding that Congress did not intend a broad construction of the discretionary decision bar).

[59] INA §242(a)(2)(B)(ii).

[60] The Ninth Circuit in *Spencer Enterprises* noted that its interpretation is quite similar to the "committed to agency discretion" doctrine under 5 USC §701(a)(2), but nevertheless distinguished it from that limitation. 345 F.3d at 690–91.

[61] *INS v. St. Cyr*, 533 U.S. 289, 298 (2001) (in finding that habeas remained to review statutory and constitutional claims in removal proceeding, the Court stated that "[f]or the INS to prevail it must overcome both the strong presumption in favor of judicial review of administrative actions and the longstanding rule requiring a clear statement of congressional intent to repeal habeas jurisdiction"); *McNary v. Haitian Refugee Center, Inc.*, 498 U.S. 479 (1991) (pattern and practice class action litigation in U.S. district court not precluded by special agricultural worker (SAW) legalization statute); *Bowen v. Michigan Academy of Family Physicians*, 476 U.S. 667, 670 (1986); *Lindahl v. Office of Personnel Management*, 470 U.S. 768 (1985); *Dunlop v. Bachowski*, 421 U.S. 560, 571 (1975); *Barlow v. Collins*, 397 U.S. 159, 166–67 (1970); *Abbott Laboratories v. Gardner*, 387 U.S. 136 (1967); *Traynor v. Turnage*, 485 U.S. 535, 541 (1988); *Perez-Martin v. Ashcroft*, 394 F.3d 752, 757 (9th Cir. 2005)

continued

The presumption may be overturned only by clear and convincing evidence that Congress intended to strip the federal courts of review.[62] In *Spencer*, the Ninth Circuit read the statute narrowly to preserve judicial review because there was no evidence that the government's broad reading to encompass all acts of discretion was intended by Congress.[63]

The government also raises the discretionary decision bar in any challenge to an IJ's or BIA's denial of the removal of conditional residency in the course of a removal proceeding. In the marriage context, USCIS has argued that decisions concerning the removal of conditional residency are purely discretionary decisions of the agency and are barred from judicial review. The courts have split on whether the IJ's or BIA's decision is subject to judicial review. The U.S. Courts of Appeals for the Third and Fifth Circuits have decided that the lifting of conditional residency is a discretionary act, thus barring judicial review.[64] The U.S. Courts of Appeals for the First and Ninth Circuits take a more nuanced view, finding that factual determinations regarding waivers—*e.g.*, the good faith marriage waiver—are subject to review under the substantial evidence test.[65] The government undoubtedly will argue that an investor whose conditional residency is not removed may not seek review in the circuit courts of appeals, although no decision has raised this issue in the EB-5 context so far.

The government also has raised in other investor litigation the typical claims of mootness, ripeness, and failure to exhaust administrative remedies.[66] In *Chang v. United States*, the government argued that the 21st Century Department of Justice Appropriations Authorization Act (DOJ Act)[67] rendered plaintiffs' retroactivity claims moot because plaintiffs now had an alternative mechanism to obtain their residency as EB-5 immigrant investors. The court properly noted that mootness is a question of law and that the moving party carries "a heavy burden of establishing that no effective relief remains for the court to provide."[68] As the government failed to demonstrate that the new statute must grant complete relief to the plaintiffs, the court found the case was not moot.[69]

The Ninth Circuit also rejected legacy INS's exhaustion argument. The court found that Subtitle B of the DOJ Act could not be applied retroactively to impose a new filing deadline that would bar plaintiffs, on exhaustion grounds, for failing to apply in a timely fashion. Because the filing deadlines of Subtitle B could not be applied retroactively, there were no filing deadlines for plaintiffs to exhaust, so they were not barred from asserting their claims in the Ninth Circuit.

The court also dismissed the government's ripeness argument. Legacy INS argued that the retroactivity claim was not ripe because plaintiffs' I-829

(citing the strong presumption of judicial review in *McNary* and *St. Cyr* and concluding that there is jurisdiction in the circuit courts to review SAW denials); *Montero-Martinez v. Ashcroft*, 277 F.3d 1137, 1141 (9th Cir. 2002) (finding there is a strong presumption of judicial review and a longstanding principle of construing ambiguities in deportation statutes in favor of aliens, thus leading to a narrow construction of preclusion statutes).

[62] *Abbott Laboratories v. Gardner*, 387 U.S. 136 (1967).

[63] In the Real ID Act of 2005, Pub. L. No. 109-13, 119 Stat. 231 (May 11, 2005), Division B §101(f), Congress clearly stated its decision that the discretionary decision bar applies to nonremoval decisions as well as removal cases and INA §242(a)(2)(B) now applies in all matters "regardless of whether the judgment, decision, or action is made in removal proceedings." INA §242(a)(2)(B). Although the new law clearly expresses Congress's intent to expand the application of INA §242(a)(2)(B)(ii) beyond removal proceedings, it does not alter the outcome in *Spencer Enterprises* because it does not affect the scope of the nonremoval statutes themselves.

[64] *Urena-Tavarez v. Ashcroft*, 367 F.3d 154, 157–61 (3d Cir. 2004) (no jurisdiction to review IJ's denial of a waiver of conditional residency under 8 USC §1186a(c)(4) because it is a discretionary decision barred from review under INA §242(a)(2)(B)(ii)); *Assad v. Ashcroft*, 378 F.3d 471, 475 (5th Cir. 2004) (following *Urena-Tavarez* and finding no jurisdiction to review good-faith marriage waiver under 8 USC §1186a(c)(4)(B) even in context of motion to reopen).

[65] *Oropeza-Wong v. Gonzales*, 406 F.3d 1135, 1141–49 (9th Cir. 2005) (8 USC §1252(a)(2)(B)(ii) did not bar the court's *continued*

jurisdiction to review whether a conditional resident in removal proceedings qualified for good faith marriage waiver under 8 USC §1186a(c)(4)(B), but IJ's denial of waiver was upheld on the merits); *Cho v. Gonzales*, 404 F.3d 96, 98–102 (1st Cir. 2005) (court had jurisdiction notwithstanding 8 USC §1252(a)(2)(B)(ii) to review whether conditional resident in removal proceedings qualified for good faith marriage waiver under §1186a(c)(4)(B); court reversed BIA for lack of substantial evidence); *Mendes v. INS*, 197 F.3d 6, 12–13 (1st Cir. 1999) (finding jurisdiction but applying the highly deferential *Elias-Zacarias* standard).

[66] *Chang v. United States*, 327 F.3d 911, 918–22 (9th Cir. 2003).

[67] DOJ Act, *supra* note 4. For a discussion of how this law was intended to help certain immigrant investors, see Stephen Yale-Loehr, "Congress Helps Stranded Immigrant Investors," 7 *Bender's Immigr. Bull.* 1306 (Nov. 1, 2002).

[68] *Chang*, 327 F.3d at 918–19.

[69] *Id.*

applications had not yet been denied. The Ninth Circuit noted, however, that ripeness is a question of law that is reviewed de novo, and "[t]his court 'does not require Damocles's sword to fall before we recognize the realistic danger of sustaining a direct injury."[70] The court adopted the "firm prediction" rule of Justice Sandra Day O'Connor in *Reno v. Catholic Social Services, Inc.*,[71] which eliminated the need to wait for the inevitable retroactive application of rules that would result in the denial of plaintiffs' I-829 applications before the court would intervene.

The government also may raise jurisdictional defenses to any challenge to the failure to grant adjustment of status to an investor with an approved I-526 petition. Typically, a person denied adjustment of status has no administrative procedure to exhaust. The application may be revisited only in a removal proceeding. However, any effort to challenge the decision of the IJ or BIA in regard to the denial of an adjustment application in a removal proceeding likely will trigger the government's claim that such challenges are barred by INA §242(a)(2)(B)(i) or its transitional predecessor, Illegal Immigration Reform and Immigrant Responsibility Act of 1996 (IIRAIRA)[72] §309(c)(4)(E). Under INA §242(a)(2)(B)(i), review is barred for "any judgment regarding the granting of relief under section . . . 1255." Again, the courts have taken different positions in regard to this bar.[73] Most courts, however, appear to accept the position that nondiscretionary decisions concerning adjustment applications, such as whether a person qualifies factually for adjustment, are not barred under this section or its predecessor.

The government also will raise jurisdictional issues when an investor, whose I-829 application has been denied, seeks review in U.S. District Court. The government will claim both that there is no review under INA §242(a)(2)(B)(i), and that if such review exists, it may be had only in the review of a final order of removal in the circuit court of appeals. But if the client has not been placed in a removal proceeding, may you proceed in district court? The government will argue that because the client *can* or *will* be placed in a removal proceeding, the district court has no jurisdiction over the case. Any effort to allow review in the district court, they will say, simply thwarts Congress' decision to channel review to the circuit courts of appeals. This thorny issue has had many different outcomes.[74] Investor's counsel, however, can argue, based upon *McNary v. Haitian Refugee Center, Inc.*[75] that Article III review may not be left to the Executive Branch's decision regarding if, or when, to put someone in removal proceedings.

In addition to jurisdictional issues, the government will always argue both *Chevron* deference and the narrow scope of substantial evidence review un-

---

[70] *Id.* at 921 (quoting *City of Auburn v. Qwest Corp.*, 260 F.3d 1160, 1171 (9th Cir. 2001)).

[71] 509 U.S. 43, 69–70 (1993) (O'Connor, J., concurring).

[72] Illegal Immigration Reform and Immigrant Responsibility Act of 1996 (IIRAIRA) (enacted as Division C of Omnibus Consolidated Appropriations Act, 1997, Pub. L. No. 104-208, §309(C)(4)(E), 110 Stat. 3009).

[73] *Compare McBrearty v. Perryman*, 212 F.3d 985 (7th Cir. 2000) (no jurisdiction where no constitutional issue raised and because of failure to exhaust removal process); *Hope v. Immigration Service (BICE)*, 349 F. Supp. 2d 490, 494–95 (E.D.N.Y. 2004) (no jurisdiction to review IJ's factual and discretionary decision to deny adjustment); *Afsharzadehyadzi v. Perryman*, 214 F. Supp. 2d 884 (N.D. Ill. 2002) (no jurisdiction under mandamus due to INA §242(a)(2)(B)(i) and failure to exhaust before IJ to consider denial of adjustment of status application for "aged-out" child); *Amoakowaa v. Reno*, 94 F. Supp. 2d 903, 905 (N.D. Ill. 2000) (no jurisdiction to challenge adjustment barred by INA §242(a)(2)(B)(i), absent constitutional claim) *with Sepulveda v. Gonzales*, 407 F.3d 59 (2d Cir. 2005) (the INA §242(a)(2)(B)(i) bar to adjustment does not extend to the nondiscretionary decision whether a person is eligible as a matter of law for adjustment under INA §245(i) even if it arises in the context of the review of a motion to reopen or
continued

---

reconsider); *Subhan v. Ashcroft*, 383 F.3d 591 (7th Cir. 2004) (neither INA §§242(a)(2)(B)(i) nor (ii) bars review of a denial of a continuance to submit an INA §245(i) application); *Korytnyuk v. Ashcroft*, 396 F.3d 272, 280–83 (3d Cir. 2005) (jurisdiction to review denial of motion to remand for adjustment is not barred by IIRAIRA §309(c)(4)(E) because it was not a discretionary decision and was not an application enumerated under the transition rule); *Billeke-Tolosa v. Ashcroft*, 385 F.3d 708 (6th Cir. 2004) (court is free to review nondiscretionary legal error where IJ looked behind the applicant's conviction to deny adjustment based upon a police report); *Medina-Morales v. Ashcroft*, 371 F.3d 520, 526–31 (9th Cir. 2004) (no judicial bar to a petition for review of a motion to reopen for adjustment under INA §§242(a)(2)((B)(i) or (ii)).

[74] *Compare, e.g., Robledo v. Chertoff*, 658 F. Supp. 2d 688, 691-94 (D. Md. 2009) [allowing district court review in widow's penalty case despite adjustment denial because petitioner sought review of the I-130 which the IJ could not review] *with Rivera-Durmaz v. Chertoff*, 456 F. Supp. 2d 943 (N.D. Ill. 2006) [respondent failed to exhaust his claim by not completing removal proceedings where his adjustment application could be raised].

[75] 498 U.S. 479 (1991)

der *INS v. Elias-Zacarias.*[76] When preparing any investor case, particularly one challenging the denial of an I-526 or I-829 petition on the merits, plaintiffs' counsel must demonstrate that the facts "compel" a contrary result and not simply that USCIS erred in reaching its conclusion.

CHOOSING THE CORRECT STRATEGY TO WIN AN IMMIGRANT INVESTOR CASE

One of the most important aspects of any EB-5 case is deciding where the suit will be brought and what issues should be raised. To some extent, a plaintiff may not have control over venue. If the case arises in the context of a removal proceeding, Congress has specified that the petition "shall be filed with the court of appeals for the judicial circuit in which the immigration judge completed the proceedings."[77] Of course, the question of where the proceedings are completed is not always clear.[78] And a party may seek to change venue if he or she has moved to another area of the United States, whether or not such move is in anticipation of future litigation.

However, a party that has some choice in the venue for federal litigation because, for example, the decision was made at a regional service center in one circuit and the person resides in another, should review the law carefully in each circuit to maximize the likelihood of success. Clearly, the circuits are quite different in their approaches to immigration matters. The U.S. Courts of Appeals for the Fourth, Fifth, Eighth, and Eleventh Circuits are quite deferential to the government, with the Eleventh Circuit being the most deferential circuit in the United States. The U.S. Courts of Appeals for the First, Second, Third, Sixth, Seventh, Ninth, and Tenth, on the other hand, are less deferential, with the Ninth Circuit generally being the least deferential to the U.S. Department of Homeland Security. A careful lawyer needs to consider this fact as well as the existing law in the circuit on both the issues the investor will address (if there is existing case law) and the precedent that the circuit applies to the type of issues (*e.g.*, retroactivity, abuse of discretion) that will be raised in the litigation.

Choosing the appropriate issues to litigate also must be a central concern of any well-prepared litigator. At times, it may be better to challenge the agency on procedural issues rather than on the merits because there is a greater likelihood of success in an indirect challenge to agency action. In *Chang v. United States*, for example, counsel was confronted with plaintiffs who had their I-526 petitions denied, plaintiffs who had their I-829 petitions denied, and plaintiffs who were likely to have their I-829 petitions denied. The decision to exclude persons with denied I-526 petitions arose out of the assessment that the best strategy for success was to argue the improper retroactive application of new INS standards. Denied I-526 petitioners were excluded from the litigation because the courts were not likely to be sympathetic to a retroactivity claim for persons whose applications had not been approved. In fact, in another EB-5 case, *Golden Rainbow Freedom Fund v. Ashcroft*, the Ninth Circuit rejected I-526 retroactivity claims brought by a provider of investor services.[79]

Also, in *Chang* it was it is unwise to challenge legacy INS on the merits of individual claims at that stage in the litigation. It was obvious that the underlying claim was not the denial of any individual I-526 or I-829 petition, but rather the criteria that the agency was applying in denying the claims. The *Chang* plaintiffs reviewed the law in each of the circuits and recognized that there was a greater chance of success, given the status of the law, in the Ninth Circuit. As *Chang* plaintiffs existed in many different areas of the United States, counsel could choose the venue of the case. As the application of the retroactive rules were the same for all plaintiffs, it made sense to initiate a class action on behalf of all I-829 petitioners affected by the retroactive application.

Another strategic issue to consider will be whether an investor whose I-829 is denied, should challenge that denial in district court or in circuit court, after a removal proceeding. Understandably, clients often do not want to wait until they are deported to challenge the government's erroneous interpretation of the law. Moreover, the government cannot be forced to place a denied investor in a re-

---

[76] 502 U.S. 478 (1992).

[77] INA §242(b)(2).

[78] *Georcely v. Ashcroft*, 375 F.3d 45, 47–49 (1st Cir. 2004) (discussing the complexity of venue questions where the hearing is in the Virgin Islands, which is governed by the Third Circuit, but the court for the Virgin Islands is in Puerto Rico, which is governed by the First Circuit).

[79] *Golden Rainbow Freedom Fund v. Ashcroft*, 2001 U.S. App. LEXIS 25482 (9th Cir. Nov. 26, 2001).

moval proceeding,[80] so the client may never get review. Nevertheless, the district court could reject the challenge on jurisdictional grounds asserting that the only method of review is through removal proceedings and a petition for review in the circuit court. Typically, litigation will center first on whether the court has jurisdiction, and if so, whether it should exercise that jurisdiction in light of potential future removal proceedings.

In the final analysis, counsel needs to review the law carefully in the circuit before initiating litigation in that circuit. He or she also needs to find ways of challenging the immigration agency's conduct that does not, at least initially, implicate judicial review of the merits of the agency's decision.

---

[80] INA §242(g); *American-Arab Anti-Discrimination Committee v. Reno*, 525 U.S. 471 (1999).

AILA
OCCUPATIONAL
GUIDEBOOK

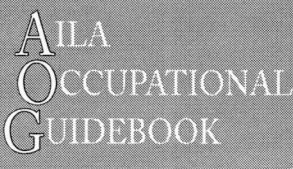

HISTORICAL ROOTS OF INVESTOR IMMIGRATION

THE EVOLUTION OF LEGAL PRECEDENT IN TREATY INVESTOR VISA CASES

*by H. Richard Sindelar III and Stephen K. Fischel**

INTRODUCTION

The authors collaborated as officials in the Visa Office (VO) of the U.S. Department of State (DOS) during the late 1970s and early 1980s, a time of significant development in the legal principles that now constitute the foundation for E-2 treaty investor visas. It is edifying to follow the evolution of investor principles from the nonpreference investor rules through the E-2 treaty investor provisions into the current EB-5 immigrant investor program. It is important to note that this was not an era in which a clear and full body of law and precedent existed. Quite the contrary, much of DOS's *Foreign Affairs Manual* (FAM) guidance on this topic was created reactively on a case-by-case basis in an uncertain milieu and under dueling pressures. Field officers sought a more detailed and impliedly stricter expostulation of the criteria, compared to political desk officers, who demanded that deference be given to trade and investment expansion as a foreign policy issue.

This article is intended to share DOS experience and sheds light on how precedent in E treaty investor visa cases has evolved, and how that evolution served as background for E visa regulations and cross-fertilization for the EB-5 permanent residence investor category in that program's own early development.

---

* This article originally appeared in the 1st edition of AILA's *Immigration Options for Investors and Entrepreneurs* (AILA 2006). It is reprinted in memory of **Stephen K. Fischel**, who served for many years as the Director of the U.S. Department of State's Office of Regulations, Legislation, and Advisory Assistance. He was a frequent speaker at national conferences on immigration law, helped negotiate several free trade agreements, including NAFTA, and had a central hand in developing many of the U.S government's immigration policies during a long career which spanned the 1970s to the 2000s.

Richard Sindelar is a partner in the law firm of Jackson Walker, LLP, an adjunct professor of American Foreign Policy at Houston's University of St. Thomas, and a former Foreign Service officer who served six years in the Department of State's Office of Legislation, Regulations, and Advisory Assistance.

BACKGROUND AND OVERVIEW

For millennia, traders plying among nations have been accorded special rights and privileges to protect them and their goods in foreign lands—typically under some protection of the king or other potentate and often in the form of notes or letters containing the royal imprimatur or seal.

The rationale behind these rights and privileges principally has been based on a belief that trade among peoples benefits all parties involved and the facilitation of trade is in the best interests of the sovereign. Nations that have encouraged international trade and have protected merchants and investors who sought to conduct business within their borders historically have been politically, economically, and often militarily the most powerful of their period. The Phoenicians, the Greeks, the Romans, the Chinese, the British, and others exemplify powerful empires that reaped the rewards of international trade.

The American Revolution was based in part on the desire of the founding fathers and the businessmen of the time to be fettered less by the Crown in all matters of trade and taxation. They wished to assure that the Colonies and not the British monarch would reap the benefits of trade in American goods.

After the War of 1812, rights and protections for both "merchants and traders" were enshrined, for the first time in the United States, in the 1815 Foreign Commerce and Navigation (FCN) Treaty between the United States and the United Kingdom,[1] and included the right to reside in the other country and "occupy houses and warehouses for the purposes of their commerce." Until this FCN treaty, local customs dictated how trade was handled; protections and rights bestowed on traders and merchants varied depending on the noblesse oblige of individual foreign rulers.

---

[1] A Convention to Regulate Commerce Between the Territories of the United States and of His Britannick Majesty (Article I), *entered into force* July 3, 1815, 8 Stat. 228, TS 110; 12 Bevans 49.

In the ensuing years, more FCN treaties were negotiated between the United States and a variety of other nations, clarifying and codifying a tradition of promoting trade by allowing merchants to move freely across international borders. Treaties were first negotiated with Costa Rica (1852)[2] and Argentina (1854)[3] and then with European nations, including Switzerland (1855)[4] and Yugoslavia (1882).[5] The rights and privileges afforded traders and merchants derived from these treaties, and interpretations of these rights usually were decided through reference to these treaties.

U.S statutes and regulations did not directly address the entry and exit rights or duties of foreign investors until §101(a)(15)(E)[6] was enacted as part of the 1952 McCarran-Walters Act, commonly known as the Immigration and Nationality Act (INA).[7] While treaty *trader* visas were issued throughout the 1900s under the authority of the treaties, treaty *investor* visas only could be issued after the enactment of the INA in 1952. INA §101(a)(15)(E) created what quickly became known as the "Treaty Trader" and "Treaty Investor" categories of business-related nonimmigrant visas, the E-1 and E-2 classifications, respectively. In the wake of World War II and the enactment of the INA, a burst of negotiation activity ensued between the United States and a host of foreign nations looking to promote trade with the new economic powerhouse. Thus the number of FCN treaties surged during the 20 years after the war.

In the 1970s, DOS's Legal Advisory Office catalogued all FCNs, and the resulting list of treaties in the FAM indicates whether each treaty accords trader and/or investor privileges to the nationals of a given FCN partner.[8] A current list of qualifying countries can be found in the FAM.[9]

Although the listed treaties established the stated right for traders and investors to live and operate their businesses in the partner country, more expansive guidance on who qualified for the visas took several decades to evolve after enactment of the INA.

This evolution occurred over what might be viewed as several "epochs" of legal development, each driven by some significant alteration to the statute or development in the field:

- Pre-1952: Sporadic federal cases sought to provide some fundamental thinking on disparate aspects of treaty individuals' activities in the United States under the FCN treaties.

- 1952–65: Explanation of the INA's treaty sections was largely limited to the promulgation of regulations thereto and some basic guidance published in the FAM for consuls in the field.

- Post-1966: Following publication of regulations relating to the former nonpreference investor category, there was a burst of court interpretations and DOS efforts to develop better guidance for consuls in terms of what constituted a qualifying investment under the nonpreference regulations.[10]

- Circa 1979–90: DOS guidance on E treaty investor/trader visas, published in the FAM and otherwise, was intensified in response to both consuls' concerns and the fast-paced computer-era changes in the ways modern executives conducted business and structured corporate investments. Some critics viewed these broad explanations, in themselves, as *new* criteria, which arguably went beyond what was specified in statute

---

[2] Treaty of Friendship, Commerce and Navigation (Article II), July 10, 1851, *entered into force* May 26, 1852, 10 Stat. 916; TS 62; 6 Bevans 1013.

[3] Treaty of Friendship, Commerce and Navigation (Article II), July 27, 1853, *entered into force* Dec. 20, 1854, 10 Stat. 1005; TS 4; 5 Bevans 61.

[4] Convention of Friendship, Commerce and Extradition (Article I), Nov. 25, 1850, *entered into force* Nov. 8, 1855, 11 Stat. 587; TS 353; 11 Bevans 894.

[5] Treaty of Commerce (Article I), Oct. 2/14, 1881, *entered into force* Nov. 15, 1882, 22 Stat. 963; TS 319; 12 Bevans 1227.

[6] INA §101(a)(15)(E).

[7] Immigration and Nationality Act of 1952 (INA), Pub. L. No. 82-414, 66 Stat. 163 (codified as amended at 8 USC §§1101 *et seq.*).

[8] For the last 20 years, the United States abandoned negotiating new FCNs and instead has negotiated bilateral investment treaties (BITs). Most of these provide specific language to extend treaty investor benefits. The current trend to negotiate free trade agreements (FTAs) also often has included treaty trader/investor provisions. But the FTAs are not treaties under U.S. law and require legislation to specifically accord treaty visa benefits to the nationals of partnering FTA countries.

[9] For an online version of the *Foreign Affairs Manual* (FAM), see *www.state.gov/m/a/dir/regs/fam/*.

[10] There was much cross-fertilization between the E-2 and nonpreference investor guidance; nonpreference investor influence on the E-2 is discussed in the following section.

and regulations, and, thus, required either statutory amendments or regulatory rulemaking, none of which the agencies had undertaken.

- Post-1990: The Immigration Act of 1990 introduced the EB-5 immigrant investor program,[11] a more complex descendant of the earlier nonpreference investor category. Furthermore, in 1991, DOS and legacy Immigration and Naturalization Service (INS) each independently proposed a comprehensive set of E treaty visa regulations; they were not reconciled and published as final regulations until 1997.[12]

INFLUENCE OF THE FORMER NONPREFERENCE INVESTOR CATEGORY

Following enactment of a new statute in 1965 that imposed a labor certification requirement for many immigrants, by regulation both DOS and legacy INS listed exceptions to the labor certification requirement. These exceptions were practical as they included persons who theoretically would not enter the labor market, such as fiancé(e)s and investors.[13] As a result, investor interpretations became more frequent and the body of guidance from DOS expanded. Many of the concepts and principles found in the current nonimmigrant treaty investor regulations were developed in the 1970s as interpretation of the nonpreference investor regulations.

The nonpreference investor regulation (which was amended several times) defined an investor as:

[A]n alien who establishes by documentary evidence, received by a consular officer after the effective date of this subparagraph, that he is seeking to enter the United States for the purpose of engaging in an enterprise in which he has invested, or is actively in the process of investing, capital totaling at least $10,000 [later raised to 40,000 in 1976 and to $100,000 in 1986], in which enterprise will employ persons in the United States who are U.S. citizens or aliens lawfully admitted for permanent residence, exclusive of the alien, his spouse and children.[14]

It should be noted that the first regulation required that the investment be substantial. The fixed dollar amount came some years after the original promulgation of the regulation. Also, the investor, for a period of time, had to prove that he or she had one year of experience or training needed to run the enterprise created or invested in by the nonpreference investor. This was a short-lived requirement.

The former nonpreference investor category, as a viable visa option, was also short-lived insofar as nonpreference visa numbers first became unavailable in 1976 and in 1978 were no longer available. Even so, many of the nonpreference investor cases provided sufficient opportunity for DOS and legacy INS to develop the concepts that the category shared with the E-2 visa category.

The early FAM notes on the nonpreference investor category provided only that the funds being invested must be in the possession and under the control of the applicant, and that "the manner of acquisition of the capital" to be invested would not disqualify an applicant from eligibility although it could cast doubt on the credibility of the asserted investment.[15]

The extensive development of the FAM notes on the nonpreference investor category increased greatly from 1975 through 1977. The FAM was updated both in 1978 and 1979 in this area, incorporating the advisory opinions rendered prior to 1975 as well as then-recent guidance from the VO. This guidance consisted of several pages addressing many of the issues that the authors, while at the VO, amplified later in the E-2 context. By 1979, the FAM notes concerning the nonpreference investor category included guidelines concerning debt and inheritance, and what the law required in terms of being "actively in the process of investing."

---

[11] See INA §203(b)(5), enacted by the Immigration Act of 1990 (IMMACT90), Pub. L. No. 101-649, §121(a), 104 Stat. 4978.

[12] The Department of State (DOS)-proposed regulation appeared at 56 Fed. Reg. 43565 (Sept. 3, 1991). The legacy Immigration and Naturalization (INS)-proposed regulation appeared at 56 Fed. Reg. 42952 (Aug. 30, 1991). The DOS final regulation appeared at 62 Fed. Reg. 48149 (Sept. 12, 1997). The legacy INS final regulation appeared at 62 Fed. Reg. 48138 (Sept. 12, 1997), corrected 62 Fed. Reg. 50435 (Sept. 25, 1997), 62 Fed. Reg. 55458 (Oct. 24, 1997), and 62 Fed. Reg. 60122 (Nov. 6, 1997). Both final regulations became effective on Nov. 12, 1997.

[13] For more information, see L. Stone, "A Synopsis of the Former Nonpreference Investor Category" (hereinafter Stone, *Synopsis*) appearing elsewhere in this volume.

[14] 22 CFR §42.91(a)(14)(ii)(D) (1972).

[15] 9 FAM 40.7(a)(14) N1.41 (1975).

Nonpreference Category—Substantiality

Prior to the 1972 revision of the regulation for the nonpreference category, which set a minimum amount of qualifying investment of $10,000, the regulation had required that the investment be "substantial"—the same standard applicable to E-2 treaty investors. Thus, many of the advisory opinions rendered in the nonpreference context formed a basis for defining "substantial" for E-2 visa purposes.

Initially, consuls tended to use a proportionality test (which was not as refined as the current treaty investor test), and substantiality was clearly a determination derived from the circumstances of the investment. Consuls had extensive discretion and based decisions on the underlying concept that the amount invested had to be substantial relative to the overall size of the business. No expansive guidance, to the authors' knowledge, was crafted for consular officers to adjudicate substantiality. Advisory opinions of that era merely relied on general principles.

It is likely that the frustration of trying to analyze substantiality led to the promulgation of the 1972 regulation that assigned a minimum amount of investment and replaced the substantiality test in nonpreference investor cases. The internal discussions as to what constituted substantial investment nonetheless constituted the basis for what later evolved into more expansive guidance of substantiality for E-2 visa purposes.

Nonpreference Category—Source of Funds

The source of funds used for the investment also was a major issue and generated many opinion requests in nonpreference investor cases. The key and almost exclusive focus of the VO regarding the source of the funds was the requirement that the investor had full possession and control over the funds to be invested. Certainly, the more expansive guidance here naturally migrated to the E-2 visa requirements. In these nonpreference investor cases, there was general latitude for the consular officer to make inquiries into the source of the monies to ensure that the investor truly controlled and possessed the funds in question. While silent about investigating the source to ensure its legitimacy, the guidance did not preclude such inquiry if a question of illegitimacy arose. Today, in all investment contexts, the requirement that funds are legitimate is either implicit or, in EB-5 cases, explicit.

The advisory opinions rendered were consistent with guidance that funds/assets inherited were considered personal, and thus, qualifying funds/assets for investment purposes. The inheritance of a business was not considered a qualifying investment for these regulations. A series of nonpreference cases based on investment in motels assisted in confirming the view that funds that were inherited or given to the investor, as well as funds that were provided by loan, qualified. Thus, the receipt of assets by gift that the recipient later invested into a qualifying business met the investment requirement. But the gift of the motel to a child would not qualify as an investment by the child under these regulations. So, the receipt of a business and the claim that the resulting ownership of the business qualifies as an investment did not amount to a qualifying investment in the nonpreference category. The same rings true in the E-2 treaty investor category.

Nonpreference Category—"At Risk"

Furthermore, the "at risk" principle was not fully developed in the FAM notes, and it certainly was not characterized as such. The notes gave sparse examples of what could qualify as investment, but these notes were woefully incomplete, as not all the advisory opinions had been introduced into the note material. When viewing everything in concert, one reaches the conclusion that the intent was to ensure that the funds invested were at risk to the investor. A loan secured by the business would not count toward the minimum investment of the $10,000 or $40,000, because it was the business assets that were at risk, and not the personal funds of the investor seeking a Green Card. The circularity of this capital financing—although a perfectly acceptable hedge against risk in the business world—was viewed as unfair in the immigrant investor context because it resulted in insufficient risk to entitle one to permanent residence.

Many applicants sought to qualify for the nonpreference category by claiming to be "actively in the process of investing" the required capital. There is a body of case precedent in the nonpreference context that interprets this language.[16] The underlying principles—proof of an actual commitment of resources, actual existence of the business, and that the proposed investment for business acquisition and operations exceeds the amount required by law—are true to both the nonpreference investor category and the E-2 treaty investor category. While the use of escrow (this arose much later in a specific E-2 case)

---

[16] *See, e.g., Matter of Lui*, 15 I&N Dec. 206 (BIA 1975); *see also* cases cited in Stone, *Synopsis, supra* note 13.

and other means of verifying committed funds to businesses were not mentioned in any guidance or likely used by applicants in the nonpreference investor context, the underlying principle of commitment to the investment is common to both the nonpreference investor category and the E-2 treaty investor category.

PRE-1979 E TREATY INVESTOR VISA GUIDANCE

For treaty investors, INA §101(a)(15)(E) provides a nonimmigrant classification for:

> an alien entitled to enter the United States under and in pursuance of the provisions of a treaty of commerce and navigation between the United States and the foreign state of which he is a national, and the spouse and children of any such alien if accompanying or following to join him:
>
> ....
>
> (ii) solely to develop and direct the operations of an enterprise in which he has invested, or of an enterprise in which he is actively in the process of investing, a substantial amount of capital.

Congress provided only scant guidance in the legislative history, as if it felt what constitutes an *investment* for the statute was obvious enough not to need further explanation. What little legislative history was placed in the record as explanation stated that Congress "intended to provide for the temporary admission of such aliens who will be engaged in developing or directing the operations of a real operating enterprise and not a fictitious paper operation."[17] The utility of this legislative history was correctly summed up by the Ninth Circuit's opinion in *Nice v. Turnage*, which stated, "We have characterized the legislative history (of the treaty investor provision) as 'of little assistance' in determining qualifications for treaty investor status."[18]

In its earlier form, the regulation concerning E-2 visa eligibility for a principal investor provided only that an investor was ineligible if he or she invested "a small amount of capital in a marginal enterprise solely for the purpose of earning a living"; and that the investor intend to depart the United States upon termination of the status.[19]

Up to this point, the existing FAM provided little guidance on investor cases. Additions made in 1975 to the E-1 and E-2 FAM notes expanded consular guidance for each, but amounted to little more than a sketchy series of simply stated instructions that did not run more than two pages per category. The E-1 notes gave a truncated list of some activities that constituted trade and mentioned the need for an actual exchange of goods. The E-2 notes were similarly sparse, and in many places cross-referenced the E-1 notes. The E-2 notes required that the enterprise "actually exist"; on the meaning of "substantial," they provided little guidance other than to say that smaller enterprises were not ruled out, and that whether the "substantial" requirement was met "depends on the nature of the enterprise and is therefore not necessarily determined by the size of the investment." The two examples given were an auto manufacturing plant and a candy making company, the former requiring more capital. The FAM also identified criteria for granting an E-2 visa for an employee qualifying as "managerial and certain technical personnel."[20]

In this void, consuls overseas were left mostly to their own devices in adjudicating E cases. Training for consuls was a mere 10-minute discussion by DOS lawyers to the junior officer class as part of what was, at that time, a morning lecture covering all NIV categories. In his early 1970s service at the embassy in Tel Aviv and the consulate general in Jerusalem, author Richard Sindelar relied mostly on his own knowledge, or lack thereof, about business and trade practices. Almost all E visas were issued if there was any evidence of investment or trade. Diamond merchants either trading with the United States or establishing offices in New York City were the most frequent recipients. After an initial reference to these sparse notes, Sindelar did not refer to the FAM at all in reaching E visa decisions thereafter, and neither did his colleagues. As later cables from the field (discussed below) eventually would make clear, consuls at posts from Germany to Japan did not refer to the FAM, finding little of use in the scant guidance.

---

[17] *See* H.R. Rep. No. 82-1365, at 44 (1952), *reprinted in* 1952 U.S.C.C.A.N. 1653, 1697, *cited in Nice v. Turnage*, 752 F.2d 431 (9th Cir. 1985).

[18] *Nice v. Turnage*, 752 F.2d at 432 (citing the court's opinion in *Kim v. INS*, 586 F.2d 713, 716 (9th Cir. 1978)).

[19] 22 CFR §41.41(a) (1975).

[20] 9 FAM 41.41 N1-9 (1975).

POST-1979 E TREATY INVESTOR VISA GUIDANCE

In 1979, a perfect storm of sorts blew in—a mix of conspiracy, media coverage, internal DOS deliberations, politics, and foreign policy pressures swirled about amidst an effort to clarify the E visa rules for field consuls.[21] By 1982, the tempest had shaped much of what still is accepted as basic E treaty visa law and guidance; it was encapsulated in the 1997 E treaty visa regulations.[22] This politically intense period culminated in a special Visa Bulletin and an All Diplomatic and Consular posts (ALDAC) instructional cable.[23]

The perfect storm formed circa 1979 in Japan.[24] Senior consuls at the Osaka Kobe Consulate General and the Tokyo Embassy, led by veteran Consul David Hobbes, shared a growing concern that too many Japanese businessmen were being issued E-1 and E-2 visas. The Japanese businessmen preferred the E-1; it was deemed superior as it came first. They soon realized that the E-2 was in many ways a more secure visa classification. The consular officers opined that this seemingly august category enshrined in international treaties was being abused by applicants who were neither truly managerial nor specialized, and that it had become indistinguishable from the more mundane B-1 business visa. The Japanese business culture of the era greatly favored E visas as better and more exalted than the routine B-1, so a large number of Japanese businessmen specifically asked for E visas for travel to the United States.[25] In addition, Japanese executives preferred to employ fellow Japanese nationals to staff their U.S. offices, and they sought E-1 or E-2 visas for all manner of U.S. positions, including those that listed duties seemingly more mundane and clerical than executive or essential. For example, a bank had sought to obtain E visas for all its tellers, not just the head teller.

Due to the paucity of guidance found at that time in the regulations and the consuls' primary reference source, the FAM,[26] the consuls informally coordinated a scheme to obtain more detailed guidance from Washington, D.C. Initially consulting among themselves, they identified cases that contained fact patterns in which, in their opinion, the business traveler lacked the qualifications necessary for an E visa, but where one would have been issued before 1979. Deliberately without fanfare, and seemingly disconnected as they arrived at DOS, these cases trickled into the Advisory Opinions Division of the VO.[27]

Crucial to the growing maelstrom, the advisory opinions rendered by the VO led to more legally precise and tighter E visa adjudications by the consuls in Japan; that, in turn, engendered consternation in the Japanese business community. Before long, these more informed, but narrower consular, E visa decisions in the field catalyzed a media story—a

---

[21] The purpose of this article is to look at the E-2 treaty investor category, but considerable cross-fertilization of issues—especially with regard to nationality and executive or essential employees—occurred between that category and the E-1 treaty trader, in which consuls raised other issues which stoked the political fires.

[22] 22 CFR §41.51, 62 Fed. Reg. 48154 (Sept. 12, 1997).

[23] Visa Bulletin, Vol. V, No. 20, DOS, Visa Office (1982), *reprinted in* 59 *Interpreter Releases* 264 (Apr. 19, 1982) (hereinafter Visa Bulletin).

[24] A subsequent German case regarding specialty bricklayers addressed which "specialized knowledge" personnel could be classified as "essential" E visa employees. It was this category of E visa employees that Japanese companies also used to staff a variety of positions in the United States.

[25] The country whose nationals request the most E visas is far and above Japan, whose nationals received 14,733 E visas or 44 percent of the total issued in FY2002. Germany was a distant second, with 2809 E visas issued that year. *See continued*

"Report of the Visa Office 2002," DOS, Bureau of Consular Affairs, DOS Publication 11075 (Dec. 2004).

[26] The consular guidance is at Volume 9 of the FAM, available at *www.state.gov/m/a/dir/regs/fam/09fam/c22752.htm*. The treaty guidance is contained at 9 FAM 41.51.

[27] By happenstance more than design, it fell to the two authors, while working in the Visa Office (VO), to research the legal issues posed and advise the consuls in Japan on the variety of cases. It is important to understand the deliberative process used by the Advisory Opinions Division. When a case was submitted to the Advisory Opinions Division, the advisory opinion process mandated a review of relevant decisions previously rendered by the VO, published administrative decisions from INS, and federal cases. The Advisory Opinions Division sought to render interpretations aligned with the legislative intent of a given provision and consistent with precedent. But E treaty cases in the federal courts, and before the Board of Immigration Appeals (BIA), and legislative history, were sparse at best. When no precedent existed, the VO tried to craft an opinion after thorough review and study of the legal issue in parallel circumstances. When no parallel legal issues were found, the VO relied on common sense and even law school hornbooks. While the process often is characterized as informal, the VO took great pains to explore all facets of the law to render the best opinion, even if these interpretative opinions—in the attempt to fill in blanks—actually seemed to break new legal ground.

"crackdown" on Japanese business bannered the major newspaper *Asahi Shimbun*. Also, the story made the front page of the *New York Times* and, of course, the *Japan Times*. This was the same era during which Japan dominated the electronics industry and was making swift headway in the automobile arena. This purported "crackdown" seen through the prism of U.S.-Japan trade relations, was viewed as another attempt by the U.S. government to limit Japanese trade in all manner of products—a form of non-tariff barrier.

Treaty visa issues thus became a public bilateral foreign policy issue, drawing the attention of the DOS's Japan desk and senior department officials, and likewise provoking interest in the halls of Japan's government, where the Japan External Trade Organization (JETRO) took the lead on the potentially explosive issue. In Washington, D.C., JETRO diplomats pressed the VO and DOS's Japan desk to return to the expansive use of E visas. The VO explained that the U.S. law had as a fundamental tenet the protection of U.S. workers, and executives needed to be executives and specialized employees needed to be truly essential.

The enormous political pressure flavored the subsequent advisory opinions and underscored trade facilitation as a fundamental raison d'etre of treaty visa implementation. Therefore, subsequent advisory opinions tended to construe the law in a generous light. But policy pressure also forced the VO to research its positions more thoroughly; whatever guidance was issued was founded in solid law and defensible as such.

In response to these numerous inquiry cables from Japan, the E treaty visa guidance evolved in several key areas. In each area, the intent of the VO was to not grow or change the law or regulations by administrative fiat. Rather, the objective was to offer more detailed explanations, with some decision tree templates, drawn from background precedential material that existed in DOS files, Board of Immigration Appeals (BIA) and federal court cases, and general business law and operational decisions on the formation and governance of corporations. Reference was made to basic corporate law in legal hornbooks, not to complex or sophisticated business or corporate law court cases.

Upon commencing this effort at the VO, the authors concluded that the existing sketchy outlines of the law did not inform consuls sufficiently well to empower them to properly adjudicate E visa cases. In most aspects, the FAM guidance to consuls had really not changed much since the days when most trade was in cotton bales and other agricultural products—a simpler era of uncomplicated shipments easily measurable from bills of lading and the like. Therefore, the areas of keenest interest among consuls were understandably areas of treaty and corporate law on which the regulations and explanatory notes in the FAM were largely silent, leaving consuls doubtful whether many E visa applicants qualified for a treaty visa. The VO work product focused on:

- The concept of "at risk" as a bellwether for determining if a qualifying, substantial investment had been made, and questions on source of funds;

- For smaller enterprises, the mirror-image concepts of substantiality and "marginal, solely for earning a living";

- Corporate control issues, such as joint ventures, franchises, and other formulations in terms of whether an investor could truly "develop and direct" the investment entity's operations as the statute required;

- Who was an "essential employee" with some skill or attribute crucial to the treaty enterprise's trade or investment prospects; and

- "Intent to return," where investors and even traders might be in the United States for many years.

"At Risk"

By 1979 and the Japanese consul issues, much effort had been expended on the concept of "at risk" and this was one of the more developed areas of guidance. When merged in a fact pattern with the issue of the "substantial" investment requirement, the "at risk" issue still drew attention. DOS never quite stated the underlying principle this way, but the VO viewed investment in the context of investing personal funds over which the alien had possession and control. Investments of personal cash and wholly owned assets were qualifying investments that put the investor at risk. The investor would assume the entire loss if the enterprise tanked. This principle guided the analysis of whether loans from banks to purchase the enterprise qualified as at risk investments. Thus, consular officers pushed the question of how an investor could be "at risk" in a variety of loan situations. The scenarios involving bank loans had in common the simple arrangement of borrowing money using the business as collateral. The VO consistently rejected these variations of loans as the individual was not personally at risk.

Certainly, the VO looked at BIA decisions for guidance.[28]

Here again, the nonpreference investor era provided materials on which to pattern an analytical interpretation. Adding in some basic corporate loan concepts to what had been developed thus far regarding "at risk" in the nonpreference setting, it was decided that proceeds of a loan would count as risk capital only in cases of signature loans where the investor was personally liable, or loans collateralized by the investor's own personal assets. Loans where the entrepreneur put up his or her own house, or stock holdings, were viewed as a legitimate way to make his or her otherwise largely illiquid holdings available in order to complete the investment deal because if the enterprise failed, the investor would, in theory, at least be forced to cash out those personal holdings in order to pay the creditor. In deciding that a signature loan (a debtor was honor-bound to repay somehow or lose his or her credit rating) was an acceptable investment vehicle, the VO relied perhaps too sanguinely on an old world view of the "honorable" world of banking and business, and harm to reputations, before the stigma of personal bankruptcy faded in the 1980s.

Again, these versions of "at risk" were intended to simplify determinations for consular adjudicators by explaining what was a bona fide, at-risk situation. They were not meant as a form of limitation on investments, although these interpretations did effectively narrow acceptable ways to invest. This interest of simplicity and accountability by the foreign investor ultimately conflicted with and diverged from acceptable business practices—the preference of any good businessperson to spread risk as widely as possible and limit a company's own risk of loss.

Source of Funds

The "at risk" concept fed into the companion issue of the source of an alien's funds. Aside from making a distinction among types of loans—secured or personal and unsecured—the VO did not focus much on the source of an alien's investment funds. Typically, banking records—wire transfers, checks drawn on overseas accounts, etc.—were sought in individual cases to show that the investment monies had come to the enterprise from some account over which the alien had control; thus, showing he or she had made the investment and had his or her own funds at stake in the investment enterprise. Bank records were easily available, and inquiry was usually not pursued beyond that point. Gifts from family members were accepted as a source of funds, so long as the gift was irrevocable by the donor.

The concern that investors could be laundering ill-gotten gains through the investment enterprise had not yet surfaced on DOS's radar and was not a consideration as the VO addressed the funding issues. Tracing the investment monies beyond that first account from which the fund transfer to the business had occurred was not something the VO sought to have consular officers do. Nonetheless, the VO contemplated that the funds could not derive from illegal activities. The question arose, in the post-1979 Iranian context with its political overlay, of whether funds spirited out of a foreign country in some way that did not comport with that country's currency or funds export laws might be questionable. But informal discussions with the Legal Advisor's office led to the conclusion that the United States should not be in the position of enforcing other countries' currency laws—a laissez-faire approach informed at least in part by the tenor of the times and the hostage taking at the Tehran Embassy.

Substantiality and Marginality

The large Japanese trading and manufacturing companies, which saw the E-2 and E-1 clarifications by the U.S. administration as a restrictionist trade tactic, drove the political storm. But many Japanese businessmen in smaller businesses sought the coveted E-2 visa as well. In the view of some consuls, these businessmen saw the E-2 as a long-term solution to the quota unavailability and demise of the nonpreference investor category. Applications involving these smaller investments led to various queries concerning when an investment might be deemed "substantial" and how to adjudicate this question.

DOS's clarifications were guided by BIA decisions, as well as a Ninth Circuit decision.[29] The goal of the VO's efforts was to give consuls more to go on in their E-2 adjudications than the sparse guidance in the FAM note referring to the *proportionality* test and its two examples.[30] The VO sought to

---

[28] *See* Visa Bulletin, *supra* note 23 (citing *Matter of Heitland*, 14 I&N Dec. 563 (1974), *Matter of Khan*, 16 I&N Dec. 138 (1977), and *Matter of Ko*, 14 I&N Dec. 349 (1973)).

[29] *Kim v. District Director*, 586 F.2d 713 (9th Cir. 1978).

[30] 9 FAM 41.41 N3 (1978 version).

develop more detailed frameworks that would allow simpler calculations about the substantiality of any given investment. To this end, the Visa Bulletin was detailed in tying together the various pieces of guidance from the BIA and the courts. Generally, beyond the E-2 visa note in the FAM, the VO resorted to the FAM's nonpreference investor guidance.

In outlining how to analyze substantiality and marginality, the Visa Bulletin guidance was based on two cases. For substantiality, the decision in a nonpreference investor case, *Matter of Heitland*,[31] informed the VO's elaborations. The case involved a nominal investment in a delivery business. The purpose of the exemption to the labor certification was based on the concept that the investor would not use the investment to enter into the skilled and unskilled labor market. The BIA said:

> The investment either must tend to expand job opportunities and thus offset any adverse impact which the alien's employment may have on the market for jobs, or must be of an amount adequate to insure, with sufficient certainty, that the alien's primary function with respect to the investment, and with respect to the economy, will not be as a skilled or unskilled laborer.

Importantly, the VO drew on *Heitland's* language to find that the dollar amount itself might be of such magnitude to be substantial on its face without weighing of proportionality.[32] This decision overruled *Matter of Finau*[33] in part because the previous standard "might lead to an unwarranted denial of the investor exemption for an alien who seeks to enter the United States for the purpose of investing a large amount of capital in an enterprise whose magnitude is such that the alien's capital contribution is relatively insignificant." This was an attempt to factor in the real world multimillion dollar investments made by large corporations, where the actual paid-in capital might be several million dollars, but only a small percentage of the overall value of, for example, a manufacturing facility, financed mostly through corporate bank loans and other financing vehicles.

Kim v. District Director, an E-2 visa case (involving a Korean investor in a small drive-through restaurant), informed on the marginality issue. The notion was that E-2 investors should not be using the treaty visa category to avoid the quotas of the immigrant visa classifications, if, in fact, they were going to work as a skilled or unskilled worker merely to support a family. Interestingly, the *Kim* court found the investment to be marginal when both the amount put in—theoretically a "substantiality" issue—and the enterprise's profitability were marginal, even though the investment enterprise created jobs for other U.S workers not in the investor's family. The impression from reading the case is that Kim did not emphasize the employment of several persons as a basis for overcoming marginality. The court seemed to focus primarily, if not exclusively, on the relatively minor net income that Kim drew from the business. DOS maintained that an investment that generated jobs for others was not "solely" for earning a living because others also earned their living from the company. This view helped a foreign investor overcome the marginality criteria.

Finally, the VO agreed with the BIA that investors should be able easily to evidence their investments. This was underscored in advisory cables at the time by reference to what became a favorite citation from *Matter of Shaw*, a nonpreference investor case, that states:

> In the United States it is difficult to establish and operate a business of any significant size without generating some documentation reflecting the affairs of the enterprise. Large purchases of equipment and inventory are rarely unaccompanied by invoices or other indicia of contractual arrangement. The market value of land, buildings, equipment and machinery can be appraised. Accounting audits can be conducted to verify the financial status of most enterprises. Finally, records required to be kept by various governmental authorities will frequently provide some indication of the nature and extent of a business venture.[34]

This case clearly speaks to the burden of the applicant to prove by submission of requisite documentation that he or she is entitled to the status sought.

Corporate Control Issues and the Joint Venture

Japanese businessmen did not always lose in the VO's deliberations. Guided by corporate governance hornbooks, the VO sorted through a variety of corporate issues that mixed aspects of nationality, corporate formation, and direction and control of the

---

[31] *Matter of Heitland*, 14 I&N Dec. 563 (1974).

[32] Visa Bulletin, *supra* note 23, at para. 15.

[33] 12 I&N Dec. 86 (BIA 1967).

[34] *Matter of Shaw*, 15 I&N Dec. 794 (BIA 1976).

investment enterprise, as required by INA §101(a)(15)(E). In arriving at simplified guidance for consuls, the VO adopted a variety of concepts that permitted flexibility in the corporate structure.

"Negative control" was the most important concept developed. The statute requires that an investor "develop and direct" the treaty enterprise. But if he or she were to not own more than 50 percent of the stock, arguably the E-2 visa holder would not be in a position to control the enterprise and, thereby, "direct" its operations, *i.e.*, make policy decisions that governed company operations.

In the real world of corporate governance, however, even minority shareholders can control company policies through various means—controlling shares actually voted, controlling the board of directors, etc. Thus, based on basic corporate law guidance, someone holding 50 percent of the shares needed at least one more share in order to adopt a board resolution or otherwise vote on company issues. Conversely, an individual holding at least 50 percent of the shares effectively could block unwanted corporate actions because he or she controlled *negatively* the crucial one share needed to adopt a resolution, leading the VO to coin the phrase "negative control."

Through the development of the "negative control" concept, the statute was interpreted to permit that era's joint venture companies to qualify their personnel for E visas.

Franchises also created an E treaty issue. Again, the issue was control, *i.e.*, who controlled the company—the investor franchisee or the franchisor company? Depending on the franchise contract entered into with a franchisor corporation, an individual franchisee's latitude of operation and decision making might be severely constrained. He or she controls the franchised corporation in theory and stock-voting practice, but the franchise contract could—in a real world view—take away a franchisee's actual independence in business decision making. Some franchise agreements detail precisely and minutely every aspect of operations, from building layout and marketing materials, to employees and products. Some even force the franchisee to purchase all supplies and materials from the franchisor, limiting any option to cut costs, a seemingly central aspect of business and business independence.

The VO had to interpret "control" in the realm of franchises when a consul sought an advisory opinion regarding the franchise arrangement of a gourmet potato fast food outlet. Here, the VO resorted to contract law and business practice to reach an interpretation consistent with the statutory mandate that a treaty investor be in control. Reference in franchise situations would be to the franchise agreement itself and the independence that document afforded the treaty investor. Practically speaking, a sliding scale was adopted. If a franchisee had latitude with the product line under the franchisor's general brand name, then requisite direction and control existed. If, on the other hand, per the agreement, close control of all aspects of operations rested with the franchisor's headquarters, down to purchases of all supplies from the franchisor at set prices, then it was felt the investor did not, in a true business sense, exercise meaningful control and direction. The direction and control criteria would not be met and a visa would be denied.[35]

Nationality

Unlike the control issue, which had opinion precedent in the nonpreference investor visa context, the nationality requirement, which is unique to the E visas, presented the greatest interpretive difficulties. Initially, the business had to be predominantly owned by nationals of the treaty country. Thus, *more than* one-half of the ownership consisted of a single treaty nationality. In the era of multinationals, this rule prohibited partnerships or joint ventures of different nationalities. That is, an equal joint venture between Japanese and British individuals would not qualify because one party did not own more than 50 percent of the venture.

Japanese businesses engaged the ambassador, who brought the matter to the highest level in DOS. The VO researched the legislative history and all relevant opinions and maintained the longstanding interpretation. The Legal Advisor's office overruled the VO, opening the way for the current rule allowing 50 percent ownership of a business to qualify that business for treaty investor status. This is a positive result.

The other nationality issue concerned nationality of companies. Treaties (and later, the implementing statutes) required aliens to possess the treaty nationality to qualify for status. In the 1800s and most of

---

[35] *See Matter of Kung*, 17 I&N Dec. 260 (Comm'r 1978) (upholding eligibility for E-2 status if the franchisee retains sufficient control over the management of the business, including the power: (i) to hire and fire employees; (ii) to set wage scales; and (iii) to set the hours of business).

the last century, the traders and investors were viewed as individuals rather than as businesses, as they were mostly individual entrepreneurs. Thus, the rules evolved in the context of the individual trader. To comply with the nationality requirements of the treaties and implementing law, the businesses, too, had to possess the nationality of the treaty country. Ownership of the business by nationals was the logical solution to determining its nationality as this entity was the legal extension of the individual(s).

This principle was well-founded before arguments arose suggesting that the place of incorporation should control the nationality requirement. While it is true that a business incorporated in Delaware is a "Delaware corporation" and, thus, a U.S. corporation, it certainly would counter the purpose of the treaty to declare all such companies American. If all foreign companies incorporated in the United States were deemed American for treaty investor purposes, then it would be impossible for them to qualify under E visa status.

The *Sumitomo v. Avagliano*[36] decision rendered by the U.S. Supreme Court furthered the "place of incorporation" debate. The Japanese company argued that since it was a Japanese company, it was not subject to U.S. laws on discrimination in the work place. The Court ruled that the business was incorporated in a state of the United States and was, therefore, a U.S. business and subject to all U.S. laws, including labor laws. This case was readily distinguished by the VO on the nationality issue as the ruling pertained to the obligation under the law of businesses incorporated and doing business in the United States rather than to an assessment of nationality for treaty purposes. To the best of the authors' recollection, the VO transmitted a communication to the field indicating that the case in no way affected the interpretation of nationality for treaty visa purposes.

The nationality requirement also was an issue regarding employees. The statute speaks only to traders and investors. The VO sent guidance stating that because the principals must possess the requisite treaty nationality, their employees must likewise possess that same nationality, as they derived employee E visa status from the employer. Certainly, persons of different nationalities, even persons from other countries with which the United States had the requisite underlying E visa treaty, could work for such enterprises, but they had to obtain some visa status other than E visa status.

Executives, Managers, and Essential Employees

David Hobbes and other consuls opined that the greatest abuse of the E visa category occurred in the numbers of employees deemed essential to the companies' U.S. operations or placed in lower managerial positions sent to the United States. In this era, it was not uncommon for Japanese employees to be found at U.S. operations, from clearly qualified senior executives, to lesser managers and employees doing mostly basic work.[37]

The VO already had developed a fairly thorough set of interpretations as to which employees were essential, courtesy of a series of meetings with representatives of a foreign treaty country company seeking to invest in a major ski resort enterprise in the United States. The original submission to DOS sought a wide variety of *essential* employees, including cooks trained in the foreign cuisine, ski instructors, and even some employees described as being specially trained in the company's particular guest relations style. The argument was that this unique entertainment enterprise, which it was at the time, provided a unique cultural experience. This cultural atmosphere could be provided only by their employees, specially selected and trained, who were circulated among the enterprise's operations globally. Having employees who spoke English accented in the style of the country was argued to be part of the guest experience. The authors recall at least 20–30 percent of the total employees were proposed to be treaty country nationals.

Over time, the ski resort's package of employees was distilled to:

- Senior managers, not every assistant managerial position (*e.g.*, the front desk manager, but not the assistant manager);

- Employees in partially managerial positions who also could be viewed as specialists in the field (the head chef, and in the context of the case, the head pastry chef, each of whom had exemplary culinary skills, but also oversaw other kitchen personnel);

- Specialist staff who would, in essence, always be needed due to their unique skills and/or their

---

[36] *Sumitomo, Inc. v. Avagliano*, 457 U.S. 176 (1982).

[37] *Id.* (addressing in part complaints filed with the Equal Employment Opportunity Commission).

knowledge of how the parent company wanted its facilities run, the unique operational style (*e.g.*, some ski instructors, usually supervisory instructors, who could impart the specific ski techniques developed and arguably unique to the treaty country);

- Employees deemed temporarily essential, but whose visa term would be limited because it was felt they could train Americans to do their jobs after some reasonable training period (*e.g.*, assistant chefs, some guest relations personnel trained in the company's unique style, etc.). This is consistent with longstanding interpretation; the lesser skilled workers could come to the United States to provide essential start-up services. Their terms were time sensitive.

By the time the advisory opinion requests arrived from the Japanese posts, the VO had begun to determine what made a specific employee either managerial or essential. One case that built on the ski resort case was that of a car assembly plant, where the Japanese company had brought in a wide variety of managers and also quite a number of technicians that the company viewed as essential to assembling its cars with the various patented parts and processes. The consul's view was that some of the positions were only secondarily managerial and too deep down the chain of command to have much opportunity to influence or direct company operations or an aspect thereof. The consul also believed that some of the purported essential employees' jobs did not really involve highly technical proprietary work, but were mere assembly jobs.

In the end, the VO developed guidance that clarified fewer executives/managers or essential employees than the Japanese had been used to sending actually met the E criteria. A sending company's representations would carry weight, but a consul should look to the substance of what the employee would actually do in a business day before deciding whether the person qualified for an E visa.

On the managerial side, a person would be eligible for an E visa if he or she handled policy decisions, directed a number of employees, possibly directed other managers (although this was not crucial), was responsible for some definable unit of the facility or office, and spent little time doing the actual work of his or her unit. A manager of a technical operation, such as a segment of an auto assembly plant, should be principally directing and overseeing the work of other technicians who perform the tasks, not actually operating an assembly machine. Hence, the senior technical supervisor of an assembly section could hold an E visa, but line foremen who worked alongside the regular technicians did not meet the manager criteria or warrant E visa issuance.

For background on essential or special skills employees, the VO reviewed the similar concepts of the L-1B specialized knowledge category. The VO found that technicians and employees who held proprietary knowledge or skills and qualified for L-1B could qualify for E visas, as possessing essential or even unique skills. Knowledge of proprietary company operational or processing techniques, *e.g.*, how a company assembled the car to achieve quality, was similarly deemed essential, but it was anticipated that most such technicians could be replaced in a predesignated period of time by American workers, after the American employees were given the opportunity to train in the techniques.

Thus, a greater number of technicians might be brought in as "essential" to the start-up of an enterprise, but their visas would be limited and the E-2 company should expect to replace these employees with Americans. The total number of E employees at a facility should naturally dwindle to the truly essential few after a couple years.

When this concept of the short-term essential employee was enshrined in the guidance cables, the Japanese companies and their attorneys tried another tactic—essential technical employees had to come each year to the facility because the car models changed each year and the patented engineering evolved, such that each year "new" proprietary knowledge was needed. The companies were unpersuasive in convincing the VO that model changes affected the assembly of new model cars in such a fundamental way. Had the manufacturer created a new and unique means of manufacturing and assembling, their arguments would have been more persuasive.

A company's operations or products could have been based on such a unique skill-set possessed by one or more of its employees that it would not have been reasonable to insist on the training of Americans. Such was the case where the embassy sought to deny an E visa to an applicant who was a craftsman of Japanese woodcut dyeing techniques for textiles. His was more an art, which included carving the wood to some extent. Research showed that very few persons had the requisite skill in the world, and most of those were Japanese nationals. Training an American in the intricate techniques, while vaguely feasible over a long haul, was not practical in real terms, so a full reciprocity E-2 as an essential employee was authorized. The VO also approved a case of a Korean artisan; his company's unique figures were often damaged in transport, so they needed someone here who could repair the artifacts. The training for such work took many years and was highly specialized.

Overall, however, the VO's interpretations ended the largely unmitigated flow of all manner of personnel to the United States, providing consuls with better guidance to distinguish which senior or essential employees were sufficiently managerial or possessed special skills to warrant E visa issuance.

Walsh-Pollard and the State Department View

In the *Walsh-Pollard* case,[38] the BIA accepted almost wholesale the VO's position on significant aspects of the E-2 criteria, including substantiality of an investment, control and direction of the enterprise, and who was an essential employee. The sending company designed a transmission based on automotive knowledge not yet taught in the United States that General Motors wanted introduced into its U.S.-manufactured product line. It was clear that these foreign workers provided essential skills, namely, technical knowledge and skills not available in the United States. Thus, they met the traditional definition for essential employees.

The nontraditional aspect of this case lay in its structure. The foreign entity created a service subsidiary by E-2 investment in the United States to whom their workers reported and by whom they were supported. The parent wholly owned this entity; thus, it met the substantiality and nationality tests. The significant difference in structure arose when GM insisted that these workers perform these specialized services on its premises rather than off-site. This difference from traditional structures led to erroneous views that the structure was a "job shop" arrangement established merely to handle a particular order rather than a commercial enterprise that would engage in ongoing business activities.

The VO found that since the foreign workers reported to and were supervised by the E-2 company officials and not GM personnel, the arrangement, albeit different, qualified for E-2 status. The BIA supported all the DOS regulations and interpretations in its case. Furthermore, DOS still continues to strongly view job shop arrangements as not qualifying for E visa status.

Intent to Return Abroad

The regulation requires that an E treaty visa-holder have intent to return abroad. Harmonizing this requirement with the practical aspects of treaty investment and trade is a conundrum. A person normally would be coming to the United States for an extensive period to pursue his or her treaty interests, and probably would maintain minimal ties with his or her home country.

The requirement that the treaty alien intend to depart upon termination of status is a longstanding regulatory requirement. The FAM already contained a brief substantive note instructing consuls that an investor or trader need not establish that he or she is proceeding to the United States for a specific temporary period of time. The note specifically instructed posts that such applicants are not required to possess a residence abroad that they have no intention of abandoning. Consuls, nevertheless, often insisted on evidence more applicable to short trips by B-1 businesspeople or B-2 tourists—family remaining behind, continuing property ownership, extensive bank accounts, a job, etc. Too many treaty visa applicants and their attorneys were complaining that E visas were being denied to otherwise well-qualified applicants where the only issue was the intent to return.

The FAM note thus was extensively revised and expanded and became one of the single longest notes under the E visa section, until the *Walsh-Pollard* notes were developed. Fundamentally, the revised note sought to dismiss the traditional concept of immigrant intent that the consul typically adjudicated, arguing that an E visa applicant might not be able to provide the usual evidence sought to demonstrate intent to return; most evidence a consul might consider was less likely to be available from a treaty visa-holder coming for a long stay. Brief consideration was given to revising the FAM note to state simply that the intent to return did not apply for treaty cases because of the practical unavailability of useful evidence of an intent far in the future. But it was decided to retain that requirement. Another view that surfaced within the VO was that even though the statute itself specifically did not address temporariness, DOS could not eliminate the standing regulatory requirement via executive fiat; this would require a statutory change.

As long as an E visa applicant made an unequivocal statement that he or she intended to return

---

[38] *Matter of Walsh and Pollard*, 20 I&N Dec. 60 (BIA 1988).

at some point when the trade or fortunes, good or bad, of the investment enterprise permitted, he or she did not need to provide other evidence of intent. To some extent this ameliorated the problem, but to this day, consuls continue to see intent to return as an E visa issue when it should not be. A pending immigrant petition or visa case might lead to further inquiry, but even then an investor or trader could be seen as intending a temporary sojourn on a current entry, with any permanent intent abiding until the approval of the petition or visa. It is also permissible to issue an E visa to an alien with a pending immigrant petition as long as he or she satisfies the consular officer that he or she plans to return to the country of nationality for immigrant visa processing.

PROMULGATION OF E VISA REGULATIONS AND THE NEW EB-5 IMMIGRANT CATEGORY

Much of the development in the FAM notes is further memorialized in the E visa regulations that were belatedly published as a final rule on September 12, 1997. Both DOS and legacy INS published final rules on the same day. As a current set of regulations is now in place, there is renewed emphasis on distinguishing between the regulations (law) and the FAM notes (guidance). Still, the regulations do not cover many scenarios and the FAM notes continue to have relevance for purposes of E visa adjudications.

Of particular interest to practitioners with a large stable of E-2 treaty investor business is the long-term impact of the EB-5 immigrant investor category that was introduced by the Immigration Act of 1990.[39] The EB-5 category presents significant questions concerning the further development of the law on investors. While the E-2 visa interpretive guidance has been an early foundation for analysis of the merits of specific EB-5 investor cases, development of additional investment criteria has shifted to EB-5 cases and to the courts and the agencies responsible for adjudicating them—primarily USCIS and possibly DOS. The 1990s witnessed a tremendous controversy in the EB-5 arena, and, in turn, a rash of reactive analysis and rulings for which binding precedent status was asserted by the government.

Practitioners fear a further evolution in the E-2 visa category that is tainted by the controversy that seems to persistently swirl around all matters involving the EB-5 category. Consuls' decision-making seems to be evolving toward a stricter view of which investments can qualify for the E-2 visa, with a higher set of standards and even valuation of the investment, seemingly driven in part by the harsh government attitude toward the EB-5 category.

SUMMARY

The FAM notes enshrine the belief that the treaty visa category promotes trade and investment as a means to help American business. They came to enshrine also the companion policy—the trade-off—that investment in the United States, to be worthy of conferring nonimmigrant or immigrant status, had to be based on an alien's significant investment for which he or she assumed personal financial risk.

Indeed, that treaty negotiators for a host of countries and the United States had drafted these treaties over the centuries to facilitate trade and investment was a guiding tenet in FAM development. Thus, it should be DOS's mission and goal—both in Washington and in the field—to facilitate the agreed-upon trade or investment. The VO, in promulgating the early guidance sought not to complicate, but to clarify and simply, realizing that most consuls are not trained specifically in business law or practices, nor in the nuances of treaty law. Templates were designed into the revised FAM to give a step-by-step paradigm for consular adjudicators to follow, in order to conduct proper analysis.

In the end, though, the perfect storm and its aftermath created greater tension between the policy of trade facilitation supported by the treaties, and the implementation of comparatively restrictionist immigration law and regulations. The Japanese businessmen's expansive views captured the treaties' spirit of trade facilitation, but ran afoul of the INA's mandate to limit beneficiaries to key personnel and the concomitant U.S interest in protecting the American worker from undue foreign labor competition. The expanded FAM guidance provided consuls with more grist when they were inspired to adopt a strict interpretation in their decision-making.

The challenge of the E visa is that gray area remains, and ever-evolving business practices require practitioners to persuade the government to address difficult questions in a meaningful and constructive way consistent with the intent of the law. Notwithstanding the amplified guidance in the FAM and the availability of the advisory opinion process, some

---

[39] Immigration Act of 1990, Pub. L. No. 101 649, 104 Stat. 4978 (IMMACT90).

qualified investors and traders still find themselves barred by consular decisions that apply restrictive rules.

Moreover, practitioners, legislators, and guidance providers need to look at the treaty trader and investor visas in the proper perspective. The treaties constitute bilateral, not multilateral, agreements, and the entire concept is 200 years old. Lawmakers should think less of stretching an antiquated, albeit effective, concept into the modern world and more of legislating a new trade/investment-based visa classification that realistically addresses the current trade environment and ever-changing business structures and practices. The trade professional category found in the NAFTA, the Chile and Singapore H-1B1 visa, and the E-3 visa are attempts to move in this direction. The authors suggest that a universal trade/investor classification be devised that provides for the international movement of certain professionals and managers in a facilitative manner. The standards should be such that they are transparent and are straightforward, allowing for expeditious consular or USCIS adjudication and processing consistent with the spirit of all trade agreements.

A SYNOPSIS OF THE FORMER NONPREFERENCE INVESTOR CATEGORY

*by Lincoln Stone**

INTRODUCTION

During its deliberations on the legislation that eventually became the fifth employment-based preference visa category (EB-5) in the Immigration Act of 1990,[1] the Senate committee ushering passage of the bill referred favorably to the regulations relating to the former nonpreference investor category.[2] The implication was that a body of law already existed, and it might serve as a resource for resolution of issues that could arise in the course of shaping policy for the EB-5 category and adjudicating individual EB-5 petitions.

Most practitioners these days know little if anything about the former nonpreference investor category, as it was a factor in immigration practice during the late 1960s and early 1970s and it went out of use entirely nearly 30 years ago. This article is a synopsis of the former nonpreference investor category, and it is intended to provide practitioners with an introduction to avenues of further research.

ORIGINS: A NARROWLY-PRESCRIBED EXEMPTION FROM LABOR CERTIFICATION

The Immigration Act of 1965[3] introduced a "nonpreference" visa category for immigrating to the United States without a family or employer sponsor. Section 212(a)(14) of the Immigration and Nationality Act (INA),[4] however, required that all immigrants who would perform skilled or unskilled labor must obtain labor certification from the Department of Labor (DOL). By regulation in 1966, the legacy Immigration and Naturalization Service (INS) specified the categories of nonpreference immigrants who would not require a labor certification because such immigrants theoretically were not seeking employment. Those who could claim they were not seeking employment included, for instance, a member of the U.S. military, a fiancé intending to marry a U.S. citizen or permanent resident, as well as an investor. The regulation allowed an alien to claim he or she was not within the purview of the statute requiring labor certification if the individual could demonstrate he or she was "an alien who [would] engage in a commercial or agricultural enterprise in which he had invested or is actively in the process of investing a substantial amount of capital."[5] The avoidance of labor certification was just as important for practitioners then as it is apt to be for practitioners today; an investor desiring to immigrate on a preference petition was subject to labor certification and would be denied a visa unless labor certification was obtained.[6]

From the initial version of the regulation providing for the nonpreference investor category, which required only three seemingly simple items of proof—(i) an "enterprise" in which the alien; (ii) had "invested or is actively in the process of investing"; and (iii) an amount of capital that could be considered "substantial"—the immigration regulators continued to tinker with the regulations by adding progressively more detail in the requirements for eligibility as a nonpreference investor. The tensions in the regulation providing for nonpreference investors—the need to ensure the protection of the U.S. worker, pitted against the desire for an immigration vehicle separate

---

* This article originally appeared in the 1st edition of AILA's *Immigration Options for Investors and Entrepreneurs* (AILA 2006).

Lincoln Stone practices immigration law in Los Angeles with Stone & Grzegorek LLP. The author thanks Eugene Flynn and Stanley Mailman for their assistance with this article.

[1] Immigration Act of 1990 (IMMACT90), Pub. L. No. 101-649, 104 Stat. 4978.

[2] S. Rep. No. 101-55, at 21 (1989). See the companion article concerning the legislative history of the EB-5 investor category, C. Perez Gonzalez et al., "Legislative History of the EB-5 Category for Immigrant Investors," elsewhere in this volume.

[3] Immigration and Nationality Act Amendments of October 3, 1965, Pub. L. No. 29-236, 79 Stat. 911.

[4] Immigration and Nationality Act of 1952 (INA), Pub. L. No. 82-414, 66 Stat. 163 (codified as amended at 8 USC §§1101 et seq.).

[5] 31 Fed. Reg. 10021 (July 23, 1966), adding to Title 8 of the Code of Federal Regulations, the section 212.8 (including §212.8(b)(4) concerning investors), entitled "Certification requirement of 212(a)(14)."

[6] *Matter of Zang*, 13 I&N Dec. 290 (Acting D.D. 1969), denying sixth-preference petition filed by investor.

and apart from having a family member or employer sponsor—gave way to a solution that resulted in raising the bar for nonpreference investors (*e.g.*, a $10,000 minimum capital investment, and the employment of at least one other U.S. worker). But that solution also had the salutary effect of providing a more definite target for nonpreference investors to meet. Over the course of the decade, the INS (and the Department of State (DOS) in its parallel regulations[7]) added further requirements for eligibility in the nonpreference investor category. Effective February 12, 1973, for example, INS required nonpreference investors to invest a minimum $10,000 in capital, and to demonstrate one year of prior experience and training.[8] Thereafter, effective October 7, 1976, citing concerns that the nonpreference investor category was being used essentially to evade the labor certification law's protection of U.S. workers, INS raised the minimum capital requirement to $40,000, required the petitioner to demonstrate that he or she was a principal manager of the enterprise, and mandated that the enterprise must create at least one job for other U.S. workers.[9] In short order, though, by late 1976, the nonpreference investor category would fall into disuse due to the oversubscription of higher preference visas.[10]

EXPERIENCE OF PRACTITIONERS

Practitioners representing investors seeking benefits under the nonpreference investor category utilized an earlier version of Form I-526, then titled "Request for Determination that Prospective Immigrant is an Investor (in order to be relieved from labor certification requirement of Section 212(a)(14) of the Immigration and Nationality Act.)" As INS had augmented the requirements for eligibility under the former nonpreference investor category, it also gradually revised Form I-526 to match the changes in the requirements of the law.[11] The nonpreference investor typically filed Form I-526 concurrently with a Form I-485 application if in the United States and seeking adjustment of status. Form I-526 also could be filed directly with the U.S. consular post abroad.

The same form number is used currently by petitioners in the EB-5 category. Practitioners will note just a few similarities between the current Form I-526 and the 1970s version of Form I-526. The principal difference is the emphasis the old Form I-526 placed on eliciting information concerning the petitioner's prior experience and training. The current Form I-526 does not request such information.[12] Note that ever since INS adopted Form I-526 for use by petitioners in the EB-5 category (with the implementing regulations of IMMACT90), the title had been changed to "Immigrant Petition by Alien Entrepreneur."

A sampling of the cases filed pursuant to the former nonpreference investor category reveals that the petitioners for the most part were owners of small businesses such as motels, gas stations, and restaurants. The investments tended to be acquisitions of existing small businesses and sole proprietorships, rather than investments in new, larger businesses.[13]

RELEVANT CONSIDERATIONS IN UTILIZING THE LAW OF THE NONPREFERENCE INVESTOR CATEGORY IN CURRENT PRACTICE

As practitioners gained more experience with the nonpreference investor category, unfavorable decisions were challenged on appeal and ended up as published decisions by the INS Associate Commissioner or the Board of Immigration Appeals (BIA). In one case, a gas station owner failed to demonstrate an "investment" by presenting evidence of funds in a bank account and contracts for purchases of gas, oil, and other merchandise because such evidence does not persuasively indicate a commitment

---

[7] 22 CFR §42.91(a)(14)(ii)(d) (1977); 22 CFR §40.7(a)(14)(iii)(C) (1987); 9 *Foreign Affairs Manual* (FAM) 40.7(a)(14) N.1.3, *as amended*, TL: Visa-1; 8-30-87.

[8] 38 Fed. Reg. 1380 (Jan. 12, 1973); 38 Fed. Reg. 8590 (Apr. 4, 1973).

[9] 41 Fed. Reg. 37566 (Sept. 7, 1976). The current 8 CFR §§212.8(b)(4), 1212.8(b)(4) continues with this formulation, as it has never been repealed. The Department of State (DOS), however, promulgated new requirements—for instance it raised the minimum capital investment to $100,000—and it began to articulate a body of legal standards applicable to investment immigration by further developing its FAM notes at 9 FAM 40.7(a)(14) N.1.3, *as amended*, TL: Visa-1; 8-30-87.

[10] *See, e.g.*, S. Mailman, "The New Regulation on Immigrant Investors," 176 *N.Y.L.J.* 68 (Oct. 6, 1976).

[11] The Form I-526, revised as of December 22, 1979, is included as Appendix A to this article.

[12] The current Form I-526 is reprinted as Appendix B to this article.

[13] The author thanks Mark Ivener for sharing excerpts from his nonpreference investor client files.

of the required funds to the business operation.¹⁴ In another case, the BIA held that the "investment" in a restaurant business is not proven by mere copies of checks claimed to be for purchases, if not accompanied by corresponding invoices for furniture and inventory.¹⁵

The BIA ruled that an investor cannot be held to be "in the process of investing" the required capital without a firm commitment of that capital. Accordingly, a landscaping service owner had not invested the minimum $10,000 where an initial $7,000 had been invested at the time of the petition filing and petitioner had intended to invest another $9,000 at a later time after visa issuance. The BIA found this arrangement to be insufficient "conditional intent."¹⁶ In a case decided with similar reasoning, the BIA held that a promissory note does not constitute the requisite firm commitment if the note provides for one date on which payment is to be made and the petitioner presents further evidence that is inconsistent with the indicated date.¹⁷ In yet another case, the BIA held that although the law would allow a petitioner to claim credit for a reasonable amount of cash deposited in a business bank account for routine business operations, the petitioner cannot prevail on a claimed investment for future business purchases of inventory where there are no contracts that would bind petitioner to expend such funds.¹⁸

One of the best available resource tools for practitioners representing investors is the DOS *Foreign Affairs Manual* (FAM). Beginning in the 1970s, and continuing to this day, the DOS Visa Office has endeavored to articulate standards for investment immigration. Not only did the Visa Office articulate in the FAM a set of standards relating to the nonpreference investor category,¹⁹ it also crafted parallel evolving standards for consular adjudication of E-2 nonimmigrant visas.²⁰ Adjudication standards for the nonimmigrant and immigrant categories, thus, in many respects, were developed in tandem as certain investment concepts were common to both categories.²¹ Indeed, the Visa Office developed E-2 visa guidelines based on BIA determinations in nonpreference investor cases, just as the Visa Office's experience with E visa adjudication informed its drafting of FAM notes for the nonpreference investor category. Consequently, the FAM notes concerning the nonpreference investor category can be viewed as at least a partial summation of the law concerning investor immigrants as it then existed.

To illustrate, one FAM note is devoted to the characteristics of an "investment." It states:

> The source of the money being invested is not material to the question of whether the applicant qualifies for the exemption, provided the funds being invested are the alien's own funds. The concept of investment connotes the placing of funds or other capital assets at risk in the hope of generating a return on the funds risked ... A consular officer may properly inquire into the source of the investment funds in this or any other case in which there is reasonable basis for questioning whether the alien actually possessed sufficient money for the asserted investment. ... An alien's personal assets and available, uninvested resources do not constitute a part of the investment....²²

From the beginning of the nonpreference investor category, the governing regulation authorized the benefit of permanent residence for an alien who presented evidence that he or she "invested or is in the process of investing." The very same language is found in the antecedent statute and regulations concerning the E-2 nonimmigrant visa category²³ as well as the statutes and regulations concerning the current EB-5 category.²⁴

Given the similarities between the language used in the two immigrant investor categories, it may be tempting to a practitioner to cite the evident parallels between the language used in the nonpreference category and the EB-5 category and to draw an adjudica-

---

¹⁴ *Matter of Ahmad*, 15 I&N Dec. 81 (BIA 1974).

¹⁵ *Matter of Shaw*, 15 I&N Dec. 794 (BIA 1976).

¹⁶ *Matter of Lui*, 15 I&N Dec. 206 (BIA 1975).

¹⁷ *Matter of Lee*, 15 I&N Dec. 408 (BIA 1975).

¹⁸ *Matter of Khan*, 16 I&N Dec. 138 (BIA 1977).

¹⁹ 9 FAM 40.7(a)(14) N.1.3, *as amended*, TL: Visa-1; 8-30-87.

²⁰ Importantly, for purposes of E visa adjudication, the FAM notes do not have the binding legal authority of regulations, as in 8 CFR §214.2(e) and 22 CFR §41.51. However, the FAM notes represent DOS's accumulated work product over the years.

²¹ *See* the companion article, S. Fischel & R. Sindelar, "The Evolution of Legal Precedent in Treaty Visa Cases," appearing elsewhere in this volume.

²² 9 FAM 40.7(a)(14) N.1.3-1, *as amended*; TL: Visa-1; 8-30-87.

²³ INA §101(a)(15)(E)(ii); 8 CFR §214.2(e); 22 CFR §41.51.

²⁴ INA §§203(b)(5)(A)(i) and 216A(d)(1)(A)(i), *as amended*.

tor's attention to the FAM notes and case law developed during the 1970s when courts decided appeals in nonpreference investor cases. Could a practitioner mine the case law and other available legal standards pertaining to the nonpreference investor category to marshal a winning argument in favor of the EB-5 petitioner seeking to remove the conditions on permanent residence? There are at least a few reasons for exercising caution when attempting to highlight the lineage from the nonpreference investor category to the EB-5 investor category.

First, it is critical to acknowledge that certain concepts common to investment immigration are best understood in the context of their actual roots. The single most important underlying consideration in shaping the law on the nonpreference investor category was the bureaucracy's objective of protecting the U.S. labor market. For example, when the category was first in use, and there was no definite dollar amount for the minimum investment, relatively smaller investments presented to the reviewing INS or consular officer the central question of whether the investment was "substantial" within the meaning of the regulation. In the circumstances, INS and consular officers no doubt perceived themselves as the front line defenders of the U.S. worker, which they were determined to protect and supposed they did so by denying nonpreference investor requests that were based on insubstantial investments. The flavor of both the regulatory modifications to the nonpreference investor category as well as the BIA decisions in cases of nonpreference investors reveals a keen interest on the part of the bureaucracy to preserve the essential thrust of the labor certification requirement. In other words, terms such as "marginality" and "substantiality" were to be viewed in nonpreference investor adjudications through the lens of the objectives of the labor certification requirement, *i.e.*, to prevent immigrants from competing in the U.S. labor market. If it appeared likely the investor might eventually compete in the U.S. labor market (as opposed to manage an enterprise of his or her own creation), then the request might be denied for the reason that the investment was only marginal or was not substantial.[25] But if, on the other hand, the investor's commitment to the enterprise is irrevocable and there are indications of likely success of the enterprise that would benefit other U.S. workers, then an investment was likely to be considered substantial and qualifying, regardless of the fact that the investor might perform unskilled tasks in the business.[26]

Whereas the clear emphasis in the law on nonpreference investors was placed on erecting legal standards that ostensibly protected the U.S. workforce from the adverse effects of allowing one additional job-seeking immigrant to the United States, the underlying considerations in the EB-5 category (and the nonimmigrant E-2 visa category) are significantly different. The EB-5 category is intended to attract foreign capital and to create jobs in the U.S. economy; the EB-5 investor is presumed to be no threat to the U.S. workforce. Similarly, the objective of the E-2 investor visa category is to facilitate reciprocal investment and trade.[27]

In a real sense, in the adjudication of cases pursuant to the nonpreference category, the decisionmakers narrowly and restrictively interpreted legal standards in order to advance the objective of protecting the U.S. worker. On the other hand, in order to effectively foster the very different objectives of the EB-5 category, adjudicators of EB-5 petitions could interpret what appear to be the same legal concepts quite differently from the way the concepts were interpreted in nonpreference investor cases. Adjudicators of EB-5 petitions, in short, might liberally construe prevailing legal standards. The upshot is that due to the widely different objectives of these investor provisions, similar language could be interpreted differently in order to further the respective underlying aims.

In deciding whether to use the analogy to nonpreference investor cases, a second consideration for the practitioner is to what extent directly applicable positive law already exists. To illustrate this particular cautionary point, there is no merit in arguing that the nonpreference investor category recognized a particular intangible asset as "capital" and, thus, the asset should also be considered capital for purposes of adjudication of an EB-5 petition. The regulations for the EB-5 category already clearly require an asset to be a tangible asset if it is to be considered

---

[25] *See, e.g., Matter of Heitland*, 14 I&N Dec. 563 (BIA 1974), *aff'd* 551 F.2d 495 (2d Cir. 1977), denying petition based on $3,400 investment for purchase of a truck to be used in a pickup and delivery business.

[26] *Matter of Ko*, 14 I&N Dec. 349 (Dep. Assoc. Comm'r 1973), approving petition based on $18,000 investment in a retail shoe business.

[27] 9 FAM 41.51 N.1, directing consular officers to adjudicate E visa applications in the spirit of facilitating economic and commercial interaction between the treaty countries.

capital.[28] Absent clear direction from Congress, the agency is free to legislate in this manner. An absurd or unreasonable result may signal the need for regulatory or statutory change, but, in the meantime, the citation by counsel to a 30-year-old nonpreference investor case will not change an adjudicator's determination to apply the directly applicable regulation in the case of an EB-5 petition.

Having noted a few limitations on using the law on nonpreference investors in current practice, one area of the EB-5 statutes and regulations that is not fully delineated and appears like it could be the subject of much future dispute is the law on removal of conditions. The statute concerning removal of conditions requires proof that the investor has "invested, or is actively in the process of investing," the requisite capital.[29] This statutory language is the same language found in the regulation on nonpreference investors.

The statute on removal of conditions, however, also requires the petitioner to prove that the requisite investment has been "sustained" throughout the period of conditional residence.[30] The regulation concerning this requirement adds ostensibly favorable "good faith" language. It states that the "sustained" requirement will be deemed satisfied if the petitioner "in good faith, has substantially met the capital investment requirement of the statute and continuously maintained his or her capital investment over the two years of conditional residence."[31]

But closer scrutiny of the regulation and the agency commentary to the regulation reveals that by way of introducing its regulation to further define what is meant by the term "sustained," legacy INS may have introduced quantitative criteria for completion of the investment. That is, according to the regulation and accompanying commentary, the term "sustained" not only involves "continuously maintaining" the investment (a natural connotation of the word "sustained"), but it also requires "substantial" compliance (which is not a natural connotation of the word "sustained"). The evident error, though, is that the regulation concerning the term "sustained" may crowd out and negate the effect of the statutory phrase "actively in the process of investing" the required capital.

One might argue on a particular set of facts that the regulation concerning the term "sustained" entirely negates the statutory language "in the process of investing." For example, at the time of filing the petition for removal of conditions, the petitioner may have invested 60 percent of the capital required by the statute, will invest another 30 percent of the capital required three months after filing the petition, and will invest the final 10 percent required by statute approximately six months after filing the petition for removal of conditions. This scenario would appear to satisfy the standard of being in the process of investing the required capital. But it is questionable whether the scenario would satisfy the "substantial" compliance part of the legacy INS regulation concerning sustained investment.

In its comment to the final regulation, legacy INS observed that "[w]hile there is no statutory requirement with respect to when the requisite capital must have been invested during the two-year period," Congress nonetheless "expressed its intent that substantially all of the requisite capital be invested by the alien entrepreneur before the expiration of the conditional resident status."[32] Legacy INS's conclusion rests on the flimsy reasoning that the statutory language "invested" is in the past tense. The reasoning of course ignores the alternative statutory language "in the process of investing." If the regulation concerning "sustained" in effect nullifies the statutory language concerning "in the process of investing" then the regulation might amount to *ultra vires* agency action.[33]

It is conceivable that the law on the nonpreference investor category—which involved the very same language of "in the process of investing"—could be used by practitioners who are faced with this knotty problem. The law on nonpreference investors is a body of law that interprets what it means to be "in the process of investing." When

---

[28] 8 CFR §204.6(e) Definitions.

[29] INA §216A(d)(1)(A)(i), *as amended*.

[30] INA §216A(d)(1)(A)(ii), *as amended*.

[31] 8 CFR §§216.6(c)(1)(iii), 1216.6(c)(1)(iii).

[32] Commentary to Final Rule, 59 Fed. Reg. 26588–89 (May 23, 1994).

[33] Note that in issuing its AAO precedent decisions concerning I-526 petitioners, the legacy Immigration and Naturalization Service (INS) invoked the same regulation concerning removal of conditions (requiring substantial completion of the investment) as an analytical basis for effectively negating the phrase "actively in the process of investing" as it appears in INA §203(b)(5)(A)(ii). *See Matter of Hsiung*, 22 I&N Dec. 201, 19 *Immigr. Rptr.* B2-106 (AAO July 31, 1998); *Matter of Izumii*, 22 I&N Dec. 169, 19 *Immigr. Rptr.* B2-32 (AAO July 13, 1998).

enacting the EB-5 category, Congress favorably cited the law on nonpreference investors.[34] A FAM note concerning the nonpreference investor category intends to provide guidance on what it means to be "actively in the process of investing." It states that the legal concept of being "actively in the process of investing" permits

> something less than a completed investment. This does not, however, include situations in which the investment is wholly prospective in nature. The essential elements are: an actual commitment of some money; evidence that the business exists, even though it may not yet be operational; evidence that the cost of acquiring or establishing the business will be at least $100,000; and evidence that the alien is in possession and control of at least $100,000.[35]

In federal court cases concerning the nonpreference investor category, where the applicant had invested additional funds in the business after the filing of the application such that the total investment exceeded the minimum capital requirement although the minimum had not been met at the time the application was filed, courts have held that the BIA may not ignore the post-application investment. Because the law authorizes the applicant to be "in the process of investing" the required capital, the post-application investment must be counted.[36]

In *Gill*, the nonpreference investor applicant had made substantial investments in his business for advertising and solicitation of sales agents. He had purchased inventory and obtained licenses to operate in several cities. He had employed a secretary and a part-time bookkeeper. The cumulative activity was indicative of a "continuing investment pattern." The court held that "[w]here probative evidence of such a pattern is present, as it is here, the plain language of 8 CFR §212.8(b)(4) requires a consideration of post-application investments in determining whether the alien has invested the requisite sum. (citations omitted) Any other interpretation would render the 'actively in the process of investing' clause a nullity."[37]

The *Gill* case, in short, stands for the proposition that a "continuing investment pattern" amounts to being in the process of investing the required capital. In these circumstances, an examiner must consider the post-application investment when determining whether the minimum capital requirement has been met. Applied to the circumstances of an EB-5 investor who is petitioning for removal of conditions, counsel should be able to argue that the compelling evidence of a continuing investment pattern amounts to being in the process of investing the required capital. This argument, which is based on the statutory language of "in the process of investing," should trump the legacy INS's restrictive regulation and commentary that strain to import the "substantial" completion concept into the meaning of what constitutes a "sustained" investment. The argument is all the more persuasive if it is supported with evidence that the investment is furthering the job-creation objectives of the EB-5 category.

CONCLUSION

Beyond pure historical interest, practitioners who represent nonimmigrant and immigrant investors are well advised to consult the body of law produced by the nonpreference investor category. A search of federal court cases, administrative decisions, and the FAM notes may prove to be a fruitful exercise in advocating a client's case.

---

[34] *See* S. Rep. No. 101-55, *supra*, note 2.

[35] 9 FAM 40.7(a)(14) N.1.3-2, *as amended*; TL: Visa-1; 8-30-87. The sum of $100,000 was required by DOS regulation at that time.

[36] *See, e.g., Gill v. INS*, 666 F.2d 390 (9th Cir. 1982).

[37] *Id.* at 393. *See also Hirunpidok v. INS*, 641 F.2d 778 (9th Cir. 1981), reversing BIA denial for failure to consider evidence of post-application investment.

APPENDIX A—FORM I-526 FROM 1979

UNITED STATES DEPARTMENT OF JUSTICE

Immigration and Naturalization Service

(Please tear off this sheet before submitting application)

REQUEST FOR DETERMINATION THAT PROSPECTIVE IMMIGRANT IS AN INVESTOR
In order to be relieved from labor certification requirement
of Section 212(a)(14) of the Immigration and Nationality Act

INSTRUCTIONS
READ INSTRUCTIONS CAREFULLY

1. *General.*—An alien seeking to live in the United States for the purpose of performing skilled or unskilled labor may become a lawful permanent resident of the United States only if the Secretary of Labor has issued a certification in the alien's behalf. Such certification may be issued only if the Secretary of Labor has determined that (a) there are not sufficient workers in the United States who are able, willing and available for the contemplated work and (b) the employment of the alien will not adversely affect the wages and working conditions of workers in the United States.

Certain persons such as close relatives of U.S. citizens or of lawful permanent resident aliens are exempt from the labor certification requirement. Also certain refugees are exempt from this requirement.

In addition, the requirement for a certification by the Secretary of Labor is not considered to be applicable to an alien who establishes that he has invested, or is actively in the process of investing, capital totaling at least $40,000 in an enterprise in the United States of which he will be a principal manager and that the enterprise will employ a person or persons in the United States who are United States citizens or aliens lawfully admitted for permanent residence, exclusive of the alien, his spouse and children.

If you believe that you qualify as an investor within the preceding paragraph and you desire to request a determination to that effect so that you will not be considered subject to the labor certification requirement, execute and submit this form with the prescribed supporting documents.

Approval of this request will establish a priority date for assignment of a non-preference visa number. It does not entitle the applicant to enter or remain in the United States. Since the availability of non-preference visa numbers vary from time to time you are advised to contact an American Consulate or this Service prior to a commitment of investment funds for current availability of visa numbers.

2. *Where to submit request.*—If you are in the United States you may submit the request on this form to an office of the Immigration and Naturalization Service only if you are eligible to apply for adjustment of status to that of a lawful permanent resident on Form I-485. In such case this form must be attached to Form I-485 and must be submitted with it to the Service office having jurisdiction over your place of residence. In all other cases you may submit the request to the American Consulate or Embassy at which you intend to apply for an immigrant visa.

3. *Supporting Documents.*—The following supporting documents must be submitted with this form:

   a. Evidence that you have invested or are actively in the process of investing capital totaling $40,000 in an enterprise located or to be located in the United States. Such evidence may be in the form of cancelled checks, receipts, bank letters, etc.

   Also

   b. Evidence that you have established or are actively in the process of establishing an enterprise in the United States. Such evidence may consist of a corporate charter, partnership agreement, license or other official authorization to engage in business, bank letters, financial statement, contracts.

   Also

   c. Evidence that you have arranged for a place in the United States at which to operate the enterprise. Such evidence may consist of a deed or lease or option to purchase or rent.

   Also

   4. Evidence that you are qualified to engage in the enterprise. This evidence may consist of letters from employers or trainers by whom you were employed or trained in jobs which qualify you to engage in the enterprise, describing the title and duties of the job including tools and equipment used, the date you started and terminated such job, and the number of hours per week you worked; letters from former business associates, contracts, invoices and other documents establishing that you have engaged in a similar enterprise, the size and location of such enterprise and the period you were so engaged; certificates, degrees, professional or journeyman licenses or other documents indicating you have been found qualified to engage in an occupation or business related to the enterprise in which you have invested or are actively in the process of investing.

4. *Rules for Documents.*—All supporting documents must be submitted in the original. If you desire to have the original returned to you, and if copies are by law permitted to be made, you may submit photostatic or typewritten copies. Photostatic copies unaccompanied by the original may be accepted if the copy bears a certification by an immigration or consular officer that the copy was compared with the original and found to be identical. A foreign document must be accompanied by a summary translation in English. The translator must certify that he is competent to translate and that the translation is accurate. A summary translation is a condensation or abstract of the text.

5. *Penalties.*—Severe penalties are provided by law for knowingly and willfully falsifying or concealing a material fact or using any false document in the submission of this form. Also a false representation may result in the denial of your application for status as a permanent resident or any other application you may make for any benefit under the immigration laws of the United States. Any statement submitted with this form is considered part of the form.

Form I-526 (Rev. 12-22-79)N

UNITED STATES DEPARTMENT OF JUSTICE
Immigration and Naturalization Service

Form approved
OMB No. 43-R0514

REQUEST FOR DETERMINATION THAT PROSPECTIVE IMMIGRANT IS AN INVESTOR
in order to be relieved from labor certification requirement
of Section 212(a)(14) of the Immigration and Nationality Act

FILL IN WITH TYPEWRITER OR PRINT IN BLOCK LETTERS WITH BALLPOINT PEN. DO NOT LEAVE ANY QUESTION UNANSWERED. When appropriate insert "None" or "Not Applicable". If you need more space to answer fully any question on this form use a separate sheet of paper this size and identify each answer with the number of the corresponding question.

I hereby declare that I am seeking to become a lawful permanent resident of the United States for the purpose of engaging in an enterprise, and that I have invested, or am actively in the process of investing, in such enterprise capital totaling at least $40,000. On the basis of such investment, I request that the labor certification requirement of Section 212(a)(14) of the Immigration and Nationality Act be considered not applicable to me.

☐ I am submitting this request as part of my application to become a lawful permanent resident of the United States

☐ I am submitting this request as part of my application for an immigrant visa

1. Name (Last in CAPS) (First) (Middle) | Alien registration number (if any) | FOR GOVERNMENT USE ONLY
   ☐ Approved ☐ Denied
   DATE OF ACTION
   DD
   DISTRICT

2. Other names used (Married woman give maiden name)

3. Place of Birth (City or town) (Country) | 4. Date of Birth (Mo/Day/Yr)

5. Present address (Number and street) (City or town) (Province or State, Zip Code) (Country)

6. Name and location of enterprise

7. Names and immigration status of partners (if applicable)

8. Percentage of partnership or stock owned by applicant. List other owners and percentage of stock owned by them.

9. Nature of enterprise (Describe briefly; include total number of persons employed or to be employed in the enterprise and relationship, if any, to the applicant. Give name, home address, immigration status and relationship of at least one employee other than your spouse and children.)

10. Show source or potential source of investment funds.

11. Check one: ☐ I have made the investment ☐ I am actively in the process of making the investment

12. The capital investment I made or am actively in the process of making consists of:
    Cash $_____
    Other $_____ (describe) _____
    Other $_____ (describe) _____
    TOTAL $_____

13. Describe briefly how you will engage in the enterprise, including the title of any job you will hold in it and the number of hours per week you will devote to the job.

Form I-526 (Rev. 12-22-79)N | RECEIVED | TRANS. IN | RET'D-TRANS. OUT | COMPLETED

APPENDIX A—FORM I-526 FROM 1979

14. EXPERIENCE—Employment or training you have had which qualify you to engage in the enterprise:
Name and address of employer or trainer
Name of Job	Date started month year	Date left month year	Kind of business
Describe in detail duties you performed, including use of tools, machines, or equipment, number of hours per week.
Name and address of employer or trainer
Name of Job	Date started month year	Date left month year	Kind of business
Describe in detail duties you performed, including use of tools, machines, or equipment, number of hours per week.

15. Describe any additional qualifications you possess for engaging in the enterprise.

16. List licenses (professional, journeyman, etc.) you have received.

17. I have attached the following documentary evidence (check each box applicable).
    - ☐ Financial statements, such as balance sheet, or profit and loss statement
    - ☐ License or other official authorization to engage in business in U.S.
    - ☐ Corporate charter or partnership agreement
    - ☐ Bank statement showing bank balance
    - ☐ Licenses received outside the U.S.
    - ☐ Other (describe briefly)
    - ☐ School records, certificates or diplomas
    - ☐ Lease or deed to premises
    - ☐ Business contracts
    - ☐ Employment letters
    - ☐ Cancelled checks
    - ☐ Receipts

18. If your native alphabet is in other than Roman Letters, write your name in your native alphabet below.

    Signature of applicant

    Date of signature

19. (Signature of person preparing form, if other than applicant) I declare that this document was prepared by me at the request of the applicant and is based on all information on which I have any knowledge.

    Address of person preparing form, if other than applicant

    Date:

    Occupation:

Form I-526 (Rev. 12-22-79)N   For sale by the Superintendent of Documents, U.S. Government Printing Office
Washington, D.C. 20402

APPENDIX B—CURRENT FORM I-526

Department of Homeland Security
U.S. Citizenship and Immigration Services

OMB No. 1615-0026; Exp. 01/31/2012
I-526, Immigrant Petition by Alien Entrepreneur

Do Not Write in This Block - For USCIS Use Only (Except G-28 Block Below)		
Classification	Action Block	Fee Receipt
Priority Date		To be completed by Attorney or Representative, if any ☐ G-28 is attached Attorney's State License No. _____
Remarks:		

START HERE - Type or print in black ink.

Part 1. Information About You

Family Name: _____   Given Name: _____   Middle Name: _____

In care of Street Number and Name: _____

Address: _____   Apt. Number: _____

City: _____   State or Province: _____   Country: _____   Zip/Postal Code: _____

Date of Birth (mm/dd/yyyy): _____   Country of Birth: _____   Social Security # (if any): _____   A # (if any): _____

If you are in the United States, provide the following information:

Date of Arrival (mm/dd/yyyy): _____   I-94 #: _____

Current Nonimmigrant Status: _____   Date Current Status Expires (mm/dd/yyyy): _____   Daytime Phone # with Area Code: _____

Part 2. Application Type *(Check one)*

a. ☐ This petition is based on an investment in a commercial enterprise in a targeted employment area for which the required amount of capital invested has been adjusted downward.

b. ☐ This petition is based on an investment in a commercial enterprise in an area for which the required amount of capital invested has been adjusted upward.

c. ☐ This petition is based on an investment in a commercial enterprise that is not in either a targeted area or in an upward adjustment area.

Part 3. Information About Your Investment

Name of commercial enterprise in which funds are invested: _____

Street Address: _____

Phone # with Area Code: _____   Business organized as (corporation, partnership, etc.): _____

Kind of business (e.g. furniture manufacturer): _____   Date established (mm/dd/yyyy): _____   IRS Tax #: _____

RECEIVED: _____   RESUBMITTED: _____   RELOCATED: SENT _____   REC'D _____

Form I-526 (Rev. 01/06/10)Y

APPENDIX B—CURRENT FORM I-526

Part 3. Information About Your Investment *(Continued)*

Date of your initial investment (mm/dd/yyyy) [   ]

Amount of your initial investment $ [   ]

Your total capital investment in the enterprise to date $ [   ]

Percentage of the enterprise you own [   ]

If you are not the sole investor in the new commercial enterprise, list on separate paper the names of all other parties (natural and non-natural) who hold a percentage share of ownership of the new enterprise and indicate whether any of these parties is seeking classification as an alien entrepreneur. Include the name, percentage of ownership, and whether or not the person is seeking classification under section 203(b)(5). **NOTE:** A "natural" party would be an individual person, and a "non-natural" party would be an entity such as a corporation, consortium, investment group, partnership, etc.

If you indicated in **Part 2** that the enterprise is in a targeted employment area or in an upward adjustment area, name the county and State: County [   ]   State [   ]

Part 4. Additional Information About the Enterprise

Type of Enterprise (check one):

☐ New commercial enterprise resulting from the creation of a new business.

☐ New commercial enterprise resulting from the purchase of an existing business.

☐ New commercial enterprise resulting from a capital investment in an existing business.

Composition of the Petitioner's Investment:

Total amount in U.S. bank account .... $ [   ]

Total value of all assets purchased for use in the enterprise......................... $ [   ]

Total value of all property transferred from abroad to the new enterprise.... $ [   ]

Total of all debt financing... $ [   ]

Total stock purchases.. $ [   ]

Other (explain on separate paper)... $ [   ]

Total $ [   ]

Income:

When you made the investment.........   Gross $ [   ]   Net $ [   ]

Now..   Gross $ [   ]   Net $ [   ]

Net worth:

When you made investment...............   Gross $ [   ]   Now $ [   ]

Form I-526 (Rev. 01/06/10)Y Page 2

Part 5. Employment Creation Information

Number of full-time employees in the enterprise in U.S. (excluding you, your spouse, sons, and daughters)

When you made your initial investment? [ ] Now [ ] Difference [ ]

How many of these new jobs were created by your investment? [ ] How many additional new jobs will be created by your additional investment? [ ]

What is your position, office, or title with the new commercial enterprise?

Briefly describe your duties, activities, and responsibilities.

What is your salary? $ [ ] What is the cost of your benefits? $ [ ]

Part 6. Processing Information

Check One:

☐ The person named in **Part 1** is now in the United States, and an application to adjust status to permanent resident will be filed if this petition is approved.

☐ If the petition is approved and the person named in **Part 1** wishes to apply for an immigrant visa abroad, complete the following for that person:

Country of nationality:

Country of current residence or, if now in the United States, last permanent residence abroad:

If you provided a United States address in **Part 1**, print the person's foreign address:

If the person's native alphabet is other than Roman letters, write the foreign address in the native alphabet:

Are you in deportation or removal proceedings? ☐ Yes (Explain on separate paper) ☐ No

Have you ever worked in the United States without permission? ☐ Yes (Explain on separate paper) ☐ No

Part 7. Signature   *Read the information on penalties in the instructions before completing this section.*

I certify, under penalty of perjury under the laws of the United States of America, that this petition and the evidence submitted with it is all true and correct. I authorize the release of any information from my records that U.S. Citizenship and Immigration Services needs to determine eligibility for the benefit I am seeking.

Signature [ ] Date [ ]

NOTE: *If you do not completely fill out this form or fail to the submit the required documents listed in the instructions, you may not be found eligible for the immigration benefit you are seeking and this petition may be denied.*

Part 8. Signature of Person Preparing Form, If Other Than Above (Sign below)

I declare that I prepared this application at the request of the above person, and it is based on all information of which I have knowledge.

Signature [ ] Print Your Name [ ] Date [ ]

Firm Name [ ] Daytime phone # with area code [ ]

Address [ ]

Form I-526 (Rev. 01/06/10)Y Page 3

LEGISLATIVE HISTORY OF THE EB-5 CATEGORY FOR IMMIGRANT INVESTORS

by Cristina Perez Gonzalez, Humberto R. Gray, and Lincoln Stone[*]

INTRODUCTION

The Immigration Act of 1990 (IMMACT90)[1] created a separate immigrant visa provision for aliens who invest substantial capital and create full-time employment for U.S. workers.[2] The foundation of this immigrant investor provision, enacted as Immigration and Nationality Act (INA)[3] §203(b)(5) and thus known as the employment-based fifth preference (EB-5) category, was established during legislative debates occurring throughout the decade leading up to the enactment. Over time, the concept of a visa for the investor shifted from a "single investor-single visa" paradigm to a comprehensive framework for utilizing foreign capital to stimulate the U.S. economy. The comments herein concentrate on the legislative history of the EB-5 category, specifically prior bills, Senate reports, congressional testimony, and other relevant correspondence between members of Congress and legacy Immigration and Naturalization Service (INS).

1982 BILL: FIRST CHAPTER OF THE DEBATE OVER AN INDEPENDENT VISA ALLOCATION FOR INVESTORS

The EB-5 investor category of IMMACT90 has roots in a Senate bill introduced in 1982, S. 2222 (1982 Bill).[4] The 1981 Report of the Select Committee on Immigration and Refugee Policy, which Congress created in 1978 to conduct a comprehensive review of U.S. immigration law and policy, overwhelmingly supported an independent category for investors based on a national interest rationale.[5] It was no surprise, therefore, that the 1982 Bill included an investor category.[6]

The investor category in the 1982 Bill would have required the immigrant "investor" applicant to establish that he or she invested, or proved to the attorney general the intention[7] to invest, substantial capital of no less than $250,000 in an enterprise in the United States. Furthermore, the applicant would have been required to demonstrate that he or she would be a principal manager, and that the enterprise would both benefit the U.S. economy and create full-time employment for no less than four eligible individuals.[8] In anticipation of the potential abuse under this category, Congress proposed adding a provision that required

---

[*] This article originally appeared in the first edition of *Immigration Options for Investors and Entrepreneurs* (AILA. 2006).

Cristina Perez Gonzalez is the founder of Perez Gonzalez, A PLC. Her practice primarily focuses in assisting foreign professionals in the technology, business, investment, athletic, and entertainment fields, in nonimmigrant and immigrant visas, labor certifications, family petitions, and naturalization. Her clientele includes professional athletes, entertainers, and business and corporate executives. Ms. Gonzalez received her J.D. from Whittier Law School in Los Angeles, and received two bachelor of arts degrees from UCLA.

Humberto Gray is the founder of Humberto R. Gray, A PLC. Since 1987, Mr. Gray has specialized in immigration law within the entertainment, sports, and business areas. He assisted in drafting the regulations for the O and P visa categories. His clientele includes professional athletes, entertainers, and business entrepreneurs. He is a member of the Board of Trustees at Whittier College. He received his J.D. from Whittier Law School, Los Angeles, and received his bachelor degree from Whittier College, Whittier, Cal.

Lincoln Stone practices immigration law in Los Angeles with Stone & Grzegorek LLP.

[1] Immigration Act of 1990 (IMMACT90), Pub. L. No. 101-649, 104 Stat. 4978.

[2] IMMACT90 §121.

[3] Immigration and Nationality Act of 1952 (INA), Pub. L. No. 82-414, 66 Stat. 163 (codified as amended at 8 USC §§1101 *et seq*.).

[4] Immigration Reform and Control Act of 1982 (1982 Bill), S. 2222, 97th Cong. (1982).

[5] Select Committee on Immigration and Refugee Policy, 97th Cong., 2nd Sess., "U.S. Immigration Policy and the National Interest," Final Report (Comm. Print 1981) (hereinafter Committee, Final Report); *see also* S. Rep. No. 101-55, at 2, 10–11 (1989).

[6] *See* §202(a)(1)(B) of the 1982 Bill (amending INA §203(b)(3)). *See also* 128 Cong. Rec. S10619, S10625 (daily ed. Aug. 17, 1982), *reprinted in* 59 Interpreter Releases 578 (Aug. 31, 1982).

[7] *Cf.* Current EB-5 law requires that an alien immigrant investor must have "invested" or be "actively in the process of investing."

[8] *See* §202(a)(1)(B) of the 1982 Bill (amending INA §203(b)(3)).

the immigrant investor to invest the requisite capital in an enterprise within one year of the date of entry. If the investor failed to do so, he or she was obligated to show good cause why such an investment was not made timely.[9]

Former Senator Alan Simpson (R-WY), then a member of the Select Committee on Immigration and Refugee Policy (Select Committee), was one of the principal supporters of the investor category in the 1982 Bill. Senator Simpson reminded Congress that the Select Committee strongly advocated increasing the number of independent or "new seed" immigrants such as investors.[10] Senator Simpson emphasized, however, that the proposed visa numbers were not specifically earmarked for investors; rather, only a ceiling had been proposed—i.e., 10 percent, or 7,500, of the total 75,000 visas proposed for the independent preference categories. Comparing the proposed investor category in the 1982 Bill with the former nonpreference investor category, Senator Simpson also emphasized that the 1982 Bill provided for more investment ($250,000 compared to $40,000) and more job creation (four employees compared to one employee).[11] Finally, while noting that family reunification was a primary purpose of the U.S. immigration system, Senator Simpson argued that improving the economy was equally as important, and that the proposed investor category should not be viewed as an "elitist" provision for the wealthy, or as a means of "buying one's way into the United States," but rather, as a significant policy shift toward attracting seed immigrants who would benefit the U.S. economy.[12]

In opposition to the proposed investor category, Senator Dale Bumpers (D-AR) argued that an independent investor category for wealthy foreigners was "odious" and "offensive" and flew "right in the face of the national character of this country."[13] While Senator Bumpers held firmly to his position, the investor category was eliminated from the 1982 Bill primarily because investors would reduce the visa allocation for family categories, which, at the time, were significantly backlogged.[14]

1989 BILL: STATING THE CASE THAT AN INVESTOR CATEGORY IS IN THE NATIONAL INTEREST

During the late 1980s, when Congress was revamping the entire immigration system, it once again seriously deliberated on enacting an immigrant investor category. The Immigration Act of 1989 (1989 Bill)[15] proposed, among other things, to overhaul the preference system for admission of immigrants to the United States.[16] The bill was designed to serve the national interest by creating immigration opportunities for individuals from nations that were shortchanged by then-current law, while maintaining the priority the United States traditionally had given to those with family connections in the United States.[17] Under then-current law, 90 percent of immigrant flows were family-related, and only 10 percent reflected "new seed" nonfamily migration.[18] The 1989 Bill was intended to strike a balance between preserving family-based categories and promoting professional and investor-based immigration. It proposed adding 54,000 visas to create an "independent" system of 120,000 visas annually.[19]

Section 103(a) of the 1989 Bill included an investor provision dressed as an "employment creation" category.[20] This section would have authorized up to 4,800 entry visas per year for qualified immigrants, who then would have been required to invest capital into a new commercial enterprise. The proposed minimum required capital investment

---

[9] See §202(d)(3) of the 1982 Bill (proposing INA §241(a)(9)(B)); see also 128 Cong. Rec. S10619, S10625 (daily ed. Aug. 17, 1982).

[10] See 129 Cong. Rec. S12385–86 (1983); see also Committee, Final Report, supra note 5.

[11] See 129 Cong. Rec. S12385–86 (1983). The former nonpreference investor category was an exception to the labor requirement created by regulation, 31 Fed. Reg. 10021 (July 23, 1966), and was useful in immigration law practice until about 1976, when visas were no longer available. It required proof of one employee other than the investor. See the companion article, L. Stone, "A Synopsis of the Former Non-Preference Investor Category," appearing elsewhere in this volume.

[12] See 129 Cong. Rec. S12385–86 (1983).

[13] Id.

[14] Senator Bumpers's amendment to eliminate the investor provision was agreed to by a vote of 51 to 46. See 129 Cong. Rec. S12385–86 (1983) (Amendment No. 1271 Senator Bumpers); 60 Interpreter Releases 418 (May 27, 1983).

[15] Immigration Act of 1989, S. 358, 101st Cong. (1989).

[16] Id.

[17] See S. Rep. No. 101-55, at 2 (1989).

[18] See id. at 5.

[19] See id.

[20] Immigration Act of 1989 §103(a), which would have created INA §203(b)(4) (as originally introduced) or INA §203(b)(5) (as passed by the Senate on July 20, 1989).

was $1 million.[21] As proposed, the investor also would have been required to create not less than 10 full-time jobs for U.S. citizens (USCs) or permanent residents.[22] Both the minimum capital and job creation requirements had been hammered out in earlier legislative debates during 1988. As initially proposed, for instance, the investor visa category would have required a $2 million minimum investment. An amendment sponsored by Senator Phil Gramm (R-TX) was approved to reduce the minimum required investment to $1 million.[23]

Congressional supporters argued that the specific goals of the investor provision in the 1989 Bill were to create new employment opportunities for U.S. workers and to infuse new capital into the United States, furthering the national interest and the economy.[24] In support of the investor provision, Senator Jesse Helms (R-NC) introduced a letter from the secretary of the North Carolina Department of Commerce that offered North Carolina as the prime example of how the United States benefited greatly from foreign investment. During the 1980s, North Carolina saw an influx of foreign investment; in 1988 alone, foreign firms invested more than $1 billion in new and expanding industrial facilities, creating more that 5,500 new jobs.[25]

Most prominent among the many opponents to the immigrant investor category was Senator Bumpers, who had succeeded in striking the investor provision from the proposed 1982 Bill. During the 1988 legislative sessions, Senator Bumpers again protested that the investor provision "violates the very marrow of the moral values of this country."[26] He was outraged particularly by "the idea of allowing somebody into this country simply because he or she happens to have a million dollars, either inherited, made in the drug cartel, regardless of where the money comes from."[27] According to Senator Bumpers, at that time, there was over $1.5 trillion of foreign investment in the United States; $1 trillion of U.S. securities were owned by foreign investors; and foreigners had already bought their way into the United States, having secured over $970 billion in holdings.[28] In response to the lofty forecasts of job creation, Senator Bumpers was most incredulous: "I will stand on my head on the dome of the Capitol on December 31 every year and wiggle my ears if that happens. Everybody knows that is nonsense."[29]

However, considering the proposed substantial increase of visa numbers across the board, Senator Bumpers had lost the earlier support he enjoyed in attacking the investor provision. Senator Edward Kennedy (D-MA), for example, pointed out that with the increase in visa numbers, the proposed investor provision would not cut into visa numbers for family immigration. Senator Simpson reiterated his earlier stance that job creation was clearly in the national interest.[30] Thus, when Senator Bumpers renewed his amendment to strike the "Fat Cat" investor provision from the proposed legislation, he could summon colorful arguments but found it difficult to secure the required votes. In the end, he did not prevail, as his amendment to strike the investor provision was defeated by a vote of 56 to 43.[31] The stage was set for the independent investor category that would appear in IMMACT90.

IMMIGRATION ACT OF 1990: A NEW INVESTOR CATEGORY THAT EMPHASIZES ATTRACTING CAPITAL AND CREATING JOBS

IMMACT90[32] was enacted on November 29, 1990, and created a fifth preference category for employment creation visas. The final allocation of visas was not to exceed 7.1 percent of the worldwide level (approximately 10,000 visas annually). It authorized visas for qualified immigrants investing $1 million and seeking to enter the United States to establish a new commercial enterprise to benefit the U.S. economy. Of the 10,000 visas, 3,000 visas were set aside for immigrants investing a minimum of $500,000 in targeted employment areas. The job creation requirement was set at 10 full-time jobs.[33] Senator Paul Simon (D-IL) envisioned the new in-

---

[21] The provision for a minimum investment of $500,000 in rural and high unemployment areas was not contained in the bill as originally introduced.

[22] See Immigration Act of 1989 §103(a).

[23] See 134 Cong. Rec. S2133–34 (1988).

[24] See S. Rep. No. 101-55, at 21(1989).

[25] See 135 Cong. Rec. S14532–34 (1989).

[26] See 134 Cong. Rec. S2126 (1988).

[27] See 135 Cong. Rec. S7768 (1989).

[28] Id. at S7769.

[29] Id. at S7770.

[30] Id. at S2127–31. See also 135 Cong Rec. S7771–72 (1989).

[31] See 135 Cong. Rec. S7775 (1989).

[32] IMMACT90, supra note 1.

[33] INA §203(b)(5).

vestor provision would generate $8 billion annually in new investment and provide 100,000 new jobs for Americans.[34]

INA §203(b)(5)—Purpose and Means

Congress was clear that the purpose of the new investor category was to create or preserve jobs for U.S. workers. This would be accomplished by attracting investment from foreign nationals seeking permanent resident status in the United States.[35]

Congress urged that the law should be interpreted as broadly as possible to accomplish these goals. In letters from Congress to legacy INS, Senators Simpson, Simon, and Kennedy emphasized that national interest required that a "flexible interpretation" of the statute should be reflected in the implementing regulations. Congress envisioned flexible methods of investment—e.g., investments in joint capital ventures; resuscitation of troubled businesses; pooled investments; and investment in targeted areas.[36] In statements made just prior to enactment of the law, Senator Simon succinctly stated: "[W]e do not want or need excessive or arbitrary industrial policy tests about what constitutes a worthwhile investment . . . we should encourage and not cripple the creativity of these enterprising immigrants."[37]

Creating Jobs

To qualify for EB-5 status, an alien must create 10 full-time jobs for USCs, permanent residents, or other immigrants lawfully authorized to work in the United States.[38] Considering that the former non-preference investor category evolved over time to require proof of creating employment for at least one U.S. worker,[39] and that the 1982 Bill proposed an investor category requiring proof of creating employment for four U.S. workers,[40] it is surprising that the enacted law requires 10 jobs. Clearly, job creation at some point became the focus of legislative sessions.

During deliberations in 1988, it was noted that an alien could come to the United States under the nonimmigrant E-2 investor visa category without job creation. Thus, to distinguish the immigrant provisions, Congress decided that it should put forth a significant requirement for job creation.[41] Soon thereafter, the proposed investor category included the requirement of creating 10 full-time jobs.

Importantly, although Congress sought to spur investment in targeted areas (i.e., rural or high unemployment areas), it maintained the requirement of 10 jobs for such investment. Congress took a different approach with respect to stimulating investment in a "troubled business," however, by urging legacy INS to promulgate a regulation enabling the investor in a troubled business to qualify for the visa if the employment levels were maintained. This provision for "saving" jobs stemmed from a post-enactment campaign by members of the Senate Judiciary Committee to sway legacy INS in writing regulations. Legacy INS adopted in its regulations the language offered by Senator Kennedy for the provision concerning investment in a troubled business.[42]

IMMACT90 does not indicate when the 10 jobs must exist. One earlier proposal stipulated that the jobs must exist within a two-year period of making the initial investment.[43] In 1989, it was recommended that the job creation take place within a reasonable time, but no longer than six months after the alien's admission to the United States.[44] But Con-

---

[34] 136 Cong. Rec. S17106, S17112 (1990) (Immigration Act of 1990, Conference Report).

[35] See 136 Cong. Rec. S7622, 7626 (1989), S. Rep. No. 101-55, at 21 (1989); see also Letter from U.S. Senate, Committee on the Judiciary, Subcommittee on Immigration and Refugee Affairs, to Gene McNary, Commissioner, INS (May 31, 1991).

[36] Letter from U.S. Senate, Committee on the Judiciary, Subcommittee on Immigration and Refugee Affairs, to G. McNary, Commissioner, INS (Apr. 12, 1991). See also Letter from U.S. Senate, Committee on the Judiciary, Subcommittee on Immigration and Refugee Affairs, to G. McNary, Commissioner, INS (Aug. 2, 1991) (submitted as a comment on proposed regulation INS No. 1434-91).

[37] 136 Cong. Rec. S17106, S17112 (1990) (Immigration Act of 1990-Conference Report).

[38] INA §203(b)(5)(A)(ii).

[39] 8 CFR §§212.8(b)(4), 1212.8(b)(4).

[40] Immigration Reform and Control Act of 1982, S. 2222 97th Cong. (1982).

[41] 134 Cong. Rec. S2119 (1988) (Immigration Act of 1988).

[42] Letter from U.S. Senate, Committee on the Judiciary, Subcommittee on Immigration and Refugee Affairs, to G. McNary, Commissioner, INS (May 31, 1991); Letter from U.S. Senate, Committee on the Judiciary, Subcommittee on Immigration and Refugee Affairs, to G. McNary, Commissioner, INS (Aug. 2, 1991) (submitted as a comment on proposed regulation INS No. 1434-91); Letter of Senator Kennedy to G. McNary, Commissioner, INS (Aug. 5, 1991), with attached proposed regulation.

[43] 134 Cong. Rec. S2119 (1988).

[44] S. Rep. No. 101-55, at 21 (1989).

gress opted not to stipulate a firm requirement on the timing of employing workers. Indeed, even the statute on removal of conditions is silent on the need to present evidence of employees.[45] Thus, although Congress viewed the job creation component to be the most important aspect of the law, it should be inferred that Congress intended to allow much latitude for alien investors to meet job creation within a reasonable period of time.

With respect to the type of business that would create jobs under IMMACT90, Congress supported a broad range. Senator Simon stated: "As long as the employment goal is met, it is unnecessary to needlessly regulate the type of business—manufacturing service, retail or the like—nor the character of the investment, corporations, partnerships, proprietors—all legal types of business ... are appropriate."[46]

Two years following introduction of the independent investor category, Congress introduced an Immigrant Investor Pilot Program to further the objectives of capital attraction and job creation. This pilot program was intended to pool investments in interrelated enterprises that would increase the employment base and economic productivity in a particular region. It allowed investors to be credited for jobs created both directly and indirectly.[47]

The Requirement of "Capital" and "Investment"

IMMACT90 requires that an alien invest (after November 29, 1990), or be actively in the process of investing, capital in a new commercial enterprise.[48] The minimum capital requirement of $1 million was agreed upon after years of debate. In the earliest proposed legislation, the investor provision required a $250,000 capital requirement.[49] Due to concern that an insubstantial amount of capital for investment purposes would result in misuse of the category, the requirement became $2 million.[50] An amendment from Senator Gramm, approved on a vote of 51 to 33, reduced the minimum capital required to a more reasonable level of $1 million.[51]

Owing to the great concern in Congress that rural areas had not experienced sound economic growth compared to the rest of the country due to difficulty in attracting investments, Senators Gramm and Rudy Boschwitz (R-MN) had proposed in the 1989 Bill to set aside 2,000 visas exclusively for investments in rural areas or areas that have an unemployment level of one and one half times the national average. The final IMMACT90 legislation, therefore, included 3,000 visas for investment in these targeted areas. The minimum capital requirement for targeted employment areas was set at $500,000.[52]

In the Senate report to the IMMACT90 legislation, Congress cited the law on the former nonpreference investor category as a guidepost for defining the technical aspects of the EB-5 category.[53] It was only after the passage of IMMACT90, when legacy INS was drafting implementing regulations, that Congress provided more guidance on what constituted capital and sufficient investment, resulting in the current definitions of "capital" and "invest," as found in the regulation at 8 Code of Federal Regulations §204.6(e). Congress was resolute that the alien investor have a personal stake in the business and that the money be at risk.[54]

Management Participation of the Alien Investor

Although IMMACT90 requires the investor to participate in the commercial enterprise, it is silent on what level of participation by the investor alien is appropriate for purposes of the EB-5 category. Earlier legislative deliberations suggested that the new category would require the investor to be a principal manager of the enterprise, along the lines of the investor in the former nonpreference investor cate-

---

[45] INA §216A.

[46] 136 Cong. Rec. S17106, S17112 (1990) (Immigration Act of 1990, Conference Report).

[47] Departments of Commerce, Justice, and State, the Judiciary, and Related Agencies Appropriations Act of 1993, Pub. L. No. 102-395, 106 Stat. 1828, as amended.

[48] INA §203(b)(5)(A)(ii).

[49] *See* Immigration Reform and Control Act of 1982, S. 2222, 97th Cong. (1982).

[50] 134 Cong. Rec. S2119 (1988) (Immigration Act of 1988); *see also* S. Rep. No 100-290, at 39 (1988).

[51] *See* 134 Cong. Rec. S2119–32 (1988) (Immigration Act of 1988); *see also* S. Rep. No 100-290, at 39 (1988); 134 Cong. Rec. S2281 (Mar. 15, 1988), *reprinted in* 65 Interpreter Releases 278 (Mar. 21, 1988).

[52] 136 Cong. Rec. S17106 (1990) (Immigration Act of 1990-Conference Report); *see also* 135 Cong. Rec. S7899 (1989) (Immigration Act of 1989); *see also* letter from U.S. Senate, Committee on the Judiciary, Subcommittee on Immigration and Refugee Affairs, to G. McNary, Commissioner, INS (Apr. 12, 1991).

[53] S. Rep. No. 101-55, at 21 (1989).

[54] Letter from U.S. Senate, Committee on the Judiciary, Subcommittee on Immigration and Refugee Affairs, to G. McNary, Commissioner, INS (Aug. 2, 1991).

gory. However, this level of activity is not required by current law. After the passage of IMMACT90, and during the legacy INS process of writing regulations, Congress encouraged legacy INS to view the management participation requirement in a flexible manner so as not to stymie investment. Congress urged legacy INS, for example, to accept limited partner investors and shareholders who engage in policy making determinations. Again, Senator Kennedy offered specific proposed regulatory language for limited partners; this language was adopted in the final legacy INS regulation.[55]

Current regulations require direct participation in the commercial enterprise by the alien investor, either on a day-to-day basis or in the mode of policy formulation. With respect to limited partners, if the investor has rights conforming to those of a limited partner under the Uniform Limited Partnership Act, the investor will satisfy the management requirement of the EB-5 category.[56]

Conditional Status

One of Congress's primary concerns when drafting the employment creation category for investors was that the law would allow the procurement of residence through fraud. Thus, the 1989 Bill included a provision designed to deter fraud.[57] Congress intended to ensure that "all aliens receiving visas in this section continue their new commercial enterprises so that the creation of U.S. jobs and the infusion of capital into the U.S. economy are sustained."[58] The statute—enacted in much the same form as initially proposed—requires a two-year conditional permanent resident status, termination of said status upon a determination that the alien does not qualify for the status, a requirement of an in-person interview, and criminal penalties for immigration-related entrepreneurship fraud.[59] Circumstances under which the status could be terminated include a finding that the business was established solely as a means of evading the immigration laws.[60]

Present law provides for removal of the conditions on residence if the petitioner invested or is in the process of investing in the commercial enterprise, sustained the investment, and created the required jobs.[61] The requirement concerning proof of jobs was added by regulation.[62]

CONCLUSION

The employment creation category for investors continues to show promise as a vehicle for attracting capital to the United States. Legislative history provides important context and is a reminder of the policy objectives that should continue to shape the interpretation and administration of the law.

---

[55] Letter of Senator Kennedy to Gene McNary, *supra* note 42.

[56] 8 CFR §204.6(j)(5).

[57] Immigration Act of 1989, S.358, 101st Cong. (1989).

[58] S. Rep. No. 101-55, at 22.

[59] *Id.*; INA §216A.

[60] S. Rep. No. 101-55 (1989); INA §216A(b)(1)(A).

[61] INA §216A(d)(1).

[62] 8 CFR §§216.6(a)(4)(iv), 1216.6(a)(4)(iv). For more information on removal of conditions, see L. Stone, "Conditional Permanent Residence and Immigration Risk for Investors," elsewhere in this volume.

AILA
OCCUPATIONAL
GUIDEBOOK

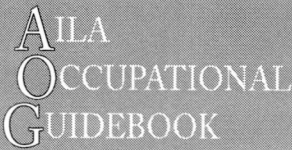

CRITICAL INTERDISCIPLINARY CONSIDERATIONS FOR IMMIGRATION COUNSEL IN REPRESENTING INVESTORS

A ROUNDTABLE ON ETHICAL CONSIDERATIONS AND PROFESSIONAL RISKS IN INVESTMENT IMMIGRATION

by Robert E. Juceam, Denyse Sabagh, and Roxana C. Bacon[*]

Editor's Comment: The Immigration Act of 1990 not only expanded the availability of "employment-based" immigration, it also dramatically impacted how many attorneys practice immigration law. For instance, the advent of the "EB-5 category" for immigrant investors led clients to turn to immigration lawyers for services in creating and operating business enterprises calling for advice and business judgment on matters well beyond legal advice based on immigration statutes and regulations. It gave rise to a mini-industry of U.S.-based entrepreneurs, developers, and promoters eager to attract capital from immigrant investors. A niche immigration law subspecialty known as investment immigration evolved. The various demands of cost-conscious clients had led to scenarios that continue to regularly raise thorny ethical questions and vexing matters of professional responsibility and discipline. We turned to some of the best and most seasoned practitioners in the immigration bar for their comments on certain scenarios that could arise in the practice of investment immigration.

DUTY OF COMPETENCE

Question: Consider among other factors that: (a) EB-5 related practice is complex due to the convergence of business, tax, accounting, and other specialties; (b) most immigration attorneys are likely to carry malpractice insurance coverage for immigration legal services but not for other legal and nonlegal work; and (c) malpractice insurance coverage for EB-5 related work may require payment of higher premiums. Assuming immigration attorneys will handle these EB-5 cases when they are presented:

(i) Must the immigration attorney be well-versed in business, tax, accounting, and related specialties in order to have the required competence? Or, can the immigration attorney reasonably rely on outside professionals to provide these competencies?

(ii) Are there provisions that can be added to the attorney-client agreement for legal services in order to beef up disclosures and/or minimize the attorney's risk?

Robert Juceam:

Answer: A lawyer who is not competent in one or more skills, subjects, or matters should not be giving advice as to those skills, subjects, or matters. There is a duty of competence under all ethics codes throughout the nation. *See, e.g.,* Restatement of the Law Governing Lawyers §26 (in handling a matter, a lawyer must have "the appropriate knowledge, time, skills and professional qualifications"). *See also* ABA Model Rule 1.1, cmt. 1; New York Disciplinary Rule (DR) 6-101.[1]

---

[*] This article originally appeared in the 1st edition of AILA's *Immigration Options for Investors and Entrepreneurs* (AILA 2006).

Robert Juceam is former president and general counsel of the American Immigration Lawyers Association (AILA) and former chair of its New York and National committees on Ethics. A founding director of the American Immigration Council (AIC, formerly the American Immigration Law Foundation), he has been recognized by numerous organizations for his pro bono work. He is Of Counsel and a former senior litigation partner at Fried, Frank, Harris, Shriver & Jacobson LLP based in New York. Barbara Gillers of Fried Frank, formerly deputy counsel to the Office of Discipline of the New York State Supreme Court Appellate Division, First Department, made material contributions to this dialog. Mr. Juceam is also a former president of AILA.

Denyse Sabagh is the chair of the Immigration Group at Duane Morris, LLP. She is a former president and general counsel of AILA and currently serves on AILA's Board of Governors. She is the former chair of the AILA EB-5 committee and is currently on the Board of Invest in the U.S., the trade organization for Regional Centers. She has been recognized by Chambers Global and the International Who's Who of Corporate Immigration Lawyers as a leading international immigration lawyer, and by Chambers USA, the Washington Post magazine, and Washingtonian magazine as one of the nations's leading immigration lawyers. She is a frequent speaker and author on a broad range of immigration law topics and recognized by the media as an immigration expert.

Roxana Bacon is Chief Counsel of U.S. Citizenship and Immigration Services (USCIS).

---

[1] There are many other sources a lawyer should consult for guidance on this and all other points made in this chapter. At a minimum, in deciding how to address the questions presented, a lawyer should consult (i) the rules in the governing jurisdiction, including any rules on conflicts of law; and (ii)

continued

A lawyer can rely on outside professionals to provide advice and services in areas of their competence, for example, accountants and others in related specialties, if the lawyer's reliance is reasonable.[2] For most purposes, the lawyer will bear the burden of proving reasonableness.

A lawyer liability risk exists where the lawyer undertakes, or the client believes the lawyer has undertaken, to give comprehensive or specific advice on a subject on which the lawyer lacks competence. Inherent in this risk is the failure of the lawyer to provide a service the lawyer in fact promised to provide. ("Complexity" will color how the courts evaluate alleged claims of malpractice.)

The lawyer can reduce liability risks by drafting a careful engagement letter to define precisely the scope of the representation, including what is *not* being undertaken. (It should also address, among other things, fees and conflicts, which are discussed below, and comply with applicable bar rules.) The primary goal of a limitation on the stated scope of the representation is to protect against a client having a reason to believe or later claiming that the lawyer promised to do some work that the lawyer did not intend or promise to do. Where the attorney has previously provided legal advice or nonlegal advice to a particular client, it is especially important to spell out in the engagement letter what the lawyer will do in the particular representation and remove any expectations that other work will be done. In some jurisdictions, a written letter of engagement is required. *See, e.g.*, 22 N.Y.C.R.R. Part 1215 (Written Letter of Engagement). Whether it is required in the governing jurisdiction, a careful engagement letter is always best practice. Some jurisdictions (*e.g.*, New York), have detailed rules governing the provision by one lawyer of legal and nonlegal services. *See* NY DR 1-106 and 1-107. *See also* New York State Bar Association Ethics Opinion 751 (Feb. 2002).

---

ethics opinions published by committees in the governing jurisdictions. Other sources are identified in the Resources List at the end of this article.

[2] *See, e.g.*, California Rules of Professional Conduct 3-110(C), attorneys may take on matters for which they lack the learning and skills required, by associating or consulting competent counsel or by acquiring sufficient learning and skill prior to performance.

Denyse Sabagh:

Answer: An immigration attorney does not need to be an expert in business, tax, or accounting to handle EB-5 cases. However, he or she must understand EB-5 issues sufficiently to spot the issue, discuss it with the client, and advise the client of the need to obtain business, tax, accounting, and other related specialty advice, if necessary. I suggest putting this advice in writing to prove that the attorney recognized the issue and addressed it with the client. Rule 1.1 of the Virginia Rules of Professional Conduct (VRPC) states that "A lawyer shall provide competent representation to a client. Competent representation requires the legal knowledge, skill, thoroughness and preparation reasonably necessary for the representation." Comment 1 of the VRPC, which discusses the legal knowledge and skill, states:

> In determining whether a lawyer employs the requisite knowledge and skill in a particular matter, relevant factors include the relative complexity and specialized nature of the matter, the lawyer's general experience, the lawyer's training and experience in the field in question, the preparation and study the lawyer is able to give the matter and whether it is feasible to refer the matter to, or associate or consult with, a lawyer so established in the field in question.

Clarify the terms of representation. If the engagement is to provide consultation and advice, solely, state it. If it is to do that and prepare and file the EB-5 petition, state it. Specifically state that the attorney is not providing business, tax, or accounting advice, if appropriate. Specifically state that the attorney is not providing a recommendation regarding the commercial viability of the business endeavor, unless the attorney has specific expertise to provide such an opinion. Specifically state that the attorney has been consulted on the legal requirements of the EB-5 category and has not provided business, tax, or accounting advice and have the client initial the particular paragraph in the agreement, if appropriate. Attach a cover letter to the retainer agreement and articulate the legal issues and recommendations provided to the client. This provides the client with a clear and concise written statement explaining the issues, problems, recommendations, and clarification that the attorney will be relying on the information provided by the client.

Roxana Bacon:

Answer: All attorneys have areas of expertise and areas in which they are less than expert. Holding ourselves out to be well-versed in the multiple legal areas involved in most EB-5 matters is courting disaster, and is not necessary. It is essential that we as immigration attorneys know enough about the business aspects of the EB-5 investment to see the big picture, know what pieces must be in place, be sure the proper protections are in writing, and watch for red flags. Beyond that, we should determine very early in the representation what our role is: Are we the quarterback for the entire investment and U.S. Citizenship and Immigration Services (USCIS) filing or are we a specialized player in a filing that will be lead by another expert? Defining your role is imperative as it dictates very different levels of responsibility and exposure. If we are quarterbacks, we need to clarify exactly what that involves in the retainer/representation letter. Among other provisions, a "quarterback letter" should include the right to retain experts as needed, the right to discharge experts as needed, the right to engage in due diligence before retaining any experts, and the right to control the sequencing and response time of the experts hired to prepare and file and approve a case. If we are to be "only" the immigration attorney, the retainer/representation letter should clarify that limited role and specifically not accept responsibility for the selection or quality of other experts.

It is very likely that an immigration expert involved in an EB-5 matter will need to work with, even retain, experts in related areas, including tax, securities, foreign business laws, and financing options. If the immigration attorney is in charge of the entire EB-5 investment, *i.e.*, is the deal's quarterback, having well-crafted agreements with each consulting expert is essential both to ensure the EB-5 deal is protected and to ensure that the immigration quarterback has only accepted liability for matters he or she intends. While each such contract must be drafted individually with the specifics of the particular deal and particular clients, generally a contract with an outside consultant should cover the following key points:

(1) Who the consultant is (are you retaining a firm or an individual?).

(2) What the consultant will do (be a source of ongoing advice or handle a specific piece?).

(3) That the consultant confirms his or her expertise. An example of language is:

> Consultant confirms that he or she is knowledgeable in the area of *** and is fully able to provide expert consulting services to (name of clients) in this area, and warrants that he or she will adhere to the professional standards applicable to his or her area of expertise during this consultation.

(4) What the fees will be, and how they will be handled—hourly or task-based? Reduction for volume or efficiency? Billed through you—the "quarterback model"—or directly to the client?

(5) Schedule for completion of work (include penalty clause for delays, etc.).

(6) Termination (be reasonable but try to control ending the agreement).

(7) Choice of laws (where are your clients best served?).

(8) Severability.

(9) Arbitration (usually much more favorable choice than litigation).

To the extent these consultant/expert contracts involve duplicate provisions, it is wise for the immigration attorney serving as quarterback to retain corporate counsel to draft the template, allowing the attorney flexibility to tailor it to specific matters without losing critical protections. If the immigration attorney is serving only as the expert and someone else is the quarterback, the attorney's agreement should still be drafted by an expert or reviewed by one who represents only you. As we tell our own clients, hiring a good attorney as early as you can is the best way to spend your legal dollars.

HAZARDS OF UNSETTLED LAW

Question: During 1998, the Administrative Appeals Office (AAO) issued four "precedent" decisions regarding adjudication of I-526 petitions. These decisions set aside earlier legacy Immigration and Naturalization Service (INS) legal opinions and memoranda that had been relied on by immigration attorneys advising clients concerning compliance with the EB-5 law. Insofar as the EB-5 category remains relatively new, it seems to be a likely candidate for even further changes as USCIS slowly gains experience through the adjudication process. What, if any, specific disclosures would you advise that the immigration attorney provide to a new client concerning this area of law?

Robert Juceam:

Answer: When a lawyer is asked to advise in a new, fast-developing, or uncertain area of the law, the concerns with regard to competence plainly arise. The lawyer should make a special effort to keep up with developments in the law, consult with more experienced colleagues, anticipate uncertainties, evaluate whether higher officials or appellate bodies could effect changes in the rules, and stay involved in professional organizations and activities that will inform the lawyer about developments. Critically, the lawyer should have a full and complete discussion with the client about the risks of rule change and how they bear on the matter.

At a minimum, the engagement letter should memorialize the discussion between the lawyer and the client of the special risks where legal doctrine is unsettled, and describe the expectations of the client. For example, the client should understand that the advice as to applicable law is current when provided. The lawyer also should make clear whether the lawyer will advise the client as developments occur. Of course, so long as the lawyer-client relationship exists, the lawyer has an obligation to inform the client of developments affecting the matter. Any ambiguity concerning whether the relationship is on-going or terminated will, in all likelihood, be resolved against the lawyer if the lawyer's conduct is contested.

Roxana Bacon:

Answer: At one time, shortly after the 1998 sea change in EB-5 processing, the EB-5 category was especially and uniquely volatile. Now, however, virtually every part of U.S. immigration law is prey to dramatic changes, often with little advance notice. Immigration has emerged in the last few years as everyone's favorite political football, and the result is great uncertainty in all aspects of the area. As evidenced by visa retrogression, sunsetting of H-1B numbers and L-1 eligibility even in the face of great demand, and tightening up the exercise of administrative discretion while broadening expedited removal and mandatory detention standards, there are no more "sure things" in the statute, the regulations, or the practice itself.

As a result, the standard explanation of the fact that both laws and their interpretation can and do change, and that the advice and opinions you give clients are accordingly also subject to change should be a sufficient note to clients. A possible introductory paragraph to anchor your own specific warning might be:

> The immigration law upon which our firm's opinions, advice, and strategy are based can be changed in a number of ways. Congress can amend or add to the underlying federal law. The agencies that enforce the law can issue different regulations. The administration can alter its internal priorities and processing. To the extent any of these changes affect your specific case, our opinions, advice, and strategy also may change. We will, of course, keep you advised of such changes and discuss them fully with you.

This language both gives the client the unsettling news that nothing is cast in stone while still providing the assurance that you will be monitoring any changes with your client's case in mind.

REPRESENTING BOTH SIDES

Question: The immigration attorney is asked by both the seller (*e.g.*, U.S.-based developer) and the buyer (*i.e.*, the immigrant investor) of a particular investment opportunity to represent them by handling all the immigration aspects of the transaction so that the buyer can secure a Green Card. This representation entails preparing and filing the required applications with USCIS, and it may involve recommending some revisions to the investment structure that the parties are contemplating.

(i) Can the attorney take on this engagement?
(ii) If yes, what should be done to minimize the risks?

Robert Juceam:

Answer: When a lawyer is asked to represent the seller (*e.g.*, a U.S.-based developer) and the buyer (*i.e.*, the immigrant investor) simultaneously in a particular matter, the usual rules regarding the representation of joint clients apply. In fact, the ethical issues raised are no different than where the lawyer represents two clients in one transaction where their interests are or may become adverse. All American jurisdictions have rules governing joint representations, and it is important to consult the rules in the governing jurisdiction before proceeding.

Many ethics counselors will counsel prophylactically not to undertake the simultaneous representation. However, properly managed, and being thoughtful about the lawyer's risk tolerance, I believe that the lawyer will be able to represent both clients in most cases after explaining the joint representation, the need for a waiver of conflicts, and the limits of the engagement, and then getting "informed consent." These understandings can be put in the engagement letter or in a separate waiver letter. In any event, the informed consent letter should cover at least the following:

(1) the scope of the joint representation;

(2) the fact that the lawyer will represent both clients and that at the time of the signing the lawyer believes that the lawyer can represent both because their interests are sufficiently aligned;

(3) a recognition of the potential need for the lawyer to withdraw if the clients' interests become adverse;

(4) how the attorney-client privilege will operate during the joint representation (including, if true in the governing jurisdiction, that in the event of a dispute between the joint clients, the attorney-client privilege will not protect against the disclosure to all joint clients of information shared during the joint representation); and

(5) other provisions that will inform the client of the limitations of the representation and reduce the risk to the lawyer.

In such dual representations, it is important that the letter reflect that the clients understood the nature of the actual and potential conflicts and consequences. A letter that does not show "informed consent" leaves the lawyer without protection when later challenged. There are volumes of material on conflicts and waivers, and the resolution of issues will be highly fact-intensive. Therefore, research appropriate to the matter should be completed in each instance of a joint representation.

Failure to follow the conflicts rules with care can result in a variety of consequences including an action for malpractice, breach of fiduciary duty, and discipline.[3]

As in all representations, the lawyer should "know the client." Taking on those who want to walk on or across the legal lines, have untested business histories, have shopped for the lawyer with the "right" opinion, or sued their prior lawyer are bad risks and absolutely "trouble" in the making in dual representation cases.

Denyse Sabagh:

Answer: Although joint representation is possible, per Bob's comments, for the typical immigration practitioner who does not as a matter of course handle these types of matters, I suggest that the most prudent course of action would be for the attorney to represent only one party or not take the engagement. The duty of loyalty to a client is clear. Representing multiple clients in a setting that potentially compromises the attorney's duty risks unethical conduct and malpractice claims.

I would not recommend representing the individual investor and the developer. The potential for conflict of interest is great. An investor's interest has the potential of being different from the developer's interest. A fundamental principle in the client-lawyer relationship is that the lawyer maintains confidentiality of information relating to the representation. The attorney representing both the investor and the developer would have confidential information about both. If the interests diverge, the attorney would be conflicted out. Loyalty is an essential element in the lawyer's relationship to a client. The general rule is that a lawyer shall not represent a client if the representation of that client will be directly adverse to another existing client unless the lawyer reasonably believes the representation will not adversely affect the relationship with the other client and each client consents after consultation. In Virginia, Rule 1.7 of the VRPC states:

> A lawyer shall not represent a client if the representation of that client may be materially limited by the lawyer's responsibilities to another client unless the lawyer reasonably believes the representation will not be adversely affected; and the client consents after consultation. When representation of multiple clients in a single matter is undertaken, the consultation shall include explanation of the implications of the common representation and the advantages and risks involved.

If the attorney insists on representation of the investor, he or she must ascertain whether a disinterested lawyer would conclude that the client should not agree to the representation under the circumstances. If so, the lawyer cannot properly ask for such agreement or provide representation on the basis of the client's consent. When more than one client is involved, the question of conflict must be resolved as to each client. As stated in the VRPC Rule 1.7, Comment (5), there may be circumstances where it is impossible to make the disclosure necessary to obtain the consent. For example, when the lawyer represents different clients in related matters and one of the clients refuses to consent to the disclosure necessary to permit the other client to make an informed decision, the lawyer cannot properly ask the latter to consent. Given these rules of profes-

---

[3] *See, e.g., Simpson v. James*, 903 F.2d 372 (5th Cir. 1990); *Milbank, Tweed, Hadley & McCloy v. Boon*, 13 F.3d 537 (2d Cir. 1994).

sional conduct, it appears that the lawyer should not represent the investor. However, if he or she does, he or she should put in writing the appropriate disclosures and obtain the appropriate consents, assuming that a disinterested lawyer deems it appropriate.

Further, unless the attorney is also a corporate attorney, he or she would not want to give advice on investment structure. It would not be in the immigration attorney's area of expertise.

Roxana Bacon:

Answer: The pitfalls of EB-5 representation have as much to do with the cases' complexity as with the fact that multiple parties in a business deal that has such high stakes are precisely the sort of multiple parties that are likely to have a falling out, making continued dual or joint representation impossible and increasing the risk that once the blame game begins, the attorney is an obvious target. The parties in an EB-5 arrangement often have differing primary goals from the beginning (in contrast to a marriage or employment-based immigration case) in that some want to make money and others want a Green Card. If the primary goals are so different that there is a significant risk that they cannot be equally represented, the ethics rules forbid accepting representation at all.

Decisions to keep a business going in the face of loss, or need for more capital, exacerbate these divergent goals, and dissension can follow quickly. The attorney who is required by professional responsibility rules to be loyal to both clients while protecting confidential information must be vigilant in identifying when the clients' goals are at odds and quick both to share that information with the clients and terminate the relationship. Trying to "save" a broken business deal by negotiating for two or more opposing clients is not just perilous practically but professionally unethical. *See* ABA Model Rules; Arizona Supreme Court Rule 42, ER 1.6 (Confidentiality of Information) and ER 1.7 (Conflict of Interest: Current Clients: . . . "Current conflict exists if . . . (2) there is a significant risk that the representation of one or more clients will be materially limited by the lawyer's responsibilities to another client . . . .").[4]

I seem to be in the middle. I agree with Denyse that no attorney should try to represent all the parties in all aspects of this hypothetical situation, but think it may be possible to simply advise on the immigration aspects as the parties do have the same goal: an investment that will be approved by USCIS. The key is to not do any of the structuring of the deal, or its restructuring, but simply to give neutral advice on whether what the other experts propose will work, and why or why not. In other words, an immigration attorney can comment on the immigration aspects of a particular investment structure, but leave the actual restructuring to other experts. Having the discipline to limit representation will be a challenge to most attorneys (so many "Type As"!), as will being firm about what will survive adjudication and what will not. But it is theoretically possible to craft a limited representation that passes ethical muster.

REPRESENTING MULTIPLE PETITIONERS

Question: A group of investors is set to invest in a project that is designed to confer immigration benefits on all of them through the EB-5 classification. A business plan details the future job creation that will be "split" among the investors. Each of them wants to hire you to represent him or her throughout the process of obtaining residence and then removing the conditions on residence.

(i) Can the attorney take on this engagement?

(ii) If yes, what can be done to minimize the potential for serious conflicts in the future?

Robert Juceam:

Answer: When a lawyer is asked to represent a group of investors, the same concerns with regard to conflicts identified in question 3 ("Representing Both Sides"), above, apply. Of course, a lawyer may represent a group of investors depending on what the investor clients are asking the lawyer to do and the client interests it may affect. If the lawyer is satisfied that group representation can be properly accomplished, then the representation should not proceed without an engagement letter and a waiver of conflicts.

Obviously, however, the lawyer cannot act for one or more of these clients to the detriment of the legal or business interests of another of these clients in the matter. So the lawyer must anticipate that one investor may pull out of the project while another needs the project to complete his or her immigration procedure. If this is likely to be the case, "best practice" is for the lawyer to decline the representation of the members of a group of investors.

---

[4] Model Rule 1.7 requires a lawyer to reasonably believe representation of one client will not adversely affect the relationship with the other client. Compare the rule in California, CRPC 3-310(C), that would permit representation of both parties if there is informed written consent.

Denyse Sabagh:

Answer: Each investor will have his own individual issues, and knowledge of one party's issues will preclude representation of others unless the parties agree to a disclosure and waiver of the conflict. If one party refuses to grant the waiver, the attorney will be conflicted out of representing the group.

The other issue raised in this question has to do with the "split" of the number of jobs. This is another potential conflict. If the requisite number of jobs is not created, one or some of the group have the potential for adverse consequences to their applications. This creates an unwaivable conflict.

Roxana Bacon:

Answer: I agree with Denyse that this scenario includes so many risks of conflict that it is not possible to see how a single attorney can remain loyal to any client. Imagine the first attorney-client conversation you have with the first investor. You would have to ask what his or her long-term goals are, what impediments he or she sees if there are delays in processing, etc. After decades of such interviews, I am certain that in a group of any size you would learn that someone has urgent family issues (marriage, divorce, birth, illness) that require a fast track at all costs and others want delay for equally urgent reasons, and you instantly have a conflict. It is so likely that the group will have divergent issues I would save time and wear and tear on the relationships you need with other investors and consultants and only accept representation of a single investor, referring the others to competent counsel.

It also is unlikely that the clients fully appreciate that a waiver of confidentiality inherent in dual representation would allow you to discuss personal matters with the group as a whole or any other member of it. For example, if Client A tells you that he wants Green Cards as soon as possible as his child has health issues best treated in the United States while Client B in the same investor group is counting on slowing the processing down as much as possible to give him time to execute his tax strategy, you are in a clear conflict and have no acceptable way to explain or resolve that conflict with the clients. This is the kind of situation the prudent lawyer wants to avoid, and underscores how important it is to evaluate any multiple-client opportunity very carefully.

HAZARDS OF INVESTMENT ADVICE

Question: Your new client wants you to help make a decision about how to invest in order to qualify for the EB-5 classification. The client has heard of an opportunity with a USCIS-designated regional center and wants your opinion about the economic merits of the investment. The client also wants your help in identifying other investments that will not only qualify for EB-5 classification but also will appreciate in value over time.

(i) What are the potential hazards?

(ii) Where should the lines be drawn in terms of what the attorney should be advising?

Robert Juceam:

Answer: A lawyer who gives advice about the economic merits of an investment is not giving legal advice. If the lawyer is competent to give economic advice, the lawyer should have a specific agreement with the client defining the scope of a separate representation as an economic or business consultant. The letter should make clear that it is not a lawyer/client relationship, that the attorney-client privilege and work product doctrines will not cover the communications between the lawyer and the client in connection with a business consultation, and other warnings. *See, e.g.*, N.Y. DR1-106 and 107, on lawyers giving nonlegal advice. *See also* ethics opinions cited in the answer to question 1 ("Duty of Competence), above.

By contrast, of course, the client may tell the lawyer how the client intends to invest and the lawyer can comment on the legal eligibility limitations that such form of investment might generate. This would be legal advice and should be covered by an engagement letter and any appropriate waivers.

There is obviously risk when the lawyer gives both legal and nonlegal advice. In hindsight, a disappointed client will be tempted to treat or claim the two functions as all erroneous legal advice. Where economic loss or similar negative business consequences occur, the more hats the lawyer wears in the matter, the more risk that a tribunal would find that the lawyer failed to perform adequately the legal undertaking.

Having engagement letters, of course, is not sufficient to protect a lawyer from liability if, in implementing the representation, the lawyer acts inconsistently with them or waives their protections.

Denyse Sabagh:

Answer: Unless an attorney considers him- or herself an expert in evaluating the economics of an investment, do not give advice. The immigration attorney may provide information about the specifics of the USCIS regional center such as background, numbers of people using the program, whether cases have been approved, etc. But, when it comes to evaluating the merits, advise the client to seek investment counseling from an expert.

The attorney should be providing advice about the legal requirements of the EB-5 program and the regional center designation. Once the attorney starts opining about the merits of the investment, the attorney opens the door to a complaint by a disgruntled client who lost his or her money based on the attorney's opinion that it was a good investment. Stick to the law and remember that is the attorney's area of expertise.

Roxana Bacon:

Answer: Stay away from giving financial advice unless you have certifications and separate malpractice insurance with limits sufficient to cover large losses. You make yourself a target for civil suits based on losses that you opined were likely not to happen. With the clarity of hindsight, clients tend to remember your opinion as fact, and will be quick to say they relied on it to their detriment. You could provide a list of all known USCIS-designated regional centers to your client with advice that expert financial advice be obtained elsewhere, and that you are happy to work with the financial consultant to answer any immigration-related issues.

If it is not clearly legal advice, STOP! Consider carefully what you are saying, how it will be perceived by the client (who likely sees you as a generic professional unlimited in expertise), and whether you have sufficiently limited and qualified your advice to bring you back to your comfort zone.

"FULL SERVICE" ATTORNEY

Question: A developer in the United States has an investment opportunity that should be appealing to foreign investors desiring a Green Card. The developer wants to hire you to represent it "soup to nuts"—advising on U.S. immigration law and how that impacts the investment structure, drafting investment agreements to be entered into between the developer and the immigrant investors, advising on marketing strategy, sending promotional brochures to investor prospects and touting the merits of the project, and representing the developer at promotional events in the United States and abroad.

(i) Which aspects of the engagement pose significant risk of liability or ethical dilemma for the immigration attorney?

(ii) May the immigration attorney, later, also decide to represent individual investors in their immigration applications?

(iii) What exposure does the attorney face if the promotional brochures are later discovered to include significant fraudulent representations?

Robert Juceam:

Answer: A lawyer hired by a developer to represent the developer "soup to nuts" in connection with the investment structure, *e.g.*, by drafting agreements, advising on marketing strategy, sending brochures, etc., faces significant risks. In addition to those discussed above, all the issues and potential liabilities that faced lawyers involved in advising on and promoting tax shelters by analogy exist here. So, in addition to liability for malpractice, the lawyer faces potential civil actions involving allegations of tortious interference with contract, fraud and misrepresentation, fraudulent conveyance, breach of contract, and intentional torts. Where one of the lawyer's aims in entering into this enterprise is economic gain from the business rather than the practice of law, the lawyer should consult another lawyer not so involved for representation on the engagement, its documentation, and for formal immigration law filings and processing.[5]

The lawyer involved in drafting and disseminating materials could face criminal, not just civil liability, exposure. For example, a lawyer who knowingly and willfully drafts any part of an EB-5 petition containing a materially false statement may be subject to criminal sanctions under 18 USC §1001. *See* 18 USC §1001 (2005) (whoever, in any matter within the jurisdiction of the executive, legislative, or judicial branch of the Government of the United States, knowingly and willfully . . . makes any materially false . . . statement or representation . . . shall be fined or imprisoned . . . ."). A lawyer who submits an EB-5 petition to the government, with the intent to commit fraud, by mail is subject to criminal sanctions under

---

[5] Of course, if the lawyer provides legal advice and also enters into a business arrangement with the client, the rules governing business transactions must be followed. *See, e.g.*, NY DR 5-104; ABA M.R. 1.8(a).

18 USC §1341 (2005) for mail fraud. In addition, INA §274C(a)(5) prohibits any person from knowingly preparing or filing any document in connection with an EB-5 application "with knowledge or in reckless disregard of the fact that such application or document was falsely made . . . ."[6]

Denyse Sabagh:

Answer: This scenario makes me nervous just reading it. There are too many land mines here. Call your malpractice carrier if you are going to get involved in this. Touting the merits of the project creates an endorsement of the project by the attorney. If it appears that the attorney recommended the project, it creates a risk for the attorney. If the project fails, the attorney could have exposure because the attorney, in essence, promoted the project as a winner. Never tout the merits of a project. Provide information, but not an opinion about commercial success.

This developer needs a corporate and securities attorney. The immigration attorney should review the documents to ensure the legal requirements of the EB-5 visa are met. But, drafting investment agreements requires expertise in aforesaid areas of law. There are various legal requirements for private offerings that must be met both inside the United States and outside of the United States.

Advising on marketing strategy crosses into the business consultant arena. Providing information about immigrant investors and their needs and requirements is helpful to a developer. However, providing a marketing strategy opens the immigration attorney to exposure as it creates an expectation that the immigration attorney is qualified to provide this advice. Sending promotional brochures to investor prospects also creates a perception that the immigration attorney is promoting the project. Again, this is conduct that could open the attorney to exposure.

If the immigration attorney in this scenario undertook the above, he or she would be crossing the line from providing strictly legal advice about immigration issues related to the EB-5 investment issues to providing corporate and securities legal advice and business advice. The rules of professional conduct require that an attorney shall provide competent representation to a client. Competent representation requires the legal knowledge, skill, thoroughness, and preparation reasonably necessary for the representation. Many of the requested duties in this case would go beyond the immigration attorney's area of expertise.

The attorney faces a bar complaint, malpractice lawsuit, lawsuit for fraud, conspiracy to commit fraud, possible racketeering violations, security violation, and other counts. If the attorney is involved in the preparation or the marketing of the development, and the representations turn out to be fraudulent, the attorney has opened the door. Some of the issues will be what did the attorney know and when, where did the attorney obtain the information, and what due diligence did the attorney undertake. The door will have been opened and the attorney could be subject to liability even if the attorney did not know about the fraudulent representations.

Roxana Bacon:

Answer: I have seen this scenario played out and it was not pretty. You should *only* represent the developer, and only in those aspects of the deal that are within your expertise as an attorney. Marketing, promoting, selling, and drafting agreements to be entered into in foreign jurisdictions should all be avoided.

The immigration attorney should give the developer "Ethics 101" so that he or she also is armed with a full understanding of the exposure that goes with actively promoting an investment scheme outside the United States. It is likely that he or she is naïve and would welcome a thorough discussion of both the points of vulnerability and your suggestions about who could best assist. In this case, any drafting of investment or corporate documents should be reviewed by counsel in the countries in which the investments will be offered. Marketing/promotions should be done by a company with successful experience in the targeted countries. And actually selling to overseas markets will require a thorough understanding of who is allowed to do that (and what kind of visa they may need), within what legal parameters, and with what consequences. Most countries do not have the laissez-faire philosophy we enjoy in the United States, but are much more restrictive about selling risky financial opportunities.

You should never represent a seller and then, later, a buyer who may need to attack the bona fides of the seller's product. The risk of a conflict is too great, and the consequences of bowing out too prejudicial to the clients. You cannot know what questions the consular officer or USCIS may have

---

[6] *See* "Ethical Issues for Immigration Lawyers," *Ethics in a Brave New World* 4, 5–7 (AILA 2004) (elaborating on INA §274C and other immigration-specific statutes).

about the deal, and you run the real risk of either illegally sharing confidential information from the developer (and remember, when you represented her, you had no other investors as clients so her information is subject to confidentiality protections) or not being able to commit the loyalty to the investor that the ethics rules require.

The promotional material risks devastating exposure. You can expect to be attacked by the investors, who will remember only that you "promised" them a great deal, and perhaps by government authorities in the country in which your promotions landed. In many countries, fraud is a criminal offense, and in virtually all, it is compensable by civil judgments that include making the defrauded person whole and adding something more as punishment. The cost of retaining counsel abroad to defend your interests is huge, and the cost of not retaining someone even greater. And of course USCIS and the Department of States (DOS) will know your name forever as someone who cannot be trusted. No one should do this unless they covet cliff-diving without any water.

THE BUSINESS PLAN

Question: In preparing the EB-5 petition for the client, the immigration attorney participated in drafting the business plan that is included in support of the petition. After the client obtains conditional residence, but before filing for removal of the conditions, the business suffers a serious downturn and the targets projected for the business in the business plan turn out to be overly optimistic.

(i) The business plan was based on client-supplied information, but it was unreasonable if one had studiously considered the competitive position of the company at the time the plan was drafted. Does the arguably irresponsible business plan put the attorney in jeopardy of sanction by the government for "misrepresentation?"

(ii) What due diligence, if any, must the attorney conduct in the circumstances?

Robert Juceam:

Answer: When a lawyer develops the economic projections, marketing strategy, and financial profiles in a business plan, the lawyer is not performing a legal service. To the extent the lawyer drafts and disseminates the client's business plan knowing an investor/client will seek immigration status based on it, the plan and other organizing documents should not contain materially false or incomplete information about matters material to the plan. The lawyer should assume that someone injured by relying on such statements will assert civil claims. Thus, the lawyer should conduct reasonable due diligence to have comfort that the material elements of the plan can be factually supported. For example, if the plan refers to an existing business, the lawyer should review the organizing documents and annual reports and filings of the business and make diligent inquiries or observations that assets needed to engage in the business exist. If the plan involves the physical development of real estate, the lawyer should determine if the key elements of the plan are in place (*e.g.*, zoning permits the development or change in zoning can likely be achieved timely, ownership or development rights in the property, etc., and appropriate disclosures are made). In general the lawyer should conduct a factual inquiry akin to the basic due diligence analysis done by a corporate deal lawyer.[7]

Denyse Sabagh:

Answer: Don't draft the business plan. A typical immigration attorney is not equipped to draft a business plan. There probably are some immigration attorneys who have MBAs and have the capability to do this; however, most don't. Don't be lulled in by a client who implores you to do it. The risks are great and the rewards are minimal. If the immigration attorney believes he or she is competent, review Bob and Roxana's suggestions.

Roxana Bacon:

Answer: Unless you also have an MBA and are insured for your business advice, do not draft business plans. As this very ordinary scenario plays out, the consequences are obvious and serious. Of course the business plan the attorney drafted puts him or her in the crosshairs of both individual and government sanctions. A good plan would not only recognize the known competitions' market positions but also include the necessary caveats and disclaimers to give the drafter protection against truly unforeseeable changes.

The due diligence is for the attorney to tell the client to retain an expert in business plans, to be sure that he or she has one that meets industry standards, and incorporates all reasonable due diligence protections. It is good to remember, and remind the client, that a bad investment yields nothing but bad results, even if it enjoys a brief honeymoon in the market.

---

[7] For sample due diligence checklists, see Alan S. Gutterman, Business Transactions Solution (West 2003).

LEGAL FEES

Question: The attorney believes she has developed a rare specialization with EB-5 cases and decides to charge all clients seeking the classification a "success fee" of $50,000 as the sole legal fee, payable in full when the visa is issued.

(i) Is this success fee permitted? What should be done by attorney to protect his- or herself in the circumstances?

(ii) Instead of the $50,000, attorney bargains for a percent of the underlying business. Is this permitted?

Robert Juceam:

Answer: "Success fees" are not prohibited, but they are subject to the general rules governing lawyer's fees, which are set forth in various ethics provisions nationally. *See, e.g.*, New York DR 2-106(a) (setting forth eight factors to determine whether a lawyer's fee is "reasonable," including the time and labor required, the fee customarily charged, and the experience, reputation, and ability of the lawyer). *See also* ABA Model Rule 1.5(a) (same factors). In some jurisdictions, the lawyer's fee agreement must be in writing. *See, e.g.*, 22 N.Y.C.R.R. Part 1215 (Written Letter of Engagement). *See also* ABA Model Rule 1.5(b) ("The scope of the representation and the basis or rate of the fee and expenses for which the client will be responsible shall be communicated to the client, preferably in writing, before or within a reasonable time after commencing the representation . . . ."). In addition, in some jurisdictions, a lawyer must offer fee arbitration to clients in civil matters, and submit to fee arbitration if a client in a civil matter requests it. *See, e.g.*, 22 N.Y.C.R.R. Part 137.

Keep in mind that the lawyer's fee will be judged in hindsight by an objective standard. Whether the fee is fixed or a percentage is immaterial. The core principles are the same. The fee must be reasonable and the parties agreed on its basis (absent quantum meruit). A small percentage of a big amount is not necessarily reasonable.

When a fee agreement is reached or modified after a representation has begun, the arrangements are scrutinized for fairness under additional rules. *See, e.g.*, NY DR 5-108 (business transactions with clients).

Denyse Sabagh:

Answer: Success fees are allowable. Rules of Professional Conduct for each state guide how attorneys' fees may be charged. VRPC Rule 1.5 requires that the lawyer's fee be reasonable. The factors to be considered in determining the reasonableness of a fee include the following: (1) the time and labor required, the novelty and difficulty of the questions involved, and the skill requisite to perform the legal service properly; (2) the likelihood, if apparent to the client, that the acceptance of the particular employment will preclude other employment by the lawyer; (3) the fee customarily charged in the locality for similar legal services; (4) the amount involved and the results obtained; (5) the time limitations imposed by the client or by the circumstances; (6) the nature and length of the professional relationship with the client; (7) the experience, reputation, and ability of the lawyer performing the services; and (8) whether the fee is fixed or contingent. In Virginia, a fee may be contingent on the outcome of the matter for which the service is rendered, except in a matter in which a contingent fee is prohibited *i.e.*, domestic relations or representing a defendant in a criminal case.

The lawyer's fee must be adequately explained to the client. It is best practice to put the agreement in writing, even for those jurisdictions that do not require written fee agreements. In Virginia, a contingent fee shall state in writing the method by which the fee is to be determined.

Roxana Bacon:

Answer: In Arizona, Arizona Supreme Court Rule 42, ER 1.5 controls attorney fees. While there is a list of factors that can be considered in determining what is "reasonable," the overarching point is that they must not be unreasonable and they must be set forth in writing to the client. The "reasonable" factors include both "skill required" and "results obtained," but any extraordinary payment such as that proposed in the hypothetical would have to overcome the fact that doubtlessly many other EB-5 attorneys with the same skill level do not charge a premium for success. Arizona does acknowledge that the eight enumerated factors are not exclusive, but their listing suggests strongly that anything outside the list will need additional explanation and authority.[8] If counsel were to collect such a large payment, the basis for it, and the full, knowing acceptance of it, would have to be in a written and signed fee agreement.

---

[8] In California, 11 factors can be considered; also, an attorney's fees must not be "unconscionable." CRPC 4-200(A), (B).

Finally, Arizona and many other states have arbitration procedures run through the state bar that encourage the resolution of fee disputes. These procedures are separate from the filing of discipline/ethics complaints, but can overlap if the nature of the ethics complaint focuses on fee issues.

FINDER'S FEES

Question: Attorneys are advised by EB-5 project promoters at legal education conferences that they can earn finder fees by referring their clients to projects.

(i) What steps must be taken by the attorney who accepts such fees?

(ii) Is it permitted to accept the finder fee and represent the client in the immigration application process?

Robert Juceam:

Answer: A lawyer referring an investor to a special investment opportunity is not giving legal advice. The ordinary duty of candor applies in providing nonlegal advice. If the lawyer is giving legal advice concerning the investment as well, then the rules governing the provision of legal and nonlegal advice in the same matter likely apply. See discussion for question 5 ("Hazards of Investment Advice"), above. In some jurisdictions, a "finder's" fee may be prohibited. In most jurisdictions, disclosure of the arrangement between the project promoter and the lawyer will have to be fully disclosed to the client. The rules governing conflicts between the interests of the lawyer and the client will apply. *See e.g.,* NY DR 5-101. *See also* NYSBA Opinion 671 (1994).

Denyse Sabagh:

Answer: As stated above, lawyers have a duty to adequately explain fees and disclose fee information to the client. Check your state rules of professional conduct to determine if a finder's fee is allowed. If it is not clear, request an opinion from bar counsel. If finder's fees are allowed, make sure that the arrangement has been fully and adequately disclosed to the client. Historically, finder's fees have been an issue in EB-5 cases. Finder's fees raise conflicts issues, appearance of impropriety, and loyalty issues. The most prudent course of action would be to decline a finder's fee.

Roxana Bacon:

Answer: What is an acceptable fee, if any, for referral of a legal case is usually handled by a state's specific rules of professional conduct. In Arizona, ER 1.5 details what can and cannot be charged, split, or made contingent. Here the referral is for investment opportunities and to a nonattorney, so the ethics rules do not directly apply. This situation is analogous to suggesting a CPA or a real estate broker to a client. However, to avoid the appearance of impropriety, it is always good policy to let the client know that you may receive a fee from the referral as it gives the client information relevant to evaluating whether he or she wants to act on that advice because it affects its impartiality.

As the attorney, you should only represent the client as an investor for immigration purposes after referring the client to the investment if the client has full disclosure, the client has received independent advice as to the bona fides of the investment separate from your referral, and the client agrees in writing to the representation. Your agreement should clarify that you made the referral but that you have no attorney-client relationship with the investment, and never have had one, and that you affirm your loyalty to represent the investor without any conflict of interest to the investor.

ADVERSE CLAIMS

Question: If you receive a letter or other notice that your representation of a party in an EB-5 action is being questioned either on the basis of malpractice or unethical conduct, what should you do?

Robert Juceam:

Answer: A lawyer receiving a disciplinary complaint, a malpractice complaint, or other notice challenging his or her professional conduct should seek legal advice immediately. In addition, the lawyer should consider, among other ethics rules, the provisions governing conflicts between lawyer and client. *See e.g.,* NY DR 5-101; ABA Model Rule 1.7. In some instances, the lawyer will have to withdraw from representing the client. In other instances, the lawyer may be able to continue the representation but will need an appropriate waiver from the client to do so. As with all other topics discussed here, the rules and case law in the governing jurisdiction must be consulted. And, of course, the lawyer should give prompt notice to his or her insurers.

Denyse Sabagh:

Answer: I agree with Bob and Roxana. I would add that you also might need to notify your malpractice carrier as there are typically notice requirements.

Roxana Bacon:

Answer: First, it is essential that you not try to respond to any claim of either malpractice or unethical conduct without at least consulting counsel expert in defending attorneys in whatever action is proposed against you. You should never respond without such outside, expert advice even if you think it is a very simple matter. Making a misstep in a disciplinary matter can have unexpected and dire consequences that can be avoided by listening and following an expert's advice.

Even before you consult counsel, get prepared. Gather all information about the file involved, prepare a chronology of events referencing documents and facts as specifically as you can, read your malpractice insurance contract and make whatever notices are required to invoke coverage, and read the applicable state ethical rules.

Next, after consulting counsel, determine your strategy and stay with it. To the extent your defense reveals weaknesses in your processes internally (written client representation agreements, identification of conflicts, fee problems) make changes to bring them into line with "best practices."

Finally, and something you can do now, before you have any adverse notices, think about what sort of support/network you have in place to review ethics issues as they arise rather than in crisis mode. Are there mentors in your jurisdiction whom you could hire or speak with for a general orientation on conflict questions (the key problem area for EB-5 representation)? Do you have a rolodex of experts with whom you have done due diligence so that you can make referrals for the business/tax/foreign law aspects of an EB-5 matter without being rushed? Does your state bar have any services that can help? Often it has ethics "hot lines" to help think through problems, and many have lists of experts in fields that lawyers frequently encounter that could form the basis of your own collection of experts for referral purposes.

LEGAL ETHICS RESOURCES

Books on Legal Ethics

1. Restatement Third, *The Law Governing Lawyers* (American Law Institute 2000, 2 vols.).
2. Geoffrey C. Hazard & W. William Hodes, *The Law of Lawyering*, 3d ed. (Aspen Law & Business 2004, 2-vol. loose-leaf).
3. Charles W. Wolfram, *Modern Legal Ethics* (West 1986).
4. ABA Center for Professional Responsibility, *Annotated Model Rules on Professional Conduct*, 5th ed. (2003).
5. Stephen Gillers and Roy D. Simon, *Regulation of Lawyers: Statutes and Standards* (Aspen Publishers 2004).
6. Roy Simon, *Simon's New York Code of Professional Responsibility Annotated* (West Group 2004).
7. Ronald D. Rotunda, *Legal Ethics: The Lawyer's Deskbook on Professional Responsibility* (ABA and West 2002).
8. Richard E. Flamm, *Lawyer Disqualification: Conflicts of Interest and Other Bases* (Banks and Jordan Law Publishing Company 2003).
9. ABA/BNA, *Lawyers' Manual on Professional Conduct* (multivolume loose-leaf).
10. Thomas Morgan, *Lawyer Law*, ABA Center for Professional Responsibility (2005).

Internet Sources for Legal Research

1. Numerous state bar and some local bar ethics opinions are available on Westlaw (databases: ABA-ETH-EO; METH-EO; NY-ETH-EO). Westlaw also has the ABA ethics opinions. Lexis has the ABA ethics opinions but only a few state bar ethics opinions. Both services have the ethics rules in every American jurisdiction.
2. ABA Center for Professional Responsibility (*www.abanet.org/cpr*).
3. LegalEthics.com (*www.legalethics.com*).
4. Cornell Legal Information Institute/American Legal Ethics Library (*www.law.cornell.edu/ethics*).
5. Freivogel on Conflicts (*www.freivogelonconflicts.com*).
6. Ethics and Lawyering Today (*www.ethicsandlawyering.com*).
7. District of Columbia Bar (*www.dcbar.org/*).
8. New York State Bar Association (*www.nysba.org*).
9. Findlaw: Ethics and Professional Responsibility (*www.findlaw.com/01topics/14ethics/index.html*).

Journals and Newsletters and Other Sources

1. *The Georgetown Journal of Legal Ethics* (Georgetown University, quarterly)
2. *New York Professional Responsibility Report* (New York Professional Responsibility Report, monthly)
3. Mary C. Daly, ed., New York Code of Professional Responsibility: Opinions, Commentary and Caselaw (Oceana, 2 vols., loose-leaf)

FEDERAL LAWS AND REGULATIONS AFFECTING THE FOREIGN INVESTOR IN THE UNITED STATES

Immigrant Investors: Creating Employment for U.S. Communities

*Updated by Doreen Edelman**

INTRODUCTION

As options for foreign investment expand and investors become more creative with their investment vehicles, legal advisors need to consider whether the U.S. government imposes any restrictions on such investments. Often the answer is "no," but lawyers providing immigration advice to the principals of such transactions should nonetheless be aware of some of the key reporting and disclosure requirements and several programs that need to be considered before an investor is given the green light to proceed.[1]

Perhaps more than any other law, the "employment creation" provisions of the Immigration Act of 1990 (IMMACT90)[2]—encouraging the immigration of individuals who seek to invest, or who are actively in the process of investing, in a new business in the United States—tie the immigration attorney more closely to the investment process itself, an activity usually performed by business attorneys. Investment-related issues include whether the investment in the business sector selected by the client is permissible and, if permissible, whether statutory reporting, disclosure, or other requirements are applicable to that investment. The latter issue is extremely important since short deadlines accompany many of the reporting requirements and civil and criminal penalties exist for negligent or willful failure to observe the deadlines.

This article describes some of the general policy issues underlying foreign investment in the United States and briefly outlines some of the key federal laws and regulations that require reporting and disclosure or otherwise affect the foreign investment process. However, this article does *not* consider applicable federal or state tax reporting requirements, *nor* does it consider the array of state prohibitions, restrictions, or other provisions that also are applicable to the foreign investment process. The primary goal of the article is to highlight some of the key investment-related laws, not to create a comprehensive compilation of every law potentially related to the investment process.

U.S. POLICY REGARDING FOREIGN INVESTMENT IN THE UNITED STATES

As a matter of policy, the United States has always welcomed foreign investors and sought to accord such investors the same fair, equitable, and nondiscriminatory treatment given to U.S. investors. In 2009, foreign investment accounted for 14 percent of all new investment in the United States.[3]

---

* **Doreen Edelman** is an attorney at Baker Donelson in Washington, D.C. and practices in the areas of international trade and foreign investment. She advises companies entering the U.S. market or establishing a presence in the United States and assists clients with global expansion strategy and legal compliance (including the Foreign Corrupt Practices Act) as well as providing counsel related to export and import issues. Ms. Edelman drafts agency, distribution and licensing agreements, prepares global business plans, establishes offshore corporations, and works with foreign counsel on behalf of U.S. entities or related parties. She can be reached at dme@bakerdonelson.com. Assistance for this article was provided by Cletus Weber, Joe Kennedy, Abbey Baker, and Harry B. Endsley, who graciously offered a previous version of this article for updating for this publication.

[1] For example, in 2006, a proposed acquisition of commercial operations at six U.S. ports by Dubai Ports World raised questions concerning national security. This action brought scrutiny upon the Committee on Foreign Investment in the United States (CFIUS). Congressional questions followed as to whether Congress could properly oversee CFIUS due to its lack of transparency. The issue of national security and its linkage to foreign investment within the United States was also raised. It was posited that U.S. security and economic concerns had changed since the events of September 11, 2001. *See* U.S. Congressional Research Service (CRS) Report for Congress, J. Jackson, "The Committee on Foreign Investment in the United States (CFIUS)" (Feb. 4, 2010), *available at* http://fas.org/sgp/crs/natsec/RL33388.pdf.

[2] Immigration Act of 1990 (IMMACT90), Pub. L. No. 101-649, §121(b)(5), 104 Stat. 4978.

[3] From 2008 to 2009, foreign direct investment declined by 57 percent.

U.S. investment policy is governed by the following principles:[4]

- **National Treatment.** Foreign investors should be given treatment that is no less favorable in like situations than domestic enterprises, except to protect national security and related interests.[5]
- **Most-Favored-Nation Status.** Foreign investors from different countries should be granted equal treatment.
- **Protection of Investor Rights.** Any expropriation of investment or abrogation of an investor's financial, physical, and intellectual property rights should be done for a public purpose, in a nondiscriminatory fashion under due process of law without violating previous contractual arrangements, and accompanied by prompt, adequate, and effective compensation.

Multilaterally, the United States has long worked to promote these principles. U.S. support in the Organization for Economic Cooperation and Development (OECD) for its Declaration on International Investment and Multinational Enterprises (1976) and its Code of Liberalisation of Capital Movements (1982) was strong. However, foreign investment often produces sharp differences over regulation between the developed and developing countries, and these foreign investment issues so far have defied consensus in international forums. In the OECD itself, during 1997 and 1998, such concerns sparked intense public opposition to the OECD's proposed agreement on investment, known as the Multilateral Agreement on Investment (MAI). Ultimately, in late 1998, the OECD Ministers were compelled to announce that they had ceased all further negotiations on the MAI.

In the "Uruguay Round" of negotiations for the World Trade Organization (WTO), negotiators successfully addressed a more limited, trade-related, agenda.[6] By adopting the Agreement on Trade-Related Investment Measures (TRIMs Agreement), the WTO members at least have a basis to deal with certain national practices, such as local content requirements, that arise in the investment context but have the effect of restricting and distorting trade in doing so. However, the measures addressed by the TRIMs Agreement are highly selective, and do not in any way attempt to regulate the entry and treatment of foreign investment.[7]

Absent a broad multilateral agreement, it is very likely that the United States and other nations will continue to liberalize foreign investment restrictions, unilaterally in competition with other countries or through the adoption of bilateral investment treaties. Under the direction of the U.S. Trade Representative (USTR), the United States is actively pursuing basic trade and investment framework agreements (TIFAs) with some countries, expanding on an existing broad network of formal bilateral investment treaties (BITs), and negotiating comprehensive free trade agreements with interested countries such as the North American Free Trade Agreement (NAFTA).[8]

While the debate over foreign direct investment in the United States has largely dissipated, or perhaps shifted to other issues, the publicly expressed concerns of the 1970s led Congress to pass legislation that increased data collection and disclosure requirements for foreign owners of U.S. assets.[9] Legislation passed in the 100th Congress granted the President the power to block foreign direct investments that the President determines could impair U.S. national security.[10] Legislation considered in the 101st Congress would have required great disclosure of foreign investment activities, and another proposal would have required reciprocal treatment in the United States for investments from countries that deny national treatment to U.S. investors.[11] Policy

---

[4] U.S. Department of State, "Foreign Direct Investment in Global Economy" (Mar. 1989).

[5] The Dubai World Ports case, mentioned *supra*, note 1, is an example of "national security" resistance to a foreign investment.

[6] *See generally* the Uruguay Round, *available at* www.wto.org/english/thewto_e/whatis_e/tif_e/fact5_e.htm.

[7] The current U.S. position is that the World Trade Organization's (WTO) Working Group on the Relationship between Trade and Investment, which was also created during the Uruguay Round, is the best vehicle to attempt to address the multitude of differences that separate the developed and developing countries, as well as those issues that divide the developed countries in the investment arena. Another WTO Agreement that can bear on the investment issue is the General Agreement on Trade in Services (GATS), which concerns the supply of services by foreign companies.

[8] *See generally* www.ustr.gov/trade-agreements. The bilateral investment treaties (BITs) program complements in part the investment protection provisions contained in more than 40 bilateral "Treaties of Friendship, Commerce, and Navigation" that the United States has been concluding for more than a century.

[9] 22 USC §§3101–3108; *see infra*, note 19.

[10] 50 App. USC §2170; *see infra*, note 55.

[11] While these pieces of legislation were never adopted, Congress, in 1990, did adopt legislation amending the International Investment and Trade in Services Survey Act, 22 USC
continued

analysts and members of Congress both have argued for prior screening of foreign investment in the United States and for selected performance requirements to govern specific investments.

Along with proposed screening measures there have been other examples of distrust of foreign investors in the United States. One can be found in the Federal Election Campaign Act of 1971 (FECA),[12] as amended by the Bipartisan Campaign Reform Act of 2002 (BCRA).[13] This act prohibits foreign nationals from participating in U.S. elections, which includes making contributions. Foreign-owned businesses are also subject to special rules under the FECA-BCRA. Although domestic corporations and partnerships must follow certain rules under these acts, those business entities owned by foreign nationals have many more restraints. This includes prohibiting foreign business owners from taking part in any political donation or decision about any such donation that the business entity might make.[14] "Rather than merely a means of regulating the influence of money on politics, this prohibition reflects a visceral fear embedded in the American psyche that un-American forces seek to manipulate and control the American political system."[15]

By and large, however, the United States continues to avoid screening, reciprocity, or performance requirements in connection with foreign investments. The U.S. approach is to utilize various foreign investment disclosure requirements that are found in selected statutes and provisions (see annexed table), as well as other laws designed to protect, broadly speaking, national security concerns, competition, and key sectors of the economy. Some important statutes and provisions are reviewed briefly below.[16]

STATUTES REQUIRING DISCLOSURE OF FOREIGN INVESTMENTS

Three of the major federal statutes that have an impact on foreign investment in the United States are information-gathering and disclosure statutes, instead of restriction statutes.

The Securities Exchange Act of 1934

The Securities and Exchange Act of 1934[17] requires disclosure of investment information in a nondiscriminatory manner from all acquirors of certain publicly held securities. The act directs any person or group acquiring more than five percent of any equity security of a 1934 Act company[18] to file a Schedule 13D form[19] with the Securities and Exchange Commission (SEC). Schedule 13D imposes no reporting requirements on the foreign investor beyond those shared by the American investor—both must disclose their citizenship and residence, the source and amount of funds used to make the purchase, and their intentions with regard to changes in control of the subject corporation.[20]

For the most part, securities laws do not treat foreign issuers differently from American issuers. There is no special form for foreign issuers who register their securities under the Securities Act of 1933,[21] which is the major federal statute concerning the initial registration of securities.

Because the securities laws of the United States require full and accurate disclosure of all material financial information, foreign issuers may face a problem if they also are offering their securities in countries that do not require such significant disclosure. This type of problem may be resolved by re-

---

§§3101–3108 (1988), discussed *infra*, to allow greater sharing of data among government agencies, and additional legislation entitled, "Foreign Direct Investment and International Financial Data Improvements Act," 22 USC §§3141–3146, requiring an annual report by the Secretary of Commerce on foreign direct investment in the United States, to be followed by a similar report by the Government Accountability Office (GAO).

[12] 2 USC §431 *et seq.*

[13] 11 CFR §100 *et seq.*

[14] *See generally* Nicholas G. Karambelas, "Examining the Law That Prohibits Foreign Nationals from Participating in U.S. Elections," *Washington Lawyer* (Feb. 2010).

[15] *Id.* at 32.

[16] Federal tax statutes that impose reporting requirements on foreign investments (*see, e.g.*, IRC §6038A) are not considered in this article nor are any applicable state restrictions.

[17] 15 USC §78 (1988).

[18] A 1934 Act company means, for this purpose, an issuer that "has total assets exceeding $1,000,000 and a class of equity security . . . held of record by five hundred or more . . . persons." 15 USC §78(l)(g)(1)(b).

[19] 15 USC §78(m)(d)(1). 17 CFR §240.13d-1 requires Schedule D to be filed within 10 days of the date of acquisition.

[20] 17 CFR §240.13d-101.

[21] 15 USC §§77a *et seq.*

questing confidential treatment by the SEC in order to protect investors.[22]

International Investment and Trade in Services Survey Act of 1976

In 1976, Congress enacted the International Investment Survey Act[23] to obtain "comprehensive and reliable information on international investment."[24] The act authorized the President to construct a "regular data collection program" with regard to foreign investment in the United States, to conduct studies and surveys, to study the adequacy of information, disclosure, and reporting requirements, and to publish statistical information.[25]

Under the act, information is collected by the Secretary of Commerce, acting through its Bureau of Economic Analysis (BEA), with respect to "direct investment," defined by the regulations to mean "the ownership or control, directly or indirectly, by one person of 10 percent or more of the voting securities of an incorporated business enterprise or an equivalent interest in an unincorporated business enterprise."[26] However, the Department of Treasury also has authority to conduct periodic comprehensive surveys of foreign "portfolio investment," which is defined as "any international investment which is not direct investment."[27] With the exception of the Securities and Exchange Act of 1934, the United States does not impose significant reporting requirements on foreign investors whose holdings fall short of this 10-percent threshold.

The BEA collects data on the operations of U.S. affiliates of foreign firms and investors through a series of initial transfer reports and periodic updates.[28] In general, the BEA requires transaction reports from U.S. affiliates at the time the foreign investment is made if the total cost of the acquisition is $3 million or more and, thereafter, quarterly reports if the total assets acquired exceed $20 million and annual reports if the total assets exceed $10 million. Purchases of residential real estate solely for personal use are exempt from reporting.[29]

Two forms are utilized by the BEA at the time that the investment is made or the transaction occurs:

- **Form BE-605.** Form BE-605 is used in connection with a foreign person's direct or indirect acquisition or establishment, of a U.S. enterprise, including a business segment, operating unit, or real estate (other than real estate purchased for personal use) of a business enterprise. The regulations require that Form BE-605 be filed by either the U.S. enterprise being purchased or the existing U.S. affiliate of the person making the acquisition.[30] In addition, a separate report must be filed for each foreign parent and information regarding foreign affiliates of the foreign parents may also be required.[31]

As provided by the forms themselves, Form BE-605 must be filed no later than 45 days after the investment transaction occurs. A civil penalty of not less than $2,500, nor more than $25,000, will lie for failure to furnish the required information.[32]

---

[22] 17 CFR §230.406.

[23] 22 USC §§3101–3108. In 1984, the statute became known as the International Investment and Trade in Services Survey Act.

[24] 22 USC §3101(b).

[25] Statistical information is collected primarily through quinquennial "benchmark surveys," which were required for the years 1980, 1987, and every fifth year thereafter. 22 USC §3103(b). The benchmark survey mandates disclosure of a multitude of information about transactions between foreign parent companies and U.S. subsidiaries, including balance sheets, income statements, trade in goods and services, employment data, taxes paid, R&D expenditures, payments arising out of technology transfers, and the like.

[26] 15 CFR §806.7(j).

[27] 15 CFR §806.7(k). Notice of surveys is published in the *Federal Register*. 31 CFR Part 129. Foreign portfolio investment generally includes items such as bank deposits, government securities, corporate bonds, and noncontrolling interests in corporate stock.

[28] In general, the reporting requirements may be categorized as:
- Quarterly reporting for qualifying reporters (Forms BE-605);
- Annual reporting for qualifying reporters (Form BE-15); and
- Quinquennial reporting in bench mark surveys (Form BE-12).

[29] 15 CFR §806.8; 15 CFR §806.15(j)(3)(A).

[30] 15 CFR §806.15(j)(3). *See* current form and instructions available at www.bea.gov/surveys/pdf/be605web08.pdf.

[31] *Id.* An exemption may be claimed if values of total assets, sales, or gross operating revenues and net income (loss) for the U.S. affiliate were each equal to or less than $60 million for the most recent reporting year or certain requirements for attenuation from foreign affiliates are met. *Available at* www.bea.gov/surveys/pdf/2010current_Reporting_Requirements.pdf.

[32] 22 USC §3105(a).

Certain "veils" that were utilized in the past to avoid disclosure of ownership information have been eliminated through regulation.[33] First, beneficial, not record, ownership is the basis of the reporting criteria for BEA reports. Thus, an owner who creates a trust, proxy, power of attorney, arrangement, or device with the purpose or effect of divesting such owner of the ownership of an equity interest as part of a plan to avoid reporting the information required by any of the BEA reports is deemed to be the owner of the equity interest.[34] Second, the U.S. affiliate of a foreign investor is required to identify the holder of bearer shares of the affiliate under certain circumstances.[35] Third, the regulations now prevent hiding foreign ownership via a "diamond holding pattern," through which the ownership of a holding company was divided into three or more entities, none having greater than a 50-percent interest in the holding company.[36] Fourth, reporting requirements now attach to estates, trusts, and other intermediaries.[37]

From the perspective of the foreign investor, it is important to stress that confidentiality under the International Investment and Trade in Services Survey Act will be strictly maintained. The act expressly provides that no information collected under its provisions may be published or released "in a manner that the person who furnished the information can be specifically identified except as provided in this section."[38] In addition, where the ultimate beneficial owner (UBO) is an individual, the U.S. affiliate need only report his or her country of residence.[39] Similarly, there is no requirement that a U.S. affiliate disclose the identity of the UBO who invests in publicly traded, as opposed to closely held, bearer shares.[40]

Agricultural Foreign Investment Disclosure Act of 1978

A large part of the public and governmental concern over foreign investment in the United States has focused on the increased foreign purchases of agricultural land. Driving up of prices in rural communities led to displacement and significant social problems. As a result, Congress, in 1978, adopted the Agricultural Foreign Investment Disclosure Act (AFIDA).[41] AFIDA requires a foreign person who acquires, disposes of, or holds any interest (other than a security interest) in agricultural land to submit a report on Form FSA-153 to the Secretary of Agriculture not later than 90 days after the date of the acquisition or transfer.[42] Form FSA-153 must be filed by: (1) any foreign person who holds, acquires or transfers any interest in agricultural property; and (2) any non-foreign person holding agricultural property who becomes a foreign person.[43]

"Agricultural property" is defined by the regulations as property in the United States currently used or if currently idle, last used within the past five years for farming, ranching, forestry, or timber production, except land not exceeding 10 acres in the aggregate if the annual gross receipts from the sale of farm, ranch, forestry, or timber products produced thereon do not exceed $1,000.[44]

Foreign persons who meet the requirements of AFIDA must submit Form FSA-153 to the office of the County Farm Service Agency where the land is located. Form FSA-153 requires disclosure of various information pertaining to the property and the owner thereof, including the following: (1) specific identification of the individual or corporate purchaser/transferee; (2) a legal description of the property; (3) the purpose for which the property will be used; (4) the type of interest held; (5) the details of the land value, including the purchase price and its

---

[33] P. Butterfield, "Who Owns America: The Adequacy of Federal Foreign Investment Disclosure Requirements," 24 Colum. J.L. & Soc. Probs. 79 (1990).

[34] 15 CFR §806.15(a)(6).

[35] 15 CFR §806.15(c).

[36] 15 CFR §806.15(a)(4).

[37] 15 CFR §806.11.

[38] 22 USC §3104(c).

[39] 15 CFR §806.15(b).

[40] 15 CFR §806.15(c).

[41] 7 USC §§3501–3508; 7 CFR §781.

[42] See 7 CFR §781-3(b). All interests must be reported except security interests, leaseholds of less than 10 years, certain future interests, easements unrelated to agricultural production, and interests solely in mineral rights. 7 CFR §781.2(c). Form FSA-153 must be filed within 90 days of acquisition or disposition if a single foreign investor holds a 10 percent or greater aggregate interest or if unrelated foreign investors together hold a 50 percent or greater aggregate interest. See www.fsa.usda.gov/wi/programs/factsheets/afida/FSA0153.pdf.

[43] 7 CFR §781.3.

[44] 7 CFR §781.2(b).

estimated current market value; and (6) if the purchaser is a corporation, information regarding any persons with substantial (10 percent) control of the purchaser.[45]

AFIDA authorizes the Secretary of Agriculture to determine the true owners of foreign and foreign-controlled organizations by requiring reports from persons in the second and third tiers of ownership of such organizations.[46]

Civil penalties of 25 percent of the fair market value of the foreign person's interest in the land in question may be imposed for persons who fail to submit reports, who submit incomplete reports, or who knowingly submit reports that are false or misleading or fail to maintain the accuracy of any submitted report. For late reports, the penalty can be one percent of the foreign person's interest in the agricultural land for each week or portion thereof that the report is late, not to exceed 25 percent of the fair market value of the foreign person's interest.[47]

LAWS THAT PROTECT THE INTEGRITY OF THE FINANCIAL SYSTEM

Reporting of International Capital and Foreign Currency Transactions, etc.

Every U.S. person must furnish information on relevant report forms if that person is engaged in: (1) any transactions in foreign exchange; (2) any transfer of credit between any person within the United States and any person outside the United States; or (3) the export or withdrawal from the United States of any currency or coin that is legal tender in the United States.[48] The Department of Treasury provides numerous report forms pertaining to a variety of transactions between foreign persons and persons subject to U.S. jurisdiction. All report forms that are relevant to a specific transaction must be separately submitted.[49]

Depending on the type of report, civil and criminal fines for failure to submit the report of up to $10,000 may be imposed, as may imprisonment of up to one year, or both.[50] The information reported remains confidential.[51]

Transportation of Currency or Monetary Instruments

Financial Crimes Enforcement Network (FinCEN) Form 105 must be submitted by any person who directly or indirectly physically transports, mails, or ships currency or other monetary instruments from the United States or into the United States in an amount exceeding $10,000.[52] The report is due at the time of such entry or departure.[53] Form 105 does not need to be submitted in connection with a transfer of funds through normal banking channels that does not involve the physical transportation of currency or monetary instruments.[54]

Civil penalties for failure to file the required report may be assessed up to the amount of the transported currency/monetary instrument. The transported currency itself also may be subject to forfeiture, in which case the civil penalty will be reduced by the amount forfeited.[55] Criminal penalties include fines of up to $500,000, and prison terms of up to 10 years.[56]

Reports of Foreign Financial Accounts

Each person subject to the jurisdiction of the United States (except a foreign subsidiary of a U.S. person) having a financial interest in, or signature or other authority over, a bank account, securities ac-

---

[45] 7 CFR §781.3(e).

[46] 7 USC §§3501(e) and (f).

[47] 7 CFR §781.4.

[48] 31 CFR §128.2(a).

[49] 31 CFR §§128.11–128.37.

[50] 31 CFR §128.4.

[51] 31 CFR §128.3.

[52] 31 USC §5316; 31 CFR §103.23(a). Currency is defined as any customarily used coin and paper money of any country, and includes U.S. notes and Federal Reserve notes, official foreign bank notes, and notes that customarily are accepted as a medium of exchange in a foreign country. 31 CFR §103.11(e). Monetary instruments consist of currency, all negotiable instruments (including personal and business checks, cashier's checks, promissory notes, traveler's checks, and money orders), and securities or stock in such form that title passes upon delivery. 31 CFR §103.11(m)(1). Monetary instruments do not include warehouse receipts or bills of lading. 31 CFR §103.11(m)(2).

[53] 31 CFR §103.27(b)(1).

[54] 31 CFR §103.23(d). Moreover, a person who is not a resident or citizen of the United States that makes shipments from abroad of currency or other monetary instruments to a bank or broker/dealer through the postal service or by common carrier is not required to submit Form 105. 31 CFR §103.23(c)(4).

[55] 31 CFR §103.58(d).

[56] 31 CFR §103.59(c). See www.fincen.gov/fin105_cmir.pdf.

count, or other financial account in a foreign country is required to report this relationship for each year in which the relationship exists to the Department of Treasury on Form 90-22.1, Report of Foreign Bank and Financial Accounts.[57]

Form 90-22.1 should be filed by June 30 of each year, and the individual also should answer questions about such accounts that appear on Part III to Schedule B of Form 1040.[58]

The principal exemption to this filing requirement is if the combined value of the foreign accounts was $10,000 or less during the preceding year or if the accounts were at a U.S. military banking facility operated by a U.S. financial institution.

LAWS THAT PROTECT NATIONAL SECURTIY

During the 1980s, there was a sharp increase in congressional concern over foreign direct investment in U.S. businesses and assets. A number of legislative proposals were considered, but the key foreign investment provision emerging from the congressional debate was Exon-Florio.[59]

The Exon-Florio provision authorizes the President, or his or her designee, to investigate foreign acquisitions to determine their effect on national security, and to take such action as the President deems appropriate to prohibit or suspend such acquisitions if the President finds that:

- There is credible evidence to believe that the foreign investor might take action that threatens to impair the national security; and
- Existing laws, other than the International Emergency Economic Powers Act and the Exon-Florio provision, do not provide adequate and appropriate authority to protect the national security.

The President may direct the Attorney General to seek appropriate judicial relief, including divestment, and the President's findings are not subject to judicial review. A later amendment to the statute requires an investigation in cases where the acquirer is controlled by or acting on behalf of a foreign government, and the acquisition could result in control of a person engaged in interstate commerce in the United States that could affect the national security of the United States.[60]

Exon-Florio was not intended to inhibit foreign direct investments in industries that are not of national security interest. Nevertheless, it potentially widens the scope of industries that fall under the national security rubric. Previous legislation barred foreign direct investment in such industries as maritime, aircraft, banking, resources, and power. Generally, these sectors were closed to foreign investors to prevent public services and public interest activities from falling under foreign control, primarily for national defense purposes.

Under Exon-Florio, however, the term national security is intended to be interpreted broadly without limitation to a particular industry. As such, it could apply to a firm in practically any industry.[61] Never-

---

[57] 31 CFR §103.24. Persons having interests in 25 or more foreign financial accounts need only note that fact on the form, and may be required to provide more detailed records regarding each account if so requested. See. www.fincen.gov/forms/files/f9022-1_fbar.pdf.

[58] Corporations also are required to file Form 90-22.1 and to complete Part L of IRS Form 1120.

[59] Pub. L. No. 100-418, §721, 102 Stat. 1107; Pub. L. No. 102-99, §8, 105 Stat. 487 (50 USC App. §2170). The Exon-Florio provision was added as §721 of the Defense Production Act of 1950 by virtue of §5021 of the Omnibus Trade and Competitiveness Act of 1988.

[60] Pub. L. No. 102-484, 106 Stat. 2315, 2463. In a recent high-profile case, Dubai Ports World, a terminal operator owned by the government of the United Arab Emirates, voluntarily submitted for investigation its proposed acquisition of certain port terminal operations.

[61] The statute does give the President or the President's designee some guidance on the factors that should be considered in taking action. These factors include, but are not limited to, domestic production needed for projected national defense requirements; the capability and capacity of domestic industries to meet national defense requirements, including the availability of human resources, products, technology, materials, and other supplies and services; the control of domestic industries and commercial activity by foreign citizens as it affects the capability and capacity of the United States to meet the requirements of national security; the potential effects of the transaction on the sales of military goods, equipment, or technology to a country that supports terrorism or proliferates missile technology or chemical and biological weapons or is a regional military threat to the interests of the United States or is on the "Nuclear Non-Proliferation-Special Country List"; the potential effects of the transaction on U.S. technological leadership in areas affecting U.S. national security; the potential national security-related effects on U.S. critical infrastructure; whether the transaction is a foreign government-controlled transaction; and the long-term projection of U.S. requirements for sources of energy and other critical resources and material. 50 USC App. §§2170(f)(1)–(11). CFIUS has considered notifications of foreign acquisi-
continued

theless, the legislative history also shows that Congress rejected proposals to expand the statute's coverage to include threats to "essential commerce" and "economic welfare," which undercuts the arguments of those who contend the term "national security" should be construed broadly enough to subsume within it notions of economic security and international competitiveness.

By Executive Order 12662 of December 27, 1988, the President designated the Committee on Foreign Investment in the United States (CFIUS) to receive notices and other information regarding acquisitions; to determine whether investigations should be undertaken; and once an investigation has been completed, to prepare a report and a recommendation to the President.[62]

The law provides a framework of a maximum 90-day review of notified transactions. This period includes 30 days to determine whether to investigate a transaction (commenced by a receipt of "written notification"),[63] 45 days to complete an investigation,[64] and a final 15 days for the President to announce his decision on the transaction.[65] If a transaction moves from the 30-day review to the formal 45-day investigation, then the President must decide its disposition.[66]

CFIUS review is initiated by receipt of a written notification of a transaction.[67] The regulations provide that notice may be given only by a party to the transaction or by a CFIUS member agency.[68] Notice from third parties is not accepted. Notification is voluntary under the Exon-Florio provision. Many foreign acquisitions do not involve issues related to national security and, consequently, parties to the transaction may decide not to notify CFIUS.[69]

In July 1989,[70] CFIUS issued proposed regulations under the Defense Production Act. Over 70 organizations commented on the regulations, which included over 700 pages of comments.[71] The Treas-

---

- Identification of the foreign parent and the ultimate beneficial owner and information on both;
- Other filings with U.S. government agencies that have been made or are contemplated;
- A list of contracts, both classified and unclassified, with Department of Defense or other U.S. government agencies; and
- The plans of the acquiring company for the U.S. company. 31 CFR §800.402.

[68] See 50 USC App. §§2170(b)(1)(C) and (D).

[69] Once a notification is received, Treasury, as the first step, decides if it is complete. If so, the 30-day review period begins. During that period, CFIUS agencies evaluate the transaction. At the end of the 30-day period, if no agencies request an investigation, the parties to the transaction are notified that there are no national security issues sufficient to warrant an investigation and that action under the Exon-Florio provision is concluded with respect to the notified transaction. If agencies decide to request an investigation, CFIUS then decides at the Assistant Secretary level whether to initiate an investigation. A decision to investigate begins the statutory investigation period, which is not to exceed 45 days. At the completion of the investigation, CFIUS must send the President a report and a recommendation. If CFIUS is unable to reach a unanimous recommendation, the Secretary of the Treasury, as chair, submits a CFIUS report to the President that sets forth the differing views and presents the issues for decision. The President then has 15 days to announce his decision on the case. See id. §2170 et seq.

[70] 54 Fed. Reg. 29744.

[71] The key concerns expressed by the commentators were the following:

- The need for a definition of, or clear guidance as to the meaning of, "national security." Neither the Exon-Florio provision and its legislative history nor the Defense Production Act defines national security. The proposed regulations left the term undefined, apparently to preserve presidential flexibility.
- The preference for a bright-line definition of "control," for example, in terms of board membership or share ownership. The proposed regulations define control functionally, in terms of the ability to make important decisions about the company.

---

tions ranging from lawn seed and tulips to defense contractors.

[62] CFIUS membership is the Secretary of the Treasury (chair), the Secretary of State, the Secretary of Defense, the Attorney General, the Secretary of Commerce, the Director of the Office of Management and Budget, the Chair of the Counsel of Economic Advisers, the U.S. Trade Representative, Director of the Office of Science and Technology Policy, Assistant to the President for National Security Affairs, Assistant to the President for Economic Policy, and the Secretary of the Department of Homeland Security. Other government agencies are included in CFIUS deliberations when a notification raises questions within their area of expertise. Id. §§2170(k)(2)(A)–(J).

[63] See id. §2170(b)(1)(E).

[64] See id. §2170(b)(2)(C).

[65] See id. §2170(d)(2).

[66] Id.

[67] Notifications to CFIUS generally include the following information:

- A description of the parties to the transaction;
- Details on the acquisition arrangements;

continued

continued

ury Department, Office of International Investment, issued final regulations in 1991.[72]

In 2007, more changes to legislation[73] ensued after the events of September 11, 2001. Congressional opposition to the Dubai Ports World's attempt to buy operations of U.S. ports and China National Offshore Oil Company Ltd.'s (CNOOC) attempted purchase of UNOCAL shook confidence in Congress's ability to provide sufficient oversight through a lack of CFIUS transparency.[74] These legislative additions expanded the scope of transactions subject to national security review as well as increased congressional reporting requirements for CFIUS. This congressional scrutiny will continue for foreign acquisitions in areas of critical technology and infrastructure.

LAWS THAT PROTECT COMPETITION

Clayton Act

The antitrust laws may prevent a particular acquisition by either domestic or foreign investors because of its effect on actual or potential competition. Section 7 of the Clayton Act is the principal statute that provides safeguards against further industrial concentrations in the United States.[75] That section prohibits any merger or acquisition by one corporation of the stock of another corporation if such action may tend substantially to lessen competition or create a monopoly in any line of commerce anywhere in the United States.

As distinguished from the earlier Sherman Act,[76] §7 of the Clayton Act allows the government to challenge anticompetitive business practices in their incipiency, before their consequences come to fruition.

Hart-Scott-Rodino

To facilitate enforcement of §7, Congress, in 1976, passed the Hart-Scott-Rodino Antitrust Improvements Act, which in part added a new §7A, providing for premerger notification.[77] The primary purpose of the premerger notification process is to allow the government sufficient opportunity to compile data concerning an impending merger, and, if that merger appears to violate §7, to facilitate obtaining a preliminary injunction against it.

In general, §7A:

- Prohibits persons, including foreign persons, from acquiring the stock or assets of other firms unless advance notice is given to the Federal Trade Commission (FTC) and the U.S. Department of Justice (DOJ);
- Establishes a 30-day waiting period after such notification, or 15 days if the tender offer is in cash;
- Exempts certain acquisitions (such as the purchase of stock for investment purposes only or the creation of subsidiaries) that pose no anticompetitive problems; and
- Authorizes up to $10,000 per day in penalties for violations of the act.

Detailed information on a prescribed form[78] must be submitted to the FTC and the DOJ. To be subject to the premerger notification provisions, either party must meet certain "size of person" requirements,[79] and the transaction must be of a certain size.[80]

- The absence of a limiting provision that would, after a period of time, remove the threat of presidential action against investors who choose not to notify.
- The status of foreign lenders who make commitments to finance an acquisition of a U.S. company, but who do not thereby acquire control or even contemplate control, absent default on loans.
- The need for special treatment for hostile transactions to take into account the fact that they are highly time-sensitive.
- The desirability of a formal fast-track procedure to enable more rapid handling of transactions that bear no relation to national security.

[72] 31 CFR §800 *et seq.*

[73] The Foreign Investment and National Security Act of 2007, Pub. L. No. 110-49, 121 Stat. 246.

[74] CRS Report for Congress, *supra* note 1.

[75] 15 USC §18.

[76] 15 USC §1.

[77] 15 USC §18a; 16 CFR §801. Pub. L. No. 94-435, 90 Stat. 1390.

[78] 16 CFR Pt. 803, Appendix.

[79] 15 USC §18A(a)(2).

[80] 15 USC §18A(a)(3). Pursuant to amendment of the statute, the Federal Trade Commission is required to revise the thresholds annually.

LAWS THAT PROTECT CLASSIFIED INFORMATION

The Executive Orders and Department of Defense regulations that constitute the National Industrial Security Program may make it difficult for foreign-controlled corporations to obtain the security clearances necessary to carry out a contract involving classified information.[81] Both a *facility* clearance and *individual* clearances for key management personnel and others who may have access to classified information are required for any company in the Untied States carrying out a classified contract.

Generally, facilities that are under "foreign ownership, control, or influence" are ineligible for facility clearances unless foreign management is excluded. A foreign-controlled U.S. subsidiary might obtain clearances by forming a "voting trust" or "proxy agreement" in which it gives up management rights, but retains rights to profits, or by formally agreeing with the U.S. government to special management arrangements that attempt to ensure the security of the classified information.

LAWS THAT PROTECT PARTICULAR SECTORS OF THE ECONOMY

Over the years, Congress has expressed its belief that certain industries are "essential" to or could affect national security and, therefore, should have limits on foreign investment. These industries include the maritime industry, the aircraft industry, banking, mining, energy, public lands, communications, government contracting, and investment regulations. A few of these specific business sectors are noted below.

Atomic Energy

The Atomic Energy Act[82] requires the issuance of a license for the operation, transfer, receipt, manufacture, production, acquisition, possession, or import or export of facilities that produce or use nuclear materials. Aliens, foreign governments, foreign corporations, or corporations owned, controlled, or dominated by such interests cannot be issued a license for any of the above activities except the export of such facilities.[83]

Radio and Television

The Communications Act[84] prohibits foreign governments and their representatives from holding any radio station license.[85] Also, aliens and their representatives, foreign chartered corporations, and foreign-owned corporations are prohibited from holding any licenses for broadcast or common carrier radio stations. (A corporation is considered "foreign owned" if any director or officer is an alien, or if more than 20 percent of its capital stock is owned or voted by aliens, a foreign government, or a foreign corporation.[86])

A domestic corporation that is foreign controlled may not hold a broadcast or common carrier license if the Federal Communications Commission finds the denial of the license to be in the public interest.[87] (A corporation is considered to be "foreign controlled" if a controlling corporation has an alien officer or if more than 25 percent of its directors are aliens or more than 25 percent of its stock is owned or voted by foreign interests.[88])

Aviation

The Federal Aviation Act (FAA) requires a carrier to obtain a license to carry persons, property, or mail between points within the United States.[89] A carrier must be a U.S. citizen to obtain such a license. To qualify a company as a U.S. citizen under the FAA, 75 percent or more of its voting interest must be owned or controlled by U.S. citizens, and the president and two-thirds or more of its management and board of directors must be U.S. citizens.[90]

---

[81] *See* Industrial Security Regulation, DoD 5220.22-R (Dec. 1985), and Industrial Security Manual for Safeguarding Classified Information, DoD 5220.22-M (Sept. 1987). The National Industrial Security Program was established by Executive Order on January 6, 1993, for the protection of classified national security information, and is under the policy direction of the National Security Council.

[82] 42 USC §2011 *et seq.*

[83] 42 USC §2133(d).

[84] Communications Act of 1934, as amended by the Telecommunications Act of 1996, Pub. L. No. 104-104, 110 Stat. 56 (1996), 47 USC §151 *et seq.*

[85] 47 USC §310(a).

[86] 47 USC §310(b)(3).

[87] 47 USC §310(d).

[88] 47 USC §310(b)(4).

[89] 49. USC §41101(a).

[90] 49 USC §40102(15).

LAWS THAT PROTECT THE U.S. TECHNOLOGY BASE

Arms Export Control Act

Under the Arms Export Control Act,[91] the Department of State promulgated implementing regulations—the International Traffic in Arms Regulations (ITAR)[92]—that were specifically amended to provide that defense firms must provide the Office of Defense Trade Controls with written notice at least 60 days prior to a planned transfer in ownership to a foreign purchaser.[93]

Such notice provides the U.S. government with the opportunity to point out to firms that, with limited exceptions, the ITAR requires a license for the transfer of technical data to a foreign person whether the recipient is within or outside the United States.[94] Licenses can be denied for foreign policy or national security reasons and, thus, may be difficult or impossible to obtain, depending on the degree of sophistication of the technical data and the nationality of the foreign investor.

Export Administration Act

The Export Administration Act of 1979, as amended,[95] authorizes the United States to restrict exports of goods and technology that would make a significant contribution to the military potential of any other country or combination of countries that would prove detrimental to the national security interests of the United States. In particular, the Department of Commerce requires firms to seek licenses for exports of "dual use" technologies. Of great concern are high performance computers, encryption technology, satellites, and certain machine tools. In 1997, the Department of Commerce determined that the mere release of technology to a foreign national was a "deemed export," vastly increasing the need for licenses."[96]

Note there is also a bar to admission to the United States for any alien who may violate U.S. laws prohibiting the export of goods, technology, or sensitive information from the United States.[97]

---

[91] 22 USC §§2751–96.
[92] 22 CFR §§120–30.
[93] 22 CFR §122.4(b).
[94] 22 CFR §125.3(c).
[95] 50. USC App. §2401 *et seq. See also* 15 CFR Part 770 ff.
[96] 15 CFR §§730–74.
[97] *See* T.L. Loke Walsh, "The Technology Alert List, Visa Mantis and Export Control: Frequently Asked Questions," 2 *Immigration & Nationality Law Handbook* 412 (AILA, 2004–05 Ed.).

FEDERAL DISCLOSURE AND REPORTING REQUIREMENTS

Statute	Agency & Form(s)	Who Files? When?	Thresholds	Penalties	What Information?	Confidentiality
International Investment and Trade in Services Survey Act of 1976 22 USC §§3101–3108 15 CFR §806	**Department of Commerce, Bureau of Economic Analysis** Initial reports (*Forms BE-13, BE-13C, and BE-14*) Quarterly reports (*Forms BE-605 and BE-606B*) Annual report (*Form BE-15*) Quinquennial report (*Form BE-12*) Industry classification (*Form BE-607*)	U.S. business enterprise U.S. person who assists or intervenes in acquisition of a U.S. business enterprise by, or who enters into a joint venture with, a foreign person (*e.g.*, attorneys, CPAs, brokers, etc.) *Report due within 45 days of investment*	Direct or indirect interest of 10% or more of voting securities of incorporated U.S. business or its equivalent Full exemption if real estate purchased for personal use; partial exemption if U.S. business enterprise has total assets of $3 million or less and owns less than 200 acres of U.S. land	Civil penalties for failure to furnish information involves civil fines not exceeding $10,000 Willful noncompliance subject to criminal fines and imprisonment	Identifying information, including ultimate beneficial ownership, and location, nature and cost of investment Information on parent's balance sheet and related data, trade between entities, employment data, and tax payments	Reports are confidential and may be used by the government only for "analytical or statistical" purposes, unless the President directs they be disseminated to other federal agencies
Agricultural Foreign Investment Disclosure Act of 1978 7 USC §§3501–3508 7 CFR §781	**Department of Agriculture, Office of Agricultural Stabilization and Conservation Service** Form FSA-153	Foreign person who acquires, disposes of, or holds an interest in U.S. "agricultural land" (other than a security interest, leaseholds less than 10 years, etc.) *Report due within 90 days of acquisition*	Must exceed 10 acres in aggregate or produce more than $1,000 annually from farming, ranching, forestry or timber production	Civil penalties up to 25% of fair market value for incomplete, false or misleading reports, or failure to update; late filings also penalized	Legal description and acreage; date of transfer and fair market value; price; legal interest conveyed and prospective use; identity of parties (*i.e.*, the true owners)	Reports are filed in Agricultural Stabilization and Conservation Service (FSA) County office and are available for public inspection ten days after filing; copy is sent to state Department of Agriculture

Currency and Foreign Transactions Reporting Act of 1970 31 USC §§321, 5311–5322 31 CFR §103 31 CFR §128	**Customs Service** **Internal Revenue Service** *Form 4790* (Customs) *Form 4789* (IRS)	Financial institutions Any person physically transporting or receiving currency or monetary instruments Any person having an interest in, or signatory or other authority over foreign financial account *Report due at time of entry or departure*	$10,000 Some exemptions applicable in case of financial institutions reporting requirements Transfer of funds by bank check, bank draft or wire transfer are exempt from the individual reporting requirement	Willful violations by financial institutions may involve civil fines from $25,000 to $100,000 Civil penalties for failure to file required report; currency and monetary instruments in transit may be subject to seizure and forfeiture Substantial criminal penalties also apply to willful violations of the Act	Financial institutions report each deposit, withdrawal, exchange of currency, or other payment by, through, or to such institution Any person who physically transports, mails or ships coins or currency or other "monetary instruments" (*e.g.*, investment securities in bearer form or registered form if endorsed in blank; promissory notes; etc.)	Reports are exempt from disclosure under Freedom of Information Act (FOIA), but may be provided by Secretary of Treasury to other agencies
Domestic and Foreign Investment Improved Disclosure Act of 1977 15 USC §78m 17 CFR §240.13d-1	**Securities and Exchange Commission** *Schedule 13D*	Any person or "group" acquiring, directly or indirectly, beneficial ownership of certain classes of securities *Report due within 10 days of date of acquisition*	5% of voting equity securities of corporation registered pursuant to Section 12 of the Act	Civil and criminal penalties under the federal securities laws	Name and address of the beneficial owner; citizenship or place of organization; source of funds; future plans	Information is public record and available for public inspection; confidential treatment may be requested
Hart-Scott-Rodino Antitrust Improvements Act of 1976 15 USC §18a 16 CFR §§801–803	**Federal Trade Commission** **Department of Justice, Antitrust Division** Notification and Report Form for Certain Mergers and Acquisitions Advance written notification of merger; 30-day waiting period before consummating transaction	Both parties to merger (acquiring party only in case of tender offer) *Report due in advance of merger or acquisition*	Transactions by which (i) one party has consolidated assets or annual sales of $100 million and other party has consolidated assets or annual sales of $10 million, and (ii) as a result of acquisition, acquiring person would have aggregate voting securities or assets of the acquired person in excess of $15 million or at least 15% of the voting securities or assets of the acquired person	Civil penalties against any person, officer, director, or partners of entity in amount not to exceed $10,000 per day Equitable relief (injunction against acquisition pending compliance)	Identity of parties; description of acquisition and assets; information related to industry and to specific business; previous acquisition information; etc.	Information is confidential and exempt from disclosure under Freedom of Information Act (FOIA); can be made public only in administrative or judicial proceeding or disclosed to committee of Congress

Defense Production Act of 1950 (Exon-Florio) 50 USC App. §2170 31 CFR §800	**Committee on Foreign Investment in the United States (CFIUS)** Written notification to CFIUS is voluntary; may trigger up to 90-day review period	Foreign investor U.S. target *Report is voluntary*	Whether foreign investor is acquiring "control" over the U.S. entity Whether foreign investor is taking action which would impair "national security"	No formal sanction for failing to file, but appropriate judicial relief is available, including the blocking of a pending transaction and the forced divestment of an already completed transaction	Description of parties, parents, transaction, other government filings, future plans, business activities of both parties, etc.	Information is confidential and exempt from disclosure under Freedom of Information Act (FOIA); can be made public only in administrative or judicial proceeding or disclosed to committee of Congress
Internal Revenue Code	**Internal Revenue Service** Form 1120 Form 5472 Form 1042 Form 1120 F Form 1040 NR	Taxpayer Reporting Corporation *Filing dates are specified by statute and/or regulation*		Civil and criminal penalties	Income, gains, losses, deductions, credits, and amount of tax; taxpayer identification; reportable transactions	
International Emergency Economic Powers Act of 1977 50 USC §§1701–1706 *See also* various regulations for assets control, sanctions, and transactions administered by Office of Foreign Assets Control, U.S. Treasury Department	**President of the United States** Formal declaration of national emergency	N.A.	In case of extraordinary and unusual threat to national security, foreign policy or economy of the U.S., President may investigate, regulate, or prohibit any transactions in foreign exchange, transfers of credit, and import or export of currency or securities; President also has broad powers with respect to any transaction involving a foreign country or national	Civil penalties not to exceed the greater of $250,000 or an amount that is twice the amount of the transaction that is the basis of the penalty Criminal penalties not to exceed $1,000,000 or 20 years imprisonment, or both	Disclosure may be required from any person before, during, or after completion of transaction, including production of books of account, records, contracts, letters, memoranda, or other papers	No formal confidentiality provision but process is nonpublic in nature

BUSINESS CONSIDERATIONS FOR INVESTORS

by Mark H. Scribner

In addition to the immigration issues foreign investors must confront while seeking status to live and work in the United States, they must also deal with business issues that affect their ability to successfully operate or invest in U.S. businesses. These business issues, though sometimes addressed generally by the investors' immigration counsel, should also be addressed on the investors' behalf (and the investment entity's behalf) by experienced business transactional counsel.

These issues can be grouped for ease of reference in the following categories: Ethical or legal practice considerations; business entity considerations/tasks; other business start-up considerations/tasks; business in practice considerations/tasks; and miscellaneous investor legal issues.

ETHICAL/LEGAL PRACTICE CONSIDERATIONS

- Immigration practitioners with clients seeking entry based on their investment into and operation of U.S. businesses must consider their clients' business interests in addition to their immigration goals.

- Immigration practitioners with foreign investor clients are urged to associate with business transactional attorneys with experience handling foreign investment matters in the United States. Separate counsel may be needed to advise the investor and the business entity. In an EB-5 project, for example, the entity is typically created by a U.S. developer/entrepreneur seeking to profit from the investors who must decide if the project is suitable for their purposes. These differing view points and the possibility of conflicts in some instances suggest that the investor should have independent business counsel.

- Immigration practitioners with foreign investor clients should advise their clients to retain a competent certified public accountant (CPA) to handle all tax and accounting issues for the investor that result from landing in the United States. This may involve the determination of tax obligations under a tax treaty between the United States and the investor's tax residence country. In addition, the CPA can assist the client with review of the business, tax, and accounting issues that may arise with any business investment project. These may include analysis of the business plan, an evaluation of the soundness of financial projections, advice on recordkeeping and assistance gathering documents for U.S. taxation purposes, tax planning and preparation and filing of Federal and State tax returns.

- Immigration practitioners with foreign investor clients should work closely with business transactional counsel and the accountant to insure that each professional is consulted at all critical stages of the investment and the business project. Whether the investor client will qualify for the visa category being pursued is dependent on many factors, including sustainability of the business. The other retained professionals will be more qualified to review with the client, including, for example, the nature of the business entity, the business interest being purchased and the capitalization of the business entity.

BUSINESS ENTITY CONSIDERATIONS/TASKS

- Consideration must be given to what type of business entity should be used for the investment. Entities that will be considered include the corporation, limited or general partnership, limited liability partnership, and the limited liability company. For example, it is critical in EB-5 cases to use an entity, and draft appropriate language in the enabling documents, that permits the EB-5 investors to be "actively involved" in the business. This required level of participation means that the business analysis must focus on how and to what extent the investor client will be involved

---

[*] **Mark H. Scribner** is a partner in the Burlington, Vermont law firm Carroll & Scribner, P.C., where he oversees the firm's commercial, corporate, and real estate practices. He has been actively involved with immigration counsel in the firm in advising sponsors and developers on structuring EB-5 projects to attract foreign investors, including drafting the securities offerings and all business agreements referenced in the offerings. Mr. Scribner also has extensive experience representing commercial lenders in the Northeast on all types of commercial loan originations, credit accommodations, and workouts. He can be reached at mscribner@cslaw.us.

- in business decisions of the entity and whether the entity gives its owners enough power to successfully meet the "active involvement" threshold (*e.g.*, will the investor be able to recommend policy, vote on significant decisions, and exercise rights normally accorded shareholders or members or partners under state law?).
- A decision must be made on what state should be used to organize, incorporate or otherwise set up the business entity.
- A decision must be made on the name of the entity and whether any fictitious name (d/b/a) will be used (*e.g.*, for marketing purposes). The name(s) must be searched in the chosen state to determine availability, to avoid confusion with other registered names, to avoid repetition of names, all to reduce the chance of denial of a name to the filing entity.
- Officers, directors, managing members, managing partners, etc. must be considered, appointed, and authorized to act on behalf of the entity. Depending on the type of investment and visa program the foreign investor is pursuing, the investor may be an owner but not a party with day-to-day decision-making authority on behalf of the entity.
- Business counsel must draft and file articles of organization (LLC or corporation) or partnership certificates (limited partnerships) with the Secretary of State for state of organization.
- Business counsel must draft and oversee adoption of the bylaws (corporation), operating agreement (LLC), or partnership agreement that will govern the operations of the entity.
- Business counsel must insure that stock, membership, or partnership certificates are issued to the investors to evidence their investment, with any restrictions on resale noted on the certificates, making mention of time or securities restrictions on resale.

OTHER BUSINESS START-UP CONSIDERATIONS/TASKS

- A business plan outlining the goals, projections, and financial analyses of the proposed entity must be drafted, reviewed, and accepted before the entity can pursue investors or other financing.
- Depending on the nature of the business investment, federal and state regulatory and disclosure requirements must be reviewed and made a part of the investment business plan.
- The CPA and business counsel will need to confer on the tax status of the entity and obtain a Federal Employer Identification Number (EIN) for the entity.
- If the foreign investor does not have a social security number (SSN), and is not work authorized, then the client should authorize the accountant to apply for the Individual Tax Identification Number (ITIN) with the Internal Revenue Service (IRS).
- The entity will need to open one or more U.S. bank accounts to accept investments, with or without escrow, and to fund operating expenses.
- The investor will need to transfer funds into the entity, and be able to document the transfer and source of funds.
- Business counsel should address any intellectual property (IP) issues that might be involved, even tangentially, with the investment or entity—copyrights, trademarks, patents, trade names, and trade secrets. Depending on the nature of the investment and project, this inquiry may include review of foreign IP filings and application approvals.
- Business counsel should consider whether other possible government filings need to be made depending on the nature of the investment and the project (*e.g.*, Department of Commerce, Department of Agriculture, Department of the Treasury's Office of Foreign Assets Control (OFAC), U.S. Customs, IRS, Securities and Exchange Commission (SEC), Department of Justice, etc.). Offerings to solicit investment, even from overseas investors, triggers SEC and state securities laws and regulations, although exemptions are typically used under Regulation D and Regulation S to avoid full-blown registrations of the offerings.
- Business counsel must review (or prepare, if representing the entity) collateral agreements needed to facilitate the investment project. These may include, for instance, the EB-5 project offering memorandum, escrow agreements for receipt of funds, real estate, licensing, distribution, loan and security agreements and management agreements.
- Determine if there are any zoning issues. May the investor operate the investment business at the desired location; can the property be used at such location for the use contemplated?

BUSINESS IN PRACTICE CONSIDERATIONS/TASKS

- Personal income tax filings with the IRS must be made annually and, possibly, more frequently if estimated tax filings are required. Entity tax filings with IRS must be made initially, quarterly and annually, depending on the nature of entity.
- The investment entity might have real property taxes, business property taxes, unemployment fund payments, and tax withholding payments on a periodic basis.
- Insurance matters for review and implementation may include premises liability insurance, workers compensation insurance, casualty insurance, and business interruption insurance. Insurance may also be a consideration in succession planning
- Recurring filings with the Secretary of State, including, for example, annual reports for corporations and limited liability companies, may be required. Business counsel or the CPA can assist on behalf of the entity.
- Business counsel must review or draft various real estate or capital lease agreements or purchase & sale agreements if investor or entity is leasing or buying real estate or capital equipment.
- Business counsel may be asked to review business contracts with customers, suppliers, etc.

MISCELLANEOUS INVESTOR BUSINESS ISSUES

- Business counsel may be asked to advise on U.S. customs issues in connection with payment of duties and taxes on products imported by the investment project.
- Business counsel may be asked to review contracts in connection with the advertising of the business, including any website production and content agreements.
- Business counsel or separate tax counsel may be asked to advise on estate planning issues for the investor and his family.
- In addition to any review in connection with business start-up, business counsel should review buy-sell agreements (corporation), operating agreements (LLC), or partnership agreements to insure that the agreement creates an "artificial" market for the sale of the investor's shares or membership/partnership interests and also provides a mechanism for the purchase of the investor's interests by other owners or the business entity, possibly using cross-purchase insurance, etc.

THE LEGAL AND NON-LEGAL PROFESSIONALS BEHIND A VIABLE EB-5 REGIONAL CENTER

by Linda Lau and Tina Lee[*]

In advising clients who wish to set up EB-5 regional centers, immigration lawyers must provide thorough counsel regarding both the regulatory requirements under the Immigrant Investor Pilot Program as well as the practical steps in constructing a regional center proposal. Many prospective regional center applicants come to the table with only basic knowledge about the EB-5 program, namely, that it is a means of connecting them to otherwise unavailable capital sources. Before launching out into the EB-5 arena, they need to understand the elements of a regional center proposal, and the professionals whose services will be needed at the proposal stage and beyond.

THE ANATOMY OF A REGIONAL CENTER PROPOSAL

The Immigrant Investor Pilot Program modifies the regular EB-5 program[1] by providing that, where the investment is made in a new commercial enterprise within a U.S. Citizenship and Immigration Services (USCIS)-approved regional center, the job creation requirement may be satisfied through proof of jobs created "indirectly" by the investment. To obtain designation from USCIS as a regional center—defined as "any economic unit, public or private, which is involved with the promotion of economic growth"[2]—an applicant must submit a proposal that clearly describes the geographic scope, business goals (including targeted industries), funding structure, promotional plan, projected indirect job creation, and overall economic impact of the planned regional center.[3]

The requisite content of a regional center proposal is generally grouped into four main components when presented to USCIS: (1) Overall Business Plan; (2) Operational Plan; (3) Economic Impact Analysis Report; and (4) Sample Agreements. As indicated by its name, the Overall Business Plan contains a narrative of the business aspects of the regional center, such as the geographic focus, target industries, planned activities, specific project profiles with timelines, applicant's background, business entity structure, and management team. Of particular interest to USCIS is the "investment plan" for each planned activity/project that supports the job projections in the economic report: how will the money invested in a project be used to capitalize and operate the project in a manner that results in the claimed creation of jobs?

The Operational Plan explains the funding structure of the regional center, anticipated capital sources including due diligence procedures with respect to foreign investment fund, allocation of funds to promotional activities, and administrative oversight procedures. The Economic Impact Analysis Report sets forth, based upon "economically or sta-

---

[*] **Linda Lau** (J.D., UCLA School of Law) currently serves on the American Immigration Lawyers Association (AILA) EB-5 Committee and is a former chair and member of the Executive Committee of AILA's Southern California chapter. Her Los Angeles-based firm, Global Immigration Law Group, specializes in U.S. and global immigration strategies for professionals and high net worth individuals. Admitted as a member of the California State Bar Association and a solicitor of England and Wales, Ms. Lau is the sole appointed U.S. agent coordinator of the Canadian and UK immigrant investor programs from Hong Kong Shanghai Bank Corporation Global Investor Immigration Services (Canada).

Tina Lee (J.D., UCLA School of Law) is a senior associate with Global Immigration Law Group. Ms. Lee focuses on EB-5 matters and has co-authored articles on this topic for AILA's 2008–09 and 2009–10 *Immigration & Nationality Law Handbook*. She was admitted to the State Bar of California in 2003.

The authors wish to acknowledge business lawyer Ron Darling, of Darling & Risbrough, LLP (Santa Ana, CA, www.darlingrisbrough.com), and economist Doug Svensson of Applied Development Economics (Walnut Creek, CA, www.adeusa.com), who provided their expert opinions for this article.

[1] *See* §203(b)(5) of the Immigration and Nationality Act (INA). In summary, the regular EB-5 program allows foreign investors to immigrate to the United States through investing capital in a new commercial enterprise that will create no fewer than 10 full time jobs for U.S. workers. The requisite capital amount is $1 million or $500,000, for an investment made in a "targeted employment area" or "rural area."

[2] 8 CFR §204.6(e).

[3] *See* 8 CFR §204.6(m).

continued

tistically valid forecasting tools,"[4] a detailed prediction of how jobs will be created indirectly through the regional center,[5] and how the regional center will positively impact the regional or national economy in general.[6] Finally, the Sample Agreements include the various legally binding documents that would be executed by a foreign investor incident to his or her investment in a regional center-based new commercial enterprise. These agreements must not only make sense from a business standpoint but also not comply with any EB-5 requirements.

All four of the components above are critical to the regional center proposal, and ideally will be crafted by qualified professionals who are familiar with the EB-5 regional center requirements. Since the immigration lawyer's role is limited to reviewing and advising on the immigration aspects of a proposed regional center, he or she should expect to work in conjunction with several other specialists in putting together a regional center proposal: a business lawyer, a securities lawyer, a business plan writer, and an economist. The immigration lawyer should be sufficiently knowledgeable in business, securities and economic models to dialogue intelligently on topics relevant to the regional center proposal.

THE BUSINESS LAWYER

At its core, an EB-5 regional center involves the establishment of various business operations and the legal rights and responsibilities that are incident thereto. It is thus critical that a regional center applicant retain a business lawyer with considerable experience in advising business clients generally, and EB-5 regional center applicants in particular. The term "regional center applicant" refers to the corporate entity that submits the regional center proposal. As an initial matter, a principal (such as a commercial developer) may need to consult the business lawyer regarding the formation of the entity that will submit the regional center proposal. Most regional center applicants are formed as Limited Liability Corporations or C Corporations. The business lawyer will ensure that the entity is duly established and that the principals are thoroughly advised as to all compliance issues. It should be noted that separate corporate and securities counsel may also be required to advise on securities law issues, and a tax professional should be consulted as to any potential tax consequences flowing from regional center operations.

A good business lawyer will help a regional center applicant fully understand all risks and responsibilities attendant with running a regional center. He or she will not only equip the applicant with well-drafted legal documents that will pass muster with USCIS, but will also provide sound practical advice on problems to anticipate in the real business world and how best to plan for them. Importantly, the experienced business lawyer will help to dispel unrealistic expectations a regional center applicant may have regarding participation in the EB-5 program. Where an applicant may come to the table with big dreams of large-scale, instant capital access, the business lawyer can step in and provide a realistic perspective and practical tools.

A business lawyer with experience in the EB-5 regional center area is the preferred choice. He or she would understand, for example, that the new commercial enterprises established within a regional center should take the form of limited partnerships, even though this investment vehicle would not typically be advisable in other contexts. This is because the limited partnership is written into the EB-5 regulations as an exception to the normal active management requirement imposed on EB-5 investors.[7]

The experienced business lawyer will be able to carefully word provisions in the limited partnership agreement pertaining to management roles and exit strategy to comply with both limited partnership law and USCIS requirements. In addition, he or she will be able to advise the regional center applicant fully concerning the general liability it will assume as general partner of the limited partnership entities, and how to avoid conflicts of interest that could arise among various limited partnerships involving similar business types.

It is best for a regional center applicant to approach a business lawyer with a well-formed business plan. Even if a written plan is not yet available, the applicant should be able to provide a description of the project with sound business justification. Starting with a mature business concept from the outset facilitates streamlined legal advice and appropriately tailored legal documents, saving an applicant time and legal fees.

---

[4] 8 CFR §204.6(m)(3)(v).
[5] 8 CFR §204.6(m)(3)(ii).
[6] 8 CFR §204.6(m)(3)(iv).

[7] See 8 CFR §204.6(j)(5).

Assuming the investment vehicle selected is a limited partnership, the business lawyer will be responsible for drafting the following investment-related legal documents to be included as samples in the regional center proposal:

- Offering Memorandum
- Statement of Risk Factors and Disclosures
- Subscription Agreement
- Limited Partnership Agreement
- Escrow Agreement (if escrow is a feature of the investment)

It should be assumed that each of the sample agreements will be carefully reviewed during the adjudication process and must be followed with respect to each EB-5 investor.

THE SECURITIES LAWYER

In addition to the business lawyer, the regional center applicant should consider retaining securities counsel to ensure that the planned investment offering(s) to EB-5 investors will not run afoul of any applicable federal or state securities regulations. Involving a separate securities lawyer may not be necessary if the business lawyer has sufficient knowledge of and experience with investment offerings made within the context of the EB-5 program. Most EB-5 investment offerings are designed as private offerings that are exempt from the requirement to register with the U.S. Securities and Exchange Commission. Since the criteria to qualify for a private offering exemption at both the federal and state levels are rigid and the potential repercussions of non-compliance tremendous, regional center applicants must ensure that their investor recruitment and admission will not violate applicable securities laws.

THE BUSINESS PLAN WRITER

The Overall Business Plan and Operational Plan are USCIS's sole source of knowledge about a proposed regional center's geographic focus, target industries, sample projects, budget, funding structure, investment plans, promotional activities and administrative oversight. Thus, the Overall Business Plan and Operational Plan must be clearly and engagingly written to incorporate all of the content needed to satisfy the relevant regulatory requirements. Ideally, the individual writing the plans will have had experience producing an Overall Business Plan and Operational Plan for a regional center proposal that was approved. In reality, most candidates do not fit this bill. A minimally qualified business plan writer would have experience writing at least some real-world business plans, and be willing and able to understand the final product envisioned in the EB-5 regional center. In addition, it is important that he or she have the flexibility to work with immigration counsel to ensure the plans written contain what USCIS is looking for.

USCIS has regularly included citations to *Matter of Ho*[8] in Requests for Evidence requiring applicants to submit more detailed overall business plans. *Matter of Ho* pertains to business plans under the regular EB-5 program and is arguably inapplicable to regional center business plans, which are more generalized and predictive in nature. Nonetheless, unless and until USCIS issues specific guidance regarding regional center business plans, the business plan writer should review the relevant language in *Matter of Ho* and aim to follow it as closely as possible. The operational plan should set forth in a detailed fashion how EB-5 investor funds will be solicited, verified for lawfulness, and then safeguarded to ensure use solely for the purpose of indirect job creation as opposed to administration of the regional center.

For many proposed regional centers, especially those involving a fund-to-fund model,[9] the total universe of projects that will take place within the regional center is unknown at the proposal stage. In

---

[8] *Matter of Ho*, 22 I&N Dec. 206 (Assoc. Comm'r, Examinations 1998) (stating, "A comprehensive business plan as contemplated by the regulations should contain, at a minimum, a description of the business, its products and/or services, and its objectives. The plan should contain a market analysis, including the names of competing businesses and their relative strengths and weaknesses, a comparison of the competition's products and pricing structures, and a description of the target market/prospective customers of the new commercial enterprise. The plan should list the required permits and licenses obtained. If applicable, it should describe the manufacturing or production process, the materials required, and the supply sources. The plan should detail any contracts executed for the supply of materials and/or the distribution of products. It should discuss the marketing strategy of the business, including pricing, advertising, and servicing. The plan should set forth the business's organizational structure and its personnel's experience. It should explain the business's staffing requirements and contain a timetable for hiring, as well as job descriptions for all positions. It should contain sales, cost, and income projections and detail the bases therefor. Most importantly, the business plan must be credible.")

[9] In the "fund-to-fund" model, EB-5 investors invest their money into a new commercial enterprise that functions as a private lender to businesses within a set list of industries.

this situation, applicants should present at least one specific planned project along with several hypothetical projects encompassing the various industries targeted by the regional center.

Where regional center applicants do not have the resources to draft plans in-house, immigration counsel should be prepared to provide referrals to qualified business plan writers who can handle the work from start to finish. Another alternative is to recommend that the applicant recruit an MBA student from a local reputable business school. In any event, the business plan writer must clearly understand that the final products will be more than broad-strokes summaries, and will require a commitment of many hours and close attention.

THE ECONOMIST

A regional center may incorporate EB-5 investor capital into its projects only to the extent justified by the projected job creation. For example, the maximum number of EB-5 investors permitted to invest in a project predicted to create 100 jobs would be 10; if the project were located in a targeted employment area, 10 investors would represent $5 million in EB-5 capital. Reliable job count predictions are a key element in a regional center proposal because they help create parameters for potential funding and also provide the framework to be used for individual investor petitions. It is therefore critical that a regional center applicant work with a qualified economist in the proposal process.

A regional center proposal must be accompanied by an economic impact analysis report satisfying the following regulatory criteria:

- Must provide in verifiable detail how jobs will be created indirectly;[10]
- Must contain a detailed prediction regarding the manner in which the regional center will have a positive impact on the regional or national economy in general, as reflected by such factors as increased household earnings, greater demand for business services, utilities, maintenance; and
- Must be supported by economically or statistically valid forecasting tools, including, but not limited to, feasibility studies, analyses of foreign and domestic markets for the goods or services to be exported, and/or multiplier tables.[11]

For an economist to render the required analysis, he or she must be provided with information on the location or geographic scope of the proposed regional center, the types of projects to be undertaken using investment money, the target market, and specifics about each project such as land use and square footage. The more complete the project description that is given, the better able an economist is to run calculations, make job count projections, and analyze regional impact factors. Even if the projects are not well-defined, concrete discussions with the economist will require at least a range of options that are likely to be pursued.

Regional center applicants may wish to consult an economist early on in the business planning process to obtain advice on how to maximize the job benefits of the project(s) to be funded in a particular location. For example, if construction of a commercial office building is planned, an economist can explain how certain types of office uses would yield a higher job count than others.

Where a regional center applicant is flexible with regard to project location as long as it is in a targeted employment area, the economist can help identify potentially qualifying sites. The regional center applicant may wish to consult with a separate economist who specializes in handling targeted employment area analysis regarding how to define a geographic scope that may be certified as a high unemployment area by the state.[12] The issue of targeted employment area is separate from the job projection issue and does not need to be included in the economic impact report.

In selecting an economist, regional center applicants should look for a qualified professional with experience preparing economic impact analysis reports for EB-5 regional centers. There is no single acceptable economic impact model under the regulations, but the economist must be able to present a clear and detailed report describing the net effect of the regional center on the economy in terms of jobs and other factors. It is important for the economist to be transparent regarding his or her thought process and the tools used in the analysis. If the principals spearheading the regional center application do not participate in an open dialogue with the economist at the proposal stage, they will not fully understand what must be demonstrated at the individual investor petition stage. Therefore, principals should seek to

---

[10] 8 CFR §204.6(m)(3)(ii).

[11] 8 CFR §204.6(m)(3)(v).

[12] *See* 8 CFR §§204.6(i) and 204.6(j)(6)(ii).

work with an economist who is interested in helping them understand the process. It is also important for the economist to cooperate with immigration counsel regarding how best to present the report and communicate the information to USCIS. Finally, as much lead time as possible should be given for the completion of the economic impact analysis so that key information is not missed and dialoguing opportunities are not lost.

THE FINAL PRODUCT

The regional center proposal, in final form, will consist of the four components described above along with a cover letter and executive summary. A sample approval letter tailored to the proposed regional center is also usually included for the adjudicator's reference. All EB-5 processing, including I-526 petitions, I-829 petitions and regional center proposals, has been centralized at the California Service Center (CSC). The processing time for regional center application adjudication is four months, according to an update from CSC staff at a public EB-5 forum held on March 16, 2010, at CSC. There is presently no form and no fee for regional center proposals, but USCIS headquarters staff announced at the March 16, 2010, EB-5 forum that the agency is in the process of creating a regional center application form.

Inquiries on pending regional center applications are made first through the National Customer Service Center, with follow-up inquiries permitted after 30 days to the general EB-5 program e-mail box, *USCIS.ImmigrantInvestorProgram@dhs.gov*. Regional center proposals can be appealed to the AAO if denied,[13] though USCIS headquarters staff indicated at an EB-5 stakeholders meeting on February 27, 2009, that the agency's approach is to work with regional center applicants as much as possible, through the Requests for Evidence process, to obtain the information required for an approval. As of April 19, 2010, there are over 91 approved regional centers.[14]

ONCE THE DESIGNATION IS OBTAINED...THEN WHAT?

It is important for applicants to understand that the approval of a regional center proposal does not by itself ensure a regional center's viability. Ongoing efforts must be made to reach out to foreign investors and to facilitate the continual progress of activities within the regional center. The regional center should take such practical steps as hiring staff fluent in the language of the targeted investors, and should be prepared to spend time and energy communicating with and servicing these investors. Care should be taken in consultation with counsel to safeguard promotional activities against the appearance of ethical compromise or the violation of applicable U.S. securities laws. Unless followed up with marketing activities that successfully direct foreign investor capital into its projects, a regional center designation is essentially useless. Further, a regional center having prolonged inactivity runs the risk of termination by USCIS on the basis that it no longer serves the purpose of promoting economic growth and job creation.[15] A regional center's inactivity would be made known to USCIS through administrative reports made by the regional center pursuant to its designation letter.

BUILDING AN EFFECTIVE MARKETING STRATEGY

According to statistics from the U.S. Department of State's Visa Office, the top five countries for EB-5 visa issuance in FY 2009 (10/1/2008–9/30/2009), based on $500,000 investment in a regional center, were as follows: China 1,803, South Korea 689, Great Britain 246, Taiwan 142, and Japan 77. For FY 2010 (beginning 10/1/2009) through May 2010, the top three countries have remained in place, with China at 486, South Korea at 151, and Great Britain at 93. Iran is fourth with 54 and India fifth with 48.

China, with a population of over 1.3 billion and a strong economy, is presently an unrivaled hub of EB-5 interest. One reason for the high interest level is that many high net worth individuals in China are parents committed to making a way for their children to study and live in the United States. By filing an immigrant investor petition with his or her children included as dependents, the parent can facilitate LPR status for the children. Where a child 21 or over is involved, the capital investment funds may be furnished by the parents so that the child can file a petition as the principal.

China is an example of how every country will have a unique culture and professional customs that

---

[13] *See* 8 CFR §204.6(m)(5).

[14] The most current list of EB-5 regional centers can be accessed via USCIS's website at *www.uscis.gov*.

[15] *See* 8 CFR §204.6(m)(6).

will affect how marketing should be carried out. Principals wishing to penetrate the China market must correctly identify who the referral source for prospective Chinese investors will be. A common misconception is that lawyers, or CPA firms, or trade associations in China are the referral source and that, therefore, efforts should be expended to reach out to such persons or groups with a marketing agenda. However, the reality in China is that immigration matters are usually handled by immigration consultancy companies that are licensed and bonded by local governments. Every province has its own special rules governing the operation of immigration consultancy companies. Unlike unlicensed *notarios* in the United States, immigration consultants in China are monitored by the government. In the past, immigration consultants have serviced large numbers of Chinese immigrant investors moving to Canada, Australia, New Zealand, and Germany. Immigration consultants are paid finder's fees by the regional center.

Regional center principals should spend time researching and interviewing immigration consultants until they find one they feel fully comfortable working with. It is a close working relationship requiring trust and open communication. Regional center principals should communicate with their immigration consultants continually to ensure that statements are not being made that could be construed as a false promise. For example, a consultant's unintentional representation as to the processing time for obtaining an immigrant visa could be problematic if the actual processing time is much longer.

Immigration law practitioners on the U.S. side may find it helpful to work alongside immigration consultants since the latter will take care of collecting requested documents and liaising with the investor, but direct dialogue should still be maintained between the investor and immigration counsel to avoid the risk of miscommunication.

A final note is that every country will have different conventions for the ownership and transfer of assets, as well as different documentation schemes and reporting requirements, which will affect the lawful source of funds analysis for each immigrant investor petition. Thus, as to source of funds, it is advisable to engage the services of a professional accountancy or investigative firm that is familiar with and experienced with regard to a particular country.[16] Such a firm would have the country-specific expertise and research tools to focus on preparing a comprehensive source of funds report to be submitted with the immigrant investor petition.

---

[16] PKF International is one such firm with extensive experience handling EB-5 source of funds analysis (*www.pkf.com/site/international*).

MARKETING AND PROMOTING EB-5 INVESTMENTS: SECURITIES ISSUES FOR REGIONAL CENTERS AND IMMIGRATION LAWYERS TO CONSIDER

*by Jennifer Mercier Moseley**

When a newly formed, start-up company needs to raise capital, it typically looks for investors by conducting an offering of its equity securities. This is no different for a regional center or limited partnership formed in connection with the regional center pilot program[1] pursuant to the EB-5 employment-creation immigrant visa category.[2] A limited partnership (or other entity) formed for the purpose of obtaining investment from foreign individuals seeking an EB-5 visa is conducting an offering of its equity securities like any other newly formed, start-up company. Therefore, it is important for regional centers to understand how U.S. securities laws affect their ability to obtain these EB-5 investors. More specifically, regional centers must learn how securities laws impact their ability to market and promote their regional center investments. In addition, both regional centers and immigration lawyers must understand how securities laws affect their ability to pay or receive, as the case may be, referral or other fees in connection with the promotion of the regional center.

REQUIREMENT TO REGISTER SECURITIES UNLESS AN EXEMPTION IS AVAILABLE

The Securities Act of 1933, as amended (the Securities Act), requires that all securities sold must be registered with the U.S. Securities and Exchange Commission (SEC) unless exempted by its rules. The Securities Act has a broad definition of what constitutes a "security." The SEC has determined that limited partnership interests and limited liability company interests are securities.[3] Thus, the offer and sale of limited partnership interests (or limited liability company interests, as the case may be) to EB-5 investors must be done either through registration or by available exemption.

EXEMPTION FROM REGISTRATION UNDER REGULATION D AND/OR REGULATION S

The common exemption used by issuers[4] who want to privately offer securities (that is, a non-public offering of securities) is Rule 506 of Regulation D promulgated under the Securities Act. In addition to providing a way to avoid the expensive and onerous task of registering the securities to be offered, Rule 506 provides an additional, and significant, advantage to the issuer: an issuer that complies with the conditions for exemption under Regulation D does not need to find a separate exemption under applicable state securities laws. Securities transactions pursuant to this regulation are exempt from any state securities registration requirements. In 1996, Congress passed the National Securities Markets Improvement Act (NSMIA) preempting state securities laws when a transaction involves "covered securities."[5] Securities exempt from registration under Rule 506 of Regula-

---

* **Jennifer Mercier Moseley** is a partner in the Birmingham, office of Burr & Forman, LLP (*www.burr.com*). She represents both public and private companies in connection with mergers and acquisitions, private securities offerings, and securities regulatory matters. Her e-mail is *jmoseley@burr.com*.

The author is not providing legal advice in this article. Please consult your own securities counsel to discuss your specific facts and the applicability of securities law.

[1] Authorized under the Departments of Commerce, Justice, and State, the Judiciary, and Related Agencies Appropriations Act of 1993, Pub. L. No. 102-395, §610, 106 Stat. 1828; S. Rep. No. 102-918 (1992).

[2] INA §203(b)(5), 8 USC §1153(b)(5).

[3] Under Section 2 of the Securities Act of 1933 (the Securities Act), a "security" includes any note, stock, bond, "investment contract" or, in general, any interest or instrument commonly known as a "security." An "investment contract" is made when a person: (i) invests money; (ii) in a common enterprise; (iii) with an expectation of profit; (iv) to be earned solely from the effort of others. The SEC has determined that interests in a limited partnership are an investment contract, and has considered limited liability company interests investment contracts as well.

[4] Under section 2(a)(4) of the Securities Act, an issuer is a person or entity who issues or proposes to issue any security. This article refers to regional centers and issuers interchangeably; if the regional center is not the issuer, the entity that is the issuer still needs to comply with securities laws.

[5] Under the National Securities Markets Improvement Act (NSMIA), however, states are still allowed to require notification of the exempt transaction and payment of a fee for such notification from the issuer.

tion D are among the transactions that are expressly listed as "covered securities."

Another exemption that a regional center may avail itself of is Regulation S promulgated under the Securities Act. An issuer that complies with the conditions under Regulation S demonstrates to the SEC that its offer and sale of securities have occurred outside of the United States. In other words, the SEC has no jurisdiction over such transactions. Unlike Regulation D, however, an issuer that relies on Regulation S as its exemption from registration must find a state-specific exemption from registration for each state whose securities laws would be applicable. Since for some states the mere fact that an issuer is organized as an entity in that state is what provides the nexus for jurisdiction over a securities offering, it is advisable that regional centers review the applicable state securities statutes to determine whether they need to find a separate state exemption for a securities offering conducted pursuant to Regulation S. Regional centers may also want to contact the applicable state securities regulators for guidance relating to their specific transaction.

An issuer that chooses to rely on Regulation S for its exemption from registration can also claim the availability of Regulation D as an exemption. However, what regional centers must understand about each of these two exemptions is that the method and manner in which a regional center markets and promotes its regional center investments will affect whether or not either (or both) of these exemptions can be claimed by the regional center. A regional center should carefully plan its marketing and promotional activities with securities laws in mind prior to taking any actions because failure to consider the conditions upon which the exemption from registration are based could cause the regional center to lose the availability of an exemption.

While there are other conditions set forth in both Regulation D[6] and Regulation S,[7] the condition in each of these regulations pertaining to the regional center's marketing and promotional activities is, practically, the most vital. This is the case because the manner in which an issuer offers or sells its securities is the condition that will most distinguish, in the case of a Regulation D offering, a private placement offering from a public distribution and, in the case of a Regulation S offering, an offshore offering from an offering in the U.S. Furthermore, it seems that if there is an area in which regional centers have not been able to create a best practices foundation as it relates to securities laws, it is in the marketing and promotion area.

MARKETING AND PROMOTING REGIONAL CENTERS

Avoiding General Solicitation Under Regulation D

Rule 502(c) of Regulation D prohibits a "general solicitation" or advertising in the offer or sale of securities under Rule 506. "General solicitation" includes any advertisement, article, notice, or other communication published in any newspaper, magazine, or similar media or broadcast over television or radio and any seminar or meeting whose attendees have been invited by the foregoing methods. This applies whether the activities are conducted in the United States or abroad, and applies to activities conducted by any third party on behalf of the issuer. In addition, sending mass e-mails, newsletters or other mailings is considered general solicitation.

If a regional center is contacting a potential investor for the first time and it has no pre-existing relationship with that investor, the regional center should take special care to ensure that any information given to the potential investor has only general terms and does not identify a specific investment opportunity. Any private placement offering comes with the dilemma of how an issuer can establish a pre-existing relationship without violating the prohibition on general solicitation. This dilemma is made more difficult by the fact that the SEC will not provide any guidelines by which issuers should and should not act if they want to avoid general solicitation. Though the SEC will review whether there has been general solicitation on a case-by-case basis, based on all the facts and circumstances surrounding a specific case, SEC no-action letters and releases provide that a pre-existing relationship can be properly formed through the use of a questionnaire to determine whether a prospective investor is an accredited investor. The SEC considers the use of accredited investor questionnaires as essential for an issuer to establish a substantive pre-existing rela-

---

[6] For a more detailed discussion of the conditions for compliance with Regulation D, see J. Moseley, A. Paparelli, L. Mark, & C. Lee, "The Relevance of U.S. Securities Laws to Immigrant Investors, EB-5 Regional Centers and Their Advisors," 14 *Bender's Immigr. Bull.* 938 (Aug. 1, 2009). Copyright 2009 LexisNexis Matthew Bender.

[7] Regional centers should consult their securities advisor to determine the applicable conditions.

tionship.[8] This 30-day "safe harbor" provides regional centers with a concrete guideline to follow. Once a pre-existing relationship has been established, a regional center may solicit a prospective investor and provide information on specific investment opportunities. Therefore, the use of these questionnaires is advisable for regional centers, and is really the only way to safely determine, and document, that a regional center is complying with Regulation D's prohibition on general solicitation.

Avoiding Directed Selling Efforts in the U.S. under Regulation S

One of the conditions upon which the availability of Regulation S is subject is that "directed selling efforts" may not be made in the United States by the issuer. "Directed selling efforts" is defined in Rule 902(c) of Regulation S as any activity undertaken for the purpose of, or that could reasonably be expected to have the effect of, conditioning the market in the United States for any of the securities being offered in reliance on Regulation S,[9] including placing an advertisement in a publication "with a general circulation in the United States"[10] that refers to the offering of securities being made in reliance upon Regulation S. Rule 902(c)(3) sets forth the limited activities that do not constitute directed selling efforts, such as providing a journalist with access to press conferences held outside of the United States, to meetings with the issuer conducted outside the United States, or to written press-related materials released outside the United States, at or in which a present or proposed offering of securities is discussed.[11] Bona fide visits to real estate, plants, or other facilities located in the United States and tours of the facilities conducted for a prospective investor by an issuer or a third party acting on its behalf also do not constitute directed selling efforts.

As with Regulation D, the practical difficulty with the prohibition on directed selling efforts under Regulation S is that many regional centers use mass e-mail and the internet to disseminate information. Clearly, if such dissemination includes information on a specific securities offering, a regional center could not claim that it has not conducted any directed selling efforts in the United States. Recognizing that issuers and their agents commonly use the internet to disseminate offering materials, the SEC published its interpretation and views regarding the use of the internet for sales pursuant to Regulation S.[12] In its release, the SEC stated that it would not view an offer as targeted at the United States. if an issuer implements adequate measures to prevent U.S. persons from participating in an offshore offer where information is distributed through the internet. Also, as with Regulation D, the SEC will determine what constitutes adequate measures based on all the facts and circumstances of a particular situation.

However, the SEC did provide certain guidelines in its release that, if an issuer were to implement at a minimum, would generally demonstrate that an issuer implemented adequate measures to ensure that its activities are not directed selling efforts. For a regional center located in the United States conducting an offering overseas, the following minimum measures must be implemented: (1) the web site includes a prominent disclaimer making it clear that the offer is directed only to countries other than the United States; (2) the issuer implements procedures that are reasonably designed to guard against sales to U.S. persons, such as by obtaining mailing addresses or telephone numbers; and (3) the issuer implements password-type procedures that are reasonably designed to ensure that only non-U.S. persons can obtain access to the offer.

REGULATION OF THIRD PARTIES WHO MARKET OR PROMOTE REGIONAL CENTERS

Most regional centers use third-party agents to make connections with potential EB-5 investors.

---

[8] In a no-action letter, the U.S. Securities and Exchange Commission (SEC) found that a 30-day waiting period should exist between the determination of accredited investor status and the date an offering is made (that is, offering materials are provided to the accredited investor). Lamp Technologies, Inc., SEC No-Action Letter, 1997 WL 282988 (May 29, 1997).

[9] Rule 901 through Rule 905, and Preliminary Notes.

[10] Publication "with a general circulation in the United States" is defined as any publication that is printed primarily for distribution in the United States, or has had, during the preceding 12 months, an average circulation in the United States of 15,000 or more copies per issue; and will encompass only the U.S. edition of any publication printing a separate U.S. edition if the publication, without considering its U.S. edition, would not constitute a publication with a general circulation in the United States.

[11] The requirements of Rule 135(e) of the Securities Act must be satisfied for this exception to apply.

[12] SEC Release Nos. 33-7516, 34-39779, IA-1710, IC-23071 (Mar. 23, 1998).

Most regional centers also offer referral fees to these third parties, such as immigration lawyers, for referring potential investors to their regional center. However, a regional center can only pay, and immigration lawyers can only receive, such referral fees if they are in compliance with securities laws. Referral fees can signal to the SEC and state securities regulators that broker-dealer activities have occurred, in which case the immigration lawyer or other third-party agent must be registered with the SEC and any applicable state securities regulatory body in order to receive these fees.

Section 15 of the Securities Exchange Act of 1934, as amended, defines a "broker" as any person engaged in the business of effecting transactions in securities. States generally define a broker-dealer as any person who effectuates or attempts to effectuate a securities transaction. Both the SEC and states will interpret the activities that qualify as "effectuating a securities transaction" broadly. Performing due diligence, negotiating terms of the offering, soliciting the investors, and handling the funds of the investors are activities that states and the SEC have found to qualify as broker-dealer activities. Though each state's securities statute must be examined for specificity, most states prohibit issuers from paying anyone in effectuating a securities transaction unless the recipient is a registered broker-dealer or agent. All states require that broker-dealers and agents register in the states in which they operate, with only a few limited exceptions. In addition, a third party who receives any transaction-based compensation in connection with a securities transaction will almost always be deemed a broker-dealer.

Many of the third parties who receive referral fees when referring potential EB-5 investors to regional centers may be doing so because they consider themselves "finders" rather than broker-dealers. However, the concept of a "finder" is really unclear under securities laws. Based on regulatory interpretations from various SEC no-action letters, it appears that a finder might be someone who nothing more than provides the name and contact information of a potential investor to the issuer, but does not do this on a regular basis. Moreover, most state securities laws do not explicitly reference finders with respect to their broker-dealer registration requirements. If the third party conducts any activities that would be considered broker-dealer activities and is not a registered broker-dealer or agent, then it cannot receive any payments for its services relating to the securities transaction. The determination of whether the activities rise to the level of broker-dealer activities will be made on a case-by-case basis by both the SEC and the applicable state securities regulatory body. In the case of immigration lawyers referring potential EB-5 investors to regional centers, unless the immigration lawyer is also a registered broker-dealer, the immigration lawyer should not accept fees for activities outside of the scope of services as an immigration lawyer without consulting a competent securities advisor.

Regional centers should also be careful when they offer such referral fees. Recent informal advisories by some regulators to issuers warn that the use of unregistered broker-dealers will render the issuer liable as an aider and abettor of securities law violations under Section 20(e) of the Securities Exchange Act of 1934. In addition, some states will impose civil and criminal penalties for issuers that compensate unregistered broker-dealers. As a result, regional centers should evaluate their policies regarding referral fees taking into consideration the prohibition on payments to unregistered broker-dealers.

WALKING THE LINE: USING BEST PRACTICES TO ACCOMPLISH BUSINESS OBJECTIVES WITHIN THE CONFINES OF SECURITIES LAWS

As outlined above, the key to compliance with Regulation D is establishing a pre-existing relationship with a prospective investor, and the key to compliance with Regulation S is establishing a relationship only with a non-U.S. person physically located outside of the United States. Though a regional center can claim exemptions under both of these regulations, it cannot use one regulation to back-stop its failure to comply with the requirements and conditions of the other regulation. The idea behind the dual exemption is that an issuer would claim exemption under Regulation S for its offers and sales outside of the United States while at the same time claiming exemption under Regulation D for its offers and sales inside the United States. This dual exemption provides an advantage to the regional center that has prospective investors that are non-U.S citizens who are residing in the United States. For the regional center that has prospective investors only outside of the United States, it still may want to consider whether Regulation D provides the better exemption because of the type and breadth of its marketing and promotional activities and applicability of state securities laws.

To create a best-practices foundation, a regional center should coordinate with its securities advisors and any third parties, such as immigration lawyers, who will act on its behalf early in the process, and certainly prior to conducting marketing and promotional activities, in order to determine which exemption is most suitable. Immigration lawyers and other third parties who work with regional centers should also consider obtaining securities advice prior to taking any actions on behalf of regional centers. Though the SEC and states will evaluate an immigration lawyer's activities and receipt of fees on a case-by-case basis, immigration lawyers who participate in marketing and promoting regional centers, whether by providing referrals, participating in discussions with the regional centers and potential EB-5 investors, or accompanying regional center staff on marketing events and trips, should ask themselves whether their activities relate to their services as an immigration lawyer or whether they are acting beyond that scope. If it is the latter, immigration lawyers should consider a policy of not accepting fees for such services, or obtaining assistance on a case-by-case basis from a securities advisor.

While it may seem like a daunting task to walk the fine line of getting the press out on a regional center in order to attract investors in the first place and still comply with securities laws, it is a manageable task if a regional center plans its marketing and promotional strategy, including its use of immigration lawyers and third parties, in advance with the assistance of its securities advisors who will know the particular facts and circumstances of the proposed offering. When it comes to ensuring compliance with an exemption from registration under securities laws, a sound strategy and thorough documentation of activities by the regional center will produce a win-win situation for the regional center and its EB-5 investors, as well as for its third-party agents.

ANTI-MONEY LAUNDERING AND OFAC SANCTIONS CONCERNS FOR IMMIGRATION PRACTITIONERS ASSISTING FOREIGN INVESTORS

by Edward J. Krauland and Jack Hayes[*]

DEVELOPMENT OF LAWS COMBATING CRIMINAL FINANCING REGIMES AND MONEY LAUNDERING

The United States has gradually increased the scope and complexity of its laws designed to combat criminal financing, money laundering, and, more recently, terrorist and weapons of mass destruction proliferation support. Congress first addressed criminal financing through its anti–money laundering laws. The first such law required only modest bank reporting.[1] The alarming growth of drug cartels in the 1980s led Congress to act more directly and impose criminal and civil penalties on persons engaging in money laundering transactions.[2]

The drug trafficking epidemic drew international concern and increased efforts to control money laundering. The United Nations held the 1987 International Conference on Drug Abuse and Illicit Traffic and then issued the 1988 U.N. Convention Against Illicit Traffic in Narcotic Drugs and Psychotropic Substances.[3]

Soon afterward, international organizations were formed to combat money laundering and to urge national governments to take coordinated or consistent legal and policy steps to detect, deter, and prosecute money laundering activity, including activity that was cross-border. Such an organization that is significant and active is the Financial Action Task Force (FATF). The United States is among 33 member countries in the FATF, which promulgates "soft law" intended to stem the flow of illicit money.[4] In 1990, the FATF issued its initial "Forty Recommendations." Endorsed by more than 130 countries, the Forty Recommendations generally set the agenda and standards for international anti–money laundering measures.[5]

Global concerns in the 1990s led to further regulation combating terrorist financing. Both Congress and the President authorized the Office of Foreign Assets Control (OFAC)[6] to seize money connected with such financing and to punish related financial transactions.[7] Congress and the President later expanded the use of OFAC regulations to control drug–, terrorist–, and weapons proliferation-related money and transactions.[8]

After the terrorist attacks of September 11, 2001, the global community renewed its efforts to detect and combat the use of laundered money for terrorist activities. Congress passed the Uniting and Strengthening America by Providing Appropriate Tools Required to Intercept and Obstruct Terrorism (USA

---

[*] **Edward Krauland** is a partner in the Washington office of Steptoe & Johnson LLP. Mr. Krauland provides immigration and visa services for corporate and individual clients. He has handled nearly all aspects and types of U.S. business visas, labor certifications, and immigrant/citizenship petitions. He has successfully pursued reconsiderations and appeals of controversial visa applications, and regularly counsels corporate clients on visa strategies and procedures that affect transboundary investments and staffing decisions, usually involving senior managers or executive personnel. Prior to joining the firm, Mr. Krauland served with the Nuclear Regulatory Commission in the area of nuclear export transactions.

[*] **Jack Hayes** is an associate in the Washington office of Steptoe & Johnson LLP. Mr. Hayes has provided economic sanctions and anti-money laundering compliance advice to clients engaged in various industries and business activities, including those related to U.S. immigration.

[1] *See* Bank Secrecy Act of 1970, Pub. L. No. 91-508, 84 Stat. 1116 (1970).

[2] *See* Money Laundering Control Act of 1986, Pub. L. No. 99-570, 100 Stat. 3207 (1986).

[3] *See* United Nations Convention Against Illicit Traffic in Narcotic Drugs and Psychotropic Substances, U.N. Doc. E/Conf.82/16 (1989), *reprinted in* 28 I.L.M. 493.

[4] *See* FATF Mandate (2004), *available at* www.fatf-gafi.org/dataoecd/46/33/35065565.pdf.

[5] *See* Review of the FATF Forty Recommendations Consultation Paper, FATF (May 30, 2002).

[6] The Office of Foreign Assets Control (OFAC) is an agency of the U.S. Department of the Treasury that enforces U.S. economic and trade sanctions. *See* OFAC homepage at www.treas.gov/offices/enforcement/ofac/.

[7] *See* Antiterrorism and Effective Death Penalty Act (AEDPA), Pub. L. No. 104-132, 110 Stat. 1232 (1996); Exec. Order No. 12947, 60 Fed. Reg. 5079 (Jan. 25, 1995).

[8] *See* Foreign Narcotics Kingpin Designation Act (Kingpin Act), Pub. L. No. 106-120, 113 Stat. 160 (1999); Exec. Order No. 12978, 60 Fed. Reg. 54579 (Oct. 24, 1995).

PATRIOT) Act of 2001, expanding government powers to fight terrorist-related activities.[9] Further, the President authorized OFAC to pursue a new class of global terrorists[10] and weapons of mass destruction proliferators and their supporters.[11] Finally, the President has authorized targeted economic sanctions against certain countries and their governments, as well as current or former officials and other politically exposed persons (PEPs). These are persons, entities, or groups who are or have been acting contrary to the foreign policy and regional security interests of the United States.

Additionally, a European Union (EU) Directive created gatekeeping roles for legal professionals across Europe.[12] These roles require lawyers to monitor and report their clients' suspected money laundering or illicit activities. The FATF amended its Forty Recommendations to reflect similar attorney "gatekeeper" requirements that should be adopted by all member countries, including the United States.[13]

In 2008, the FATF promulgated risk-based guidance for lawyers to provide them with assistance in conducting appropriate client due diligence in accordance with the ethical duty of client confidentiality.[14] The American Bar Association's (ABA) House of Delegates also passed Resolution 300 to support the legal profession conducting risk-based client due diligence in a manner consistent with FATF's guidelines and that does not conflict with the attorney-client relationship and ethical requirements imposed by state authorities on lawyers.[15]

In today's regulatory environment, lawyers dealing with the movement of money and people in the United States face significant potential liability. Law enforcement authorities closely monitor immigration and financial flows from abroad. Accordingly, lawyers who represent foreign nationals making investments in the United States, including immigration practitioners, must exercise great care to understand the source of financing for transactions, to know who their clients are, the nature of the money being invested, and to comply with U.S. laws and regulations as outlined generally below.[16]

DEALING WITH STOLEN MONEY: 18 USC §§1956–57

Generally

U.S. anti–money laundering laws extend potential criminal and civil liability to lawyers that knowingly conduct activities involving illicit money.[17] Sections 1956 and 1957 of the U.S. Code, Title 18 set out the offenses constituting "money laundering" under U.S. law.

Lawyers have been convicted for their involvement with money laundering, either for themselves or on behalf of clients. For example, in August 2009 an immigration attorney, Kenneth L. Rothey, 70, pleaded guilty and was sentenced to 14 months imprisonment for conspiracy to engage in visa fraud, encouraging Chinese aliens to unlawfully enter the United States, and money laundering.[18]

Elements

Section 1956

Subsection (a)(1) extends liability for transactions using illicit money (Transaction Provision). Liability extends to any person: (1) who knows a financial transaction involves the proceeds of some form of felony; (2) where the funds involved in the

---

[9] See Uniting and Strengthening America by Providing Appropriate Tools Required to Intercept and Obstruct Terrorism Act of 2001, Pub. L. No. 107-56, 115 Stat.; USA PATRIOT Improvement and Reauthorization Act of 2005, Pub. L. No. 109-107; 120 Stat. 195.

[10] See Exec. Order No. 13224, 66 Fed. Reg. 49079 (Sept. 25, 2001).

[11] See Exec. Order No. 13382, 70 Fed. Reg. 38567 (July 1, 2005).

[12] See Council Directive 2001/97/EC, 2001 O.J. (L 344) 76.

[13] See The Forty Recommendations, Recommendations 4-25, FATF (2003).

[14] See Risk-Based Approach (RBA) Guidance for Legal Professionals (2008), available at www.fatf-gafi.org/dataoecd/5/58/41584211.pdf.

[15] See American Bar Association (ABA) Section of Real Property, Trust, and Estate Law, Report to the House of Delegates: Task Force On Gatekeeper Regulation and The Profession, available at www.abanet.org/leadership/2008/annual/recommendations/ThreeHundred.doc.

[16] This article is not legal advice, and does not cover the extensive detail, complexity, and breadth of U.S. anti–money laundering and anti-terrorism laws and regulations. Specific legal advice should be obtained for any transaction or situation, based on the specific facts and a detailed legal assessment.

[17] See, e.g., United States v. Tarkoff, 242 F.3d 991, 995 (11th Cir. 2001) (upholding defendant attorney's money laundering conviction).

[18] Plea Agreement as to Kenneth L. Rothey, Criminal No. H-05-113, Case No. 4:05-cr-001113, Docket No. 230 (S.D. Tex. Aug. 18, 2009).

financial transaction in fact were the proceeds of a Specified Unlawful Activity; and (3) conducts or attempts to conduct the transaction with one of the following elements of scienter:

- intent to promote a "Specified Unlawful Activity," 18 USC §1956(a)(1)(A)(i);
- intent to evade specified Internal Revenue Code sections, 18 USC §§1956(a)(1)(A)(i);
- knowledge of a design to conceal some information about the funds or property involved, 18 USC §1956(a)(1)(B)(i); or
- knowledge of a design to avoid a transaction reporting requirement, 18 USC §1956(a)(1)(B)(ii).

Subsection (a)(2) creates liability for illicit transportation of money (Transportation Provision). Liability extends where a person: (1) transports or attempts to transport across U.S. borders; (2) monetary instruments or funds; and (3) with one of the following elements of scienter:

- intent to promote the carrying on of a Specified Unlawful Activity, 18 USC §1956(a)(2)(A); or
- knowledge that the instrument or fund represents the proceeds of some unlawful activity and knowledge that the transportation is designed in whole or in part to:
  - conceal the characteristics of the proceeds of Specified Unlawful Activity, 18 USC §1956 (a)(2)(B)(i); or
  - to avoid a federal or state currency transaction reporting requirement, 18 USC §1956(a)(2) (B)(ii).

Finally, subsection (a)(3) creates liability for intentional acts done in the context of police stings (Sting Provision). Liability extends where a person: (1) conducts or attempts to conduct a financial transaction involving property which is; (2) represented by a federal law enforcement officer as: (a) the proceeds of Specified Unlawful Activity; or (b) property used to conduct or facilitate specified unlawful activity; and (3) acts with the intent to

- promote Specified Unlawful Activity, 18 USC §1956(a)(3)(B)(A);
- conceal the characteristics of the proceeds of Specified Unlawful Activity, 18 USC §1956 (a)(3)(C); or
- avoid a state or federal transaction reporting requirement, 18 USC §1956(a)(3)(B).

Section 1957

Section 1957 extends liability to: (1) any person engaging in a monetary transaction in the United States or for a U.S. person[19] engaging in any monetary transaction anywhere; (2) knowing the money involved is criminally derived; and (3) where the money is actually property derived from a Specified Unlawful Activity and valued in excess of $10,000.[20]

Culpable Acts

Liability under §§1956 and 1957 requires defendants to either perform a transaction or to transport money. The §1956 Transaction and Sting provisions require a financial transaction, which includes a purchase, sale, loan, pledge, gift, transfer, delivery, or other disposition executed through: (1) the movement of funds; (2) the use of a monetary instrument; (3) title transfer; or (4) the use of a financial institution.[21]

Section 1957 applies more narrowly to monetary transactions involving more than $10,000, which include only standard banking transactions through or to a financial institution: deposit, withdrawal, transfer, or exchange of funds or monetary instruments.[22] Because almost all transactions by established companies and individual investors from abroad involve payments to or from bank accounts, most business or investment transactions encountered by U.S. immigration practitioners representing foreign investors are covered under these provisions.

Finally, transportation required by the §1956 Transportation provision includes virtually any movement of money, including wire transfers.[23]

In *Cuellar*, the Supreme Court directly addressed the transportation element of §1956, holding that the government need not prove the defendant attempted to make illegal funds appear legitimate, but that it must prove that the defendant did more than merely

---

[19] 18 USC §3077 defines "United States person" to include "a corporation organized under the laws of the United States . . . and a foreign subsidiary of such corporation." Section 1957 of Title 18 specifically incorporates the definition of "United States person" set forth at 18 USC § 3077.

[20] *See* 18 USC §1957(a). *See also United States v. Caruso*, 948 F. Supp. 382, 390 (D.N.J. 1996) (listing elements for §1957 offenses).

[21] *See* 18 USC §1956(c)(4).

[22] *See* 18 USC §1957(d)(1).

[23] *See United States v. Piervinzanzi*, 23 F.3d 670, 678 (2d Cir. 1994).

hide the funds during transport.[24] To sustain a conviction, the government must prove that a defendant knew that a purpose of the transportation was to conceal or disguise the "nature, the location, the source, the ownership, or the control" of funds.

Again, the breadth of these U.S. laws is vast, and prosecutors are aggressively utilizing these provisions to prosecute individuals involved in money laundering activities. These provisions also provide for the seizure and forfeiture of the assets involved in money laundering offenses, which is another attractive feature for prosecutors and law enforcement agents to investigate and charge money laundering offenses, even though severe forfeiture penalties may be more difficult to sustain under *Bajakajian*.[25] With the increasing focus on money laundering in support of narcotics trafficking, other cross-border criminal conduct, and terrorist activity, including a focus on relatively small dollar transactions, attorneys representing or assisting in foreign investor immigrant/nonimmigrant visa matters need to be mindful of suspicious activities and take appropriate steps to avoid legal risks (as discussed below).

Scienter Elements

Knowledge

Liability under the §1956 Transaction and Transportation Provisions and §1957 require knowledge that proceeds stem from illicit funds. Courts may apply a conscious avoidance or willful blindness standard to the knowledge elements under §§1956 and 1957.[26] Many Circuits have allowed the use of sufficient circumstantial evidence to prove the required knowledge.[27]

Under §1956(c)(1), a person must have knowledge that the property involved in a financial transaction represents the proceeds of "some form of unlawful activity," defined to mean felonious conduct.[28] The person need not know the specific criminal activity from which the proceeds are derived. Courts have rejected assertions that the defendant must know that criminal conduct constituted a felony rather than a misdemeanor.[29]

Section 1957(a) requires that the offender "knowingly engages or attempts to engage in a monetary transaction in criminally derived property." The defendant must know that the proceeds originated from some criminal conduct but not necessarily the specific criminal activity involved. This knowledge can be satisfied without the defendant having designed the transaction.[30]

Intent to Promote a Specified Unlawful Activity

All three §1956 provisions extend liability for intent to promote a Specified Unlawful Activity. Such intent has been demonstrated where defendants associated themselves with a specified criminal venture for the purpose of its advancement.[31] Intent to promote, therefore, is stricter than the threshold knowledge element, which requires only that the defendant knew that the money was derived from some criminal activity. Liability under this intent element does not require traditional money laundering activities. Rather, defendants need only intend to promote a Specified Unlawful Activity (discussed below).

Intent to Engage in Conduct that Would Evade Specified Internal Revenue Code Sections

The §1956 Transaction Provision extends liability to defendants who intend to engage in acts that would evade tax laws, or otherwise defraud or mis-

---

[24] *See Cuellar v. United States*, 128 S. Ct. 1994, 2002–06 (2008) (defendant did not violate the statute when he merely hid of $81,000 in a trunk of a car during transportation, even with substantial efforts at concealment).

[25] *United States v. Bajakajian*, 118 S. Ct. 2028 (1998) (abrogating a $357,144 forfeiture judgment as a violation of the Eighth Amendment).

[26] *See United States v. Bornfield*, 145 F.3d 1123, 1123–32 (10th Cir. 1998) (affirming money laundering conviction where evidence showed that defendant accountant "conspicuously avoided actual knowledge" of illegal source of funds).

[27] *United States v. Hall*, 434 F.3d 42, 50 (1st Cir. 2006) (proof may be based on circumstantial evidence); *see also United States v. Pizano*, 421 F.3d 707, 723 (8th Cir. 2005); *United States v. Henry*, 325 F.3d 93, 104 (2d Cir. 2003); *United States v. Prince*, 214 F.3d 740, 760 (6th Cir. 2000).

[28] Section 1956(c)(1) defines "some form of unlawful activity" to mean felonious conduct.

[29] *See United States v. Hill*, 167 F.3d 1055, 1066 (6th Cir. 1999) (prosecution need not prove defendant knew precise nature (felony or misdemeanor) of the unlawful activity).

[30] *See United States v. Hemmingson*, 157 F.3d 347, 355 (5th Cir. 1998) (defendant need not design money laundering scheme but must know transaction was conducted to conceal illegal funds)

[31] *See United States v. Gibson Specialty Co.*, 507 F.2d 446, 449 (9th Cir. 1974) (interpreting the Travel Act, which imposes a similar scienter element).

lead the Internal Revenue Service (IRS).[32] The language "intent to engage" suggests that defendants are culpable even where they do not know that their actions violated the tax laws.[33]

Intent, or Knowledge of a Design, to Conceal Some Information About the Funds or Property Involved

Liability extends under the §1956 Transaction and Transportation Provisions where a defendant knew of another transactor's design "to conceal" information.[34] Liability extends under the §1956 Sting Provision where a defendant intends "to conceal" information him- or herself.[35]

Courts have split on whether intent or knowledge of a scheme to conceal must include intent or knowledge of a scheme to create the appearance of legitimate wealth. For example, the Tenth Circuit acquitted a defendant of money laundering charges because his use of illicit funds to pay a mortgage and buy a horse was for personal use, and was not to create the appearance of legitimate wealth.[36] The court explained that money laundering was a crime of concealment, not a crime of spending money.[37]

Conversely, the Eleventh Circuit has held that §1956 punished all attempts to conceal money, not just those that create the appearance of legitimate wealth.[38] The court explained that the text of §1956 requires only that defendants conceal the source of the proceeds of "Specified Unlawful Activity" and says nothing regarding the appearance of legitimate wealth.[39] Accordingly, *Abbel* upheld the conviction of two attorneys who made transactions on behalf of their client who himself was involved in criminal activity.[40] The court explained that because the payments were not in the client's name, the transaction effectively concealed the source of the funding for the transaction.[41]

Intent, or Knowledge of a Design, to Avoid a Transaction Reporting Requirement

Liability extends under the §1956 Sting provision where defendants intend to avoid transactions themselves, 18 USC §1956(a)(3)(C), and under the Transaction and Transportation provisions where they knew of the intent of other parties to the transactions to conceal information, 18 USC §§1956(a)(1)(B)(ii), (a)(2)(B)(ii).

Specified Unlawful Activity

Specified Unlawful Activities (SUA) include a very broad list of foreign and domestic crimes that occur in whole or part in the United States.[42] The U.S. offenses listed as SUAs include racketeering offenses, violent crimes, terrorism, Foreign Corrupt Practices Act offenses (*e.g.*, bribery), embezzlement, bank fraud, narcotics trafficking, foreign tax offenses, and export control or economic sanctions violations.[43] SUAs also include foreign crimes involving controlled substances, certain violent crimes, any form of fraud against a foreign bank, bribery of a public official, certain smuggling or export control violations, and any other offenses with respect to which the United States would be required by treaty to extradite the alleged offender or submit the case for prosecution.[44] In sum, it is safe to assume that almost any illegal or felonious activity may be covered by the definition of SUA.

Even unlisted crimes may form the predicate for SUAs.[45] In *Pasquantino*, the Court held that a scheme to defraud the Canadian government of tax revenue could form the basis of liability of the federal wire fraud statute.[46] In turn, participation in wire fraud can form the basis of liability under the money laundering statutes.[47]

---

[32] *See* 18 USC §1956(a)(1)(A)(ii); 26 USC §§7201, 7206.

[33] The statute does not prohibit tax evasion itself, but rather financial transactions conducted in the course of committing criminal tax evasion. *See, e.g., United States v. Zanghi*, 189 F.3d 71, 81 (1st Cir. 1999) (defendant violated statute by withdrawing company funds as "loan repayment" to avoid taxation).

[34] *See* 18 USC §1956(a)(2)(B)(i).

[35] *See* 18 USC §§1956(a)(2)(B)(i), (a)(3)(B).

[36] *See United States v. Garcia-Emanuel*, 14 F.3d 1469, 1477 (10th Cir. 1994).

[37] *See id.* at 1475.

[38] *See United States v. Abbel*, 271 F.3d 1286, 1298 (11th Cir. 2001), *questioned on other grounds by Cuellar*, 128 S. Ct. at 2002–06 (2008).

[39] *See id.*

[40] *See id.* at 1304.

[41] *See id.* at 1298.

[42] *See* 18 USC §1956(c)(7).

[43] *See id.*

[44] *See* 18 USC §1956(c)(7)(B).

[45] *See Pasquantino v. United States*, 125 S. Ct. 1766, 1771 (2005).

[46] *See id.*

[47] *See id.* at 1787 (Ginsburg., J. dissenting on other grounds).

Proceeds of a Crime and Criminally Derived Property

The anti-money laundering statute targets "proceeds of a crime" under §1956 and "criminally derived property" under §1957. Proceeds include valuables beyond money.[48]

In *Santos*, a divided Supreme Court considered whether the term "proceeds" under §1956(a)(1) means "receipts" or "profits."[49] A plurality of four Justices held both terms were equally plausible in light of the legislative history. Therefore, based on the rule of lenity as a canon of statutory construction, the plurality required that "proceeds" be construed as "profits" of the criminal activity.[50] Justice Stevens concurred in the judgment, including relying on the rule of lenity, but his opinion did permit proceeds to mean receipts when the legislative history reflected a congressional intent to do so, such as for the sale of contraband and operations of organized crime groups.[51] The other four Justices dissented on the basis that the "primary definition" of proceeds is "the total amount brought in," customarily construed as receipts.[52]

Penalties

Section 1956 imposes both criminal and civil penalties. Section 1956 extends criminal fines up to $500,000 or twice the value of the property involved in the transaction, whichever is greater, or imprisonment up to 20 years, or both.[53] Violators of §1956 are also liable for civil penalties up to twice the value of the property involved in the transaction or $10,000, whichever is greater.[54]

A violator of §1957 can be criminally punished by fine or imprisonment for not more than 10 years, or both. Courts may impose fines up to twice the amount of the criminally derived property involved in the transaction, or $250,000.[55]

Also, courts apply criminal and civil forfeiture statutes to property involved in a transaction that violates §§1956–57.[56]

RESTRICTED TRANSACTIONS

Generally

The Office of Foreign Assets Control (OFAC) of the U.S. Department of the Treasury implements economic restrictions directed at ending financial support and business activities for (1) certain countries and (2) specified individuals and entities engaged in certain activities or acting as agents of restricted countries. In addition, certain OFAC economic restrictions apply to entities where there is a significant ownership interest by governments identified under (1), and individuals and entities identified under (2).

OFAC imposes comprehensive economic sanctions on the countries and governments of Cuba, Iran, and Sudan. These sanctions prohibit the furnishing of services to Cuban nationals,[57] wherever located in the world, or to persons in Iran.[58] Services are also prohibited to persons in Sudan, except most transactions are permitted with respect to persons located in certain "Specified Areas" of Sudan.[59]

OFAC restricts transactions and services benefiting designated entities, groups, and individuals, including those that are involved in terrorism, narcotics trafficking, and proliferation of nuclear, chemical, and biological weapons. Such persons and entities are known as Specially Designated Nationals (SDNs). OFAC also prohibits transactions with and blocks the property of SDNs (including current or former government officials) in or affiliated with certain countries acting contrary to U.S. foreign policy objectives, such as by threatening regional stability, undermining democratic institutions, or contributing to humanitarian suffering, violence, and civil unrest. These targeted sanctions cover SDNs related

---

[48] *See, e.g., United States v. Estacio,* 64 F.3d 477, 481 (9th Cir. 1995) ("proceeds" include fraudulently obtained lines of credit).

[49] *United States v. Santos,* 128 S. Ct. 2020 (2008).

[50] *See id.* at 2022, 2025.

[51] *See id.* at 2030.

[52] *See id.* at 2035–37; *see also* J. Gurulé, "Does "Proceeds Really Mean "Net Profits"? The Supreme Court's Efforts to Diminish the Utility of the Federal Money Laundering Statute," 7 Ave Maria L. Rev. 339 (Spring 2009).

[53] *See* 18 USC §§1956(a)(1), (2), and (3).

[54] *See* 18 USC §1956(b)(1).

[55] *See* 18 USC §1957(b).

[56] *See* 18 USC §§981–82.

[57] *See* 31 CFR §515.302.

[58] *See* 31 CFR §560.204.

[59] *See* 31 CFR §§538.205, 538.320 (including Southern Sudan, Southern Kordofan/Nuba Mountains State, Blue Nile State, Abyei, Darfur, and "marginalized areas" in and around Khartoum).

to the Balkans, Belarus, Burma (Myanmar), Ivory Coast, Democratic Republic of the Congo, Iraq, Liberia, Lebanon, North Korea, Syria, and Zimbabwe.[60]

Finally, under several economic sanctions programs, OFAC also restricts U.S. persons from having any business dealings or providing services with entities in which specified SDNs have an ownership interest of 50 percent or more. Such entities are themselves deemed to be "blocked property", thereby triggering the restriction on U.S. persons having any dealing with such "property". For example, if an individual identified as a terrorist SDN were to own 60 percent of a company in the United Kingdom, a U.S. person (including an attorney) could have no dealings with the UK company absent a specific authorization from OFAC.

As OFAC generally defines transactions or services to include legal services, these regulations directly affect attorneys practicing in any area within the United States, or U.S. persons who are attorneys practicing abroad. Generally speaking, the OFAC regulations apply to any person inside the United States, any company incorporated within the United States (and its foreign-located branch offices), and any U.S. citizen or lawful permanent resident, wherever located in the world.

The restrictions on providing services to, and on engaging in transactions involving the property or interests in property of, restricted governments, entities, or persons, are very broad. Unless a general authorization or license exemption applies, U.S. persons must obtain a license from OFAC prior to providing such services or dealing in property of these restricted countries, governments, persons, or SDNs. Services can include almost any type of activity that confers a benefit. Property is broadly deferred to include any type of tangible or intangible real, personal, contractual, or financial asset. Interest is defined to mean any interest (not necessarily a legal interest), whether past, present, future, or contingent.

OFAC publishes a list, which it updates regularly via its website and *Federal Register* notices, identifying SDNs.[61] The SDN List contains thousands of individuals, entities, business, and organizations in or affiliated with the countries or activities noted above. However, many SDNs are not located or resident in these countries. Some SDNs may be resident in or nationals of countries having extensive and friendly commercial ties with the United States. (Indeed, OFAC has begun to list individuals and entities located inside the United States.)

As discussed below, an important compliance step for lawyers and other U.S. persons is to verify the identity of their clients or persons with whom they are dealing and to check their names against the SDN List before entering into any engagement, rendering any services, or accepting any money or other asset or property. The SDN List can be accessed at the OFAC website.[62]

Elements

Under the International Emergency Economic Powers Act (IEEPA)

IEEPA authorizes OFAC to regulate transactions that the President deems an extraordinary threat and subject of national emergency.[63] The President has designated the following as special national security threats:

- Specially Designated Narcotics Traffickers (SDNT);[64]
- Specially Designated Terrorists (SDT);[65]

---

[60] *See* Exec. Order No. 13219, 66 Fed. Reg. PAGE (June 29, 2001) and 31 CFR §588 (BALKANS); Exec. Order No. 13405, 71 Fed. Reg. 35485 (June 20, 2006) and 31 CFR §548 (BELARUS); Exec. Order No. 13448, 72 Fed. Reg. 60223 (Oct. 23, 2007) and 31 CRR §537 (BURMA); Exec. Order No. 13413 (Oct. 27, 2006) (CONGO); Exec. Order No. 13396 (Feb. 7, 2006) (IVORY COAST); Exec. Order No. 13441, 72 Fed. Reg. 43499 (Aug. 3, 2007) (LEBANON); Exec. Order No.13348, 69 Fed. Reg. 44885 (July 27, 2004) and 31 CFR §593 (LIBERIA); Exec. Order No. 13438, 72 Fed. Reg. 39719 (Jul. 19, 2007) and 31 CFR §575 (IRAQ); Exec. Order No. 13460, 73 Fed. Reg. 8991 (Feb. 15, 2008) and 31 CFR §542 (SYRIA); Exec. Order No. 13469, 73 Fed. Reg. 43841 (Jul. 29, 2008) and 31 CFR §541 (ZIMBABWE).

[61] *See* Specially Designated Nationals and Blocked Persons List, *available at www.ustreas.gov/offices/enforcement/ofac/sdn/index.shtml*.

[62] *See* discussion *infra*, "OFAC Licenses Limited Legal Services to Designated Entities."

[63] *See* 50 USC §1701(a).

[64] For a list of Specially Designated Narcotics Traffickers (SDNTs), see Exec. Order No. 12978, 60 Fed. Reg. 54579 (Oct. 21, 1995) and 31 CFR §36.312.

[65] For a list of Specially Designated Terrorists (SDTs), see Exec. Order No. 12947, 60 Fed. Reg. 5079 (Jan. 25, 1995) and 31 CFR §595.311; Exec. Order No. 13099, 63 Fed Reg. 45167 (Aug. 25, 1998).

- Specially Designated Global Terrorists (SDGT);[66] and
- Proliferation of Weapons of Mass Destruction (NPWMD).[67]

IEEPA typically extends liability to any U.S. person engaging in transactions or otherwise dealing in property or interests in property of these SDNs. IEEPA also generally prohibits any person from dealing with "property subject to U.S. jurisdiction" in which there is an "interest" by these SDNs.

OFAC has broad discretion in interpreting and applying these laws and regulations. It is at its core an enforcement agency of the U.S. Department of the Treasury, and with the significant focus on combating money laundering in connection with cross-border criminal activities, OFAC has increased its investigators and civil enforcement activities. Penalty actions and settlements are posted to its website, and in a few instances, OFAC has imposed penalties on law firms for violating U.S. economic sanctions directed at specific countries.

Under the Antiterrorism and Effective Death Penalty Act (AEDPA)

AEDPA[68] regulates transactions with Foreign Terrorist Organizations (FTO), as designated by the U.S. Department of State. Liability extends to any person who knowingly provides material support to an FTO, with knowledge of either the organization's designation as a FTO or the FTO's unlawful activities that caused its designation.[69]

Also, AEDPA regulates transactions with terrorism list governments. Liability extends to any U.S. person who knowing—or having reasonable cause to know—that a country is designated under §6(j)(3) of the Export Administration Act of 1979,[70] engages in a financial transaction with the government of that country. The current countries that are on the terrorism list are Cuba, Iran, North Korea, Sudan, and Syria. The current OFAC regulations do *not* restrict normal financial transactions with the governments of North Korea and Syria. However, U.S. persons cannot engage in any financial transactions with any of these governments that the U.S. person knows or has reasonable cause to believe poses a risk of furthering terrorist acts in the United States.[71]

Under the Foreign Narcotics Kingpin Designation Act (Kingpin Act)

The Kingpin Act extends liability for transactions with a Significant Foreign Narcotics Trafficker (SFNT). Liability extends for any transaction or dealing by a U.S. person, or within the United States, that involves in property or interests in property of any SFNT.[72]

Under the False Statement Statute

Criminal liability extends to any person who: (1) knowingly and willfully falsifies, conceals, covers up, or makes false statements; or (2) conceals materials facts, when dealing with OFAC in connection with matters under it jurisdiction.[73]

Culpable Acts

Liability under the OFAC regulations requires U.S. persons to engage in transactions, dealings, or material assistance with restricted countries, governments, FTOs, or SDNs, including but not limited to SDNTs, SDTs, SDGTs, NPWMDs, and their supporters. Regardless of the terminology, these regulations cover legal services so as to impose a risk of liability on lawyers who render commercial or immigration services to such restricted countries, persons, or entities.[74]

OFAC also defines transactions and material support to include actions or conspiracies for the purpose, effect, or intent of evading or avoiding restrictions placed on services for such restricted countries, persons, or entities.[75] In *Holder v. Humanitarian Law Project*, the Supreme Court held that 18 USC §2339B, which makes if a federal crime

---

[66] For a list of Specially Designated Global Terrorists (SDGTs), see Exec. Order No. 13224 (Sept. 25, 2001) and 31 CFR §594.310.

[67] For a list of Proliferation of Weapons of Mass Destruction (NPWMDs), *see* Exec. Order No. Order No. 13382, 70 Fed. Reg. 38567 (July 1, 2005) and 31 CFR §544.

[68] Antiterrorism and Effective Death Penalty Act of 1996, Pub. L. No. 104-132, 110 Stat. 1214 (AEDPA).

[69] *See* 18 USC §2339B(a)(1).

[70] 50 USC App. 2405.

[71] *See* 18 USC §2332d(a); 31 CFR §596.504.

[72] *See* 21 USC §1904.

[73] *See* 18 USC §1001.

[74] *See* 31 CFR §§595.406(b) (application to SDT), 598.406 (application to SFNT); 18 USC §§2339A(b), 2239B(g)(4) (material support to Foreign Terrorist Organizations (FTOs) includes "expert advice").

[75] *See* 31 CFR §§536.204 (application to SDNT), 594.205 (SDGT), 595.205 (SDT), 596.201 (countries), 597.204 (FTO), 598.204 (SFNT).

to "knowingly provid[e] material support or resources to a foreign terrorist organization" is not unconstitutionally vague.[76] Interpreting the definition of material support, which includes "training," "expert advice or assistance," "service," and "personnel" further defined by 18 USC §2339A, the Court found that Congress enacted limiting definitions in the statute for these terms that "provide[s] a person of ordinary intelligence fair notice of what is prohibited" (as well as knowledge requirements discussed below) and therefore sufficiently addressed vagueness concerns.

Scienter

Civil Liability

Most of the prohibitions on dealing with restricted countries, persons, or entities are subject to both civil and criminal enforcement. OFAC has typically taken a strict liability approach to civil enforcement actions. Therefore, even unwitting, unknowing, or negligent involvement with restricted countries, persons, or entities can create civil liability for U.S. persons, including attorneys. If OFAC believes that a violation has occurred, it is typical that some type of civil financial penalty is imposed, regardless of whether one had any knowledge or reason to know of the restricted activity.

Knowledge Under AEDPA for Criminal Liability

The knowledge element of AEDPA regulations requires defendants to know that they are transacting with or providing material support or resources to a terror-related entity designated by the U.S. Government or to know of the entity's unlawful activities that would lead to designation as a terror-related entity.[77]

The courts had previously split on whether AEDPA requires a defendant to know only that he or she was providing support, or whether AEDPA requires a defendant to have specific intent to support further illegal activity.

A federal district court in Florida adopted the latter reading and required specific intent to further future unlawful activity.[78] The court explained that AEDPA's broad reach implicated a wide host of innocent activities and potentially violated the Fifth Amendment's requirement that a defendant have guilty knowledge.[79] To avoid this constitutional infirmity, the court narrowed AEDPA's reach through a specific intent requirement.[80]

Both the Fourth and Ninth Circuits have refused to read a specific intent requirement into AEDPA.[81] These courts considered and rejected First Amendment overbreadth and vagueness challenges to AEDPA. They did not consider the federal district court's personal guilt rationale.

In *Holder*, the Supreme Court held that criminal liability, as applied to speech, can arise for knowingly providing material support to an FTO, and in doing so, rejected an interpretation that would require proof that a defendant intended to further terrorist or criminal goals of the FTO.[82] In reviewing 18 USC §2339B, and comparing it to 18 USC §§2339A and 2339C, the Court ruled that Congress chose "knowledge" about an FTO's connection to terrorism, not specific intent to further its terrorist activities, as the mental state necessary for a violation. The Court noted that certain speech-related activities not related to terrorist or criminal activities, such as training FTOs to use international law to resolve disputes peacefully, teaching members of FTOs to petition the United Nations for relief, and engaging in political advocacy on behalf of displaced persons affiliated with FTOs, could be considered criminal activities as material support, provided that they were not undertaken independently, but performed in coordination with, or at the direction of, an FTO. The Court reasoned that Congress sought to cut off nearly all forms of material support to FTOs, even if benign. Since this was a pre-enforcement review of a criminal statute, however, the Court would not speculate as to whether engaging in the stated activities actually constituted criminal violations.

---

[76] *See Holder v. Humanitarian Law Project*, No. 08-1498, 561 U.S. __ (2010).

[77] *See Humanitarian Law Project v. DOJ*, 352 F.3d 382, 403 (9th Cir. 2003) (application under AEDPA), *vacated in part on other grounds at Humanitarian Law Project v. United States DOJ*, 393 F.3d 902, 903 (9th Cir. 2004) (*en banc*), *certiorari granted by Humanitarian Law Project v. Holder*, 130 S. Ct. 49 (2009); *United States v. Al-Arian*, 329 F. Supp. 2d 1294, 1340 (M.D. Fla. 2004) (application under IEEPA).

[78] *See Al-Arian*, 329 F. Supp. 2d at 1340.

[79] *Id.* at 1338–39.

[80] *Id.* at 1339.

[81] *See Humanitarian Law Project v. U.S. DOJ*, 393 F.3d 902, 903 (9th Cir. 2004) (*en banc*).

[82] *See supra*, note 76.

The Willful Standard Under IEEPA and the Kingpin Act

IEEPA and the Kingpin Act extend criminal penalties for willful violations.[83] Courts apply slightly different willful *mens rea* standards for IEEPA violations. Courts may consider a defendant's knowledge of unlawful conduct sufficient to satisfy the willful element, even absent a showing that the defendant knew of the specific legal restrictions.[84] However, in *Homa*, the Second Circuit found that previous OFAC warning letters to the defendant, and the defendant's use of code to hide his transactions, provided sufficient evidence to show that he knew he was violating IEEPA regulations.[85] In other words, the courts can allow a jury to consider circumstantial evidence to find a willful violation of a specific legal requirement or restriction.

Some courts have required that defendants have intent to further future unlawful activity, or to have a specific intent to violate a known legal regime or duty.[86] A Florida district court explained that by reading a specific intent element into "willful," the court avoided potential First and Fifth Amendment problems caused by the statute's broad reach.[87]

The Kingpin Act also extends criminal penalty for willful neglect.[88] No reported cases discuss this mens rea element for the Kingpin Act.

OFAC Licenses Limited Legal Services to Designated Entities

Licensed lawyers may provide specified but circumscribed legal services to SDNs described above.[89] However, in most instances, the types of legal services authorized by OFAC are limited to sanctions compliance advice and assistance with the OFAC regulations, litigation, or services considered to be *pro bono*. Commercial legal services or support for SDNs, such as receiving personal funds into escrow, helping with the visa processing paper work, and overseeing the foreign national's compliance with a visa program, are not authorized.

OFAC is unlikely to issue a specific authorization or license for SDN-related legal services that are not specifically identified in the regulations. Moreover, even if legal services may be authorized by the appropriate regulatory provision, OFAC typically requires the attorney to obtain a specific license (via an application to OFAC) in order to receive payment.

Absent a specific OFAC license, generally speaking any moneys, assets, or property received by an attorney from a restricted country, government, person, or SDN would be considered blocked property, which the attorney would need to place into a special blocked account. Upon receiving such property, the attorney would be obligated to file a report to OFAC within 10 days.[90] Failure to do so constitutes an independent violation of the OFAC regulations, where required.

OFAC Licenses for Immigrant Visas

Relevance to EB-5 Investor Immigrants

Anti-money laundering and OFAC sanctions compliance concerns are particularly relevant to lawyers engaged in processing the EB-5 category of visas. For the applicant to qualify for U.S. permanent residence status under EB-5, the foreign national generally must invest at least $500,000 into a new or existing business which benefits the U.S. economy and creates full-time employment for at least 10 U.S. workers.

USCIS Denial of EB-5 Applications for Iranians

Recently, U.S. Citizenship and Immigration Services (USCIS) has denied EB-5 visa petitions on behalf of Iranian citizens, citing OFAC regulations as the basis because: (1) the source of funds was of Iranian origin; (2) a U.S. person would be offering employment to an Iranian person, located in Iran, seeking to invest in the United States; and/or (3) the applicant's funds, in the normal course of being

---

[83] See 50 USC §1705(b) (IEEPA penalties); 21 USC §1906 (Kingpin Act penalties).

[84] See *United States v. Homa Int'l Trading Corp.*, 387 F.3d 144, 147 (2d Cir. 2004) (upholding IEEPA conviction where jury instruction appropriately described willful mens rea).

[85] *Id.*

[86] See *Al-Arian*, 329 F. Supp. 2d at 1341; see also *United States v. Soussi*, 316 F.3d 1095, 1103 (10th Cir. 2002) (upholding sufficiency of evidence in an IEEPA conviction where jury could conclude that the defendant acted with the purpose of avoiding the statutory requirements).

[87] See *Al-Arian*, 329 F. Supp. 2d at 1341.

[88] See 21 USC §1906.

[89] See 31 CFR §§536.506 (application to SDNTs), 594.506 (SDGTs), 595.506 (SDTs), 597.505 (FTOs), 598.506 (SFNTs).

[90] See 31 CFR §501.603.

transferred out of Iran and destined ultimately for the United States, may have involved Iranian banks listed as SDNs by OFAC.

No OFAC Approval Needed for Iranian EB-5 Applications?

In response to these denials, some advocates have argued to OFAC that the Iranian Transaction Regulations (ITR) should be read to provide the necessary authorization for U.S. persons to engage in EB-5-related activities without a specific license. Specifically, 31 CFR §560.505(c) provides a general authorization for the importation of Iranian-origin services and activities related to numerous visa categories.[91] Because Iranians can emigrate to the United States and engage in economic development activity as employees, owners, or partners of U.S. businesses under the general authorization of 31 CFR §560.505(a), such activity arguably should not constitute unlawful importation of or dealing in Iranian-origin services, and there should be no basis for claiming that visa-related activities by U.S. persons "facilitate" an unlawful activity by providing a prohibited service to Iran.[92]

Indeed, many visa petitions require: (1) U.S. person sponsorship, contracting, and involvement; (2) funds and personal information to be transferred into the United States; and (3) legal and other professionals (such as human resources professionals, or employment placement services) to support the visa petition. Since these activities are necessary and incidental to the process of obtaining a bona fide visa, whether entering the United States as lawful immigrants or nonimmigrants, it has been argued to OFAC that such services should be authorized so that U.S. lawyers may engage in these activities under the general authorization of 31 CFR §560.505.

Moreover, advocates have argued to OFAC that the limited involvement of certain Iranian banks in transferring assets or holding assets prior to transfer from Iran should not preclude the investment of funds into the United States under the EB-5 immigrant visa program. First, the fact that banks are located in Iran does not preclude the ability for funds from these banks to be invested into the United States or otherwise to be held by U.S. financial institutions or U.S. persons.[93] Second, should certain Iranian banks be designated as NPWMDs or SDGTs, and have indirect, limited, or fleeting involvement with the transfer of funds, this arguably does not mean that a private Iranian immigrant's funds are restricted from or blocked in the U.S. banking system because there would be no SDN bank "interest" in the funds.

Informal OFAC Position

We understand OFAC has determined that the general authorization of 31 CFR §560.505(c) does not cover legal services related to or asset transfers in connection with EB-5 petitions from Iranians. Rather, OFAC has implemented a specific licensing policy for Iranians who are resident in Iran and/or whose assets will originate from Iran in connection with EB-5 visa petitions. It appears that OFAC has taken a licensing interest in Iranian petitions given the amount of funds necessary to transfer for EB-5 qualification and a likely U.S. Government concern in verifying the identity and source of assets of the applicants.[94] At this time it is not clear whether OFAC has limited this policy only to Iranian EB-5 immigrants—theoretically it also could apply to Cuban nationals wherever located or certain persons in Sudan—or if it could also apply to all other immigrant visa petition categories for Iranian persons.

However, we also understand that OFAC has informally determined that if: (1) an Iranian national is ordinarily resident outside of Iran; *and* (2) the assets necessary to fund the EB-5 immigrant visa will not originate from Iran or are already in the United States, then a license may not be required.

Specific OFAC Licenses—EB-5 Visas for Iranians

To seek specific licenses for EB-5 visas, applicants have submitted to OFAC specific information about the intending investor to be considered for determining whether an approval should be granted. This information could include full name, place of birth, date of birth, Iranian national iden-

---

[91] "Persons otherwise qualified for a visa under categories E-2 (treaty investor) . . . and all immigrant visa categories are authorized to carry out in the United States those activities for which such a visa has been granted by the U.S. State Department...[.]"

[92] *See* 31 CFR §560.208.

[93] *See* 31 CFR §560.516 (authorizing U.S. depository institutions to receive and handle funds originating from Iran).

[94] *See, e.g.*, Guidance to Financial Institutions on the Increasing Money Laundering Threat Involving Illicit Iranian Activity, FIN-2007-A001 (Oct. 16, 2007), *available at www.fincen.gov/statutes_regs/guidance/pdf/guidance_fi_increasing_mlt_iranian.pdf*.

tification number, passport number, address, telephone number, information about the source of assets and how funds will be (or have been) transferred out of Iran to the United States, and/or prior petitions to USCIS or approval by USCIS of petitions (*i.e.*, I-526). Copies of identity cards, passports, and résumés also may be submitted.

We understand that OFAC has approved specific licenses for individual EB-5 applicants from Iran. These licenses typically stipulate quarterly reporting requirements to OFAC regarding the EB-5 immigration status of the Iranians.

However, OFAC has noted that the EB-5-related licenses do not cover assets received from or through blocked Iranian banks. In particular, licensees have been cautioned that U.S. persons are generally prohibited from engaging in transactions, directly or indirectly, with Iranian banks designated as NPWMDs, including but not limited to Bank Saderat, Bank Sepah, Bank Mellat, Bank Melli, Future Bank B.S.C., or the Export Development Bank of Iran, and that the licenses approved do not authorize funds transferred from or through these blocked banks, even if the transactions may be otherwise permitted under the ITR.[95] Consequently, lawyers should take these restrictions into account when considering how to structure monetary transfers for EB-5 applications—and potentially other visa category petitions—from Iran in connection with petitions to USCIS and applications to OFAC.

Record Keeping and Reporting

Any legal services provided pursuant to an OFAC authorization or license to a restricted country, person, or entity are subject to recordkeeping, and in some instances, reporting obligations. Generally speaking, lawyers (like any U.S. person) who engage in transactions that are authorized by OFAC must maintain records of the services provided, payments received, and transactions for a period of five years from the conclusion of the service.[96] In addition, for any services involving litigation, administrative proceedings, or dispute resolution, the attorney may be required to provide copies of pleadings or filings to OFAC. The relevant regulations should be consulted for any such requirements, depending on the nature of the filings, if any. Finally, OFAC can demand information or reports. Any such demand would present potential conflicts with the attorney-client privilege and/or ethical obligations to maintain client confidences, depending on the nature of the information requested.

Penalties

IEEPA

Criminal IEEPA violations carry fines up to $1,000,000, up to 20 years' imprisonment, or both.[97] Civil IEEPA violations carry fines of twice the value of the transaction, or up to $250,000, whichever is greater.[98]

AEDPA

Transactions with FTOs in violation of the AEDPA subject violators to fines, or up to 15 years' imprisonment, or both, and life imprisonment if the crime causes the death of any person.[99] Transaction with terrorism-list countries in violation of AEDPA subjects violators to fines, or up to 10 years' imprisonment, or both.[100]

Kingpin Act

The Kingpin Act provides fines, criminal penalties of up to 10 years' imprisonment, and civil penalties of up to $1 million.[101]

False Statements to OFAC

Providing false statements carries criminal penalties of up to five years' imprisonment, or, if the offense involves international or domestic terrorism, imprisonment up to 8 years, and up to a $10,000 fine, or both.[102]

Criminal Fines Generally

All felonies are subject to penalty under 18 USC §3571, which provides for fines in the greater of the amount of $250,000, or twice the pecuniary gain from the violation.

---

[95] Note that no Presidential blocking order applies to banks designated under OFAC's IRAN program and pursuant to the ITR.

[96] See 31 CFR §501.601.

[97] See 50 USC §1705(b).

[98] See id. at §1705(a).

[99] See 18 USC §2339B(a)(1).

[100] See 18 USC §2332d.

[101] See 21 USC §1906.

[102] See 18 USC §1001.

CURRENCY TRANSACTION REPORTING

Introduction

Under the Bank Secrecy Act and related U.S. anti-money laundering laws, various financial institutions, types of business (such as casinos), and even individuals or other types of businesses (including attorneys and law firms) may be required to file reports with the U.S. government relating to certain types of financial transactions in which they engage. Most pertinent to attorneys and law firms would be Report of Cash Payments over $10,000 Received in a Trade or Business, or IRS Form 8300, and the Financial Crimes Enforcement Network (FinCEN) at the U.S. Department of the Treasury. Form 8300 must be filed: (1) by any person engaged in a business or trade (which would include attorneys); (2) who in the course of conducting that business or trade (such as rendering legal services); and (3) receives more than $10,000 in cash in one transaction, or two or more related transactions within a 12-month period. Anyone engaged in such a cash transaction must complete and submit a Form 8300 to the IRS at the location identified in the instructions to Form 8300. Note that the reporting requirement applies to cash, defined to mean U.S. or foreign coin and currency. It does not cover payments by personal or corporate check.

Nor would Form 8300 cover a cashier's check, money order, traveler's check, or bank draft if such instruments are used to pay for legal services as to make an investment in the United States, unless one is aware that such a money instrument is being used in an attempt to avoid the reporting of a cash transaction.

Cash transactions of less than $10,000 are considered related and therefore must be considered together for purposes of the reporting requirement if: (1) the cash transactions occur within 24 hours of one another; or (2) if the recipient knows or has reason to know that each cash transaction is one in a series of connected transactions, regardless of the time period over which they occur.

Reports are to be filed within 15 calendar days of the date the cash was received. If more than one related transaction is involved, the report must be filed based on the date the $10,000 threshold is exceeded.

Failure to file a required report can result in civil penalties up to $25,000 or more, if the failure is the result of intentional disregard of the reporting requirement. Criminal penalties are also available, including imprisonment of up to five years, as well as fines up to $250,000 for individuals or $500,000 for businesses.

EVOLVING GATEKEEPING REGIMES

Generally

European and FATF Gatekeeper Initiatives impose reporting requirements for legal professionals who *suspect* their clients are involved in some type of illegal activity. These Gatekeeper requirements generally extend the type of *suspicious activity reporting* requirements—applicable to financial institutions for many years under anti-money laundering laws—to legal professionals. While there are some limits to the scope of the reporting obligations imposed on lawyers in the EU and elsewhere, including an exception for privileged communications, these reporting requirements pose significant challenges to lawyers to whom they apply. The ABA has adopted a resolution opposing mandatory reporting obligations for lawyers, and an ABA Task Force on Gatekeeper Regulation and the Profession has vigorously advocated to the U.S. government agencies and FATF against any reporting requirement that would jeopardize the attorney-client privilege, the ethical duties of confidentiality and loyalty, or otherwise compromise the attorney-client relationship.[103] Nonetheless, non-U.S. Gatekeeper laws may foreshadow increased regulations of lawyer activities in the United States.[104]

These developing international norms could fundamentally alter attorney-client relationships. Reporting requirements undermine the loyalty and confidentiality owed every client, potentially conflict with the attorney-client privilege, and increase the financial burdens and compliance procedures that typically accompany governmental regulation.[105] Thus far, the U.S. government has not adopted any type of Gatekeeper reporting requirement for lawyers. Various state bar rules do permit disclosure of confidential client information in specified circumstances, but none appear to require disclosure of client confidential information in circumstances that

---

[103] *See* various materials, position papers, and comments at *www.abanet.org/crimjust/taskforce*.

[104] *See* ABA Task Force on Gatekeeper Regulation and the Profession at *www.abanet.org/crimjust/taskforce/*.

[105] *See* R. Gregory, "The Lawyer's Role: Will Uncle Sam Want You In The Fight Against Money Laundering and Terrorism?" 72 *UMKC L. Rev.* 23, 24 (2003) (hereinafter Gregory).

raise *suspicions* of money laundering activity. To date, the principal regulatory initiative of the U.S. government has been an April 9, 2003, Advance Notice of Proposed Rulemaking, issued by the U.S. Department of the Treasury, FinCEN, seeking public comment on the possible application of certain anti–money laundering compliance requirements, pursuant to the USA PATRIOT Act, on persons involved in real estate settlements and closings. It is likely that any such rulemaking will include real estate lawyers; however, the proposed anti–money laundering compliance requirements would not include any mandatory reporting requirements. FinCEN has not, as of the date of this article, taken any further rulemaking activity. Even if the U.S. government does not adopt Gatekeeper international norms, however, these rules outside the United States may influence the level of care necessary under existing anti-money laundering U.S. laws.

This section below discusses the Gatekeeper initiative suggested by FATF.

Customer Identification

Gatekeeper Initiative regimes require attorneys to comply with customer due diligence (CDD) requirements whenever they engage in activities potentially and commonly involved with money laundering.[106]

Lawyers should verify the identity of the customer and beneficial owner before or during the course of establishing a business relationship or conducting transactions for occasional customers. CDD under the FATF Recommendations requires customer identification whenever legal professionals: (1) establish business relations; (2) carry out designated suspect transactions; (3) suspect customers are engaging in money laundering or terrorist financing; or (4) doubt the veracity or adequacy of previously obtained customer identification data.[107]

CDD forbids lawyers from creating anonymous accounts or accounts in obviously fictitious names. To eliminate client anonymity, CDD requires legal professionals to: (1) verify the customer's identity using reliable, independent source documents, data, or information; (2) take reasonable measures to verify the identity of the beneficial owners to the financial institution's satisfaction, including understanding the customer's ownership and control structure; (3) obtain information on the purpose of the business relationship; and (4) conduct ongoing CDD and scrutiny of transactions to ensure that the transactions being conducted are consistent with the institution's knowledge of the customer, its business, and its risk profile, including, where necessary, the source of funds.[108]

Areas for Heightened Risk and Diligence

Under the FATF Recommendations, lawyers should increase diligence when dealing with PEPs (*e.g.*, foreign government officials and close relatives thereof). Increased diligence requires: (1) appropriate risk management systems to determine whether the customer is a PEP; (2) senior management approval for establishing business relationships with such customers; (3) reasonable measures to establish the source of wealth and source of funds; and (4) enhanced ongoing monitoring of the business relationship.[109]

The FATF also recommends that lawyers investigate complex, unusually large transactions and all unusual patterns of transactions that have no apparent economic or visible lawful purpose.[110]

These Recommendations are generally consistent with existing U.S. policy applicable to U.S. financial institutions, and they are precedent steps to take more generally for those engaged in cross-border transactions as noted earlier. OFAC requires licenses for lawyers dealing with high risk persons identified on the SDN list.[111] Further, general U.S. anti-money laundering laws apply to lawyers who participate in transactions that appear to conceal some characteristic of illicit money.

Suspicious Transactions Reporting (STR)

Most controversial are the FATF Recommendations relating to reporting requirements for legal professionals who suspect their clients are involved with illicit activity, terrorist property, or cross-border criminal financing.[112] Further, the FATF recommends that lawyers investigate and document

---

[106] *See* The Forty Recommendations, Recommendation 12(d), FATF (2003); *see also infra*, "Substance of the Guidance."

[107] *Id.* at Recommendation 5.

[108] *Id.*

[109] *Id.* at Recommendation 6.

[110] *Id.* at Recommendation 11.

[111] *See* discussion *supra*, "OFAC Licenses Limited Legal Services to Designated Entities."

[112] *See* The Forty Recommendations, at Recommendation 13.

suspicious transactions for authorities and auditors.[113] A "no tipping off" rule compounds the problems of reporting, because it prevents an attorney from informing a client about any reports that are filed regarding the client's activities.[114]

Exemption from Reporting for Privileged Materials

The FATF recommends exemptions from reporting obligations for lawyers, if the relevant information was obtained in circumstances subject to professional secrecy or legal professional privilege.[115] The attorney-client privilege exemption does not eliminate concerns for lawyer reporting requirements, however, as the privileged and nonprivileged distinction is unlikely to be clean or workable.[116]

ABA Resolution 300

Pursuant to Resolution 300, passed in August 2008, the House of Delegates provided that the ABA: (1) urges Congress to refrain from enacting federal legislation that would regulate lawyers through anti-money laundering initiatives; (2) recommends that lawyers conduct risk-based CDD in a manner that does not conflict with ethical requirements and regulations imposed by state authorities; (3) and supports the development of voluntary guidance for lawyers on conducting appropriate CDD to help avoid involvement in money laundering.[117]

Development of Lawyer Guidance

In collaboration with the private sector, the FATF formulated stand-alone Lawyer Guidance (Guidance) for the legal profession on implementing anti-money laundering compliance to improve understanding of the recommendations directed at lawyers, which culminated in October 2008.[118]

The FATF agreed not to impose a mandatory STR regime and the "no tipping off" rule on lawyers, leaving the decision to individual countries about whether to adopt a risk-based or rules-based approach to STRs for legal professionals. The FATF also agreed with the lawyers' group that beneficial ownership identification should be styled as a risk-based analysis, and that lawyers should not be required to identify their clients' beneficial ownership.[119]

Substance of the Guidance

The Guidance applies to lawyers only when they "prepare for and carry out" transactions or activities for their client concerning one of five specifically enumerated categories: (1) buying and selling of real estate; (2) managing of client money, securities, or other assets; (3) management of bank, savings, or securities accounts; (4) organization of contributions for the creation, operation, or management of companies; and (5) creation, operation, or management of legal persons or arrangements, and buying and selling of business entities.

Based on the applicability of these specific categories, the Guidance recommends that lawyers engage in an appropriate risk-based analysis, considering country risk, client risk, and service risk. The Guidance acknowledges that there is no international concurrence regarding which particular jurisdictions or regions represent a higher risk, but it has developed a profile of high-risk countries or locations, including those that are subject to sanctions and identified as being tax havens, having significant levels of corruption or weak anti-money laundering laws, engaging in cross border criminal activity, or supporting terrorism. The Guidance contemplates lawyers developing their own risk criteria to determine whether a particular client poses a high risk, as well as the potential risk presented by the specific services offered by a lawyer.

The FATF's risk-based approach outlined in the Guidance allows for a certain amount of flexibility by lawyers, depending on the practice, size, scale, and expertise of the legal professional. Nonetheless, the Guidance recommends that all lawyers consider if the client and work would be "unusual, risky, or suspicious." In this regard, the Guidance identifies factors that may influence the risk assessment, such as the reputation and publicly available information about a client, as well as the regularity or duration of

---

[113] *Id.* at Recommendation 11.

[114] *Id.* at Recommendation 13.

[115] *Id.* at Recommendation 12.

[116] *See* Gregory, *supra* note 105, at 24. *See also* ABA Task Force on Gatekeeper Regulation and Professional Responsibility.

[117] *Supra* note 15.

[118] *See* Financial Action Task Force, Chairman's Summary: Rio de Janeiro Plenary (Oct. 15–17, 2008), *available at* www.fatf-gafi.org/dataoecd/31/49/41521461.pdf.

[119] FATF noted that if a lawyer's client is a politically exposed person (PEP), a high-risk client, then the lawyer will need, but is not required, to conduct thorough customer due diligence regarding beneficial ownership issues. *See supra* note 14, at 13, 26–27.

a client relationship. Based on these variables, enhanced or reduced CDD may be warranted.

GENERAL COMPLIANCE TIPS FOR ATTORNEYS

In accordance with the existence of U.S. anti-money laundering and anti-terrorist support laws, the OFAC economic sanctions regulations, cash transaction reporting requirements, and the evolving Gatekeeper Initiatives, the FATF Recommendations and Guidance operate to place a premium on "know-your-client" due diligence for attorneys providing legal services, including immigration practitioners assisting clients with investor visas and transactions. For purposes of minimizing risk of legal liability under these legal regimes, basic proactive compliance should consist of some or all of the following elements:

- Screening client names against the OFAC SDN List, as well as possibly other U.S. government restricted-persons lists, such as the General Services Administration Excluded Parties List, the Commerce Department's Denied Parties List and Entities List, and the State Department Disbarred Parties List (all of which are available via the Internet by searching the name of the list or by software screening providers);

- Undertaking client identification and verification steps, including the collection of residence and personal background, and determining to the best of one's ability the source of any funds, assets, or property to be used in an investment supporting the visa application;

- Understanding and confirming the details of the investor's business plans, investments, and entrepreneurial activities in the United States, both during the visa petition process and after visas are approved;

- Conducting appropriate CDD to include public database and press searches, investigation of any PEP-related connections, financial status and wherewithal (including bank references), business background, and any association with countries or organizations subject to U.S. economic sanctions or embargoes, and, if possible, criminal background checks;

- Identifying whether lawyers or their law firm might be vulnerable to being used for money laundering or terrorist financing activity, including but not limited to the (1) characteristics of the firm's client base; (2) types of transactions in which the firm frequently engages; (3) jurisdictions in which the firm does business; and (4) manner in which financial accounts are opened and maintained for clients.

- Training and education for lawyers or other firm personnel regarding how to recognize "red flags" of suspicious money laundering or illicit activity, as well as how to alert appropriate personnel if apparent red flags are detected.

Attached to this article are some tools and sample checklists to assist with due diligence on client intake. The bottom line is that immigration practitioners, like all lawyers, need to be careful, watchful for red flags, and conduct appropriate due diligence consistent with the legal requirements and risks presented by the anti–money laundering, anti-terrorism, and sanctions laws outlined herein.

APPENDIX 1: COMPLIANCE MATERIALS

Compliance Procedures

Before working with any new client or opening a new matter for an existing client, the partner responsible for the client/matter must certify on the case opening form that there are no reasonable grounds to suspect money laundering. Before making such a certification, the partner must:

- have reasonable evidence of the identity of the client (see Appendix 2 for detailed requirements), which must be placed on the client file; *and*

- exercise *due diligence* in considering whether the circumstances give rise to any reasonable grounds to suspect money laundering (considering factors including but not limited to those set out in Appendix 3)—in some cases, it may be necessary to conduct due diligence on parties other than the client in order to determine that there are no reasonable grounds to suspect money laundering.

Employees with reasonable grounds to suspect money laundering by clients shall report such suspicions to the money launder compliance officer (MLCO). The MLCO will respond to such reports by:

- informing all employees, unless authorized by the MLCO, (a) not to do any further work for the client in question and (b) not to inform the client in any way that suspicions of money laundering have been raised;

- promptly work with the employee raising the suspicions and other appropriate employees to complete the form set out at Appendix 4 and gather any other relevant information.

Acknowledgment and Training

The firm will conduct periodic training to familiarize employees with anti-money laundering requirements and employees will acknowledge familiarity with this policy on an annual basis using the form set out at Appendix 3.

APPENDIX 2: SUGGESTIONS FOR IDENTIFICATION INFORMATION FOR NEW CLIENTS

A. Individuals/Private Clients

1. Prospective clients should be interviewed personally wherever possible to identify the true name, correct current address, and date of birth. Such identity should be checked against a document of a reputable source bearing a photograph (*e.g.*, a current full valid passport or national identity card).

2. Address and identity in non-face-to-face situations can be verified by credit reference agency search, electoral roll, local telephone directory, original utility or tax bills, passports or identity cards, or personal home visits.

3. Verify the source of funds to be used on any investment or commercial transaction.

B. NYSE or NASDAQ Listed Corporate Clients

No further verification will be needed over and above normal commercial checks and due diligence if the company is:

1. Quoted on the NYSE or NASDAQ; or

2. Known to be a subsidiary of such a company; or

3. A member of a U.S.-recognized investment exchange.

C. Unquoted U.S. Corporate Clients

In the case of U.S. unquoted corporate clients, you need to consider obtaining the following documentation:

1. Original or certified copy of the certificate of incorporation;

   An inquiry via a business information service;

   Evidence that any individual representing the company has the necessary authority to do so also should be sought and retained;

   A letter from the auditors of the company in some circumstances;

   In the case of a U.S. private company whose directors are not known to the firm, the identity of:

   (a) at least two directors/company secretary/shareholders; and/or

   (b) at least two persons authorized to act on behalf of the company should be verified in line with the requirements for individuals/private clients;

   A visit to the place of business also may be made to confirm the true nature of the business activities;

   A copy of the latest annual report or audited financial statement.

D. U.S. Corporate Clients Other Than Those Above

In the case of unincorporated businesses or partnerships where none of the partners or individuals are known to the attorney, the attorney should identify one or more of the principal/partners in line with the requirements for private clients as referred to in A above.

The attorney may also:

(a) make a credit reference agency search or take a banker's reference; and

(b) for partnerships, verify the identity of one or more of the directors/partners in line with the requirements for individuals/private clients as referred to in A above.

E. Non–U.S. Listed Companies

No further verification will be needed over and above normal commercial checks and due diligence if the company is:

1. Quoted on a recognized investment exchange in a country with equivalent financial markets regulations to the United States; or

   Known to be a subsidiary of such a company; or

   A member of a U.S.-recognized exchange.

F. Non–U.S. Companies that Do Not Fall Within the Above Categories

1. Comparable documents to those required for U.S. unquoted corporate clients should be obtained;

   The identity of at least one of the principal directors and shareholders of the company or the sole director where applicable, in accordance with the requirements of private clients should be verified;

   Evidence of individual(s) who have significant influence and financial control and authority should be sought and retained;

   Take particular care where verifying the legal existence of the company and to ensure the authority of any person purporting to act on behalf of the company;

   Ensure that the company exists for legitimate trading or economic purposes and is not merely a shell or "brass plate" company where the controlling principals cannot be identified;

   Conduct equivalent company searches to those that would be obtained in the United States;

   Request a letter confirming the existence and identity of the clients from local counsel/auditors.

G. Trust, Fiduciary, and Nominee Accounts

These are popular vehicles for money laundering due to the scope for avoiding identification of ownership of funds and property.

The following procedures should be adhered to:

1. Establish the identity of the underlying beneficiary;

   Establish the source of monies and the nature of the transaction;

   Ensure that payments are made only in accordance with the terms of the trust deed and that they are properly authorized in writing by the trustee;

   Particular care should be taken where the accounts are in offshore locations with strict bank secrecy or confidentiality rules.

APPENDIX 3: TIPS ON HOW TO SPOT A MONEY LAUNDERING TRANSACTION

Signs to watch out for include:

1. **Unusual settlement or investment requests**

   Settlement by cash of any large transaction involving the purchase of property or any other investment should give rise to caution. Payment by way of third party check or money transfer where there is a variation between the account holder, the signatory, and a prospective investor should give rise to the need for additional enquiries.

2. **Unusual instructions**

   Care always should be taken when dealing with a client who has no discernible reason for using the firm's service, *e.g.*,. clients with distant addresses who could find the same service nearer their home base; or clients whose requirements do not fit into the normal pattern of the firm's business and could be more easily serviced elsewhere.

3. **Large sums of cash**

   Always be cautious when requested to hold large sums of cash in your client account, either pending further instructions from the client or for no other purpose than for onward transmission to a third party.

4. **The secretive client**

   A personal client who is reluctant to provide details of his identity, residence, or background, reason for investment, business plan, or intended activities in the United States relating to the investment. Be particularly cautious about the client that you do not meet in person.

5. **Suspect territory**

   Caution should be exercised whenever a client is introduced by an overseas bank, other investor, or third party based in countries where production of drugs or drug trafficking may be prevalent, where terrorist activity is prevalent, or where there is a connection to an OFAC-sanctioned country (*see* 31 CFR Chapter V or OFAC website).

6. **General**

   You should consider whether further information is required where:

   (i) amounts to settle clients' transactions are received from some person other than the client or are received from a different account to that previously used by the client; or

   (ii) an agent is being used for no apparent purpose; or

   (iii) funds or assets received come from multiple sources or through convoluted, highly structured/tiered transactions.

APPENDIX 4: EXAMPLE OF PRO FORMA MONEY LAUNDERING SUSPICIOUS CLIENT/MATTER REPORT FORM

FOR INTERNAL USE ONLY

1. **NAME OF CLIENT/S:**

   ....

   ....

   Aliases/Trading Names

   ....

   ....

2. **ADDRESS** (including postcode, telephone, fax, and contact name):

   ....

   ....

   ....

3. **DATE OF BIRTH (or date of incorporation):**

   ....

4. **SUMMARY OF AND DATE OF INSTRUCTIONS FOR INVESTMENT TRANSACTION:**

   ....

5. **IF NOT ACTING AS PRINCIPAL**

   a) Name of Principal:

   ....

   b) Address of Principal:

   (including postcode, fax, and contact name)

   ....

   ....

   ....

6. **EVIDENCE OF IDENTITY OF CLIENT:**
   Attached   YES/NO:..

7. **VALUE OF INVESTMENT AND DESCRIPTION:**

   ....

8. **NAME AND ADDRESS OF INTRODUCER:**

   ....

   ....

....

(letter of introduction attached)
YES/NO..

9. **SOURCE OF FUNDS**

   Cash/Bank/Securities/Other:

   ....

   Amount, type, source and destination:

   ....

   Independent verifications obtained?

   ....

10. **ANY REASON FOR SUSPICION OF ILLICIT OR UNLAWFUL ACTIVITY:**

    ....

11. **SCREENING CONDUCTED AGAINST OFAC SDN LIST AND RESULTS**

    YES/NO:...
    (a) Were any positive hits investigated and resolved; if so, description and date of resolutions
    YES/NO:...

12. **IF RESTRICTED COUNTRY, PERSON, OR ENTITY WAS OFAC LICENSE OBTAINED, OR AUTHORIZATION CONFIRMED; DESCRIBE**

    YES/NO:...
    (a) If yes, ensure that an OFAC authorization is received for payments, a recordkeeping system established, and all records are maintained for five years after conducting the representation.

13. **IS ANY INFORMATION RECEIVED SUBJECT TO PROFESSIONAL PRIVILEGE?**
    Applicable   YES/NO:...

An Overview of Business Entities

by Paul Applebaum[*]

There are many alternatives available to the entrepreneur in choosing an entity for a new business. Each entity has its business advantages and disadvantages. The organizational forms fall into two broad categories: "corporate" entities and "noncorporate" entities. The choice of entity may have a profound effect upon liability, taxation, complexity of creation and termination, management capabilities, and cost of running the business. The form of entity may also have profound visa implications. Following is a brief description of the different forms a business entity may take.

SOLE PROPRIETORSHIP

In General

A sole proprietorship is a business that is owned and operated by one person. The sole proprietorship is the simplest form of ownership to start and terminate and is often employed at the start of a new business. However, the sole proprietorship may involve difficulties in planning a transfer of the business and in estate planning for the owner.

---

[*] *Author's Note:* This article offers some general guidelines to consider in choosing a business entity and should not be construed as providing legal, tax, accounting, or other professional advice. Anyone considering starting a business or forming a business entity is urged to consult his or her own attorney and other professional advisors prior to doing so. This article is written with particular reference to Illinois law. Laws of other states may vary.

Paul Applebaum is executive vice president and general counsel of Shure Incorporated, a leading manufacturer of microphones and other audio electronic products, headquartered in Niles, IL. Prior to joining Shure, Mr. Applebaum was a partner in the law firm of Seyfarth Shaw LLP. He has extensive experience in complex mergers and acquisitions, dispositions, joint ventures, venture capital investments, private placements of securities, commercial sales and marketing, and other commercial transactions. Mr. Applebaum was the co-author of the publication *Illinois Corporate Practice and Forums* and has been a guest lecturer at Loyola University Chicago, School of Law. Mr. Applebaum received a B.A., magna cum laude, in 1984 from the University of Illinois, and a J.D. in 1998 from the University of Chicago Law School. Mr. Applebaum is a member of the Illinois Bar.

This noncorporate form of business may appeal to someone concerned with keeping organizational costs low. It is often the form utilized by an individual starting a new business, such as a small or part-time business or a service business. However, it affords no protection against liability, as it is not recognized as a separate entity from the owner for most purposes.

Assets and Liabilities

In a sole proprietorship, the owner personally finances the business and has the right to manage the business. Accordingly, he or she is entitled to all of the profits of the business and is liable for all debts the business incurs. Liability of the owner also stretches to the acts of employees and the obligations of the business. The sole proprietor's assets may be protected to some extent by appropriate liability insurance.

Transfer of Interest

Transfer of interest in a sole proprietorship seems simple in that the sale of a sole proprietorship is accomplished by selling the assets used in the business. Yet, the transaction is treated as separate sales for each asset, rendering the transfer of interest in a sole proprietorship slightly complex.

Formalities

Generally, in creating a sole proprietorship, no filings or other formalities are necessary. Yet, if the owner opts to use a trade name or an assumed name, he or she must file a certificate in the county in which the business is located.

Tax Considerations

The choice of sole proprietorship as a form of business has no immediate tax consequences. The net income or loss and other tax items of the business are passed through to the owner and reported on the owner's individual tax return. The sole proprietor's income should be reported on Schedule C of his or her personal federal tax return.

The sole proprietor does not receive wages subject to social security tax, but he or she may be subject to self-employment tax, depending on whether he or she also earns wages subject to the social security tax.

Advantages of Sole Proprietorship

- Very few formal steps are necessary to set up the business. The costs of forming the business are relatively low.

- The owner has the freedom to make decisions and take action without consulting partners, investors, or board members.

- The owner does not face the risk of one partner obligating another. There are relatively few reporting requirements for a sole proprietorship. When seeking credit from lenders, both the assets of the owner and the business may be considered.

- The owner does not face the double taxation[1] that corporations could potentially face.

- The owner may freely transfer the business.

Disadvantages of Sole Proprietorship

- The personal liability of the owner is unlimited.

- If the owner dies, the business shuts down and its assets become part of the owner's estate. The owner's resources are the only equity that goes into the business.

- The owner may be placed in a higher tax bracket due to the fact that the profits of the business are taxable to the owner. As a result, funds available to the business in the future may be reduced.

GENERAL PARTNERSHIP

In General

A general partnership, another basic noncorporate form, is a business entity made up of two or more people or entities in which each partner is entitled to participate in the partnership's management. The owners of a partnership may be individuals, corporations, estates, trusts, and other legal and quasi-legal entities.

A general partnership is often a form of business utilized when a sole proprietor aspires to expand the business by bringing in a new investor or co-owner. It is also typically used by two or more people interested in forming a low-risk business financed with personal assets. Because the formation of a general partnership is relatively simple and because insurance can provide some liability protection, the partnership often is still the choice of professionals. The partnership form also may be beneficial for corporations or other limited liability entities entering into joint ventures because the corporation or other entity already enjoys limited liability. With regard to tax considerations, the partnership is often an excellent choice of entity, particularly if the business will be closely held, *i.e.*, held by only a few individuals or entities. Yet, the benefits of partnership decrease with the increase in number of owners due to administration and limited liability problems.

Assets and Liabilities

Generally, the partners own the business assets, and each partner is subject to unlimited personal liability for business debts and obligations. Usually, a partnership agreement states the manner in which profits and losses are to be shared. Profits are shared equally amongst partners if there is not a partnership agreement.

Transfer of Interest

Generally, the transferability of partnership interest is limited to situations where there is unanimous consent of the other partners, unless the partnership agreement stipulates otherwise. In most cases, partners do not want to have an unknown person become a partner and, thus, do not provide for free transferability in the partnership agreement.

Formalities

In many states, the only formal requirement for a general partnership is the filing of a certificate in the county where the partnership will do business. In naming the partnership, owners may use an assumed name or the names of some or all of the partners. The partners may not, however, use the name of someone who is not a member of the partnership. When a partner leaves the partnership, he or she is obligated to notify the creditors. If the partner fails to do so, he or she may be liable for additional debt.

Although no written organizational documents are required for a partnership, a written organizational document is highly recommended and usually used for planning purposes. In the absence of a contrary agreement among the partners, the law imposes certain rules to govern the organization and operation of the partnership. But those rules may not reflect the optimal outcome from the perspective of the partners.

---

[1] Double taxation occurs in a C corporation when the corporation's income is taxed and then the individual stockholders are taxed on the subsequent distribution of such income to them in the form of a dividend.

Tax Considerations

Generally, no income tax is imposed on partnerships. Instead, the partnership's income is passed through and taxed to the partners. The partners include their percentage share of the income or loss on their own income tax forms, regardless of the payment of income to the partner. A partner's basis in the partnership is adjusted to account for the passing through of tax items and for distributions. Income items passed through increase the basis, and loss and deduction items passed through decrease the basis.

The partnership is a relatively advantageous form of business for federal income tax purposes. One advantage of the partnership over the C corporation[2] is that partners may deduct any partnership losses on their own income tax returns. Another important advantage is that the partnership is not subject to the double taxation that the C corporation may face. Some advantages the partnership has over the S corporation[3] include the ability to pass through losses and exclude distributions to the extent of a partner's basis plus debt and allowance of tax-advantageous allocations of tax items.

Although the partnership is not a separate legal entity for tax purposes, it has quasi-entity status in that it must file information returns. Moreover, tax items such as income and deductions are passed through to the partners only after they are determined at the partnership level.

Advantages of a General Partnership

- Because a general partnership is jointly owned, the owners share responsibility and control.
- There are relatively few legal requirements involved in forming a general partnership.
- Decision-making may be informal, unless otherwise indicated in the partnership agreement.
- Capital may be invested in the form of cash, property, or services.
- Generally, a partnership is cheaper and simpler to organize and operate than a corporation.
- Partners have a great deal of flexibility in structuring the ownership and management of their partnership.

Disadvantages of a General Partnership

- Each partner faces unlimited liability (or general liability) for debt and other obligations, including liability for the acts of other partners acting as agents of the partnership without authorization.
- The partnership interests are not freely transferable.
- The death, bankruptcy, withdrawal, or other dissociation of a partner may cause the dissolution of the partnership or force the purchase of the dissociated partner's interest.
- Each partner is liable for actions by the other partners.
- If there are several partners, management can be difficult.
- Transfer of interest in a partnership is more complicated than transfer of corporate interest.
- Transfers of partnership can have adverse tax effects for incoming and continuing partners.

LIMITED PARTNERSHIP

In General

Limited partnerships (LPs) are partnerships formed by two or more persons or entities having one or more general partners and one or more limited partners. LPs may be useful for the entrepreneur who needs to raise capital while retaining complete control over the venture.

Assets and Liabilities

The general partner of an LP has general or unlimited liability. Limited partners have no liability for the obligations of the partnership except to the extent of their capital contributions (*i.e.*, limited liability). The exception to this general rule is when the limited partner participates in the control of the business.

Transfer of Interest

LP interests are subject to the restrictions on transferability contained in the partnership agreement.

Formalities

Formation of an LP involves certain formalities. The LP must file a Certificate of Limited Partnership in the state in which it wishes to organize. Annual reports or filings are due once a year in certain states (*e.g.*, Illinois and Delaware); however, Massachusetts does not require a limited partnership to file an annual report.

---

[2] *See infra* text.
[3] *See infra* text.

Tax Considerations

LPs are generally not taxed separately. A limited partnership's income is passed through to the individual partners, and the partners are taxed on their portion of the income of the limited partnership. Most other tax considerations are similar to those of a general partnership.

Advantages of LP

- Limited liability for limited partner investors.
- Ease of transferability of partnership interest.
- Continuity of existence.
- Can separate ownership/governance rights.
- Partners have a great deal of flexibility in structuring the ownership and management of their partnership.

Disadvantages of LP

- Unlimited personal liability for general partner.
- Limited control by limited partner investors.
- Interests may be "securities" and, therefore, issuances and transfers of interests must comply with applicable federal and state securities laws.
- Agreements and tax issues are generally complex.

LIMITED LIABILITY PARTNERSHIP

In General

Limited liability partnerships (LLPs) are general partnerships that have been registered as limited liability partnerships. The LLP's basic structure is similar to that of the general partnership, but the LLP allows partners to benefit from partial limited liability. Like general partnerships, management is not centralized.

LLPs are often the choice of entity of professionals who wish to reduce the risk of professional liability. In particular, the LLP is appropriate for partnerships that cannot operate as limited partnerships because of the active conduct of the partners in the business.

Assets and Liabilities

The LLP form of business entity is, to some degree, protected from the traditional liabilities of a partner in a general partnership. In an LLP, each partner is protected from the acts and omissions of the other partners. However, partners in an LLP may still be liable for their own acts and omissions as well as the acts and omissions of the employees who are under their direct control. Partners also retain liability to the LLP's outside creditors.

Transfer of Interest

The LLP is virtually identical to the general partnership with regard to transfer of interest.

Formalities

Formation of an LLP involves certain formalities. The LLP must file papers with the applicable Secretary of State's Office in the jurisdiction in which the LLP is organized annually or every other year, depending upon the law of the jurisdiction in which the LLP is organized. Additionally, the name of the partnership must end with one of various authorized terms, such as "Registered Limited Liability Partnership" or "LLP."

Tax Considerations

The tax considerations of an LLP are generally similar to the tax considerations of a general partnership and of a limited liability company (LLC). Thus, the LLP may enjoy flow-through taxation rather than the double taxation that C corporations may face.

Advantages of LLP

- Partners are subject to limited tort and contract liability.
- Formation of an LLP is less formal and expensive than formation of a corporation.
- Owners of the LLP retain decision-making power.
- LLPs are generally not subject to double taxation.

Disadvantages of LLP

- Because partners are not generally responsible for other partners' liabilities, a negative atmosphere may result.
- The partners who practice in riskier areas may feel exposed.
- Some LLPs opt to use contribution agreements in an effort to balance the risks among the partners.
- LLPs do not have perpetual existence.

C CORPORATION

Corporations in General

Virtually all corporations are formed under state law. They are commonly referred to as a "C" corporation or an "S" corporation, depending on whether the corporation is federally taxed under Subchapter C or Subchapter S under the Internal Revenue Code.

C Corporations in General

A C corporation is a legal entity formed as a separate existence from its shareholders. Corporations offer employees various fringe benefits. For instance, owner-employees may often deduct health insurance premiums paid by the corporation from corporate income. Also, corporate-defined benefit plans may offer better retirement options and benefits than noncorporate plans.

This form of business is one typically chosen where the business risk is significant and the owners want to reduce their personal liability. Corporations also are generally formed when the owners want to raise additional capital while maintaining management responsibilities. The corporate form is a wise choice if business is conducted in several jurisdictions or if many types of businesses are conducted. Also, this form is one typically chosen when multiple transfers of interests are anticipated or when the business is expected to continue indefinitely.

Assets and Liabilities

Generally, the corporation provides more protection against personal liability than a sole proprietorship or a general partnership. In a corporation, capital is raised by sale of stock, and the shareholders of a corporation are subject to limited liability. A notable exception occurs when the corporate veil is pierced. Generally, piercing of the corporate veil and the resulting liability of shareholders occurs in a closely held corporation where shareholders have commingled corporate and personal funds or neglected to pay employee withholdings or sales tax, or where other corporate formalities required by the state of incorporation are not followed.

Transfer of Interest

Interests in a corporation are generally freely transferable in the absence of a restriction imposed by agreement or by the corporation's governing instruments. In fact, corporations (both C and S) have the most freely transferable interests of all of the forms of business. Transfers of shares may be restricted by an agreement among the shareholders in a closely held corporation or by its certificate of incorporation or bylaws. Transfers also may be restricted under federal and state securities laws, particularly in cases where shareholders are not actively involved in the company's operation and the shares are not registered with the Securities and Exchange Commission (SEC).

Formalities

There are many formalities associated with creating and operating a corporation. Although the requirements vary by jurisdiction, there are some general requirements all corporations must meet. To form a corporation, an incorporator must file articles of incorporation or a certificate of incorporation and pay the requisite state fees and prepaid taxes with the appropriate state agency, which is usually the Secretary of State. Written bylaws should be adopted. The shareholders, the owners of a corporation, must elect directors. The directors are responsible for management and policy decisions of the corporation and for appointing officers who operate the day-to-day affairs of the corporation. Additionally, annual meetings must be held, and corporate minutes of the meetings must be maintained.

The corporation should issue stock to its shareholders and keep enough capital on hand to cover any foreseeable business debts or obligations. A C corporation may issue various types of stock, signifying that the C corporation offers maximum flexibility in allocation of control and in varying the nature of the shareholders' ownership in the corporation.

Tax Considerations

A C corporation is taxed as a separate legal entity. It pays taxes at its own corporate income tax rates and files its own corporate tax forms (IRS Form 1120) every year. If the profits are distributed to shareholders as dividends, there may be double taxation because dividends are taxable as income to shareholders. However, most small corporations rarely distribute dividends. Instead, owner-employees are paid salaries and fringe benefits that are deductible to the corporation. Consequently, only the owner-employees pay any income taxes on the business income, and double taxation rarely occurs. Although double taxation can be prevented or minimized through planning, the possibility of double taxation is a major disincentive for choosing the C corporation form of business.

Transfers of interest have no effect on the corporation or the shareholders who are not parties to the transfer in regard to taxes. A corporate transfer of interests is the least complicated for tax purposes compared to other forms of business entities.

Advantages of a C Corporation

- Owners' liability is limited to the capital they contributed.
- The corporation exists perpetually, notwithstanding the death of a shareholder.
- Interests may be transferred with ease.
- A corporation has centralized management, so the corporation may hire people with the expertise that the owners may be lacking.
- The corporation, being an independent legal entity, may own property in its own name.
- Capital contributions are relatively flexible.
- The corporation may easily raise capital by selling additional shares.

Disadvantages of a C Corporation

- Formation of a corporation is comparatively complicated and can be expensive.
- There are relatively many formalities involved in operating a corporation.
- Corporate profits may be subject to double taxation.
- The corporate form may be subject to closer supervision by regulatory bodies than other forms of business.
- The tax cost of changing from a C corporation to an S corporation and the tax cost of disincorporating could be daunting.

S CORPORATION

In General

For nontax purposes, S corporations are virtually identical to C corporations. One major difference between C and S corporations is that it is more difficult to qualify for S corporation status. In order to qualify, a corporation must have no more than 100 shareholders who are individuals, although certain trusts and estates may qualify. All of the shareholders must be U.S. citizens or have U.S. tax resident status. If shares are sold or transferred to a shareholder who is a foreign national, the corporation loses its S corporation status and is treated as a C corporation. Moreover, that corporation may not return to S corporation status for a minimum of five years.

If the corporate form is chosen for nontax reasons such as limited liability, then the S corporation is often favored over the C corporation because of the pass-through tax treatment of the S corporation. If the corporate form is not a preferred choice due to nontax considerations, then tax considerations favor a choice of the sole proprietorship, partnership, or LLC over the S corporation. The S corporation may generally not be used for publicly held entities due to the 75-shareholder limit of the S corporation.

Assets and Liabilities

Treatment of assets and liabilities in an S corporation is substantially identical to a C corporation.

Transfer of Interest

The S corporation is virtually identical to the C corporation in regard to the nontax aspects of transfers of interest. The tax difference is a result of the pass-through status of the S corporation. A shareholder of a C corporation is taxed only upon receiving a distribution from the corporation. In other words, the C corporation shareholder is not taxed unless he or she receives a distribution after the interest is transferred. On the other hand, the S corporation shareholder must report a share of the corporation's income, losses, deductions, and other credits accruing after the transfer date, irrespective of whether or not he or she has received a distribution.

Formalities

An S corporation must follow the same state formalities as does a C corporation (*i.e.*, filing articles of incorporation and paying requisite fees). In addition, an S corporation must make a special tax election under subchapter S of the Internal Revenue Code by submitting IRS Form 2553. Thereafter, an S corporation must file an IRS Form 1120-S to report its annual income each year.

The S corporation may have only one class of stock. However, the stock may carry different voting rights. All shareholders must consent to become an S corporation.

Tax Considerations

The main distinction between an S corporation and a C corporation is in taxation. Like partnerships and LLCs, profits and losses of an S corporation are passed through the corporation and reported on the individual tax returns of the shareholders. In other words, in an S corporation, profits and losses are not taxed at the corporate/business level as they would be in a C corporation, and double taxation is thus avoided. Additionally, if losses are expected early on, the passing through of profits and losses permits the shareholders to offset the losses of the business against their income from other sources.

Advantage of S Corporation

- Owners retain the limited liability of a corporation and the tax treatment of a partnership.

Disadvantages of S Corporation

- An S corporation may have only one class of stock, though differences in voting rights are permitted.
- Qualifying for S corporation status, both initially and on an ongoing basis, can be difficult.
- Changing from a C corporation to an S corporation can be complicated and costly.
- All shareholders must be U.S. citizens or have U.S. tax resident status (*i.e.*, no non-resident alien shareholders).

LIMITED LIABILITY COMPANY

In General

A limited liability company is a hybrid of a partnership and a corporation in that it allows the "pass-through" tax treatment and flexibility in structuring of a partnership and the limited liability of shareholders of a corporation. Owners or "members" manage and control the LLC, unless the articles of organization provide for management by a "manager," who is not necessarily also a member. (state limited liability company statutes also now commonly allow single-member LLCs.) However, unlike a limited partnership, in which at least one partner manages and controls and has unlimited liability, the LLC form does not require any member or manager to have unlimited liability. State limited liability company statutes govern LLCs through "default" rules that generally operate in the absence of contrary provisions in the articles of organization or operating agreement. For example, membership in the LLC occurs only with the consent of all of the members, unless the articles of organization or the operating agreement provide otherwise. Similar to other corporate entities, the LLC is a separate legal entity from its members.

LLCs are formed when the owners wish to reduce the risk of personal liability while avoiding double taxation. Flexibility in structuring ownership and management is also a major draw. LLCs may choose to have the centralized management of a corporation or the decentralized management of a partnership. The LLC's operating agreement should set out how the LLC is structured.

Assets and Liabilities

Owners of an LLC are subject to limited liability similar to that of shareholders in a corporation, unless otherwise specified in the LLC's operating agreement.

Transfer of Interest

LLC statutes specify that transfer of an interest may occur by unanimous or majority consent of members, absent a contrary provision in the articles or operating agreement. However, absent the required consent or compliance with any other procedure set forth in the articles of organization or operating agreement, a transfer of a member's interest to a nonmember does not give the transferee all the rights and powers of a member, such as the right to participate in management. Rather, the transferee only has a right to the transferor's share of distributions to members and certain other limited rights. Note that because transferability restrictions on LLCs may effectively limit who can use them, LLCs are generally more popular with smaller groups of investors.

Formalities

In order to form an LLC, articles of organization must be executed and filed with the Secretary of State. The articles of organization must specify the date on which the LLC will terminate, though many states now allow perpetual existence. An operating agreement should also be executed.

Tax Considerations

With regard to federal income tax, a domestic LLC may elect, if it has at least two members, to be taxed as either a corporation or a partnership. If this choice is not made, the LLC is treated as a partnership. A single-member LLC is disregarded for federal income tax purposes.

Upon termination by liquidation, liquidating distributions to members are generally nontaxable to the extent of the members' basis. In contrast, corporations suffer substantial tax consequences upon liquidation.

Advantages of LLC

- Capital may be invested in the form of cash, property, or services.
- Owners are not personally liable for the company's debts and obligations.
- LLCs offer a highly flexible management system and business structure.

Disadvantages of LLC

- An LLC may be relatively costly and technical to form.
- There has been some inconsistency between states in the way LLCs are treated.
- Ownership in the LLC is not freely transferable.
- An LLC does not necessarily have continuous existence. Limited liability company statutes specify that, unless otherwise provided in the articles of organization or in the operating agreement of an LLC, the LLC is dissolved upon the occurrence of certain events specified in the statute. Those events often include such things as the death, withdrawal, resignation, or expulsion of a member.
- LLCs are relatively new in the United States, and thus, there remains some uncertainty regarding legal and tax ramifications of the LLC.

ACCOUNTING FOR INVESTOR-BASED IMMIGRATION: MORE TO IT THAN JUST FEDERAL TAX RETURNS

by Christopher K. Zilafro[*]

Introduction	339
Accounting Information Systems	340
Overview of Financial Statements	340
Background of Modern U.S. Accounting	342
Generally Accepted Accounting Principles	343
Common GAAP Departures	343
Financial Statement Qualities	344
Accounting Policies	344
Other Comprehensive Basis of Accounting	345
Understanding the Differences Among "Compiled," "Reviewed," and "Audited" Financial Statements	345
Entity Types	347
Understanding Equity Accounts	349
Reporting Changes in Equity Accounts	350
Understanding the Differences Between Net Income and Cash Flow	350
Use of Income Tax Returns	351
Deciphering Income Tax Returns	353
Relationships between Schedules K, L, M-1, and M-2 of Form 1065 and the Schedule K-1 Capital Account Reconciliation	355
Initial Investment	357
Summary	357

INTRODUCTION

U.S. Citizenship and Immigration Services (USCIS) regulations concerning investor-based immigration petitions require a review of financial information from sources that may include income tax returns, audited financial statements, and other financial data evidencing the investor-petitioner's initial and ongoing capital investment. The accurate presentation of financial documentation concerning the valuation of assets contributed to a business, as well as the financial status of a business, is critical to eligibility. Moreover, at the end of the two-year conditional permanent residence period in EB-5 cases, the investor must demonstrate that the investment and the enterprise have been sustained. An understanding of financial documentation, therefore, is essential to preparing petitions that will qualify the investor for immigration benefits.

Of course, the reality is that immigration lawyers interested in working with investors and entrepreneurs may not be familiar with the details of accounting systems or financial or tax accounting concepts in particular—and may not have time to devote to learning the many facets of these disciplines. Nonetheless, at a minimum, it is critical to understand that there are many legitimate combinations of systems and methods of accounting used in business. This awareness alone can be very valuable in identifying potential ways to help clients address Requests for Evidence (RFE), or developing a response for overturning denials based on financial factors.

For example, in cases where USCIS believes the data analyzed per the entity's tax returns are insufficient in proving the case, it is critical to remember that tax returns are just one source of the entity's accounting information and that there may exist other completely legitimate (and sometimes, even more appropriate) sources of information that USCIS has accepted in assessing the financial or economic facts of the case when the information reported on the entity's tax returns failed to provide the necessary support.

Toward that end, this article provides an overview of the differences that exist among accounting methods, reporting documents, and entity types, and it introduces the nuances of the accounting and tax treatment of information concerning investment activity. This article also will familiarize the reader with U.S. accounting principles in general, creating a context in which to understand an entity's application of these principles in particular. Understanding both is essential for proper identification and analysis of the applicant's investment and the entity's financial performance. Frequent reference is made to generally accepted accounting principles (GAAP), a term that is used in USCIS regulations.

For the sake of clarity and brevity, because many additional accounting and tax issues arise when assets other than cash (such as receivables, inventory, equipment, buildings, land, or other long-lived assets) are contributed in exchange for stock or a partnership interest, this discussion is primarily limited

---

[*] **Christopher Zilafro** is a certified public accountant in Los Angeles. His expertise is in forensic accounting and taxation. Prior to forming his practice, he was in the audit department of Peat, Marwick, Mitchell & Co. (now KPMG).

to measuring investments of cash in non–publicly traded companies.

ACCOUNTING INFORMATION SYSTEMS

There are several systems of accounting through which to interpret accounting information for a particular business, including:

- Book/Economic Accounting;
- Cash Flow Accounting;
- Budgetary Accounting;
- Management Accounting;
- Tax Accounting;
- Operational Accounting; and
- Regulatory Accounting.

Book/economic accounting comprises the activities necessary for an entity's management to prepare financial statements. Information regarding the economic events of transactions affecting the financial position of a business is identified, measured, recorded, and then communicated in an entity's financial statements. Financial statements represent models of the entity's financial position, and are the link between the accounting detail of the business activities and the financial reporting to users/decision-makers. Such internal statements are either "unaudited," or may be compiled, reviewed, or audited in an engagement involving a certified public accountant (CPA).

OVERVIEW OF FINANCIAL STATEMENTS

The financial statements and related items of an entity will provide the primary source of information concerning the status of the applicant's investment. It is essential, where possible, to utilize a complete set of statements when analyzing the financial activity of an entity, and avoid reliance on a single statement. In reviewing a complete set of financial statements, it is also important to understand the flow of information between the statements and, thus, to establish that the individual statements "articulate" or agree with one another.

A standard set of financial statements will include all of the following: balance sheet, income statement, statement of cash flows, and disclosures and notes to financial statements.

In presenting financial information, current year financial statements are presumed to be more useful if financial statements for one or more prior years also are presented for comparative purposes. Although prevailing accounting standards do not require such presentation, comparative financial statements often help readers more clearly understand the nature and trends of current changes affecting an entity. Furthermore, they emphasize that the business is an ongoing entity and the current period is just one of a number of periods in its history.[1]

The Financial Accounting Standards Board's (FASB) Statement of Financial Accounting Concepts (SFAC) No. 6, *Elements of Financial Statements*, defines the broad classifications of items found in the financial statements to include the following:

- *Assets.* Probable future economic benefits obtained or controlled by a particular entity as a result of past transactions or events. The common characteristic of all assets (economic resources) is service potential or future economic benefits.

- *Liabilities.* Probable future sacrifices of economic benefits arising from present obligations of a particular entity to transfer assets or provide services to other entities in the future as a result of past transactions or events.

- *Equity (or net assets).* Residual interest in the assets of an entity that remains after deducting its liabilities. In a business enterprise, the equity is the ownership interest.

- *Investment by Owners.* Increases in net assets of a particular enterprise resulting from transfers to it from other entities of something of value to obtain or increase ownership interests (or equity) in the enterprise. Assets are most commonly received as investments by owners, but this may include services or satisfaction or conversion of liabilities of the enterprise.

- *Distributions to Owners.* Decreases in net assets of a particular enterprise that result from transferring assets, rendering services, or incurring liabilities by the enterprise to owners. Distributions to owners decrease ownership interests (or equity) in an enterprise.

- *Revenues.* Actual or expected cash inflows (or the equivalent) that have occurred or will eventuate as a result of an entity's major or central operations.

- *Expenses.* Outflows or other using up of assets or incurrence of liabilities (or a combination of both) from delivering or producing goods, ren-

---

[1] Financial Accounting Standards Board (FASB) Accounting Standards Codification (ASC) 205, *Presentation of Financial Statements*.

dering services, or carrying out other activities that constitute the entity's ongoing major or central operations.

- *Gains.* Increases in equity (net assets) from peripheral or incidental transactions of an entity and from all other transactions and other events and circumstances affecting the entity, except those that result from expenses or distributions to owners.
- *Losses.* Decreases in equity (net assets) from peripheral or incidental transactions of an entity and from all other transactions and other events and circumstances affecting the entity, except those that result from expenses or distributions to owners.

Balance Sheet

The balance sheet presents assets, liabilities, and owners' equity at a point in time (usually the business year end), at book value. Book value represents cost less depreciation and other non-cash charges in accordance with accounting principles. The balance sheet provides an indication of the assets available to conduct business operations and the scope of operations. A series of balance sheets can reveal the financial soundness of a company's structure. The basic balance sheet equation is stated:

Assets = Liabilities + Equity

When reviewing the balance sheet, remember that it is based on historical transactions. In accounting, the historical cost principle dictates that most assets and liabilities should be recorded at their historical cost. The term historical cost refers to the original cost of an asset at the time of purchase or payment as opposed to its saleable value, replacement value, or value in present or alternative use. As a result, reported amounts typically will not correspond to the market value of an enterprise.

Current assets are those that will be realized in cash, sold, or used within one year (or operating cycle, if longer). Current liabilities are obligations that will be liquidated by using current assets or creating other current liabilities. Classified balance sheets distinguish current assets and current liabilities from other assets and liabilities and are more useful to readers than unclassified balance sheets because they present information that owners, lenders, and investors frequently use to measure a company's liquidity. The difference between current assets and current liabilities provides some indication of a company's liquidity and solvency.

Fixed assets are recorded at historical cost less an estimate for depreciation that may not bear any resemblance to fair market value (FMV). This is especially true with respect to land assets, since FMV may be many times the land's original cost.

Understanding and interpreting the changes to the entity's financial position occurring between balance sheet dates can be accomplished primarily by analyzing the income statement and statement of cash flows.

Income Statement

The income statement presents revenues, expenses, gains, losses, and income over a period of time—typically one year. The income statement is one of the basic financial statements necessary to present a company's financial position and results of operations in conformity with prevailing accounting standards. FASB Accounting Standards Codification (ASC) 225, *Income Statement*, states that the statement of income and the statement of retained earnings (separately or combined) are designed to reflect, in a broad sense, results of operations.

Each income statement item may be categorized as revenue, expense, gain, or loss. Classifying amounts as revenues, expenses, gains, or losses varies among companies depending on the nature of each company's operations. Although there are few strict rules for presenting these items in the income statement, GAAP requires the following to be presented separately:

- Extraordinary items;
- Unusual or infrequent items;
- Discontinued operations of a component of an entity;
- Cumulative effects of accounting changes;
- Equity in operations in investees; and
- Goodwill (excess of the purchase price over the net amounts assigned to the acquired entity's assets and liabilities) impairment losses.

The income statement measures the performance in the entity's assets and liabilities by reporting the changes during the period of measurement (normally 12 months). It also measures a company's sales (revenue), expenses, and earnings over the specified time period.

Income statements provide a good indicator of a company's financial health and performance, since earnings and trends in earnings are important indicators of a company's profitability. Changes or trends in financial position, as indicated on income statements, should provide an indication whether the company is experiencing growth or is in decline.

In some cases, small businesses may be able to produce only an income statement generated specifically for tax purposes. As will be addressed later, the income statement may not have been prepared based on GAAP.

Statement of Cash Flows

A statement of cash flows shows the changes in an entity's cash and cash equivalents during a specific period. It should be presented as a basic financial statement when the financial statements are prepared in accordance with GAAP. A statement of cash flows may be presented, but is not required if the financial statements are not prepared in accordance with GAAP.[2]

A statement of cash flows has five basic elements:

- Cash flows from operating activities;
- Cash flows from investing activities;
- Cash flows from financing activities;
- Net change in cash during the period; and
- Supplemental disclosure of non-cash investing and financing activities.

All cash receipts and payments should be classified as operating, investing, or financing activities. Non-cash transactions involving investing and financing activities, such as acquiring assets by assuming liabilities, should be disclosed separately rather than within the body of the statement.

Cash flows from operating activities represent the cash effects of transactions resulting from the company's normal operations for delivering goods for sale and providing services. The amounts are derived from activities that enter into the determination of net income.

Cash flows from investing activities include: lending money and collecting on loans; acquiring and selling or disposing of securities that are not cash equivalents; and acquiring and selling or disposing of productive assets that are expected to generate revenue over a long period of time.

Cash flows from financing activities include: obtaining resources from owners and providing them with a return on, and return of, their investment; obtaining resources from creditors; repaying the short- and long-term borrowings; or settling the obligation.

Non-cash investing and financing transactions result from issuing an ownership interest in exchange for non-cash consideration, and from stock dividends or distribution of property as dividends.

Disclosures and Notes to Financial Statements

Notes are an integral part of financial statements and should be used to present material disclosures required by GAAP that are not presented in the statements. A summary of significant accounting policies is usually the first note to the financial statements, and is required by GAAP when financial statements that purport to present financial position, results of operations, or cash flows are issued.

BACKGROUND OF MODERN U.S. ACCOUNTING

The era of modern financial reporting and the authoritative body of principles that we refer to as GAAP began with America's rise to industrial power at the end of the 19th century, as investors' interests in the opportunities found in emerging markets furthered the need for additional financial information, greater disclosure, and increased regulation.

Under the Securities Exchange Act of 1934, the U.S. Securities and Exchange Commission (SEC) has statutory authority to establish financial accounting and reporting standards for publicly held companies. In April 1938, the SEC delegated authority to establish accounting standards to the private sector, and encouraged establishment of private standard-setting bodies through the American Institute of Certified Public Accountants (AICPA).[3]

In 1973, the FASB was formed. The FASB is officially recognized as authoritative by the SEC[4] and by the AICPA.[5] Since 1973, the Financial Accounting Standards Board (FASB) has been the designated organization in the private sector for establishing standards of financial accounting and reporting that govern the preparation of financial reports.

In the United States, accounting standards have been developed and have evolved primarily to meet

---

[2] FASB ASC 230, *Statement of Cash Flows*.

[3] Accounting Series Release No. 4.

[4] Financial Reporting Release No. 1, Section 101; reaffirmed in U.S. Security and Exchange Commission's April 2003, Policy Statement.

[5] Rule 203, Rules of Professional Conduct, *as amended* May 1973, and May 1979.

the needs of participants in the capital markets. As a result, in responding to accounting questions pertaining to U.S. immigration regulations, when analyzing and summarizing data using statements prepared on a GAAP basis, the information may not provide the same level of usefulness.

GENERALLY ACCEPTED ACCOUNTING PRINCIPLES

GAAP encompasses the conventions, practices, rules, and procedures necessary to define accepted accounting practice at a particular time. It includes not only broad guidelines of general application, but also detailed practices and procedures. Those conventions, rules, and procedures provide a standard by which to measure financial presentations.[6]

GAAP includes the measurement and disclosure principles that apply to all financial statements, except those prepared on an Other Comprehensive Basis of Accounting (OCBOA). In short, GAAP generally governs the recognition of transactions and dictates the numbers and other information that must be presented in financial statements.

The International Accounting Standards Committee (IASC), formed in 1973 to develop global accounting standards, recently created a new standard-setting body called the International Accounting Standards Board (IASB); it gained the endorsement of both the SEC and FASB. Important progress already has been made toward a convergence of national and international accounting standards—a shared objective of these organizations—as evidenced by the existing similarities in the conceptual frameworks of the FASB and IASC. While the principles of GAAP are generally the same across the world, there remain significant differences in GAAP for each country. It is important to keep this distinction in mind in performing analysis on any non-U.S. companies. References in this article are made only to U.S. GAAP.

COMMON GAAP DEPARTURES

Notwithstanding the benefits that GAAP provides to financial reporting, possibilities exist for differences in stating the financial condition and performance of the same entity. Further, many small companies and much of the internal reporting figures used by larger companies do not conform to GAAP. More significantly, many decision-makers are not fluent in GAAP.

Because of the nature of accrual versus cash accounting, as it is possible to misrepresent earnings by not matching revenue with expenses, it also is possible to distort the investor's present equity position by overstating an entity's net income (or understating losses). This can result in distributions representing a potential return of capital and not distributions of profits, or characterizing taxable distributions as tax-neutral loans.

When analyzing financial statements and/or other accounting data, it is important to have an awareness of potential departures, misstatements, and inconsistencies to accurately comprehend the nature of both a company's and an individual's investment activity. Although effectively identifying the extent of any differences that exist between GAAP and non-GAAP prepared statements may not be possible apart from an in-depth analysis, awareness of many of the common differences that exist can be effective in analyzing the entity's financial information.

GAAP departures common to the financial statements of many nonpublic companies include:

- *Basis of accounting.* Financial statements that are prepared on a tax or cash accounting basis versus the accrual basis required by GAAP.
- *Unrecorded revenue.* Tendency of the owner in some industries to understate cash sales to minimize tax liability.
- *Inadequate allowance for bad debts.* Companies with a large volume of credit sales may have exposure in this area. Owners tend to be overly optimistic about the collectability of their accounts receivable. This also could be true of employee or related-party receivables.
- *Failure to record obsolete, slow moving, or damaged inventory.* This is especially common with manufacturers, retailers, or distributors with large inventories of numerous products.
- *Understated inventories.* Some small businesses may try to understate inventories to reduce income taxes. This is especially true for companies without perpetual inventory systems.
- *Unrecorded prepaid expenses.* Prepaid items are sometimes expensed to save on income taxes.
- *Obsolete, damaged, or abandoned equipment still shown in the financial statements.* Companies with large investments in fixed assets are

---

[6] American Institute of Certified Public Accountants (AICPA), Statement on Auditing Standards (SAS) No. 69, AU Section 411, *The Meaning of Present Fairly in Conformity With Generally Accepted Accounting Principles.*

more likely to have this problem, especially if they have not inventoried those assets recently.

- *Small tools that have been expensed.* Manufacturing companies may have large numbers of small tools or supplies that were expensed when purchased. Those items should be added back, if material.

- *Unrecorded liabilities.* This is a common problem with interim financial statements when late bills are not recorded in the correct accounting period.

- *Failure to record capital lease obligations.* Certain leases, especially those involving large trucks or heavy equipment, normally should be classified as capital leases under GAAP. In those cases, both the asset and lease obligation would be recorded on the balance sheet.

- *Failure to accrue for wages, employee benefits, and vacation/sick pay.* This can be a material liability if the company has a large workforce.

- *For construction contractors, failure to use percentage-of-completion accounting.* This is a common problem for small contractors who keep their general ledger on a completed-contract basis for tax purposes.

- *Impairment of long-lived assets.* Failure to reduce the carrying amount of the impaired asset and charge current period net income for the recognized impairment loss equal to the difference between the asset's carrying amount and fair value.

- *Related-party transactions.* Financial dealings with related parties pertaining to revenue and expenses often will require adjustment to fair market values if not stated on arm's length terms.

FINANCIAL STATEMENT QUALITIES

The FASB's goal in setting standards is to enhance the usefulness of the information that entities report in financial statements to investors and creditors. In assessing whether the usefulness of information would be enhanced, the FASB considers the "qualitative characteristics" that make accounting information useful to investors and creditors.

FASB Concept Statement No. 2, *Qualitative Characteristics of Accounting Information*, identifies those qualitative characteristics, defines them, and explains how they interact with each other. It states that in order to be useful, financial information has to be both *relevant* and *reliable*—concepts referred to as primary qualities.

Additional characteristics, referred to as secondary qualities, are *comparability* and *consistency*. Interacting with the primary and secondary qualities are constraints that are presented when developing accounting information.

Constraints

These consist of determining the *cost/benefit* of information (intended usefulness of the information should not exceed the related cost to develop it), *materiality level* (keeping in mind the degree to which the transaction is big enough to matter), and the principle of *conservatism* (understating, not overstating, net income and net assets for significant uncertainties and contingencies).

Note that while the "qualitative characteristics" enhance the usefulness of financial information to investors and creditors, they do not necessarily answer the material questions in an immigrant investor petition. In reviewing GAAP-based financial statements for investment or credit decisions, an omission or misstatement of an item may not be material under GAAP. However, an error may be material in determining the present balance of the petitioner's equity investment in the enterprise. For example, over the two-year conditional period, an overstatement of an asset discovered and the subsequent "writedown" may not be material to the overall balance sheet of an entity, or the statements taken as a whole in terms of GAAP, but the writedown and corresponding charge to current year net income would impact the petitioner's capital balance.

ACCOUNTING POLICIES

Accounting policies are the specific accounting principles and methods of applying those principles that an entity uses to prepare its financial statements. The accounting methods used by a business may be determined by various factors—*e.g.*, the entity's size and cost constraints, the method's usefulness to management, specific industry regulations, or requirements imposed by an investor/creditor.

Applying GAAP often involves choosing from a number of acceptable accounting principles and methods. Selecting one alternative over another may result in significantly different financial results. Consequently, FASB ASC 235, *Notes to Financial Statements*, requires an entity to disclose its significant accounting policies when a balance sheet, income statement, or statement of cash flows is presented. An accounting policy is significant if it materially affects the determination of financial position, cash flows, or results of operations. In particular, FASB ASC 235 requires disclosing accounting principles and methods that involve any of the following:

- A selection from existing acceptable alternatives;
- Industry peculiarities; and
- Unusual or innovative application of GAAP.[7]

The format of the disclosure (including the location) is flexible. However, FASB ASC 235 states that it is preferable to title the information "Summary of Significant Accounting Policies" and present it in a separate summary preceding the notes or in the first note to the financial statements.[8]

OTHER COMPREHENSIVE BASIS OF ACCOUNTING

Due to the growing complexity and expense of GAAP-based financial statements for small businesses, despite the governmental directives, many entities will not have GAAP-based financial statements that are either compiled, reviewed, or audited by an independent CPA. As an alternative to GAAP, these entities may have financial statements prepared on an Other Comprehensive Basis of Accounting (OCBOA). The most widely used OCBOA methods include tax basis, cash basis, and modified cash basis statements. One difference to note between OCBOA-prepared Financial Statements and GAAP-based statements is that OCBOA-prepared Financial Statements may not include a statement of cash flow.

The interest in OCBOA statements continues to increase for several reasons. First, information contained in OCBOA statements is often more intuitive to owners and managers of privately held companies. OCBOA statements offer cost savings compared with preparation of GAAP-based financial statements, and an increasing number of external users, including banks and insurance companies, have begun to show acceptance of such statements.

For many companies, neither GAAP– nor OCBOA-prepared financial statements will be available, limiting documentation available for analysis to the entity's income tax returns, internally prepared financial statements, and other supporting accounting information.

Under these circumstances, it is important to understand the differences and limitations that may exist between the entity's internally prepared financial statements and other forms of financial documentation, including the potential departures from GAAP.

Because of the accounting conventions necessary for developing financial statements (*e.g.*, the assignment of estimated useful lives to assets for the purpose of charging periodic depreciation), book/economic accounting can distort what is actually happening in the business. It also is not particularly susceptible to certain detailed financial analyses, as the limited number of accounts frequently combines transactions that are more easily analyzed if separated. In many cases, in order for accounting information to yield relevant data on which sound decisions can be based, book/economic accounting must be adjusted to address the informational needs of the decision-maker.

Adjustments may be necessary on items reported on both the balance sheet and the income statement. Balance sheet adjustments include adjustments for non-operating and excess assets, and for loans to/from related parties. Income statement adjustments often will require normalization of compensation and fringe benefits for an owner or family members that are above or below reasonable levels. Profitable companies may pay part of their profits to owners as excess compensation, or they may pay family members who are no-show employees. Marginal companies may underpay their owners to improve their bottom lines.

UNDERSTANDING THE DIFFERENCES BETWEEN "COMPILED," "REVIEWED," AND "AUDITED" FINANCIAL STATEMENTS

If the financial statements have been compiled, reviewed, or audited by a CPA, the financial statements should be accompanied by an accountant's report that describes the CPA's level of service and indicates whether the financial statements contain departures from GAAP. There are three general types of engagements.

Compiled Statements

Compilation engagements are engagements in which a CPA receives information supplied by the client and arranges it into proper financial statement form in accordance with GAAP, without attempting to express any assurance on those statements. The CPA is concerned that the assembly of information is arithmetically correct; however, the CPA does not attempt to verify the accuracy or completeness of the information provided.

---

[7] FASB ASC 235-10-50-1 and 50-3.
[8] FASB ASC 235-10-50-6.

In a compilation engagement, the CPA is not required to make inquiries of management or perform other procedures to verify, corroborate, or review information supplied by the client.

Compiled financial statements are common for a majority of small companies or companies that do not have reporting requirements to a bank or other creditors.

Reviewed Statements

In a review engagement, the CPA goes beyond putting client information together. The CPA also makes certain inquiries of management and performs analytical procedures. However, in a review, the CPA is not required to understand the company's internal control, test the accounting records, observe inventory, confirm receivables, or obtain other corroborating evidence, as is required in an audit.

Review engagements are distinguishable from audits in that the scope of review is less than that of an audit and, therefore, the level of assurance provided is lower. A review consists primarily of enquiry, analytical procedures, and discussion related to information supplied to the public accountant by the enterprise with the limited objective of assessing whether information being reported on is plausible within the framework of appropriate criteria.

Audited Statements

In an audit engagement, the CPA goes beyond a review, and on a test basis, examines evidence supporting the amounts and disclosures in a company's financial statements.

The objective of an independent, external audit in accordance with generally accepted auditing standards (GAAS) is to express an opinion on whether an entity's financial statements present fairly, in all material respects, its financial position, results of operations, and cash flows in conformity with GAAP. This is the highest form of assurance. The auditor performs the audit with an attitude of professional skepticism and seeks reasonable assurance as to whether the financial statements are free of material misstatement.

Materiality and audit risk affect the application of GAAS, especially the fieldwork and reporting standards, and are reflected in the auditor's standard report. The auditor must make judgments about materiality and audit risk in determining the nature, timing, and extent of procedures to apply, and in evaluating the results.

The concept of "materiality" recognizes that some matters, but not all, are important for fair presentation of the financial statements in conformity with GAAP. Materiality judgments are made in light of surrounding circumstances and involve qualitative and quantitative considerations.

"Audit risk" is the risk that an auditor may unknowingly fail to modify the opinion on materially misstated financial statements.[9] The exercise of due professional care allows the auditor to provide only reasonable, not absolute, assurance that the financial statements are free of material misstatement, whether caused by error or fraud. Thus, an audit performed in accordance with GAAS does not eliminate audit risk.[10]

The existence of audit risk is recognized by the statement in the auditor's standard report that the auditor obtains reasonable assurance about whether the financial statements are free of material misstatement.

Types of Audit Reports

- *Unqualified opinion.* An unqualified opinion states that the financial statements present fairly, in all material respects, the financial position, results of operations, and cash flows of the entity in conformity with GAAP.

- *Explanatory language added to the auditors' standard report.* Although not affecting the auditor's unqualified opinion, certain circumstances may require that the auditor add an explanatory paragraph to the report.

- *Qualified opinion.* A qualified opinion states that, except for the effects of the matter(s) to which the qualification relates, the financial statements present fairly, in all material respects, the financial position, results of operations, and cash flows in conformity with GAAP.

- *Adverse opinion.* An adverse opinion states that the financial statements do not present fairly the financial position, results of operations, or cash flows of the entity in conformity with GAAP.

GAAS—The Reporting Standards

There are 10 GAAS consisting of three general standards, three standards of field work, and four standards of reporting. These standards set the ob-

---

[9] AICPA Professional Standards, AU Section 312, *Audit Risk and Materiality in Conducting an Audit.*

[10] AICPA Professional Standards, AU Section 230, *Due Professional Care in the Performance of Work.*

jectives of audit procedures.[11] The four standards of reporting are as follows:

(1) *The report shall state whether the financial statements are presented in accordance with GAAP.*

Financial statements should:

- Use principles that have general acceptance;
- Use principles that are appropriate in the circumstances;
- Include adequate disclosure;
- Classify and summarize information in a reasonable manner; and
- Reflect underlying events and transactions within an acceptable range.

(2) *The report shall identify those circumstances in which such principles have not been consistently observed in the current period in relation to the preceding period.*

The financial statement user has the right to expect that changes in the account balances have resulted from transactions, not changes in principle. Management has the responsibility to disclose the effects of changes in principle, and the auditors' report should include an additional paragraph when a material change in principle has occurred.

(3) *Informative disclosures in the financial statements are to be regarded as reasonably adequate unless otherwise stated in the report.*

Presenting statements in conformity with GAAP includes adequate disclosure of material matters related to form, arrangement, and content of the statements and notes. If management omits information required by GAAP, if practicable, the auditor should provide the necessary disclosures in the report and express a qualified or adverse opinion.[12]

(4) *The report shall contain either an expression of opinion regarding the financial statements, taken as a whole, or an assertion to the effect that an opinion cannot be expressed. When an overall opinion cannot be expressed, the reasons therefore should be stated. In all cases in which an auditor's name is associated with the financial statements, the report should contain a clear indication of the character of the auditor's work, if any, and the degree of responsibility the auditor is taking.*

The objective of the fourth standard is to prevent misinterpretation of the degree of responsibility the auditor is assuming when his or her name is associated with financial statements.

"Taken as a whole," as referred to in the fourth standard of reporting, applies equally to a complete set of financial statements, to an individual financial statement, and to financial statements for different periods presented comparatively.

The auditor may express an unqualified opinion on one of the financial statements, and express a qualified or adverse opinion or disclaim an opinion on others if circumstances warrant.

Exercising Professional Skepticism in Analyzing Data

The professional standards promulgated by the AICPA require sufficient relevant data be obtained to afford a reasonable basis for conclusions or recommendations in relation to any professional services performed. When examining underlying information, a member must use professional judgment and exercise independence, integrity, and objectivity.[13] This standard requires professional skepticism when analyzing the work of others.

When analyzing the documentation supporting the investor-petitioner's investment, although it is the client's responsibility to provide honest representations, it is best done through the provision of objective data. Inability to produce records, as well as the presence of multiple sets of books and records, would be causes for concern.

ENTITY TYPES

Although there are many different types of entities, most business undertakings are conducted as corporations, partnerships, limited liability companies (LLCs), or sole proprietorships. Following is an overview of the different entity types and the equity/capital accounts commonly utilized in the entity's system of accounting.

Corporations

Corporations are business entities created under state law. For corporations, the equity section of the balance sheet generally consists of the following accounts:

---

[11] AICPA Professional Standards, AU Section 150, *Generally Accepted Auditing Standards.*

[12] AICPA Professional Standards, AU Section 431, *Adequacy of Disclosure of Financial Statements.*

[13] AICPA Code of Professional Conduct ET section 100.

- Common Stock;
- Additional Paid-in Capital;
- Preferred Stock;
- Treasury Stock; and
- Retained Earnings.

S Corporations

S corporations are hybrid corporations that combine some of the tax advantages of a partnership with the liability protection of a corporation. Start-up businesses often consider S corporation status because profits and losses are passed through to the shareholders with no corporate tax imposed.

Generally, S Corporations use the same equity accounts as regular (C) corporations. However, because an S corporation's retained earnings may consist of items that have not been taxed previously, the retained earnings account of an S corporation is often separated into additional components used primarily to determine the taxability of distributions to stockholders.

Partnerships

Unlike corporations, partnerships do not issue stock to their owners. Also, partnerships do not retain earnings and losses, but pass them through to each partner. As a result, partnerships do not use accounts for common stock, additional paid-in capital, or retained earnings to record partners' equity. While they differ slightly by type of partnership (general, limited, or limited liability partnership), they usually maintain the following accounts for each partner:

- Partner's Capital;
- Partner Contributions; and
- Partner Drawings.

General Partnerships

General partnerships are associations of two or more persons as co-owners to carry on a business for profit. The co-owners personally share the risks and rewards of all phases of the business. Because of tax rules and regulations, partnerships are increasingly complex entities. Each partner is jointly and severally liable for the partnership's obligations. Like proprietorships, a partner's personal assets can be seized to satisfy partnership debts.

Limited Partnerships

Limited partnerships are similar to general partnerships, except that one or more of the partners has limited exposure to loss. This form of organization is a legal device that enables limited partners to be investors in a partnership, normally limiting their liability to the extent of their investment and enabling any general partners to manage and control day-to-day operations. A general partner's assets can be seized to satisfy debts of the limited partnership.

Limited Liability Partnerships

Limited liability partnerships (LLPs) are a special type of partnership that exists under applicable state law. Relatively new, LLPs were enacted in response to the concern that a partner of a professional firm can be held liable for the malpractice of another partner in the same firm. LLPs are an alternative available in some states that do not allow professional firms to organize as LLCs.

Limited Liability Companies

LLCs are business entities created under state law that can be used in all states. LLCs are owned by members and combine the tax advantages of a partnership with the liability protection of a corporation. As a result, the LLC structure is often compared to an S corporation. In many cases, LLCs are more flexible than S corporations. The major drawbacks of LLCs are that laws are new and relatively untested in non-tax matters, and members of LLCs that conduct an active business generally will be subject to self-employment tax. Each state establishes its own LLC rules and characteristics. The following accounts typically are used for each LLC member:

- Member's Capital;
- Member Contributions; and
- Member Drawings.

Sole Proprietorships

A proprietorship is the simplest form of business organization. It is an unincorporated business owned entirely by one individual. Unlike a corporation or partnership, a proprietorship is not a separate legal entity. Its assets and liabilities are personal assets and liabilities of its owner, and its income and expense are reported on the owner's personal income tax return. Accounts used for proprietors consist of the following:

- Proprietor's Capital; and
- Proprietor's Drawings.

The proprietor's drawing account is used to record distributions made to the proprietor during the year (including the cost of any items purchased for the proprietor's personal, rather than business, use). At the end of the tax year, the drawing account is "closed" to the proprietor's capital account.

UNDERSTANDING EQUITY ACCOUNTS, INCLUDING RETAINED EARNINGS

Following the contribution of cash by the owner to a business, a stockholder or partnership/member interest is exchanged representing an ownership interest in the respective entity, evidenced by the number of shares held or percentage interest in the entity. For corporations, the stockholder's respective share of the book value/accounting value of the corporate stock is determined by dividing net book value (assets minus liabilities) by the total number of shares issued and multiplying book value per share times the number of shares held by the stockholder. For partnerships and limited liability companies, the interest held in the entity is reflected in the respective capital account balances maintained for each partner/member.

No matter if the entity is a corporation, partnership, or sole proprietorship, many of the same concepts apply to stockholders' equity, partners' equity, and proprietorship's equity. The components of stockholders' equity include contributed capital (capital stock, additional paid-in capital, and stock subscriptions receivable), retained earnings, and treasury stock. For partners' equity and proprietorship's equity, the equity sections typically include a capital account, contribution account, and a drawing account.

In terms of reviewing financial statements to ascertain the amount of the petitioner's total investment in the business, changes in the entity's equity accounts should be analyzed from the initial investment period forward, including any increases or decreases to contributed capital and accumulated net profits (or losses) and any distributions of those profits. This may require statements covering several financial periods.

Stockholders' equity represents the owners' interests in a corporation's assets and liabilities. It is the residual amount of the corporation's assets less liabilities, and it results from owner contributions, cumulative undistributed profits, and cumulative losses. Stockholders' equity consists of the following accounts:

Contributed Capital

Contributed capital represents the investments made by the owners. It consists of amounts paid by owners when the company issues its stock, and amounts arising from subsequent transactions with owners. Contributed capital includes capital stock and additional paid-in capital.

Capital Stock

Capital stock represents the legal capital provided by stockholders. It is the minimum investment in the business that must, under state law, be retained for the protection of creditors. Capital stock may consist of common or preferred shares.

Common stock is the basic share issued and confers upon its owner the right to (a) vote on corporate matters; (b) share in profits; (c) purchase a proportionate share of additional common stock issued; and (d) share in the corporation's assets upon liquidation. Generally, unless restricted by the terms of the issuance, common stockholders control the corporation. The articles of incorporation will indicate whether the common stock is par value stock (determining the minimum price per share), or no par stock (with or without a stated or assigned value).

Preferred stock represents amounts raised by owners without sharing in the voting rights and equity participation as owners of common stock, and carries certain specified preferences or privileges (defined in the corporation's charter) over common stock.

When capital stock is issued, its par value (stated value in the case of no-par stock) is recorded to common or preferred stock and any proceeds received in excess of par or stated value are recorded to additional paid-in capital. (Most common stocks issued today do not have par values.)

Additional Paid-in Capital

Additional paid-in capital represents contributed capital in excess of legal capital. Consequently, it is affected by capital-related transactions such as selling stock at an amount in excess of par or stated value, and capitalizing retained earnings, for example, as a result of issuing stock dividends.

Retained Earnings

Retained earnings represent the undistributed earnings of an entity retained to finance future operations. Retained earnings is increased by the net earnings of the corporation, and decreased by net losses of the corporation and dividends paid to preferred and common stockholders. Other changes in retained earnings include adjustments to the opening balance as a result of prior period adjustments of certain changes in accounting principle.

Treasury Stock

At times, a corporation may repurchase common stock from its stockholders. The reacquired stock, or treasury stock, does not represent an asset of a corporation. Instead, it is reported in the balance sheet as a reduction of stockholder's equity because the corporation is, in effect, returning capital to stockholders. Shares of treasury stock are either reissued to new stockholders or cancelled.

The following chart summarizes the descriptions commonly used for balance sheet reporting of equity/capital items:

Entity	Balance Sheet Descriptions	Section
C Corporations	Common Stock Additional Paid-in Capital Preferred Stock Treasury Stock Retained Earnings	Stockholders' Equity Section
S Corporations	Common Stock Additional Paid-in Capital Accumulated Earnings and Profits Accumulated Adjustments Account Previously Taxed Income Other Adjustments Account Tax Timing Adjustments Other Retained Earnings	Stockholders' Equity Section
General Partnerships, Limited Partnerships, LLPs	Partner's Capital Partner Contributions Partner Drawings	Partners' Equity Section
LLCs	Member's Capital Member Contributions Member Drawing	Members' Equity Section
Sole Proprietorships	Proprietor's Capital Proprietor's Drawing	Proprietor's Equity Section

REPORTING CHANGES IN EQUITY ACCOUNTS

Companies are required to disclose changes in the separate accounts comprising stockholders' equity—including retained earnings—when they present both a balance sheet and income statement.[14]

The accounting standards do not require a separate statement of retained earnings as a basic financial statement, but do require that changes in equity during a reporting period be disclosed.[15] This disclosure requirement can be accomplished by preparing a separate financial statement (*e.g.*, a statement of retained earnings or a statement of changes in equity), by combining these disclosures within the body of another financial statement (*e.g.*, a combined statement of income and retained earnings), or by presenting these disclosures in the notes to the financial statements. There is no requirement for a separate statement of retained earnings in GAAP-based financial statements, nor in financial statements prepared under some other comprehensive basis of accounting (OCBOA).[16]

Changes in Retained Earnings

When there are no changes in stockholders' equity accounts other than retained earnings, disclosure of changes in retained earnings is typically accomplished by one of the following methods:

- A combined statement of income and retained earnings;
- Presentation in the stockholders' equity section of the balance sheet; or
- A separate statement of retained earnings.

Changes in Other Elements of Stockholders' Equity

When changes occur in stockholders' equity accounts other than retained earnings, most companies disclose the changes in a statement of stockholders' equity. The principal advantage of presenting all changes in stockholders' equity in one statement is that it allows users to understand the interrelationships of the accounts and changes therein.

As with presenting changes in retained earnings, changes in each element of stockholders' equity may be disclosed in separate statements, on the face of the balance sheet, in the notes to the financial statements, or any combination of the above.

UNDERSTANDING THE DIFFERENCES BETWEEN NET INCOME AND CASH FLOW

An understanding of an entity's cash flows is essential, since, for most entities, several differences exist between the net income figures reported for a period, and the amount of cash that actually flows through the entity for the same period. These differences are often due to 1) the accounting treatment of non-cash items used in the determination of net in-

---

[14] FASB ASC 505-10-50-2.
[15] *Id.*

[16] Statement on Standards for Accounting and Review Services (SSARS) No. 9.

come, such as deducting expenses for depreciation and amortization, and 2) accounting accruals that are made by the entity in recognizing income before cash is actually received or expenses before cash payments are made.

The measure of available cash is the difference between total cash income and the total of all required cash outlays. This is commonly referred to as "free cash flow". Required cash outlays include amounts of capital expenditures required to maintain the entity's productive capacity and may include payment of dividends to shareholders or distributions to partners.

Aspects of a particular case may focus on an entity's ability to pay for certain specified expenditures, which deal with questions of the entity's available cash (and not the sufficiency of earnings). In these cases, an understanding of an entity's cash flows will be informative as to whether the entity had sufficient cash available to pay the particular items throughout the period.

USE OF INCOME TAX RETURNS

When information from an entity's income tax returns is used as the basis for investor applications and compliance, it is important to recognize the differences that may exist in accounting for investment activity between the information reported on the entity's financial statements (whether audited, reviewed, compiled, or internally prepared) and the information reported on the entity's income tax returns.

The income tax basis of accounting follows the provisions of the federal income tax law. It covers a range of reporting alternatives, from cash to full accrual, depending on the nature of the taxpayer and, in some circumstances, the taxpayer's elections. On the other hand, the entity's financial statements may differ significantly due to the accounting decisions made by the entity.

The Internal Revenue Service (IRS) requires that taxable income be computed under the method of accounting on the basis of which a taxpayer regularly computes income for purposes of keeping its books. This is referred to as the "book conformity requirement."[17]

A taxpayer's accounting records (books) for purposes of applying the conformity requirement may include its regular books of account and other records and data necessary to support the entries in those books and on its tax returns. These records include applicable reconciliations between book and tax income that are maintained as part of the accounting records.[18]

A taxpayer's accounting methods must be used consistently and must reflect income clearly.[19] The IRS has broad powers to prescribe accounting methods when it determines that income has not been reflected clearly. Accounting methods include not only the taxpayer's overall method, such as cash or accrual, but also the special methods used to determine the tax treatment of specific items.

From the perspective of the IRS, acceptable accounting methods by which taxpayers can compute their taxable income include any of the following:[20]

- Cash receipts and disbursements method;
- An accrual method;
- Any other method permitted or required by a specific Internal Revenue Code (IRC) section;[21] or
- Any combination of these methods permitted under regulations (a hybrid method).

The following chart identifies the line item for disclosure of the accounting method used for computing taxable income:

Entity Type	Federal Income Tax Return
Corporations: C Corporations S Corporations	Form 1120, Schedule K, Line 1 Form 1120S, Schedule B, Line 1
Partnerships/ LLCs/LLPs	Form 1065, Pg. 1, Line H
Sole Proprietorships	Form 1040, Schedule C, Line F

The following is an overview of the federal income tax returns, including the primary forms and schedules used to report financial information for corporations, partnerships, and sole proprietorships.

Corporations

C corporations are required annually to file IRS Form 1120, "U.S. Corporation Income Tax Return."

---

[17] Internal Revenue Code (IRC) §446(a).

[18] Treasury Reg. 1.446-1(a)(4).

[19] IRC §446(b).

[20] IRC §446(c).

[21] For example, the percentage-of-completion method for long-term contracts generally required by IRC §460(a).

Form 1120 is a four-page form that includes the following information:

- Page 1 contains information concerning the corporation's income, deductions, and tax payments.
- Page 2 consists of schedules that support amounts on page 1. Schedule A calculates cost of goods sold; Schedule C calculates dividend income and special deductions; and Schedule E reports compensation of corporate officers.
- Page 3 consists of Schedules J and K. Schedule J calculates the corporation's income tax provision, and Schedule K requests corporate information that includes method of accounting and business activity classification.
- Page 4 is in reference to Schedules L, M-1, and M-2. Schedule L contains information concerning the corporation's balance sheet at the beginning and end of its fiscal year. Schedule M-1 is a reconciliation of income (or loss) reported on the corporation's books to the income reported on page 1 of the return. Schedule M-2 reflects the changes in the corporation's capital account during the year.

S Corporations

For federal income tax purposes, S corporations are required to file Form 1120S, "U.S. Income Tax Return for an S Corporation." Form 1120S is a four-page form that requires completion of the following information:

- Page 1 reports information for sales, costs of sales, wages and salaries and other items for the determination of ordinary income or loss from business activities (non-separately stated income and deductions), and tax payments.
- Page 2 consists of schedules that support amounts reported on page 1. Schedule A calculates cost of goods sold, and Schedule B is used for reporting other information about the corporation.
- Page 3 contains Schedule K, which summarizes the corporation's income, deductions, and credits reportable by the shareholders. It presents amounts for both non-separately and each separately stated item.
- Page 4 is in reference to Schedules L, M-1, and M-2. Schedule L contains information concerning the corporation's balance sheet at the beginning and end of its fiscal year. Schedule M-1 is a reconciliation of income (or loss) reported on the corporation's books to the ordinary income reported on page 1 of the return. Schedule M-2 reflects the changes in the corporation's accumulated adjustments, other adjustments, and previously taxed income during the year.

In addition to Form 1120S, S corporations are required to prepare a Schedule K-1 (Form 1120S), "Shareholder's Share of Income, Credits, and Deductions," for each person who was a shareholder during the year. Schedule K-1 reports a particular shareholder's pro-rata share of amounts reported on Schedules K and M-2 of Form 1120S.

Partnerships

For federal income tax purposes, partnerships are required to file Form 1065, "U.S. Partnership Return of Income." Form 1065 is a four-page form that includes the following:

- Page 1 reports information for sales, costs of sales, wages and salaries and other items comprising ordinary income or loss from business activities (non-separately stated income and deductions).
- Page 2 consists of Schedules A and B. Schedule A is a detail of the cost of goods sold calculation. Schedule B requests certain nonfinancial information about the partnership.
- Page 3 refers to Schedule K. Schedule K is primarily a summary of the partnership's income, deductions, and credits reportable by the partners. It presents amounts for both non-separately and each separately stated item.
- Page 4 is in reference to Schedules L, M-1, and M-2. Schedule L contains information concerning the partnership's balance sheet at the beginning and end of its fiscal year. Schedule M-1 is a reconciliation of income (or loss) reported on the partnership's books to the income reported on page 1 of the return. Schedule M-2 reflects the changes in the partners' capital account during the year.

In addition to form 1065, partnerships are required to prepare a Schedule K-1 (Form 1065), "Partner's Share of Income, Credits, and Deductions," for each person who was a partner during the year. Schedule K-1 reports a particular partner's pro-rata share of amounts reported on Schedules K and M-2 of Form 1065.

Proprietorships

Because a sole proprietorship is not a separate taxable entity for tax purposes, proprietorship income or loss is included in the proprietor's personal income tax return. Generally, all proprietorship income and expenses, other than capital gains and losses, employee benefits paid for the proprietor, and proprietor retirement plan contributions should be reported on Schedule C (Form 1040), "Profit or Loss from Business."

A separate Schedule C must be prepared for each proprietorship. Gains or losses from disposal of proprietorship capital assets (such as securities) are reported on Form 4797, "Sales of Business Property," and Schedule D (Form 1040), "Capital Gains and Losses." For tax reporting purposes, there is no requirement to present a balance sheet.

Schedule C is a five-part form consisting of the following:

- Part I contains information about the proprietorship's gross receipts, returns and allowances, cost of goods sold, and other income.
- Part II includes information about the proprietorship's expenses and computes the business's net income or loss.
- Part III calculates the cost of goods sold amount reported in Part I.
- Part IV requests information on the proprietorship's vehicle expenses (if the proprietor is not required to file Form 4562, "Depreciation and Amortization").
- Part V requests an itemized list of "other expenses" reported in Part II.

DECIPHERING INCOME TAX RETURNS: PARTNERSHIP CAPITAL ACCOUNTS, ALLOCATIONS, AND BASIS

Creating and operating a partnership usually involves transfers of property or services from partners to the partnership. Under GAAP, partnerships should record assets or services contributed by partners at their fair market values. For tax purposes, the partnership's basis in the contributed property is generally the contributing partner's adjusted basis in the property. For contribution of services, the amount depends on the whether the partner receives an immediate interest in partnership capital in exchange for contributing services, or if the partner receives only an interest in future profits in exchange for contributing services.

Partner contributions are recorded in the corresponding partner's partner contributions account. Distributions to partners are recorded in each partner's partner drawings account. At the end of the year, partner drawings and partner contributions are closed by transferring the balance to each partner's capital account (along with each partner's pro-rata share of partnership income or loss). As a result, partner's capital accounts are increased by partner contributions and partnership income, and decreased by partnership losses and distributions.

After partner drawings and partner contributions accounts are closed, partner's capital accounts should reflect each partner's interest in the net assets of the partnership.

For tax purposes, a partnership's basis in contributed property is the same as the contributing partner's tax basis in the property. Thus, subject to certain exceptions, partners generally will recognize no gain or loss when they contribute property (including money) to the partnership.

A partnership may distribute cash or property to a partner as a current (non-liquidating) distribution or as a distribution in complete liquidation of a partner's interest. The distributions reduce partner's basis in the partnership (but not below zero). Generally, a partner does not recognize taxable gain when the partnership makes current distributions of cash or property unless the partner receives cash in an amount exceeding the tax basis of his or her partnership interest. Partners do not recognize a taxable gain when they receive a property distribution in complete liquidation of their partnership interests. Partners can recognize a loss on current or liquidating distributions if only cash, receivables, and inventory are distributed and the partnership's tax basis in those items is greater than the tax basis of his or her partnership interest.

Capital Accounts Used in Tax Returns

The partnership capital accounts reported on Form 1065 should agree with the partnership's primary books and records. If the partnership maintains its primary books and records on a GAAP basis, capital accounts should be reported on a GAAP basis. If the partnership keeps its books using some other accounting system, such as the tax basis of accounting, capital accounts should be reported using tax basis accounting.[22]

The following is a summary of the basic differences between capital accounts maintained on a book and tax basis.

Book-Basis Capital Accounts

Each partner has a separate capital account that represents the equity the partner has in the partnership. The partners' share of equity is the amount that would be received if the partnership was liquidated and all the assets were sold at their book value, all liabilities were

---

[22] Form 1065, Instructions for Schedule K-1 and Schedule L.

paid, and the net proceeds distributed. Based on the agreement between the partners, as the partnership conducts trade or business, the capital accounts will increase or decrease based on how they will share in partnership profits and losses. The following is a general summary of items affecting the book capital account:[23]

    Fair Market Value (FMV) of asset or cash contributed
- Liabilities on asset assumed by partnership
= Initial book capital account balance
+ Additional cash and property (at FMV) contributed by partner
+ Allocations of partnership income or gain
+ Allocations of partnership tax-exempt income
- Cash distributed to the partner
- FMV of property distributed to partner net of liabilities secured by the property
- Allocations of nondeductible partnership expenses
- Allocations of partnership losses and deductions
= Book capital account balance at end of year

Tax-Basis Capital Accounts

In contrast to the book approach to maintaining the partnership capital accounts, a partnership's books may be maintained on the tax basis of accounting, which will reflect the adjusted basis of the assets contributed and property distributed instead of FMV. The following is a general summary of items affecting the capital account maintained on the tax basis of accounting:[24]

    Adjusted basis of asset or cash contributed
- Liabilities on asset assumed by partnership
+ Gain recognized by partner (if any) on contributed property
= Beginning tax-basis capital account
+ Additional cash or property at adjusted basis contributed by partner
+ Allocations of partnership income or gain
+ Allocations of partnership tax-exempt income
- Cash distributed to the partner
- Adjusted basis of property distributed to partner net of liabilities secured by the property
- Allocations on nondeductible partnership expenses
- Allocation of partnership losses and deductions
= Tax-basis capital account balance at end of year

Book capital accounts reflect the FMV of property at contribution date and tax-basis capital accounts reflect the adjusted basis. Book-capital accounts reflect the FMV of the property at the date of distribution and tax-basis capital accounts reflect the adjusted basis of the property at the date of distribution. The capital account balances are reported on Schedule K-1 under Item N, the balance sheet on Schedule L, and Schedule M-2 of Form 1065.

Because any of several different methods can be used to report partners' capital accounts, users should not rely automatically on the Schedule K-1 capital account information to be an accurate calculation of either a partner's tax-basis or book capital account unless the user has specific knowledge of how the return was prepared.

Economic versus Tax Allocations

Generally, partnerships have a written partnership agreement that sets out the partners' duties and the allocation to those partners of the partnership's economic and tax items. The partnership agreement governs both the allocation of economic items among the partners (dictating how partners agree to divide the partnership's economic results) and the allocation of taxable income, gain, loss, deduction, and credit among the partners. However, tax allocations cannot be made independently of the corresponding economic results of the partnership and should follow the related economic allocations made under the partnership agreement.[25]

The basic rule is that tax allocations must be made to reflect the manner in which the partners have agreed to share the economic benefit or burden corresponding to the taxable income, gain, loss, deduction, or credit that is allocated.

Many partnerships allocate income, losses, and deductions on a pro-rata basis, but some partnerships make special allocations. If special allocations are made that are independent of the economic results of the partnership, there is a risk, upon audit, that these allocations will not be respected by the IRS.

In order for partnership allocations to be respected by the IRS, they either must meet the objective standards outlined under the substantial economic effect rules, or the allocations must be made

---

[23] IRS Partnership Audit Technique Guide.
[24] Id.

[25] IRC §704(a).

in accordance with the partners' interests in the partnership, a more subjective requirement.

The rules for determining whether a tax allocation has substantial economic effect and for determining a partner's interest in the partnership are similar. The purpose of both tests is to ensure each tax allocation matches the partners' agreed allocations of the corresponding economic results according to their economic agreement.

Basis in Partnership Taxation

Documentation supporting the investment activity may include tax-basis information provided by the investor-petitioner. Basis has two separate applications in partnership taxation. Inside basis is the basis of the partnership in its assets. Outside basis is the basis of the partner in the partnership interest.

Basis has an impact on every partnership transaction and is the tax record used to track virtually every partnership transaction. Basis is the key to determining gain and loss on distributions, the basis of distributed property, and gain or loss on the disposition of a partnership interest. Basis also limits the partner's ability to deduct losses that flow through from the partnership. The determination of basis is the reason liabilities are important in partnership taxation.

RELATIONSHIPS BETWEEN SCHEDULES K, L, M-1, AND M-2 OF FORM 1065 AND THE SCHEDULE K-1 CAPITAL ACCOUNT RECONCILIATION

Schedule K

Schedule K (Form 1065, "Partners' Distributive Share Items") summarizes the various partnership tax items allocated to each of the partners on their Schedules K-1. Schedule K ties Form 1065 together with Schedules K-1. For example, Schedule K includes partnership trade or business ordinary income (from Form 1065, Page 1, line 22) on line 1, and a portion of this amount is then reported on line 1 of each of the partner's Schedules K-1.

Schedule K-1

Schedule K-1 (Form 1065, "Partner's Share of Income, Credits, and Deductions") is completed for each person who was a partner during the year. Schedule K-1 reports on a particular partner's pro-rata share of amounts reported on Schedule K.

In addition, Schedule K-1 reflects all economic activity during the year that affects the partner's capital interest. Item N of Schedule K-1 ("Partner's Capital Account Analysis") should reflect a partner's pro-rata share of amounts reported on Schedule M-2 under the partner's capital account analysis section. Allocable amounts from Schedule M-2 include increases and decreases to the partner's total capital during the year.

Item N of Schedule K-1 includes five line items:

Line 1		Beginning Capital Account Balance
Line 2	+	Capital contributed during the year
Line 3	+/–	Current year increase or decrease
Line 4	–	Withdrawals or distributions
Line 5		Ending Capital Account Balance

The capital accounts shown on item N of Schedule K-1 are often tax-basis capital accounts, determined using a tax-basis partnership balance sheet. It is not uncommon for the Schedule K-1 capital accounts to be based on IRC §704(b) safe harbor book principles, or on GAAP. From the disclosure on Schedule K-1, it is important to note the accounting method upon which the Schedule K-1 capital accounts have been prepared.

The Schedule K-1 capital account analysis for all partners should agree to amounts presented on Schedules K, L, M-1, and M-2 of Form 1065.

The amounts in the capital account analysis Item N on the partners' Schedules K-1 should equal the amounts on the corresponding lines of Schedule M-2 on Form 1065, page 4. Specifically:

Schedule K-1 Item N	Corresponding Lines in Schedule M-2
Lines 1 and 2	Should equal partner's share of lines 1 and 2, respectively
Line 3	Should equal partner's share of lines 3, 4, and 7
Line 4	Should equal partner's share of line 6
Line 5	Should equal partner's share of line 9

In some situations, the only way to be sure Schedule K-1 has been prepared properly is to reconcile the amounts reported on the various Schedule K-1 lines to the amounts in the partner's Schedule K-1 capital account reconciliation.

All "profit and loss" items (based on the partnership's accounting methods used in maintaining capital accounts) for the year should flow through the capital account analysis. Any regular tax item of income, gain, loss, or deduction passing through to the partner (other than guaranteed payments) should be included in item N, line 3 "current year increase (decrease)" of the Schedule K-1.

Schedule L

Instructions to Schedule L (Form 1065) state that the balance sheet should agree with the entity's books and records. For example, if the partnership's books and records are kept on a GAAP basis, the Schedule L balance sheet also should be reported on a GAAP basis.

Schedule L is found on the following IRS forms by entity type:

Entity	Form
Corporations	Form 1120 and 1120S, Page 4
Partnerships/LLCs/LLPs	Form 1065, Page 4
Sole Proprietorships	Not used

Schedule M-1

Schedule M-1 ("Reconciliation of Income [Loss] per Books With Income [Loss] per Return") is designed to reconcile book partnership income reported on Schedule L to line item amounts reported on Schedule K (and on each partner's Schedule K-1).

Differences between net income per the books and taxable income from the tax return are reported on Schedule M-1 of the entity's tax return (or Schedule M-3 for corporations with assets of $10 million or more).

Schedule M-1 ties the partnership's book income to the taxable income or loss shown on the analysis of net income (loss) at the top of page 4 of Form 1065. However, even if the partnership uses tax-basis accounting, reconciling items often appear on Schedule M-1.

The following is an overview of Schedule M-1 line items including examples of book/tax differences:

Line 1—Book Income (or Loss)
Line 2—Income Subject to Tax Not Recorded on Books in the Current Year
- Prepaid interest received;
- Prepaid rent received;
- Prepaid subscriptions; and
- Realized capital gains on previously accrued trading security gains.

Line 4—Expenses Recorded on Books Not Deducted on the Return
- Book depreciation in excess of tax depreciation;
- Travel and entertainment expenses in excess of deductible amounts;
- Reserves for warranty expenses;
- Bad debt expense when tax reporting uses specific charge-off method;
- Allowances for returns not recognized for tax purposes until occurrence; and
- Differences in amortization of intangible assets.

Line 6—Income Recorded on Books Not Included on the Return
- Unrepatriated income from foreign subsidiaries;
- Rent prepaid in a prior period;
- Tax-exempt interest (permanent difference); and
- Accrued capital gains on trading securities not yet realized.

Line 7—Deductions Not Charged Against Book Income in the Current Year
- Tax depreciation in excess of book depreciation;
- Compensation related to the exercise of non-qualified stock options; and
- Realized capital losses on previously accrued trading security losses.

Schedule M-2

Schedule M-2 of Form 1065 is a detail of total partner capital from the beginning of the tax year to the end. The sum of the amounts from all partners' Schedules K-1 should equal the total partnership amount on the corresponding line of Schedule M-2.

Allocable amounts from Schedule M-2 include increases and decreases to the partner's total capital during the year.

Schedule M-2 and Schedule L should agree and reflect the basis of book accounting.

Schedule M-2 ("Analysis of Partners' Capital Accounts") includes nine line items (check line numbers to schedule):

Line 1	Beginning balance
Line 2a	Cash contributed
Line 2b	Property contributed
Line 3	Net income or loss per books
Line 4	Other increases
Line 5	Subtotal
Line 6a	Cash distributed
Line 6b	Property distributed
Line 7	Other decreases

Line 8   Subtotal
Line 9   Ending balance

The amounts in the capital account analysis on the partnership's Schedule M-2 on Form 1065, page 4, should equal the aggregate amounts of the corresponding lines on the partners' Schedules K-1. (See chart under Schedule K-1, *supra*.)

INITIAL INVESTMENT

Although the focus on this article has been ongoing compliance, documentation necessary to establish the applicant's original investment often requires going beyond financial statement representation to tracing and examining supporting information from the originating source documents, including bank statements, wire-transfer instructions, and reconciliations to the books and records of the designated entity. This is necessary to determine:

- That the transaction was completed and investor balance reflects all cash transactions;

- That the designated entity possesses all the rights of ownership and has disclosed any obligations stemming from the cash investment;

- That the cash investment has been properly valued and any necessary allocation was made correctly (holding foreign currency may require additional analysis); and

- That existence or occurrence of the cash investment can be substantiated; negotiable securities are confirmed; and inquiries made regarding other transactions and written or oral arrangements, such as contingent liabilities, lines of credit, compensating balances, security agreements, and direct liabilities on loans.

In order to verify the investment information, it may be necessary to trace the initial deposit(s) from the originating source. Researching bank statements, deposit slips, and transaction searches before and after the investment in question will often prove helpful in verifying investment data.

SUMMARY

Activity of the entity should be monitored and reviewed over the two-year conditional permanent residence period to determine that the investment satisfies the legal standard for removal of the conditions. The primary sources for this information are the detailed books and records of the entity and the financial statements. The financial statements are prepared from a selection of various accounting principles and methods, which may be based on GAAP or OCBOA.

After the initial investment is made, accounting for the applicant's investment will vary due to entity type, accounting policies, industry regulations, and the nature and extent of any distributions, loans, salaries, employee benefits, and related-party transactions. In situations where financial statements are not available or appear unreliable, review of applicant information may be limited to tax returns, accounting detail, and other filings. Keep in mind that while immigration applications require specific dollar amounts in response to questions surrounding a petitioner's investments and a company's net worth, arriving at appropriate figures in response to these questions will require a detailed case-by-case analysis of the individual's and company's available reporting information.

TAX IMPLICATIONS OF AND PLANNING FOR IMMIGRANT AND NONIMMIGRANT VISAS

by Albert S. Golbert and Miriam J. Golbert[*]

Introduction 359
General U.S. Federal Income Tax Rules 360
Overview and Importance of Estate Tax Planning 361
Determination of Tax Residency Status 363
Immigration vs. Nonimmigration: View From the
  Tax Bridge 367
Federal Estate Taxation of Foreigners 368
U.S. Situs Property 373
Noncitizen Spouses Qualified Domestic Trust 375
Pre-Immigration Planning Issues 383
Pre-residence Income Tax Planning (Summary) 388
Post-Residence Income Tax Planning/Reporting: Dual
  Residence 389
Federal Estate/Gift Taxation And Planning Opportunities . 390
Departure Planning 391
Conclusion 394
U.S. Gift Tax Treaties in Force 394
U.S. Estate Tax Treaties in Force 394

---

[*] The original version of this article was adapted from a *Special Edition* of the *California International Practitioner* in 2004, and published with the permission of the State Bar of California International Law Section. The authors have updated the material for this volume.

Albert Golbert is a principal in Golbert & Associates in Los Angeles and has more than 50 years of experience practicing law in Europe, the Far East, and California in the areas of international business law and taxation. He has written four books and over 50 articles on these subjects, and has been a leader in the State and Los Angeles County Bar Associations Sections of International Law and Taxation. He was certified as a Specialist in Taxation Law by the California Board of Legal Specialization of the State Bar of California in 1973 and has taught at the USC Law Center, Loyola Law School, UC Davis, UCLA, Southwestern University School of Law, and Whittier Law School.

Miriam Golbert has practiced law in Los Angeles for more than 28 years in the areas of estate planning, taxation of trusts and estates, probate, trust administration, conservatorships, and guardianships. Since 2001, she has been a partner in Glaser, Weil, Fink, Jacobs, Howard & Shapiro, LLP, where she concentrates on estate planning for high net-worth individuals, noncitizens, and nonresidents. She is co-author of Marshall & Garb, *California Probate Procedure* (5th ed.), and has taught estate and gift taxation and wills and trusts at Loyola Law School and Laverne College of Law.

INTRODUCTION

Tax planning should ideally be coordinated with the immigration planning for all employment and investment-related visas. Although most immigration practitioners are familiar with the term *residency* for immigration purposes and some for customs purposes, all practitioners who deal with aliens—whether they be *resident* or *nonresident* aliens for immigration or business law purposes—should have at least some familiarity with the term for purposes of U.S. taxation, lest they do their clients a grave disservice! Since the Tax Reform Act (TRA) of 1984 (which added §7701(b) to the Internal Revenue Code (IRC or the Code[1]), it has become easier for the non-tax specialist to offer guidance to clients on questions of U.S. tax residency.

Prior to the TRA, a knowledge of tax jurisprudence and practice is required to opine on the issue of tax residence. Since January 1, 1985, the issues are essentially statutory and generally capable of ascertainment by a practitioner who is not a tax specialist. There are, as always, sensitive issues of statutory interpretation. Nevertheless, the following should provide the non-tax practitioner with the essential basic information to determine whether an alien client has already become a U.S. resident for income or estate[2] and gift taxation, or both (one can be *resident* for income taxation and *nonresident* for estate and gift taxation), and to determine whether to

---

[1] Unless otherwise noted, all references to IRC or Code hereinafter are to the Internal Revenue Code of 1986, as amended.

[2] The enactment of the Economic Growth and Tax Relief Reconciliation Act of 2001, forecast major changes to the transfer tax system beginning in 2010. The estate and generation-skipping transfer taxes (but not the gift tax) are repealed for 2010. Unless modified by Congress, the transfer tax rules in effect prior to the implementation of the 2001 Act will be revived in 2011. Because of the short duration of the repeal, estate tax issues and generation-skipping transfer tax issues are discussed in this article as if the repeal were not in effect. The reader should understand that the rules will again be in effect as of January 1, 2011, but should also be aware that there may be congressional changes during the period leading up to January 1, 2011.

recommend that an alien consult a tax practitioner (and not leave it to the alien to make an uninformed decision for himself or herself!).

The classification by the immigration laws of aliens as either *immigrant* or *nonimmigrant* are not necessarily a helpful distinction for tax purposes.

- Immigrants, often referred to as *permanent residents* or *aliens lawfully admitted for permanent residence*, are generally treated as residents, at least for federal income tax purposes.[3]

- Nonimmigrants, typically persons not necessarily seeking to enter the United States on other than a temporary basis, may nevertheless be treated as resident for federal income tax purposes. Illegal immigrants may also become tax residents under the rules outlined below.

This discussion will focus on U.S. income, estate and gift tax issues, and probate concerns for nonresident aliens. Because aliens who are residents in the United States for estate and gift tax purposes (*i.e.*, U.S. domiciliaries, as discussed below) are treated like U.S. citizens for federal estate[4] and gift tax purposes, their estate and probate concerns will not be extensively considered. However, the last two sections of this article consider: (1) various pre-immigration planning concerns for the alien contemplating becoming a U.S. resident for income, estate, and gift tax purposes; and (2) the 1996 federal tax legislation applicable to the outbound use of foreign trusts.

This article does not address tax, probate, and heirship rules under the laws of foreign jurisdictions, or under the laws of the various states. However, the laws of an alien client's home jurisdiction will frequently dictate what planning is appropriate for the individual's U.S. activities and investments. Often the U.S. estate planner must coordinate his or her efforts with advisers in the home jurisdiction.

GENERAL U.S. FEDERAL INCOME TAX RULES [5]

Aliens considered nonresident for U.S. income tax purposes are taxed only on their U.S. source income (which may or may not be alleviated by applicable tax treaties) and income effectively connected to their U.S. trade or business.

Aliens considered resident for U.S. income tax purposes are subject to U.S. income taxation on their worldwide income. In addition, a number of other detrimental tax consequences follow the acquisition of residency for U.S. income taxation:

- any U.S. corporation owned by an alien may be classified as a personal holding company with its attendant U.S. tax consequences;

- a foreign corporation may be classified as a foreign personal holding company,[6] a passive foreign investment company or a controlled foreign corporation with attendant U.S. tax consequences, including reporting obligations;

- the application of IRC §367 where the alien makes a property transfer to a foreign entity;

- U.S. grantor trust provisions apply to an alien settling a foreign situs trust; and

- an alien beneficiary of a foreign situs trust may become subject to U.S. tax on his or her aliquot share of the income from such trust if the alien were the settlor,[7] or the trust were a *foreign grantor* trust or if the settlor is deceased and the alien beneficiary is considered to be a U.S. tax resident.

Foreign investors often *think* they want *Green Cards* (or evidence of permanent residence, *viz.*, I-551 status), but often would settle for something less committed if they derive significant income from sources foreign to the United States, and fully un-

---

[3] IRC §7701(b)(1)(A)(i).

[4] The exception is that there are special marital deduction rules that apply to transfers to noncitizen spouses while the estate tax is in effect. *See infra* discussion on "Noncitizen Spouses Qualified Domestic Trust."

[5] *Vide*: Albert S. Golbert, "Taxation of Aliens: A Practitioner's Guide," 1 *The California International Practitioner* 22, for a more complete discussion of the federal income tax residency rules (hereinafter Golbert, "Taxation of Aliens").

[6] The foreign personal holding company (FPHC) rules have been repealed for tax years of foreign corporations beginning after December 31, 2004, and tax years of U.S. shareholders whose tax year ends with or within the FHPC's tax year. American Jobs Creation Act of 2004, Pub. L. No. 108-357.

[7] *Vide* footnote 19 and accompanying text, *infra*.

derstood the effect of such status on their ex-U.S. source income liable to taxation.[8]

On the other hand, certain investors and intending immigrants (regardless of the temporary nature of their current visa status) may have no fear of U.S. taxation as it appears almost salubrious when compared to that to which they may be subject in their country of origin. These aliens will, nevertheless, benefit from tax advice in order to claim treaty protection, if any, and to benefit from available tax credits against their U.S. liability for income taxes paid in other countries.[9]

Benefits of residency status include:

- the deductibility of foreign source losses against U.S. source income;
- the ability to file a joint return and entitlement to other deductions, exclusions, and credits unavailable to a nonresident; and
- the ability to minimize or avoid altogether foreign taxes on foreign source income under the extensive U.S. tax treaty network.

OVERVIEW AND IMPORTANCE OF ESTATE TAX PLANNING

Beginning in 2011, federal estate taxes in the United States will be imposed at a maximum rate of 55[10] percent.[11] Moreover, again in 2011 the generation-skipping transfer tax[12] will seek to impose two taxes on a wealthy individual's federal estate before that estate can pass from the decedent to his grandchildren. Thus, a grandchild would stand to receive only about 20 percent of a foreign client's estate, if the two taxes (estate and generation-skipping transfer) are imposed.

The thoughtful adviser for foreign clients often must be the one to raise estate tax concerns, since the concepts involved in estate planning, especially U.S. estate planning, may be totally unfamiliar to the foreign client. Some foreign countries do not impose estate and gift taxes and have procedures for transferring assets to beneficiaries that are quite different from the procedures in the United States. Moreover, even brief and limited U.S. contacts may create potential estate, as well as income, tax exposure for the foreign client. Fortunately for the foreign client, most federal estate tax liability can be avoided, or substantially mitigated, provided the client carefully plans his or her U.S. activities in advance. The need for advance planning becomes even more acute for the foreign client planning to immigrate to the United States. As discussed further below, perhaps 90 percent or more of the U.S. estate and gift tax planning for a foreign client will focus on two fundamental concepts:

First: Avoiding U.S. residency (*i.e.*, U.S. domicile); and

Second: Avoiding ownership of U.S. situs assets.

Nonresident Aliens

For federal estate tax purposes, the estate of a nonresident alien includes only defined U.S. situs property at the time of his or her death.[13] Estates of nonresident aliens, dying on or after November 10, 1988, incur estate tax liability at the same rates imposed on estates of U.S. citizens and residents (*i.e.*, in 2011 up to a maximum rate of 55 percent).[14]

---

[8] While most foreign investors are not averse to paying U.S. taxation on their U.S. source income, they are often most upset to learn that they may be liable for U.S. taxation on their non–U.S. source income as well!

[9] For example, Iranian immigrants who correctly declared and paid U.S. federal income taxes on their Iran-sourced income in the 1970s were able to claim foreign expropriation losses when their Iranian properties were seized in the 1980s. Such losses were not available to those whose status did not require that they declare (or, who otherwise failed to declare) such income.

[10] *See* IRC §2001(c)(2).

[11] Under the Economic Growth and Tax Relief Reconciliation Act of 2001, Pub. L. No. 107-16 (2001 Act), there will be no estate tax in 2010 unless Congress seeks retroactively to impose an estate tax in 2010, but this provision remains in effect only for one year unless re-enacted. *See* discussion of the 2001 Act, below. Note also that the 2001 Act contains many new provisions and modifications of existing provisions, which will affect estate and gift tax planning. They are too numerous to discuss in detail in this article.

[12] IRC §§2601 *et seq. Note*: Beginning in 2004, the generation-skipping tax exemption amount for any calendar

continued

year is equal to the estate tax applicable exclusion amount under §2010(c) for that calendar year.

[13] IRC §2103.

[14] IRC §2101(b). *But see supra*, note 10. For estates of decedents dying in 2005, the top estate and gift tax rate is 47 percent (on amounts over $2 million). For decedents dying prior to November 10, 1988, the maximum estate tax rate on nonresident aliens was 30 percent. *See* Technical and Miscellaneous Revenue Act of 1988 (TAMRA), Pub. L. No. 100-647, §5032.

Nonresident alien donors now also incur federal gift tax at the same rates applicable to U.S. citizens and residents on their gifts of U.S. situs property. Significantly, for the application of the federal gift tax to nonresident aliens, the definition of U.S. situs gifts is much more limited than the definition of U.S. situs property, which is included in the taxable estate of a nonresident alien decedent; the nonresident alien donor incurs federal gift tax only on gifts of real and tangible (not intangible) personal property situated in the United States.[15]

The nonresident alien decedent is generally entitled to a $13,000 credit against his or her federal estate tax liability.[16] Notwithstanding the several modifications in the exemption available to U.S. citizens and residents, the exemption and credit available to nonresident aliens has not changed. Significantly, unlike domestic donors, the nonresident alien donor is not entitled to any unified credit against his or her gift tax liability.[17]

The United States has entered into estate and gift tax treaties with other countries that may alter the rules with respect to aliens from the signatory countries.[18]

U.S. Citizens and Resident Aliens

U.S. citizens and resident aliens are subject to federal estate tax on their worldwide assets.[19] Similarly, federal gift tax applies to worldwide gifts of a U.S. citizen or resident alien.[20] While a credit is available to the domestic decedent against the federal estate tax for foreign estate or similar death taxes paid to a foreign country on assets located in that country,[21] no credit is available for foreign gift taxes. U.S. citizens and resident aliens receive an applicable exclusion for estate tax purposes of $1 million in 2011. and 2005. Step-up and step-down basis will end and modified carryover basis will apply for property acquired from a decedent after December 31, 2009.[22] Record-keeping becomes extremely important. The available aggregate basis increase will be limited to $1.3 million, with an additional *spousal* basis increase of $3 million.[23]

Estate and gift taxes have now been officially "de-linked." Effective in 2002, the exemption for gift tax purposes was increased to $1 million and it will remain at that amount,[24] notwithstanding the increase in the applicable exclusion for estate tax purposes and notwithstanding repeal of the estate tax (for one year) in 2010. Section 901 of the Economic Growth and Tax Relief Reconciliation Act of 2001 (2001 Act)[25] is a sunset provision whereby all provisions of and amendments made by the 2001 Act cease to apply after December 31, 2010, and all provisions will revert to their status as of the date of enactment, unless the provisions are re-enacted by Congress.

Transfers to Spouses: Qualified Domestic Trust

For federal estate and gift tax purposes, a marital deduction is generally allowed for property passing to the decedent's or donor's spouse.[26] But, in the case of a spouse who is not a U.S. citizen, the marital deduction for federal estate tax purposes is allowed only for property passing to the spouse in a "qualified domestic trust" (QDOT),[27] a trust having some but not all of the benefits of the better-known QTIP (marital deduction trust applicable to certain transfers in trust to spouses who are U.S. citizens). The purpose of the QDOT is to assure that the assets passing to the noncitizen spouse are subject to federal estate tax upon the spouse's death. The rules and planning considerations with respect to the QDOT are discussed further below. Moreover, no gift tax deduction under §2523 is available for gifts to noncitizen spouses, but annual tax-free gifts to a noncitizen spouse of $100,000 are permitted.[28] A nonresident alien can take advantage of the marital deduction for gifts to a spouse who is a U.S. citizen.[29]

---

[15] IRC §§2501(a)(2), 2511(a).

[16] IRC §2102(c).

[17] IRC §2505(a).

[18] The United States currently has eight gift tax treaties in force and 17 estate tax treaties in force. *See* Lists of Treaties in Force at the end of this article.

[19] IRC §2031(a).

[20] IRC §2511(a).

[21] IRC §2014.

[22] IRC §1014(f), *as amended by* 2001 Act, §541.

[23] New IRC §1022. These amounts will be indexed for inflation.

[24] *See* IRC §2505(a)(i). The top gift tax rate under the 2001 Act will be 35 percent after 2009.

[25] Pub. L. No. 107-16.

[26] IRC §§2056(a), 2523(a).

[27] IRC §2056(d). *See* IRC §2056A.

[28] IRC §2523(i). This sum is adjusted annually for cost-of-living increases.

[29] IRC §2523(i), *as amended by* Omnibus Budget Reconciliation Act of 1989, Pub. L. No. 101-239, §7815(d)(2) (1989 Act).

DETERMINATION OF TAX RESIDENCY STATUS

Is the Client Foreign? An Overview.

Different rules apply for federal income tax purposes, federal estate, and gift tax purposes to determine whether an alien is a resident or nonresident of the United States. The fact that an alien constitutes a resident for income tax purposes under §7701(b), discussed below, does not necessarily mean that the alien will be treated as a resident for federal estate and gift tax purposes. Familiarity with the definitions of resident alien for both federal income tax purposes and federal estate and gift tax purposes are advisable for anyone representing individual alien clients with U.S. activities or investments.

Lawful Permanent Resident

An alien individual would be deemed to be a U.S. resident for income tax purposes when lawful permanent residence (Green Card status) has been acquired pursuant to the Immigration and Nationality Act (INA),[30] or falls within the terms of the *substantial presence test*.

Nonresident Alien

If neither of these tests is met, the alien is deemed to be a *nonresident alien* for purposes of U.S. income taxation.[31]

Lawful Permanent Resident Test

If an alien individual has been granted the status of lawful permanent resident under the INA, is physically present in the United States even one day in a calendar year following receipt of such status, and the same has not been surrendered, revoked nor administratively or judicially determined to have been lost or abandoned, then such individual is treated as a resident alien of the United States for the full calendar year. For Green Card holders, income tax residency is totally divorced from the length of physical presence in the United States. Hence, one who returns to the United States only a few days each year to maintain permanent residence status for INA purposes may be a resident alien for income tax purposes.[32]

Substantial Presence Test

This is essentially a numerical test satisfied if an alien is physically present in the United States for a certain number of days either in a current calendar year or over a three-year sequence, as follow:

- if the alien is physically present in the United States for 183 days or more during the calendar year; or
- if the sum of the days the alien is physically present in the United States during the current calendar year plus one-third the number of days the alien is physically present in the United States during the preceding calendar year plus one-sixth the number of days the alien is physically present in the United States during the second preceding calendar year, equals or exceeds 183 days (*i.e.*, whether the alien has been in the United States, on average, 122 days or more over the three-year period). An alien is treated as physically present in the United States on a given day if physically present at any time during such day. Thus, the day of arrival as well as the day of departure will count.

Exempt Individuals

An alien is treated as not being present in the United States on any day such individual is treated as an exempt individual. There are four categories:

Foreign Government Related Individuals

These include individuals holding, generally, an A visa or one that the Secretary of State determines represents full-time diplomatic or consular status; individuals who are full-time employees of an international organization (generally G-4 visa holders); and individuals who are members of the immediate family (spouse or child) of an individual described above. Domestics, apparently, are not included, nor does the exemption include nongovernmental income.

---

[30] Immigration and Nationality Act of 1952, Pub. L. No. 82-414, 66 Stat. 163 (*codified as amended at* 8 USC §§1101 *et seq.*) (INA).

[31] By definition, a U.S. citizen can *never* be deemed to be nonresident for income tax purposes (even if *residing abroad*) because a citizen cannot ever be termed an *alien*. Neither does this rule apply to estates and trusts nor to estate and gift taxation.

[32] If such individual is a *dual resident* of the United States and a country with which the United States has a tax treaty, the issue may be resolved by recourse to the treaty tie-breaker provisions of the treaty. However, any permanent resident seeking to claim such treaty benefits is required to take a treaty-based return position by filing a tax return.

Teachers and Trainees

The presence of any individual temporarily in the United States under INA §101(a)(15)(J) (other than a student) is disregarded for substantial presence test purposes if he or she:

- has substantially complied with the visa requirements (by not accepting employment in violation of the visa terms); and

- has not claimed exemption for any two calendar years during the preceding six calendar years as a teacher, trainee, or student.

This exemption applies for only two years, and J visa-holders will be treated as resident in the third and subsequent calendar year periods if they spend at least 183 days in the United States.

Students

Individuals who are temporarily present in the United States under INA §§101(a)(15)(F) or 101(a)(15)(J), and who substantially comply with the requirements of such status, may claim exemption from the substantial presence test as a teacher, trainee, or student for five calendar years. Each such person will be treated as a resident alien in the sixth calendar year unless, in addition to substantial compliance with the terms of the visa, it can be shown that the alien student has no intention of residing permanently in the United States. For an F visa holder without income, it is immaterial whether the exemption applies. However, if an F visa holder is the recipient of foreign source income, it is important that substantial compliance be maintained, or that tax planning be effected, in order, alternatively, to avoid resident status or U.S. taxation of such foreign source income.

Professional Athletes Present for Charitable Sports Events

A professional athlete is one who is temporarily present in the United States to compete in a charitable sports event as described in the Code.

Exceptions from Substantial Presence

Individual with Medical Condition

An individual with a medical condition is not treated as present in the United States on any day if such individual was unable to leave the United States due to a medical condition that arose while the individual was present in the United States. On the other hand, an alien who comes to the United States for medical treatment and stays long enough to satisfy the substantial presence test will be treated as a resident alien of the United States.

Commuters From Canada and Mexico

Regular commuters from Canada and Mexico are not treated as being present in the United States on any day on which they commute. In order for this exemption to apply, the alien must have a place of residence in Canada or Mexico from which he or she regularly commutes to a place of employment in the United States.

Days in Transit

For an individual in transit between two points outside the United States, physical presence in the United States for less than 24 hours shall be disregarded for purposes of the substantial presence test.

The 31-Day Exception

An alien individual present in the United States for less than 31 days in any calendar year is not treated as a resident alien of the United States for such calendar year under the substantial presence test.

The Closer Connection (*Tax Home*) Exception

An alien who is present in the United States for fewer than 183 days in the current calendar year, but who qualifies as a resident alien under the substantial presence test, will be treated as a nonresident alien for the current calendar year, provided that the following conditions obtain:

- The alien individual establishes that for the current calendar year he or she has a *tax home*[33] in a foreign country and has a closer connection with such foreign country than with the United States;[34] and

- The alien individual neither had an application pending for adjustment of status nor took other steps to apply for status as a lawful permanent

---

[33] The term *tax home* has the same meaning it has in IRC §911(d)(3), which, in turn, refers to IRC §162(a)(20) relating to travel expenses while away from home.

[34] The Secretary of the Treasury has issued regulations requiring aliens claiming the foreign tax home exemption to file annual statements setting forth the basis on which such exemption is claimed. A passive claim of exemption is inadequate, and the alien will have to file a timely tax return (1040NR) in order to do so. *See* Reg. §301.7701(b)-8 with regard to the statement that must be filed by an alien individual claiming the closer connection exception pursuant to Reg. §301.7701(b)-2.

resident of the United States at any time during the calendar year.

The filing of U.S. Citizenship and Immigration Services (USCIS) Form I-130 by a relative of the alien is disregarded for purposes of the closer connection/tax home exception that becomes unavailable only when the alien individual takes an affirmative step to seek permanent resident alien status (*e.g.*, by filing USCIS Form I-485). The filing of an application for Labor Certification (Form ETA 9089) by a prospective employer would probably be sufficient to void the exception since the alien must sign Form ETA 9089.[35]

Tax Residence Under Income Tax Treaties

Determination of the fact of *residence* under the laws of one country will have no direct effect on such finding under the laws of another. Most countries tax residents on their worldwide income, thereby possibly subjecting (in the absence of applicable tax credits, if any) an unfortunate alien found to be considered resident in two (or more!) countries to double taxation. Modern income tax treaties contain *tie-breaker* provisions addressing the problem of dual residence and proffer solutions. The request by an alien to the *Competent Authority* under such a treaty[36] may, however, trigger a USCIS enquiry into the possible abandonment of permanent residence status.

Residence for Estate and Gift Tax Purposes

The Concept of Domicile

The test under §7701(b) for determining income tax residency is a relatively straightforward, mechanical one. That is not the case for determining whether an alien is a resident of the United States for federal estate and gift tax purposes. An alien for these purposes is determined to be a resident where he or she maintains his or her domicile. Whether a person is a domiciliary or nondomiciliary of the United States depends on the person's intentions. The Treasury Regulations provide:

A *resident* decedent is a decedent who, at the time of his death, had his domicile in the United States . . . . A person acquires a domicile in a place by living there, for even a brief period of time, with no definite present intention of later removing therefrom. Residence without the requisite intention to remain indefinitely will not suffice to constitute domicile, nor will intention to change domicile effect such a change unless accompanied by an actual removal. . . .

A *nonresident* decedent is a decedent who, at the time of his death, had his domicile outside of the United States under [these] principles. . . .[37]

Domicile requires not only residency, but an intent to remain permanently.[38] Thus, an alien individual may be a resident for U.S. income tax purposes, but a nondomiciliary for estate and gift tax purposes.[39] However, if the individual intends to remain in the United States on a permanent basis, he or she will be a domiciliary of the United States.

Though the alien's intention is of paramount importance in determining his or her domicile, the courts and tax authorities must often rely upon extrinsic evidence in order to determine the alien's domicile, particularly when the issue arises in an estate tax context.[40] Among other items, consideration should be given to the location and relative importance of dwellings maintained by the alien inside and outside the United States, the location of the alien's valued personal possessions, and the location of the alien's family, friends, and important social contacts. It is possible for an individual to give up his or her domicile and establish a domicile in a new location, but the case law establishes a presumption that the old domicile continues where a change of domicile is alleged.[41]

Thus, if an alien wishes to establish that he or she is not a U.S. domiciliary, care must be taken to minimize U.S. contacts and to evidence the alien's

---

[35] There are relatively complex rules for determining the beginning and ending dates of residency as well as anti-avoidance rules. *See* Golbert, "Taxation of Aliens," *supra* note 5.

[36] Under U.S. income tax treaties, the Commissioner of Internal Revenue has been designated the U.S. Competent Authority.

[37] Treas. Reg. S 20.0-1(b).

[38] *Estate of Jan W. Nienhuys*, 17 T.C. 1149 (1952).

[39] *Commissioner v. Patino*, 186 F.2d 962 (4th Cir. 1950); *Stallforth v. Helvering*, 77 F.2d 548 (1935), *cert. denied*, 296 U.S. 606.

[40] *See, e.g., Estate of Valentine v. Commissioner*, 21 B.T.A. 1971 (1930), *acq.* X-1 C.B. 4, 67; *Jellinek v. Commissioner*, 36 T.C. 826 (1961), *acq.* 1964-1 C.B. 4.

[41] *Estate of Bloch-Sulzberger*, 6 TCM 1201, 1203 (1947); *Mitchell v. United States*, 88 Wall. 350; *Estate of Rienhuys*, 17 T.C. 1149, 1159 (1952).

intent to maintain his or her permanent home in a foreign country. If possible, the alien should actually maintain a home in a foreign country, as well as a current driver's license and voting rights in the foreign country. Similarly, the alien should prepare a will declaring his or her country of domicile.

The duration of an alien's stay in the United States will not necessarily be determinative of his or her status as a domiciliary or nondomiciliary of the United States.[42]

U.S. Possession Residents

A decedent who was a U.S. citizen and a resident of a U.S. possession at the time of his or her death is generally considered, for estate tax purposes, as a U.S. citizen.[43] However, the decedent will be considered a nonresident alien if he or she acquired his or her U.S. citizenship solely by reason of: (1) his or her being a citizen of the possession; or (2) his or her birth or residence within the possession.[44]

Impact of Estate and Gift Tax Treaties

The potential for double taxation of the same assets by the United States and a second country may clearly arise for U.S. citizens and residents because they are subject to estate and gift taxation on their worldwide assets. In addition, the potential for double taxation may arise even with respect to nonresident aliens because of conflicting rules in the United States and foreign jurisdictions on the situs of property and the domicile of the decedent or of the beneficiary. Bilateral estate and gift tax treaties are designed to mitigate the potential for double taxation.[45]

Older estate and gift treaties[46] attempted to mitigate the potential for double taxation by focusing on the situs of the property and by limiting taxation to the jurisdiction in which the property was located.[47] More modern treaties place more emphasis on the domicile of the taxpayer.[48] They generally provide that the country of the transferor's domicile may tax estates and gifts and generation-skipping transfers on a worldwide basis, but must credit the tax paid to the other state on the basis of the location or situs of the property.

The Organization for Economic Cooperation and Development (OECD) and the Treasury Model Conventions contain specific rules to determine the domicile of the taxpayer. However, the treaties generally do not attempt to modify the definition of domicile given by one of the contracting countries. The determination of a single domicile for purposes of the estate and gift tax treaties is important since the country of domicile has the primary right to tax transfers or deemed transfers of property wherever located, other than real property, business property of a permanent establishment, and assets pertaining to a fixed base, which are subject to local primary tax jurisdiction.

Under the OECD Model Convention, a person is domiciled in one treaty country if his or her estate or gift, under the law of that state, is liable to tax therein by reason of the domicile, residence, or place of management of that person or any other criterion of similar nature. A person is not considered domiciled in one country if his or her estate or gift is taxable in that country only with respect to property situated therein.[49]

As with income tax treaties, estate and gift tax treaties generally contain "tie breaker" rules to determine the domicile of the taxpayer in case he or she is considered domiciled in both countries.[50] *Residence* pursuant to U.S. federal estate and gift tax rules may be summarized as follows:

- residence for estate and gift tax purposes is the equivalent of *domicile*;
- domicile requires physical presence in a particular place coupled with an intent to make that place a fixed and permanent home;

---

[42] *See Estate of Valentine v. Commissioner*, 21 H.T.A. 197 (1930), *acq.* X-1 C.B. 4, 67 (five years of absence from the United States not sufficient to establish domicile abroad). *But see Cooper v. Reynolds*, 24 F.2d 150 (D. Wyo. 1927) (decedent held to be a U.S. domiciliary when he died accidentally shortly after arriving in the United States where the facts indicated that he intended to reside permanently in the United States).

[43] IRC §2209.

[44] *Id.*

[45] *See* Lists of Treaties in Force at the end of this article.

[46] *See, e.g.*, OECD Model Draft Convention for the Avoidance of Double Taxation With Respect to Taxes on Estate and Inheritances, Paris 1966.

[47] *See, e.g.*, UK-U.S. Gift and Estate Tax Treaty, Article 9.

[48] *See, e.g.*, OECD Model Double Taxation Convention on Estate and Inheritances and on Gifts, Paris 1982; Treasury Department, Model Estate and Gift Tax Treaty, 1980.

[49] OECD Model Convention, Art. 4(1).

[50] *See, e.g.*, OECD Model Convention, Art. 4(2), and Treasury's Model Convention, Art. 4.2.

- a person may have more than one residence, but only one domicile.[51] Hence, it is possible for an individual to be resident in one place and domiciled in another;

- different jurisdictions may reach different conclusions with respect to the place of such domicile and the decision of one is not binding on the other;[52] and

- although the tests of residence and domicile differ, U.S. courts will probably apply the tests extant prior to IRC §7701(b) (*i.e.*, pre-1985) in determining a conflict between the two.

None of the foregoing discussion applies to U.S. citizens subject to U.S. taxation on worldwide income as well as to federal estate and gift taxation regardless of the *residence* of the U.S. citizen.

IMMIGRATION VS. NONIMMIGRATION: VIEW FROM THE TAX BRIDGE

Since 1990, the expansion of the tax base has been affected by the shift of policy away from family unification to the attraction of investors and skilled immigrants. If this expansion is accomplished by would-be immigrants, they will become tax residents. Persons seeking to avoid tax resident status should continue to enter the United States in nonimmigrant status.

Since 1990, immigration bills have been clearly tilted toward those who seek immigrant status:

- Visas available for employment-based immigration increased from 54,000 annually to 140,000;

- Foreign investors may now gain access to immigration visas by the act of investing in a U.S. trade or business; and

- Hong Kong immigration has been facilitated and has increased exponentially.

In addition to the changes affecting immigration, a number of changes impact upon nonimmigrant areas. These are particularly important for tax motivated aliens purposefully seeking to enter the United States in a status that will not, *ipso facto*, cause them to become U.S. tax residents. Moreover, employers should also be made aware of effect of tax residency on their employees, in that many executives agree to work for temporary periods in the United States in consideration of a *tax equalization* agreement pursuant to which the employer agrees to reimburse the employee the amount of additional taxes caused by virtue of the acceptance of such *foreign* (to the employee) assignment. If the employee gets caught in the web of global U.S. taxation without proper tax planning and advice, it may be his or her employer who will be obligated to effect reimbursement!

H-1B Visas

The H-1B visa was designed to permit employers to gain authorization for the temporary employment of professional workers. Although the requirements for the visa were made more stringent and the annual number of H-1B admissions originally capped at 65,000, the requirement that the alien maintain a residence abroad was deleted. From the standpoint of tax planning, if the alien fails to maintain a residence abroad, the *foreign tax home* exception to the physical presence test will be lost and the number of days such alien is permitted annually to stay in the United States without being treated as a tax resident is reduced from 182 to 121! Moreover, retention of the foreign residence will be important to the alien in maintaining foreign domicile for U.S. gift and estate tax purposes.

In addition to the foregoing tax considerations, if the alien is successful in maintaining a foreign *tax home*, he or she may be allowed to deduct *away from home* expenses while in the United States that would include qualified lodging and costs of meals and travel.[53]

In addition to other restrictions, the H-1B visa also requires the employer to make certain attestations and public disclosures that some foreign entities may find unpalatable. Hence, the choice of nonimmigrant visa will require more complete analysis than that which has typically been associated with it, *i.e.*, the *whatever will work* school of immigration practice should be closed for the duration. In this regard, various requirements for qualifying for L and E visas have been eased and such visas are viable and often more appropriate alternatives to the H visa. For example:

Treaty Trader/Treaty Investor (E) Visas

The E visa (E-1 Treaty Trader and E-2 Treaty Investor) allows individuals who are nationals of a foreign country that is a signatory of a treaty of

---

[51] *Cf. supra* note 24 and accompanying text.

[52] *Id.*

[53] IRC §911(d)(3), referring to IRC §162(a)(2). *Cf.* Treas. Reg. §1.911-2(d), which provides that a tax home is an individual's regular or principal place of business.

commerce and navigation with the United States to enter as nonimmigrants to "carry on substantial trade, including trade in services or trade in technology" or to "develop and direct the operations of an enterprise in the United States in which they have invested, or are actively in the process of investing, a substantial amount of capital."

Moreover, such visas also are available to countries such as Australia and Sweden under Bilateral Investment Treaties and to Canada and Mexico under the North American Free Trade Agreement (NAFTA).

L-1 Visas

The L-1 visa permits the transfer of managers, executives, or persons of specialized knowledge who have been continuously employed for at least one out of the past three years preceding his or her application for admission by the same firm or corporation or an affiliate or subsidiary thereof to enter the United States temporarily to continue to render services to the same employer or a subsidiary or affiliate thereof in a capacity that is managerial, executive or involves specialized knowledge.

Like H-1Bs, L-1s are not subject to the usual nonimmigrant requirement that a residence be maintained abroad that the alien has no intent to abandon.

Moreover, the alien need not be employed by the petitioning U.S. employer on a full-time basis (INS Operations Instructions (OI) 214.2(l)(5)(ii)(B)), making the L-1 an ideal visa for executives of foreign-based parent companies who need to travel to the United States on frequent and extended periods of time to oversee the operations of a U.S. subsidiary but who wish to remain a nonresident for U.S. income tax purposes.

O Visas

O visas are for foreign individuals of extraordinary ability in the arts, sciences, education, business, or athletics and for certain aliens accompanying or assisting them, and their family members, according to INA §101(a)(15)(O).

The O-1 is for the principal alien with "extraordinary" ability, and the individual is required to have sustained national or international acclaim and must be seeking to enter the United States to work in his or her field.

FEDERAL ESTATE TAXATION OF FOREIGNERS

Overview

Once it is determined that the alien client is a nondomiciliary of the United States, it must be determined what assets will be included in the nonresident's gross estate and be taxable for federal estate tax purposes. The taxable gross estate of the foreign decedent is then reduced by certain permitted deductions. The federal estate tax imposed on the nondomiciliary's net taxable estate is calculated according to the same tax rate schedule applicable to U.S. citizens and residents, but the nondomiciliary receives a substantially smaller federal estate tax credit against the resulting liability (*i.e.*, $60,000 of exemption for the nondomiciliary versus an exemption of $1 million available to a U.S. citizen or resident in 2011).[54]

Determination of Gross Estate

Property Situated in United States

The taxable estate of a foreign domiciliary includes only the foreign decedent's property that is situated in the United States. The situs rules for determining where property is situated for federal estate tax purposes are discussed below. While the nondomiciliary's property situated outside of the United States does not enter into his or her taxable federal estate, the amount of his or her non-U.S. property (*i.e.*, the size of his or her "entire gross estate")[55] may be relevant for other purposes (*e.g.*, for purposes of calculating allocable deductions).[56]

Parallel to Estates of U.S. Citizens and Residents

Aside from excluding property situated outside the United States, the federal taxable estate of the foreign decedent would generally be determined according to the regular federal estate tax rules applicable to U.S. citizens and residents. For example, the rules of §§2035 through 2038, which draw certain recently or incompletely transferred assets back into the estate of a domestic decedent, would be applicable to draw similar assets into the foreign decedent's federal estate, provided the transferred assets were

---

[54] *See* IRC §§2101, 2102(b), and 2106.
[55] *See* Treas. Reg. §20.2103-1.
[56] *Id. See also* IRC §2106(b).

situated in the United States at the time of the transfer or upon the date of death.[57]

Deductions

General Allocation

An allocable portion of the administration and other expenses of the foreign decedent's worldwide estate are deductible from the aggregate amount of the foreign decedent's U.S. situs property, provided the expenses would be deductible for purposes of calculating the net taxable estate of a domestic decedent.[58] The portion of these expenses allocable to the U.S. situs assets is found by multiplying the deductions of the worldwide estate by a fraction the numerator of which is the fair market value of the U.S. situs assets and the denominator of which is the fair market value of the worldwide assets.[59] In order to be permitted a deduction for the allocable share of deductions, the executor of the foreign decedent must disclose the value of the foreign decedent's non-U.S. situs assets.[60]

Charitable Deductions

Charitable deductions for bequests to domestic charitable corporations and trusts that will use the gifts for charitable purposes in the United States are deductible in full, without any prior allocation between assets located within and without the United States.[61]

Debt

The gross fair market value of U.S. situs assets encumbered by nonrecourse debt will be reduced by the amount of the debt on the date of death.[62] Generally, recourse debt of the decedent will be allocated between the domestic and foreign situs assets of the decedent for purposes of determining the decedent's net taxable estate.[63]

Transfers to Spouse

The Technical and Miscellaneous Revenue Act of 1988 limited the ability of domestic decedents to transfer their property and obtain tax deferral if the spouse is not a citizen of the United States. These rules apply equally to foreign nonresident alien decedents.[64] Prior to the 1988 law change, the foreign decedent was not allowed a marital deduction.[65] In order to take advantage of the marital deduction, a foreign decedent must transfer U.S. assets to a noncitizen spouse through a QDOT. On the other hand, the foreign decedent will be entitled to the full marital deduction, without regard to the existence of a QDOT, for transfers to a spouse who is a U.S. citizen.

Credits

Unified Credit

The nonresident decedent's estate is allowed a credit of $13,000 (equal to an exemption of $60,000) against the base federal estate tax liability under §2101.[66] A decedent from a U.S. possession who is treated as a nonresident alien under §2209 for federal estate tax purposes is entitled to a credit equal to the greater of either: (1) $13,000; or (2) the portion of $46,800 which the value of the decedent's U.S. situs gross estate bears to the value of his or her worldwide gross estate.[67]

If an estate treaty obligation so requires, the foreign decedent from the treaty country is entitled to an estate tax credit equal to that portion of the applicable credit amount as the value of the decedent's U.S. situs gross estate bears to the value of his or her

---

[57] Treas. Reg. §20.2104-1(b). *But see* LTR 9507044 (May 31, 1994) (in a technical advice memorandum, the Service concludes, under §2104(b), that a foreign decedent (DOD: Aug. 16, 1991), who had a retained life interest in a foreign trust, must include in her taxable U.S. estate the fair market value of all the trust's assets, even though the trust held only foreign situs assets at the time of the decedent's death, since the decedent had funded the inter vivos trust in 1923 with only U.S. situs assets; the ruling concludes that because U.S. situs assets were transferred to the trust initially, §2104(b) taints the trust's assets indefinitely, even if the U.S. assets are sold and reinvested in foreign situs assets).

[58] Treas. Reg. §20.2106-1(a).

[59] IRC §2106(a); Treas. Reg. §20.2106-2(a)(2).

[60] IRC §2106(b); Treas. Reg. §20.2106-1(b).

[61] IRC §2106(a)(2). *See* Tech. Adv. Memo 199925043 (Mar. 8, 1999) where a full deduction was allowed under §2106 for an NRA's bequest to a foreign hospital. The Service allowed the interpretation of the governing instrument to refer to the hospital's U.S. affiliate so as to permit the deduction in full.

[62] *Estate of Harcourt Johnstone v. Commissioner*, 19 T.C. 44 (1952).

[63] *See Rodiek v. Helvering*, 87 F.2d 328 (2d Cir. 1937).

[64] IRC §2106(a)(3). *See* "Pre-Immigration Planning Issues" section, below.

[65] *See* Treas. Reg. §20.2106-1(b) [obsolete].

[66] IRC §2102(c)(1).

[67] IRC §2102(c)(2).

worldwide gross estate.[68] The amount of the credit so allowed must be further reduced for the amount of any credit allowed the decedent for gift tax purposes.

Other Credits

The estate of the foreign decedent was previously entitled to a credit for state death taxes allocable to the U.S. situs assets.[69] The foreign decedent's estate is also entitled to the §2012 credit for gift taxes previously paid on gifts included in the value of the donor's gross estate on his or her death. Similarly, the foreign decedent's estate is entitled to a credit under §2013 for estate taxes paid on prior transfers.

Significantly, the foreign decedent's federal estate is not generally entitled to a credit for foreign death taxes under §2014. The absence of the foreign death tax credit for the nonresident alien decedent is appropriate since the foreign death tax credit is available only for foreign death taxes attributable to foreign situs property and federal estate tax only applies to the U.S. situs property of a foreign decedent.[70] The legislation in 1996 provides for a credit for foreign death taxes imposed on the estate of certain former citizens who gave up their U.S. citizenship for tax avoidance purposes.[71]

Generation-Skipping Transfer Tax

Overview

The generation-skipping transfer tax (GST) imposes a tax payable either when:

- a trust that skips a generation below the grantor undergoes a taxable termination or distribution to the grantor's grandchildren (or other specified "skip person"s);[72] or

- when an individual makes a direct transfer to a skip person.[73]

Every individual currently has a GST exemption equal to the applicable exclusion amount under IRC §2010(c) for the year in question.[74] Note also that because the GST tax is a flat rate equal to the maximum estate and gift tax rate in effect at the time of the GST transfer (multiplied by the inclusion ratio), the increases or reduction in the estate tax rates will cause a corresponding increase or reduction in the GST tax rate. Note also that under current law, when the estate tax is fully phased out in 2010, the GST tax will also be phased out.

Regulations Address NRA Transfers

Treasury regulations contain a specific section addressing the application of the GST tax to transfers by nonresidents, noncitizens of the United States (NRAs).[75] For these purposes, an individual is a resident or citizen of the United States if the individual is a resident or citizen of the United States for purposes of the Chapter 11 estate tax or Chapter 12 gift tax (*i.e.*, the U.S. domiciled alien is a U.S. resident). The Treasury regulations address the application of the GST tax to transfers of both U.S. situs and non-U.S. situs property by NRAs.

U.S. Situs Property

On December 26, 1995, Treasury issued final regulations that revised substantially the Treasury's position with respect to transfers by nonresidents, not citizens of the United States.[76] The proposed regulations had made transfers subject to the GST tax if the transferor was a nonresident alien and the transferred property was situated in the United States because of either estate or gift tax rules. Under the final regulations, a transfer will be subject to the GST rules under the following circumstances: (1) for direct skips, only to the extent that the transfer is subject to U.S. estate or gift taxes within the meaning of Treasury regulations §26.2652-1(a)(2);[77] or (2) for taxable distributions and taxable terminations, only to the extent that the initial transfer of property to the trust by an NRA transferor was subject to estate or gift tax within the meaning of Treasury regulations §26.26521(a)(2).[78] If a single trust created by an NRA is in part subject to chapter 13 and in part not subject to chapter 13, the GST exposure is determined by the application of an *applica-*

---

[68] IRC §2102(c)(3).

[69] IRC §§2102(a), 2102(b). Note that under the 2001 Act, the State Death Tax Credit (SDTC) has been repealed and in 2005, the SDTC was replaced by a deduction under new IRC §2058.

[70] IRC §2014 (a).

[71] IRC §2107(c)(2). This legislation is discussed in "United States Situs Property," below.

[72] *See* IRC §2613.

[73] IRC §2601 *et seq.*

[74] IRC §2631(c).

[75] Treas. Reg. §26.2663-2.

[76] *Id.*

[77] *See* Treas. Reg. §26.2663-2(b)(1).

[78] *See* Treas. Reg. §26.2663-2(b)(2).

ble fraction to establish the taxable and nontaxable portions of the trust.

Impact of Estate Tax Treaties

The United States has 17 estate tax treaties in force with foreign countries.[79] As mentioned above, estate tax treaties generally contain situs rules that may vary from those of the IRC. Furthermore, treaties generally tend to allocate jurisdiction to tax to the state in which the decedent was domiciled and not to the state in which the property is located. The treaties provide major exceptions for real property and business property associated with permanent establishment or a fixed base. With respect to these types of property, treaties generally allocate jurisdiction to tax to the state in which the property is located.

Moreover, estate tax treaties may increase the availability of the credit for estate taxes paid to the other contracting state[80] and allow a marital deduction[81] to the estate of decedents domiciled outside the United States. Finally, estate tax treaties generally contain a nondiscrimination clause.

Gift Taxation of Foreigners

Taxable Gifts

A nonresident alien donor is subject to gift tax on transfers of only real property and tangible personal property situated within the United States.[82] The rules for determining where property is situated and whether it constitutes tangible or intangible property are considered below.[83] The GST should apply to a nonresident alien's lifetime gifts of tangible U.S. situs property to skip persons.

Annual, Spousal, and Support Gifts

Foreign donors of U.S. situs real estate or tangible personal property can take advantage of the annual exclusion of only $13,000 per donee exclusion for gifts of present interests in property.[84] A spouse who is not a citizen of the United States may no longer benefit from the unlimited marital deduction for gifts between citizen spouses under IRC §2523.[85] However, the noncitizen spouse can receive annual gifts of up to $100,000 (as indexed annually for cost-of-living increases) tax-free, provided, in the case of gifts made after June 29, 1989,[86] the gift would have otherwise qualified for the marital deduction.[87] These limitations on gifts to noncitizen spouses apply to donors who are U.S. citizens and resident aliens, as well as nonresident aliens. The 1989 Act clarified that the marital deduction is available for a nonresident alien's transfers to a spouse who is a U.S. citizen.[88]

A foreign donor should be able to take advantage of the gift tax exclusion for transfers by gift on behalf of another individual to educational institutions and medical care providers to pay for educational and medical expenses.[89]

No Gift Splitting

The benefit of §2513, which permits a donor to elect with his or her spouse to treat a gift as being made one-half by each of them, is expressly limited to spouses who are citizens or residents of the United States at the time of the gift and, therefore, is not available to a nonresident alien donor.[90]

---

[79] *See* Lists of Treaties in Force at the end of this article.

[80] *See, e.g.*, Art. 9, United States—United Kingdom Estate and Gift Treaty, C.C.H. Tax Treaties, ¶8228. *See also* Tech. Adv. Memo 9750002 (Aug. 20, 1997), permitting the estate of a Canadian citizen domiciled in Canada who died in 1992 to claim benefits under the Revised Protocol to the 1980 U.S.-Canada Income Tax Convention for estate property with a U.S. situs. Similarly, on December 14, 1998, the United States and Germany signed a Protocol amending the December 3, 1980, Convention of Estates, Inheritances, and Gifts that will go into force upon exchange of instruments of ratification, but to a limited extent, the Protocol will be applicable to decedents dying after November 10, 1988. The provisions include a limited U.S. estate tax marital deduction for noncitizen spouses, a pro-rata unified credit (or exemption equivalent) for property within the United States.

[81] *See, e.g.*, Art. 8, United States—United Kingdom Estate and Gift Treaty, C.C.H. Tax Treaties, ¶8228H.

[82] IRC §§2511(a), 2501(a)(2). But see IRC §2501(a)(3) for the special rule permitting gifts of U.S. intangible assets of 10-year tax expatriates to be taxed. *See* "United States Situs Property" section, below.

[83] *See* "United States Situs Property" section, below.

[84] *See* IRC §2503(b). The annual exclusion has increased in 2002 by reason of indexing for inflation.

[85] IRC §2523(i).

[86] 1989 Act, §7815(d)(1)(B).

[87] IRC §2523(1)(2) (post-1989 Act). *See* IRC §2523(b) (life estates or terminable interest).

[88] 1989 Act, §7815(d)(2).

[89] *See* IRC §2503(e).

[90] IRC §2513(a)(1).

No Unified Credit

While the standard, domestic estate and gift tax credits can be applied against gift tax (as limited by the Code Section) or estate tax (as provided in IRC §2010), the nonresident alien donor is not entitled to any standard credit against his or her federal gift tax liability.

1996 Legislation: U.S. Donee Report

In conjunction with the federal tax legislation revising the rules applicable to the tax treatment of foreign trusts, Congress in 1996 imposed a reporting obligation generally on U.S. persons receiving foreign gifts or bequests of more than $10,000 during the year.[91] A §501(c) tax-exempt organization is not required to report such gifts.[92] The Internal Revenue Service (IRS) requires a U.S. trust to report gifts made in trust. A U.S. person who fails to report foreign gifts is subject to a penalty of 5 percent of the amount of the gift for each month that the failure to report continues, to a maximum of 25 percent.[93] Further, in the absence of the required report, Treasury can determine the tax treatment of the unreported gift (*e.g.*, treatment as a taxable distribution of a foreign trust's current or accumulated income).[94] The history of the legislation provides that Treasury's exercise of this authority should receive a high degree of deference and will be subject to judicial review only under an arbitrary and capricious standard.[95] The concern of the Treasury Department and Congress was that otherwise, taxable distributions from foreign trusts would be mischaracterized by U.S. recipients as nontaxable gifts or bequests. Such concern was heightened by the 1996 legislation's general repeal of the foreign grantor trust rules.[96]

In Notice 97-34,[97] the Service provided guidance with respect to the reporting requirements for the foreign trust and foreign gift provisions of §§6039F and 6048. Section VI of the Notice pertains to "foreign gifts." Foreign gifts are defined as any amount received from a person other than a U.S. person that the recipient treats as a gift, but excludes qualified transfers within §2503(e)(2) relating to transfers for educational or medical expenses, or any distribution properly reported under §6048(e). Reporting is to be made on IRS Form 3520. Sufficient information is required for the Service to determine whether the gift is truly a gift or whether it is income. Form 3520 does not require the foreign donor to be identified, unless the donor is a foreign corporation or a foreign partnership.

Notwithstanding the statute, the Service has modified the reporting thresholds. Aggregate gifts from nonresident aliens or foreign estates are to be reported only if the total exceeds $100,000 during the taxable year. In such case, each gift in excess of $5,000 is to be identified, but the donor does not have to be identified. Aggregate gifts from foreign corporations and partnerships in excess of $10,000 ($11,000, as adjusted for inflation, for gifts in 2002) are to be reported. In this case, the donor must be identified.[98] The Notice provides aggregation rules for gifts from related parties or entities.[99]

Gift Tax Treaties

The United States has entered into eight gift tax treaties.[100] As in the case of estate tax treaties, gift tax treaties usually confer general jurisdiction to tax to the state in which the donor is domiciled and not to the state where the property is located. Important exceptions to the general rule are provided for real property and for business assets of a permanent establishment or a fixed base, which may be taxed in the state in which the property is located. Gift tax treaties may confer on donors domiciled in the treaty country the right to use a portion of the unified credit (or its equivalent) to offset gift tax liability.[101] Gift tax treaties may also allow a marital deduction to foreign donors domiciled in foreign jurisdictions

---

[91] The 1996 legislation on foreign trusts was in the Small Business Job Protection Act, Pub. L. No. 104-188, §§1901 *et seq.* (hereinafter SBA 96). The 1996 legislation amending the 10-year expatriation tax regime of IRC §§2017, 2501(a)(3), and 877 was the Health Insurance Portability and Accountability Act, Pub. L. No. 104-191, §511 (hereinafter HIA 96). *See* IRC §6039F, as added by SBA 96, §1905(a).

[92] IRC §6039F(a).

[93] *Id.* at §6039F(c).

[94] *Id.*

[95] *See, e.g.,* Staff of Joint Comm. on Taxation, 104th Cong. 2d Sess., General Explanation of Tax Legislation Enacted in the 104th Congress 276 (Comm. Print 1996) (hereinafter 104th Congress Bluebook).

[96] *See* IRC §672(f), *as amended by* SBA 96.

[97] 1997-1 C.B. 422.

[98] *Id.* Notice 97-34 at Section VI.B.1 and 2.

[99] *Id.* at Section VI.B.3.

[100] *See* Lists of Treaties in Force at the end of this article.

[101] United States-Japan Estate and Gift Tax Treaty (Apr. 16, 1954).

and may expand the availability of the charitable deduction.[102]

U.S. SITUS PROPERTY

Overview

Only the nonresident alien decedent's property situated in the United States is subject to the federal estate tax; a nonresident alien donor is subject to federal gift tax only on gifts of real estate and tangible personal property situated in the United States. Thus, it is crucial to review the nonresident alien's property holdings, classify them properly, and determine their situs.

Real Estate Interests

The situs of real estate is determined by its physical location.[103] It must be determined what law resolves the classification of property interests and whether specific interests in land constitute real property under the applicable law.[104] Security interests[105] and leasehold interests[106] have not generally been held to constitute real property.

Tangible Personal Property

The situs of tangible personal property is determined by its physical location at the time of death.[107] However, tangible personal property that is in transit and has obtained only a temporary situs in the United States will not be subject to U.S. estate tax. Thus, in *Delaney v. Murchie*,[108] the First Circuit determined that personal jewelry in the possession of a nonresident alien who died during a temporary visit to the United States was not situated in the United States for federal estate tax purposes.

For both estate and gift tax purposes, the IRS takes the position that currency is tangible personal property and is subject to federal gift tax if it is gifted within the United States and is subject to federal estate tax to the extent it is located in the United States on the date of the foreign decedent's death.[109] The IRS has ruled that even currency that is held in a bank safety deposit box in the United States on the date of the foreign decedent's death will have a U.S. situs and not fall within the bank deposit exception discussed below.[110]

Code Exclusions

Overview

Though certain property would clearly be situated in the United States under the generally applicable principles, the IRC deems certain property to have a situs outside the United States, so a foreign decedent's estate will not incur federal estate tax on the transfer of these assets.[111]

Works of Art

Works of art owned by nonresident aliens will not be deemed to be property within the United States if the works of art are imported into the United States solely for exhibition by a nonprofit public gallery or museum and were on exhibition at the nonprofit gallery or museum (or in transit with respect to that exhibition) at the time of the owner's death.[112]

Deposits

A foreign decedent's deposits with domestic banks and savings institutions or amounts held by insurance companies will not be subject to estate tax, unless the deposits are effectively connected with the conduct of a trade or business within the United States.[113] Deposits with foreign branches of U.S. banking corporations or partnerships will not

---

[102] United States-France Estate and Gift Tax Treaty (Nov. 24, 1978).

[103] Treas. Reg. §§20.2104-1(a)(1), 20.2105-1(a)(1), 25.2511-3(b)(1).

[104] *Morgan v. Commissioner*, 309 U.S. 78 (1940). *See Estate of Perigny v. Commissioner*, 9 T.C. 782 (1947), *nonacq.*, and *Fair v. Commissioner*, 91 F.2d 218 (3d Cir. 1937), in which unusual rights in land were held to constitute real property.

[105] *See Estate of Tarafa y Armas v. Commissioner*, 37 H.T.A. 19 (1938), *acq.* 1938-1 C.B. 30.

[106] *Estate of Perigny v. Commissioner*, 9 T.C. 782 (1947), *nonacq.*

[107] Treas. Reg. §§20.2104-1(a)(2), 20.2105-1(a)(2), 25.2511-3(b)(1.).

[108] 177 F.2d 444 (1st Cir. 1949).

[109] *See* Treas. Reg. §20.2104-1(a)(7). *But see* IRC §2105(b), discussed below (special exclusion for bank-type deposits).

[110] Rev. Rul. 55-143, 1955-1 C.B. 465.

[111] IRC §2105.

[112] IRC §2105(c); Treas. Reg. §20.2105-1(b).

[113] IRC §§2105(b)(1), 871(i)(3). In Tech. Adv. Memo 9748004 (Aug. 19, 1997), the Service ruled that the interest of a decedent in a unit investment trust (UIT) was not an asset situated in the United States for estate tax purposes under IRC §2105(b)(3). However, shares in three regulated investment companies (RIGs) were includable in his U.S. estate (as U.S. situs assets) for estate tax purposes.

be deemed to constitute property within the United States.[114] Significantly, the benefits of these rules do not extend to cash held in domestic brokerage firms. Funds held by the Treasury do not qualify for this exception.[115]

Portfolio Debt

Portfolio debt obligations issued by U.S. obligors after July 18, 1984, the date of enactment of the Tax Reform Act of 1984, are also deemed to be property situated outside the United States.[116]

Debt of 80/20 Companies

Debt obligations issued by U.S. corporations (so-called "80/20 companies") that meet the "80 percent foreign business requirement" of §861(c)(1) will also not be treated as U.S. situs property for estate tax purposes.[117] For this purpose, debt obligations of a domestic corporation generally are not considered U.S. situs property so long as the corporation derives at least 80 percent of its gross income from the conduct of an active foreign business during the three years prior to the foreign decedent's death.

Insurance Proceeds

Insurance proceeds received on a policy on the life of a foreign decedent are deemed to be property situated outside the United States.[118] Since a life insurance policy is an intangible, foreign donors can generally make gifts of life insurance policies that are issued by domestic life insurance companies without incurring gift tax liability.[119]

Payments under an annuity contract do not fall within the life insurance exception and, therefore, an annuity payable by a domestic person has been treated as U.S. situs property.[120]

Intangible Personal Property

Overview

Foreign donors' gifts of intangible personal property are not subject to gift taxation.[121] There is an important exception to this rule for tax-motivated former citizens during the 10-year period after their loss of U.S. citizenship. For these individuals, gifts of U.S.-situs intangible personal property are subject to a new transfer tax.[122]

Interests in Entities

Corporations

The stock of a domestic corporation is deemed situated within the United States, while stock of a foreign corporation is deemed situated outside the United States regardless of where the stock certificates are located or the source of the corporation's income.[123] The situs rules for corporations are a key planning tool in the international area. These rules permit nonresident aliens to hold their U.S. situs assets, including U.S. real estate and shares of domestic corporations, through foreign corporations and avoid federal estate tax, as well as gift tax on transfers of the shares of the foreign corporation. Attention to corporate formalities is required. If these formalities are not followed, the corporation may be disregarded, and the U.S. situs assets in the corporation may be treated as owned by the nonresident alien shareholders.[124]

Partnerships

The IRS has ruled that a partnership interest has its situs where the partnership business is conducted.[125] Notwithstanding the IRS's position, proper treatment of partnership interests is unclear. Where a foreign entity, which held U.S. assets, terminated by operation of foreign law on the death of the foreign decedent, and the entity's assets were distributable to the estate of the deceased partner, the Second Circuit held that the foreign decedent's

---

[114] IRC §2105(b)(2).

[115] Rev. Rul. 56-421, 1956-2 C.H. 602.

[116] IRC §2105(b)(3). *See* IRC §871(h). *But see* PLR 9422001 (Feb. 16, 1993) (short-term obligations not portfolio obligations).

[117] IRC §§2104(c), 861(a)(1)(A).

[118] IRC §2105(a).

[119] *See* IRC §2501(a)(2).

[120] *Guarantee Trust Co. v. Commissioner*, 16 B.T.A. 314 (1929).

[121] *But see* IRC §2501(a)(3).

[122] *See* "Caveat re: Expatriation" under "Federal Estate/Gift Taxation and Planning Opportunities" section, below.

[123] IRC §2104(a); Treas. Reg. §§20.2104-4(a)(5), 20.2105-1(f); Rev. Rule 54-407, 1954-2 C.B. 657.

[124] *Fillman v. United States*, 355 F.2d 632 (Ct. Cl. 1966).

[125] Rev. Rul. 55-701, 1955-2 C.B. 836.

estate is subject to federal estate tax on a pro rata portion of the entity's U.S. assets.[126]

Foreign Entities

Extreme care must be taken in dealing with interests in foreign entities where the foreign entities hold U.S. situs property.[127] Consideration should be given to obtaining an opinion of foreign counsel to determine whether the entity will terminate upon the nonresident alien's death and what rights the nonresident alien holds in the assets held by the foreign entity.

Debt Obligations

Except for the special exceptions for portfolio obligations, deposit-type obligations, and obligations of 80/20 companies, as discussed above, debt obligation of a U.S. person, the United States, or a state or any political subdivision of the United States, will constitute U.S. situs property.[128] Obligations of foreign debtors generally have their situs outside the United States even if the foreign debtor is engaged in a U.S. trade or business.

Benefits from a pension or other retirement plan would most likely be treated as debt obligations and have their situs where the plan trustees reside. Similarly, claims of an income beneficiary to undistributed income on the date of the beneficiary's death are claims against the trustee that would probably have its situs where the trustee resides or in the jurisdiction in which a corporate trustee is incorporated.

NONCITIZEN SPOUSES QUALIFIED DOMESTIC TRUST

Overview

Under IRC §2056, a federal estate tax marital deduction is available for assets passing outright to a surviving spouse, for assets passing to a general power of appointment trust for the benefit of the surviving spouse, for assets passing to an "estate trust" and for assets passing to a "qualified terminable interest property trust" (a QTIP Marital Deduction Trust) for the benefit of the surviving spouse. After November 10, 1988, a marital deduction is disallowed for assets passing to a spouse who is not a U.S. citizen. This means that estate taxes are payable on transfers at death to a noncitizen spouse—a situation markedly different from assets passing to a citizen spouse in which transfers are generally free of estate tax under the provisions of IRC §§2056(a), 2056(b)(5), and 2056(b)(7). Why the change and the singling out of noncitizen spouses? Legislative history reveals that Congress was fearful that noncitizen surviving spouses would move themselves and the assets they received offshore and that the tax deferral goals of the estate tax marital deduction would be thwarted.[129] The IRC does, however, provide an exception to the requirement that estate tax be paid on the death of the first spouse if the surviving spouse is a noncitizen. The exception is that the transfer to or for the benefit of the surviving spouse must be to a "qualified domestic trust" (QDOT) established for the benefit of the noncitizen surviving spouse.[130] The goal of the QDOT legislation is to provide tax deferral, but also to ensure that estate taxes are paid: (1) when principal distributions are made from the QDOT; (2) when the Trust ceases to qualify as a QDOT; or (3) at the time of death of the surviving spouse, whichever is the first to occur.

For purposes of the rules governing transfers to a noncitizen spouse, the citizenship, residency, or nonresidency of the decedent is irrelevant. Thus, a nonresident alien for U.S. situs assets (as well as a U.S. citizen or resident for their worldwide assets) may establish (and should consider establishing) a QDOT under §2056A for assets passing to a noncitizen spouse. Section 2056A was added in 1988 by TAMRA,[131] revised by the 1989 Act[132] and the Revenue Reconciliation Act of 1990 (1990 Act)[133] and applies to decedents dying after November 10, 1988.[134]

---

[126] *Sanchez v. Bowers*, 70 F.2d 715 (2d Cir. 1934).

[127] *See* the "check-the-box" regulations. Treas. Reg. §301.7701-2 (T.D. 8697). The regulations are issued under §7701(a), which sets forth definitions under the IRC, including the estate, gift, and GST tax rules. Thus, it would appear that a foreign entity's tax treatment under the regulations should control for federal estate and gift purposes.

[128] IRC §2104(c).

[129] In the legislative history, Congress pointed out that "[p]roperty passing to an alien surviving spouse is less likely to be includible in the spouse's estate, since to avoid taxation on the worldwide estate, the spouse need only give up U.S. residence." H.R. Rep. No. 795, 100th Cong., 2d Sess. 592 (1988).

[130] IRC §2056(d).

[131] TAMRA, §5033(a)(2).

[132] 1989 Act, §7815(d).

[133] Pub. L. No. 101-508, §11702(g)(2).

[134] 1989 Act, §7817.

A QDOT is an irrevocable trust into which assets passing from the decedent for the benefit of his or her noncitizen surviving spouse are placed. The trust may be formed under the estate plan of the deceased spouse, or it may be created by the surviving spouse. Its primary goal is to defer the estate tax otherwise payable on the death of the first spouse where the surviving spouse is a non–U.S. citizen, but also to ensure proper payment of taxes. The QDOT provides some of the benefits that the better-known QTIP Trust provides for transfers in trust for the benefit of a citizen spouse. The QDOT is not, however, identical to a QTIP; there are substantial restrictions that apply to distributions to or for the benefit of the noncitizen surviving spouse, as further explained below.

On January 5, 1993, the Service published extensive proposed regulations with respect to the requirements of QDOTs under §2056A.[135] On August 21, 1995, and November 29, 1996, the Service published final regulations with respect to the requirements for QDOTs under §2056A.

Requirements for QDOT

IRC §2056A imposed four requirements in order for a trust to qualify as a QDOT:

- The trust instrument must require that at least one trustee be a U.S. citizen or domestic corporation (U.S. trustee).

- The trust instrument must require that no distribution (other than a distribution of income) may be made from a QDOT unless the U.S. trustee has the right to withhold from such distribution the tax imposed by §2056A on the distribution.

- The trust must meet requirements of future regulations to be promulgated to ensure collection of any tax imposed by §2056A(b);[136] and

- An election under §2056A(d) must be made by the executor on the decedent's federal estate tax return.[137]

Reformation of nonqualifying QDOT trusts is available if permitted under the instrument. Any such reformation must be completed by the time (including extensions) prescribed for filing the decedent's estate tax return. Where a judicial proceeding is required, the judicial proceeding must be commenced on or before the due date (determined with regard to extensions) for filing the decedent's federal estate tax return.[138] The trust must be treated as a QDOT at all times, even before the reformation is completed.[139]

Post-Death Transfers to QDOT

Any property passing from the decedent to the surviving spouse, including probate and nonprobate assets,[140] is treated as passing to the spouse in a QDOT if: (1) the property is transferred to a QDOT before the date on which the federal estate tax return is required to be filed; or (2) the property is irrevocably assigned by the spouse to a QDOT on or before the date on which the federal estate tax return is required to be filed and the assignment is enforceable under local law.[141]

More on Post-Death Transfers to a QDOT

The Service has provided extensive regulations on the subject of non-trust marital transfers.[142] If: (1) property passes to a spouse by bequest, devise, operation of law, or pursuant to an annuity or other similar plan or arrangement; and (2) such property would otherwise qualify for the marital deduction except that it does not pass to a QDOT, the property can be treated as passing to the spouse in a QDOT under certain conditions. Either: (1) the property must actually be transferred to a QDOT before the estate tax return is filed (and such transfer must occur on or before the last date prescribed by law that

---

[135] PS-102-88, 1993-4 IRB 48.

[136] IRC §2056A(a)(2).

[137] IRC §2056A(a)(3).

[138] IRC §2056(d)(5).

[139] Reg. §20.2056A-4(a)(1), (2). Letter Ruling 9845015 (Aug. 7, 1998) concerned a charitable remainder trust (CRUT) established post-death under a settlement between the surviving spouse and the decedent's estate. The CRUT also qualified as a QDOT. After the settlement, a payment was made from the estate to the CRUT and then to the spouse to compensate him or her for the delay in funding. The payment to the spouse was characterized as an income payment and not a distribution of principal subject to the additional estate tax under §2056A. The Service further ruled that if, during the term of the CRUT, there were unitrust distributions that were not trust income for trust accounting purposes, and the trustee withheld a portion of the distribution to pay the additional estate tax, the spouse would be treated as having received the entire unitrust amount for federal income tax purposes.

[140] *E.g.*, joint tenancy property transferred by operation of law, life insurance payable to the noncitizen spouse, assets passing by intestacy, and assets passing directly under a will.

[141] IRC §2056(d)(2)(B).

[142] Treas. Reg. §20.2056A-4(b).

the QDOT election may be made);[143] or (2) the property must be assigned to a QDOT under an enforceable, irrevocable written agreement made on or before the return is filed or on or before the last date prescribed by law for making the QDOT election. The transfer or assignment may be made by the spouse, by the spouse's legal representative if the spouse is incompetent, or by the personal representative of the spouse if the spouse has died.

The QDOT to which the property is to be transferred may be created in one of several ways. It may be created by the decedent (during life or by will), it may be created by the spouse, or it may be created by the executor. If only property passing from the decedent directly to the surviving spouse is to be allocated to the QDOT, the "transferee QDOT" is not required to be in a form that would qualify for the marital deduction under §2056(a) of the Code; however, if other property is or has been bequeathed to the QDOT by the decedent, the QDOT must meet all of the requirements for the marital deduction under §2056(a) of the Code.[144]

It should be noted that property assigned or transferred to a QDOT by the surviving spouse is treated as passing to a QDOT *solely* for purposes of §2056(d)(2)(A). For all other purposes (*i.e.*, income, estate, generation-skipping taxes), the surviving spouse is treated as the transferor of the property.[145] For example, if property passes to a noncitizen surviving spouse by operation of law (for example, the property is vested in the spouses as "joint tenancy with right of survivorship"), the noncitizen spouse receiving the property as the surviving joint tenant is entitled to create a QDOT and make a transfer of the property to it, retaining an income interest for life with the remainder perhaps to children or grandchildren. With such a transfer by the spouse to a QDOT, there may be a reportable gift by the spouse of the actuarial value of the remainder interest in the QDOT, unless the spouse makes the transfer an "incomplete gift" (for example, retaining a power of appointment over the assets at death). Notwithstanding the possible lifetime gift on the creation of the QDOT, the assets in the QDOT will be included in the estate of the surviving spouse under §2036(a)(1) (transfers with retained life estate). It should be noted that the estate may be entitled as well to a credit for tax on prior transfers under §2013 if the QDOT property is included in both the estate of the deceased spouse and the estate of the surviving spouse for federal estate tax purposes.[146]

Note, however, that there is a special exception to the valuation rules of §2702 for transfers to a QDOT, that is, the QDOT created by the surviving spouse does not have to qualify as a charitable remainder annuity trust (CRAT) or a charitable remainder trust (CRUT).[147]

Protective Assignments

Under certain circumstances, protective assignments to a QDOT may be made. The regulations cite as permissible circumstances: (1) a bona fide will contest; (2) a bona fide issue concerning the residency or citizenship of the decedent or the surviving spouse; (3) a bona fide issue as to whether or not an asset or portion thereof is includable in the decedent's gross estate; or (4) a bona fide issue as to the amount or nature of property the surviving spouse is entitled to receive. The protective assignment is made in writing and signed by the assignor under penalty of perjury on or before the date on which the estate tax return is due and on or before the last date prescribed by law that the QDOT election may be made. The election must identify specific assets to

---

[143] Section 2056A(d) provides that the election must be made on a return filed no later than one year after the time prescribed by law, including extensions, for filing the estate tax return.

[144] Treas. Reg. §§20.2056A-2(b), 20.2056A-4(b). On February 15, 2001, the Treasury issued a proposed regulation, 20.2056A-13, which would permit a marital trust, as well as a QDOT, to qualify for the marital deduction under the income distribution rules if it was in conformity with state law that provides for the reasonable apportionment between income and remainder beneficiaries based upon a "total return" concept. If and when issued in the form of a final regulation, the provision will be applicable to trusts after that date. Reg. §20.2056A-5 would also be amended.

[145] *Id.* §20.2056A-4(b)(5).

[146] There is an exception to the rules of §2702 (special valuations rules for interests in trusts in the case of transfer of interests). Section 2702 would generally treat the value of any retained interest by a transferor (here the noncitizen surviving spouse) as zero in the determination of the value of a gift in trust, unless the retained interest is "qualified interest, that is, generally, a 'unitrust'" interest or an annuity trust interest. Treas. Reg. §25.2702-1(c)(8) exempts from the general rule of §2702 a transfer or assignment by a noncitizen surviving spouse of property to a QDOT where the surviving spouse retains an interest (for example, an income interest) in the transferred property that is not a "qualified interest" under §2702 and the transfer is not described in §2702(a)(3)(A)(ii) or §2702(c)(4).

[147] IRC §2702-1(c)(8) and Treas. Reg. §25.2702-1(c)(8).

which the protective election applies and state the basis for the protective election. The protective election may be made on the basis of a formula, such as the minimum amount necessary to reduce the estate tax to zero. Once made, a protective election cannot be revoked.[148]

Difficult to Transfer Assets

The regulations recognized that there are certain assets as to which it may be difficult or impossible to make an irrevocable assignment to a QDOT under federal law, state law, or foreign law or the terms of the plan or arrangement itself. Where such nonassignable assets exist (or are treated as such under the regulations), such as in the case of a nonassignable annuity under a qualified or nonqualified plan, if the surviving spouse agrees to be bound by the provisions of the regulations,[149] the property will be treated as passing in the form of a QDOT. The cited regulations permit the surviving spouse to remit the §2056A estate tax on the corpus portion of each annuity payment received, or to agree to roll over the corpus portion of each annuity payment to a QDOT.[150]

The Bank, Bond, or Letter of Credit Requirement

Summary of Requirement

In order to ensure collection of the QDOT tax, the regulations[151] impose what have come to be known as the Bank, Bond, or Letter of Credit Requirements. These regulations frequently impose complex requirements in order for a trust to qualify as a QDOT. If the fair market value of the QDOT is in excess of $2 million calculated without reduction for indebtedness, the QDOT: (1) must have a bank trustee (as banks are defined in §581); (2) must furnish a bond in favor of the IRS equal to 65 percent of the fair market value of the QDOT assets, again determined without regard to indebtedness; or (3) must furnish an irrevocable letter of credit issued by a bank equal to the same 65 percent of the fair market value of the QDOT assets. The forms of bond and letter of credit are set forth in detail in the regulations.[152]

The regulations make it clear that a QDOT can alternate between the bank trustee, bond, or letter of credit, so long as one of them is in place at all times.[153] In order to determine whether the QDOT has exceeded the $2 million threshold, the fiduciary may elect to exclude up to $600,000 in value attributed to residential real property and related furnishings held for use by the spouse.[154] If the value of the QDOT is $2 million or less, the bank, bond, or letter of credit requirements are waived if the trust instrument provides that no more than 35 percent of the fair market value of the trust assets, determined annually on the last day of the taxable year, will consist of real property located outside the United States.[155] The regulations have modified the original rule so that a trust, which at any time exceeds 35 percent foreign real property, will not automatically cease to qualify as a QDOT. If the trust again meets the requirements by the end of the next taxable year, or if the bank, bond, or letter of credit requirements are then in place, the trust will continue to qualify. If either the bond or letter of credit is drawn upon, neither the U.S. Trustee nor any other person can seek return of any part of the remittance until April 15 of the calendar year following the year in which the draw is made upon the bond or letter of credit. If a return is made, the refund is without interest.

---

[148] Treas. Reg. §20.2056(b)(8).

[149] *Id.* §20.2056A-4(c)(2), (3).

[150] In Priv. Ltr. Rul. 9623063 (Mar. 13, 1996), the Service analyzed the applicability of the marital deduction QDOT rules and §408 to a request to approve the rollover by a surviving spouse (not a U.S. citizen) of the decedent's community property one-half interest in three Individual Retirement Accounts (IRAs) of which the spouse was the named beneficiary. The Service concluded that so long as the rollover accounts remained subject to a QDOT agreement embodying the requirements of the statute and then Temp. Treas. Reg. §20.2056A-2T, each rollover IRA would constitute the corpus of a QDOT and the marital deduction was available. In Letter Ruling 9746049 (Aug. 15, 1997), distributions from an IRA that were rolled over into a QDOT were subject to Reg. §20.2056A-5(c)(2), the rules defining "income." In this case, the spouse did not receive the IRA in the form of an annuity. More interestingly, distributions from the corpus of the QDOT to reimburse the spouse for income taxes on the corpus distributions from the IRA were not subject to the QDOT tax.

[151] Treas. Reg. §20.2056A-2(d).

[152] *Id.* §20.2056A-2(d)(1)(B), (C).

[153] *Id.* §20.2056A-2(d)(1). (A U.S. branch of a foreign bank may act so long as another U.S. Trustee acts with the foreign trustee.) *Id.* §20.2056A-2(d)(1)(i)(A).

[154] *Id.* §20.2056A-2(d)(1)(iv).

[155] *Id.* §20.2056A-2(d)(1)(ii).

1996 Regulations

In General

The regulations issued with respect to the security arrangements under §2056A were issued as Temporary Regulations on August 21, 1995.[156] On November 29, 1996, the regulations were made permanent.[157] They now impose both stringent and precise requirements with respect to the security arrangements required under a QDOT.[158] In addition, the preface to the 1996 Regulations includes a summary of the significant comments to the Temporary Regulations and the reason for accepting or rejecting the comments in the Final Regulations.[159]

Specifics

Among the more important matters covered in the preface are the following:

- In order to eliminate drafting difficulties with respect to the security arrangements, the regulations pertaining to such requirements may now be incorporated into the trust document by reference.[160] In addition, to provide further guidance for those who wish to specify the required provisions, the Service has published Revenue Procedure 96-54[161] to provide sample language of the governing instrument requirements.

- Both the regulations and the preface thereto make it clear that a QDOT may alternate among the three security arrangements, so long as, at any given time, one of the three arrangements is in effect.[162] Moreover, if a bank trustee is serving and if the QDOT switches to an alternate security arrangement, a bank need not continue as trustee, so long as the U.S. Trustee requirement is fulfilled.[163]

- Substantial numbers of comments were received pertaining to the fact that, in determining the $2 million threshold (where the bank, bond, or letter of credit requirements are imposed), the assets are valued at their gross value, without reduction for indebtedness. In addition, the bond or letter of credit, where imposed, is to be 65 percent of gross fair market value, again without regard to indebtedness. Comments suggested that indebtedness be taken into account in determining the threshold of the bank, bond, or letter of credit requirements. The Treasury declined to take this step in the 1996 Regulations.[164]

- Under the Temporary Regulations, the term "finally determined" is utilized in connection with the fair market value of trust assets passing to a QDOT.[165] Comments suggested that the regulations provide a definition of the term "finally determined," a definition that has now been provided. The value of assets will be finally determined with the earliest to occur of the following:

  – The entry of a decision, judgment, decree or other order by any court of competent jurisdiction that has become final;

  – The execution of a closing agreement made under §7121;

  – Any final disposition by the Service of a claim for refund;

  – The issuance of an estate tax closing letter (if no claim for refund is filed); or

  – The expiration of the statute of limitation for assessment with respect to decedent's estate tax liability.[166]

The regulations provide that in order to qualify as a QDOT, the trust must be maintained and administered under the laws of a state of the United States or the District of Columbia.[167] The trust instrument

---

[156] Temp. Treas. Reg. §20.2056A-2T, promulgated by T.D. 8644, 1996-1 C.B. 200.

[157] 202 T.D. 8686, 1996-2 C.B. 152.

[158] Treas. Reg. §20.2056.

[159] T.D. 8686, 1996-2 C.B.

[160] *Id.*

[161] 1996-2 C.B. 386. See, for example, Letter Ruling 199918039 where the Service approved a QDOT that incorporated the sample paragraphs of Rev. Proc. 96-54. In the same Ruling, the Service approved the transfer of a commercial building to a corporation formed under the laws of a foreign country in exchange for stock and stated that the stock could be transferred to the QDOT. Note also that the classification of the trust as a "foreign trust" under IRC §7701(a)(31)(B) did not preclude it from qualifying as a QDOT.

[162] Treas. Reg. §20.2056A-2(d)(1).

[163] T.D. 8686, 1996-2 C.B. 152.

[164] *Id.*

[165] Temp. Treas. Reg. §20.2056A-2T.

[166] T.D. 8686, 1996-2 C.B. 152; Treas. Reg. §20.2056-2(d)(1)(iii).

[167] Treas. Reg. §20.2056A-2(a) (replacing Temp. Treas. Reg. §20.2056A-2T). The 1996 Regulations apply to estates of decedents dying after February 19, 1996, except where the special rules applying to incompetency or irrevocable trusts are applicable). *See* Treas. Reg. §20.2056A-2(d)(6).

may, however, be executed under the laws of a foreign jurisdiction, so long as the foreign instrument designates the law of a state or the District of Columbia as governing the administration and such designation is effective under the laws of the designated jurisdiction.[168]

Guidance on Bank, Bond, or LLC Requirement

The main purpose of the 1996 Final Regulations was to finalize the security arrangements required of QDOTs in order to ensure collection of the tax. As mentioned above, those Regulations distinguish between QDOTs having assets in excess of $2 million and those having assets of $2 million or less.

Where the security arrangements of Treasury Regulations §20.2056A-2(d) are required, one of the security arrangements must remain in effect until the trust ceases to function as a QDOT and any tax liability under §2056A is finally determined and paid, or is finally determined to be zero.[169]

For purposes of determining whether the $2 million threshold has been met, the executor may exclude up to $600,000 in value attributable to real property (wherever located) and related furnishings that are owned by the QDOT and are used or held for use by the surviving spouse at all times. The regulations make it clear that this exception includes the principal residence and one other residence. Any such residence must not be rented, even when not occupied by the surviving spouse. The term "residence" includes appurtenant structures and land not in excess of that which is "reasonably appropriate" for residential purposes.[170] Related furnishings means furniture, furnishings, and items commonly used in the residence, but specifically excludes rare art work, valuable antiques, and automobiles.[171] The residence exclusion election may be made on the federal estate tax return on which the QDOT election is made, by a written statement identifying the property or properties being excluded and claiming the exclusion, or at a later time during the lifetime of the spouse.[172]

If the personal residence exclusion has been claimed and the residence is later sold or ceases to be used or held for the use of the surviving spouse, the U.S. Trustee is required to file a statement on Form 706-QDT by April 15 of the calendar year following the event which terminates the residence exception.[173] The statement must describe whether the proceeds will be used for the timely purchase[174] of a new residence for the spouse, and, if not, the steps that will be taken to comply with the QDOT rules.[175] The personal residence exclusion may be shifted from one residence to another during the lifetime of the spouse so long as the new or other residence is in the same or in another QDOT and qualifies under the residence-exclusion rules. Moreover, the exclusion may be utilized at a later date, to the extent not originally claimed on the federal estate tax return when filed.[176]

Qualification of Other Security Arrangements

The regulations recognize that additional published guidance may be necessary on the subject of what security arrangements besides the bank, bond, or letter of credit requirements will be accepted. Once published, a QDOT meeting such alternate plan or arrangement will be treated as a QDOT. In the interim, taxpayers may submit requests for private letter rulings requesting approval of an alternate plan or arrangement to ensure collection of the tax.[177]

Anti-Abuse, Miscellaneous Provisions

The regulations provide anti-abuse rules, look-through rules, and multiple-QDOT rules (for determining the $2 million threshold) in order to ensure that appropriate security arrangements are in place, and that the tax will be collected upon the trust ceasing to qualify as a QDOT or upon the death of the surviving spouse.[178]

Income Distributions; Taxable Events

Under §2056A(b)(3), a spouse may receive all of the QDOT income, and there is no QDOT tax on distributions of income to the surviving spouse. Income has the meaning given the term by §643(b) of the Code (*i.e.*, trust accounting income).[179] One of the

---

[168] Treas. Reg. §20.2056A-2(a).

[169] *Id.* §§20.2056A-2(d)(1)(i)(B) and (C); 20.2056A-2(d)(1)(iii).

[170] *Id.* §20.2056A-2(d)(1)(iv)(A).

[171] *Id.* §20.2056A-2(d)(1)(iv)(E).

[172] *Id.* §20.2056A-2(d)(1)(iv)(A).

[173] *Id.* §20.2056A-2(d)(1)(iv)(F).

[174] *See id.* §20.2056A-2(d)(1)(iv)(G) (within 12 months of the date of the sale).

[175] *Id.* §§20.2056A-2(d)(3)(i), (ii), and (iii).

[176] *Id.* §20.2056A-2(d)(1)(iv)(G).

[177] *Id.* §20.2056A-2(d)(4).

[178] *Id.* §§20.2056A-2(d)(1)(v), (ii)(A) and (B).

[179] IRC §2056A(c)(2).

principal differences between a Q-TIP Marital Trust and a QDOT is that certain distributions to the spouse, particularly of principal or corpus, are subject to the QDOT tax imposed by §2056A.[180] The tax is generally to be withheld from the distribution by the U.S. trustee and is reported on IRS Form 706-QDT. If the tax is not withheld but is paid out of other assets, constituting the corpus of the QDOT, any tax so paid is treated as an additional distribution to the spouse in the year so paid.[181] This tax is imposed at the decedent's (rather than the surviving spouses) bracket. No QDOT tax is imposed on any income distribution to the spouse or on any principal distribution to the spouse on account of "hardship."[182] The term "hardship" is defined as an immediate and substantial financial need relating to the spouse's health, maintenance, education or support, or the health, maintenance, education or support of any person that the surviving spouse is legally obligated to support.[183] The hardship dispensation will not be applicable if the amount may be obtained from sources reasonably available to the surviving spouse, such as publicly traded stock or certificates of deposit (Closely held business interest, real estate, and tangible personal property will not be considered sources that are reasonably available to the surviving spouse.) Even though hardship distributions are nontaxable, such distributions are to be reported on Form 706QDT,[184] possibly to permit the Service to make a determination of whether the distribution did, in fact, constitute a hardship distribution.

The QDOT estate tax is also imposed on the fair market value of the property remaining in the trust at the time of the surviving spouse's death or on any earlier date that the trust ceases to have at least one trustee who is a U.S. Trustee or to meet other QDOT requirements under the regulations.[185]

The QDOT Tax

Computation of Tax

The amount of the estate tax imposed with respect to the QDOT is the additional estate tax that would be due if the property subject to the tax had been included in the decedent spouse's estate.[186] If a taxable event occurs before the estate tax on the decedent's estate is finally determined, a tentative tax is imposed using the highest estate tax rate in effect on the date of the decedent's death.[187] When the decedent's estate tax liability is finally determined, the excess of the tentative tax over the estate tax as finally determined is allowed as a refund or a credit, with interest, provided the refund or credit is claimed not more than one year after the date on which the final determination is made.[188]

Multiple QDOTs

If there is more than one QDOT with respect to a decedent, the amount of estate tax imposed as to any trust must be calculated on the basis of the highest estate tax rate in effect on the date of the decedent's death, unless a U.S. Trustee becomes the "Designated Filer." The nomination of the Designated Filer is made on the federal estate tax return or the first Form 706-QDT that is filed by its prescribed date. The Designated Filer is responsible for filing all returns and paying the tax due from all QDOT trusts pertaining to the decedent.[189]

Payment of Tax

The QDOT estate tax is imposed: (1) on the value of trust property remaining at the date of death of the surviving spouse; (2) on the value of trust property at such time as the trust no longer qualifies as a QDOT; or (3) on QDOT distributions during the calendar year.[190] The tax due by reason of the surviving spouse's death is due and payable nine months after the date of death or cessation of qualified status.[191] The QDOT tax on distributions is due and payable on the 15th day of the fourth month following the calendar year in which the taxable event occurs.[192]

Basis of Property Distributed from a QDOT

Any distribution during the lifetime of the surviving spouse with respect to which the QDOT tax is paid is treated as a transfer by gift for purposes of determining the basis of the property. The QDOT

---

[180] *Id.* §2056A(b).
[181] Treas. Reg. §20.2056A-5(b).
[182] IRC §2056A(b)(3).
[183] Treas. Reg. §20.2056A-5(c).
[184] *Id.* §20.2056A-5(c).
[185] IRC §§2056A(b)(1)(B), (4).

[186] IRC §2056A(b)(2).
[187] *Id.* §2056A(b)(2)(B).
[188] *Id.*
[189] Treas. Reg. §20.2056A-9.
[190] IRC §2056A(b)(1), (4).
[191] *Id.* §§2056A(b)(5)(B), (b)(4).
[192] *Id.* §2056A(b)(5)(A).

tax is treated as a gift tax and the basis of the distributed property is increased by an amount equal to the proportion of the tax paid that the net appreciation in the property bears to the distribution.[193]

Spouse Becomes Citizen or Reduces Credit

Necessity for QDOT May End

The estate tax on a QDOT will cease to apply if the surviving spouse becomes a U.S. citizen, and one of the following conditions is met:[194]

- The spouse was a U.S. resident at all times after the decedent's death and at all times before becoming a U.S. citizen; or

- No taxable distributions are made from the QDOT before the spouse becomes a U.S. citizen (regardless of the residency status of the spouse).

The U.S. trustee must notify the Service (and certify in writing) that the spouse has become a citizen and file a final Form 706-QDT on or before April 15 of the calendar year following the year the spouse becomes a citizen (unless an extension is granted).[195] If the spouse becomes a citizen, if the spouse has not been a U.S. resident at all times after the death of the decedent, and if a tax has been imposed under §2056A(b)(1)(A) with respect to any distribution from the QDOT before the spouse becomes a citizen, the QDOT tax under §2056A(b)(1) will cease to apply to QDOT's distributions after the spouse becomes a citizen, only if the spouse elects to treat any reduction in the §2056A estate tax due, as a result of the decedent spouse's unified credit, and amounts subject to the decedent spouse's lower tax brackets, as a reduction in the surviving spouse's unified credit for purposes of determining the spouse's tax bracket for gifts in the year citizenship is granted and for subsequent years.[196]

Handling Assets Pending Naturalization of Surviving Spouse

The issue may arise as to what is the status of assets transferable directly to a noncitizen spouse where citizenship will be obtained only after the due date of the estate tax return, including extensions. It appears preferable that the surviving spouse establish a QDOT before the return's extended due date, so estate tax can be calculated on a timely filed return with the benefit of the marital deduction for the property passing outright to the decedent's surviving noncitizen spouse. Conceivably, the estate return could be filed delinquent, after the surviving spouse is naturalized, since §2056(d)(4) treats the property passing to the surviving spouse as passing to a U.S. citizen if the surviving spouse becomes a U.S. citizen before the day on which the estate tax return is made. For this purpose, a timely return is considered filed on the last date that the return is required to be filed, including extensions, and a late return is considered filed on the date that it is actually filed.[197] Thus, the transfer appears to be a qualifying transfer to a citizen spouse even though the estate tax return is filed delinquent only after the spouse is naturalized.

Further, under the QDOT rules, as discussed, if property has passed directly to the surviving spouse, the property is treated as passing to the spouse in a QDOT if the property is transferred by the spouse to the QDOT, or the property is irrevocably assigned to the QDOT, prior to the date the Form 706 is filed and on or before the last date the QDOT election can be made.[198] Thus, the spouse may have a back-up position to set up a QDOT within a year, if he or she does not obtain U.S. citizenship within that period. The QDOT election is made on the estate tax return, provided such return is filed not more than one year after the extended due date.[199] If a timely return is not filed, the QDOT election must be made on the first federal estate tax return filed after the due date.[200] Therefore, if the Form 706 is not filed by the due date (including extensions), the QDOT election must be included on the next filed return and that return must be filed within one year of the due date (including extensions). If the Form 706 is filed by the due date, the QDOT election should be included

---

[193] *See* Treas. Reg §20.2056A-12 and Treas. Reg. §1.1015-5(c)(4).

[194] Treas. Reg. §20.2056A-10(a)(1). See Private Letter Ruling 9848007 (July 27, 1998), where the spouse became a citizen prior to any taxable distributions from the QDOT and had resided in the United States at all times since the death of the decedent. In such event, distributions were not subject to the Section 2056A estate tax.

[195] IRC §6081.

[196] *Id.* §2056A(b)(12); Treas. Reg. §20.2056A-10(b).

[197] *See* Treas. Reg. §20.2056A-1(b).

[198] *See* IRC §2056(d)(2); Treas. Reg. §20.2056A-1(a).

[199] IRC §2056A(d).

[200] Treas. Reg. §20.2056A-3(a).

in the timely filed return. (However, it does not appear that a valid QDOT election can be made if no QDOT is in existence when the return is filed). If the QDOT election is not included in the timely return, it may be possible to file a "supplemental"[201] Form 706 to report the creation of the QDOT and to make the QDOT election, if such return is filed within one year of the extended due date. The IRS has granted extensions for making late QDOT elections in such circumstances under §9100.[202]

There are always hazards to filing a late return, and the authors do not believe that filing a delinquent return to await a surviving spouse's naturalization would ever be the preferred course of action. Chief among these hazards may be the loss of the ability to make the QTIP election for a spousal trust, if the QTIP election is not made on a timely filed return.[203] Other significant tax issues may be raised. If the entire estate does not pass to the spouse (that is, a federal estate tax on some portion of the estate is due), will late filing penalties (or late payment penalties) apply?

The QDOT and the 2001 Act

The 2001 Act provides that in applying the §2056A estate tax with respect to a surviving spouse dying before January 1, 2010, the following will occur:

- The estate tax under §2056A(b)(1) will continue to be imposed on property remaining in the QDOT as of the noncitizen spouse's death if the noncitizen spouse dies before January 1, 2010.

- The estate tax under §2056A(b)(i)(A) on distributions of principal (not on account of hardship) to a noncitizen spouse will continue to be imposed on distributions made before January 1, 2021.[204]

---

[201] The instructions to Form 706 provide that "if you find that you must change something on a return that has already been filed, you should file another Form 706 and write 'Supplemental Information' across the top."

[202] See PLR 9834013 (July 24, 1998) (granting, pursuant to Treas. Reg. 20.2056A-4(b)(6), an extension of time to make the QDOT election and to irrevocably assign the assets to the QDOT, when the timely filed Form 706 did not report the QDOT, but a supplemental Form 706, filed within one year of the due date of the return, did so). See also PLR 200910019 (Nov. 20, 2008), granting a 60-day extension for spouse to make a protective election to her QDOT.

[203] See Treas. Reg. §20.2056A-4(b).

[204] New IRC §2210, 2001 Act §501(a).

PRE-IMMIGRATION PLANNING ISSUES

Overview

The nonresident alien client should undertake pre-immigration planning if he or she is contemplating establishing income tax residence or estate and gift tax domicile in the United States. It is appropriate to coordinate U.S. pre-immigration planning with foreign counsel to assure that planning which is undertaken to save future federal taxes will not create a current foreign tax liability for the foreign client.

One major thrust of pre-immigration planning for the foreign client should be to accelerate the foreign client's transfer of assets out of his or her estate prior to the time he or she establishes domicile in the United States and to accelerate receipt of gain on appreciated assets retained in the estate.

Foreign Trusts

General

A trust could be established in a suitable foreign jurisdiction, and the nonresident alien could transfer assets to such trust. Planning will be required to address the changes made by the 1996 foreign trust tax legislation.

Use of Grantor Trusts

Old Law

Prior to new foreign trust tax legislation in 1996, a common planning technique for wealthy individuals who had family members immigrating to the United States was to have a wealthy relative parent or grandparent who is not immigrating to the United States establish an offshore trust to provide for the U.S. beneficiaries. The trust would be maintained as a grantor trust during the settlor's lifetime.[205]

Tax Treatment

Prior to the 1996 legislation, grantor trust rules under §§671 through 678 generally applied to foreign (or domestic) trusts created by foreign grantors. Thus, as described above, it would often be beneficial for a nonresident alien who is likely to remain a nonresident alien to establish the grantor trust for

---

[205] See IRC §§671–679 (grantor trust rules for treating the income of such trust as the income of the grantor (or certain other persons)). But see IRC §672(f), as amended by 1904(a), Small Business Act (general repeal of grantor trust rules with respect to foreign grantors), discussed below.

domestic beneficiaries, rather than a non-grantor trust. Non–U.S. source income of the trust would often be tax-free to both the grantor and the trust. Furthermore, the grantor trust could make distributions of the income to the U.S. beneficiaries free of income tax and subject to gift tax only if the distribution was in the form of tangible U.S. situs property.

On the other hand, income distributions to the domestic beneficiaries of a non-grantor trust could constitute distributable net income (DNI) that would be taxable to the domestic beneficiaries and potentially subjected to a large interest charge pursuant to §668, to the extent the income had been accumulated.

1996 Law

REPEAL OF FOREIGN GRANTOR TRUSTS

IRC §672(f), as amended by the 1996 Small Business Act, generally repeals the ability of foreign grantors to take advantage of the foreign grantor trust rules for U.S. beneficiaries as described above.

Under the new provision, the grantor trust rules will only apply to the extent his or her application results in income being taken into account, directly or indirectly, through entities, in computing the income of a U.S. citizen, a U.S. resident, or a domestic corporation.[206] However, exceptions are created to this general rule where the grantor retains the power to re-vest title in him- or herself to trust property, so long as this power to revoke is exercisable solely by the grantor or by the grantor with the consent of a related or subordinate party who is subservient to the grantor.[207] Alternatively, the grantor trust rules continue to apply if the only amount distributable from the trust, whether income or corpus, during the lifetime of the grantor, are amounts distributable to the grantor or his or her spouse.[208] The provision also excludes application to compensatory trusts whose distributions would be taxable as compensation for services. This exclusion appears to leave intact the ability to utilize foreign rabbi-type grantor trusts to pay for deferred compensation to U.S. service providers.[209]

The repeal of the foreign grantor trust rules is generally effective as of the date of enactment of the provision (*i.e.*, Aug. 20, 1996).

PRE-IMMIGRATION TRANSFERS

The 1996 legislation amended IRC §679 to provide that a foreign grantor who becomes a U.S. resident within five years after transferring property to a foreign trust will be treated for purposes of IRC §679 (and reporting under IRC §6048) as if he or she had made the transfer to the trust at the start of his or her U.S. residency.[210] Treasury's concern was that foreigners who are immigrating to the United States to become U.S. citizens or residents would set up foreign trusts for beneficiaries who are also moving to the United States. Prior to the revisions, such a trust could then accumulate income tax-free offshore and be accessed by beneficiaries, particularly during periods of non–U.S. residency. The new provision applies to transfers of property after February 6, 1995.

IRC §679 is a grantor trust rule under which a U.S. person who directly or indirectly transfers property to a foreign trust is attributed the income with respect to the property that he or she transfers if the trust during the year had a U.S. beneficiary. Thus, the effect of the provision will be, in many circumstances, to require foreigners immigrating to the United States to create their pre-immigration trusts more than five years before U.S. tax residency commences.

INDIRECT TRUST CREATIONS

In revising IRC §672(f), Congress retained prior IRC §672(f)(1), which provides that where a U.S. beneficiary previously made direct or indirect transfers of property to the foreign grantor of a trust (where the foreign grantor would be treated as the

---

[206] IRC §672(f)(1).

[207] IRC §672(f)(2).

[208] *Id.*

[209] A Rabbi Trust is a deferred compensation arrangement in the form of an irrevocable grantor trust to which an employer *continued*

makes contributions to finance a promised deferred benefit to an employee. The trust assets are placed outside the reach of the corporate employer, but they remain within the reach of the corporation's general creditors. If the participant retires while the corporation is solvent, the benefits are payable to the participant according to the formula set up in the trust or a collateral instrument. Because the trust income and principal can be used to satisfy the corporation's creditors, the IRS has ruled that the trust is a grantor trust and the corporation is the owner of the trust assets for federal income tax purposes. The Rabbi Trust takes its name because the first private letter ruling (PLR 8113117) involved a deferred compensation arrangement established by a synagogue for its rabbi.

[210] IRC §679(a)(4).

owner of the trust under the grantor trust rules), then the beneficiary would be treated as the grantor to the extent of the beneficiary's prior transfers.[211] The beneficiary's gifts of $10,000 or less per year to the donor that are excluded from taxable gifts under IRC §2503(b) are ignored for purposes of this rule. Further, the 1996 legislation clarifies that sales by the U.S. beneficiary to the foreign grantor for full and adequate consideration are ignored for purposes of applying this rule.

Impact of Loss of Grantor Trust Status

If the 1996 legislation repealing foreign grantor trusts applies or the trust otherwise ceases to constitute a grantor trust (*e.g.*, after the settlor's death), distributions of DNI to domestic beneficiaries will be subject to federal income tax as received and, potentially, to adverse throw-back and interest charge rules.[212]

Powers of Appointment

If the nonresident alien holds a general power of appointment over trust property, the power should be exercised, if possible, before the nonresident alien establishes a U.S. domicile. Similarly, any general power of appointment over U.S. situs property should be exercised before a nonresident alien's death, so long as an inter vivos transfer of the property would not attract gift tax. Once again, in order to avoid federal gift tax, any tangible U.S. situs property should be converted to intangible property before the power is exercised.

Subsequent Gifts and Bequests

Once the nonresident alien establishes U.S. domicile, gifts and bequests that would come to the alien from the family members still living abroad might be directed to the resident alien's children and other heirs, in order to avoid later U.S. gift, estate, and GST taxes that might be imposed if the resident alien were to receive the property and subsequently retransfer it.

Current Outbound Foreign Trust Tax Legislation

Increased Compliance and New Reporting Obligations

In proposing the legislation to modify the tax treatment of foreign trusts, the Administration was motivated, in part, by the belief that the use of offshore trusts with respect to U.S. taxpayers was proliferating. Treasury was concerned that existing reporting and compliance requirements were not adequate to disclose the existence of these foreign trusts, to enforce existing tax treatment of such trusts, and to distinguish between taxable and nontaxable transactions. Treasury was particularly concerned about the visible marketing of asset-protection trusts, and it sensed that billions of dollars of assets had been transferred to offshore asset-protection trusts, but only a tiny fraction of those assets were being reported under the grantor trust rules by the U.S. taxpayers (actual or potential debtors) creating the trusts. On August 20, 1996, the Small Business Act, which included the foreign trust legislation, became law.[213] A major thrust of the foreign trust legislation, with respect to the outbound use of foreign trusts that had U.S. grantors or U.S. beneficiaries, was to substantially increase the reporting requirements with respect to foreign trusts and, as importantly, to substantially increase the penalties for a failure to report. To this end, the legislation completely revises the information-reporting requirements with respect to foreign trusts under §6048.

Reportable Events

Under IRC §6048, as revised, the grantor, transferor, or executor (a so-called "responsible party") is required to notify the Service of certain "reportable events."[214] This report must provide the information that the Service will require by regulations, including the amount of money or other property transferred to the trust and the identity of the trust, and each trustee and trust's beneficiary (or class of beneficiaries).[215] The report is required on or before the 90th day after a reportable event. Reportable events include: (1) the creation of any foreign trust by a U.S. person; (2) the transfer of any money or property, directly or indirectly, to a foreign trust by a

---

[211] Now recodified as IRC §672(f)(5).

[212] *See* IRC §§662–668. Further, 1996 legislative changes to the tax treatment of outbound use of foreign trusts are discussed in "Post-Residence Income Tax Planning/Reporting: Dual Residence" section, below.

[213] Pub. L. No. 104-188.

[214] IRC §§6048(a)(1), (4).

[215] IRC §6048(a)(2).

U.S. person, including a transfer by reason of death; and (3) the death of a U.S. citizen or resident if the person was treated as the owner of any portion of a foreign trust under the grantor trust rules or any portion of the foreign trust is included in the gross estate of the decedent.[216] Fair market value sales and transfers in exchange for a consideration of at least equal to the value of the transferred property are generally excepted transfers for which reporting is not required.[217]

Annual Reports

A U.S. person who will be treated as the owner of any portion of a foreign trust under the grantor trust rules is required to ensure that the trust files an annual return, providing a full accounting of the trust's activities for the taxable year.[218]

Beneficiary Reports

A U.S. person who directly or indirectly receives a distribution from a foreign trust is required to make a return with respect to the trust, reporting the aggregate amount of the distributions received during the year.[219] As a back stop to the beneficiary reporting requirements, Congress enacted the new foreign gift and bequest reporting requirements under §6039F. These provisions, discussed above, generally require reporting of gifts in excess of $10,000. In the absence of the Service being provided adequate records to determine the proper treatment of a U.S. beneficiary's distribution from a foreign trust, the Service is to treat the distribution as an accumulation distribution, subject to the throw-back rules and §6069 interest charge.[220] The distribution will be treated as allocable for purposes of §668 (the throw-back rules) to a number of years equal to one-half the number of years that the trust has been in existence.[221] The impact of these rules, where adequate information is not provided by the foreign trust, is to treat all of the distributions as throw-back distributions, rather than distributions of the current year's DNI, so that the §669 interest charge applies.

Appointment of Limited Agent for Audit

Unless the foreign trust appoints a U.S. person to act as its limited agent for purposes of conducting a tax audit and for purposes of issuing and enforcing a summons, Treasury is permitted to determine the amount of the trust income that is reportable by a U.S. person under the grantor trust rules as Treasury shall determine.[222]

Effective Date

IRC §6048 reporting provisions are generally effective for reportable transactions occurring after August 20, 1996, for grantor trust reporting for taxable years of U.S. persons beginning after December 31, 1995, and for U.S. beneficiary reporting with respect to distributions received after August 20, 1995.

Increased Penalties

A person who fails to provide the required §6048 notice with respect to the transfer of property to a foreign trust, or a distribution by a foreign trust to a U.S. person, will be subject to a penalty equal to 35 percent of the amount that should have been reported (*i.e.*, generally the value of the property involved in the transaction).[223] Failure to provide the required annual reporting of the trust activities results in an initial penalty equal to five percent of the reportable amount.[224] An additional $10,000 penalty is imposed for the continued failure to report for each 30-day period beginning 90 days after Treasury notification of the failure to report under §6048. The total penalties are not permitted to exceed the gross reportable amount.

Changes to §679

Deemed Transfers

The legislation revised the exception for transfers to trusts by a sale or exchange at fair market value.[225] Under the revised rule, only those transfers of property to the trust in exchange for a consideration at least equal to the fair market value of the transferred property are excluded. Consideration other than cash is to be taken into account at its fair market value. However, except as provided in regulations, any obligation of (or guaranteed by) the

---

[216] IRC §6048(a)(3).

[217] *But see* IRC §679(a)(3), discussed below (ignoring certain debt obligations received in sales, for purposes of determining whether there was a fair market value transfer).

[218] IRC §6048(b)(1).

[219] IRC §6048(c).

[220] IRC §6048(c)(2).

[221] IRC §6048(c)(2)(B).

[222] IRC §6048(b)(2)(A).

[223] IRC §6677.

[224] IRC §6677(b).

[225] *See* IRC §679(a)(2)(B), pre– and post-legislation.

trust, the grantor, a beneficiary's trust, or a person related to a grantor or beneficiary of the trust within the meaning of §6043(i)(2)(H) is to be ignored for purposes of determining whether or not the transfer was in exchange for consideration at least equal to the fair market value of the transferred property.[226] Principal payments by a trust on an obligation are to be taken into account for purposes of determining the portion of the trust attributable to the property transferred; thus, principal payments appear to reduce the portion of the trust's income that will be attributed to the U.S. transferor to the trust.

The impact of this rule will be to limit the ability of U.S. beneficiaries to utilize aggressive valuation positions to foster the rapid build-up of foreign trusts in which they or other family members have an interest.

Pre-Immigration Trust

As to pre-immigration trusts, as discussed above, §679 was amended to provide that a foreign grantor who becomes a U.S. resident within five years after transferring property to a foreign trust is treated for purposes of §679 as if he or she had made the transfer to the trust at the start of his or her U.S. residency.

Conversely, a beneficiary is not treated as a U.S. person for purposes of §679 if the beneficiary becomes a U.S. person more than five years after the funding of the trust.[227] This latter rule is a favorable rule for taxpayers, particularly in light of §679(b) which provides that the foreign trust's transferor will be treated as having income equal to the entire undistributed net income of the trust, once the trust acquires a U.S. beneficiary, where it did not previously have a U.S. beneficiary.

Loans to U.S. Beneficiaries

The 1996 legislation provides that, unless otherwise provided in regulations, a foreign trust that makes a loan of cash or marketable securities directly or indirectly to the U.S. grantor or beneficiary of the trust (or a U.S. person related to such a grantor or beneficiary), then, the amount of the loan will be treated as a distribution by the trust to the grantor or beneficiary.[228] A person is related to another person for these purposes if the parties are related under §267 or 707(b); family attribution under §267(c)(4) is applied as if the family of an individual includes the spouses of members of the family.[229]

Increased Interest Charge

Prior to the 1996 legislation, §668 imposed only a flat six percent simple interest charge, rather than a market rate of interest, on the U.S. tax deferral associated with accumulation distributions from a foreign trust to U.S. beneficiaries.[230] Under the 1996 legislation, the simple six percent interest charge under §668 is increased and pegged to the compounding interest charge imposed on tax underpayments under §6621, which is a market rate of interest.

Trust Situs

New Rule

Treasury believed that the existing multifactor test[231] of whether a trust should be considered to be a domestic or foreign trust failed to provide a "bright-line" determination of a trust's status and, as a result, it could and was being manipulated to provide tax benefits or to avoid reporting obligations.

The 1996 legislation amends §7701(a)(30) to provide that a trust is to be treated as a U.S. person only if a U.S. court can exercise primary supervision over the administration of the trust and if one or more U.S. persons have the authority to control all substantial decisions of the trust.

Excise Tax on Expatriating Trusts

Treasury was concerned that substantial domestic trusts might convert into foreign trusts and took the position that such a conversion does not constitute an outbound transfer from a domestic trust to a foreign trust. A transfer from a domestic trust to a foreign trust is a trans-

---

[226] IRC §679(a)(3).

[227] IRC §679(c)(3).

[228] IRC §643(i).

[229] IRC §643(i)(2)(B).

[230] See IRC §§667(a)(3), 668.

[231] See B.W. Jones Trust v. Commissioner, 46 H.T.A. 531 (1942), aff'd, 132 F.2d 914 (4th Cir. 1943); Maximov v. United States, 373 U.S. 49 (1963); Rev. Rul. 60-181, 1960-1 C.B. 257; Rev. Rul. 70-242, 1970-1 C.B. 89; Rev. Rul. 87-61, 1987-2 C.B. 219. Among the factors considered are: (i) the country under whose laws the trust was created; (ii) the nationality/residency of the settlor; (iii) the nationality/ residency of the trustees; (iv) the nationality/residency of the beneficiaries; (v) the situs of the trust's administration; and (vi) the situs of the trust's corpus. IRC §7701(a)(31) provides a circular definition of a "foreign trust": A trust whose foreign source income that is not effectively connected with the conduct of a U.S. trade or business is not includable in gross income for U.S. tax purposes.

fer that subjects the appreciation in the domestic trust's assets to the 35 percent excise tax under §1491.

The 1996 legislation amends §1491 to provide that a non-foreign trust that becomes a foreign trust will be treated for purposes of §1491 as having transferred, immediately before becoming a foreign trust, all of its assets to a foreign trust.[232] As a result, §1491 will apply to the conversion of the domestic trust into a foreign trust. The 1996 legislation also revises the penalties for a failure to report a §1491 transaction, by applying the revised IRC §6677 penalties, described above,[233] as if the failure to report the §1491 transaction were a failure to file a required notice under §6048(a).

The excise tax was repealed by the Taxpayer Relief Act of 1997, Pub. L. No. 105-34, §1131(a), effective August 5, 1997. The 1997 Act amended §684(a) to require recognition of gain on transfers by a U.S. person to a foreign trust or estate to the extent of the excess of the fair market value of the property so transferred over the adjusted basis of the property in the hands of the transferor. The gain recognition rule did not apply to a transfer of appreciated property by a U.S. citizen to a foreign trust, to the extent that *any person* was treated as the owner of the trust under the grantor trust rule.[234] The 2001 Act subsequently amends §684 again. Under the 2001 Act, the gain recognition rule is expanded to include post-2009 transfers by a U.S. person to *a nonresident alien*. However, it will not apply to a post-2009 transfer of appreciated property by a U.S. citizen to a foreign trust, to the extent that *any U.S. person* is treated as the owner of the trust under the grantor trust rules.[235]

Notice 96-65

In Notice 96-65,[236] the Service granted additional time to comply with the new domestic trust criteria set forth in IRC §7701(a)(30)(B). Such action was necessary in order to avoid the imposition of then-extant IRC §1491's 35-percent excise tax on those trusts that were not able to meet the new definition of the domestic trust (*e.g.*, by having a foreign trustee who partially controlled substantial positions of the trust). The Service recognized that certain existing domestic trusts might have difficulty meeting the new domestic trust criteria prior to the new legislation's effective date for trust years beginning after December 31, 1996.

PRE-RESIDENCE INCOME TAX PLANNING (SUMMARY)

Prior to the advent of tax residency, aliens have available to them a number of alternatives not available to U.S. citizens or other tax residents:

Establishment of Foreign Situs Trusts

Congress has closed the door on most foreign situs trusts with U.S. beneficiaries, especially when settled by an intending immigrant. However, they may still be viable for grandparents or other relatives, provided, essentially, the trust remains revocable during the life of the settlors, or when there are *no* U.S. beneficiaries. When correctly established, such foreign situs trusts may have the effect of removing the trust income from U.S. taxation in the hands of the current beneficiaries, and of avoiding the generation skipping estate tax consequences inherent in the descent and distribution of assets of U.S. domiciliaries.[237]

Acceleration of Income or Gain

To the extent possible and practicable, an intending immigrant or tax resident should accelerate receipt of income prior to entry into the United States for such purpose, especially if such income would be subject to lower (or *nil*) taxation abroad. Additionally, investments should be liquidated prior to coming to the United States in order that the prior appreciation not be subject to U.S. capital gain taxation. Regularly traded (appreciated) stocks could be sold and the gain realized prior to U.S. entry—even if the proceeds were immediately reinvested in the same securities (which would result in a step-up in basis so that only future gain would be subject to U.S. taxation). It also permits the alien to enjoy the gain on an asset capable of producing future earn-

---

[232] IRC §1491 (obsolete).

[233] IRC §1494(c) (obsolete). *See* Notice 97-18, 1997-10 IRB 1 (guidance on reporting and penalty exposure on transfers to foreign entities under Sections 1491 through 1494).

[234] IRC §684(a)–(b), applicable to transfers on or before December 31, 2009.

[235] IRC §684(a)–(b), as applicable to transfers after December 31, 2009.

[236] 1996-52 IRB 1.

[237] IRC §672(f), as amended by the 1996 Small Business Act, generally repeals the ability of foreign grantors to take advantage of the foreign grantor trust rules for U.S. beneficiaries. See IRC §672(f)(4), for the narrow exceptions and discussion in the text, above.

ings on the basis of a multiple of such earnings rather than subject the earnings (and future gain) to U.S. taxation when earned (or sold) later.

Timing Issues

By picking up the visa (permanent or nonimmigrant) outside of the United States, an alien may, with proper planning, defer or accelerate U.S. tax residency. When the sale of a principal residence is involved, IRC §1034 (revoked) will no longer obtain to defer recognition of gain if the foreign residence is sold after U.S. tax residence obtains. This result may be avoided by advising the alien to sell his or her foreign home *before* entering the United States in immigrant status, in which case the gain will *not* be subject to tax in this country. Other aliens may, because of the political climate at *home*, wish to accelerate tax residence in order to obtain possible U.S. tax benefits to be derived in the case of future foreign expropriation losses.[238]

Income Splitting

The partitioning of foreign and domestic (non–real property) assets amongst the members of the family of intending immigrants has long been a method of reducing the overall tax rate on productive assets. This, obviously, is a more efficacious tool when tax rates are progressively steeper than they are currently. However, similar results may also obtain through the use of foreign and, with certain limitations, domestic trusts (which are subject to the so-called *kiddie tax*—applying parents' rates to the income of minor children and affecting as well U.S. trusts for minors).

POST-RESIDENCE INCOME TAX PLANNING/REPORTING: DUAL RESIDENCE

During the first year of U.S. tax residence, it may be the case that the new resident may be able to claim dual residence status by virtue of a tax treaty (providing a tie-breaker provision) or by reason of the residency starting date.

An alien who acquires U.S. residence under the substantial presence test, but who was not a U.S. resident in the prior year, begins U.S. residency on the first day during the calendar year when he or she was physically present in the United States. An alien may be present in the United States for up to 10 days without triggering the residency starting date if the individual is able to establish a closer connection to a foreign tax home for that period. If the alien is physically present in the United States for 183 days or more in the current year, the foreign tax home exception will not spare him or her from the substantial presence test. Hence, there would be dual residence for an alien who meets the substantial presence test and is treated as a tax resident in a foreign tax home.

An alien who acquires U.S. residency under the lawful permanent resident (Green Card) test, but who was not a U.S. resident in the prior calendar year begins residency on the first day during the calendar year when he or she was physically present in the United States as a lawful permanent resident of the United States. The nominal presence exception does not apply. Again, dual residence will obtain and the alien will not be subject to tax in respect of the portion of the year preceding the alien's U.S. residence.

An alien and spouse may, however, make an election[239] to file a joint income tax return for the entire tax year in order to obtain the split income advantages and lower rates provided by the Code. However, any benefits of dual residency would be forfeited and the alien subject to U.S. tax on worldwide income for the entire tax year. The ability to use this election would clearly be dependent on the alien's having received *timely* tax counsel in order to have effected appropriate tax planning techniques such as income acceleration above discussed.

An employee in the United States for less than one year is typically considered temporarily away from home and entitled to the *away from home* provisions of the Code (*i.e.*, the ability to deduct expenses of lodging, travel, meals, *etc.*). The Service will also treat as temporary an individual who intends to return to his or her foreign tax home within two years.[240]

---

[238] Such losses may be subject to adjustment to the extent of future recovery. IRC §§80, 165(g), 166, 172(b)(1)(A), (B), (D), (d)(2), (h), 1212(a), 1231, 1351, 6167, and 6503(e).

[239] Per IRC §§6013(g) and (h).

[240] *Vide* note 18, *supra*. N.B. Federal Insurance Contributions Act (FICA or Social Security) tax is generally applicable to compensation paid for services performed in the United States. Compensation earned by employees of foreign governments and specified international organizations is exempt from FICA taxation, as are the earnings of aliens in F-1, J-1, or M-1 status from *authorized* employment. Moreover, a number of so-called Social Security Totalization Agreements have been negotiated with foreign countries exempting the

continued

Report Interests in Foreign Financial Accounts[241]

A U.S. person (for federal tax purposes) who has a financial interest in, or signature or other authority over, any financial accounts in a foreign country, if the aggregate value of these accounts exceeds $10,000 at any time during the calendar year, must report those accounts each year by filing Form TD F 90-22.1 with the Department of the Treasury on or before June 30 of the succeeding year. The act adds to existing penalties for failure to file TD F 90-22.1 a civil penalty of up to $10,000 that can be imposed without regard to willfulness. The penalty will not apply if income from the account has been properly reported on the U.S. person's income tax return and there was reasonable cause for the failure to report. In the case of a willful violation, however, the new penalty increases to the greater of $100,000 or 50 percent of the account balance. This civil penalty is effective for violations occurring after October 22, 2004.

FEDERAL ESTATE/GIFT TAXATION AND PLANNING OPPORTUNITIES

If an alien dies domiciled in the United States, his or her worldwide estate is subject to U.S. estate tax, regardless of the location of the assets.[242]

If an alien having a foreign domicile dies, his or her estate is subject to U.S. estate taxation only in respect of property with a U.S. situs, *viz.*, real property, stocks and bonds of U.S. issuers.[243]

While, as a general rule, an individual has but one domicile, courts in different jurisdictions have each found that a decedent died domiciled in its jurisdiction, thus subjecting the unfortunate estate to taxation on its worldwide assets.[244] While an alien lawfully admitted for permanent residence may indeed harbor an intention to return to the *old sod* to retire, thus retaining his or her domicile of origin, a facts and circumstances test will surely be applied to this issue upon death and each, the United States and the decedent's domicile of origin, may well find the decedent to have died its domiciliary! Nevertheless, the finding in such a case that the decedent had a foreign domicile would not affect the obligation of the decedent to pay federal income taxes on his or her worldwide income.

As in the case of income tax planning, estate tax planning for aliens should also be effected prior to acquiring U.S. residence. Thereafter, it is fraught with many of the same problems that beset tax planning for U.S. citizens. By timely transfer, the intending immigrant may avoid subsequent U.S. gift and estate taxation on foreign situs real, tangible, and intangible property. Moreover, U.S. real property interests may be converted to *intangible* property interests by incorporation and gift of the shares free from U.S. gift taxation.[245] Again, appropriate use of foreign situs trusts may, in certain narrow cases, also assist in providing relief from future U.S. estate and gift taxation.[246]

After acquiring U.S. domicile, the alien will be subject to the unified U.S. gift and estate tax regime. However, there are limitations on the unlimited deduction available as between U.S. citizen spouses when one or both of the spouses are resident aliens. In order to defer taxation on the portion of the decedent's estate left to an alien spouse, the same must be left to a qualified domestic trust (QDT).[247] To the extent the new immigrant expects to receive gifts or distributions from foreign individuals or estates, it may be efficacious to suggest that the same be transferred outright or in trust to his or her children (or, grandchildren) so as to avoid U.S. gift or, later, generation skipping taxes on such distributions from a U.S. estate.[248]

---

earnings of the citizens of each in the territory of the other from Social Security taxes for periods up to five years. These Agreements should be reviewed prior to collection of FICA taxes from nationals of such countries.

[241] American Jobs Creation Act of 2004, Pub. L. No. 108-357. Following an amnesty period (which expired Oct. 15, 2009) for filing foreign bank and financial account reports (FBARs), the Treasury Department has stepped up enforcement of FBARs' civil and *criminal* provisions and their harsh penalties.

[242] IRC §2031(a).

[243] IRC §§2103, 2104.

[244] *In re Dorrance*, 115 N.J. Eq. 268, 170 A. 601, *Dorrance's Estate*, 309 Pa. 151, 163 A. 303, *cert. denied*, *Dorrance v. Pennsylvania*, 287 U.S. 660 and 288 U.S. 617 (1932); *Dor-*
continued

---

rance v. Thayer-Martin, 116 N.J. Law 362, 184 A. 743, *cert. denied*, 298 U.S. 678 (1935). *Cf. Texas v. Florida*, 306 U.S. 398 (1938).

[245] IRC §2501(a)(2).

[246] *Vide* note 16, *supra*, and accompanying text.

[247] IRC §2056A.

[248] *N.B.* There is no statutory regime for the crediting of foreign gift taxes to the U.S. estate tax liability of a decedent. Such credit is based upon reciprocity (IRC §2014(h)) and/or
continued

Although not deductible for income tax purposes, contributions to foreign charities are deductible from a U.S. estate for gift and estate tax purposes.[249]

DEPARTURE PLANNING

The tax regime for the departing alien is an attractive one if properly used. Like that for the inbound alien, however, it is fraught with pitfalls, and professional tax advice will prove beneficial.[250] Examples include:

Tax-free Sale of Principal Residence

Prior to 1997, it was possible, by making the appropriate election, for a resident alien to sell his or her U.S. residence and acquire a new one abroad, deferring thereby any tax on the gain.[251] In this manner, the basis of the new residence abroad would have a carryover basis (that of the rollover U.S. property), and no gain would be realized until disposition of the foreign residence. If the alien were no longer a U.S. tax resident at the time of such disposition, he or she would not be subject to U.S. tax on the gain.[252] Currently, the Code provides an exclusion of $250,000 of gain realized from the sale of a principal residence ($500,000 in the case of qualifying couples) utilized as such for at least two years prior to the date of sale. This exclusion does not *apply to any sale or exchange by an individual if the treatment provided by* (the expatriation provisions of IRC) *§877(a)(1) applies to such individual*.[253] Hence, sale of a principal residence should occur prior to abandonment of the resident alien's status as such.

Deferral of Capital Gain

The deferred disposition of an intangible capital asset (other than of a USRPI or asset used within the preceding 10 years in a U.S. trade or business) until a tax year when the alien is no longer resident or actively engaged in the conduct of a trade or business in the United States (and is physically present in the United States fewer than 183 days) should produce gain free from U.S. taxation.[254]

Deferral of Compensation

Deferred income for services performed abroad may escape U.S. taxation if paid to an alien after relinquishment of U.S. residence status.[255] Deferral of receipt of U.S. source income or income attributable to services performed when the alien was a U.S. tax resident (whether through delay of payment or from a Deferred Compensation Plan) until a year when an alien is no longer resident or otherwise engaged in a U.S. trade or business, will ordinarily be fully subject to U.S. taxation as if received while the alien were resident, and not at the 30 percent (or lower tax treaty) withholding tax rate.[256]

Gifts to a Spouse

A resident alien may make unlimited tax-free gifts of U.S. situs real, tangible, and intangible property to a U.S. citizen spouse and gifts of up to $100,000 per year to a resident alien spouse, tax-free. Such gifts would be subject to gift tax if made after relinquishing U.S. tax residence.

Caveat Re: Expatriation

U.S. citizens or long-term residents who relinquish their U.S. citizenship or green cards or are treated as a residents of a foreign country under the provisions of a tax treaty between the United States and the foreign country, and who do not waive treaty benefits applicable to residents of the foreign country, will both be treated for tax purposes as if they were former citizens of the United States. A *long-term resident* is an individual who has been a lawful

---

estate and gift tax treaty (IRC §§170.642(C), 2055, 2106(a)(2), and 2522).

[249] IRC §§170, 642(C), 2055, 2106(a)(2), and 2522.

[250] Note also that aliens who have more than eight years of U.S. tax residence and who are *expatriating* by renouncing their permanent residence status for presumed tax reasons, fall under an entirely different set of rules that are outside the scope of this paper. *See* IRC §877(a)(1).

[251] IRC §1034 (repealed). *Cf.* note 20, *supra*, and accompanying text.

[252] If such sale does not qualify for rollover, *e.g.*, if the alien were no longer *resident*, he or she could be subject to a tax liability for the disposition of a *U.S. Real Property Interest (USRPI)* per IRC §897 (created by the Foreign Investor Tax Act of 1980 (FIRPTA).

[253] *See* IRC §121(e).

---

[254] IRC §§871(a)(2), 897. In the absence of an applicable U.S. tax treaty, installment sale of an asset used in the active conduct of a U.S. trade or business within 10 years after cessation of use, will trigger capital gains tax even if no installments are received by the departing alien until he or she is no longer *resident* for U.S. tax purposes. IRC §§453 and 864(c)(6) and (7).

[255] IRC §§871(a) and (f).

[256] IRC §§871(a) and (f).

permanent resident of the United States in at least eight taxable years during the period of 15 taxable years ending with the year in which the individual relinquishes his or her U.S. green card or commences to be treated as a resident of a foreign country.

The Heart Act of 2008[257] marks a dramatic change for those individuals who choose to relinquish U.S. citizenship or terminate status as a long-term U.S. permanent resident. New Internal Revenue Code §§877A and 2801 are effective immediately and affect certain U.S. citizens who expatriate and certain long-term U.S. residents who terminate U.S. residency on or after June 17, 2008. For ease of reference, individuals who fall into either category are referred to herein as "expatriates."

Unlike the situation under current law, in which an expatriating individual can often make financial and other arrangements to avoid additional U.S. taxes, under the new law the imposition of U.S. taxes upon and following expatriation will be unavoidable in many cases (particularly with respect to covered expatriates with substantial unrealized gain in their investment portfolios and heirs who are either U.S. citizens or residents).

The most notable changes effectuated by the new law are as follows: (1) imposition of a new "mark-to-market" exit tax; (2) elimination of the 10-year alternate income, gift, and estate tax regimes that formerly applied to expatriates; and (3) imposition of a new transfer tax payable by U.S. citizens and residents who receive gifts or bequests from expatriates.

Summary of Prior Law

Generally, under Code §877, expatriates who met certain conditions were subject to an alternate U.S. income tax regime for a 10-year period after the date of expatriation, during which they were required to file annual information returns and pay U.S. tax on certain items of income not otherwise taxable to nonresident aliens (*e.g.*, capital gains on the sale of U.S. stock). In addition, such expatriates were subject, during the 10-year post-expatriation period, to U.S. gift and estate tax on the transfer of a broader array of assets than other nonresident aliens.

Also, under prior law, if any such expatriate were physically present in the U.S. for more than 30 days in any given year during the 10-year post-expatriation period, he or she would be treated for tax purposes as a U.S. citizen or resident for that taxable year. As a result, such individual would be subject *that year* to: (i) U.S. income tax on worldwide income earned; (ii) U.S. gift tax if he or she transferred any worldwide assets by gift; and (iii) U.S. estate tax on worldwide assets if he or she died.

These rules will continue to apply to individuals who expatriated from the United States prior to June 17, 2008. They will not apply, however, to individuals who expatriate on or after that date.

Summary of New Law

Applicability of New Law

The new law applies to so-called "covered expatriates," who are defined under new Code §877A as individuals who: (1) are either U.S. citizens who relinquish U.S. citizenship or long-term U.S. residents (*i.e.*, individuals holding a green card for at least 8 of the prior 15 years) who terminate U.S. residency; *and* (2) meet one of the following requirements:

- Average annual net income tax liability for the five preceding years ending before the date of the loss of U.S. citizenship or residency termination that exceeds $139,000 (as indexed for inflation);

- Net worth of $2,000,000 or more on such date; or

- Failure to certify under penalties of perjury that he or she has complied with all U.S. federal tax obligations for the preceding five years, or failure to submit such evidence of compliance as the Secretary may require.

The various instances in which a U.S. citizen will be deemed to have relinquished U.S. citizenship are set forth in IRC §877A(g)(4). A long-term U.S. resident will be treated as having terminated his or her U.S. residency if his or her green card is revoked, if it is administratively or judicially determined that he or she has abandoned lawful permanent resident status, and in certain other unique circumstances.

Certain individuals who either are born with dual citizenship or who relinquish U.S. citizenship prior

---

[257] The 1996 legislation amending the 10-year expatriation tax regime of IRC §§2017, 2501(a)(3) and 877 was the Health Insurance Portability and Accountability Act, Pub. L. No. 104-191, which was again modified in 2008 by H.R. 6081, the Heroes Earnings Assistance and Relief Tax Act of 2008 (the Heart Act), passed by Congress on May 22, 2008, and signed into law by the President on June 17, 2008. The Heart Act adds new Sections 877A and 2108 to the Code. *See also* IRC §6039F, as added by SBA 96, §1905(a).

to age 18½ are exempt from covered expatriate status, provided they meet certain additional requirements.

Exit Tax

GENERAL DESCRIPTION

Under the new law, covered expatriates are not subject to the above-described 10-year alternate U.S. income, gift and estate tax regimes, and will not be deemed to be U.S. residents for tax purposes if they are physically present in the United States for more than 30 days in any given year following expatriation.

Instead, covered expatriates will now be subject to "mark-to-market" deemed sale rules under which they will be treated as if they sold their worldwide assets for fair market value on the day before expatriation.

Gain from the deemed sale is taken into account at the time of expatriation without regard to other Code provisions. Loss is also taken into account at that time to the extent otherwise provided in the Code, except that the wash sale rules of Code §1091 do not apply. Net gain on the deemed sale is taxable to the extent that it exceeds $600,000 (indexed for inflation). For example:

If a covered expatriate owns $5 million in total assets with an aggregate income tax basis of $1 million, then such individual will be required to pay tax on a deemed gain of $3.4 million (*i.e.*, $4 million gain minus the $600,000 exemption) in connection with his or her expatriation.

It is unclear under the new law whether expatriates will be required to pay the exit tax upon departure from the United States, or with a tax return timely filed during the calendar year following expatriation.

For purposes of determining the tax imposed under the mark-to-market rules, assets held by an individual on the day that he or she became a U.S. resident shall be treated as having a basis on that date of not less than the fair market value of such assets on that date. A covered expatriate can make an irrevocable election for this particular rule not to apply. It appears that this rule will apply retroactively to individuals who became U.S. residents before the effective date of the Act.

ELECTION TO DEFER EXIT TAX

A covered expatriate may elect to defer payment of the exit tax imposed on the deemed sale of property, so long as he or she furnishes a bond or other adequate security to the IRS. Interest is charged for the deferral period at the rate normally applicable to individual underpayments. The election is irrevocable and is made on a property-by-property basis.

SPECIAL RULES

Deferred Compensation Items. If a covered expatriate holds an interest in an "eligible deferred compensation item," the payor must deduct and withhold from a "taxable payment" to the expatriate a tax equal to 30 percent of such payment. This withholding requirement replaces any withholding requirement under prior law.

An "eligible deferred compensation item" is any deferred compensation item with respect to which: (1) the payor is either a U.S. person or a non-U.S. person who elects to be treated as a U.S. person for purposes of withholding and meets other requirements; and (2) the covered expatriate notifies the payor of his status as a covered expatriate and irrevocably waives any claim of withholding reduction under any treaty with the United States.

If the deferred compensation item is not an eligible deferred compensation item, an amount equal to the present value of the covered expatriate's deferred compensation item is treated as having been received by him or her on the day before the expatriation date. Adjustments are made for subsequent distributions to take into account this treatment. Furthermore, such deemed distributions are not subject to early distribution tax.

Tax-Deferred Accounts. If a covered expatriate holds any interest in a specified tax-deferred account (*e.g.*, an IRA, 529 Plan, etc.) prior to expatriation, such covered expatriate is treated as having received a distribution of his or her entire interest in such account on the day before the expatriation date. Again, appropriate adjustments are made for subsequent distributions to take into account this treatment, and the deemed distributions are not subject to early distribution tax.

Interests in Trusts. Grantor trusts. The assets held by any portion of a trust that is a grantor trust for income tax purposes with respect to a covered expatriate are subject to the mark-to-market exit tax.

Nongrantor trusts. The exit tax does not apply to the portion of a trust that is a nongrantor trust for income tax purposes. Instead, with respect to any direct or indirect distribution from such trust to a covered expatriate, the trustee must deduct and withhold from the distribution an amount equal to 30 percent of the portion of the distribution that would have been includible in the gross income of the covered expatriate if the covered expatriate had not expatriated. If the nongrantor trust distributes appreciated property to a covered expatriate, the trust must recognize gain as if the property were then sold to the covered expatriate at its fair market value. It is not clear how these provisions will apply to foreign nongrantor trusts.

Transfer tax. Under new Code §2801, U.S. citizens and residents who receive any bequests, or any gifts in excess of the annual gift tax exclusion amount, from a covered expatriate will be liable for a transfer tax at the highest applicable estate or gift tax rate.

Note, however, that the transfer tax does not apply with respect to transfers: (i) reported on a timely filed U.S. gift or estate tax return; or (ii) for which a marital or charitable deduction would otherwise be allowed.

Special rules apply to transfers in trust. If a covered expatriate makes a gift or bequest to a domestic trust, the trust must pay the transfer tax. If, in contrast, a covered expatriate makes a gift or bequest to a foreign trust, the foreign trust is not subject to the transfer tax; rather, the transfer tax will be payable if and when assets attributable to the gift or bequest made by the covered expatriate to the foreign trust are distributed to a recipient who is a U.S citizen or resident.

The new expatriation law represents a substantial change from prior law. Accordingly, any individuals who are thinking about relinquishing their U.S. citizenship or residency, and their advisors, should familiarize themselves with the new rules before proceeding. It should also be noted that it is not clear that the *exit* tax created by IRC §877A will be creditable against income tax liabilities of the expatriate, as it is not a tax on income or a tax in lieu of such a tax.

CONCLUSION

Effective tax planning and stand-up comedy have much in common. Essentially, it is all in the timing. As an oft-quoted German immigrant is supposed to have said: *I' bin too soon old und too late schmart*! It is one thing to learn from one's own mistakes; it is another to expect a client to pay for them. It is hoped that the foregoing will have the salutary effect of raising the tax consciousness of the immigration specialist as well as of the generalist who delves from time to time in immigration matters, hopefully eliciting thereby future timely enquiry and assistance on behalf of their clients from tax professionals whose interest in well serving the immigration client dovetails quite perfectly with those of the immigration practitioner. Like taxes themselves, tax professionals are a necessary evil; and, as with the ubiquitous American Express card, foreign clients should never leave home without one.

U.S. GIFT TAX TREATIES IN FORCE
- Australia
- Austria
- Denmark
- France
- Germany
- Japan
- Sweden
- United Kingdom

U.S. ESTATE TAX TREATIES IN FORCE
- Australia
- Austria
- Canada (pre-1985 decedents)
- Denmark
- Finland
- France
- Germany
- Greece
- Ireland
- Italy
- Japan
- Netherlands
- Norway
- South Africa
- Sweden
- Switzerland
- United Kingdom

AILA
OCCUPATIONAL
GUIDEBOOK

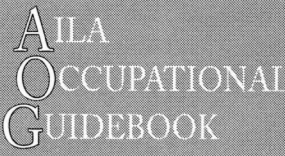

COMPARATIVE INVESTMENT IMMIGRATION

ENTREPRENEURS AND INVESTORS—AUSTRALIA

*by Robert J. Walsh**

INTRODUCTION

The current Australian Labor Government, elected in November 2007, has continued the emphasis of the previous long-standing Coalition Government in pursuing a migration policy based on skills rather than on family relationships, seeking to attract individuals to migrate to Australia with employment-based skills, business capabilities or capacity to invest funds in government bonds. Prior to this policy shift, which commenced in 1996, skilled migrants accounted for approximately 30 percent of the total Non-Humanitarian Migration Program. Under the policy emphasis on skilled migration, the percentages allocated between skilled and family migration have almost reversed. In 2008–09, over 67 percent of visas in the Non-Humanitarian Migration Program were allocated to skilled migrants and in 2009–10, 64 percent of visas have been allocated to skilled migrants.[1] In 2009–10 there has been a re-balancing of skills migration toward those individuals who are sponsored by an employer or a state or territory government or those who have an occupation on the Critical Skills List.[2] In early 2010, the Australian government announced further changes to the skilled migration program which will give even greater emphasis to skilled occupations considered by the government to be critical to the Australian economy and society. These occupations will include engineering professionals, medical practitioners and nurses, as well as specialist information technology occupations. Those who are not sponsored by an employer or by a state or territory government or who are not in one of the highly sought after occupational groups are likely to be no longer eligible to migrate to Australia. Announcements on the details of the new arrangements for this aspect of skilled migration are expected to commence at the end of April 2010.

The number of business skills visas for business people or investors available in 2009–10 has increased by about five percent over the previous year.[3] This represents a further modest increase in the year-to-year numbers for business skills visas with the total number of business skills visas increasing from 1,982 visas in 2002–03 to the planned figure of 7,800 in 2009–10, which has now been capped at 6,530 places.[4]

Business skills migration to Australia has been a somewhat problematic area for successive Australian governments as the relatively low numbers illustrate. It is not an area of migration that is enthusiastically embraced by either Coalition or Labor governments. There have been a number of major revisions of business skills migration policy since the early 1990s. The current framework introduced in March 2003 and modified in April 2010[5] has an emphasis on a two-stage process leading to permanent residence with concessions for those business people willing to establish a business away from Australia's major metropolitan areas. While this program has been more successful than its predecessors in meeting the policy objectives of a business skills migration program, it has also led to a small take-up rate despite the low financial thresholds for potential applicants, which were increased in April 2010. This should be contrasted to the general skills-based programs where numbers have climbed significantly, noting the trimming of numbers in the current year's

---

* **Robert Walsh** is the Managing Partner of Fragomen in Australia and is located in Sydney. Robert is an experienced commercial lawyer with significant experience in providing immigration and other legal advice to companies in sectors such as financial services, mining and resources, information technology and telecommunications, retail, science and engineering, and health. He is a member of American Immigration Lawyers Association (AILA), the Immigration and Nationality Law Committee of the International Bar Association, American Chamber of Commerce, the International Law Committee of the Law Council of Australia, and the Migration Institute of Australia.

[1] For full details of the number of visas available in all programs, see *www.immi.gov.au/media/statistics/statistical-info/visa-grants/migrant.htm*.

[2] For a full list of occupations on the Critical Skills List, see *www.immi.gov.au/skilled/general-skilled-migration/pdf/critical-skills-list.pdf*.

[3] Migration Program Statistics—*www.immi.gov.au/media/statistics/statistical-info/visa-grants/migrant.htm*.

[4] For the capping of business skills visa numbers for 2009–10, see *www.comlaw.gov.au/ComLaw/Legislation/LegislativeInstrument1.nsf/all/whatsnew/5FBF9614B703A98CCA*.

[5] See *www.immi.gov.au/skilled/business/_pdf/businesschanges.pdf*.

program, with little public anxiety and full allocation of places each year.

The current approach to business skills migration in Australia is a significant refinement of the previous model reflecting concerns with some policy failings that had been identified in the previous arrangements. There are now concerns in Australia with the current business skills rules that the program is not attracting the individuals most likely to make a significant contribution to the Australian economy. The previously low financial thresholds coupled with the two-stage approach to attaining permanent residence have perhaps been perversely turning away business people with larger amounts of capital to invest in favor of high net worth programs in countries, such as the United Kingdom. In addition, the lack of a true entrepreneur visa category is frequently viewed as a weakness in the Australian business skills program and there are concerns on the operation of the program as it relates to senior managers.

As a result of these concerns and the fact the current rules have been in place for some seven years, the Department of Immigration and Citizenship (the Department) has been conducting a review of the business skills program which has led to the changes implemented effective April 19, 2010. These changes have increased a number of the financial thresholds for net business and personal assets for the first stage provisional business skills visas and the percentage of ownership interests held by applicants for eligibility for most of the first and second stages of business skills visas. In addition, the senior management option for one of the state-sponsored categories of business skills has been removed. More generally, in 2009 the government commenced "the task of constructing a long-term planning framework for migration so that future levels of immigration remain in the best interests of Australia." This task will now be complemented by the larger review of population-growth issues to be undertaken by the newly appointed Minster for Population in the Australian government. It is expected that both these reviews will impact policy decisions for all migration categories, including business skills migration. It is expected that these reviews will take up to 12 months to be completed.[6]

---

[6] See media releases issued by Senator the Hon. Chris Evans, Minister for Immigration and Citizenship, on Sept. 23, 2009, at *www.minister.immi.gov.au/media/media-releases/2009/ ce09091.htm* and by the Hon. Kevin Rudd, Prime Minister, on Apr. 3, 2010, at *www.pm.gov.au/node/6614.*

AUSTRALIAN BUSINESS SKILLS PROGRAM

The Business Skills visa classes are a subcategory within the skilled stream of Australia's Non Humanitarian Migration Program. The Business Skills visa classes include categories for business owners, senior executives, and investors. There are other visa categories for migrants who already have established a business in Australia, either with or without sponsorship from state or territory governments. As illustrated above, the various business skills visas make up less than 10 percent of visa approvals in the total skilled program. Despite the small numbers, it has been the stated policy of successive governments to seek to attract successful business people and investors to migrate to Australia.

Current Australian Government Policy on Business Skills Migration

Some of the key features of the current arrangements for business skills migration, which have been in effect since 2003 and had been designed to address serious concerns with the previous rules, are:

Staged Approach to Permanent Residence

A central feature of the current business skills visa categories is a two-staged approach to obtaining permanent residence. For the majority of potential business migrants, the business skills visas were made provisional rather than granting immediate permanent residence in the first instance. The provisional visas are valid for four years. Once requisite business or investment levels have been achieved over a certain period of time, an application for permanent residence can then be made.

A direct pathway to permanent residence is now only available for a limited number of potential business migrants of extremely high caliber who have an outstanding track record of business success and who have high-level support of the relevant state or territory government.

The policy rationale behind the staged approach to permanent residence was the Department's finding that a significant percentage of business skills migrants were not settling in Australia. Instead, they would activate their permanent residence visas by entering Australia and then return to their country of origin without spending appropriate time in Australia to make any attempt to establish a business in Australia. The staged approach to permanent residence provides greater certainty that business skills migrants would engage in a predetermined level of business and investment activities, thereby ensuring an inflow of capital into Australia.

Moreover, holders of the provisional business skills visas are not eligible for Medicare benefits or for other social security and welfare services. Access to Medicare benefits then became a motivation to achieve permanent residence through establishing a business or maintaining investment activities.

The Independent Executive temporary residence visa, which generally attracted business migrants who could not meet the higher threshold criteria of the Business Skills category, was abolished. It was probably the closest Australia has come to having a visa category for entrepreneurs, in that it was based more on potential and, with its lower financial criteria, not on clearly defined levels of business experience.

The main criteria for the Independent Executive visa was that the business person have net assets of AUD$250,000[7] (or an appropriate lower amount depending on the business plan), for the purpose of establishing, or buying into a business and managing that business on a day-to-day basis. Personal attributes and background consistent with the nature of the proposed business were also required. Once a successful business had been established, many Independent Executives applied for permanent residence. However, the Department noted that many holders of the Independent Executive visas were unable to meet the thresholds for a permanent residence application.[8]

Since March 1, 2003, individuals have been prohibited from making new applications for the 457 Independent Executive visa. Individuals who already hold a 457 Independent Executive visa are able to continue to apply for an extension of their status.

While there were widely recognized concerns with the Independent Executive visa, the continued lack of a visa category for entrepreneurs or business people with good ideas, but a lower level of available capital and actual business experience, is perceived by some to be an ongoing weakness of the business skills regime in Australia.

State or Territory Government Sponsorship

Another key feature of the current business skills visa arrangements is the emphasis on sponsorship by an Australian state or territory government, complemented by lower threshold criteria where such sponsorship is achieved.

Sponsorship provides Australian states and territories with a greater opportunity to attract prospective business migrants to their respective state or territory. This has led to competition between certain state and territory governments to promote their state or territory as a destination for business skills migrants. While there is debate on the benefits of migration from time to time, the overall consensus of commentators in Australia is that migration is positive for the country despite additional costs for public services, including infrastructure.[9]

The impact of state and territory sponsorship and the lower thresholds where such sponsorship is available is illustrated in the proportionately higher numbers of successful visas in the sponsored categories than in the unsponsored categories.

Regional Settlement of Business Migrants

Almost 80 percent of migrants are settling in the major metropolitan areas of New South Wales, Queensland, and Western Australia. The concern of other smaller states and territories is that they are not receiving their fair share of business migrants and cannot reap the economic benefits. Victoria and South Australia, for example, have both formalized a comprehensive marketing strategy to improve their market share position in this area.[10] Other less populous states and territories also have implemented similar strategies and support mechanisms to attract investors and other business migrants.

New South Wales, in light of concerns about resource and infrastructure costs in absorbing a large proportion of migrants in and around Sydney, did not support business skills migration for some years. However, more recently New South Wales has de-

---

[7] As the legal requirements to migrate to Australia in the business skills program are expressed in Australian dollars (AUD), all dollar values in this article are given in AUD. At the time of writing, AUD1.00 was valued at approximately USD0.93. With this exchange rate, for example, AUD250,000 would be equal to USD232,464. The current exchange rate between AUD and USD at any particular time would need to be confirmed.

[8] Department of Immigration and Multicultural and Indigenous Affairs (DIMIA), Submission to the Joint Standing Committee on Foreign Affairs and Trade (Trade Subcommittee), Inquiry into "Enterprising Australia—Planning, Preparing and Profiting from Trade and Investment" (Mar. 2001).

[9] See, for example, DIMIA, "The Impact of Permanent Migrants on the State and Territory Budgets" (May 2002).

[10] Economic Development Committee, "Inquiry into the Economic Impact of Business Migration on Victoria," No. 8 Session (May 1998).

cided to provide sponsorship for business migrants to live both in Sydney and elsewhere in the state.

CURRENT BUSINESS SKILLS VISA REQUIREMENTS[11]

The current arrangements for business skills migrants in Australia are divided between visas available for individuals who wish to establish a business or participate in an existing business as an owner and manager, and those prepared to invest in state or territory government bonds for four years while assessing longer-term business or investor opportunities in Australia.

Business Background and Business Ownership Interest Requirements

There are two key concepts relating to the business background of, and to the ownership interests held by, applicants for both provisional and permanent residence business skills visas. The two key concepts are:

- "qualifying business"; and
- "main business."[12]

A "qualifying business" for the purposes of meeting the criteria for most business skills visas is an enterprise operated for making a profit though the provision of goods and/or services to the public, but not the provision of rental property and it must not be operated primarily for speculative or passive investment.

A "main business" is an actively operating business providing goods and/or services to the public where:

- the applicant for the relevant business skills visa maintains, or has maintained, direct and continuous involvement in the management of the business from day to day and in making decisions affecting the overall direction and performance of the business; and
- the value of the business skills visa applicant's ownership interest in the business is or was:
  - at least 10 percent of the total value of the business if the business is operated by a publicly listed company; or
  - at least 30 percent of the total value of the business if the business is not operated by a publicly listed company and the annual turnover of the business is AUD$400,000 or more; or
  - at least 51 percent of the total value of the business if the business is not operated by a publicly listed company and the annual turnover of the business is AUD$400,000 or less.

Common General Requirements Across All Business Skills Visa Categories

There are a number of common requirements across all business skills visa categories. These include:

Age Requirement

The age limit of 45 years for applicants for business skills visas who are not sponsored is a reflection of the Department's research that shows people 45 years of age or older have a net negative impact on the Australian economy over their lifetime. For example, most people incur most of their medical costs in the later years of life.[13]

For those visas sponsored by a state or territory government, the age limit is raised to 55 years of age. It is possible for applicants who are 55 years of age or more to obtain sponsorship by a state and territory government. However, any such applicant must demonstrate that they will bring exceptional economic benefit to the relevant state or territory.

English Language Requirement

There is also a minimum English language proficiency of vocational English for the main applicant for business skills visas.

For state– or territory-sponsored visas, there is no formal English requirement for the main applicant. However, as the application must be lodged in English, and if an interview is required, it is likely to be detrimental to a successful outcome where the applicant does not possess some English language ability.

Family members are not required to have English language ability, but where any family member over the age of 18 years has less than functional English, an additional application fee must be paid.[14]

---

[11] A summary of the requirements for business skills visas is provided at the end of this article.

[12] See Regulation 1.03 and Regulation 1.11 of Migration Regulations 1994.

[13] *Procedure Advice Manual 3*, "Policy and Procedural instructions for officers administering migration law."

[14] The second installment of the visa application charge, as of July 1, 2009, is AUD$3,510.

Health and Character Requirements

All applicants, including family members, must meet the relevant health and character requirements. These generally consist of medical and chest x-ray examinations, including HIV testing and police clearance certificates for all jurisdictions where applicants over 16 years of age have lived for more than 12 months in the 10 years before the time of application.

Only one category of business skills visa leads to permanent residence in the first instance: the Business Talent (subclass 132) visa. The relevant criteria for that category are:

- the applicant must have had a successful business career;
- for each of at least two of the last four fiscal years, he or she (and his or her spouse) have held net assets in a qualifying business(es), to a value of not less than AUD$400,000;
- for each of at least two of the last four fiscal years, the applicant's main business(es) had an annual turnover of at least AUD$3 million;
- the applicant's business and personal assets (or those of the applicant and his or her spouse) together have a net value of not less than AUD$1.5 million and are capable of being transferred to Australia within two years; and
- the applicant must be sponsored by a state or territory government.

All other applicants for business skills migration to Australia, either to establish or participate actively in a business in Australia or to invest in state or government bonds, must go through a two-stage process to achieve permanent residence.

Business Skills Migration: Establishing or Participating in a Business—First Stage

The specific criteria for the subclass 160 Business Owner (Provisional) and subclass 163 State/Territory Sponsored Business Owner (Provisional),[15] and the subclass 161 Senior Executive (Provisional) and subclass 164 State/Territory Sponsored Senior Executive (Provisional)[16] are set out below:

For subclass 160 and subclass 163 visas, the following criteria must be met:

- the applicant has overall had a successful business career;
- for each of at least two of the last four fiscal years, he or she (and his or her spouse) have held net assets in a qualifying business(es) to a value of not less than AUD$200,000 (this criteria only applies to subclass 160 applicants);
- for each of at least two of the last four fiscal years, the applicant's main business(es) had an annual turnover of at least AUD$500,000 (reduced to AUD$300,000 in the case of subclass 163 applicants); and
- the applicant's business and personal assets (or those of the applicant and his or her spouse) together have a net value of not less than AUD$800,000 and are capable of being transferred to Australia within two years (reduced to AUD$500,000 in the case of subclass 163 applicants).

For subclass 161 and subclass 164, the following criteria must be met:

- for each of at least two of the last four fiscal years, the applicant has occupied a position in the three highest levels of the management structure of the business and was responsible for the strategic policy development affecting a major component or a wide range of operations of that major business; and
- the applicant's business and personal assets (or those of the applicant and his or her spouse) together have a net value of not less than AUD$800,000 and are capable of being transferred to Australia within two years (reduced to AUD$500,000 in the case of subclass 164 applicants).

Business Skills Migration: Establishing or Participating in a Business—Second Stage

Holders of certain business skills provisional visas may apply to remain permanently in Australia in a number of subclasses:

The subclass 890 Business Owner and subclass 892 State/Territory Sponsored Business Owner[17] visas are the usual second-stage pathway to permanent residence for holders of first-stage business

---

[15] Item 1202A of Schedule 1 and Regulations 160 and 163 of Schedule 2 of the Migration Regulations 1994.

[16] Item 1202A of Schedule 1 and Regulations 161 and 164 of Schedule 2 of the Migration Regulations 1994.

[17] Item 1104B of Schedule 1 and Regulations 890 and 892 of Schedule 2 of the Migration Regulations 1994.

skills visas, such as the subclass 160, 161, 163 or 164 visas. The criteria for these visas are:

- the applicant has had, and continues to have, an ownership interest in at least one actively operating main business in Australia for at least two years before applying;
- in the 12 months before the application is made, the applicant's main business(es) in Australia had an annual turnover of AUD$300,000 (reduced to AUD$200,000 in the case of subclass 892 applicants);
- all Australian Business Numbers have been obtained and all Business Activity Statements have been submitted to the Australian Taxation Office;
- throughout the 12 months immediately before the application is made, the applicant's main business(es) employed at least two full-time employees, each of whom is not the applicant or a member of the applicant's family and is an Australian citizen or permanent resident or a New Zealand passport holder (in the case of subclass 892 applicants, this criteria is satisfied if the business employed one eligible employee); and
- the net value of the applicant's business and personal assets in Australia (or those of the applicant and his or her spouse) has been at least AUD$250,000 throughout the 12 months immediately before the application is made.

Another pathway to permanent residence is through the Established Business in Australia (subclass 845)[18] visa. The applicant, who must hold a substantive temporary residence visa, must show that:

- he or she, either individually or together with his or her spouse, has had net assets in Australia of least AUD$250,000, of which the net assets in his or her main business are no less than AUD$100,000 for at least the last 12 months before the date of lodging the application;
- he or she, either individually or together with his or her spouse, has an ownership interest in a main business in Australia for the last 18 months before the date of lodging the application;
- he or she has been actively involved in and responsible for the overall management and performance of his or her main business;
- he or she has been physically present in Australia for nine out of the last 12 months before the date of lodging the application;
- he or she has had a successful business career; and
- he or she would score at least 105 points on the points test.

In the Regional Established Business in Australia sponsored by a state/territory regional authority (subclass 846)[19] category, the applicant, who must hold a subclass 457 visa, must show that:

- he or she, either individually or together with his or her spouse, have net assets in Australia of least AUD$200,000, of which the net assets in his or her main business are not less than AUD$75,000;
- he or she, either individually or together with his or her spouse, have an ownership interest in a main business for the last two years before lodging the application;
- the main business must have had an annual turnover of at least AUD$200,000 in each of the two years before lodging the application, or exported goods or services of a value of at least AUD$100,000 in each of the last two years;
- the applicant has been actively involved in and responsible for the overall management and performance of his or her main business;
- he or she has been physically present in Australia for one out of the last two years before the date of lodging the application;
- he or she has had a successful business career; and
- he or she would score at least 105 points on the points test.

In announcing the higher percentages for business ownership interests held by applicants in a main business(es) on April 19, 2010, an exemption from the higher thresholds was announced for applicants for subclass 890, 892, 845, and 846 second-stage permanent residence visas where the applicants had purchased a business prior to the change in the thresholds.

Business Skills Migration: Business Migrants Wishing to Invest in Government Bonds— First Stage

Business skills visas relevant to business investors to enter Australia to take up investment activities are

---

[18] Item 1104A of Schedule 1 and Regulations 845 of Schedule 2 of the Migration Regulations 1994.

[19] Item 1104A of Schedule 1 and Regulation 846 of Schedule 2 of the Migration Regulations 1994.

the subclass 162 Investor (Provisional)[20] or subclass 165 State/Territory Sponsored Investor (Provisional).[21] These subclasses are intended for business migrants with a broader business and investment skills profile than that targeted by the other business skills subclasses and who wish to take longer to assess future business or investment activities in Australia but who are able to invest their own funds in government bonds for four years. Both visas enable the holders to travel to, enter, and remain in Australia for a provisional period of up to four years.

Under the former Investment Linked visa categories, the high level of investment that was required was considered to be an indication of a business person's commitment to settle in Australia in the longer term. The migrant was not required to make any other investment in Australia during or after the three-year investment period. Some viewed the Investment Linked visa as a "buy a visa" category. Investment Linked visa holders were surveyed at 36 months after arrival to measure their business contribution to Australia. Survey data for 1996–97, arrivals showed that only 23 percent of Investment Linked visa holders were engaged in business three years after arrival.[22] Rejection rates for this visa class were also high and varied from 30 percent to 50 percent in 2003.[23] For these reasons the criteria were changed to the current requirements whereby the individual must have broad business or investment experience as well as funds available to invest in government bonds for four years.

The basic requirements for the subclass 162 Investor (Provisional) visa,[24] without state or territory sponsorship, are that the applicant:

- has a demonstrated record of business management skill or eligible investment activity, for example, a senior management role in a qualifying business with 10 percent ownership or managing investments with a net value of at least AUD$1,500,000;

- is able to make a designated investment[25] of AUD$1,500,000 in the relevant state or territory government bonds for four years;

- has had, for the two years before application, net personal assets valued at least AUD$2,250,000; and

- has a genuine and realistic intention to continue to maintain business or investment activity in Australia after the designated investment has matured.

For the subclass 165 State/Territory Sponsored Investor Provisional visa,[26] the basic requirements are that the applicant has:

- sponsorship by a state or territory government;

- a demonstrated record of business management skill or eligible investment activity, for example, a senior management role in a qualifying business holding a 10 percent ownership or managing investments with a net value of at least AUD$750,000;

- made a designated investment of AUD$750,000 in the relevant state or territory government bonds for four years;

- for the two years before application, net personal assets that were valued at least AUD$1,125,000; and

- a genuine and realistic intention to continue to maintain business or investment activity in Australia after the designated investment has matured.

Business Skills Migration: Business Migrants Who Have Invested in Government Bonds—Second Stage

The basic requirements for subclass 891 Investor visa and 893 State/Territory Sponsored Investor visa[27] (permanent residence) are that a business investor must:

- be the primary holder of a subclass 162 Investor Provisional visa or corresponding subclass 165 State/Territory Sponsored Investor (Provisional) visa for at least two years in the four years immediately before the application is made;

---

[20] Regulation 162 of Schedule 2 of the Migration Regulations 1994.

[21] Regulation 165 of Schedule 2 of the Migration Regulations 1994.

[22] DIMIA, "Improving the Performance of Business Skills Migrants," Canberra (2002).

[23] DIMIA, "Improving the Performance of Business Skills Migrants," Canberra (2002).

[24] Item 1202A of Schedule 1 and Regulation 162 of Schedule 2 of the Migration Regulations 1994.

[25] Designated Investment is specified by Gazette Notice 25, of June 29, 2005, for the purposes of Regulation 5.19A of the Migration Regulations 1994.

[26] Item 1202A of Schedule 1 and Regulation 165 of Schedule 2 of the Migration Regulations 1994.

[27] Item 1104B of Schedule 1 and Regulations 891 and 893 of Schedule 2 of the Migration Regulations 1994.

- have state or territory sponsorship (for subclass 893 State/Territory Sponsored Investor visa);
- have a genuine and realistic commitment to continue to maintain business or investment activity in Australia; and
- have held a designated investment continuously for at least four years.

POST-ARRIVAL MONITORING AND VISA CANCELLATIONS FOR BUSINESS SKILLS VISA HOLDERS

Australia is one of the few countries that undertake detailed post-arrival monitoring of business migrants. The requirement for business migrants to participate in post-arrival monitoring is legislated within the Migration Act 1958. Business owners and senior executives are surveyed at 24– and 36-month intervals after initial arrival. At the time of the survey, business migrants are required to provide information on their business activities or their efforts to engage in business. Investors may be asked to complete a monitoring survey to assist the Department in reporting on outcomes of the business skills program.

The cancellation provisions under Section 134 of the Migration Act 1958 (the Act) provide a legislative framework where a permanent resident visa of a business migrant who does not comply with the requisite level of investment or business activity could be cancelled under Section 134 of the Act.

Section 134 of the Act also relates to business skills migrants who have become holders of Resident Return Visas. This is in order to prevent a business skills visa holder applying for a Resident Return visa in an effort to circumvent the visa cancellation provisions. The Migration Act provides that business skills visa holders who did not comply with the appropriate level of investment or business activity after permanent residence was granted and who subsequently obtained a Resident Return visa or were issued with a notice of intention to cancel the business skills visa, remained subject to Section 134.

The visa must not be cancelled if the visa holder has made a genuine effort to obtain a substantial business ownership in a business in Australia or to use their skills to actively participate at a senior level in the day-to-day management of a business. The Migration Act sets out the relevant considerations that may be taken into account in determining whether the visa holder has made a genuine effort to establish a business in Australia. A visa holder must be given written notice that it is proposed to cancel the visa, and the visa holder must be invited to make representations as to why the visa should not be cancelled. Any adverse information that is made known to the Department at any stage of the visa cancellation process must be notified to the visa holder, who must then be given the opportunity to respond. A decision to cancel a business skills visa is reviewable by the Administrative Appeals Tribunal.[28]

Business investors who do not maintain the required level of investment in Australia may also be subject to visa cancellation. Where an investor withdraws his or her designated investment ahead of time, there are arrangements in place for the Department to be informed.

TEMPORARY RESIDENCE FOR SELF-FUNDED RETIREES

The subclass 405 Retirement Investor visa[29] may be appropriate in circumstances where a business person or a retired person is 55 years or older, is unable to meet the criteria for any of the provisional business skills visas, and does not wish to establish a business or participate in a business, but still wishes to be able to live in Australia.

The subclass 405 Retirement Investor visa is a temporary residence visa valid for four years at a time, but with no pathway to permanent residence. However, retiree investors may apply for subsequent four-year subclass 405 Retirement Investor visas at the end of each visa validity period. The criteria for subsequent applications are streamlined, and there is no limit on the number of times a retiree investor may apply to remain in Australia, providing he or she continues to meet the criteria.

State or territory sponsorship is mandatory for the subclass 405 Retirement Investor visa. Currently, all states and territories are participating in the Retirement Investor program.

The investment criterion for the subclass 405 Retirement Investor visa is closely linked to sponsorship by the state or territory government. If the retiree investor is willing to invest and live in the state or territory providing the sponsorship, the designated investment is AUD$500,000, and the retiree

---

[28] *See* Subdivision G of the Migration Act 1958 (Cth), made up of sections 134–37.

[29] Item 1212B of Schedule 1 and Regulation 405 of Schedule 2 of the Migration Regulations 1994.

investor must have access to a net annual income of AUD$50,000.

If the retiree investor does not live in the state or territory providing the sponsorship, the designated investment is increased to AUD$750,000 and the retiree investor must have access to a net annual income of AUD$65,000.

Being a temporary residence visa, there is no access to Medicare benefits. The retiree investor must maintain adequate private health insurance throughout the validity period of the visa. The retiree investor is able to work up to 20 hours a week.

ENTREPRENEUR VISAS

Australia has not had a specific "entrepreneur" visa for many years. As indicated by the demise of the subclass 457 Independent Executive visa, it appears that a specific entrepreneurial visa category is no longer in line with the Australian government's policy shift in assessing possible business skills migrants. The current arrangements have clear preference for demonstrated successful business or investment performance rather than based on potential for future business achievement by an entrepreneur or a businessperson without clearly demonstrated business experience and capital to invest. To some extent, the state and territory sponsored business skills visas with their lower threshold criteria meet some of this need, but the preference is still for established, experienced business people. At least from the point of view of the lower thresholds for the various business skills visa categories, it is arguable that for potential applicants from countries with currencies that are strong against the Australian dollar, these categories could be seen to be attractive to such entrepreneurs. However in reality, this has not been the case. Australia could do well to consider a form of well-regulated visas for entrepreneurs who are prepared, have the means, and the aptitude to undertake business activity in a defined sector, for example, in biotechnology or IT-related industries.

CONCLUSION

The Business Skills migration arrangements introduced on March 1, 2003, marked a substantial departure from the previous arrangements. The current arrangements are somewhat restrictive with the emphasis on a two-stage path to permanent residence for most business skills migrants. While encouraging business skills migrants to consider locating in less populous states and territories or in areas of lower economic activity appears to be paying dividends, the business skills area is not one of the shining success stories of Australia's generally well-regarded skilled migration program. Despite some increasing numbers of business skills visas being approved where the applicant has state or territory government sponsorship, and a number of the state and territory governments having instituted active campaigns to attract Business Skills migrants to their jurisdictions, generally successive Australian governments have not given any emphasis to developing a flourishing Business Skills migration program. The changes made in April 2010 bring the thresholds for business and personal assets to more realistic levels and address some integrity issues, but more needs to be done if this ambivalent area of migration policy is to be given the policy settings to enable it to make a significant contribution to the Australian economy, which remains a stated intention of the program.

SUMMARY OF REQUIREMENTS FOR AUSTRALIAN BUSINESS SKILLS VISAS

This table is a summary of the requirements and should not be relied on without reference to the Migration Regulations 1994

Visa subclass	Net Assets in Qualifying Business (2 out of 4 yrs) AUD$	Business Annual Turnover (2 out of 4 yrs) AUD$	Net Business & Personal Assets AUD$	Other specific requirements[1]
Temporary Visas				
Business Owner (Provisional) 160	200,000	500,000	800,000	• Overall successful business career. • Requisite level of ownership interest in main business(es)
State/Territory Sponsored Business Owner (Provisional) 163		300,000	500,000	• Sponsored by State or Territory; • Overall successful business career; • Requisite level of ownership interest in main business(es)
Senior Executive (Provisional) 161		50 million	800,000	Have been in the three top levels of major business (turnover: AUD$50 million) for at least 2 out of 4 years.
State/Territory Sponsored Senior Executive (Provisional) 164		10 million	500,000	Have been in the three top levels of major business (turnover: AUD$10 million) for at least 2 out of 4 years.
Investor (Provisional) 162			2.25 million (for 2 years)	• 3 years experience managing business/investment; • One in five years: managing and 10% ownership in qualifying business OR actively managing investments valued at AUD$1.5million; • Designated investment of AUD$1.5 million for four years; • Genuine and realistic intention to continue to maintain business or investment activity in Australia after the designated investment has matured.
State/Territory Sponsored Investor (Provisional) 165			1.125 million (for 2 years)	• Sponsorship by State or Territory; • 3 years experience managing business/investment; • Designated investment of $750,000 for four years; • One in five years: managing/10% in qualifying business OR managing investments 750k; • Genuine and realistic intention to continue to maintain business or investment activity in Australia after the designated investment ahs matured.
Permanent Visas				
Business Talent (Residence) 132	400,000 (for 2 years)	3 million (for 2 years)	1.5 million	• Sponsorship by State or Territory. • Successful business career;
Established Business in Australia (Residence) 845	100,000 in Australia (Last 12 months)		250,000	• Successful business career; • Ownership interest in a main business in Australia for 18 months prior to applying; • Actively involved/responsible for the overall management and performance of main business; • Physically present in Australia for 9 out of 12 months before applying; • Score at least 105 points on points test.
State/Territory Sponsored Regional Established Business in Australia 846	75,000 in Australia	200,000 or exported goods or services of a value of 100,000 (last 2 years)	200,000	• Sponsorship by State or Territory; • Successful business career; • Ownership interest in a main business in Australia for 2 years prior to applying; • Actively involved in and responsible for the overall management and performance of main business; • Physically present in Australia for 1 out of 2 years before applying; • Score at least 105 points on points test.
Business Owner (Residence) 890	100,000 in Australia	300,000	250,000 (last 12 months)	• Continued ownership interest in an actively operating main business in Australia for 2 years prior to applying; • Employed 2 full time employees throughout 12 months prior to applying; • Obtained all Australian Business Numbers and submitted all Business Activity Statements to Australian Taxation Office.
State/Territory Sponsored Business Owner (Residence) 892	75,000 in Australia (last 12 months)	200,000 (or exceptional circumstances)	250,000 (last 12 months)	• Sponsorship by State or Territory; • Employed 1 full time employee throughout 12 months prior to applying. Must meet 2 of the assets in main business, net business and personal assets or employment criteria.
Investor (Residence) 891	–	–	–	• Holder of a Subclass 162 visa for 2 years in the 4 years before applying; • Designated investment made & held for 4 years; • Genuine and realistic commitment to continue to maintain business or investment activity in Australia.
State/Territory Sponsored Investor (Residence) 893	–	–	–	• Sponsorship by State or Territory; • Holder of a Subclass 165 visa for 2 years in the 4 years before applying; • Designated investment made & held for 4 years; • Genuine and realistic commitment to continue to maintain business or investment activity in Australia.

---

[1] General requirements relating to ownership interests in the applicant's main business(es), age, English language ability, history of acceptable business activities, notification to state or territory body, declaration that obligations on business skills visa holders are understood, health and character are discussed in the article.

CANADIAN IMMIGRATION FOR INTERNATIONAL INVESTORS AND ENTREPRENEURS IN THE CURRENT GLOBAL ECONOMY

by David L.P. Garson and Lainie M. Appleby[*]

INTRODUCTION

It is an understatement to say that there has been a worldwide upheaval in both international banking and real estate. Nevertheless, Canada has remained somewhat more stable than other parts of the world. This is due to the nature of the rules and regulations that surround and protect our banking and mortgage industries.

Generally, Canada is more conservative with regard to its investment environment. This extends to Canada Immigration's Investor and Entrepreneur categories. The Canadian immigration programs available to investors and entrepreneurs are reviewed regularly to ensure that they operate appropriately. The variety of business immigration programs, coupled with excellent socialized health care, urban safety, and a high quality of life make Canada an ideal option for investor and entrepreneurial immigrants.

Canada's immigration programs can be broken down into the federal categories and the provincial categories, neither of which are subject to an annual limit or "cap." Under the Federal immigration scheme, business immigrants can qualify as Investors, Entrepreneurs, or Self-Employed applicants. Investors and Entrepreneurs will be discussed below. Each of Canada's provinces has recently devised its own Provincial Nominee Program with various categories that may be applicable to an investor or entrepreneur. The Province of Quebec has jurisdiction over its own immigration laws, regulations, and programs.

Canada's Federal Business Immigration Program

The laws and regulations that govern the federal business immigration programs emanate from the Immigration and Refugee Protection Act[1] and the corresponding Immigration and Refugee Protection Regulations.[2] There is an investor category and an entrepreneur category.

Applicants applying in the investor category must meet the following criteria:

- Demonstrate business experience;
- Have a minimum net worth of CND$800,000 that was obtained legally; and
- Make an investment of CND$400,000 with the government.

More specifically, "business experience" is defined as having at least two years of business experience in the past five years. The two years of experience must be comprised of one of the following:

- two one-year periods of experience in the management of a qualifying business[3] and the control of a percentage of equity[4] of the

---

[*] **David L.P. Garson** is a founding partner of the immigration law firm Guberman, Garson, Bush in Toronto, Canada. He is a Certified Specialist in immigration law and has been practicing exclusively in the area for over 18 years.

Lainie M. Appleby is a lawyer at Guberman, Garson, Bush in Toronto. Her practice is limited to immigration matters and immigration has been her focus since the start of her career.

[1] Immigration and Refugee Protection Act (IRPA), S.C. 2001, c. 27.

[2] Immigration and Refugee Protection Regulations (IRPR), SOR/2002-227.

[3] IRPR, *supra* note 2, at s.88(1):

"qualifying business" means a business—other than a business operated primarily for the purpose of deriving investment income such as interest, dividends or capital gains—for which, during the year under consideration, there is documentary evidence of any two of the following:

(a) the percentage of equity multiplied by the number of full-time job equivalents is equal to or greater than two full-time job equivalents per year;

(b) the percentage of equity multiplied by the total annual sales is equal to or greater than $500,000;

(c) the percentage of equity multiplied by the net income in the year is equal to or greater than $50,000; and

(d) the percentage of equity multiplied by the net assets at the end of the year is equal to or greater than $125,000.

[4] *Id.* "Percentage of equity" means:

(a) in respect of a sole proprietorship, 100 percent of the equity of the sole proprietorship controlled by a foreign national or [his or her] spouse or common-law partner;

(b) in respect of a corporation, the percentage of the issued and outstanding voting shares of the capital stock

continued

qualifying business during the period beginning five years before the date of application for a permanent resident visa and ending on the day a decision is made on the application; or

- two one-year periods of experience in the management of at least five full-time job equivalents per year in a business during the period beginning five years before the date of application for a permanent resident visa and ending on the day a decision is made on the application; or

- a combination of a one-year period of experience described in subparagraph (i) and a one-year period of experience described in subparagraph (ii).

The investments are overseen by Citizenship and Immigration Canada. At the conclusion of a five-year period, the CND$400,000 investment is returned without interest.

Once an applicant demonstrates that he or she is able to meet the basic investor definition, the applicant is also required to demonstrate that he or she can achieve 35 points on the basis of the following criteria:

Selection Criteria	Maximum Points
Education	25
Business experience	35
Age	10
Ability in English and/or French	24
Adaptability	6
TOTAL	100

As 35 points are awarded for business experience, it is a given that a suitable applicant will obtain enough points.

In contrast to the Investor category, which does not require any active involvement in the investment, the Entrepreneur category provides opportunities for immigration to Canada for applicants with a desire to open, establish, and run an enterprise. An entrepreneur must attain a minimum of 35 points based upon the government's selection criteria and meet the definition of having operated a "qualifying business."

of the corporation controlled by a foreign national or [his or her] spouse or common-law partner; and

(c) in respect of a partnership or joint venture, the percentage of the profit or loss of the partnership or joint venture to which a foreign national or [his or her] spouse or common-law partner is entitled.

An "entrepreneur" is a foreign national who has business experience, a minimum net worth of CND$300,000 and the intention and ability to establish a qualifying Canadian business. The entrepreneur must control 33.3 percent or more of a qualifying business and provide active and ongoing management of the business. The entrepreneur's business must create one full-time job for a Canadian citizen or permanent resident, aside from the entrepreneur and his or her family members. The entrepreneur must meet these conditions for a period of at least one year within three years after the day on which the entrepreneur becomes a permanent resident in Canada. Proof of compliance and reporting to Citizenship and Immigration Canada are required at intervals of six months (for the purpose of reporting residential address) and between 18 and 24 months after landing to provide evidence of efforts to comply with the conditions within the three-year period.

To prove that a "qualifying Canadian business"[5] has been established, the entrepreneur must provide evidence of two of the following:

the percentage of equity multiplied by

(a) the number of full-time job equivalents is equal to or greater than two full-time job equivalents per year; or

(b) the total annual sales is equal to or greater than CND$250,000; or

(c) the net income in the year is equal to or greater than CND$25,000; or

(d) the net assets at the end of the year are greater than CND$125,000.

Provincial Nominee Programs for Investor and Entrepreneurial Immigrants

Each province is entitled to set its own criteria in attracting immigrants based on its economic and labor needs.[6] Therefore, not all provinces have a program geared towards investors or entrepreneurs. The provinces that do are Manitoba,[7] New Brunswick,[8] Newfoundland/Labrador,[9] Ontario,[10] Prince

---

[5] *Id.*

[6] IRPA, *supra* note 1, at ss. 9(1), 15(2), 20(2); IRPR, *supra* note 2, at ss. 87(1), (2).

[7] *Provincial Nominee Program for Business,* Government of Manitoba, *www.gov.mb.ca/ctt/invest/pnp-b/index.html* (June 23, 2009).

[8] *Provincial Nominee Program—Business Plan Applicants,* Government of New Brunswick, *www.gnb.ca/Immigration/ Information/businessapplicants-e.asp* (June 23, 2009).

Edward Island,[11] Saskatchewan,[12] the Yukon,[13] and British Columbia.[14]

Manitoba

In Manitoba, qualifying business applicants must meet the following criteria:

- Minimum personal net worth: CND$350,000;
- Minimum amount of equity of investment in Manitoba of CND$150,000;
- Demonstrated business experience or a minimum of three years' experience in a senior management role of a successful company. In a partnership situation, the applicant must have a minimum of 33.3 shares and play an active management role in the business;
- Conducted an exploratory visit to Manitoba to investigate business opportunities and examine the Manitoba lifestyle for a minimum of seven days.

If a business application is approved by the province of Manitoba, the applicant is required to make a CND$75,000 cash deposit to the government of Manitoba, guaranteeing the establishment or purchase of a business in Manitoba within two years of becoming a landed immigrant. The cash deposit is refunded when the total investment is made and the intended business is established according to the business plan that was submitted to the province.

New Brunswick

The province of New Brunswick's plan states that, in addition to meeting the evaluation criteria, an applicant must also attain 50 points on the province's business points system. Other considerations include: previous management experience with proven success as a senior executive and/or business owner within three out of the past five years; possession of business skills that are relevant to the business that will be pursued in New Brunswick; and a knowledge of French or English that is sufficient to understand and communicate with the New Brunswick officials in the course of an interview. A successful applicant will be required to demonstrate that he or she has sufficient funds to finance the first phase of the planned business venture without third-party assistance and to support his or her family for a period of up to two years. A minimum personal net worth of CND$350,000 is required and the investment required varies depending upon the business plan; however, the investment cannot be less than CND$125,000. The New Brunswick Business Plan applicant must participate in the business in an active managerial role and commit to settling permanently in New Brunswick. A signed declaration of intention to live and work in New Brunswick is required, as is a mandatory five-day exploratory visit.

Newfoundland/Labrador

In Newfoundland/Labrador, there are opportunities for immigrant applicants who intend to be self-employed and wish to start a new business or purchase an existing business. The category is known as Immigration Entrepreneur. Priority will be given to cases that fall into industries noted on the provinces Strategic Sector List[15] and a pre-assessment must be submitted prior to the actual application. Individuals applying as Immigration Entrepreneurs must meet the following requirements:

- Possess a minimum of five years of senior managerial or direct entrepreneurial experience in a business similar to the one proposed for Newfoundland/Labrador;
- Possess a minimum net worth of $450,000 CND, including liquid assets of at least $350,000 CND.

Immigrant Entrepreneurs in Newfoundland/Labrador must be prepared to make a minimum direct investment of CND$200,000 in equity in order to establish a new enterprise or purchase an eligible existing business. The applicant is required to sign a

---

[9] *Immigrant Entrepreneur Category,* Newfoundland and Labrador Canada Provincial Nominee Program, Office of Immigration and Multiculturalism, Department of Human Resources, Labor and Employment, *www.nlpnp.ca/entrepreneur.html* (June 23, 2009).

[10] *Opportunities Ontario: Investors,* Ontario Immigration, *www.ontarioimmigration.ca/english/PNPInvestors.asp* (June 23, 2009).

[11] *Prince Edward Island Provincial Nominee Program,* The Government of Prince Edward Island, *www.gov.pe.ca/immigration/index.php3?number=1014385* (June 23, 2009).

[12] *Entrepreneurs, Immigration,* Government of Saskatchewan, *http://www.immigration.gov.sk.ca/entrepreneur/* 23-JUN-09.

[13] *Yukon Business Nominee Program,* Government of Yukon, *www.economicdevelopment.gov.yk.ca/general/ynp.html#ent* (June 23, 2009).

[14] *Provincial Nominee Program: Business Immigrants,* Government of British Columbia, *www.aved.gov.bc.ca/provincialnominee/businessimmigrants/welcome.htm* (June 23, 2009).

[15] Knowledge-based industries; manufacturing; natural resources; agriculture & agrifood; healthcare; tourism; creative & cultural industries; fisheries.

Performance Agreement setting out the terms of the investment required and submit it along with $100,000 CND. An exploratory visit of a duration allowing the applicant to conduct research relating to the proposed business and have an interview with a Program Officer is required. As well, the submission of a business plan is mandatory.

Ontario

The relevant program for international investors and entrepreneurs in Ontario is called the Investors stream. It is an ideal category to consider for companies establishing or expanding operations in Ontario. In order to initiate this type of application, an interested investor should contact the Ministry of Ontario that is relevant to the industry in which business will be conducted. For instance, an investor with expertise in Information Technology should contact the Ministry of Research and Innovation. If the relevant Ministry endorses the proposed investment, an Investment Endorsement Form, along with the endorsed business proposal is forwarded to Opportunities Ontario, the government entity responsible for overseeing the Ontario Provincial Nominee Program. At a minimum, the investment must be CND$3,000,000 and create at least five permanent full-time positions for Canadian citizens or permanent residents in Ontario. Unlike the Federal Investor Program, this is not a passive investor program.

The number of foreign individuals who can make application under an approved Investment Endorsement Form depends upon the number of jobs that will be created for Canadians. Below is the current schedule outlining the number of foreign applications that can be received on the basis of the extent of job creation by the investment:

Number of jobs created as a result of the investment	Number of jobs created for Canadian citizens or permanent residents located in Ontario	Number of nominee positions investors can request
	5	1
8	6	2
10	7	3
12	8	4
14	9	5
16	10	6
26	15	11
36	20	16
46	25	21
54+	29+	25

The foreign applicants who are eligible to submit an application as a Nominee resulting from an Investment Endorsement must be working in a skilled occupation; be coming to Canada to work on a full-time basis; and receive a wage the is consistent with Canadian labor standards. In addition, the applicant's presence in Canada must be necessary to the long-term success of the investment.

Prince Edward Island

As of this time, the province of Prince Edward Island (PEI) only has an Immigration Entrepreneur Provincial Nominee program. The Immigrant Partner Category, which is also relevant to international investors and entrepreneurs, has been temporarily suspended.

To be eligible in the Immigrant Entrepreneur Category, applicants must meet the following criteria:

- possess a minimum net worth of CND$400,000;
- invest a minimum of CND$200,000 to establish a new enterprise or purchase a minimum of 33 percent of an existing business;
- provide a business plan;
- provide a CND$100,000 business investment deposit, which is held in escrow and returned to the applicant after one year's residency and the establishment of the business;
- provide CND$25,000 in escrow with the Government of PEI as a good faith deposit. This is returned after the applicant has resided for one year in PEI.
- possess suitable age, education, language skills and transferrable management skills.

The business in which the Immigrant Entrepreneur is involved must be established or purchased within two years of becoming a permanent resident. Prior to filing the case, a pre-assessment must be filed and subsequent to that, the immigrant entrepreneur is required to make an exploratory visit of three to five business days upon receiving an invitation to do so.

Saskatchewan

The Saskatchewan Provincial Nominee Program also has a category for entrepreneurs. In order to be eligible, the applicant must have a minimum of three years of entrepreneurial business ownership or business management experience, in addition to net worth of CND$300,000. At least 80 percent of the net worth must be verified as being accumulated legally. The minimum investment is CND$150,000 to start a new business or buy an existing business outright. The applicant must intend to own at least

33.3 percent of the business. If the ownership percentage is less than 33.3 percent, an investment of CND$1,000,000 is required. Regardless of the percentage of ownership or the amount of investment, active day-to-day management of the enterprise is required. A deposit of CND$75,000 into a trust account is needed, as is a signed Performance Agreement that is based upon the Business Establishment Plan. The deposit is refunded if the applicant meets the conditions of the performance agreement within two years of becoming a permanent resident in Canada.

Further, the Province of Saskatchewan evaluates the applicant's intention according to a Points Grid. Fifty-five points out of one hundred must be awarded in order to be eligible. The intent grading criteria include visit, business contacts, business development, home ownership, English competency, community/family contacts, and commitment. Points awarded within each category range from five points to 20 points. For instance, in the business development category, zero points are awarded if the applicant has no knowledge of business sectors and opportunities in Saskatchewan, whereas an applicant who has made a legal or financial commitment towards establishing a business will receive 20 points. While interviews are not mandatory, an interview may be requested should the province be seeking additional information.

Yukon

The Yukon maintains an entrepreneur category included among its Provincial Nominee offerings. Although the business can be established in any sector, as in Newfoundland/Labrador, there are priority sectors,[16] and specific sectors have been designated as non-priority,[17] unless the related product would provide significant benefits to the Yukon. An eligible business may be a new business or based upon the purchase of an existing business. The business plan that is submitted must identify all benefits to the Yukon.

In order to be eligible as an entrepreneur under the Yukon scheme, a prospective applicant must:

- invest a minimum of CND$150,000 equity into a Yukon business;
- have a personal net worth of CND$250,000;
- demonstrate knowledge and understanding of the Yukon and its economy;
- have reasonable communication skills; and
- be able to demonstrate that he or she has the necessary experience and education to follow through on the business plan.

British Columbia

The province of British Columbia also has Provincial Nominee Programs geared to business immigration. This is the most expansive of the provincial nominee programs for business immigrants. There are three available categories: Business Skills, Regional Business, and Strategic Projects. The requirements for each program are contrasted in the table on the following page and pertain to the establishment of an eligible business.

For the purposes of the Provincial Nominee Program in British Columbia, an eligible business is one that is operating in order to earn a profit from active income that is generated through the provision of products or services. The business in question must have a strong potential for long-term commercial viability and should have the potential to create significant economic benefits to the province in the following sectors:

- manufacturing/processing
- exports
- tourism
- research development/technology.

Alternatively, the business can help in developing new approaches to traditional business; transfer of skills and technology; or service an underserviced market. Business immigrants providing proposals pertaining to expanding business with the Asia Pacific region, using wood infested with the Mountain Pine Beetle or contributing to its related community economies, partnering with First Nations, or involving alternative energy, clean technology, information technology, new media, life science will receive priority. That said, there are also a significant number of excluded businesses, including but not limited to bed and breakfasts, pawnbrokers, real estate development, and pornography. In the Vancouver and Abbotsford Area, convenience stores, video stores, gas stations, dry cleaning, and most franchise operations are excluded.

For all of the Provincial Nominee Programs, the initial filing is with the province selected by the applicant. If the province approves the applicant, a

---

[16] Manufacturing; Value-Added Processing; Forestry; Tourism Products, Attractions, Services and Facilities; Energy; Mining/Mineral Development; Agriculture; Cultural Industries; Film and Video Production; Information Technology.

[17] Sectors designated as non-priority include retail.

"provincial nomination" is provided and the applicant then files the second phase of the processing with the Canadian Consulate General, Embassy, or High Commission responsible for the applicant's place of residence or citizenship. At that time, the matter is evaluated for compliance with all admissibility criteria, including medical and criminal.

	Business Skills[a]	Regional Business[b]	Strategic Projects[c]
Investment Required	CND $400,00	CND $200,000	CND $500,000
Job Creation for Canadians or Permanent Residents	3	1	3 for each applicant put forward by company
Ownership Interest	33.3 percent of the equity	33.3 percent of the equity	Minimum equity investment of CND $500,000 and incorporate a Canadian subsidiary or register an extra-provincial company to operate the business
Level of Participation	Active and on-going participation in day-to-day management and direction	Active and on-going participation in day-to-day management and direction	Establish or purchase and expand an eligible business in BC
Background Requirements of Applicant	• Possess skills necessary to establish and operate a viable business in BC • Legally obtained personal net worth of $800,000 • Sufficient unencumbered personal funds to make the investment • Viable business proposal	• Possess skills necessary to establish and operate a viable business in BC • Legally obtained personal net worth of $400,000 • Sufficient unencumbered personal funds to make the investment • Viable business proposal	The foreign applicants must be essential senior personnel who can establish/ expand or operate the business
Signed Commitments to the Province of British Columbia	Performance Agreement and, if seeking "fast track"[18] nomination, a Deposit Agreement	Performance Agreement and, if seeking "fast track" nomination, a Deposit Agreement	Performance Agreement

[a] Personal investment in an eligible business anywhere in B.C.; aside from the principal applicant, a key staff member may be a co-applicant.
[b] Personal investment in an eligible business outside of Vancouver or Abbotsford.
[c] For foreign-controlled companies establishing an eligible business with the entry of up to five foreign managerial/professional/technical staff as applicants.

Quebec's Business Immigration Program

As mentioned at the outset, the Province of Quebec has jurisdiction over its own immigration laws, regulations, and programs that are governed by An Act Respecting Immigration to Quebec[19].

For the Quebec entrepreneur program, in order to be eligible an applicant must have:

- legally obtained net assets of at least CND$300,000

---

[18] The Fast Track option offers immediate nomination for permanent residence, if a conditionally refundable CND$125,000 deposit is provided to the Province of British Columbia. The deposit will be refunded (without interest) when the terms and conditions of the Performance Agreement and Deposit Agreement are met.

[19] An Act Respecting Immigration to Quebec, R.S.Q., c.I-02.

- at least two years' full-time experience running and managing a profitable business with at least a 25 percent ownership stake within the five-year period preceding the application.

An entrepreneurial applicant can file an application on the basis of creating or acquiring a business that he or she will manage, or participate in the management of, on a daily basis. The applicant and/or his or her spouse must control 25 percent of the equity with a value of at least CND$100,000. Alternatively, an entrepreneur and/or his or her spouse can acquire a 25 percent interest in a business with a value of $100,000 and be involved in managing or participating in the management on a daily basis. The province of Quebec also considers factors such as age, background training, language skills, knowledge of Quebec, any steps taken to acquire a Quebec business, and the applicant's ability to carry through with the proposed business.

For at least one of the three years subsequent to becoming a permanent resident, the applicant must demonstrate that a business has been created or acquired, that he or she holds a 25 percent capital equity valued at $100,000, and participates in the daily operation of the business. Further, the business must permanently employ a Quebec resident who is not a family member for at least 30 hours per week.

The Quebec investor program is very similar to the Federal Investor program as it is based on a five-year investment of CND$400,000 that is guaranteed by the province of Quebec. In order to be eligible, the applicant solely or with his or her spouse, must demonstrate a legally obtained net worth of CND$800,000 and have appropriate management experience in a business that employed two full-time staff. The management experience must have been accrued over two years within the past five-year period.

CONCLUSION

As a result of these various programs, in 2008 there were a total of 11,902 investor and entrepreneur immigrants to Canada, including their family members, under the Federal Investor and Entrepreneur business immigration programs. There were 22,418 Provincial Nominee Immigrants, including family members, for all provincial nominee programs inclusive of the business categories, but exclusive of a Quebec Immigration programs.[20] One of the reasons for the dramatic difference between the federal and provincial programs is that the provincial nominee cases are generally processed more quickly.

The best program for an applicant depends upon many factors, including his or her financial resources, as well as the "personality" and cultural/social/business fabric of each province. Of course, the primary consideration is the monetary eligibility for a program, as summarized in the following table.

Program	Personal Net Worth	Minimum Investment
Federal • Investor • Entrepreneur	• CND$800,000 • CND$300,000	• CND$400,000 • varies
Manitoba	CND$350,000	CND$150,000
New Brunswick	CND$350,000	CND$125,000
Newfoundland/ Labrador	CND$450,00	CND$200,000
Ontario	n/a – require referral from another Ontario Ministry as program is primary intended for large corporations	CND$3,000,000
Prince Edward Island	CND$400,000	CND$200,000
Saskatchewan	CND$300,000	CND$150,000
Yukon	CND$250,000	CND$150,000
British Columbia • Business Skills • Regional Business • Strategic Projects	• CND$800,000 • CND$400,000 • n/a - intended for foreign controlled companies incorporating a Canadian subsidiary of registering and extra-provincial company	• CND$400,000 • CND$200,000 • CND$500,00

After determining an applicant's financial ability to participate in a program, his or her relevant experience and other eligibility criteria can be considered.

---

[20] Citizenship and Immigration Canada, "Facts & Figures 2008 —Immigration Overview: Permanent and Temporary Residents," *available at www.cic.gc.ca/english/resources/ statistics/facts2008/index.asp.*

The breadth and scope of programs in Canada available to the international investor or entrepreneur is impressive. With investment categories ranging from CND$150,000 to CND$3,000,000, there are options available for smaller businesses as well as large corporations. Net-worth considerations for some programs are variable, depending upon the venture proposed. In sum, opportunities are diverse, as is Canada's cultural and physical landscape.

HONG KONG RESIDENT VISAS FOR ENTREPRENEURS AND INVESTORS[*]

by Eugene Chow[**]

INTRODUCTION

The United States, Canada, Australia, New Zealand as well as the United Kingdom have traditionally been attractive immigration destinations because they are stable democracies which offer a high quality of life.

However, with the global financial recession and the collapse of the real estate markets in many of the western economies, one economy that has been very resilient has been the People's Republic of China, which in turn has benefited Hong Kong as the Special Administrative Region has become increasingly integrated with the Mainland economy.

With its proximity to China and its low tax regime, Hong Kong has become a very attractive alternative jurisdiction for residency based on investment, not only for many People's Republic of China nationals but also for business people and entrepreneurs from North America and Western Europe, as well as nationals of developing countries.

Hong Kong is a strategic gateway to the many business opportunities in Mainland China, and it has a well-established infrastructure, a free economy, and a simple and low tax regime. It has no capital gains tax, no tax on dividends and interest income from bank deposits, no sales tax, and it completely abolished estate tax effective February 11, 2006.

Assessable profits of corporations are now at 16.5 percent while the standard salaries tax, at 15 percent, is among the lowest in the world.

EMPLOYMENT (ENTRY FOR INVESTMENT) VISAS

Until the launching of the Capital Investment Entrant Scheme in October of 2003 (discussed below), Hong Kong immigration policy only permitted investors coming to Hong Kong to join in or set up an active business to qualify for resident visas.

While this visa category contemplates an investment by the applicant, the visa itself, if approved, is simply indicated as an "employment visa," similar to the visa granted to employees sponsored by an employer, except that the internal record file of the applicant with the Hong Kong Immigration Department (HKID) will indicate that the visa is based upon investment in Hong Kong.

Obtaining approval of an employment ("entry for investment") visa is much more onerous than obtaining an employment visa as a professional under employer sponsorship and involves different considerations.

The essential criteria for the approval of an employment (entry for investment) visa by HKID is whether the business in which the investor has invested is of substantial benefit to the economy of the Hong Kong Special Administrative Region (HKSAR).

The Hong Kong Immigration Department has issued a Guidebook for Entry for Investment (to establish/join in business) in Hong Kong.[1] In an employment (entry for investment) application, the applicant must submit evidence that he has a good education background, good technical qualifications, proven professional activities and relevant experience, and

---

[*] Updated from an article by Mr. Chow which appeared in the conference CD of the International Bar Association's 4th Biennial Global Immigration Law Conference (Nov. 2009). Copyright © 2010, Eugene Chow. All rights reserved. An earlier version of this article titled "Investment-Related Hong Kong Resident Visas" was originally published in *Immigration Options for Investors and Entrepreneurs* 413 (AILA 2006).

[**] **Eugene Chow** is the principal of Chow King & Associates, a Hong Kong-based firm specializing in U.S., Hong Kong, and international immigration matters. Mr. Chow is a graduate of Pennsylvania State University and obtained his J.D. from Boston College Law School. He has been in practice for more than 33 years and has been a California Board Certified Specialist in Immigration Law since 1989. He is listed in *An International Who's Who of Corporate Immigration Lawyers*, *Who's Who of the Law (Hong Kong & China)*, and has been an annual contributing author to all 17 editions of the American Immigration Lawyers Association's (AILA) *The Visa Processing Guide: Process and Procedures at U.S. Consulates and Embassies*. He also served as an Associate Editor and contributing author to AILA's "Thinking Beyond Borders: 2004 Global Immigration Summit Handbook" as well as *Immigration Options for Investors and Entrepreneurs* (AILA 2006).

[1] Form ID(E)1000, "Guidebook for Entry for Investment (to establish/join in business) in Hong Kong"—English Version (last revision date May 6, 2009), *available at* www.immd.gov.hk/ehtml/id(e)1000.htm.

achievements. There is no prescribed minimum amount required to be invested, nor is there a minimum number of jobs that have to be created. However, a successful application almost always includes evidence provided to the HKID that local jobs have been created or will be created by the business within a reasonable time and that local vendors and suppliers will benefit from the commercial activities of the investor's company.

The actual amount of capital invested to qualify for an investment visa will depend on the nature of the business. At a minimum, the business should be sufficiently capitalized to finance the start-up costs, including the securing of physical premises, the hiring of one to two local employees, and the fulfillment of the short-term cash flow needs of the company as its business activities get underway.

Thus, depending on the nature of the business and the nationality and background of the investor,[2] it is possible to invest as little as US$50,000 (HK$390,000) to US$100,000 (HK$780,000) and still qualify for an employment (investment) visa. This does not mean, however, that a one-man trading business operating out of a home on a shoe-string budget, or a sublease of a small part of an office with limited capital at risk which generates modest revenues will be approved.

In general, if the investor has less than HK$1 million (US$128,205) invested, the application will be much more closely scrutinized. In any event, an investment applicant must, at a minimum, demonstrate that he or she has made a long-term commitment to Hong Kong by executing a commercial lease for adequate business premises, provide documentary evidence of the business entity created, demonstrate that it has been adequately capitalized for the type of business activities it is embarking on, and provide a detailed and comprehensive business plan to explain how that business will substantially benefit Hong Kong in the long term.

In this regard, the HKID will also require a business profile, an explanation of the mode of operation of the business, a listing of its business connections in Hong Kong and overseas, proof of business activities (such as letters of credit, bills of lading, shipment papers, contracts/agreements reached and realized), a full résumé of the applicant's background, as well as a full description of the post to be taken up by the applicant, along with letters of support from local business associates, vendors, providers of service, manufacturers, and documents verifying the financial standing and source of finance of both the applicant and his or her company, including bank account statements, bank reference statements, banking facilities letters, and financial statements.

Entry Scheme not Available to Certain Nationalities

The employment entry for investment category is not available to nationals of Afghanistan, Albania, Cambodia, Cuba, Laos, Korea (Democratic People's Republic of), Nepal, or Vietnam.

Note that Chinese residents of the Mainland are also not eligible to apply, but overseas Chinese nationals holding People's Republic of China passports may apply if (a) the applicant has permanent residence overseas; or (b) the applicant has been residing for over one year immediately before the submission of the application ("overseas" means places outside the Mainland, the Macao Special Administrative Region (SAR) and Hong Kong SAR) **and** the application is submitted from overseas.

DIRECT FILING WITH THE HONG KONG IMMIGRATION DEPARTMENT

While an application can be filed through the nearest Chinese embassy or consulate in the applicant's home country, in practice it is much more expedient to file for an employment (entry for investment) visa directly with the HKID from offshore if the applicant has already set up the business entity, capitalized it, and undertaken sufficient business activities to make a strong case that the investor's business would substantially benefit the Hong Kong Special Administrative Region economically.

To apply for entry for investment, the applicant must nominate a local sponsor, which can be a company or an individual.

An entry for investment application thus can be filed from overseas where the applicant either has a local Hong Kong business partner involved in the business he has set up or has hired a local Hong Kong employee to manage and run the day-to-day operations or a local representative serving as a director of the company, who can readily respond to any follow up requests for information from the HKID. Typically, this approach is favored by an investor who has been traveling in and out of Hong

---

[2] While all applicants are supposed to meet the same criteria officially, in the writer's experience, well-educated Americans, Canadians, and nationals of Western European countries with strong prior professional/business experience seem to have a more relaxed standard applied to them.

Kong for business meetings during the start-up phase of the Hong Kong business, but who now finds it necessary to acquire a visa to live and work in Hong Kong so that he or she can be based there to manage and direct the business and to help formulate strategic expansion plans as well as to develop additional business relationships and opportunities.

A business entity which may seem small and marginal may nevertheless be of substantial benefit to the economy of the HKSAR because it is the buying, liaison, or representative office of a substantial and reputable overseas company that has given the investor's newly established business the full financial support of the overseas entity or perhaps where well-established, reputable, and reliable Hong Kong customers and suppliers are in place already.

If the business is already well established and has audited financial statements and a good track record, the applicant can be readily approved for the employment (entry for investment) visa simply on the basis of his or her shareholdings in the business enterprise. In this case, once the application is approved, the visa/entry permit label can be picked up by the applicant's representative in Hong Kong and couriered to the applicant and his or her family so that they affix the labels into their passports and enter directly as "employment" and dependent visa holders.

EXTENSION OF STAY

Persons who have been admitted for investment are allowed to remain in the HKSAR on employment status. They may apply for extension of stay for investment within four weeks before their limit of stay expires provided they continue to meet the eligibility criteria. The first two extensions are granted for two years, while the third, and all subsequent extensions, are granted for three years each. This is much like a U.S. Treaty Investor (E-2) visa, which can be indefinitely renewed so long as the investor remains actively involved in the business. However, most persons admitted in this category will opt not to apply for further extensions but will, instead, apply for the "right of abode" (or permanent residency) after seven years of "ordinary residence" in employment (investment) status. This way, their business and status will not be subject to further immigration control unless they leave Hong Kong for a continuous period of three years or more.

DEPENDENT VISAS

The investor's spouse and unmarried children under the age of 18 are permitted the same period of stay based on the sponsorship of the investor so long as there is reasonable proof that a genuine relationship exists between the dependents and the sponsor and the principal applicant is able to support the dependents' living at a standard well above the subsistence level and provide them with suitable accommodation in the HKSAR. Under current immigration policy, dependents of all employment-visa holders (including entry for investment) may work in any capacity in Hong Kong without obtaining HKID permission.

THE CAPITAL INVESTMENT ENTRANT SCHEME

The Capital Investment Entrant Scheme is a passive investment scheme launched by the Hong Kong Government on October 27, 2003, to attract investors prepared to make a substantial capital investment in Hong Kong but who do not wish to set up, join in, or run a business themselves.

According to the Hong Kong Immigration Department's latest statistics, as of December 31, 2009, HK$42.06 billion of new capital has been invested in the city since the inception of the program as a result of the approval of 5,953 applicants out of a total of 9,894. Financial assets such as shares and securities account for HK$29.76 billion, with the remaining HK$12.30 billion invested in property.[3] In addition, 1,268 applicants have received notification of their "approval-in-principle" but have not yet completed their investment.

Chinese nationals with permanent residence overseas account for the largest number of applications, 6,642 of the total 8,861 applications to date. Foreign nationals account for another 1,546 applications while Taiwan residents made 414 applications.

Eligibility Criteria

Under the Rules for the Capital Investment Entrant Scheme, Form ID(E)968,[4] an applicant must be at least 18 years of age and prove that he or she has net assets of at least HK$6.5 million to which he or she is absolutely beneficially entitled for the two years immediately preceding his or her application.

The applicant must also invest at least HK$6.5 million (US$833,334) in either real property or other per-

---

[3] Statistics on the Capital Investment Entrant Scheme, www.immd.gov.hk/ehtml/hkvisas_13_19.htm.

[4] Form ID(E)968, "Rules for Capital Investment Entrant Scheme—English Version," available at www.immd.gov.hk/ehtml/id(e)968.htm.

missible financial assets such as equity shares in Hong Kong Stock Exchange-listed companies, debt securities denominated in Hong Kong dollars issued or guaranteed by the HKSAR Government, certificates of deposit denominated in Hong Kong dollars issued by authorized institutions under the Banking Ordinance, subordinated debt, or eligible collective investment schemes (*i.e.*, unit trusts or mutual funds) managed by a corporation licensed under the Securities and Futures Ordinance and authorized by the Securities and Futures Commission for sale to the public in Hong Kong.

The scheme is applicable to foreign nationals (except for nationals of Afghanistan, Albania, Cuba, and the Democratic People's Republic of Korea); Macao SAR residents; Chinese nationals who have obtained permanent resident status in a foreign country; stateless persons who have obtained permanent resident status in a foreign country with proven re-entry facilities; and Taiwan residents.

Compared to the investment programs of other jurisdictions, the Capital Investment Entrant Scheme of Hong Kong is extremely flexible, as an investor can choose an investment portfolio amongst a wide range of permissible assets and may switch his or her investment within the class of permissible assets at any time.

Any investments in permissible investment asset classes made six months before the entrant's submission of his or her application to the HKID, or within six months after the granting of approval in principle by the HKID, may be counted toward the minimum investment threshold amount.

Applicants must also have no adverse (criminal or security) record in Hong Kong or their home country and country of residence, and be able to demonstrate they are able to support themselves and their dependents without relying on any return on the permissible investment assets, employment, or public assistance in Hong Kong.

Entrants under this scheme who invest in real estate must remain the absolute beneficial owner of the real estate and maintain a net equity of HK$6.5 million. If the real estate is sold and the proceeds are reinvested in another real property, it must be reinvested within three months. If the proceeds of the sale of the real estate are to be reinvested in specified financial assets, they must be reinvested within two months.

The Director of Immigration must also be notified in writing of any changes regarding the absolute beneficial ownership of, or legal title to, or any mortgage of the real estate which forms the basis of the applicant's acquisition of capital investment entrant status.

Entrants who acquired their status by investing in specified financial assets are not permitted to realize or cash in any capital appreciation of the qualifying portfolio. On the other hand, if the value of the portfolio falls below the original HK$6.5 million, no topping up is required either.

However, rental income from a qualifying property and cash dividend income and interest income derived from permissible financial assets can be retained by the entrant and need not be "ring-fenced" under the scheme. The entrant may also switch his investments from one permissible asset class to another (*e.g.*, from real estate to financial assets or vice versa) so long as the earlier proceeds from the sale of the initial assets are reinvested.

In the case of investment outside of real estate, there is an annual reporting requirement on the composition and value of the qualifying portfolio. Since an applicant who decides to invest in specified financial assets rather than real estate must open a designated account in his or her own name with a single "financial intermediary" that can be managed on either a self-directed basis by the applicant or at the discretion of the financial intermediary, any reporting requirements would be handled by the financial intermediary.

A "financial intermediary" must be an authorized institution as defined in the Banking Ordinance, or a licensed corporation under the Securities and Futures Ordinance.

In contrast to the United States, Hong Kong has set out its welcome mat for foreign investors. Like the United States and other leading jurisdictions, Hong Kong is concerned that the source of the funds invested in Hong Kong is "clean." Accordingly, the applicant is required to show he or she has had uninterrupted control over at least HK$6.5 million throughout the two years immediately preceding his or her application. Thus, persons who suddenly win the lottery or receive a "gift" from a benefactor will not be eligible to apply until the funds have been under their control for at least two years.

Unlike other jurisdictions, the HKID has not become fixated on income tax returns and business records to establish the legal source of the funds, recognizing that many legitimate high net worth individuals may have income from investments that are either not subject to taxation or tax exempt and thus, not necessarily reflected in tax returns or business records.

Application Procedure

The application for Residence under the Capital Investment Entrant Scheme is submitted on Form ID(E)97 and asks for the applicant's personal particulars, including educational attainment and professional/technical qualifications. The employment record/business experience of the applicant for the past five years is also required along with disclosures concerning any prior entries to Hong Kong, any criminal conviction, and a local reference (if available).

In addition, the applicant must provide supporting documents of his or her personal net assets for the two years preceding the application, including bank deposits, real estate, and other assets such as stocks, equities, or debt securities, and indicate whether he or she has invested or intends to invest in real estate in Hong Kong or in specified financial assets. He or she must also furnish the contact details of a financial intermediary if one has been appointed.

As a result of a significant increase in the number of applications, it now takes about six months for a case to be approved. To help streamline the procedure and to shorten the processing time, with effect from March 16, 2009, applicants may engage a Certified Public Accountant (CPA) to issue a report that they meet the requirement of paragraph 2.1(b) of the Rules for the Capital Investment Entrant Scheme, including evidence that they have net assets or net equity to which they are absolutely beneficially entitled with a market value of not less that HKD6.5M throughout the two years immediately preceding the date they submit their applications. This is an optional arrangement; whether or not a CPA is engaged will not affect the outcome of the application although a CPA report demonstrating that the asset requirements have been met is expected to reduce the processing time.

After evaluating the application and receiving security clearances, a successful applicant who has already invested the required threshold amount will be issued a visa label which he or she can affix into his or her passport for entry and, upon presentation of the visa at the port of entry, will be initially granted a two-year period of stay.

Approval in Principle

If the applicant has not perfected his or her investment but has shown that he or she meets the eligibility criteria, he or she will be granted approval in principle and can enter Hong Kong on visitor status for three months. Once proof is furnished that the requisite minimum threshold investment has been made, formal approval will be initially granted for two years.

Dependents

A spouse and unmarried dependent children under 18 years of age are permitted to accompany the principal applicant, provided that the principal is capable of supporting and accommodating his or her dependents without having to rely on any return on the permissible investment assets, employment, or public assistance in Hong Kong.

Thereafter, extensions in two-year increments will be granted provided the entrant can demonstrate to the HKID that he or she continues to meet the eligibility criteria and the portfolio maintenance requirements in the Capital Investment Entrant Rules. Thus, it is important to keep a record of every change to the entrant's investment portfolio for extension of stay purposes.

It is important to note that at the time of the application for extension of stay, the applicant must provide proof that he or she continues to meet the eligibility criteria as well as the portfolio-maintenance requirements.

The portfolio-maintenance and "ring-fencing" requirements are imposed to ensure that the entrant does not reduce his investment commitment and has only transacted in the "Permissible Investment Asset Classes" as detailed at *www.immd.gov.hk/ehtml/hkvisas_13_5.htm.*

Upon completion of not fewer than seven years of continuous ordinary residence in Hong Kong, the capital investment entrant and his or her dependents may apply for the right of abode in Hong Kong in accordance with the law. Chinese citizens who have the right of abode in the HKSAR are eligible for an HKSAR passport.

According to statistics released by the HKID, from the time of the October 2003 launch of the program until December 31, 2009, a total of 9,894 applications were received by HKID. Out of these, 5,953 were approved and 1,268 have been granted "approval in principle."

Mainland China investors who do not have overseas permanent resident status are officially barred from participation in the Capital Investment Scheme because of foreign exchange control rules that the HKSAR Government must uphold and respect as part of "One Country, Two Systems."

However, many mainland residents have been able to establish eligibility to apply by first acquiring permanent resident status in another overseas jurisdiction, such as The Gambia or New Zealand. They do so not because those locales are their ultimate destination of choice, but instead as a stepping stone to establish residency in Hong Kong. In Hong Kong, they can enjoy the benefits of a low tax jurisdiction and continue overseeing their businesses in China while accumulating residency toward right of abode and an HKSAR passport that offers visa-free access or visa-on-arrival privileges to some 140 countries.

CONCLUSION

With globalization and the escalating fear of terrorism in the post-9/11 world, there has been a dampening of enthusiasm for migration to the traditionally popular Western destinations by high net-worth individuals because of security concerns along with high tax considerations.

Increasingly, this writer is encountering more and more high net-worth U.S. citizens and Europeans who are either applying for Hong Kong employment (entry for investment) visas or participating in the Capital Investment Entrant Scheme because of the flexibility of the program. This program has also become a haven for high net-worth individuals in the financial industry who have relocated to Hong Kong but are unable to extend their employment visas because they have lost their jobs and not yet been able to secure new employment.

These individuals are attracted to Hong Kong as not only a low tax jurisdiction and a safe haven from terrorism, but also as a world-class international financial center and strategic location ideally suited to take advantage of the trade and direct investment opportunities in China. This is especially so with the signing of the Closer Economic Partnership Arrangement (CEPA) between the Central People's Government and the HKSAR which provides for preferential access to the Mainland market and reduced tariffs for certain enterprises and individuals in Hong Kong, whether locally or foreign-owned.

After seven years of residence, some of these individuals have qualified for right of abode in Hong Kong and applied for naturalization as HKSAR citizens, which can be readily approved if these foreign nationals are prepared to renounce their present country of nationality.

NEW ZEALAND RESIDENCY FOR INVESTORS

by Eugene Chow[*]

INTRODUCTION

When advising clients seeking alternative destinations for investment immigration, most practitioners of immigration law in the United States will usually only venture as far as Canada. However, lawyers practicing overseas with a substantial client base in the People's Republic of China, Taiwan, and other parts of Asia have often looked to New Zealand as an attractive alternative.

This article[1] will provide an overview of the New Zealand Migrant Policy for the two categories of investors which took effect on July 27, 2009, explain the procedures for applying under the respective categories, and examine whether some of the salient features of the New Zealand "Investor Plus" and "Investor" categories have made New Zealand a more desirable destination.

A discussion of the new "Entrepreneur Plus" visa category, which came into effect November 30, 2009, and provides a faster track to residency for migrants who have been actively taking part in business and contributing to New Zealand's development, and the "Entrepreneur Visa Category" are beyond the scope of this article.

Overseas lawyers who may wish to represent a client on a New Zealand immigration matter should take note, however, that under the Immigration Advisers Licensing Act 2007, effective May 4, 2009, anyone who provides immigration advice in New Zealand must obtain a license to advise, assist, or represent a person on an immigration matter related to New Zealand and anyone based offshore giving New Zealand immigration advice must also be licensed as of May 4, 2010.

While lawyers admitted to practice in New Zealand are exempted from licensing, it is otherwise an offence for anyone not exempt to knowingly provide immigration advice without a licence, which offence may be punishable by a fine of up to NZ$100,000 (about US$71,414) and/or as much as seven years in prison.

Giving people publicly available information (*e.g.*, information on the Immigration New Zealand website) is not classified as "immigration advice" under the Act. As the Immigration New Zealand website publishes comprehensive information about immigration requirements, including the Immigration New Zealand Operations Manual, merely providing information obtained from the website or the Operations Manual would not amount to providing immigration advice.[2]

However, beyond providing general information, it would be prudent for foreign immigration lawyers with clients interested in obtaining professional advice to refer their clients to either a New Zealand lawyer with immigration expertise or a licensed immigration adviser.

MIGRANT INVESTMENT POLICY

Under New Zealand's current Migrant Investment Policy, an applicant may apply under either the "Investor Plus" (Investor 1 Category) or the "Investor" (Investor 2 Category).

INVESTOR PLUS (INVESTOR 1 CATEGORY)

The requirements for Investor 1 Category are more flexible in that there is no maximum age limit, no English language required, no business experi-

---

[*] **Eugene Chow** is the principal of Chow King & Associates, a Hong Kong-based firm specializing in U.S., Hong Kong, and international immigration matters. Mr. Chow is a graduate of Pennsylvania State University and obtained his J.D. from Boston College Law School. He has been in practice for more than 33 years and has been a California board-certified specialist in immigration law since 1989. He is listed in *An International Who's Who of Corporate Immigration Lawyers*, *Who's Who of the Law (Hong Kong & China)*; has been an annual contributing author to all 17editions of the American Immigration Lawyers Association's (AILA) *The Visa Processing Guide: Process and Procedure at U.S. Consulates and Embassies*. He also served as an Associate Editor of AILA's *Thinking Beyond Borders: 2004 Global Immigration Summit Handbook* as well as *Immigration Options for Investors and Entrepreneurs* (AILA 2006).

[1] The primary source of information for this article is from Immigration New Zealand's website at *www.immigration.govt.nz/migrant/stream/invest/migrantinvestment/requirements* as well as the Immigration New Zealand Operations Manual, which are available online at *www.immigration.govt.nz/opsmanual/index.htm*.

[2] Immigration Advisers Authority website: *www.iaa.govt.nz/*.

ence required, and no settlement funds required so long as the applicant invests NZ$10 million (about US$7.13 million) for three years and spends at least 73 days in New Zealand in each of the last two years of the three-year investment period.

Criteria for Approval

To be granted permanent residence under the Investor Plus (Investor 1 Category), the applicant must:

- Meet health and character requirements;
- Nominate funds and/or assets equivalent to at least NZ$10 million (about US$7.13 million) to be invested in an acceptable investment(s);[3]
- Provide evidence of ownership of the funds and/or assets and that they have been earned or acquired legally;
- Be able to transfer the investment funds through the banking system to New Zealand.

Application Procedure

An applicant interested in migrating under the Investor Plus (Investor 1 Category) must complete INZ 1163 and send it to the Business Migration Branch of Immigration New Zealand, P.O. Box 3705, in Wellington, New Zealand, along with supporting documents and an application fee of NZ$3,400 (about US$2,428).

If Immigration New Zealand is satisfied that the applicant meets the requirements for residence, the application will be approved in principle. Residence visas will then be granted to the applicant and his family members[4] once the applicant provides evidence that the investment funds have been transferred to New Zealand and placed in acceptable investments, provided a New Zealand address where the applicant can be contacted by mail after arrival, and has paid the appropriate migrant levy.

A residence visa valid for 12 months from the date of issue will then be issued and upon arrival, the applicant will be granted a returning resident's visa initially valid for two years from the date of first entry.

A residence visa is issued subject to certain requirements under Section 18A of the Immigration Act 1987. This is similar to the conditional lawful permanent residency granted to U.S investors under §203(b)(5) of the U.S. Immigration & Nationality Act, who are required to petition for removal of conditions within the 90-day period immediately preceding the second anniversary of their admission to the U.S. as a conditional lawful permanent resident. In the case of an Investor Plus immigrant, these requirements are that the investment funds must be retained in an "acceptable investment" for three years, and that the principal applicant must stay in New Zealand 73 days per year in each of the final two years of the three-year investment period.

Three months before the second anniversary of the investment period, Immigration New Zealand will write the applicant asking him to furnish evidence that he has retained acceptable investment(s) in New Zealand for the past two years and spent the requisite minimum time in New Zealand in the second year of the investment period. Upon furnishing satisfactory evidence he has met the requirements, the applicant and his family will be eligible for a subsequent returning resident's visa (RRV) valid for up to two years.

If the applicant fails to satisfy the Section 18A requirements, his residence permit will be revoked under Section 20(1)(d) of the Immigration Act 1987.

Three months before the third anniversary of his prescribed investment period, the applicant will again be asked for evidence that he has retained acceptable investment(s) in New Zealand for the remaining time of his investment period and spent the required 73 days in New Zealand for the remaining year of his investment period. Upon furnishing evidence of compliance, the principal applicant and his

---

[3] An "acceptable investment" is defined as an investment capable of a commercial return invested in New Zealand currency in lawful enterprises or managed funds which has the potential to contribute to New Zealand's economy. While investments in bonds issued by the New Zealand Government or bonds issued by new Zealand firms traded in the New Zealand Debt Securities Market (NZDX) or equity in New Zealand firms (public or private including managed funds) would qualify, an investment in a residential property development or an investment in a deposit-taking financial institution (*e.g.*, banks or finance companies) would not qualify (*http://glossary.immigration.govt.nz/acceptableinvestment.htm*).

[4] "Family members" are defined to include not only the spouse of a legal marriage but a "partner" in a civil union or a de facto relationship, whether of the same or opposite sex, so long as the relationship is genuine and stable, *i.e.*, where both people in the partnership have been living together for
continued

at least 12 months, as well as dependent child up to age 24. *See infra* notes 5 and 6.

family will be eligible for indefinite returning resident's visas.

INVESTOR (INVESTOR 2 CATEGORY)

Unlike the Investor Category, the Investor 2 Category is more stringent in that all applicants (the applicant, his partner[5] and dependent children[6]) must meet English language requirements and the principal applicant must have at least three years of business experience. While a lesser amount of investment funds are required (NZ$1.5 million, about US$1.07 million), the required investment period is longer (four years), and the applicant must also have NZ$1 million (about US$.7 million) in settlement funds. In addition, the principal applicant is required to spend at least 146 days in New Zealand in each of the last three years of the four-year investment period.

Criteria for Approval

To summarize, to be granted permanent residence under the Investor 2 Category, an applicant must:

- Invest NZ$1.5 million (about US$1.07 million) in New Zealand over a period of four years;
- Prepare NZ$1 million (about US$.7 million) in settlement funds;
- Have at least three years of business experience;
- Be 65 years old or younger at the time he or she applies for residence;
- Spend at least 146 days in New Zealand in each of the last three years during the four-year investment period;
- Meet English language, health, and character requirements; and
- Demonstrate that he or she intends, and has the ability to successfully settle in and make contributions to New Zealand.

Application Procedure

Expression of Interest

The application procedure for the Investor (Investor 2 Category) consists of two stages. The first stage involves the submission of an Expression of Interest (EOI) form that will be used as the basis for a points-based judgment as to the ability of a potential investor migrant to contribute to New Zealand businesses. The second stage only takes place if the applicant's EOI form has been accepted and only if the New Zealand government sends an invitation to apply, at which point the investor applicant can submit an application along with relevant supporting documentation.

A person interested in migrating as an investor to New Zealand must complete and submit the EOI Form (INZ 1165) to the Business Migration Branch, Immigration New Zealand, P.O. Box 3750, Wellington, New Zealand, along with a filing fee of NZ$460 (about US$328).

The EOI Form is a 20-page form that asks for very comprehensive information about the principal applicant, as well as his or her family, so that Immigration New Zealand can assess whether the applicant is likely to meet the criteria for residence under this category. No evidence needs to be submitted with the EOI; it is only if the EOI is accepted and the applicant is invited to apply that documentary evidence supporting the claims made in the EOI are required.

Character Requirements

The applicant and his or her family are required to answer detailed questions of character, including questions about past criminal violations or convictions, past immigration violations, removals from any country, or past refusal of entry or visas to any country, whether the applicant or any of his or her family members are currently under investigation or wanted by any law enforcement agency in any country, and whether the applicant has belonged to any groups that may raise security concerns. Applicants assessed to be within the prohibited classes of persons described under Section 7(1) of the Immigration Act 1987 cannot be accepted.

---

[5] In addition to a person legally married, New Zealand Immigration recognizes as a "partner" persons in a civil union or a de facto relationship, whether of the same or opposite sex, so long the relationship is genuine and stable, *i.e.*, where both people in the partnership have been living together for at least 12 months. Immigration Regulations 1999 reg 20, R2.1.10, R2.1.15 (*www.immigration.govt.nz/opsmanual/5191.htm*).

[6] A dependent child can be up to 24 years of age so long as he or she is single and without child(ren) of his or her own. The child need not live with the principal applicant or the principal applicant's partner so long as he or she relies totally or substantially on the principal applicant or on the principal applicant's partner for financial support. Immigration Regulations 1999, reg 20 R2.1.30 (*www.immigration.govt.nz/opsmanual/5191.htm*).

Character Waivers

Persons assessed to be within a prohibited class as described above (A5.25 of the Administration Chapter of the Immigration New Zealand Operations Manual[7]), may be granted character waivers even though they normally would be ineligible for residence visas. Whether a character waiver will be granted depends on the surrounding circumstances of the application and the weighing of the relevant factors outlined in A5.25.1b, c, and d of the Administration Chapter of the Immigration New Zealand Operations Manual.[8] These factors include a consideration of: the seriousness of the offence, whether there is more than one offence, the significance of the false, misleading, or forged information (if applicable) and whether the applicant has a reasonable/credible explanation if in supplying or withholding such information he or she did not intend to deceive the Immigration New Zealand, how long ago the relevant event occurred, whether the applicant has immediate family lawfully and permanently in New Zealand, whether the applicant has strong emotional or physical ties to New Zealand, and whether the applicant's potential contribution to New Zealand will be significant.

In the case of someone who is a member of a proscribed organization with objectives or principles that express hostility against certain groups of people on the basis of color, race, or ethnic or national origin, or has publicly made speeches that one race or color or ethnic or national origin group is inferior, Immigration New Zealand will consider the length of time since the applicant has publicly expressed such views or was a member of such a group or organization, whether the applicant still holds such views and the extent to which the applicant was involved in publishing such views, and the extent of his or her involvement in the organization or group.

In cases where a character waiver is possible, the EOI may be accepted although the applicant will be required to provide a police certificate along with other relevant information to enable Immigration New Zealand to fully consider the case.

Health Requirements

There also are detailed questions about health conditions to ensure that the applicant and his or her family meet an acceptable standard of health for residence in New Zealand. Immigration New Zealand may decline an application for residence based on an unacceptable standard of health. This pertains to those applicants whose health will likely impose considerable costs on New Zealand's health services (specific conditions are listed in Appendix 10 of the Immigration New Zealand Operations Manual). However, medical waivers are available for some health conditions if all other requirements for approval have been met.

English Language Requirements

The principal applicant is required to explain how he or she meets the minimum standard of English set forth in NZIS 1060, English Language Information (either an English background or an IELTS test report with an overall band score in the IELTS General or Academic Modules to earn at least one point for English ability).

IELTS is the International English Language Testing System, jointly managed by the University of Cambridge Local Examinations System (UCLES), the British Council, and IDP Education Australia (IELTS Australia). IELTS is an international test that provides an assessment of ability in English, its General and Academic Modules provide band totals (test results) showing overall ability, as well as performance in listening, reading, writing, and speaking.

The principal applicant's partner and/or children aged 16 and over who will be included in the residence application may either meet the minimum standard of English or must be willing to pre-purchase English language (ESOL) tuition and attend English language classes once they arrive in New Zealand.

Business Experience

Finally, the applicant is required to identify the type of business/industry in which he or she has worked, the past job titles/positions he or she has held, and provide detailed descriptions of past work experience. The applicant also is asked to explain why he or she considers that work experience to meet the definition of "business experience."

Under BJ 5.30.1a of Immigration New Zealand's Operations Manual, "business experience" is recognized if it is experience in planning, organization, control, senior change-management, direction-setting and mentoring acquired through ownership of or management level experience in a lawful business enterprise that has at least five full-time em-

---

[7] *www.immigration.govt.nz/opsmanual/11635.htm.*
[8] *Id.*

ployees and an annual turn-over of NZ$1 million (about US$.7 million).

A principal applicant must own at least 25 percent of a business to be considered an "owner" and a "lawful business enterprise" is defined as an organization that operates lawfully in a commercial environment with the goal of returning a profit and is not set up primarily for passive or speculative purposes. BJ5.30.1b and c.

The length of business experience is determined on the basis of at least 30 hours per week, and credit for part-time business experience may be given on a proportional basis. Thus, if an applicant has worked 15 hours per week for eight years, this would be equivalent to four years' business experience based on a 30-hour week. BJ5.30.5.

Investment Funds

The principal applicant is then asked to state what kind of investment he or she proposes undertaking, whether he or she can demonstrate ownership over the funds to be invested in New Zealand, the type and location of the funds and/or assets that will be used for investment and settlement, and to explain in detail how the investment funds and/or assets were earned or acquired.

Selection from EOI Pool

To enter into the EOI Pool, the applicant must meet prerequisites for health, character, English language, age, business experience, investment funds and settlement funds, and have a minimum points score of 20 or more.

There is no pass mark for EOIs being selected from the pool in order to be issued an invitation to apply for residence. EOIs will be selected from the pool according to their points ranking in sufficient numbers to suit the places available under the Investor 2 Category at time of selection.[9]

The Investor 2 Category has a cap of 300 approved applications per year. As this is a new program which only started operating in July, 2009, it is uncertain whether the entire quota will be taken up. Obviously, people with the highest total points will be selected from the pool. Thus, the more points an applicant can claim for English language ability, business experience, the younger he or she is, and the more he or she is prepared to invest, the better the chances of being issued an invitation to apply.

Invitation to Apply

If invited to apply, Immigration New Zealand will send the applicant an application form which must be completed and submitted to the Business Migration Branch within three months of the date of the letter inviting the applicant to apply, along with a filing fee of NZ$3,400 (about US$2,428). In the most recent round of selection of EOIs, which took place on March 3, 2010, nine EOIs were selected with all EOIs with a claim of between 20–84 points selected.[10]

When the application is submitted, evidence must be provided to substantiate all of the claims made in the EOI.

Under Section K2, page 8, of the Investor (Investor 2 Category) Guide (INZ 1164), Immigration New Zealand suggests the following documents as acceptable evidence of business experience:

- Business registration;
- Company financial statements;
- Company tax returns and tax records;
- Shareholder certificates or proof of ownership of business;
- Pay slips;
- Job specifications;
- Job assessments;
- Personal tax returns;
- Letters of appointments;
- Certificates of service;
- Strategic planning documents;
- References from employers on company letterhead, stating position(s) and dates of employment, and giving the contact phone number and address of the employer.

If the applicant worked part time, he or she must show the actual weekly hours worked.

The applicant also must provide documents showing the applicant owns net funds and assets equivalent to the required investment funds, that he or she earned or acquired the funds legally, and pro-

---

[9] www.immigration.govt.nz/migrant/stream/invest/migrantinvestment/MigrantInvestmentPolicyQAs.htm.

[10] www.immigration.govt.nz/migrant/general/generalinformation/news/eoimigrantinvestmentpolicy.htm.

vide proof of the applicant's earnings for the last five years.

If the funds/assets come from earnings from earlier years, appropriate information from earlier years will be required.

When the funds and/or assets have been given by a donor, the applicant is required to show that the donor legally acquired the funds and/or assets.

APPROVAL IN PRINCIPLE

Once approved in principle, the Investor Category applicant must show that the required funds have been transferred to New Zealand, and generally follow the same procedures as an Investor Plus Category applicant except that the ESOL training tuition fee(s) must be paid for any family member aged 16 and over included in the application who has not satisfied the English language requirements.

Similar to the Investor Plus immigrant, an Investor Category immigrant arriving in New Zealand after being issued a residence visa is subject to certain requirements under Section 18A of the Immigration Act 1987.

For the Investor Category immigrant, these requirements are that his funds invested in New Zealand be retained for a period of four years, and that he spends a minimum period of 146 days in New Zealand for each of the last three years during the four-year investment period.

CONCLUSION

The world is a global economy, and business investors and entrepreneurs today are highly mobile and simply do not remain "settled" in one single place.

In the experience of the author, most wealthy Asian business immigrants do not immigrate for economic reasons (this is especially true for a destination such as New Zealand), but for "quality of life" reasons, educational opportunities for their children, as a hedge against political uncertainty in their home countries, or to obtain a passport for ease of travel because of visa-free privileges once they become nationals of their destination countries.

While New Zealand may be legitimately concerned about the lack of commitment by some of the Asian business immigrants while their families are enjoying New Zealand's education, health, and social services, the reality is that immigrants do contribute substantially to the New Zealand economy through the transfer of substantial capital and assets into New Zealand, even if they do not spend a substantial amount of time there.

The Migrant Investment Policy's creation of two categories of investors was designed to attract financial capital to New Zealand by providing residence to those prepared to make a significant contribution to New Zealand's economy while at the same time an attempt at accommodating the wealthy migrant's desire for mobility by reducing the period of time the Investor Plus immigrant and the Investor Category immigrant is required to live in New Zealand.

The removal of an age limitation and the English language barrier for the Investor Plus Category and the downgrading of the importance of English language for the Investor Category, along with a reduced investment amount as well as the prescribed minimum period of investment are welcome changes to the previous Business Immigration Policy.

From 2002–03 to 2008–09, 16,743 people (5,102 principal applicants) were approved for residence through the Business Immigration Policy (which included the Entrepreneur Category and the Active Investor Migrant Policy comprised of three subcategories: General (Active) Investor, Professional Investor, and Global Investor. The main source countries were China (5,707), South Korea (4,243), and the United Kingdom (2,156). Over the past three years, the number of business migrants dropped from 1,257 in 2006–07 to 413 in 2008–09. However, the number of business migrants from the United Kingdom remained relatively steady, with 166 (40 percent) in 2008–09.[11]

Since 2005–06, the overall number of approvals through the Business Immigration Policy has dropped substantially, from 3,440 to 413 in 2008–09.[12] In addition to the English language requirement, the drop in approvals can be attributed to the requirement that principal applicants had to retain investment funds in New Zealand for a five-year period, and to make New Zealand their main home during the five-year investment period.[13]

In 2008–09, only 33 people were approved for residence through the Investor Category. While Chi-

---

[11] Migration Trends and Outlook 2008/09, at 64 (New Zealand Government, IMSED Research, Department of Labour 2009).

[12] Migration Trends and Outlook 2008/09 (New Zealand Government, IMSED Research, Department of Labour 2009).

[13] *Id.* at 62.

na had 1,958 approvals in 2002–03, 715 approvals in 2003–04, and 545 approvals in 2004–05, this had declined to 44 in 2005–06 and to only 6 in 2008–09.[14]

According to data contained in a report current to March 7, 2010, prepared by the Business Information Services Department of Labour (Immigration),[15] 20 applications have been accepted in the Investor Plus Category for 2009–10 to date and 177 in the Investor Category. This compares quite favorably with the 42 cases in the former General Investor 2007 Category in 2008–09 and 7 cases in the former Global Investor 2007 that year and to the 42 and 4 cases in these categories accepted in 2007–08.[16]

While the new Migrant Investment Policy is not a resounding success, it is a vast improvement from the previous policy which had deterred Asian investor immigrants while increasing intake from a politically favored country such as the United Kingdom.

These changes, however, are insufficient to make New Zealand a truly attractive destination for wealthy Asian immigrants when compared with competing jurisdictions such as Hong Kong and Singapore, both of which have much more flexible investment programs and no minimum residency requirements in order to maintain status.

---

[14] Table 6.5, Source Country of Investor Category approvals 2002/03–2008/09, Migration Trends and Outlook 2008/2009 (New Zealand Government, IMSED Research, Department of Labour 2009).

[15] Table R6, Residence Accepted by Financial Year from July 1, 1997 to March 6, 2010 (*www.immigration.govt.nz/NR/rdonlyres/319625F1-8DFA-47F1-B953-AECFF52EF54F/0/R7ResidenceAppsAcceptedforProcessingbyFY08Mar2010.pdf*).

[16] *Id.*

UNDERSTANDING INVESTMENT-BASED IMMIGRATION TO THE UNITED KINGDOM

by Linda Lau[*]

INTRODUCTION

High net worth individuals around the world possess the means to establish mobile lifestyles for themselves and their families. Given their resources and needs, they are generally willing and able to consider a variety of investment-based immigration options that include both the United States as well as other nations. The United Kingdom is often an appealing alternative to the United States because of its status as a major English-speaking country with a global influence and European context. Thus, U.S. immigration law practitioners servicing an upper echelon clientele will expand their capacity to assist clients by understanding the UK investor visa category. Should a client choose the United Kingdom as the target destination, the well-informed U.S. practitioner will be able to work effectively alongside a UK immigration practitioner to facilitate the UK application process.

OVERVIEW OF UK INVESTOR VISA CATEGORY

The UK investor visa category took effect in 1994 and was most recently retooled in June 2008 as part of a major overhaul of the UK immigration system. Since June 2008, "high net worth individuals making a substantial financial investment to the UK"[1] fall under Tier 1 of a five-tier, points-based system into which all classes other than family settlement are organized. Under the system, Tier 1 is assigned to highly skilled migrants, entrepreneurs, and investors; Tier 2 to various subcategories of sponsored skilled workers; Tier 3 to low-skill workers needed to fill temporary labor shortages[2]; Tier 4 to students; and Tier 5 to temporary workers including young people sponsored under the Youth Mobility Scheme. The five tiers and subcategories thereunder each entail different qualifying criteria and entitlements, and eligibility in all cases is based on earning a sufficient number of points tied to objective criteria. Tier 1 Investors are exempted from the English language requirement imposed on all other visa categories.

It is noted that while the 2008 changes radically restructured the immigration system, they did not alter the fundamental eligibility criteria under the investor visa category other than to restate them in a points-based format. The criteria are twofold.[3] First, a Tier 1 Investor applicant must have (a) at least £1 million of his/her own money that is held in a regulated financial institution[4] such as HSBC, and is disposable in the UK[5]; or (b) personal assets amounting to a net worth of at least £2 million, along with £1 million that he or she has borrowed from a regulated UK bank, which funds are held in a regulated financial institution and disposable in the UK. Funds or assets belonging to an investor's spouse, civil partner or unmarried or same-sex partner can be considered as the investor's own as long as it can be

---

[*] **Linda Lau** (J.D., UCLA School of Law) is a 2009–10 American Immigration Lawyers Association (AILA) EB-5 Committee member and a former chair and member of the Executive Committee of AILA's Southern California chapter. Her Los Angeles-based firm, Global Immigration Law Group, specializes in U.S. and global immigration strategies for professionals and high net worth individuals. She is admitted as a member of the California State Bar Association and a solicitor of England and Wales. **Tina Lee** (J.D., UCLA School of Law) assisted in writing this article. Ms. Lee is admitted to practice in California and is a senior associate at Global Immigration Law Group.

[1] *See* UK Immigration Rules, par. 245O. The rules can be accessed online through the UK Border Agency's website, at *www.ukba.homeoffice.gov.uk/policyandlaw/immigration law/immigrationrules/*.

[2] Implementation of Tier 3 has been suspended indefinitely according to the UK Border Agency. See *www.ukba. homeoffice.gov.uk/managingborders/managingmigration/ apointsbasedsystem/howitworks*.

[3] *See* UK Immigration Rules, par. 42–50 for the complete requirements.

[4] *See* UK Immigration Rules, Appendix A, par. 47: "A regulated financial institution is one which is regulated by the appropriate regulatory body for the country in which the financial institution operates. For example, where a financial institution does business in the UK, the appropriate regulator is the Financial Services Authority."

[5] *See* UK Immigration Rules, Appendix A, par. 48: "Money is disposable in the UK if all of the money is held in a UK based financial institution or if the money is freely transferable to the UK and convertible to sterling."

proven that the investor has control over the funds and is free to invest them.[6] In such cases, the partner must give permission for the applicant to control the money in the United Kingdom and a document confirming this must be submitted with the application.

Second, the applicant must, within three months of being granted entry to the UK as a Tier 1 Investor, invest a minimum of £750,000 of his or her money in the UK by way of UK government bonds, share capital, or loan capital in active and trading UK-registered companies other than those engaged principally in property investment. The investment must be maintained in order to be eligible for permanent residence.

In terms of points, the minimum number that must be achieved is 75. An initial applicant who satisfactorily shows possession of £1 million disposable funds in the UK, either by the "money of his own" or net worth-plus-loan route, scores 75 points. An applicant seeking an extension of Tier 1 Investor classification will be awarded 30 points for having met the initial £1 million disposable funds test, 30 points for having invested the minimum £750,000 in the UK, and 15 points for having made the requisite investment within three months of obtaining entry as a Tier 1 Investor and maintaining the investment for the totality of the initial entry period.

THE PATH TO RESIDENCY AND CITIZENSHIP

The immigration process for Tier 1 Investor applicants begins with the submission of an application and supporting documents to the UK Border Agency, via the appropriate consulate, requesting "entry clearance."[7] If the applicant is in the United States lawfully in a status other than visitor, he or she may submit the application through a UK consulate in the United States.[8] Depending on whether the applicant is a "visa national"[9] or "non-visa national," entry clearance will be in the form of either a visa or an entry certificate in the passport that permits admission to the UK. The application and evidence are reviewed according to the point system described earlier.

If the application and documents are in order, the application is decided at the local consulate and the investor is granted entry clearance for a period of three years. One significant substantive change in the investor category is that Tier 1 Investors (and their dependents) who enter the UK under the new 2008 rules may work in the UK,[10] whereas employment was not permitted under the older rules.

At the end of the initial three-year period, the investor may apply for "leave to remain" for an additional two-year period. Neither the initial entry clearance nor leave to remain equate to permanent residence, technically termed "indefinite leave to remain" (ILR). Before discussing the rules regarding permanent residence and citizenship, it is important to note that effective July 2011, the path to UK citizenship will be drastically changed pursuant to legislation passed by the UK government on July 21, 2009. The current regime will only apply to those who hold ILR or are in the process of applying for ILR at the time the new provisions are implemented. Such persons will have until July 2013 to apply for UK citizenship under the current criteria.

Under current law, ILR may be sought only after the investor has spent a continuous period of five years in the UK, demonstrates that the original investment has been maintained, and meets requirements for English language proficiency and knowledge of life in the UK. The investor may apply for naturalization as a British citizen after spending 12 months in the UK under ILR, provided that during the five-year period immediately prior to applying, the investor was not outside the UK for more than 450 days and not more than 90 days in the last 12 months. They will be able to apply under the current rules for up to a two-year period i.e., up until July 2013.

Under the new law effective July 2011, ILR will no longer be available. Instead, the five-year period spent as a Tier 1 Investor will be called "Temporary Residence," and will be followed by a period of "Probationary Citizenship" upon passing English language and knowledge of life in the UK tests. Probationary Citizenship, which refers to further temporary leave to remain in the UK while working toward permanent residence or citizenship, will be granted for a minimum of one and a maximum of five years. During the Proba-

---

[6] See UK Immigration Rules, Appendix A, par. 49.

[7] See UK Immigration Rules, par. 245P.

[8] Presently, visa applications are processed in the United states only at the Los Angeles, Chicago, and New York consular posts. Jurisdictional information is listed at www.visainfoservices.com/Pages/Welcome.aspx.

[9] Visa nationals are those who require a visa to enter the UK based on their nationality. See UK Immigration Rules, Appendix 1, for a listing of visa-subject countries.

[10] Employment may not be as a doctor in training. UK Immigration Rules, par. 245(R)(a)(iii).

tionary Citizenship period, the investor may apply for naturalization after a minimum of one year provided that all requirements are met. Among the new and more stringent requirements, naturalization applicants may only be outside of the UK a maximum of 90 days per year during the qualifying period. Also, there will be an "active citizenship" component requiring participation in volunteer or community work recognized by the government, likely for a total of 50 hours. Should the investor opt for Permanent Residence instead of Citizenship, he or she must hold Probationary Citizenship for a minimum of three years before applying. Permanent Residents may apply for Citizenship at a later date. Guidance and rules implementing the new law have not yet been published.[11]

The new law is designed to "incentivize migrants to become active members of society as they proceed on the journey to citizenship," as well as improve their integration into British society by steering them "to complete their journey to citizenship."[12] Accordingly, immigration counsel should thoroughly understand the long-term goals of Tier 1 Investor applicants and provide a realistic view of how easily they can be attained.

The following diagram summarizes the timeline for a Tier 1 (Investor) to achieve permanent residence or citizenship under the new law:

DEPENDENT ELIGIBILITY

The Partner and Child of a Tier 1 Investor may apply for entry clearance, leave to remain, and ILR at the same time as the investor. "Partner" includes spouses, civil partners, and unmarried or same-sex partners who have been living together in a relationship similar to marriage or civil partnership for at least two years. For ILR, the Partner must have been living together in the UK with the investor for at least two years in a marriage or civil partnership, or a relationship similar to marriage or civil partnership, and must demonstrate sufficient knowledge of the English language and knowledge of life in the UK. The "Child" of the Tier 1 Investor must be under 18 years of age on the date of application or, if over 18, have last been granted leave to remain as the child of the investor. The Child must not be married or in a civil partnership, or have formed an independent family unit or, be leading an independent life. Additionally, both parents must apply at the same time as the Child as a general rule. The same requirements apply to ILR, and the Child must, in addition, pass the English language and life in the UK tests.[13]

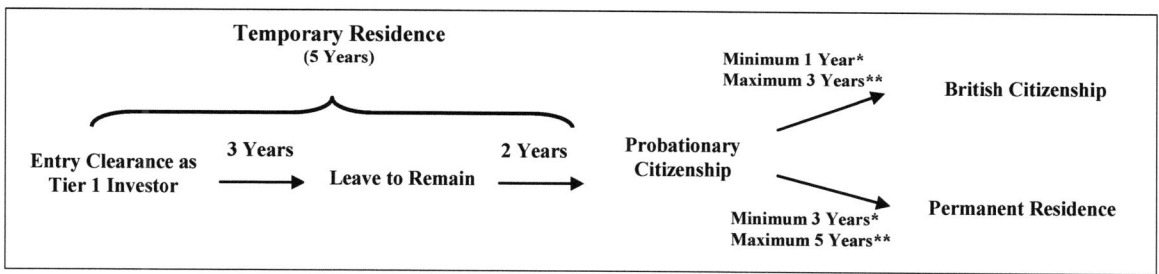

* with "active citizenship"
** without "active citizenship"

---

[11] An overview of the new citizenship law has been published by the UK Border Agency, at *www.ukba.home office.gov.uk/sitecontent/documents/aboutus/consultations/pathtocitizenship/*.

[12] *See* the UK Border Agency's "Impact Assessment of Earned Citizenship Proposals Borders, Citizenship and Immigration Bill," p. 4, *available at www.ukba.homeoffice.gov.uk/sitecontent/documents/policyandlaw/legislation/bci-act/*.

[13] *See* UK Immigration Rules, par. 319A–319K.

Like the Tier 1 Investor applicant, the investor's dependents may also work as long as employment is not as a doctor in training.[14] For purposes of citizenship, residency and other requirements are assessed on an individual basis, so the dependents of an investor must independently qualify under the new citizenship rules to take effect in July 2011.

EFFICIENCY AND TRANSPARENCY

According to the processing time report for all decisions made in December 2009,[15] the processing times for Tier 1 visa applications were as follows:

	2 days	3 days	5 days	10 days	15 days	30 days	60 days	90 days	120 days	Total decisions made
British Consulate General in Los Angeles	0%	40%	68%	87%	98%	100%	100%	100%	100%	80
British Consulate-General in Chicago	21%	34%	62%	90%	100%	100%	100%	100%	100%	32
British Consulate-General in New York	49%	57%	71%	94%	97%	98%	100%	100%	100%	71

While the report does not address the Tier 1 Investor subcategory separately, the processing times attest to a high level of efficiency, with a substantial number being processed in a matter of weeks. Even accounting for time delays due to security checks, 100 percent of the applications are decided within 60 days. The efficiency reflects the streamlined application process in which applicants are provided with a clear list of supporting documents required for approval.[16] Also, the manner in which processing times are organized and accessible to the public attest to the transparency of the UK program.

COMPARATIVE SNAPSHOT OF THE UK AND U.S. INVESTOR PROGRAMS

A brief comparison of the UK and U.S. investor immigration programs will enable immigration law practitioners from either country to assess which option best fits their clients' needs. Moreover, a study of the UK system can offer valuable insight into how the U.S. program might be improved.

Under the U.S. scheme, investment-based immigration is achieved through the EB-5 (employment-based fifth preference visa) program administered by the U.S. Citizenship and Immigration Services (USCIS).[17] Generally speaking, EB-5 eligibility is predicated on a minimum at-risk[18] investment of $500,000 or $1,000,000 in capital into a new commercial enterprise in the United States that, within roughly a two-year period, will create 10 new[19] full-time positions for qualifying U.S. workers. Whether the minimum investment amount can be $500,000 depends on whether the investment location is within a "targeted employment area."[20] The employment creation requirement may be satisfied through a showing of jobs "created indirectly" where the investment is in connection with a USCIS-designated regional center.[21]

EB-5 immigrant investor classification is requested through filing an immigration petition (on Form I-526), the approval of which allows the investor to then apply for conditional residence. Assuming the application is approved, the investor is admitted to the U.S. as a conditional permanent, meaning initial admission is for a period of two years as opposed to the initial admission period of 10 years granted to

---

[14] See UK Immigration Rules, par. 319D(b)(iii).

[15] Posted online at www.ukvisas.gov.uk/en/howtoapply/processingtimes.

[16] See www.ukvisas.gov.uk/en/howtoapply/infs/inf23pbs investor#14536494.

[17] See Immigration and Nationality Act (INA) §203(b)(5) et seq., and Title 8, Code of Federal Regulations (8 CFR) Parts 204.6 et seq. and 216.6 et seq.

[18] See 8 CFR §204.6(j)(2) and Matter of Izummi, 22 I&N Dec. 169, 19 Immigr. Rep. B2-32 (Assoc. Comm'r, Examinations 1998).

[19] For a "troubled business," maintenance of pre-investment jobs may be counted toward the employment creation requirement. See 8 CFR §204.6(j)(4)(ii).

[20] See 8 CFR Parts 204.6(e) and 204.6(f)(2).

[21] See 8 CFR §204.6(m)(7). A periodically updated list of U.S. Citizenship and Immigration Services (USCIS)-designated regional centers is published at www.uscis.gov/portal/site/uscis/menuitem.5af9bb95919f35e6 6f614176543f6d1a/?vgnextoid=d765ee0f4c014210VgnVCM 100000082ca60aRCRD&vgnextchannel=facb83453d4a3210 VgnVCM100000b92ca60aRCRD.

most other permanent residents. The investor can obtain "permanent" residence only if he or she satisfies the requirements for the removal of conditions, sought by filing a Form I-829 prior to the end of the two-year conditional residence period. Approval of the I-829 approval hinges primarily on proof that the requisite jobs have been created within the conditional period.

The above summary is by no means meant as a thorough discussion of the highly complex EB-5 program. It is a starting point, however, for highlighting some major differences between the U.S. and UK investor programs suggesting the superiority of the latter.

First, there is no employment creation requirement under the UK's Tier 1 Investor category. The UK system attaches a job creation requirement to the Tier 1 Entrepreneur category,[22] but the value of a Tier 1 Investor's economic contribution to the UK is not measured in terms of job creation. This reflects the idea that the deployment of funds into government bonds or UK-registered companies creates a ripple effect that stimulates the economy as a whole. The EB-5 program partially espouses the "ripple effect" notion with respect to regional center investments[23], but ultimately insists on job creation being the ultimate indicator, in part because it conflates the concepts of investor and entrepreneur.

Second, under the UK program, Tier 1 Investors can qualify by investing in UK government bonds or providing loans to UK-registered companies. By nature, government bonds are clearly connected to activities targeting economic and social improvements. Similarly, viable companies routinely utilize loan capital to sustain and grow competitive businesses. Unlike EB-5 investors who are subject to a strictly interpreted "at risk" requirement that only allows equity investments, Tier 1 Investors do not have to demonstrate that their investment is a gamble in order to reasonably show that their money will benefit the UK economy. It is debatable whether the U.S. risky equity investment approach furthers the policy of benefitting the U.S. economy in the long term.

Third, the UK program does not require investors to demonstrate the source of their funds as long as they can demonstrate the funds have been held in an institution regulated by the Financial Services Authority, or a bank regulated by the home regulator, for at least three months preceding the application. If this cannot be demonstrated, prescribed documents are provided to show the source of the funds, *e.g.* deed of gift. The Border Agency does not accord discretionary authority to officers regarding the source-of-funds issue. Government-regulated banks have a vested interest in guarding against unlawful activities and are better equipped to handle the vetting of funds. By building in the requirement that investor funds be from a regulated bank in or outside of the UK, the UK program is able to safeguard source-of-funds concerns as well as efficiency.

A final difference to be discussed in this article is in how an investor reaches permanent residence and citizenship in the UK versus the United States. Under the EB-5 program, an investor obtains two-year conditional permanent residence immediately on entry and then has the opportunity to seek true permanent residence within 90 days before the two years expires. A Tier 1 Investor in the UK is not granted permanent residence, conditional or otherwise, until he or she spends five years in Tier 1 Investor status. While UK law stipulates a longer path to permanent residence and eventual citizenship, the path is fairly predictable because the investor's investment will likely be stable throughout the five-year period. Not so with the EB-5 program. The reality is that EB-5 investors must meet such onerous requirements to achieve the removal of conditions on residence that their short-lived resident status has questionable value. If a start-up investment enterprise plays out the common scenario of failing or growing at a slow pace during the first two years of operations, the investor will be denied permanent residence despite his or her good-faith investment and best efforts. When all is said and done, the Tier 1 Investor is more often like the proverbial tortoise that reaches the finish line.

CONCLUSION

Since September 2009, the USCIS Office of Policy and Strategy has been conducting an EB-5 program assessment that includes a comparative study of other investment immigration programs, including the UK program.[24] As the project was due for completion at the end of February 2010, USCIS's conclusions remain to be seen. It is hoped that the

---

[22] *See* UK Immigration Rules, Appendix A, par. 32–41.

[23] *See* 8 CFR §204.6(m).

[24] *See* "USCIS Q&A from Stakeholder Session with AILA EB-5 Committee and Invest in the USA" (Dec. 14, 2009), item no. 4, *published on* AILA InfoNet at Doc. No. 10010462 (*posted* Jan. 4, 2010), and reproduced at Appendix H.

EB-5 program will learn from the UK's reasonable and streamlined model, so that existing hindrances to EB-5 participation can be minimized or eliminated. However the verdict may lie, practitioners of U.S. immigration law will benefit from keeping a broad perspective that readily considers and understands global options for their investor clients.

TABLE OF APPENDICES

A. AAO Precedents

1. *Matter of Soffici*, 22 I&N Dec. 158 (Assoc. Comm'r, Examinations 1998), AILA InfoNet Doc. No. 98070290 437

2. *Matter of Izummi*, 22 I&N Dec. 169 (Assoc. Comm'r, Examinations 1998), AILA InfoNet Doc. No. 98082091 449

3. *Matter of Ho*, 22 I&N Dec. 201 (Assoc. Comm'r, Examinations 1998), AILA InfoNet Doc. No. 98081291 481

4. *Matter of Hsiung*, 22 I&N Dec. 206 (Assoc. Comm'r, Examinations 1998) AILA InfoNet Doc. No. 98081290 491

B. Federal Court Decisions

- *Chang v. United States*, 327 F.3d 911 (9th Cir. 2003), AILA InfoNet Doc. No. 03043045 497

C. USCIS/INS Memos

1. USCIS Memorandum, W. Yates, "Establishment of an Investor and Regional Center Unit" (Jan. 19, 2005), AILA InfoNet Doc. No. 05012663 529

2. Legacy INS Memorandum, M. Pearson, "EB-5 Field Memorandum No. 9: Form I-829 Processing" (Mar. 3, 2000), AILA InfoNet Doc. No. 00060702 533

3. USCIS Memorandum, W. Yates, "Amendments Affecting Adjudication of Petitions for Alien Entrepreneur" (June 10, 2003), AILA InfoNet Doc. No. 03061744 555

4. USCIS Memorandum, D. Neufeld, "EB-5 Entrepreneurs—Job Creation and Full-Time Positions (AFM Update AD 09-04)" (June 17, 2009), AILA InfoNet Doc. No. 09061964 559

5. USCIS Memorandum, D. Neufeld, "Adjudication of EB-5 Regional Center Proposals and Affiliated Form I-526 and Form I-829 Petitions; Adjudicator's Field Manual (AFM) Update to Chapters 22.4 and 25.2 (AD09-38)" (Dec. 11, 2009), AILA InfoNet Doc. No. 09121561 567

D. USCIS *Adjudicator's Field Manual*

1. Chapter 22, Section 22.4: Employment Creation Entrepreneur Cases 591

2. Chapter 25, Section 25.2: Entrepreneurs 605

E. Highlights, GAO Report on Immigrant Investors

- U.S. Government Accountability Office (GAO) Report to Congressional Committees, "Immigrant Investors: Small Number of Participants Attributed to Pending Regulations and Other Factors," No. GAO-05-256 (Apr. 2005), AILA InfoNet Doc. No. 05040475 619

F. CIS Ombudsman Report

- Office of the CIS Ombudsman, "Employment Creation Immigrant Visa (EB-5) Program Recommendations" (Mar. 18, 2009), AILA InfoNet Doc. No. 09031868 621

G. USCIS Response to Ombudsman Report

- USCIS Memorandum, M. Aytes, "Response to Recommendation 40, Employment Creation Immigrant Visa (EB-5) Program Recommendations" (June 12, 2009), AILA InfoNet Doc. No. 09061770 639

H. USCIS Q&A from Stakeholder Session

- USCIS Q&A from Stakeholder Session with AILA EB-5 Committee and Invest in the USA" (Dec. 14, 2009), AILA InfoNet Doc. No. 10010462 643

I. Index of Online Resources, *compiled by* Susan Pilcher 659

APPENDIX A-1: *MATTER OF SOFFICI*

In re SOFFICI, Petitioner

In Visa Petition Proceedings

A76 472 614

Designated as a precedent by the Commissioner, June 30, 1998.
(Decided by the Associate Commissioner, Examinations, June 25, 1998.)

(1) A petitioner under § 203(b)(5) of the Immigration and Nationality Act cannot establish the requisite investment of capital if he lends the money to his new commercial enterprise.

(2) Loans obtained by a corporation, secured by assets of the corporation, do not constitute capital invested by a petitioner. Not only is such a loan prohibited by 8 C.F.R, § 204.6(e), but the petitioner and the corporation are not the same legal entity.

(3) A petitioner's personal guarantee on a business's debt does not transform the business's debt into the petitioner's personal debt.

(4) A petitioner must present clear documentary evidence of the source of the funds that he invests. He must show that the funds are his own and that they were obtained through lawful means.

(5) A petitioner who acquires a pre-existing business must show that the investment has created, or at least has a reasonable prospect of creating, 10 full-time positions, in addition to those existing before acquisition. The petitioner must, therefore, present evidence concerning the pre-acquisition level of employment. Simply maintaining the pre-acquisition level of employment is not sufficient, unless the petitioner shows that the pre-existing business qualifies as a "troubled business."

ON BEHALF OF PETITIONER: LARRY J. BEHA
888 SE 3RD AVENUE
SUITE 400
FORT LAUDERDALE FL 33316

The preference visa petition was approved by the Director, Texas Service Center, who certified the decision to the Associate Commissioner for Examinations for review. The decision of the director will be reversed.

The petitioner seeks classification as an alien entrepreneur pursuant to section 203(b)(5) of the Immigration and Nationality Act, 8 U.S.C. § 1153(b)(5). The director determined that the petitioner had adequately

158

Interim Decision #3359

established that he was actively in the process of investing the requisite amount of capital. The director further found that the investment would result in full-time positions for not fewer than 10 qualifying employees.

In response, counsel urges the Administrative Appeals Office to affirm the director's decision. He asserts that the petitioner's investment exceeds one million dollars and points out that the hotel is commercially active. He states that the petitioner's investment has already created at least 10 full-time jobs.

Section 203(b)(5)(A) of the Act provides classification to qualified immigrants seeking to enter the United States for the purpose of engaging in a new commercial enterprise:

> (i) which the alien has established,
>
> (ii) in which such alien has invested (after the date of the enactment of the Immigration Act of 1990) or, is actively in the process of investing, capital in an amount not less than the amount specified in subparagraph (C), and
>
> (iii) which will benefit the United States economy and create full-time employment for not fewer than 10 United States citizens or aliens lawfully admitted for permanent residence or other immigrants lawfully authorized to be employed in the United States (other than the immigrant and the immigrant's spouse, sons, or daughters).

MINIMUM INVESTMENT AMOUNT.

The petitioner indicates that the petition is based on an investment in an existing business located in a targeted employment area, for which the required amount of capital invested has been adjusted downward.

8 C.F.R. § 204.6(e) states, in pertinent part, that:

> *Targeted employment area* means an area which, at the time of investment, is a rural area or an area which has experienced unemployment of at least 150 percent of the national average rate.

The petitioner's company, Ames Management, Inc., does business as a Howard Johnson Hotel located at 950 South Federal Highway in Stuart, Florida. The City of Stuart is in Martin County. The petitioner has submitted a March 1996 letter from the Florida Department of Labor and Employment Security indicating that Martin County qualified as a rural area in 1995. In addition, the Ft. Pierce metropolitan statistical area, which encompassed Martin County, experienced a sufficiently high unemployment rate to qualify as a targeted employment area in 1995.

A petitioner has the burden to establish that his enterprise does business in an area that is considered "targeted" as of the date he files his petition.

Interim Decision #3359

The fact that a business may be located in an area that was once rural, for example, does not mean that that area is still rural. The letter from the Florida Department of Labor and Employment Security contains the following statement: "This listing will only remain in effect until 1996 annual averages are available in early 1997." The petitioner here filed his Form I-526 in January 1998, and his data are at least a year, if not two years, out of date.

The Service has nevertheless independently obtained current employment information from the Florida Department of Labor and Employment Security. While Martin County is no longer a rural area, the "Ft. Pierce-Port St. Lucie" metropolitan statistical area does constitute an area of high unemployment; all of Martin County is contained in this new metropolitan statistical area. Therefore, the amount of capital necessary to make a qualifying investment in this matter is $500,000.

THE PETITIONER HAS NOT MADE, AND IS NOT IN THE PROCESS OF MAKING, A QUALIFYING INVESTMENT OF CAPITAL.

8 C.F.R. § 204.6(e) states, in pertinent part, that:

> *Capital* means cash, equipment, inventory, other tangible property, cash equivalents, and indebtedness secured by assets owned by the alien entrepreneur, provided the alien entrepreneur is personally and primarily liable and that the assets of the new commercial enterprise upon which the petition is based are not used to secure any of the indebtedness.
>
> *Commercial enterprise* means any for-profit activity formed for the ongoing conduct of lawful business including, but not limited to, a sole proprietorship, partnership (whether limited or general), holding company, joint venture, corporation, business trust, or other entity which may be publicly or privately owned. This definition includes a commercial enterprise consisting of a holding company and its wholly-owned subsidiaries, provided that each such subsidiary is engaged in a for-profit activity formed for the ongoing conduct of a lawful business. This definition shall not include a non-commercial activity such as owning and operating a personal residence.
>
> *Invest* means to contribute capital. A contribution of capital in exchange for a note, bond, convertible debt, obligation, or any other debt arrangement between the alien entrepreneur and the new commercial enterprise does not constitute a contribution of capital for the purposes of this part.

8 C.F.R. § 204.6(j) states, in pertinent part, that:

> (2) To show that the petitioner has invested or is actively in the process of investing the required amount of capital, the petition must be accompanied by evidence that the petitioner has placed the required amount of capital at risk for the purpose of generating a return on the capital placed at risk. Evidence of mere intent to invest, or of prospective investment arrangements entailing no present commitment, will not suf-

160

Interim Decision #3359

fice to show that the petitioner is actively in the process of investing. The alien must show actual commitment of the required amount of capital. Such evidence may include, but need not be limited to:

(i) Bank statement(s) showing amount(s) deposited in United States business account(s) for the enterprise;

(ii) Evidence of assets which have been purchased for use in the United States enterprise, including invoices; sales receipts; and purchase contracts containing sufficient information to identify such assets, their purchase costs, date of purchase, and purchasing entity;

(iii) Evidence of property transferred from abroad for use in the United States enterprise, including United States Customs Service commercial entry documents, bills of lading and transit insurance policies containing ownership information and sufficient information to identify the property and to indicate the fair market value of such property;

(iv) Evidence of monies transferred or committed to be transferred to the new commercial enterprise in exchange for shares of stock (voting or nonvoting, common or preferred), Such stock may not include terms requiring the new commercial enterprise to redeem it at the holder's request; or

(v) Evidence of any loan or mortgage agreement, promissory note, security agreement, or other evidence of borrowing which is secured by assets of the petitioner, other than those of the new commercial enterprise, and for which the petitioner is personally and primarily liable.

(3) To show that the petitioner has invested, or is actively in the process of investing, capital obtained through lawful means, the petition must be accompanied, as applicable, by:

(i) Foreign business registration records;

(ii) Corporate, partnership (or any other entity in any form which has filed in any country or subdivision thereof any return described in this subpart), and personal tax returns including income, franchise, property (whether real, personal, or intangible), or any other tax returns of any kind filed within five years, with any taxing jurisdiction in or outside the United States by or on behalf of the petitioner;

(iii) Evidence identifying any other source(s) of capital; or

(iv) Certified copies of any judgments or evidence of all pending governmental civil or criminal actions, governmental administrative proceedings, and any private civil actions (pending or otherwise) involving monetary judgments against the petitioner from any court in or outside the United States within the past fifteen years.

Purchase of the hotel.

Ames Management, Inc. filed its articles of incorporation with the State

Interim Decision #3359

of Florida on June 27, 1997. All 1000 authorized shares were issued to the petitioner in July 1997. On October 31, 1997, Ames Management purchased a Howard Johnson's Motor Lodge for the sale price of $2.4 million, paid as follows: $25,000 in earnest money, consisting of a $10,000 initial deposit and a subsequent $15,000 deposit; $705,298.79 brought to settlement; and $1.7 million borrowed from 1st United Bank.

In a document entitled Sources of Investment Funds, the petitioner stated that the money used to purchase the hotel came from two sources. Approximately $450,000 were transferred to Barnett Bank from Argentina over the period 1994 to 1997; these funds "originated from personal savings and a sale of a house." An additional $500,000 were transferred from Argentina in December of 1996; these funds originated from the sale of "our business." The petitioner explained that, for both sources, "[t]hese monies were loaned to me by my father and I loaned them back to my company Ames Management, Inc. It has not been stipulated when I should return the funds."[1]

The balance sheet for the petitioner's hotel, dated November 30, 1997, confirms that the business's liabilities include long-term loans, totaling $922,136.09, payable to the shareholder (the petitioner), *See also* the Continuing and Unconditional Subordination of Debt discussed below. The accompanying "Transactions by Account" breaks down the amount, date, and destination of each loan. It is clear from this document that the $25,000 in earnest money and the $705,298.79 brought to the settlement table are mere loans from the petitioner to Ames Management. As specified in the definition of "invest" set forth in 8 C.F.R. § 204.6(e), debt arrangements between a petitioner and his business do not constitute qualifying contributions of capital. Therefore, the $730,298.79 paid toward the purchase of the hotel cannot be considered to be an "investment" by the petitioner.

Ames Management financed the balance of the purchase price, or $1.7 million, through 1st United Bank. According to the Mortgage and Security Agreement, the loan is secured by the hotel and all of its contents, including inventory, accounts, leases, the franchise agreement, furniture, patio umbrellas, landscaping, etc. First, it should be noted that a loan obtained by a corporation is not the same as a loan obtained by an individual, and it cannot be said that this loan through 1st United Bank is an investment of the *petitioner's* personal capital. Second, even if it were assumed, arguendo, that the petitioner and Ames Management were the same legal entity for purposes of this proceeding, indebtedness that is secured by assets of the enterprise is specifically precluded from the definition of "capital." *See* 8 C.F.R. § 204.6(e).

---

[1] The petitioner has not disclosed the terms of the loan from his father, and it is not known if, for example, it is secured by assets of Ames Management.

Counsel points out that the petitioner has personally guaranteed the payment of the loan. In a Continuing and Unconditional Subordination of Debt dated October 31, 1997, Ames Management and the petitioner agreed that all debts owed by Ames to 1st United would receive priority; all obligations owed by Ames to the petitioner would be subordinated to those owed to 1st United. In case of default by Ames with regard to its loan from 1st United, the petitioner would not seek or accept payment from Ames with regard to Ames's debts to the petitioner. In an Unconditional and Irrevocable Guaranty of Payment, also dated October 31, 1997, the petitioner agreed to make the mortgage payments if Ames Management did not. 1st United would have the right to proceed against the petitioner without first proceeding against Ames Management or against any property securing the note.

As the guarantee does not **obligate** 1st United to proceed against the petitioner, it does not prohibit 1st United from first seeking payment from the business.[2] The petitioner's personal guarantee of payment does not change the character of the mortgage; the assets of Ames Management are still primarily securing the mortgage. As such, the $1.7 million that the mortgage represents cannot properly be considered an investment of the petitioner's capital.

Purchase of the van, pre-opening expenses, and corporate accounts.

On November 1, 1997, Ames Management purchased a van to be used as the hotel shuttle. The petitioner made a down payment of $8,000 and Ames Management financed the balance of $17,477.06 through Primus. Counsel and the petitioner count this van as part of the petitioner's investment. The loan through Primus does not constitute a qualifying investment of capital because it is secured by the van itself, which is an asset of Ames Management; moreover, it is not an investment of the *petitioner's* capital because it is a loan obtained by Ames and not by the petitioner.

The $8,000 down payment also does not qualify as an "investment" of the petitioner's funds; according to the Transactions by Account referenced above, it is part of the $922,136.09 in long-term loans payable to the petitioner. In other words, the $8,000 must be repaid to the petitioner.

Counsel and the petitioner include bank accounts and pre-opening expenses as investments in Ames Management. The pre-opening expenses of $44,836.09, however, appear on the Transactions by Account and are part of the long-term loans payable to the petitioner. The amounts transferred to the bank accounts also appear on the Transactions by Account as long-term loans and therefore cannot constitute qualifying investments.

---

[2]It is not clear why, in the event of default, 1st United would prefer to research and pursue the petitioner's personal assets, which are not specified in the guarantee and which do not total $1.7 million, in lieu of seizing the easily accessible hotel itself.

Interim Decision #3359

Resources to invest.

As discussed above, the petitioner has not made a qualifying investment in Ames because the amounts he has paid on behalf of Ames are mere loans to Ames, prohibited by the regulations. It should be noted that the petitioner has not documented that he has the means to begin the process of investing, either. He submits a personal net worth report as of November 30, 1997, purporting to show that his net worth is $761,747.02. It is not clear who prepared this report, and the report contains certain irregularities. For example, the hotel, which belongs to Ames Management, is counted among the petitioner's personal assets. Also, the mortgage held by Ames Management is included among the petitioner's personal liabilities. On the other hand, the hotel van owned by Ames Management is correctly omitted from the report. In effect, with this personal net worth report the petitioner is attempting to show that he has sufficient wealth to invest in the hotel because he has invested in the hotel. Subtracting the hotel entries leaves the petitioner's alleged net worth at $61,747.02.

The petitioner counts the funds in various personal bank accounts as part of his personal assets. A letter and bank statements from Barnett Bank reveal that the petitioner has held *joint* accounts with his father since October 1994. It is not possible to determine what portions of these accounts belong to the petitioner's father and what portions to the petitioner. Unlike the situation of a husband and wife, funds in a pooled joint account cannot be attributed to only one person.

A letter from Bank Boston states that, since April 1997, "Ames Resources Limited maintains an International Private Banking Relationship" with BankBoston. The petitioner is the secretary of Ames Resources Limited, and the account has always had balances in the mid seven figures. These funds belong to Ames Resources Limited, a corporation, and do not belong to the petitioner, an individual. Furthermore, "Ames Resources Limited" is not the same thing as "Ames Management, Inc.," and at most, this letter indicates that the petitioner serves as an officer at a separate corporation in addition to his own corporation, and that this separate corporation has a bank account with BankBoston.

Source of funds.

The source of the funds lent to the petitioner (and in turn lent to Ames Management) has also not been adequately documented. The petitioner claims that the first $450,000 came from personal savings and the sale of "a house." The second $500,000 came from the sale of "our business." No documentation, such as a sales contract or deed establishing ownership and price, has been submitted regarding the house or the business. Such documentation is relevant to the question of whether the funds have been lawfully obtained, which is a requirement under 8 C.F.R. § 204.6(j)(3).[3] Simply going on record without supporting documentary evidence is not sufficient for purposes of meeting the burden of proof in these proceedings. *See Matter of Treasure Craft of California*, 14 I&N Dec. 190 (Reg. Comm. 1972).

In summary, the petitioner has failed to demonstrate that he has invested, or is actively in the process of investing, the requisite amount of capital obtained by lawful means. The amounts referenced by the petitioner either do not constitute qualifying "capital," because they are not his, or have not been properly "invested," because they are debt arrangements between the petitioner and his business. Even if the petitioner and Ames were to be considered one and the same entity, the loans obtained by Ames from other banks would not be considered qualifying capital because they are secured by assets of the business. The petitioner has also failed to document the source of his funds other than to say that the funds are a loan from his father.

THE PETITIONER HAS FAILED TO ESTABLISH A NEW COMMERCIAL ENTERPRISE.

8 C.F.R. § 204.6(h) states that the establishment of a new commercial enterprise may consist of:

(1) The creation of an original business;

(2) The purchase of an existing business and simultaneous or subsequent restructuring or reorganization such that a new commercial enterprise results; or

(3) The expansion of an existing business through the investment of the required amount, so that a substantial change in the net worth or number of employees results from the investment of capital. Substantial change means a 40 percent increase either in the net worth, or in the number of employees, so that the new net worth, or number of employees amounts to at least 140 percent of the pre-expansion net worth or number of employees. Establishment of a new commercial enterprise in this manner does not exempt the petitioner from the requirements of 8 C.F.R. § 204.6(j)(2) and (3) relating to the required amount of capital investment and the creation of full-time employment for ten qualifying employees. In the case of a capital investment in a troubled business, employment creation may meet the criteria set forth in 8 C.F.R. § 204.6(j)(4)(ii).

---

[3] A petitioner must also establish, pursuant to 8 C.F.R. § 204.6(e), that funds invested are his own. The petitioner has already conceded that the funds lent to Ames are not his; the funds belong to his father and must be repaid.

Interim Decision #3359

8 C.F.R. § 204.6(e) states that:

> *Troubled business* means a business that has been in existence for at least two years, has incurred a net loss for accounting purposes (determined on the basis of generally accepted accounting principles) during the twelve- or twenty-four month period prior to the priority date on the alien entrepreneur's Form I-526, and the loss for such period is at least equal to twenty percent of the troubled business's net worth prior to such loss. For purposes of determining whether or not the troubled business has been in existence for two years, successors in interest to the troubled business will be deemed to have been in existence for the same period of time as the business they succeeded.

Although Ames Management was incorporated in 1997, it is the job-creating business that must be examined in determining whether a new commercial enterprise has been created. The Howard Johnson's Motor Lodge purchased by Ames Management had been in operation for approximately 24 years and was an ongoing business at the time of purchase; Ames Management, doing business as Howard Johnson Hotel, has merely replaced the former owner.

The petitioner has provided no documentation whatsoever to establish that the Howard Johnson's was a "troubled business," as defined above, prior to his purchase. He also does not claim that he will expand the hotel by 40 percent as provided in 8 C.F.R. § 204.6(h)(3). The petitioner has not shown the degree of restructuring and reorganization required by 8 C.F.R. § 204.6(h)(2); the hotel has always been a Howard Johnson and is still a Howard Johnson today. A few cosmetic changes to the decor and a new marketing strategy for success do not constitute the kind of restructuring contemplated by the regulations, nor does a simple change in ownership. Therefore, it cannot be concluded that the petitioner has created a new commercial enterprise.

THE PETITIONER HAS NOT ESTABLISHED THE REQUISITE EMPLOYMENT CREATION.

8 C.F.R. § 204.6(j)(4) discusses job creation, and states:

> (i) *General.* To show that a new commercial enterprise will create not fewer than ten (10) full-time positions for qualifying employees, the petition must be accompanied by:

> (A) Documentation consisting of photocopies of relevant tax records, Form I-9, or other similar documents for ten (10) qualifying employees, if such employees have already been hired following the establishment of the new commercial enterprise; or

> (B) A copy of a comprehensive business plan showing that, due to the nature and projected size of the new commercial enterprise, the need for not fewer than ten (10) qualifying employees will result, including approximate dates, within the next two years, and when such employees will be hired.

Interim Decision #3359

> (ii) *Troubled business*. To show that a new commercial enterprise which has been established through a capital investment in a troubled business meets the statutory employment creation requirement, the petition must be accompanied by evidence that the number of existing employees is being or will be maintained at no less than the pre-investment level for a period of at least two years. Photocopies of tax records, Forms I-9, or other relevant documents for the qualifying employees and a comprehensive business plan shall be submitted in support of the petition.

8 C.F.R. § 204.6(e) states, in pertinent part:

> *Employee* means an individual who provides services or labor for the new commercial enterprise and who receives wages or other remuneration directly from the new commercial enterprise...This definition shall not include independent contractors.
>
> *Full-time employment* means employment of a qualifying employee by the new commercial enterprise in a position that requires a minimum of 35 working hours per week.

In a letter dated January 15, 1998, the petitioner states that Ames Management employs 23 full-time United State citizens or lawful permanent residents. It also employs part-time employees on an as-needed basis, as well as multiple subcontractors.

Section 5.1.19 of the Agreement for Sale and Purchase refers to an Exhibit H containing the payroll of the Howard Johnson's Motor Lodge as of the date of the petitioner's purchase. The petitioner has furnished copies of the neatly-labeled exhibits, but the only document between Exhibit G and Exhibit I is an unlabeled, one-page worksheet. This worksheet, for the 1997 quarter to date, merely provides the amount of taxes withheld, wages paid, etc. It does not name any of the employees or specify the positions held or hours worked, although it does mention the number of employees as 29.

To show the current level of employment at the hotel, the petitioner has supplied the payroll journal for the period ending November 28, 1997. Assuming that this journal reflects one week of work and not two, only 16 individuals clearly worked at least the minimum 35 hours to be considered full-time employees.[4] Another three were paid salaries and not by the hour, while the last three worked fewer than 35 hours and must be considered part-time employees. The petitioner has submitted a Form I-9 for one other person who was hired after the date of the payroll journal. At most, the hotel employs 20 full-time workers. The petitioner has not established that this figure constitutes either the maintenance of the previous level of full-time

---

[4] If the payroll journal reflects *two* weeks of work instead of one, then only two individuals worked at least the minimum 70 hours to be considered full-time employees.

Interim Decision #3359

employment or the addition of 10 new, full-time positions. As noted above, the hotel previously had 29 employees of unknown designation.

If a petitioner has not already created the requisite number of positions, he must submit a comprehensive business plan clearly demonstrating that the business will need the applicable level of employment. 8 C.F.R. § 204.6(j)(4)(i)(B), The plan must contain a timetable for hiring and must be credible. The petitioner has provided a Marketing Plan 1998 for the hotel. The plan discusses, in detail, the petitioner's marketing strategies and employee-incentive programs, among other things. It does not address the issue of hiring, however. While the plan states that a new position will be created in sales, the person named to occupy this position, Janet Mills, has been working at the hotel since 1994.

CONCLUSION.

In conclusion, the petitioner is ineligible for classification as an alien entrepreneur because he has failed to show that he has invested, or is actively in the process of investing, the requisite amount of money. In every transaction, he has attempted to distance himself from making an actual investment in Ames Management by instead becoming Ames Management's creditor. The petitioner has not shown that Ames Management has been established with anything but loans; in essence, the petitioner has attempted to create something from nothing. The petitioner has further failed to demonstrate that he has established a "new" commercial enterprise, and he has failed to show that his business has or will engage in either employment maintenance or employment creation.

The burden of proof in these proceedings rests solely with the petitioner. Section 291 of the Act, 8 U.S.C. § 1361. The petitioner has not met that burden. Accordingly, the petition is denied.

ORDER: The decision of the director is reversed. The petition is denied.

APPENDIX A-2: *MATTER OF IZUMMI*

Interim Decision #3360

In re IZUMMI, Petitioner

In Visa Petition Proceedings

A76 426 873

Decided by the Associate Commissioner, Examinations, July 13, 1998.

(1) Regardless of its location, a new commercial enterprise that is engaged directly or indirectly in lending money to job-creating businesses may only lend money to businesses located within targeted areas in order for a petitioner to be eligible for the reduced minimum capital requirement.

(2) Under the Immigrant Investor Pilot Program, if a new commercial enterprise is engaged directly or indirectly in lending money to job-creating businesses, such job-creating businesses must all be located within the geographic limits of the regional center. The location of the new commercial enterprise is not controlling.

(3) A petitioner may not make material changes to his petition in an effort to make a deficient petition conform to Service requirements.

(4) If the new commercial enterprise is a holding company, the full requisite amount of capital must be made available to the business(es) most closely responsible for creating the employment on which the petition is based.

(5) An alien may not receive guaranteed payments from a new commercial enterprise while he owes money to the new commercial enterprise.

(6) An alien may not enter into a redemption agreement with the new commercial enterprise at any time prior to completing all of his cash payments under a promissory note. In no event may the alien enter into a redemption agreement prior to the end of the two-year period of conditional residence.

(7) A redemption agreement between an alien investor and the new commercial enterprise constitutes a debt arrangement and is prohibited under 8 C.F.R. § 204.6(e).

(8) Reserve funds that are not made available for purposes of job creation cannot be considered capital placed at risk for the purpose of generating a return on the capital being placed at risk.

(9) The Service does not pre-adjudicate immigrant-investor petitions; each petition must be adjudicated on its own merits.

(10) Under 8 C.F.R. § 204.6(e), all capital must be valued at fair market value in United States dollars, including promissory notes used as capital. In determining the fair market value of a

169

Interim Decision #3360

promissory note, it is necessary to consider, among other things, present value.

(11) Under certain circumstances, a promissory note that does not itself constitute capital may constitute evidence that the alien is "in the process of investing" other capital, such as cash. In such a case, the petitioner must substantially complete payments on the promissory note prior to the end of the two-year conditional period.

(12) Whether the promissory note constitutes capital or is simply evidence that the alien is in the process of investing other capital, nearly all of the money due under the promissory note must be payable within two years, without provisions for extensions.

(13) In order for a petitioner to be considered to have established an original business, he must have had a hand in its actual creation.

ON BEHALF OF PETITIONER: MAURICE INMAN/FREDRICK W. VOIGTMANN
1925 CENTURY PARK EAST, 16TH FLOOR
LOS ANGELES, CA 90067

DISCUSSION

The preference visa petition was denied by the Director, Texas Service Center, who certified the decision to the Associate Commissioner for Examinations for review. The decision of the director will be affirmed.

The petitioner seeks classification as an alien entrepreneur pursuant to section 203(b)(5) of the Immigration and Nationality Act, 8 U.S.C. § 1153(b)(5), and section 610 of the Appropriations Act of 1993. The director determined that the petitioner had failed to establish that he had placed the requisite capital at risk. The director made the following findings: $30,000 of the claimed contribution would be used for the expenses of the Partnership rather than being infused into the subsidiary commercial enterprise for the purpose of employment creation; the majority of the remaining capital would not be available for job creation because the Partnership was required to maintain it in reserves; part of the petitioner's capital contribution was not an investment because it was made in exchange for a debt arrangement; and another part of the petitioner's contribution would derive from guaranteed annual interest payments received from the Partnership.

In response, the petitioner submits two separate briefs, two supplemental briefs, and numerous exhibits. He contends that the director's decision misstates existing facts and mischaracterizes the provisions of the American Export Limited Partnership ("AELP") investor program. The petitioner also complains that the director's decision fails to mention, distinguish, or "explain away" approvals of other AELP petitions by both the Texas Service Center and Vermont Service Center; furthermore, the director's decision fails to mention, distinguish, or "explain away" prior Service opin-

Interim Decision #3360

ions and communications that directly supported and authorized the use of various features of the AELP program. The petitioner states that, even if the director had been correct in denying the petition, certain new amendments to the partnership plan should cause the Administrative Appeals Unit (AAU) to approve his petition.

Oral argument was granted in this case, and during his presentation counsel reiterated the points made in the brief. Counsel emphasized that the petitioner had made an investment by executing and delivering the promissory note for $500,000; the schedule of future payments under the note was irrelevant.

Section 203(b)(5)(A) of the Act provides classification to qualified immigrants seeking to enter the United States for the purpose of engaging in a new commercial enterprise:

> (i) which the alien has established,
>
> (ii) in which such alien has invested (after the date of the enactment of the Immigration Act of 1990) or, is actively in the process of investing, capital in an amount not less than the amount specified in subparagraph (C), and
>
> (iii) which will benefit the United States economy and create full-time employment for not fewer than 10 United States citizens or aliens lawfully admitted for permanent residence or other immigrants lawfully authorized to be employed in the United States (other than the immigrant and the immigrant's spouse, sons, or daughters).

The petitioner indicates that the petition is based on an investment in a new business in a targeted employment area for which the required amount of capital invested has been adjusted downward. In addition, the business is located in an area designated as a "regional center" authorized to participate in the Immigrant Investor Pilot Program.

THE PETITIONER HAS NOT DEMONSTRATED THAT AELP IS ENGAGING IN APPROVED REGIONAL-CENTER ACTIVITIES IN TARGETED EMPLOYMENT AREAS

8 C.F.R. § 204.6(e) states, in pertinent part, that:

> *Targeted employment area* means an area which, at the time of investment, is a rural area or an area which has experienced unemployment of at least 150 percent of the national average rate.

8 C.F.R. § 204.6(j)(6) states that:

> If applicable, to show that the new commercial enterprise has created or will create employment in a targeted employment area, the petition must be accompanied by:

Interim Decision #3360

> (i) In the case of a rural area, evidence that the new commercial enterprise is principally doing business within a civil jurisdiction not located within any standard metropolitan statistical area as designated by the Office of Management and Budget, or within any city or town having a population of 20,000 or more as based on the most recent decennial census of the United States; or
>
> (ii) In the case of a high unemployment area:
>
> (A) Evidence that the metropolitan statistical area, the specific county within a metropolitan statistical area, or the county in which a city or town with a population of 20,000 or more is located, in which the new commercial enterprise is principally doing business has experienced an average unemployment rate of 150 percent of the national average rate; or
>
> (B) A letter from an authorized body of the government of the state in which the new commercial enterprise is located which certifies that the geographic or political subdivision of the metropolitan statistical area or of the city or town with a population of 20,000 or more in which the enterprise is principally doing business has been designated a high unemployment area. The letter must meet the requirements of 8 C.F.R. § 204.6(i).

On October 19, 1995, American Export Partners, LLC ("AEP") filed its articles of organization with the State of South Carolina. On March 25, 1996, AELP filed its certificate of limited partnership with the State of South Carolina, and AEP was designated as AELP's general partner. Both AEP and AELP are located in Charleston, South Carolina.

In a letter dated February 8, 1995, the Assistant Commissioner for Adjudications designated AEP a regional center and specified that individuals could file petitions with the Service "for new commercial enterprises located within the eight-county coastal areas, or Lowcountry, of South Carolina." On June 14, 1995, the Acting Assistant Commissioner for Adjudications expanded the geographical area covered by the AEP regional center to include 22 other counties in South Carolina.

The petitioner has presented evidence that many, but not all, of the counties within this regional center were considered rural in 1995 and qualified at that time as targeted employment areas.[1]

In his brief, the petitioner explains that AELP has established a commercial credit corporation subsidiary, American Commercial and Export Credit Company, Inc., with its co-venturer, Resurgens Capital & Investment. This credit company makes asset-based loans and engages in receivables financing for small export companies "located throughout South Carolina and the southeastern United States." The capital provided by the alien investors to AELP is used to purchase stock in the credit com-

---

[1] Of the 22 new counties added to the regional-center area, Aiken, Edgefield, Lexington, Richland, and Sumter counties were not targeted employment areas in 1995.

Interim Decision #3359

of Florida on June 27, 1997. All 1000 authorized shares were issued to the petitioner in July 1997. On October 31, 1997, Ames Management purchased a Howard Johnson's Motor Lodge for the sale price of $2.4 million, paid as follows: $25,000 in earnest money, consisting of a $10,000 initial deposit and a subsequent $15,000 deposit; $705,298.79 brought to settlement; and $1.7 million borrowed from 1st United Bank.

In a document entitled Sources of Investment Funds, the petitioner stated that the money used to purchase the hotel came from two sources. Approximately $450,000 were transferred to Barnett Bank from Argentina over the period 1994 to 1997; these funds "originated from personal savings and a sale of a house." An additional $500,000 were transferred from Argentina in December of 1996; these funds originated from the sale of "our business." The petitioner explained that, for both sources, "[t]hese monies were loaned to me by my father and I loaned them back to my company Ames Management, Inc. It has not been stipulated when I should return the funds."[1]

The balance sheet for the petitioner's hotel, dated November 30, 1997, confirms that the business's liabilities include long-term loans, totaling $922,136.09, payable to the shareholder (the petitioner), *See also* the Continuing and Unconditional Subordination of Debt discussed below. The accompanying "Transactions by Account" breaks down the amount, date, and destination of each loan. It is clear from this document that the $25,000 in earnest money and the $705,298.79 brought to the settlement table are mere loans from the petitioner to Ames Management. As specified in the definition of "invest" set forth in 8 C.F.R. § 204.6(e), debt arrangements between a petitioner and his business do not constitute qualifying contributions of capital. Therefore, the $730,298.79 paid toward the purchase of the hotel cannot be considered to be an "investment" by the petitioner.

Ames Management financed the balance of the purchase price, or $1.7 million, through 1st United Bank. According to the Mortgage and Security Agreement, the loan is secured by the hotel and all of its contents, including inventory, accounts, leases, the franchise agreement, furniture, patio umbrellas, landscaping, etc. First, it should be noted that a loan obtained by a corporation is not the same as a loan obtained by an individual, and it cannot be said that this loan through 1st United Bank is an investment of the *petitioner's* personal capital. Second, even if it were assumed, arguendo, that the petitioner and Ames Management were the same legal entity for purposes of this proceeding, indebtedness that is secured by assets of the enterprise is specifically precluded from the definition of "capital." *See* 8 C.F.R. § 204.6(e).

---

[1] The petitioner has not disclosed the terms of the loan from his father, and it is not known if, for example, it is secured by assets of Ames Management.

Interim Decision #3360

Also, the regional-center designation in this case was granted for most of the counties in South Carolina. It did not extend to Georgia or Florida. While AELP is located in South Carolina, neither the credit company extending the actual loans nor the companies receiving the loans are located within the regional center. Therefore, the petitioner must establish direct employment creation.

The petitioner states in his brief that the Service had expressly permitted the use of the subsidiary credit corporation as a vehicle for making loans to export-related businesses not related to the regional center. He refers to a letter dated September 27, 1995, from the Chief of the Immigrant Branch, Adjudications, who was asked whether the customers of an export credit corporation needed to be located within the region covered by the regional-center designation. The Chief's response did not directly address this question; instead, he stated, "Although the regional center should focus on a geographical area, there is no requirement in either the statute or the regulations that the exports generated under the Pilot Program be **produced or manufactured** within the area designated by the regional center," (emphasis added).[4] The petitioner concludes that the credit company may extend loans to any export-related company located anywhere.

Such an interpretation renders the geographical limitation of a regional center meaningless. The definition of "regional center" in 8 C.F.R. § 204.6(e) requires that the economic unit be involved in "improved regional productivity." 8 C.F.R. § 204.6(m)(3)(i) states that, in order to gain approval as a regional center, an entity must describe clearly how it will promote economic growth through "improved regional productivity." If neither the credit company nor the export-related businesses are located in the regional center, it is difficult to see how the productivity within the regional center is being improved.[5]

As the subsidiary credit corporation's actual and proposed loan activities benefit companies outside the geographical area covered by the regional-center designation granted in this case, the petitioner must estab-

---

[4] Not all export-related businesses produce or manufacture their own goods. For example, if a bank located within the regional center were to lend money to a company that exported chicken parts to Russia, the chickens would not have to have been raised within the specific geographical area; the export company would have to be located within the area, however. Similarly, the bank could permissibly lend money to a company located in the geographical area that exported cosmetics, jeans, and American rice to Japan; these products would likely not have been produced or manufactured within the area. It is not sufficient for just the bank, or the bank's primary shareholder, to be located in the regional center

[5] Even if the credit company here were located within the regional center rather than in Atlanta, the arrangement would still not qualify. The only improved regional productivity would concern the salaries of a few loan officers; this is not what was intended by the regional-center provisions.

174

Interim Decision #3360

lish direct employment creation; he cannot rely on indirect employment creation. For the sake of argument, however, the AAU will analyze the investment portion of this case using his claim of indirect employment creation.

CERTAIN REVISIONS TO THE PARTNERSHIP AGREEMENT CANNOT BE ACCEPTED

Subsequent to the issuance of the director's decision, counsel has submitted numerous revisions to AELP's limited partnership agreement. He explains that the revisions are in the form of Stage I and Stage II amendments.

The original partnership agreement had been prepared and executed in March of 1996, prior to the creation of an initial payment option of $120,000. When the $120,000 option was added to AELP's program in the fall of 1996, AELP neglected to amend the partnership agreement. As a result, many provisions within the documents signed by this petitioner contradict provisions within the official partnership agreement. The Stage I amendments are intended to correct these inconsistencies.

In addition, after the attorneys for AELP obtained a copy of a memorandum issued in December of 1997 by the Service's Office of General Counsel ("OGC"), "the Limited Partnership Agreement of AELP was further amended to restructure, amend or eliminate some or all of [the] 'objected-to' provisions." These Stage II amendments, counsel continues, should render the instant petition approvable.

A petitioner must establish eligibility at the time of filing; a petition cannot be approved at a future date after the petitioner becomes eligible under a new set of facts. *See Matter of Katigbak*, 14 I&N Dec. 45, 49 (Comm. 1971), Therefore, a petitioner may not make material changes to a petition that has already been filed in an effort to make an apparently deficient petition conform to Service requirements.

Counsel states that petitions have previously been amended to reflect program changes and to cure defects in the original documents. He refers to a 1995 case in which the center director had correctly found that the business at issue did not constitute a troubled business. At oral argument in that case, counsel presented a completely different business plan that abandoned the troubled-business claim and substituted a plan to create a new business instead. This new business plan formed the basis of an approval. The case referenced by counsel, however, resulted in an unpublished decision that did not have any precedential value, procedural or otherwise. Furthermore, the AAU acknowledges that acceptance of the new business plan at such a late date was improper and erroneous.

In the case at hand, the AAU will recognize the Stage I amendments to the extent that they cause the partnership agreement to conform to the other

Interim Decision #3360

agreements that this petitioner had originally executed and submitted with his Form I-526. The AAU will make no determination as to the adequacy or inadequacy of the Stage II amendments, as they are irrelevant in this proceeding; the Service cannot consider facts that come into being only subsequent to the filing of a petition. *See Matter of Bardouille*, 18 I&N Dec. 114 (BIA 1981). If counsel had wished to test the validity of the newest plan, which is materially different from the original plan, he should have withdrawn the instant petition and advised the petitioner to file a new Form I-526. The case shall be analyzed only on the basis of the original documents and the revisions that correct the original inconsistencies.

THE PETITIONER HAS NOT MADE A QUALIFYING "INVESTMENT"

8 C.F.R. § 204.6(e) states, in pertinent part, that

> *Capital* means cash, equipment, inventory, other tangible property, cash equivalents, and indebtedness secured by assets owned by the alien entrepreneur, provided the alien entrepreneur is personally and primarily liable and that the assets of the new commercial enterprise upon which the petition is based are not used to secure any of the indebtedness. All capital shall be valued at fair market value in United States dollars, ...

> *Commercial enterprise* means any for-profit activity formed for the ongoing conduct of lawful business including, but not limited to, a sole proprietorship, partnership (whether limited or general), holding company, joint venture, corporation, business trust, or other entity which may be publicly or privately owned. This definition includes a commercial enterprise consisting of a holding company and its wholly-owned subsidiaries, provided that each such subsidiary is engaged in a for-profit activity formed for the ongoing conduct of a lawful business. This definition shall not include a non-commercial activity such as owning and operating a personal residence.

> *Invest* means to contribute capital. A contribution of capital in exchange for a note, bond, convertible debt, obligation, or any other debt arrangement between the alien entrepreneur and the new commercial enterprise does not constitute a contribution of capital for the purposes of this part.

8 C.F.R. § 204.6(j) states, in pertinent part, that:

> (2) To show that the petitioner has invested or is actively in the process of investing the required amount of capital, the petition must be accompanied by evidence that the petitioner has placed the required amount of capital at risk for the purpose of generating a return on the capital placed at risk. Evidence of mere intent to invest, or of prospective investment arrangements entailing no present commitment, will not suffice to show that the petitioner is actively in the process of investing. The alien must show actual commitment of the required amount of capital. Such evidence may include, but need not be limited to:
>
> (i) Bank statement(s) showing amount(s) deposited in United States business

Interim Decision #3360

account(s) for the enterprise;

(ii) Evidence of assets which have been purchased for use in the United States enterprise, including invoices; sales receipts; and purchase contracts containing sufficient information to identify such assets, their purchase costs, date of purchase, and purchasing entity;

(iii) Evidence of property transferred from abroad for use in the United States enterprise, including United States Customs Service commercial entry documents, bills of lading and transit insurance policies containing ownership information and sufficient information to identify the property and to indicate the fair market value of such property;

(iv) Evidence of monies transferred or committed to be transferred to the new commercial enterprise in exchange for shares of stock (voting or nonvoting, common or preferred), Such stock may not include terms requiring the new commercial enterprise to redeem it at the holder's request; or

(v) Evidence of any loan or mortgage agreement, promissory note, security agreement, or other evidence of borrowing which is secured by assets of the petitioner, other than those of the new commercial enterprise, and for which the petitioner is personally and primarily liable.

Counsel states that the petitioner has made an investment of $500,000 in the form of a $500,000 promissory note. This note provides for an initial deposit of $120,000 into an escrow account, to be released to the partnership upon approval of the immigrant visa, five annual payments of $18,000, and a final balloon payment of $290,000.

Initial Partnership expenses

On October 14, 1997, Wells Fargo Bank notified the petitioner that his funds in the amount of $120,000 had been received and deposited into a custody account for the Partnership. According to section 2.A(3) of the investment agreement, the petitioner agreed to instruct counsel, as trustee of his escrow account, "immediately to release US$30,000 as a refundable advance for initial expenses of the Partnership"; the remaining $90,000 would be released upon approval of the visa application. As pointed out by the director on page 4 of his decision, the use of the $30,000 for Partnership costs and expenses meant that the full $500,000 would not be "infused into the commercial enterprise for the purpose of employment creation."

In response, the petitioner states that it is possible that the director objected to the expenses being released from the escrow account and that the director might not have objected if the expenses had been paid after the funds were released from escrow. Regardless of the timing of the payment, the ultimate payee is the Partnership, the petitioner maintains. The timing

177

Interim Decision #3360

of the payment, however, was not the director's objection. The director cited 8 C.F.R. § 204.6(j)(2) in stating that the required amount of capital must be placed at risk "for the purpose of generating a return on the capital placed at risk." As the payment of initial Partnership expenses and costs was not the type of profit-generating activity contemplated by the regulations, no more than $470,000 could be considered to have been "invested."

The petitioner argues that fees and expenses incurred in the process of raising capital are customary and reasonable. For example, when businesses go to banks for money, the banks charge processing fees, points, appraisal fees, and other expenses that are included in the debt. The petitioner continues:

> It is absurd to suggest that there is no cost to creating an immigrant investor program (attorneys fees, accountant fees, and administrative fees), there is no cost to raising money in the market place (finders fees, immigration consultant fees, forwarding fees, and so forth); and that there are no ongoing administrative and operating expenses during the initial start up phase of the business (rent, utilities, telephones, fax machines, office furniture, personnel costs, executive salaries, etc.), We live in a world of reality, not "make believe."

The petitioner refers to AELP's subsidiary credit company having retained an expert in asset-based loans for an annual salary "in excess of $200,000." What is important, the petitioner emphasizes, is that the money spent by AELP on initial expenses is in furtherance of the Partnership business.[6]

While points and processing fees are often financed, they are considered an amount over and above the original loan amount. To illustrate, when a person intends to obtain a mortgage for $200,000, he can choose to pay the points and fees separately or he can choose to finance them. If he chooses to finance the fees, the principal on his mortgage is no longer just $200,000 but something more. In the investor context, the Service is not prohibiting the payment of Partnership expenses; rather, the Service is finding that if AELP wishes to have the limited partners pay these expenses, these expenses must be paid in addition to the $500,000.

The petitioner explains that AELP deducts its operating expenses of $30,000, and the remaining funds go to the subsidiary credit corporation. The credit corporation then deducts its own expenses and the leftover money is contributed to a lending fund from which the loans to export companies are made. The petitioner contends that the new commercial enter-

---

[6]Nevertheless, counsel appears to be prepared to abandon these numerous arguments. In his brief on behalf of the petitioner, counsel states that if the AAU finds that providing for the payment of initial expenses from and out of capital contributed by the investor is improper, then AELP will immediately amend its partnership agreement to eliminate the provision from its program.

prise here is the Partnership, AELP, and an investment of $500,000 in AELP constitutes an investment of $500,000 in the new commercial enterprise, "It was never AELP's intent...that 100% of the funds contributed by the foreign national investors would flow through the partnership and into the credit corporation for lending to U.S. export businesses." After AELP and the credit corporation deduct tens of thousands of dollars for their "expenses," however, it is not clear how much of the original money is made available for loans.

It could perhaps be argued that, when the owner of a corporation pays a million dollars for shares in his business and earmarks the money for equipment, inventory, and working capital, some of the working capital will in fact be spent on initial salaries and expenses. In the partnership scenario, the new commercial enterprise is the partnership, and it too will need to spend money on initial salaries and expenses. The Service distinguishes these two situations in that, in the former example, the employment-creating entity is spending the money. In the latter example, the employment-creating entity never receives the money spent on the partnership's expenses. Especially where indirect employment creation is being claimed, and the nexus between the money and the jobs is already tenuous, the Service has an interest in examining, to a degree, the manner in which funds are being applied. **The full amount of money must be made available to the business(es) most closely responsible for creating the employment upon which the petition is based.**[7] The Service does not wish to encourage the creation of layer upon layer of "holding companies" or "parent companies," with each business taking its cut and the ultimate employer seeing very little of the aliens' money.

In his brief on behalf of the petitioner, counsel claims that the deduction of AELP's and the credit company's expenses had previously been disclosed to, and approved by, the Service when the Service approved the general partner's designation as a regional center. The focus of an inquiry into the designation of a regional center, however, has to do with whether proposed activities will improve regional productivity through increased exports; it has nothing to do with the propriety of various business expenses and how they are funded. Counsel also claims that the same facts were disclosed within the past few months, both in writing and during a conference attended by AELP representatives and Service attorneys. Disclosure, though, does not mandate approval.

---

[7] Whether or not $500,000 must be made available for the loans to export companies or whether $500,000 must merely be made available to the credit corporation extending the loans, it is clear that making $500,000 available to **AELP** is not sufficient. AELP's primary purpose is apparently to locate potential alien investors. AELP does not extend the loans to the export companies and is not the entity most closely engaged in employment creation, indirect or otherwise.

Interim Decision #3360

In his brief on behalf of the petitioner, counsel cites a 1995 case in which the Vermont Service Center had questioned whether $80,000 or $90,000 set aside for fees could be considered an investment of capital. On May 25, 1995, the Administrative Appeals Unit approved the case. Counsel further states, "During oral argument an AAU official stated that it was proper to deduct such fees from the amount of the capital contributed by the investor without thereby reducing the investor's contribution of capital."

The decision rendered by the AAU in that case did not specifically address the issue of fees. In addition, the decision in that case was unpublished and has no precedential value.

Annual payments

According to section 2B of the investment agreement executed by the petitioner, the petitioner must make five annual cash payments of $18,000 each, totalling $90,000, commencing one year from the date he is admitted to the Partnership.

Section 3 of the investment agreement, however, states, "I shall receive a return on the cash I have contributed to the Partnership in the amount of 12% per annum, payable annually, commencing one year from the date I am admitted to the Partnership as a Limited Partner and ending five years thereafter."[8] The petitioner would also receive a share of any profits exceeding this 12-percent return. The partnership agreement explains that the percentage return is computed on the basis of the total cash contributed at the time the distribution is made. In other words, the petitioner's first annual distribution would be at least $14,400 (12 percent of $120,000, plus any additional profits), his second annual distribution at least $16,560 (12 percent of $138,000), his third at least $18,720, his fourth at least $20,880, and his fifth at least $23,040.

In effect, the $90,000 that the petitioner's annual payment obligation represents would require very little in new, personal funds. To make his first annual payment of $18,000, the petitioner would have to contribute no more than $3,600 of his own funds to the $14,400 (or more) he would receive from the Partnership. To make his second payment, the petitioner would have to contribute no more than $1,440 of his own funds to the $16,560 he would receive from the Partnership. The petitioner's third, fourth, and fifth payments, however, would be entirely covered by his guaranteed distributions from the Partnership; in fact, the petitioner would be at least $8,640 ahead for these last three years.

---

[8]The original partnership agreement, however, provides that this return is 10 percent per year, payable for **four** years. Counsel does not submit a Stage I amendment for this inconsistency.

Interim Decision #3360

The petitioner's obligation to make his annual payments is conditioned upon the Partnership making the guaranteed annual distributions to the petitioner.[9] As such, these annual payments do not constitute a contribution of capital.[10]

The petitioner refers to the OGC memorandum of December 19, 1997, which had criticized the use of profits generated by a business to meet obligations under a promissory note. The petitioner contends that he is entitled to use his guaranteed return for whatever purpose he desires, and it would be absurd to segregate dividends or profits in a special account to guarantee that they would not be used to make payments on the note.

The AAU does not at this time reach the issue of whether it is ever appropriate for a business to distribute profits to an alien who still owes money to the business. The problem addressed here is that the annual returns are **guaranteed**. The fact that title to that money changes hands does not change the essence of the transaction; as the director pointed out in his decision, the Partnership receives no infusion of new funds from the petitioner.

Another problem with guaranteed annual distributions is the source of the distributions. As the petitioner concedes on page 70 of his brief, "[i]t is unlikely that the business will be immediately profitable from the lending activities contemplated by AELP and its credit corporation subsidiary." Since there is never a guarantee that the Partnership will generate sufficient profits during any given year to pay each investor his 12-percent guaranteed distribution, the possibility exists that the distributions may be drawn from the contributions of future limited partners (thereby necessitating the acquisition of more and more limited partners) or from the contributions already made (thereby depleting the initial contributions).

At pages 70 and 71 of his brief on behalf of the petitioner, counsel counters, "The payment of this guaranteed return is an obligation of the partnership which may or may not be met. If the partnership does not have the ability to make such annual payments, they will not be made." As mentioned earlier, this is directly contradicted by section 2.C of the investment agreement, which provides that the failure of the Partnership to make the

---

[9]Section 2.C of the investment agreement states, "In the event of the bankruptcy, the insolvency, or the failure of the partnership to pay the annual return on capital, to pay the sell option price, or to pay any judgment, the Partnership shall be deemed to be in breach of its obligations to the Limited Partners under the American Export Limited Partnership Agreement, and I, as a Limited Partner, shall have no further obligations to the Partnership, and furthermore, I shall not be obligated to make any further cash payments under the Limited Partnership Agreement, this Investment Agreement or the Promissory Note."

[10]At most, one could argue that the petitioner must make an initial outlay of $5,040 for the first two payments; but because this amount would be more than offset by the last three guaranteed distributions from the Partnership, this initial outlay is, in effect, a loan. 8 C.F.R. § 204.6(e) specifies that contributions of money in exchange for debt arrangements do not qualify as "investments."

181

Interim Decision #3360

annual distributions is considered a breach of the Partnership's obligations and will cause the petitioner not to have to make any further cash payments.

The petitioner states that Service administrative case law exists supporting a petitioner's application of guaranteed annual returns paid by a partnership toward meeting the petitioner's obligation to make annual payments to the partnership. The petitioner cites an unpublished AAU decision from 1995 involving the "C&W Hotel Management program." While the center director's decision in that case had referred to a provision in the business plan stating that four annual payments might come from the profits of the business, the center director did not note whether these so-called "profits" were in the form of *guaranteed* returns (which would then have no direct connection to profit, as discussed above), and he did not make any finding as to the propriety of this provision. Review of the AAU decision reveals no reference whatsoever to annual returns or annual payments. Therefore, it cannot be said that the AAU has specifically sanctioned the use of guaranteed annual returns toward meeting obligations to make annual payments. More significantly, the AAU decision in question was unpublished and has no binding precedential authority.[11]

The petitioner points to an internal Service memorandum issued on October 20, 1997, by the Office of Adjudications. This memorandum stated that in some cases, guaranteed interest payments were made through outside loans or from capital contributed by other investors; as not all businesses could be profitable immediately, a contractual provision for guaranteed payments may, in certain cases, be consistent with a genuine investment.[12] This memorandum was a general statement of policy and did not analyze any particular fact patterns. Indeed, the statements in the memorandum were qualified with the words "may" and "in certain cases." Given the confusing statements contained in the memorandum, and the lack of guidelines provided, this memorandum provides no assistance in resolving the present case.

In short, because the petitioner is guaranteed annual distributions from the Partnership of at least 12-percent for five years, which would yield him $93,600, the petitioner's five annual payments totalling $90,000 under the promissory note cannot be considered a qualifying contribution of capital.[13]

---

[11] The AAU recognizes that the Service has approved plans that may have contained guaranteed annual returns. If so, such approvals were in error for the reasons stated in this decision.

[12] This recent memorandum was superseded by a subsequent memorandum dated March 11, 1998, however.

[13] In apparent recognition of the fact that the petitioner is not contributing capital through the five annual payments, the investment agreement provides, at section 6, that if the conditions of the petitioner's permanent resident status are not removed, the Partnership will refund the petitioner $120,000. Presumably, by the time the petitioner applied for removal of his conditions, he would have made at least one of the annual payments and contributed $138,000.

Interim Decision #3360

The petitioner has effectively shifted the risk of loss of the $90,000 from himself to the Partnership.

Redemption agreement

Section 4 of the investment agreement provides, "after the sixth anniversary of my admission to the Partnership, I, as a limited partner, may exercise a sell option under which I have the **right to require** the Partnership to purchase from me my limited partnership interest," (emphasis added).[14] The sell-option price is equal to the petitioner's total contributed capital, less the first six payments, plus a pro rata share of profits. In other words, the sell-option price is $290,000 plus profits. Or, to look at it from the petitioner's perspective, the price of permanent resident status is $116,400 minus profits; as discussed above, the five annual payments are more than fully covered by the annual distributions and do not require any expenditure on the part of the petitioner. At the same time, the Partnership may exercise a buy option for the same price.[15]

Section 4 of the investment agreement specifies that the sell-option price is "payable as soon as the sell option is exercised." Section 8.05C of the original partnership agreement, however, states that the price is payable 180 days after the exercise of the sell option. The revised partnership agreement, instead of conforming to the investment agreement, reiterates the 180-day deadline. While the Stage I amendments were intended to reflect the actual intent of the parties, the petitioner has not executed a new investment agreement or otherwise indicated that he agrees with the new partnership agreement and is willing to wait 180 days.

It is not clear whether the petitioner is obligated actually to make the last payment of $290,000 if he exercises his sell option; both his responsibility to pay and his right to sell ripen at the same time. Section 8.05C of the partnership agreement provides that once the Partnership pays the sell-option price, "all amounts owed under such Selling Limited Partner's Investor Note shall be deemed satisfied by the Partnership..." Similarly, under section 8.06C, after the Partnership pays the buy-option price, "all

---

[14]The original partnership agreement states that the sell option is exercisable after five years; the revised agreement, pursuant to a Stage I amendment, states that the sell option is exercisable after six years in the case of a limited partner who makes an initial cash payment of $120,000.

[15]Section 8.06 of the original partnership agreement states that this "buy option" is exercisable after **three** years. Pursuant to Stage II amendments, the partnership agreement now states that the buy option is exercisable one year after the petitioner completes his payments under the note, or **seven** years. The revised partnership agreement also mentions sell-option prices of "$410,000? $290,000?" [sic],

Interim Decision #3360

amounts due and owing under the Investor Note shall be discharged by the Partnership..." It is not known what amount would still be owed if the petitioner is obligated to pay the $290,000 prior to the exercise of the buy or sell option. If the petitioner can avoid making this last payment by exercising his sell option, this amount of $290,000 cannot be considered to have been placed at risk.

Even if the petitioner is obligated to make this balloon payment prior to exercising his sell option, the $290,000 still cannot be said to be at risk because it is guaranteed to be returned, regardless of the success or failure of the business. If the investment agreement executed by the petitioner is controlling, then the moment he made this last payment, the petitioner could exercise his sell option, and the money would be immediately returned; the amount of $290,000 would never be at risk. If the partnership agreement is controlling, then the petitioner's agreement to make this payment of $290,000 is, in essence, a debt arrangement in which he provides funds in exchange for an unconditional, contractual promise that it will be repaid later at a fixed maturity date (six months later). Such an arrangement is specifically prohibited by the regulations. *See* 8 C.F.R. § 204.6(e).

In its opinion dated December 19, 1997, OGC engaged in a lengthy discussion of the factors evidencing debt and equity in the context of tax law; the opinion cited various tax cases and concluded that the debt characteristics of a plan such as AELP's outweighed any equity characteristics. The AAU finds such a discussion unnecessary and not particularly helpful with respect to this matter. The considerations at issue here are not the same as those of a court attempting to ascertain whether a business is attempting to evade taxes. Furthermore, the businesses examined in those tax cases were standard businesses not created for the purpose of enabling aliens to obtain immigration benefits. As counsel conceded at oral argument, potential alien investors are

> not going to make this investment, under *any* circumstances, unless they get a green card. If anybody ever suggests that this is a wonderful investment and they're going to make it without getting lawful permanent residence, they're lying and they're crazy; they're brain-damaged, all right? Nobody is gonna do this without getting a green card. That was the intent of the law. That's the carrot; that's the quid pro quo.

In other words, AELP has created a program to which most people would be unwilling to subscribe.[16] A discussion of the numerous debt and equity factors set forth in the tax cases unnecessarily complicates the

---

[16]This, by itself, raises the question of whether the AELP plan is a genuine investment. If normal investors would be unwilling to participate in this program because the chance for a net monetary gain does not exist, then it is logical to conclude that the hoped-for "profit" inherent in this program is the green card itself.

Interim Decision #3360

attempt to ascertain the true substance of the transaction. Very simply, the payment of the $290,000 constitutes a straight loan; the petitioner would be making this money available to AELP with the contractual expectation that it would be returned to him six months later. The risk that the petitioner might not receive payment if the Partnership fails is no different from the risk any business creditor incurs.

Counsel states on page 30 of his brief on behalf of the petitioner, "The payment of the sell-option price was dependent upon the Partnership's ability and willingness to pay. Thus, substantial risk existed in that the Partnership might be unable or unwilling to pay the investor." At oral argument, counsel claimed that the redemption provisions were entirely unenforceable; no partner could bring a lawsuit to enforce them. Aside from the question of why not, counsel's statements raise questions of good faith. For AELP to entice aliens to invest in AELP by promising them redemption rights, but then for counsel (who is counsel for both AELP and the petitioner) to suggest in his brief that AELP might not be "willing" to honor the redemption rights, and to add at oral argument that the redemption provisions are not enforceable anyway, is disturbing. While most normal investors in the business world realize that they risk losses due to business downturns, the aliens participating in AELP may not realize that their attorney believes that their risk instead involves the refusal of their attorney's other client to comply with the written contract it executed with them. The Service cannot endorse illusory promises and does not recognize this type of "risk" as the kind of risk contemplated by 8 C.F.R. § 204.6(j)(2).

More importantly, the AAU must look to the plain language of the documents executed by the petitioner and not to subsequent statements of counsel; these documents provide the petitioner with the right to redemption and a certain price. As mentioned earlier, section 2.C of the investment agreement specifies that the failure of AELP to pay the sell-option price constitutes a breach of AELP's obligations to its limited partners.

In its memorandum of September 10, 1993, OGC stated its opinion at page 8 that it was "entirely appropriate for an alien to enter into an agreement with the investment fund whereby the seller agrees to repurchase the investor's shares upon, but not before, removal of the conditional basis of the alien's permanent residence." OGC qualified this statement by adding that such a redemption agreement "may not be used as a vehicle to avoid or reduce the risk of capital loss to the alien investor during the two-year period of conditional residency." To ensure that the capital remained at risk during the two-year period, OGC believed that the repurchase agreement should expressly provide that the price of the shares to be resold could not exceed the fair market value of the shares at the time of repurchase; "[a]ny other repurchase arrangement would impermissibly shift the risk of loss from the investment from the alien to the party promising to buy back the alien's interest in the investment." In a subsequent memorandum dated

Interim Decision #3360

June 27, 1995, OGC explained at page 10 that such a redemption agreement was permissible "since the alien risks losing all or part of his own capital in the event the fair market value of the investment has fallen at the time of the repurchase."

The AAU does not entirely agree with the opinions of OGC. To enter into a redemption agreement at the time of making an "investment" evidences a preconceived intent to unburden oneself of the investment as soon as possible after unconditional permanent resident status is attained. This is conceptually no different from a situation in which an alien marries a U.S. citizen and states, in writing, that he will divorce her in two years. The focus here is on the green card and not on the business. Despite counsel's repeated claims that the Service's current position is hurting U.S. workers and U.S. businesses, and despite counsel's accusations regarding the Service's allegedly cavalier attitude toward them, one could argue that an alien who enters into a redemption agreement considers the continued success of the U.S. workers and U.S. businesses secondary. His primary concern is obtaining permanent resident status for as little money as possible.

For the alien's money truly to be at risk, the alien cannot enter into a partnership knowing that he already has a willing buyer in a certain number of years, nor can he be assured that he will receive a certain price. Otherwise, the arrangement is nothing more than a loan, albeit an unsecured one.

The fair-market-value limitation on the sale price referenced by OGC, while well-intended, is not workable. It is not clear how this fair market value would be determined. For example, at page 31 of his brief on behalf of the petitioner, counsel discusses the two five-year payment options offered by AELP prior to the offering of the $120,000 option subscribed to by this petitioner. "Since the AELP sell-option prices were either $150,000 or $140,000 less than the $500,000 cash contribution recently completed, it seemed obvious that the sell-option prices would be substantially below fair market value." The only reason this would be "obvious" would be if counsel already knew what the fair market value would be in five years. True fair market value cannot be known five years in advance. Fair market value assumes the existence of a market. In this case, no public market exists for the AELP partnership interest. The sale of the partnership interest would not be an arms-length transaction, and the valuation of the parties would not reflect a true fair market value.

The AAU does not find that an alien investor may never sell back his partnership interest. Rather, the AAU finds that, prior to completing all his cash payments under a promissory note (whether to the partnership or to some third-party lender), an alien investor may not enter into any agreement granting him the right to sell his interest back to the partnership. In no event may he enter into such an agreement prior to the end of the two-year period of conditional residence. An investment assumes that a risk exists. The

Interim Decision #3360

alien must go into the investment not knowing for sure if he will be able to sell his interest at all after he obtains his unconditional permanent resident status; and if he is successful in selling his interest, the sale price may be disappointingly low (or surprising high and more than what he paid), This way, the alien risks both gain and loss. To allow otherwise transforms the arrangement into a loan.[17]

The petitioner contends that the AAU, in the unpublished C&W decision from 1995, had previously considered the issue of whether a structure identical to AELP's constituted a debt arrangement. According to the petitioner, the Vermont Service Center had found that the plan in question appeared to represent a good-faith commitment on a debt agreement, and representatives of the AAU "advised that they had analyzed the investment agreements and had concluded that the C&W program did not constitute a debt arrangement." "The C&W decision reversing the Vermont Service Center and ordering that the petitions be approved rejects the argument that this structure constitutes a debt arrangement," the petitioner continues.

The petitioner misreads the decisions. The Vermont Service Center's statement regarding a "good faith commitment on a debt agreement" was a reference to a comment in the Federal Register from someone suggesting that the Service "should state in the regulations that a good faith commitment on a debt agreement, *which is secured by the alien entrepreneur's assets*, should suffice to meet the requirement that the alien entrepreneur has, in good faith, substantially met the capital investment requirement..." (emphasis added). In other words, the "debt agreement" referred to by the Vermont Service Center was the promissory note executed by the *petitioner*, who had agreed to make cash payments to the partnership; as such, the "debt" at issue was the petitioner's debt to the partnership, not the partnership's subsequent debt to the petitioner. Neither the center decision nor the AAU decision specifically considered whether the investment structure at issue involved a prohibited debt arrangement (i.e., loan) as is at issue here. Neither decision made reference to a sell option.

The petitioner points to another program, which he calls the "Pardini/Tony Roma program." According to the petitioner's counsel, the California Service Center stated, in a notice of intent to deny, that the effect of the partnership arrangement appeared to be "a series of loans called investments made by the Limited Partners, the foreign investors, to the General Partner who is to be repaid by the General Partners at 10% interest." Brief at 54. Counsel claims that, in his response, he set forth the AAU decision in C&W; "[t]he AAU's rejection of the debt arrangement argument proved persuasive to the California Service Center, which in turn rejected

---

[17]More precisely, the AAU finds that the AELP plan contains, as one of its many features, a loan of $290,000. This amount of $290,000 cannot be considered an "investment."

Interim Decision #3360

the 'debt' argument and approved the Pardini/Tony Roma investor petitions."

As noted above, the AAU's C&W decision did not address the issue of loans extended by the limited partners to the partnership. Therefore, the California Service Center would have been in error if it had relied on the C&W decision to conclude that the Tony Roma plan did not involve an impermissible debt arrangement. Moreover, the C&W decision was unpublished and, even if it were relevant to Tony Roma or to this case, would not have any binding precedential value. Furthermore, even if the Service has, in the past, approved petitions that contained redemption agreements, these approvals were in error because the Service now recognizes that such agreements are in fact debt arrangements.

> The petitioner also refers to an internal Service memorandum from October 20, 1997, in which appears the following statement:
> On the other hand, absent evidence to the contrary, where the agreement does not specifically grant the investor the option to sell or the new commercial enterprise to buy out the investment before the balloon payment is due, an adjudicator may not deny the petition based on a finding that the investor will not exercise a sell (or the new commercial enterprise a buy-out) option before the due date on the balloon payment.

This statement makes no sense and certainly does not support the petitioner's contentions. The petitioner characterizes this memorandum as "all-important"; far from being "all-important," this memorandum was meant only to provide general policy statements, not to analyze specific fact patterns.[18]

As far as the petitioner's criticism that the Texas Service Center's decision in this case failed to mention, distinguish, or explain away the above prior decisions and OGC opinions, it is not clear why the center director would reference them at all. Neither of the above decisions had any precedential value, and neither case originated from the Texas Service Center. OGC memoranda, as counsel himself stated after oral argument, are merely opinions. OGC is not an adjudicative body and is in the position only of being an advisor; as such, adjudicators are not bound by OGC recommendations. *See* 8 C.F.R. § 103.1(b)(1).

Because the petitioner here has entered into an agreement to pay $290,000 in exchange for a promise that he can receive the $290,000 back six months later, he has in effect entered into a debt arrangement as prohibited by 8 C.F.R. § 204.6(e).[19] The $290,000 cannot be considered to have been properly "invested" and is not at risk.

---

[18] Furthermore, as mentioned earlier, this memorandum was superseded by another memorandum less than five months later.

[19] Again, this is assuming that the partnership agreement is the controlling document. If the investment document executed by this petitioner is controlling, then the money must be returned immediately and not after six months.

Interim Decision #3360

Cash reserves

The definitions section and section 4.04 of the original partnership agreement state that the general partner may deposit portions of the limited partners' capital contributions, designated as "reserve funds," in escrow or sub-escrow accounts. According to section 4.04.A(i) of the agreement, the banks holding these accounts shall invest the funds "in securities or other financial instruments and obligations in amounts sufficient to satisfy the requirements of **Section 8.05**," (emphasis in original). Section 4.04.B adds that the general partner "shall deposit with the Banks from the Initial Cash Payments sufficient Reserve Funds to satisfy the Partnership obligations under **Section 8.05** and to defray such costs and expenses of the Partnership as determined by the General Partner," (emphasis in original), Section 8.05 of the partnership agreement is entitled "Limited Partner Sell Option" and sets forth the timing and price of the sell option.

Section 4.03.B explains that after all the requirements of section 4.04.B are satisfied, any funds remaining from the initial cash payments and all subsequent capital contributions may be used to meet the obligations of the Partnership, as determined by the general partner in its sole discretion, with any excess to be used in the business of the Partnership.

In other words, pursuant to the above sections of the original partnership agreement, the general partner would be obligated to deposit sufficient portions of the initial $120,000 and/or the remaining $380,000 into the reserve funds such that the deposits and their earnings (from securities or other financial instruments) would enable the Partnership to fulfill its own obligations to buy back Partnership interests. The creation and maintenance of these reserve funds take priority over any other use of the capital contributions. Under these terms, any leftover money would be used for other Partnership obligations, and whatever was left thereafter would then be used for business activities. As the director stated in his decision, these reserve funds are, by agreement, not available for purposes of job creation and therefore cannot be considered capital placed at risk for the purpose of generating a return on the capital being placed at risk.

In his brief, the petitioner claims, "It is estimated in the business plans of AEP [the general partner] that no more than 10% of the total amount invested will ever be placed in bank accounts as reserves." The petitioner argues that since the sell-option price is $290,000, the initial payment of $120,000 and the installment payments totalling $90,000 would never become the subject of reserve accounts because they would yield an insufficient amount ($210,000) to cover the sell-option price. As such, these payments would be able to be used fully by the Partnership. Furthermore, the petitioner points out that if all of the limited partners' initial contributions and annual payments had been withheld as cash reserves, the subsidiary credit corporation could not have extended the

Interim Decision #3360

loans that it has.[20]

First, the partnership agreement states that the reserve funds are supposed to be invested in securities and other financial instruments, so the amount withheld from the capital contributions would not necessarily have to be $290,000. Second, the reserve provisions do not say that the reserves deducted from the contributions of a limited partner must be used to pay the sell-option price to that same limited partner; reserves drawn from later partners could conceivably be used to help pay the sell-option price to earlier partners.

Third, the reserve provisions probably have more significance as far as the final balloon payment of $290,000 than with respect to the initial payments. This final payment might have to be returned to the limited partner within six months, and the Partnership has a contractual obligation under sections 4.04.A(i) and 4.04.B to reserve sufficient funds to meet its redemption obligation of $290,000.[21] This is assuming, of course, that the partnership agreement is controlling; if the investment agreement executed by the petitioner is controlling, the money would be returned immediately instead of six months later.

In his brief, the petitioner states that in 1992 a Service official had delivered to counsel a model EB-5 investor petition that had been approved; at oral argument, counsel added that he was assured that if he followed this model petition, his petitions would also be approved. According to the petitioner, the one million dollars in capital invested in that case "would create reserves for inventory, working capital, expansion, and other partnership expenses, in the sum of *$450,000*. Thus, the model petition established that $450,000 of the $1,000,000 to be invested, or 45%, would be set aside as bank reserves."

The record does not contain a copy of this "model petition," and the AAU cannot ascertain whether the cash reserves in that case were mandatory or inadvertent, temporary or long-term. The opinions of one Service official, moreover, cannot work to remove from the AAU's jurisdiction the authority to review individual cases. *See* 8 C.F.R. § 103.1(f)(3)(iii). The Service does not pre-adjudicate investor petitions;[22] each petition must be adjudicated on its own merits. The fact that a particular petition (which did not result in a precedent decision) was considered qualifying in 1992, when the Service was less experienced with these types of cases, has no bearing

---

[20]The credit company has only extended four loans to date, totalling $1,361,000. Capital contributions of $500,000 from the 95 previously-approved petitioners would yield $47.5 million available for loans.

[21]Even if, after six years, the petitioner elected to remain in the Partnership instead of exercising his redemption option, the reserve provisions would still preclude the capital from being placed at risk during the two-year conditional period, as required by the regulations.

[22]Cf. 8 C.F.R. § 214.2(l)(2)(ii) regarding non-immigrant L-1 blanket petitions.

Interim Decision #3360

on whether the reserve provisions in question here should also be considered qualifying.

> Counsel explains in his brief on behalf of the petitioner:
>
> It was discovered by AELP that the Limited Partnership Agreement may be interpreted to require the creation of reserves in order to enable the Partnership to perform its obligation to pay the sell-option price to investors who exercised the sell-option obligations. It was never the intention of the Partnership to require the maintenance of reserves for this purpose.

Therefore, he states, pursuant to Stage I amendments the reserve provisions have since been eliminated.

The plain language of section 4.04.B of the original partnership agreement, however, clearly states that the general partner "shall" deposit sufficient reserves for the purpose of enabling the Partnership to meet its obligations under the sell-option agreement; the reference to the section pertaining to the sell option is even in bold face. It is difficult to imagine what the intent of this provision could be other than to require the creation and maintenance of reserves for such purpose. The assertion that the deletion of the reserve provisions is a Stage I amendment is not well taken; this revision does not conform the partnership agreement to the investment agreement executed by the petitioner and is a material change in position from the original partnership agreement. It is more in the nature of an unacceptable Stage II amendment.[23] (See earlier discussion of revisions to the partnership agreement.) Even if the issue of cash reserves were the sole ground for denial, the elimination of the cash-reserve requirement could not form the basis of an approval of *this* petition.

Fair market value of promissory note, schedule of payments

As stated in 8 C.F.R. § 204.6(e), **all** capital must be valued at fair market value in United States dollars. Counsel claims that the petitioner has made a capital contribution of $500,000 because he has executed a promissory note for $500,000. One issue to be examined when determining the fair market value of a promissory note is whether it is adequately secured.

According to the Secured Promissory Note executed by the petitioner on October 14, 1997, the obligation of the petitioner to make payments is secured by the petitioner's personal assets, "which are identified in the Attachment hereto." The promissory note does not include any document entitled "Attachment," although the record does contain a Summary of Bank Account Balances. This summary does not specify that the bank

---

[23] The investment agreement is silent as to cash reserves.

Interim Decision #3360

accounts listed are securing the note.

The summary and accompanying bank statements verify that the petitioner's accounts at Sumitomo Bank in Japan contained a total of $42,376.70 as of October 3, 1997; the petitioner's savings accounts at Sanwa Bank in Japan contained a total of $500,558.60 as of October 6, 1997; the petitioner's checking account at Sanwa Bank in California contained $70,985.80 as of October 10, 1997; and the petitioner's account at South Bay Bank in California contained $51,500 as of October 14, 1997. The Summary states that these accounts represent a total of $665,421.10 in funds.[24]

Assuming, arguendo, that the bank accounts do constitute the security for the promissory note, the petitioner has not demonstrated how AELP could reach the funds in the overseas accounts if the petitioner were to default, and it is not clear what expenses and effort would be involved. In the absence of such information, and in the absence of any details regarding the laws of Japan and the enforceability, by U.S. entities, of security interests taken in Japanese bank accounts, the petitioner has failed to establish that the security interest in the foreign accounts has any value.

More importantly, funds in bank accounts can easily be dissipated. As none of the above accounts is, for example, an escrow account or trust account in favor of AELP, no guarantee exists that the money contained in the accounts would remain there for the entire six years over which the petitioner would be obligated to make payments on the promissory note. For this reason, too, the petitioner has failed to show that his promissory note is adequately secured.

The fair market value of a promissory note also depends on the terms of the note itself. The petitioner contends that the promissory note at issue here is for $500,000, not $380,000; he urges the Service not to view his contribution as an initial payment of $120,000, plus annual payments totalling $90,000, plus a balloon of $290,000. The petitioner states that the regulations allow him either to have already invested or to be in the process of investing the requisite amount of capital. Therefore, the petitioner could either pay all $500,000 now or pay it over time. The regulations do not require that a petitioner pay extra to compensate for the fact that money paid now is worth more than money paid later, he argues. The petitioner points out that, at the time an alien investor seeks to remove the conditions of his permanent resident status, he need only demonstrate that he has "substantially" complied with the investment requirement. The petitioner main-

---

[24] It should be noted that the bank balances are for completely different dates, and it is not known if money was transferred among the various accounts and some of the funds double-counted. The petitioner did not provide transactions histories, and only one bank statement specifies the date on which the account was opened.

Interim Decision #3360

tains that by delivering the executed promissory note for the full $500,000, he has already made the full investment, and the schedule of payments is irrelevant.

The petitioner has failed to demonstrate that his promissory note, if it is to be considered capital, has a fair market value equal to its face value of $500,000. The question to be asked is what a third party would pay for the petitioner's note. In the real business world, promissory notes, such as mortgages, are regularly sold and are regularly discounted; present value is always relevant. The petitioner has submitted no evidence whatsoever as to the fair market value of his promise to finish paying $500,000 over six years.[25] In fact, applying standard formulae for computing the fair market value of annuities and future payments, the present value of five annual payments of $18,000 plus a payment due in six years of $290,000 plus a completed payment of $120,000 would be approximately $375,000 instead of $500,000.[26]

Under certain circumstances, a promissory note that does not itself constitute capital could instead constitute evidence that the petitioner is "in the process of investing" other capital, such as cash. In that situation, 8 C.F.R. § 216.6(c)(1)(ii) requires that a petitioner substantially complete his payments on the note prior to the end of the two-year conditional period. In the present case, however, the promissory note is not evidence that the petitioner is in the process of investing $500,000 of cash. As discussed earlier, the five $18,000 annual payments are covered by the guaranteed annual distributions. The $290,000 balloon payment is not due until well after the two-year period.

In administering this program, the Service has a responsibility to ensure that the requisite amount of money is actually paid by the petitioners. Over the years, the Service has observed that the terms of promissory notes have grown progressively longer; AELP, for example, started with due dates of four and five years, while the petitioner's payment plan, a more recent AELP development, involves six years. The schedule of payments under a promissory note, whether the note is used as capital or as evidence of a

---

[25] As noted earlier, it is not actually clear that the petitioner is in fact obligated to complete all of his payments prior to exercising his sell option. If the petitioner can avoid making the last payment of $290,000 by simply exercising his sell option at the time the payment is due, any purchaser of the note could not count on receiving this last payment and would further discount the value of the note. In addition, as discussed earlier, section 2.C of the investment agreement provides that the petitioner is not obligated to make any further payments on the note in the event of the Partnership's bankruptcy (voluntary or involuntary) or failure to make any of its own payments; this further reduces the value of the promissory note to a third-party purchaser.

[26] As discussed above, the note in this case would be further discounted for other reasons, such as the lack of adequate security.

Interim Decision #3360

commitment to invest, is relevant to the issue of whether a petitioner has, in good faith, committed the requisite amount of his personal funds. It is also relevant to the issue of the amount of funds at risk and available to the job-creating enterprise(s). Therefore, at a minimum, nearly all of the money due under a promissory note must be payable within two years, without provisions for extensions.[27] To allow otherwise would permit the admission of aliens who, by the terms of their investment plans, would be ineligible for removal of the conditions of their permanent resident status. *See* 8 C.F.R. § 216.6(c)(1)(iii).

If the instant petition were to be approved, the petitioner would have paid at most $123,600 of his own funds at the time he sought removal of the conditions of his permanent resident status.[28] This is far short of the requisite $500,000 and hardly evidences a good-faith commitment of funds. As noted above, the petitioner has also failed to show that the promissory note is adequately secured and that it otherwise has an adequate fair market value.

Source of funds

8 C.F.R. § 204.6(j) states, in pertinent part, that:

(3) To show that the petitioner has invested, or is actively in the process of investing, capital obtained through lawful means, the petition must be accompanied, as applicable, by:

(i) Foreign business registration records;

(ii) Corporate, partnership (or any other entity in any form which has filed in any country or subdivision thereof any return described in this subpart), and personal tax returns including income, franchise, property (whether real, personal, or intangible), or any other tax returns of any kind filed within five years, with any taxing jurisdiction in or outside the United States by or on behalf of the petitioner;

(iii) Evidence identifying any other source(s) of capital; or

(iv) Certified copies of any judgments or evidence of all pending governmental civil or criminal actions, governmental administrative proceedings, and any private civil actions (pending or otherwise) involving monetary judgments against the petitioner from any court in or outside the United States within the past fifteen years.

---

[27] The petitioner must still show that the promissory note is adequately secured and that the promissory note has an adequate fair market value.

[28] §§ 216A(c)(1) and (d)(2) of the Act provide that such a petition must be filed within the 90-day period preceding the second anniversary of a petitioner's admission as a conditional permanent resident.

Interim Decision #3360

While the record contains a letter from Wells Fargo Bank dated October 14, 1997, acknowledging the receipt of $120,000 and advising the petitioner that the funds had been deposited into a custody account, the record does not reveal from where these funds originated. It is not known if the money came from the petitioner's overseas accounts, from his U.S. accounts, or from some other source. As the petitioner has not documented the path of the funds, such as by wire-transfer records, the petitioner has failed to meet his burden of establishing that the initial $120,000 were his own funds. *See Matter of Soffici*, 22 I&N Dec. 158 (Comm. 1998).

The petitioner has also failed to document the source of the hundreds of thousands of dollars in his bank accounts. The petitioner is 30 years old and, according to counsel, began his "entrepreneurial activities" in May 1993. The petitioner is said to be the president of a company that imports and sells vintage Levis jeans in Japan.

The only evidence of earnings contained in the record consists of two documents from the Director of Nerima Higasi Taxation Office. These documents indicate that, for the taxable year of June 3, 1996, to May 31, 1997, South Bay Trading Japan, Inc., declared Y12,674,887 in corporate income and paid Y3,992,100 in taxes. Counsel states that, applying an exchange rate of 122 Japanese yen to one U.S. dollar, the company's taxable income was $103,892.52 for this period. After subtracting taxes paid, however, the net income of South Bay Trading was approximately $71,170.

Furthermore, this figure says nothing about the *petitioner's* level of income that year, and the petitioner has not submitted any documentation about his level of income during other years. Assuming that the petitioner had taken all of South Bay's net income for himself, and assuming that the petitioner's business activities had been just as successful in the previous three years, and assuming that the petitioner had had no living expenses, he could have saved no more than $300,000; counsel claims that the petitioner's bank accounts contain over $650,000. Therefore, the petitioner has failed to meet the requirements of 8 C.F.R. § 204.6(j)(3).

Estoppel and reliance considerations

In his brief on behalf of the petitioner, counsel refers to instances in which he was supposedly guaranteed that his clients' petitions would be approved. Counsel states that in 1992 he was given a model petition and advised that if he patterned his investment structures in the same way, his clients' petitions would be approved.

In the fall of 1996, counsel met with "the Senior INS representative in charge of immigrant investor programs" and this person

> expressly approved the $120,000 initial payment option, the six year schedule of payments in the sell-option or redemption agreement available after all of the payments

195

Interim Decision #3360

> have been made. The only limitation placed upon any of these provisions was that the redemption agreement could not be exercised until all of the payments had been made by the investor.

Brief at 46. Counsel states, at page 14, "Thereafter, INS kept its word. Approximately 95 petitions of AELP were approved by INS including over 50 petitions involving the initial payment option of $120,000." The opinions of a single Service official, however, are not binding, and as stated earlier, no Service officer has the authority to pre-adjudicate an immigrant-investor petition.

Counsel states that he has submitted 11 different partnership plans to the Service and that they are all identical; since the first petitions were approved, the Service is bound to approve the petition at issue here. Counsel further claims that on more than 30 occasions, he had been promised that no "changes" would be made except by formal rulemaking. Counsel is saying, in effect, that the approval of his programs is nonreviewable except upon a writing of formal regulations. Opinions purportedly expressed by a few Service officials cannot remove the AAU's regulatory authority to review these cases. To say that an agency's knowledge cannot grow, and that an agency is prohibited from benefiting from its experience, is unreasonable.

The petitioner argues that the OGC opinion of December 19, 1997, constitutes a rule change that the Service is now retroactively applying in violation of the Administrative Procedure Act ("APA"). Brief at 4-7, 114-43; Second Supplemental Brief at 5-12. This OGC opinion, however, is not a "rule." Under the APA, a rule is a binding legal principle "designed to implement, interpret or prescribe law or policy." 5 U.S.C. § 551. As noted in the OGC opinion itself, the opinion in no way modifies existing law, but is intended merely to provide guidance to the Service in understanding many factual issues that have arisen over the years with respect to immigrant-investor petitions. Providing this type of guidance is the very mission of OGC, as specifically provided at 8 C.F.R. § 100.2(a)(1) and 103.1(b)(1). These regulations do not delegate any authority to OGC to establish binding legal principles or to exercise any other rulemaking power. Neither the AAU nor other Service adjudicators, therefore, are bound to follow the OGC opinion of December 19, 1997. The AAU's decision in this case is based entirely on the application of longstanding statutory and regulatory law to the facts presented in this petition.

The petitioner incorrectly argues that the Service should be estopped from finding that his investment plan is inconsistent with § 203(b)(5) of the Act and the relevant regulations. The Supreme Court has never upheld a claim that a Government agency may be estopped from deciding a case before it, such as this case, in accordance with the law. *See Office of Personnel Management v. Richmond*, 496 U.S. 414, 422 (1990).

Interim Decision #3360

Furthermore, even if estoppel were applicable to the Service under these circumstances, the petitioner has completely failed to establish the requisite elements therefor. For example, the petitioner has shown no affirmative misconduct on the part of the Service.

Moreover, the petitioner has not shown that he has detrimentally relied on any prior representation by a Service official. First, no basis exists for a claim that the petitioner or his counsel "reasonably" or "justifiably" believed that informal discussions between counsel and any Service officer were an acceptable substitute for following the normal rules applicable to the filing and adjudication of investor-visa petitions. It is basic immigration law that the only way to obtain a determination on eligibility for immigrant-investor classification is to file a petition with the Service. *See* section 204(a)(1)(F); 8 C.F.R. § 2.1 and 204.6(a), Furthermore, the Service may approve a petition only if the Service makes a formal adjudication "[a]fter an investigation of the facts in each case," that the alien is eligible for the classification sought, § 204(b) of the Act.

In addition, even if the petitioner were able to establish reasonable reliance, he has not shown that he has done so to his detriment. For example, according to the investment plan, the petitioner is only obligated to pay the required investment upon the approval of his visa petition. Brief at 29.

THE PETITIONER HAS NOT ESTABLISHED A NEW COMMERCIAL ENTERPRISE

8 C.F.R. § 204.6(h) states that the establishment of a new commercial enterprise may consist of:

(1) The creation of an original business;

(2) The purchase of an existing business and simultaneous or subsequent restructuring or reorganization such that a new commercial enterprise results; or

(3) The expansion of an existing business through the investment of the required amount, so that a substantial change in the net worth or number of employees results from the investment of capital. Substantial change means a 40 percent increase either in the net worth, or in the number of employees, so that the new net worth, or number of employees amounts to at least 140 percent of the pre-expansion net worth or number of employees. Establishment of a new commercial enterprise in this manner does not exempt the petitioner from the requirements of 8 C.F.R. § 204.6(j)(2) and (3) relating to the required amount of capital investment and the creation of full-time employment for ten qualifying employees. In the case of a capital investment in a troubled business, employment creation may meet the criteria set forth in 8 C.F.R. § 204.6(j)(4)(ii).

8 C.F.R. § 204.6(e) states that:

Troubled business means a business that has been in existence for at least two years,

Interim Decision #3360

> has incurred a net loss for accounting purposes (determined on the basis of generally accepted accounting principles) during the twelve- or twenty-four month period prior to the priority date on the alien entrepreneur's Form I-526, and the loss for such period is at least equal to twenty percent of the troubled business's net worth prior to such loss. For purposes of determining whether or not the troubled business has been in existence for two years, successors in interest to the troubled business will be deemed to have been in existence for the same period of time as the business they succeeded.

According to the plain language of § 203(b)(5)(A)(i) of the Act, a petitioner must show that he is seeking to enter the U.S. for the purpose of engaging in a new commercial enterprise that **he** has established. As counsel maintains, the new commercial enterprise at issue here is AELP. AELP, however, was established on March 25, 1996. The petitioner executed the various partnership documents on October 14, 1997. The petitioner did not indicate, at Part 4 of the Form I-526, in what way he was creating a new enterprise.

While AELP is a new commercial enterprise, in that it was formed after November 29, 1990, the petitioner had no hand in its creation and was not present at its inception.[29] Therefore, the petitioner must demonstrate that he will restructure or reorganize AELP to the degree that a new business will result, or he must demonstrate that he will expand AELP's net worth or number of employees by 40 percent, or he must demonstrate that AELP is a troubled business as defined above.

AELP was an ongoing business prior to the petitioner executing the investment agreement, and it intends to continue in its current form; therefore, the petitioner has not established the requisite restructuring or reorganization. As the petitioner has noted on numerous occasions, 95 investors have previously been approved with respect to AELP. Taking his claims at face value, and assuming that all 95 investors have made capital investments of $500,000, it is not possible for this petitioner to expand AELP by 40 percent with a single "investment" of $500,000. Finally, the petitioner has not submitted evidence to show that AELP has suffered the degree of loss in net worth specified by 8 C.F.R. § 204.6(e) to qualify as a troubled business; in addition, AELP was not in existence for at least two years prior to the time the petitioner signed the investment agreement.

The AAU recognizes that the Service has previously approved petitions involving plans in which limited partners joined partnerships over varying periods of time. Experience has shown, however, that some of these pool-

---

[29] It could perhaps be argued that the date of filing of the Certificate of Limited Partnership was not the date of AELP's creation, that AELP is still in the process of being created, and that therefore the petitioner is part of the original creation of AELP. If so, the petition has been filed prematurely; the Act requires that the petitioner "has established" the commercial enterprise already. Accomplishment of a business's purposes would be too speculative if it was based on successfully attracting unidentified future investors.

Interim Decision #3360

ing arrangements are being used to circumvent the establishment requirement set forth by Congress.

The petitioner has failed to show that **he** has established a new commercial enterprise, as required by § 203(b)(5)(A)(i) of the Act.

THE PLAN DOES NOT MEET THE EMPLOYMENT-CREATION REQUIREMENT

8 C.F.R. § 204.6(j)(4)(i) states:

> To show that a new commercial enterprise will create not fewer than ten (10) full-time positions for qualifying employees, the petition must be accompanied by:
>
> (A) Documentation consisting of photocopies of relevant tax records, Form I-9, or other similar documents for ten (10) qualifying employees, if such employees have already been hired following the establishment of the new commercial enterprise; or
>
> (B) A copy of a comprehensive business plan showing that, due to the nature and projected size of the new commercial enterprise, the need for not fewer than ten (10) qualifying employees will result, including approximate dates, within the next two years, and when such employees will be hired.

8 C.F.R. § 204.6(g) deals with multiple investors and states, in pertinent part:

> (1) The establishment of a new commercial enterprise may be used as the basis of a petition for classification as an alien entrepreneur by more than one investor, provided each petitioning investor has invested or is actively in the process of investing the required amount for the area in which the new commercial enterprise is principally doing business, and provided each individual investment results in the creation of at least ten full-time employees.
>
> (2) The total number of full-time positions created for qualifying employees shall be allocated solely to those alien entrepreneurs who have used the establishment of the new commercial enterprise as the basis of a petition on Form I-526. No allocation need be made among persons not seeking classification under section 203(b)(5) of the Act or among non-natural persons, either foreign or domestic. The Service shall recognize any reasonable agreement made among the alien entrepreneurs in regard to the identification and allocation of such qualifying positions.

As discussed earlier, the petitioner has failed to demonstrate that the subsidiary credit corporation has extended loans in the past to export-related businesses located within the geographical limitation of the regional center. Similarly, the credit corporation's loan prospects do not appear to involve businesses within the geographical limitation. No reason exists to believe that this petitioner's money will be lent to businesses within the geographical area. Therefore, he must establish direct employment creation.

199

Interim Decision #3360

The petitioner has failed to show that AELP has hired or will hire a sufficient number of employees to allocate 10 full-time positions to each of the 95 previously-approved petitioners as well as to this petitioner and the remaining 64 petitioners whose cases have not been decided.

CONCLUSION

In his brief, counsel states, "INS is supposed to *grant* immigrant investor petitions, not to *deny* them. INS is to interpret the laws and regulations liberally and generously so as to achieve [this] Congressional purpose." He presents statistics showing that, of the total number of visas made available, only six percent has been used. The fact that counsel considers this category to be under-utilized is irrelevant. The alien-entrepreneur classification is for a special kind of person, and it is not surprising that, notwithstanding the random number fixed by Congress, few people have both the financial means and the entrepreneurial spirit to apply. The Service will not eviscerate the meaning of the regulations or the essence of the law simply to "fill up" the numbers. The measure of success or failure of the EB-5 program is not the number of petitions granted; rather, it is the extent to which proper compliance is achieved and genuine investments are made.

Counsel continues, "Failing to comply reflects adversely upon INS as having failed to properly communicate to those attempting to comply, that which is necessary to comply." The foregoing decision should offer some guidance as to what is necessary to comply.

The burden of proof in these proceedings rests solely with the petitioner. Section 291 of the Act, 8 U.S.C. § 1361. The petitioner has not met that burden. Accordingly, the petition is denied.

ORDER: The decision of the director is affirmed. The petition is denied.

APPENDIX A-3: *MATTER OF HO*

In re HO, Petitioner

In Visa Petition Proceedings

WAC 98 072 50493

Decided by the Associate Commissioner, Examinations, July 31, 1998.

(1) Merely establishing and capitalizing a new commercial enterprise and signing a commercial lease are not sufficient to show that an immigrant-investor petitioner has placed his capital at risk. The petitioner must present, instead, evidence that he has actually undertaken meaningful concrete business activity.

(2) The petitioner must establish that he has placed his own capital at risk, that is to say, he must show that he was the legal owner of the invested capital. Bank statements and other financial documents do not meet this requirement if the documents show someone else as the legal owner of the capital.

(3) The petitioner must also establish that he acquired the legal ownership of the invested capital through lawful means. Mere assertions about the petitioner's financial situation or work history, without supporting documentary evidence, are not sufficient to meet this requirement.

(4) To establish that qualifying employment positions have been created, INS Forms I-9 presented by a petitioner must be accompanied by other evidence to show that these employees have commenced work activities and have been hired in permanent, full-time positions.

(5) In order to demonstrate that the new commercial enterprise will create not fewer than 10 full-time positions, the petitioner must either provide evidence that the new commercial enterprise has created such positions or furnish a comprehensive, detailed, and credible business plan demonstrating the need for the positions and the schedule for hiring the employees.

ON BEHALF OF PETITIONER: JOHN L. SUN
3550 WILSHIRE BOULEVARD, SUITE 1250
LOS ANGELES, CA 90010-2413

DISCUSSION

The preference visa petition was approved by the Director, California Service Center, who certified the decision to the Associate Commissioner for Examinations for review. The decision of the director will be reversed.

The petitioner seeks classification as an alien entrepreneur pursuant to section 203(b)(5) of the Immigration and Nationality Act, 8 U.S.C. § 1153(b)(5), The director determined that the petitioner had already invest-

206

Interim Decision #3362

ed the requisite amount of capital, apparently obtained through lawful means. The director further found that, while the business had only two employees at the time of her decision, the business plan called for at least eight more employees within the next 12 months.

The petitioner has chosen not to respond.

Section 203(b)(5)(A) of the Act provides classification to qualified immigrants seeking to enter the United States for the purpose of engaging in a new commercial enterprise:

(i) which the alien has established,

(ii) in which such alien has invested (after the date of the enactment of the Immigration Act of 1990) or, is actively in the process of investing, capital in an amount not less than the amount specified in subparagraph (C), and

(iii) which will benefit the United States economy and create full-time employment for not fewer than 10 United States citizens or aliens lawfully admitted for permanent residence or other immigrants lawfully authorized to be employed in the United States (other than the immigrant and the immigrant's spouse, sons, or daughters).

The petitioner indicates that the petition is based on the creation of a new business located in a targeted employment area, for which the required amount of capital invested has been adjusted downward.

MINIMUM INVESTMENT AMOUNT

8 C.F.R. § 204.6(e) states, in pertinent part, that:

Targeted employment area means an area which, at the time of investment, is a rural area or an area which has experienced unemployment of at least 150 percent of the national average rate.

On December 18, 1997, King's Wheel Corp. filed its articles of incorporation with the State of California. According to the petitioner, who is the president, director, and chief executive officer of the corporation, King's Wheel will import steel and aluminum automobile wheels from Taiwan and market them in the United States as a wholesaler. On December 20, 1997, the petitioner signed a lease on behalf of King's Wheel for an "office and warehouse" located at 350 W. Artesia Boulevard in Compton, California.

Compton is in Los Angeles County, and the most current information available from the California Employment Development Department indicates that all of Los Angeles County is an area of sufficiently high unemployment to qualify as a targeted area. Therefore, the amount of capital necessary to make a qualifying investment in this matter is $500,000.

Interim Decision #3362

INVESTMENT OF QUALIFYING CAPITAL

8 C.F.R. § 204.6(e) states, in pertinent part, that:

> *Capital* means cash, equipment, inventory, other tangible property, cash equivalents, and indebtedness secured by assets owned by the alien entrepreneur, provided the alien entrepreneur is personally and primarily liable and that the assets of the new commercial enterprise upon which the petition is based are not used to secure any of the indebtedness, ...
>
> *Commercial enterprise* means any for-profit activity formed for the ongoing conduct of lawful business including, but not limited to, a sole proprietorship, partnership (whether limited or general), holding company, joint venture, corporation, business trust, or other entity which may be publicly or privately owned. This definition includes a commercial enterprise consisting of a holding company and its wholly-owned subsidiaries, provided that each such subsidiary is engaged in a for-profit activity formed for the ongoing conduct of a lawful business. This definition shall not include a non-commercial activity such as owning and operating a personal residence.
>
> *Invest* means to contribute capital. A contribution of capital in exchange for a note, bond, convertible debt, obligation, or any other debt arrangement between the alien entrepreneur and the new commercial enterprise does not constitute a contribution of capital for the purposes of this part.

8 C.F.R. § 204.6(j) states, in pertinent part, that:

> (2) To show that the petitioner has invested or is actively in the process of investing the required amount of capital, the petition must be accompanied by evidence that the petitioner has placed the required amount of capital at risk for the purpose of generating a return on the capital placed at risk. Evidence of mere intent to invest, or of prospective investment arrangements entailing no present commitment, will not suffice to show that the petitioner is actively in the process of investing. The alien must show actual commitment of the required amount of capital. Such evidence may include, but need not be limited to:
>
> (i) Bank statement(s) showing amount(s) deposited in United States business account(s) for the enterprise;
>
> (ii) Evidence of assets which have been purchased for use in the United States enterprise, including invoices; sales receipts; and purchase contracts containing sufficient information to identify such assets, their purchase costs, date of purchase, and purchasing entity;
>
> (iii) Evidence of property transferred from abroad for use in the United States enterprise, including United States Customs Service commercial entry documents, bills of lading and transit insurance policies containing ownership information and sufficient information to identify the property and to indicate the fair market value of such property;
>
> (iv) Evidence of monies transferred or committed to be transferred to the new com-

Interim Decision #3362

mercial enterprise in exchange for shares of stock (voting or nonvoting, common or preferred), Such stock may not include terms requiring the new commercial enterprise to redeem it at the holder's request; or

(v) Evidence of any loan or mortgage agreement, promissory note, security agreement, or other evidence of borrowing which is secured by assets of the petitioner, other than those of the new commercial enterprise, and for which the petitioner is personally and primarily liable.

On December 30, 1997, the sum of $515,000 was transferred from an unidentified bank account to one of King's Wheel's business accounts at Cathay Bank, and the business account was credited $514,995. On January 5, 1998, the petitioner obtained 500,000 of the one million authorized shares of King's Wheel; the petitioner indicates that these shares were in exchange for $500,000.

Capital at risk

Even though the petitioner owns only half of the authorized shares in King's Wheel, he is the sole shareholder thus far. He is also the only officer of the corporation. As such, the petitioner exercises sole control over the corporation's activities; whether the business proceeds according to plan or whether, for example, the business returns the petitioner's money is the petitioner's decision alone. Therefore, the petitioner cannot meet his at-risk requirement by merely depositing funds into a corporate account.

The business plan indicates that sales would commence in three to six months from the date of submission of the petition (January 12, 1998), yet the petitioner has not undertaken the necessary preparations to meet this deadline. The petitioner has not submitted evidence that King's Wheel has purchased inventory or office equipment. The petitioner has not shown that he has entered into negotiations with potential suppliers of wheels abroad, nor has he even identified who his potential suppliers are. The petitioner has not provided evidence that he has identified or entered into negotiations with potential buyers within the United States. The petitioner has not even furnished evidence that he has contracted with the suppliers of local utilities, such as the telephone or electric companies. The petitioner has not adequately explained how the business will go about spending the $500,000 that have been placed into its account. Although the petitioner has signed a lease for King's Wheel's showroom, the lease contains an escape clause at section 14, allowing King's Wheel to assign the lease or sublet the property with consent from the landlord.

The regulations provide that a petition must be accompanied by evidence that the petitioner has placed the required amount of capital at risk for the purpose of generating a return on the capital placed at risk. A mere

Interim Decision #3362

deposit into a corporate money-market account, such that the petitioner himself still exercises sole control over the funds, hardly qualifies as an active, at-risk investment.[1] Simply formulating an idea for future business activity, without taking meaningful concrete action, is similarly insufficient for a petitioner to meet the at-risk requirement. Before it can be said that capital made available to a commercial enterprise has been placed at risk, a petitioner must present some evidence of the actual undertaking of business activity; otherwise, no assurance exists that the funds will in fact be used to carry out the business of the commercial enterprise. This petitioner's de minimis action of signing a lease agreement, without more, is not enough.

Source of funds

8 C.F.R. § 204.6(j) states, in pertinent part, that:

> (3) To show that the petitioner has invested, or is actively in the process of investing, capital obtained through lawful means, the petitioner must be accompanied, as applicable, by:
>
> (i) Foreign business registration records;
>
> (ii) Corporate, partnership (or any other entity in any form which has filed in any country or subdivision thereof any return described in this subpart), and personal tax returns including income, franchise, property (whether real, personal, or intangible), or any other tax returns of any kind filed within five years, with any taxing jurisdiction in or outside the United States by or on behalf of the petitioner;
>
> (iii) Evidence identifying any other source(s) of capital; or
>
> (iv) Certified copies of any judgments or evidence of all pending governmental civil or criminal actions, governmental administrative proceedings, and any private civil actions (pending or otherwise) involving monetary judgments against the petitioner from any court in or outside the United States within the past fifteen years.

To show that he has invested his own capital obtained through lawful means, the petitioner has furnished copies of bank statements showing that as of December 12, 1997, he had NT$1,339,447 (less than US$41,000[2]) on deposit at the Bank of Taiwan, and as of December 23, 1997, an individual named "Ho Wang Chung-Chia, Theresa Wang" had NT$6,255,844.52

---

[1] King's Wheel has two accounts at Cathay Bank: the money-market account into which the $514,995 were deposited and a commercial checking account containing $3,100. The petitioner has not shown any activity in either account.

[2] This figure assumes an exchange rate of NT$32.68 = US$1, which appears in the materials submitted by the petitioner. The current exchange rate is closer to NT$34.27 = US$1. WASHINGTON POST, July 21, 1998, at C10.

Interim Decision #3362

(US$191,427.31) on deposit at the First Commercial Bank. The petitioner has also submitted a letter from the United World Chinese Commercial Bank indicating that he holds 506,000 shares of capital stock in the bank, and as of December 22, 1997, those shares were worth NT$30,866,000. A letter from United Orthopedic Corporation states, "Mrs. Ho Wang Chung-Chia, also known as Theresa Wang has invested N.T.$1,000,000 in United Orthopedic Corp." On December 19, 1997, Ms. Chung-Chia Ho Wang's single unit on the 11th floor of an 18-story, 147-unit condominium in Taiwan was appraised at NT$6,502,348 (less than US$199,000).

The petitioner asserts that Chung-Chia Ho Wang is his wife; however, he has submitted no documentation, such as a marriage certificate, to substantiate this claim.[3] Even if Ms. Wang is the petitioner's wife, and even if her assets can be considered joint property, the petitioner has failed to establish the source of the funds transferred to the King's Wheel money-market account, totalling $515,000. Prior to the date of transfer, neither Taiwanese bank account contained sufficient funds; in fact, the two accounts together contained less than $250,000. Neither the petitioner nor Ms. Wang has sold any shares of stock in the Taiwanese corporations, and Ms. Wang appears still to own the condominium unit. As stated earlier, the wire-transfer receipt does not reveal from what bank account(s) the funds originated.

Furthermore, while the petitioner claims to have been a medical doctor in Taiwan, he has not presented any evidence of his having engaged in this occupation, nor has he provided any documentation regarding his level of income. The petitioner explains that, through his medical practice and investments, he has accumulated "liquid assets" of approximately US$1.4 million, and therefore the source of his $500,000 is lawful. The above documentation does not reflect $1.4 million in liquid assets; moreover, simply going on record without supporting documentary evidence is not sufficient for purposes of meeting the burden of proof in these proceedings. *See Matter of Treasure Craft of California*, 14 I&N Dec. 190 (Reg. Comm. 1972).

EMPLOYMENT CREATION

8 C.F.R. § 204.6(j)(4)(i) states:

To show that a new commercial enterprise will create not fewer than ten (10) full-time positions for qualifying employees, the petition must be accompanied by:

(A) Documentation consisting of photocopies of relevant tax records, Form I-9, or

---

[3]The real-estate appraisal indicates that Ms. Wang's name changed to "Ho" after marriage, but "Ho" is a common Chinese name.

Interim Decision #3362

> other similar documents for ten (10) qualifying employees, if such employees have already been hired following the establishment of the new commercial enterprise; or
>
> (B) A copy of a comprehensive business plan showing that, due to the nature and projected size of the new commercial enterprise, the need for not fewer than ten (10) qualifying employees will result, including approximate dates, within the next two years, and when such employees will be hired.

8 C.F.R. § 204.6(e) states, in pertinent part:

> *Employee* means an individual who provides services or labor for the new commercial enterprise and who receive wages or other remuneration directly from the new commercial enterprise...This definition shall not include independent contractors.
>
> *Full-time employment* means employment of a qualifying employee by the new commercial enterprise in a position that requires a minimum of 35 working hours per week.
>
> *Qualifying employee* means a United States citizen, a lawfully admitted permanent resident, or other immigrant lawfully authorized to be employed in the United States including, but not limited to, a conditional resident, a temporary resident, an asylee, a refugee, or an alien remaining in the United States under suspension of deportation. This definition does not include the alien entrepreneur, the alien entrepreneur's spouse, sons, or daughters, or any nonimmigrant alien.

As evidence that two positions have already been created, the petitioner has submitted two Forms I-9 completed just three days prior to the date he signed the Form I-526 petition. The business plan calls for the hiring of eight employees within the next 12 months: a secretary, an accounting clerk, a truck driver, two warehouse people, and three salespersons.

With respect to the two persons identified in the Forms I-9, the petitioner has not explained what positions they occupy, and it is not known whether they work full- or part-time or whether they work at all. Forms I-9 verify, at best, that a business has made an effort to ascertain whether particular individuals are authorized to work; they do not verify that those individuals have actually begun working. In the absence of such evidence as paystubs and payroll records showing the number of hours worked, the petitioner has not met his burden of establishing that he has created full-time employment within the United States.

In addition, as the business plan fails to reveal what these two individuals do, it is not altogether clear that they would still be needed once sales commenced and the business progressed beyond its "planning stage." The petitioner has not demonstrated that he has created permanent employment.

According to 8 C.F.R. § 204.6(j)(4)(i)(B), if a petitioner has not already met the employment-creation requirement, he must submit a comprehensive business plan from which it is clear that the business will in fact require

Interim Decision #3362

10 qualifying employees within the next two years. To be "comprehensive," a business plan must be sufficiently detailed to permit the Service to draw reasonable inferences about the job-creation potential. Mere conclusory assertions do not enable the Service to determine whether the job-creation projections are any more reliable than hopeful speculation.

A comprehensive business plan as contemplated by the regulations should contain, at a minimum, a description of the business, its products and/or services, and its objectives. The plan should contain a market analysis, including the names of competing businesses and their relative strengths and weaknesses, a comparison of the competition's products and pricing structures, and a description of the target market/prospective customers of the new commercial enterprise. The plan should list the required permits and licenses obtained. If applicable, it should describe the manufacturing or production process, the materials required, and the supply sources. The plan should detail any contracts executed for the supply of materials and/or the distribution of products. It should discuss the marketing strategy of the business, including pricing, advertising, and servicing. The plan should set forth the business's organizational structure and its personnel's experience. It should explain the business's staffing requirements and contain a timetable for hiring, as well as job descriptions for all positions. It should contain sales, cost, and income projections and detail the bases therefor.[4] Most importantly, the business plan must be credible.

Certainly no astute investor would place half a million or a million dollars into a business that he had not thoroughly researched. Creating a comprehensive business plan as described above is normal practice for any businessman seeking to operate a viable business. Without knowing whether a business is feasible and has the potential for long-term survival, neither the petitioner nor the Service can reasonably conclude that it will create permanent, full-time employment. It is not too onerous to ask a petitioner who has not yet met the employment-creation requirement to submit to the Service a real business plan. Other administrative agencies, such as the Small Business Administration, and private financial institutions routinely require the submission of detailed business plans before extending loans to businesses. Permanent resident status is no less significant a matter than a loan.

The petitioner's four-page "business plan" is wholly inadequate and fails to meet the petitioner's burden of showing that he will create 10 permanent, full-time positions within the next two years.

---

[4] The Service recognizes that each business is different and will require different information in its business plan. These guidelines, therefore, are not all-inclusive.

Interim Decision #3362

CONCLUSION

The petitioner is ineligible for classification as an alien entrepreneur because he has failed to establish that he has made an active, at-risk investment and has failed to clarify the source of his funds. The petitioner has further failed to demonstrate clearly that his proposed business will result in the requisite employment creation.

The burden of proof in these proceedings rests solely with the petitioner. Section 291 of the Act, 8 U.S.C. § 1361. The petitioner has not met that burden. Accordingly, the petition is denied.

ORDER: The decision of the director is reversed. The petition is denied.

APPENDIX A-4: *MATTER OF HSIUNG*

Interim Decision #3361

In re HSIUNG, Petitioner

In Visa Petition Proceedings

A76 854 232

Decided by the Associate Commissioner, Examinations, July 31, 1998.

(1) A promissory note secured by assets owned by a petitioner can constitute capital under 8 C.F.R. § 204.6(e) if: the assets are specifically identified as securing the note; the security interests in the note are perfected in the jurisdiction in which the assets are located; and the assets are fully amenable to seizure by a U.S. note holder.

(2) When determining the fair market value of a promissory note being used as capital under 8 C.F.R. § 204.6(e), factors such as the fair market value of the assets securing the note, the extent to which the assets are amenable to seizure, and the present value of the note should be considered.

(3) Whether a petitioner uses a promissory note as capital under 8 C.F.R. § 204.6(e) or as evidence of a commitment to invest cash, he must show that he has placed his assets at risk. In establishing that a sufficient amount of his assets are at risk, a petitioner must demonstrate, among other things, that the assets securing the note are his, that the security interests are perfected, that the assets are amenable to seizure, and that the assets have an adequate fair market value.

(4) A petitioner engaging in the reorganization or restructuring of a pre-existing business may not cause a net loss of employment.

ON BEHALF OF PETITIONER: ROBERT LUBIN
8229 BOONE BOULEVARD
SUITE 610
VIENNA, VA 22182

DISCUSSION

The preference visa petition was denied by the Director, Nebraska Service Center, who certified the decision to the Associate Commissioner for Examinations for review. The petitioner has chosen not to respond. The decision of the director is affirmed.

The petitioner seeks classification as an alien entrepreneur pursuant to section 203(b)(5) of the Immigration and Nationality Act, 8 U.S.C. § 1153(b)(5), The petitioner is one of 14 "investors" in Imedix, Inc. Imedix was established on June 16, 1997, for the purpose of structuring, purchas-

201

Interim Decision #3361

ing, reorganizing, and upgrading health-care facilities in targeted areas of the United States. No clinics have yet been acquired, but the petitioner estimates that 27 clinics will employ approximately 194 employees.

The director determined that the petitioner had failed to make an active, at-risk investment in that the project was not even in the start-up phase; Imedix had not conducted any sort of business or financial analysis and had not engaged in any discussions with health-care facilities, state health officials, or real-estate agents, for example. The director also found that the required amount of capital had not been placed at risk and that the petitioner had failed to show that he was investing his own funds, obtained through lawful means. The director was further unable to ascertain a reasonable basis for Imedix's determination that it would create 194 positions, as this estimate was given without reference to medical needs of specific communities to be served.

After review of the evidence contained in the record, the decision of the director is found to be correct. Beyond the director's decision, other issues must be addressed. The affirmance of the director's decision is based not only on the director's findings but also on the findings discussed below.

The first issues concern the petitioner's payment agreement and his claimed assets abroad. As stated by the director, the petitioner agreed, pursuant to this payment agreement, to make an initial payment of $50,000, another payment within 30 days after the petition was approved, a payment of $200,000 one year after entry into the United States, and a final payment of $200,000 prior to the removal of the conditions of permanent resident status. The petitioner agreed to secure the principal sum of $500,000 by an assignment of his property having a net fair market value of $500,000.

The petitioner's claimed investment is in the form of a promissory note. A promissory note can constitute "capital" under 8 C.F.R. § 204.6(e) if the note is secured by assets owned by the petitioner. These assets must be specifically identified as securing the note. Furthermore, any security interest must be perfected to the extent provided for by the jurisdiction in which the asset is located,[1] and the asset must be fully amenable to seizure by a U.S. note holder.[2]

---

[1]This office notes that the Office of General Counsel ("OGC") has previously stated its opinion that the regulations do not require that indebtedness meet the requirements for secured transactions under Article 9 of the Uniform Commercial Code ("UCC"); similarly, OGC has stated that the regulations do not require that the lender perfect his security interest. Memorandum from Paul W. Virtue to Louis D. Crocetti, Jr. (June 27, 1995), *reprinted in* 72 INTERP. REL. 1209 (September 1, 1995), While the regulations do not specifically require that a promissory note be secured under the UCC, merely "identifying" assets as securing a loan, without perfecting the security interest, is not meaningful since the note holder cannot be assured that the identified assets will remain available for seizure in the event of default.

[2]See below for a discussion concerning the seizure of assets.

Interim Decision #3361

The petitioner has submitted no evidence that a security interest has been recorded in any particular property, and the promissory note does not even identify what assets are securing it. In addition, as the director stated in her decision, the petitioner has not established that the assets he claims to own in Taiwan are in fact his. The bank accounts at the Bank of Taiwan, containing NT$5,736,012 (US$199,613 as of September 3, 1997, according to counsel), belong to Dustin Hsiung; the petitioner has not demonstrated that he and Dustin Hsiung are the same person. The real estate in Taiwan, appraised at NT$11,167,843 (US$388,640 as of September 3, 1997), belongs to Ping-Hsiu Liu; the petitioner has not demonstrated that he and Ping-Hsiu Liu are the same person. Therefore, even if these assets were properly securing the note, the note does not meet the definition of "capital" because the petitioner has not shown that it is secured by his assets.

Assuming arguendo that the note at issue here did constitute "capital," the regulations at 8 C.F.R. § 204.6(e) further provide that all capital must be valued at fair market value in United States dollars. Whether a promissory note has a fair market value equivalent to its face value depends on many factors, including the value of the assets securing the note. The Taiwanese real estate, appraised at $388,640, is subject to a mortgage of NT$7,000,000 (approximately US$201,180). The net value of this real estate, then, is approximately $187,460. Assuming that the petitioner has made his initial payment of $50,000, assuming that the real estate and the money in the bank accounts (which contain $199,613) are his, and assuming that these assets do secure the promissory note, the net result is that a $450,000 obligation is being secured by only $387,073 in assets.[3] This is not sufficient to meet the fair-market-value requirement of the regulations.

The fair market value of a promissory note also depends on the amenability of the assets securing the note to seizure. Both the bank account and real estate are located abroad. In order for foreign assets, including real estate, to be considered as acceptable security, a petitioner must establish that the laws of the foreign country in which the assets are located would recognize, and permit execution of, a judgment of a court of the United States or of any State with respect to the foreign assets.[4] In the alternative, the petitioner must establish that the courts of that foreign country would themselves recognize and enforce the promissory note absent the judgment of an American court. Otherwise, the promissory note would clearly not have the value attributed to it by the petitioner. The petitioner here has not

---

[3] The current exchange rate is closer to NT$34.27 = US$1. WASHINGTON POST, July 21, 1998, at C10. At this exchange rate, the net value of the assets is only US$288,994.89.

[4] This, for example, could take the form of a transfer of ownership of the property to the creditor or it could take the form of a court-ordered liquidation and transfer of assets to the creditor.

Interim Decision #3361

presented any evidence as to Taiwanese law regarding the seizure of assets.

Even if assets can be reached under the laws of the applicable foreign country, considerable expense and effort would be involved in pursuing them. These factors would reduce the fair market value of a promissory note secured by foreign assets. It is not clear to what extent the value of the petitioner's promissory note should be reduced since the petitioner has not submitted any evidence as to the cost of enforcing a judgment against his purported property.

The fair market value of a promissory note further depends on its *present* value. *Matter of Izumii,* 22 I&N Dec. 169 (July 13, 1998), Money received today is worth more than money received tomorrow, and promissory notes are routinely discounted in recognition of this principle. A petitioner who bases his claim of investment on a promissory note must demonstrate that the promissory note has a fair market value equal to the amount of the investment. A petitioner cannot merely claim that his promissory note for $500,000 is worth $500,000, even if the note is properly secured with personal assets, amenable to seizure, of sufficient fair market value. This petitioner has not furnished evidence of the present value of his promissory note and has therefore failed to meet his burden.

To establish that the petitioner has invested, or is actively in the process of investing, he must show that he has placed the required amount of capital at risk.[5] 8 C.F.R. § 204.6(j)(2), The petitioner here has not shown that his assets are at risk. As discussed above, the petitioner has failed to demonstrate the following: that the bank accounts and real estate in Taiwan allegedly securing the note belong to him; that these assets are in fact securing the note; that any security interest in these assets has been perfected to the extent provided for under Taiwanese law; and that these assets are amenable to seizure. In addition, even if the petitioner had established ownership of these assets, he still has not shown that the requisite amount of money is at risk; he has failed to demonstrate that the assets in Taiwan have a total net fair market value of $500,000 (or $450,000 if he has already made his first payment of $50,000), and he has failed to allow for the estimated costs of seizing the assets should the need arise.

A further issue to be addressed concerns the petitioner's statement that Imedix plans to engage in "structuring, purchasing, reorganizing and upgrading health care facilities." Although the petitioner could argue that Imedix is the new commercial enterprise at issue here, the clinics Imedix claims it will purchase are pre-existing, ongoing businesses. Through his

---

[5]This applies regardless of whether the petitioner is claiming that his promissory note is itself capital or whether he claims that it is merely evidence that he is in the process of investing cash. An actual commitment does not exist if the petitioner's assets are not at risk. *See* 8 C.F.R. § 204.6(j)(2).

204

Interim Decision #3361

company's business activities, a petitioner cannot directly cause a net loss of employment. It is not known if the projected figure of "194" employees represents the maintenance of the former levels of employment at the unidentified clinics (in the case of troubled businesses), the addition of 10 new positions per investor, or an actual loss of employment.

ORDER: The decision of the director is affirmed. The petition is denied.

APPENDIX B: *CHANG V. INS*

FOR PUBLICATION
UNITED STATES COURT OF APPEALS FOR THE NINTH CIRCUIT

WEN-WAN CHANG; TSUNG-MING CHANG; CHIAO-YING CHANG; YI YUAN CHIANG; HSIEN-MING HSIEH; SHU-CHUAN HSIEH; PEI-CHEN HSIEH; SUNG DUCK KONG; HYE RA KONG; HYUN JUNG KONG; MIN SUK KONG; YEI-CHIEN LAI; YU KUEI LAI; YEN CHIH LAI; CHEN JU LAI; YOON SIK LEE; JONG HEE LEE; EUNG JUN LEE; SANG EUN LEE; EUNG SANG LEE; CHENG-HSIUNG SHE; HUI WEN SHE; TZU MING SHE; ALABAMA ALMARK, LP; ALABAMA BAILEY LP; ALABAMA COOSA LP; ALABAMA DALLAS LP; ALABAMA DENIM LP; ALABAMA MILLRY LP; ALABAMA PRO SPORTS LP; ALABAMA RIVE RUN LP; C & W HOTEL LP; DELAWARE MILFORD LP; GEORGIA ALMARK LP; LOUISIANA LASEVILLA LP; MISSISSIPPI BASS LP; MISSISSIPPI MAGEE LP; MISSISSIPPI MCT LP; MISSISSIPPI NEELY LP, Maryland Limited Partnerships; MISSISSIPPI TEES LP, a Mississippi Limited Partnership; NATIONAL STEAK RESTAURANTS LP; NORTH CAROLINA K-BARB LP; NORTH CAROLINA RUSSELL-HARVELLE HOSIERY LP; PENNSYLVANIA LOUNGEWEAR LP;

No. 01-56266
D.C. No.
CV-99-10518-GHK

5619

5620 CHANG v. UNITED STATES

RECAP FUND I LP; RECAP FUND V LP; RPC FUND I LP; SOUTH CAROLINA MANUFACTURING LP; TENNESSEE LAFAYETTE LP; WTC FUND I LP; UNITED STATES EXPORT FUND I LP, Maryland Limited Partnerships,
   Plaintiffs-Appellants,

v.

UNITED STATES OF AMERICA,
   Defendant-Appellee.

WEN-WAN CHANG; TSUNG-MING CHANG; CHIAO-YING CHANG; YI YUAN CHIANG; HSIEN-MING HSIEH; SHU-CHUAN HSIEH; PEI-CHEN HSIEH; SUNG DUCK KONG; HYE RA KONG; HYUN JUNG KONG; MIN SUK KONG; YEI-CHIEN LAI; YU KUEI LAI; YEN CHIH LAI; CHEN JU LAI; YOON SIK LEE; JONG HEE LEE; EUNG JUN LEE; SANG EUN LEE; EUNG SANG LEE; CHENG-HSIUNG SHE; HUI WEN SHE; TZU MING SHE; ALABAMA ALMARK, LP; ALABAMA BAILEY LP; ALABAMA COOSA LP; ALABAMA DALLAS LP; ALABAMA DENIM LP; ALABAMA MILLRY LP; ALABAMA PRO SPORTS LP; ALABAMA RIVE RUN LP; C & W HOTEL LP; DELAWARE MILFORD LP;

No. 01-56379
D.C. No.
CV-99-10518-GHK
OPINION

CHANG v. UNITED STATES   5621

GEORGIA ALMARK LP; LOUISIANA LASEVILLA LP; MISSISSIPPI BASS LP; MISSISSIPPI MAGEE LP; MISSISSIPPI MCT LP; MISSISSIPPI NEELY LP, Maryland Limited Partnerships; MISSISSIPPI TEES LP, a Mississippi Limited Partnership; NATIONAL STEAK RESTAURANTS LP; NORTH CAROLINA K-BARB LP; NORTH CAROLINA RUSSELL-HARVELLE HOSIERY LP; PENNSYLVANIA LOUNGEWEAR LP; RECAP FUND I LP; RECAP FUND V L; RPC FUND I LP; SOUTH CAROLINA MANUFACTURING LP; TENNESSEE LAFAYETTE LP; WTC FUND I LP; UNITED STATES EXPORT FUND I LP, Maryland Limited Partnerships,
        Plaintiffs-Appellees,

v.

UNITED STATES OF AMERICA,
        Defendant-Appellant.

Appeal from the United States District Court
for the Central District of California
George H. King, District Judge, Presiding

Argued and Submitted
February 10, 2003—Pasadena, California

Filed April 29, 2003

Before: Betty B. Fletcher and Michael Daly Hawkins, Circuit Judges, and David C. Bury, District Judge.*

Opinion by Judge B. Fletcher

*The Honorable David C. Bury, United States District Judge for the District of Arizona, sitting by designation.

COUNSEL

Ira J. Kurzban, Kurzban, Kurzban, Weinger & Tetzili, Miami, Florida, for the plaintiff-appellant-cross-appellee.

John C. Cunningham, Senior Litigation Counsel, and Heather Phillips, Attorney, Office of Immigration Litigation, Civil Division, U.S. Department of Justice, Washington, D.C., for the defendant-appellee-cross-appellant.

OPINION

B. FLETCHER, Circuit Judge:

Plaintiff-Appellants are seven "Immigrant Investors" who have participated in the "EB-5" program, which grants lawful permanent resident ("LPR") status in the United States to those who make qualifying investments under the Immigrant Investor Law ("IIL"), 8 U.S.C. §§ 1153(b)(5), 1186b; 8 C.F.R. §§ 204.6, 216.6.[1] Appellants complain that in 1998,

---

[1] The twenty-nine limited partnerships in which the Immigrant Investors invested were plaintiffs in the original action and are listed on the Notice of Appeal, but no appeal is taken from the district court's ruling denying them standing. Six of the Immigrant Investors among them have a total of sixteen dependents who are also nominal Appellants. The term "Appellants" will refer only to the Immigrant Investors.

after their investment proposals and business plans had been approved and they and their dependents had moved to the United States, the Immigration and Naturalization Service ("INS") changed the rules of the EB-5 program. Appellants contend that the INS applied these new rules to reject their applications at a stage in the process that called only for confirmation that they had fulfilled their part of the originally approved bargain. The government counters, *inter alia*, that new amendments to EB-5 in November, 2002 render the instant case moot and establish a new exhaustion requirement for some plaintiffs.

We hold that the recent amendments to EB-5 neither render this case moot nor establish an additional administrative appeal that plaintiffs must exhaust before obtaining judicial review. We hold further that the district court erred in finding that the claims of six Appellants were not ripe for adjudication and, therefore, that the district court should analyze whether a plaintiffs' class should be certified. Finally, we hold that the district court correctly rejected the motion to dismiss the retroactivity claim on the pleadings. It erred, however, in remanding to the INS. Because the analysis involves solely questions of law, we conduct the retroactivity analysis ourselves and conclude that the 1998 changes in the EB-5 rules are impermissibly retroactive as applied to the evaluation of Appellants' petitions to remove the conditions on their permanent residency.

I. *FACTUAL AND PROCEDURAL BACKGROUND*

Appellants have applied to become lawful permanent residents ("LPRs") under the EB-5 program, which grants such status to Immigrant Investors who create jobs for United States workers.[2] EB-5 requires prospective Immigrant Inves-

---

[2] To qualify for the program, applicants must invest $1,000,000 (or half that amount in certain targeted areas) in new enterprises that create at least ten full-time permanent jobs for U.S. workers. 8 U.S.C. § 1153(b)(5)(A)(i)-(iii), (C). Other requirements also apply, including some of those at issue in this case.

tors to file "I-526" petitions seeking approval of their submitted investment and business plans. After approval, Immigrant Investors and their dependents may enter the country as conditional LPRs. EB-5 requires the Immigrant Investors to file a second petition, an "I-829," between 21 and 24 months after the first petition. The INS is to approve the I-829 petition, and grant unconditional LPR status, if it finds that the petitioner made no material misrepresentations in the I-526 petition and complied with the EB-5 requirements. 8 C.F.R. §§ 204.6, 216.6.

The INS approved Appellants' initial I-526 petitions between July 1996 and July 1997. Upon approval, Appellants and their families moved to the United States with conditional LPR status. However, Appellants' I-526 petitions contained features that the INS now believes contravene the terms of the IIL program. For example: 1) Appellants were not partners at the inception of the limited partnerships in which they invested, 2) they were guaranteed the right to redeem their full investments after they received permanent residency, 3) they were guaranteed a return on their investments, 4) their promissory notes were insufficient because they were valued at face value and did not adequately reveal the personal assets securing the notes, and 5) they were permitted to make balloon payments to their limited partnerships or to continue making payments on their promissory notes beyond the end of their two-year conditional residency periods.[3] At the time the INS approved Appellants' I-526 petitions, these features were not considered by the INS to be disqualifying, but the INS has since declared that by structuring their investments in these ways Appellants had transformed them into loans.

AIS, the private agency that had recruited Appellants and channeled their investments into the limited partnerships, had

---

[3] For ease of reference, we will refer to all of the contested features of Appellants' investments as "redemption agreements and related provisions."

conferred with the INS to ensure its investment packages were acceptable. It made some changes as a result of its inquiries, and was assured that any further changes in the IIL would involve notice and comment rulemaking and apply prospectively. Ultimately, however, the INS instead established new rules for EB-5 applicants through a set of "precedent decisions" rejecting the appeals of other new applicants' I-526 petitions. The pertinent case for our purposes is *Matter of Izummi*, 22 I. & N. Dec. 169, Interim Decision (BIA) 3360 (1998), which held *inter alia* that Immigrant Investors' I-526 petitions could not be approved if the Immigrant Investors were not partners at the inception of a partnership or if their investment plans featured a redemption agreement or related provisions. Had the criteria announced in these decisions been in effect at the time Appellants filed their I-526 petitions, the petitions would not have been approved.

The precedent decisions were issued subsequent to the INS's approval of Appellants' I-526 petitions. However, the INS applied the new criteria to the Appellants' I-829 petitions. Prior to the district court hearing, it denied Appellant Yi Yuan Chiang's petition, as well as those of other similarly-situated non-plaintiffs, and placed the six other Appellants' petitions on indefinite "administrative hold." The INS argues that, based on the precedent decisions, a review of Appellants' I-829 petitions will not allow it to certify that Appellants have complied with the legal requirements of EB-5.

Appellants brought suit to force consideration of their I-829 petitions based solely on the criteria that were in effect when their I-526 petitions were approved. They argue that the INS should review the I-829 petitions only for whether they made material misrepresentations in their I-526 petitions and whether they executed their proposed plans. Appellants asked the district court (1) to estop the INS from applying its current interpretation of EB-5 to their I-829 petitions because it had approved their I-526 petitions, (2) to rule that the INS did not follow required Administrative Procedure Act notice and comment procedures for changing its rules governing EB-5, and (3) to rule that applying the new interpretations of the EB-5 law and regulations promulgated in the precedent decisions to their I-829 petitions would be impermissibly retroactive. They also sought certification as a class action.

The INS challenged the justiciability of Appellants' claims and moved for judgment on the pleadings pursuant to Federal Rule of Civil Procedure 12(c). The district court dismissed the claims of all petitioners except Chiang as not ripe and dismissed the motion for certification of a plaintiffs' class as moot. It granted the government's 12(c) motion on Chiang's estoppel and APA claims, but denied the motion on the retroactivity claim, holding that an analysis applying the factors presented in *Montgomery Ward & Co. v. FTC*, 691 F.2d 1322 (9th Cir. 1982), was appropriate. It remanded this claim to the INS for the agency to develop the record and conduct such an analysis.[4]

Appellants appeal the rulings on ripeness, mootness as to class certification, and the dismissal of their APA and estoppel claims. In its counterclaim, the government appeals the remand to the INS for a retroactivity analysis. The government also asserts that this court has no jurisdiction to consider Chiang's claim because 8 U.S.C. § 1186b mandates that appeals be pursued solely through the INS's administrative appeals process; it contends that the substantive issues raised by Chiang may reach this court only after being rejected by the INS in a removal proceeding. Appellants argue that this

---

[4]This is not a typical remand, but rather an invitation to the agency to reconsider its position that the precedent decisions could be applied to those in Chiang's position in light of the claim of impermissible retroactivity. The INS had previously refused a proposal for a voluntary remand to conduct such an analysis, contending that it had no statutory right to consider "hardship factors" in evaluating I-829 petitions, and stating that such arguments should be raised in removal proceedings. It reiterates these arguments in the current proceedings.

court has no jurisdiction to hear the government's counterclaim because the remand to the INS is not a final order.

On November 2, 2002, after this appeal was filed, Congress enacted the "21st Century Department of Justice Appropriations Authorization Act." Pub. L. No. 107-273, 116 Stat. 1758. "Subtitle B" of the act amended the Immigration and Naturalization Act and created a new class of "eligible aliens" who, like Appellants, had obtained approval of their I-526 petitions between January 1, 1995 and August 31, 1998, had conditional LPR status, and had filed their I-829 petitions on time. Under the statute, these eligible aliens may have their I-829 petitions approved under relaxed standards. If their I-526 petitions contained no material misrepresentations and their conditions were satisfied, they are given additional time, up to when the Attorney General makes his determination as to their eligibility, to bring their business ventures into compliance with the EB-5 program as changed by the new precedent decisions. Subtitle B also provides that aliens like Appellant Chiang, whose I-829 petitions have already been rejected, may reopen their cases by filing for reconsideration by January 1, 2003.

The government argues that Appellants' claims are moot because the November 2002 "Subtitle B" amendments grant all appropriate relief in this case. It further argues that Chiang's claim should be dismissed for failure to exhaust his administrative remedies if he did not meet the January 1 deadline for invoking the new appeal procedures of Subtitle B. Finally, the government argues that the appeals of all Appellants but Chiang were not ripe for consideration by the district court because the INS had not yet denied their I-829 applications.

We consider these arguments in turn.

II. *ISSUES PRESENTED ON APPEAL*

A. *Subtitle B*

1. *Mootness*

[1] Mootness is a question of law reviewed *de novo. Biodiversity Legal Found. v. Badgley*, 284 F.3d 1046, 1053 (9th Cir. 2002). A case properly brought in the first instance is rendered moot when "interim relief or events have completely and irrevocably eradicated the effects of the alleged violation." *County of Los Angeles v. Davis*, 440 U.S. 625, 631 (1979). The party asserting mootness carries a heavy burden of establishing that no effective relief remains for the court to provide. *GATX/Airlog Co. v. United States District Court*, 192 F.3d 1304, 1306 (9th Cir. 1999). Were Appellants' only claims that they were denied permanent LPR status because they purportedly violated EB-5's requirements by entering limited partnerships subsequent to their formation, the government would have a strong argument for mootness. But the crux of this case, and the focus of the INS's concern, is the presence of redemption agreements and related provisions in Appellants' investment plans. Appellants' I-829 petitions still stand to be rejected, under Subtitle B, if they are not in compliance with the INS's current construction of EB-5 in this respect as well.[5] Because this court has the capacity to grant relief by declaring that the ban on redemption agreements and related provisions could not be applied to Appellants at all, this case is not moot.

---

[5]The government argues that Subtitle B affords Appellants the opportunity, even now, to comply with the new regulations. But doing so could require an EB-5 petitioner who had already recouped his investment through a redemption agreement to rapidly collect as much as $1,000,000 and reinvest it in a company under terms that, he argues, were not required of him at the time his I-526 petition was approved. This is not an equivalent substitute for the relief requested from this court.

2. *Exhaustion*

Appellants have sought to certify a class action. The government argues that the claim of anyone whose I-829 petition was denied, but who did not file to reopen his or her case by January 1, 2003, should be dismissed as unexhausted; he or she would of necessity thus be excluded from such a proposed class.[6] In deciding whether such petitioners must be excluded from any certified class, we must ask whether and how exhaustion should apply when a new law grants a class of applicants 60 days after its enactment to initiate a new appeals process or else waive all further right to pursue administrative or judicial relief, including pending judicial relief. Whether administrative remedies must be exhausted is a question of law reviewed *de novo. Rumbles v. Hill*, 182 F.3d 1064, 1067 (9th Cir. 1999).

a. *Does Subtitle B establish a new exhaustion requirement?*

We do not face the question here of whether Congress may enact legislation explicitly extinguishing the right of a class of plaintiffs to sue the government by creating a new administrative remedy that must be invoked within a limited time period to preserve the right. The government's argument is that, by setting a 60-day limit, Congress did so *implicitly.* Even if Congress could preempt civil suits against the government by suddenly setting imminent deadlines for plaintiffs to avail themselves of such administrative channels in order to retain standing,[7] it does not follow that the courts should

---

[6] We do not know whether Chiang filed to reopen his petition by that deadline. But given the number of others who were similarly situated, the question of whether, after enactment of Subtitle B, they must be excluded from any possible proposed class is nevertheless before us. Unlike Chiang, they would not all be involved in a pending lawsuit. The likelihood of some not having known of or met the deadline is high.

[7] Subtitle B is contained in a large appropriation bill. Whether Appellant Chiang and those similarly situated knew of its imminent deadline in sufficient time to react to it, we can say with certainty only that this court did not. The government's motion to dismiss for mootness reached this court on January 21, 2003, precisely twenty days after the deadline expired and twenty days before this case was heard.

apply the principle of exhaustion to require that outcome where Congress's intent to do so is at best implicit. We avoid the issue here because we need only apply well-established principles addressing retroactive application of law.

In the government's view, while Subtitle B granted Chiang and those similarly situated new rights, it also removed others: Chiang gained the right to pursue a new administrative remedy, but immediately lost the right to pursue permanent residence under the rules extant when his I-526 petition was approved. He also would lose the right to pursue relief of any kind if he failed to file a petition by January 1, 2003. Because Congress did not explicitly express its intention to make the statute retroactive, we must ask if Subtitle B, so construed, had an impermissible retroactive application upon Chiang and others whose I-526 approvals are jeopardized by the rejection of their I-829s and the expiration of Subtitle B's deadline. If we find an impermissible retroactive application, we must construe Subtitle B not to impose a new exhaustion requirement on appellants and those similarly situated.

b. *Applicable principles of retroactivity analysis*: Retroactive application of statutes is disfavored in the absence of clear contrary Congressional intent. *See, e.g., Martin v. Hadix,* 527 U.S. 343, 352 (1999); *Landgraf v. USI Film Prods.,* 511 U.S. 244, 270 (1994). Whether a statute has a retroactive effect is a fairly straightforward question: it is retroactive if it alters the legal consequences of acts completed before its effective date. *Miller v. Florida,* 482 U.S. 423, 430 (1987). Specifically, a statute has retroactive effect when it "takes away or impairs vested rights acquired under existing laws, or creates a new obligation, imposes a new duty, or attaches a new disability, in respect to transactions or considerations already past." *Landgraf,* 511 U.S. at 269. In considering a law's retroactive effect, the court's analysis is to be guided by three "familiar considerations" that the Supreme Court has clearly enunciated: reasonable reliance, fair notice, and settled expectations. *Id.* at 270.

As the Supreme Court emphasizes in *INS v. St. Cyr*, 533 U.S. 289 (2001), the test set forth in *Landgraf* " 'does not purport to define the outer limit of impermissible retroactivity' " but instead "simply describes several 'sufficient,' as opposed to 'necessary,' conditions for finding retroactivity." *Id.* at 321 n.46 (quoting *Hughes Aircraft Co. v. United States ex rel. Schumer*, 520 U.S. 939, 947 (1997)).[8] In short, *Landgraf* requires that a court conduct a two-pronged analysis: first, the court must ask whether a law imposes new negative consequences on past actions; second, the court must ask whether those consequences are imposed without fair notice, or in a manner that undermines reasonable reliance or upsets settled expectations.

c. *Application of retroactivity principles to Subtitle B*: Subtitle B, as portrayed by the government, attached a new disability to the previous actions of Immigrant Investors who entered into limited partnerships after their initial formation by establishing a deadline for them to file a form initiating administrative review of their case or lose all right to seek relief. It also imposed a new exhaustion requirement on eligible aliens whose I-829 petitions were rejected for any reason. These actions eliminated what we conclude below is the right of an Immigrant Investor whose I-829 petition had been rejected due to application of the precedent decisions to appeal that decision to district court. This retroactive application of Subtitle B was imposed in violation of the right to fair notice.

---

[8]No single consideration is essential. Retroactivity analysis under *Landgraf* requires independent analysis of whatever factors may apply, any of which can ground a finding of impermissible retroactive application. *See, e.g., Landgraf*, 511 U.S. at 275, 282 (independently assessing reasonable reliance and fair notice); *United States v. Velasco-Medina*, 305 F.3d 839, 849-50 (9th Cir. 2002) (independently assessing fair notice and settled expectations). Reasonable reliance may itself be based upon a quid pro quo, as in *St. Cyr*, 533 U.S. at 320-25 or merely on assurances as to the current status of the law, *see, e.g., Hughes Aircraft*, 520 U.S. at 951-52.

The government knew precisely which individuals had had their I-829 petitions rejected based on the rules from the precedent decisions; it had done the rejecting. It also had, at the least, relatively current information about how to contact them. And yet, beyond publication of the potentially life-altering one-sentence deadline within a massive appropriations bill, the government indicated at oral hearing that it took no steps to notify these individuals that they had no more than sixty days to preserve any possibility of judicial review of their case. The government may not take away such rights without fair notice. We do not explore whether providing a longer amount of time, or announcing the new policy more prominently, or individually notifying those to be affected — since the government had that information readily at hand — would have been necessary or sufficient to constitute fair notice. But taking the right of judicial review away from perhaps unrepresented individuals by imposing such a precipitous deadline is a prohibited retroactive application of law.

[2] We therefore construe Subtitle B not to impose an additional exhaustion requirement on those whose I-829 petitions had been rejected before the statute's effective date, but who did not file to reopen their cases by the January 1, 2003 deadline. On remand, the district court must consider certifying classes without respect to whether prospective class members have or have not availed themselves of the opportunity for relief under Subtitle B.[9]

B. *Ripeness of claims of Appellants other than Chiang*

Ripeness is a question of law reviewed *de novo*. *Daniel v.*

---

[9]The government argues that the motion for class certification was untimely under local circuit rules. But the motion was not denied for this reason, and the court never suggested that it would be; the stated reason for dismissal was mootness. In any event, Plaintiffs had filed a motion to enlarge the time for filing, which the district court never ruled upon due to its mootness ruling.

County of Santa Barbara, 288 F.3d 375, 380 (9th Cir. 2002). It turns on the constitutional consideration of "whether the plaintiffs face a realistic danger of sustaining a direct injury" from the challenged act, *City of Auburn v. Qwest Corp.*, 260 F.3d 1160, 1171 (9th Cir. 2001) (internal quotation marks omitted), and on the prudential considerations of whether the issue is fit for decision and whether parties will suffer hardship if the court declines to consider it. *Id.* at 1172-73. This court "does not require Damocles's sword to fall before we recognize the realistic danger of sustaining a direct injury." *Id.* at 1171. Here, the INS has already failed to act upon Plaintiffs' I-829 petitions within the 90-day period required by statute. 8 C.F.R. § 216.6(c)(1). It is undisputed that Appellants' I-829 petitions will be rejected if the standards of the precedent decisions are applied to them.

As the district court noted, ordinarily under *Reno v. Catholic Social Services, Inc.*, 509 U.S. 43 (1993) a formal denial of an alien's application on the disputed grounds is required, but if denial is certain review will not be barred based on ripeness. *Id.* at 69-71 (O'Connor concurring). In *Freedom to Travel Campaign v. Newcomb*, 82 F.3d 1431, 1436 (9th Cir. 1996), this court expressly adopted the "firm prediction" rule from Justice O'Connor's *Catholic Social Services* concurrence, which eliminates the need to await an inevitable application of a regulation to a plaintiff before determining a claim to be justiciable.

Prudential considerations also favor review. The issues remaining are legal and do not require further factual development. The uncertain state of the law is sufficient hardship to prompt judicial review, *see Thomas v. Union Carbide Agric. Prods. Co.*, 473 U.S. 568, 581 (1985), but Appellants' businesses are also suffering from lack of clarity about their prospects. Delay injures Appellants' hopes for obtaining permanent residence status, and if their position is indeed futile, they would best abandon their present course and start again. Nothing is gained from postponement, either from the aliens' or the government's perspective. Accordingly, the district court erred when it dismissed the claims of the Appellants other than Chiang as not ripe for review. Ripeness is not a bar to this action, and the district court must consider the merits of class certification.

C. *Subject matter jurisdiction to review denial of Chiang's I-826 petition*

The government argues that EB-5 sets forth an administrative process requiring that appeals of the rejection of I-829 petitions take place solely through removal hearings, and thus that the district court had no jurisdiction to hear Chiang's claim. This raises the questions of whether the APA requires that these administrative review procedures be exhausted before an appeal is brought to the district court, and whether the administrative review process offered by the INS is adequate. Subject matter jurisdiction is a question of law reviewed *de novo. Delta Savings Bank v. United States*, 265 F.3d 1017, 1024 (9th Cir. 2001).

1. *Must administrative review be exhausted?*

The district court properly asserted jurisdiction to review the denial of Chiang's I-829 petition because 8 U.S.C. § 1186b (INA § 216A) does not state that review of such a denial must occur exclusively in removal proceedings. Absent language foreclosing immediate judicial review, a district court's subject matter jurisdiction is unaffected by the availability of non-mandatory administrative procedures. *See, e.g., Darby v. Cisneros*, 509 U.S. 137, 154 (1993) ("[W]here the APA applies, an appeal to 'superior agency authority' is a prerequisite to judicial review *only* when expressly required by statute or when an agency rule requires appeal before review and the administrative action is made inoperative pending that review.") (emphasis in original). The government reads the language of 8 U.S.C. § 1186b(c)(3)(D) — "[A]ny alien whose permanent residence status is terminated under subparagraph (C) may request a review . . . in a proceeding to remove the alien" — as establishing an exclusive review process. However, while this language permits an alien to elect initial administrative review, it does not expressly mandate that course.

Given the courts' deference to agency interpretation of their governing statutes, however, see *Chevron U.S.A., Inc. v. Natural Resources Defense Council*, 467 U.S. 837, 842-45 (1994), we do not end our analysis here. If the INS's interpretation of § 1186b(c)(3)(D) were to be accepted, administrative review would still be required only if that review provides an adequate remedy. See *Bowen v. Massachusetts*, 487 U.S. 879, 901 (1988) (finding that a statute providing for administrative review does not bar relief, since the "doubtful and limited relief available . . . is not an adequate substitute for review in the District Court.") We therefore consider the adequacy of the administrative review.

2. Is administrative review adequate?

In *Winterberger v. General Teamsters Auto Truck Drivers & Helpers*, 558 F.2d 923 (9th Cir. 1977), we stated:

> Ordinarily, a court possesses jurisdiction to review an . . . administrative-like proceeding whether or not the aggrieved party has exhausted administrative remedies. But as a matter of sound policy, courts usually decline to intercede and in most instances act within their discretion in doing so. However, there are occasions when a court is obliged to exercise its jurisdiction and is guilty of an abuse of discretion if it does not, the most familiar examples perhaps being when resort to the administrative route is futile or the remedy inadequate.

Id. at 925 (citations omitted). In assessing whether this court has jurisdiction, "the Administrative Procedure Act's gener-

5640	CHANG V. UNITED STATES

ous [judicial] review provisions must be given a hospitable interpretation." *Abbott Laboratories v. Gardner*, 387 U.S. 136, 140-141 (1967) (internal quotation marks omitted). The Supreme Court has repeatedly upheld an aggrieved party's prompt access to the district court when it provides greater redress and broader opportunity to develop a claim than is available in a more limited statutory scheme. *See, e.g., Bowen*, 487 U.S. at 904; *McNary v. Haitian Refugee Ctr., Inc.*, 498 U.S. 479, 496-97 (1991); *Bowen v. Michigan Acad. of Family Physicians*, 476 U.S. 667, 670 (1986).

Here Appellants' access to removal proceedings is an inadequate substitute for prompt access to judicial review. The denial of an I-829 petition is a final and non-appealable agency action, *see* 5 U.S.C. § 704, with immediate concrete injuries. Upon termination of LPR status, aliens must surrender their "Permanent Resident Cards" upon request and cannot lawfully work in the country without special documentation that can be revoked at any time. 8 C.F.R. § 216.6(d)(2). The clock begins to run on their period of "unlawful presence" in the country, which can lead to their exclusion from the country for up to ten years. 8 U.S.C. § 1182(a)(9)(B). Furthermore, because the INS need not commence removal proceedings immediately, conditioning aliens' access to an Article III court on their first having undergone removal proceedings would leave them in limbo in the interim. Should they lose an appeal, final orders of removal carry an additional ten-year bar to seeking readmission to the United States. *Id.* § 1182(a)(9)(A)(ii).

Removal proceedings are not designed to develop an adequate record for judicial review of the issues at stake for these appellants, but rather to test the veracity of the petition, which is not what is at issue in this case. *See id.* § 1186b(c)(3)(D) ("[T]he burden of proof shall be on the Attorney General to establish . . . that the facts and information . . . alleged in the petition are not true with respect to the qualifying commercial enterprise.")

The immigration judge in removal proceedings cannot hear the sorts of claims at issue here, which include whether equitable relief is available, whether APA notice and comment was required before promulgating new rules, and whether constitutional claims challenging the rule of law applied in their case. Such claims lie outside the scope and jurisdiction of the immigration judges and the BIA. For example, the BIA has held that even though district courts may apply the doctrine of equitable estoppel against the INS — relief requested in this case — administrative judges may not. *Matter of Hernandez-Puente*, 20 I. & N. Dec. 335, 338-39 (BIA 1991). The BIA has likewise disclaimed authority to adjudicate APA claims, also at issue in this case. *See Matter of Hector Ponce de Leon-Ruiz*, 21 I. & N. Dec. 154, 165 (BIA 1996) ("[The BIA does not] assess[ ] regulatory compliance with the APA, . . . [and should make no] observations in this area where we lack expertise. We ourselves are exclusively a creature of the Attorney General's regulations, and we have properly left it to the courts to resolve questions of APA compliance."). Finally, the BIA has also disclaimed authority to consider constitutional claims in removal hearings. *See Matter of Cenatice*, 16 I. & N. Dec. 162, 166 (BIA 1977) ("[I]t is not within the province of this Board to pass upon the constitutionality of the statutes it administers, but rather is solely within the power and capacity of the United States courts to declare them unconstitutional."). As a result, removal hearings would not establish a record on the critical issues; statutory appeal would be to our court.

The limitation on the scope of removal proceedings is particularly problematic because we would be limited to this inadequate record by 8 U.S.C. § 1252(b)(4)(A): "With respect to review of an order of removal . . . the court of appeals shall decide the petition only on the administrative record on which the order of removal is based." Furthermore, 8 U.S.C. § 1252(b)(4)(B) mandates that "administrative findings of fact are conclusive unless any reasonable adjudicator would be compelled to conclude to the contrary." Cases requiring factual development beyond the scope of removal proceedings are generally channeled to the district court, which will afford more full appellate review. *See, e.g., Mohammadi-Motlagh v. INS*, 727 F.2d 1450, 1452-53 (9th Cir. 1984) ("The BIA lacked authority to hear and determine these factual issues and did not do so. We are therefore without jurisdiction to consider these claims. They must be raised in the first instance in the district court."). Given the above, we hold that even if the APA did require that administrative remedies be exhausted before recourse to Article III courts, removal proceedings are not adequate for this purpose.

3. *Ripeness of Chiang's claim.*

The government argues that Chiang's claim is not yet ripe for adjudication, because he has not yet been subjected to the removal process, and urges that this court wait to rule on this issue until he appeals from a removal order. For reasons expressed in our previous discussion of ripeness, and because we find the removal process inadequate to the task at hand, we hold that Chiang's appeal was ripe for adjudication, and that the district court properly exercised jurisdiction over it.

D. *Improper Retroactive Effect*

The district court dismissed Chiang's claims that the precedent decisions violated APA notice and comment rulemaking provisions and were barred by estoppel, but it refused to dismiss Chiang's claim that the precedent decisions were improperly retroactive. The district court remanded Chiang's I-829 petition to the INS to apply factors presented in *Montgomery Ward & Co. v. FTC*, 691 F.2d 1322 (9th Cir. 1982) for determining the propriety of retroactively applying the precedent decisions.

1. *Jurisdiction.*

Appellants assert that this court lacks jurisdiction to consider the government's counterclaim because the district court's remand to the INS for a retroactivity analysis is not a final and appealable order, but interlocutory. We construe the remand as a decision to require exhaustion of administrative remedies. "The basic purpose of the exhaustion doctrine is to allow an administrative agency to perform functions within its special competence — to make a factual record, to apply its expertise, and to correct its own errors so as to moot judicial controversies." *Parisi v Davidson*, 405 U.S. 34, 37 (1972). Since record development is unnecessary and the INS has no special expertise to do the retroactivity analysis, we interpret the remand to be an offer to the agency to correct its error. We review for abuse of discretion the decision of the court to require exhaustion. *See Pension Benefit Guar. Corp. v. Carter & Tillery Enters.*, 133 F.3d 1183, 1187 (9th Cir. 1998).

The Supreme Court instructs that final order jurisdiction is to be given a "practical rather than a technical construction," *Gillespie v. U.S. Steel Corp.*, 379 U.S. 148, 152 (1964). One justification for hearing interlocutory appeals is to avoid a "totally wasted proceeding below." *Stone v. Heckler*, 722 F.2d 464, 467 (9th Cir. 1983). Here, the INS contends that it has no authority to apply the *Montgomery Ward* factors outside of a removal proceeding, and no such proceeding has come before it.

We are persuaded by the government's argument that, given the INS's stance, a remand to that agency now would simply waste judicial resources. The INS holds fast to its position that it cannot conduct such an analysis outside of a removal proceeding, and there is no need to force it to do so. *See Young v. Reno*, 114 F.3d 879, 881-82 (9th Cir. 1997) (noting exception to exhaustion requirement where recourse within the agency is futile); *Winterberger*, 558 F.2d at 925. "An abuse of discretion occurs if the court applies the correct law to facts which are not clearly erroneous but rules in an irrational manner." *United States v. Sherburne*, 249 F.3d 1121, 1125-26 (9th Cir. 2001) (internal quotation marks omitted). While the district judge was admirably solicitous of the

5644   CHANG V. UNITED STATES

INS in offering it the opportunity to conduct a retroactivity analysis in the first instance, wasting judicial resources by remanding to the INS for it to do what it firmly states it may not and will not do is irrational, even if well-motivated. The district court was itself fully capable of doing what it asked the INS to do against its will. The remand was thus an abuse of discretion. We accept jurisdiction over the interlocutory appeal to decide the retroactivity claim.

2. *Reaching the retroactivity analysis*

[3] In refusing to dismiss Appellants' claim on the pleadings, the district court stated:

> [I]n denying Plaintiff Chiang's I-829 petition, the INS relied largely on principles announced in the Precedent Decisions. In effect, having already approved Plaintiff Chiang's investment program by virtue of its approval of his I-526 petition, the INS effectively changed the rules of the game by judging Plaintiff Chiang's I-829 petition under the Precedent Decisions even though Plaintiff Chiang had not altered his previously approved investment program, and had not acted in a way which would otherwise justify denial of the I-829, but for the Precedent Decisions.

The district court's findings of fact are not clearly erroneous. We agree with its consequent analysis. The government raises three arguments as to why a retroactivity analysis is inappropriate, each of which is unavailing.

    a. *Retroactive application is not a "hardship factor"*. While the government continues to argue that retroactivity is a "hardship factor" that has no place in analysis of I-829 petitions, the district court correctly noted that *Montgomery Ward* did not involve applying hardship factors, but "a wholly different analysis . . . that examines degree of burden on the parties." A finding of impermissible retroactivity would not waive compliance with the new EB-5 requirements as a matter of beneficence due to hardship, but would refuse to impose the new requirements because Appellants had the legal right to have their petitions "grandfathered" under the previous standards.

b. *A finding of retroactive application is not foreclosed by prior case law.* We reject the government's contention that the question of improper retroactive application of the precedent decisions against Appellants was resolved in *R.L. Investment Limited Partners v. INS*, 273 F.3d 874 (9th Cir. 2001) (*"RLILP"*) (adopting in full the district court's decision in *R.L. Investment Limited Partners v. INS*, 86 F. Supp. 2d 1014 (D. Haw., 2000)).[10] The *RLILP* plaintiffs were not situated similarly to Appellants in the instant case: as their I-526 petitions had not been approved, they had no reliance interest comparable to that of Appellants. They challenged the prospective application of the precedent decisions to their new unapproved I-526 applications, on the basis that the INS had violated the APA in changing what they contended was its longstanding policy of allowing redemption agreements and related provisions. By contrast, because Appellants' own I-526 petitions had been approved, and they had acted relying on that approval, a different mix of considerations guide the appropriate analysis. Furthermore, *RLILP*'s holding that the precedent decisions did not "effect a change in existing law" applied only to 8 C.F.R. § 204.6, which governs review of I-526 petitions. The question we face is whether applying the precedent decisions to I-829 petitions effects a change in 8 C.F.R. § 216.6, which governs review of I-829 petitions. This

---

[10] The opinion of our court came down after the district court opinion in this case. Because the argument that the INS's rules were retroactive had not been raised before the district court, the appellate panel rejected it as defaulted without reaching the merits. *RLILP*, 273 F.3d at 874-75.

5646   CHANG v. UNITED STATES

question is analytically distinct from that before the *RLILP* court.[11]

c. I-829 applications need not receive ab initio *review*. The crux of the government's position is that the *Montgomery Ward* retroactivity concerns do not apply to EB-5 applications, because EB-5 requires a "fresh demonstration of compliance with statutory standards at the I-829 stage." However, if I-526 approval is decoupled from I-829 approval, then petitioners whose I-526 petitions had been approved would have no reasonable reliance that the rules set out in 8 C.F.R. § 216.6 would not change in midstream. If, on the other hand, approval of the I-526 petition was an official provisional approval of the petitioner's plan, contingent on its effectuation, then a retroactivity analysis is required.

[4] The EB-5 statute requires that each I-829 petition "shall contain facts and information demonstrating that — (A) a commercial enterprise was established by the alien; (B) the alien invested or was actively in the process of investing the requisite capital; and (C) the alien sustained [these actions] throughout the period of the alien's residence in the United States." 8 U.S.C. § 1186b(d)(1). In 8 C.F.R. § 216.6(d), examples of the appropriate documentation include tax returns, to show that the enterprise was in fact established; an audited financial statement, to show that the alien had actually invested; and bank statements, invoices, receipts, contracts, business licenses, and payroll records to show that the petitioner had sustained the actions throughout the two year conditional residence period. This is in marked contrast to the documentation requirements of 8 C.F.R. § 204.6(j), governing

---

[11]It is also immaterial that, as the government argues, "the final result of an adjudicatory proceeding will [always] have a retroactive effect on the positions of parties to that proceeding," because Appellants were not parties to the precedent decisions. However, the fact that Appellants were not parties to the precedent decisions does not obviate the need for a retroactivity analysis; rules generated through adjudications are not exempt from such analysis.

approval of the I-526 petition. We will not review the several pages of requirements listed in this subsection; suffice it to say that they require a much more comprehensive documentation of the petitioner's plans and resources.

[5] The language of 8 U.S.C. § 1186b(d)(1) and the contrast between the documentation requirements of the regulations at each stage of the approval process strongly support the view that I-829 approval is a procedure intended to confirm that the petitioner fulfilled the plan set out in the I-526 petition. The government's contention that I-829 approval proceeds *ab initio* — and that I-526 approval therefore may not be relied upon as setting forth a plan that, if followed, will lead to I-829 approval — is not sustainable. The government argues that I-526 approval neither guarantees nor predicts I-829 approval, but the latter is clearly untrue. I-526 approval does not guarantee I-829 approval — the petitioner might not successfully "sustain the actions . . . throughout the period of . . . residence" — but it certainly predicts it. No one obtains I-829 approval without prior I-526 approval. The government provides no reason to believe that the combination of I-526 approval, successful execution of the approved plan, and absence of material misrepresentation in the I-526 petition — all characteristics that Appellants claim apply to them — was not an excellent predictor of I-829 approval up until the precedent decisions appeared.

[6] We conclude that Appellants reasonably relied on the application of 8 C.F.R. § 216.6 extant when their I-526 petitions were approved. We conclude that the INS's refashioning of 8 C.F.R. § 216.6 into an independent *ab initio* assessment of Appellants' satisfaction of the EB-5 program standards raises serious retroactivity concerns.

d. *Initial retroactivity analysis may be conducted by this court*. For the above reasons, we affirm the district court's refusal to dismiss the retroactivity claim. We further conclude that the record is already sufficiently developed to allow us to undertake the retroactivity analysis. The parties briefed the issue of retroactivity and application of the *Montgomery Ward* factors and argued the issue before the district court. "Although we ordinarily do not consider an issue not passed upon below, the decision to resolve a question for the first time on appeal is one left primarily to the discretion of the courts of appeals. . . . It is sometimes appropriate for an appellate court to pass on issues of law that the trial court did not consider." *City of Auburn*, 260 F.3d at 1173 (citations and internal quotation marks omitted). Application of the *Montgomery Ward* factors is now purely a matter of applying the law. We are as well situated as the district court to perform this retroactivity analysis. We elect to do so.

3. *Merits of the retroactivity claim*

[7] In *Montgomery Ward*, this court adopted the five-factor analytical framework set forth in *Retail, Wholesale and Department Store Union v. NLRB*, 466 F.2d 380, 390-93 (D.C. Cir. 1972). This test balances a regulated party's interest in being able to rely on the terms of a rule as it is written against an agency's interest in retroactive application of an adjudicatory decision:

> Among the considerations that enter into a resolution of the problem are (1) whether the particular case is one of first impression, (2) whether the new rule represents an abrupt departure from well established practice or merely attempts to fill a void in an unsettled area of law, (3) the extent to which the party against whom the new rule is applied relied on the former rule, (4) the degree of the burden which a retroactive order imposes on a party, and (5) the statutory interest in applying a new rule despite the reliance of a party on the old standard.

Montgomery Ward & Co. v. FTC, 691 F.2d 1322, 1333 (9th Cir. 1982).

[8] The present case is one of first impression, which weighs in the government's favor. But the next two factors weigh heavily in Appellants' favor. The INS's history of approving I-829 petitions without respect to the presence of redemption agreements and related provisions was a well established practice. The approval of Appellants' own I-526 petitions containing such provisions shows that this practice continued at least until shortly before the publication of the precedent decisions; the rules introduced in those decisions were an abrupt departure. Appellants also relied on their understanding that their business and investment plans conformed to the requirements of EB-5. They sold businesses, uprooted from their homelands, and moved to the U.S. They had assurance that the redemption agreements and related provisions in their business plans would not obstruct their applications for permanent residency.

[9] We now turn to balancing the burdens on the parties. The new regulations impose a substantial burden upon Appellants. Appellants are given a choice: either they invest or commit to reinvest large sums of money immediately, or they and their dependents must leave the United States. The latter course would mean starting the process of applying to the EB-5 program over again, with uncertain results, or possibly subject to bar on re-entry given their deemed unlawful presence in the United States. Either alternative involves substantial sacrifice.

The government argues that Appellants have suffered no burden, since they can ask for their money back from the limited partnerships in which they invested. But the burden at issue is not merely whether Appellants can now recoup their investments if they have not already done so. It also involves whether the time and expense put into their good faith efforts to obtain LPR status will have been squandered. The government also argues that to the extent that Appellants severed ties to their home countries, they did so at their own risk and not on the basis of any assurances from the INS. This argument misses the point in an instructive way. Appellants sought no guarantee of success, but a contingent promise that, if they held up their end of the bargain by fulfilling the terms of their approved I-526 petitions, they would obtain the LPR status promised by the EB-5 program. This was not unreasonable.

[10] Against the burdens on Appellants weighs the factor of the INS's statutory interest in applying the new rule to these Appellants and those similarly situated. That interest is insufficiently substantial to outweigh the other factors. We do not fault the INS for determining that its earlier approvals of I-526 petitions interpreted the EB-5 program in ways that arguably contravened Congressional intent. It then closed what it considered to be a set of loopholes. We will assume *arguendo* that its initial policy was mistaken and its remedial efforts justified.

The consequences of the INS's mistake are not overwhelming. If a class action is certified, approximately 250 Immigrant Investors and perhaps 350 more of their dependents may be granted permanent residency. The government has never argued that this class of Immigrant Investors did not act in good faith, nor that the efforts they undertook to avail themselves of the EB-5 program were negligible. From Appellants' perspective, the INS's approving and receiving the benefits of their investments, only to renege on the promise of LPR status once those benefits were garnered, must seem very unfair. It is hard to imagine how the INS has a compelling statutory interest in such an outcome. Congress has not repealed the EB-5 program; it still intends for it to continue. The reputation and integrity of the EB-5 program is ill-served by the proposition that INS approval of an I-526 petition as satisfying EB-5's requirements cannot be relied upon.

[11] On balance, after applying the *Montgomery Ward* factors, we conclude that the application of the INS's intended change in the function of I-829 review is impermissibly retroactive as applied to Appellants.

4. *Implications of the retroactivity analysis*

Ultimately, the INS's fundamental argument is simply that it is not authorized to certify that Appellants' I-829 petitions satisfy the requirements of EB-5 in light of the precedent decisions. The INS's position that it cannot grandfather Appellants' petitions under its previous construction of EB-5 of its own accord is understandable. But, the INS certainly *can* do so pursuant to a court order requiring that in reviewing the I-829 petitions of those whose I-526 petitions had already been approved, it may not apply the rules introduced in the 1998 precedent decisions because such action fails the balancing test of *Montgomery Ward*.

Because we rule that the INS may not apply the rules introduced in the precedent decisions in evaluating Appellants' I-829 petitions, we need not address Appellants' estoppel and APA notice and comment claims, as they would afford Appellants no additional relief even were we to reverse the district court.

III. CONCLUSION

All of Appellants' claims were ripe, none were moot, no further exhaustion of the administrative process was necessary, and no statute ousted our jurisdiction. We also have jurisdiction over the government's counterclaim.

Retroactive application of the new rules adopted by the 1998 precedent decisions to Appellants' I-829 petitions is impermissible. The INS may not apply the rules established in the 1998 precedent decisions in reviewing the I-829 petitions of those whose I-526 petitions had been approved before those new rules were promulgated. The remaining issue in this case is whether one or more plaintiffs' classes should be certified; we remand back to the district court for that determination. This panel will retain jurisdiction over all future appeals deriving from these claims. Costs are taxed against the United States. The decision of the district court is

AFFIRMED IN PART, REVERSED IN PART, VACATED IN PART, AND REMANDED WITH INSTRUCTIONS.

APPENDIX C-1: YATES MEMO OF 1-19-05

U.S. Department of Homeland Security
20 Massachusetts Ave
Washington, DC 20529

U.S. Citizenship and Immigration Services

HQPRD 70/6.2.8

Interoffice Memorandum

To: All Service Center Directors
Regional Directors

From: William R. Yates
Associate Director
Operations

Date: JAN 1 9 2005

Re: <u>Establishment of an Investor and Regional Center Unit</u>

PURPOSE

Effective the date of this memo, oversight for policy and regulation development, field guidance, form design, case auditing, and training regarding Regional Center adjudications and associated investor petitions within the EB-5 Investor Program, shall reside with PRD/Investor and Regional Center Unit (IRCU). Given the well documented past abuses in the alien investor program, and the complexity and sensitivity of the issues and factors relating to both Regional Centers as well as with individual alien investor cases, there is a need for effective oversight, coordination and uniform standards governing all aspects of EB-5 matters.

DISCUSSION

PRD/IRCU will maintain liaison and regularly consult with Headquarters Service Center Operations (SCOPS), Field Operations (OFO), Administrative Appeals Office (AAO), as well as with the Texas and California Service Centers with respect to the Immigrant Investor Pilot Program, Regional Centers, I-526 and I-829 alien investor petitions. In addition, PRD/IRCU will work directly with both SCOPS and the Office of Fraud Detection and National Security (FDNS) to enhance the integrity of the EB-5 program.

This action is a major step in CIS' establishment of a nationwide and coordinated adjudicative alien investor EB-5 program, which will strengthen and protect the integrity of the program while promoting the intent of Congress to encourage investment and increase employment within the United States. The IRCU's functions and responsibilities are as follows:

1. Sole adjudicative jurisdiction for Regional Center applications pursuant to the Immigrant Investor Pilot Program for purposes of approval, denial and Requests for Evidence (RFE's).

2. Monitor and follow up on the actions of approved Regional Centers to ensure compliance with the terms, scope, and conditions of their approval/designation relative to their approved business plans and indirect job creation methodologies.

Establishment of an Investor and Regional Center Unit
HQPRD 70/6.2.8
Page 2

4. Monitor and be responsible for the policy coordination relating to CIS wide I-526 and related I-829 Immigrant Investor cases.

5. In coordination with SCOPS, conduct quarterly evaluations and an annual analysis of Regional Center activities in terms of number of alien investors, aggregate investment capital, average value of investments per alien investor, aggregate total of direct and indirect jobs per each regional center, and review total number of alien investors petitioning through each regional center per year.

6. Coordinate with the SCOPS and FDNS, to develop program and process integrity improvements and assessments for purposes of strengthening fraud detection and preventing abuses of the program by mala fide promoters and investors.

7. In coordination with SCOPS, develop and update Executive Level Review Criteria (ELRC) for purposes of identifying and selecting I-526 and I-829 Regional Center affiliated cases to review and/or adjudicate for both audit and "special handling" to verify consistent application of applicable regulations and policies, and to provide oversight, guidance and provide priority adjudication of sensitive high visibility cases.

8. In coordination with SCOPS conduct random and focused audits and quality assurance reviews of individual and groups of both Regional Center affiliated I-526 and I-829 cases, and non-Regional Center affiliated cases, in accordance with ELRC procedures.

9. In coordination with SCOPS, conduct both Regional Center and EB-5 regulatory/policy training for CAO's and DAO's adjudicating individual EB-5 alien petitions as well as petitions affiliated with a regional center.

10. Maintains and updates the USCIS web content on the EB-5 program and Pilot Program information.

Attached is the mission and organizational structure for PRD/IRCU.

POINT OF CONTACT

For additional information and clarification of this action, please contact Thomas Cook, Director, HQPRD, at (202) 514-2685.

CC: Carlos Iturregui, HQOPS
Dominick Gentile, HQREC
Michael Aytes, HQIU
Robert Devine, HQOCC
Robert Wiemann, AAO
Terry O'Reilly, HQOFO
Don Crocetti, HQFDNS

Attachment

Attachment

Investor and Regional Center Unit Mission and Organization

Mission:

The Investor and Regional Center Unit (IRCU) is a special project team within the Business and Trade Branch, Office of Program and Regulations Development. The new unit has oversight for all policy and regulatory development, form design and training regarding the EB-5 Program and Regional Center adjudications.

To carry out its mission, IRCU works closely with the Office of Service Center Operations (SCOPS), the California and Texas service centers, field offices, and the Department of State's Bureau of Consular Affairs in the administration of the law, and clarifying processing procedures regarding the adjudication of I-526 and related I-829 alien investor petitions. IRCU maintains liaison and works closely with SCOPS and the Office of Fraud Detection and National Security related to EB-5 and regional center program integrity, fraud detection and prevention.

IRCU provides outreach to the business community, professional associations and coordinates with DHS and other federal agencies as directed, and participates on panels and public forums about the EB-5 program, regulations, and policies.

IRCU Organizational Structure Within PRD

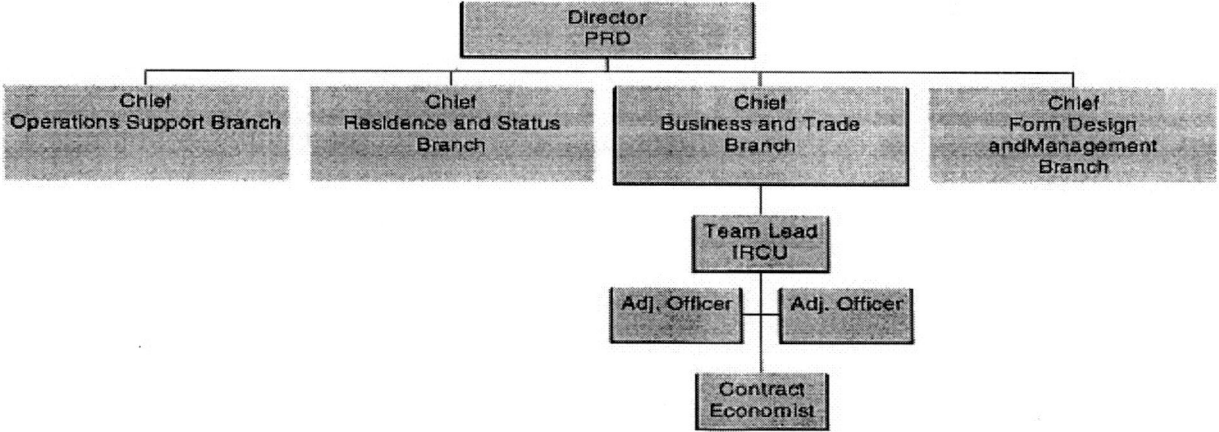

APPENDIX C-2: PEARSON MEMO OF 3-3-00

U.S. Department of Justice
Immigration and Naturalization Service

425 I Street NW.
Washington, DC 20536

MAR 3 2000

EB-5 FIELD MEMORANDUM NUMBER 9: FORM I-829 PROCESSING

MEMORANDUM FOR ALL REGIONAL DIRECTORS,
        ALL SERVICE CENTER DIRECTORS,
        DISTRICT DIRECTORS (INCLUDING FOREIGN),
        DIRECTORS, DOTF, GLYNCO AND ARTESIA

FROM: Michael A. Pearson
             Executive Associate Commissioner
             Office of Field Operations

SUBJECT: <u>AFM Update: Immigrant Investor Petitions – Form I-829 Adjudication</u>

     This memorandum updates the Adjudicators Field Manual (AFM) to provide guidance on the adjudication of petitions on Form I-829, Petition by Entrepreneur to Remove the Conditions. In addition, this memorandum provides the status of certain other EB-5 matters and reminds all Immigration and Naturalization Service (Service) offices that the Service remains committed to having these complex matters adjudicated by specially trained and experienced officers. The AFM is updated by adding appendices which include a list of frequently asked questions about Form I-829, a model notice of automatic termination of status, and four model Notices to Appear (Form I-862). These policies and procedures are effective immediately and will be included in the AFM in the next release of INSERTS.

     This memorandum reflects the complexity of certain EB-5 petitions and the INS' commitment to provide specialized training to Service personnel who adjudicate these petitions. All Service personnel are reminded that the "hold" on the adjudication of certain EB-5 petitions implemented pursuant to the March 19, 1998 field memorandum is over.

     1. In Chapter 25 of the Adjudications Field Manual, section 25.2 is added to read as follows:

25.2 Removal of Conditions for Section 203(b)(5) Immigrants

     (a) **Commitment to Trained and Experienced Officers.** All Service offices must ensure that only specially trained and experienced officers who understand the guidance provided in recent precedent decisions and field instructions adjudicate EB-5 petitions. Therefore, all

Memorandum for Regional Directors, etc.
Subject: AFM Update: Immigrant Investor Petitions--Form I-829 Adjudication

Service offices should review procedures, e.g., annual rotations and processing timelines, to ensure a careful and thorough adjudication. Training in the adjudication of petitions filed on Form I-829, Petition by Entrepreneur to Remove Conditions, is being scheduled at this time for district office adjudicators. If a district, service center, or regional office is referred a Form I-829 and is without a trained and experienced officer, the office should follow the procedures outlined in this memorandum. In addition, all such offices must ensure that the officers adjudicating petitions on Form I-829 have received training in the Marriage Fraud Amendment System (MFAS).

Service center directors in Texas and California, regional directors and district directors in offices with a high volume of Form I-829 petitions shall designate a trained and experienced officer as an EB-5 POC to facilitate the review and management of petitions on Form I-829 in accordance with these instructions. For purposes of clarity in these instructions, the term "service center director" includes the service center EB-5 POC and the term "district director" includes the district EB-5 POC.

(b) **Failure to File Form I-829**. These instructions provide procedures consistent with those provided for the adjudication of Form I-751, Petition to Remove Condition on Residence (for alien spouse) where possible. Under 8 CFR 216.6(a), immigrant investors in conditional resident status must submit Form I-829 to the appropriate service center within the 90-day period immediately preceding the second anniversary of his or her admission to the United States as a conditional permanent resident. A conditional resident's failure to properly file Form I-829 within the time period prescribed in the statute and the regulations will result under 8 CFR 216.6(a)(5) in the automatic termination of the conditional resident's status and initiation of removal proceedings.

Service officers are reminded that, in accordance with the Notice in the Federal Register at 63 Fed. Reg. 67135, published on, and in effect since, December 4, 1998, the service centers in Vermont and Nebraska no longer have jurisdiction over EB-5 matters. Form I-829 petitions are to be filed at either (1) the Texas Service Center if the new commercial enterprise is located, or will principally be doing business, in the areas previously covered by the Vermont and Texas Service Centers or (2) the California Service Center if the new commercial enterprise is located, or will principally be doing business, in the areas previously covered by the Nebraska and California Service Centers.

However, to facilitate timely notification, immediately upon publication of this memorandum, the Nebraska and Vermont Service Centers will generate a printout from the MFAS to determine those conditional residents whose I-526's were approved by those centers who have failed to file timely Form I-829s to have the conditions on their status removed in accordance with Section 216A(c) of the Immigration and Nationality Act (the Act). Termination of conditional status for failure to file to remove the conditions during the proper period is

Memorandum for Regional Directors, etc. Page 3
Subject: AFM Update: Immigrant Investor Petitions--Form I-829 Adjudication

automatic by law and by regulations. This one time procedure is necessary to avoid excess movement of files that may result in undue delay and due to service resource concerns.

Where it is determined that Form I-829 has not been timely filed, the appropriate service center director shall issue the attached standard notice which states that the failure to file has resulted in the automatic termination of the alien's status. (See Appendix 22-3). The alien's MFAS file shall be updated as "Automatic Termination" and the notice of automatic termination generated. Where such alien is unrepresented, the original notice of automatic termination is to be sent to the alien whose conditional resident status has been automatically terminated. Where such alien is represented, the notice shall be sent to the attorney or representative of record. Two copies of the notice of automatic termination are to be placed in the A-file. The A-file will be routed to the mailroom with instructions to forward the file to the Office of Adjudications of the Service District Office with jurisdiction over the location of the conditional resident's last known address for issuance of the NTA. The service center shall update CIS and RAFACS to indicate that the files have been transferred.

Hereafter, each service center shall generate weekly a printout from the MFAS to determine those conditional residents within their respective jurisdictions who have failed to file timely Form I-829 to have the conditions on their status removed in accordance with Section 216A(c) of the Act. The Nebraska Service Center will forward this report to the California Service Center weekly for issuance of the standard notice. Likewise, the Vermont Service Center will forward this report to the Texas Service Center weekly for issuance of the standard notice. Thereafter, the service centers will use standard letters to respond to all inquiries regarding the termination of conditional resident status. The letter will direct inquiries to the District Counsel's Office of the Service District Office to which the A-file was transferred.

(c) **Receipt of Form I-829**. Parallel to the procedures for processing Form I-751, Petition to Remove Conditions on Residence, upon receipt of Form I-829, the service center director shall issue the conditional resident a fee receipt notice on Form I-797 that includes the following paragraph:

> Your Permanent Resident Card (Form I-551), also known as a "green card," is extended one (1) year – employment and travel is authorized during this extension. Processing your petition for removal of conditions will require a minimum of one hundred and twenty (120) days. Thirty (30) days before the expiration of this extension, if you have not received approval of your petition, please contact the district office nearest to where you are living for further documentation for employment and/or travel purposes.

(d) **Adjudication of Form I-829 By Service Center. (1) Initial Review of Form I-829.** A service center director in receipt of a timely filed petition on Form I-829 may approve the petition without an interview, issue a request for further evidence that can be provided in writing,

Memorandum for Regional Directors, etc.
Subject: AFM Update: Immigrant Investor Petitions--Form I-829 Adjudication

Page 4

or refer it for an adjudication (with or without the interview) by a district office under 8 CFR 216.6(d).

The service center director must initially review the petition in order to determine which course to take. The petition must be adjudicated with the A-file and normal procedures are to be followed for requesting the A-file (see paragraph (e) for procedures in the event of delay in receipt of a requested A-file). In addition, the director is to follow normal procedures for consultation and referral to operational and investigative units where this is appropriate. If necessary, such units may coordinate the referral of a petition on Form I-829 to the Department of Treasury's Financial Crimes Enforcement Network (FINCEN) with a request for appropriate research.

(2) **Approval of Form I-829 by the Service Center Director.** A service center director may approve a petition on Form I-829 if he or she is satisfied that the petition establishes the requirements for removal of the conditions under 8 CFR 216.6(c)(1), enumerated at paragraph (f)(5) of this memorandum. If the petition is approved, the service center director will remove the conditions on the conditional resident's status as of the second anniversary of his or her admission as a conditional resident. Written notice of the decision must be provided to the conditional resident if he or she is not represented; however, if the conditional resident is represented as evidenced by a duly executed Form G-28, the notice must be provided to the attorney or representative of record only. Pursuant to 8 CFR 216.6(d)(1)) the notice must require the conditional resident to report to the appropriate district office for processing for a new permanent resident card, Form I-551. At the district office, the conditional resident shall surrender any permanent resident card previously issued and receive interim documentation valid for 12 months in the form of either a temporary I-551 stamp in his or her unexpired foreign passport (if the expiration date of the passport is one year or more), or a Form I-94 containing a temporary I-551 stamp and his or her photograph. The district director should follow normal procedures for card production.

(3) **Request for Evidence.** A service center director may also issue a request for additional evidence (RFE). An RFE must be based on a determination by the service center director that, in his or her discretion, in order to approve or refer the petition, the conditional resident must provide further documentation or answer certain questions in writing. In such a case, any questions posed must be stated with specificity. If the questions cannot be answered in writing, the petition must be referred for an interview. An RFE is not appropriate if the petition is clearly deniable on grounds other than those for which the RFE might be issued. Under 8 CFR 103.2(b)(8), a conditional resident is to be provided 12 weeks to respond to an RFE. Upon receipt of the conditional resident's response to the RFE, the service center director must approve or refer the Form I-829 petition.

(4) **Determination that Referral to District Office is Appropriate.** The service center

Memorandum for Regional Directors, etc.
Subject: AFM Update: Immigrant Investor Petitions--Form I-829 Adjudication

director should refer a petition on Form I-829 to a district director if the initial review of the petition, or the response to a request for additional evidence, reveals that:

(A) under the regulation at 8 CFR 216.6(c)(1), the requirements for removal of conditions have not been met and the case should be denied without an interview; or that

(B) an interview is necessary to approve or deny the petition.

A recommendation that the petition be denied without an interview is appropriate where the service center director determines that there is no material issue of fact in dispute and that the petition does not meet the requirements of the law and the regulations. In such a case, it should be clear that an interview is unlikely to produce evidence to alter a decision to deny the petition.

Section 216A(d)(3) of the Act provides the Attorney General with authority to waive the deadline for an interview or the interview itself, if that is appropriate. Accordingly, an interview is not required to either approve or deny the petition; neither is an interview a benefit that the alien may request. Under current regulations, both service center and district directors have authority in appropriate cases to waive the interview and adjudicate the petition. However, a service center director only has authority to waive an interview if the petition appears to be approvable on its face; he or she cannot waive the interview if the petition appears deniable. As discussed in paragraph 5, below, the recommendation that accompanies the referral should include the service center director's recommendations regarding whether an interview is necessary to approve or deny the petition.

(5) **Service Center Recommendation.** (A) <u>Denial Without Interview</u>. A service center director who refers a Form I-829 petition to a district director with a recommendation that <u>the requirements for removal of conditions are not met and the case should be denied without an interview</u> (see paragraph 4, above) shall forward the petition as directed by the regional EB-5 POC with:
- a memorandum reviewing the petition and explaining the reasons for his or her recommendation, in particular, the reasons why an interview is unnecessary for the denial of the petition.

(B) <u>Adjudication With Interview</u>. A service center director who refers a Form I-829 petition with a recommendation that <u>an interview is necessary to approve or deny the petition</u> (see paragraph 4, above) shall forward the petition as directed by the regional EB-5 POC with:
- a memorandum reviewing the petition and explaining the reasons for his or her specific recommendation; and
- a list of recommended questions that should be answered in an interview in order to approve or deny the petition.

(e) **Regional EB-5 POC Coordination.** Each regional director shall designate an officer

Memorandum for Regional Directors, etc.
Subject: AFM Update: Immigrant Investor Petitions--Form I-829 Adjudication

in his or her respective regional office to receive appropriate training and to coordinate the management of petitions on Form I-829 within his or her region. The responsibilities of the regional EB-5 POC include determining to which district office the service center director will forward the petition; coordinating the referral with the proper district director; ensuring that the petition is adjudicated by a trained district office adjudicator in accordance with these instructions, and; keeping a record of the distribution of cases within his or her region. In addition, the regional EB-5 POC is responsible for assisting an adjudications officer who has not received a requested A-file from a service center or district office within 30 days of a request (see paragraph (d)(1) of this field memorandum). In such a case, if a CIS file transfer request (FTR) screen indicates that no file transfer was initiated (FTI) after 30 days, the regional EB-5 POC must contact the regional POC for records at the File Control Office and coordinate the transfer of the requested file. The regional EB-5 POC shall also coordinate the referral of substantive questions received from service centers and district offices to the Headquarters Immigration Services Division (HQISD) for a responsive review.

Prior to forwarding a file for referral, the service center director shall contact the appropriate regional EB-5 POC at the number located at Appendix 22-4. When contacted by a service center director, the regional EB-5 POC shall consult with the district office having jurisdiction over the location of the alien entrepreneur's commercial enterprise in the United States. If there is a trained officer at that location, the regional EB-5 POC shall direct the service center director to forward the petition to that office. If there is no trained officer at that location, the regional EB-5 POC shall consult with district offices as necessary to direct the referral of the case in accordance with the availability, and expeditious use, of trained and experienced district office adjudicators. The regional EB-5 POC shall consider whether a district director without a trained and experienced officer prefers to detail in such an officer from another district office or has other preferences, e.g. for a telephonic or video interview.

In a specific case, a district director may determine and recommend to the regional EB-5 POC that, due to the limited availability of trained district office adjudicators, he/she must delegate his or her authority to a district director with a trained and experienced officer. A delegation of authority must be clear and in writing. In such cases, the regional EB-5 POC is responsible for ensuring that a written delegation of authority from the district director with jurisdiction is transmitted by fax or mail to the district director under whose authority the interview will be performed.

In all cases, once a district office is selected to perform the adjudication, the regional EB-5 POC will direct the service center director to forward the case file by certified mail or express mail service to that office flagged in red marker "to the attention of the district EB-5 POC." The service center director must record the referral of the case in MFAS in accordance with routine procedures.

Memorandum for Regional Directors, etc.
Subject: AFM Update: Immigrant Investor Petitions--Form I-829 Adjudication

(f) Adjudication of Form I-829 by District Office.

(1) Procedures for Currently Received Form I-829s. Upon issuance of this memorandum, district offices with Form I-829 petitions prepared and transmitted in a manner that is NOT consistent with the procedures outlined in this memorandum must return those files to the appropriate service center, with the A-file, marked to the attention of the EB-5 POC and, in red, "I-829 return." The district director must update CIS accordingly. In accordance with the Notice in the Federal Register, 63 FR 67135, published on December 4, 1998, effective immediately, the Vermont and Nebraska Service Centers no longer have jurisdiction over EB-5 matters. Form I-829 petitions shall be returned to:

  (A) the Texas Service Center if the new commercial enterprise is located, or will principally be doing business, in the areas previously covered by the Vermont and Texas Service Centers; or

  (B) the California Service Center if the new commercial enterprise is located, or will principally be doing business, in the areas previously covered by the Nebraska and California Service Centers.

When a Form I-829 file is returned to the California or Texas Service Center, the district office must manually send the petitioner, or the attorney or representative of record if the petitioner is represented, a notice of the file transfer. The notice of file transfer should inform that, if necessary, the conditional resident may take the receipt notice to the nearest district office and receive evidence of status in accordance with the procedures set forth in paragraph (g).

In addition, the Vermont and Nebraska Service Centers are instructed to forward any outstanding Form I-829 petitions to the Texas and California Service Centers. Upon receipt of a returned file, the Texas and California Service Centers are instructed to prepare and transmit the file with the required recommendation through a regional EB-5 POC in accordance with these instructions.

(2) Initial Review of Form I-829 Transmitted in Accordance with these Instructions. District offices that receive a petition on Form I-829 prepared and transmitted in accordance with these instructions may approve or deny the petition with or without an interview. The district director must initially review the petition in order to determine whether or not an interview will be conducted and that the necessary written delegation of authority is in the case file. In adjudicating the petition, the district director may accept or reject the service center director's recommendation.

Memorandum for Regional Directors, etc.
Subject: AFM Update: Immigrant Investor Petitions--Form I-829 Adjudication

Page 8

> (3) **Waiver of the Interview.** A district director may waive the interview if an interview is not necessary because either:
>
>> (A) the petition is approvable and the requirements for removal of the conditions are established; or
>>
>> (B) the petition is deniable because on its face those requirements are not established.

Therefore, to waive the interview and approve or deny the petition, the district director must be satisfied that the initial review of the petition demonstrates that the requirements for the removal of conditions are met or not met and an interview can provide no information relevant to that finding and, therefore, will serve no purpose. If the interview is waived, the petition must be annotated and MFAS updated in accordance with routine procedures.

> (4) **The Form I-829 Interview.** If an interview is necessary to approve or deny the petition, the district director will offer the conditional resident the option of traveling to the district office for a face-to-face interview or, if available, participating telephonically or by video conferencing. The interviewing officer shall create a record of the interview that responds to the service center director's memorandum and sets forth new or additional information or issues arising from the interview. The officer who conducts the interview shall render a final adjudication of the Form I-829 and recommend a decision to the district director in accordance with his or her findings. If a conditional resident fails to appear for an interview, the alien's permanent resident status shall be terminated automatically in accordance with the procedures outlined at 8 CFR 216.6(b)(3).

> (5) **Approval of Form I-829 by the District Director.** A district may approve a petition on Form I-829 if he or she is satisfied that the petition establishes that the requirements for the removal of the conditions have been met under 8 CFR 216.6(c)(1), namely that:
>
>> (A) a commercial enterprise was established by the conditional resident;
>>
>> (B) the conditional resident invested or was actively in the process of investing the requisite capital;
>>
>> (C) the conditional resident sustained the establishment and investment activities throughout the relevant period of his or her residence in the United States, i.e., the conditional resident, in good faith, substantially met the capital investment requirement of the statute and continuously maintained his or her capital investment over the two years of conditional residence; and

Memorandum for Regional Directors, etc. Page 9
Subject: AFM Update: Immigrant Investor Petitions--Form I-829 Adjudication

> (D) the conditional resident created or can be expected to create within a reasonable period of time ten full-time jobs to qualifying employees.

In addition, pursuant to section 216A(c)(3) of the Act, it must also be determined that the facts and information contained in the petition are true.

(6) Action by District Director upon Approval. If, after initial review or after the interview, the petition is approved, the district director will remove the conditions on the conditional resident's status as of the second anniversary of his or her admission as a conditional permanent resident. The district director must provide written notice of the decision to the conditional resident if he or she is not represented; however, if the conditional resident is represented as evidenced by a signed G-28, the notice must be provided to the attorney or representative of record only. Pursuant to 8 CFR 216.6(d)(1), the notice must require the conditional resident to report to the appropriate district office for processing of a new permanent resident card, Form I-551. At that time the conditional resident shall surrender any permanent resident card previously issued and shall receive temporary evidence of lawful permanent resident status in accordance with paragraph (d)(2) of this section. The district director shall ensure that the file, including all relevant documents, for example, a delegation of authority or a record of the interview, is returned to the appropriate service center director. Normal procedures should be followed for entering the decision into MFAS and card production.

(7) Derogatory information. In accordance with 8 CFR 216.6(c)(2), if the review of the petition, or the interview itself, reveals derogatory information concerning the requirements for removal of conditions (see paragraph (5)), the district director shall provide the conditional resident the opportunity to rebut such information. A 30-day period from the date of issuance is a reasonable period of time within which to allow the petitioner to submit a rebuttal. This opportunity to rebut provided by 8 CFR 216.6(c)(2) does not entail a notice of intent to deny. Rather the district director shall issue a Form I-72, Form Letter for Returning Deficient Applications/Petitions, with a short explanation of the derogatory information, a request that the conditional resident respond only to that information, and the date the response is due. This will provide the conditional resident with an opportunity to rebut only that information on the Form I-72. Derogatory information should be limited to information that the alien has not previously had an opportunity to address and the opportunity to rebut should not reopen the entire case. The opportunity to rebut shall also be provided if it is determined that the entrepreneur obtained his or her investment funds through other than legal means (such as through the sale of illegal drugs).

If no unresolved derogatory information is present, the petition shall be approved pursuant to the procedures outlined in paragraph (f)(6) of this section of the Field Manual. See also 8 CFR 216.6(c)(2).

Memorandum for Regional Directors, etc.
Subject: AFM Update: Immigrant Investor Petitions--Form I-829 Adjudication

If the conditional resident fails to overcome such derogatory information or evidence that the investment funds were obtained through other than legal means, the director may deny the petition in accordance with paragraph (f)(8) of this section, terminate the conditional resident's status, and issue a Notice To Appear (NTA) (See Appendix 22-2).

For example, the interview may reveal that a conditional resident has created positions for only seven full time employees. If, in rebuttal, the conditional resident states that he or she intends to create three additional positions at an indefinite time in the future, the petition has not met the requirements of the regulations and the petition should be denied. On the other hand, an interview may reveal that while a conditional resident has created positions for ten full time employees, only nine are actually working. The conditional resident may present rebuttal information by demonstrating that he or she actively recruited the tenth employee, and the tenth employee is expected to be hired and begin employment imminently. The director may, after considering this information as well as all of the evidence supporting the petition as a whole, determine that such a petition is approvable.

If derogatory information <u>unrelated</u> to any of the requirements for removal of conditions is identified during the course of the interview (for example, an arrest or criminal conviction), such information shall be forwarded to the investigations unit for appropriate action, and no opportunity to rebut shall be provided.

(8) Denial of Form I-829 by the district director. A district director must deny a petition on Form I-829 if the petition does not establish the requirements for removal of conditions listed in 8 CFR 216.6(c)(1). If, after initial review or after the interview, the district director denies the petition, he or she shall provide written notice to the conditional resident if he or she is not represented. However, if the conditional resident is represented, the district director shall provide written notice of the decision to the conditional resident's attorney or representative of record only. No appeal shall lie from this decision. The conditional resident may seek review of the district director's decision in removal proceedings. In issuing this denial notice, the district director shall:

(A) advise the conditional resident of the specific reasons for the denial and that:

--the conditional resident's status, and that of his or her spouse or children, is terminated as of the date of the decision and, in the case of a conditional resident that is not represented, that an NTA is attached, or, in the case of a represented conditional resident, that an NTA will be served separately upon the alien;

--the conditional resident is instructed to surrender to the district office any permanent resident card, Form I-551, previously issued by the Service and request temporary evidence of conditional residence; and

Memorandum for Regional Directors, etc. Page 11
Subject: AFM Update: Immigrant Investor Petitions--Form I-829 Adjudication

--there is no appeal from the decision, although the conditional resident may seek review of the decision in removal proceedings;

(B) issue and serve an NTA together with the notice if the conditional resident is not represented (if the conditional resident is represented, the notice should be sent only to the attorney or the representative of record and the NTA should be sent to the conditional resident) in accordance with the routine procedures (See Appendix 22-2) and with proper service of the NTA to the Executive Office of Immigration Review;

(C) enter the denial information into MFAS.

(D) ensure that the A-file includes all relevant documents, for example, a delegation of authority or a record of the interview, and is forwarded to the appropriate Office of the District Counsel. An office of the district or regional counsel with questions regarding this field memorandum should contact the Office of the General Counsel at the number for that office at Appendix 22-4.

(9) **Grounds for Denial of Form I-829**. A district director may deny Form I-829 on the following grounds:

(A) <u>Denial due to alien's failure to meet the statutory and regulatory requirements as a factual matter.</u> The Service lacks authority to grant a Form I-829 petition if the petition does not meet the statutory and regulatory requirements. This is true even if the Service granted the original I-526 petition in error and the petitioner has complied with the investment plan outlined in the Form I-526. If a director determines, after initial review of the Form I-829 petition, or referral for an interview, that the petition on its face does not meet the statutory and regulatory requirements, the petition must be denied.

(B) <u>Denial due to features discussed in the June 26, 1998, field memorandum.</u> Special procedures referenced in the June 26, 1998, field memorandum should be followed when a district director determines that a Form I-829 should be denied solely because one or more of the seven features discussed therein, and precluded under the recently issued precedent decisions, were present in the Form I-526. (If the petition is deniable for any other reason, for example because the conditional resident did not meet the job creation or preservation requirement or the new commercial enterprise has failed or is no longer viable, then the Service will follow normal procedures for denying a petition.) In a case deniable solely for one of the seven features discussed in the June 26, 1998, field memorandum, the conditional resident will be given an opportunity to file a new Form I-526 based upon the same job-creating or job-preserving business enterprise and business plan as in the original Form I-526 petition but with changes made to the financing of the business plan, while the Service suspends issuance of a decision to deny his or her Form

Memorandum for Regional Directors, etc.
Subject: AFM Update: Immigrant Investor Petitions--Form I-829 Adjudication

I-829. This would allow conditional residents who exercise this option to remain in the United States in conditional resident status while their new petition is pending. A decision on the pending Form I-829 would be issued once adjudication of the Form I-526 is completed. Should the Service grant the new Form I-526 petition, the conditional resident could seek to obtain an immigrant visa from a consular officer abroad and return to the United States to begin a new 2-year period of conditional residence. Thus, for cases falling under this paragraph, the district director shall issue a notice of intent to deny that shall state the reasons for the issuance of the notice of intent to deny and shall advise the conditional resident of the following:

- If he or she files, with the service center having jurisdiction over the location of the new commercial enterprise, a new petition on Form I-526, with the fee, within 90 days of the date of the notice of intent to deny, and this new petition does not contain the defects in the original filing, the Service will suspend issuance of a denial of his or her Form I-829 until it has adjudicated the new Form I-526. Concurrently, the conditional resident should send a copy of both the new Form I-526 and proof of filing to the district director of the district office that issued the notice of intent to deny. Exercising this option will allow the conditional resident to remain in the United States in conditional resident status during the adjudication of the new petition. Should the new petition be approved, however, he or she will be required to depart the United States to file for an immigrant visa and obtain authorization for a new 2-year conditional resident period from a consular officer abroad, since, pursuant to section 245(f) of the Act, conditional residents cannot apply within the United States for adjustment of status.

- If he or she does not file a new Form I-526 within 90 days of the date of the notice of intent to deny, the Service will proceed to deny the Form I-829 on the merits of the petition and issue a Notice to Appear for removal proceedings.

- If he or she does exercise the option to file a new Form I-526, the conditional resident must agree to continue to provide the same opportunities for employment for the entire new conditional resident period. In addition, the new petition that is filed must be based upon:
  - an investment in the same job-creating or job-preserving United States business as the original petition;
  - a business plan that is the same as in the original petition and that was sufficient and was otherwise fully complied with in the original petition throughout the two-year conditional period; and
  - the same job-creating or job-preserving United States business that actually created or preserved the required number of jobs.

Memorandum for Regional Directors, etc.
Subject: AFM Update: Immigrant Investor Petitions--Form I-829 Adjudication

Page 13

The only change that may be made in the new petition is in the financing of the business plan.

- In the new Form I-526 petition that is filed under these procedures, the conditional resident must recognize that the original request to remove the conditions on the conditional resident's status was deniable or subject to denial because the original petition did not comply with the law and the regulations.

- If the new Form I-526 petition is denied, the Service will proceed to deny the Form I-829 on the merits of the petition and issue a Notice to Appear for removal proceedings.

- If the new Form I-526 petition is approved, the conditional resident must, within 60 days of the date of the approval notice, submit to the service center director of the service center where the new Form I-526 was approved a completed and signed Form I-407, Abandonment by Alien of Status as Lawful Permanent Resident, abandoning his or her permanent resident status, and his or her expired Form I-551, Permanent Resident Card, if still in his or her possession. Upon receipt of Form I-407, the Service will proceed to deny the Form I-829 for failure to prosecute. Once this denial is issued, the alien will no longer be in lawful status and will begin to accrue time unlawfully present in the United States for purposes of section 212(a)(9)(B)(i) of the Act. The alien should promptly depart the United States to avoid any adverse consequences under the Act and file for an immigrant visa with a consular office abroad. The Form I-407 must be received by the service center by the close of business on the last day of the 60-day period.

If the Service does not receive Form I-407 by the close of the 60-day time period, the Service will proceed to deny the Form I-829 on the merits of the petition and issue a Notice to Appear for removal proceedings.

- When filing for a new immigrant visa with a consular officer abroad, the alien should provide to the consular officer a copy of the notice of intent to deny, a copy of the Form I-407, evidence of the date of departure from the United States (e.g., boarding pass), and evidence of the approval of the new Form I-526 petition, in addition to any documentation required by the consular officer for visa processing.

- Finally, if admission for a new two-year conditional period is authorized by the consular officer and the alien is admitted to the United States as a conditional resident, he or she will be required to comply with all the requirements of the law, including the employment creation requirements, so that the jobs previously

Memorandum for Regional Directors, etc.
Subject: AFM Update: Immigrant Investor Petitions--Form I-829 Adjudication

Page 14

created or preserved by the new commercial enterprise are sustained throughout the new 2-year conditional period.

MFAS should be appropriately updated and the case file placed in a holding area, or holding cabinet, marked "EB-5 I-829 90 day hold" during the response period. At the end of the 90-day period, the district director shall determine whether a response has been received and, if so, whether that response provides evidence that a new petition has been filed in accordance with the notice. If no response is received, the district director shall proceed to prepare and issue the denial and the NTA in accordance with the procedures outlined above. If a new petition is filed in accordance with the notice, the district director shall forward the original file to the service center director with jurisdiction over that filing. The service center director must promptly adjudicate the petition pursuant to the guidelines provided in recent precedent decisions and field instructions.

For those conditional residents whose new Form I-526 petitions are approved, the service center director shall mail the approval notice to the conditional resident if unrepresented or, if represented, to the attorney or representative of record and record the approval of the new petition in CLAIMS. The service center director shall place the file in a holding cabinet, marked "EB-5 60-day hold" during the 60-day period in which the alien must submit Form I-407 (and Form I-551, if any) before departing the United States and filing for a new immigrant visa at a consular office abroad. Immediately after the end of the 60-day period, the service center director will determine whether the alien submitted Form I-407. If the alien failed to submit the Form I-407, the service center director shall transfer the alien's file to the district office for issuance of a denial of the Form I-829 on the merits of the petition and a Notice to Appear. If it is determined that the alien submitted the Form I-407, the service center director shall transfer the alien's file with a copy of Form I-407 to the district office that issued the notice of intent to deny Form I-829 for issuance of a denial of the Form I-829 for failure to prosecute. MFAS must be updated accordingly. Form I-407, in the original, shall be forwarded to the Texas Service Center for additional processing. Upon the admission of an alien based upon the new immigrant visa, immigration officers shall ensure that a new A number is not created, but that the prior A number is assigned to the alien's new immigrant visa.

(C) <u>Denial due to fraud or other criminal grounds.</u> When a district director determines that a petition may be deniable for fraud or other criminal grounds, the Form I-829 petition shall be referred to the district's investigations branch with specific requests for a benefit fraud investigation. The district director may also coordinate the referral of a Form I-829 petition to FINCEN with a request for appropriate research. The district director shall make no disposition of the petition until he or she obtains a report of the results of the referral or investigation.

(g) **<u>Extension of Status for Conditional Residents with Pending or Denied Forms</u>**

Memorandum for Regional Directors, etc.
Subject: AFM Update: Immigrant Investor Petitions--Form I-829 Adjudication

I-829. Service officers are advised that no extension of status can be given to an alien who has not filed a Form I-829, unless the district director accepts a late petition based upon the alien's showing of good cause in accordance with 8 CFR 216.6(a)(5).

Upon receipt of a properly filed Form I-829, the Service is authorized by 8 CFR 216.6(a)(1) to extend automatically a conditional resident's status, if necessary, until such time as a service center or district director has adjudicated the petition. Therefore, if necessary, a district immigration information officer (IIO) in receipt of a request for documentation for travel or employment purposes from a petitioner who requires an extension of status based on a filed Form I-829 shall check the status of the petitioner on MFAS. If the Form I-829 has been denied, the IIO should check DACS to determine if an NTA has been issued. If no NTA has been issued, the IIO must ensure that the petitioner is issued an NTA through Investigations or Adjudications, depending on the policy of the district office.

If the Form I-829 is still pending or it has been denied but no final order of removal has been entered, the IIO must collect the expired Permanent Resident Card and issue either:

(A) a temporary I-551 stamp with a 12-month expiration date in the petitioner's unexpired, foreign passport (if the expiration date of the passport is one year or more), or

(B) if the petitioner is not in possession of an unexpired foreign passport, a Form I-94 (arrival portion) containing a temporary I-551 stamp with a 12-month expiration date and a photograph of the petitioner.

The IIO must use the same conditional resident status code initially issued to the petitioner and grant the status for an additional 12 months. Documentation of conditional resident status must be issued until a final order of removal is issued. An order of removal is final if a decision is not appealed or, if appealed, when the appeal is dismissed by the Board of Immigration Appeals.

Where the Form I-829 has been denied for failure to appear for an interview, the alien's permanent resident status will be automatically terminated. Temporary evidence of permanent resident status as stated above should only be issued if the conditional resident's status is restored as described in 8 CFR 216.6(b)(3).

(h) **Lawful Permanent Residents whose Conditions have been Removed.** Service Officers are reminded that, as stated in the field memorandum of June 26, 1998, absent a finding of fraud or other improper acts, the Service will not initiate recission proceedings in the cases of aliens who have obtained lawful permanent resident status (without conditions) based on petitions that may have not complied with the statute and regulations, as discussed in the General Counsel's memorandum of December 19, 1997.

Memorandum for Regional Directors, etc.
Subject: AFM Update: Immigrant Investor Petitions--Form I-829 Adjudication

2. The AFM Table of Contents is revised and a new Appendix 22-1 is added to read as follows:

Appendix 22-1

FREQUENTLY ASKED QUESTIONS ABOUT FORM I-829

1. **What is the Form I-829?** Form I-829, Petition by Entrepreneur to Remove the Conditions, is a petition that must be filed by an alien entrepreneur, or immigrant investor, in conditional permanent resident status under section 203(b)(5) of the Immigration and Nationality Act.

2. **What is the Form I-829 used for?** Section 203(b)(5) provides an alien entrepreneur/investor with a 2-year period of conditional residence to invest the required capital in a new commercial enterprise that the alien has established. In addition, in the 2-year period the alien entrepreneur/investor must create full-time employment for the required number of United States workers. (United States workers may be citizens, aliens lawfully admitted for permanent residence or other immigrants lawfully authorized to be employed in the United States, other than the petitioner and immediate family members). Form I-829 is used by an alien entrepreneur/investor at the end of the 2-year conditional period to request removal of the conditions on his or her lawful permanent resident status.

3. **When is Form I-829 filed?** It must be filed within the 90-day period preceding the second anniversary of the conditional resident's admission to the United States or adjustment of status as a conditional resident.

4. **Where is Form I-829 filed?** Form I-829 must be filed with the INS service center having jurisdiction over the location of the alien entrepreneur/investor's commercial enterprise in the United States. On December 4, 1998, the Service published a Federal Register Notice announcing that all petitions related to alien entrepreneur/ immigrant investor classification were to be filed at the newly defined jurisdictional areas of either the Texas Service Center or the California Service Center (63 FR 67135).

Petitions on Form I-829 are filed (1) with the Texas Service Center if the new commercial enterprise is located, or will principally be doing business, in the geographic area previously under the jurisdiction of the Vermont and Texas Service Centers or (2) with the California Service Center if the new commercial enterprise is located, or will principally be doing business, in the geographic area previously under the jurisdiction of the California and Nebraska Service Centers.

The Nebraska and Vermont Service Centers no longer have jurisdiction over Form I-829. The Nebraska and Vermont Service Centers were authorized to forward EB-5 petitions to the Texas and California Service Centers if necessary due to incorrect filing for a

Memorandum for Regional Directors, etc.
Subject: AFM Update: Immigrant Investor Petitions--Form I-829 Adjudication

60-day period following December 4, 1998. (That time period has expired.)

5. **What are the mailing addresses for these new filing locations?** The current mailing addresses for these petitions and applications are as follows: for the California Service Center, 24000 Avila Road, 2nd floor (P.O. Box 10526), Laguna Niguel, California 92607-0526; for the Texas Service Center, P.O. Box 852135, Mesquite, Texas, 75185-2135.

6. **What is the fee for Form I-829?** To be considered properly filed, Form I-829 must be accompanied by the fee required under 8 CFR 103.7(b)(1), which is $345.

7. **What other documents are filed with Form I-829?** Under 8 CFR 216.6(a)(4), the petition for removal of conditions must be accompanied by evidence that:
- a commercial enterprise was established by the alien entrepreneur/investor;
- the alien entrepreneur/investor invested or was actively in the process of investing the requisite capital;
- the alien entrepreneur/investor sustained the actions at (1) and (2) throughout the period of his or her residence in the United States, and;
- the alien entrepreneur/investor created or can be expected to create within a reasonable time ten full-time jobs for qualifying employees.

8. **Are the entrepreneur/investor's spouse and child required to file separate applications?** Under 8 CFR 216.6(a), they should be included in the conditional resident's petition on Form I-829, at Part 3. Children who have reached the age of twenty-one, children who have married during the period of conditional permanent residence, and the former spouse of an entrepreneur, who was divorced from the entrepreneur during the period of conditional residence, may be included in the conditional resident's petition or may file a separate petition on Form I-829.

9. **Will entrepreneurs/investors remain in status after they file Form I-829?**
Under 8 CFR 216.6(a), upon receipt of a properly filed Form I-829, the alien's conditional permanent resident status shall be extended automatically, if necessary, until such time as the director has adjudicated the petition. The Form I-829 receipt notice will state that the conditional resident's Form I-551, Permanent Resident Card, is extended for one year. If the petition is not adjudicated within this time period, the conditional resident, if necessary, should contact the district office nearest to where he or she is living thirty (30) days before the Form I-551 expiration date is reached for further documentation regarding status and employment.

10. **Can entrepreneurs/investors travel after filing Form I-829?**
Under 8 CFR 216.6(a)(3), an alien entrepreneur who has filed Form I-829 is authorized to

Memorandum for Regional Directors, etc.
Subject: AFM Update: Immigrant Investor Petitions--Form I-829 Adjudication

travel outside the United States and return if in possession of appropriate documentation. The regulation at 8 CFR 211.1(a)(5) authorizes admission if an alien presents an expired Form I-551, Permanent Resident Card, accompanied by a filing receipt issued within the previous 6 months for a Form I-829, if seeking admission or readmission after a temporary absence of less than 1 year. (Some filing receipts may authorize travel for up to 1 year.) Waivers from visa requirements may be obtained under 8 CFR 211.1(b). District offices are authorized to issue (a) a temporary I-551 stamp with a 12-month expiration date in the petitioner's unexpired, foreign passport (if the expiration date of the passport is one year or more), or (b) if the petitioner is not in possession of an unexpired foreign passport, a Form I-94 (arrival portion) containing a temporary I-551 stamp with a 12-month expiration date and a photograph of the petitioner. An alien entrepreneur may wish to contact his or her local INS district office to discuss the travel planned and determine the routine procedures of that office for obtaining such necessary travel documentation. If necessary, thirty (30) days before the expiration of the Form I-829, the conditional resident should contact the district office nearest to where he or she is living for such documentation for purposes of travel outside of the United States.

3. The AFM Table of Contents is revised and a new Appendix 22-2 is added to read as follows:

Appendix 22-2

MODEL NOTICES TO APPEAR (NTAs) – Note: The allegations must be appropriately modified in the case of NTAs issued for derivatives (i.e., spouse and children).

FOR IMMIGRANT ENTREPRENEUR TERMINATED DUE TO FAILURE TO FILE FORM I-829 (for District Office use)

A. **Termination of Conditional Permanent Residence** (Entry on Immigrant Visa)
ALLEGATIONS:

1. You are not a citizen or national of the United States;
2. You are a native of _____ and a citizen of _____;
3. On _____, you were lawfully admitted to the United States for permanent residence on a conditional basis based on your engagement/investment in a new commercial enterprise known as _____;
4. Your status was terminated on _____ because you failed to properly file the Request for Removal of Conditions (Form I-829).

CHARGE:
Section 237(a)(1)(D)(i) of the Immigration and Nationality Act (Act), as amended, in that after admission or adjustment as an alien lawfully admitted for permanent residence on a conditional basis under section 216A of the Act your status was terminated under such respective section.

Memorandum for Regional Directors, etc. Page 19
Subject: AFM Update: Immigrant Investor Petitions--Form I-829 Adjudication

B. Termination of Conditional Permanent Residence   (Adjustment)
ALLEGATIONS:

1. You are not a citizen or national of the United States;
2. You are a native of _____ and a citizen of _____;
3. You were admitted to the United States at _____ as a nonimmigrant;
4. On _____ your status was adjusted to that of a permanent resident on a conditional basis based upon your engagement/investment in a new commercial enterprise known as _____.
5. Your status was terminated on _____ because you failed to file a Request to Remove Conditions (Form I-829).

CHARGE:

Section 237(a)(1)(D)(i) of the Immigration and nationality Act (Act), as amended, in that after admission or adjustment as an alien lawfully admitted for permanent residence on a conditional basis under Section 216A of the Act your status was terminated under such respective section.

FOR IMMIGRANT INVESTOR/ALIEN ENTREPRENEUR TERMINATED DUE TO SUBSTANTIVE DENIAL OF FORM I-829 (for DISTRICT OFFICE use)

C. Termination of Conditional Permanent Residence   (Entry on Immigrant Visa)
ALLEGATIONS:

1. You are not a citizen or national of the United States;
2. You are a native of _____ and a citizen of _____;
3. On _____, you were lawfully admitted to the United States for permanent residence on a conditional basis based on your engagement/investment in a new commercial enterprise known as _____;
4. Your Request for Removal of Conditional Residence was denied by the District Director on _____ because you failed to meet the requirements necessary to remove the conditions on your status.

CHARGE:
Section 237(a)(1)(D)(i) of the Immigration and Nationality Act (Act), as amended, in that after admission or adjustment as an alien lawfully admitted for permanent residence on a conditional basis under section 216A of the Act your status was terminated under such respective section.

D. Termination of Conditional Permanent Residence   (Adjustment)

Memorandum for Regional Directors, etc.
Subject: AFM Update: Immigrant Investor Petitions--Form I-829 Adjudication

Page 20

ALLEGATIONS:

1. You are not a citizen or national of the United States;
2. You are a native of _____ and a citizen of _____;
3. You (entered without inspection, were paroled, or were admitted to the United States at _____ _____ as a nonimmigrant) (specify);
4. On _____ your status was adjusted to that of a permanent resident on a conditional basis based on your engagement/investment in a new commercial enterprise known as _____;
5. Your Request for Removal of Conditional Residence was denied by the District Director on _____ because you failed to meet the requirements necessary to remove the conditions on your status.

CHARGE:

Section 237(a)(1)(D)(i) of the Immigration and Nationality Act (Act), as amended, in that after admission or adjustment as an alien lawfully admitted for permanent residence on a conditional basis under section 216A of the Act your status was terminated under such respective section.

4. The AFM Table of Contents is revised and a new Appendix 22-3 is added to read as follows:

Appendix 22-3

MODEL NOTICE OF AUTOMATIC TERMINATION OF CONDITIONAL RESIDENCE OF IMMIGRANT INVESTOR/ALIEN ENTREPRENEUR BASED UPON FAILURE TO PROPERLY FILE FORM I-829 PETITION.

Notice of Conditional Resident Status Termination

A review of the records of the Immigration and Naturalization Service (Service) reveals that you were admitted to the United States as a conditional permanent resident on [insert date of admission or adjustment].

In accordance with the provisions of section 216A(c)(2) of the Immigration and Nationality Act (the Act), you were required to file a petition (Form I-829) requesting removal of the conditional basis of residence between [insert date 21 months after date of admission or adjustment] and [insert date 24 months after date of admission or adjustment]. As of this date, the Service has no record that you have filed such a petition.

Therefore, in accordance with the provisions of Section 216A(c)(2)(A) of the Act, the permanent residence status previously accorded you is hereby terminated as of [insert date 24 months after date of admission or adjustment].

Memorandum for Regional Directors, etc.
Subject: AFM Update: Immigrant Investor Petitions--Form I-829 Adjudication

All privileges that you have derived from the status, including the privileges to reside and work in the United States, are terminated concurrently.

A Notice to Appear is attached, or will be forwarded under separate cover to you. Your file is being forwarded to the Office of District Counsel of the INS District Office having jurisdiction over the location of your last known address. All inquiries should be made to the District Counsel Office.

In accordance with section 216A(c)(2)(B) of the Act, you may request review of this determination in removal proceedings. In those proceedings, you shall have the burden of proving your compliance with the requirement to file the petition (Form I-829) within the designated period.

Sincerely,

Director

5. The AFM Table of Contents is revised and a new Appendix 22-4 is added to read as follows:

Appendix 22-4

POINTS OF CONTACT FOR EB-5 CASES

Questions about ADJUDICATIONS issues may be directed to Katharine A. Lorr at HQADN, (202) 353-8177.

Questions about INVESTIGATIONS issues may be directed to Maryann Maillet at HQINV (202) 514-0747.

Questions about legal issues from regional or district counsel offices may be directed to Susan Mathias at HQCOU, (202) 514-2895.

Questions from service center directors or district directors regarding the procedures outlined in these instructions may be directed to the regional EB-5 POC at the following numbers: Western Regional Office – 949-360-3314; Central Regional Office – 214-767-7430; Eastern Regional Office – 802-660-5036.

APPENDIX C-3: YATES MEMO OF 6-10-03

U.S. Department of Justice
Immigration and Naturalization Service

HQ40/6.1.3

425 I Street NW
Washington, DC 20536

JUN 1 0 2003

MEMORANDUM FOR: SERVICE CENTER DIRECTORS
BCIS FIELD OFFICE DIRECTORS
DIRECTOR, NATIONAL BENEFITS CENTER

FROM: William R. Yates
Acting Associate Director for Operations
Bureau of Citizenship and Immigration Services
Department of Homeland Security

SUBJECT: Amendments Affecting Adjudication of Petitions for Alien Entrepreneur (EB-5)

The purpose of this memorandum is to provide interim guidance on certain changes affecting the adjudication of Form I-526, Immigrant Petition by Alien Entrepreneur, and Form I-829, Petition by Alien Entrepreneur to Remove Conditions, that were pending or filed on or after November 2, 2002. On November 2, 2002, the President signed into law the Twenty-First Century Department of Justice Appropriations Authorization Act (Public Law 107-273), which, among other things, mandated a review of cases in which the alien entrepreneur filed a Form I-526 petition that was approved after January 1, 1995 and prior to August 31, 1998, and timely filed an I-829 petition prior to November 2, 2002.

In addition to cases described above, the new law also affects the adjudication of Form I-526 petitions pending or filed on or after November 2, 2002, the date on which the law was enacted. Changes brought about by the new law include the following:

1. Chapter 2, section 11036 of Public Law 107-273, (Subtitle B) amends the law at sections 203(b)(5) and 216A of the Immigration and Nationality Act (INA) so that an alien entrepreneur is no longer required to establish a commercial enterprise.

MEMORANDUM FOR SERVICE CENTER DIRECTORS, ET.AL. Page 2
SUBJECT: Amendments Affecting Adjudication of Petitions, etc.

This modifies 8 CFR § 204.6(h)(l), regarding the creation of an original business. Adjudicators, however, should still inquire as to whether the petitioner personally established the commercial enterprise because if not, then the adjudicator must inquire as to the number of jobs at the time the petitioner acquired the business since petitioner still has to create 10 <u>new</u> jobs.

2. In addition, the new law did not remove the requirement that the commercial enterprise be "new," as defined in 8 CFR § 204.6(e). Under this definition, an enterprise must have been established after November 29, 1990 in order to be "new". The regulations at 8 CFR 204.6(h)(3), which describe "the establishment of a new commercial enterprise", have been superceded in part by Public Law 107-273 due to the removal of the requirement that the alien entrepreneur establish the commercial enterprise. Nonetheless, this section is still relevant in that it describes under what circumstances a commercial enterprise in existence prior to November 29, 1990 will be considered to be "new" for the purposes of this law. Specifically, enterprises that have been expanded or substantially reorganized continue to meet the definition of "new" regardless of when the commercial enterprise was actually created. Accordingly:

   - A business established prior to November 29, 1990 may be considered a new commercial enterprise under 8 C.F.R. § 204.6(e) and (h) if since that date it has been expanded so that a substantial change in the net worth or number of employees has occurred. Substantial change means a 40 percent increase in either the net worth or the number of employees.

   - In addition, a commercial enterprise established prior to November 29, 1990 will be considered to be new under 8 C.F.R. § 204.6(e) and (h) if since that date it has been restructured or reorganized so that a new commercial enterprise results.

3. With respect to cases where the alien entrepreneur filed a Form I-526 petition after August 31, 1998, the new law does not permit such an alien entrepreneur to meet the requirements for the removal of conditions by combining investments in multiple commercial enterprises. The investment of capital in only one commercial enterprise remains a requirement for these cases.

4. Section 11035 of Chapter 2 amends section 203(b)(5) of the INA to include a definition of "full-time" employment, which is defined as a position that requires at least 35 hours of service per week at any time.

MEMORANDUM FOR SERVICE CENTER DIRECTORS, ET.AL.   Page 3
SUBJECT: Amendments Affecting Adjudication of Petitions, etc.

5. Public Law 107-273 has not changed the definitions of qualifying employee under 8 C.F.R. § 204.6(e), which continues to mean United States citizens, aliens lawfully admitted for permanent residence or other immigrants lawfully authorized to be employed in the United States, not including members of the alien entrepreneur's immediate family or household employees.

6. Section 11036 of Chapter 2 amends section 216A of the INA to include "limited partnership" within the term "commercial enterprise."

Form I-526 and I-829 petitions pending or filed on or after November 2, 2002 should be adjudicated in accordance with the changes specified in this memorandum. Previous EB-5 field guidance memorandums and regulations remain in effect, barring any changes specified above. Questions regarding this memorandum may be directed through appropriate channels to Morrie Berez or Joseph Holliday in BCIS Operations.

APPENDIX C-4: NEUFELD MEMO OF 6-17-09

U.S. Department of Homeland Security
U.S. Citizenship and Immigration Services
Office of Domestic Operations
Washington, DC 20529

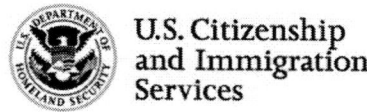

U.S. Citizenship and Immigration Services

HQDOMO 70/6.1.8
AD09-04

Memorandum

To: SERVICE CENTER DIRECTORS
REGIONAL DIRECTORS
DISTRICT DIRECTORS
FIELD OFFICE DIRECTORS
NATIONAL BENEFIT CENTER DIRECTOR

From: Donald Neufeld /S/
Acting Associate Director, Domestic Operations

Date: June 17, 2009

Subject: <u>EB-5 Alien Entrepreneurs - Job Creation and Full-Time Positions (AFM Update AD 09-04)</u>

1. Purpose

This AFM update provides United States Citizenship and Immigration Services (USCIS) personnel with instructions related to the timing of job creation and the meaning of "full-time" positions in the EB-5 program.

The AFM update clarifies that each petitioner must submit a business plan, along with their Form I-526, Immigrant Petition by Alien Entrepreneur, which provides an accounting of the required number of qualifying jobs that will be created within the two-year period of conditional residency. This AFM update also clarifies that there may be some flexibility with respect to the timing of job creation at the Form I-829, Petition by Entrepreneur to Remove Conditions, stage. Finally, this AFM update clarifies the meaning of full-time position as it relates to job creation.

The AFM update conforms the filing locations with the Federal Register Notice dated January 9, 2009, 74 Fed. Reg. 912-913.

2. Relevant Laws

INA § 203(b)(5) creates a class of immigrant visas (EB-5) for individuals who invest a specified amount of capital in the United States and who will "create full-time employment

Clarification of Two-Year Period the Meaning of Full-Time Positions for Job Creation by EB-5 Alien Entrepreneurs
HQDOMO 70/6.1.8 AD09-04
Page 2

for not fewer than 10" qualified employees. INA § 216A places conditions upon the permanent resident status of aliens admitted in the EB-5 classification that must be removed at the end of a two-year period of conditional residency. In order to have the conditions removed, EB-5 visa holders must file a Form I-829 that demonstrates that the petitioner is, among other requirements, "conforming to the requirements of INA § 203(b)(5)." INA § 216A(d)(1)(B).

Consistent with the two-year period of conditional residency, USCIS regulations generally require evidence to obtain approval of a Form I-526, including a business plan that demonstrates that jobs will be created within the two-year period of conditional residence. 8 C.F.R. § 204.6(j)(4)(i)(B).

USCIS regulations relating to the removal conditions from the lawful permanent resident status of alien entrepreneurs status provide that a petitioner must demonstrate that "the alien has created or can be expected to create within a reasonable period of time" the required jobs. 8 C.F.R. § 216.6(c)(1)(iv).

3. Field Guidance Summary

Effective immediately, USCIS personnel are directed to comply with the following instructions, as set forth in revisions to the *Adjudicator's Field Manual* (AFM) noted in section 5, as summarized below.

For purposes of the Form I-526 adjudication and the job creation requirements, USCIS will deem the two-year period described in 8 C.F.R. § 204.6(j)(4)(i)(B) to commence six months after the adjudication of the Form I-526. USCIS officers should ensure that the business plan filed with the Form I-526 reasonably demonstrates that the requisite number of jobs will be created by the end of this two-year period.

For Regional Center petitions and for purposes of indirect job creation, USCIS officers may consider economic models that rely on certain variables to show job creation and the amount of investment to determine whether the required infusion of capital or creation of direct jobs will result in a certain number of indirect jobs.

USCIS also has concluded that direct and indirect construction jobs that are created by the petitioner's investment and that are expected to last at least 2 years may now count as permanent jobs for Form I-526 and I-829 purposes.

4. Use

This AFM update is intended solely for the guidance of USCIS personnel in performing their duties relative to adjudications. It is not intended to, does not, and may not be relied upon to create any right or benefit, substantive or procedural, enforceable at law or by any individual or other party in removal proceedings, in litigation with the United States, or in any other

Clarification of Two-Year Period the Meaning of Full-Time Positions for Job Creation by EB-5 Alien Entrepreneurs
HQDOMO 70/6.1.8 AD09-04
Page 3

form or manner. In addition, the instruction and guidance in this AFM update is in no way intended to and does not prohibit enforcement of the immigration laws of the United States.

5. **Contact Information**

Questions related to this memorandum should be directed to Joseph P. Whalen, USCIS Headquarters Office of Service Center Operations, through appropriate supervisory channels.

6. **Field Guidance and AFM Update**

Chapter 22.4(c)(4)(D) of the AFM is amended to number it as three subsections and include the new subsections (ii) and (iii) at the end of Paragraph (D) and prior to the Note.

(D) **Job Creation.**

(i) The petition must be supported with evidence the new commercial enterprise will create no fewer than 10 full-time positions (or the equivalent). ....

****

(ii) **Clarification of the Two-Year Period for Job Creation.**

(a) Petitioners who are filing a Form I-526 must submit "a comprehensive business plan showing that, due to the nature and projected size of the new commercial enterprise, the need for not fewer than ten (10) qualifying employees will result, including approximate dates, within the next two-years, and when each employee will be hired." 8 C.F.R. § 204.6(j)(4)(i)(B) (emphasis added). The requirement for a business plan that shows jobs will be created in two years applies to all Form I-526 petitions, including those filed under the Regional Center Program, that will rely on indirect job creation to satisfy the statutory employment creation requirement.

The regulations, however, do not clearly state when the two-year period commences for purposes of adjudicating the Form I-526. The reference to a two-year period relates to the two-year period of conditional residence, and the time requirement of 8 C.F.R. § 204.6(j)(4)(i)(B) is intended to ensure that aliens seeking to enter the United States on EB-5 visas have a legitimate and feasible plan to create jobs as required by the statute within that period of conditional residence. Nevertheless, at the time of adjudication of Form I-526, the alien entrepreneur will not have attained conditional permanent residence, and the officer adjudicating Form I-526 cannot be certain when the period of conditional residence will in fact commence.

USCIS has determined that the average processing times for EB-5 petitioners filing for immigrant visas via consular processing and EB-5 petitioners filing

Clarification of Two-Year Period the Meaning of Full-Time Positions for Job Creation by EB-5 Alien Entrepreneurs
HQDOMO 70/6.1.8 AD09-04
Page 4

for adjustment of status is approximately six months. Accordingly, in order to best approximate the two-year period of conditional residence, the two-year period described in 8 C.F.R. § 204.6(j)(4)(i)(B) will be deemed to commence six months after the adjudication of Form I-526. USCIS officers should ensure that the business plan filed along with Form I-526 reasonably demonstrates that the requisite number of jobs will be created by the alien's investment by the end of the two-year period that commences six months after the adjudication of the petition. If, in the future, processing times significantly change, this paragraph may be amended.

(b) **Special considerations for Regional Center based I-526 petitions**:

(i) Aliens filing I-526 petitions for investments to be made through a regional center may use reasonable methodologies to establish the number of jobs created. 8 C.F.R. § 204.6(j)(4)(iii). However, some of the economic models may not expressly consider temporal aspects of job creation, and will not be able to conclusively state that indirect jobs will be created within two years. In such circumstances, officers should first explore whether there are reasonable and/or accepted temporal assumptions that can be attributed to the particular economic model and consider such assumptions in determining compliance with the two-year requirement.

For example, the RIMSII handbook states the following about the RIMSII economic model, which is often used to demonstrate indirect job creation:

> RIMS II, like all I-O models, is a "static equilibrium" model, so impacts calculated with RIMS II have no specific time dimension. However, because the model is based on annual data, it is customary to assume that the impacts occur in 1 year. For many situations, this assumption is reasonable.

This assumption supports the conclusion that the indirect jobs will be created within the requisite two-year period.

If, however, there are no reasonable and/or accepted temporal assumptions that can be made with respect to a particular economic model, USCIS may presume that the jobs will be created within the required period of time provided that the alien can demonstrate compliance with paragraph (ii) below.

(ii) Many economic models used to demonstrate indirect job creation rely on certain assumptions or variables to show the requisite job creation. For example, a model might demonstrate that the requisite jobs will be created

Clarification of Two-Year Period the Meaning of Full-Time Positions for Job Creation by EB-5 Alien Entrepreneurs
HQDOMO 70/6.1.8 AD09-04
Page 5

> if a Regional Center infuses $10 million into a particular industry. Similarly, a model might demonstrate that, using accepted multipliers, the creation of 100 direct jobs will result in a certain number of indirect jobs. Under such circumstances, the I-526 petition should demonstrate that the required infusion of capital or the creation of the direct jobs will occur within two years.

Nothing in this paragraph should be construed to alter in any way the current adjudication procedures. Officers may review the evidence required by the petitioner to demonstrate the number of jobs that will be created by the investment. For example, Form I-526s filed under the Regional Center Program which rely on indirect job creation must also comply with the evidentiary requirements of 8 C.F.R. § 204.6(j)(4)(iii) to demonstrate the number of jobs created. Officers may also continue to determine the reasonableness of a business plan to ensure that the jobs are likely to be created.

(iii) **Clarification of the Meaning of Full-Time Position.**

Section 203(b)(5) of the INA requires that the investment in a new commercial enterprise will create full-time employment for not fewer than 10 qualified employees. The INA further defines full-time employment as "employment in a position that requires at least 35 hours or service per week at any time, regardless of who fills the position." USCIS has interpreted the full-time employment requirement to exclude jobs that are intermittent, temporary, seasonal or transient in nature. See, e.g., Spencer Enterprises v. U.S., 229 F.Supp.2d 1025 (E.D.Cal. 2001). For example, historically, construction jobs have not been counted toward job creation because they are seen as intermittent, temporary, seasonal and transient rather than permanent.

USCIS, however, now interprets that direct and indirect construction jobs that are created by the petitioner's investment and that are expected to last at least 2 years, inclusive of when the petitioner's I-829 is filed, may now count as permanent jobs. Although employment in some industries such as construction or tourism can be intermittent, temporary, seasonal or transient, officers should not exclude jobs simply because they fall into such industries. Rather, the focus of the adjudication should be on whether the position, as described in the petition, is continuous full-time employment rather than intermittent, temporary, seasonal or transient. For example, if a petition reasonably describes the need for general laborers in a construction project that is expected to last several years and would require a minimum of 35 hours per week over the course of that project, the positions would meet the full-time employment requirement. However, if, for example, the same project called for electrical workers to provide services during three to four five week periods over the course of the project,

Clarification of Two-Year Period the Meaning of Full-Time Positions for Job Creation by EB-5 Alien Entrepreneurs
HQDOMO 70/6.1.8 AD09-04
Page 6

such positions would be properly deemed to be intermittent and not meet the definition of full-time employment.

Generally, it is the position that is critical to the full-time employment criterion, not the employee. Accordingly, the fact that the position may be filled by more than one employee does not exclude a position from consideration as full-time employment. For example, the positions described above would not be excluded from being considered full-time employment if the general laborers needed to fill the positions varied from day to day or week to week as long as the need for the position remains constant. This interpretation is consistent with 8 C.F.R. § 204.6(e), which, as part of the regulatory definition of full-time employment includes job sharing arrangements.

It is important to note, however, that this new interpretation does not override the regulatory definitions of employee and full time employment at 8 C.F.R. § 204.6(e). Thus, the positions must still be filled by qualifying employees, and such positions may not be filled by independent contractors. In addition, multiple part time positions may not be combined to create one full time position.

2. Chapter 25.2(e)(1) of the AFM is amended to include the following new paragraph at the beginning of Paragraph (1). The existing Paragraph (1) will now become Paragraph (2) and so on.

   (1) **Initial Review.** Form I-829 petition is intended to examine whether the alien entrepreneur has satisfied the conditions of his admission to the United States. Primarily, USCIS is determining whether the alien has invested the requisite capital and created the requisite jobs through that investment. Form I-829 petition is to be filed within 90 days prior to the second anniversary of the alien's admission to the United States in conditional resident status.

3. Chapter 25.2(e)(4)(D) of the AFM is amended to include the following new paragraphs at the end of Paragraph (D).

   Recognizing that circumstances may change after an alien secures admission to the United States, USCIS chose to implement INA § 216A with some "flexibility." See, 59 FR 1317-01, 1317-18 (Jan. 10, 1994) (proposed rule). Consistent with this flexibility, USCIS provides that Form I-829 must contain evidence that the petitioning alien "has created or can be expected to create within a reasonable time ten full-time jobs for qualifying employees." 8 C.F.R. § 216.6(a)(4)(iv).

   In making the "reasonable time" determination, officers should consider the evidence submitted along with the petition that demonstrates when the jobs are expected to be created, the reasons that the jobs were not created as predicted in Form I-526,

Clarification of Two-Year Period the Meaning of Full-Time Positions for Job Creation by EB-5 Alien Entrepreneurs
HQDOMO 70/6.1.8 AD09-04
Page 7

> the nature of the industry or industries in which the jobs are to be created, and any other evidence submitted by the petitioner.
>
> If after considering the evidence, the officer determines that the jobs are more likely than not going to be created within a reasonable time, Form I-829 should be approved consistent with 8 C.F.R. § 216.6(d)(1) if the petitioner is otherwise eligible to have his or her conditions removed. If, however, the officer determines that the jobs will not be created within a reasonable period of time, Form I-829 should be denied consistent with 8 C.F.R. § 216.6(d)(2).

4. Chapters 22.4(b), 25.2(a), 25.2(b), 25.2(g)(1), and 25.2(i)(2)(C) of the AFM are revised to reference that all petitions and applications related EB-5 immigrant classifications and Regional Center proposals must be filed at the California Service Center (CSC).

   Chapter 22.4(b) [fourth bullet]

   - The petition must be filed with the California Service Center.

   Chapter 25.2(a)

   California Service Center director, regional directors and field office directors in offices with a high volume of Form I-829s shall designate an EB-5 trained and certified officer as an EB-5 point of contact (POC) to facilitate the review and management of Form I-829. For purposes of clarity in these instructions, references to service center management and field office management includes the appropriate EB-5 POC.

   Chapter 25.2(b)

   Officers are reminded that, in accordance with the Notice in the Federal Register at 74 Fed. Reg. 912-913, published on, and in effect since, January 9, 2009, Form I-829 petitions are to be filed with the California Service Center.

   Chapter 25.2(g)(1)

   All such Form I-829s shall be returned to the California Service Center.

   Chapter 25.2(i)(2)(C)

   The California Service Center shall generate weekly a printout from the MFAS to determine those conditional residents within its jurisdiction who have failed to file a timely Form I-829 to have the conditions on their status removed in accordance with section 216A(c) of the Act and will take the actions described above in this section to terminate the status of such conditional residents and their dependents.

Clarification of Two-Year Period the Meaning of Full-Time Positions for Job Creation by EB-5 Alien Entrepreneurs
HQDOMO 70/6.1.8 AD09-04
Page 8

5. The *AFM* **Transmittal Memoranda** button is revised by adding a new entry, in numerical order, to read:

AD 09 -04 (02-xx-2009)	**Chapter 22.4(c)(4)(D)** **Chapter 22.4(b)** **Chapter 25.2(a)** **Chapter 25.2(b)** **Chapter 25.2(e)(1)** **Chapter 25.2(g)(1)** **Chapter 25.2(i)(2)(C)**	This memorandum adds five paragraphs at the end of **Chapter 22.4(c)(4)(D)**; adds a new first paragraph to Chapter 25.2(e)(1); adds three new paragraphs at the end of Chapter 25.2(e)(1); and makes changes to both Chapter 22.4 and 25.2 to reference that all EB-5 petitions and applications are now filed with the California Service Center all in the AFM.

APPENDIX C-5: NEUFELD MEMO OF 12-11-09

U.S. Department of Homeland Security
U.S. Citizenship and Immigration Services
Office of Domestic Operations (MS-2010)
Washington, DC 20529-2010

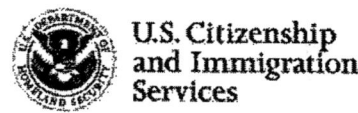

U.S. Citizenship and Immigration Services

HQ 70/6.2
AD 09-38

DEC 11 2009

Memorandum

TO: Field Leadership

FROM: Donald Neufeld
Acting Associate Director, Domestic Operations

SUBJECT: Adjudication of EB-5 Regional Center Proposals and Affiliated Form I-526 and Form I-829 Petitions; Adjudicators Field Manual (AFM) Update to Chapters 22.4 and 25.2 (AD09-38)

I. Purpose

This memorandum provides instruction to California Service Center (CSC) personnel involved in the adjudication of EB-5 Regional Center Proposals, and affiliated Forms I-526, Immigrant Petition by Alien Entrepreneur and Forms I-829, Petition by Entrepreneur to Remove Conditions. This memorandum rescinds in its entirety the USCIS memorandum, *Establishment of an Investor and Regional Center Unit*, dated January 19, 2005, and provides guidance regarding:

- The timing of the adjudication of EB-5 eligibility issues;
- The procedures to be used when there appears to be a material change in circumstances relating to an eligibility issue following the issue's prior adjudicative resolution;
- Targeted Employment Area (TEA) determinations;
- How an alien may seek approval of a new Form I-526 petition in order to change the focus of his or her investment to a new capital investment project or commercial enterprise; and
- The respective EB-5 program responsibilities of CSC and Service Center Operations (SCOPS) personnel.

This memorandum also addresses the issue of communication with non-USCIS individuals or entities regarding case specific information.

II. Background

Adjudication of EB-5 Regional Center Proposals and Affiliated Form
I-526 and Form I-829 Petitions; Adjudicators Field Manual (AFM) Update to Chapters
22.4 and 25.2 (AD09-38)
Page 2

The Immigrant Investor Program, also known as "EB-5", was created by Congress in 1990 under § 203(b)(5) of the Immigration and Nationality Act (INA) to stimulate the U.S. economy through job creation and capital investment by alien investors. Alien investors have the opportunity to obtain lawful permanent residence in the United States for themselves, their spouses, and their minor unmarried children by making a certain level of capital investments and associated job creation or preservation.

There are two distinct EB-5 pathways for an alien investor to gain lawful permanent residence, the Basic Program and the Regional Center Pilot Program. Both programs require that the alien investor make a capital investment of either $500,000 or $1,000,000 (depending on whether the investment is in a TEA or not) in a new commercial enterprise located within the United States. The new commercial enterprise must create or preserve 10 full-time jobs for qualifying U.S. workers within two years of the alien investor's admission to the United States as a Conditional Permanent Resident (CPR).[1] When making an investment in a new commercial enterprise affiliated with a USCIS-designated regional center under the Regional Center Pilot Program, an alien investor may satisfy the job creation requirements of the program through the creation of either direct or indirect jobs. Notably, an alien investing in a new commercial enterprise under the Basic Program may only satisfy the job creation requirements through the creation of direct jobs.

Note: *Direct jobs* are those jobs that establish an employer-employee relationship between the newly established commercial enterprise and the persons that they employ.

---

[1] The statutory framework for the EB-5 program can be found at INA sections 203(b)(5) and 216A, which were modified by:
- Section 610 of Pub. L. 102-395, as amended by section 116(a)(l) of Pub. L. 105-119 and section 402(a) of Pub. L. 106-396;
- Section 4 of Pub. L. 108-156, relating to the Regional Center Pilot Program; and
- Sections 11031-11034 of the 21st Century Department of Justice Appropriations Authorization Act, Pub. L. 107-273, relating to certain aliens with conditional resident status who filed I-829 petitions before November 2, 2002.

The regulatory framework for the EB-5 program can be found at 8 CFR 204.6 and 8 CFR 216.6.

There are also four EB-5 precedent decisions:
- *Matter of Soffici*, 22 I&N Dec. 158 (BIA 1998);
- *Matter of Izummi*, 22 I&N Dec. 169 (BIA 1998). **Note:** Pub. L. 107-273 eliminated the requirement set forth in *Izummi* that, in order for a petitioner to be considered to have "created" an original business, he or she must have had a hand in its actual creation. Under the new law, an alien may invest in an existing business at any time following its creation, provided he or she meets all other requirements of the regulations;
- *Matter of Hsiung*, 22 I&N, Dec. 201 (BIA 1998); and
- *Matter of Ho*, 22 I&N Dec. 206 (BIA 1998).

Adjudication of EB-5 Regional Center Proposals and Affiliated Form
I-526 and Form I-829 Petitions; Adjudicators Field Manual (AFM) Update to Chapters
22.4 and 25.2 (AD09-38)
Page 3

Indirect jobs are the jobs held by persons who work outside the newly established commercial enterprise. For example, indirect jobs include employees of the producers of materials, equipment, and services that are used by the commercial enterprise. There is also a sub-set of indirect jobs that are calculated using economic models that are known as induced jobs. *Induced jobs* are those jobs created when direct and indirect employees go out and spend their increased incomes on consumer goods and services.

Under the Regional Center Pilot Program, an individual or entity must file a Regional Center Proposal[2] with the CSC to request USCIS approval of the proposal and designation of the entity that filed the proposal as a regional center. A "Regional Center" is defined as any economic unit, public or private, engaged in the promotion of economic growth, improved regional productivity, job creation and increased domestic capital investment. The Regional Center Proposal must provide a framework within which individual alien investors affiliated with the regional center can satisfy the EB-5 eligibility requirement and create qualifying EB-5 jobs.

The Regional Center Proposal may also include copies of the commercial enterprise's organizational documents, capital investment offering memoranda, and transfer of capital mechanisms for the transfer of the alien investor's capital into the job creating enterprise so that USCIS may determine if they are in compliance with established EB-5 eligibility requirements. Providing these documents may facilitate the adjudication of the related I-526 petitions by identifying any issues that could pose problems when USCIS is adjudicating the actual petitions. For example, if a new commercial enterprise's limited partnership (LP) agreement contains a redemption clause guaranteeing the return of the alien investor's capital investment, then the alien investor's capital investment will not be a qualifying "at-risk" investment for EB-5 purposes. Likewise, if the LP agreement requires the payment of fees from the alien investor's capital investment of $1,000,000 (or $500,000 if in a TEA) to such extent that the investment will be eroded below the qualifying level, preventing the full infusion of sufficient capital into the job creating enterprise, then the alien investor's capital investment will not meet the required EB-5 level of investment. The approval of a Regional Center Proposal containing defects such as these is not in the best interest of the prospective regional center or the USCIS EB-5 program as the end result will most likely be the denial of the individual alien investor's Form I-526 petition.

Any individual Form I-526 and Form I-829 petitions claiming new commercial enterprise affiliation with a regional center and thus EB-5 eligibility based on indirect job creation must be denied if they are filed prior to the approval of the Regional Center Proposal.

---

[2] USCIS is developing a Regional Center Proposal form through the standard Office of Management and Budget (OMB) form development process. The new form will require the submission of a filing fee for the filing of an initial Regional Center Proposal and for Proposal Amendments that are filed subsequent to the initial approval and designation of the regional center. There is no filing fee for the submission of Regional Center Proposals and Proposal Amendments at the present time.

Adjudication of EB-5 Regional Center Proposals and Affiliated Form
I-526 and Form I-829 Petitions; Adjudicators Field Manual (AFM) Update to Chapters
22.4 and 25.2 (AD09-38)
Page 4

Each alien investor must file an individual Form I-526 petition to establish his or her eligibility for classification as an EB-5 alien investor under either the Basic Program or the Regional Center Pilot Program. If the Form I-526 petition is approved, then the alien must file a Form I-485, Application to Register Permanent Residence or Adjust Status, to adjust status in the United States, or apply for an immigrant visa abroad, in order to obtain CPR status. The alien investor must file a Form I-829 petition within the 90-day period immediately preceding the two-year anniversary of his or her admission to the United States or adjustment of status as a CPR. The Form I-829 petition must demonstrate that all of the terms and conditions of the EB-5 program have been met by the alien investor in order for the conditions on his or her permanent residence to be removed.

III. Rationale for Updated Field Guidance

A. Streamlining EB-5 Case Processing.

USCIS wishes to streamline the Regional Center Proposal and EB-5 petitioning processes. Distinct EB-5 eligibility requirements must be met at each stage of the EB-5 immigration process. If USCIS evaluates and approves certain aspects of an EB-5 investment, that favorable determination should generally be given deference at a subsequent stage in the EB-5 process. However, a previously favorable decision may not be relied upon in later proceedings where, for example, the underlying facts upon which a favorable decision was made have materially changed, there is evidence of fraud or misrepresentation in the record of proceeding, or the previously favorable decision is determined to be legally deficient.

USCIS is aware that there are times when Immigration Service Officers (ISOs) question whether a previously established EB-5 eligibility requirement has been met at a later stage in the process even though the facts of the case have not changed. USCIS is also aware that some designated regional centers have subsequently made material alterations to documentation initially provided in support of the regional center proposal. For example, there have been cases where a regional center has made significant changes to the organizational documentation, the transfer of capital mechanisms, or other aspects of the new commercial enterprise after approval of the regional center proposal. This documentation was changed to such a degree that it no longer resembled the documentation upon which USCIS based the approval of the Regional Center Proposal, and it appeared that the new commercial enterprise would no longer comply with EB-5 Program requirements.

In some instances, the adjudication of EB-5 petitions has been prolonged due to the issuance of requests for evidence (RFEs) that inappropriately seek to revalidate previously favorable determinations. Likewise, the finalization of EB-5 petitions have

Adjudication of EB-5 Regional Center Proposals and Affiliated Form
I-526 and Form I-829 Petitions; Adjudicators Field Manual (AFM) Update to Chapters
22.4 and 25.2 (AD09-38)
Page 5

been delayed due to the material alteration of documentation vetted during the Regional Center Proposal Process, requiring that previously decided issues be re-adjudicated within the EB-5 petitioning processes. This has prompted USCIS to deny EB-5 petitions.[3] Information provided in support of EB-5 petitions may also prompt USCIS to reopen a Regional Center Proposal and ultimately terminate the regional center designation under 8 CFR 204.6(m)(6) if the regional center is shown to be operating in a manner not in accordance with section §610(a) of Public Law 102-395.

In light of the above, USCIS is incorporating guidance into the AFM that highlights the adjudicative issues to be resolved at each stage of the Regional Center Proposal and EB-5 petitioning processes. In addition, the guidance outlines the factors that should be in place in order to revisit previously approved EB-5 eligibility requirements at a later stage in the process. USCIS is also adding guidance into the AFM update that explains how a regional center may provide an exemplar Form I-526 with the supporting documentation required by 8 CFR 204.6 in order to determine if the documentation is EB-5 compliant, and thus can generally be favorably acted upon if submitted unaltered in support of an actual Form I-526 petition.

B. Changes in Form I-526 Business Plans.

USCIS is aware that some EB-5 aliens may encounter difficulties when unforeseen circumstances cast doubt on the achievement of the requisite job creation as outlined in an approved Form I-526 petition. This may occur when the job creating capital investment project or commercial enterprise that was relied upon for the approval of the Form I-526 petition fails, or otherwise cannot be completed, within the alien's two-year period of conditional residence. The statutory structure of the EB-5 program and relevant precedent decisions limit an alien entrepreneur's options when a planned investment project fails. The capital investment project identified in the business plan in the approved Form I-526 petition must serve as the basis for determining at the Form I-829 petition stage whether the requisite capital investment has been sustained throughout the alien's two year period of conditional residency and that at least ten jobs have been or will be created within a reasonable period of time as a result of the alien's capital investment.[4] The business plan in the Form I-526 petition may not be materially changed after the petition has been filed.[5] In addition, USCIS may not act favorably on requests to delay the filing or adjudication of Form I-829 petitions beyond the timeframes outlined in INA section 216A(d)(2) and 8 CFR 216.6(a) and (c).

---

[3] EB-5 petitioners must establish eligibility as of the date of filing of the petition. See 8 CFR 103.2(b)(1), (12); *Matter of Katigbak*, 14 I&N Dec. at 49. Note also that a petitioner may not make material changes to a petition that has already been filed in an effort to make an apparently deficient petition conform to USCIS requirements. *Matter of Izummi*, 22 I&N Dec. at 175.

[4] See 8 CFR 216.6(c).

[5] See *Matter of Izummi*, 22 I&N Dec. 169 (BIA 1998) and 8 CFR 103.2(b).

Adjudication of EB-5 Regional Center Proposals and Affiliated Form
I-526 and Form I-829 Petitions; Adjudicators Field Manual (AFM) Update to Chapters
22.4 and 25.2 (AD09-38)
Page 6

As a result, USCIS is incorporating guidance into the AFM outlining the procedures for an ISO to follow when adjudicating:
- A new Form I-526 petition seeking to change the capital investment and job creation scheme outlined in an alien's previously filed Form I-526 petition; and
- If such new Form I-526 petition is approved, a Form I-485 application requesting re-adjustment of status.

C. Communication with EB-5 External Stakeholders.

It is critically important that all USCIS staff involved in the EB-5 Program understand that any case-specific communication with non-agency stakeholders may not be considered in the adjudication of an application or petition unless it is included in the record of proceeding of the case. USCIS may only provide information about specific cases to:
- The affected party in the proceeding; and
- The representative of the affected party, if any, who is identified on a properly executed Form G-28.[6] The agency will only recognize one attorney of record at a time as reflected in the most current Form G-28 available in the record.[7]

If USCIS receives evidence about a specific case from anyone other than an affected party or his or her representative, such information is not part of the record of proceeding and cannot be considered in adjudicative proceedings, unless the affected party has been given notice of such evidence and, if such evidence is derogatory, he or she has been given an opportunity to respond to the evidence as required in 8 CFR 103.2(b)(16). Note that the opinion of a USCIS official outside of the adjudicative process is not binding and no USCIS officer has the authority to pre-adjudicate a Regional Center Proposal or an EB-5 petition. *Matter of Izummi*, 22 I&N Dec. at 196.

In light of the above, USCIS staff is directed to include in the record of proceeding copies of all case-specific written communication with external stakeholders involving receipt of information relating to specific EB-5 Regional Center Proposals or individual petitions pending on or after the date of this memorandum. In the very limited instances where oral communication takes place between USCIS staff and external stakeholders regarding specific EB-5 cases, the conversation must either be recorded, or detailed minutes of the session must be taken and included in the record of proceeding. As provided above, if the documentary or oral evidence was not provided by the affected party or his or her representative, the party must be notified of the evidence.

---

[6] See 8 CFR 103.3(a)(iii)(B), 103.2(a)(3). See also sections §§551(14) and 557(d) of the Administrative Procedures Act (APA).

[7] See 8 CFR 292.4(a) providing for substitution of counsel via subsequent execution and submission of a new G-28. See also 8 CFR 292.5(a) and (b), 103.2(a)(3), and 103.2(b)(11), all of which refer to a singular "attorney" or "representative" permitted to represent the petitioner or applicant.

Adjudication of EB-5 Regional Center Proposals and Affiliated Form
I-526 and Form I-829 Petitions; Adjudicators Field Manual (AFM) Update to Chapters
22.4 and 25.2 (AD09-38)
Page 7

The EB-5 program maintains an e-mail account at
USCIS.ImmigrantInvestorProgram@dhs.gov for external stakeholders to use when
seeking general EB-5 program information, inquiring about the status of pending cases,
or requesting the expedite of a pending EB-5 case. USCIS personnel are instructed to
direct all case-specific and general EB-5 related communications with external
stakeholders through this email account, or through other established communication
channels, such as the National Customer Service Center (NCSC), or the USCIS Office of
Public Engagement.

USCIS believes that transparency in the administration of this program is critical to its
success. USCIS is aware that some external stakeholders routinely contact SCOPS HQ
personnel with questions regarding general EB-5 eligibility issues. SCOPS HQ has
routinely responded directly to the external stakeholders in accordance with the EB-5
oversight authority delegated to the Investor and Regional Center Unit in the USCIS
memorandum, *Establishment of an Investor and Regional Center Unit*, dated January 19,
2005. Unfortunately this method of communication is very resource intensive and only
serves to inform the external stakeholders who contact SCOPS HQ. USCIS is formally
rescinding the January 19, 2005, memo. SCOPS HQ will no longer respond to questions
from external stakeholders regarding EB-5 eligibility issues that have not been vetted
through the National Customer Service Center at (800) 375-5283, the EB-5 email account
at USCIS.ImmigrantInvestorProgram@dhs.gov, or are raised through other established
USCIS communication channels.

EB-5 eligibility issues that are raised through the EB-5 email account will be reviewed by
the CSC EB-5 staff who will:
- Respond to those that involve routine EB-5 questions; and
- Raise issues involving novel adjudicative questions to SCOPS HQ personnel.

SCOPS HQ will publish EB-5 FAQs and in some cases, policy memoranda, on the
USCIS website to address novel adjudicative issues raised by external stakeholders. This
method of communication will promote transparency and the free flow of EB-5 related
information in a manner that makes all EB-5 external stakeholders privy to the
information, not just a select few.

IV. Field Guidance

USCIS EB-5 program staff are directed to follow the guidance provided in this
memorandum in the adjudication of all Regional Center Proposals and EB-5 petitions
pending or filed as of the date of this memo.

V. AFM Update

The Adjudicator's Field Manual is revised as follows:

Adjudication of EB-5 Regional Center Proposals and Affiliated Form
I-526 and Form I-829 Petitions; Adjudicators Field Manual (AFM) Update to Chapters
22.4 and 25.2 (AD09-38)
Page 8

1. Chapter 22.4(a)(2) of the AFM is revised to read as follows:

    (2) Regional Center Pilot Program.

    (A) Program Overview. The Regional Center Pilot Program was first instituted in 1992. Three thousand of the 10,000 total available EB-5 visas are set aside for aliens who invest in a USCIS designated "regional center" in the United States organized "for the promotion of economic growth, including improved regional productivity, job creation, and increased domestic capital investment." Section 610 of Pub. L. 102-395, as amended by section 116(a)(I) of Pub. L. 105-119 and section 402(a) of Pub. L. 106-396.

    An alien investing in a new commercial enterprise affiliated with and located in a regional center is not required to demonstrate that the new commercial enterprise itself directly employs ten U.S. workers; a showing of indirect job creation and improved regional productivity will suffice. Implementing regulations for the Pilot Program are found at 8 CFR 204.6(m).

    Note: *Direct jobs* are those jobs that establish an employer-employee relationship between the commercial enterprise and the persons that they employ. Regional centers typically use the RIMS II or IMPLAN economic models to determine the number of indirect jobs that will be created through investments in the regional center's investment projects. *Indirect jobs* are the jobs held by persons who work for the producers of materials, equipment, and services that are used in a commercial enterprise's capital investment project, but who are not directly employed by the commercial enterprise, such as steel producers or outside firms that provide accounting services. There is a sub-set of indirect jobs that are calculated using economic models that are known as induced jobs. *Induced jobs* are those jobs created when direct and indirect employees go out and spend their increased incomes on consumer goods and services.

    A Regional Center Proposal must be filed with the CSC to request USCIS approval of the proposal and designation of the entity that filed the proposal as a regional center. A "Regional Center" is defined as any economic unit, public or private, engaged in the promotion of economic growth, improved regional productivity, job creation and increased domestic capital investment. The Regional Center Proposal must demonstrate that capital investments made by individual alien investors within the geographic area of the regional center will satisfy the EB-5

Adjudication of EB-5 Regional Center Proposals and Affiliated Form
I-526 and Form I-829 Petitions; Adjudicators Field Manual (AFM) Update to Chapters
22.4 and 25.2 (AD09-38)
Page 9

eligibility requirements in order to create qualifying EB-5 jobs. The Regional Center Proposal should also demonstrate that the new commercial enterprise's organizational documents, capital investment offering memoranda, and transfer of capital mechanisms for the transfer of the alien investor's capital into the job creating enterprise are in compliance with established EB-5 eligibility requirements.

(B) <u>Regional Center Proposal EB-5 Eligibility Requirements</u>. Regional Center Proposals must demonstrate the following EB-5 eligibility requirements in order to be approved:

(i) A clearly identified, contiguous geographical area for the regional center. If the regional center proposal bases its predictions regarding the number of direct or indirect jobs that will be created through EB-5 investments in the regional center, in whole or in part, by offering investment opportunities to EB-5 investors with the reduced $500,000 threshold, then the Targeted Employment Areas (TEAs), Rural Areas (areas with populations under 20,000 people) and areas of high unemployment (areas with unemployment rates 150% or more of the national rate), should be identified. Note: An alien filing a regional center affiliated Form I-526 must still establish that the investment will be made in a TEA at the time of filing of the alien's Form I-526 petition, or at the time of the investment, whichever occurs first, to qualify for the reduced $500,000 capital investment threshold.

(ii) A detailed description of how EB-5 capital investment within the geographic area of the regional center will create qualifying EB-5 jobs, either directly or indirectly. This analysis must be supported by economically and statistically valid forecasting tools, including, but not limited to, feasibility studies, analyses of foreign and domestic markets for the goods or services to be exported [if any], and/or multiplier tables.

(iii) A detailed prediction of the proposed regional center's predicted impact regionally or nationally on household earnings, greater demand for business services, utilities, maintenance and repair, and construction both within and outside of the geographic area of the proposed Regional Center.

(iv) A description of the plans to administer, oversee, and manage the proposed Regional Center, including but not limited to how the regional center will:

Adjudication of EB-5 Regional Center Proposals and Affiliated Form
I-526 and Form I-829 Petitions; Adjudicators Field Manual (AFM) Update to Chapters
22.4 and 25.2 (AD09-38)
Page 10

- Be promoted to attract EB-5 alien investors, including a description of the budget for the promotional activity;
- Identify, assess and evaluate proposed immigrant investor projects and enterprises;
- Structure its investment capital, e.g., whether the investment capital to be sought will consist solely of alien investor capital or a combination of alien investor capital and domestic capital, and how the distribution of the investment capital will be structured, e.g. loans to developers, venture capital, etc.; and
- Oversee all investment activities affiliated with, through or under the sponsorship of the proposed Regional Center.

(C) The Regional Center Proposal may also include an "exemplar" Form I-526 petition that contains copies of the commercial enterprise's organizational documents, capital investment offering memoranda, and transfer of capital mechanisms for the transfer of the alien investor's capital into the job creating enterprise. USCIS will review the documentation to determine if they are in compliance with established EB-5 eligibility requirements. Providing these documents may facilitate the adjudication of the related I-526 petitions by identifying any issues that could pose problems when USCIS is adjudicating the actual petitions. For example, if a new commercial enterprise's limited partnership (LP) agreement contains a buy-back agreement (i.e. a redemption clause guaranteeing the return of the alien investor's capital investment), then the alien investor's capital investment will not be a qualifying "at-risk" investment for EB-5 purposes. Likewise, if the LP agreement requires the payment of fees from the alien investor's capital investment of $1,000,000 or $500,000, respectively, to the extent that the investment will be eroded below the qualifying level, preventing the full infusion of the capital into the job creating enterprise, then the alien investor's capital investment will not meet the required EB-5 level of investment. The approval of a Regional Center Proposal containing defects such as these is not in the best interest of the prospective regional center or the USCIS EB-5 program as the end result will most likely be the denial of the individual alien investor's Form I-526 petition.

Any individual Form I-526 and Form I-829 petitions claiming new commercial enterprise affiliation with a regional center and thus EB-5 eligibility based on indirect job creation must be denied if they are filed prior to the approval of the regional center's Regional Center Proposal.

(D) Regional Center Proposal and Amendment Request Processing.
There are two general workflows for the adjudication of Regional Center

Adjudication of EB-5 Regional Center Proposals and Affiliated Form
I-526 and Form I-829 Petitions; Adjudicators Field Manual (AFM) Update to Chapters
22.4 and 25.2 (AD09-38)
Page 11

>Proposals, one for Initial Regional Center Proposals and one for Regional Center Amendment requests. ISOs adjudicate cases within these workflows in "first in, first out" order, unless an expedite request is granted by the CSC director in accordance with the routine expedite criteria that is used for all cases filed with USCIS.
>
>(E) <u>Amended Regional Center Proposals</u>.
>
>>(i) <u>Amendments Due to Material Changes in EB-5 Related Organizational Structure or Capital Investment Instruments</u>. Designated regional centers may elect to file an amended Regional Center Proposal and receive an updated approval of the regional center designation prior to the filing of individual EB-5 petitions that use supporting documentation relating to EB-5 eligibility issues that has been materially altered or is inconsistent with the documentation used as the basis for the approval of the regional center designation. Doing so, may assist in the streamlining of the adjudication of affiliated individual EB-5 petitions, as the altered documentation may otherwise need to be re-evaluated within the individual EB-5 petitions to determine if they still EB-5 compliant.
>>
>>(ii) <u>Other Amendments</u>. Some Regional Center Proposals are approved for an industry segment using a hypothetical investment project in order to demonstrate how an actual investment project will be capitalized and operate in a manner that will create at least 10 direct or indirect jobs per alien investor. Individual Form I-526 petitions are then filed with copies of the business plan for the hypothetical investment project as well as the regional center's actual investment project. If the actual investment project is not different in a material way from the exemplar investment project, then the job creating efficacy of the investment project, if carried through as specified in the business plan will generally be established.
>>
>>Regional centers may opt to file an amendment of their Regional Center Proposal in order to eliminate the uncertainty as to whether the actual investment project is different in a material way from the exemplar investment project that was approved in the Regional Center Proposal. The filing of these amendments is in the best interest of the EB-5 program as it may assist in the streamlining of the adjudication of the individual Form I-526 petitions. These amendments should be supported by detailed documentation relating to the actual investment project. Once approved, then only the documentation relating to the actual approved project would be provided in support of the Form I-526

Adjudication of EB-5 Regional Center Proposals and Affiliated Form
I-526 and Form I-829 Petitions; Adjudicators Field Manual (AFM) Update to Chapters
22.4 and 25.2 (AD09-38)
Page 12

>petition, eliminating the uncertainty regarding whether the actual project meets EB-5 eligibility requirements.
>
>A regional center may also file an amendment in order to provide an exemplar Form I-526 with the supporting documentation required by 8 CFR 204.6 in order for USCIS to determine if the documentation is EB-5 compliant, and thus facilitate adjudication of an actual but identical Form I-526 petition, if the evidence of record otherwise establishes EB-5 eligibility.
>
>**Note:** If the Regional Center requirements are met and a determination of eligibility is made, then the favorable determination regarding regional center eligibility requirements for the capital investment structure and job creation should generally be given deference and not revisited in the adjudication of individual EB-5 petitions, as long as the underlying facts upon which the favorable decision was made remain unchanged. The CSC EB-5 program manager should be notified to determine the appropriate action to take if an ISO discovers during the adjudication of an EB-5 petition that:
>- Documentation relating to the regional center's capital investment structure or job creation methodologies, or the exemplar Form I-526 petition has materially changed since the most recent approval of the regional center designation;
>- The record contains evidence of fraud or misrepresentation; or
>- The evidence of record indicates that the previously favorable decision to approve the regional center proposal (or amendment) to include the determination that the exemplar Form I-526 petition is EB-5 compliant was legally deficient.

2. Chapter 22.4(c)(3) of the AFM is revised to read as follows:

(3) <u>General Review</u>. Review the Form I-526 petition for completeness and signature of the petitioner.

- Verify that the name given in Part 1 (Information about you) is identical to the signature in Part 7 (Signature block).

- Remember that the petition can only be signed by the petitioner and not by his or her authorized representative.

The following EB-5 eligibility requirements must be established in the Form I-526 petition:

Adjudication of EB-5 Regional Center Proposals and Affiliated Form
I-526 and Form I-829 Petitions; Adjudicators Field Manual (AFM) Update to Chapters
22.4 and 25.2 (AD09-38)
Page 13

- The capital investment is in a new commercial enterprise;

- If the petitioner claims that the capital investment qualifies for the reduced capital investment threshold of $500,000, that the new commercial enterprise is located in a TEA;

- The investment capital was obtained by the alien through lawful means;

- The required amount of capital has been fully committed to the new commercial enterprise;

- The new commercial enterprise will create not fewer than 10 full-time positions; and

- The alien investor will be engaged in the management of the new commercial enterprise.

Note: If the new commercial enterprise identified in the petition is affiliated with a regional center, then the petitioner must provide with the Form I-526 petition a copy of the regional center's:

- Most recently issued approval letter; and
- Documentation relating to its approved capital investment structure and job creation methodology.

If the evidence provided remains unchanged from the documentation that was the basis for the approval of the regional center proposal, then the prior approval of the capital investment structure and the job creation methodology should generally be given deference. The CSC EB-5 program manager should be notified to determine the appropriate action to take if an ISO discovers during the adjudication of Form I-526 petition that:
- Documentation relating to the regional center's capital investment structure or job creation methodologies has materially changed since the approval of the regional center designation;
- The record contains evidence of fraud or misrepresentation; or
- The evidence of record indicates that the previously favorable decision to approve the regional center proposal (or amendment) to include the determination that the exemplar Form I-526 petition is EB-5 compliant was legally deficient.

3. Chapter 22.4(c)(4)(D)(iii) of the AFM is revised to read as follows:

Adjudication of EB-5 Regional Center Proposals and Affiliated Form
I-526 and Form I-829 Petitions; Adjudicators Field Manual (AFM) Update to Chapters
22.4 and 25.2 (AD09-38)
Page 14

> (iii) <u>Clarification of the Meaning of Full-time Position</u>. Section 203(b)(5) of the INA requires that the investment in a new commercial enterprise will create full-time employment for not fewer than 10 qualified employees. The INA further defines full-time employment as "employment in a position that requires at least 35 hours or service per week at any time, regardless of who fills the position." Adjudicating ISOs should keep the following points in mind when determining if positions meet this requirement:
>
> - Economic input/output (I/O) models, such as RIMS II or IMPLAN, used to evaluate the calculation of the number of <u>indirect jobs</u> (including <u>induced jobs</u>) created through a commercial enterprise affiliated with a regional center do not distinguish between full-time and part-time jobs. In other words, the job creation results of the multipliers in the economic I/O models do not distinguish between the full-time and part-time nature of the positions. Therefore, the number of <u>indirect jobs</u> quantified through the I/O model analysis will be considered to be full-time and qualifying for EB-5 purposes. Accordingly, determinations regarding whether jobs qualify as "full-time" are only relevant to the analysis of <u>direct jobs</u> created by a commercial enterprise claiming the creation of <u>direct jobs</u> as a result of the EB-5 capital investment.
>
> - USCIS has interpreted the full-time employment requirement to exclude jobs that are intermittent, temporary, seasonal or transient in nature. See, e.g., <u>Spencer Enterprises v. U.S.</u>, 229 F.Supp.2d 1025 (E.D. Cal. 2001). Historically, construction jobs have not been counted toward job creation because they are seen as intermittent, temporary, seasonal and transient rather than permanent. USCIS, however, now interprets that direct construction jobs may now count as permanent jobs if they:
>   - Are created by the petitioner's investment; and
>   - Are expected to last at least two years, inclusive of when the petitioner's Form I-829 is filed.
>
> Although employment in some industries such as construction or tourism can be intermittent, temporary, seasonal or transient, officers should not exclude jobs simply because they fall into such industries. Rather, the focus of the adjudication should be on whether the direct positions, as described in the petition, are continuous full-time employment rather than intermittent, temporary, seasonal or transient.

Adjudication of EB-5 Regional Center Proposals and Affiliated Form
I-526 and Form I-829 Petitions; Adjudicators Field Manual (AFM) Update to Chapters
22.4 and 25.2 (AD09-38)
Page 15

>**For example**, if a petition reasonably describes the need to directly employ general laborers in a construction project that is expected to last several years and require a minimum of 35 hours per week over the course of that project, the positions would meet the full-time employment requirement. However, if the same project called for electrical workers to provide services as direct employees during three to four five week periods over the course of the project, such positions would be properly deemed to be intermittent and not meet the definition of full-time employment.

- Generally, it is <u>the position</u> that is critical to the full-time direct employment criterion, not <u>the employee</u>. Accordingly, the fact that the position may be filled by more than one employee does not exclude a position from consideration as full-time employment.

    >**For example**, the positions described in the above bullet would not be excluded from being considered full-time employment if the general laborers needed to fill the positions varied from day to day or week to week, as long as the need to directly employ general laborers in the position remains constant. This interpretation is consistent with 8 CFR 204.6(e), which includes job sharing arrangements as part of the regulatory definition of full-time employment.

- It is important to note, however, that this interpretation does not override the regulatory definitions of employee and full-time employment at 8 CFR 204.6(e). Thus, direct jobs must still be filled by qualifying employees and not by independent contractors. Positions filled by independent contractors are not qualifying direct jobs and may only be credited for EB-5 job creation purposes in petitions involving commercial enterprises that are affiliated with a regional center. In addition, multiple part-time positions may not be combined to create one full-time position, unless those part-time jobs can be shown to be part of a job-sharing arrangement.

- Full-time employment relating to the creation of direct jobs as defined in 8 CFR 204.6(e) means year-round employment and not seasonal full-time employment. Full-time employment consists of 35 hours a week. Seasonal positions do not qualify for purposes of the full-time employment requirement for <u>direct jobs</u>.

Adjudication of EB-5 Regional Center Proposals and Affiliated Form
I-526 and Form I-829 Petitions; Adjudicators Field Manual (AFM) Update to Chapters
22.4 and 25.2 (AD09-38)
Page 16

4. Chapter 22.4(c)(4)(F) of the AFM is revised to read as follows:

> (F) <u>New Commercial Enterprise in a Targeted Employment Area (TEA)</u>. A TEA is <u>either</u> a rural area or an area experiencing a high unemployment rate at the time of the capital investment or the time of filing of the Form I-526 petition, whichever occurs first. If the petitioner shows that the area where he or she is investing is a rural area, the petitioner need not also establish that the area has high employment. Conversely, if the area is a high unemployment area, the petitioner need not also show that it is a rural area.
>
> INA 203(b)(5)(B) and 8 CFR 204.6(e) require that in order to establish eligibility for the reduced EB-5 investment threshold of $500,000, the area in which the alien makes a capital investment must qualify as an rural area or an area of high unemployment when the investment is made. <u>Matter of Soffici</u>, 22 I&N Dec. 158 (BIA 1998) provides in pertinent part that:
>
>> A petitioner has the burden to establish that his enterprise does business in an area that is considered "targeted" as of the date he files his [Form I-526] petition. The fact that a business may be located in an area that was once rural, for example, does not mean that the area is still rural.
>
> A conflict between the statutory and regulatory requirements, and <u>Matter of Soffici</u> may arise when an alien makes a capital investment at a point in time prior to the filing of the Form I-526 petition when the area in which the investment is made qualifies as a TEA, only to have the area no longer qualify as a TEA at the time of filing of the Form I-526 petition. In order to promote predictability in the capital investment process and to reconcile the potential conflict outlined above, ISOs must identify the appropriate date to examine in order to determine that the alien's capital investment qualifies for the reduced $500,000 threshold according to the following "if, then" table:

TEA "if then" Table	
If the Investment…	Then…
Is made into the commercial enterprise's job creating project prior to the filing of the Form I-526 petition…	The TEA analysis should focus on whether the location of the investment qualifies as a TEA at the time of the investment.
Has yet to be committed to the commercial enterprise's job	The TEA analysis should focus on whether the location of the

Adjudication of EB-5 Regional Center Proposals and Affiliated Form
I-526 and Form I-829 Petitions; Adjudicators Field Manual (AFM) Update to Chapters
22.4 and 25.2 (AD09-38)
Page 17

creating project at the time of filing of the I-526, i.e. is still in escrow or is otherwise not irrevocably invested into the commercial enterprise pending the approval of the I-526 petition…	investment qualifies as a TEA at the time of the filing of the I-526 petition.

Note: In some instances, an alien may request eligibility for the reduced investment threshold based on the fact that other EB-5 aliens who previously invested in the same project qualified for the $500,000 minimum investment, even though the area did not qualify at the time of the instant alien's investment or the filing of his or her Form I-526. Each alien must establish that his or her capital investment qualifies for the reduced investment threshold, and cannot rely on previous TEA determinations made based on facts that have subsequently changed.

Note also that the area where the new commercial enterprise is located may qualify as a TEA at the time the capital investment is made or the I-526 petition is filed, (whichever occurs first), but may cease to qualify by the time the Form I-829 petition is filed. Changes in population size or unemployment rates within the area during the alien investor's period of conditional permanent residence are acceptable as increased job creation is the primary goal of the EB-5 program.

> (i) <u>Rural Area Defined</u>. The term "rural area" means any area that is both outside of a metropolitan statistical area (MSA) and outside of a city or town having a population of 20,000 or more based on the most recent decennial census of the United States. See INA § 203(b)(5)(B)(iii) and 8 CFR §204.6(j)(6)(i). MSAs are designated by the Office of Management and Budget and can be found at www.census.gov.

> (ii) <u>Definition of High Unemployment Area</u>. The term "high unemployment area" means an area which has experienced unemployment of at least 150 percent of the national average rate. See INA § 203(b)(5)(B)(ii). The I-526 petitioner must demonstrate that, at the time the capital investment is made or the petition is filed (whichever occurs first), there has been an unemployment rate of at least 150% of the national unemployment rate within the MSA or other non-rural area in which the commercial enterprise that will create or preserve jobs is located. This should be based on the most recent information available to the general public from federal or state governmental sources as of the time the I-526 petition is submitted.

Adjudication of EB-5 Regional Center Proposals and Affiliated Form
I-526 and Form I-829 Petitions; Adjudicators Field Manual (AFM) Update to Chapters
22.4 and 25.2 (AD09-38)
Page 18

In some instances I-526 petitioners may claim high unemployment in only a portion or portions of a geographic area or political subdivision for which distinct unemployment data is not readily available to the general public from federal or state governmental sources. This may be indicative of an attempt by the petitioner to "gerrymander" a finding of high unemployment when in fact the area does not qualify as being a high unemployment area. Such a claim is not sufficient to establish that the area is a high unemployment area unless it is accompanied by a designation from an authorized authority of the state government. (State designations are discussed below in (iii) of this section.)

The Bureau of Labor Statistics (BLS) provides data regarding the national average rate of unemployment at www.bls.gov/cps/. BLS's **Local Area Unemployment Statistics (LAUS)** program produces monthly and annual unemployment and other labor force data for census regions and divisions, states, counties, metropolitan areas, and many cities, by place of residence. This information can be found at www.bls.gov/lau/. States, the District of Columbia, and the U.S. territories may also publish local area unemployment statistics on their government websites.

(iii) <u>State Designation of a High Unemployment Area</u>. The state government of any state of the United States may designate a particular geographic area or political subdivision located within a metropolitan statistical area or within a city or town having a population of 20,000 or more within such a state as an area of high unemployment. Before any such designation is made, an official of the state must notify USCIS of the agency, board, or other appropriate governmental body of the state which shall be delegated the authority to certify that the geographic or political subdivision is a high unemployment area. Evidence of such a designation, including a description of the boundaries of the geographic or political subdivision and the method or methods by which the unemployment statistics were obtained, may be submitted in support of the Form I-526 petition in lieu of other documentary evidence of high unemployment in the area where the new commercial enterprise is located. See 8 CFR 204.6(i). The statistics used in the analysis must reflect the national and local unemployment rates for these regions at the time of the alien investor's capital investment. See 8 CFR 204.6(e).

The designation of high unemployment areas are within the purview of each U.S. state governor, or if applicable, his or her designee. USCIS

Adjudication of EB-5 Regional Center Proposals and Affiliated Form
I-526 and Form I-829 Petitions; Adjudicators Field Manual (AFM) Update to Chapters
22.4 and 25.2 (AD09-38)
Page 19

personnel have no substantive authority to question or challenge such high unemployment designations, and therefore must rely on the high unemployment designations that conform to the requirements outlined above that are made by a U.S. state governor or his or her designee. ISOs should notify the CSC EB-5 program manager and seek guidance regarding how to address the TEA issue in petitions that contains a state designation letter that does not conform to the requirements of 8 CFR 204.6(i), utilizes statistics that do not reflect the national and local unemployment rates at the time of the alien investor's capital investment, or has been issued by an official of a state that has not notified USCIS regarding who in the state government has the authority to issue such designations.

Note: State designations of high unemployment areas also include designations issued by the appointed government body with authority to make such certifications by the governors of the U.S. territories or the mayor of the District of Columbia.

5. Chapter 22.4(c)(4)(G) of the AFM is added as follows:

(G) Eligibility Requirements for the Review of a Form I-526 Petition that Seeks Consideration of a Business Plan that Differs from the Business Plan in a Previously Approved Form I-526 Petition.

Some EB-5 aliens may encounter difficulties when unforeseen circumstances cause the achievement of the requisite job creation outlined in the Form I-526 petition to be cast in doubt. This may occur when the job creating capital investment project or commercial enterprise that was relied upon for the approval of the Form I-526 petition fails or otherwise cannot be completed within the alien's two-year period of conditional residence. The structure of the EB-5 program is inflexible in that the capital investment project identified in the business plan in the approved Form I-526 petition must serve as the basis for determining at the Form I-829 petition stage whether the requisite capital investment has been sustained throughout the alien's two year period of conditional residency and that at least ten jobs have been or will be created within a reasonable period of time as a result of the alien's capital investment. The business plan in the Form I-526 petition may not be materially changed after the petition has been filed. In addition, USCIS may not act favorably on requests to delay the filing or adjudication of Form I-829 petitions beyond the timeframes outlined in 8 CFR 216.6(a) and (c).

Adjudication of EB-5 Regional Center Proposals and Affiliated Form
I-526 and Form I-829 Petitions; Adjudicators Field Manual (AFM) Update to Chapters
22.4 and 25.2 (AD09-38)
Page 20

The following "if, then" table explains how an EB-5 investor can seek consideration of a business plan that differs from the business plan in a previously approved Form I-526 petition.

New Form I-526 Petition "If, Then" Table	
If...	Then...
The alien wishes to change the business plan from the business plan outlined in a previously filed Form I-526 petition...	S/he may file a new Form I-526 petition with fee that is supported by the new business plan and addresses all requirements of the I-526 petition.
If the new Form I-526 Petition is Filed...	Then...
Before the alien adjusts status (AOS) or is issued an immigrant visa (IV)...	The new petition, if approved, will be the basis for the AOS or the IV and the new business plan will be used as the basis for evaluating EB-5 eligibility at the I-829 stage.
After the alien adjusts status or is issued an IV, but before the due date of the filing of the I-829 petition (90 days prior to the end of the two-year CPR period).	Upon approval of the new Form I-526 petition, S/he may file Form I-407 with a Form I-485 adjustment application. The prior CPR status will be terminated and the new AOS application will be approved, if otherwise approvable, granting a new two year period of CPR status. The new I-526 petition will be used as the basis when evaluating eligibility at the I-829 stage. If the new Form I-526 is denied, then the alien will have to file the I-829 petition and use the initial Form I-526 petition as the basis for the eligibility evaluation in the Form I-829 petition.
After the alien adjusts status or is issued an IV on or after the due date for the filing of the I-829 petition.	If the new I-526 is approved, S/he may request the withdrawal of the initial I-829 petition and file an AOS application. The prior CPR status will be terminated and the new AOS application will be approved, if otherwise approvable, granting a new two year period of CPR status. The new I-526 petition will be used as the

Adjudication of EB-5 Regional Center Proposals and Affiliated Form
I-526 and Form I-829 Petitions; Adjudicators Field Manual (AFM) Update to Chapters
22.4 and 25.2 (AD09-38)
Page 21

	basis when evaluating eligibility at the second I-829 stage.
	If the new I-526 petition is denied, then the initial Form I-829 petition will be adjudicated using the project plan in the initial I-526 petition as the basis for the initial I-829 eligibility evaluation.
Note: Dependents will have to file I-407s at the same time as required for the principals as well as Form I-485 applications in order to terminate their CPR status and be "re-adjusted" to CPR anew. The dependents must be eligible to be classified as EB-5 dependents at the time of the filing of new Form I-485 application, i.e. the dependents must be the spouse or unmarried child under the age of 21 years of the EB-5 principal alien	

6. Chapter 25.2(e)(4) of the AFM is revised by adding new paragraph (E) to read as follows:

> (E) <u>I-829 Consideration of Form I-526 EB-5 Eligibility Requirements.</u> Pursuant to section 216A(c)(3) of the Act, USCIS must determine that the facts and information contained in the petition are true. ISOs should generally give deference to the approval of EB-5 eligibility requirements previously made in the alien investor's Form I-526 petition and affiliated regional center designation, as applicable, if the facts presented in the earlier proceedings remain unchanged to include:
>
> - The new commercial enterprise's capital investment structure;
>
> - That the commercial enterprise qualifies as "new" for EB-5 purposes;
>
> - If the commercial enterprise is affiliated with a regional center, the direct and indirect job creation methodology;
>
> - If the Form I-526 petition was approved for reduced capital investment threshold of $500,000, that the new commercial enterprise was located in a TEA at the time of filing of the Form I-526, and;
>
> - That the alien investor's investment capital was lawfully obtained.
>
> The CSC EB-5 program manager should be notified to determine the appropriate action to take if an ISO discovers during the adjudication of the Form I-829 petition that:

Adjudication of EB-5 Regional Center Proposals and Affiliated Form
I-526 and Form I-829 Petitions; Adjudicators Field Manual (AFM) Update to Chapters
22.4 and 25.2 (AD09-38)
Page 22

- Documentation relating to the regional center's capital investment structure or job creation methodologies or the eligibility requirements favorably decided-upon in the Form I-526 petition have materially changed post-approval of the regional center designation or Form I-526 petition;
- The record contains evidence of fraud or misrepresentation; or
- The evidence of record indicates that the previously favorable decision to approve the regional center proposal (or amendment) was legally deficient.

If the documentation of record presents material inconsistencies that impact the alien investor's EB-5 eligibility, then ISOs should require the petitioner to resolve the inconsistencies prior making a favorable determination in the case. It is incumbent upon the petitioner to resolve any inconsistencies in the record by independent objective evidence. Any attempt to explain or reconcile such inconsistencies will not suffice unless the petitioner submits competent objective evidence pointing to where the truth lies. *Matter of Ho*, 19 I&N Dec. 582, 591 (BIA 1988).

Note: EB-5 petitioners must establish eligibility as of the date of filing of the petition. See 8 CFR 103.2(b)(1), (12); *Matter of Katigbak*, 14 I&N Dec. at 49. Note also that a petitioner may not make material changes to a petition that has already been filed in an effort to make an apparently deficient petition conform to USCIS requirements. *Matter of Izummi*, 22 I&N Dec. at 175.

7. The AFM **Transmittal Memoranda** button is revised by adding a new entry, in numerical order, to read:

AD09-38	Chapter 22 and Chapter 25	This memorandum revises Chapters 22 and 25 of the *Adjudicator's Field Manual (AFM)* by amending sections 22.4 and 25.2 to clarify issues pertaining to EB-5 (Immigrant Investor) Regional Center Proposal petitions for classification (Form I-526) and petitions for removal of conditions (Form I-829).

VI. Use

This memorandum is intended solely for the instruction and guidance of USCIS personnel in performing their duties relative to adjudications. It is not intended to, does

Adjudication of EB-5 Regional Center Proposals and Affiliated Form
I-526 and Form I-829 Petitions; Adjudicators Field Manual (AFM) Update to Chapters
22.4 and 25.2 (AD09-38)
Page 23

not, and may not be relied upon to create any right or benefit, substantive or procedural, enforceable at law or by any individual or other party in removal proceedings, in litigation with the United States, or in any other form or manner.

VII. Questions

Questions regarding this memorandum should be directed through appropriate channels to Alexandra Haskell in the Business and Employment Services Team of Service Center Operations.

Distribution List:

    Regional Directors
    Service Center Directors
    District Directors
    Field Office Directors
    National Benefits Center Director
    Chief, Service Center Operations
    Chief, Field Operations

APPENDIX D-1: ADJUDICATOR'S FIELD MANUAL, CHAPTER 22.4 EMPLOYMENT CREATION ENTREPRENEUR CASES

22.4 Employment Creation Entrepreneur Cases.

(a) General. In 1990, Congress created the Employment Creation Immigrant Visa Category (EB-5). Section 121(a) of Public Law 101-649 (Nov. 29, 1990). Section 203(b)(5) of the Immigration and Nationality Act, as amended, allows for admission to permanent residence on a two-year conditional basis to qualified aliens who will contribute to the economic growth of the United States by investing in U.S. businesses and creating needed employment opportunities. In 2002, Congress amended the EB-5 statute. Those amendments are discussed in paragraph (h), below.

(1) *Basic (Non-Pilot Program) Provisions.* Section 203(b)(5) of the Act authorizes up to 10,000 visas each fiscal year to alien entrepreneurs (along with their spouses and unmarried minor children) who have invested or are actively in the process of investing in a new commercial enterprise.

The new commercial enterprise may take any lawful business form, including a limited partnership, and must both benefit the U.S. economy and directly create full-time employment for not fewer than 10 "qualifying employees," defined as U.S. citizens, lawful permanent residents, or certain other immigrants lawfully authorized to be employed. Noncommercial activities, including home ownership, do not qualify. In general, the Act established a threshold investment amount of one million U.S. dollars ($1,000,000.00). In order to encourage the investment in new enterprises located in areas that would most benefit from employment creation, section 203(b)(5)(B) of the Act sets aside on an annual basis 3,000 of the available 10,000 EB-5 visas for qualified aliens who have made investments in "targeted employment areas." Such targeted employment areas are defined in the Act to include rural areas and areas which have experienced high unemployment. The investment amount for investing in a targeted employment area is currently set at five hundred thousand dollars ($500,000.00).

(2) *Regional Center Pilot Program.* [Revised by 12/11/09, AD09-38]

(A) *Program Overview.* The Regional Center Pilot Program was first instituted in 1992. Three thousand of the 10,000 total available EB-5 visas are set aside for aliens who invest in a USCIS designated "regional center" in the United States organized "for the promotion of economic growth, including improved regional productivity, job creation, and increased domestic capital investment." Section 610 of Pub. L. 102-395, as amended by section 116(a)(*l*) of Pub. L. 105-119 and section 402(a) of Pub. L. 106-396.

An alien investing in a new commercial enterprise affiliated with and located in a regional center is not required to demonstrate that the new commercial enterprise itself directly employs ten U.S. workers; a showing of indirect job creation and improved regional productivity will suffice. Implementing regulations for the Pilot Program are found at 8 CFR 204.6(m).

Distributed by AILA Publications (American Immigration Lawyers Association, 2010)

Note: *Direct jobs* are those jobs that establish an employer-employee relationship between the commercial enterprise and the persons that they employ. Regional centers typically use the RIMS II or IMPLAN economic models to determine the number of indirect jobs that will be created through investments in the regional center's investment projects. *Indirect jobs* are the jobs held by persons who work for the producers of materials, equipment, and services that are used in a commercial enterprise's capital investment project, but who are not directly employed by the commercial enterprise, such as steel producers or outside firms that provide accounting services. There is a sub-set of indirect jobs that are calculated using economic models that are known as induced jobs. *Induced jobs* are those jobs created when direct and indirect employees go out and spend their increased incomes on consumer goods and services.

A Regional Center Proposal must be filed with the CSC to request USCIS approval of the proposal and designation of the entity that filed the proposal as a regional center. A "Regional Center" is defined as any economic unit, public or private, engaged in the promotion of economic growth, improved regional productivity, job creation and increased domestic capital investment. The Regional Center Proposal must demonstrate that capital investments made by individual alien investors within the geographic area of the regional center will satisfy the EB-5 eligibility requirements in order to create qualifying EB-5 jobs. The Regional Center Proposal should also demonstrate that the new commercial enterprise's organizational documents, capital investment offering memoranda, and transfer of capital mechanisms for the transfer of the alien investor's capital into the job creating enterprise are in compliance with established EB-5 eligibility requirements.

(B) *Regional Center Proposal EB-5 Eligibility Requirements.* Regional Center Proposals must demonstrate the following EB-5 eligibility requirements in order to be approved:

(i) A clearly identified, contiguous geographical area for the regional center. If the regional center proposal bases its predictions regarding the number of direct or indirect jobs that will be created through EB-5 investments in the regional center, in whole or in part, by offering investment opportunities to EB-5 investors with the reduced $500,000 threshold, then the Targeted Employment Areas (TEAs), Rural Areas (areas with populations under 20,000 people) and areas of high unemployment (areas with unemployment rates 150% or more of the national rate), should be identified. Note: An alien filing a regional center affiliated Form I-526 must still establish that the investment will be made in a TEA at the time of filing of the alien's Form I-526 petition, or at the time of the investment, whichever occurs first, to qualify for the reduced $500,000 capital investment threshold.

(ii) A detailed description of how EB-5 capital investment within the geographic area of the regional center will create qualifying EB-5 jobs, either directly or indirectly. This analysis must be supported by economically and statistically valid forecasting tools, including, but not limited to, feasibility studies, analyses of foreign and domestic markets for the goods or services to be exported [if any], and/or multiplier tables.

(iii) A detailed prediction of the proposed regional center's predicted impact regionally or nationally on household earnings, greater demand for business services, utilities, maintenance and repair, and construction both within and outside of the geographic area of the proposed Regional Center.

(iv) A description of the plans to administer, oversee, and manage the proposed Regional Center, including but not limited to how the regional center will:

- Be promoted to attract EB-5 alien investors, including a description of the budget for the promotional activity;

- Identify, assess and evaluate proposed immigrant investor projects and enterprises;

- Structure its investment capital, e.g., whether the investment capital to be sought will consist solely of alien investor capital or a combination of alien investor capital and domestic capital, and how the distribution of the investment capital will be structured, e.g. loans to developers, venture capital, etc.; and

- Oversee all investment activities affiliated with, through or under the sponsorship of the proposed Regional Center.

(C) The Regional Center Proposal may also include an "exemplar" Form I-526 petition that contains copies of the commercial enterprise's organizational documents, capital investment offering memoranda, and transfer of capital mechanisms for the transfer of the alien investor's capital into the job creating enterprise. USCIS will review the documentation to determine if they are in compliance with established EB-5 eligibility requirements. Providing these documents may facilitate the adjudication of the related I-526 petitions by identifying any issues that could pose problems when USCIS is adjudicating the actual petitions. For example, if a new commercial enterprise's limited partnership (LP) agreement contains a buy-back agreement (i.e. a redemption clause guaranteeing the return of the alien investor's capital investment), then the alien investor's capital investment will not be a qualifying "at-risk" investment for EB-5 purposes. Likewise, if the LP agreement requires the payment of fees from the alien investor's capital investment of $1,000,000 or $500,000, respectively, to the extent that the investment will be eroded below the qualifying level, preventing the full infusion of the capital into the job creating enterprise, then the alien investor's capital investment will not meet the required EB-5 level of investment. The approval of a Regional Center Proposal containing defects such as these is not in the best interest of the prospective regional center or the USCIS EB-5 program as the end result will most likely be the denial of the individual alien investor's Form I-526 petition.

Any individual Form I-526 and Form I-829 petitions claiming new commercial enterprise affiliation with a regional center and thus EB-5 eligibility based on indirect job creation must be denied if they are filed prior to the approval of the regional center's Regional Center Proposal.

(D) *Regional Center Proposal and Amendment Request Processing.* There are two general workflows for the adjudication of Regional Center Proposals, one for Initial Regional Center Proposals and one for Regional Center Amendment requests. ISOs adjudicate cases within these workflows in "first in, first out" order, unless an expedite request is granted by the CSC director in accordance with the routine expedite criteria that is used for all cases filed with USCIS.

(E) Amended Regional Center Proposals.

(i) *Amendments Due to Material Changes in EB-5 Related Organizational Structure or Capital Investment Instruments.* Designated regional centers may elect to file an amended Regional Center Proposal and receive an updated approval of the regional center designation prior to the filing of individual EB-5 petitions that use supporting documentation relating to EB-5 eligibility issues that has been materially altered or is inconsistent with the documentation used as the basis for the approval of the regional center designation. Doing so, may assist in the streamlining of the adjudication of affiliated individual EB-5 petitions, as the altered documentation may otherwise need to be re-evaluated within the individual EB-5 petitions to determine if they still EB-5 compliant.

(ii) *Other Amendments.* Some Regional Center Proposals are approved for an industry segment using a hypothetical investment project in order to demonstrate how an actual investment project will be capitalized and operate in a manner that will create at least 10 direct or indirect jobs per alien investor. Individual Form I-526 petitions are then filed with copies of the business plan for the hypothetical investment project as well as the regional center's actual investment project. If the actual investment project is not different in a material way from the exemplar investment project, then the job creating efficacy of the investment project, if carried through as specified in the business plan will generally be established.

Regional centers may opt to file an amendment of their Regional Center Proposal in order to eliminate the uncertainty as to whether the actual investment project is different in a material way from the exemplar investment project that was approved in the Regional Center Proposal. The filing of these amendments is in the best interest of the EB-5 program as it may assist in the streamlining of the adjudication of the individual Form I-526 petitions. These amendments should be supported by detailed documentation relating to the actual investment project. Once approved, then only the documentation relating to the actual approved project would be provided in support of the Form I-526 petition, eliminating the uncertainty regarding whether the actual project meets EB-5 eligibility requirements.

A regional center may also file an amendment in order to provide an exemplar Form I-526 with the supporting documentation required by 8 CFR 204.6 in order for USCIS to determine if the documentation is EB-5 compliant, and thus facilitate adjudication of an actual but identical Form I-526 petition, if the evidence of record otherwise establishes EB-5 eligibility.

Note: If the Regional Center requirements are met and a determination of eligibility is made, then the favorable determination regarding regional center eligibility requirements for the capital investment structure and job creation should generally be given deference and not revisited in the adjudication of individual EB-5 petitions, as long as the underlying facts upon which the favorable decision was made remain unchanged. The CSC EB-5 program manager should be notified to determine the appropriate action to take if an ISO discovers during the adjudication of an EB-5 petition that:

- Documentation relating to the regional center's capital investment structure or job creation methodologies, or the exemplar Form I-526 petition has materially changed since the most recent approval of the regional center designation;
- The record contains evidence of fraud or misrepresentation; or
- The evidence of record indicates that the previously favorable decision to approve the regional center proposal (or amendment) to include the determination that the exemplar Form I-526 petition is EB-5 compliant was legally deficient.

(b) Governing Factors. 8 CFR 204.6(a) cites several governing factors which you must consider. They are:

- A visa petition must be filed;
- A fee for filing the petition is required;
- Before the petition is considered properly filed, the petition must be signed by the petitioner and the initial supporting documentation required by this section must be attached;
- The petition must be filed with the California Service Center; [Revised by 6/17/09, AD09-04]
- The appeal of a denial of this petition is to the Administrative Appeals Office; and
- The approval of the petition is valid indefinitely, provided that the investment remains qualifying.

(c) Preliminary Action. (after petition has been accepted and fee paid).

(1) *When to Create a File.* If the alien petitioner is in the United States, search for an existing "A" file. If none exists, create one. If the beneficiary is not in the United States, no file should be created, unless the petition is to be denied.

(2) *Priority Date.* The priority date of a petition for classification as an alien entrepreneur is the date the petition is properly filed with USCIS.

(3) *General Review.* [Revised by 12/11/09, AD09-38] Review the Form I-526 petition for completeness and signature of the petitioner.

- Verify that the name given in Part 1 (Information about you) is identical to the signature in Part 7 (Signature block).
- Remember that the petition can only be signed by the petitioner and not by his or her authorized representative.

The following EB-5 eligibility requirements must be established in the Form I-526 petition:

- The capital investment is in a new commercial enterprise;
- If the petitioner claims that the capital investment qualifies for the reduced capital investment threshold of $500,000, that the new commercial enterprise is located in a TEA;
- The investment capital was obtained by the alien through lawful means;
- The required amount of capital has been fully committed to the new commercial enterprise;
- The new commercial enterprise will create not fewer than 10 full-time positions; and

– The alien investor will be engaged in the management of the new commercial enterprise.

Note: If the new commercial enterprise identified in the petition is affiliated with a regional center, then the petitioner must provide with the Form I-526 petition a copy of the regional center's:

– Most recently issued approval letter; and

– Documentation relating to its approved capital investment structure and job creation methodology.

If the evidence provided remains unchanged from the documentation that was the basis for the approval of the regional center proposal, then the prior approval of the capital investment structure and the job creation methodology should generally be given deference. The CSC EB-5 program manager should be notified to determine the appropriate action to take if an ISO discovers during the adjudication of Form I-526 petition that:

– Documentation relating to the regional center's capital investment structure or job creation methodologies has materially changed since the approval of the regional center designation;

– The record contains evidence of fraud or misrepresentation; or

– The evidence of record indicates that the previously favorable decision to approve the regional center proposal (or amendment) to include the determination that the exemplar Form I-526 petition is EB-5 compliant was legally deficient.

(4) *Review of Supporting Documents.* When reviewing the documentation submitted in support of the petition you should keep in mind the following factors:

(A) *Investment in a New Commercial Enterprise.* Whether the alien creates an original business, purchases an existing business, expands an existing business, or joins with a pool of investors who have already invested in an existing business, his or her action must be taken after November 29, 1990. The statute requires it, and the definition of the word "new" means created after November 29, 1990.

Note: You should be aware that, although pooled investment arrangements are specifically permitted under the current regulations, historically, there have been serious problems associated with certain pooled arrangements, resulting in a Department of Justice Office of the Inspector General investigation and a number of successful criminal prosecutions.

If the petitioner submits evidence that the new commercial enterprise was a result of simultaneous or subsequent restructuring or reorganization of an existing business, the commercial enterprise that is the result of this action must be a new legal entity. Thus, there are three ways to invest in a new commercial enterprise: creation of brand new business, purchase of an existing business, or expansion of an existing business. You must keep in mind that in order for the business to qualify as a new commercial enterprise, any of the above actions must have taken place after November 29, 1990.

You must look at the evidence presented to demonstrate the date of creation of the business to determine whether it is a "new" commercial enterprise. In general, the business must have been created AFTER November 29, 1990. If the business was created BEFORE November 29, 1990, it cannot qualify, unless the petitioner can demonstrate expansion of the business after November 29, 1990. If the business was created prior to November 29, 1990, issue a RFE explaining this requirement, and requesting evidence relating to post-November 29, 1990, expansion.

To qualify for creation based on expansion, the petitioner must invest the required capital in the existing business, and demonstrate that the investment has increased, by 40 percent, either the number of employees or the net worth of the business. The petitioner will still be required to employ ten additional employees before the conditional basis of his or her EB-5 permanent resident status may be removed.

(B) *Investing the Required Amount of Capital.* You should always be aware that the statutory requirements of investing the prescribed amount of capital and the creation of new jobs apply no matter how the alien seeks to demonstrate investment in a new commercial enterprise. These requirements apply even if the alien is investing in a new commercial enterprise that purchases an existing business. The alien is still obligated to show that he or she has invested the prescribed amount of capital (some of which would probably be the purchase price of the old company) and that 10 new jobs would be created in addition to the employees of the purchased company. A mere intent to invest does not suffice for EB-5 purposes. The petitioner must actually have committed the capital to the new commercial enterprise.

Note: "Capital" is defined to include cash, equipment, inventory, other tangible property, cash equivalents and indebtedness secured by assets owned by the alien provided that he or she is personally and primarily liable and the assets of the new commercial enterprise are not used to secure any of the indebtedness. If the alien uses a secured note, the alien must be able to show that this note has a real cash value, and that the total value of all capital invested, including the note, has a cash value equal to or greater than the statutory minimum.

Note also: As discussed below, all of the requisite capital must go directly into the new commercial enterprise; amounts paid for "administrative fees, attorneys' fees," "finders' fees" and other types of expenses not directly paid into the new commercial enterprise will not count towards the minimum investment amount.

Note further: The term "invest" is defined as a contribution of capital. In determining whether the full amount of capital has been invested, adjudicators should be aware that proceeds that are left (*i.e.,* "reinvested") in the business do not count toward meeting the minimum investment requirement. Further, adjudicators should be aware that an EB-5 petitioner must make an equity investment in the commercial enterprise; a mere loan from the alien shareholder or partner to the business does not qualify as an investment of capital for purposes of the EB-5 statute. Thus, contributions of funds to the commercial enterprise, in exchange for a note, bond, convertible debt, obligation, or any other debt arrangement, cannot be counted toward meeting the minimum capital requirement. Balance sheets, including those incorporated into tax returns, generally, but not necessarily, should reflect the amount of equity versus debt contributed to the commercial enterprise. The determination as to what constitutes debt or equity is, in the final analysis, a question of fact, and not simply a matter of what is reflected on a balance sheet.

(C) *Investment of Capital Obtained Through Lawful Means.* The regulation at 8 CFR 204.6(j)(3) indicates that the petitioner is to submit documentation "as applicable" that investment capital has been obtained through lawful means. Since it is often difficult to determine the source of the capital used for the investment, there is no clear-cut answer as to how far back the petitioner should go to establish that he or she has met this requirement. In making your determination, you should exercise sound judgment. Obviously, if you have reason to believe that more documentation is necessary, it should be requested.

An individual who is operating as a sole proprietor cannot count his or her personal bank account as committed funds. The regulation refers specifically to funds in business bank accounts, not personal bank accounts. This applies to all cases, including sole proprietorships. Funds in a personal bank account are not necessarily committed to the new commercial enterprise.

(D) *Job Creation.* [Revised by 6/17/09, AD09-04]

(i) The petition must be supported with evidence the new commercial enterprise will create no fewer than 10 full-time positions (or the equivalent).

(ii) Clarification of the Two-Year Period for Job Creation.

(a) Petitioners who are filing a Form I-526 must submit "a comprehensive business plan showing that, due to the nature and projected size of the new commercial enterprise, the need for not fewer than ten (10) qualifying employees will result, including approximate dates, within the next two-years, and when each employee will be hired." 8 C.F.R. §204.6(j)(4)(i)(B) (emphasis added). The requirement for a business plan that shows jobs will be created in two years applies to all Form I-526 petitions, including those filed under the Regional Center Program, that will rely on indirect job creation to satisfy the statutory employment creation requirement.

The regulations, however, do not clearly state when the two-year period commences for purposes of adjudicating the Form I-526. The reference to a two-year period relates to the two-year period of conditional residence, and the time requirement of 8 C.F.R. §204.6(j)(4)(i)(B) is intended to ensure that aliens seeking to enter the United States on EB-5 visas have a legitimate and feasible plan to create jobs as required by the statute within that period of conditional residence. Nevertheless, at the time of adjudication of Form I-526, the alien entrepreneur will not have attained conditional permanent residence, and the officer adjudicating Form I-526 cannot be certain when the period of conditional residence will in fact commence.

USCIS has determined that the average processing times for EB-5 petitioners filing for immigrant visas via consular processing and EB-5 petitioners filing for adjustment of status is approximately six months. Accordingly, in order to best approximate the two-year period of conditional residence, the two-year period described in 8 C.F.R. §204.6(j)(4)(i)(B) will be deemed to commence six months after the adjudication of Form I-526. USCIS officers should ensure that the business plan filed along with Form I-526 reasonably demonstrates that the requisite number of jobs will be created by the alien's investment by the end of the two-year period that commences six months after the adjudication of the petition. If, in the future, processing times significantly change, this paragraph may be amended.

(b) Special considerations for Regional Center based I-526 petitions:

(i) Aliens filing I-526 petitions for investments to be made through a regional center may use reasonable methodologies to establish the number of jobs created. 8 C.F.R. §204.6(j)(4)(iii). However, some of the economic models may not expressly consider temporal aspects of job creation, and will not be able to conclusively state that indirect jobs will be created within two years. In such circumstances, officers should first explore whether there are reasonable and/or accepted temporal assumptions that can be attributed to the particular economic model and consider such assumptions in determining compliance with the two-year requirement.

For example, the RIMSII handbook states the following about the RIMSII economic model, which is often used to demonstrate indirect job creation:

RIMS II, like all I-O models, is a "static equilibrium" model, so impacts calculated with RIMS II have no specific time dimension. However, because the model is based on annual data, it is customary to assume that the impacts occur in 1 year. For many situations, this assumption is reasonable.

This assumption supports the conclusion that the indirect jobs will be created within the requisite two-year period.

If, however, there are no reasonable and/or accepted temporal assumptions that can be made with respect to a particular economic model, USCIS may presume that the jobs will be created within the required period of time provided that the alien can demonstrate compliance with paragraph (ii) below.

(ii) Many economic models used to demonstrate indirect job creation rely on certain assumptions or variables to show the requisite job creation. For example, a model might demonstrate that the requisite jobs will be created if a Regional Center infuses $10 million into a particular industry. Similarly, a model might demonstrate that, using accepted multipliers, the creation of 100 direct jobs will result in a certain number of indirect jobs. Under such circumstances, the I-526 petition should demonstrate that the required infusion of capital or the creation of the direct jobs will occur within two years.

Nothing in this paragraph should be construed to alter in any way the current adjudication procedures. Officers may review the evidence required by the petitioner to demonstrate the number of jobs that will be created by the investment. For example, Form I-526s filed under the Regional Center Program which rely on indirect job creation must also comply with the evidentiary requirements of 8 C.F.R. §204.6(j)(4)(iii) to demonstrate the number of jobs created. Officers may also continue to determine the reasonableness of a business plan to ensure that the jobs are likely to be created.

(iii) *Clarification of the Meaning of Full-Time Position.* [Revised by 12/11/09, AD09-38] Section 203(b)(5) of the INA requires that the investment in a new commercial enterprise will create full-time employment for not fewer than 10 qualified employees. The INA further defines full-time employment as "employment in a position that requires at least 35 hours or service per week at any time, regardless of who fills the position." Adjudicating ISOs should keep the following points in mind when determining if positions meet this requirement:

- Economic input/output (I/O) models, such as RIMS II or IMPLAN, used to evaluate the calculation of the number of indirect jobs (including induced jobs) created through a commercial enterprise affiliated with a regional center do not distinguish between full-time and part-time jobs. In other words, the job creation results of the multipliers in the economic I/O models do not distinguish between the full-time and part-time nature of the positions. Therefore, the number of indirect jobs quantified through the I/O model analysis will be considered to be full-time and qualifying for EB-5 purposes. Accordingly, determinations regarding whether jobs qualify as "full-time" are only relevant to the analysis of direct jobs created by a commercial enterprise claiming the creation of direct jobs as a result of the EB-5 capital investment.

- USCIS has interpreted the full-time employment requirement to exclude jobs that are intermittent, temporary, seasonal or transient in nature. *See, e.g., Spencer Enterprises v. U.S.,* 229 F.Supp.2d 1025 (E.D. Cal. 2001). Historically, construction jobs have not been counted toward job creation because they are seen as intermittent, temporary, seasonal and transient rather than permanent. USCIS, however, now interprets that direct construction jobs may now count as permanent jobs if they:

- Are created by the petitioner's investment; and

- Are expected to last at least two years, inclusive of when the petitioner's Form I-829 is filed.

    Although employment in some industries such as construction or tourism can be intermittent, temporary, seasonal or transient, officers should not exclude jobs simply because they fall into such industries. Rather, the focus of the adjudication should be on whether the direct positions, as described in the petition, are continuous full-time employment rather than intermittent, temporary, seasonal or transient.

    For example, if a petition reasonably describes the need to directly employ general laborers in a construction project that is expected to last several years and require a minimum of 35 hours per week over the course of that project, the positions would meet the full-time employment requirement. However, if the same project called for electrical workers to provide services as direct employees during three to four five week periods over the course of the project, such positions would be properly deemed to be intermittent and not meet the definition of full-time employment.

- Generally, it is the position that is critical to the full-time direct employment criterion, not the employee. Accordingly, the fact that the position may be filled by more than one employee does not exclude a position from consideration as full-time employment.

    For example, the positions described in the above bullet would not be excluded from being considered full-time employment if the general laborers needed to fill the positions varied from day to day or week to week, as long as the need to directly employ general laborers in the position remains constant. This interpretation is consistent with 8 CFR 204.6(e), which includes job sharing arrangements as part of the regulatory definition of full-time employment.

- It is important to note, however, that this interpretation does not override the regulatory definitions of employee and full-time employment at 8 CFR 204.6(e). Thus, direct jobs must still be filled by qualifying employees and not by independent contractors. Positions filled by independent contractors are not qualifying direct jobs and may only be credited for EB-5 job creation purposes in petitions involving commercial enterprises that are affiliated with a regional center. In addition, multiple part-time positions may not be combined to create one full-time position, unless those part-time jobs can be shown to be part of a job-sharing arrangement.

- Full-time employment relating to the creation of direct jobs as defined in 8 CFR 204.6(e) means year-round employment and not seasonal full-time employment. Full-time employment consists of 35 hours a week. Seasonal positions do not qualify for purposes of the full-time employment requirement for direct jobs.

Note: You must also keep in mind that full-time employment as defined in 8 CFR 204.6(e) means year-round employment and not seasonal full-time employment. Full-time employment consists of 35 hours a week. Regulations permit the combining of certain part-time positions to equal one full-time equivalent position for purposes of meeting the job creation requirement. Seasonal positions do not qualify for purposes of the full-time employment requirement.

(E) *Alien Petitioner Engaged in the Management of the New Enterprise.* The alien petitioner must be involved in the new enterprise by either exercising managerial control of the day-to-day operations or through policy formulation. The alien petitioner cannot just invest in the new enterprise; he or she must be involved in the new enterprise. An alien must be "actively involved in the business;" a purely passive investor may not qualify for the EB-5 classification. See 8 CFR 204.6(j)(5). While an alien may seek EB-5 qualification on the basis of an investment in a limited partnership, under current regulations, even he or she, as a limited partner, must have a certain level of involvement in the running of the business. Under 8 CFR 204.6(j)(5)(iii), if the alien is a limited partner, he or she must have been granted all (*i.e.*, not simply some) of the rights, powers, and duties granted to the other limited partners in the partnership in order to be considered sufficiently engaged in the business.

(F) *New Commercial Enterprise in a Targeted Employment Area (TEA).* [Revised by 6/17/09, AD09-04] A TEA is either a rural area or an area experiencing a high unemployment rate at the time of the capital investment or the time of filing of the Form I-526 petition, whichever occurs first. If the petitioner shows that the area where he or she is investing is a rural area, the petitioner need not also establish that the area has high employment. Conversely, if the area is a high unemployment area, the petitioner need not also show that it is a rural area.

INA 203(b)(5)(B) and 8 CFR 204.6(e) require that in order to establish eligibility for the reduced EB-5 investment threshold of $500,000, the area in which the alien makes a capital investment must qualify as an rural area or an area of high unemployment when the investment is made. *Matter of Soffici*, 22 I&N Dec. 158 (BIA 1998) provides in pertinent part that:

A petitioner has the burden to establish that his enterprise does business in an area that is considered "targeted" as of the date he files his [Form I-526] petition. The fact that a business may be located in an area that was once rural, for example, does not mean that the area is still rural.

A conflict between the statutory and regulatory requirements, and *Matter of Soffici* may arise when an alien makes a capital investment at a point in time prior to the filing of the Form I-526 petition when the area in which the investment is made qualifies as a TEA, only to have the area no longer qualify as a TEA at the time of filing of the Form I-526 petition. In order to promote predictability in the capital investment process and to reconcile the potential conflict outlined above, ISOs must identify the appropriate date to examine in order to determine that the alien's capital investment qualifies for the reduced $500,000 threshold according to the following "if, then" table:

TEA "if then" Table	
If the Investment...	Then...
Is made into the commercial enterprise's job creating project prior to the filing of the Form I-526 petition...	The TEA analysis should focus on whether the location of the investment qualifies as a TEA at the time of the investment.
Has yet to be committed to the commercial enterprise's job creating project at the time of filing of the I-526, i.e. is still in escrow or is otherwise not irrevocably invested into the commercial enterprise pending the approval of the I-526 petition...	The TEA analysis should focus on whether the location of the investment qualifies as a TEA at the time of the filing of the I-526 petition.

Note: In some instances, an alien may request eligibility for the reduced investment threshold based on the fact that other EB-5 aliens who previously invested in the same project qualified for the $500,000 minimum investment, even though the area did not qualify at the time of the instant alien's investment or the filing of his or her Form I-526. Each alien must establish that his or her capital investment qualifies for the reduced investment threshold, and cannot rely on previous TEA determinations made based on facts that have subsequently changed.

Note also that the area where the new commercial enterprise is located may qualify as a TEA at the time the capital investment is made or the I-526 petition is filed, (whichever occurs first), but may cease to qualify by the time the Form I-829 petition is filed. Changes in population size or unemployment rates within the area during the alien investor's period of conditional permanent residence are acceptable as increased job creation is the primary goal of the EB-5 program.

(i) *Rural Area Defined.* The term "rural area" means any area that is both outside of a metropolitan statistical area (MSA) and outside of a city or town having a population of 20,000 or more based on the most recent decennial census of the United States. See INA §203(b)(5)(B)(iii) and 8 CFR §204.6(j)(6)(i). MSAs are designated by the Office of Management and Budget and can be found at *www.census.gov.*

(ii) *Definition of High Unemployment Area.* The term "high unemployment area" means an area which has experienced unemployment of at least 150 percent of the national average rate. See INA §203(b)(5)(B)(ii). The I-526 petitioner must demonstrate that, at the time the capital investment is made or the petition is filed (whichever occurs first), there has been an unemployment rate of at least 150% of the national unemployment rate within the MSA or other non-rural area in which the commercial enterprise that will create or preserve jobs is located. This should be based on the most recent information available to the general public from federal or state governmental sources as of the time the I-526 petition is submitted.

In some instances I-526 petitioners may claim high unemployment in only a portion or portions of a geographic area or political subdivision for which distinct unemployment data is not readily available to the general public from federal or state governmental sources. This may be indicative of an attempt by the petitioner to "gerrymander" a finding of high unemployment when in fact the area does not qualify as being a high unemployment area. Such a claim is not sufficient to establish that the area is a high unemployment area unless it is accompanied by a designation from an authorized authority of the state government. (State designations are discussed below in (iii) of this section.)

The Bureau of Labor Statistics (BLS) provides data regarding the national average rate of unemployment at *www.bls.gov/cps/.* BLS's Local Area Unemployment Statistics (LAUS) program produces monthly and annual unemployment and other labor force data for census regions and divisions, states, counties, metropolitan areas, and many cities, by place of residence. This information can be found at *www.bls.gov/lau/.* States, the District of Columbia, and the U.S. territories may also publish local area unemployment statistics on their government websites.

(iii) *State Designation of a High Unemployment Area.* The state government of any state of the United States may designate a particular geographic area or political subdivision located within a metropolitan statistical area or within a city or town having a population of 20,000 or more within such a state as an area of high unemployment. Before any such designation is made, an official of the state must notify USCIS of the agency, board, or other appropriate governmental body of the state which shall be delegated the authority to certify that the geographic or political subdivision is a high unemployment area. Evidence of such a designation, including a description of the boundaries of the geographic or political subdivision and the method or methods by which the unemployment statistics were obtained, may be submitted in support of the Form I-526 petition in lieu of other documentary evidence of high unemployment in the area where the new commercial enterprise is located. See 8 CFR 204.6(i). The statistics used in the analysis must reflect the national and local unemployment rates for these regions at the time of the alien investor's capital investment. See 8 CFR 204.6(e).

The designation of high unemployment areas are within the purview of each U.S. state governor, or if applicable, his or her designee. USCIS personnel have no substantive authority to question or challenge such high unemployment designations, and therefore must rely on the high unemployment designations that conform to the requirements outlined above that are made by a U.S. state governor or his or her designee. ISOs should notify the CSC EB-5 program manager and seek guidance regarding how to address the TEA issue in petitions that contains a state designation letter that does not conform to the requirements of 8 CFR 204.6(i), utilizes statistics that do not reflect the national and local unemployment rates at the time of the alien investor's capital investment, or has been issued by an official of a state that has not notified USCIS regarding who in the state government has the authority to issue such designations.

Note: State designations of high unemployment areas also include designations issued by the appointed government body with authority to make such certifications by the governors of the U.S. territories or the mayor of the District of Columbia.

(G) Eligibility Requirements for the Review of a Form I-526 Petition that Seeks Consideration of a Business Plan that Differs from the Business Plan in a Previously Approved Form I-526 Petition. [Added by 6/17/09, AD09-04]

Some EB-5 aliens may encounter difficulties when unforeseen circumstances cause the achievement of the requisite job creation outlined in the Form I-526 petition to be cast in doubt. This may occur when the job creating capital investment project or commercial enterprise that was relied upon for the approval of the Form I-526 petition fails or otherwise cannot be completed within the alien's two-year period of conditional residence. The structure of the EB-5 program is inflexible in that the capital investment project identified in the business plan in the approved Form I-526 petition must serve as the basis for determining at the Form I-829 petition stage whether the requisite capital investment has been sustained throughout the alien's two year period of conditional residency and that at least ten jobs have been or will be created within a reasonable period of time as a result of the alien's capital investment. The business plan in the Form I-526 petition may not be materially changed after the petition has been filed. In addition, USCIS may not act favorably on requests to delay the filing or adjudication of Form I-829 petitions beyond the timeframes outlined in 8 CFR 216.6(a) and (c).

The following "if, then" table explains how an EB-5 investor can seek consideration of a business plan that differs from the business plan in a previously approved Form I-526 petition.

New Form I-526 Petition "If, Then" Table	
If...	Then...
The alien wishes to change the business plan from the business plan outlined in a previously filed Form I-526 petition...	S/he may file a new Form I-526 petition with fee that is supported by the new business plan and addresses all requirements of the I-526 petition.
If the new Form I-526 Petition is Filed...	Then...
Before the alien adjusts status (AOS) or is issued an immigrant visa (IV)...	The new petition, if approved, will be the basis for the AOS or the IV and the new business plan will be used as the basis for evaluating EB-5 eligibility at the I-829 stage.
After the alien adjusts status or is issued an IV, but before the due date of the filing of the I-829 petition (90 days prior to the end of the two-year CPR period).	Upon approval of the new Form I-526 petition, S/he may file Form I-407 with a Form I-485 adjustment application. The prior CPR status will be terminated and the new AOS application will be approved, if otherwise approvable, granting a new two year period of CPR status. The new I-526 petition will be used as the basis when evaluating eligibility at the I-829 stage. If the new Form I-526 is denied, then the alien will have to file the I-829 petition and use the initial Form I-526 petition as the basis for the eligibility evaluation in the Form I-829 petition.
After the alien adjusts status or is issued an IV on or after the due date for the filing of the I-829 petition.	If the new I-526 is approved, S/he may request the withdrawal of the initial I-829 petition and file an AOS application. The prior CPR status will be terminated and the new AOS application will be approved, if otherwise approvable, granting a new two year period of CPR status. The new I-526 petition will be used as the basis when evaluating eligibility at the second I-829 stage. If the new I-526 petition is denied, then the initial Form I-829 petition will be adjudicated using the project plan in the initial I-526 petition as the basis for the initial I-829 eligibility evaluation.
Note: Dependents will have to file I-407s at the same time as required for the principals as well as Form I-485 applications in order to terminate their CPR status and be "re-adjusted" to CPR anew. The dependents must be eligible to be classified as EB-5 dependents at the time of the filing of new Form I-485 application, i.e. the dependents must be the spouse or unmarried child under the age of 21 years of the EB-5 principal alien.	

(d) Approval of the Petition..

    (1) Affix the approval stamp on the Form I-526 and sign.

(2) An approved visa petition should be sent to the specified embassy or consul or if petitioner is requesting adjustment, then the petition should be routed (with file) to the main file shelf waiting request by field office.

(3) Keep a record of statistics (approvals, denials, returned, etc.)

(4) Update CLAIMS with appropriate information. Do not place on clerical hold unless there is documentation to be sent back to the petitioner.

(e) Action to be Taken if the Petition is Denied. Denial decisions will be prepared on Form I-292, usually with the reference "SEE ATTACHMENTS." The attached pages will cover the specific grounds for denial as determined from the evidence. Form M-188 (on appeals and motions) and Form I-290B will be attached to all visa petition denials. It is essential that any denial you prepare be premised solely on the evidence submitted. Refer in your denial to controlling statutes and regulations. Where the decision is motivated by or governed by any published decisions, reference to those decisions must be made in the approved format. Your decision should be written in direct and comprehensible language. All reasons for denial should be included. In all denial cases, an "A" file must be used to house the petition and supporting documents. Copies of the decision must be sent to the petitioner and any attorney of record. Once your supervisor has signed off your denial, CLAIMS should be updated to reflect that the case has been denied.

(f) Revocation of Petitions. Visa petitions approved under section 204 of the Act may be revoked under the provisions of section 203(e) or section 205 of the Act.

(g) Precedent Decisions. The following precedent decisions relate to employment creation petitions:

In re Soffici, ID #3359 (Commr, 1998). (1) A petitioner under section 203(b)(5) of the Act cannot establish the requisite investment of capital if he lends the money to his new commercial enterprise. (2) Loans obtained by a corporation, secured by assets of the corporation, do not constitute capital invested by a petitioner. Not only is such a loan prohibited by 8 CFR 204.6(e), but the petitioner and the corporation are not the same legal entity. (3) A petitioner's personal guarantee on a business's debt does not transform the business's debt into the petitioner's personal debt. (4) A petitioner must present clear documentary evidence of the source of the funds that he invests. He must show that the funds are his own and that they were obtained through lawful means. (5) A petitioner who acquires a pre-existing business must show that the investment has created, or at least has a reasonable prospect of creating, 10 full-time positions, in addition to those existing before acquisition. The petitioner must, therefore, present evidence concerning the pre-acquisition level of employment. Simply maintaining the pre-acquisition level of employment is not sufficient, unless the petitioner shows that the pre-existing business qualifies as a "troubled business."

In re Izumii, ID #3360 (Assoc. Commr, 1998). (1) Regardless of its location, a new commercial enterprise that is engaged directly or indirectly in lending money to job creating businesses may only lend money to businesses located within targeted areas in order for a petitioner to be eligible for the reduced minimum capital requirement. (2) Under the Immigrant Investor Pilot Program, if a new commercial enterprise is engaged directly or indirectly in lending money to job-creating businesses, such job-creating businesses must all be located within the geographic limits of the regional center. The location of the new commercial enterprise is not controlling. (3) A petitioner may not make material changes to his petition in an effort to make a deficient petition conform to USCIS requirements. (4) If the new commercial enterprise is a holding company, the full requisite amount of capital must be made available to the business(es) most closely responsible for creating the employment on which the petition is based. (5) An alien may not receive guaranteed payments from a new commercial enterprise while he owes money to the new commercial enterprise. (6) An alien may not enter into a redemption agreement with the new commercial enterprise at any time prior to completing all of his cash payments under a promissory note. In no event may the alien enter into a redemption agreement prior to the end of the two-year period of conditional residence. (7) A redemption agreement between an alien investor and the new commercial enterprise constitutes a debt arrangement and is prohibited under 8 CFR 204.6(e). (8) Reserve funds that are not made available for purposes of job creation cannot be considered capital placed at risk for the purpose of generating a return on the capital being placed at risk. (9) USCIS does not pre-adjudicate immigrant investor petitions; each petition must be adjudicated on its own merits. (10) Under 8 CFR 204.6(e), all capital must be valued at fair market value in United States dollars, including promissory notes used as capital. In determining the fair market value of a promissory note, it is necessary to consider, among other things, present value. (11) Under certain circumstances, a promissory note that does not itself constitute capital may constitute evidence that the alien is "in the process of investing" other capital, such as cash. In such a case, the petitioner must substantially complete payments on the promissory note prior to the end of the two-year conditional period. (12) Whether the promissory note constitutes capital or is simply evidence that the alien is in the process of investing other capital, nearly all of the money due under the promissory note must be payable within two years, without provisions for extensions.

Note: In 2002, Congress eliminated the requirement set forth in *Izumii* that, in order for a petitioner to be considered to have "created" an original business, he or she must have had a hand in its actual creation. Under the new law, an alien may invest in an existing business at any time following its creation, provided he or she meets all other requirements of the regulations.

In re Hsiung, ID #3361 (Assoc. Commr, 1998). (1) A promissory note secured by assets owned by a petitioner can constitute capital under 8 CFR 204.6(e) if: the assets are specifically identified as securing the note; the security interests in the note are perfected in the jurisdiction in which the assets are located; and the assets are fully amenable to seizure by a U.S. note holder. (2) When determining the fair market value of a promissory note being used as capital under 8 CFR 204.6(e), factors such as the fair market value of the assets securing the note, the extent to which the assets are amenable to seizure, and the present value of the note should be considered. (3) Whether a petitioner uses a promissory note as capital under 8 CFR 204.6(e) or as evidence of a commitment to invest cash, he must show that he has placed his assets at risk. In establishing that a sufficient amount of his assets are at risk, a petitioner must demonstrate, among other things, that the assets securing the note are his, that the security interests are perfected, that the assets are amenable to seizure, and that the assets have an adequate fair market value. (4) A petitioner engaging in the reorganization or restructuring of a preexisting business may not cause a net loss of employment.

In re Ho, ID #3362 (Assoc. Commr, 1998). (1) Merely creating and capitalizing a new commercial enterprise and signing a commercial lease are not sufficient to show that an immigrant investor petitioner has placed his capital at risk. The petitioner must present, instead, evidence that he has actually undertaken meaningful concrete business activity. (2) The petitioner must establish that he has placed his own capital at risk; that is to say, he must show that he was the legal owner of the invested capital. Bank statements and other financial documents do not meet this requirement if the documents show someone else as the legal owner of the capital. (3) The petitioner must also establish that he acquired the legal ownership of the invested capital through lawful means. Mere assertions about the petitioner's financial situation or work history, without supporting documentary evidence, are not sufficient to meet this requirement. (4) To establish that qualifying employment positions have been created, Forms I-9 presented by a petitioner must be accompanied by other evidence to show that these employees have commenced work activities and have been hired in permanent, full-time positions. (5) In order to demonstrate that the new commercial enterprise will create not fewer than 10 full-time positions, the petitioner must either provide evidence that the new commercial enterprise has created such positions or furnish a comprehensive, detailed, and credible business plan demonstrating the need for the positions and the schedule for hiring the employees.

Note: There are also a number of precedent decisions that pertain to old (pre-1978) immigrant investor provisions under the former non-preference immigrant visa category. While some of these decisions may be interesting from a historical perspective, they have little or no relevance to the "employment creation" investor category created by IMMACT 90 and should not be relied upon when adjudicating post IMMACT 90 cases.

(h) November 2, 2002 Amendments to EB-5. On November 2, 2002, the President signed into law certain amendments to the EB-5 program. Title I, subtitle B of Division C of the Twenty-First Century Department of Justice Appropriations Authorization Act (the "2002 DOJ Appropriations Act)," sections 11031-37 of Public Law 107-273.

On June 10, 2003, USCIS issued interim policy guidance regarding changes effected by the new law. Memorandum from William R. Yates, HQ40/6.1.3, entitled "Amendments Affecting Adjudication for Alien Entrepreneur (EB-5)" (the "Yates Memorandum"). The Yates Memorandum provides that:

As before, the commercial enterprise must be "new," that is, have been created after November 29, 1990. *See* 8 CFR 204.6(e). Section 11036 of the law does, however, eliminate the previous requirement that an alien personally have "established," that is, have had a personal hand in, the creation of the new commercial enterprise. Under the 2002 DOJ Appropriations Act, the alien need only "sustain" his or her investment in a pre-existing commercial enterprise. This effectively allows multiple investments in the same commercial enterprise at any time, provided that the alien still creates ten new positions for qualifying U.S. workers jobs and meets all other EB-5 requirements are complied with. The law applies to both pending I-526 and I-829 petitions filed on that date or thereafter. This provision modifies 8 CFR 204.6(h)(1), regarding the creation of an original business.

Note: The 2002 DOJ Appropriations Act does not change the requirement that the commercial enterprise create 10 new jobs. In order to determine whether the commercial enterprise actually has created ten new positions, adjudicators must first determine whether the petitioner personally created the commercial enterprise and, if the petitioner did not create the business, the number of jobs there were in the existing business at the time the petitioner acquired the business.

Note Also: The 2002 DOJ Appropriations Act supercedes, in part, 8 CFR 204.6(h)(3), which describes "the establishment of a new commercial enterprise," due to the removal of the requirement that the alien entrepreneur establish the new commercial enterprise. Section 204.6(h)(3) of the Act continues, however, to be relevant in that it describes the circumstances under which a commercial enterprise in existence prior to November 29, 1990 will be considered "new" for purposes of the law. Enterprises that have been expanded or substantially reorganized, as described above, will continue to meet the definition of "new" regardless of when the commercial enterprise was actually created.

As was the case by regulation before November 2, 2002, a new commercial enterprise may include a limited partnership.

Full-time employment is defined as employment that requires at least 35 hours of service per week "at any time," regardless of who fills the position. This provision does not change the requirement that, in order to be "full-time," the job created may not be seasonal. If the enterprise employs individual workers on a temporary basis, it can meet the "full-time" requirement only if the job itself is permanent in nature and will be staffed year-round by qualified U.S. workers for the requisite 35 hours per week. For example, an enterprise which is staffed by qualifying workers on one-year contracts would qualify only if, upon expiration of a particular contract, the enterprise, without break, continues to employ the same or another U.S. worker in that same position.

With the limited exception of certain persons eligible for a "second opportunity" to make a qualifying investment (discussed below) under the 2002 DOJ Appropriations Act, as before, a petitioner may invest capital, for purposes of EB-5, in only one commercial enterprise. A petitioner who filed a Form I-526 petition after August 31, 1998 therefore may not qualify for removal of conditions if he or she has invested in multiple commercial enterprises.

The 2002 DOJ Appropriations Act does not change the definition of "qualifying employee."

The 2002 DOJ Appropriations Act also provides a second opportunity for certain aliens whom USCIS believes failed to make a qualifying investment, now to satisfy USCIS that they have done so, provided certain conditions are met. Persons specifically covered by this provision of the 2002 law may invest in the same or a new commercial enterprise, or even a combination of the two. This second opportunity is limited, however, to cases where the alien's EB-5 petition does not contain any material misrepresentation. Persons eligible for this "second chance" to comply with the statute and regulations are those whose Form I-526 petitions were approved between January 1, 1995 and August 31, 1998. The 2002 DOJ Appropriations Act also contains provisions with respect to certain aliens who applied for immigrant visas or adjustment of status prior to November 2, 2002, but did not obtain or were not granted conditional resident status.

Note: The 2002 Appropriations Act is NOT an amnesty program; the statute merely provides certain aliens with a second chance to establish that they have made a qualifying investment. Conditions may not be removed with respect to any of these persons unless they can establish, at the end of their two-year period of conditional residence, that they meet all applicable requirements for removal of conditions.

Regulatory guidance will be forthcoming as to how cases covered by the 2002 Appropriations Act are to be handled.

APPENDIX D-2: ADJUDICATOR'S FIELD MANUAL, CHAPTER 25.2 ENTREPRENEURS

25.2 Entrepreneurs. [Revised by 12/21/06]

(a) Commitment to Trained and Experienced Officers. All USCIS offices must ensure that only officers who have been specially trained and certified by USCIS Headquarters EB-5 program management adjudicate EB-5 immigrant investor casework. In addition, all such offices must ensure that the officers adjudicating petitions on Form I-829 have received training in the Marriage Fraud Amendment System (MFAS).

California Service Center director, regional directors and field office directors in offices with a high volume of Form I-829s shall designate an EB-5 trained and certified officer as an EB-5 point of contact (POC) to facilitate the review and management of Form I-829. For purposes of clarity in these instructions, references to service center management and field office management includes the appropriate EB-5 POC. [Revised by 6/17/09, AD09-04]

(b) Filing the Form I-829. These instructions provide procedures consistent with those provided for the adjudication of Form I-751, Petition to Remove Conditions on Residence (for alien spouse) where possible. Under 8 CFR 216.6(a), immigrant investors in conditional resident status must file a Form I-829 at the appropriate service center within 90 days prior to the second anniversary of their admission to the United States as a conditional permanent resident.

Note: The instructions in this memorandum and AFM section update also apply to processing I-829s for spouses and dependent children pursuant to 8 CFR 216.6(a)(1) and (6) (i.e. derivatives, who subsequent to obtaining conditional resident status are: (1) children who are married, (2) former spouses who are divorced from the principal, and (3) widow or widowers of the principal alien investor).

Officers are reminded that, in accordance with the Notice in the *Federal Register* at 74 Fed. Reg. 912-913, published on, and in effect since, January 9, 2009, Form I-829 petitions are to be filed with the California Service Center. [Revised by 6/17/09, AD09-04]

See Chapters 25.2(i)(1)(A) and 25.2(i)(2) below for procedures when a Form I-829 has not been timely filed.

(c) Receipt of Form I-829. Parallel to the procedures for processing Form I-751, Petition to Remove Conditions on Residence, upon receipt of Form I-829, the service center director shall issue the conditional resident a fee receipt notice on Form I-797 that includes the following paragraph:

Your Permanent Resident Card (Form I-551), also known as a "green card," is extended one (1) year – employment and travel is authorized during this extension. Processing your petition for removal of conditions will require a minimum of one hundred and twenty (120) days. Thirty (30) days before the expiration of this extension, if you have not been notified by USCIS of a decision on your petition, please contact the field office nearest to where you are living for further documentation for employment and/or travel purposes.

(d) Notice. A receipt notice and any written notice of any decision, request for evidence (RFE) or interview appointment should be provided to the conditional resident if he or she is not represented.

However, for other than receipt notices, if the conditional resident is represented as evidenced by a signed Form G-28, the notice should be sent to the attorney or representative of record and, in the case of a denial or termination of conditional resident status, to the conditional resident as well.

Any transfer notice should state that as necessary the conditional resident may take his or her receipt notice to the nearest field office and receive evidence of status in accordance with procedures set forth in paragraph (k) below.

(e) Adjudication by a Service Center. With respect to a properly filed Form I-829, a service center may approve the petition or issue an RFE. Service center directors also have now been delegated the authority to deny a Form I-829 if the eligibility requirements under section 216A and 8 CFR 216.6(c) have not been met or refer it to a field office for adjudication. **See Notes below.** There is no appeal of a denial of a Form I-829; however, a conditional resident may seek review of the decision in removal proceedings. 8 CFR 216.6(d)(2). [Revised by 6/17/09, AD09-04]

NOTE: Section 216A(d)(3) of the Act provides USCIS with authority to waive the deadline for an interview or the interview itself, if that is appropriate. Accordingly, an interview is not required to either approve or deny the petition. Under current regulations, both service center and district directors have authority in appropriate cases to waive the interview and adjudicate the petition.

However, in the past, a service center director only had authority to waive an interview if the petition was approvable. A service center director could not waive the interview if the petition appeared to be deniable.

With the issuance of this AFM Update, the authority to waive the interview and deny the Form I-829 has been delegated to Service Center Directors. Service Center Directors may waive the interview and deny the petition if they determine that, upon review of the petition supporting evidence, the conditional resident has not met the eligibility requirements for removal of the conditions.

NOTE: The guidance provided in this AFM Update does not pertain to the denial of Form I-829s for those aliens who may qualify for benefits based on the provisions of the 21st Century Department of Justice Appropriations Authorization Act of 2001, Public Law 107-273, 116 Stat. 1757 (Nov. 2, 2002). Until such time as regulations are promulgated implementing the procedures regarding the denial of Form I-829s affected by Public Law 107-273, such cases will be not be denied by service center or field office directors.

(1) *Function of Form I-829.* A Form I-829 petition is intended to examine whether the alien entrepreneur has satisfied the conditions of his admission to the United States. Primarily, USCIS is determining whether the alien has invested the requisite capital and created the requisite jobs through that investment. Form I-829 petition is to be filed within 90 days prior to the second anniversary of the alien's admission to the United States in conditional resident status.

(2) *Initial Review.* The service center must initially review the petition in order to determine which course to take. The petition must be adjudicated with the A-file and normal procedures are to be followed for requesting the A-file (see paragraph (f) for procedures in the event of delay in receipt of a requested A-file).

In addition, the service center is to follow normal procedures for consultation and referral to operational and investigative units such as the Office of Fraud Detection & National Security (FDNS) if the facts of the case warrant it and where appropriate. If necessary, such units may coordinate the referral of a Form I-829 to the Department of Treasury's Financial Crimes Enforcement Network (FINCEN) with a request for appropriate research.

(3) *Request for Evidence.* In situations where required initial evidence is submitted but does not establish eligibility, USCIS may deny the petition for ineligibility. 8 CFR 103.2(b)(8)(iii).

Alternatively, USCIS may request more evidence. USCIS may assign flexible times for petitioners to submit a response to a request for evidence (RFE). AFM Appendix 10-9 sets general timeframes for applicants or petitioners to respond RFEs. However, the maximum time to respond cannot exceed 12 weeks. 8 CFR

103.2(b)(8)(iv). See AFM Chapter 25.2 for instructions regarding receipt of a conditional resident's response to an RFE.

- If an applicant or petitioner does not respond to an RFE by the required date, USCIS may summarily deny the application or petition as abandoned or deny the application or petition on the record. However, it is a better practice for USCIS to deny the application or petition for both reasons.

* * *.

If the questions on the RFE cannot be answered in writing, the petition must be referred for an interview.

Note: See Chapter 10.5 for a detailed explanation of requests for evidence and responses to a notice to deny.

(4) *Derogatory Information.* In accordance with 8 CFR 216.6(c)(2), if the review of the petition, or the interview itself, reveals derogatory information concerning the requirements for removal of conditions, the service center shall provide the conditional resident with the opportunity to rebut such information pursuant to paragraph (h) of this instruction.

(E) *Form I-829 Consideration of Form I-526 EB-5 Eligibility Requirements.* [Added by 12/11/09, AD 09-38] Pursuant to section 216A(c)(3) of the Act, USCIS must determine that the facts and information contained in the petition are true. ISOs should generally give deference to the approval of EB-5 eligibility requirements previously made in the alien investor's Form I-526 petition and affiliated regional center designation, as applicable, if the facts presented in the earlier proceedings remain unchanged to include:

- The new commercial enterprise's capital investment structure;
- That the commercial enterprise qualifies as "new" for EB-5 purposes;
- If the commercial enterprise is affiliated with a regional center, the direct and indirect job creation methodology;
- If the Form I-526 petition was approved for reduced capital investment threshold of $500,000, that the new commercial enterprise was located in a TEA at the time of filing of the Form I-526, and;
- That the alien investor's investment capital was lawfully obtained.

The CSC EB-5 program manager should be notified to determine the appropriate action to take if an ISO discovers during the adjudication of the Form I-829 petition that:

- Documentation relating to the regional center's capital investment structure or job creation methodologies or the eligibility requirements favorably decided-upon in the Form I-526 petition have materially changed post-approval of the regional center designation or Form I-526 petition;
- The record contains evidence of fraud or misrepresentation; or
- The evidence of record indicates that the previously favorable decision to approve the regional center proposal (or amendment) was legally deficient.

If the documentation of record presents material inconsistencies that impact the alien investor's EB-5 eligibility, then ISOs should require the petitioner to resolve the inconsistencies prior making a favorable determination in the case. It is incumbent upon the petitioner to resolve any inconsistencies in the record by independent objective evidence. Any attempt to explain or reconcile such inconsistencies will not suffice unless the petitioner submits competent objective evidence pointing to where the truth lies. *Matter of Ho,* 19 I&N Dec. 582, 591 (BIA 1988).

Note: EB-5 petitioners must establish eligibility as of the date of filing of the petition. See 8 CFR 103.2(b)(1), (12); *Matter of Katigbak,* 14 I&N Dec. at 49. Note also that a petitioner may not make material changes to a petition that has already been filed in an effort to make an apparently deficient petition conform to USCIS requirements. *Matter of Izummi,* 22 I&N Dec. at 175.

(5) *Approval.* The service center may approve a Form I-829 if USCIS is satisfied that the conditional resident has met all the requirements for the removal of the conditions as specified under Section 216A of the Act and 8 CFR 216.6(c)(1), namely that:

(A) a commercial enterprise was established by the conditional resident;

(B) the conditional resident invested or was actively in the process of investing the requisite capital;

(C) the conditional resident sustained the establishment and investment activities throughout the relevant period of his or her residence in the United States (*i.e.,* the conditional resident, in good faith, substantially met the capital investment requirement of the statute and continuously maintained his or her capital investment over the two years of conditional residence); and

(D) the conditional resident created or can be expected to create within a reasonable period of time ten full-time jobs for qualifying employees. (**Note**: in the case of a "troubled business" as defined in 8 CFR 204.6(j)(4)(ii), the conditional resident must establish that he or she maintained the number of existing employees at no less than the pre-investment for the previous two years.)

In addition, pursuant to section 216A(c)(3) of the Act, USCIS must also determine that the facts and information contained in the petition are true. Recognizing that circumstances may change after an alien secures admission to the United States, USCIS chose to implement INA 216A with some "flexibility." See, 59 FR 1317 at 1, 18 (Jan. 10, 1994) (proposed rule). Consistent with this flexibility, USCIS provides that Form I-829 must contain evidence that the petitioning alien "has created or can be expected to create within a reasonable time 10 fulltime jobs for qualifying employees." 8 CFR 216.6(a)(4)(iv).

In making the "reasonable time" determination, officers should consider the evidence submitted along with the petition that demonstrates when the jobs are expected to be created, the reasons that the jobs were not created as predicted in Form I-526, the nature of the industry or industries in which the jobs are to be created, and any other evidence submitted by the petitioner.

If after considering the evidence, the officer determines that the jobs are more likely than not going to be created within a reasonable time, Form I-829 should be approved consistent with 8 CFR 216.6(d)(1) if the petitioner is otherwise eligible to have his or her conditions removed. If, however, the officer determines that the jobs will not be created within a reasonable period of time, Form I-829 should be denied consistent with 8 CFR 216.6(d)(2).

(6) *Action upon Approval.* If the petition is approved, the service center will remove the conditions on the conditional resident's status as of the second anniversary of his or her admission as a conditional permanent resident. 8 CFR 216.6(d).

If biometrics have not already been collected at an Application Support Center (ASC), the conditional resident must be notified to report for processing of a new permanent resident card (Form I-551). Normal procedures should be followed for entering the decision into MFAS and for card production.

(7) *Denial.* The service center may deny a petition if the initial review of the petition or review of a response to a request for initial and/or additional evidence reveals that the requirements for removal of conditions, as prescribed under Section 216A of the Act and the regulation at 8 CFR 216.6(c)(1), have not been met and the service center adjudicator determines that the case can be denied without an interview.

(A) *Grounds for Denial.* USCIS may deny a Form I-829 on the following grounds:

(i) *Denial Due to Alien's Failure to Meet the Statutory and Regulatory Requirements as a Factual Matter.* USCIS lacks authority to grant a Form I-829 if the petition does not meet the statutory and regulatory requirements. If the service center director determines that the conditional resident has not established eligibility to have the conditions removed under the statute and regulations, the petition must be denied.

(ii) *Denial due to fraud or other criminal grounds.* When it is determined that a petition may be deniable for fraud or other criminal grounds, the Form I-829 must first be referred to the FDNS POC in the service center in accordance with the Fraud Detection Standard Operating Procedures.

The processing site may also coordinate the referral of a Form I-829 to FINCEN with a request for appropriate research. USCIS shall not make a final decision on the petition until a report of the results of the referral or investigation is obtained.

In most instances, if the decision to deny the petition is based on derogatory information considered by the service center of which the petitioner is unaware, he or she shall be advised of this fact and offered an opportunity to rebut the information and present evidence in his or her own behalf prior to a final decision being rendered by USCIS. See 8 CFR 103.2(b)(16)(i).

(B) *Action upon Denial.* The service center director shall provide written notice in accordance with 8 CFR 216.6(d)(2) if the petition is denied and shall follow established procedures for the issuance of an NTA to initiate removal proceedings. No appeal shall lie from this decision. The conditional resident may seek review of the decision to deny the petition in removal proceedings. In issuing this denial notice, the service center director shall:

(i) Advise the conditional resident of the specific reasons for the denial and that:

- the conditional resident's status, and that of his or her spouse or children, is terminated as of the date of the decision;
- the conditional resident must surrender to the field office any permanent resident card, Form I-551, previously issued by legacy INS or USCIS; and
- there is no appeal from the decision, although the conditional resident may seek review of the decision in removal proceedings;

(ii) Follow established procedures for the issuance of an NTA to initiate removal proceedings.

(iii) Enter the denial information into MFAS.

(iv) Ensure that the A-file includes all relevant documents and is forwarded to the appropriate office.

(8) *Referral to Field Office.* The service center director may refer a Form I-829 to a field office if he or she determines that referral is appropriate and that an interview is necessary to adjudicate the petition and render a decision in the case.

When transferring a Form I-829 to a field office, the service center should indicate the basis for referral in a memorandum to the field office. In that memorandum, the service center also may specifically recommend that an interview be conducted as part of the field office's review and adjudication.

Such a recommendation must: (i) be clearly identified in the memorandum, (ii) detail the reasons for the interview recommendation, and (iii) include specifics as to questions the service center recommends the field office ask the conditional resident during the interview.

After coordination with the regional EB-5 POC, service centers shall transfer the referred cases to the assigned field office by express mail, flagging it in red marker "**to the attention of the EB-5 POC.**" The service center must record the referral of the case in MFAS in accordance with routine procedures and update the Central Index System (CIS) accordingly.

(f) Regional Office Coordination. Each regional director shall designate an officer in their regional office to coordinate the management of Form I-829s within each region's jurisdiction. The responsibilities of the regional EB-5 POCs include:

(1) Determining appropriate field offices to receive Form I-829s;

(2) Coordinating referral procedures;

(3) Ensuring that Form I-829s referred to field offices are adjudicated by EB-5 trained and certified field office adjudicators;

(4) Facilitating the return of petitions to service centers as appropriate; and

(5) Keeping track of Form I-829 processing and cases within the jurisdiction of the region.

The regional EB-5 POC is also responsible for assisting when a requested A-file has not been received within the appropriate period of time and for requesting A-files according to established procedures.

The regional EB-5 POC shall keep a list of field offices with trained EB-5 adjudicators, and shall coordinate service center referrals of Form I-829s to the field offices. The regional EB-5 POCs shall direct the referral in accordance with the availability of trained EB-5 adjudicators at the appropriate field office, and may direct the

Chapter 25 • Adjudicator's Field Manual

referral of a Form I-829 to another office as necessary or to coordinate the detail of trained EB-5 adjudicators as required.

In a specific case, field management may determine and recommend to the regional EB-5 POC that, due to the limited availability of EB-5 trained adjudicators in a particular area, the field office director should delegate his or her authority to another field office director to complete the interview and adjudication of the case.

Such delegation of authority must be clear and in writing. In such cases, the regional EB-5 POC is responsible for ensuring that a written delegation of authority from the field office director with jurisdiction is transmitted by fax, mail, or e-mail (with hard-copy of e-mail placed in the file) to the field office director under whose authority the interview and adjudication will be performed.

(g) Adjudication by a Field Office. With respect to a properly filed Form I-829, a field office may approve the petition, issue a request for further evidence, conduct an interview, or deny the petition if the petition is deniable because the eligibility requirements have not been met. A field office may also refer a Form I-829 back to the appropriate service center for processing if the case has not been previously reviewed by a trained and certified service center EB-5 adjudicator.

Note: Field offices may not deny Form I-829s that are covered by Pub. L. 107-273. See note under Chapter 25.2(b).

(1) *Procedures for a Form I-829 Not Referred According to Instructions.* Field offices that receive Form I-829s transmitted in a manner that is NOT consistent with the procedures outlined herein should return those files to the service center, with the A-file, marked to the attention of the service center EB-5 POC and, in red, "Form I-829 return". The field office must update CIS accordingly.

All such Form I-829s shall be returned to the California Service Center. [Revised by 6/17/09, AD09-04]

Field offices receiving a Form I-829 that does not contain the recommendation required under paragraph (e)(7) should return the I-829 to the sending service center. Upon receipt of a returned file, the service centers are instructed to prepare and transmit the file with the required recommendation directly to the field office while simultaneously notifying the regional office EB-5 POC of the file transfer in accordance with these instructions.

When a Form I-829 file is returned to the service center, the field office must notify the conditional resident or representative pursuant to section (1) of this paragraph. The notice of file transfer should state that as necessary, the conditional resident may take the receipt notice to the nearest field office and receive evidence of status in accordance with the procedures set forth in paragraph (k).

(2) *Initial Review.* Field offices may approve or deny the petition with or without an interview. A field office director, or his or her delegate, must initially review the petition in order to determine whether or not an interview will be conducted.

In adjudicating the petition, the field office may accept or reject the service center director's recommendation for interview and/or for suggested questions to ask the conditional resident during the interview to establish eligibility when the district director determines upon review of the record that the petition is approvable.

Pursuant to 8 CFR 216.6(b)(1), a field office may waive the interview on the Form I-829 and adjudicate the case. If the interview is waived, the petition must be annotated and MFAS updated in accordance with routine procedures. The field office director may also schedule the applicant for an interview, within 90 days of the date on which the petition was properly filed. 8 CFR 216.6(b)(2).

Instead of proceeding to approve or deny a case based on a determination that an interview is not essential to the adjudication and thus should be waived, a field office director may return a Form I-829 to a service center for adjudication if the initial review reveals that:

– The case was not reviewed by a trained and certified service center EB-5 adjudicator;

– An interview is not necessary; or

– The petition is deniable because the eligibility requirements for approving the petition have not been met.

All such returns must be made in coordination with the appropriate regional EB-5 POC. When a Form I-829 file is returned to the service center, the field office must manually send the petitioner, or the attorney or representative of record if the petitioner is represented, a notice of the file transfer.

(3) *Interview.* If an interview is necessary to approve or deny the petition, the field office director will notify the conditional resident of the location and date of the scheduled interview.

The interviewing officer shall create a record of the interview, placing a memorandum in the file that responds to the issues raised in the service center director's referral memorandum as well as sets forth any new or additional information or issues arising from the interview.

The officer who conducts the interview shall render a final adjudication of the Form I-829 and recommend a decision to the field office director. If a conditional resident fails to appear for an interview, the alien's permanent resident status shall be terminated automatically in accordance with the procedures outlined at 8 CFR 216.6(b)(3).

(4) *Request for Evidence.* A field office may issue a request for initial evidence or additional evidence (RFE).

An RFE must be based on a determination that initial evidence, additional evidence or explanations are necessary to the adjudication of the petition. Any questions posed must be stated with specificity.

If the questions cannot be answered in writing, the petition must be referred for an interview. An RFE is not required if there is evidence of ineligibility in the record and the petition is clearly deniable. 8 CFR 103.2(b)(8).

If the conditional resident was issued an RFE for initial evidence by the field office and failed to respond to the request, the petition will be considered abandoned and denied in accordance with 8 CFR 103.2(b)(13). Under 8 CFR 103.2(b)(8), field offices should provide the conditional resident the specified period of time for response to an RFE.

(5) *Derogatory Information.* In accordance with 8 CFR 216.6(c)(2), if the review of the petition, or the interview itself, reveals derogatory information concerning the requirements for removal of conditions, the field office shall provide the conditional resident with the opportunity to rebut such information. See paragraph (h) below.

(6) *Approval.* A field office director may approve a Form I-829 if satisfied that the conditional resident has met all the requirements for the removal of the conditions as specified under section 216A of the Act and 8 CFR 216.6(c)(1), namely that:

   (A) a commercial enterprise was established by the conditional resident;

   (B) the conditional resident invested or was actively in the process of investing the requisite capital;

   (C) the conditional resident sustained the establishment and investment activities throughout the relevant period of his or her residence in the United States (*i.e.*, the conditional resident, in good faith, substantially met the capital investment requirement of the statute and continuously maintained his or her capital investment over the two years of conditional residence); and

   (D) the conditional resident created or can be expected to create within a reasonable period of time ten full-time jobs for qualifying employees. (**Note**: in the case of a "troubled business" as defined in 8 CFR 204.6(j)(4)(ii), the conditional resident must establish that he or she maintained the number of existing employees at no less than the pre-investment for the previous two years.)

   In addition, pursuant to section 216A(c)(3) of the Act, the field office director must also determine that the facts and information contained in the petition are true.

(7) *Action upon Approval.* If the petition is approved, the field office will remove the conditions on the conditional resident's status as of the second anniversary of the alien entrepreneur's admission as a conditional permanent resident.

If the conditional resident's biometrics have not already been collected at an ASC, the conditional resident must be notified to report for processing of a new permanent resident card.

Chapter 25 • Adjudicator's Field Manual

The field office shall ensure that the file, including all relevant documents, is returned to the appropriate service center director. Normal procedures should be followed for entering the decision into MFAS and for card production.

(8) *Denial.* A field office director may deny a petition if the initial review of the petition, the information obtained during the interview, or review of a response to a request for initial and/or additional evidence reveals that the requirements for removal of conditions, as prescribed under section 216A of the Act and the regulation at 8 CFR 216.6(c)(1), have not been met. The decision to deny a petition will be issued and signed by the appropriate district office director or his or her designee in accordance with standard field office practice.

> (A) *Grounds for Denial.* USCIS may deny a Form I-829 on the following grounds:
>
>> (i) *Denial Due to Alien's Failure to Meet the Statutory and Regulatory Requirements as a Factual Matter.* USCIS lacks authority to grant a Form I-829 if the petition does not meet the statutory and regulatory requirements. If the field office director determines that the conditional resident has not established eligibility to have the conditions removed under the statute and regulations, the petition must be denied.
>>
>> (ii) *Denial due to fraud or other criminal grounds.* When it is determined that a petition may be deniable for fraud or other criminal grounds, the Form I-829 must first be referred to the FDNS POC in the field office in accordance with the Fraud Detection Standard Operating Procedures.
>
> The processing site may also coordinate the referral of a Form I-829 to FINCEN with a request for appropriate research.
>
> USCIS shall not make a final decision on the petition until a report of the results of the referral or investigation is obtained.
>
> In most instances, if the decision to deny the petition is based on derogatory information considered by the field office director of which the petitioner is unaware, he or she shall be advised of this fact and offered an opportunity to rebut the information and present evidence in his or her own behalf prior to a final decision being rendered by USCIS. See 8 CFR 103.2(b)(16)(i).
>
> (B) *Action upon Denial.* The field office director shall provide written notice in accordance with 8 CFR 216.6(d)(2) if the petition is denied and shall follow established procedures for the issuance of an NTA to initiate removal proceedings. No appeal shall lie from this decision. The conditional resident may seek review of the decision to deny the petition in removal proceedings. In issuing this denial notice, the field office director shall:
>
>> (i) Advise the conditional resident of the specific reasons for the denial and that:
>
> - the conditional resident's status, and that of his or her spouse or children, is terminated as of the date of the decision and, in the case of a conditional resident that is not represented;
> - the conditional resident must surrender to the field office any permanent resident card, Form I-551, previously issued by legacy INS or USCIS; and
> - there is no appeal from the decision, although the conditional resident may seek review of the decision in removal proceedings;
>
>> (ii) Follow established procedures for the issuance of an NTA to initiate removal proceedings;
>>
>> (iii) Enter the denial information into MFAS.
>>
>> (iv) Ensure that the A-file includes all relevant documents and is forwarded to the appropriate office.

(h) Derogatory Information. If, in accordance with 8 CFR 216.6(c)(2), derogatory information is revealed during the adjudication of the Form I-829, USCIS shall provide the conditional resident with an opportunity to rebut such information through issuance of an RFE or a Notice of Intent to Deny (NOID).

The field office shall issue a Form I-72 Form Letter for Returning Deficient Applications/Petitions or the service center shall issue a Form I-797 notice, with a short explanation of the derogatory information, requesting that the conditional resident respond to the derogatory information and other issued identified in the RFE or NOID noting the date the response is due.

Derogatory information should be limited to information that the alien has not previously had an opportunity to address and the opportunity to rebut should not reopen the entire case. The opportunity to rebut shall also be provided if it is determined that the entrepreneur obtained his or her investment funds through other than legal means (such as through the sale of illegal drugs).

Depending on the response to a Form I-72, Form I-797 or NOID, a conditional resident may or may not be able to overcome the derogatory information.

Example 1: An interview may reveal that a conditional resident has created positions for only seven full-time employees.

If, in rebuttal, the conditional resident (CR) states that he or she intends to create three additional positions at an indefinite time in the future, the CR has not met the requirements of the regulations and the petition should be denied.

If, in rebuttal, the CR provides credible evidence that demonstrates recruitment for the three remaining full-time positions, that the positions are in the process of being posted and actively recruited, and that they clearly will be filled, approval may be considered.

Example 2: An interview may reveal that while a CR claims to have created positions for ten full-time employees, only nine are actually working.

The CR may present rebuttal information by demonstrating that he or she actively recruited the tenth employee, and the tenth employee is expected to be hired and begin employment.

USCIS may determine, after considering this information as well as all of the evidence supporting the petition as a whole, that such a petition is approvable.

If the conditional resident fails to overcome the derogatory information or evidence that the investment funds were obtained through other than legal means, USCIS may deny the petition in accordance with 8 CFR 216.6(d), terminate the conditional resident's status, and follow established procedures relating to the issuance of an NTA to initiate removal proceedings.

If derogatory information *unrelated* to any of the requirements for removal of conditions is identified during the course of an interview or review of the petition (for example, an arrest or criminal conviction or other egregious public safety issue), such information shall be referred to the Office of Fraud Detection and National Security (FDNS) in accordance with Fraud Detection Standard Operating Procedures for appropriate action.

Any action on the petition should be held until FDNS determines whether a referral for investigation should be made to Immigration and Border Enforcement (ICE) or no further action is required based on the information provided.

(i) Termination of Conditional Resident Status..

(1) *Grounds for Termination.* USCIS may automatically terminate an alien's conditional resident status in the following instances:

(A) *Failure to Timely File a* Form I-829. Generally, when a conditional resident fails to properly file a Form I-829 within the 90-day period immediately preceding the second anniversary of the date on which the alien obtained lawful permanent residence, the alien's status will automatically terminate.

USCIS will issue a notice of termination and follow established procedures for the issuance of an NTA to initiate removal proceedings. There is no appeal from an automatic termination on this ground but the alien can seek review of the decision in removal proceedings. See 8 CFR 216.6(a)(5).

(B) *Failure to Appear for Interview on a* Form I-829. Generally, if a conditional resident fails to appear for interview on a Form I-829, his or her conditional resident status will be automatically terminated as of the second anniversary of the date on which the alien obtained lawful permanent residence.

USCIS will issue a notice of termination and follow established procedures for the issuance of an NTA to initiate removal proceedings. The field office director may reschedule or waive the interview requirement if the alien establishes good cause for the failure to appear. See 8 CFR 216.6(b)(3).

Chapter 25 • Adjudicator's Field Manual

(2) *Action on Termination for Failure to Timely File.* Where it is determined that Form I-829 has not been timely filed, the appropriate service center or field office shall:

(A) Issue a notice which states that the failure to file has resulted in the automatic termination of the alien's status;

(B) Update the alien's MFAS file to reflect "Automatic Termination" and the notice of automatic termination shall be generated and mailed to the alien's last known address; and

(C) Follow established procedures for the issuance of an NTA to initiate removal proceedings, ensure that the A-file includes all relevant documents and is forwarded to the appropriate office with jurisdiction over the alien's last known address.

The California Service Center shall each generate weekly a printout from the MFAS to determine those conditional residents within its jurisdictions who have failed to file a timely Form I-829 to have the conditions on their status removed in accordance with section 216A(c) of the Act and will take the actions described above in this section to terminate the status of such conditional residents and their dependents. [Revised by 6/17/09, AD09-04]

(j) Form I-829 Withdrawal Requests. Pursuant to 8 CFR 103.2(b)(6), a petitioner may withdraw a Form I-829 at any time until a decision is issued by USCIS. However, a withdrawal may not be retracted.

The petitioner must request the withdrawal of the Form I-829 in writing. The written request may be executed by the petitioner and/or his or her attorney or representative of record.

The petitioner's conditional lawful permanent resident status and that of his or her spouse and any children shall be terminated as of the second anniversary of the date on which the alien obtained this status. In such cases, USCIS shall follow established procedures for the issuance of an NTA to initiate removal proceedings.

(k) Extension of Status for Conditional Residents with a Pending or Denied Form I-829. Officers are advised that no extension of status can be given to an alien who has not timely filed a Form I-829, unless USCIS accepts a late petition based upon the alien's showing of good cause in accordance with 8 CFR 216.6(a)(5).

Upon receipt of a properly filed Form I-829, USCIS is authorized by 8 CFR 216.6(a)(1) to extend automatically a conditional resident's status, if necessary, until such time as USCIS has adjudicated the petition.

Therefore, if necessary, a field immigration information officer (IIO) in receipt of a request for documentation for travel or employment purposes from a petitioner who requires an extension of status based on a filed Form I-829 shall check the status of the petitioner in MFAS.

If the Form I-829 has been denied, the IIO should check DACS to determine if an NTA has been issued and follow established procedures for the issuance of an NTA to initiate removal proceedings.

If the Form I-829 is still pending or has been denied but no final order of removal has been entered, the IIO must collect the expired Permanent Resident Card and follow established procedures for providing a temporary extension of the alien's conditional resident status.

Documentation of conditional resident status must be issued until a final order of removal is issued. An order of removal is administratively final if a decision is not appealed or, if appealed, when the appeal is dismissed by the Board of Immigration Appeals.

Where the Form I-829 has been denied for failure to properly file a timely Form I-829 or for failure to appear for an interview, the alien's permanent resident status will be automatically terminated. Temporary evidence of permanent resident status as stated above should only be issued if the conditional resident's status is restored as described in 8 CFR 216.6(a)(5) and 8 CFR 216.6(b)(3).

(*l*) Lawful Permanent Residents Whose Conditions have been Removed. Officers are reminded that, as stated in the field memorandum of June 26, 1998, absent a finding of fraud or other improper acts, USCIS will not initiate rescission proceedings in the cases of aliens who have obtained lawful permanent resident status (without conditions) based on petitions that may have not complied with the statute and regulations, as discussed in the General Counsel's memorandum of December 19, 1997.

(m) Adjudication of Form N-400, Applications for Naturalization when a Form I-829 Is Pending with the Service Center or Field Office..

(1) *General.* The procedures for adjudicating a Form N-400 for a conditional resident (CR) who still has a Form I-829 pending at a service center or field office differ depending on whether the Form I-829 is subject to Pub. L. 107-273 or standard EB-5 procedures under Section 216A of the Act and 8 CFR 216.6.

Before taking any final action on a Form N-400, the naturalization adjudicator should confirm whether the case is subject to Pub. L. 107-273 by contacting the Chief Adjudications Officer, Foreign Trader, Investor, and Regional Center Program (FTIRCP), Headquarters for further instructions. The FTIRCP will coordinate any action with the relevant service center or regional office EB-5 POC.

(2) *Public Law Cases.* Form I-829s filed by conditional residents are subject to Pub. L. 107-273 if the Form I-526 was approved after January 1, 1995 and prior to August 31, 1998, and the Form I-829 was timely filed prior to November 2, 2002.

Even if the Form I-829 was denied before November 2, 2002, the Form I-829 falls under the Pub. L. provisions if a motion to reopen was filed before January 2, 2003.

Section 11033 of Pub. L. 107-273 states that USCIS cannot deny any of these applications until implementing regulations have been published. As a result, these cases generally must remain pending until the regulations are published and USCIS commences its review of them pursuant to such regulations.

(3) *Identifying EB-5 Cases Prior to Adjudication of the Form N-400.* Generally, EB-5 CRs will have one of the following EB-5 classification codes: N51-N58, T51-T53, T56-T58, I51-I53, I56-I58, C51-C53, C56-C58, R51-R53, or R56-R58.

If a CR has a status in the "N" series, the service center or field office adjudicator should first check the U.S. Department of Justice Executive Office for Immigration Review (EOIR) system to see if the person has been ordered removed by the Immigration Judge and then follow the March 3, 2000 *EB-5 Field Memo Number 9: Form I-829 Processing* and the January 18, 2005 *Memo on Extension of Status for Conditional Residents with Pending or Denied Form I-829s Subject to Public Law 107-273*.

The E51- E58 classification codes are given only once the conditions are removed.

If an adjudicator checks the Central Index System (CIS) history and only sees an E51-E58 classification without the alien previously having a conditional classification (i.e. C51-C58, T51-T58, I51-I58, R51-R58), the adjudicator should then check the A-file to determine if there was a classification error at the time of admission or adjustment or if the error was in updating CIS. This issue must be resolved before moving forward on the adjudication of the N-400.

(4) *Eligibility to File for Naturalization While a Form I-829 is Pending.* A conditional resident who has timely filed a Form I-829 may submit a Form N-400 prior to the adjudication of the Form I-829. Section 216A(e) of the Act and the regulations at 8 CFR 216.1 allow a conditional resident to apply for naturalization and the conditional resident may file a Form N-400 whether or not the Form I-829 filed by the CR has been adjudicated.

(5) Scheduling of the Naturalization Interviews for EB-5 Cases.

(A) *Non-Public Law Cases.* Field offices or service centers may schedule for interview Form N-400s for non-Public Law cases as provided in subparagraph 6(ii)(C) below.

(B) *Public Law Cases.* Except as provided in subparagraph 6(A) below, field offices or service centers will not schedule for interview any Public Law cases where a Form N-400 has been filed and the Form I-829 is still pending.

If a case has already been scheduled for interview, but the applicant has not yet appeared, the field office or service center with the Form N-400 should de-schedule the interview.

The California Service Center (CSC) also will de-schedule in Claims 4 the examination of any naturalization applicant who has not had his or her conditional resident status removed and whose Form I-829 is subject to Pub. L. 107-273.

Field offices or other service centers should forward any such Form N-400s to the California Service Center to the EB-5 POC for consolidation with the A-file containing the Form I-829. USCIS will not permit a Pub. L. 107-273 case with a pending Form N-400 to proceed to initial interview (even after all required background checks have been completed) until the conditions have been removed.

(6) *Adjudicating the Form N-400 if the Form I-829 is Pending.* For Form N-400s that are pending adjudication prior to the effective date of this memorandum, service centers and field offices should ascertain the current status of the Form I-829 prior to proceeding with a final adjudication of the N-400.

NOTE: An N-400 shall not be approved under any circumstances prior to the adjudication of a pending Form I-829 and the removal of conditions on the CR's status, unless the applicant has obtained lawful permanent resident status (LPR) through another avenue or is eligible to naturalize based on military service under section 329 of the Act.

(A) N-400 filed with a pending I-829 where the applicant has since obtained LPR status on other grounds (applies to all EB-5 cases, including Pub. L. 107-273 cases). An alien who is already a CR cannot seek to obtain LPR status, based on other grounds, through filing of an application for adjustment of status while in the United States. Section 245(d) of the Act; 8 CFR 245.1(c)(5).

However, if the alien's CR status is properly terminated prior to filing of a subsequent application for adjustment of status, USCIS may, in its discretion, adjust the alien to LPR status again, if the alien remains admissible, has an immigrant visa immediately available, and favorable exercise of discretion to adjust is warranted. If the alien's CR status has not been terminated or rescinded, the alien may only obtain LPR status again via consular processing and admission to the United States on a new immigrant visa.

A CR is eligible for naturalization and may be interviewed, notwithstanding a currently pending I-829, if he or she visa processed abroad and reentered on a new immigrant visa, or subsequently adjusted status on other grounds (*e.g.,* marriage to a U.S. citizen) after termination of the original CR status. The naturalization adjudicator should refer the pending Form I-829 to their supervisor for further instructions on how to close out the original Form I-829 and document that the CR status on which it was based was either terminated, rescinded, or superseded by a subsequent admission on an immigrant visa.

(B) N-400 filed with a pending Form I-829 where the applicant has not obtained LPR status on other grounds.

Public Law Cases Where Form N-400 *Interview has Already Occurred.* If prior to the effective date of this AFM update (12-21-2006), an applicant has appeared for examination on his or her Form N-400 but is still a CR, the field adjudicator must ensure that the Form I-829 is adjudicated prior to a final decision on the Form N-400.

If the Form I-829 cannot be approved and, because the Form I-829 is subject to Pub. L. 107-273, also cannot be denied, the Form N-400 may still be denied under Section 318 of the Act (along with any other applicable ground that may be the basis for a finding of ineligibility for naturalization), when review of the A-file by a fully trained EB-5 adjudicator reveals that the applicant did not properly obtain EB-5 status or that the Form I-829 would not be approvable due to the applicant's failure to comply with the EB-5 requirements.

A report of the analyses and findings made by the EB-5 service center adjudicator who reviewed the entire case file will be forwarded to the field office adjudicator to support the Form N-400 denial.

Sample Denial Language for Applications Subject to Pub. L. 107-273. When the field adjudicator determines that the Form N-400 must be denied, the field adjudicator may use the following language to address the issue of ineligibility under section 318 of the Act.

* * * *

Except as otherwise specifically provided, no person shall be naturalized unless he or she has been lawfully admitted to the United States for permanent residence in accordance with all applicable provisions of the Immigration and Nationality Act (INA). See INA §318. The term "lawfully admitted for permanent residence" is defined as "the status of having been lawfully accorded the privilege of residing permanently in the United States as an immigrant in accordance with the immigration laws, such status not having changed." INA §101(a)(20).

A person may only be naturalized if he or she was granted resident status in accordance with the immigration laws, and not if status was obtained by mistake, fraud, or otherwise not in compliance with the law. *Matter of Koloamatangi,* 23 I&N Dec 548, 550 (2003) (holding that "the term 'lawfully admitted for permanent residence' did not apply to aliens who had obtained their permanent residence by fraud, or had otherwise not been entitled to it"); see also, *Arellano-Garcia v. Gonzales,* 429 F.3d 1183 (8th Cir. 2005) (holding that an alien who received permanent residency status by a mistake could not be considered an alien "lawfully admitted for permanent residence"); *Lai Haw Wong v. INS,* 474 F.2d 739 (9th Cir. 1973) (same).

You were accorded conditional resident status pursuant to the Employment Creation immigrant visa category under INA §203(b)(5). To qualify under this immigrant visa category, an alien must invest $1,000,000 (or $500,000 in certain targeted areas) of lawfully obtained capital such as cash, inventory or other tangible property. In addition, the alien's investment must create at least ten full-time jobs for United States citizens, lawful permanent residents, or other immigrants lawfully authorized to be employed in the United States. A review of your file reflects that you did not make the required investment and/or create the required number of full-time jobs. Thus, your admission to the United States was not in accordance with all applicable provisions of the INA and you are therefore ineligible for naturalization.

* * * *

The language suggested above should be modified to address the specific circumstances in each case (for example, to account for N-400 applicants who were EB-5 derivatives).

(C) *Applications not subject to Pub. L. 107-273.* The field adjudicator may conduct the naturalization examination, but must immediately contact the service center with jurisdiction over the Form I-829 before taking any final action.

Only officers fully trained and certified in EB-5 law, procedures, and the relevant precedent decisions may adjudicate Form I-829s. As a result, the field adjudicator conducting the naturalization examination shall not attempt to adjudicate the Form I-829, but instead must contact the appropriate service center or regional office EB-5 POC to obtain adjudication of the Form I-829 before proceeding with a determination on the Form N-400.

Once the Form I-829 is adjudicated, including the appropriate update in MFAS, the field adjudicator may proceed with the adjudication of the Form N-400. If the service center approves the Form I-829, the service center will update MFAS. If the Form I-829 is approved, the Form N-400 may be granted if the applicant is otherwise eligible for naturalization.

If the Form I-829 is denied, the Form N-400 must be denied based on Section 318 of the Act because the applicant no longer has the required lawful permanent resident status.

Because 8 CFR 336.1(a) requires that "the Service shall serve a written notice of denial upon an applicant for naturalization no later than 120 days after the date of the applicant's first examination on the application...", it is imperative that the service center or field office with jurisdiction over the Form I-829 adjudicate it expeditiously so that if the Form I-829 is denied, denial of the Form N-400 can occur within the 120-day timeframe.

APPENDIX E: HIGHLIGHTS, GAO REPORT ON IMMIGRANT INVESTORS

*The entire report is posted on the AILA InfoNet (www.aila.org) at Doc. No. 05040475

GAO

United States Government Accountability Office

Report to Congressional Committees

April 2005

IMMIGRANT INVESTORS

Small Number of Participants Attributed to Pending Regulations and Other Factors

GAO-05-256

April 2005

IMMIGRANT INVESTORS

Small Number of Participants Attributed to Pending Regulations and Other Factors

Highlights of GAO-05-256, a report to congressional committees

Why GAO Did This Study

In 1990, Congress established an investor visa category, referred to as EB-5, whereby immigrants are granted conditional residence and after 2 years, permanent residence status in the United States if they invest in a commercial enterprise that will benefit the U.S. economy and create at least 10 full-time jobs. The Basic Pilot Program Extension and Expansion Act of 2003 (P.L. 108-156) mandates that GAO provide certain information regarding the EB-5 employment category. In response to the mandate, this report provides information on immigrant participation, including the number of participants, their countries of origin, and the number who sought U.S. citizenship. Also, this report includes information about the types of business established and where they were established.

What GAO Recommends

To better achieve the economic benefits of the EB-5 visa category, GAO recommends that the Secretary of the Department of Homeland Security finalize and issue regulations necessary to provide final adjudication to those cases dependent on these regulations.

In commenting on our recommendation, DHS stated that the regulations have been, and remain a priority within the department.

www.gao.gov/cgi-bin/getrpt?GAO-05-256.

To view the full product, including the scope and methodology, click on the link above. For more information, contact Paul Jones at (202) 512-8777 or jonesp@gao.gov.

What GAO Found

The number of visas granted under the EB-5 category has been a small fraction of the approximately 10,000 allocated annually by the authorizing legislation. According to State Department records, a total of 6,024 visas have been issued to immigrant investors and their dependents since 1992. As of June 2004, 653 investors (not including dependents) had met this immigration category's requirements and received permanent legal resident status.

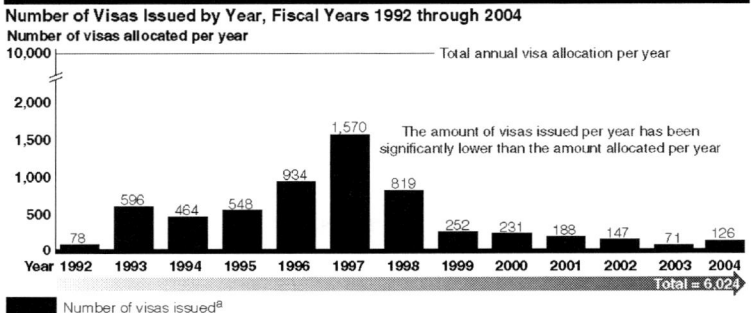

Number of Visas Issued by Year, Fiscal Years 1992 through 2004

Source: GAO analysis of State Department data.

ªSince decisions for applications are not necessarily rendered the same year they are received, numbers of visas issued in a year may be from applications submitted in prior years.

The immigration officials and lawyers who represent immigrant investors that we interviewed attribute the low participation to the rigorous application process and the uncertainty of meeting the requirements that can result in the permanent residency benefit. They also cited, as a potentially negative impact on future applicants, the failure to issue implementing regulations to adjudicate hundreds of EB-5 permanent residence applications that have left investors in conditional resident status—some for as long as 10 years. In 2002, Congress mandated that the regulations be issued by March 2003. The regulations were initially drafted but continue to be under review by the Department of Homeland Security. DHS cited many difficult and competing demands associated with establishing the new department and meeting its mission challenges as reasons the regulations have not been completed.

About 83 percent of investors and their dependents who were granted permanent resident status through the EB-5 category are from Asia. EB-5 participants have invested an estimated $1 billion in a variety of businesses (e.g., hotels/motels, manufacturing, restaurants, real estate, and farms). GAO estimates that 41 percent of the businesses were established in California.

United States Government Accountability Office

APPENDIX F: CIS OMBUDSMAN REPORT OF 3-18-09

Office of the
Citizenship and Immigration Services Ombudsman

U.S. Department of Homeland Security
Mail Stop 1225
Washington, DC 20528-1225

EMPLOYMENT CREATION IMMIGRANT VISA (EB-5) PROGRAM RECOMMENDATIONS

March 18, 2009

The Citizenship and Immigration Services Ombudsman, established by the Homeland Security Act of 2002, provides independent analysis of problems encountered by individuals and employers interacting with U.S. Citizenship and Immigration Services, and proposes changes to mitigate those problems.

I. EXECUTIVE SUMMARY

The Citizenship and Immigration Services Ombudsman (Ombudsman) has reviewed the United States Citizenship and Immigration Services (USCIS) policies and processes concerning the Employment Creation EB-5 immigrant visa,[1] and formed several recommendations that USCIS should implement to stabilize and energize the program.

In passing employment creation legislation, Congress sought to attract entrepreneurial immigrants to the United States who would invest capital to create jobs for U.S. workers, and thereby stimulate the economy.[2]

Congress allocates approximately 10,000 immigrant visas per year to the EB-5 category (including derivative visas for the spouses and minor children of investors), although less than 1,000 visas are used annually.[3] This underutilization is caused by a confluence of factors, including program instability, the changing economic environment, and more inviting immigrant investor programs offered by other countries.

In recognition of the present turmoil in the U.S. economy, it is incumbent upon USCIS to take all necessary and appropriate steps to facilitate a healthy, vigorous, and smooth-running employment creation immigrant visa program.

---

[1] Immigration and Nationality Act (INA) § 203(b)(5); 8 U.S.C. § 1153(b)(5).

[2] Immigration Act of 1990, Pub. L. No. 101-649 (Nov. 29, 1990).

[3] Between 1992 and 2004, 6,024 EB-5s were issued, which averaged approximately 500 per year. Government Accountability Office, Immigrant Investors: Small Number of Participants Attributed to Pending Regulations and Other Factors, p. 2 (Apr. 2005) (GAO-05-256). "The bill's supporters predicted that about 4,000 millionaire investors, along with family members, would sign up, bringing in $4 billion in new investments and creating 40,000 jobs [annually]." *See* Al Kamen, "An Investment in American Citizenship; Immigration Program Invites Millionaires to Buy Their Way In," Washington Post, (Sept. 29, 1991).

Citizenship and Immigration Services Ombudsman

Recommendation from the CIS Ombudsman to the Director, USCIS
March 18, 2009
Page 2 of 17

For these reasons, the Ombudsman recommends that USCIS:

1. **Finalize regulations to implement the special 2002 EB-5 legislation which offers a certain subgroup[4] of EB-5 investors a pathway to cure deficiencies in their previously submitted petitions.**

2. **Issue Standard Operating Procedures (SOPs) for Form I-526 (Immigrant Petition by Alien Entrepreneur) and Form I-829 (Petition by Entrepreneur to Remove Conditions) that specifically direct EB-5 adjudicators to not reconsider or re-adjudicate the indirect job creation methodology in Regional Center cases, absent clear error or evidence of fraud.**

3. **Designate more EB-5 Administrative Appeals Office (AAO) decisions as precedent/adopted decisions to provide stakeholders, investors, and adjudicators a better understanding of the application of existing USCIS regulations to given factual circumstances.**

4. **Engage in formal rulemaking to further develop rules that will promote stakeholder and investor confidence as well as predictability in adjudicatory processes.**

5. **Form an inter-governmental advisory group to consult on domestic business, economic, and labor considerations relevant to EB-5 adjudications.**

6. **Offer a Special Handling Package option to EB-5 investors for faster adjudication of Forms I-526, I-829, and related applications for a higher fee.**

7. **"Prioritize" the review and processing of all Regional Center EB-5 related petitions and applications to foster the immediate creation and preservation of jobs.[5]**

8. **Establish a program to promote the EB-5 program overseas in coordination with the U.S. Departments of State and Commerce.**

---

[4] This subgroup includes only those EB-5 investors whose Forms I-526 (Immigrant Petition by Alien Entrepreneur) were filed and/or approved between January 1, 1995, and before August 31, 1998. *See* 21st Century Department of Justice Appropriations Authorization Act, §§ 11031-37, Pub. L. No. 107-273 (Nov. 2, 2002).

[5] "Priority" processing is authorized by the Basic Pilot Program Extension and Expansion Act of 2003, Pub. L. No. 108-156 (Dec. 3, 2003).

Citizenship and Immigration Services Ombudsman

Recommendation from the CIS Ombudsman to the Director, USCIS
March 18, 2009
Page 3 of 17

II. BACKGROUND

Purpose and Terms of the EB-5 Program

Pursuant to INA § 203(b)(5), Congress established the fifth employment-based (EB-5) preference category in 1990 for immigrants seeking to enter the United States to engage in a commercial enterprise that will benefit the U.S. economy and directly create[6] at least ten full-time jobs.[7] The minimum qualifying investment amount is $500,000 for commercial enterprises located within a rural area[8] (or targeted employment area),[9] and is otherwise $1,000,000.[10]

Congress allocated 10,000 immigrant visas annually for this employment-based preference category. Figure 1 depicts actual EB-5 usage from FY 1998 through FY 2007.

---

[6] A qualifying investment in a new commercial enterprise must create full-time employment for at least ten U.S. citizens, lawful permanent residents, or other immigrants lawfully authorized to be employed in the United States. INA § 203(b)(5)(a)(ii); 8 U.S.C. § 1153(b)(5)(A)(ii); *see also* 8 C.F.R. § 204.6(j)(4)(i) (2008). The investor and his/her immediate family, as well as lawful nonimmigrant employees, are excluded from the ten-person employment calculation. 8 C.F.R. § 204.6(e) (2008). Special rules also allow for making a qualifying investment where the investment serves to maintain jobs that might otherwise be lost in a troubled business (i.e., an existing business over two years old that has incurred a net loss exceeding 20 percent of its net worth during the 12 or 24 month period preceding a Form I-526 petition filing). 8 C.F.R. §§ 204.6(e), 204.6(j)(4)(i)(B)(ii) (2008).
[7] INA § 203(b)(5)(A)(ii); 8 U.S.C. § 1153(b)(5)(A)(ii).
[8] "Rural area" is defined as "any area other than an area within a metropolitan statistical area or within the outer boundary of any city or town having a population of 20,000 or more (based on the most recent decennial census of the United States)." INA § 203(b)(5)(B)(iii); 8 U.S.C. § 1153(b)(5)(B)(iii); *see also* 8 C.F.R. § 204.6(e) (2008).
[9] "Targeted employment area" means that "at the time of the investment, a rural area or an area which has experienced high unemployment (of at least 150 percent of the national average rate)." INA § 203(b)(5)(B)(ii); 8 U.S.C. § 1153(b)(5)(B)(ii); *see also* 8 C.F.R. § 204.6(j)(6) (2008).
[10] INA § 203(b)(5)(C)(i); 8 U.S.C. § 1153(b)(5)(C)(i).

Citizenship and Immigration Services Ombudsman

Recommendation from the CIS Ombudsman to the Director, USCIS
March 18, 2009
Page 4 of 17

Figure 1: U.S. EB-5 Immigrant Visa Utilization (Principals + Derivatives), FY 1998-2007

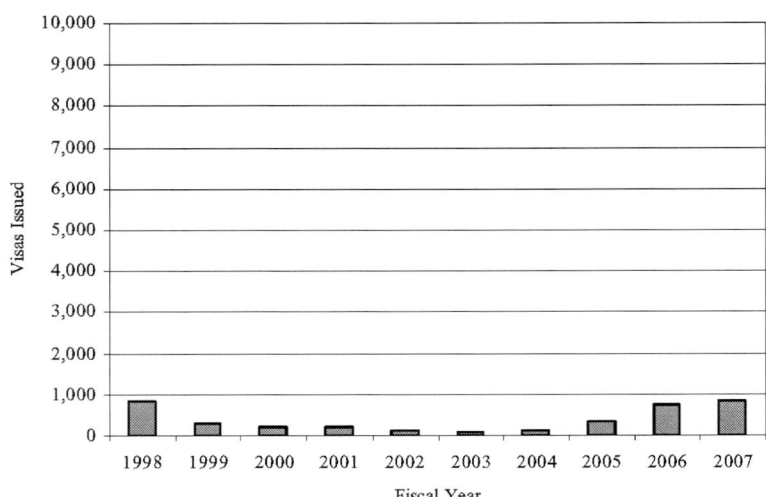

Source: DHS Office of Immigration Statistics, "2007 Yearbook of Immigration Statistics," Table 6 at p. 18, http://www.dhs.gov/ximgtn/statistics/index.shtm (accessed Feb. 19, 2009).

A Senate Committee Report stated that the EB-5 provision was "intended to provide new employment for U.S. workers and to infuse new capital in the country, not to provide immigrant visas to wealthy individuals. . . ."[11]

The legislative history suggests that Congress anticipated that as many as 4,000 foreign investors and their families would seek U.S. lawful permanent residence (LPR or "green card" status), bringing in fresh investment funds totaling an estimated $4 billion and creating 40,000 jobs annually.[12]

Pilot Regional Center Program

To encourage use of the EB-5 visa category, Congress established the Immigrant Investor Pilot Program in 1993 and set aside 3,000 of the allocated 10,000 visas for investors who invest within designated "regional centers."[13] This program eventually became referred to as the "Regional

---

[11] S. Rep. No. 55, 101st Cong., 1st Sess. at 21 (1989).

[12] *See* Al Kamen, "An Investment in American Citizenship; Immigration Program Invites Millionaires to Buy Their Way In," Washington Post, (Sept. 29, 1991).

[13] The original set-aside was 300 visas annually. *See* Departments of Commerce, Justice, State, the Judiciary, and Related Agencies Appropriation Act of 1993, Pub. L. No. 102-395 (Oct. 6, 1992). In 1997, Congress increased the set-aside to 3,000 annually. *See* Departments of Commerce, Justice, and State, the Judiciary, and Related Agencies Appropriation Act of 1998, Pub. L. No. 105-119 (Nov. 26, 1997). A "regional center" is defined as "any economic

Citizenship and Immigration Services Ombudsman

Recommendation from the CIS Ombudsman to the Director, USCIS
March 18, 2009
Page 5 of 17

Center Pilot," and legislation was introduced in 2008 to make the Regional Center Pilot permanent.[14] Under the pilot, foreign investors can pool their investments into Regional Centers which make large investments that create jobs. Regional Center investors are permitted to demonstrate through "reasonable methodologies" that their investment resulted in the creation of ten or more direct or indirect jobs. More specifically, investors within EB-5 Regional Centers are permitted to use statistical formulas and models to demonstrate a correlation between their investment of capital into a specific business and indirect jobs created in other businesses within the greater community. In Regional Center cases, these indirectly generated jobs may be used to satisfy the job creation requirement.

According to the Congressional Research Service, the South Dakota International Business Institute's Dairy Economic Region program (SDIBI South Dakota Dairy) provides an EB-5 Regional Center story that illustrates how the successful implementation of an EB-5 program can positively impact a community.[15] Approved in June 2005, the SDIBI South Dakota Dairy program attracted more than 60 immigrant investors who infused approximately $30 million into the South Dakota economy. Their combined investment was leveraged to secure approximately $90 million in bank financing for various dairy investment projects. These EB-5 investments directly created 240 jobs. Using RIMS II[16] modeling to predict the correlation between monies invested and employment creation, the combined investment also is credited with generating an additional 638 indirectly-created jobs, and over $360 million in additional funds to the region.[17]

According to the SDIBI South Dakota Dairy Director, the "paramount" EB-5 program issue is whether "USCIS [has] sufficient resources to quickly adjudicate EB-5 immigrant visa petitions. If the adjudication process is too long . . . the opportunity cost may make a South Dakota dairy investment unappealing to foreign investors."[18] Similar sentiments were expressed to the

---

unit, public or private, which is involved with the promotion of economic growth, including increased export sales, improved regional productivity, job creation, and increased domestic capital investment." 8 C.F.R. § 204.6(e) (2008).

[14] *See* S. 2751, a Senate bill co-sponsored by Senators Patrick Leahy (D-VT) and Arlen Specter (R-PA) on March 12, 2008. Although the EB-5 Regional Center Pilot program was not made permanent in the 110th Congress, bipartisan support did exist to ensure that the pilot did not expire at the end of the 2008 fiscal year. A short extension of the Regional Center Pilot (through March 6, 2009) was thus included in the Consolidated Security, Disaster Assistance, and Continuing Appropriations Act, 2009, Pub. L. No 110-329 (Sept. 30, 2008). Following passage of a five day extension, on March 11, 2009, President Obama signed the Omnibus Appropriations Act extending the EB-5 Regional Center Pilot sunset date to September 30, 2009. Accordingly, the 111th Congress may yet again take up the question of extending the pilot, or making the program permanent, later this year.

[15] *See* Chad C. Haddal, "Foreign Investor Visas: Policies and Issues," pp. 31-32, Congressional Research Service (Jan. 29, 2007).

[16] RIMS II is the upgraded version of the original Regional Industrial Multiplier System (RIMS) created by the U.S. Department of Commerce, Bureau of Economic Analysis, and is used in public and private sector project planning as a model to predict regional output, earnings, and employment in specific geographic and industrial settings. *See* "Regional Multipliers from the Regional Input-Output Modeling Systems (RIMS II): A Brief Description;" www.bea.gov/regional/rims/brfdesc.cfm (accessed Jan. 8, 2009).

[17] *See supra* note 15.

[18] *Id.* at p. 32.

Citizenship and Immigration Services Ombudsman

Recommendation from the CIS Ombudsman to the Director, USCIS
March 18, 2009
Page 6 of 17

Ombudsman by other stakeholders. They emphasized that the EB-5 program generally, and the Regional Center Pilot particularly, needs stability and predictability to attract foreign investors.

Foreign Competition and Response

It is generally understood that in enacting the EB-5 provisions contained within the Immigration Act of 1990,[19] Congress intended to establish an immigrant investment program to rival those enacted by other countries, specifically Canada and Australia.[20] However, by the time the EB-5 program became law, Canada's Immigrant Investor program was in existence for four years (since 1986). See Figure 2 below for use of this program.

Figure 2: Canada's Immigrant Investor Visa Utilization (Principals + Derivatives), CY 1998-2007

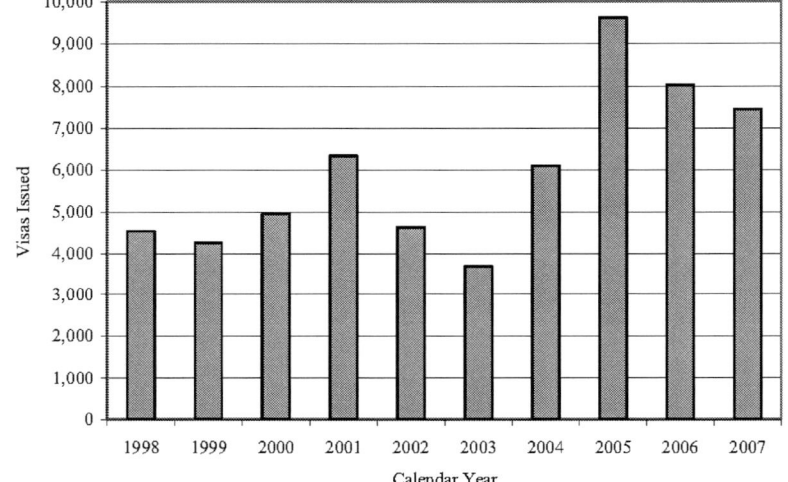

Source: Citizenship & Immigration Canada Facts and Figures 2007: Immigration Overview-Permanent and Temporary Residents, p. 19, www.cic.gc.ca (accessed Feb. 19, 2009).

Under the Canadian program, foreign business persons establish eligibility by proving that they have "two years of business experience," a net worth of at least CDN $800,000, and by affirmatively expressing that they are willing to deposit CDN $400,000 into designated government guaranteed securities for a period of five years.[21] Unlike the EB-5 program, the

---

[19] *See supra* note 2.

[20] *See* 136 Cong. Rec. 17106, 112 (Oct. 26, 1990) (Senator Paul Simon (D-IL) arguing that the United States should "learn from and build upon the track record and experiences of Governments of Canada and Australia who have had great success in attracting talented people through their investor visa programs.")

[21] *See* Citizenship and Immigration Canada, "Investors;" www.cic.gc.ca (accessed Feb. 18, 2009). Invested funds are used by the federal government to generate new employment opportunities for Canadian citizens, and in turn, the foreign investor is granted permanent resident status, and provided a government promissory note representing a

Citizenship and Immigration Services Ombudsman

Recommendation from the CIS Ombudsman to the Director, USCIS
March 18, 2009
Page 7 of 17

Canadian Immigrant Investor program is a passive program: a qualifying investor is not required to open a business, or hire and manage employees. Rather, the investment itself is assumed to spur significant economic activity and create jobs.

Uncertainty Has Plagued the EB-5 Program From Its Inception

Initial delay in the issuance of EB-5 rules, followed by changes in interpretation of the rules, has led to uncertainty in the EB-5 program since inception.

Between 1993 and 1997, the Immigration and Naturalization Service (INS) issued General Counsel interpretive guidance on key legal issues, which was received favorably by several private sector companies specifically formed to develop investment project opportunities for EB-5 investors.

The number of EB-5 immigrant visas issued increased from 583 in FY 1993 to 1,361 visas in FY 1997. However, informal General Counsel guidance in the mid-1990s permitted investors to obtain status without actually committing their entire investment amount to the business.[22]

Concerns of insider access, suspicions of abuse, misrepresentation, and fraud surfaced in the mid-1990s at the same time that the EB-5 program was experiencing its most significant usage. Some of these concerns were later proven in a federal court case leading to convictions for immigration fraud, wire fraud, money laundering, and conspiracy against the principals and officers of an EB-5 investment business then operating as Interbank.[23] The defendants in the case attracted $21 million in investment funds from foreign investors who were seeking to lawfully obtain green card status through the EB-5 program. The fraudulent investment scheme involved the juggling of funds through an offshore financial institution, and the production and use of fake bank statements used in connection with underlying I-526 petitions filings. However,

---

debt obligation to return the full CDN $400,000 in five years (without interest). *Id.* There has never been a governmental default on these obligations, and because of their reliability, Canadian financial institutions are willing to partially finance the required investment. *See* Jeffrey S. Lowe, "Canada's Immigrant Investor Program," Research Solutions (Dec. 2007). Interestingly, the qualifying investment may be delayed until as late as the eve of the date of visa issuance. *See* Citizenship and Immigration Canada "Operating Procedure Manual (OP 9 Investors)" at 9.2 (Aug. 8, 2008); www.cic.gc.ca (accessed Feb. 18, 2009). In the ten-year period between 1998 and 2007, according to Citizenship & Immigration Canada, 16,213 principal foreign nationals have invested in direct qualifying funds in Canada. *See* Citizenship & Immigration Canada Facts and Figures 2007: Immigration Overview—Permanent and Temporary Resident, p. 19; http://www.cic.gc.ca/english/resources/statistics/menu-fact.asp (accessed Feb. 5, 2009). Based on the total number of principal foreign nationals and the qualifying investment of CDN $400,000, Canada has benefited from CDN $6,485,200,000 through its Immigrant Investor program.

[22] *See* INS General Counsel Memorandum, "Sections 203(b)(5) (EB-5) and 216A of the Immigration and Nationality Act," HQCOU 70/6.1 & 70/9-P (Dec. 19, 1997). This 1997 Memorandum clarified and provided new guidance disallowing such practices.

[23] *See* U.S. v. O'Connor, 158 F. Supp. 2d 697, 723-38 (E.D. Va 2001).

Citizenship and Immigration Services Ombudsman

Recommendation from the CIS Ombudsman to the Director, USCIS
March 18, 2009
Page 8 of 17

none of the individual 216 EB-5 investors were found complicit in the fraud. In fact, most of the foreign investors suffered a total loss of their funds and were not granted green cards.[24]

In 1998, the USCIS Administrative Appeals Office (AAO)[25] issued four precedent decisions[26] that altered the previously issued guidance and substituted new and more restrictive interpretations of the law. These changes caused much concern among current and potential EB-5 investors, and introduced new and significant uncertainties into the EB-5 program.

Figure 3: Changes in Selected EB-5 Legal Guidance

Issue	Pre-1998 AAO Decisions	Post-1998 AAO Decisions
Establishment of "new" enterprise	Business must be created after November 1990	Investor must personally be involved in establishment of business [27 C]
Source of funds	General representation and proof of legal generation of fund accepted	Legal generation of funds must be traced with particularity [A,C&D]
Promissory notes	Considered at face value; no limit on duration; need not be perfected; foreign collateral acceptable	Must prove fair market value;[C] duration generally restricted to two years;[C] must be perfected;[B] foreign collateral must be seizable [B] and marketable[C]
Guaranteed returns	Permitted generally	Prohibited[C]
Redemption provisions	Permissible but may not exercise until after two year conditions lifted	Impermissible to enter redemption agreement within two-year conditional period[C]

[A] Matter of Soffici, 22 I&N Dec. 158 (Assoc. Comm'r Examinations 1998).
[B] Matter of Hsiung, 22 I&N Dec. 201 (Assoc. Comm'r Examinations 1998).
[C] Matter of Izummi, 22 I&N Dec. 169 (Assoc. Comm'r Examinations 1998).
[D] Matter of Ho, 22 I&N Dec. 206 (Assoc. Comm'r Examinations 1998).

Following issuance of the AAO's precedent decisions, EB-5 visa applications dropped dramatically. Between FY 1998 and FY 2008, USCIS had an average approval rate of approximately 44 percent, as shown in Figure 4 below.

---

[24] *See* U.S. v. O'Connor, 321 F. Supp. 2d 722, 725 (E.D. Va 2004).
[25] The AAO is the appellate body within USCIS with primary authority to review most service center decisions.
[26] Matter of Soffici, 22 I&N Dec. 158 (Assoc. Comm'r Examinations 1998); Matter of Izummi, 22 I&N Dec. 169 (Assoc. Comm'r Examinations 1998); Matter of Hsiung, 22 I&N Dec. 201 (Assoc. Comm'r Examinations 1998); Matter of Ho, 22 I&N Dec. 206 (Assoc. Comm'r Examinations 1998). Precedent decisions are those decisions specially designated to provide controlling legal principles and interpretations which are "binding on all Service employees in the administration of the Act." 8 C.F.R. § 103.3(c) (2008).
[27] Congress abolished the establishment criterion though legislative action in 2002 when it passed the 21st Century Department of Justice Appropriations Authorization Act. *See supra* note 4 at § 11036.

Citizenship and Immigration Services Ombudsman

Recommendation from the CIS Ombudsman to the Director, USCIS
March 18, 2009
Page 9 of 17

Figure 4: Form I-526 Approvals and Denials by USCIS (Principals Only), FY 1998-2008

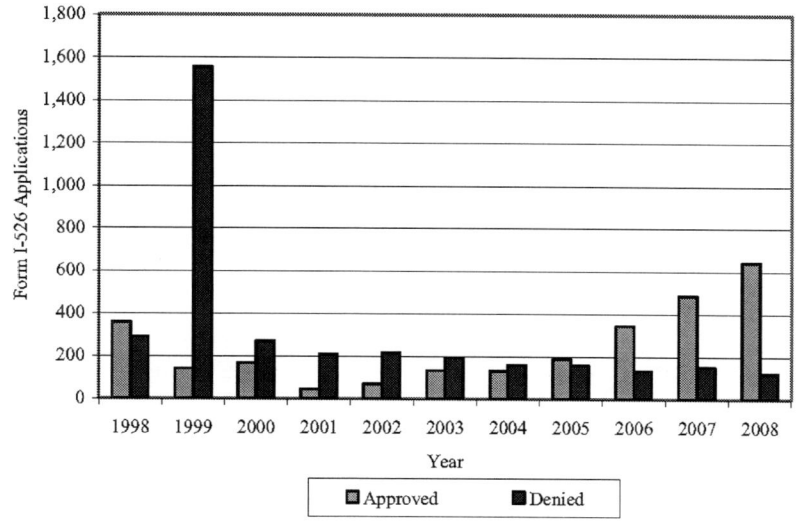

Source: USCIS Performance Analysis System Data, as of October 2008.

Many potential investors decided not to go forward with their EB-5 investments and filings. In addition, USCIS took action to remove some existing investors from the United States based on the retroactive application of the principles set forth in the precedent decisions. While most investors lost legal challenges, one group of affected investors did successfully challenge the retroactive application of these decisions in one federal court. In reversing the denials, the court found:

> [Investors] relied on their understanding that their business and investment plans conformed to the requirements of EB-5. They sold businesses, uprooted from their homelands, and moved to the U.S.... [They] sought no guarantee of success, but a contingent promise that, if they held up their end of the bargain ... they would obtain LPR status promised by the EB-5 program. This was not unreasonable.... The reputation and integrity of the EB-5 program is ill-served by the proposition that INS approval of an I-526 petition as satisfying EB-5's requirements cannot be relied upon.[28]

---

[28] Chang v. U.S., 327 F.3d 911, 928-29 (9th Cir. 2003).

Citizenship and Immigration Services Ombudsman

Recommendation from the CIS Ombudsman to the Director, USCIS
March 18, 2009
Page 10 of 17

In 2002, the President signed special legislation that attempted to rectify the situation.[29] However, new regulations needed to implement this legislation remain outstanding, and these cases cannot be adjudicated until final rules are issued. As a result, approximately 700 investors, most of whom are at the condition removal stage, have had their immigration status placed on hold, some since 1995.[30] This long delay has adversely impacted these affected investors (and their derivative family members) who have been unable to fully integrate into the United States.

It is widely believed that the EB-5 program has never truly fulfilled Congress' expectations. Experts may differ on the cause, but citing to input from USCIS officials and immigration attorneys, a 2005 Government Accountability Office (GAO) report attributed:

> ... low participation to a series of factors that led to uncertainty among potential investors. These factors include an onerous application process; lengthy adjudication periods; and the suspension of processing of over 900 EB-5 cases -- some of which date to 1995 -- precipitated by a change in [USCIS'] interpretation of regulations regarding financial [qualifications.][31]

Citing the same GAO report, the Congressional Research Service's 2005 report to Congress on "Federal Investor Visas: Policies and Issues," stated that EB-5 visa underutilization can be traced to:

> [T]he rigorous nature of the LPR investor application process and qualifying requirements; the lack of expertise among adjudicators; uncertainty regarding adjudication outcomes; negative media attention on the LPR investor program; lack of clear statutory guidance; and lack of timely application processing and adjudication.[32]

In 2005, USCIS established an EB-5 unit at USCIS headquarters, the Investor and Regional Center Unit (IRCU),[33] and announced the agency's intention to re-invigorate the EB-5

---

[29] *Supra* note 4. Immigrant investors affected by the retroactively applied 1998 AAO decisions were provided an additional two years to demonstrate that they made a supplemental investment, and in combination, that they met the minimum required qualifying investment and created and/or preserved ten jobs.

[30] Information provided by USCIS to the Ombudsman (Jan. 30, 2008).

[31] Immigrant Investors: Small Number of Participants Attributed to Pending Regulations and Other Factors, p.3 GAO-05-256 (Apr. 2005).

[32] *Supra* note 15 at p. 8.

[33] The IRCU reviews and approves the submissions of applicants seeking Regional Center designation. Applicants are required to provide a "detailed prediction regarding the manner in which the [R]egional [C]enter will have a positive impact on the regional and national economy...." 8 C.F.R § 204.6(m)(3)(iv) (2008). The proposal must be supported by "economically or statistically valid forecasting tools, including, but not limited to, feasibility studies ... and/or multiplier tables." 8 C.F.R. § 204.6(m)(3)(v) (2008). "To show that 10 or more jobs are actually created indirectly by the business, reasonable methodologies may be used. Such methodologies may include ...

Citizenship and Immigration Services Ombudsman

Recommendation from the CIS Ombudsman to the Director, USCIS
March 18, 2009
Page 11 of 17

program.[34] In the last few years, the EB-5 immigrant visa category has attracted the interest of high net-worth investors seeking to immigrate to the United States. USCIS reported to the Ombudsman that it received 1,257 Form I-526 petitions in FY 2008.

Despite a recent upswing in EB-5 filings, as discussed below, the Ombudsman has heard from stakeholders that USCIS' decision to consolidate EB-5 adjudications at the California Service Center (CSC)[35] has rekindled concerns within the EB-5 investor community.

Case Processing Procedures

To acquire an EB-5-based green card, an investor must first make a qualifying investment, and then file a Form I-526 petition (and supporting documents) with USCIS. Once the Form I-526 is approved, an investor who is in the United States in lawful nonimmigrant status may file a Form I-485 (Application to Register Permanent Residence or Adjust Status).[36] Upon approval of the Form I-485, the investor is afforded conditional lawful permanent resident status, which is valid for two years.

If the investor is outside the United States when the Form I-526 petition is approved, the U.S. Department of State's National Visa Center will process the EB-5 immigrant visa through the local U.S. consular post with jurisdiction over the place of residence. The EB-5 immigrant visa is used to enter the United States, which commences the two-year conditional lawful permanent resident status.

Regardless of whether the investor adjusted to conditional green card status while living in the United States, or acquired such status through consular processing, approximately 21 months later the investor must file a Form I-829 to remove the conditional status. In addition, petitioners must also provide supporting documents to establish that they have satisfied all EB-5 qualifying conditions. Upon approval, a new ten-year unconditional green card is issued.

Prior to October 1, 2008, EB-5 related Form I-526 and Form I-829 filings were divided between the Texas Service Center (TSC) and the CSC as part of USCIS' bi-specialization initiative. USCIS announced last year that beginning on October 1, 2008, all Form I-526 and I-829 petitions would be adjudicated at the CSC.[37]

---

economically or statistically valid forecasting devices which indicate the likelihood that the business will result in increased employment." 8 C.F.R. § 204.6(m)(7)(ii) (2008).
[34] USCIS Interoffice Memorandum, "Establishment of An Investor and Regional Center Unit" (Jan. 19, 2005).
[35] "Change in Filing Location for EB-5-Related Petitions and Applications and Regional Center Proposals," 74 Fed. Reg. 912 (Jan. 9, 2009).
[36] The spouse and minor children of the investor may also file for green card status by filing separate Form I-485 applications.
[37] *Supra* note 35.

Citizenship and Immigration Services Ombudsman

Recommendation from the CIS Ombudsman to the Director, USCIS
March 18, 2009
Page 12 of 17

The Ombudsman met with EB-5 product line managers and adjudicators at the TSC and CSC in August 2008 regarding the scheduled consolidation of EB-5 adjudications at the CSC. At that time, there were two EB-5 adjudicators at the TSC, each with over ten years of experience. The Ombudsman learned that neither of these seasoned TSC EB-5 adjudicators would relocate to the CSC to continue work on EB-5 filings. However, these seasoned adjudicators trained ten CSC adjudicators who now supplement the EB-5 unit.

The CSC advised the Ombudsman that it expects the new complement of CSC EB-5 adjudicators to reduce processing times. Final transition of all EB-5 related adjudications and oversight to the CSC, including IRCU functions, occurred in January 2009.

Recent EB-5 Stakeholder Meetings and Feedback

Stakeholders advised the Ombudsman that they are concerned about delays in EB-5 processing times and the impact on existing investors. Specifically, some expressed concern[38] that adjudicators who are new to the complex EB-5 product line may seek to review previously settled guidance, or request new types of evidence from investors.[39]

USCIS met with an EB-5 regional center trade association group in Washington on September 22, 2008. There were four themes highlighted by EB-5 stakeholders at this meeting: program institutionalization, program enforcement, minimization of program risk, and a need to increase program predictability.

Stakeholders believe that USCIS should not re-adjudicate the indirect job creation methodology when reviewing individual Form I-526 and I-829 petitions. Since that meeting, USCIS advised the Ombudsman in December 2008 that the agency is continuing to review I-829s to determine if the originally presented methodology is valid and appropriate, and whether the projected jobs were created or will be created within two years.[40]

---

[38] These concerns were raised by individual stakeholders with the Ombudsman in informal discussions in the fall of 2008, and in an Ombudsman-hosted a public teleconference on September 26, 2008, "EB-5 Investor Visas: Opportunities and Challenges."

[39] In the past, the AAO has endorsed a "hypertechnical" review of certain issues, including source and path of funds. See Matter of [Redacted], EAC 98 229 50661, Vermont Service Center (AAO Jan. 18, 2005) ("'hypertechnical' requirements for establishing the lawful source of an investor's funds serve a valid government interest....") *citing* a Ninth Circuit decision, Spencer Enterprises, Inc., v. United States, 229 F. Supp. 2d 1025, 1040 (E.D. Cal. 2001), *aff'd* 345 F. 3d 683 (9th Cir. 2003).

[40] USCIS has sent mixed messages on the question of whether and when an EB-5 investor must prove that the qualifying Regional Center investment satisfied the law's job creation requirement. In an October 22, 2008, letter to Senator Patrick J. Leahy (D-VT), Chairman of the Senate Committee on the Judiciary, USCIS stated that a business plan that relies on an indirect job creation methodology, but does not forecast the generation of the jobs within the two-year period that an investor is afforded conditional LPR status, is insufficient. Yet the same letter, citing 8 C.F.R. § 216.6(a)(4)(iv) (2008), states that the regulations do allow some flexibility for USCIS to remove the conditions on an investor's LPR status based upon a showing that the forecasted "jobs will be created within a reasonable time." Note that the cited regulation concerns the adjudication of Form I-829 and in fact does not

Citizenship and Immigration Services Ombudsman

Recommendation from the CIS Ombudsman to the Director, USCIS
March 18, 2009
Page 13 of 17

III. ANALYSIS

Based upon the foregoing discussion, EB-5 program administration has historically lacked continuity. For the EB-5 program to realize its full potential, it is essential that USCIS establish a regulatory and administrative environment to promote investor confidence that the program can be relied upon.

Accordingly, the Ombudsman makes the following recommendations to USCIS:

1. Quickly Finalize the Special Legislation Regulations.

USCIS drafted proposed regulations to implement the EB-5 special legislation in 2002,[41] but these proposed rules remain in internal rulemaking review processes with the USCIS Office of Chief Counsel.[42] Adjudicators in the field indicate that they are ready to address these long-pending I-829 petitions to remove condition cases, but need final action on the regulations to move forward. Continued delay negatively impacts adjudicators and USCIS as a whole, as hours of customer service time are spent addressing congressional and direct customer inquiries on these cases. Finalization of these proposed regulations is overdue.

For these reasons, the Ombudsman recommends that USCIS finalize regulations to implement the special 2002 EB-5 legislation which offers a certain subgroup[43] of EB-5 investors a pathway to cure deficiencies in their previously submitted petitions.

2. Do Not Re-adjudicate the Job Creation Methodology Question.

USCIS should issue Standard Operating Procedures (SOPs) for Form I-526 and Form I-829 adjudications that specifically instruct adjudicators that they are not to reexamine the job methodology issue. Repeat questioning, debate, and re-adjudication of complex economic models and analyses used to prove the ten full-time job creation requirement unnecessarily uses USCIS resources and results in adjudication delays. Eliminating this re-examination may result in increased speed and predictability in adjudications, and allow adjudicators more time to focus on other factual matters. The adoption of SOPs should yield greater regularity in process, and consequently, build confidence in EB-5 project developers and attract potential foreign national entrepreneurs.

---

specifically state that the investor must prove that the required jobs be created and filled within the two-year conditional LPR period initially granted to the EB-5 investor.

[41] *Supra* note 27.
[42] Information provided by USCIS to the Ombudsman (Jan. 30, 2008).
[43] This subgroup includes only those EB-5 investors whose Form I-526 petition was filed and/or approved between January 1, 1995 and August 31, 1998.

Citizenship and Immigration Services Ombudsman

Recommendation from the CIS Ombudsman to the Director, USCIS
March 18, 2009
Page 14 of 17

Developers and investors should be able to rely on the rules applicable at the time they make their investments and expect the government not to revisit those rules when it adjudicates their cases. Accordingly, once the agency reviews the indirect job methodology presented by a developer in its submission seeking USCIS designation as an approved Regional Center, the issue should be considered conclusively established, absent clear error or fraud.

For these reasons, the Ombudsman recommends that USCIS issue Standard Operating Procedures (SOPs) for Form I-526 and Form I-829 that specifically direct EB-5 adjudicators to not reconsider or re-adjudicate the indirect job creation methodology in Regional Center cases, absent clear error or evidence of fraud.

3. Issue More EB-5 Precedent/Adopted[44] Decisions.

Although the EB-5 visa category and the Regional Center pilot program have been in existence for over 15 years, many key terms have not been clearly defined by USCIS. Such ambiguity contributes to entrepreneur anxiety and uncertainty about the program, and ultimately to underutilization of this visa category. AAO issuance of additional precedent/adopted decisions would clarify USCIS' interpretation of key EB-5 terms and policies within specific fact patterns, and assist the business community, investors, and EB-5 adjudicators. For example:

- **Definition of Restructuring.** Current regulations do not define what level of restructuring or reorganization is required to render the purchase of an existing business a "new enterprise" under the EB-5 provisions. The AAO has held that simply buying and changing the legal name and/or the legal form of the business entity alone is insufficient to qualify the business as a "new enterprise."

- **Designation of High Unemployment Area and Effect of Later Changes in Unemployment Rate.** Clarification is needed on which government office(s) is/are appropriate to designate an area as a qualified "high unemployment area." The EB-5 legislation permits a lower ($500,000) threshold investment in areas so defined. In addition, clarification is needed on what impact an improvement in the unemployment rate would subsequently have on an investor who invested in a formerly designated "high unemployment area." The lack of clarity in these matters might cause investors to avoid investing in areas which could otherwise benefit from an infusion of foreign capital and related job creation.

For these reasons, the Ombudsman recommends that USCIS designate more EB-5 Administrative Appeals Office (AAO) decisions as precedent/adopted decisions to provide

---

[44] USCIS adopted decisions are AAO decisions that the USCIS Director proactively identifies and considers binding policy guidance on USCIS personnel, and must be followed in all cases involving similar issues. *See generally* Ombudsman Recommendation #20 (FR2005-20).

Citizenship and Immigration Services Ombudsman

Recommendation from the CIS Ombudsman to the Director, USCIS
March 18, 2009
Page 15 of 17

stakeholders, investors, and adjudicators a better understanding of the application of existing USCIS regulations to given factual circumstances. The Ombudsman suggests that USCIS issue additional EB-5 precedent/adopted decisions as an interim measure until completion of formal rulemaking, as outlined in Recommendation #4 below.

4. EB-5 Rulemaking Is Needed.

The time is ripe to take a fresh look at how USCIS can best implement congressional intent in establishing the EB-5 category.

Given that four significant EB-5 precedent decisions[45] effectively established extra-regulatory interpretations of law, the Ombudsman further recommends that USCIS initiate formal EB-5 rulemaking to advance a new set of rules to replace the combination of existing rules and controlling precedent decisions.[46]

By engaging in formal rulemaking, USCIS will have a chance to reinvigorate the EB-5 program.

For these reasons, the Ombudsman recommends that USCIS engage in formal rulemaking to further develop rules that will promote stakeholder and investor confidence as well as predictability in adjudicatory processes.

5. Form An EB-5 Advisory Group.

USCIS should form an EB-5 inter-governmental advisory group composed of selected representatives from the Departments of Commerce, Treasury, State, Labor, and possibly, the Small Business Administration. Without recommending that these agencies have any adjudicatory role in determining the merits of an application or petition, this group should meet regularly to consult with USCIS on Regional Center designations, and to address other business, economic, and labor issues which impact the EB-5 program.

Some of the specific matters which the inter-governmental advisory group could provide invaluable insight and assistance with include: the examination of Regional Center submissions for such designation, including the business plan; the financial instruments described; the designation of high unemployment areas; and the validity of "indirect job methodologies" advanced by EB-5 project developers. Additional issues might include: appropriate levels of due diligence related to program integrity; the availability and reasonableness of requesting particular financial documents and/or asset identification; and issues surrounding the path of funds.

---

[45] *Supra* note 26.
[46] To avoid further confusion or inequity, the regulations concerning new EB-5 filings should not be made retroactive.

Citizenship and Immigration Services Ombudsman

Recommendation from the CIS Ombudsman to the Director, USCIS
March 18, 2009
Page 16 of 17

For these reasons, the Ombudsman recommends that USCIS form an inter-governmental advisory group to consult on domestic business, economic, and labor considerations relevant to EB-5 adjudications.

6. Offer A Special Handling Processing Option To EB-5 Investors.

High net-worth individuals who are willing to risk in excess of $500,000 in an investment in the United States require program predictability. Such entrepreneurs frequently make significant financial decisions in a matter of hours or days, and existing EB-5 case processing timeframes simply do not mesh well with the pace of progress expected in the business world. The Ombudsman notes that this is not a new concern -- the time USCIS takes to adjudicate these filings has been regularly mentioned as a source of difficulty by stakeholders and investors. This issue was specifically raised by stakeholders during a public meeting with USCIS in Washington in September 2004. It also was the subject of an April 6, 2005, letter from House Judiciary Committee Chairman James Sensenbrenner to then USCIS Director Eduardo Aguirre, requesting that USCIS process EB-5 cases more quickly by instituting a premium processing option, as well allowing for concurrent filing.[47] The Ombudsman recognizes that it may be impractical for USCIS to institute the standard 15-day[48] premium processing $1,000 upgrade option[49] for these complex EB-5 filings. However, USCIS may formulate an appropriately priced specialized handling option that is operationally sound (e.g., 60 days).

For these reasons, the Ombudsman recommends that USCIS offer a Special Handling Package option to EB-5 investors for faster adjudication of Forms I-526, I-829, and related applications for a higher fee.

7. "Prioritize" Processing of Regional Center Related Filings.

Section 4 of the Basic Pilot Program Extension and Expansion Act of 2003 states: "[i]n processing [EB-5] petitions ... the Secretary of Homeland Security may give priority to petitions filed by aliens seeking admission under the pilot program...."[50] Timely adjudications are of critical importance to EB-5 investors. Given the current state of the U.S. economy, USCIS should exercise this discretion and "prioritize" Regional Center filings.

Additionally, as a matter of administrative discretion, the Ombudsman suggests that USCIS consider accelerating its review and adjudication of all new applications seeking Regional Center approval and designation. In these difficult times, many communities nationwide could benefit from investments in newly created Regional Centers.

---

[47] *Supra* note 15 at p. 26, citing to Chairman Sensenbrenner letter. "Concurrent filing" refers to the ability to simultaneously file Form I-485 along with Form I-526, rather than to file this form sequentially after the Form I-526 is approved. Existing regulations do not currently permit concurrent filing of these forms.
[48] 8 C.F.R. § 103.2(f) (2008).
[49] INA § 286(u); 8 U.S.C. § 1356(u).
[50] *Supra* note 5 (emphasis supplied).

AILA InfoNet Doc. No. 09031868. (Posted 3/18/09)

Citizenship and Immigration Services Ombudsman

Recommendation from the CIS Ombudsman to the Director, USCIS
March 18, 2009
Page 17 of 17

For these reasons, the Ombudsman recommends that USCIS "prioritize" the review and processing of all Regional Center EB-5 related petitions and applications to foster the immediate creation and preservation of jobs.

8. Actively Promote the EB-5 Program.

Visible support by USCIS of the EB-5 program generally, and the Regional Center Pilot Program specifically, would send a strong signal to entrepreneurs, financiers, and stakeholders that the United States is open for business and intends to welcome immigrant investors. Sending such a signal, in coordination with its adoption of the other recommendations in this study, would likely encourage individuals and interests to look at the EB-5 program.

Just as corresponding immigration components in other countries actively promote their immigrant investor programs globally,[51] USCIS should actively support the U.S. EB-5 program.

For these reasons, the Ombudsman recommends that USCIS establish a program to promote the EB-5 program overseas in coordination with the U.S. Departments of State and Commerce.

IV. CONCLUSION

The underutilization of the EB-5 visa category is principally caused by significant regulatory and administrative obstacles, as well as by uncertainties that undermine investor and stakeholder confidence. Given current economic conditions, by adopting these recommendations USCIS will send a message that it accepts, understands, and will implement Congress' intention that the EB-5 program serve as an employment creation engine for our nation.

---

[51] Among others, Canada, Australia, New Zealand, Poland, and the United Kingdom have investor programs that offer high net-worth individuals the opportunity for permanent resident status. Some are more active than others in terms of marketing. One of the most active is Canada, where the equivalent organization to USCIS, Citizenship & Immigration Canada (CIC), actively promotes and sponsors initiatives to strengthen its Immigrant Investor Program. In 2004, CIC reported that immigrant investors contributed CDN $211 million in funds that were used to create employment opportunities for Canadians. "Annual Report to Parliament on Immigration, 2005;" http://www.cic.gc.ca/english/resources/publications/annual-report2005/section3.asp (accessed Dec. 22, 2008).

APPENDIX G: USCIS RESPONSE TO OMBUDSMAN REPORT [AYTES MEMO OF 6-12-09]

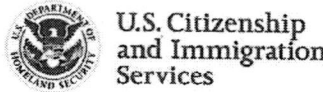

U.S. Department of Homeland Security
U.S. Citizenship and Immigration Services
Office of the Director (MS 2000)
Washington, DC 20529-2000

U.S. Citizenship and Immigration Services

Memorandum

TO: Richard Flowers
Acting Citizenship and Immigration Services Ombudsman

FROM: Michael Aytes /S/ **June 12, 2009**
Acting Deputy Director

SUBJECT: Response to Recommendation 40, Employment Creation Immigrant Visa (EB-5) Program Recommendations

Recommendation

The CIS Ombudsman recommends that USCIS:

- Finalize regulations to implement the special 2002 EB-5 legislation which offers a certain subgroup of EB-5 investors a pathway to cure deficiencies in their previously submitted petitions;

- Issue Standard Operating Procedures (SOPs) for Form I-526 (Immigrant Petition by Alien Entrepreneur) and Form I-829 (Petition by Entrepreneur to Remove Conditions) that specifically direct EB-5 adjudicators to not reconsider or re-adjudicate the indirect job creation methodology in Regional Center cases, absent clear error or evidence of fraud;

- Designate more EB-5 Administrative Appeals Office (AAO) decisions as precedent/adopted decisions to provide stakeholders, investors, and adjudicators a better understanding of the application of existing USCIS regulations to given factual circumstances;

- Engage in formal rulemaking to further develop rules that will promote stakeholder and investor confidence as well as predictability in adjudicatory processes;

- Form an inter-governmental advisory group to consult on domestic business, economic, and labor considerations relevant to EB-5 adjudications;

- Offer a Special Handling Package option to EB-5 investors for faster adjudication of Forms I-526, I-829, and related applications for a higher fee;

Response to Recommendation 40
Page 2

- "Prioritize" the review and processing of all Regional Center EB-5 related petitions and applications to foster the immediate creation and preservation of jobs, and;

- Establish a program to promote the EB-5 program overseas in coordination with the U.S. Departments of State and Commerce.

USCIS Response

1. **Finalize regulations to implement the special 2002 EB-5 legislation which offers a certain subgroup of EB-5 investors a pathway to cure deficiencies in their previously submitted petitions.**

USCIS is actively working to finalize and publish regulations regarding EB-5 investors affected by the 2002 EB-5 legislation. The rule has already been reviewed by the U.S. Department of Homeland Security's (DHS) Office of General Counsel (OGC), and the agency is attempting to streamline the current draft as well as incorporate substantive decisions that are not subject to OGC's review. During the past year or so the agency was directed to issue several rulemakings that were designated as priority rules for the Department of Homeland Security, including rules related to H-1B, H-2A, H-2B, I-9, TN, and T and U Adjustment of Status; therefore, the agency could not finalize this EB-5 rule. USCIS will urge the Department to put this rule on the priority list as many of the investors are in the process of litigating their right to citizenship.

2. **Issue Standard Operating Procedures (SOPs) for Form I-526 (Immigrant Petition by Alien Entrepreneur) and Form I-829 (Petition by Entrepreneur to Remove Conditions) that specifically direct EB-5 adjudicators to not reconsider or re-adjudicate the indirect job creation methodology in Regional Center cases, absent clear error or evidence of fraud.**

USCIS concurs with the intent of this recommendation to the extent that EB-5 adjudicators should not re-adjudicate the indirect job creation methodology for Regional Center cases absent clear error or evidence of fraud. USCIS will, however, continue to review the I-829 petitions to ensure that all measurable variables and assumptions that underlie the indirect job creation methodology have, in fact, been met. For example, an investor may make a proposal to create a shopping center that would be leased to various businesses. At the I-526 stage, the investor may claim that this proposal would result in the hiring of a certain number of employees by the tenant-businesses and that a certain number of indirect jobs would be created as well. USCIS must ensure that the tenant jobs have substantially been filled to support the indirect job count. This is not re-adjudicating the job creation methodology, merely, verification of an assertion previously made during the I-526 stage. In the alternative, if the job creation was based on total expenditure of capital to create the shopping center, USCIS must make sure that the full amount has, in fact, been invested in the job creating enterprise to support the job count.

USCIS regulations provide some flexibility to respond to changed circumstances at the time the I-829 is filed by permitting the conditions to be removed from the alien investor's permanent residence based upon a showing that the jobs will be created within a reasonable time. USCIS has encouraged stakeholders to contact the agency should they have any concerns about how the agency

Response to Recommendation 40
Page 3

has applied the reasonable timeframe standard at the Form I-829 stage. USCIS will confer internally to develop additional training sessions for adjudicators rather than issue SOPs or policy guidance via the AFM for Forms I-526 and I-829.

3. **Designate more EB-5 Administrative Appeals Office (AAO) decisions as precedent/adopted decisions to provide stakeholders, investors, and adjudicators a better understanding of the application of existing USCIS regulations to given factual circumstances.**

USCIS concurs with the intent of this recommendation, but believes that it is more beneficial to issue new policies through formal rulemaking or policy guidance which would provide examples of certain factual circumstances via the AFM. On occasion, USCIS will certify unique or novel decisions to the AAO for clarification on certain issues. Unfortunately, issuing a precedent decision is a multi-department and time-consuming process.

4. **Engage in formal rulemaking to further develop rules that will promote stakeholder and investor confidence as well as predictability in adjudicatory processes.**

USCIS acknowledges that the regulations governing the EB-5 Program need to be updated. During the past 20 months the agency was directed to issue several rules that were designated as priorities by the previous presidential administration. USCIS met these challenges despite limited resources, and we are continuing with rulemaking efforts that are agency priorities. USCIS will re-examine its current resources in relation to its ability to promulgate new regulations versus statutory mandates and other existing priority regulations which are currently in progress.

5. **Form an inter-governmental advisory group to consult on domestic business, economic, and labor considerations relevant to EB-5 adjudications.**

USCIS is exploring the possibility of developing an inter-governmental advisory group to discuss operational and policy issues with respect to domestic business, economic, and labor considerations relevant to EB-5 adjudications. USCIS will advise the CIS Ombudsman if a group is convened.

6. **Offer a Special Handling Package option to EB-5 investors for faster adjudication of Forms I-526, I-829, and related applications for a higher fee.**

USCIS concurs with this recommendation. USCIS Service Center Operations recently advised attendees at the EB-5 quarterly stakeholders meeting that the agency is committed to offering Premium Processing Service for some or all EB-5 form types in the future. However, because of the complexity of the issues presented by EB-5 petitions, the agency does not believe that it is possible to provide Premium Processing Service for EB-5 petitions under the current statutory scheme.[1] The agency believes that a longer processing time as well as an increase in the premium processing fee may be necessary before EB-5 petitions will be eligible for Premium Processing Service. In

---

[1] Currently the Premium Processing Service provides a 15 calendar day processing time for an additional cost of $1000.

AILA InfoNet Doc. No. 09061770. (Posted 06/17/09)

Response to Recommendation 40
Page 4

addition, the agency intends to meet the targeted cycle times before it pursues adding EB-5 applications to Premium Processing Service.

7. "Prioritize" the review and processing of all Regional Center EB-5 related petitions and applications to foster the immediate creation and preservation of jobs.

USCIS currently prioritizes the review and processing of all Regional Center-affiliated petitions and will continue to do so. Regional Center-affiliated petitions are separated and assigned to specific officers who are trained to complete such specialized adjudications. With the increased number of staff dedicated to the processing of I-526 and I-829 petitions,[2] we fully anticipate that the cycle times will continue to decrease. Recently, we requested that stakeholders include a copy of the Regional Center approval notice when submitting petitions and applications. This will enable our contractor to easily identify the Regional Center cases and segregate them so that they can be worked more quickly.

8. Establish a program to promote the EB-5 program overseas in coordination with the U.S. Departments of State and Commerce.

USCIS believes that this suggested initiative focuses more on high-level promotional efforts rather than operational matters. USCIS is responsible for administering immigration benefits and not necessarily for promoting increased commercial enterprises within the United States. For this reason, USCIS believes that other agencies and departments, such as the U.S. Department of Commerce, would be better suited to promote such a program. However, USCIS may potentially discuss the promotion of the program within the proposed inter-governmental advisory group or in other cross-cutting department panels.

---

[2] There are currently 16 officers dedicated to adjudicating EB5-related petitions (Form I-526 and Form I-829). There were previously only 2 officers assigned to adjudicating EB5-related petitions.

APPENDIX H: USCIS Q&A OF 12-14-09

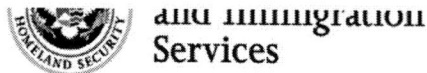

Questions and Answers

December 14, 2009

American Immigration Lawyers Association EB-5 Committee and Invest In the USA (IIUSA)

Introduction

Below are the questions posed by the American Immigration Lawyers Association and Invest in the USA and the answers provided by USCIS during a stakeholder session held on December 14, 2009.

Questions and Answers

1. **Question:** What is the status of the idea of instituting premium processing for I-526s?

   Response: As noted in the September 2009 EB-5 Stakeholder's Q&A, USCIS will not consider instituting premium processing for I-526 petitions until a full year has passed since the consolidation of all EB-5 case processing at the CSC, so USCIS will not take up the examination of this issue until the second quarter of 2010. EB-5 related premium processing will only be instituted if it is determined that sufficient resources are available to adjudicate EB-5 petitions accompanied by premium processing requests in the manner required by the premium processing program.

2. **Question:** What EB-5 memos are being drafted and on what topics? When do you think they will be issued?

   Response: USCIS has recently published policy and procedural EB-5 guidance regarding a variety of topics which should include TEA determinations, the timing of adjudication of EB-5 eligibility issues, and the procedures for filing amended I-526 petitions, etc.

3. **Question:** At the September EB-5 stakeholders meeting, USCIS officials stated that the agency is in the process of updating EB-5 materials on its web site to include an FAQ regarding the EB-5 pilot program. What is the status of that FAQ?

   Response: The "Frequently Asked Questions" (FAQ) will be published soon. The draft FAQ is being revised to include new FAQs that relate to the newly published guidance.

4. **Question:** What is the status of the EB-5 study being conducted by the USCIS Office of Policy and Strategy? When will that be finalized?

   Response: This study is intended to assess the economic impact of the EB-5 program, compare the U.S. immigrant investor program to similar programs in Canada, UK, and Australia, and review the

1

EB-5 adjudication process. Work on this project began in September 2009. Delays in security clearance processing and data availability resulted in the period of performance being extended from November 30, 2009 to February 28, 2010. While the tasks to be performed as part of the study are now progressing smoothly, the specific date upon which the study will be concluded cannot be determined at this time.

Statistical/Informational Questions

5. **Question:** Please provide statistics for I-526 and I-829 filings, approvals and denials for FY 2009 and FY 2010 so far.

    Response: USCIS only has FY 2009 statistics to provide at this time.

FY 2009	Receipt	Approved	Denied
Form I-526	1028	966	163
Form I-829	437	335	55

6. **Question:** What are the current processing times for I-526 and I-829 petitions?

    Response: Form I-526 and I-829 petitions are within the established processing time target of five months.

7. **Question:** Please provide the correct URL for the current list of all approved EB-5 regional centers, since the USCIS web site has recently been revised.

    Response: This is the URL:
    http://www.uscis.gov/portal/site/uscis/menuitem.5af9bb95919f35e66f614176543f6d1a/?vgnextoid=d765ee0f4c014210VgnVCM100000082ca60aRCRD&vgnextchannel=facb83453d4a3210VgnVCM100000b92ca60aRCRD

    The page can be accessed through navigating from the www.uscis.gov page as follows:

    From the main page click on:
    1) "Working in the U.S.";
    2) "Permanent Workers";
    3) "Employment-Based Immigration: Fifth Preference EB-5"
    4) "Immigrant Investor Regional Centers"

8. **Question:** How many EB-5 regional center applications have been approved as of November 15, 2009?

    Response: There are currently 75 approved Regional Centers. See question #10 for directions to the list of approved regional centers on USCIS' website.

9. **Question:** How many EB-5 regional center applications are pending at the CSC?

    Response: There are less than 50 regional center applications pending at the CSC.

10. **Question:** It was reported at the AILA EB-5 conference in San Francisco that over 4,100 EB-5 immigrant visa numbers were used last fiscal year. The USCIS has estimated in the past that over

APPENDIX H: USCIS Q&A OF 12-14-09

90% of all EB-5 petitions are filed through regional centers. If so, that means that more than 3,000 EB-5 visas were issued last year for investors investing through regional centers, more than the 3,000 number specified in the EB-5 statute. Please confirm that the USCIS and the State Department have authority to issue more than 3,000 EB-5 visas per year for investors filing through regional centers. Please also confirm that the USCIS has authority to approve more than 3,000 I-526 petitions per year filed through regional centers, and describe how the USCIS interprets the appropriations act "set aside" of 3,000 visas for regional centers in terms of USCIS operations in a fiscal year in which it may receive more than 3,000 regional center-based I-526 petitions and in which the 10,000 limit for the overall EB-5 preference category appears likely to be reached.

Response: USCIS interprets the set aside of visas to ensure that a minimum of 3,000 visas are available for regional center based applicants. We do not see the set aside as limiting the number of visas that can be granted to regional center based applicants.

Case Adjudication/Legal Issue Questions

11. **Question**: At the last EB-5 stakeholders meeting in September, USCIS officials mentioned a new procedure for notifying the agency if an I-526 is approved and subsequently there is a change in the commercial enterprise's business plan, such that an investor needs to invest in a new commercial enterprise in the same or different regional center.

    a. What exactly is the procedure for notifying USCIS of such a change?
    b. Is the procedure different if the change occurs:
       - Before I-526 approval?
       - After I-526 approval but before acquisition of conditional residence?
       - After acquisition of conditional residence but before filing the I-829?
       - After filing the I-829?
    c. Does the procedure differ depending upon whether the 10 jobs have been created by the time the I-829 must be filed?
    d. If an amended I-526 must be filed, does it extend the time for filing the I-829? Does it extend the time for job creation? If the amended I-526 is approved with a new business plan with revised job creation timeline, does this mean that USCIS will accept less than total job creation at the I-829 phase?
    e. If the I-829 is filed, will adjudication be deferred pending action on the amended I-526?
    f. If the I-829 is filed and no amended I-526 has been filed, but the necessary jobs have been created, will the I-829 be denied? If so, can the amended I-526 be accompanied by a new I-829?
    g. Does an amended I-526 require a new filing fee?

    Response: Please see the newly published Adjudication Field Manual Update AD09-38, which addresses this issue.

12. **Question**: If a business plan provides for investments in multiple job-creating businesses over time, and if the commercial enterprise moves the money from one job-creating business to another consistent with the business plan, does every such movement of funds require an amended I-526?

    Response: In Matter of Ho, the Administrative Appeals Office held that a "comprehensive business plan as contemplated by the regulations should contain, at a minimum, a description of the business, its products and/or services, and its objectives." The business plan that is required for the Form I-526 petition is the road map to determining whether the capital investment has been made, that the proposed capital investment project is feasible, and that the requisite number of jobs have or can reasonably be expected to be created at the Form I-829 petition stage. A business plan that is submitted in support of a Form I-526 petition that is affiliated with a regional center must be in accordance with the USCIS-approved capital investment activities of the regional center. A Form I-526 petition business plan as contemplated above must have sufficient detail regarding the proposed multiple investment activities and must specifically provide for investment in multiple job-creating businesses over time in order for USCIS to determine that it is feasible. The business plan must also demonstrate that the requisite jobs will be created through the succession of capital investments through the commercial enterprise. Such a business plan may help to form the basis for the approval of the Form I-526 petition. In such an instance, an amended petition would not be required as long as the capital investment activities conducted by the EB-5 alien are in keeping with the approved business plan.

13. **Question:** Can an EB-5 investor use funds unrelated to the EB-5 investment to purchase insurance from a third party (e.g., Lloyd's of London) in which insurance proceeds would be paid to the investor if the commercial enterprise fails to repay the investor? Assume the third party is unrelated to the commercial enterprise or a regional center.

    Response: Yes, as long as the alien investor's capital is "at risk", and the indemnity policy does not constitute a redemption agreement or a guaranteed buy-back arrangement for the alien investor's investment in the commercial enterprise. A determination as to whether a specific indemnity policy is contrary to the statutory and regulatory requirements has to be made on a case-by-case basis.

14. **Question:** If an EB-5 investor/petitioner uses a professional employer organization (PEO) to administer payroll for his employees, does this meet EB-5 job creation requirements? As a general matter, a PEO exists only to administer payroll, benefits, communications policies and other administrative employer functions. The petitioner-established commercial enterprise controls the work of the employees, and provides the funds to the PEO to pay the employees.

    The EB-5 regulations define an "employee" as one who receives wages "directly from the new commercial enterprise." 8 C.F.R. § 204.6(e). Because the PEO's wage payment to employees comes directly from compensation paid by the commercial enterprise, arguably the commercial enterprise is still "directly" paying the employees. But in another sense, the payment may be deemed indirect in that it is made through the PEO. We urge you to look through the PEO to find that in fact, the employees are paid by the commercial enterprise into which the petitioner has made the required investment. Form should not be elevated over substance.

    USCIS previously addressed this issue in the H-1B context. In a December 20, 2000 letter to Kary Ann Woodward, Esq., Efren Hernandez opined that "it is clear that an entity can file an H-1B petition on behalf of an alien even though the alien's salary is paid from another source, provided that an employer-employee relationship exists. The existence of the employer-employee relationship can be demonstrated by evidence establishing that the entity has control over the H-1B nonimmigrant even though the alien's salary is paid from another source." Again, the EB-5 commercial enterprise and only the commercial enterprise controls the employee's work. The EB-5 commercial enterprise is also solely providing the payroll funds.

APPENDIX H: USCIS Q&A OF 12-14-09

The USCIS letter in the H-1B context makes sense. We urge USCIS to adopt the same view in the EB-5 context. Many companies find it more economical to hire PEOs to handle the administrative/personnel side of running the company, so that it can focus on the company's core business and technologies. As a result, an industry of PEOs has arisen. By using a PEO, a commercial enterprise can expand more efficiently, having outsourced an aspect of management to professionals specializing in that particular function. Please see the list of benefits provided on the National Association of Professional Employer Organization's (NAPEO) website: http://www.napeo.org/peoindustry/benefits.cfm.

We also understand that some USCIS employees receive pay checks issued by the Department of Agriculture, and that many of the employee management functions are administered by professionals in CBP. Such employers are still clearly USCIS employees, however.

Response: The PEO concept may possibly be acceptable within the EB-5 context in certain instances. However, as the scope and nature of PEO contractual relationships vary greatly, the approvability of such an arrangement for EB-5 purposes would have to be decided on a case-by-case basis through a review of the specific evidence of record.

15. **Question:** Please consider accepting a declaration from the employer of the created jobs concerning the number of full-time positions employed and an attestation that the employer has properly completed Forms I-9 concerning such employees. USCIS can coordinate with ICE to perform any desired audits of I-9s to discover and sanction any violations or any identity theft by workers who may turn out to be unauthorized. A policy requiring investors to present I-9 forms and not to receive credit for jobs filled by workers who misrepresented themselves as authorized is beyond the scope of the EB-5 program. USCIS demands for individual workers' I-9s, especially in an indirect employment context, would seem to violate guidance issued by the Justice Department's Office of Special Counsel for Immigration-Related Unfair Employment Practices. Please comment.

    Response: The initial evidence to provide in support of EB-5 petitions regarding whether the jobs were created is identified in 8 CFR 204.6(j)(4) and 8 CFR 216.6(a)(4)(iv). 8 CFR 103.2(b)(2) provides the regulatory framework for the submission of secondary evidence and affidavits. Note that the EB-5 statutory requirement at INA §203(b)(5)(A)(ii) clearly requires that the EB-5 investment must create full time employment for "not fewer than 10 United States citizens or alien lawfully admitted for permanent residence or other immigrants lawfully authorized to be employed in the United States." With respect to direct jobs, it is the EB-5 investor's burden to demonstrate that the jobs created by the investment qualify under this statutory provision.

16. **Question:** To the extent USCIS will require individual I-9 forms, will an I-526 or I-829 be denied where the requisite 10 full-time positions have been created but, unbeknownst to the investor, one or more of the employees occupying those positions at any given time may not in fact be a permanent resident or citizen? Will the investor be given an opportunity to replace any such worker before final adjudication of the petition? Is it sufficient that the full-time positions are created?

    Response: As noted, above, it is not sufficient that the EB-5 alien simply create at least 10 full-time jobs. Congress through enacting INA §203(b)(5)(A)(ii) clearly requires that the EB-5 investment must create full time employment for "not fewer than 10 United States citizens or alien lawfully admitted for permanent residence or other immigrants lawfully authorized to be employed in the

United States." With respect to direct jobs, it is the EB-5 investor's burden to demonstrate that the jobs created by the investment qualify under this statutory provision. EB-5 investors' should determine whether the jobs that they have created are EB-5 compliant before filing the Form I-829 petition.

17. **Question:** What steps, if any, must an investor take to ascertain the citizenship or permanent residence of a direct employee beyond the proper completion of an I-9 form?

    Response: The burden is on the EB-5 investor to demonstrate that the incumbents in the direct jobs to be credited for EB-5 purpose have been created for qualifying employees, e.g. United States citizens, LPRs, refugees or asylees. As noted above, EB-5 investors' should determine whether the jobs that they have created are EB-5 compliant before filing the Form I-829 petition.

18. **Question:** At the EB-5 stakeholders meeting in September, USCIS officials indicated that they are consulting with the Treasury Department's Office of Foreign Asset Control (OFAC) to determine when an OFAC license may be required in EB-5 matters. What is the status of this issue? Does USCIS or OFAC have any general guidance to educate us on this issue?

    Response: USCIS has engaged OFAC on issues related to several cases that are currently pending with USCIS. USCIS cannot speak about the particulars of those cases in this forum. Prospectively, EB-5 investors who may be subject to limitations governed by OFAC should reach out to OFAC to obtain a license or clarification that no license is required before filing a petition with USCIS.

19. **Question:** Pursuant to 8 C.F.R. § 204.6(i), please confirm that a targeted employment area (TEA) may consist of a geographic area designated by a governor's delegate, that is described by a collection of wards, census tracts, and/or other political descriptions (such as sets of city blocks), even when the precise location of a particular commercial enterprise is located in a ward or census tract that does not by itself have an unemployment rate of 150% of the national average.

    Response: The regulation at 8 CFR 204.6(i) provides that a state government may designate a particular geographic or political subdivision located within a metropolitan statistical area or within a city or town having a population of 20,000 or more within such state as an area of high unemployment (at least 150% of the national average rate.) The following reasoning for involving states in this process was noted in legacy INS' final rule implementing the initial EB-5 regulations, *Employment-Based Immigrants*, [56 FR 60897]:

    Twelve commenters called for the Service to change the definition of targeted employment area. **The Service cannot, of course, alter the statutory definition of targeted employment area.** The Service has concluded, however, that the designation of smaller geographic or political areas within metropolitan statistical areas or within cities or towns with a population of 20,000 or more as areas of high unemployment would comport with the intent of Congress regarding targeted employment areas. **[emphasis added]**

    This part of the rule contains a method for the designation of such geographic or political areas as areas of high unemployment. Under the final rule, a state government may delegate to any agency, board, or other appropriate state governmental entity the authority to certify that geographic or political subdivisions of non-rural areas within the state qualify as areas of high unemployment. The delegation must be reported to the Immigration and Naturalization Service through the Associate Commissioner for Examinations prior to the issuance of any area designation. The evidence of such area designations that a state provides to a prospective alien entrepreneur should include a description of the boundaries of the geographic or political subdivision and the method or methods by which the unemployment statistics were obtained.

This part is not intended to place any unnecessary burden upon any state. With respect to geographic and political subdivisions of this size, however, the Service believes that the enterprise of assembling and evaluating the data necessary to select targeted areas, and particularly the enterprise of defining the boundaries of such areas, should not be conducted exclusively at the Federal level without providing some opportunity for participation from state or local government. This part of the rule is merely intended to afford the states a method by which particular areas of high unemployment within their boundaries may qualify as "targeted," and to allow alien entrepreneurs the opportunity to invest in such areas under the targeted employment area guidelines, including lowered investment amounts.

Based upon the reasoning provided in the final rule, state-issued TEA designations under 8 CFR 204.6(i) must be in accordance with the statutory definition of targeted employment in INA §203(b)(5)(B), which requires that a targeted area either be "rural" or an "area of high unemployment." Further, 8 CFR 204.6(i) does not provide states with the authority to make TEA designations regarding whether a certain area qualifies as "rural". Any state TEA designation must involve the assembly and evaluation of data in a manner sufficient to arrive at a defensible finding of high unemployment within the bounds of the area to be designated in a manner that is in keeping with the statutory requirement. That is why 8 CFR 204.6(i) provides that state designations be accompanied by a description of the boundaries of the geographic areas, and explain the method or methodologies by which the unemployment statistics were obtained. While state governments clearly have the authority to make TEA designations, states governments do not have the authority to designate areas as high unemployment that do not in reality qualify as a targeted area under INA §203(b)(5)(B).

It appears that this question solicits confirmation from USCIS that state-sanctioned attempts to "gerrymander" a finding of high unemployment that is not in accordance with the statutory requirement, through the cobbling together of various portions of political subdivisions so that an investment in a commercial enterprise in a location that is not a high unemployment area would ultimately qualify as one, is an acceptable business practice for EB-5 purposes. On its face, this supposition blatantly frustrates the congressional intent behind INA §203(b)(5)(B). As such, USCIS cannot confirm that this is an acceptable business practice for states to use in making TEA designations.

20. **Question:** An EB-5 investor invests in a company that operates several retail outlets. The company's headquarters office is in a designated TEA, but the retail stores directly owned and operated by the company are not in TEAs. Assume 5 jobs will be created in the headquarters location and 5 jobs will be created at retail stores that are not in TEAs. How much money must the investor invest: $500,000 or $1 million?

    Response: This question cannot be answered in the abstract without a clear presentation of the facts in the record of proceeding. Whether a particular case with this fact pattern can be approved is dependent upon a review of the specific evidence of record.

Regional Center Questions

21. **Question:** Optional project pre-approval procedures: If an existing regional center has a new project, is there a procedure in existence to have USCIS pre-approve the project before EB-5 investors invest in the project? USCIS officials mentioned the possibility of such a procedure at the September EB-5 stakeholders meeting, and indicated at AILA's October 19 EB-5 conference that the USCIS will now accept and adjudicate such requests. Details remain lacking, however. For example:

    - What exactly is the procedure? USCIS officials appeared to indicate two alternatives: filing a "dummy" I-526 petition or filing an amendment to the regional center. How do these procedures differ?
    - Is there currently a form and a fee? If not, how does a regional center file a request to have a project pre-approved? How will the CSC mailroom know how to handle such requests without a fee or form?
    - What documents need to be submitted? Is a comprehensive I-526 business plan sufficient, or does the regional center need to also submit the corporate documents the investors will read and sign as part of the project?
    - What is the processing time, given that investment projects are very time sensitive?
    - If USCIS believes changes are necessary before the project is approved, is there a procedure for dialogue to discuss the feasibility of the changes and possibly to clarify any ambiguities or misunderstandings?
    - What form will the pre-approval take? Will the USCIS issue a letter confirming the pre-approval or an approval notice on Form I-797?
    - What is the effect of project pre-approval? We suggest that the approval be attached to the investors' I-526 petitions without the need for the investor to submit all of the documentation that was submitted by the regional center to have the project pre-approved, akin to the Blanket L approval notice. Does USCIS agree?

    Response: Please see the newly published Adjudication Field Manual Update AD09-38, which addresses this issue.

22. **Question:** At the October 19, 2009, AILA EB-5 conference in San Francisco, CSC officials indicated that an acceptable EB-5 investment in a regional center context may consist of an equity investment in a commercial enterprise that in turn makes a loan with the invested capital to a borrower. CSC officials also appeared to state at the conference that the commercial enterprise could receive a guarantee from a third party that the borrower would repay the borrowed funds to the commercial enterprise. Please confirm that this is acceptable. It should be, since even a third party may not be able to pay the guarantee (e.g., AIG). Similarly, the borrower may not be able to repay the commercial enterprise, even if it receives money from the third party (e.g., General Motors). Also, does it matter whether the third party guarantor is a private insurer, bonding company, or a government entity?

    Response: Yes, there is currently nothing in the statute or regulations to preclude the guarantee from the third party as long as the alien investor's capital is still "at risk", and the arrangement does not constitute a redemption agreement or a guaranteed buy-back arrangement for the alien investor's investment in the commercial enterprise. A determination as to whether a specific third party guarantee is contrary to the statutory and regulatory requirements has to be made on a case-by-case basis.

23. Question: For regional center projects, do indirect jobs created outside the regional center's geographic area count? For example, a regional center may be approved for Los Angeles County. The regional center's first project may be a bakery located in Los Angeles County, and direct jobs are created in that county. The economic model, however, may not specify where indirect jobs are created. The flour distributing company that has to hire an additional employee to transport flour to the Los Angeles bakery may be located in Riverside County, for example. We believe that an indirect job in such circumstances should count for EB-5 purposes. Please confirm.

Response: Section 610(a) of the Departments of Commerce, Justice, and State, the Judiciary, and Related Agencies Appropriations Act, 1993 (8 U.S.C. 1153 note), as amended states that: "A regional center shall have jurisdiction over a limited geographic area, which shall be described in the proposal and consistent with the purpose of concentrating pooled investment in defined economic zones." While the regulation at 8 CFR 204.6(m)(3) provides that each regional center must describe "how the regional center focuses on a geographical region of the United States," USCIS interprets the statutory and regulatory prescribed focus to mean that the economic analysis methodology used by regional centers should also be focused on job creation within the bounds of the regional center. [See also Matter of Izummi.] As a result, a regional center should file an amended proposal seeking an expansion of the geographic area of the regional center if it wishes to include job creation within its economic models in areas outside of the bounds of the regional center.

Note: Regional economic impact models have limitations; one of the biggest is that they ARE regional in nature, so if most of the direct inputs are not locally produced the user of the model must account for this in their calculations. Problems occur when people misuse models like RIMS II by using data that is not limited to the area that is the focus of the regional center, but then claim job creation within the bounds of a regional center. The BEA defines geographic region as the area that will supply the majority of the direct inputs of production (including labor). So, if in the above example, if the RIMS II data for Los Angeles County was used in the economic impact analysis it will not tell you about an indirect job in Riverside County or any other County. The use of economic data, such as RIMS II input/output tables for areas outside of the bounds of the regional center does not accurately assess the impact of economic activity within the regional center.

24. Question: We understand that the USCIS generally wants "relocated" jobs discounted from the final job count set forth in regional center economic reports. Is the ban on "relocated" jobs limited to jobs relocated within the regional center? For example, if a large architecture firm moved offices from New York City to San Francisco, would those relocated jobs count for EB-5 purposes since San Francisco would benefit from an increase in jobs? What if a large employer attests in writing to the USCIS that it must (because of shortage of office space or other reasons) relocate jobs to another state unless new office space (partly funded with EB-5 investment money) is constructed in the regional center? Can the jobs staying in the regional center be counted towards the EB-5 job creation requirements? (Assume this is not a troubled business.)

Response: USCIS is unaware of any statutory or regulatory requirement, or of any vetted and published policy guidance that addresses the "discounting of relocated jobs" within a regional center's economic analysis. As noted in the response to question #26, USCIS expects regional centers to comply with the statutory requirement regarding "concentrating pooled investment in defined economic zones" by limiting the focus of the economic impact of capital investment projects conducted within the regional center to the approved geographic boundaries of the regional center.

This question asks that if a large architecture firm moved offices from New York City to San Francisco, would those relocated jobs count for EB-5 purposes since San Francisco would benefit from an increase in jobs? The answer is no, because jobs that were in existence prior to the alien investor's capital investment into the commercial enterprise cannot be credited towards the requisite creation of 10 jobs per each alien investor. If the business qualifies as a "troubled business", then the relocated jobs could be considered as part of the existing job threshold in determining whether the architecture firm's jobs were retained pursuant to 8 CFR 204.6(j)(4)(ii).

25. **Question**: Please confirm that an investor in a troubled business in a regional center can count the indirect jobs associated with the preservation of the jobs that are preserved in the troubled business.

    Response: In theory, Yes. However, a determination as to whether a specific business plan and supporting economic analysis is compliant with the statutory and regulatory EB-5 requirements has to be made on a case-by-case basis.

26. **Question**: Where a new commercial enterprise such as a large mixed-use commercial real estate development wishes to file a regional center application after some EB-5 investors have already invested in the same project under the regular EB-5 program, please confirm that it is permissible for a regional center proposal to be submitted for the new commercial enterprise in this situation as long as the economic impact analysis report indicates that the number of direct jobs already allocated to EB-5 investors under the regular program are not "double-counted" for subsequent investors under the regional center program.

    Response: Yes, as long as the jobs are not "double-counted."

27. **Question**: At the September EB-5 stakeholders meeting, USCIS headquarters staff stated that in the EB-5 regional center context, a "fund of funds" (i.e. mutual fund) model may not be feasible if it involves investment funds being disbursed across a large number of projects that makes it hard to trace job creation. Please confirm that by contrast, as long as all of the EB-5 money is invested into a single job-creating project, it is permissible for investment funds to be invested into a holding company, which then invests into a non-wholly owned subsidiary formed to operate and develop the job-creating project, notwithstanding 8 C.F.R. § 204.6(e), which provides that the definition of "commercial enterprise" includes "a commercial enterprise consisting of a holding company and its wholly-owned subsidiaries."

    Response: Yes. However, a scheme such as this may not be feasible unless the regional center properly documents the scheme at the regional center proposal stage. If a regional center wishes to build such complexity into its capital investment scheme, then any such initial or amended regional center proposal should contain sufficient documentation and analysis for each category of projects in order to demonstrate EB-5 compliance with the required capital investment and job creation. The scheme must be designed in a manner that is sufficiently transparent to enable USCIS to track each individual EB-5 investor's capital investment into the commercial enterprise and into the job-creating investment projects to enable USCIS to make a determination as to whether each alien's investment was sustained and to determine the allocation of jobs amongst the multiple EB-5 investors.

APPENDIX H: USCIS Q&A OF 12-14-09

28. **Question:** Will USCIS recognize investment in a fund that will capitalize or lend money to numerous business projects with one or more companies and allow the investors in the fund to aggregate the job creation of all of the projects (as long as no job is allocated to more than one investor)? If not, why not, and on what legal basis? And if not, how similar or related must a set of economic activities be to be considered one project for purposes of the job-tracking requirement?

    Response: See the answer to question #30.

I-526 Questions

29. **Question:** Please clarify what constitutes a "new commercial enterprise" and "creation of an original business" for purposes of 8 C.F.R. § 204.6(h). That regulation states that the establishment of a new commercial enterprise may exist in three circumstances, including the "creation of an original business." 8 C.F.R. § 204.6(e) defines "new" as being established after November 29, 1990. Assume a company was created in 1991 and has been in existence ever since. An EB-5 investor plans to invest in the company now. Does the investor's investment qualify under 8 C.F.R. § 204.6(h)(1) (creating an original business) without needing to meet the requirements of expansion of an existing business under 8 C.F.R. § 204.6(h)(3) or restructuring/reorganization under 8 C.F.R. § 204.6(h)(2)? Is it correct that expansion of an existing business under 8 C.F.R. § 204.6(h)(3) or restructuring/reorganization under 8 C.F.R. § 204.6(h)(2) are only necessary to meet when the business entity was created after November 29, 1990? Also, must evidence of restructuring or expansion be submitted with the I-526, or should this evidence be submitted with the I-829?

    Response: Section 11036 of the 21st Century Department of Justice Appropriations Authorization Act, Public Law No. 107-273, eliminated the requirement than an EB-5 alien must be involved in the establishment of a new commercial enterprise. Rather, the amended statutory requirement only requires that the alien investor must invest in the new commercial enterprise. As a result, while the regulation at 8 CFR 204.6(h) is longer in effect with regard to the establishment of the new commercial enterprise, the regulatory requirement regarding what constitutes a "new commercial enterprise" remains in effect.
    This question has several parts to it, as follows:

    a. **Question:** 8 C.F.R. § 204.6(e) defines "new" as being established after November 29, 1990. Assume a company was created in 1991 and has been in existence ever since. An EB-5 investor plans to invest in the company now. Does the investor's investment qualify under 8 C.F.R. § 204.6(h)(1) (creating an original business) without needing to meet the requirements of expansion of an existing business under 8 C.F.R. § 204.6(h)(3) or restructuring/reorganization under 8 C.F.R. § 204.6(h)(2)?

        Response: The alien investor does not have to have been involved in the creation of the commercial enterprise as noted above. Yes, the alien's investment would qualify without the need to show that the "new" commercial enterprise was "expanded" or "restructured/reorganized" under 8 CFR 204.6(h)(2) and (3).

    b. **Question:** Is it correct that expansion of an existing business under 8 C.F.R. § 204.6(h)(3) or restructuring/reorganization under 8 C.F.R. § 204.6(h)(2) are only necessary to meet when the business entity was created after November 29, 1990?

        Response: The expansion of an existing business under 8 C.F.R. § 204.6(h)(3) or restructuring/reorganization under 8 C.F.R. § 204.6(h)(2) are only necessary to meet when the commercial enterprise was created **before, not after,** November 29, 1990?

c. **Question:** Also, must evidence of restructuring or expansion be submitted with the I-526, or should this evidence be submitted with the I-829?

Response: The evidence must be submitted with the Form I-526 petition, and if the transaction is not yet completed at the time of the filing of the Form I-526 petition, then additional evidence must be provided in support of the Form I-829 petition to show that the commercial enterprise that was established prior to November 29, 1990 was expanded, or restructured/reorganized in accordance with 8 CFR 204.6(h)(2) and (3).

30. **Question:** Please confirm how USCIS treats job creation where the new commercial enterprise purchases the assets of a distressed corporation for the purposes of revitalization. For example, if the new commercial enterprise purchases a commercial property, such as a shopping mall, that at the time of purchase has only 20% of its tenants in operation because the other 80% went out of business, please confirm that the job creation requirement would be met by showing that alien investment into the new commercial enterprise resulted in the creation of 10 jobs per investor, provided only that the job count does not include jobs associated with the tenants that were in operation at the time the shopping mall was purchased.

    Response: It is not possible to confirm whether the job creation requirement would be met, based on the limited information provided above. Such a case would have to be evaluated by a review of the specific evidence in the record, which may or may not establish that the job creation requirement would be met. Further, based on this fact pattern, such an investment would have to be made through a petition affiliated with a regional center as the job creation appears to depend on the crediting of indirect jobs.

31. **Question:** What factual scenarios have been approved as a "restructuring or reorganization" sufficient to create a new commercial enterprise under 8 C.F.R. § 204.6(h)(2)? For example, if an EB-5 investor buys a company that was created before Nov. 29, 1990 and then folds it into his own holding company as a subsidiary, is that a restructuring or reorganization? If not, what counts as a restructuring or reorganization?

    Response: USCIS does not maintain records independent of the individual EB-5 case files that document the factual scenarios that have been approved for a particular EB-5 eligibility requirement. However, it was held in Matter of Soffici, that the petitioner in that case did not show the degree of restructuring and reorganization required by 8 CFR 204.6(h)(2). In that case, the commercial enterprise was a hotel that had always been operated as a Howard Johnson and was still a Howard Johnson at the time of the issuance of the decision. Matter of Soffici also held that a few cosmetic changes to the decor and a new marketing strategy for success did not constitute the kind of restructuring contemplated by the regulations, nor did a simple change in ownership. It is not possible to state whether the abbreviated scenario outlined above would be qualifying. The question may not be answered in the abstract without a review of the specific evidence of record.

32. **Question:** Please confirm that if a new commercial enterprise's business operations involve acquiring (out of bankruptcy or bank foreclosure portfolio) and renovating an incomplete or abandoned commercial building, completion or renovation of the building by the new commercial enterprise will be treated as a new business for EB-5 purposes. If not, what arrangements would be necessary to allow the project to be treated as a new commercial enterprise?

Response: See the response to question #32 for a description regarding what constitutes a "new" commercial enterprise. Acquiring assets that are not currently being used in business operations by any other entity is unrelated to whether a commercial enterprise is "new" for EB-5 purposes.

33. **Question:** 8 C.F.R. § 204.6(j)(1) states that an I-526 petition must be accompanied by evidence that the EB-5 investor has invested "or is actively in the process of investing" the required money. Similarly, 8 C.F.R. § 216.6(a)(4)(ii) requires an investor at the I-829 stage to show that he has invested or "was actively in the process of investing" the required capital. The quoted langue would seem to indicate that an investment of $100,000 cash before filing the I-526 petition, plus a promise to pay another $400,000 (payable before the I-829 must be filed) would satisfy the EB-5 regulations. What is the USCIS' position on this question?

    Response: EB-5 capital investment and job creation requirements typically involve a separate analysis. However, if the job creation is predicated on the infusion of EB-5 capital into a given capital investment project in order to realize indirect job creation, then the economic analysis would have to account for the timing of the infusion of capital in order to demonstrate that the indirect jobs would be created within a reasonable time. Any "promise to pay" due at a date in time post-filing of the I-526 petition must meet the requirements for promissory notes specified in Matter of Izumii and Matter of Hsiung, and must show that at the time of filing the I-526 petition that the capital is at risk, the lawful source of the capital, and that the alien has legal ownership of the capital per Matter of Ho.

34. **Question:** Please explain how USCIS applies the preponderance of the evidence standard in adjudicating lawful source of funds in I-526 petitions.

    Response: As we stated at a previous stakeholders meeting, in adjudicating all eligibility requirements in EB-5 related petitions, officers use the preponderance of the evidence standard. It is difficult to answer this question in the abstract without looking at the specific evidence of record.

    As we stated previously, if for example, an officer issues an RFE related to the lawful source of funds, the petitioner should respond to the request in a timely manner. The petitioner may choose not to provide all of the requested evidence and request a decision on the merits if he or she believes that eligibility has been established by the evidence already in the record or that the request is not proper. See 8 CFR 103.2(b)(11).

    Separately from the adjudicative process, if there are repeated cases in which you believe that an RFE is improperly issued, you may send an e-mail to the EB-5 mailbox. USCIS will investigate the matter and, if necessary, will take appropriate action.

I-829 Questions

35. **Question:** Based on the USCIS June 17, 2009 memo regarding EB-5 job creation, it is our understanding that USCIS has accepted the use of economic models that are based on infusion of capital into a particular industry. Please confirm that if such a model is used to calculate job projections at the I-526 stage, an investor would receive credit for job creation at the I-829 stage simply by establishing that he/she invested the requisite amount into the new commercial enterprise, and that the new commercial enterprise spent that capital, regardless of any data about actual job creation.

Response: This form of capital investment involves more than simply investing a certain amount of investment dollars into a particular industry. An important aspect to any economic analysis model is the feasibility and quality of the business plan that is the basis for determining the appropriate inputs into an economic model, such as RIMS II, IMPLAN, etc. If the infusion of capital occurs according to the approved business plan and economic analysis, and the capital investment scheme comes to fruition in the manner outlined in the business plan, then the economic data provided in support of the Form I-526 petition regarding indirect job creation may be sufficient to demonstrate the creation of the indirect jobs without the submission of further data about job creation at the Form I-829 petition stage.

36. **Question:** What factors are considered in determining whether the necessary jobs will be created within a "reasonable time" in adjudicating an I-829 petition, per 8 C.F.R. § 216.6(a)(4)(iv)? Section 25.2(e)(4)(D) of the Adjudicator's Field Manual lists some factors in making the reasonable time determination, but how do CSC adjudicators apply those factors in actual cases? For example, what if a regional center has an approved job creation methodology, proof that the investment has gone into the project, and has leased up the project but the tenants have not moved in when the I-829 is filed? What if the project is almost but not completely leased? Will USCIS approve an I-829 in such a case? If so, what documentation would be required?

    Response: CSC adjudicators follow the guidance put forth in the Adjudicator's Field Manual (AFM) at section 25.2(e)(4)(D), which states:

    In making the "reasonable time" determination, officers should consider the evidence submitted along with the petition that demonstrates when the jobs are expected to be created, the reasons that the jobs were not created as predicted in Form I-526, the nature of the industry or industries in which the jobs are to be created, and any other evidence submitted by the petitioner.

    If after considering the evidence, the officer determines that the jobs are more likely than not going to be created within a reasonable time, Form I-829 should be approved consistent with 8 CFR 216.6(d)(1) if the petitioner is otherwise eligible to have his or her conditions removed. If, however, the officer determines that the jobs will not be created within a reasonable period of time, Form I-829 should be denied consistent with 8 CFR 216.6(d)(2).

    CSC adjudicators apply the factors outlined above when analyzing the facts in each individual case using the preponderance of evidence standard. Note: It is not possible to answer "what if" questions such as this question in the abstract. Whether a particular case will be approved is dependent upon the determination of eligibility, based upon the specific evidence of record.

37. **Question:** If an I-829 petition is denied because of a determination that the jobs will not be created within a reasonable time or because the investor was not aware of the need to file an amended I-526 petition, will the investor be placed into removal proceedings in order to renew the I-829 before an immigration judge? What are USCIS' procedures to place an EB-5 investor in removal proceedings? We have heard stories of EB-5 investors waiting months before a notice to appear is issued. During that time, what is the investor's status until the removal proceedings are initiated? If the investor or a family member is outside the United States, what document will be issued to enable the investor or family member to be reunited with the remainder of the family or to appear in the removal proceeding?

Response: In accordance with 8 CFR 216.6(d)(2), if after review of the petition, the director denies the petition, he or she shall place the investor in removal proceeding by issuing a Notice to Appear (NTA). The investor may seek review of the petition during removal proceedings. Petitions are sent to CSC's NTA unit after the denial of the petition. The NTA unit prepares the NTA and issues it to the investor via mail. The investor's lawful permanent resident status and that of his or her dependent spouse and children are terminated as of the date of the director's written decision. Generally an NTA is not issued if USCIS determines that an investor or a family member is out of the United States and their status is terminated. If an investor or a family member is out of the United States at the time that their status is terminated, then he or she will be put into removal proceedings at the time of their application for admission. An alien investor retains conditional resident status and is entitled to proof of that status while he or she obtains review of the USCIS termination in removal proceedings.

38. **Question:** Many USCIS Field Offices refuse to stamp passports of people who have pending I-829s with temporary evidence of permanent resident status with I-551 stamp, on the ground that I-829 receipt notice should suffice for work and travel purposes. However, this view does not take into account the fact that CPB often wants to see temporary stamps. Will you issue a memo to all USCIS Field Offices telling them that all pending I-829 applicants should get their permanent resident stamps in their passports?

    Response: USCIS is in the process of updating the language regarding this issue on the Form I-829 receipt notice which will resolve this issue.

APPENDIX I: INDEX OF ONLINE RESOURCES

Compiled by Susan Pilcher (last visited 7/9/10) *

CURRENCY EXCHANGE RATES

Online currency conversion tool:

www.oanda.com

INTERNATIONAL TAX REPORTING REQUIREMENTS

Concise information about tax reporting requirements for businesses and individuals worldwide:

www.deloitte.com/view/en_GX/global/services/tax/international-tax/international-tax-and-business-guides/index.htm

DUE DILIGENCE RESOURCES (U.S. DEPARTMENTS OF TREASURY AND COMMERCE):

Government lists of prohibited, debarred, and sanctioned persons and entities:

www.bis.doc.gov/complianceandenforcement/liststocheck.htm

Treasury's Office of Foreign Asset Control program information regarding sanctions programs prohibiting or regulating transactions involving specified nations, including links to applicable rules:

www.treas.gov/offices/enforcement/ofac/programs/

USCIS AGENCY INFORMATION

www.uscis.gov/

Current links or navigation paths through *www.uscis.gov/*:

- Agency summary of eligibility criteria and required initial evidence
  - Home > Working in the United States > Permanent Workers > Employment-Based Immigration: Fifth Preference EB-5
- Agency list of USCIS-approved Regional Centers & contacts
  - Home > Working in the United States > Permanent Workers > Employment-Based Immigration: Fifth Preference EB-5 > Immigrant Investor Regional Centers [*Ed. note*: final link in upper right corner, or search within the EB-5 section on "Immigrant Investor Regional Centers"]

---

* **Susan L. Pilcher** is of counsel to the firm of Carroll & Scribner, P.C. in Burlington, VT, where her general immigration practice includes a substantial focus on EB-5 and investment-related matters. Ms. Pilcher's professional background includes nearly a decade of full-time law teaching, including general and specialized immigration law courses, at the University of Arkansas School of Law (Fayetteville), a federal court clerkship in San Diego, commercial law practice, and many years of diverse and rewarding experience representing clients in virtually all types of immigration-related matters. She obtained her J.D. with distinction from Stanford Law School, where she served as managing editor of the *Stanford Law Review*. Ms. Pilcher has published and lectured extensively on immigration law topics, and she is active in agency liaison functions for the American Immigration Lawyers Association.

- This is the agency's new location for posting minutes or Q&As from stakeholder information sessions, such as the 12/14/09 EB-5 Stakeholder Teleconference
  - Home > Resources > Public Engagement > Public Engagement National Events [browse by date or search on "EB-5" and/or "Immigrant Investor"]
- June 17, 2009, Neufeld Memorandum re: Job Creation and EB-5 Adjudications (amending AFM)
  - *www.uscis.gov/files/nativedocuments/eb5_17jun09.pdf*
- December 11, 2009, Neufeld Memorandum re: Regional Center-Based Adjudications of I-526 and I-829 Petitions (amending AFM)
  - *www.uscis.gov/USCIS/Laws/Memoranda/Static%20Files%20Memoranda/Adjudicating%20of%20EB-5_121109.pdf*

OTHER FEDERAL AGENCY INFORMATION

Searchable Census Bureau database for state, city, and town population and county/MSA affiliation data:
http://quickfacts.census.gov/qfd/index.html

Census Bureau's current lists of Metropolitan Statistical Areas:
www.census.gov/population/www/metroareas/metrodef.html

Census Bureau's population estimates for cities and towns:
www.census.gov/popest/cities/SUB-EST2008-4.html

Department of Labor's unemployment statistics:
www.bls.gov/bls/unemployment.htm

INTEREST GROUPS/LISTSERVES

Membership-based organization—The Association to Invest in USA:
www.iiusa.org

SUBJECT-MATTER INDEX
IMMIGRATION OPTIONS FOR INVESTORS AND ENTREPRENEURS, 2ND ED.

A

AAO. *See* **Administrative Appeals Office**
ABA Model Rules of Professional Conduct
   foreign exchange violations and, 136
Ability to pay
   EB-1-3 visas, 39
   H-1B visas, 8–9
Academic fields
   outstanding professors and researchers (EB-1-2), 34–37
Accounting issues. *See also* **Financial Accounting Standards Board (FASB)**
   generally, 339–357
   accounting policies, 344–345
   additional paid-in capital, 349
   adverse opinion, 346
   audit reports, types of, 346
   background of modern accounting, 342–343
   balance sheet, 341
   business entity, types of, 347–348
   cash flow
      net income vs., 350–351
      statement, 342
   contributed capital, 349
   equity accounts, 349–350
      reporting changes in, 350
   explanatory language added to audit, 346
   financial statements, 340–341
      comparing "compiled," "reviewed," and "audited" statements, 345–346
      disclosures and notes, 342
      FASB standards, 344
   generally accepted accounting principles (GAAP), 343
      common departures, 343–344
   generally accepted auditing standards (GAAS), 346–347
   income statement, 341–342
   income tax returns, 351–355
      basis in partnership taxation, 355
      capital accounts, 353–354
      economic vs. tax allocations, 354–355
      Schedules K and K-1, 355–356
      Schedule L, 356
      Schedule M-2, 356
      tax-basis capital accounts, 354
   information systems, 340
   initial investment, 357
   net income vs. cash flow, 350–351
   Other Comprehensive Basis of Accounting (OCBOA), 345
   qualified opinion, 346
   retained earnings, 349
   reporting changes in, 350
   treasury stock, 349–350
   unqualified opinion, 346
***Adjudicator's Field Manual* (AFM).** *See also* **Neufeld Memo**
   sole owner/investor context for H-1B visas, 8
Adjustment of status
   investors (EB-5), 76, 218
Administrative Appeals Office (AAO)
   "at risk" capital for EB-5 investors, 114–118, 125
   engineering and product design not construed as research activities, 35
   national interest waivers, 42
Administrative Procedure Act (APA)
   review of agency actions as arbitrary, capricious, or abuse of discretion, 195, 219–220
Adverse opinion
   accounting issues, 346
Advertising contracts
   U.S. counsel advising on, 295
AEDPA. *See* **Antiterrorism and Effective Death Penalty Act**
Agreement on Trade-Related Investment Measures (TRIMs Agreement)
   scope of, 280
Alien influence and control over job opportunity
   generally, 45–58
   audit triggered, 50–52
      documentation requested, 52–53
   employer with only a few employees, 51
   Modular Container test, 46, 53
      alien's familial relationship not precluding labor certification, 49
      alien's investment, managerial involvement, or familial relationship precluding labor certification, 47–48
      alien's investment or involvement not precluding labor certification, 48–49
      BALCA cases after, 47–49
      BALCA cases prior to, 46–47
American Bar Association (ABA)
   House of Delegates Resolution 300 (Aug. 2008), 310, 323
American Institute of Certified Public Accountants (AICPA)
   accounting standards, 342, 347
Anti-money laundering. *See* **Money laundering**
Antiterrorism and Effective Death Penalty Act (AEDPA)
   Foreign Terrorist Organizations (FTOs) and terrorism list governments, transactions with, 316
   knowledge for criminal liability, 317
   penalties, 320

Arms Export Control Act
   defense firms' notice of transfer in ownership to foreign purchaser, 289
Atomic energy
   laws to protect from foreign interests, 288
"At risk" capital
   EB-5 investors, 92, 113–118
   for EB-5 investors, 92, 113–118
      Ho decision (AAO), 117–118, 125, 179–180
      Izummi decision (AAO), 114–117, 125, 179–180
      regulatory sources, 113–114
   nonpreference investor category, 232–233
Attorneys
   ethical considerations for. *See* Ethical considerations
   Lawyer Guidance (FATF), 323–324
Attorney's fees
   investors (EB-5) representation, 275–276
Audits
   alien's influence and control over job opportunity, 50–52
      documentation requested, 52–53
   financial audits
      explanatory language added to, 346
      types of, 346
Australia
   business skills program, 397–404
      cancellation of visa, 404
      current visa requirements, 400–404
      post-arrival monitoring, 404
      requirements summary, 406
   E-3 visas, specialty workers from, 243
   entrepreneur visas, 405
   temporary residence for self-funded retirees, 404–405
Aviation
   laws to protect from foreign interests, 288

B

B visas
   applications by potential EB-5 petitioners, purpose of, 140
Background check on clients
   due diligence, 119
Balance sheet
   described, 341
Benefit requirements
   investor (EB-5) to benefit U.S. economy, 65
   substantial benefit for exceptional ability EB-2 visas, 41
Bipartisan Campaign Reform Act of 2002 (BCRA)
   prohibition on foreign national contributions to U.S. elections, 281
Board of Alien Labor Certification Appeals (BALCA)
   alien's influence and control over job opportunity, 45–58
Board of Immigration Appeals (BIA)
   removal appeals to, 220

Bona fide commercial or entrepreneurial undertaking
   E-2 visas, 18
Bona fide job opportunities. *See* **Alien influence and control over job opportunity**
Bureau of Economic Analysis (BEA)
   collection of data on foreign investment in U.S., 282–283
Bureau of Labor Statistics (BLS)
   high unemployment areas established by, 109
Business entities
   accounting systems, 347–348
   choice of type, 293–294
   overview of types, 331–338. *See also* Corporations; Limited liability companies (LLCs); Limited liability partnerships (LLPs); Limited partnerships (LPs); Partnerships; S corporations; Sole proprietorships
Business management. *See* **Managerial capacity; Managers**

C

Campaign contributions
   BCRA prohibition on foreign national contributions to U.S. elections, 281
Canadians
   business immigration program, 407–408
      Quebec, 412–413
   commuters and tax liability, 364
   E-2 visas
      change of status denied, 27
      disqualified if strike or lockout in labor dispute, 25
   investor immigration, 407–414
   provincial nominee programs for investor and entrepreneurial immigrants, 407–412
Capital
   accounting standards
      additional paid-in capital, 349
      contributed capital, 349
   "at risk." *See* "At risk" capital
   E-2 visas, investor's possession and control of invested funds, 15–16
   EB-5 investor capital
      expending all of, 178–180
      legal acquisition of, 67–68, 93, 119–129, 131–132
      required amount of capital investment, 174
      shortfall of capital investment, 175–177
      source of funds, 93, 120–125, 174–175
   income tax returns, capital accounts, 353–354
   money laundering, relevance to, 318–319
   source of funds
      legal precedent, 232, 236
      nonpreference investor category, 232
Capital gain deferral
   departure planning, 391
Capital stock
   described, 349

Cash flow
  net income vs., 350–351
  statement, 342
C corporations. *See* **Corporations**
***Chang* decision (9th Cir.)**
  retroactive application of rules to investors' I-829 petitions when they followed previous rules, 195–196, 224
Change of status
  E-2 visas, 27
Checklists
  investors (EB-5), 90
***Chevron* deference**
  validity of agency decisions, 220, 223–224
Chile
  H-1B1 visas, 243
China. *See* **People's Republic of China (PRC)**
Circuit Courts
  deferential levels of, 224
  removal appeals to, 220
Citizenship
  illegal procurement, effect on EB-5 status, 219
Classified information
  laws to protect, 288
Clayton Act
  prevention of acquisition by either domestic or foreign investors, 287
Closely held corporations
  alien with interest in, audit triggered, 50
  defined, 50
Compensation deferral
  departure planning, 391, 393
Competition
  laws to protect, 287
Conditional permanent residents
  investors (EB-5), 165–191. *See also* Form I-829
    agency actions transforming conditions to permanent residence, 168–171
    statutory framework, 166–168
    termination grounds, 167, 218
  with pending I-829 petitions, 72, 75
Conflict of interest
  representing both U.S.-based developer and immigrant investor, 268–270
  representing multiple petitioners, 270–271
Consular post applications
  E-2 visas, 27
Consultants for EB-5 investors
  business plan writer, 299–300
Control over job opportunity, 45–58. *See also* **Alien influence and control over job opportunity**
Corporations
  accounting system, 347–348
  choice of entity type for foreign investors, 293–294
  equity/capital reporting, 350
  H-1B visas for when petitioner is sole owner and operator of, 6–7
  income tax returns, 351–352
  overview, 335–336
  stock, situs rules for nonresident aliens, 374
Criminal fines. *See* **Penalties**
Cuba
  OFAC economic sanctions on, 314
Currency and Foreign Transactions Reporting Act of 1970
  provisions of, 291
Currency transactions
  Fin-CEN Form 105 for transportation of currency or monetary instruments, 284
  PRC currency exchange, 135–136
  reporting requirements, 291, 321
  Russia currency exchange, 141
Customer identification
  FATF recommendations, 322, 326–327
Customs
  U.S. counsel advising on, 295

D

Debt
  estate tax, 369, 375
Defense Production Act of 1950 (Exon-Florio)
  provisions of, 292
De novo review
  Chevron deference to agency decisions, 220
  removal appeals, 220
Department of Homeland Security Appropriations bill (2009)
  extension of EB-5 pilot program, 80
Dependents
  E-2 nonimmigrants, 25–26
  Hong Kong, 417, 419
  UK, 431–432
Discretionary decision bar
  government defense, 222
District Office
  Form I-829 adjudication, 72
Domestic and Foreign Investment Improved Disclosure Act of 1977
  provisions of, 291
Dual nationality
  E status, 14
  income tax, 389
Due diligence
  background check on clients, 119
  business planning, retention of expert, 274

E

E-1 visas
  employees of E-1 businesses seeking E-2 visas, 21–24
  history and background, 230–231
  Japanese investors, 234–235
  tax planning issues for immigrant and nonimmigrant visas, 368–369

E-2 visas
- ability to develop and direct business, 20–21
- bona fide commercial or entrepreneurial undertaking, 18
- change of status, 27
- consular post applications, 27
- dependents of E-2 nonimmigrants, 25–26
- eligibility requirements, 13–14
- employees of E-1 businesses seeking, 21–24
    - essential skills, 22–23
    - executive or supervisory character, 21–22
    - general requirements, 21
    - short-term need, 23
- franchised businesses, 21
- history and background, 230–231
- incidental activities, 25
- intention to depart United States, 24–25
- investor's possession and control of invested funds, 15–16
- irrevocable commitment of investment, 16
- Japanese investors, 234–235
- marginal investments, 19–20
- Mexicans and Canadians disqualified if strike or lockout in labor dispute, 25
- nationality of treaty country required for applicant, 14–15
- new businesses, 16
- nonpreference investor category, 247–250
- other financial transactions as investments, 16–18
- relevant authorities, 13–14
- renewals, 27
- retained earnings, applicability to, 17–18
- risk of investment, 16
- smaller businesses, 13–29
- substantial investment, 18
- tax planning issues for immigrant and nonimmigrant visas, 368–369
- treaty of Freedom, Commerce, and Navigation (FCN), 14
    - list of treaty countries, 28–30
- validity period and admission period, 26
- where to apply, 26–27

E-3 visas
- specialty workers from Australia, 243

Earnings
- from petitioner's business, as source of EB-5 funds, 121
- in unlawful status, as source of EB-5 investor funds, 128

EB-1-2 visas
- outstanding professors and researchers, 34–37

EB-1-3 visas
- multinational executives and managers, 31, 37–39
    - compared with EB-5 investor program, 88–89

EB-1(A) visas
- extraordinary ability in sciences, art, or business, 32–34

EB-2 visas
- exceptional ability in sciences, art, or business, 39–41
- national interest waiver, 41–43

EB-5 Alien Entrepreneurs—Job Creation and Full-Time Positions (USCIS memorandum 2009). *See* **Neufeld Memo**

EB-5 investors
- generally, 61–90
- areas restricted for foreign investment, 65
- attorney advice, 298–299
- background, 105
- benefiting U.S. economy, 65
- business plan writer, 299–300
- capital and source of funds. *See* Capital
- checklist for qualifying, 90
- from China (PRC), 131–137
- compared with multinational executives and managers (EB-1-3), 88–89
- comparison of UK investor program, 432–433
- congressional involvement. *See* 21st Century Department of Justice Appropriations Act of 2002
- creating or saving jobs. *See* Job creation
- economists, 300–301
- ethical considerations for attorneys, 76. *See also* Ethical considerations
- expanding existing business, 63–64
- federal court rulings, 83, 194–195
- fraud and misrepresentation, 73, 75
- initial evidence to be submitted, 67–69, 82
- INS restrictive standard of adjudication, 81
- investing. *See* Capital; "Investing" or "actively in the process of investing"
- legislative history, 257–262
    - 1982 Bill, 257–258
    - 1989 Bill, 258–259
- litigation over, 217–225
    - *Chevron* deference, 220, 223–224
    - clear and convincing evidence to preclude judicial review, 221–222
    - discretionary decision bar, 222
    - failure to naturalize conditional resident and five-year period for citizenship has accrued, 221
    - federal court litigation, 219–221, 224
    - government defenses, 221–224
    - jurisdictional issues, 223
    - mandamus to compel adjudication of petition, 220
    - mootness, ripeness, and failure to exhaust administrative remedies, 195, 222–223
    - removal proceeding precluding review, 223
    - substantial evidence standard, 220–221, 223–224
    - typical issues, 217–219
    - winning strategy, 224–225
- managerial capacity of investor, 69, 93–94
- money laundering, relevance to, 318–319
- new commercial enterprise, 63, 92
    - division of commercial enterprise into two or more legal entities, 198–199
    - "engaging" in, 64

initial evidence for, 67
nonpreference investor category as predecessor to, 245–256
onerous burden of requirements, 73–74, 82
partnerships, 63
pilot program, 62, 66, 70, 80–87, 89, 146–147. *See also* Form I-526
pooling arrangements, 64, 84, 186
procedures, 67–69
qualified immigrants, 62–63
quota, 80
reform recommendations, 190–191
regional centers. *See* Regional centers
removal of conditions, 71–72, 75, 94, 154–155, 165–191. *See also* Form I-829
    litigation over, 217
restructuring existing business, 63
revisiting residency issues, 219
from Russia, 139–143
statutory requirements, 62, 81
targeted employment areas. *See* Targeted employment areas
termination of status, 72–73
top 5 countries for visa issuance, 301–302
troubled businesses, 66–67, 188
    initial evidence for, 69
2002 law, effect of, 74–76
unlawful status of petitioner, 128

Elections
BCRA prohibition on foreign national contributions to U.S. elections, 281

Employer-employee relationship
H-1B petitions, 55–56
validity of
    for EB-1-2 visas, 36–37
    for EB-2 visas, 41
    for H-1B visas, 6–7

Employment agreements
with owners/beneficiaries, 7

Employment authorization (EAD)
dependents of E-2 nonimmigrants, 25

Employment-based immigration. *See* **EB visas**

Entrepreneurs. *See also* **specific countries**
generally, 3
E-2 visas, 18

Equity accounts
accounting issues, 349–350
reporting changes in, 350

Escrow
"investing" (EB-5), 92

Estate planning
tax considerations, 361–362, 390–391
U.S. counsel advising on, 295

Estate tax. *See* **Taxes**

Ethical considerations
investors (EB-5) representation, 76, 136, 265–278, 293
    adverse claims of malpractice or unethical conduct, 276–277

drafting business plan, 274
duty of competence, 265–267
finder's fees, 276
"full service" attorney, 272–274
investment advice and economic merits, 271–272
legal fees, 275–276
representing both U.S.-based developer and immigrant investor, 268–270
representing multiple petitioners, 270–271
resources, 278
source of funding, 310
unsettled law, advice to clients regarding, 267–268
suspicious activity reporting, 321–322, 325

European Union (EU)
anti-money laundering directive, 310
gatekeeping regimes, 321

Exceptional ability
defined, 39
sciences, art, or business (EB-2 status), 39–41

Executives
multinational executives (EB-1-3), 31, 37–39

Exhaustion of administrative remedies
denial of I-829 petition, 195, 222–223

Exit tax
departure planning, 393

Expanding existing business
EB-5 investors, 63–64

Expatriation
tax effect of, 391–392

Export Administration Act of 1979
restrictions on exports of goods and technology related to military potential of foreign countries, 289

Extraordinary ability
defined, 32
O-1 visas, 11
priority workers (EB-1(A)), 32–34

F

False Statement Statute
criminal liability under, 316
penalties, 320

Familial relationship of alien
audit response, 54
audit triggered, 50
defined, 50
not precluding labor certification, 49
precluding labor certification due to alien's influence, 47–48

Family-sponsored immigrants
generally, 3

FATF. *See* **Financial Action Task Force**

Federal Election Campaign Act of 1971 (FECA)
prohibition on foreign national contributions to U.S. elections, 281

Financial Accounting Standards Board (FASB)
Accounting Standards Codification

ASC 225, Income Statement, 340
ASC 235, Notes to Financial Statements, 344–345
Concept Statement No. 2, Qualitative Characteristics of Accounting Information, 344
establishment and role of, 342
Statement of Financial Accounting Concepts (SFAC) No. 6, *Elements of Financial Statements,* 340

Financial Action Task Force (FATF)
combating money laundering, 309, 310
gatekeeping regimes, 321–323
    ABA Resolution 300, 323
    customer identification, 322, 326–327
    due diligence, heightened standard, 322, 325
    Lawyer Guidance, 323–324
    privileged materials, reporting exemption for, 323
    suspicious transactions reporting (STR), 322–323, 325

Financial Crimes Enforcement Network (Fin-CEN)
advance notice of proposed rulemaking on real estate settlements and closings, 322
Form 105 for transportation of currency or monetary instruments, 284
reporting of currency transactions, 321

Financial statements
accounting standards, 340–341
    FASB standards, 344
comparing "compiled," "reviewed," and "audited" statements, 345–346
disclosures and notes, 342

Finder's fees
ethical considerations, 276

Fines. *See* **Penalties**

***Foreign Affairs Manual* (FAM)**
development of, 229–242
DOS guidance on E treaty investor/trader visas, 230–231

Foreign business records
as evidence of investment funds (EB-5), 120

Foreign Commerce and Navigation (FCN) Treaties
history of, 229–230

Foreign exchange transactions
reporting of, 284–285

Foreign financial accounts
reporting of, 284–285

Foreign investments
disclosure requirements in U.S. law, 281–284
    Agricultural Foreign Investment Disclosure Act of 1978 (AFIDA), 283–284, 290
    International Investment and Trade in Services Survey Act of 1976, 282–283, 290
    Securities Exchange Act of 1934, 281–282
laws to protect classified information, 288
laws to protect competition, 287
laws to protect national security, 285–287
laws to protect particular sectors of economy, 288
laws to protect U.S. technology base, 289
reporting of foreign financial accounts, 284–285
restricted areas, 65

Foreign Narcotics Kingpin Designation Act. *See* **Kingpin Act**

Foreign Terrorist Organizations (FTOs)
AEDPA provisions on transactions with, 316

Foreign Trader, Investor and Regional Center Program
creation of, 77, 85

Form 90-22.1 (Treasury Department)
Report of Foreign Bank and Financial Accounts., 285

Form 105 (Fin-CEN)
transportation of currency or monetary instruments, 284

Form 8300 (IRS)
reporting of currency transactions, 321

Form ETA-9089
answers triggering audit, 50–51

Form I-94
E-2 visa entry, 26

Form I-485
filed with Form I-526 (1970s version), 246

Form I-526. *See also* **Immigrant Investor Pilot Program**
1970s version, request for determination as investor exempt from labor certification, 246, 251–253
current form (reproduced), 254–256
guidance for completing, 94–96, 98–100
initial assessment for, 91
investor (EB-5) pilot program, 70, 71, 74, 75, 80–87, 146–147
mandamus to compel adjudication of petition, 220
new or amended form, filing due to material change in business plan, 159–161, 181–183
procedure for new I-526, 162

Form I-829. *See also* **EB-5 investors**
approval of petition, 172
change in business plan, choice to file I-829 or new I-526, 161–162
denial of petition, 172, 182–183, 193–215
    Chang decision (9th Cir.), 195–196, 224
    effect of, 162–163
    exhaustion of administrative remedies, 195, 222–223
    federal court action, 194–195
    immigration court review, 193
    motions to reopen or reconsider, 193–194
    review of, 193–197
    Steenblik case (C.D. Cal.), 197, 203–215
    typical issues, 218
documentation required, 197–198
guidance for completing, 96–97, 101–103
legal authorities, 172–174
mandamus to compel adjudication of petition, 220
notice of USCIS decision, 172
petition to remove conditions on EB-5 investor, 71–72, 81–87, 94, 128–129, 170, 171–190
procedure, 171–172
revisiting residency issues, 219
revisiting targeted employment areas, 174, 195

Form I-864
affidavit of support, 50

Franchises
    E-2 visas, 21
Fraud and misrepresentation
    Immigration Marriage Fraud Amendments of 1986 (IMFA), 166
    investors (EB-5), 73, 75, 197
Free trade agreements
    U.S. pursuit of, 280
Funding source. *See* **Capital**

G

Generally accepted accounting principles (GAAP)
    common departures, 343–344
    described, 343
Generally accepted auditing standards (GAAS)
    described, 346–347
Gifts
    as source of investment funds (EB-5), 122–123
Gift tax. *See* **Taxes**
Government Accountability Office (GAO)
    study of EB-5 program, 62, 84, 191

H

H-1B visas
    ability to pay, 8–9
    definition of "research," 35
    employer defined for purposes of, 5
    Neufeld Memo and, 6–7, 37
    owner/beneficiary situations, 5
    owner/manager situations, 9
    Requests for Evidence (RFEs), 6–7
    size of the business, 9
    student founders of businesses, 3
    tax planning issues for immigrant and nonimmigrant visas, 368
H-1B1 visas
    Chile and Singapore, 243
Hart-Scott-Rodino Antitrust Improvements Act of 1976
    premerger notification, 287
    provisions of, 291
HEART Act of 2008
    expatriation, effect of, 392
"High unemployment" test
    targeted employment areas for EB-5 investors, 108–112
***Ho* decision (AAO)**
    "at risk" capital for EB-5 investors, 117–118, 125, 179–180
Hong Kong
    capital investment entrant scheme, 417–420
    dependent visas, 417, 419
    direct filing with Hong Kong Immigration Department, 416–417
    employment (entry for investment) visas, 415–416
    extension of stay, 417
    investor and entrepreneur resident visas, 415–420

I

IIEPA. *See* **International Emergency Economic Powers Act of 1977**
Illegal Immigration Reform and Immigrant Responsibility Act of 1996 (IIRAIRA)
    bar to review, 223
Immigrant Investor Pilot Program. *See also* **Form I-526**
    generally, 62, 66, 70, 80–87, 89, 146–147, 186–190
Immigration Act of 1965
    nonpreference investor category, 245
Immigration Act of 1990 (IMMACT90)
    EB-5 status, 79, 231
        capital and investment requirement, 261
        conditional status, 262
        job creation requirement, 260–261
        lawful permanent residence status on a conditional basis, 166
        legislative history, 259–262
        management participation of alien investor, 261–262
        purpose of, 260
    statutory framework, 79–80
Immigration and Nationality Act (INA)
    §203(b)(5)(a)(ii), job creation requirements, 153
    §203(b)(5) for investor visas, 62
    §212(a)(3)(A)(ii) inadmissibility due to unlawful activity, 140
    §212(a)(14) labor certification requirement, 245
    history of, 230
Immigration Marriage Fraud Amendments of 1986 (IMFA)
    lawful permanent residence status on a conditional basis, 166
Income tax. *See* **Taxes**
Influence over job opportunity. *See* **Alien influence and control over job opportunity**
Inheritance
    as source of investment funds (EB-5), 123
Insurance
    considerations for foreign investors, 295
Intention to depart United States
    E-2 visas, 24–25
    tax planning. *See* **Taxes**
Internal Revenue Code
    provisions on reporting foreign investments, 292
International Emergency Economic Powers Act of 1977 (IEEPA)
    elements, 315–316
    extraordinary and unusual threat to national security or economy, 292
    penalties, 320
    willful standard, 318

International Traffic in Arms Regulations (ITAR)
    defense firms' notice of transfer in ownership to foreign purchaser, 289

Intracompany transfers
    L-1 visas, 9–10

"Investing" or "actively in the process of investing" (EB-5). *See also* **Capital**
    generally, 64–65, 91–92, 174–180
    "at risk" capital, 92, 113–118
    country-specific problems, 127–128
    currency transfer laws, 126–127
    earnings from petitioner's business, 121
    earnings while in unlawful status, 128
    escrow, 92
    evidence for, 67, 93, 119–120
    expending all EB-5 investor capital, 178–180
    foreign business records as evidence, 120
    gifts, 122–123
    income tax returns as evidence, 120
    inheritance, 123
    legal acquisition of capital, 67–68, 93, 119–129, 131–132
    loans, 121–122, 200–201
    real estate transactions, 123–124
    required amount of capital investment, 174
    retirement funds, 124
    sale of business assets, 124
    shortfall of capital investment, 175–177
    source of funds, 93, 120–125, 174–175
    sustained investment throughout period of conditional residence, 180–183
    tracing path of funds from petitioner to EB-5 enterprise, 125–127, 140–142
    transactions, 123
    wealth accumulation, 124–125

Investment advice
    ethical considerations for attorney giving, 271–272

Investment policies, U.S.
    OECD's Declaration on International Investment and Multinational Enterprises (1976) and Code of Liberalisation of Capital Movements (1982), 280
    principles of, 280

Investor and Regional Center Unit (IRCU). *See* **Foreign Trader, Investor and Regional Center Program**

Investors. *See also* **EB-5 investors; E visas**
    generally, 3
    investment of alien
        not precluding labor certification, 48–49
        precluding labor certification, 47–48
    not defined as employees, 45

Iran
    OFAC approval of EB-5 applications, 319–320
    OFAC economic sanctions on, 314
    source of funds of EB-5 investors from, 175, 318–319

Izummi **decision (AAO)**
    "at risk" capital for EB-5 investors, 114–117, 125, 179–180
    crediting indirect employment, 150

J

Japanese investors
    E-1 or E-2 visas, 234–235

Job creation (EB-5)
    generally, 65–67, 80, 85–87, 93, 146–147
    agency-imposed job creation requirement, 183–190
    background, 153–154
    crediting indirect employment, 149–150
    employment eligibility of U.S. workers, 184–185
    expressio unius est exclusio alterius, 169
    failure to create jobs or delay in creation, 153–163
    initial evidence for, 68–69
    reasonable time for, 185–186
    review of I-829 petitions where jobs have not been created, 87
    targeted employment areas. *See* **Targeted employment areas**
    timing of job creation, 86–87, 147–149, 155–157

Job descriptions
    of owners/beneficiaries, 7–8
    size of the business and, 9

Job opportunity and offers. *See* **Alien influence and control over job opportunity; Offers of employment**

Judicial review
    government arguments to preclude under INA §242(a)(2)(B)(ii), 221
    mandamus to compel adjudication of I-526 or I-829 petition, 220

K

Kingpin Act
    penalties, 320
    transactions with Significant Foreign Narcotics Trafficker (SFNT), 316
    willful standard, 318

Knowledge
    AEDPA criminal liability, 317
    L-1B visas specialized knowledge, 10
    stolen money, 312, 313

L

L-1 visas
    intracompany transfers, 9–10
    new office provisions, 10–11
    tax planning issues for immigrant and nonimmigrant visas, 368

L-1A visas
    compared to EB-1-3 visas, 37–38

Neufeld Memo, not applicable to, 8
L-1B visas
    extensions, 11
    specialized knowledge, 10
Labor certification
    alien's investment, managerial involvement, or familial relationship precluding, 47–48
    exemption for nonpreference investor category, 245–256
        utilizing in current practice, 246–250
Lawful permanent residents (LPRs)
    conditional permanent residents with pending I-829 petitions, 72, 75
    without labor certification, using EB-1 and EB-2 visas, 31–43
Legal precedent
    "at-risk" capital, 232–233, 235–236
    background and overview, 229–231
    corporate control issues and joint ventures, 237–238
    creation of EB-5 immigrant investor category, 242
    executives, managers, and essential employees, 239–241
    intent to return abroad, 241–242
    nationality of treaty country, 238–239
    nonpreference investor category, 231–233
        "at-risk" capital, 232–233
        source of funds, 232
        substantiality, 232
    post-1979 treaty investor visa guidance, 234–242
    pre-1979 treaty investor visa guidance, 233
    promulgation of E visa regulations, 242
    source of funds, 232, 236
    substantiality and marginality, 236–237
    in treaty investor visa cases, 229–243
    Walsh-Pollard case and E-2 criteria, 241
Limited liability companies (LLCs)
    accounting system, 348
    choice of entity type for foreign investors, 293–294
    equity/capital reporting, 350
    income tax returns, 351
    interests treated as securities, 303
    investors (EB-5), 92
    overview, 337–338
Limited liability partnerships (LLPs)
    accounting system, 348
    choice of entity type for foreign investors, 293
    equity/capital reporting, 350
    income tax returns, 351
    overview, 334
Limited partnerships (LPs)
    accounting system, 348
    choice of entity type for foreign investors, 293–294
    interests treated as securities, 303
    investors (EB-5), 69, 92
    overview, 333–334
LLCs. *See* **Limited liability companies**
LLPs. *See* **Limited liability partnerships**

Loans
    investment funds for EB-5 from, 121–122, 200–201
Local Area Unemployment Statistics (LAUS) program
    high unemployment areas established by, 109–110
LPs. *See* **Limited partnerships**

M

Malpractice claims
    in investors (EB-5) representation, 276–277
Managerial capacity
    E-2 visas, ability to develop and direct business, 20–21
    EB-5 investors, 69, 93–94
Managers
    managerial involvement of alien
        not precluding labor certification, 48–49
        precluding labor certification, 47–48
    multinational executives and managers (EB-1-3), 31, 37–39
        compared with EB-5 investor program, 88–89
Mandamus
    to compel adjudication of I-526 or I-829 petition, 220
Marginal investments
    E-2 visas, 19–20
McCarran-Walters Act of 1952
    history of, 230
Mergers
    premerger notification, 287
Mexicans
    commuters and tax liability, 364
    disqualified from E-2 visas if strike or lockout in labor dispute, 25
***Modular Container* test**
    alien influence and control over job opportunity, 46, 53
        alien's familial relationship not precluding labor certification, 49
        alien's investment, managerial involvement, or familial relationship precluding labor certification, 47–48
        alien's investment or involvement not precluding labor certification, 48–49
    BALCA cases after, 47–49
    BALCA cases prior to, 46–47
    bona fide job opportunity, 46, 53
Money laundering
    compliance tips for attorneys, 324–325
    development of laws, 309–310
    as inadmissibility grounds, 140
    penalties, 314
    proceeds of crime and criminally derived property, 314
    pro forma suspicious client/matter report form, 329–330
    relevance to EB-5 investors, 318–319
    restricted transactions, 314–320
    signs of, 328

Mootness

stolen money, 310–314
    culpable acts, 311–312
    elements, 310–311
    intent, or knowledge of design, to avoid transaction reporting requirement, 313
    intent, or knowledge of design, to conceal information about funds or property involved, 313
    intent to engage in conduct to evade tax law, 312–313
    intent to promote specified unlawful activity, 312
    knowledge, 312
    scienter, 312–313
    Specified Unlawful Activities (SUA), 313–314
suspicious activity reporting, 321–322

Mootness
government defense, 222–223

N

National Industrial Security Program
foreign-controlled corporations obtaining security clearances, 288

National Interest Waiver (NIW)
EB-2 visas, 41–43

National Securities Markets Improvement Act (NSMIA)
preemption of state securities laws, 303

National security. *See also* **Terrorism and counterterrorism**
laws to protect, 285–287

Net income
cash flow vs., 350–351

Neufeld Memos
business plan, no material changes after filing petition, 157–159, 169–170, 181–183
    procedure for filing new I-526 petition, 162
guidance of, 5, 6–7, 37, 55–58, 87, 169–170
job creation requirements, 145–146, 154, 169, 187–188
    timing of job creation, 147–149, 155–156
new challenges created by, 219
strategies for dealing with, 7–8

New commercial enterprises. *See also* **Startups**
EB-5 investors, 63, 92
    division of commercial enterprise into two or more legal entities, 198–199
    "engaging" in, 64
    initial evidence for, 67

New offices
L-1 visas, 10–11

New Zealand
migrant investment policy
    Investor 1 Category, 421–423
    Investor 2 Category, 423–426
residency for investors, 421–427

Nonpreference investor category
labor certification exemption for, 245–256

Notice to Appear
denial of I-829 petition triggering, 172

O

O-1 visas
extraordinary ability, 11

Offers of employment
NIW route to permanent residence, job offer not required, 42
outstanding professors and researchers (EB-1-2), 36
with owners/beneficiaries, 7

Office of Foreign Assets Control (OFAC)
culpable acts, 316–317
IEEPA authorization, 315–316
licenses for immigrant visas (EB-5), 318–320
scienter, 317–318
Specially Designated Nationals (SDNs), prohibited transactions with, 314–315
    legal services authorized, 318
    list of SDNs, 315
terrorist financing, 309
transactions restrictions and sanctions, 314–317

Organizational charts
owner/beneficiary's place within company, 8

Organized crime
memberships as inadmissibility grounds, 140

Other Comprehensive Basis of Accounting (OCBOA)
described, 345

O visas
tax planning issues for immigrant and nonimmigrant visas, 368

Owners/beneficiaries
EB-1-3 visas, 39
H-1B denials, 5–8

Owners/managers
specialty occupations, 9

P

Partnerships. *See also* **Limited liability partnerships (LLPs); Limited partnerships (LPs)**
accounting system, 348
alien with interest in
    audit triggered, 50
    in situs, gift taxation, 374–375
choice of entity type for foreign investors, 293–294
EB-5 investors, 63
equity/capital reporting, 350
income tax returns, 351, 352
    Schedules K and K-1, 355–356
    Schedule L, 356
    Schedule M-2, 356
investors (EB-5), 63, 92
overview, 332–333

PATRIOT Act of 2001
counterterrorism goals, 309–310

Penalties
  AEDPA, 320
  Agricultural Foreign Investment Disclosure Act of 1978, 290
  criminal fines generally, 320
  Currency and Foreign Transactions Reporting Act of 1970, 291
  failure to report currency transactions, 321
  False Statement Statute, 320
  Fin-CEN Form 105 for transportation of currency or monetary instruments, 284
  IEEPA, 320
  International Investment and Trade in Services Survey Act of 1976, 290
  Kingpin Act, 320
  money laundering, 314
  outbound foreign trust tax legislation, 386

People's Republic of China (PRC)
  consular processing in, 136–137
  EB-5 petitioners from, 131–137, 301–302
  legal acquisition of capital, 131–132
    creative approaches to, 134–135
    currency exchange, 135–136
  tax system, 132–134
    business tax, 134
    consumption tax, 134
    corporate income tax, 133
    individual income tax, 132
    sole proprietors, 132
    VAT (value-added tax), 133–134
  third-party accounting proving source of funds, 134

Performance review process
  of owners/beneficiaries, 8

Permanent residency. *See* **Lawful permanent residents (LPRs)**

PERM regulations
  alien's influence and control over job opportunity, 45
  audit triggered, 50

Petitioning
  employer petitioning for
    exceptional ability (EB-2, Schedule A, Group II), 40–41
    multinational managers and executives (EB-1-3), 39
    outstanding professors and researchers (EB-1-2), 34–37
  self-petitioning by extraordinary ability priority workers (EB-1(A)), 33

Pilot program. *See* **Immigrant Investor Pilot Program**

Pooling arrangements
  EB-5 investors, 64, 84, 186

Principal residence
  tax-free sale, 391

Privileged materials
  reporting exemption for, FATF recommendation, 323

Professors
  outstanding professors and researchers (EB-1-2), 34–37

Q

Qualified domestic trusts (QDOTs)
  estate tax, 362, 369
    anti-abuse provisions, 380
    bank, bond, or letter of credit requirement, 378–380
    computation of tax, 381–382
    difficulty in transferring assets, 378
    income distributions, 380–381
    noncitizen spouses, 375–376
    post-death transfers, 376–377
    protective assignments, 377–378
    spouse becoming citizen, 382–383

Qualified opinion
  audit, 346

Quota
  EB-5 investors, 80

R

Radio and television
  laws to protect from foreign interests, 288

Real estate transactions
  considerations for foreign investors, 295
  Fin-CEN advance notice of proposed rulemaking on settlements and closings, 322
  as source of investment funds (EB-5), 123–124

Regional centers (EB-5 investors)
  generally, 69–71, 80, 82–83, 151, 297–302
  affiliated petitions, 186–190
  approval of application, 301
  best practices and securities law compliance, 306–307
  defined, 186
  final proposal for application, 301
  hiring immigration consultants, 302
  marketing and promoting EB-5 investments, 302, 303–307, 304–307
  Regulation D and Regulation S, 303–305
  third parties who market or promote, 305–306

Regulation D
  avoiding general solicitation under, 304–305
  exemption of securities from registration, 303–304
  Rule 502(c), 304
  Rule 506, 303–304

Regulation S
  avoiding directed selling efforts in U.S. under, 305
  exemption of securities from registration, 303–304

Removal of conditions (EB-5). *See also* **Form I-829**
  generally, 71–72, 75, 94, 154–155, 165–191
  litigation over, 217

Removal proceeding
  precluding review of EB-5 status, 223
  termination of conditional resident status, 172, 220–221

Reporting
  of currency transactions (Fin-CEN), 321
  of foreign exchange transactions, 284–285

Requests for Evidence (RFEs)
of foreign financial accounts, 284–285
Requests for Evidence (RFEs)
Form I-829 petitions, 71–72, 156–157, 165, 175
H-1 visas and, 6–7
increase in, 5
Research
defined, 35
outstanding professors and researchers (EB-1-2), 34–37
Retained earnings
accounting standards, 349
applicability to E-2 visas, 17–18
reporting changes in, 350
Retirement funds
as source of investment funds (EB-5), 124
Retroactive application of new standards
I-829 petitions, 195–196, 218–219
Ripeness
government defense, 222–223
Risk of investment
E-2 visas, 16
"Rural area" test
targeted employment areas for EB-5 investors, 107–108
Russia
barred by potentially illegal activities, 139–140
corporate governance law, 141
corruption, effect of, 141–142
currency exchange, 141
EB-5 petitioners from, 139–143
Embassy in Moscow interviews, 142
Labor Book as confirmation of work experience, 142
public records, 142
residential registration system *(propiska),* 142
tax law, 141
tracking path of funds, 140–142

S

Sale of business assets
as source of investment funds (EB-5), 124
Sanctions
counterterrorism goals, 310
Scienter
OFAC, 317–318
stolen money, 312–313
S corporations
accounting system, 348
equity/capital reporting, 350
income tax returns, 351, 352
overview, 336–337
Secretary of State filings
considerations for foreign investors, 295

Securities
registration, 303
exemption under Regulation D and/or Regulation S, 303–304
Securities Act of 1933
registration requirement, 303
Securities and Exchange Commission (SEC)
authority, 342
Securities Exchange Act of 1934
aider and abettor violations under §20(e), 306
disclosure requirements in U.S. law, 281–282
SEC authority, 342
Self-petitioning
extraordinary ability priority workers (EB-1(A)), 33
Singapore
H-1B1 visas, 243
Size of business
H-1B visas, 9
Smaller businesses
E-2 visas, 13–29
Sole proprietorships
accounting system, 348
alien with interest in, audit triggered, 50
equity/capital reporting, 350
H-1B visas, 5
income tax returns, 351, 352–353
investors (EB-5), 92
overview, 331–332
Source of funds. *See* **Capital**
Specialized knowledge
L-1B visas, 10
Spousal transfers
departure planning, making gifts, 391
estate tax and qualified domestic trusts, 362, 369, 375–376
gift tax, 371
Startups
considerations for foreign investors, 294
EB-1-3 visas and, 38
investors (EB-5), new commercial enterprise requirement, 63, 92
NIW challenges, 42
Steenblik **case (C.D. Cal.)**
denial of I-829 petition, 197, 203–215
Stock
capital stock, 349
situs rules for nonresident aliens, 374
treasury stock, 349–350
Stolen money
generally, 310–314
culpable acts, 311–312
elements, 310–311
intent, or knowledge of design, to avoid transaction reporting requirement, 313
intent, or knowledge of design, to conceal information about funds or property involved, 313
intent to engage in conduct to evade tax law, 312–313
intent to promote specified unlawful activity, 312

knowledge, 312
scienter, 312–313
Specified Unlawful Activities (SUA), 313–314
Substantial benefit requirement
for exceptional ability EB-2 visas, 41
Substantial evidence standard
administrative findings of fact, 220–221, 223–224
Substantial investment
E-2 visas, 18
Sudan
OFAC economic sanctions on, 314
Suspicious transactions reporting (STR)
applicable to lawyers, 321–322, 325
FATF recommendations, 322–323, 325

T

Targeted employment areas (EB-5 investors)
generally, 66, 69, 80, 85, 87–88, 91, 105–112
city or town with population exceeding 20,000, 107
defined, 105
"high unemployment" test, 108–112
metropolitan statistical areas (MSAs), 106–107
revisiting in adjudicating I-829 petition, 174, 195
"rural area" test, 105–108
Taxes
choice of entity. *See* specific types of entities (*e.g.*, Limited liability companies, Corporations, etc.)
departure planning, 391–394
    capital gain deferral, 391
    compensation deferral, 391, 393
    exit tax, 393
    expatriation, effect of, 391–392
    principal residence, tax-free sale, 391
    spousal gifts, 391
estate tax
    charitable deductions, 369
    credits, 369–370
    debt, 369
    deductions, 369
    exclusions, 373–374
    generation-skipping transfer tax (GST), 370–371
    gross estate, determination of, 368–369
    nonresident aliens, 361–362, 368–372
    planning, 361–362, 390–391
    residency status, determination of, 365–367
    spousal transfers and qualified domestic trusts, 362, 369, 375–376
    tax treaties, effect of, 371, 394
    unified credit, 369–370
    U.S. citizens and resident aliens, 362
    U.S. situs property, 373–375
federal income tax rules, 360–361
gift tax
    annual, spousal, and support gifts, 371
    exclusions, 373–374
    generation-skipping transfer tax (GST), 371
    intangible personal property, 374–375
    nonresident aliens, 371–373
    planning opportunities, 390–391
    reporting requirement for donee, 372
    residency status, determination of, 365–367
    splitting gifts, 371–372
    tax treaties, effect of, 372–373, 394
    unified credit not applicable, 372
    U.S. situs property, 373–375
income tax, 351–355
    basis in partnership taxation, 355
    capital accounts, 353–354
    dual residence, 389
    economic vs. tax allocations, 354–355
    evidence of funds for EB-5 investors, 120
    interests in foreign financial accounts, 390
    Schedules K and K-1, 355–356
    Schedule L, 356
    Schedule M-2, 356
    tax-basis capital accounts, 354
information systems, 340
initial investment, 357
intent to engage in conduct to evade tax law, 312–313
IRS filings, 295
planning issues for immigrant and nonimmigrant visas, 359–394
    H-1B visas, 368
    L-1 visas, 368
    O visas, 368
    pre-immigration planning, 383–388
    treaty trader/treaty investor (E) visas, 368–369
pre-immigration planning
    foreign trusts, 383–385
    income tax planning prior to residence, 388–389
    interest charges, 387
    loans to U.S. beneficiaries, 387
    outbound foreign trust tax legislation, 385–387
    post-U.S. domicile gifts and bequests, 385
    powers of appointment, 385
    trust situs, 387–388
residency status, determination of, 363–367
    athletes present for charitable sporting events, 364
    Canadian or Mexican commuters, 364
    day in transit, 364
    estate and gift taxes, 365–367
    exempt individuals, 363–364
    G-4 visas, employees of international organization, 363
    income tax planning prior to residence, 388–389
    individuals with medical condition, 364
    lawful permanent residents (LPRs), 363
    nonresident aliens, 363
    students, 364
    substantial presence test, 363
    tax home exception, 364–365
    tax treaties, effect of, 365
    teachers and trainees, 364

Tax Reform Act of 1984 (TRA)
    31-day exception, 364
    U.S. possession residents, 366
    A visas, diplomatic or consular status, 363
Tax Reform Act of 1984 (TRA)
    tax residency issues, 359
Tax treaties
    estate tax, 371, 394
    gift tax, 372–373, 394
TEAs. *See* **Targeted employment areas; Targeted employment areas (EB-5 investors)**
Technology
    laws to protect U.S. technology base, 289
Terrorism and counterterrorism
    AEDPA, 316
    IEEPA, 292, 315–316
    USA PATRIOT Act of 2001, 309–310
Treaties
    estate tax, 371, 394
    Freedom, Commerce, and Navigation (FCN), 229–230
        E-2 visas, 14
            list of treaty countries, 28–30
    gift tax, 372–373, 394
Treaty investors. *See* **E-2 visas**
Treaty traders. *See* **E-1 visas**
TRIMs Agreement
    scope of, 280
Troubled businesses
    investors (EB-5), 66–67, 69, 188
Trusts
    foreign trusts, pre-immigration planning, 383–388
    QDOTs. *See* Qualified domestic trusts
21st Century Department of Justice Appropriations Act of 2002
    enactment of, 62, 74, 83–84

U

U.N. Convention Against Illicit Traffic in Narcotic Drugs and Psychotropic Substances
    money laundering and, 309
United Kingdom
    comparison of U.S. and UK investor programs, 432–433
    dependents, 431–432
    investor visa category, 429–430
    path to residency and citizenship, 430–431
    processing time, 432
Universities
    outstanding professors and researchers (EB-1-2), 34–37
Unqualified opinion
    audit, 346
USA PATRIOT Act of 2001
    counterterrorism goals, 309–310
U.S. Trade Representative (USTR)
    role of, 280

V

Visa Waiver Permanent Program Act of 2000
    extension of EB-5 pilot program, 80

W

Wealth accumulation
    as source of investment funds (EB-5), 124–125
Willful standard
    IEEPA, 318
    Kingpin Act, 318
World Trade Organization (WTO)
    Agreement on Trade-Related Investment Measures (TRIMs Agreement), 280